NOTES

ON THE

OLD TESTAMENT

EXPLANATORY AND PRACTICAL

BY

ALBERT BARNES

ENLARGED TYPE EDITION

EDITED BY

ROBERT FREW, D.D.

ISAIAH
VOL. I

BAKER BOOK HOUSE
GRAND RAPIDS, MICHIGAN

Library of Congress Catalog Card Number: 55-11630

ISBN: 0-8010-0538-8

First Printing, May 1950
Second Printing, November 1955
Third Printing, September 1960
Fourth Printing, September 1962
Fifth Printing, July 1964
Sixth Printing, September 1966
Seventh Printing, June 1968
Eighth Printing, March 1969
Ninth Printing, June 1971
Tenth Printing, September 1972

PRINTED IN THE UNITED STATES OF AMERICA

EDITOR'S PREFACE.

So long as the church endures, shall the genius and eloquence of the son of Amoz be held in admiration. On the ruins of once flourishing empires and cities, his credentials are written; and the more these ruins are explored, and compared with his prophetic pages, the deeper will the conviction grow, that the inspiration of God is there. In a sceptical age like the present, it cannot but be of great advantage to direct the minds of our youth to *demonstrations* like these. But Isaiah has still nobler themes than the downfall of empires. The grand subjects of this "fifth evangelist" are the person and character, and reign and glory of Christ; the triumphs of the church; the restoration of the Jews; and conversion of the world; and these are presented in a style that is by turns simple, beautiful, tender, sublime, impetuous. The majesty of Isaiah has never been surpassed.

This exposition of the prophet originally appeared in three large octavos; it was subsequently condensed by the author, and re-issued in two volumes of smaller size. From this second and latest edition, the present reprint has been made. The reader will recognize in it the same easy and perspicuous style, the same racy illustrations, the same prevailing good sense, and general fullness of exposition, that have made the author the most popular of modern commentators. He makes no pretence, indeed, to very profound or original criticism. But while there is necessarily less of this than in works written professedly for the scholar, there is much more of it than is usually found in popular commentaries. The sense of the original is always carefully ascertained, and made the basis of exposition; but while the merely philological inquiry is, for the most part, carried so far as to satisfy, it is never pushed to the length of tedium or fatigue. Thus a happy medium has been secured, and a commentary produced, acceptable alike to the scholar and the Christian. It is, perhaps, not too much to say that it is the most readable and generally useful commentary on Isaiah in the English language. The scholarship of Alexander is doubtless more exact and profound, and his exegesis more independent; but his book is for scholars, and for scholars alone. It deals principally in philological criticism; its avowed aim is briefly to present the true sense, along with a condensed historical synopsis of opinion. Very nearly the same may be said of Henderson, Lowth, Stock, and Noyes. The illustration in all of them is too scant to satisfy, and the public instructor in search of available materials for lectures on Isaiah, will consult them in vain; but in these volumes will be found, in union with judicious criticism, a satisfying copiousness of illustration. In the archæological department particularly, the author excels, having added to the stores of Gesenius and other diligent cultivators of this field, much additional matter from the works of modern travellers. This feature of the book greatly enhances its value, and lends to it a peculiar charm ; it is especially fitted to captivate the young, and allure them to studies which they are but too apt to imagine repulsive and dry. The author, indeed, has been blamed for disproportionate attention to this part of his subject ; but readers generally will thank him for that attention, and think with himself that it is perhaps the capital excellence of the work. Yet the author has by no means prosecuted this part of his subject to the injury of other parts. The Messianic prophecies, which form so marked a portion of Isaiah, have due care bestowed on them, and the evangelical interpretation is throughout skilfully and successfully maintained. The author, indeed, does not exalt anything into a type or prediction of Christ merely because it occurs in the writings of a prophet ; but, on the other hand, he has no rationalistic bias inclining him to explain away such prophecies as the Church has all along applied to the Messiah. His good sense never forsakes him. The sobriety of his judgment is seen in the manner in which he deals with the questions of the literal restoration of the Jews, and the personal reign of Christ. If the advocates of these doctrines are not satisfied with his conclusions, they will seldom or never find reason to complain of his candour.

The peculiarities of this edition are the careful revision to which the text has been subjected ; additional Notes where these were required ; references to supplementary Notes in former volumes, under those places where the author's views were supposed to be at variance with the received theology of our church and country ; to which must be added very many additional pictorial illustrations. Numerous errors, in the Hebrew text particularly, had crept into the American edition ; these have been corrected ; and care has been taken to present the pointed Hebrew throughout with due accuracy. The supplementary Notes would have been perhaps more numerous, but for the fact that the author's peculiarities had been reviewed at length in the New Testament volumes, and therefore a simple reference seemed all that was needed. The aim, from the first, has been to supply no more Notes than were absolutely required, that the author might appear in his own dress, with as little foreign admixture as possible.

May this work be abundantly blessed. May it revive in our land, and especially in our youth, a taste for the literature of the Bible, deepen in their minds the conviction of its inspiration, and dispose them to its study.

PREFACE TO THE FIRST EDITION.

It is with unaffected diffidence that this work is offered to the patronage of the Christian public. It has been prepared amidst the toils and responsibilities of a most laborious pastoral charge, and at such intervals as could be secured without seeming to infringe on the direct and immediate duties demanded in my station. Those hours have been, with scarcely an exception, the early morning hours ; and whatever may be the manner in which this book may be received by the public, whether it shall or shall not contribute in any degree to advance the knowledge of the truth, and the love of the sacred Scriptures, its preparation, by requiring me to commence each day with the direct contemplation of an interesting portion of inspired truth, has for four years constituted one of the most delightful parts of my work. It is the production of many a laborious, but many a pleasant, hour ; and while I desire to render thanks to the Giver of life and health, that he has granted me strength to engage in these studies, I shall ever look back with gratitude to the deeply interesting moments in which I have been endeavouring to illustrate the ' Visions of Isaiah.'

When I commenced the work, I designed nothing farther than an *enlargement* of Lowth on Isaiah. It occurred to me that it might be useful to retain his Notes as a *basis*, with some additional illustrations. But this plan was soon abandoned ; and no other use has been made of Lowth than that which is common with other writers. Valuable as are his Notes, and beautiful as is his version, yet it was soon perceived, or thought to be perceived, that greater usefulness might be secured by enlarging the plan, and making a work entirely new. Very valuable helps have been furnished, since the time of Lowth, for the illustration of the Hebrew prophets ; and it was deemed desirable to avail myself of them all, so far as it was in my power. Most of those helps will be found enumerated in the list of works on Isaiah, at the close of the Introduction, § 8.

Some of the reasons which led to the wish to illustrate Isaiah, are the following : (1.) He is one of the most beautiful and sublime of the sacred writers. (2.) In some respects his writings are among the most difficult portions of the Old Testament. (3.) His prophecies are so closely connected with interesting historical events, and furnish so much opportunity of illustration from archæology, oriental customs, and the investigations of modern travellers, that it is highly desirable that all the light should be thrown upon them which is possible from these sources. (4.) The fulfilment of prophecy is perhaps more clear.

minute, and striking in Isaiah than in any other of the prophets; and a commentary, therefore, on his writings, compared with the present state of the countries to which his prophecies refer, as reported by modern travellers, and especially with the record of the life, and doctrines, and death of Christ, will constitute itself a demonstration of the divine origin of the sacred Scriptures, and may be made one of the best antidotes against infidelity. It is impossible, it is believed, with an honest mind, to compare the predictions of Isaiah respecting Babylon, Moab, Tyre, and Idumea, with the travels of Volney, Burckhardt, Seetzen, Sir R. K. Porter, Maundrell, Laborde, and Stephens, without the fullest conviction that he who uttered these predictions, two thousand and five hundred years since, was divinely inspired. It is impossible to believe that this could have been the result of political sagacity; it is equally impossible to believe that it could have been produced by chance or conjecture. And, in like manner, it is impossible to compare his full, minute, and glowing descriptions of the Messiah, with the life of the Lord Jesus Christ; to collate minutely and critically, for example, the prophecies in the ixth, the xith, the xxxvth, the liid, the liiid chapters, with what actually occurred in the life, the sufferings, and the death of the Redeemer, without the fullest conviction that he was permitted to see, in distinct vision, events which were to take place in future times. No man can be a close student of Isaiah, and remain an infidel; no man can study his writings with prayer, who will not find his faith confirmed, his heart warmed, his mind elevated and purified, and his affections more firmly fixed on the beauty of the everlasting truth of God.

But the main reason which led to the selection of Isaiah as a subject of exposition was, his strongly evangelical character, and the fact, that he, more than any other prophet, has unfolded the future glories, and predicted the triumphs of the church on earth. He has been usually styled 'the fifth Evangelist;' and it is certain that there was vouchsafed to him a clearer view of the universal spread of the gospel, and of the blessedness of the reign of the Messiah, than was granted to any other of the ancient prophets. It was this characteristic mainly which has prompted to this attempt to make his sentiments more widely known, and more clearly understood. In an age distinguished, more than any other since that of the apostles, for efforts for the conversion of the whole world to God, nothing will so entirely fall in with the leading characteristics and efforts of the times as an attempt to establish some just views of the right interpretation of the prophecies on this subject. Men will put forth great and noble exertions when the object is clearly defined, and when they have some distinct view of what it is possible to attain. A right apprehension of what *is to be* on earth, will do much to form the plans and shape the efforts of those who seek the world's conversion. It will do much to suppress unauthorized hopes, to repress wild and visionary schemes, and to secure well-founded and judicious efforts to accomplish the object. A correct understanding of the prophecies, therefore, is necessary to direct those who are forming plans for the conversion of the world, and to uphold the hands and to encourage the hearts of those who are engaged in practically executing the work.

There is one advantage on this subject, in contemplating the *entire* prophecies in a book, above what would arise from *selecting* the portions which relate to the final triumph of the gospel, and forming a commentary on them exclusively. As the predictions now stand in the prophets, they are intermingled with predictions respecting *other* events which have been strikingly and clearly fulfilled. The mind is carried forward therefore *amidst demonstrations ;* the certain conviction of the mind that the predictions respecting Babylon, Tyre, Moab, and Idumea *have been fulfilled,* is carried to the contemplation of the predictions respecting things yet to come. The mind ranges amidst proofs of the divine origin of the book which is examined ; and these proofs strengthen the faith in regard to the events which are yet to come. He performs some service for his generation, who contributes in any degree to unfold the meaning of the ancient predictions, and to show to the Christian church what the world yet will be ; and he who contributes in any manner so to blend the arguments for the past fulfilment of prophecy with the predictions of what is yet to be on earth, does not live entirely in vain. It is doubtless with this view that the predictions respecting the Messiah, and the final universal triumph of the gospel, are *scattered along* and *intermingled with* predictions that relate to events that would be of more immediate fulfilment. The student of the prophecies thus walks amidst the monuments of their truth which time has set up along his way;—not much unlike the traveller who is seeking a distant land amidst much that is obscure and uncertain ; who encounters rapid streams and lofty crags and hills ; whose paths lead through dense and entangled forests ; but who yet finds every now and then monuments erected which show him that the road *has* been travelled, and which prove that the same path which others have trod will lead him to the place which he desires to reach. He who has attentively examined Isaiah, and compared the predictions respecting events which are now passed, with their fulfilment, is not likely to be a man whose faith will be shaken in regard to the reality of the inspiration of the Book of God, or to the final prevalence of religion all over the world. As an illustration of the influence of Isaiah in forming the opinions of Christians in regard to the character of the better days which are to bless the world, we may advert to the fact that the views of most Christians respecting the Millennium are probably derived from this prophet; and that even after the revelations of the New Testament, if we wish to obtain full and clear conceptions of what the world is yet to be under the reign of the Prince of Peace, we instinctively turn to the glowing visions of the son of Amoz. It has been one of the constant and earnest prayers of the author of these Notes, that his labours may contribute to the confirmation of the faith of Christians in respect to the final triumph of Christianity; and to the augmentation of their zeal in spreading the gospel around the world.

In the fulfilment of this design, as well as to exhibit the true meaning of the prophet, I have availed myself of all the helps within my reach, to show that the prophecies pertaining to events already passed, have been minutely and strikingly fulfilled. In these portions of the book, my first aim has been to settle, as well as I could, the exact sense of the prophet by philological investigation, and then to adduce the testimony of modern travellers in regard to the *present* condition of the countries so described. Modern travellers have contributed much to the confirmation of the truth of the prophetic statements; and if these Notes have *any* value above what is found in the common expositions of Isaiah, it is probably in this respect. In illustration of this, reference may be made to the prophecies respecting Babylon, Moab, Damascus, Tyre and Idumea, in the xiiith, xivth, xvth, xvith, xviith, xxxiiid, and xxxivth chapters.

In the preparation of these Notes I have availed myself of all the aids within my reach. The books from which I have derived most assistance are WALTON'S POLYGLOTT; the Critici Sacri; Poole's Synopsis; Calmet's Dictionary; Vitringa; Rosenmüller; Calvin; Gesenius; Jerome; Bochart's Hierozoicon; Taylor's Heb. Con.; Lowth's and Noyes' Versions; Keith on the Prophecies; Newton on the Prophecies; Hengstenberg's Christology; and the writings of oriental travellers to which I have had access. I have also derived considerable aid from the Biblical Repository, and from Prof. Bush's Scripture Illustrations.

This work is committed now to the Christian public with the fervent prayer that it may do good. The public—for whose favourable regards thus far in life I have had abundant reason to be grateful—will receive kindly what is kindly meant. It is not *right* to deprecate criticism, for every man who makes a book subjects himself, of his own choice, to the free remarks of all who may choose to notice his productions. His works, henceforward, whatever they may be, belong not to himself alone, but to the public at large; and no author has a right to complain if his style, his opinions, his arguments, his illustrations, are freely examined. For such examination he should be grateful, come from what quarter it may—if it help him to amend his style, to correct his errors, to suggest better illustrations, to remove obscurity, to advance sounder arguments, and in any way to make his works more worthy of the patronage of the public. *He* has a right to demand only that criticisms should be in the spirit of Christian love—that they should not be made *for the sake* of criticism, and that they should not be carping or petulant. He has a right to ask that those who examine his positions should *presume* that he has bestowed labour and thought on them, and that labour and thought should be reciprocated in judging of them before they are condemned. He has a right to expect that assertion in regard to his opinions should not be deemed sufficient to supply the place of argument; and that the uttering of an opinion *ex cathedra* should not be allowed to take the place of a candid and prayerful investigation of the meaning of words, and phrases, and figures of speech; of a careful inquiry into whatever in archæology, philology, geography, or travels, may throw light on the meaning of God's word. Argument should meet argument; thought conflict with thought; and truth should be elicited by manly, liberal, and candid discussion. The only object should be truth; and every author should be thankful to any man who will suggest to him what he had forgotten; communicate what to him was unknown; correct or refute what was erroneous; and thus make him more useful to his fellow-men.

It is not improper, however, as a matter of mere justice to myself, to suggest one other thing to those who may be disposed to examine this work. A man burdened with the cares and toils of a pastoral office, has not the advantages of preparing a work for the public which they have who are favoured with the entire command of their time, or whose professional duties *require* them to pursue a course of study that shall be in accordance with what they may choose to submit to the press. The pastors of the churches, for whose use more especially this work is intended, will know how to appreciate this remark ; and they who know the toils of that office will not judge unkindly or severely of what is designed as a means of enlarging the sphere of usefulness in which a man is placed ; or of contributing in any, the humblest degree, to illustrate the truth of the Bible, to confirm the churches in its inspiration, to unfold its beauties, and to aid in the exposition of truth. Lord Bacon has said, 'I HOLD EVERY MAN TO BE A DEBTOR TO HIS PROFESSION ;' and they who appreciate the force of this remark will look with kindness on every effort to enlarge the sphere of the usefulness of those who are by their office expositors of the word of God.

With these remarks, this work is committed to the world. The desires of my heart will be gratified if it is the means, in any degree, of confirming the faith of man in the inspiration of the Divine oracles, and of hastening the triumphs of that day when ' the wilderness and the solitary place shall be glad, and the desert shall rejoice and blossom as the rose,' and when ' the ransomed of JEHOVAH shall return and come to Zion with songs, and everlasting joy upon their heads.' Isa. xxxv. 1, 10.

ALBERT BARNES.

Philadelphia, Nov. 14, 1838.

PREFACE TO THE SECOND EDITION.

Since the publication of the first edition of this work, I have twice carefully revised it. In doing this, while the main features of the exposition have been retained, I have endeavoured to render it more worthy of the patronage of the Christian public. I have availed myself of all the criticisms made on it which I have seen, and have adopted all the suggestions which appeared to me to be well founded. My principal aim has been to *condense* the work as much as possible, by removing redundant words, and by excluding whatever did not contribute to the elucidation of the Prophet. The work was originally published in three large octavo volumes. By using a different type ; by the omission of the 'New Translation' inserted in the former edition, and by the abridgments which have been made, I am now able to present it in a much narrower compass, and at a price which will make it much more easy to procure it. It may perhaps be of interest to some to know that in revising it, I have stricken out matter, besides the 'New Translation,' to the amount of about one hundred and twenty octavo pages, and have introduced new matter to the amount of about fifty pages. In a few places additions of considerable extent have been made. For the *new* matter I am under special obligations to the Biblical Researches of Dr. Robinson, and Mr. Smith, and to the work of Wilkinson on the Manners and Customs of the Ancient Egyptians. By the aid of the 'Researches' I have been enabled to correct several places relating to the geography of Palestine, and to throw important light on several passages of the Prophet. I have, in fact, incorporated in the Notes all that I have found in that invaluable work which seemed to me to illustrate in any way the writings of Isaiah, and as nothing better can be hoped for on the Holy Land, this part of the work may be considered to be complete. The favourable manner in which the first edition was received made it obligatory on me to do all that I could to make it more worthy of patronage, and again I commit it to the world, with the hope that it may contribute in some degree to the illustration of this sublime and beautiful portion of the inspired volume.

ALBERT BARNES.

Washington Square, Philadelphia, June 23. 1845.

INTRODUCTION.

§ 1. *Division of the Books of the Old Testament.*

THE Jews early divided the books of the Old Testament into three parts—the *Law*, the *Prophets*, and the *Hagiographa*, or holy writings. The *Law* comprised the five books of Moses; and the priority was given to this division because it was the first composed, as well as on account of its containing their civil and ecclesiastical constitution, and their oldest historical records. The *Prophets* comprised the second and the largest division of the sacred writings of the Jews. This portion comprehended the books of Joshua, Judges, 1 and 2 Samuel, 1 and 2 Kings, which were called the *former prophets ;* and Isaiah, Jeremiah, Ezekiel, and the books from Hosea to Malachi, which were called the *latter prophets.* Daniel has been excluded from this portion by the later Jews, and assigned to the third division, because they regard him not as a prophet, but as an historical writer. Formerly his work was doubtless included in the second division. The third portion, *the Hagiographa*, comprises the Psalms, Proverbs, Job, Song of Solomon, Ruth, Lamentations, Ecclesiastes, Esther, Daniel, Ezra and Nehemiah, and the two books of Chronicles. This division of the Old Testament is as old as the time of our Saviour, for he refers to it in Luke xxiv. 44. The Jews attribute the arrangement and division of the canonical books to Ezra. They say that he was assisted in this by one hundred and twenty men who constituted 'a great Synagogue ;' that Daniel, and his three friends, Shadrach, Meshach, and Abednego, were of this number; and that Haggai and Zechariah, together with Simon the Just, also were connected with it. But this statement is known to be erroneous. From the time of Daniel to the time of Simon the Just, not less than two hundred and fifty years intervened (Alexander on the Canon, pp. 26, 27); and of course all these persons could not have been present. It is not, however, improbable that Ezra may have been assisted by learned and pious men who aided him in the work. What Ezra *did* is indeed unknown. It is the general opinion that he collected and arranged the books which now compose the Old Testament ; that perhaps he wrote some of the historical books, or compiled them from fragments of history and documents that might have been in the public archives (comp. the ANALYSIS of Isa. ch. xxxvi.); and that he gave a finish and arrangement to the whole. As Ezra was an inspired man, the arrangement of the sacred books, and the portions which he may have added, have thus the sanction of Divine authority. There is no evidence, however, that Ezra *completed* the canon of the Old Testament. Malachi lived after him, and in the first book of Chronicles (ch. iii.) the genealogy of the sons of Zerubbabel is carried down to the time of Alexander the Great—about one hundred and thirty years subsequent to the time of Ezra. The probability is, therefore, that Ezra *commenced* the arrangement of the books, and that the canon of the Old Testament was completed by some other hand.

The 'prophets' were divided into *the former* and *the latter*. Among the latter, Isaiah has uniformly held the first place and rank. This has been assigned him not because he prophesied before all the others. He indeed preceded Ezekiel and Jeremiah, but Jonah, Amos, and Hosea were his contemporaries. The precedence has been given to his prophecies over theirs, probably for two reasons; first, on account of their length, dignity, and comparative value; and secondly, because formerly the minor prophets were bound in one volume, or written on one roll of parchment, and it was convenient to place them *together*, and they all had a place, therefore, after Isaiah. At all times his prophecies have been regarded as the most important of any in the Old Testament; and by common consent they have been deemed worthy of the principal place among the Jewish writings.

§ 2. *Life of Isaiah, and the Characteristics of his Writings.*

Of the time in which Isaiah lived, little more is known than he has himself told us. In the superscription to his book (ch. i. 1), we are told that he was the son of Amoz, and that he discharged the prophetic office under the reign of the kings Uzziah, Jotham, Ahaz, and Hezekiah. In regard to those times, and the character of the period in which they reigned, see Introduction, § 3. It is evident also from the prophecies themselves, that he delivered them during the reign of these kings. In ch. vi. 1, it is expressly said that he had a vision of JEHOVAH in the year in which Uzziah died. Of course he must have commenced his prophetic labours at least as early as during the last year of that king. If that chapter or vision was not designed as an inauguration of the prophet, or an induction into the prophetic office (see Notes on the chapter), and if his prophecies were collected and arranged as they were delivered, then it will follow that the previous chapters (i.–v.) may have been delivered in the reign of Uzziah, and perhaps some time before his death. There is no express mention made of his uttering any prophecies in the time of Jotham. Hengstenberg and others suppose that the prophecies in ch. ii.–v. were delivered during his reign. But of this there is no conclusive evidence. He might not have *recorded* anything during his reign; though he may, as a public preacher, have been engaged in the prophetic office in another mode. His writings themselves contain evidence that he was engaged in the prophetic office in the reign of Ahaz. See ch. vii., seq. That he was engaged in the prophetic office during the reign of Hezekiah we learn from chs. xxxvi.–xxxix. We have an explicit statement that he was occupied in his prophetic work until the fifteenth year of Hezekiah, at the commencement of which the ambassadors from Babylon came up to Jerusalem to congratulate him on his recovery from his illness; ch. xxxix. Uzziah died, according to Calmet, 754 years before Christ. Isaiah must therefore have occupied the prophetic office at least from 754 years before Christ to 707 years before Christ, or forty-seven years ; that is, under Uzziah one year, under Jotham sixteen years, under Ahaz sixteen years, and under Hezekiah fourteen years. It is not known at what age he entered on the prophetic office. It is probable that he lived much longer than to the fifteenth year of Hezekiah. In 2 Chron. xxxii. 32, it is said that ' the rest of the acts of Hezekiah ' were ' written in the vision of Isaiah ;' and this statement obviously implies that he survived him, and wrote the acts of his reign up to his death. As Hezekiah lived fourteen or fifteen years after this (Isa. xxxviii. 5. comp. 2 Kings xviii. 2), this would make the period of his public ministry to extend to at least sixty-one or sixty-two years. If he survived Hezekiah, he probably lived some time during the reign of Manasseh. This supposition is confirmed, not indeed by any direct historical record in the Old Testament, but by all the traditional accounts which have been handed down to us. The testimony of the Jews, and of the early fathers, is uniform that he was put to death by Manasseh by being sawn asunder. The main alleged offence was, that he had said that he had seen JEHOVAH, and that for this he ought to die, in accordance with the law of Moses (Ex. xxxiii. 20), ' No man shall see me and live.' If he lived to the time of Manasseh, and especially if he prophesied under him, it is probable the true reason why he was put to death was, that he was offensive to the monarch and his court.

The circumstances which render the supposition probable that he lived under Manasseh, and that he was put to death by him by being sawn asunder, are the following. (1.) The fact which has been stated above that he lived to complete the record of the reign of Hezekiah, and of course survived him. (2.) The testimony of the Jewish writers. There is, indeed, much that is fabulous in their writings, and even in connection with the truths which they record, there is much that is puerile and false ; but there is no reason to doubt the main *facts* which they relate. Josephus, indeed, does not expressly state that he was slain by Manasseh, but he gives an account of the reign of Manasseh which renders it probable that *if* Isaiah were then alive he would have been put to death. Thus he says (Ant. B. x. ch. iii. § 1) that ' he barbarously slew all the righteous men that were among the Hebrews ; nor would he spare the prophets, for he every day slew some of them, till Jerusalem was overflown with blood.' In the Talmud the following record occurs :—' Manasseh put Isaiah to death. The Rabbi said, he condemned him, and put him to death ; for he said to him, Moses, thy Lord said, No man shall see me and live (Ex. xxxiii. 20), but thou hast said, I saw the Lord upon a throne high and lifted up (Isa. vi. 1). Moses, thy Lord said, Who will make the Lord so near that we can call to him ; but thou hast said, Seek the Lord while he may be found, call upon him while he is near (lv. 6). Moses, thy Lord said, The number of thy days will I fulfil (Ex. xxii. 26); but thou hast said, I will add to thy days fifteen years (xxxviii. 5),' etc. See Gesenius Einlei. p. 12. The testimony of the Jews on this subject is uniform. Michaelis (Preface to Isaiah) has referred to the following places in proof on this point. Tract. Talmud. *Jabhamoth*, fol. 49; *Sanhedrin*, fol. 103; *Jalkut*, part ii. fol. 38; *Schalscheleth Hakkab.* fol. 19. Raschi and Abarbanel in their commentaries give the same statement. (3.)

The testimony of the early Christian writers is the same.   Justin Martyr, in
his dialogue with Trypho the Jew (p. 349), speaking of Isaiah, says, ὃν πρίονι
ζύλῳ ἐπρίσατε, 'whom ye sawed asunder with a wooden saw.'—Tertullian (do
patientia, c. 14) says, His patientiae viribus secatur Esaias.—Lactantius (lib.
iv. c. 2) says, Esais, quem ipsi Judaei serrâ consectum crudelissime necaverunt.
—Augustine (de Civit. Dei, lib. 18, c. 24) says, 'the prophet Isaiah is reputed
to have been slain by the impious King Manasseh.'   Jerome (on Isa. lvii. 1)
says, that the prophet prophesied in that passage of his own death, for 'it is
an undisputed tradition among us, that he was sawn asunder by Manasseh,
with a wooden saw.'   These passages and others from the Jewish writers, and
from the fathers, are to be found in Michaelis' Preface to Isaiah ; in Gesenius'
Introduction ; and in Carpzov. Crit. Sacr.   In a matter of simple fact, there
seems to be no reason to call this testimony in question.   It is to be remembered that Jerome was well acquainted with Hebrew, that he dwelt in Palestine, and no doubt has given the prevalent opinion about the death of Isaiah.
(4.) The character of Manasseh was such as to make it probable that if Isaiah
lived at all during his reign, he would seek his death.   In 2 Kings xxi. 16, it
is said of him that he 'shed innocent blood very much, till he had filled Jerusalem from one end to another.'   This account is in entire accordance with
that of Josephus, quoted above.   In the early part of his reign, it is recorded
that he did evil, and especially that he reared the high places and the altars
of idolatry which Hezekiah had destroyed, and endeavoured to restore again
the abominations which had existed in the time of Ahab.   2 Kings xxi. 2, 3.
It is scarcely credible that such a man as Isaiah would see all this done without
some effort to prevent it; and it is certain that such an effort would excite the
indignation of Manasseh.   If, however, he cut off the righteous men of Jerusalem, as Josephus testifies, and as the author of the books of Kings would
lead us to believe, there is every probability that Isaiah would also fall a
sacrifice to his indignation.   It is not necessary in order to this to suppose
that Isaiah appeared much in public; or that, being then an old man, he
should take a prominent part in the transactions of that period.   That we
have no *recorded* prophecy of that time, as we have of the times of Uzziah,
Ahaz, and Hezekiah, leaves it probable that Isaiah had withdrawn from the
more public functions of the prophetic office, and probably (see § iv. of this
Introduction) had given himself to the calm and holy contemplation of future
and better times under the Messiah.   But still his sentiments would be known
to the monarch ; and his influence while he lived among the people may have
been materially in the way of the designs of Manasseh.   Manasseh, therefore, may have regarded it as necessary to remove him, and in the slaughter
of the good men and prophets of his time, there is every probability that
Isaiah would be made a victim.   (5.) It affords some confirmation of this
statement that Paul (Heb. xi. 37) affirms of some of the ancient saints, that
they were 'sawn asunder.'   There is not in the Old Testament any express
mention of any one's being put to death in this manner; but it has been common with all expositors, from the earliest periods, to suppose that Paul had
reference to Isaiah.   The universal tradition on this subject among the
Hebrews makes this morally certain.   It is certain that Paul could not have

made such an enumeration unless there was a well-established tradition of some one or more who had suffered in this manner; and all tradition concurs in assigning it to Isaiah. (6.) The character of the second part of the prophecies of Isaiah (chs. xl.–lxvi.) accords with this supposition. They are *mainly* employed in depicting the glories of a future age; the blessedness of the times of the Messiah. They bespeak the feelings of a holy man who was heart-broken with the existing state of things; and who had retired from active life, and sought consolation in the contemplation of future blessings. No small part of those prophecies is employed in lamenting an existing state of *idolatry* (see particularly chs. xl. xli. lvi. lvii. lxv.), and the prevalence of general irreligion. Such a description does not accord with the reign of Hezekiah; and it is evidently the language of a man who was disheartened with prevailing abominations, and who, seeing little hope of immediate reform, cast his mind forward into future times, and sought repose in the contemplation of happier days. How *long* he lived under Manasseh is unknown; and hence it is not possible to ascertain his age when he was put to death. We may reasonably suppose that he entered on his prophetic office as early as the age of twenty. From Jer. i. 6, we learn that an earlier call than this to the prophetic office sometimes occurred. On this supposition he would have been eighty-two years of age at the death of Hezekiah. There is no improbability, therefore, in the supposition that he might have lived ten or even fifteen years or more, under the long reign of Manasseh. The priest Jehoiada attained the great age of one hundred and thirty years, 2 Chron. xxiv. 15. Isaiah lived evidently a retired and a temperate life. It is the uniform tradition of the oriental Christians that he lived to the age of one hundred and twenty years ; see Hengstenberg's Christol. vol. i. p. 278.

Where he lived is not certainly known ; nor are many of the circumstances of his life known. His permanent residence, in the earlier part of his prophetic life, seems to have been at Jerusalem. During the reign of the ungodly Ahaz, he came forth boldly as the reprover of sin, and evidently spent a considerable part of his time near the court, ch. vii. seq. His counsels and warnings were then derided and disregarded. Hezekiah was a pious prince, and admitted him as a counsellor, and was inclined to follow his advice. In his reign he was treated with respect, and he had an important part in directing the public counsels during the agitating occurrences of that reign. If he lived in the time of Manasseh, he probably retired from public life; his counsel was unsought, and if offered, was disregarded. It is evident that he did not *entirely* withdraw from his office as a reprover (chs. lvi.–lviii), but his main employment seems to have been to contemplate the pure and splendid visions which relate to the happier times of the world, and which constitute the close of his prophecies, chs. xl.–lxvi.

Of the family of Isaiah little is known. The Jewish writers constantly affirm that he was of noble extraction, and was closely connected with the royal family. The name of his father was Amoz, or *Amotz*—אָמוֹץ ; not the prophet Amos, as some have supposed, for *his* name in Hebrew is עָמוֹס, Amos. Amoz, or Amotz, the father of Isaiah, the Jews affirm to have been the brother of Amaziah the son of Joash, king of Judah, 2 Kings xiv. 1. Thus D. Kimchi on Isa. i. 1, writes, 'We are ignorant of his family, from what tribe he was, except that our doctors have handed it down by tradition that Amotz and Amaziah were brothers.' And thus R. Solomon says, ' It is handed down to us from our ancestors that Amotz and Amaziah were brothers.' The same is said also by R. Levi (in Megilla, c. i. fol. 10); and by Abarbanel, Pref. fol. 1 (quoted by Michaelis, Pref. to Isa.) In this supposition there is nothing improbable; and the fact that he was admitted so freely to the counsels of Hezekiah, and that he went so boldly to Ahaz (ch. vii. 1, seq.), may seem to give some countenance to the idea that he was connected with the royal family. His father was evidently well known; see ch. i. 1, and elsewhere, where his name is introduced. Indeed, it is not improbable that most of the prophets were descended from families that were highly respectable, as they generally mention the name of their father as a name that is well known; comp. Ezek. i. 3; Jer. i. 1; Hos. i. 1; Joel i. 1; Jonah i. 1; Zeph. i. 1; Zec. i. 1. In the other prophets the name of the *father* is omitted, probably because he was obscure and unknown. It is morally certain that Isaiah was not connected with the Levitical order, since if he had been, this would have been designated as in Jer. i. 1; Ezek. i. 3. The wife of Isaiah is called a prophetess (ch. viii. 3), and it is supposed by some that she had the spirit of prophecy; but the more probable opinion is, that the wives of the prophets were called prophetesses, as the wives of the priests were called priestesses. On the question whether he had more than one wife, see Notes on chs. vii. viii. Two sons of Isaiah are mentioned, both of whom had names fitted to awaken religious attention, and who were in some sense the pledges of the fulfilment of divine predictions. The name of the one was ' SHEAR-JASHUB ' (ch. vii. 3), the meaning of which is, *the remainder shall return*—designed, undoubtedly, to be a sign or pledge that the remnant of the Jews who should be carried away *at any time* would return; or that the whole nation would not be destroyed and become extinct. This was one of the *axioms*, or fundamental points in all the writings of this prophet; and whatever calamity or judgment he foretold, it was always terminated with the assurance that the nation should be still ultimately preserved, and greatly enlarged, and glorified. This idea he seems to have resolved to keep as much as possible before the minds of his countrymen, and to this end he gave his son a name that should be to them a pledge of his deep conviction of this truth. The name of the other is MAHER-SHALAL-HASH-BAZ (ch. viii. 1), *haste to the spoil; haste to the prey*—a name significant of the fact that the Assyrian (ch. vii.) would soon ravage and subdue the land, or would extensively plunder the kingdom of Judea. Tradition says that the death of Isaiah occurred in Jerusalem, near the fountain of Siloam. Just below this fountain and opposite to the point where Mount Ophel terminates, is a large mulberry-tree, with a terrace of stones surrounding its trunk, where it is said Isaiah was sawn asunder; Robinson's Bib. Research, i. 342. The tradition further is, that his body was buried here, whence it was removed to Paneas near the sources of the Jordan, and from thence to Constantinople in the year of our Lord 442.

Great respect was paid to Isaiah and his writings after his death. It is evident that Jeremiah imitated him (comp. Notes on chs. xv. xvi.); and there is abundant evidence that he was studied by the other prophets. The estimate in which he was held by the Lord Jesus, and by the writers of the New Testament, will be shown in another part of this Introduction ; see § viii. Josephus (Ant. B. xi. ch. i. § 2) says that Cyrus was moved by the reading of Isaiah to the acknowledgment of the God of Israel, and to the restoration of the Jews, and to the rebuilding of the temple. After stating (§ 1) the decree which Cyrus made in favour of the Jews, he adds, ' This was known to Cyrus by his reading the book which Isaiah left behind him of his prophecies ; for this prophet had said that God had spoken thus to him in a secret vision, " My will is that Cyrus, whom I have appointed to be king over many and great nations, send back my people to their own land, and build my temple." This was foretold by Isaiah one hundred and forty years before the temple was demolished. Accordingly, when Cyrus read this, and admired the divine power, an earnest desire and ambition came upon him to fulfil what was so written ; so he called for the most eminent Jews that were in Babylon, and said to them, that he gave them leave to go back to their own country, and to rebuild their city Jerusalem and the temple of their God.' In this passage of Josephus there is an undoubted reference to Isa. xliv. 28; ' That saith of Cyrus, He is my Shepherd, and shall perform all my pleasure, even saying to Jerusalem, Thou shalt be built ; and to the temple, Thy foundation shall be laid ;' comp. ch. xlv. 1, seq. On the genuineness of this passage of Josephus see Whiston's Note. It is justly remarked (see Jahn's observation, quoted by Hengstenberg, Christol. i. 279) that this statement of Josephus furnishes the only explanation of the conduct of Cyrus towards the Jews. It is only a commentary on Ezra i. 2, where Cyrus says, ' JEHOVAH the God of heaven and earth hath given me all the kingdoms of the earth ; and he hath charged me to build him an house at Jerusalem which is in Judah.' It is incredible that Cyrus should not have seen the prophecy (Isa. xliv. 28) respecting himself before he made this proclamation.

The writings of the fathers are full of the praise of Isaiah. Jerome says of him that he is not so much to be esteemed a prophet as an Evangelist. And he adds, ' he has so clearly explained the whole mystery of Christ and the church, that you will regard him not as predicting future events, but as composing a history of the past.' In his Epistle ad Paulinum he says, ' Isaiah seems to me not to have composed a prophecy, but the gospel.' And in his Preface he says, ' that in his discourse he is so eloquent, and is a man of so noble and refined elocution, without any mixture of rusticity, that it is impossible to preserve or transfuse the beauty of his style in a translation ;' comp. the Confess. of Augus. ix. 5; De Civita. Dei. lib. viii. c. 29. Moses Amyraldus said of Isaiah that he ' seems to thunder and lighten ; he seems to confound and mingle not Greece, as was formerly said of Pericles ; not Judea, and the neighbouring regions, but heaven and earth and all the elements ;' see Michælis Pref. to Isa. p. 8, 9, 10; comp. Joseph. Ant. B. x. c. 3; Sirach ch. xlviii. 22.

' The style of Isaiah,' says Hengstenberg, Christol. vol. i. p. 281, ' is in general characterized by simplicity and sublimity ; in the use of imagery, he holds an intermediate place between the poverty of Jeremiah and the exuberance of Ezekiel. In other respects his style is suited to the subject, and changes with it. In his denunciations and threatenings he is earnest and vehement ; in his consolations and instructions, on the contrary, he is mild and insinuating ; in the strictly poetic passages, full of impetuosity and fire. He so lives in the events he describes, that the future becomes to him as the past and the present.'

It is now generally conceded that a considerable portion of Isaiah, like the other prophets, is poetry. For the establishment of this opinion, we are indebted mainly to Bishop Lowth. 'It has,' says he, (Prelim. Diss. to Isaiah) 'I think, been universally understood that the prophecies of Isaiah were written in prose. The style, the thoughts, the images, the expressions, have been allowed to be poetical, and that in the highest degree ; but that they were written in verse, in measure, in rhythm, or whatever it is that distinguishes as poetry the composition of those books of the Old Testament which are allowed to be poetical, such as Job, the Psalms, and the Proverbs, from the historical books, as mere prose, this has never been supposed, at least has not been at any time the prevailing feeling.'

The main object of Lowth, in his Preliminary Dissertation, was to demonstrate that the prophecies of Isaiah have all the characteristics of Hebrew poetry ; a position which he has abundantly established, and which is admitted now by all to be correct. For a more extended view of the nature of Hebrew poetry, the reader may consult my Introduction to the Book of Job, pp. xxxix–liv.

In all ages Isaiah has been regarded as the most sublime of all writers. He is simple, bold, rapid, elevated ; he abounds in metaphor, and in rapid transitions ; his writings are full of the sublimest figures of rhetoric, and the most beautiful ornaments of poetry. Grotius compares him to Demosthenes. 'In his writings we meet with the purity of the Hebrew tongue, as in the orator with the delicacy of the Attic taste. Both are sublime and magnificent in their style ; vehement in their emotions ; copious in their figures ; and very impetuous when they describe things of an enormous nature, or that are grievous and odious. Isaiah was superior to Demosthenes in the honour of illustrious birth.' Comm. on 2 Kings xix. 2. It may be added here, that although his writings are not so ancient as those of Moses, or as those of Homer and Hesiod, yet they are more ancient than most of the admired classic productions of Greece, and are far more ancient than any of the Latin classics. As an *ancient writer* he demands respect. And laying out of view altogether the idea of his inspiration, and his *religious* character, he has a claim as a poet, an orator, a writer of eminent beauty and unrivalled sublimity, to the attention of those who are seeking eminence in literature. No reason can be given why in a course of mental training, Isaiah, and the language in which he wrote, should be neglected, while Hesiod and Homer, with the language in which they wrote, should be the objects of admiration and of diligent culture. In no book, perhaps, can the mere man of taste be more gratified than in the study of Isaiah ; by no writings would the mind be more elevated in view of the beautiful and the sublime, or the heart be more refined by the contemplation of the pure. Few, very few of the Greek and Latin classic writers can be put into the hands of the young without endangering the purity of their morals; but Isaiah may be studied in all the periods of youth, and manhood, and age, only to increase the virtue of the heart and the purity of the imagination, at the same time that he enriches and expands the understanding. And while no one who has just views of the inestimable value of the Greek and Latin classics in most of the respects contemplated in education, would wish to see them banished from the schools, or displaced from seminaries of learning, yet the lover of ancient writings; of purity of thought and diction ; of sweet and captivating poetry; of the beautiful and sublime in writing ; of perhaps the oldest language of the world, and of the pure sentiments of revelation, may hope that the time will come when the Hebrew language shall be deemed worthy of culture in American schools and colleges as well as the Latin and Greek ; and that as a part of the training of American youth, Isaiah may be allowed to take a place *at least* as honourable as Virgil or Homer—as Cicero or Demosthenes. It is indeed a melancholy reflection which we are compelled to make on the seminaries of learning in our land—a Christian land—that the writings of the Hebrew prophets and poets have been compelled to give place to the poetry and the mythology of the Greeks; and that the books containing the only system of pure religion are required to defer to those which were written under the auspices of idolatry, and which often express sentiments, and inculcate feelings, which cannot be made to contribute to the purity of the heart, or be reconciled with the truth as revealed from heaven. As specimens of taste; as models of richness of thought and beauty of diction ; as well as for their being the vehicles in which the knowledge of the only true religion is conveyed to man, these writings have a claim on the attention of the young. Were the writings of Isaiah mere human compositions ; had they come down to us as the writings of Demosthenes and Homer have done ; and had they not been connected with *religion*, we may be permitted to express the belief, that the Jewish *classics, with* the classics of Greece and Rome, would have been allowed an honourable place in all the seminaries of learning, and in all the public and private libraries of the land.

§ 3. *The Times of Isaiah.*

Isaiah, as we have seen, lived for the greater part of a century, and possibly even more than a century. It is probable also that for a period of more than seventy years he exercised the prophetic office. During that long period, important changes must have occurred ; and a knowledge of some of the leading events of his time is necessary to understand his prophecies. Indeed a simple knowledge of historical facts will often make portions of his prophecies clear which would be otherwise entirely unintelligible.

The kingdom of Israel, which during the reigns of David and Solomon had been so mighty and so magnificent, was divided into two separate kingdoms 990 years before Christ, or two hundred and forty years before Isaiah entered on his prophetic office. The glory of these kingdoms had departed ; and they had been greatly weakened by contentions with each other, and by conflicts with surrounding nations. In a particular manner, the kingdom of Israel, or

Samaria, or Ephraim, or the ten tribes, as it was indiscriminately called, had been governed by a succession of wicked princes ; had become deeply imbued with idolatry, and had so far provoked God as to make it necessary to remove them to a foreign land. It was during the time in which Isaiah discharged the duties of the prophetic office that that kingdom was utterly overturned, and the inhabitants transplanted to a distant country. In the year 736 before Christ, or not far from twenty years after Isaiah entered on his work, Tiglath-Pileser king of Assyria slew Rezin king of Damascus, the ally of Pekah the king of Samaria ; and he entered the land of Israel, and took many cities and captives, chiefly in Gilead and Galilee, and carried many of the inhabitants to Assyria ; 2 Kings xvi. 5–9 ; Amos i. 5 ; 2 Kings xv. 29 ; 1 Chron. v. 26. This was the first captivity of the kingdom of Israel. Shalmaneser succeeded Tiglath-Pileser as king of Assyria B.C. 724. In the year 721 B.C. he besieged Samaria, and after a siege of three years he took it. He carried beyond the Euphrates the inhabitants which Tiglath-Pileser had not removed, and placed them in cities there ; 2 Kings xvii. 3–18 ; Hos. xiii. 16 ; 1 Chron. v. 26. This was the end of the kingdom of Israel, after it had subsisted two hundred and fifty-four years. Isaiah exercised the prophetic office during about thirty of the last years of the kingdom of Israel. But his residence was principally at Jerusalem ; and not many of his predictions have reference to the kingdom of Israel. Most of his prophecies which have reference to the Jews relate to the kingdom of Judah, and to Jerusalem.

The kingdom of Judah, whose capital was Jerusalem, had greatly declined from the splendour and magnificence which had existed under David and Solomon. It had been greatly weakened by the revolt of the ten tribes, and by the wars in which it had been engaged with the kingdom of Samaria, as well as with surrounding nations. Though its kings were superior in virtue and piety to the kings of Israel, yet many of them had been unworthy to be the descendants of David, and their conduct had exposed them greatly to the divine displeasure.

When Isaiah entered on his prophetic office the throne was occupied by Uzziah ; or as he is elsewhere called, Azariah. He succeeded his father Amaziah, and was sixteen years old when he came to the throne, and reigned fifty-two years. He began his reign in the year 809 B.C., and of course his reign extended to the year 757 B.C. His general character was that of integrity and piety. He was a worshipper of the true God, yet he did not remove the groves and high places which had been established in the land for idolatrous worship. He greatly strengthened Jerusalem ; was successful in his wars with the Philistines, with the Arabians, and the Ammonites, and extended his kingdom somewhat into surrounding regions. Near the close of his life he was guilty of an act of rashness and folly in claiming as a monarch the right of going into the temple of the Lord, and of burning incense on the altar. For this sin he became a leper and remained so till his death ; 2 Kings xv ; 2 Chron. xxvi. He was of course regarded as unclean, and was obliged to dwell by himself in a separate house ; 2 Chron. xxvi. 21. During this period, the affairs of the government were administered by his son Jotham ; 2 Chron. xxvi. 21. It is probable that Isaiah exercised the prophetic office but for a short time, perhaps for a single year, during the reign of Uzziah. None of his prophecies can be certainly proved to relate to his reign except that contained in the sixth chapter. It is more natural, however, to suppose that those in the previous five chapters were delivered in his reign.

Uzziah, or Azariah, was succeeded by his son Jotham. He ascended the throne at the age of twenty-five, and reigned sixteen years in Jerusalem. The general character of Jotham was like that of his father. He was upright; and he was not guilty of idolatry. Yet the high places were not removed; the groves still remained : and the state of the people was corrupt ; 2 Kings xv. 32–36 ; 2 Chron. xxvii. 1–9. He carried forward the plan which his father had commenced of fortifying the city (2 Chron. xxvi. 3), and of enlarging and beautifying his kingdom. In a particular manner, he is said to have built a high gate to the house of the Lord, and to have fortified Ophel ; 2 Chron. xxvi. 3. Ophel was a mountain or *bluff*, which was situated between Mount Zion and Mount Moriah. From the base of this mountain or bluff flowed the waters of Siloam. This bluff was capable of being strongly fortified, and of contributing much to the defence of the city, and accordingly it became one of the strongest places in Jerusalem. Jotham also built cities, and castles, and towns in the mountains and forests of Judea (2 Chron. xxvi. 4), and it is evident that his great aim was to beautify and strengthen his kingdom. The principal wars in which he was engaged were with the Ammonites, whom he subdued, and laid under tribute ; 2 Chron. xxvi. 5.

It was during the reign of Jotham that very important events occurred in the vast empire of the East. The ancient empire of the Assyrians which had governed Asia for more than thirteen hundred years was dissolved on the death of Sardanapalus in the year 747 before Christ. Sardanapalus was distinguished for sloth and luxury. He sunk into the lowest depths of depravity ; clothed himself as a woman ; spun amidst the companies of his concubines ; painted his face and decked himself as a harlot. So debased was he, that his reign became intolerable. He became odious to his subjects and particularly to Arbaces the Mede, and to Belesis the Babylonian. Belesis was a captain, a priest, and an astrologer ; and by the rules of his art, he took upon him to assure Arbaces that he should dethrone Sardanapalus, and become lord of all his dominions. Arbaces hearkened to him, and promised him the chief place over Babylon if his prediction proved true. Arbaces and Belesis promoted a revolt, and the defection spread among the Medes, Babylonians, Persians, and Arabians, who had been subject to the Assyrian empire. They mustered an army of not less than four hundred thousand men, but were at first defeated by Sardanapalus, and driven to the mountains ; but they again rallied and were again defeated with great slaughter, and put to flight towards the hills. Belesis, however, persisted in the opinion that the gods would give them the victory, and a third battle was fought, in which they were again defeated. Belesis again encouraged his followers ; and it was determined to endeavour to secure the aid of the Bactrians. Sardanapalus supposing victory was secure, and that there could be no more danger, had returned to his pleasures, and given himself and his army up to riot and dissipation. Belesis and Arbaces, with the aid of the Bactrians, fell upon the army, sunk in inglorious ease, and

entirely vanquished it, and drew Sardanapalus without the walls of his capital.
Here, closely besieged, he sent away his three sons and two daughters into
Paphlagonia. In Nineveh he determined to defend himself, trusting to an
ancient prophecy, " that Nineveh could never be taken till the river became
her enemy ; " and as he deemed this impossible, he regarded himself as secure.
He maintained his position, and resisted the attacks of his enemies for two
years, until the river, swelled by great rains, rose and overflowed a considerable part of it. Regarding his affairs as now desperate, he caused a vast pile
of wood to be raised in a court of his palace, in which he placed his gold and
silver and royal apparel, and within which he enclosed his eunuchs and concubines, and retired within his palace, and caused the pile to be set on fire,
and was consumed himself with the rest ; Universal History, Anc. Part, vol.
iii. pp. 354–358. Edit. Lond. 1779.

From this kingdom, thus destroyed, arose the two kingdoms of Assyria, as
mentioned in the Scriptures, and of Babylonia. Arbaces, who, according to
Prideaux, is the same as Tiglath-Pileser (comp. however Universal History,
vol. v. 359), obtained a large part of the empire. Belesis had Babylon,
Chaldea, and Arabia. Belesis, according to Prideaux (Connex. book i. p.
114), was the same as Nabonassar, or Baladan (see Note on ch. xxxix. 1); and
was the king from whom was reckoned the famous era of Nabonassar com-
mencing in the 747th year before the Christian era. It is not improbable
that there was some degree of dependence of the Babylonian portion of the
empire on the Assyrian ; or that the king of Babylon was regarded as a
viceroy to the king of Assyria, as we know that among the colonists sent by
Shalmaneser to people Samaria after the ten tribes were carried away, were
some from Babylon, which is there mentioned in such a manner as to leave
the impression that it was a province of Assyria ; 2 Kings xvii. 24. The
kingdom of Babylon, however, ultimately acquired the ascendency, and the
Assyrian was merged into the Chaldean monarchy. This occurred about one
hundred years after the reign of Nabonassar, or Baladan, and was effected by
an alliance formed between Nabopolassar and Cyaxares the Median ; see Rob.
Cal. Art. Babylonia ; comp. Note on ch. xxxix. 1. It should be observed,
however, that the history of the Assyrian empire is one of the obscurest portions of the ancient history ; see the article Assyria in Rob. Calmet.

There is not any decided evidence that Isaiah delivered any prophecies
during the reign of Jotham. Most commentators have supposed that the
prophecies in ch. ii.—v. were delivered during his reign ; but there is no internal proof to demonstrate it ; see the Analysis of these chapters.

Jotham was succeeded by Ahaz. He was the twelfth king of Judah. He
came to the throne at the age of twenty years, and reigned in Jerusalem
sixteen years, and of course died at the age of thirty-six. He ascended the
throne, according to Calmet, 738 years before the Christian era ; see 2 Kings
xvi. 2 ; 2 Chron. xxviii. 5. The character of Ahaz was the reverse of that of
his father ; and, excepting Manasseh his grandson, there was not probably a
more impious prince that sat on the throne of Judah. Nor was there a reign
that was on the whole more disastrous than his. A statement of his deeds of
evil, and a brief record of the calamitous events of his reign, is given in 2 Chron.

xxviii. and in 2 Kings xvi. He imitated the kings of Israel and Samaria in all manner of abominations and disorders. He early made images of Baalim. He burnt incense in the valley of Hinnom to idol gods, and burnt his children in the fire. He established idolatrous places of worship in every part of the land ; and caused the worship of idols to be celebrated in the groves, and on all the hills in Judea. As a consequence of this idolatry, and as a punishment for his sins and the sins of the nation, his kingdom was invaded by the joint forces of the kings of Syria and of Samaria. A large number of captive Jews were carried to Damascus ; and in one day Pekah the king of Samaria killed one hundred and twenty thousand, and took captive two hundred thousand more whom he purposed to carry captive to Samaria. This he would have done but for the remonstrance of the prophet Obed, who pled with him, and represented the impropriety of his carrying his brethren into bondage ; and at his solicitation, and from the apprehension of the wrath of God, the captives were returned to Jericho, and set at liberty ; 2 Chron. xxviii. 15. It was at this juncture, and when Ahaz trembled with alarm at the prospect of the invasion of the kings of Syria and Samaria, that he resolved to call in the aid of the Assyrian, and thus to repel the apprehended invasion. Though he had been able to defeat the united armies of Syria and Samaria once (2 Kings xvi. 5), yet those armies again returned, and Ahaz in alarm determined to seek the aid of Assyria. For this purpose he sent messengers, with terms of most humble submission and entreaty, and with the most costly presents that his kingdom could furnish, to secure the alliance and aid of Tiglath-Pileser the king of Assyria ; 2 Kings xvi. 7, 8. It was at this time, when Ahaz was so much alarmed, that Isaiah met him at the conduit of the upper pool in the highway of the fuller's field (Isa. vii. 3, 4,) and assured him that he had no occasion to fear the united armies of Syria and Samaria ; that Jerusalem was safe, and that God would be its protector. He assured him that the king- doms of Syria and Samaria should not be enlarged by the accession and con- quest of the kingdom of Judah (Isa. vii. 7–9) ; and advised Ahaz to ask a sign, or demonstration, from JEHOVAH that this should be fulfilled ; Isa. vii. 10, 11. Ahaz indignantly, though with the appearance of religious scruple, said that he would *not* ask a sign, vii. 12. The *secret* reason, however, why he was not solicitous to procure a sign from JEHOVAH was, that he had formed an alliance with the king of Assyria, and scorned the idea of recognizing his dependence on JEHOVAH.—Isaiah, therefore, proceeded (vii. 13, seq.) to assure him that JEHOVAH would himself give a sign, and would furnish a demonstration to him that the land would be soon forsaken of both the kings which Ahaz dreaded ; see Notes on ch. vii. Isaiah then proceeded to state the consequences of this alliance with the king of Assyria, and to assure him that the result would be, that, under the pretence of aiding him, he would bring up his forces on the land of Judah, and spread devastation and ruin, and that Jerusalem only would be spared ; Isa. vii. 17, seq. and ch. viii. The prophecy respecting the speedy removal of the two kings of Syria and Samaria was accomplished ; see Notes on ch. vii. 16. At about the same time the kingdom of Judah was threatened with an invasion from the Edomites and Philistines ; 2 Chron. xxviii. 17, 18 In this emergency Ahaz had recourse to his old ally the king of Assyria ;

2 Chron. xxviii. 20, 21. To secure his friendship, he made him a present obtained from the temple, from his own house, and from the princes ; 2 Chron. xxviii. 21. The king of Assyria professedly accepted the offer ; marched against Rezin the king of Syria, took Damascus, and slew Rezin, agreeably to the prediction of Isaiah, ch. vii. 16. While Tiglath-Pileser was at Damascus, Ahaz visited him, and being much charmed with an altar which he saw there, he sent a model of it to Urijah the priest to have one constructed like it in Jerusalem ; 2 Kings xvi. 10, seq. This was done. Ahaz returned from Damascus ; offered sacrifice on the new altar which he had had constructed, and gave himself up to every species of idolatry and abomination ; 2 Kings xvi. 12, seq. He offered sacrifice to the gods of Damascus, on the pretence that they had defended Syria, and might be rendered propitious to defend his own kingdom (2 Chron. xxviii. 23); he broke up the vessels of the temple, shut up the doors, and erected altars to the heathen deities in every part of Jerusalem ; 2 Chron. xxviii. 24, 25. He thus finished his inglorious reign in the thirty-sixth year of his age, and was buried in the city of Jerusalem, but not in the sepulchres of the kings, on account of his gross abominations ; 2 Chron. xxviii. 27.

The prediction of Isaiah (ch. vii. viii.) that his calling in the aid of the king of Assyria would result in disaster to his own land, and to *all* the land except Jerusalem (Note, ch. viii. 8), was not accomplished in the time of Ahaz, but was literally fulfilled in the calamities which occurred by the invasion of Sennacherib in the times of Hezekiah ; see Notes on ch. viii. and ch. xxxvi. –xxxix.

It is not *certainly* known what prophecies were delivered by Isaiah in the time of Ahaz. It is certain that those contained in ch. vii. viii. and ix. were uttered during his reign, and there is every probability that those contained in ch. x. xi. xii. were also. Perhaps some of the subsequent predictions also were uttered during his reign.

Ahaz was succeeded by his son Hezekiah, one of the most pious kings that ever sat on the throne of David. He was twenty-five years old when he began to reign, and he reigned twenty-nine years ; 2 Chron. xxix. 1. His character was the reverse of that of his father ; and one of the first acts of his reign was to remove the evils introduced in the reign of Ahaz, and to restore again the pure worship of God. He began the work of reform by destroying the high places, cutting down the groves, and overturning the altars of idolatry. He destroyed the brazen serpent which Moses had made, and which had become an object of idolatrous worship. He ordered the doors of the temple to be rebuilt, and the temple itself was thoroughly cleansed and repaired ; 2 Kings xviii. 1–6. 2 Chron. xxix. 1–17. He restored the observance of the Passover, and it was celebrated with great pomp and joy (2 Chron. xxx. seq.), and he restored the regular worship in the temple as it was in the time of Solomon ; 2 Chron. xxviii. 18. Successful in his efforts to reform the religion of his country, and in his wars with the Philistines (2 Kings xviii. 8), he resolved to cast off the inglorious yoke of servitude to the king of Assyria ; 2 Kings xviii. 7. He refused, therefore, to pay the tribute which had been promised to him, and which had been paid by his father Ahaz. As might have been expected, this resolution excited the indignation of the king of Assyria, and led to the resolution to compel submission. Sennacherib, therefore, invaded the land with a great army; spread desolation through no small part of it; and was rapidly advancing towards Jerusalem. Hezekiah saw his error, and, alarmed, he sought to avoid the threatened blow. He, therefore, put the city in the best possible posture of defence. He fortified it; enclosed it with a second wall; erected towers; repaired the fortification Millo in the city of David; stopped all the fountains; and made darts and shields that the city might be defended; 2 Chron. xxxii. 1–8. He endeavoured to prepare himself, as well as possible to meet the mighty foe; and he did all that he could to inspire confidence in God among the people; Notes on Isa. xxii. 9–11. Yet as if not quite confident that he could be able to hold out during a siege, and to resist an army so mighty as that of Sennacherib, he sent ambassadors to him, acknowledged his error, and sued for peace. Sennacherib proposed that he should send him three hundred talents of silver, and thirty talents of gold, and gave the *implied* assurance that if this were done his army should be withdrawn; 2 Kings xviii. 13, 14. Hezekiah readily agreed to send what was demanded; and to accomplish this he emptied the treasury, and stripped the temple of its ornaments; 2 Kings xviii. 15, 16. Sennacherib *then* went down to Egypt (see Notes on ch. xxxvi. xxxvii.), and was repelled before Pelusium by the approach of Tirhakah king of Ethiopia, who had come to the aid of the Egyptian monarch. On his return, Sennacherib sent messengers from Lachish, and a portion of his army to Jerusalem to demand its surrender; Isa. xxxvi. 2. To this embassy no answer was returned by the messengers of Hezekiah (Isa. xxxvi. 21, 22); and the messengers of Sennacherib returned again to him to Libnah; Note on Isa. xxxvii. 8. At this period, Sennacherib was alarmed by the rumour that Tirhakah, whom he had so much reason to dread, was advancing against him (Isa. xxxvii. 9), and he again sent messengers to Hezekiah to induce him to surrender, intending evidently to anticipate the news that Tirhakah was coming, and to secure the conquest of Jerusalem without being compelled to sit down before it in a regular siege. This message, like the former, was unsuccessful. Hezekiah spread the case before Jehovah (ch. xxxvii. 15–20), and received the answer that Jerusalem was safe. Sennacherib advanced to attack the city; but in a single night 185,000 of his men were destroyed by an angel of the Lord, and he himself fled to his capital, where he was slain by his two sons; ch. xxxvii. 36–38.

These events were among the most important in Jewish history. Isaiah lived during their occurrence; and a large portion of his prophecies from ch. xiv. to ch. xxxix. are occupied with allusions to and statements of these events. He gave himself to the work of preparing the nation for them; assuring them that they would come, but that Jerusalem should be safe. He seems to have laboured to inspire the mind of Hezekiah and the minds of the people with confidence in God, that when the danger should arrive, they might look to him entirely for defence. In this he was eminently successful; and Hezekiah and the nation put unwavering confidence in God. An accurate acquaintance with the causes, and the various events connected with the overthrow of Sennacherib is indispensable to a clear understanding of Isaiah; and these causes and events I have endeavoured to present in Notes on the several chapters which refer to that remarkable invasion. Soon after this, Hezekiah became dangerously ill; and Isaiah announced to him that he must die; Isa. xxxviii. 1. Hezekiah prayed to God for the preservation of his life, and an assurance was given to him that he should live fifteen years longer; Isa. xxxviii. 5. In attestation of this, and as a demonstration of it, the shadow on the sun-dial of Ahaz was made to recede ten degrees ; see Notes on ch. xxxviii. 8.

Hezekiah, after his signal success over his foe, and the entire deliverance of his kingdom from the long dreaded invasion, and his recovery from the dangerous illness, became eminently prosperous and successful. He was caressed and flattered by foreign princes ; presents of great value were given him, and he encompassed himself with the usual splendour and magnificence of an oriental monarch ; 2 Chron. xxxii. 23, 27, 28. As a consequence of this, his heart was lifted up with pride ; he gloried in his wealth, and magnificence, and even became proud of the divine interposition in his favour. To show what was in his heart, and to humble him, he was left to display his treasures in an ostentatious manner to the ambassadors of Merodach-Baladan king of Babylon (2 Chron. xxxii. 25, 31), and *for this* received the assurance that all his treasures and his family should be carried in inglorious bondage to the land from whence the ambassadors came ; 2 Kings xx. 12–18; Notes on Isa. xxxix. The remnant of the life of Hezekiah was peace ; Isa. xxxix. 8. He died at the age of fifty-four years ; and was buried in the most honoured of the tombs of the kings of Judah (2 Chron. xxxii. 33) ; and was deeply lamented by a weeping people at his death.

The reign of Hezekiah stretched through a considerable portion of the prophetic ministry of Isaiah. A large part of his prophecies are, therefore, presumed to have been uttered during this reign. It is probable that to this period we are to attribute the entire series from ch. xiii. to ch. xxxix. inclusive. The *most* important of his prophecies, from ch. xl. to ch. lxvi., I am disposed to assign to a subsequent period—to the reign of Manasseh. The reasons for this may be seen, in part, in § 2 of this Introduction.

Hezekiah was succeeded by his son Manasseh. The reasons for thinking that any part of the life of Isaiah was passed under the reign of this wicked prince have been stated above. He was the fifteenth king of Judah, and was twelve years old when he began to reign, and reigned fifty-five years. It was during his reign, and by him, as it is commonly supposed, that Isaiah was put to death. He forsook the path of Hezekiah and David, restored idolatry, worshipped the idols of Canaan, rebuilt the high places which Hezekiah had destroyed, set up altars to Baal, and planted groves to false gods. He raised altars to the whole host of heaven even in Jerusalem and in the courts of the temple, made his son pass through the fire to Moloch, was addicted to magic and divination, set up the idol of Astarte in the house of God, and caused the people to sin in a more aggravated form than had been done by the heathen who had formerly inhabited the land of Canaan. To all this he added cruelty in the highest degree, and 'shed innocent blood very much, till he had filled Jerusalem from one end to another.' Probably most of the distinguished men of piety were cut off by him, and among them, it is supposed, was Isaiah ; see 2 Kings xxi.; 2 Chron. xxxiii.

So great were his crimes that God brought upon the land the king of Assyria, who took Manasseh from the hiding place where he sought a refuge amidst briers and thorns, and bound him, and carried him to *Babylon* (2 Chron. xxxii. 11),—another proof that Babylon was at this time a dependent province of the Assyrian monarchy. In Babylon, Manasseh repented of his sins and humbled himself, and he was again returned to his land and his throne. After his restoration he removed the worship of idols, and re-established the worship of JEHOVAH. He built a wall on the west side of Gihon, and extended it around to Mount Ophel, and put Jerusalem in a posture of defence. He broke down and removed the altars which he had erected in Jerusalem, and in the temple ; and he removed all traces of idolatrous worship except the high places, which he suffered still to remain. There is evidence of his reformation ; and the latter part of his reign appears to have passed in comparative happiness and virtue.

It was only during the early part of his reign that Isaiah lived, and there is in his prophecies no express mention made of Manasseh. If he lived during any part of it, it is evident that he withdrew entirely, or nearly so, from the public exercise of his prophetic functions, and retired to a comparatively private life. There is evidently between the close of the xxxixth chapter of his prophecy, and the period when the latter part of his prophecies commences (ch. xl.) an interval of considerable duration. It is not a violation of probability that Isaiah after the death of Hezekiah, being an old man, withdrew much from public life ; that he saw and felt that there was little hope of producing reform during the impious career of Manasseh ; and that, in the distress and anguish of his soul, he gave himself up to the contemplation of the happier times which should yet occur under the reign of the Messiah. It was during this period, I suppose, that he composed the latter part of his prophecies, from the xlth to the lxvith chapter. The nation was full of wickedness. An impious prince was on the throne. Piety was banished, and the friends of JEHOVAH were bleeding in Jerusalem. The nation was given up to idolatry. The kingdom was approaching the period of its predicted fall and ruin. Isaiah saw the tendency of events ; he saw how hopeless would be the attempt at reform. He saw that the captivity of Babylon was hastening on, and that the nation was preparing for that gloomy event. In this dark and disastrous period, he seems to have withdrawn himself from the contemplation of the joyless present, and to have given his mind to the contemplation of happier future scenes. An interval perhaps of some ten or fifteen years may be supposed to have elapsed between his last public labours in the time of Hezekiah, and the prophecies which compose the remainder of the book. During this interval he may have withdrawn from public view, and fixed his mind on the great events of future times. In his visions he sees the nation about to go into captivity. Yet he sees also that there would be a return from bondage, and he comforts the hearts of the pious with the assurance of such a return. He announces the name of the monarch by whom that deliverance would be accomplished, and gives assurance that the captive Jews should again return to their own land. But he is not satisfied with the announcement of this comparatively unimportant deliverance. With that he connects a far greater and more important deliverance, that from sin, under the Messiah. He fixes his eye, therefore, on the future glories of the kingdom of God ; sees the long promised Messiah; describes his person, his work, his doctrine, and states in glowing language the effects of his coming on the happiness and destiny of mankind. As he advances in his prophetic descriptions, the deliverance from Babylon seems to die away and is forgotten ; or it is lost in the contemplation of the event to which it had a resemblance—the coming of the Messiah—as the morning star is lost in the superior glory of the rising sun. He throws himself forward in his descriptions ; places himself *amidst* these future scenes, and describes them as taking place around him, and as events which he saw. He thinks and feels and acts as if *in* that period ; his mind is full of the contemplation ; and he pours out, in describing it, the most elevated language and the sublimest thoughts. It was in contemplations such as these, I suppose, that he passed the close of his life ; and in such visions of the glorious future, that he sought a refuge from the gloom and despondency which must have filled a pious mind during the early part of the reign of the impious and blood-thirsty Manasseh.

Isaiah was cotemporary with the prophets Jonah, Hosea, and Micah. They, however, performed a less important public part, and were not favoured with visions of the future glory of the church, like his. In a single chapter, however, the same language is used by Isaiah and by Micah ; see Isa. ii. 2–4 ; comp. Micah iv. 1–4. In which prophet the language is original, it is impossible now to determine.

The period of the world in which Isaiah lived was in some respects a *forming* period. We have seen that it was during his life that the kingdom of Assyria, which had so long swayed a sceptre of entire dominion over the East, began to wane, and that its power was broken. The kingdom of Babylon, which ultimately became so vast and mighty, and which destroyed Assyria itself, was established during his life on a basis that secured its future independence and grandeur. The kingdom of Macedon, whose rise was followed by so great events under the emperor Alexander, was founded about the time when Isaiah began his prophetic life (B.C. 814), by Caranus. Carthage had been founded about half a century before (B.C. 869); and Rome was founded during his life, B.C. 753. Syracuse was built by Archias of Corinth, during his life, B.C. 769. It is of some importance in recollecting the events of ancient history to *group* them together, and some advantage may be derived to the student from connecting these events with the name and life of Isaiah.

The following tables, copied mainly from Jahn's Biblical Archaeology, will give a correct view of the principal chronological events in the time of Isaiah, and may be of use in the correct understanding of his prophecies.

TABLE I.

B.C.	JUDAH.	ISRAEL.	ASSYRIA.	MEDIA.	BABYLON.	OTHERS.
825	Amaziah.	Jeroboam II. 41 yrs.		Arbaces, 29 years.		
814		*Jonah*, the prophet.				Mace- donia.
811	Uzziah, 52 years.	*Amos*, the prophet.				
797					Interreg- num, 79 yrs.	
784		*Hosea*, the prophet. Interreg- num, 12 ys.				
773		Zechariah, 6 months. Shallum, 1 month.	Phul, 21 yrs.			
772		Menahem, 10 years.				
761	*Isaiah*.	Pekahiah, 2 years.				
759	Jotham, 16 years. *Micah*.	Pekah, 20 years.				
753			Tiglath- Pileser, 19 years.			Rome.
747					Nabonassar 14, or Mero- dach-Bala- dan.	
743	Ahaz, 16 ys.					
740			Conquers Da- mascus, Gali- lee & Gilead.			
739		Interreg- num, 9 yrs.				
734			Shalmaneser, 14 years.		Nadius, 2 years.	
730		Hosea, 9 ys.			Porus, 5 ys.	
728	Hezekiah, 29 years.				Jugaeus, 5 years.	
722		OVERTHROW OF ISRAEL.				

TABLE II.

B.C.	JUDAH.	ASSYRIA.	MEDIA.	BABYLON.
721	Hezekiah.			
720		Sennacherib, 7 ys.		
718			Dejoces, 53 yrs.	
714		Senn. in Judea.		
713		Essar-haddon, 35 years.		
709				Arkianus, 5 yrs.
704				Interreg. 2 yrs.
702				Belibus, 3 years.
699	Manasseh, 55 ys.			Apronadius, 6 yrs.
693				Rigebelus, 1 yr.
692				Messomordacus, 4 years.

§ 4.   *Divisions of Isaiah.*

Various modes of classifying the prophecies of Isaiah have been proposed, in order to present them in the most lucid and clear manner.   Gesenius divides the whole into four parts, exclusive of the historical portion (ch. xxxvi.–xxxix.); the first, comprising ch. i.–xii.; the second, ch. xiii.–xxiii.; the third, ch. xxiv.–xxxv.; and the fourth, ch. xl.–lxvi.   Horne proposes the following division : Part I. ch. i.–v.; II. ch. vii.–xii.; III. ch. xiii.–xxiv.; IV. ch. xxiv.–xxxiii.; V. ch. xxxvi.–xxxix.; VI. ch. xl.–lxvi.; see his Introduction, vol. ii. 157, seq.   Vitringa divides the book into the following portions :—

I. PROPHETIC.

(1.) Five prophetic addresses directly to the Jews, including the Ephraimites, reprehending, denouncing, and accusing them, ch. i.–xii.

(2.) Eight addresses or prophetic discourses, in which the destiny of foreign nations is foretold, particularly the destiny of Babylon, Philistia, Moab, Syria, Assyria, Ethiopia, Egypt, Arabia and Tyre, ch. xiii.–xxiii.

(3.) Penal judgments against the Jews and their foes, with ample promises of the final preservation and future prosperity of the Jews, ch. xxiv.–xxxvi.

(4.) Four consolatory addresses, respecting the coming of the Messiah, and particularly describing the events which would be introductory to it; especially the liberation from the captivity at Babylon, ch. xl.–xlix.

(5.) A description of the coming and work of the Messiah—his person his doctrines, his death, and the success of the gospel and its final triumph, ch. xlix.–lxvi.

II. HISTORIC.   The events recorded in ch. xxxvi.–xxxix.

The natural and obvious division of Isaiah is into two parts, the first of which closes with the xxxixth chapter, and the latter of which comprises the remainder of the book (xl.–lxvi).   In this division the latter portion is regarded as substantially a *continuous* prophecy, or an *unbroken* oracle or vision, relating to far distant events, and having little reference to existing things at the time when Isaiah lived, except the implied censures which are passed on the idolatry of the Jews in the time of Manasseh.   The main drift and scope, however, is to portray events to come—the certain deliverance of the Jews from the bondage in Babylon, and the higher deliverance of the world under the Messiah, of which the former was the *suggester* and the *emblem.*

The former part (ch. i.–xxxix.) comprises a collection of independent prophecies and writings composed at various periods during the public ministry of the prophet, and designed to produce an *immediate* effect on the morals, the piety, the faith, and the welfare of the nation.   The general drift is, that Jerusalem was secure ; that the kingdom of God on earth could not be destroyed ; that however much his people might be subjected to punishment for their sins, and however long and grievous might be their calamities, and however mighty their foes, yet that the kingdom of God could not be overturned, and his promises set at nought.   Hence in all the predictions of judgment and calamity ; in all the reproofs for crime, idolatry, and sin ; there is usually found a *saving clause*,—an assurance that the people of God would finally triumph, and be secure. And hence so large a portion of this division of the book is occupied with a prophetic statement of the entire and utter overthrow of the formidable states, nations, and cities with which they had been so often engaged in war, and which were so decidedly hostile to the Jews. The prophet, therefore, goes over in detail these cities and nations, and depicts successively the destruction of the Assyrians, of Babylon, Tyre, Moab, Damascus, Edom, &c., until he comes to the triumphant conclusion in ch. xxxv. that ALL the enemies of the people of God would be destroyed, and his kingdom be established on an imperishable basis under the Messiah ; see Notes on ch. xxxv. This is the scope of this part of the prophecy ; and this is the reason why there is such fearful denunciation of surrounding nations. In the course of the predictions, however, there are frequent reproofs of the Jews for their sins, and solemn warnings and assurances of judgments against *them ;* but there is the uniform assurance that they should be delivered, as a people, from all bondage and calamity, and be restored to ultimate freedom and prosperity.

This part of the book comprises the prophecies which were uttered during the reigns of Uzziah, Jotham, Ahaz, and Hezekiah ; see § 3. For convenience it may be divided in the following manner :—

FIRST. Independent prophecies, relating to Judah and Israel, ch. i.–xii. These are seven in number.

I. Reproof of national crimes, ch. i.

II. JUDAH, its sins, ch. ii. iii. iv.

III. JUDAH, a vineyard, ch. v.

IV. VISION OF JEHOVAH, ch. vi.

V. AHAZ ; impending calamity ; prediction of the birth and character of the Messiah, ch. vii. viii. ix. 1–7.

VI. SAMARIA, ch. ix. 8–21 ; x. 1–4.

VII. SENNACHERIB ; deliverance from him ; advent and work of the Messiah, ch. x. 5–34 ; xi. xii.

SECOND. Independent prophecies, mainly relating to surrounding nations which had been regarded as hostile to the Jews, or which were their natural enemies, or which for their sins were to be cut off to make way for the introduction and permanent establishment of the kingdom of God, ch. xiii.–xxiii. These prophecies are fourteen in number, and relate to the following kingdoms and people.

VIII. BABYLON, ch. xiii. xiv. 1–27.

IX. PHILISTIA, ch. xiv. 28–32.

X. MOAB, ch. xv. xvi.

XI. DAMASCUS, ch. xvii. 1–11.

XII. SENNACHERIB, ch. xvii. 12–21.

XIII. NUBIA, or ETHIOPIA, ch. xviii.

XIV. EGYPT, ch. xix.

XV. EGYPT and ASSYRIA, ch. xx.

XVI. The destruction of BABYLON, ch. xxi. 1–10.

XVII. DUMAH OR IDUMEA, ch. xxi. 11, 12.

XVIII. Arabia, ch. xxi. 13–17.

XIX. Jerusalem, when about to be besieged by Sennacherib, ch. xxii. 1–14.

XX. The fall of Shebna, and the promotion of Eliakim, ch. xxii. 15–25.

XXI. Tyre, ch. xxiii.

Third. Independent prophecies, relating mainly to the times of Hezekiah, and to the prospect of the Assyrian invasion under Sennacherib ; with a statement of the ultimate safety of the people of God, and the overthrow of all their enemies, ch. xxiv.–xxxv. These prophecies are eight in number, and relate to the following events.

XXII. Desolation of the land of Judea, its delivery and triumph, ch. xxiv.–xxvii.

XXIII. Ephraim to be destroyed, and Judah preserved, ch. xxviii.

XXIV. The siege and deliverance of Jerusalem, ch. xxix.

XXV. An alliance with Egypt condemned, ch. xxx.

XXVI. Denunciation on account of the contemplated alliance with Egypt, ch. xxxi.

XXVII. The virtuous and yet unsuccessful reign of Hezekiah, ch. xxxii.

XXVIII. The destruction of the Assyrian army, ch. xxxiii.

XXIX. The destruction of Edom, and of all the enemies of God, and the final triumph and security of the people, ch. xxxiv. xxxv.

Fourth. The historical portion (ch. xxxvi.–xxxix.), relating to the destruction of Sennacherib, and the sickness and recovery of Hezekiah.

One great cause of the difficulty of understanding Isaiah arises from the manner in which the division into chapters has been made. This division is known to be of recent origin, and is of no authority whatever. It was first adopted by Cardinal Hugo in the 13th century, who wrote a celebrated commentary on the Scriptures. He divided the Latin Vulgate into chapters nearly the same as those which now exist in the English version. These chapters he divided into smaller sections by placing the letters A, B, C, &c., at equal distances from each other in the margin. The division into verses is of still later origin. It was made by Stephens on a journey from Lyons to Paris in 1551, and was first used in his edition of the New Testament. The Jews formerly divided the books of the Old Testament into greater and smaller sections.

It is obvious that these divisions are of no authority ; and it is as obvious that they were most injudiciously made. A simple glance at Isaiah will show that prophecies have been divided in many instances which should have been retained in the same chapter ; and that prophecies, and parts of prophecies, have been thrown into the same chapter which should have been kept distinct. It is not usually difficult to mark the commencement and the close of the prophecies in Isaiah ; and an indication of such a natural division throws material light on the prophecy itself. The proper divisions have been indicated above.

§ 5. *The Historical Writings of Isaiah.*

It is evident that Isaiah wrote more than we have in the book which bears his name. In 2 Chron. xxvi. 22, it is said, ' Now the rest of the acts of Uzziah, first and last, did Isaiah the prophet, the son of Amoz, write.' But the only portion of the book of Isaiah which can with any *certainty* be referred to the time of Uzziah is chapter vi. And even if, as we may suppose, the five previous chapters are to be referred to his time, yet they contain no historical statement ; no record of public events sufficient to constitute a history of ' the acts of Uzziah, first and last.' It is therefore morally certain that there were other writings of Isaiah which we have not in this collection of his prophecies.

Again, in 2 Chron. xxxii. 32, it is said, ' Now the rest of the acts of Hezekiah, and his goodness, behold, they are written in the vision of Isaiah the prophet, the son of Amoz.' In the book of Isaiah we have a record of some very important events connected with the life of Hezekiah ; see ch. xxxvi.–xxxix. But there is no formal *record* of the events of the early part of his reign, or of his death. What is said relates to the invasion of Sennacherib (ch. xxxvi. xxxvii.) ; to the sickness and recovery of Hezekiah (ch. xxxviii.) ; and to the visit of the ambassadors from Babylon, ch. xxxix. But this would scarcely deserve to be called a record, or history of his ' acts,' and his ' goodness,' (marg. *kindnesses*) ; that is, his doings or plans of beneficence to promote the happiness and piety of his people. It is not, however, on this passage so much that reliance is to be placed to prove that he wrote other documents, as on the passage quoted from 2 Kings.

In regard to these historical records which are not now found in the book of Isaiah, there can be but two opinions.

(1.) One is, that they are lost ; that they formed a part of the record of his times which was then of value, and which was lost when more full and complete records were made in the books of Kings and Chronicles. Many such writings are mentioned which are now lost, or which are not found under the names of their authors. Thus we have accounts of the writings of Gad, and Iddo the Seer, and Nathan, and the prophecy of Ahijah the Shilomite, and the book of Jehu (1 Chron xxix. 29 ; 2 Chron. ix. 29 ; xx. 34 ; 1 Kings xvi. 1) ; all of which are now lost, unless they have come down to us under some other name. Nor is there any improbability that some portions of the once inspired writings are lost. They may have been inspired to accomplish a certain object ; and, when that object was gained, they may have been lost or destroyed as not farther necessary, or as superseded by superior clearness of revelation. No man can tell why it should be regarded as more improbable that divine communications which are *written* should be lost when they have accomplished their purpose, than it is that divine communications *spoken* should be lost. In the mere act of writing there is no peculiar sacredness that should make it necessary to preserve it. And yet no one can doubt (comp. John xxi. 25) that a very large portion of what our blessed Lord spoke, who always spoke inspired truth, is now irrecoverably lost. It never was recorded ; and there can be no impropriety in supposing that portions of truth that have been recorded have likewise perished. The whole Bible will be consumed in the conflagration of the last day—but truth will live. God has preserved, with remarkable care, as much truth as he saw was necessary to illuminate and edify his church to the end of time. There is, however, no indispensable necessity of supposing that *in fact* any part of the sacred record has been destroyed. For,

(2.) The records which were made by Isaiah, Iddo, Nathan, Abijah, &c., may have been public documents that were laid up in the archives of the state, and that were subsequently *incorporated* into the historical books which we now have. It is probable that the history of each reign was recorded by a prophet, a scribe, or a *historiographer;* see Note, Isa. xxxvi. 3. From the following extract from the travels of Mr. Bruce, it is evident that such an officer is known in modern times as attached to a court. The extract will also be descriptive of the duties of such an officer, and perhaps may be regarded as descriptive of some of the functions discharged by the prophets. 'The king has near his person an officer who is meant to be his HISTORIOGRAPHER. He is also keeper of his seal ; and is *obliged to make a journal of the king's actions, good or bad, without comment of his own upon them.* This, when the king dies, or at least soon after, is delivered to the council, who read it over, and erase every thing false in it, whilst they supply every material fact that may have been omitted, whether purposely or not.' Travels, vol. ii. p. 596. Such a record is also kept of all the sayings and purposes of the Emperor of China by an officer appointed for this purpose. It is carefully made, and sealed up during his life, and is not opened until he dies. This is regarded in that empire as an important public security that the Emperor will say or do nothing that he will be unwilling should be known by posterity; see Edin. Ency., Art. China. It would seem probable, therefore, that this is an oriental custom extensively prevalent. There is every reason to believe that a part of these royal biographies, or records of important events in each reign, were written by prophets ; see the Analysis of Isa. xxxvi. These records would be deposited in the archives of state, and would be regarded as authentic documents, and placed under the custody of proper officers. When the connected history of the nation came to be written ; when the books of the 'Kings' and the 'Chronicles' were composed, nothing would be more natural than to take these documents or historical records, and arrange and embody them *as a part* of the sacred history. They may have been incorporated entire into the narratives which we now have ; and the name of the writer simply referred to as the *authority* for the document, or to preserve the recollection of the original author of each fragment or part of the history. This I regard as by far the most probable supposition ; and if this be correct, then we have still substantially the portions of history which were composed by Isaiah, Gad, &c., and they have been, with perhaps some slight changes necessary to constitute a continuous narrative, or to supply some omissions, incorporated into the historical records which we now possess. These requisite changes may have been made by Ezra when the canon of the Old Testament was .completed. The reasons for this opinion may be seen more at length in the Analysis of chapter xxxvi.

§ 6. *Quotations of Isaiah in the New Testament.*

Isaiah refers more fully to the times of the Messiah than any other of the prophets. It is natural, therefore, to expect to find his writings often quoted or appealed to in the New Testament. The frequency of the reference, and the manner in which it is done, will show the estimate in which he was held by the Saviour, and by the apostles. It may also contribute in some degree to the explanation of some of the passages quoted to have them convenient for reference, or for examination. The meaning of Isaiah may be often determined by the inspired statement of the event referred to in the New Testament ; and the meaning of a New Testament writer likewise by a reference to the passage which he quotes. In regard to these quotations, also, it may be of use to bear in remembrance that a portion is made directly and literally from the Hebrew, and agrees also with the Septuagint version, or is in the words of the Septuagint ; a portion agrees with the Hebrew in sense but not in words ; a portion is made from the Septuagint translation even when the Septuagint differs from the Hebrew ; and in some cases there is a bare allusion to a passage. It may be useful to furnish a classification of the entire passages which are quoted in the New Testament, under several heads, that they may be seen at one view, and may be compared at leisure. For this selection and arrangement, I am mainly indebted to Horne. Intro. vol. ii. p. 343, seq.

I. Quotations agreeing exactly with the Hebrew.

Isa. liii. 4.	. quoted in .	Matt. viii. 17.
Isa. liii. 12.	. . . .	Mark xv. 28; Luke xxii. 37.
Isa. liii. 1.	. . . .	John xii. 38; comp. Rom. x. 16.
Isa. lii. 15.	. . . .	Rom. xv. 21.
Isa. xxii. 13.	. . . .	1 Cor. xv. 32.
Isa. xxv. 8.	. . . .	1 Cor. xv. 54.
Isa. xlix. 8.	. . . .	2 Cor. vi. 2.
Isa. liv. 1.	. . . .	Gal. iv. 27.
Isa. viii. 17, 18.	. . .	Heb. ii. 13.

II. Quotations nearly agreeing with the Hebrew.

Isa. vii. 14.	. quoted in	Matt. i. 23.
Isa. vi. 9, 10.	. . . .	Matt xiii. 14, 15; comp. Acts xxviii. 26; Mark iv. 12; Luke viii. 10.
Isa. liv. 13.	. . . . . .	John vi. 45.
Isa. lxvii. 1, 2.	. . . . . .	Acts vii. 49, 50.
Isa. xlix. 6.	. . . . . .	Acts xiii. 47.
Isa. lii. 5.	. . . . . .	Rom. ii. 24.
Isa. i. 9.	. . . . . .	Rom. ix. 29.
Isa. viii. 14.	. . . . . .	Rom. ix. 33.
Isa. lii. 7.	. . . . . .	Rom. x. 15.
Isa. lxv. 1, 2.	. . . . . .	Rom. x. 20, 21.
Isa. xxix. 14.	. . . . . .	1 Cor. i. 19.
Isa. xl. 13.	. . . . . .	1 Cor. 2. 16.
Isa. xxxviii. 11, 12.	. . Comp. Rom. xi. 34.	1 Cor. xiv. 21.
Isa. xl. 6, 7, 8.	. . . . . .	1 Pet. i. 24, 25.
Isa. liii. 9.	. . . . . .	1 Pet. ii. 22.
Isa. liii. 5.	. . . . . .	1 Pet. ii. 24.
Isa. viii. 12, 13.	. . . . . .	1 Pet. iii. 14, 15.

III. *Quotations agreeing with the Hebrew in sense, but not in words.*

Isa. xl. 3, 4, 5.   Matt. iii. 3.   Comp. Mark i. 3.   Luke iii. 4–6.
Isa. xlii. 1–4.   .   .   .   .   Matt. xii. 18–21.
Isa. lix. 7, 8.   .   .   .   .   Rom. iii. 15–17.
Isa. x. 22, 23.   .   .   .   .   Rom. ix. 27, 28.
Isa. xlv. 23.   .   .   .   .   Rom. xiv. 11.
Isa. xi. 10.   .   .   .   .   Rom. xv. 12.
Isa. lii. 11, 12.   .   .   .   .   .   .   2 Cor. vi. 17.

IV. *Quotations which give the general sense, but which abridge, or add to it.*

Isa. vi. 9, 10.   .   .   John xii. 40; Matt. xiii. 14, 15; Mark iv. 12.
                                              Luke viii. 10; Acts xxviii. 26.
Isa. xxix. 10.   .   .   .   .   .   .   Rom. xi. 8.

V. *Quotations which are taken from several different places.*

Isa. xxvi. 16; viii. 14.   .   quoted in   .   Rom. ix. 33.
Isa. xxix. 10; vi. 9; Ezek. xii. 2.   .   .   .   Rom. xi. 8.
Isa. lxii. 11; Zech. ix. 9.   .   .   .   .   Matt. xxi. 5.

VI. *Quotations differing from the Hebrew, but agreeing with the Septuagint.*

Isa. xxix. 13.   .   .   .   .   Matt. xv. 8, 9.
Isa. lv. 3.   .   .   .   .   Acts xiii. 34.

VII. *Quotations in which there is reason to suspect a different reading in the Hebrew, or that the words were understood in a sense different from that expressed in our Lexicons.*

Isa. lx. 1, 2.   .   .   .   .   .   .   Luke iv. 18, 19.
Isa. liii. 7, 8.   .   .   .   .   .   .   Acts viii. 32, 33.
Isa. lix. 20, 21.   .   .   .   .   .   Rom. xi. 26, 27.
Isa. lxiv. 4.   .   .   .   .   .   .   1 Cor. ii. 9.
Isa. xlii. 2, 4.   .   .   .   .   .   ,   Matt. xii. 18, 21.

VIII. *Allusion to a passage in Isaiah.*

Isa. xii. 3.   .   .   .   .   .   .   John viii. 37, 38.

IX. *Quotations made from the Septuagint.*

Many of the passages above referred to are made also from the Septuagint, when that version agrees with the Hebrew. I refer here to a few passages which have not been noted before. The apostles wrote in the Greek language, and for the use of those among whom the Septuagint was extensively used. Occasionally, however, they quoted directly from the Hebrew, that is, made a *translation* themselves, or quoted according to the general sense. *All* the quotations that are in accordance with the Septuagint, or that vary from it, may be seen in Horne's Introd. vol. ii. p. 387, 428.

X. *Quotations which differ from the Hebrew, and the Septuagint, and which were perhaps taken from some version or paraphrase, or which were so rendered by the sacred writers themselves.*

So numerous are these quotations, and so entirely do the writings of Isaiah harmonize with those of the New Testament, that it may be regarded almost as an indispensable part of the work of explaining the New Testament to explain Isaiah. They seem to be parts of the same work; and an exposition of the apostles and evangelists can hardly be deemed complete without the accompaniment of the evangelical prophet.

§ 7. *The Character and Nature of Prophecy.*

1. The words prophet and prophecy are used in the Bible in a larger sense than they are commonly with us. We have attached, in common usage, to the word prophet, the idea simply of one who foretels future events, προφήτης from προόφημι *to speak before, to foretel.* To a correct understanding of the prophetic functions, and of the writings of the prophets, however, it is necessary to bear in remembrance that the office of foretelling future events comprised but a small portion of their public duties. They were the messengers of God to his people and to the world; they were appointed to make known his will; to denounce his judgments; to rebuke the crimes of rulers and people; to instruct in the doctrines of religion; and generally to do whatever was needful in order effectually to promulgate the will of God. The prophet was, therefore, a man who was commissioned to teach and rebuke kings and nations, as well as to predict future events. With the idea of a prophet there is *necessarily* connected the idea that he spoke not his own thoughts, but that what he uttered was received directly from God in one of the modes in which that will was made known. He was God's ambassador to men; and of course was a man who was raised up or designated by God himself. He was not *trained* for this office, since a man could not be trained for inspiration; though it was a matter of fact that several of the prophets were taken from the ' school of the prophets,' or from among the ' sons of the prophets;' 1 Kings xx. 35; 2 Kings ii. 3, 5, 7, 15; iv. 1, 38; v. 22; vi. 1. Yet the choice from among them of any one to perform the functions of the prophet under divine inspiration, seems to have been incidental, and not in a uniform mode. A large part of the prophets had no connection with those schools. Those schools were doubtless usually under the direction of some inspired man, and were probably

designed to train those educated there for the functions of public teachers, of
for the stations of learning under the theocracy; but they could not have been
regarded as intended to train for that office which depended wholly on the direct
inspiration of God.

The word rendered prophet, נָבִיא *Nábi̇̂*, is derived from נָבָא *Nábâ*, not
used in Kal, which is probably, according to Gesenius, the same as נָבַע *Nábăng*
—the ע *Ayin* being softened into *Aleph* א —and which means to boil up, to
boil forth, as a fountain; hence to pour forth words as they do who speak with
fervour of mind, or under divine inspiration. The word, therefore, properly
means, to speak under a peculiar fervour, animation, inspiration of mind produced by a divine influence; to speak, either in foretelling future events, or
denouncing the judgments of God when the mind was full, and when the excited
and agitated spirit of the prophet poured forth words as water is driven from
the fountain.

But the word also denotes all the forms or modes in which the prophet communicated the will of God, or discharged the functions of the prophetic office.
Hence it is used to denote, (1) the predicting of future events (see Taylor's
Heb. Con. or Cruden); (2) to speak in the name of God, or as his messenger,
and by his authority, Ex. vii. 1; iv. 16; (3) to chant or sing sacred praises to
God while under a divine influence—1 Sam. x. 11; xix. 20; 1 Chron. xxv. 2,
3—because this was often done by the inspired prophets; (4) to rave, as e. g.
to utter the frantic ravings of the prophets of Baal, 1 Kings xviii. 29; 1 Sam.
xviii. 10. This latter meaning is in accordance with the customs among the
heathen, where the prophet or the prophetess professed to be full of the divine
influence, and where that influence was manifested by writhings and contor-
tions of the body, or by a pretended suspension of the powers of conscious
agency, and the manifestation of conduct not a little resembling the ravings
of delirium. Hence the Greeks applied the word μαντις, *mantis* (from μαίνομαι
to be mad, to rave, to be delirious) to the frenzied manner of the soothsayers,
prophetic oracles, &c. It is possible that the true prophets, occasionally under
the power of inspiration, exhibited similar agitations and spasmodic affections
of the body (comp. Num. xxiv. 4; Ezek. i. 28; Dan. x. 8–10; 1 Sam. xix. 24;
Jer. xx. 7), and that this was imitated by the false prophets. The two main
ideas in the word *prophecy* relate, (*a*) to the prediction of future events, and
(*b*) to declaring the will of God, denouncing vengeance, threatening punishment,
reproving the wicked, &c., under the influence of inspiration, or by a divine
impulse.

II. In order to obtain a clear idea of the nature of prophecy, it is important
to have a correct apprehension of the *modes* in which God communicated his
will to the prophets, or of the manner in which they were influenced, and
affected by the prophetic *afflatus* or inspiration. Of course all the light which
can be obtained on this subject is to be derived from the Scriptures; but the
subject is involved still in much obscurity. Perhaps the following will include
all the modes in which the will of God was made known to the prophets, or in
which they received a knowledge of what they were to communicate to others.

(1.) A direct commission by an audible voice from heaven, spoken in a solemn
manner, and in circumstances in which there could be no doubt of the call.

Thus Moses was called by God at the Bush, Ex. iii. 2–6; Isaiah in the temple, Isa. vi. 8, seq.; Samuel by God, 1 Sam. iii. 4, 6, 8, 10; Jeremiah, Jer. i. 4, Ezek. i. 3; and perhaps Joel, i. 1, Amos, i. 1, Jonah, Jon. i. 1, Micah, Mic. i. 1, &c. In these cases there was no doubt on the mind of the prophet of his call, as it was usually in such circumstances, and probably in such a manner, as to leave the fullest demonstration that it was from God. There is no evidence, however, that the whole message was usually communicated to the mind of the prophet in this manner. Perhaps the first call to the prophetic office was made in this mode, and the nature of the message imparted in the manner that will be specified soon. All that is essential to the correct understanding of this is, that there was a clear designation to the prophetic office.

(2.) The will of God was made known by dreams. Instances of this kind are common in the sacred Scriptures, as one of the earliest modes of communication between God and the soul. The idea seems to be that the senses were locked up, and that the soul was left free to hold communication with the invisible world, and to receive the expressions of the will of God. The belief that God made known his will in this manner was by no means confined to the Jewish nation. God informed Abimelech in a dream that Sarah was the wife of Abraham, Gen. xx. 3, 6. Joseph was early favoured with prophetic dreams, which were so clear in their signification as to be easily interpreted by his father and brethren, Gen. xxxvii. 4, 5, 6. The butler and baker in Egypt both had dreams predicting their future destiny, Gen. xl. 5; and Pharaoh had a dream of the future condition of Egypt, which was interpreted by Joseph, Gen. xli. 7, 25. God spake to Jacob in a dream, Gen. xxxi. 11; and it was in a dream that he made his promise to impart wisdom to Solomon, 1 Kings iii. 5. Nebuchadnezzar had dreams respecting his future destiny, and the kingdoms that should arise after him, Dan. ii. 1, 5; and the will of God was made known to Daniel in a dream, Dan. i. 17; vii. 1. God expressly declared that he would make known his will by dreams. Num. xii. 6: 'If there be a prophet among you, I the Lord will make myself known to him in a vision, and will speak unto him in a dream.' Thus also in Joel ii. 28: ' Your sons and your daughters shall prophesy, your old men shall dream dreams, your young men shall see visions.' The false prophets pretended also to have dreams which conveyed to them the will of God. The ancient belief on this subject is expressed in a most sublime manner in the language of Elihu as addressed to Job:—

> For God speaketh once,
> Yea, twice, when man regardeth it not ;
> In a dream, in a vision of the night,
> When deep sleep falleth upon men,
> In slumberings upon the bed—
> Then he openeth the ears of men,
> And sealeth up for them admonition,
> That he may turn man from his purpose,
> And remove pride from man.
>
> Ch. xxxiii. 14—17.

It is now impossible to determine in what way God thus communicated his will ; or how it was known that the thoughts in sleep were communicated by God ; or what criterion the prophet or other person had, by which to distinguish these from common dreams. The *certainty* that they were from God is demonstrated by the fact that the event was accurately fulfilled, as in the case of Joseph, of Pharaoh, of Nebuchadnezzar, of Daniel. There is no instance in which the will of God seems to have been communicated to Isaiah in this manner; and it is not needful to my purpose to pursue this part of the inquiry any further. The mode in which the will of God was made known to Isaiah was mainly, if not entirely, by *visions*, ch. i. 1; and that mode will demand a more full and distinct examination. It may just be remarked here, that no man can demonstrate that God *could* not convey his will to man in the visions of the night, or in dreams; or that he could not then have access to the soul, and give to the mind itself some certain indications by which it might be known that the communication was from him. It is possible that the mode of communicating the will of God by the *dream* חֲלוֹם *hhălōm*—did not differ *essentially* from the mode of *the vision*—חִזָּיוֹן—*hh zōn*—by causing a *vision* of the subject as in a landscape to pass before the mind.

(3.) The prophets were brought under such an influence by the divine Spirit as to overpower them, and while in this state the will of God was made known to them. In what way his will was *then* communicated we may not be able to determine. I speak only of an overpowering influence which gave them such views of God and truth as to weaken their animal frame, and as, in some instances, to produce a state of *ecstacy*, or a *trance*, in which the truth was made to pass before them by some direct communication which God had with their minds. In these cases, in some instances at least, the communication with the external world was closed, and God communicated his will immediately and directly. Reference to this is not unfrequently made in the Scriptures, where there was such a powerful divine influence as to prostrate the frame, and take away the strength of the body. Thus in Ezek. i. 3, 'The hand of JEHOVAH was then upon me.' Cornelius à Lapide remarks on this passage, that 'the prophets took their station by the side of a river, that in the stillness and delightful scenery around them they might, through the soft pleasing murmur of the waters, be refreshed, enlivened, and prepared for the divine ecstacies.' Bib. Repository, vol. ii. p. 141. It is more natural, however, to suppose that they did not court or solicit these influences, but that they came upon them by surprise. Jer. xx. 7, 'Lord, thou hast persuaded me, and I have suffered myself to be persuaded; thou hast been too strong for me, and hast prevailed.' This influence is referred to in 1 Sam. xix. 20, 'The Spirit of God was upon the messengers [of Saul] and they also prophesied.' In 1 Sam. xix. 24, the *power* of the prophetic impulse is indicated by the fact that it led Saul to strip off his clothes, probably his robes, and to prophesy in the same manner as Samuel; and in the statement that 'he lay down naked all that day, and all that night,' under the prophetic impulse.

The *effect* of this strong prophetic impulse on the body and the mind is indicated in the following passages. It is said of Abraham in Gen. xv. 12, when he had a vision, 'Behold terror and great darkness came upon him.' It was evinced in a remarkable manner in the case of Balaam, Num. xxiv. 4, 16. It is said of him, that he 'saw the vision of the Almighty, falling *into a trance* (LXX. "who saw the vision of God ἐν ὕπνῳ, *in sleep*,") but having his eyes open.' He was probably overcome, and fell to the ground, and yet his eyes were open, and *in* that state he uttered the predictions respecting Israel. The same effect is indicated in regard to John, Rev. i. 17, ' And when I saw him, I fell at his feet as dead.' So of Ezekiel (ch. i. 28, ' And when I saw it, I fell upon my face, and I heard a voice of one that spoke.' And in a more remarkable manner in the case of Daniel (ch. x. 8), ' Therefore I was left alone, and saw this great vision, and there remained no strength in me; for my comeliness was turned in me into corruption, and I retained no strength.' And again (ch. viii. 27), ' And I Daniel fainted, and was sick certain days.' That there was a remarkable agitation of the body, or suspension of its regular functions so as to resemble in some degree the ravings of delirium, is apparent from 2 Kings ix. 11; Jer. xxix. 26. The nature of the strong prophetic impulse is perhaps indicated also in the expression in 2 Pet. i. 21, ' Holy men of God spake as they were moved—(φερόμενοι—*borne along, urged, impelled*) by the Holy Ghost.'

That it was supposed that the prophetic impulse produced such an effect on the body as is here represented, is well known to have been the opinion of the heathens. The opinion which was held by them on the subject is stated in a beautiful manner by Plato : ' While the mind sheds its light around us, pouring into our souls a meridian splendour, we being in possession of ourselves, are not under a supernatural influence. But after the sun has gone down, as might be expected, an ecstasy, a divine influence, and a frenzy falls upon us. For when the divine light shines, the human goes down ; but when the former goes down, the latter rises and comes forth. This is what ordinarily happens in prophecy. Our own mind retires on the advent of the divine Spirit ; but after the latter has departed, the former again returns.' Quoted in Bib. Repos. vol. ii. p. 163. In the common idea of the Pythia, however, there was the conception of derangement, or raving madness. Thus Lucan :—

> ——Bacchatur demens aliena per antrum
> Colla ferens, vittasque Dei, Phœbacaque serta
> Erectis discussa comis, per inania templi
> Ancipiti cervice rotat, spargitque vaganti
> Obstantes tripodas, magnoque exaestuat igne
> Iratum te, Phœbe, ferens.   *Pharsalia*, V.

' She madly raves through the cavern, impelled by another's mind with the fillet of the god, and the garland of Phœbus, shaken from her erected hair: she whirls around through the void space of the temple, turning her face in every direction ; she scatters the tripods which come in her way, and is agitated with violent commotion, because she is under thy angry influence, O Apollo.' Virgil has given a similar description of a demoniacal possession of this kind:—

> ——Ait: Deus, ecce, Deus! cui talia fanti
> Ante fores, subitò non vultus, non color unus,
> Nec comptae mansere comae; sed pectus anhelum,
> Et rabie fera corda tument: majorque videri
> Nec mortale sonans; afflata est numine quando
> Iam propriore Dei.   *Æneid*. vi. 46, seq.
>
> I feel the god, the rushing god! she cries—
> While thus she spoke enlarged her features grew
> Her colour changed, her locks dishevelled flew.

> The heavenly tumult reigns in every part,
> Pants in her breast and swells her rising heart;
> Still spreading to the sight the priestess glowed,
> And heaved impatient of the incumbent god.
> Then to her inmost soul, by Phœbus fired,
> In more than human sounds she spoke inspired.   *Pitt.*
> See also *Æneid.* vi. 77, seq.

From all such mad and unintelligible ravings the true prophets were distinguished. The effect of inspiration on the physical condition of their bodies and minds may be expressed in the following particulars. (*a*.) It prostrated their strength; it threw them on the ground, as we have seen in the case of Saul, and of John, and was attended occasionally with sickness, as in the case of Daniel. There seems to have been such a view of God, and of the events which were to come to pass, as to take away for a time their physical strength. Nor is there any thing improbable or absurd in this. In the language of Prof. Stuart (Bib. Repos. ii. p. 221), we may ask, ' Why should not this be so? How could it be otherwise than that the amazing disclosures sometimes made to them should affect the whole corporeal system? Often does this happen when one and another scene opens upon us in a natural way, and which has respect merely to things of the present world. But when the future glories of the Messiah's kingdom were disclosed to the mental eye of a prophet or a seer, when the desolation of kingdoms, and the slaughter of many thousands, the subjugation and massacre of God's chosen people, famine, pestilence, and other tremendous evils were disclosed to his view, what could be more natural than that agitation, yea, swooning, should follow in some cases?' It may be added, that in the experience of Christians in modern times the elevated views which have been taken of God, of heaven, of the hopes of glory, and of the plan of salvation, have produced similar effects on the bodily frame. *Any* deep, absorbing, elevated emotion may produce this state. ' The flesh is weak,' and that there *may* be such a view of glory or of calamity; such hope or fear; such joy or sorrow as to prostrate the frame and produce sickness, or faintness, is nothing more than what occurs every day. (*b*.) There is no evidence that the true prophets were divested of intelligent consciousness so that they were ignorant of what they uttered ; or that the Spirit made use of them *merely* as organs, or as unconscious agents to utter his truth. They everywhere speak and act as men who understood what they said, and do not rave as madmen. Indeed, the very fact to which I have adverted, that the view of future events had such an effect as to take away their strength, shows that they were conscious, and had an intelligent understanding of what they saw, or spoke. That the prophet had *control* of his own mind ; that he could speak or not as he pleased ; that he acted as a conscious, voluntary, intelligent agent, is more than once intimated, or expressly affirmed. Thus in one of the strongest cases of the overpowering nature of the inspiration which can be adduced—the case of Jeremiah—it is intimated that the prophet *even then* was a voluntary agent, and could speak or not, as he pleased. The *strength* of this overpowering agency is intimated in Jer. xx. 7.

> Thou didst allure me, O JEHOVAH, and I was allured;
> Thou didst encourage me, and didst prevail;

1 am become a laughing stock every day,
Ridicule hath spent its whole force upon me.

Blayney's Trans.

And yet, in immediate connection with this, the prophet *resolved* that he would cease to prophesy, and that he would no more speak in the name of JEHOVAH.

Then I said, I will not make mention of him,
Nor speak any more in his name;
But his word was in my heart as a burning fire shut up in my bones,
And I was weary with forbearing,
And I could not stay.   ver. 9.

This proves, that Jeremiah was, even under the full power of the prophetic impulse, a free and conscious agent. If he was a mere passive instrument in the hands of the Spirit, how could he determine no more to prophesy? And how could he carry this purpose into execution, as he actually did for a while? But this inquiry has been settled by the express authority of the apostle Paul. He affirms, in a manner which leaves no room to doubt, that the prophets were conscious agents, and that they had control over their own minds, when he says (1 Cor. xiv. 32), ' the spirits of the prophets are subject to the prophets ; ' and on the ground of this he requires those who were under the prophetic inspiration to utter their sentiments in such a manner as not to produce confusion and irregularity in the churches, 1 Cor. xiv. 29–31, 33, 40. How could he reprove their disorder and confusion, if they had no control over the operations of their own minds ; and if they were not conscious of what they were uttering? The truth seems to have been that they had the same control over their minds that any man has ; that they were urged, or impelled by the Spirit to utter the truth, but that they had power to refuse ; and that the exercise of this power was subjected to substantially the same laws as the ordinary operations of their minds. The true idea has been expressed, probably, by Bishop Lowth. ' Inspiration may be regarded not as suppressing or extinguishing for a time the faculties of the human mind, but of purifying, and strengthening, and elevating them above what they would otherwise reach.' Nothing can be more rational than this view; and according to this, there was an essential difference between the effect of true inspiration on the mind, and the wild and frantic ravings of the pagan priests, and the oracles of divination. Every thing in the Scriptures is consistent, rational, sober, and in accordance with the laws of the animal economy ; every thing in the heathen idea of inspiration was wild, frantic, fevered, and absurd. (*c.*) It may be added, that this is the common view of prophecy which prevailed among the fathers of the church. Thus Epiphanius says, ' In whatever state the prophets have said, they have been accompanied with an intelligent state of mind ; ' Ad. Haeres. Mont. c. 4. Jerome in his Preface to Isaiah says, ' Nor indeed, as Montanus and insane women dream, did the prophets speak in an ecstasy, so that they did not know what they uttered, and, while they instructed others, did not themselves understand what they said.' Chrysostom says, ' For this is characteristic of the diviners, to be in a state of frenzy, to be impelled by necessity, to be driven by force, to be drawn like a madman. A prophet, on the contrary, is not so ; but utters his communication with sober intelligence, and in a sound state of mind, knowing what he says,' Homil. xxix. in Ep. ad Cor., Bib. Repos. ii. 141.

(4.) The representation of future scenes was made known to the prophets by VISIONS. This idea may not differ from the two former, except that it intimates that *in* a dream, and *in* the state of prophetic ecstasy, events were made known to them not by *words*, but by causing the scene to pass before their mind or their mental visions, *as if* they saw it. Thus the entire series of the prophecies of Isaiah is described as a VISION in ch. i. 1, and in 2 Chron. xxxii. 32. It is of importance to have a clear understanding of what is implied by this. The name *vision* is often elsewhere given to the prophecies, Num. xxiv. 4, 16; 1 Sam. iii. 1; 2 Sam. vii. 17; Prov. xxix. 18; Obad. i. 1; Isa. xxi. 2; xxii. 1, 5; Jer. xiv. 14; Lam. ii. 9; Ezek. vii. 13; Dan. ii. 19; vii. 2; viii. 1, 13, 16, 17, 26; ix. 21, 23, 24; x. 1, 7, 8, 14, 16; 2 Chron. ix. 29; Ezek. i. 1. The prophets are called *Seers* רֹאִים *rōyìm;* and חֹזִים *Ihōzim*, and their prophecies are designated by words which denote that which *is seen,* as מַחֲזֵה הַדִּיוֹן חָזוֹן מַרְאֶה, &c.—all of which are words derived from the verbs rendered *to see,* חָזָה and רָאָה. It would be unnecessary to quote the numerous passages where the idea of *seeing* is expressed. A few will show their general characters. They may be *classified* according to the following arrangement.

(*a.*) Those which relate to an *open* vision, a distinct and clear *seeing*, 1 Sam. iii. 1: ' And the word of the LORD was precious in those days ; there was no open vision '—חָזוֹן נִפְרָץ—no vision spread abroad, common, open, public, usual. It was a rare occurrence, and hence the divine communications were regarded as peculiarly precious and valuable.

(*b.*) Those which pertain to the prophetic ecstasy, or trance—probably the more usual, and proper meaning of the word. Num. xxiv. 3, 4, ' The man whose eyes are open hath said ; he hath said which heard the words of God, which saw the vision of the Almighty, falling, but having his eyes open.' Num. xxiv. 17, ' I see him, but not now; I behold him, but not near ; there shall come a Star out of Jacob, and a Sceptre shall rise out of Israel.' That is, I see, or have a vision of that Star, and of that Sceptre *in the distance*, as if looking on a landscape, and contemplating an indistinct object in the remote part of the picture. Thus Ezek. i. 1, ' The heavens were opened, and I saw the visions of God ; ' viii. 3.; xl. 2, ' In visions he brought me to the land of Israel,' comp. Luke i. 22.

(*c.*) Instances where it is applied to DREAMS: Dan. ii. 19, 28; iv. 5; vii. 2; viii. 1, 13, 16, 17, 26, 27; ix. 21, 23, 24; Gen. xlvi. 2, ' God spake to Israel in visions of the night,' Job. iv. 13.

(*d.*) Instances where the prophets represent themselves as standing on a *watch-tower*, and looking off on a distant landscape to descry future and distant events.

> 'I will stand upon my watch,
> And will set me upon the tower,
> And will watch to see what he will say unto me,
> And what I shall answer when I am reproved.'   Habak. ii. 1.

' For thus hath the Lord said unto me, Go, set a watchman, let him declare what he seeth ;' Notes, Isa. xxi. 6; comp. ver. 8, 11 ; Micah vii. 4 ; comp.

Jer. vi. 17; Ezek. iii. 17; xxxiii. 7. In these passages, the idea is that of one who is stationed on an elevated post of observation, who can look over a large region of country, and give timely warning of the approach of an enemy

The general idea of prophecy which is presented in these passages, is that of a scene which is made to pass before the mind like a picture, or a landscape, where the mind contemplates a panoramic view of objects around it, or in the distance ; where, as in a landscape, objects may appear to be grouped together, or lying near together, which may be in fact separated a considerable distance. The prophets described those objects which were presented to their minds as they *appeared* to them, or as they seem to be drawn on the picture which was before them. They had, undoubtedly, an intelligent consciousness of what they were describing ; they were not mad, like the priestesses of Apollo ; they had a clear view of the *vision,* and described it as it appeared to them. Let this idea be kept in mind, that the prophets saw IN VISION ; that probably the mode in which they contemplated objects was somewhat in the manner of a *landscape* as it passes before the mind, and much light and beauty will be cast on many of the prophecies which now seem to be obscure.

III. From the view which has now been taken of the nature of prophecy, some important remarks may be made, throwing additional light on the subject.

(1.) It is not to be expected that the prophets would describe what they saw in all their connections and relations ; see Hengstenberg, in Bib. Repos. ii. p. 148. They would present what they saw as we describe what we witness in a landscape. Objects which *appear* to be near, may be in fact separated by a considerable interval. Objects on the mountain side may seem to lie close to each other, between which there may be a deep ravine, or a flowery vale. In describing or painting it, we describe or paint the points that appear ; but the ravine and the vale cannot be painted. They are not seen. So in a prophecy, distant events may appear to lie near to each other, and may be so described, while *between* them there may be events happy or adverse, of long continuance and of great importance.

(2.) Some SINGLE VIEW of a future event may attract the attention and engross the mind of the prophet. A multitude of comparatively unimportant objects may pass unnoticed, while there may be one single absorbing view that shall seize upon, and occupy all the attention. Thus in the prophecies which relate to the Messiah. Scarcely any one of the prophets gives any connected or complete view of his entire life and character. It is some single view of him, or some single event in his life, that occupies the mind. Thus at one time his birth is described ; at another his kingdom ; at another his divine nature ; at another his sufferings ; at another his resurrection ; at another his glory. *The prophetic view is made up, not of one of these predictions, but of all combined;* as the life of Jesus is not that which is contained in *one* of the Evangelists, but in all combined. Illustrations of this remark might be drawn in abundance from the prophecies of Isaiah. Thus in ch. ii. 4, he sees the Messiah as the Prince of Peace, as diffusing universal concord among all the nations, and putting an end to war. In ch. vi. 1–5, comp. John xii. 41, he sees him as the Lord of glory, sitting on a throne, and filling the temple. In ch. vii. 14, he

sees him as a child, the son of a virgin. In ch. ix. 1, 2, he sees him as having
reached manhood, and having entered on his ministry, in the land of Galilee
where he began to preach. In ch. ix. 6, 7, he sees him as the exalted Prince,
the Ruler, the mighty God, the Father of eternity. In ch. xi. he sees him as
the descendant of Jesse—a tender sprout springing up from the stump of an
ancient decayed tree. In ch. xxv. 8, he sees him as destroying death, and
introducing immortality; comp. 1 Cor. xv. 54. In ch. xxxv. the happy effects
of his reign are seen ; in ch. liii. he views him as a suffering Messiah, and contemplates the deep sorrows which he would endure when he should die to make
atonement for the sins of the world. Thus in all the prophets we have one
view presented at one time, and another at another ; and the entire prediction
is made up of *all* these when they are combined into one. It may be observed
also of Isaiah, that in the first part of his prophecy the idea of an exalted or
triumphant Messiah is chiefly dwelt upon ; in the latter part, he presents more
prominently the idea of the suffering Messiah. The reason may have been,
that the object in the first part was to console the hearts of the nation under
their deep and accumulated calamities, with the assurance that their great
Deliverer would come. In the latter part, which may not have been published
in his life, the idea of a suffering Messiah is more prominently introduced. This
might have been rather designed for posterity than for the generation when
Isaiah lived ; or it may have been designed for the more pious individuals in
the nation rather than for the nation at large, and hence, in order to give a *full*
view of the Messiah, he dwelt then on his sufferings and death ; see Hengstenberg's Christol. vol. i. pp. 153, 154.

(3.) Another peculiarity, which may arise from the nature of prophecy as
here presented, may have been that the mind of the prophet glanced rapidly
from one thing to another. By very slight associations or connections, as they
may now appear to us, the mind is carried from one object or event to another ;
and almost before we are aware of it, the prophet seems to be describing some
point that has, as appears to us, scarcely *any* connection with the one which
he had but just before been describing. We are astonished at the transition,
and perhaps can by no means ascertain the *connection* which has subsisted in
view of the mind of the prophet, and which has led him to pass from the one
to the other. The mental association to us is lost or unseen, and we deem him
abrupt, and speak of his rapid transitions, and of the difficulties involved in the
doctrine of a double sense. The views which I am here describing may be
presented under the idea of what may be called THE LAWS OF PROPHETIC SUGGES-
TION ; and perhaps a study of those laws might lead to a removal of most of the
difficulties which have been supposed to be connected with the subject of a
spiritual meaning, and of the double sense of the prophecies. In looking over
a landscape ; in attempting to describe the objects as they lie in view of the
eye—if that landscape were not seen by others for whom the description is
made—the transitions would seem to be rapid, and the objects might seem to
be described in great disorder. It would be difficult to tell why this object was
mentioned in connection with that ; or by what laws of association the one was
suggested by the other. A house or tree ; a brook, a man, an animal, a valley,
a mountain, might all be described, and between them there might be no appa-

rent laws of close connection, and all the real union may be that they lie in the same range, in view of him who contemplates them. The *laws of prophetic suggestion* may appear to be equally slight ; and we may not be able to trace them, because we have not the entire view or grouping which was presented to the mind of the prophet. We do not see the associations which in his view connected the one with the other. To him, there may have been no double sense. He may have described objects singly as they appeared to him. But they may have lain near each other. They may have been so closely grouped that he could not separate them even in the description. The words appropriate to the one may have naturally and easily fallen into the form of appropriate description of the other. And the objects may have been so contiguous, and the transition in the mind of the prophet so rapid, that he may himself have been scarcely conscious of the change, and his narrative may seem to flow on as one continued description. Thus the object with which he commenced, may have sunk out of view, and the mind be occupied entirely in the contemplation of that which was at first secondary. Such seems to have been, in a remarkable manner, the peculiarity of the mind of Isaiah. Whatever is the object or event with which he *commences*, the description usually *closes* with the Messiah. His mind glances rapidly from the object immediately before him, and fixes on that which is more remote, and the first object gradually sinks away; the language rises in dignity and beauty; the mind is full, and the description proceeds with a statement respecting the Prince of Peace. This is not double sense: it is RAPID TRANSITION under the laws of PROPHETIC SUGGESTION; and though at first some object immediately before the prophet was the subject of his contemplation, yet before he closes, his mind is totally absorbed in some distant event that has been presented, and his language is designedly such as is adapted to that. It would be easy to adduce numerous instances of the operation of this law in Isaiah. For illustration we may refer to the remarkable prophecy in ch. vii. 14; comp. ch. viii. 8; ix. 1–7. See Notes on those passages. Indeed, it may be presented, I think, as one of the prominent characteristics of the mind of Isaiah, that in the prophetic visions which he contemplated, the Messiah always occupied some place ; that whatever prophetic landscape, so to speak, passed before him, the Messiah was always in some part of it ; and that consequently wherever he *began* his prophetic annunciations, he usually *closed* with a description of some portion of the doctrines, or the work of the Messiah. It is this law of the mental associations of Isaiah which gives such value to his writings in the minds of all who love the Saviour.

(4.) It follows from this view of prophecy, that the prophets would speak of occurrences and events as they appeared to them. They would speak of them as actually present, or as passing before their eyes. They would describe them as being what they *had* seen, and would thus throw them into the past tense, as we describe what we have seen in a landscape, and speak of what we *saw*. It would be comparatively infrequent, therefore, that the event would be described as *future*. Accordingly we find that this is the mode actually adopted in the prophets. Thus in Isa. ix. 6, ' Unto us a child *is* born, unto us a son *is* given.' Isa. xlii. 1, ' Behold my servant whom I *uphold*, mine elect in whom

my soul *delighteth.*' So in the description of the sufferings of the Messiah : ' He *is* despised.' ' He *hath* no form or comeliness,' ch. liii. 2, 3. Thus in ch. xiv. 1–8, Cyrus is addressed as if he were personally present. Frequently events are thus described as *past*, or as events which the prophet *had seen* in vision. ' The people that walked in darkness *have seen* a great light ; they that dwell in the land of the shadow of death, upon them hath the light shined,' ch. ix. 2. So especially in the description of the sufferings of the Messiah : ' As many *were* astonished at thee.' ' His visage *was* so marred.' ' He *hath* borne our griefs.' ' He *was* oppressed, and he *was* afflicted.' ' He *was* taken from prison.' ' He *was* cut off out of the land of the living.' ' He *made* his grave,' &c. &c.; Isa. lii. 14, 15; liii. 4–9. In some cases, also, the prophet seems to have placed himself in vision *in the midst* of the scenes which he describes, or to have taken, so to speak, a station where he might contemplate a part as past, and a part as *yet to come.* Thus in Isa. liii. the prophet seems to have his station *between* the humiliation of the Saviour and his glorification, in which he speaks of his sufferings as *past,* and his glorification, and the success of the gospel, as *yet to come;* comp. particularly ver. 9–12. This view of the nature of prophecy would have saved from many erroneous interpretations ; and especially would have prevented many of the cavils of sceptics. It is a view which a man would be allowed to take in describing a landscape ; and why should it be deemed irrational or absurd in prophecy ?

(5.) From this view it also follows, that the prophecies are usually to be regarded as seen *in space* and not *in time ;* or in other words, the time would not be actually and definitely marked. They would describe the *order*, or the succession of events ; but between them there might be a considerable, and an unmeasured interval of time. In illustration of this we may refer to the idea which has been so often presented already—the idea of a landscape. When one is placed in an advantageous position to view a landscape, he can mark distinctly the *order* of the objects, the succession, the *grouping.* He can tell what objects appear to him to lie *near* each other ; or what are apparently in juxtaposition. But all who look at such a landscape know very well that there are objects which the eye cannot take in, and which will not be exhibited by any description. For example, hills in the distant view may seem to lie *near* to each other ; one may seem to rise just back of the other, and they may appear to constitute parts of the same mountain range, and yet *between* them there may be wide and fertile vales, the *extent* of which the eye cannot measure, and which the mind may be wholly unable to conjecture. It has no means of measuring the distance, and a description of the whole scene as it *appeared* to the observer would convey no idea of the distance of the intervals. So in the prophecies. Between the events seen in vision there may be long intervals, and the length of those intervals the prophet may have left us no means of determining. He describes the scene as it appeared to him in vision. In a *landscape* the distance, the length, the nature of these intervals might be determined in one of three ways : (1) by the report of one who had gone over the ground and actually *measured* the distances ; (2) by going ourselves and measuring the distances ; or (3) by a revelation from heaven. So the *distance of time* occurring between the events seen in vision by the prophets, may be determined either by the actual *admeasurement* as the events occur, or by direct revelation either made to the prophet himself, or to some other prophet. Accordingly we find in the prophecies these facts. (*a*) In many of them there are no marks of *time*, but only of *succession*. It is predicted only that one event should succeed another in a certain order. (*b*) Occasionally the time of some *one* event is marked in the succession, as e. g. the time of the death of the Messiah, in Dan. ix. 26, 27. (*c*) Events are apparently connected together, which in fact were to be separated by long intervals. Thus Isaiah ch. xi. makes the deliverance which was to be effected by the Messiah, to follow immediately the deliverance from the yoke of the Assyrians, without noticing the long train of intermediate occurrences. And in the same manner Isaiah, Hosea, Amos, and Micah very often connect the deliverance under the Messiah with that which was to be effected from the captivity at Babylon, without noticing the long train of intermediate events. There was such a resemblance between the two events that, by the laws of *prophetic suggestion*, the mind of the prophet glanced rapidly from one to the other, and the description which *commenced* with the account of the deliverance from the Babylonish captivity, *closed* with the description of the triumphs of the Messiah. And yet not one of the prophets ever intimate that the Messiah would be the leader from the exile at Babylon. (*d*) The *time* is sometimes revealed to the prophets themselves, and they mark it distinctly. Thus to Jeremiah it was revealed that the exile at Babylon would continue seventy years (ch. xxv. 11, 12), and although this event had been the subject of revelation to other prophets, yet to no one of them was there before an intimation of the *time* during which it was to continue. So also of the *place*. That the Jews would be carried away to a distant land if they were disobedient, had been predicted by Moses, and threatened by many of the prophets ; and yet there was no intimation of the *place* of their bondage until the embassy of the king of Babylon to Hezekiah, and the sin of Hezekiah in showing them his treasure, led Isaiah to declare that *Babylon was the place* to which the nation was to be carried ; see Notes on Isa. xxxix. 6. Marks of time are thus scattered, though not very profusely, through the prophecies. They were, on the whole, so definite as to lead to the general expectation that the Messiah would appear about the time when Jesus was born ; see Notes on Matt. ii.

(6.) It is a consequence of this view also, that many of the prophecies are obscure. It is not to be expected that the *same* degree of light should be found in the prophecies which we have now. And yet so far as the prophecy *was* made known, it might be clear enough ; nor was there any danger or need of mistake. The facts themselves were perfectly plain and intelligible ; but there was only a partial and imperfect development of the facts. The *fact*, e.g. that the Messiah was to come ; that he was to be born at Bethlehem ; that he was to be a king ; that he was to die ; that his religion was to prevail among the nations ; and that the Gentiles were to be brought to the knowledge of him, were all made known, and were as clear and plain as they are now. Much is known now, indeed, of the *mode* in which this was to be done which was not then ; and the want of this knowledge served to make the prophecies appear obscure. We take the information which we *now* have, and go back to the times when the prophecies were uttered, and finding them obscure, we seem to infer that because *all* was not known, *nothing* was known. But we are to remember that *all* science at the beginning is elementary ; and that knowledge on all subjects makes its advances by slow degrees. Many things in the prophecies were obscure, in the sense that there had been only a partial revelation ; or that only a few facts were made known ; or that the time was not marked with certainty ; and yet the facts themselves may have been as clear as they are now, and the *order of succession* may have been also as certainly and clearly determined. The *facts* were revealed ; the manner in which they were to occur may have been concealed.

It may be added here, in the words of Prof. Stuart, ' that many prophecies have respect to kingdoms, nations, and events, that for thousands of years have been buried in total darkness. In what manner they were fulfilled we know not ; when, we know not. We do not even know enough of the geography of many places and regions that are named in them, to be able to trace the scene of such fulfilment. Customs, manners, and many other things alluded to by such prophecies, we have no present means of illustrating in an adequate manner. Of course, and of necessity, then, there must be more or less in all such prophecies, that is obscure to us.' Bib. Repository, vol. ii. p. 237.

§ 8. *Works illustrative of Isaiah.*

Probably no book of the Bible has occupied so much the attention of critics, of commentators, and of private Christians, as Isaiah. The beauty, grandeur, and power of his prophecies ; their highly evangelical character ; the fact that they are so frequently quoted in the New Testament ; the number and minuteness of his predictions in regard to cities and kingdoms ; as well as the intrinsic difficulty of many portions of his writings, all have contributed to this. Of the numerous works which may be consulted in reading, or in explaining Isaiah, the following are among the principal :

I. THE ANCIENT VERSIONS.

(1.) The Septuagint, so called from the seventy interpreters who are supposed to have been engaged in it. This is the most ancient, and in some respects the most valuable of all the versions of the Bible, and was formerly esteemed so valuable as to be read in synagogues and in churches. Much uncertainty exists in regard to the *real* history of this version. According to the common Jewish legend respecting it, Ptolemy Philadelphus, who reigned king of Egypt from 284 to 246 B. C., formed the wish, through the advice of his librarian, Demetrius Phalerius, to possess a Greek copy of the Jewish Scriptures, for the Alexandrian Library, and sent to Jerusalem for this object. The Jews sent him a Hebrew manuscript, and seventy-two men of learning to translate it. They all laboured together, being shut up in the island of Pharos, where having agreed on the translation by mutual conference, they dictated it to Demetrius, who wrote it down, and thus in the space of seventy-two days the whole was finished. This legend is given in an epistle said to have been written by Aristeas, to his brother in Alexandria. Josephus also relates the story, Ant. xii. II. 2–14, But it has every mark of fiction ; and an examination of the Septuagint itself will convince any one that it was not all made by the same persons, or at the same time. The most probable supposition is, that after the Jews had settled in great numbers in Egypt, and had in some measure forgotten the Hebrew Language, a Greek version became necessary for the public use in their temple there (Notes, Isa. xix. 18), and in their synagogues. There is no improbability that this was done under the sanction of the Sanhedrim, or Council of LXXII. in Egypt, and that it thus received its name and authority. The translation was probably commenced about 250 years before Christ. The Pentateuch would be first translated, and the other books were probably translated at intervals between that time and the time of Christ. ' The Pentateuch is best translated, and exhibits a clear and flowing Greek style ; the next in rank is the translation of Job and the Proverbs ; the Psalms and the Prophets are translated worst of all, and indeed often without any sense. Indeed, the real value of the Septuagint, as a version, stands in no sort of relation to its reputation.'—*Calmet.* ' Isaiah has had the hard fate to meet a translation unworthy of him, there being hardly any book of the Old Testament that is so ill rendered in that version as Isaiah.'—*Lowth.* The authority of this version, however, soon became so great as to supersede the use of the Hebrew among all the Jews who spoke Greek. It was read in the synagogues in Egypt, and was gradually introduced into Palestine. It had the highest reverence among the Jews, and was used by them everywhere ; and is the version that is most commonly quoted in the New Testament. From the Jews the reputation and authority of this version passed over to Christians, who employed it with the same degree of credence as the original. The *text* of this version has suffered greatly, and great efforts have been made to restore it ; and yet probably after all these efforts, and after all the reputation which the version has enjoyed in former times, there has not been any where, or scarcely in any language, any version of the Scriptures that is more incorrect and defective than the Septuagint. Probably there is *no* version from which, as a whole, a more correct idea would not be derived of the real meaning of the sacred Scriptures, and this is true in a special manner of Isaiah. It is valuable as the oldest version ; as having been regarded with so much respect in former times : and as, notwithstanding its faults, and the imperfection of the text, throwing much light on various parts of the Old Testament. But as an *authority* for correcting the Hebrew text, it is of little or no value. The history of the Septuagint may be seen in Hody, de Biblior. Textibus orig. Ox. 1705; Horne's Intro. vol. ii. 163, seq.; Prideaux's Connexions ; Walton's Proleg. c. ix. § 3–10; Isaac Vossius de LXX. Inter. Hag. Com. 1661; and Brett, Diss. on the Septuagint, in Watson's Theo. Tracts, vol. iii. p. 18, seq.

(2.) The Latin Vulgate—the authorized version of the Papal communion. When Christianity had extended itself to the West, where the Latin language was spoken, a version of the Scriptures into that language became necessary. In the time of Augustine there were several of these, but only one of them was adopted by the church. This was called *common vulgata*, because it was made from the common Greek version, η κοινή. In modern times this version is often called *Itala*, or the Italic version. This version, in the Old Testament, was made literally from the Septuagint, and copied all its mistakes. To remedy the evils of this, and to give a correct translation of the Scriptures, Jerome undertook a translation directly from the Hebrew. He went to Palestine and enjoyed the oral instructions of a learned Jew. He availed himself of all the labours of his predecessors, and furnished a translation which surpassed all that preceded his in usefulness. In the seventh century this version had supplanted all the old ones. It was the first book ever printed. By the Council of Trent, it was declared to be 'authentic'—and is the authorized or standard version of the Papists; and is regarded by them as of equal authority with the original Scriptures. This version is allowed generally to be a very faithful translation; and it undoubtedly gives a much more correct view of the original than the Septuagint.

(3.) The Syriac versions. Of these there are two, both of which are of Christian origin; having been made by Christians of the Syrian church who dwelt in Mesopotamia. The earliest, and most celebrated of these is the Peshito; i. e. *the clear*, or *the literal*. It is the authorized version of the Syrian church, and is supposed by them to have been made in the time of Solomon. It was probably made in the first century. It follows, in general, the Hebrew literally; and is VERY VALUABLE as an aid in ascertaining the meaning of the Hebrew Scriptures. The other Syriac version was made from the Septuagint about the year 616, for the use of the Monophysites. It is of value, therefore, only for the interpretation of the Septuagint. It is the former of these which is printed in the Polyglotts. Of the latter no portion has been printed except Jeremiah and Ezekiel, 1787, and Daniel, 1788. —*Calmet.*

(4.) The Arabic versions. The Scriptures have been at various times translated into Arabic. After the time of Mohammed, the Arabic became the common language of many of the Jews, and of numerous bodies of Christians in the East. Sometimes the translations were made from the Hebrew, sometimes from the Septuagint, from the Peshito, or the Vulgate. The version of R. Saadias Gaon, director of the Jewish Academy at Babylon, was made in the tenth century. It comprised originally the Old Testament; but there have been printed only the Pentateuch, and Isaiah. The Pentateuch is found in the Polyglotts. Isaiah was published by Paulus in 1791. The Mauritanian version was made in the thirteenth century, by an Arabian Jew, and was published by Erpenius in 1629. The Arabic version in the Polyglotts was made by a Christian of Alexandria, and was made from the Septuagint.—*Robinson.* Of course these are of little value in illustrating the Hebrew text. The chief and great value of the Arabic consists in the light which is thrown upon the meaning of Hebrew words, phrases, and customs, from the Arabic language, manners, and literature.

(5.) The Targums or Chaldee versions. All these are the works of Jews living in Palestine and Babylon, from a century before Christ, to the eighth, or ninth century after. They bear the name *Targum*, i. e. *translation*. They comprise the Targum of Onkelos on the Pentateuch; of Jonathan Ben Uzziel on the historical books, and the prophets; of Jerusalem on the Pentateuch ; and of smaller and separate Targums on the books of Daniel, Ezra, and Nehemiah. That of Jonathan Ben Uzziel, which was made about the time of the Saviour, and which includes Isaiah, is far inferior to that of Onkelos. It often wanders from the text in a wordy, allegorical explanation; admits many explanations which are arbitrary, and especially such as honour the Pharisees ; and often gives a *commentary* instead of a translation ; see Gesenius, Comm. uber den Isa. Einl. § 11. It is valuable, as it often gives a literal translation of the Hebrew, and adheres to it closely, and as it gives a statement of what was the prevailing interpretation of the sacred writings in the time when it was made. It may, therefore, be used in an argument with the modern Jews, to show that many of the passages which they refuse to refer to the Messiah were regarded by their fathers as having a relation to him.

The more modern versions of the Scriptures are evidently of little or no use in interpreting the Bible, and of no authority in attempting to furnish a correct text. On the general character of the versions above referred to, the reader may consult Horne's Intro. vol. ii. 156, seq. ; Gesenius, Einl. § 10–20.

II. COMMENTARIES. The following are among the principal, which may be referred to in illustration of Isaiah :

(1.) Commentarius in Librum Prophetiarum Isaiæ, Cura et Studio Campegii Vitringa, 2 vol. fol. 1714, 1720, 1724. This great work on Isaiah first appeared at Leuwarden in 1714. It has been several times reprinted. Vitringa was professor of theology at Franecker, and died in 1722. In this great work, Vitringa surpassed all who went before him in the illustration of Isaiah ; and none of the subsequent efforts which have been made to explain this prophet have superseded this, or rendered it valueless. It is now indeed indispensable to a correct understanding of this prophet. He is the fountain from which most subsequent writers on Isaiah have copiously drawn. His excellencies are, great learning ; copious investigation ; vast research ; judicious exposition ; an excellent spirit, and great acuteness. His faults—for faults abound in his work—are (1.) Great diffuseness of style. (2.) A leaning to the allegorical mode of interpretation. (3.) A minute, and anxious, and often fanciful effort to find something in history that accords with his view of each prediction. Often these parts of his work are forced and fanciful ; and though they evince great research and historical knowledge, yet his application of many of the prophecies must be regarded as wholly arbitrary and unsatisfactory. (4.) He did not seem to be fully acquainted with the poetic and figurative character of the prophetic style. Hence he is often forced to seek for fulfilment of particular expressions when a more complete acquaintance with the character of that style would have led him to seek for no such minute fulfilment. Yet no one can regard himself as furnished for a correct and full examination of Isaiah, who is not in possession of this elaborate work.

(2.) The collection of commentaries in the Critici Sacri, 9 vols. fol. This great work contains a collection of the best commentaries which were known at the time in which it was made. Valuable critical notes will be found in the commentary of Drusius, and occasional remarks of great value in the brief commentary of Grotius. Grotius is the father of commentators ; and especially on the New Testament, he has furnished more *materials* which have been worked up into the recent commentaries, than all other expositors united. He is especially valuable for the vast amount of classical learning which he has brought to illustrate the Scriptures. His main faults are, a want of spirituality, and a laxness of opinions ; but no man who wishes to gain a large and liberal view of the sacred writings, will deem his library complete who has not the commentary of this great man. His notes, however, on Isaiah and the Old Testament generally, are very brief.

(3.) The same work abridged and arranged by Poole, in 5 vols. fol. This work has often been reprinted, and is well known as Poole's Synopsis. It is a work of great labour. It consists in arranging in one continuous form the different expositions contained in the work last mentioned. With all the learning and labour expended on it, it is, like most other abridgements, a work which will make him who consults it regret that an abridgement had been attempted, and sigh for the original work. It is an arrangement of *opinions*, without any *reasons* for those opinions as they existed in the minds of the original authors. To a man disposed to collect *opinions* merely, this work is invaluable ; to a man who wishes to know on what opinions are based, and what is their true value, it will be regarded generally as of comparatively little use. The original work—the Critici Sacri—is of infinitely more value than this Synopsis by Poole.

(4.) The commentary of Calvin. This may be found in his works printed at Amsterdam in 1667. This commentary on Isaiah was originated in discourses which were delivered by him in his public ministry, and which were committed to writing by another hand, and afterwards revised by himself. The critical knowledge of Calvin was not great ; nor does he enter minutely into criticisms, or philology. He aims at giving the sense of Isaiah, often somewhat in the form of a paraphrase. There is little criticism of words and phrases ; little attempt to describe customs, or to illustrate the geography of the places referred to ; and there is often in the writings of this great man a want of vivacity and of point. But he is judicious and sound. His practical remarks are useful ; and his knowledge of the human heart, and his good sense, enabled him to furnish a commentary that is highly valuable.

(5.) Rosenmüller on Isaiah. This distinguished and very valuable work was first published in 1793, in three parts, and afterwards in a completely revised edition in 1810, in three volumes. The merit of Rosenmüller consists in his great learning ; in his cautious and careful collection of all the materials which existed to throw light on the prophet ; and in his clear and simple arrangement and statement. The *basis* of this work is indeed Vitringa ; but Rosenmüller is by no means confined to him. He has gathered from all sources what he regarded as necessary to an explanation of the prophet. He is judicious in his criticisms ; and not rash and reckless in attempting to modify and amend the text. He does not resemble Grotius, who is said to have 'found Christ nowhere ;' but he is almost always, particularly in the first part, an advocate for the Messianic interpretation. There can be found nowhere a more valuable collection of *materials* for an understanding of Isaiah than in Rosenmüller.

(6.) Philologisch-Kritischer und Historischer Commentar über den Isaiah, von W. Gesenius, 3 Th. Leipzig, 1821. 'The commentary of Gesenius has not rendered superfluous the work of Rosenmüller. Gesenius has certainly been more independent in ascertaining the meaning of words, and in this respect has rendered a great service to the prophet. His diligence has considerably increased the materials of exegesis by collecting a number of striking parallel passages, especially from Arabian and Syrian writers, which though not numerous, have been very accurately read. His historical illustrations, especially of the prophecies relating to foreign nations, are for the most part very valuable ; and his acuteness has made new discoveries.'—*Hengstenberg.* The great value of Gesenius consists in his explanation of words and phrases ; in his bringing to bear his vast learning in the Hebrew, and the cognate languages, to an explanation of the prophet ; in his acuteness and skill in philological investigations ; and in his use of illustrations of customs, geography, &c., from modern travellers. A favourable specimen of his manner of exposition may be seen in his commentary on the prophecy respecting Moab, ch. xv. xvi. This is translated in the Biblical Repository for January 1836. See also a translation of ch. xvii. 12–14. xviii. 1–7, in the Biblical Repository for July, 1836. Of this exposition Prof. Stuart says, 'I consider it the only successful effort which has been made, to unravel the very difficult passage of which it treats. I consider it a kind of *chef d' œuvre* among the philological efforts of this distinguished writer ; ' Bib. Rep. July, 1836, p. 220. For the general merits of Gesenius, see the article ' Hebrew Lexicography,' by Prof. Stuart, in Bib. Repository, 1836, p. 468, seq.

(7.) Isaiah ; a New Translation with a Preliminary Dissertation, and Notes, Critical, Philological, and Explanatory. By Robert Lowth, D. D., Lord Bishop of London. This very beautiful translation of Isaiah was first published in London, in quarto, in 1778, and has been several times reprinted. A German translation was published by M. Koppe, with notes and additions, at Göttingen, 1779, 1780, in 4 vols. 8vo. It is the *only* work in English, with which I am acquainted, of any very great value on Isaiah ; and it will doubtless continue to hold its rank as a standard work in sacred literature. Of all the interpreters of Isaiah, Lowth has probably most clearly discerned the true nature of the prophetic visions ; has been enabled most clearly to apprehend and express the sense of the prophet ; and has presented a translation which has been universally admired for its beauty. The faults of the work are, that his translation is often too paraphrastic ; that he indulges in great caprice of criticism ; that he often changes the Hebrew text on very slight authority ; and that there is a want of copiousness in the notes for the purpose of those who would obtain a full and accurate view of Isaiah. Lowth made good use of the aids which in his time might be derived from the researches of Oriental travellers. But since his time, this department of literature has been greatly enlarged, and important light has been thrown upon many passages which in his time were obscure.

(8.) A new translation of the Hebrew Prophets, arranged in chronological order. By George Noyes, Boston, 1833. This work professes to be simply a literal translation of the prophets, without an extended commentary. A very few notes are appended. The translation is executed with great skill and fidelity, and gives in general very correctly the meaning of the original. The translator has availed himself of the labours of Gesenius, and of the other modern critics. For a further view of this work, see North American Review for January, 1838.

(9.) Esaias ex recensione Textus Hebraei, ad fidem Codd. et verss. Latine, vertit, et Notas subjecit, J. C. Doederlin. Altdorf, 8vo. 1780. Norimbergæ, 1789.

(10.) The Book of the Prophet Isaiah, in Hebrew and English. The Hebrew text metrically arranged, the translation altered from that of Bishop Lowth. By the Right Rev. Joseph Stock, D. D., Bishop of Killala, 1804, 4to. 'There is a variety of notes, critical and explanatory, supplied partly by the translator, and partly by others. Many of these are uncommonly valuable for their depth and acuteness, and tend to elucidate in a high degree the subject matter of these prophecies;' British Critic, vol. xxviii. p. 466.

(11.) Lectures on the Prophecies of Isaiah, by Robert Macculoch. London, 1791, 4 vols. 8vo.

(12.) Hierozoicon, Sive de animalibus Sacræ Scripturæ. Auctore Samuele Bocharto. Folio, Lond. 1663. This great work has been several times reprinted. It is a work of immense research and learning; and is invaluable to all who desire to obtain a knowledge of the subjects on which it treats. Great use may be made of it in the interpretation of the Scriptures; and its authority has often been used in the following translation and notes. There is repeated mention of *animals* in Isaiah; and in no other work known to me can so accurate and valuable a description of those animals be found as in Bochart.

(13.) Christology of the Old Testament and a commentary on the Predictions of the Messiah, by the prophets. By E. W. Hengstenberg, Doctor of Phil. and Theol., Professor of the latter in the University of Berlin. Translated from the German by Reuel Keith, D. D. Alexandria, 1836. For a notice of Prof. Hengstenberg, and the character of his writings, see Biblical Repository, vol. i. p. 21. The first vol. of this work was published in 1829 It is a very valuable accession to sacred literature, and should form a part of every theological library. It evinces great learning; accurate research; and is deeply imbued with the spirit of piety. Its fault on Isaiah is, that there are many parts of this prophet which should be regarded as predictions of the Messiah, which are not noticed, or so regarded in his work. His expositions of those parts which he *has* examined (Isa. ii. iv. vii. viii. 23. ix. 1–6. xi. xii. xl. seq.) are very valuable.

(14.) Oriental Travellers. In regard to these, the main design is not usually to demonstrate the truth of the predictions of the prophets, or to furnish formal expositions of the meaning of the passages of Scripture. The illustration of the sacred writings which is to be derived from them, is mainly incidental, and often is as far as possible from the intention of the traveller himself. The illustrations which are derived from these travels, relate particularly to manners, rites, customs, usages, modes of travelling, conversation, and laws; to the animals which are mentioned in the Bible; to houses, articles of dress and furniture; and more especially to the fulfilment of the prophecies. In this respect almost a new department pertaining to the truth of the Bible has been opened by the researches of modern travellers. Many of the older commentaries were exceedingly defective and unsatisfactory for the want of the information which can now be derived from such researches; and the principal advance which can be anticipated in the interpretation of the prophecies, is probably to be derived from this source. In this respect such researches are invaluable, and particularly in the exposition of Isaiah. Some of the most complete and irrefragable demonstrations of the inspiration of the sacred writings are furnished by a simple comparison of the predictions with the descriptions of places mentioned by modern travellers. In this work, I have endeavoured to embody the results of these inquiries in the notes. As an illustration of the kind of aid to be expected from this quarter, I may refer to the notes on ch. xiii. xiv. respecting Babylon; ch. xv. xvi. respecting Moab; ch. xxiii. of Tyre; and ch. xxxiv. xxxv. of Edom. Perhaps no part of the world has excited more the attention of travellers than those where the scenes of Scripture history and of prophecy are laid. Either for commercial purposes, or by a natural desire to visit those parts of the earth which have been the scenes of sacred events, or by the mere love of adventure, most of the places distinguished either in history or in prophecy have been recently explored. The sites of Babylon, Nineveh, Tyre, Damascus, and Jerusalem have been examined; Lebanon, Egypt, Arabia, and Palestine in general have been visited; and even Moab and Arabia have been traversed. The ancient land of Idumea, long deemed inaccessible, now Arabia Petræa, has been explored by Burckhardt, by Captains Irby and Mangles, by Laborde, and still more recently by our own countrymen, Mr. Stephens, and by Messrs. Smith and Robinson. The capital of that once celebrated kingdom has been discovered and examined after it had been unknown for ages, and a most striking fulfilment of the sacred predictions has thus been furnished; see Notes on ch. xvi. and xxxiv. Perhaps there is no department of sacred learning that promises so much to illustrate the Scriptures, as that of modern travels. It is to be remembered (to use the words of Prof. Bush), that as ' the Bible, in its structure, spirit, and costume, is essentially an Eastern book, it is obvious that the natural phenomena and the moral condition of the East should be made largely tributary to its elucidation. In order to appreciate fully the truth of its descriptions, and the accuracy, force and beauty of its various allusions, it is indispensable that the reader, as far as possible, separate himself from his ordinary associations, and put himself by a kind of mental transmutation into the very circumstances of the writers. He must set himself down in the midst of Oriental scenery—gaze upon the sun, sky, mountains and rivers of Asia—go forth with the nomade tribes of the desert—follow their flocks—travel with their caravans—rest in their tents—lodge in their khans—load and unload their camels—drink at their watering places—pause during the heat of the day under their palms—cultivate the fields with their own rude implements—gather in or glean after their harvests—beat out and ventilate the grain in their open threshing floors—dress in their costume—note their proverbial or idiomatic forms of speech, and listen to the strain of song or story with which they beguile their vacant hours ; ' Pref. to **Illustrations of the Scriptures.** To use the words of a late writer in the London Quarterly Review, ' we confess that we have felt more surprise, delight, and conviction in examining the account which the travels of Burckhardt, Mangles, Irby, Leigh, and Laborde have so recently given of Judea, Edom, &c., than we have ever derived from any similar inquiry. It seems like a miracle in our own times. Twenty years ago, we read certain portions of the prophetic Scriptures with a belief that they were true, because other similar passages had, in the course of ages, been proved to be so, and we had an indistinct notion that all these (to us) obscure and indefinite denunciations had been— we know not very well when or how—accomplished ; but to have graphic descriptions, ground plans and elevations, showing the actual existence of all the heretofore vague and shadowy denunciations of God against Edom, does, we confess, excite our feelings, and exalt our confidence in prophecy to a height that no *external* evidence has hitherto done. Here we have, bursting upon our age of incredulity, by the labours of accidental, impartial, and sometimes incredulous witnesses, the certainty of existing facts, which fulfil what were hitherto considered the most vague and least intelligible of all the prophecies. The value of one such contemporaneous proof is immense.' ' It is,' to use the language of the Biblical Repository (vol. ix. pp. 456, 457), ' *sensible* evidence, graven on the eternal rocks, and to endure till those rocks shall melt in the final catastrophe of earth. The exactness between the prediction and the fulfilment is wonderful. The evidence for the truth of the prophecies is sometimes said to be cumulative ; but here we have a new volume at once opened to our view; a sudden influx of overpowering light. It is a monumental miracle, an attestation to the truth of God wrought into the very framework of the globe ; ' Review of Laborde's Journey to Petra. It may be added, that the sources of information on these interesting subjects are becoming very numerous, and already leave little to be desired. To see this, it is sufficient to mention the following :—Roberts' Oriental Illustrations ; Maundrell's Journey from Aleppo to Jerusalem ; Volney's Travels through Egypt and Syria ; Mariti's Travels through Cyprus, Syria and Palestine ; Russell's Natural History of Aleppo ; Clarke's Travels in the Holy Land ; Burckhardt's Travels in Syria ; ———— Travels in Nubia and Egypt ; Keppel's Narrative of a Journey from India to England ; Morier's Journey through Persia ; Jowett's Christian Researches ; Burnes' Travels in Bokhara ; Laborde's Journey to Petra, and the travels of Chandler, Pococke, Shaw, Pitts, Niebuhr—the ' prince of travellers'—Porter, Seetzen ; from all of whom valuable illustrations may be derived, and confirmations of the truths of the Scripture prophecies. Of all the works of this description, the most valuable for an accurate exposition of the Scriptures, in relation to the geography of the Holy Land, is the recent work of our own countrymen—' Biblical Researches in Palestine, Mount Sinai, and Arabia Petræa,' a journal of Travels in the year 1838, by E. Robinson and E. Smith, 3 vols. 8vo, 1841.

THE BOOK

OF

THE PROPHET ISAIAH.

CHAPTER I.

ANALYSIS OF THE CHAPTER.

THIS chapter contains, I. the Inscription or title to the whole book of Isaiah (ver. 1); and, II. an entire prophecy respecting the land of Judah. In regard to the title see the Notes on ver. 1.

The remainder of the chapter (ver. 2-31) comprises a single prophecy, complete in itself, and evidently delivered on a single occasion. It has no immediate connection with that which follows, though it may have been delivered about the same period. When it was delivered is not known. We are informed (ch. vi. 1) that the vision of Jehovah, which Isaiah had in the temple, occurred during the last year of the reign of Uzziah. The only indication which we can have of the time when this prophecy was uttered, is to be derived from its *location*, and from the accordance of its contents with the state of things in Judea. It is evident that the author of the arrangement, whoever he was, regarded it as properly placed in the order of time before the account of the vision of Jehovah, i.e. as having been uttered before the death of Uzziah. Nor are the contents of such a nature as to render it improbable that the collector has followed the natural order in which the prophecies were delivered. On some accounts, indeed, it might better be regarded as spoken during the reign of Ahaz; but at any time of the Jewish history in which Isaiah lived, it is not an inappropriate description of the character of the Jewish people. There is one internal indication indeed that it was not delivered in the time of Ahaz. Ahaz had filled the land with the groves and altars of idolatry. See the Introduction, § 3. But this prophecy does not allude to idolatry, as the leading and characteristic sin. It is a description of a people who still kept up the *form* of the worship of Jehovah; of a people deeply depraved indeed, and suffering under the tokens of the Divine displeasure, but who were professedly the worshippers of the true God. It is descriptive of a time when the nation was distinguished for *hypocrisy* rather than *idolatry*. It naturally falls, therefore, into the time of Uzziah, or Jotham—as it cannot be supposed that if delivered during the reign of Hezekiah, it would be so far misplaced as to constitute the introductory chapter to the whole series of prophecies. In regard to the *time* when it was uttered, and the *time* to which it refers, there have been very different opinions. Abarbanel, Grotius, and Rosenmuller, suppose that it refers to the times of Uzziah, De Wette supposes that it relates to the reign of Jotham; Piscator, Hensler, Arnold, regard it as relating to the reign of Ahaz; and Jarchi, Vitringa, and Eichhorn, refer it to the times of Hezekiah. In such a variety of opinion it is impossible to fix the time with any certainty. Nor is it very material. It was not an inappropriate description of the general character of the Jewish people; and there can be no doubt that there were times during the long prophetic life of Isaiah, when it would be found to accord fully with the condition of the nation. Unhappily, also, there are times in the church now, when it is fully descriptive of the character of the professed people of God, and it contains truths, and fearful denunciations, not less appropriate to them, than they were to the people who lived in the time of Isaiah.

The prophecy is highly objurgatory and severe in its character. It is made up of reproof, and of assurances that the evils which they were suffering were for their hypocrisy, and other sins. It commences with a solemn and very sublime address to heaven and earth to witness the deep depravity, and the pervading corruption of the land of Judah. It was such as was adapted to attract the attention, and to amaze all beings in heaven and on earth, v. 2-4. The prophet then proceeds to state that the existing calamities of the nation had been inflicted on account of their sins, and that for those sins the land was laid waste, v. 5-9. Yet they kept up the appearance of religion. They were constant and regular, externally, in offering sacrifices. But their character was deeply hypocritical. The services of God were so false and hollow, that he spurned and despised them. They were a weariness to him, and a burden, v. 10–15. The prophet then calls on the sinful nation to turn from their sins, and to seek God, with the assurance that he was willing to re-admit them to his favour; to pardon all their crimes, and to receive them as his own children, v. 16–20. If they did not do it, he assures them that heavier judgments would come upon them than they had yet experienced,

v. 21–25; and that God would so deal with them as to effect a change in the nation, and to restore the happier and purer state of things existing in former days. The wicked would be punished, and Zion would be redeemed, v. 26–31.

THE vision *a* of Isaiah, the son of Amoz, which he saw concerning Judah and Jerusalem, in the days *b* of Uzziah, Jotham, Ahaz, *and* Hezekiah, kings of Judah.

a Num.12.6.   *b* 2Ch.26.32.

---

1. *The vision.* The first verse evidently is a *title*, but whether to the whole book or only to a part of it has been questioned. As it stands here, however, it seems clearly intended to include the entire book, because it embraces all that was seen during the reigns of Uzziah, Jotham, Ahaz, and Hezekiah; that is, during the whole prophetic life of the prophet. The same title is also given to his prophecies in 2 Chron. xxxii. 32: 'Now the rest of the acts of Hezekiah, and his goodness, behold they are written in the vision of Isaiah.' Vitringa supposes that the former part of this title, 'the vision of Isaiah,' was at first affixed to the single prophecy contained in the first chapter, and that the latter part was inserted afterwards as an introduction to the whole book. This might have been done by Isaiah himself if he collected his prophecies into a volume, or by some other inspired man who collected and arranged them; see the Introduction to ch. xxxvi. —The word *vision*, חָזוֹן *hhăzōn*, denotes properly that which is *seen*, from the verb, חָזָה *hhăzâ*, to see, to behold. It is a term which is often used in reference to the prophecies of the Old Testament; Num. xii. 6; xxiv. 4; 1 Sam. iii. 1; Ps. lxxxix. 19; Dan. ii. 19; vii. 2; viii. 1; Nah. i. 1; Gen. xv. 1; Isa. xxi. 2; xxii. 1. Hence the prophets were anciently called *Seers*, as those who *saw* or witnessed events which were yet to come; comp. 1 Sam. ix. 9: 'He that is now called a Prophet was beforetime called a *Seer*;' 1 Sam. ix. 11, 18, 19; 1 Chron. ix. 22; xxix. 29; 2 Kings xviii. 13. In these *visions* the objects probably were made to pass before the mind of the prophet

as *a picture*, in which the various events were delineated with more or less distinctness, and the prophecies were spoken, or recorded, as the visions appeared to the observer. As many events could be represented only by *symbols*, those symbols became a matter of record, and are often left without explanation. On the nature of the prophetic visions, see Introduction, § 7. (4.) ¶ OF ISAIAH. The name Isaiah יְשַׁעְיָהוּ from יֵשַׁע *Yĕsha'* — salvation, help, deliverance—and יְהֹוָה *Yehovâ* or JEHOVAH, means 'salvation of JEHOVAH,' or 'JEHOVAH will save.' The Vulgate renders it ISAIAS; the LXX. Ἡσαίας *Esaias*. This is also retained in the New Testament; Mat. iii. 3; iv. 14; xii. 17; xv. 7; Mar. vii. 6; Luke iv. 17; John xii. 39; Acts viii. 28; Rom. ix. 27, &c., &c. In the book of Isaiah itself we find the form יְשַׁעְיָהוּ *Yesha'yâhu*, but in the inscription the Rabbins give the form יְשַׁעְיָה *Yesha'yâ*. It was common among the Hebrews to incorporate the name JEHOVAH, or a part of it, into their proper names; see Note on ch. vii. 14. Probably the object of this was to express veneration or regard for him—as we now give the name of a parent or friend to a child; or in many cases the name may have been given to record some signal act of mercy on the part of God, or some special interposition of his goodness. The practice of incorporating the name of the God that was worshipped into proper names was common in the East. Thus the name *Bel*, the principal idol worshipped in Babylon, appears in the proper names of the kings, as Belshazzar, &c.; comp. Note ch. xlvi. 1. It is not known that the name was given to Isaiah

2 Hear, *a* O heavens; and give ear, O earth; for the LORD hath spoken: I have nourished and brought up children,*b* and they have rebelled against me:

a De.32.1,Je.2 12.Mi.1.2.   *b* ch.63.16.

with any reference to the nature of the prophecies which he would deliver; but it is a remarkable circumstance that it coincides so entirely with the design of so large a portion of his predictions. The substance of the latter portion of the book, at least, is the *salvation* which Jehovah would effect for his people from their oppressors in Babylon, and the far mightier deliverance which the world would experience under the Messiah. ¶ *The son of Amoz.* See the Introduction, § 2. ¶ *Concerning Judah.* The Jews after the death of Solomon were divided into two kingdoms; the kingdom of Judah, and of Israel, or Ephraim. The kingdom of *Judah* included the tribes of Judah and Benjamin. Benjamin was a small tribe, and it was not commonly mentioned, or the name was lost in that of Judah. The kingdom of Israel, or Ephraim, included the remaining ten tribes. Few of the prophets appeared among them; and the personal ministry of Isaiah does not appear to have been at all extended to them. ¶ *Jerusalem.* The capital of the kingdom of Judah. It was on the dividing line between the tribes of Judah and Benjamin. It is supposed to have been founded by Melchizedek, who is called king of Salem (Gen. xiv. 18), and who is supposed to have given this name *Salem* to it. This was about 2000 years before Christ. About a century after its foundation as a city, it was captured by the *Jebusites,* who extended its walls and built a citadel on Mount Zion. By them it was called Jebus. In the conquest of Canaan, Joshua put to death its king (Josh. x. 23), and obtained possession of the town, which was jointly occupied by the Hebrews and Jebusites until the latter were expelled by David, who made it the capital of his kingdom under the name of *Jebus-Salem,* or, for the sake of easier pronunciation by changing the ב B into ר R, *Jerusalem.* After the revolt of the ten tribes, it of course became the capital of the kingdom of Judah. It was built on hills, or rocks, and was capable of being strongly fortified, and was well adapted to be the capital of the nation. For a more full description of Jerusalem, see Notes on Mat. ii. 1. The vision which is here spoken of as having been seen respecting Judah and Jerusalem, pertains only to this chapter; see ch. ii. 1. ¶ *In the days of Uzziah.* In the *time,* or during the *reign* of Uzziah; 2 Chron. xxvi.; comp. Intro. § 3. He was sixteen years old when he began to reign, and reigned fifty-two years. It is not affirmed or supposed that Isaiah began to prophesy at the *commencement* of his reign. The first part of the long reign of Uzziah was prosperous. He gained important victories over his enemies, and fortified his kingdom; 2 Chron. xxvi. 5–15. He had under him an army of more than three hundred thousand men. But he became proud—attempted an act of sacrilege—was smitten of God, and died a leper. But though the kingdom under Uzziah was flourishing, yet it had in it the elements of decay. During the previous reign of Joash, it had been invaded and weakened by the Assyrians, and a large amount of wealth had been taken to Damascus, the capital of Syria; 2 Chron. xxiv. 23, 24. It is not improbable that those ravages were repeated during the latter part of the reign of Uzziah; comp. Isa. i. 7. ¶ *Jotham.* He began to reign at the age of twenty-five years, and reigned sixteen years; 2 Chron. xxvii. 1, 2. ¶ *Ahaz.* He began to reign at the age of twenty, and reigned sixteen years. He was a wicked man, and during his reign the kingdom was involved in crimes and calamities; 2 Chron. xxviii. ¶ *Hezekiah.* He was a virtuous and upright prince. He began his reign at the age of twenty-five years, and reigned twenty-nine; 2 Chron. xxix; see the Introduction § 3.

2. *Hear, O heavens.* This is properly the beginning of the prophecy. It is a sublime commencement; and is of a highly poetic character. The heavens and the earth are summoned to bear witness to the apostacy, ingratitude, and deep depravity of the chosen people of God. The address is expressive of deep feeling,—the bursting forth

of a heart filled with amazement at a wonderful and unusual event. The same sublime beginning is found in the song of Moses, Deut. xxxii. 1:

Give ear, O ye heavens, and I will speak;
And hear, O earth, the words of my mouth.

comp. Ps. iv. 3, 4. Thus also the prophets often invoke the hills and mountains to hear them; Ezek. vi. 3: 'Ye mountains of Israel, hear the words of the Lord God: Thus saith the Lord God to the mountains, and to the hills, and to the rivers, and to the valleys;' comp. Ezek. xxxvi. 1. 'Be astonished, O ye heavens, at this, and be horribly afraid, be ye very desolate, saith the Lord,' Jer. ii. 12. By the *heavens* therefore, in this place, we are not to understand the *inhabitants* of heaven, i. e. the angels, any more than by *the hills* we are to understand the *inhabitants* of the mountains. It is high poetic language, denoting the *importance* of the subject, and the remarkable and amazing truth to which the attention was to be called. ¶ *Give ear. O earth.* It was common thus to address the earth on any remarkable occasion, especially any one implying warm expostulation, Jer. v, 19; xxii. 29; Micah i. 2; vi. 2; Isa. xxxiv. 1; xlix. 13. ¶ *For.* Since it is Jehovah that speaks, all the universe is summoned to attend; comp. Ps. xxxiii. 8, 9: 'Let all the earth fear the Lord; let all the inhabitants of the world stand in awe of him. For he spake and it was done; he commanded and it stood fast.' ¶ *The* LORD.—יְהוָה *Yehōvâ*, or JEHOVAH. The small *capitals* used here and elsewhere throughout the Bible, in printing the word LORD, denote that the original word is JEHOVAH. It is derived from the verb הָיָה *hâyâ, to be;* and is used to denote *being*, or the fountain of being, and can be applied only to the true God; comp. Ex. iii. 14: 'And God said unto Moses, I AM THAT I AM,' אֶהְיֶה אֲשֶׁר אֶהְיֶה; Ex. vi. 3; Num. xi. 21; Isa. xlvii. 8. It is a name which is never given to idols, or conferred on a creature; and though it occurs often in the Hebrew Scriptures, as is indicated by the small capitals, yet our translators have retained it but four times; Ex. vi. 3; Ps. lxxxiii. 18; Isa. xii. 2; xxvi. 4. In *combination*, however, with

other names, it occurs often. Thus in *Isaiah*, meaning the salvation of Jehovah; *Jeremiah*, the exaltation or grandeur of Jehovah, &c.; comp. Gen. xxii. 14: 'Abraham called the name of the place *Jehovah-jireh*,' Ex. xvii. 15; Judg. vi. 24; Ezek. xlviii. 35. The Jews never pronounced this name, not even in reading their own Scriptures. So sacred did they deem it, that when it occurred in their books, instead of the word JEHOVAH, they substituted the word ADONAI, אֲדֹנָי *Lord.* Our translators have shown respect to this feeling of the Jews in regard to the sacredness of the name; and hence, have rendered it by the name of LORD—a word which by no means conveys the sense of the word JEHOVAH. It would have been an advantage to our version if the word JEHOVAH had been retained wherever it occurs in the original. ¶ *I have nourished.* Heb. *I have made great;* גִּדַּלְתִּי. In Piel, the word means *to make great, to cause to grow;* as e. g. the hair; Num. vi. 5, plants, Isa. xliv. 14; then to educate or bring up children; Isa. xlix. 21, 41, 13; 2 Kings x. 6. ¶ *And brought up.* רוֹמַמְתִּי *rōmamtī*, from רוּם *rûm*, to lift up or exalt. In Piel it means to bring up, nourish, educate; Isaiah xxiii. 4. These words, though applied often to the training up of children, yet are here used also to denote the *elevation* to which they had been raised. He had not merely trained them up, but he had trained them up to *an elevated station;* to peculiar honour and privileges. ¶ *Children.* Heb. בָּנִים *bânim—sons.* They were the adopted children of God; and they are represented as being weak, and ignorant, and helpless as children, when he took them under his fatherly protection and care; Hos. xi. 1: 'When Israel was a child, then I loved him, and called my son out of Egypt;' comp. Note, Mat. ii. 15; Isa. lxiii. 8–16. ¶ *They have rebelled.* This complaint was often brought against the Jews; comp. Isa. lxiii. 10; Jer. ii. 6, 7, 8.—This is the sum of the charge against them. God had shown them peculiar favours. He recounted his mercy in bringing them out of Egypt; and on the ground of this, he demanded obedience and love; comp. Ex. xx. 1, 2, 3. And yet they

3 The ox[a] knoweth his owner, and the ass his master's crib : *but* Israel doth not know, my people doth not consider.

4 Ah, sinful nation, a people laden [1] with [b] iniquity, a seed of evil-doers, children that are corrupters ! they have forsaken the LORD, they have provoked the Holy One of Israel unto anger, they are [2]gone away backward.

a Jer.8.7. 1 *of heaviness.* *b* Mat.11.21.
2 *alienat. d, or separated,* Ps.58.3.

---

had forgotten him, and rebelled against him. The Targum of Jonathan, an ancient Chaldee version, has well expressed the idea here. ' Hear, O heavens, which were moved when I gave my law to my people : give ear, O earth, which didst tremble before my word, for the Lord has spoken. My people, the house of Israel, whom I called sons,—I loved them,—I honoured them, and they rebelled against me.' The same is true substantially of all sinners; and alas, how often may a similar expostulation be made with the professed people of God !

3. *The ox,* &c. The design of this comparison is to show the great stupidity and ingratitude of the Jews. Even the least sagacious and most stupid of the animals, destitute as they are of reason and conscience, evince knowledge and submission far more than the professed people of God. The ox is a well known domestic animal, remarkable for patient willingness to toil, and for submission to his owner. ¶ *Knoweth his owner.* Recognizes, or is submissive to him. ¶ *The ass.* A well known animal, proverbial for dulness and stupidity. ¶ *His master's crib.* אֵבוּס from אָבַס *âbâs,* to heap up, and then to fatten. Hence it is applied to the stall, barn, or crib, where cattle are fed, or made fat ; Job xxxix. 9 ; Prov. xiv. 4. The ass has sufficient knowledge to understand that his *support* is derived from that. The idea is, that the ox was more submissive to laws than the Jews ; and that even the most stupid animal better knew whence support was to be derived, than they did the source of their comfort and protection. The ass would not wander away, and the ox would not rebel as they had done. This comparison was very striking, and very humiliating, and nothing could be more fitted to bring down their pride. A similar comparison is elsewhere used. Thus, in Jer. viii. 7, the Jews are contrasted with the stork : ' Yea, the stork in the heaven knoweth her appointed times : and the turtle [dove], and the crane, and the swallow, observe the time of their coming ; but my people know not the judgment of the Lord.' This idea has been beautifully expressed by Watts :

The brutes obey their God,
And bow their necks to men ;
But we more base, more brutish things,
Reject his easy reign.

Comp. Hos. xi. 4. ¶ *But Israel.* The name *Israel,* though after the division of the tribes into two kingdoms specifically employed to denote that of the ten tribes, is often used in the more general sense to denote the whole people of the Jews, including the kingdom of Judah. It refers here to the kingdom of Judah, though a name is used which is not inappropriately characteristic of the whole people. ¶ *Doth not know.* The Latin Vulgate, the Septuagint, and the Arabic, add the word ' me.' The word *know* is used in the sense of *recognizing* him as their Lord ; of acknowledging him, or submitting to him. ¶ *Doth not consider.* Heb. Do not *understand.* They have a stupidity greater than the brute.

4. *Ah! sinful nation.* The word rendered ' ah !'— הוֹי *hoy*—is not a mere exclamation, expressing astonishment. It is rather an interjection denouncing threatening, or punishment. ' Wo to the sinful nation.' Vulg. ' Vae genti peccatrici.' The corruption pertained to the *nation,* and not merely to a part. It had become general. ¶ *Laden with iniquity.* The word translated *laden*— כָּבֵד—denotes properly any thing *heavy,* or burdensome ; from כָּבַד *kâbhâdh, to be heavy.* It means that they were oppressed, and borne down with the *weight* of their sins. Thus we say, Sin sits *heavy* on the conscience. Thus Cain said, ' My punishment is greater than I can bear ;' Gen. iv. 13. The word

5 Why *a* should ye be stricken
any more? ye will ¹revolt more and

a Je.2.30.   1 *increase revolt.*

more. The whole head is sick, and
the whole heart faint.

is applied to an *employment* as being
burdensome; Exod. xviii. 18: 'This
thing is too *heavy* for thee.' Num. xi.
14: 'I am not able to bear all this people alone; it is too *heavy* for me.' It is
applied also to a *famine*, as being heavy,
severe, distressing. Gen. xii. 10: 'For
the famine was *grievous* (כָּבֵד *heavy*) in
the land;' Gen. xli. 31. It is also applied
to *speech*, as being heavy, dull, unintelligible. Ex. iv. 10: 'I am slow (heavy
כְּבַד) of speech, and of a slow (heavy כְּבַד)
tongue.' It is not applied to *sin* in the
Scriptures, except in this place, or except in the sense of making atonement
for it. The idea however is very striking—that of a *nation*—an entire people,
bowed and crushed under the enormous
weight of accumulated crimes. To pardon iniquity, or to *atone* for it, is represented by *bearing it*, as if it were a heavy
burden. Ex. xxviii. 38, 43, 'That
Aaron may *bear* the iniquity of the holy
things.' Lev. x. 17: 'God hath given
it you to *bear* the iniquity of the congregation.' Lev. xxii. 9; xvi. 22; Num.
xviii. 1; Isa. liii. 6: 'Jehovah hath laid
on him the iniquity of us all.' 11: 'He
shall *bear* their iniquities.' 1 Pet. ii.
24: 'Who his own self bare our sins
in his own body on the tree.' ¶ *A seed.*
זֶרַע *zĕrā'*, from זָרַע *zārā'*, to sow, to
scatter, to disperse. It is applied to
seed sown in a field; Judg. vi. 3; Gen.
i. 11, 12; xlvii. 23; to plants set out, or
engrafted; or to planting, or transplant-
ing a nation. Isa. xvii. 10: 'And thou
shalt *set it* [תִּזְרָעֶנּוּ shalt sow, or plant it]
with strange slips.' Hence it is applied
to children, posterity, descendants, from
the resemblance to seed sown, and to a
harvest springing up, and spreading.
The word is applied by way of eminence
to the Jews, as being THE *seed* or posterity of Abraham, according to the
promise that his seed should be as the
stars of heaven; Gen. xii. 7; xiii. 15,
16; xv. 5, 18; xvii. 7, &c. ¶ *Children.*
Heb. *sons*—the same word that is used
in ver. 2. They were the adopted people or sons of God, but they had now become corrupt. ¶ *That are corrupters.*

מַשְׁחִיתִים *măshhĭthăm*, from שָׁחַת *shăh-
hăth*, to destroy, to lay waste, as an invading army does a city or country;
Josh. xxii. 33; Gen. xix. 13. To destroy a vineyard; Jer. xii. 10. To break
down walls; Ezek. xxvi. 4. Applied to
conduct, it means to *destroy*, or lay
waste virtuous principles; to break
down the barriers to vice; to corrupt
the morals. Gen. vi. 12: 'And God
looked upon the earth, and it was *corrupt*—נִשְׁחָתָה;—for all flesh had corrupted his way—הִשְׁחִית—upon the
earth;' Deut. iv. 16; xxxi. 29; Judg.
ii. 19. They were not merely corrupt
themselves, but they corrupted others
by their example. This is always the
case. When men become infidels and
profligates themselves, they seek to
make as many more so as possible.
The Jews did this by their wicked lives.
The same charge is often brought against
them; see Judg. ii. 12; Zeph. iii. 7.
¶ *They have provoked.* Heb. נִאֲצוּ.
'They have *despised* the Holy One;'
comp. Prov. i. 30; v. 12; xv. 5. Vulg.
'They have *blasphemed.*' Septuagint,
παρωργίσατε. 'You have *provoked* him
to anger.' The meaning is, that they
had so *despised* him, as to excite his
indignation. ¶ *The Holy One of Israel.*
God; called the Holy One of Israel because he was revealed to them as *their*
God, or they were taught to regard him
as the sacred object of their worship.
¶ *They are gone away backward.*
Lowth: 'They have turned their backs
upon him.' The word rendered *they are
gone away*, נָזֹרוּ *năzŏrū*, from זוּר *zūr*,
means properly, *to become estranged;
to be alienated.* Job. xix. 13: 'Mine
acquaintance are verily *estranged* from
me.' It means especially that declin-
ing from God, or that alienation, which
takes place when men commit sin; Ps.
lxxviii. 30.

5. *Why, &c.* The prophet now, by
an abrupt change in the discourse, calls
their attention to the *effects* of their
sins. Instead of saying that they *had*
been smitten, or of saying that they
had been punished *for their sins*, he

assumes both, and asks why it should be repeated. The Vulgate reads this: 'Super quo—on what part—shall I smite you any more?' This expresses well the sense of the Hebrew—עַל־מֶה —*upon what;* and the meaning is, 'what part of the body can be found on which blows have not been inflicted? On every part there are traces of the stripes which have been inflicted for your sins.' The idea is taken from a body that is all covered over with *weals* or marks of blows, and the idea is, that the whole frame is one continued bruise, and there remains no sound part to be stricken. The particular chastisement to which the prophet refers is specified in ver. 7–9. In ver. 5, 6, he refers to the calamities of the nation, under the image of a person wounded and chastised for crimes. Such a figure of speech is not uncommon in the classic writers. Thus Cicero (de fin. iv. 14) says, 'quae hic reipublicae vulnera imponebat hic sanabat.' See also Tusc. Quaes. iii. 22; Ad Quintum fratrem, ii. 25; Sallust; Cat. 10. ¶ *Should ye be stricken.* Smitten, or punished. The manner in which they *had* been punished, he specifies in ver. 7, 8. Jerome says, that the sense is, 'there is no medicine which I can administer to your wounds. All your members are full of wounds; and there is no part of your body which has not been smitten before. The more you are afflicted, the more will your impiety and iniquity increase.' The word here, תֻּכּוּ *thŭkkū*, from נָכָה, means to smite, to beat, to strike down, to slay, or kill. It is applied to the infliction of punishment on an individual; or to the judgments of God by the plague, pestilence, or sickness. Gen. xix. 2: 'And they *smote* the men that were at the door with blindness.' Num. xiv. 12: 'And I will *smite* them with the pestilence.' Ex. vii. 25: 'After that the Lord *had smitten* the river,' i.e. had changed it into blood; comp. verse 20; Zech. x. 2. Here it refers to the judgments inflicted on the nation as the punishment of their crimes. ¶ *Ye will revolt.* Heb. You will *add* defection, or revolt. The effect of calamity, and punishment, will be only to increase rebellion. Where the heart is right with God, the tendency of affliction is to humble it, and lead it more and more to God. Where it is evil, the tendency is to make the sinner more obstinate and rebellious. This effect of *punishment* is seen every where. Sinners revolt more and more. They become sullen, and malignant, and fretful; they plunge into vice to seek temporary relief, and thus they become more and more alienated from God. ¶ *The whole head.* The prophet proceeds to specify more definitely what he had just said respecting their being *stricken.* He designates each of the members of the body—thus comparing the Jewish people to the human body when under severe punishment. The word *head* in the Scriptures is often used to denote the *princes, leaders,* or *chiefs* of the nation. But the expression here is used as a figure taken from the human body, and refers solely to the *punishment* of the people, not to their *sins.* It means that *all* had been smitten—all was filled with the effects of punishment—as the human body is when the head and all the members are diseased. ¶ *Is sick.* Is so smitten—so punished, that it has become sick and painful. Heb. לָחֳלִי—*for sickness,* or *pain.* The preposition לְ denotes a *state,* or condition of any thing. Ps. lxix. 21. 'And in [לְ] my thirst, they gave me vinegar to drink.' The expression is *intensive,* and denotes that the head was entirely sick. ¶ *The whole heart faint.* The *heart* is here put for the whole region of the chest or stomach. As when the head is violently pained, there is also sickness at the heart, or in the stomach, and as these are indications of *entire* or *total* prostration of the frame so the expression here denotes the perfect desolation which had come over the nation. ¶ *Faint.* Sick, feeble, without vigour, attended with nausea. Jer. viii. 18: 'When I would comfort myself in my sorrow, my heart is faint within me;' Lam. i. 22. When the body is suffering; when severe punishment is inflicted, the effect is to produce languor and faintness at the seat of life. This is the idea here. Their punishment had been so severe for their sins, that the heart was languid and feeble—still keeping up the figure drawn from the human body.

6 From the sole of the foot even unto the head *there is* no soundness in it ; *but* wounds, and bruises, and putrifying sores : they have not been closed, neither bound up, neither mollified with ointment.[1]

1 or, *oil.*

6. *From the sole of the foot,* &c. Or as we say, ' from head to foot,' that is, in every part of the body. There may be included also the idea that this extended from the lowest to the highest among the people. The Chaldee paraphrase is, ' from the lowest of the people even to the princes—all are contumacious and rebellious.' ¶ *No soundness.* מְתֹם *methôm,* from תָּמַם *thâmăm,* to be perfect, sound, uninjured. There is no part unaffected ; no part that is sound. It is all smitten and sore. ¶ *But wounds.* The precise shade of difference between this and the two following words may not be apparent. *Together,* they mean such wounds and contusions as are inflicted upon man by scourging, or beating him. This mode of punishment was common among the Jews ; as it is at the East at this time. Abarbanel and Kimchi say that the word here rendered *wounds* (פֶּצַע, a verbal from פָּצַע to wound, to mutilate), means an open wound, or a cut from which blood flows. ¶ *Bruises.* חַבּוּרָה *hhăbbŭrâ.* This word means a contusion, or the effect of a blow where the skin is not broken ; such a contusion as to produce a swelling, and livid appearance ; or to make it, as we say, black and blue. ¶ *Putrifying sores.* The Hebrew rather means *recent,* or *fresh* wounds ; or rather, perhaps, a running wound, which continues fresh and open ; which cannot be cicatrized, or dried up. The LXX. render it elegantly πληγὴ φλεγμαίνουσα, a swelling, or tumefying wound. The expression is applied usually to inflammations, as of boils, or to the swelling of the tonsils, &c. ¶ *They have not been closed* That is, the lips had not been pressed together, to remove the blood from the wound. The meaning is, that nothing had been done towards healing the wound. It was an unhealed, undressed, all-pervading sore. The art of medicine, in the East, consists chiefly in external applications ; accordingly the prophet's images in this place are all taken from surgery. Sir John Chardin, in his note on Prov. iii. 8,

' It shall be health to thy navel, and marrow to thy bones,' observes, that the comparison is taken from the plasters, ointments, oils, and frictions, which are made use of in the East in most maladies. ' In Judea,' says Tavernier, ' they have a certain preparation of oil, and melted grease, which they commonly use for the healing of wounds.' *Lowth.* Comp. Note on ch. xxxviii. 21. ¶ *Neither mollified with ointment.* Neither made *soft,* or *tender,* with ointment. Great use was made, in Eastern nations, of *oil,* and various kinds of unguents, in medicine. Hence the good Samaritan is represented as pouring in *oil* and wine into the wounds of the man that fell among thieves (Luke x. 34) ; and the apostles were directed to anoint with oil those who were sick ; James v. 14 ; comp. Rev. iii. 18. ¶ *Ointment.* Heb. *oil.* שָׁמֶן. The oil of olives was used commonly for this purpose. The whole figure in these two verses relates to their *being punished* for their sins. It is taken from the appearance of a man who is severely beaten, or scourged for crime ; whose wounds had not been dressed ; and who was thus a continued bruise, or sore, from his head to his feet. The *cause* of this the prophet states afterwards, ver. 10, seq. With great skill he first reminds them of what they saw and knew, that they were severely punished ; and then states to them the *cause* of it. Of the calamities to which the prophet refers, they could have no doubt. They were every where visible in all their cities and towns. On these far-spreading desolations, he fixes the eye distinctly first. Had he *begun* with the statement of their *depravity,* they would probably have revolted at it. But being presented with a statement of their sufferings, which they all saw and felt, they were prepared for the statement of the cause.—To find access to the consciences of sinners, and to convince them of their guilt, it is often necessary to remind them first of the calamities in which they are actually

7 Your country *is* desolate,*a* your cities *are* burned with fire: your land, strangers devour it in your

a Deut. 28.51.

presence, and *it is* desolate, as overthrown[1] by strangers.

8 And the daughter of Zion is

1 *the overthrow of.*

involved; and then to search for the cause. This passage, therefore, has no reference to their moral character. It relates solely to their punishment. It is often indeed adduced to prove the doctrine of depravity; but it has no direct reference to it, and it should *not* be adduced to prove that men are depraved, or applied as referring to the moral condition of man. The account of their *moral* character, as the cause of their calamities, is given in ver. 10–14. That statement will fully account for the many woes which had come on the nation.

7. *Your country is desolate.* This is the *literal* statement of what he had just affirmed by a figure. In this there was much art. The figure (ver. 6) was striking. The resemblance between a man severely beaten, and entirely livid and sore, and a land perfectly desolate, was so impressive as to arrest the attention. This had been threatened as one of the curses which should attend disobedience; Lev. xxvi. 33:

And I will scatter you among the heathen,
And will draw out a sword after you:
And your land shall be desolate,
And your cities waste.

Comp. ver. 31, 32; Deut. xxviii. 49–52. It is not certain, or agreed among expositors, to what time the prophet refers in this passage. Some have supposed that he refers to the time of *Ahaz*, and to the calamities which came upon the nation during his reign; 2 Chron xxviii. 5–8. But the probability is, that this refers to the time of Uzziah; see the Analysis of the chapter. The reign of Uzziah was indeed prosperous; 2 Chron. xxvi. But it is to be remembered that the land had been ravaged just before, under the reigns of Joash and Amaziah, by the kings of Syria and Israel; 2 Kings xiv. 8–14; 2 Chron. xxiv.; xxv.; and it is by no means probable that it had recovered in the time of Uzziah. It was lying under the effect of the former desolation, and not improbably the enemies of the Jews were even then hovering around it, and possibly still in the

very midst of it. The kingdom was going to decay, and the reign of Uzziah gave it only a temporary prosperity. ¶ *Is desolate.* Is desolation. שְׁמָמָה *shemâmâ.* This is a Hebrew mode of emphatic expression, denoting that the desolation was so universal that the land might be said to be entirely in ruins. ¶ *Your land.* That is, the *fruit*, or *productions* of the land. Foreigners consume all that it produces. ¶ *Strangers* זָרִים *zârîm*, from זוּר *zûr*, to be alienated, or estranged, ver. 4. It is applied to *foreigners*, i. e. those who were not Israelites, Ex. xxx. 33; and is often used to denote an enemy, a foe, a barbarian; Ps. cix. 11:

Let the extortioner catch all that he hath,
And let the *strangers* plunder his labour.

Ezek. xi. 9; xxviii. 10; xxx. 12; Hos. vii. 9; viii. 7. The word refers here particularly to the Syrians. ¶ *Devour it.* Consume its provisions. ¶ *In your presence.* This is a circumstance that greatly heightens the calamity, that they were compelled to look on and witness the desolation, without being able to prevent it. ¶ *As overthrown by strangers.* כְּמַהְפֵּכַת זָרִים—from הָפַךְ *hâphakh*, to turn, to overturn, to destroy as a city; Gen. xix. 21–25; Deut. xxix. 22. It refers to the changes which an invading foe produces in a nation, where every thing is subverted; where cities are destroyed, walls are thrown down, and fields and vineyards laid waste. The land was as if an invading army had passed through it, and completely overturned everything. Lowth proposes to read this, 'as if destroyed by an inundation;' but without authority. The desolation caused by the ravages of foreigners, at a time when the nations were barbarous, was the highest possible image of distress, and the prophet dwells on it, though with some appearance of repetition.

8. *And the daughter of Zion. Zion*, or *Sion*, was the name of one of the hills on which the city of Jerusalem was built. On this hill formerly stood the

left as *a cottage in a vineyard,* | as a lodge in a garden of cucumbers, as a besieged city.

a Lam.2.6.

city of the *Jebusites,* and when David took it from them he transferred to it his court, and it was called the city of David, or the holy hill. It was in the southern part of the city. As Zion became the residence of the court, and was the most important part of the city, the name was often used to denote the city itself, and is often applied to the whole of Jerusalem. The phrase 'daughter of Zion' here means Zion itself, or *Jerusalem.* The name *daughter* is given to it by a personification in accordance with a common custom in Eastern writers, by which beautiful towns and cities are likened to young females. The name *mother* is also applied in the same way. Perhaps the custom arose from the fact that when a city was built, towns and villages would spring up round it—and the first would be called the *mother-city* (hence the word metropolis). The expression was also employed as an image of *beauty,* from a fancied resemblance between a beautiful town and a beautiful and well-dressed woman. Thus Ps. xlv. 13, the phrase *daughter of Tyre,* means Tyre itself; Ps. cxxxvii. 8, *daughter of Babylon,* i. e. Babylon; Isa. xxxvii. 22, 'The virgin, the daughter of Zion;' Jer. xlvi. 2; Isa. xxiii. 12; Jer. xiv. 17; Num. xxi. 23, 32, (Heb.); Jud. xi. 26. *Is left.* נוֹתְרָה. The word here used denotes left as *a part* or *remnant* is left—not left *entire,* or *complete,* but in a weakened or divided state. ¶ *As a cottage.* Literally, *a shade,* or *shelter*—כְּסֻכָּה *kesŭkkâ,* a temporary habitation erected in vineyards to give shelter to the grapegatherers, and to those who were appointed to *watch* the vineyard to guard it from depredation; comp. Note Matt. xxi. 33. The following passage from Mr. Jowett's 'Christian Researches,' describing what he himself saw, will throw light on this verse. 'Extensive fields of ripe melons and cucumbers adorned the sides of the river (the Nile). They grew in such abundance that the sailors freely helped themselves. Some guard, however, is placed upon them. Occasionally, but at long and desolate intervals, we may observe a little hut,

made of reeds, just capable of containing one man ; being in fact little more than a fence against a north wind. In these I have observed, sometimes, a poor old man, perhaps lame, protecting the property. It exactly illustrates Isa. i. 8.' 'Gardens were often probably unfenced, and formerly, as now, esculent vegetables were planted in some fertile spot in the open field. A custom prevails in Hindostan, as travellers inform us, of planting in the commencement of the rainy season, in the extensive plains, an abundance of melons, cucumbers, gourds, &c. In the centre of the field is an artificial mound with a hut on the top, just large enough to shelter a person from the storm and the heat ;' Bib. Dic. A.S.U. The following cut will convey a clear idea of such a cottage.

LODGE IN A GARDEN OF CUCUMBERS.

Such a cottage would be designed only for a *temporary* habitation. So Jerusalem seemed to be left amidst the surrounding desolation as a temporary abode, soon to be destroyed. ¶ *As a lodge.* The word *lodge* here properly denotes a place for *passing the night,* but it means also a *temporary abode.* It was erected to afford a shelter to those who guarded the enclosure from thieves, or from jackals, and small foxes. 'The jackal,' says Hasselquist, 'is a species of mustela, which is very common in Palestine, especially during the vintage,

9 Except *a* the LORD of hosts had left unto us a very small remnant, we should have been as Sodom,*b* *and* we should have been like unto Gomorrah.

a Lam.3.22. Rom.9.29.
b Gen.19.24.

and often destroys whole vineyards, and gardens of cucumbers. ¶ *A garden of cucumbers.* The word *cucumbers* here probably includes every thing of the *melon* kind, as well as the cucumber. They are in great request in that region on account of their cooling qualities, and are produced in great abundance and perfection. These things are particularly mentioned among the luxuries which the Israelites enjoyed in Egypt, and for which they sighed when they were in the wilderness. Num. xi. 5: ' We remember—the cucumbers and the melons,' &c. The cucumber which is produced in Egypt and Palestine is large—usually a foot in length, soft, tender, sweet, and easy of digestion *(Gesenius)*, and being of a cooling nature, was peculiarly delicious in their hot climate. The meaning here is, that Jerusalem seemed to be left as a temporary, lonely habitation, soon to be forsaken and destroyed. ¶ *As a besieged city.* כְּעִיר נְצוּרָה. *Lowth.* ' As a city taken by siege.' *Noyes.* " ' So is the delivered city.' This translation was first proposed by Arnoldi of Marburg. It avoids the incongruity of comparing a city with a city, and requires no alteration of the text except a change of the vowel points. According to this translation, the meaning will be, that all things round about the city lay desolate, like the withered vines of a cucumber garden around the watchman's hut ; in other words, that the city alone stood safe amidst the ruins caused by the enemy, like the hut in a gathered garden of cucumbers." *Noyes.* According to this interpretation, the word נְצוּרָה *netzûrâ* is derived not from עוּר *tzūr,* to besiege, to press, to straiten ; but from נָעַר *nâtzăr,* to preserve, keep, defend ; comp. Ezek. vi. 12. The Hebrew will bear this translation ; and the concinnity of the comparison will thus be preserved. I rather prefer, however, the common interpretation, as being more obviously the sense of the Hebrew, and as being sufficiently in accordance with the design of the prophet. The idea then is, that of a city straitened by a siege, yet standing as a temporary habitation, while all the country around was lying in ruins. Jerusalem, alone preserved amidst the desolation spreading throughout the land, will resemble a temporary lodge in the garden—itself soon to be removed or destroyed. The essential idea, whatever translation is adopted, is that of the solitude, loneliness, and temporary continuance of even Jerusalem, while all around was involved in desolation and ruin.

9. *Except, &c.* It is owing entirely to the mercy of God, that we are not like Sodom. The prophet traces this not to the goodness of the nation, not to any power or merit of theirs, but solely to the mercy of God. This passage the apostle Paul has used in an argument to establish the doctrine of divine sovereignty in the salvation of men ; see Note Rom. ix 29. ¶ *The Lord.* Heb. JEHOVAH. Note ver. 2. ¶ *Of hosts.* צְבָאוֹת *Tzebhâôth*—the word sometimes translated *Sabaoth* ; Rom. ix. 29 ; James v. 4. The word means literally *armies* or *military hosts.* It is applied however to the *angels* which surround the throne of God ; 1 Kings xxii. 19 ; 2 Chron. xviii. 18 ; Ps. ciii. 21 ; and to *the stars* or constellations that appear to be marshalled in the sky ; Jer. xxxiii. 22 ; Isa. xl. 26. This *host,* or the " host of heaven," was frequently an object of idolatrous worship ; Deut. iv. 19 : xvii. 3 ; 2 Kings xvii. 16. God is called JEHOVAH *of hosts* because he is at the head of all these armies, as their leader and commander ; he marshals and directs them —as a general does the army under his command. ' This,' says Gesenius, ' is the most common name of God in Isaiah, and in Jeremiah, Zechariah, and Malachi. It represents him as the ruler of the hosts of heaven, i.e., the angels and the stars. Sometimes, but less frequently, we meet with the appellation Jehovah, *God* of hosts. Hence, some suppose the expression *Jehovah of hosts* to be elliptical. But it is not a correct

10 Hear the word of the LORD, ye rulers of Sodom; give ear unto the law of our God, ye people of Gomorrah:

11 To what purpose *a* is the multitude of your sacrifices unto me? saith the LORD: I am full of the

a Ps.50.8,&c. Amos 5 21,22.

---

assertion that Jehovah, as a proper name, admits of no genitive. But such relations and adjuncts as depend upon the genitive, often depend upon proper names. So in Arabic, one is called *Rebiah of the poor* in reference to his liability.' The name is given *here*, because to save any portion of a nation so wicked implied the exercise of the same power as that by which he controlled the hosts of heaven. ¶ *Remnant.* A small part—that which is left. It means here, that God had spared a portion of the nation, so that they were not entirely overthrown. ¶ *We should have been as Sodom,* &c. This does not refer to the *character* of the people, but to their *destiny.* If God had not interposed to save them they would have been overwhelmed *entirely* as Sodom was; comp. Gen. xix. 24, 25.

10. *Hear the word of the Lord.* The *message* of God. Having stated the *calamities* under which the nation was groaning, the prophet proceeds to address the rulers, and to state the *cause* of all these woes. ¶ *Ye rulers of Sodom.* The incidental mention of Sodom in the previous verse gives occasion for this beautiful transition, and abrupt and spirited address. Their character and destiny were almost like those of Sodom, and the prophet therefore openly addresses the rulers as being called to preside over a people like those in Sodom. There could have been no more severe or cutting reproof of their wickedness than to address them as resembling the people whom God overthrew for their enormous crimes.

11. *To what purpose.* לָמָּה לִי. 'What is it to me; or what profit or pleasure can I have in them?' God here replies to an *objection* which might be urged by the Jews to the representation which had been made of their guilt. The objection would be, that they were strict in the duties of their religion, and that they even abounded in offering victims of sacrifice. God replies in this and the following verses,

that all this would be of no use, and would meet with no acceptance, unless it were the offering of *the heart.* He demanded righteousness; and without that, all external offerings would be vain. The same sentiment often occurs in the Old Testament.

Hath Jehovah as great delight in burnt-offerings
　　and sacrifices
As in obeying the voice of the Lord?
Behold, to obey is better than sacrifice,
And to hearken than the fat of rams.
　　　　　　　　　　　1 Sam. xv. 22

To what purpose shall frankincense be brought
　　unto me from Sabah?
Or the rich aromatic reed from a far country?
Your burnt-offerings are not acceptable,
Nor your sacrifices pleasant unto me.
　　　　　　　　Jer. vi. 20. *Blaney.*

For I desired mercy and not sacrifice;
And the knowledge of God more than burnt-
　　offerings.　　　　　Hosea vi. 6.
I hate, I despise your solemn feast days,
And I will not smell in your solemn assemblies;
Though ye offer me your burnt-offerings,
And your meat-offerings,
I will not accept them;
Neither will I regard the thank-offerings of your
　　fat beasts.
Take thou away from me the noise of thy songs;
For I will not hear the melody of thy viols.
But let judgment run down as waters,
And righteousness as a mighty stream.
　　　　　　　　　　Amos v. 21—24.

¶ *Is the multitude.* There was no deficiency in the amount of offerings. It was admitted that they complied in this respect with the requirements of the law; and that they offered an *abundance* of sacrifices, so numerous as to be called a *multitude*—רֹב *rŏbh,* a vast number. Hypocrites abound in outward religious observances just in proportion to their neglect of the spiritual requirements of God's word; comp. Matt. xxiii. 23. ¶ *Your sacrifices.* וּבְחֵיכֶם *zĭbhhhēkhĕm,* from זָבַח, to slay; especially to slay for sacrifice. The word used here denotes any sacrifice which was made by blood; but is distinguished from the burnt-offering from the fat, that this was not entirely consumed. It is applied to the sin-offering, trespass-offering, thank-offering. The word also stands opposed to the offerings which burnt-offerings of rams, and the fat of fed beasts; and I delight not in the blood of bullocks, or of lambs, or of ¹ he-goats.

12 When ye come to ²appear before me, who hath required this at your hand to tread my courts?

1 great he-goats.　　　2 be seen.

were made *without* blood (מִנְחָה *mĭn-ḥâ*). Any offering that consisted in an animal that was slain came under this general denomination of *sacrifice*, Ex. x. 25; Lev. xvii. 8; Num. xv. 5. ¶ *Burnt-offerings.* עֹלוֹת *ŏlŏth*, from עָלָה, *âlâh*, to go up, ascend. It is applied to a sacrifice that was wholly consumed, or made to ascend on an altar. It answers to the Greek ὁλόκαυστον— *holocaust*, that which is entirely consumed. Such offerings abounded among the Hebrews. The burnt-offering was wholly consumed on the altar, excepting the skin and the blood. The blood was sprinkled round the altar, and the other parts of the animal which was slain, were laid upon the altar and entirely burned; see Lev. i. This was commonly a *voluntary* offering; and this shows their zeal to comply with the external forms of religion. ¶ *I am full.* שָׂבַעְתִּי, I am *satiated*. The word is usually applied to food and drink, denoting satisfaction, or satiety. It is used here with great force, denoting that their offerings had been so numerous and so incessant, that God was *satiated* with them. It means that he was weary, tired, disgusted with them. Thus, in Job vii. 4: 'I am full—שָׂבַעְתִּי—of tossings to and fro unto the dawning of the day.' Prov. xxv. 17:

Withdraw thy foot from thy neighbour's house, Lest he be weary (Heb. *full*) of thee, and hate thee.

¶ *Fat, &c.* They were required to offer, not the lame, or the diseased (Deut. xv. 21; xvii. 1; Lev. xvii. 20; Mal. i. 7, 8); and God admits here that they had *externally* complied with this requirement. The fat was burned on the altar. ¶ *I delight not.* That is, I delight not in them when offered without the heart; or I delight not in them in comparison with works of righteousness; see Amos v. 21–24; Ps. iv. 9–13; li. 16–19.

12. *When you come to appear before me.* The temple was in Jerusalem, and

was regarded as the *habitation*, or *dwelling-place*, of the God of Israel. Particularly, the most holy place of the temple was deemed the place of his sacred abode. The Shekinah—from שָׁכַן *shâkhăn, to dwell*—the visible symbol of his presence, rested on the cover of the ark, and from this place he was accustomed to commune with his people, and to give responses to their requests. Hence, 'to appear before God,' Heb. 'to be seen before my face,' לִרְאוֹת פְּנֵי for פְּנֵי אֶת, means to appear in his temple as a worshipper. The phrase occurs in this sense in the following places: Exod. xxxiv. 23, 24; Deut. xxxi. 11; 1 Sam. i. 22; Ps. xlii. 3. ¶ *Who hath required this.* The Jews were required to appear there to worship God (Exod. xxiii. 17; Deut. xvi. 16); but it was not required that they should appear with that spirit and temper. A similar sentiment is expressed in Ps. l. 16. ¶ *At your hand.* From you. The emphasis in this expression is to be laid on *your.* 'Who has asked it of *you?*' It was indeed the duty of the humble, and the sincere, to tread those courts, but who had required such hypocrites as *they* were to do it? God sought the offerings of pure worshippers, not those of the hypocritical and the profane. ¶ *To tread my courts.* The *courts* of the temple were the different *areas* or open spaces which surrounded it. None entered the temple itself but the priests. The people worshipped God in the *courts* assigned them around the temple. In one of those courts was the altar of burnt-offerings; and the sacrifices were all made there; see Notes on Matt. xxi. 12. *To tread his courts* was an expression therefore, equivalent to, to worship. To *tread the courts* of the Lord here, has the idea of profanation. Who has required you to tread those courts with this hollow, heartless service? It is often used in the sense of *treading down*, or *trampling on*, 2 Kings vii. 17–20; Dan. viii 7–10; Isa. lxiii. 3–16.

13 Bring no more vain oblations: *a* incense is an abomination unto me; the new moons and sabbaths,

a Lu.11.42.

the calling of assemblies, I cannot away with; *it is* [1] iniquity, even the solemn meeting.

1 *or, grief.*

13. *Bring no more.* God does not intend absolutely to forbid this kind of worship, but he expresses his strong abhorrence of the *manner* in which it was done. He desired a better state of mind; he preferred purity of heart to all this external homage. ¶ *Vain.* Heb. '*offering of vanity*'—שָׁוְא *shâv*—offerings which were hollow, false, deceitful, and hypocritical. ¶ *Oblations.* מִנְחַת *minhhâth.* This word properly denotes a gift, or present, of any kind (Gen. xxxii. 13), and then especially a *present* or *offering* to the Deity, Gen. iv. 3–5. It does not denote a *bloody* offering, but what is improperly rendered in the Old Testament, a *meat-offering* (Lev. ii. 1; vi. 14; ix. 17)—an offering made of flour or fruits, with oil and frankincense. A small part of it was burned upon the altar, and the remainder was eaten by Aaron and his sons with salt, Lev. ii. 1, 9, 13. The proper translation would have been *meal* or *flour-offering* rather than *meat-offering,* since the word *meat* with us now denotes animal food only. ¶ *Incense.* More properly *frankincense.* This is an aromatic or odoriferous gum, which is obtained from a tree called *Thurifera.* Its leaves were like those of a pear-tree. It grew around Mount Lebanon, and in Arabia. The gum was obtained by making incisions in the bark in dog-days. It was much used in worship, not only by the Jews, but by the heathen. When burned, it produced an agreeable odour; and hence it is called a sacrifice of sweet smell, an odour acceptable to God; comp. Phil. iv. 18. That which was burned among the Jews was prepared in a peculiar manner, with a mixture of sweet spices. It was offered by the priest alone, and it was not lawful to prepare it in any other way than that prescribed by the law: see Ex. xxx. 34, &c. ¶ *Is an abomination.* Is hateful, or an object of abhorrence; that is, as it was offered by them, with hollow service, and with hypocritical hearts. ¶ *The new moons.*

On the appearance of the new moon, in addition to the daily sacrifices, two bullocks, a ram, and seven sheep, with a meal-offering, were required to be offered to God, Num. x. 10; xxviii. 11–14. The new moon in the beginning of the month Tisri (October), was the beginning of their civil year, and was commanded to be observed as a festival, Lev. xxiii. 24, 25. The appearance of the new moon was announced by the blowing of silver trumpets, Num. x. 10. Hence the annual festival was called sometimes, 'the memorial of the blowing of trumpets.' The time of the appearance of the new moon was not ascertained, as with us, by astronomical calculation; but persons were stationed, about the time it was to appear, on elevated places in the vicinity of Jerusalem, and when it was discovered, the trumpet was sounded. Moses did not command that this should be observed as a festival except at the beginning of the year, but it is not improbable that the Jews observed each return of the new moon as such. ¶ *And sabbaths.* שַׁבָּת *shăbbâth,* from שָׁבַת *shâbăth,* to cease to do anything; to rest from labour. The words here used are all in the singular number, and should have been rendered 'the new moon, and the sabbath, and the calling of the assembly;' though used in a collective sense. The sabbaths here refer not only to the weekly sabbaths, but to *all* their days of rest. The word *sabbath* means properly a day of rest (Gen. ii. 2, 3); and it was applied not only to the seventh day, but particularly to the beginning and the close of their great festivals, which were days of unusual solemnity and sacredness, Lev. xvi. 31; xxiii. 24–39. ¶ *The calling of assemblies.* The solemn convocations or meetings at their festivals and fasts. ¶ *I cannot away with.* Heb. לֹא אוּכַל —I cannot bear, or endure. ¶ *It is iniquity.* That is, in the way in which it is conducted. This is a strong emphatic expression. It is not merely evil, and tending to evil; but it is *ini-*

14 Your new moons and your appointed feasts my soul hateth: they are a trouble unto me; I am weary to bear *them*.

15 And when ye *a* spread forth your hands I will hide mine eyes from you; yea, when ye [1]make

a Mic.3.4.	1 *multiply prayer.*

quity itself. There was no mixture of good. ¶ *Even the solemn meeting.* The word which is here used—עֲצָרָה—comes from the verb עָצַר *âtzar,* which signifies *to shut up,* or *to close;* and is applied to the solemnities which con-*cluded* their great feasts, as being periods of unusual interest and sacredness. It was applied to such solemnities, because they *shut up,* or *closed* the sacred festivals. Hence that day was called *the great day of the feast,* as being a day of peculiar solemnity and impressiveness; see Note, John vii. 37; comp. Lev. xxiii. 3–36. In the translation of this word, however, there is a great variety in the ancient versions. Vulg., ' Your assemblies are iniquitous.' LXX., 'Your new moons, and sabbaths, and great day, I cannot endure; fasting and idleness,' Chald. Paraph., ' Sacrifice is abominable before me; and your new moons, and sabbaths, *since you will not forsake your sins, so that your prayer may be heard in the time of your assembling.*' Syriac, ' In the beginning of your months, and on the sabbath, you convene an assembly, but I do not eat that [*i.e.,* sacrifices] which has been obtained by fraud and violence.' The English translation has, however, probably expressed the correct sense of the Hebrew.

14. *Your appointed feasts.* That is, your assemblies convened on *regular set times*—מוֹעֵד *moēdh,* from יָעַד *yâădh, to fix, to appoint.* Hengstenberg (Chris. iii. p. 87) has shown that this word (מוֹעֲדִים) is applied in the Scriptures only to the sabbath, passover, pentecost, day of atonement, and feast of tabernacles. Prof. Alexander, *in loc.* It is applied to those festivals, because they were fixed by law to certain periods of the year. This verse is a very impressive repetition of the former, as if the soul was full of the subject, and disposed to dwell upon it. ¶ *My soul hateth.* I hate. Ps. xi. 5. The nouns נֶפֶשׁ *nephesh, soul,* and רוּחַ *rŭăhh, spirit,* are often used to denote the *person*

himself, and are to be construed as *I.* Thus, Isa. xxvi. 9: ' With my soul have I desired thee in the night; yea, with my spirit within me will I seek thee early;' that is, ' I myself seek thee; I myself do desire thee.' So the phrase, ' deliver my soul,'—נַפְשִׁי—that is, *deliver me,* Ps. xxii. 20; lxxxiv. 3; lxxxvi. 13, 14; *that thy soul may bless me,* Gen. xxvii. 19; *his soul shall dwell at ease,* Ps. xxv. 13; comp. Num. xi. 6; Lev. xvi. 29; Isa. lv. 2, 3; Job. xvi. 4. So the word *spirit:* ' Thy watchfulness hath preserved my spirit '—רוּחִי—Job x. 12; comp. Ps. xxxi. 6; 1 Kings xxi. 5. The expression here is emphatic, denoting *cordial* hatred: *odi ex animo.* ¶ *They are a trouble.* טֹרַח *tōrăhh.* In Deut. i. 12, this word denotes a *burden,* an oppressive load that produces weariness in bearing it. It is a strong expression, denoting that their acts of hypocrisy and sin had become so numerous, that they became a heavy, oppressive load. ¶ *I am weary to bear them.* This is language which is taken from the act of carrying a burden till a man becomes weary and faint. So, in accordance with human conceptions, God represents himself as *burdened* with their vain oblations, and evil conduct. There could be no more impressive statement of the evil effects of sin, than that even Omnipotence was exhausted as with a heavy, oppressive burden.

15. *Ye spread forth your hands.* This is an expression denoting the act of *supplication.* When we ask for help, we naturally stretch out our hands, *as if* to receive it. The expression therefore is equivalent to ' when ye pray, or implore mercy.' Comp. Ex. ix. 29; xvii. 11, 12; 1 Kings viii. 22. ¶ *I will hide mine eyes,* &c. That is, I will not attend to, or regard your supplications. The Chaldee Paraphrase is, ' When your priests expand their hands to pray for you.' ¶ *Your hands,* &c. This is given as a reason why he would not hear. The expression *full of blood,*

many prayers, I will not hear: your hands are full of ¹blood.

16 Wash ª you, make you clean, put away the evil of your doings

1 *bloods.*   a Jer.4.14.

from before mine eyes; cease ᵇ to do evil;

17 Learn to do well: seek judgment, ²relieve the oppressed; judge

b 1Pet.3.11.   2 or, *righten.*

denotes crime and guilt of a high order —as, in murder, the hands would be dripping in blood, and as the stain on the hands would be proof of guilt. It is probably a figurative expression, not meaning literally that they were murderers, but that they were given to rapine and injustice ; to the oppression of the poor, the widow, &c. The sentiment is, that *because* they indulged in sin, and came, even in their prayers, with a determination still to indulge it, God would not hear them. The same sentiment is elsewhere expressed ; Ps. lxvi. 18 : ' If I regard iniquity in my heart, the Lord will not hear me ; ' Prov. xxviii. 9: ' He that turneth away his ear from hearing the law, even his prayer shall be abomination ; ' Jer. xvi. 10–12 ; Zech. vii. 11, 12 ; Prov. i. 28, 29. This is the reason why the prayers of sinners are not heard.—But the truth is abundantly taught in the Scriptures, that if sinners will forsake their sins, the *greatness* of their iniquity is no obstacle to forgiveness ; Isa. i. 18 ; Matt. xi. 28 ; Luke xvi. 11–24.

16. *Wash you.* This is, of course, to be understood in a moral sense ; meaning that they should put away their sins. Sin is represented in the Scriptures as *defiling* or *polluting* the soul (Ezek. xx. 31; xxiii. 30; Hos. v. 8; ix. 4); and the removal of it is represented by the act of washing ; Ps. li. 2: ' Wash me thoroughly from mine iniquity, and cleanse me from my sin ; ' Jer. iv. 14 : ' O Jerusalem, wash thine heart from wickedness, that thou mayest be saved ; ' Job ix. 30 ; 1 Cor. vi. 11 ; Heb. x. 22 ; 2 Peter ii. 22 ; Rev. i. 5; vii. 14. It is used here in close connection with the previous verse, where the prophet says that their *hands were filled with blood.* He now admonishes them to *wash away* that blood, with the implied understanding, that *then* their prayers would be heard. It is worthy of remark, also, that the prophet directs them to do this *themselves.* He addresses them as moral agents, and as

having ability to do it. This is the uniform manner in which God addresses sinners in the Bible, requiring them to put away their sins, and to make themselves a new heart.* Comp. Ezek. xviii. 31, 32. ¶ *The evil of your doings.* This is a Hebraism, to denote *your evil doings.* ¶ *From before mine eyes.* As God is omniscient, to put them away from before *his* eyes, is to put them away altogether. To pardon or forgive sin, is often expressed by *hiding it ;* Ps. li. 9 :

Hide thy face from my sins.

¶ *Cease to do evil.* Comp. 1 Peter iii. 10, 11. The prophet is specifying what was necessary in order that their prayers might be heard, and that they might find acceptance with God. What he states here is a universal truth. If sinners wish to find acceptance with God, they must come renouncing *all* sin ; resolving to put away *every* thing that God hates, however dear it may be to the heart. Comp. Mark ix. 43–47.

17. *Learn to do well.* To *learn* here is *to become accustomed to,* to practise it. *To do well* stands opposed to all kinds of evil. ¶ *Seek judgment.* The word *judgment*—מִשְׁפָּט—here means *justice.* The direction refers particularly to *magistrates,* and it is evident that the prophet had them particularly in his view in all this discourse. Execute justice between man and man with impartiality. The word *seek*—דִּרְשׁוּ— means to pursue, to search for, as an object to be gained ; to regard, or care for it, as the main thing. Instead of seeking gain, and bribes, and public favour, they were to make it an object of intense interest to do justice. ¶ *Relieve*—אַשְּׁרוּ—literally, *make straight,* or *right* (margin, *righten*). The root—אָשַׁר *ashăr*—means *to proceed, to walk*

* See the subject of moral inability discussed in the Notes and Supplementary Notes, under 1 Cor. ii. 14; Gal. v. 17. The author's language here is certainly unguarded.

the fatherless; plead for the widow.

18 Come now, and let us reason *a*

forward in a direct line; and bears a relation to יָשָׁר *yâshăr,* to be straight. Hence it often means to be successful or prosperous—to go straight forward to success. In Piel, which is the form used here, it means to *cause* to go straight ; and hence, applied to leaders, judges, and guides, to conduct those under their care in a straight path, and not in the devices and crooked ways of sin ; Prov. xxiii. 19 :

Hear thou, my son, and be wise,
And guide (אַשֵּׁר *make straight*) thine heart in the way.

¶ *The oppressed.* Him to whom injustice has been done in regard to his character, person, or property ; comp. Notes on ch. lviii. 6. ¶ *Judge the fatherless.* Do justice to him—vindicate his cause. Take not advantage of his weak and helpless condition—his ignorance and want of experience. This charge was particularly necessary on account of the *facilities* which the guardians of orphans have to defraud or oppress, without danger of detection or punishment. Orphans have no experience. Parents are their natural protectors ; and therefore God especially charged on their guardians to befriend and do justice to them; Deut. xxiv. 17 : ' Thou shalt not pervert the judgment of the stranger, nor the fatherless, nor take the widow's raiment to pledge.' ¶ *Plead for.* Contend for her rights. Aid her by vindicating her cause. She is unable to defend herself ; she is liable to oppression ; and her rights may be taken away by the crafty and designing. It is remarkable that God so often insists on this in the Scriptures, and makes it no small part of religion ; Deut. xiv. 29 ; xxiv. 17 ; Ex. xxii. 22 : ' Ye shall not afflict any widow, or fatherless child.' The ancient views of piety on this subject are expressed in the language, and in the conduct of Job. Thus, *impiety* was said to consist in oppressing the fatherless and widow :

They drive away the ass of the fatherless,
They take the widow's ox for a pledge.
Job xxiv. 3.

together, saith the LORD : though your sins be as scarlet, they shall be

He evil-entreateth the barren that beareth not,
And doeth not good to the widow.　Ver. 21.

Job's own conduct was an illustration of the elevated and pure views of ancient piety :

When the ear heard me, then it blessed me ;
And when the eye saw me, it gave witness to me;
Because I delivered the poor that cried,
And the fatherless,
And him that had none to help him.
The blessing of him that was ready to perish came upon me ;
And I caused the widow's heart to leap for joy.
Job xxix. 11–13.

See also Jer. vii. 6; Mal. iii. 5; Jas. i. 27. Hence God is himself represented as the vindicator of the rights of the widow and orphan :

A father of the fatherless,
And a judge of the widows,
Is God in his holy habitation.　Ps. lxviii. 5.
Leave thy fatherless children, I will preserve them alive;
And let thy widows trust in me.
Jer. xlix. 11.

18. *Come now.* This is addressed to the nation of Israel; and the same exhortation is made to all sinners. It is a solemn act on the part of God, submitting the claims and principles of his government to *reason,* on the supposition that men *may* see the propriety of his service, and of his plan. ¶ *Let us reason together.* וְנִוָּכְחָה from יָכַח, not used in Kal, but in Hiphil ; meaning to *show,* to *prove.* Job xiii. 15: ' Surely I will *prove* my ways (righteous) before him ;' *i.e.,* I will justify my ways before him. Also *to correct, reprove, convince,* Job xxxii. 12 ; *to rebuke, reproach, censure,* Job vi. 25; *to punish,* Job v. 17; Prov. iii. 12; *to judge, decide,* Isa. xi. 3; *to do justice,* Isa. xi. 4; or *to contend,* Job xiii. 3; xvi. 21; xxii. 4. Here it denotes the kind of contention, or argumentation, which occurs in a court of justice, where the parties reciprocally state the grounds of their cause. God had been addressing magistrates particularly, and commanding them to seek judgment, to relieve the oppressed, to do justice to the orphan and widow ; all of which terms are taken from courts

as white as *a* snow; though they be

a Ps.51.7.

red like crimson, they shall be as wool.

of law. He here continues the language, and addresses them as accustomed to the proceedings of courts, and proposes to submit the case as if on trial. He then proceeds (vers. 18–20), to adduce the *principles* on which he is willing to bestow pardon on them ; and submits the case to them, assured that those principles will commend themselves to their reason and sober judgment. ¶ *Though your sins be as scarlet.* The word used here—שָׁנִים *shânim*—denotes properly a bright red colour, much prized by the ancients. The Arabic verb means to *shine*, and the name was given to this colour, it is supposed by some, on account of its splendour, or bright appearance. It is mentioned as a merit of Saul, that he clothed the daughters of Israel in *scarlet*, 2 Sam. i. 24. Our word *scarlet*, denoting a bright red, expresses the colour intended here. This colour was obtained from the eggs of the *coccus ilicis*, a small insect found on the leaves of the oak in Spain, and in the countries east of the Mediterranean. The cotton cloth was dipped in this colour *twice;* and the word used to express it means also *double-dyed*, from the verb שָׁנָה *shânâ, to repeat.* From this *double-dying* many critics have supposed that the name given to the colour was derived. The interpretation which derives it from the sense of the Arabic word *to shine*, however, is the most probable, as there is no evidence that the *double-dying* was peculiar to this colour. It was a more *permanent* colour than that which is mentioned under the word *crimson*. White is an emblem of innocence. Of course *sins* would be represented by the opposite. Hence we speak of crimes as *black*, or *deep-dyed*, and of the soul as *stained* by sin. There is another idea here. This was a *fast*, or *fixed* colour. Neither dew, nor rain, nor washing, nor long usage, would remove it. Hence it is used to represent the *fixedness* and *permanency* of sins in the heart. No human means will wash them out. No effort of man, no external rites, no tears, no sacrifices,

no prayers, are of themselves sufficient to take them away. They are *deep fixed* in the heart, as the scarlet colour was in the web of cloth, and an almighty power is needful to remove them. ¶ *Shall be as white as snow.* That is, the deep, fixed stain, which no human power could remove, shall be taken away. In other words, sin shall be pardoned, and the soul be made pure. White, in all ages, has been the emblem of innocence, or purity ; comp. Ps. lxviii. 14; Eccl. ix. 8; Dan. vii. 9; Matt. xvii. 2; xxviii. 3; Rev. i. 14; iii. 4, 5; iv. 4; vii. 9, 13. ¶ *Though they be red.* The idea here is not materially different from that expressed in the former part of the verse. It is the Hebrew poetic form of expressing substantially the same thought in both parts of the sentence. Perhaps, also, it denotes *intensity*, by being repeated ; see Intro. § 8. ¶ *Like crimson*, כַּתּוֹלָע. The difference between *scarlet* and *crimson* is, that the former denotes a *deep red; the* latter a deep red slightly tinged with *blue*. Perhaps this difference, however, is not marked in the original. The *purple* or *crimson* colour was obtained commonly from a shell-fish, called *murex*, or *purpura*, which abounded chiefly in the sea, near Tyre; and hence the *Tyrian dye* became so celebrated. That, however, which is designated in this place, was obtained, not from a shell-fish, but a worm (Heb. תּוֹלָע *tôlâ*), snail, or conchylium—the *Helix Janthina* of Linnæus.* This colour was less per-

---

* *Helix Janthina* is a mollusc or shell-fish, called the violet snail. It inhabits the deep sea in warm latitudes, and, when the water is calm,

Helix Janthina.

may be seen in large numbers floating on its surface. By the Heb. תּוֹלָע *tôlâ*, is probably meant the *Coccus ilicis* of Linnæus, which attains the size and form of a pea, is of a violet black colour, covered with a whitish powder, adhering to plants, chiefly various species of oak, and so

19 If ye be willing and obedient, ye shall eat the good of the land:

20 But if ye refuse and rebel, ye shall be devoured with the sword:

for the mouth of the Lord *a* hath spoken *it*.

21 How is the faithful city be-

a Lev. 26.33.

manent than the *scarlet;* was of a *bluish* cast; and is commonly in the English Bible rendered *blue.* It was employed usually to dye *wool,* and was used in the construction of the tabernacle, and in the garments of the high-priest. It was also in great demand by princes and great men, Judg. viii. 26; Luke xiv. 19. The prophet has adverted to the fact that it was employed mainly in dying *wool,* by what he has added, ' *shall be as wool.*' ¶ *As wool.* That is, as wool *undyed,* or from which the colour is removed. Though your sins appear as deep-stained, and as permanent as the fast colour of crimson in wool, yet they shall be removed—as if that stain should be taken away from the wool, and it should be restored to its original whiteness.

19. *If ye be willing.* If you submit your wills, and become voluntary in your obedience to my law. ¶ *And obedient.* Heb. If you will *hear; i.e.,* my commands. ¶ *Ye shall eat,* &c. That is, the land shall yield its increase; and you shall be saved from pestilence, war, famine, &c. The productions of the soil shall no more be devoured by strangers, ver. 7; comp. Notes on ch. lxv. 21–23. This was in accordance with the promises which God made to their fathers, and the motives to obedience placed before them, which were drawn from the fact, that they should possess a land of distinguished fertility, and that obedience should be attended with eminent national prosperity. Such an appeal was adapted to the infancy of society, and to the circumstances of the people. It should be added, however, that with this they connected the idea, that God would be *their* God and Protector; and, of course, the idea that all the blessings resulting from that fact would be theirs; Ex. iii. 8: ' And I am come down to deliver them out of the hand of the Egyptians, and to bring

closely resembling grain, that its insect nature was not known for many centuries, &c.—*Kitto's Cyclop.,* Art. *Purple.*

them up out of that land unto a good land and a large, unto a land flowing with milk and honey;' comp. Ex. iii. 17; xiii. 5; Deut. xxviii. 1–9. In accordance with this, the *language* of promise in the New Testament is, that of inheriting the earth, *i.e.,* the land, Note, Matt. v. 5. The expression here means, that if they obeyed God they should be under his patronage, and be prospered. It refers, also, to ver. 7, where it is said, that strangers devoured the land. The promise here is, that if they were obedient, this calamity should be removed.

20. *But if ye refuse, ye shall be devoured with the sword.* Your enemies shall come in, and lay waste the land. This prediction was fulfilled, in consequence of their continuing to rebel, when the land was desolated by Nebuchadnezzar, and the nation was carried captive to Babylon. It illustrates a *general* principle of the Divine government, that if men persevere in rebelling against God, they shall be destroyed. The word *devour* is applied to the *sword,* as if it were insatiable for destruction. Whatever *destroys* may be figuratively said to *devour;* see Notes on ch. xxxiv. 5, 6; comp. Isa. v. 24; Lam. ii. 3; Ezek. xv. 4; Joel ii. 3; Re. xi. 5—where *fire* is said to devour. ¶ *The mouth of the Lord.* Jehovah himself This had been spoken by the mouth of the Lord, and recorded, Lev. xxvi. 33:

And I will scatter you among the heathen,
And will draw out a sword after you;
And your land shall be desolate,
And your cities waste.

On these points God proposed to *reason;* or rather, perhaps, these principles are regarded as *reasonable,* or as commending themselves to men. They are the great principles of the Divine administration, that if men obey God they shall prosper; if not, they shall be punished. They commend themselves to men as just and true; and they are seen and illustrated every where.

21. *How is.* This is an expression

come an harlot! *it* was full of judgment; righteousness lodged in it; but now murderers.

a Jer.2.20,21.

22 Thy silver is become dross, thy wine mixed with water:

23 Thy princes *are* rebellious, and companions of thieves: every

of *deploring*, or *lamenting*. It indicates that that had occurred which was matter of grief. The prophet had stated the principles of the Divine government; had urged the people to reason with God; and had affirmed his willingness to pardon. But it was seen that they *would not* repent. They were *so* wicked and perverse, that there was no hope of their reformation. His mind is full of this subject; he repeats the charge of their wickedness (21-23), and states what *must be* the consequences. ¶ *The faithful city.* Jerusalem. It is represented here under the image of *a wife*—once faithful to her husband; once a devoted and attached partner. Jerusalem *was* thus once. In former days, it was the seat of the pure worship of God; the place where his praise was celebrated, and where his people came to offer sincere devotion. In the Scriptures, the *church* is often represented under the image of a wife, to denote the tenderness and sacredness of the union; Hos. ii. 19, 20; Isa. lxii. 5; liv. 6; Rev. xxi. 9. ¶ *An harlot.* She has proved to be false, treacherous, unfaithful. The unfaithfulness of the people of God, particularly their idolatry, is often represented under the idea of unfaithfulness to the marriage contract; Jer. iii. 8, 9; v. 7; xiii. 27; xxiii. 14; Ezek. xvi. 32; xxiii. 37; Hos. ii. 2; iv. 2. ¶ *It was full of judgment.* It was distinguished for *justice* and righteousness. ¶ *Lodged in it.* This is a figurative expression, meaning that it was characterized as a righteous city. The word רָלִין is from כּוּן *lün*, to pass the night, to remain through the night (Gen. xix. 2); and then to lodge, to dwell; Ps. xxv. 13; Job xvii. 2; xxix. 19. In this place it has the sense of *abiding, remaining, continuing permanently.* Jerusalem was *the home* of justice, where it found protection and safety. ¶ *Now murderers.* By *murderers* here are meant probably unjust judges; men who did not regard the interests of the poor,

the widow, and the orphan; and who therefore, by a strong expression, are characterized as murderers. They had displaced justice from its home; and had become the permanent inhabitants of the city; comp. Note, ver. 15.

22. *Thy silver.* The sentiment in this verse, as it is explained by the following, is, thy princes and people have become corrupt, and polluted. Silver is used here to denote what should have been more valuable—virtuous princes. ¶ *Dross.* This word—סִיג—means the *scoriae*, or baser metal, which is separated from the purer in smelting. It is of little or no value; and the expression means, that the rulers had become debased and corrupt, as if pure silver had been converted wholly to dross. ¶ *Thy wine.* Wine was regarded as the most pure and valuable drink among the ancients. It is used, therefore, to express that which *should have been* most valued and esteemed among them —to wit, their rulers. ¶ *Mixed with water.* Diluted, made weak. According to Gesenius, the word rendered *mixed*—מָחוּל *mâhül*—is from מָחַל *mâhäl*, the same as מוּל *mül*, to circumcise; and hence, by a figure common with the Arabians, to *adulterate*, or dilute wine. The word does not occur in this sense elsewhere in the Scriptures, but the connection evidently requires it to be so understood. Wine mixed with water is that which is weakened, diluted, rendered comparatively useless. So with the rulers and judges. They had lost the strength and purity of their integrity, by intermingling those things which tended to weaken and destroy their virtue, pride, the love of gifts, and bribes, &c. Divested of the figure, the passage means, that the rulers had become wholly corrupt.

23. *Thy princes, &c.* This is an explanation of the previous verse. Princes mean here those attached to the royal family; those who by rank, or office, had an influence over the

one loveth gifts, and followeth after rewards: they judge not the father-less, neither doth the cause of the widow come unto them.

24 Therefore saith the Lord, the LORD of hosts, the mighty One of Israel, Ah, I will ease *a* me of mine

a Deut.28.63; Eze.5.13.

people. ¶ *Rebellious.* Against God. The corruption of a nation commonly begins with the rulers. ¶ *Companions of thieves.* That is, they connive at the doings of robbers; and they do not bring them to justice; they are their accomplices, and are easily bribed to acquit them. ¶ *Every one loveth gifts.* Every magistrate can be *bribed.* ¶ *Followeth after rewards.* רֹדֵף. This word denotes the act of *pursuing after* in order to obtain something; and means here that they made it an object to obtain rewards by selling or betraying justice. They sell justice to the highest bidder. No more distressing condition of a people can be conceived than this, where justice could not be secured between man and man, and where the wicked could oppress the poor, the widow, and the orphan, as much as they pleased, because they knew they could bribe the judge. ¶ *They judge not.* They do not render justice to; ver. 17. The Chaldee has well expressed the sense of a part of this verse: 'They say, each one to his neighbour, Favour me in my judgment, or do me good in it, and I will recompense you in your cause.' ¶ *The cause of the widow come unto them.* Or, rather, come *before* them. They would not take up her cause, but rather the cause of those who were esteemed able to offer a bribe, and from whom a gift might be expected, if a decision was made in their favour.

24. *Therefore saith the Lord, &c.* The prophet having stated the guilt of the nation, proceeds to show the consequences of their crimes; or to foretell what would happen. The name of God is repeated, to attract attention; to fill the mind with awe; and to give emphasis to the solemn sentence which was about to be uttered. ¶ *The Lord.* אָדוֹן. This word properly denotes *master, lord, owner.* Gen. xxiv. 9: *Lord over his whole house.* 1 Kings xvi. 24: *Owner of the hill Samaria.* It is applied here to JEHOVAH, not as a peculiar title, or as one of the names which he

assumes to himself, but as owner, proprietor, master, ruler of the nation. The word, when applied to God as one of his peculiar titles, has the form of an ancient plural termination, אֲדֹנָי *ădōnâi.* The root is probably דּוּן *dhûn,* to judge, which in ancient times was also closely connected with the idea of *ruling.* ¶ *The Lord of hosts.* JEHOVAH—ruling in the hosts of heaven, and therefore able to accomplish his threatenings; Note, ver. 9. ¶ *The mighty One of Israel.* He who had been their defender in the days of their peril; who had manifested his mighty power in overthrowing their enemies; and who had shown, therefore, that he was able to inflict vengeance *on them.* ¶ *Ah.* הוֹי. This is an expression of *threatening.* It is that which is used when an *affront* is offered, and there is a purpose of revenge; see ver. 4. ¶ *I will ease me.* This refers to what is said in ver. 14, where God is represented as *burdened* with their crimes. The Hebrew word is, I will be consoled, or comforted—*i.e.,* by being delivered from my foes—אֶנָּחֵם from נָחַם, in Niphil, to suffer pain, to be grieved; and hence, to have pity, to show compassion. In Piel, to console or comfort one's-self; to take revenge. The idea included in the word is that of *grief* or *distress,* either in beholding the sufferings of others, or from some injury received from others. Hence, in Piel, it denotes to obtain relief from that distress, either by aiding the distressed object, or by taking revenge. In both instances, the mind, by a law of its nature, finds relief. The passion expends itself on its proper object, and the mind is at ease. It is used here in the *latter* sense. It is an instance where God uses the language which men employ to denote *passion,* and where they obtain relief by *revenge.* When applied to God, it is to be understood in accordance with *his* nature, as implying simply, that he would punish them; comp. Note on ver. 13. It means that he had been *pained* and *grieved* by their crimes;

adversaries, and avenge me of mine enemies:

25 And *a* I will turn my hand upon thee, and purely ¹ purge away

a Mal.3.3.

thy dross, and take away all thy tin:

26 And I will restore thy judges as at the first, and thy counsellors

¹ *according to pureness.*

---

his patience had been put to its utmost trial; and now he would seek relief from this by inflicting due punishment on them. An expression explaining this may be seen in Ezek. v. 13: 'Then shall mine anger be accomplished, and I will cause my fury to rest upon them, and *I will be comforted.*' Also, Deut. xxviii. 63: 'As the Lord rejoiced over you, to do you good; so the Lord will rejoice over you, to destroy you.' ¶ *Mine adversaries.* The enemies to his law and government among the rebellious Jews. The expression in this verse is a remarkable instance of God's adapting himself to our apprehension, by using our language. Instances occur often in the Scriptures where language expressive of human passions is applied to God; and as human language must be employed in revelation, it was indispensable. But those expressions are not to be understood as they are when applied to the passions of men. In God, they are consistent with all that is pure, and glorious, and holy, and should be so understood. The Chaldee renders this verse, 'I will console the city of Jerusalem; but woe to the impious, when I shall be revealed to take vengeance on the enemies of my people.' But this is manifestly a false interpretation; and shows how reluctant the Jews were to admit the threatenings against *themselves.*

25. *And I will turn my hand upon thee.* This expression is capable of two significations. The hand may be stretched out for two purposes, either to inflict punishment, or to afford help and protection. The phrase here refers evidently to the latter, to the act of redeeming and restoring his people, ver. 26, 27. The idea may be thus expressed: 'I will stretch out my hand to punish my enemies (ver. 24), and will *turn my hand* upon thee for protection, and recovery.' ¶ *Purge away.* This refers to the process of smelting, or purifying metals in the fire. It means, I will

remove all the dross which has accumulated (ver. 22), and will make the silver pure. This was commonly done by fire; and the idea is, that he would render his own people pure by those judgments which would destroy his enemies who were intermingled with them. ¶ *Purely.* The original word here—כַּבֹּר *kabbor*—has been commonly understood to mean, *according to purity; i.e.,* effectually or entirely pure. Thus it is translated by the Septuagint, and by the Latin Vulgate. But by the Chaldee it is translated, 'I will purify thee as with *the herb borith.*' The word *may* mean *lye, alkali,* or *potash,* (Job ix. 30); and it may mean also *borax*—a substance formed of alkali and boracic acid, much used in purifying metals. The essential idea is, I will make you effectually, or entirely pure. ¶ *Thy tin.* Tin is with us a well-known white metal. But the word used here does not mean *tin.* It denotes the *stannum* of the ancients; a metal formed of lead mixed with silver ore. Here it means, I will take away all the impure metal mixed with thee; varying the idea but little from the former part of the verse.

26. *And I will restore,* &c. That is, I will give you such judges as the nation had in former days—in the times of Moses, Joshua, &c. Most of the charges in this chapter are against the *magistrates.* The calamities of the nation are traced to *their* unfaithfulness and corruption, ver. 17–23. God now says that he will remove this cause of their calamity, and give them pure magistrates. ¶ *Thy counsellors.* Thy advisers; that is, those occupying places of trust and responsibility. *When* this should be, the prophet does not say. The Jewish commentators suppose that he refers to the time after the return from captivity, and to such men as Zerubbabel, Ezra, and Nehemiah; and to the times of Hyrcanus and Herod. Jerome supposes that the times of the Messiah are referred to. It is impos-

as at the beginning: afterward thou
shalt be called, The city of righteousness, The faithful city.

1 *or, they that return of her.*

27 Zion shall be redeemed with
judgment, and her converts [1] with
a righteousness.

a 1 Cor. 1. 30.

sible to determine which is the correct
opinion; though, as the Babylonish captivity was the *punishment* of those
national sins which the prophet was
denouncing, it is more probable that he
refers to the time immediately *succeeding* that punishment, when the nation
would be restored. I am inclined, therefore, to the opinion, that the prophet
had reference solely to the prosperity
of the Jewish nation, under a succession of comparatively virtuous princes,
after the Babylonish captivity. ¶ *Thou
shalt be called,* &c. The principal *cause*
of your wickedness and calamity, *i.e.*
your unfaithful rulers being removed
and punished, you shall afterwards be
distinguished as a city of righteousness.
¶ *The faithful city.* That is, faithful to JEHOVAH—faithful in keeping his
laws, and maintaining the rites of his
religion as formerly; comp. ver. 21.

27. *Zion.* See Note, ver. 8. The
word *Zion* here is used to designate
the whole Jewish people to whom the
prophet had reference; that is, the
inhabitants of Judah and Jerusalem,
ver. 1. ¶ *Shall be redeemed.* The
word used here—פָּדָה—is employed in
two senses in the Scriptures. It implies
always the idea of *deliverance,* as from
captivity, danger, punishment, slavery,
sin. But this idea occurs (1) sometimes
without any reference to a *price* paid,
but simply denoting to deliver, or to
set at liberty; and (2) in other instances
the price is specified, and then the word
occurs under the strict and proper sense
of redeem; *i.e.,* to rescue, or deliver,
by a ransom price. Instances of the
former general sense occur often; as
e.g., to deliver from slavery without
mention of a price; Deut. vii. 8: 'The
LORD loved you, and *redeemed* you out
of the house of bondmen.' See also Jer.
xv. 21; xxxi. 11. The idea of delivering
in any way from danger occurs often;
Job v. 20: 'In famine he shall *redeem*
thee from death, and in war from the
power of the sword;' 1 Kings i. 29:
'As Jehovah liveth, that hath *redeemed*

my soul out of all distress.' 1 Sam. iv.
9. But the word often occurs in connection with the mention of the *price,*
and in this sense the words rendered
redeem are commonly used in the New
Testament; see Ex. xiii. 13; Num.
xviii. 15, 16, 17; comp. Gal. iii. 13.
1 Pet. i. 18; Rev. v. 9; Eph. i. 17.
Matt. xx. 28; 1 Tim. ii. 6. In these
last places, the blood of Christ, or his
atoning sacrifice, is mentioned as the
price, or the *valuable consideration,* by
which deliverance from sin is effected;
comp. Note, ch. xliii. 3. In the case
now before us, however, the word is used
in the *general* sense, to denote that God
would *rescue* and save his people from
the calamities and judgments to which
they were to be subjected on account of
their sins. Though they were to be
taken captive for their sins, yet they
should again be delivered and restored
to their land. The Septuagint evidently
so understands it: 'Her captivity
shall be saved with judgment and
with mercy.' The Chaldee Paraphrase
renders it in a manner somewhat similar: 'But Zion, when judgment shall
have been accomplished in her, shall be
redeemed; and they who keep the law
shall be returned to it in righteousness.'
¶ *With judgment.* In a righteous, just
manner. That is, God shall evince his
justice in doing it; his justice to a
people to whom so many promises had
been made, and his justice in delivering
them from long and grievous oppression.
All this would be attended with the displays of *judgment,* in effecting their
deliverance. This might be evinced (1)
in keeping his promises made to their
fathers; (2) in delivering an oppressed
people from bondage; and (3) in the
displays of *judgment* on the nations
necessary in accomplishing the deliverance of the Jews. This is the common
interpretation. It *may be,* however,
that the expression does not refer to
the *character of God,* which is not at
all the subject of discourse, but to the
character *of the people* that should be

28 And the [1] destruction of the transgressors and of the sinners *shall be* together, [a] and they that

1 *breaking.*   a Ps.125.5; Lu.12.45,46.

forsake [b] the LORD shall be consumed.

29 For they shall be ashamed of

b Zeph.1.6.

redeemed. Before, the nation was corrupt; after the captivity, they would be just. Zion should be redeemed; and the effect of that redemption would be, that the people would be reformed, and holy, and just. This does not refer, properly, to redemption by the Lord Jesus, though it is equally true that that will be accomplished with justice, *i.e.*, in entire consistency with the character of a just and holy God. ¶ *Her converts.* This is an unhappy translation. The Hebrew here means simply, ' they that return of her ' (marg.); that is, those who return from captivity. It is implied that *all* would not return —which was true—but those who *did* return, would come back in righteousness. ¶ *With righteousness.* This refers to the *character* of those who shall return. The prediction is, that the character of the nation would be reformed (ver. 26); that it would be done by means of this very captivity; and that they who returned would come back with a different character from the nation at the time that Isaiah wrote. They would be a reformed, righteous people. The character of the nation was greatly improved after the captivity. Their propensity to idolatry, in a particular manner, was effectually restrained; and probably the character of the people *after* the captivity, for morals and religion, was not inferior to the best periods of their history before.

28. *And the destruction.* Heb. שֶׁבֶר —the *breaking,* or *crushing,* i.e., the *punishment* which was about to come upon them; comp. Lam. ii. 11; iii. 47; Prov. xvi. 18. ¶ *Of the transgressors. Revolters,* or those that rebel against God. ¶ *And of the sinners.* Of all the sinners in the nation, of all kinds and degrees. ¶ *Together.* At the same time with the redemption of Zion. ¶ *Shall be consumed.* יִכְלוּ, from כָּלָה *kâlâ,* to be completed, or finished ; to be consumed, wasted away ; to vanish, or disappear. It denotes complete and

entire extinction ; or the *completing* of any thing. It is applied to a cloud of smoke, that entirely dissolves and disappears :

As the cloud is *consumed* and vanisheth away:
So he that goeth down to the grave shall come
    up no more.   Job vii. 9.
But the wicked shall perish,
And the enemies of the Lord shall be as the fat
    of lambs ;
They shall *consume,*
Into smoke shall they *consume* away.
                Ps. xxxvii. 20.

It is applied to *time,* as vanishing and disappearing (Job vii. 6) ; and to the destruction or perishing of men ; Jer. xvi. 4; Ezek. v. 13. The idea is that of *complete* and *entire* consumption and destruction, so that *none shall be left.* Applied to future punishment, it means that the destruction of sinners shall be total and complete. There shall be no sinner who shall not be destroyed ; and there shall be none destroyed whose destruction shall not be entire and total. The expression here refers to the heavy calamities which were about to come upon the guilty nation, but it is *as* descriptive of the future punishment that shall come upon the wicked.

29. *For they shall be ashamed.* That is, when they see the punishment that their idolatry has brought upon them, they shall be ashamed of the folly and degradation of their worship. Moreover, the gods in which they trusted shall yield them no protection, and shall leave them to the disgrace and confusion of being forsaken and abandoned. ¶ *Of the oaks. Groves,* in ancient times, were the favourite places of idolatrous worship. In the city of Rome, there were thirty-two groves consecrated to the gods. Those were commonly selected which were on hills, or high places ; and they were usually furnished with temples, altars, and all the implements of idolatrous worship. Different kinds of groves were selected for this purpose, by different people. The *Druids* of the ancient Celtic nations in Gaul, Britain, and Germany, offered their worship in

the oaks which ye have desired, and | ye shall be confounded for the gardens that ye have chosen.

---

groves of *oak*—hence the name *Druid*, derived from δρῦς, *drus*, an oak. Frequent mention is made in the Scriptures of groves and high places; and the Jews were forbidden to erect them; Deut. xvi. 21; 1 Kings xvi. 23; 2 Kings xvi. 4; Ezek. vi. 13; xvi. 16, 39; Ex. xxxiv. 13; Judg. iii. 7; 1 Kings xviii. 19; Isa. xvii. 8; Mic. v. 14. When, therefore, it is said here, that they should be ashamed of the *oaks*, it means that they should be ashamed of their *idolatrous worship*, to which they were much addicted, and into which, under their wicked kings, they easily fell. Their calamities were coming upon them mainly for this idolatry.—It is not certainly known what species of tree is intended by the word translated *oaks*. The LXX. have rendered it by the word *idols*—ἀπὸ τῶν εἰδώλων αὐτῶν. The Chaldee, 'ye shall be confounded *by the groves of idols*.' The Syriac version also has *idols*. Most critics concur in supposing that it means, not the *oak*, but the *terebinth* or *turpentine* tree— a species of fir. This tree is the *Pistacia Terebinthus* of Linnæus, or the common turpentine tree, whose resin or juice is the Chian or Cyprus turpentine, used in medicine. The tree grows to a great age, and is common in Palestine. The *terebinth*—now called in Palestine the but'm-tree—'is not an evergreen, as is often represented; but its small, feathered, lancet-shaped leaves fall in the autumn, and are renewed in the spring. The flowers are small, and are followed by small oval berries, hanging in clusters from two to five inches long, resembling much the clusters of the vine when the grapes are just set. From incisions in the trunk there is said to flow a sort of transparent balsam, constituting a very pure and fine species of turpentine, with an agreeable odour like citron or jessamine, and a mild taste, and hardening gradually into a transparent gum. The tree is found also in Asia Minor, Greece, Italy, the south of France, and in the north of Africa, and is described as not usually rising to the height of more than twenty feet.'—

Robinson's *Bib. Researches*, iii. 15, 16. It produces the nuts called the pistachio nuts. They have a pleasant, unctuous taste, resembling that of almonds, and they yield in abundance a sweet and pleasant oil. The best Venice turpentine, which, when it can be obtained pure, is superior to all the rest of its kind, is the produce of this tree. The following cut will give an idea of the appearance of the *terebinth*.

TURPENTINE TREE. *(Pistacia Terebinthus.)*

The Hebrew word אֵילִים *ēlim*, from אֵיל *ēl*, or more commonly אֵלָה *ēlâ*, seems to be used sometimes as the Greek δρῦς is, to denote *any* large tree, whether evergreen or not; and especially any large tree, or cluster of trees, where the worship of idols was celebrated. ¶ *Which ye have desired.* The Jews, until the captivity at Babylon, as all their history shows, easily relapsed into idolatry. The meaning of the prophet is, that the punishment at Babylon would be so long and so severe as to make them *ashamed* of this, and turn them from it. ¶ *Shall be confounded.* Another word meaning to be ashamed. ¶ *For the gardens.* The places planted with trees, &c., in which idolatrous worship was practised. 'In the language of the Hebrews, every place where plants and trees were cultivated with greater care than in the open field, was called a garden. The idea of such an enclosure was certainly borrowed from the garden of Eden, which the

30 For ye shall be as an oak whose leaf fadeth, and as a garden that hath no water.

31 And the strong shall be as tow, and the maker of it as a spark, and they shall both burn together, and none shall quench *them*.

bountiful Creator planted for the reception of his favourite creature. The garden of Hesperides, in Eastern fables, was protected by an enormous serpent ; and the gardens of Adonis, among the Greeks, may be traced to the same origin ; for the terms *horti Adonides*, the gardens of Adonis, were used by the ancients to signify gardens of pleasure, which corresponds with the name of Paradise, or the garden of Eden, as *horti Adonis* answers to the garden of the Lord. Besides, the gardens of primitive nations were commonly, if not in every instance, devoted to religious purposes. In these shady retreats were celebrated, for a long succession of ages, the rites of pagan superstition.'—*Paxton*. These groves or gardens were furnished with the temple of the god that was worshipped, and with altars, and with every thing necessary for this species of worship. They were usually, also, made as shady and dark as possible, to inspire the worshippers with religious awe and reverence on their entrance ; comp. Note, lxvi. 17.

30. *For ye*, &c. The mention of the *tree* in the previous verse, gives the prophet occasion for the beautiful image in this. They had desired the oak, and they should be like it. *That*, when the frost came, was divested of its beauty, and its leaves faded, and fell ; so should their beauty and privileges and happiness, as a people, fade away at the anger of God. ¶ *A garden that hath no water.* That is therefore withered and parched up ; where nothing would flourish, but where all would be desolation—a most striking image of the approaching desolation of the Jewish nation. In Eastern countries this image would be more striking than with us. In these hot regions, a constant supply of water is necessary for the cultivation, and even for the very existence and preservation of a garden. Should it want water for a few days, every thing in it would be burnt up with neat and totally destroyed. In all gardens, therefore, in those regions,

there must be a constant supply of water, either from some neighbouring river, or from some fountain or reservoir within it. To secure such a fountain became an object of indispensable importance, not only for the coolness and pleasantness of the garden, but for the very existence of the vegetation. Dr. Russell, in his *Natural History of Aleppo*, says, that ' all the gardens of Aleppo are on the banks of the river that runs by that city, or on the sides of the rill that supplies their aqueduct ;' and all the rest of the country he represents as perfectly burnt up in the summer months, the gardens only retaining their verdure, on account of the moistness of their situation.

31. *And the strong.* Those who have been *thought* to be strong, on whom the people relied for protection and defence —their rulers, princes, and the commanders of their armies. ¶ *As tow.* The coarse or broken part of flax, or hemp. It means here that which shall be easily and quickly kindled and rapidly consumed. As tow burns and is destroyed at the touch of fire, so shall the rulers of the people be consumed by the approaching calamities. ¶ *And the maker of it.* This is an unhappy translation. The word פֹּעֲלוֹ *may be* indeed a participle, and be rendered ' its maker,' but it is more commonly *a noun*, and means his *work*, or his *action*. This is its plain meaning here. So the Latin Vulgate, the Septuagint, and the Chaldee. It means, that as a spark enkindles tow, so *the works* or *deeds* of a wicked nation shall be *the occasion* or *cause* of their destruction. The ambition of one man is the cause of his ruin ; the sensuality of a second is the cause of his ; the avarice of a third is the cause of his. These passions, insatiable and ungratified, shall be the occasion of the deep and eternal sorrows of hell. So it means here, that the crimes and hypocrisy of the nation would be the real cause of all the calamities that would come upon them as a people. ¶ *Shall both burn together.*

CHAPTER II.

ANALYSIS OF CHAPTERS II. III. IV.

THE prophecy in this and the two following chapters, constitutes one continued discourse. At what time it was delivered is not known, and cannot be ascertained by the prophecy itself. Bishop Lowth supposes it was in the time of Jotham, or Uzziah, and this opinion is probably correct; for it is to be presumed that in collecting the prophecies, those would be placed first which were first delivered. Besides, the prophecy relates to a time of prosperity, when the fruits of commerce abounded, and did much to corrupt the people (see ch. ii. 7, 16, 20; iii. 18–23), and this accords best with the time of Uzziah, or the time of Jotham. Some have referred it to the return from Babylon, others to the times of the Messiah. The description in ch. ii. 2–4, and iv. 5, 6, cannot easily be referred to any other times than those of the Messiah.

The main scope of the prophecy is, to denounce the crimes which prevailed in the time when it was delivered; to threaten certain punishment for these crimes; and to assure the nation that there would be happier times when those crimes should have received their appropriate punishment, and when the nation should be reformed. The prophecy has relation solely to the kingdom of Judah, ch. ii. 1. The prophet opens the prophecy (ch. ii. 2) by a brief but striking statement of the happy period when the Messiah should come, and the happy influence of his advent, ch. ii. 2–4. It would seem, in looking at the entire prophecy, as if he had been contemplating the sins of the nation which then abounded, until his heart was sickened, and he involuntarily cast his mind forward to brighter and happier days when these things should cease, and the Messiah should reign in his glory. See Introduction, § 7. The future times of the Messiah he exhibits, by showing (ch. ii. 2) that the benefits of the true religion would be extended to all people, and would be so conspicuous as to attract their attention, as if the temple, the place of the worship of the true God, should be made conspicuous in the sight of all nations. It would excite a deep interest, and a spirit of earnest inquiry every where (ver. 3), and the effect of his reign would be to put an end to wars, and to introduce ultimately universal peace (ver. 4). In view of that, the prophet (ver. 5) exhorts all the people to turn from their sins, and to walk in the light of Jehovah. This leads him to a statement of the crimes which he would seem to have been contemplating, and the punishment which must follow from their prevalence. The statement of the crimes and their punishment is somewhat intermingled, but they may be exhibited so as to be contemplated separately and distinctly.

Crimes.

Forsaking Jehovah;
Patronage of soothsayers;
Alliance with strangers (ver. 6);
Accumulation of treasures;
Preparation of war-chariots (ver. 7);
Universal and debasing idolatry (ver. 8, 9).

Punishments.

God would so judge them as to produce universal consternation (ver. 10).

He would humble their pride, and bring them low (ver. 11, 12).

He would smite and destroy all their wealth, and the sources of national corruption and depravity (ver. 13–17).

He would entirely destroy the idols (ver. 18).

He would produce universal terror and alarm (ver. 19–21).

In view of these heavy judgments, the prophet calls on the people (ver. 22) to cease to trust in men, since all were mortal, and unworthy of their confidence.

In chapter iii., the description of the punishment of the nation is continued (ver. 1–15), intermingled with the account of their sins.

The spark and the flame from the kindled flax mingle, and make one fire. So the people and their works would be enkindled and destroyed together. They would burn so rapidly, that nothing could extinguish them. The meaning is, that the nation would be punished; and that all their works of idolatry and monuments of sin would be the occasion of their punishment, and would perish at the same time. The *principle* involved in this passage teaches us the following

things:—(1.) That the wicked, however mighty, shall be destroyed. (2.) That their works will be the *cause* of their ruin—a cause necessarily leading to it. (3.) That the works of the wicked—all that they do and all on which they depend—shall be destroyed. (4.) That this destruction shall be final. Nothing shall stay the flame. No tears of penitence, no power of men or devils, shall *put out* the fires which the works of the wicked shall enkindle.

There would be calamity, the removal of the means of support, and the removal of the men in whom the nation had reposed confidence (ver. 1–4).

There would be oppression, and a violation of, and disregard of all the proper laws of social life (ver. 5).

There would be a state of anarchy and calamity, so that no one would be willing to be a leader, or undertake to remove the difficulties of the nation, or hold an office of trust (ver. 6, 7).

Jerusalem would be ruined (ver. 8).

The cause of this was pride and hypocrisy (ver. 8, 9).

The prophet states the principles of the Divine administration—that it should be well with the righteous, but ill with the wicked (ver. 12–15).

The rulers of the nation were corrupt and oppressive (ver. 12–15).

The chapter closes (ver. 16–26) with a graphic description of the gaiety, pride, and folly of the female part of the Jewish community, and with the assurance that they would be involved in the calamities which were coming upon the nation.

Chapter iv. is a continuation of the same prophecy. It contains the following parts:—

1. A statement of the general calamity of the nation, indicated by the fact that the *men* would be destroyed, and that the women would apply to the few that remained that they might be called by their name, and their reproach be taken away (ver. 1).

2. At that future time there would be a looking to the Messiah; a feeling that God only could interpose and save them; and a high estimate placed on the 'Branch of Jehovah'—the Messiah, to whom alone they could look for deliverance (ver. 2).

3. The people would turn to God, and there would be a reformation from their national sins (ver. 3, 4). The judgments of Jehovah would be effectual to the removal of the peculiar crimes

which the prophet had denounced, and the nation would become holy.

God would, in that future time, become the protector of his people, and the symbols of his presence and protection would be manifest every where in the midst of them (ver. 5, 6).

It is evident, therefore, that this prophecy was uttered when the nation was proud, haughty, and hypocritical; when they had been successfully engaged in commerce, and when the means of luxury abounded; when the national pride and vanity were manifested in dress, and luxury, and in the oppressive acts of the rulers; when general disorder and anarchy prevailed, and when a part of the nation at least was idolatrous. The entire prophecy may be regarded as a condemnation of these sins, and a solemn declaration that *for* these sins, wherever they prevail, the judgments of God will be poured out on a people. The prophecy, also, contemplates happier and purer times, and contains the assurance that the *series* of judgments which God would bring on a guilty people would *ultimately* have the effect to purify them, and that all these crimes and calamities would be succeeded by the pure and peaceful reign of the Messiah. It is in accordance with the manner of Isaiah, when he surveys existing crimes; when he sees the degradation of his countrymen, and is deeply distressed; when he portrays the judgments that must *certainly* come upon them; and when, as if sickened with the contemplation of their crimes and calamities, his mind seeks repose in the contemplation of the purer and happier period when the Messiah should reign, and peace, prosperity, and purity should prevail.

THE word that Isaiah the son of Amoz saw concerning Judah and Jerusalem.

2 And ᵃit shall come to pass in the last days, *that* the mountain of the Lord's house shall be

a Mic.4.1,&c.

CHAPTER II.

1. *The word.* This indicates that this is the commencement of a new prophecy. It has no immediate connection with the preceding. It was delivered doubtless at a different time, and with reference to a different class of events. In the previous chapter the term *vision* is used (ver. 1), but the meaning is substantially the same. The term *word* רְבַּד *dâbâr*, denotes a

command, a promise, a doctrine, an oracle, a revelation, a message, a thing, &c. It means here, that Isaiah foresaw certain *future events* or *things* that would happen in regard to Judah and Jerusalem. ¶ *Judah*, &c.; see Notes, ch. i. 1.

2. *In the last days.* בְּאַחֲרִית הַיָּמִים *beʾahhărith hăyyâmim.* In the *after* days; in the *futurity* of days; *i.e.*, in the time to come. This is an expres-

established[1] in the top of the mountains, and shall be exalted above

the hills; and all [a] nations shall flow unto it.

sion that often occurs in the Old Testament. It does not of itself refer to any *particular* period, and especially not, as our translation would seem to indicate, to the end of the world. The expression properly denotes *only future time* in general. But the prophets were accustomed to concentrate all their hopes on the coming of the Messiah. They saw his advent as giving character, and sublimity, and happiness to all coming times. Hence the expression came to denote, by way of eminence, the times of the Messiah, and is frequently used in the New Testament, as well as the Old, to designate those times; see Acts ii. 17; comp. Joel ii. 28; Heb. i. 2; 1 Pet. i. 5, 20; 1 John ii. 18; Gen. xlix. 1; Mic. iv. 1; Deut. iv. 30; Jer. xlviii. 47; Dan. xi. 28. The expressions which follow are figurative, and cannot well be interpreted as relating to any other events than the times of the Messiah. They refer to that future period, then remote, which would constitute the *last* dispensation of things in this world—the *last* time—the period, however long it might be, in which the affairs of the world would be closed. The patriarchal times had passed away; the dispensation under the Mosaic economy would pass away; the times of the Messiah would be the *last* times, or the last dispensation, under which the affairs of the world would be consummated. Thus the phrase is evidently used in the New Testament, as denoting the *last* time, though without implying that that time would be short. It might be longer than *all* the previous periods put together, but it would be the *last* economy, and under that economy, or *in* that time, the world would be destroyed, Christ would come to judgment, the dead would be raised, and the affairs of the world would be wound up. The apostles, by the use of this phrase, never intimate that the time would be short, or that the day of judgment was near, but only that *in* that time the great events of the world's history would be consummated and

closed; comp. 2 Thess. ii. 1–5.—This prophecy occurs in Micah (ch. iv. 1–5) with scarcely any variation. It is not known whether Isaiah made use of Micah, or Micah of Isaiah, or both of an older and well-known prophecy. Hengstenberg (*Chris.* i., pp. 289, 290) supposes that Isaiah copied from Micah, and suggests the following reasons:—1. The prediction of Isaiah is disconnected with what goes before, and yet begins with the copulative *Vav* ְ, *and.* In Micah, on the contrary, it is connected with what precedes and follows. 2. In the discourses of the prophets, the promise usually follows the threatening. This order is observed by Micah; in Isaiah, on the contrary, the promise contained in the passage precedes the threatening, and another promise follows. Many of the older theologians supposed that the passages were communicated alike by the Holy Spirit to both writers. But there is no improbability in supposing that Isaiah may have availed himself of language used by Micah in describing the same event. ¶ *The mountain of the Lord's house.* The temple was built on mount Moriah, which was hence called the mountain of the Lord's house. The temple, or the mountain on which it was reared, would be the object which would express the public worship of the true God. And hence, to say that that should be elevated higher than all other hills, or mountains, means, that the worship of the true God would become an object so conspicuous as to be seen by all nations; and so conspicuous that all nations would forsake other objects and places of worship, being attracted by the glory of the worship of the true God. ¶ *Shall be established.* Shall be fixed, rendered permanent. ¶ *In the top of the mountains.* To be in the top of the mountains, would be to be *conspicuous,* or seen from afar. In other words, the true religion would be made known to all people. ¶ *Shall flow unto it.* This is a figurative expression, denoting that they would be converted to the true re-

3 And many people shall go and say, Come *a* ye, and let us go up to the mountain of the LORD, to the house of the God of Jacob: and he will teach us of his ways, and we will walk in his paths; for out of Zion *b* shall go forth the law, and the word of the LORD from Jerusalem.

a Jer.31.6; 50.5; Zec.8.21,23.　　*b* Lu.24 47.

---

ligion. It indicates that they would come in multitudes, like the flowing of a mighty river. The idea of the *flowing* of the nations, or of the movement of many people towards an object like a broad stream, is one that is very grand and sublime; comp. Psal. lxv. 7. This cannot be understood of any period previous to the establishment of the gospel. At no time of the Jewish history did any events occur that would be a complete fulfilment of this prophecy. The expressions evidently refer to that period elsewhere often predicted by this prophet (Isa. xi. 10· xlii. 1, 6; xlix. 22; liv. 3; lx. 3, 5, 10; lxii. 2; lxvi. 12, 19), when *the Gentiles* would be brought to the knowledge of the true religion. In Isa. lxvi. 12, there occurs a passage remarkably similar, and which may serve to explain this:

'Behold I will extend peace to her [to Zion] as a river;
And the glory of the Gentiles like a flowing stream.'

Under the Messiah, through the preaching of the apostles and by the spread of the gospel, this prophecy was to receive its full accomplishment.

3. *And many people shall go.* This denotes a prevalent *desire* to turn to the true God, and embrace the true religion. It is remarkable that it speaks of an inclination among them *to seek* God, as if they were satisfied of the folly and danger of their ways, and felt the necessity of obtaining a better religion. In many cases this has occurred. Thus, in modern times, the people of the Sandwich Islands threw away their gods and remained without any religion, as if waiting for the message of life. Thus, too, the heathen not unfrequently come from a considerable distance at missionary stations to be instructed, and to receive the Bible and tracts. Perhaps this is to be extensively the mode in which Christianity is to be spread. God, who has all power over human hearts, may excite the heathen to anxious inquiry; may show them the folly of their religion; and may lead them to this *preparation* to embrace the gospel, and this disposition to *go* and seek it. He has access to all men. By a secret influence on the understanding, the heart, and the conscience of the heathen, he can convince them of the folly of idolatry and its vices. He can soften down their prejudices in favour of their long-established systems; can break down the barriers between them and Christians; and can dispose them to receive with joy the messengers of salvation. He can raise up, among the heathen themselves, reformers, who shall show them the folly of their systems. It cannot be doubted that the universal triumph of the gospel will be preceded by some such remarkable preparation among the nations; by a secret, silent, but most mighty influence from God on the heathen generally, that shall loosen their hold on idolatry, and dispose them to welcome the gospel. And the probability that this state of things exists already, and will more and more, should be an inducement to Christians to make more vigorous efforts to send every where the light of life. ¶ *He will teach us of his ways.* He will make us acquainted with his will, and with the doctrines of the true religion. ¶ *For out of Zion.* These are the words of the *prophet*, not of the people. The prophet declares that the law would go from Zion; that is, Zion would be the centre from which it would be spread abroad; see Note, ch. i. 8. Zion is put here for Jerusalem, and means that the message of mercy to mankind would be spread *from* Jerusalem. Hence the Messiah commanded his disciples to tarry 'in Jerusalem until they should be endued with power from on high.' Luke xxiv. 49. Hence, also, he said that repentance and remission of sins should 'be preached among all nations, *beginning at Jerusalem* '—

4 And he shall judge among the | nations, and shall rebuke many

perhaps referring to this very passage in Isaiah; Luke xxiv. 47. ¶ *The law.* This is put here for the doctrines of the true religion in general. The law or will of God, under the reign of the Messiah, would proceed from Zion. ¶ *The word of the Lord.* The message of his mercy to mankind ; that which he has *spoken* respecting the salvation of men.—The truth which is here taught is, *that Zion or the church is the source of religious truth, and the centre of religious influence in the world.* This is true in the following respects :— (1.) Zion was the source of religious truth to the ancient world. Knowledge was gained by travel ; and it is capable of about as clear demonstration as any fact of ancient history, that no inconsiderable part of the knowledge pertaining to God in ancient Greece was obtained by intercourse with the sages of distant lands, and that the truths held in Zion or Jerusalem thus radiated from land to land, and mind to mind. (2.) The church is now the centre of religious truth to the world around it. (*a.*) The world by its philosophy never originates a system of religion which it is desirable to retain, and which conveys any just view of God or the way of salvation. (*b.*) The most crude, unsettled, contradictory, and vague opinions on religion prevail in this community called ' *the world.*' (*c.*) If *in* this community there are any opinions that are true and valuable, they can in most instances be traced to *the church.* They are owing to the influence of the pulpit ; or to an early training in the Bible ; or to early teaching in the Sabbath-school, or to the instructions of a pious parent, or to the *general* influence which Christianity exerts on the community. (3.) The church holds the power of *reformation* in her hands, every cause of morals advancing or retarding as she enters into the work, or as she withdraws from it. (4.) The heathen world is dependent on the church for the knowledge of the true religion. There are *no* systems of truth that start up on a pagan soil. There is no elastic energy in a heathen mind.

There is no recuperative power to bring it back to God. There is no *advance* made toward the truth in any heathen community. There is no well-spring of life to purify the soul. The effect of time is only to deepen the darkness, and to drive them farther from God. They only worship mere shapeless blocks ; they bow down before worse looking idols ; they enter less elegant and more polluted temples. The idols of the heathen are not constructed with half the skill and taste evinced two thousand years ago; nor are their temples built with such exquisite art. No idol of the heathen world now can compare with the statue of Minerva at Athens; no temple can be likened to the Parthenon ; no sentiment of heathenism in China, India, or Africa, can be compared with the views of the sages of Greece. The heathen world is becoming worse and worse, and if ever brought to better views, it must be by a *foreign* influence; and that influence will not go forth from philosophy or science, but *from the church.* If light is ever to spread, it is to go forth from Zion ; and the world is dependent on *the church* for any just knowledge of God and of the way to life. The ' law is to go forth from Zion ; ' and the question whether the millions of the human family are to be taught the way to heaven, is just a question whether the church can be roused to diffuse abroad the light which has arisen on her.

4. *And he shall judge.* Or he shall exercise the office of a judge, or umpire. This *literally* refers to the God of Jacob (ver. 3), though it is clear that the meaning is, that he will do it by the Messiah, or under his reign. One office of a judge is to decide controversies ; to put an end to litigations, and thus to promote peace. The connection shows that this is the meaning here. Nations that are contending shall be brought to peace by the influence of the reign of the Messiah, and shall beat their swords into ploughshares. In other words, the influence of the reign of the Messiah shall put a period to wars, and reduce contending nations to peace. ¶ *And*

people; and they *a* shall beat their swords into ploughshares; and their

a Ps.46.9; Hos.2.18.

shall rebuke. Shall *reprove* them for their contentions and strifes.

Lowth: 'Shall work conviction in many peoples.'
Noyes: 'He shall be a judge of the nations,
And an umpire of many kingdoms.'

He shall show them the evil of war; and by reproving them for those wicked passions which cause wars, shall promote universal peace. This the gospel every where does; and the tendency of it, if obeyed, would be to produce universal peace. In accordance with predictions like these, the Messiah is called the Prince of Peace (Isa. ix. 6); and it is said that of his peace there shall be no end; Isa. ix. 7. ¶ *And they shall beat,* &c. They shall change the arts of war to those of peace; or they shall abandon the pursuits of war for the mild and useful arts of husbandry; comp. Ps. xlvi. 9; Hos. ii. 20. A similar prophecy is found in Zech. ix. 10. The following extracts may serve to illustrate this passage :—' The Syrian plough, which was probably used in all the regions around, is a very simple frame, and commonly so light, that a man of moderate strength might carry it in one hand. Volney states that in Syria it is often nothing else than the branch of a tree, cut below a bifurcation, and used without wheels. The ploughshare is a piece of iron, broad but not large, which tips the end of the shaft. So

MODERN ORIENTAL PLOUGH.—From Fellow's Asia Minor.

a, the plough; *b,* the pole; *c,* the handle or plough-tail, *d d d,* shares; *a e,* yokes; *f,* the goad, or instrument for driving.

much does it resemble the short sword used by the ancient warriors, that it may, with very little trouble, be converted into that deadly weapon; and when the work of destruction is over, reduced again to its former shape, and

spears into [1] pruning-hooks: nation shall not lift up sword against

[1] or, *scythes.*

applied to the purposes of agriculture.' ¶ *Their spears.* Spears were much used in war. They were made of wood, with a sharpened piece of iron or other metal attached to the end. The pruning-hook, made for cutting the limbs of vines or trees, is, in like manner, a long piece of wood with a crooked knife attached to it. Hence it was easy to convert the one into the other. ¶ *Pruning-hooks.* Hooks or long knives for trimming vines. The word here, however, means any thing employed in *reaping* or *mowing,* a sickle, or a scythe, or any instrument to *cut with,* as well as a pruning-hook. These figures, as images of peace, are often used by the prophets. Micah (iv. 4) has added to this description of peace in Isaiah, the following :

But they shall sit
Every man under his vine,
And under his fig-tree;
And none shall make them afraid:
For the mouth of Jehovah hath spoken it.

Joel (iii. 10) has reversed the figure, and applied it to war prevailing over peace :

Beat your ploughshares into swords;
And your pruning-hooks into spears.

The same emblems to represent peace, which are here used by Isaiah, also occur in heathen poets. Thus Martial; Epigr. xiv. 34:

Falx ex ense.
Pax me certa ducis placidos conflavit in usus,
Agricolae nunc sum, militis ante fui.

So Virgil; Georg. 1, 507:

Squalent abductis arva colonis,
Et curvae rigidum falces conflantur in ensem.

So also Ovid; Fast. 1, 699:

Sarcula cessabunt, versique in pila ligones.

¶ *Nation shall not lift up,* &c. This is a remarkable prediction of universal peace under the gospel. The prediction is positive, that the time will come when it shall prevail. But it has not yet been fully accomplished. We may remark, however, in relation to this:

nation, neither shall they learn war any more.

5 O house of Jacob, come ye, and let us walk *a* in the light of the LORD

a Eph.5.8.   1 or, *more than.*

6 Therefore thou hast forsaken thy people, the house of Jacob, because they be replenished ¹from the east, and *are* soothsayers *b* like the Philistines, and they ²please

b Deut.18.14.   2 or, *abound with.*

(1.) That the tendency of the gospel is to promote the arts, and to produce the spirit of peace. (2.) It will dispose the nations to do right, and thus to avoid the occasions of war. (3.) It will fill the mind with horror at the scenes of cruelty and blood that war produces. (4.) It will diffuse honour around the arts of peace, and teach the nations to prize the endearments of home and country, and the sweet scenes of domestic life. (5.) Just so far as it has influence over princes and rulers, it will teach them to lay aside the passions of ambition and revenge, and the love of conquest and 'glory,' and indispose them to war. (6.) The tendency of things now is towards peace. The laws of nations have been established under the gospel. Difficulties can even now be adjusted by negotiation, and without a resort to arms. (7.) Wars are far less barbarous than they were formerly. The gospel has produced humanity, mildness, and some degree of justice even in war. It has put an end to the unmerciful treatment of prisoners; has prevented their being sold as slaves; has taught even belligerents not to murder women and children. (8.) Nothing remains to be done to make peace universal but to send the gospel abroad through every land. When that is done, the nations will be disposed to peace; and the prophet, therefore, has predicted the universal prevalence of peace *only* when all nations shall be brought under the influence of the gospel.

5. *O house of Jacob.* This is a direct address, or exhortation, of the prophet to the Jews. It is made in view of the fact that God had gracious purposes towards them. He intended to distinguish them by making them the source of blessings to all nations. As this was to be their high destiny, he exhorts them to devote themselves to him, and to live to his honour. The word *house* here means the *family,* or *nation.* The

phrase is applied to the Jews because their tribes were descended from the twelve sons of Jacob. ¶ *Let us walk.* Let us *live.* The word *walk* is often used to denote human life or conduct; comp. ver. 3; Rom. vi. 4; viii. 1; 1 Cor. v. 7; Gal. vi. 16, &c. ¶ *In the light of the* LORD. The sense of this is: Let us obey the commandments of JEHOVAH; or, as the Chaldee expresses it, 'Let us walk in the doctrine of the law of the Lord.' The idea may be thus expressed: 'Let us not walk in the darkness and error of sin and idolatry, but in the light or instruction which God sheds upon us by his law. He teaches us what we should do, and let us obey him.' *Light* is often, in the Scriptures, thus put for instruction, or teaching; comp. Note, Matt. iv. 16; John i. 4; also, Eph. v. 8.

6. *Therefore.* The prophet proceeds in this and the following verses, to state the reasons of their calamities, and of the judgments that had come upon them. Those judgments he traces to the crimes which he enumerates—crimes growing chiefly out of great commercial prosperity, producing pride, luxury, and idolatry. ¶ *Thou hast forsaken.* The address is changed from the exhortation to the house of Jacob (ver. 5) to God, as is frequently the case in the writings of Isaiah. It indicates a state where the mind is full of the subject, and where it expresses itself in a rapid and hurried manner. ¶ *Hast forsaken.* Hast withdrawn thy protection, and given them over to the calamities and judgments which had come upon them. ¶ *They be replenished.* Heb. They are *full.* That is, these things abound. ¶ *From the East.* Marg. *More than the East.* The meaning of the expression it is not easy to determine. The word translated *East,* קֶדֶם, denotes also *antiquity,* or that which is *of old,* as well as the East. Hence the LXX. render it, 'their land is, *as of old,* filled.' The Chaldee, 'their land is filled with idols *as at the*

themselves in the children of strangers. [b]

7 Their [b] land also is full of silver and gold, neither *is there any* end

beginning.' Either idea will suit the passage ; though our translation more nearly accords with the Hebrew than the others. The *East, i.e.,* Arabia, Persia, Chaldea, &c., was the country where astrology, soothsaying, and divination particularly abounded ; see Dan. ii. 2; Deut. xviii. 9–11. ¶ *And* are *soothsayers.* Our word *soothsayers* means *foretellers, prognosticators,* persons who pretend to predict future events *without inspiration,* differing in this from true prophets. What the Hebrew word means, it is not so easy to determine. The word עֹנְנִים *ōnĕnīm* may be derived from עָנָן *ānān, a cloud*—and then would denote those who augur from the appearance of the clouds, a species of divination from certain changes observed in the sky ; comp. Lev. xix. 26: ' Neither shall ye—*observe times.'* 2 Kings xxi. 6. This species of divination was expressly forbidden ; see Deut. xviii. 10, 11, 12 : ' There shall not be found among you any one that useth divination, or *an observer of times,* or an enchanter,' &c. Or the word may be derived from עַיִן *ain, an eye,* and then it will denote those who fascinate, enchant, or bewitch by the eye. It is probable that the word includes *augury, necromancy,* and *witchcraft,* in general —all which were expressly forbidden by the law of Moses ; Deut. xviii. 10–12. ¶ *Like the Philistines.* The Philistines occupied the land in the south-west part of Palestine. The LXX. use the word *foreigners* here, as they do generally, instead of the Philistines. ¶ *And they please themselves.* The word here used—שָׂפֵק—means literally *to clap the hands* in token of joy. It may also mean, *to join the hands, to shake hands,* and then it will signify that they *joined hands* with foreigners; that is, they made compacts or entered into alliances with them contrary to the law of Moses. The LXX. seem to understand it of unlawful marriages with the women of surrounding nations—τέκνα πολλὰ ἀλλόφυλλα ἐγενήθη αὐτοῖς ; comp. Neh. xiii. 23. It means probably, in

general, that they entered into improper alliances, whether they were military, matrimonial, or commercial, with the surrounding nations. The words *children of strangers* may mean, with the descendants of the foreigners with whom Moses forbade any alliances. The Jews were to be a separate and peculiar people, and, in order to this, it was necessary to forbid all such foreign alliances ; Ex. xxiii. 12–15; Ps. cvi. 3, 5 ; Ezra ix.

7. *Their land also is full of silver and gold.* This *gold* was brought chiefly from Ophir. Solomon imported vast quantities of silver and gold from foreign places ; 2 Chron. viii. 18 ; ix. 10; 1 Chron. xxix. 4; comp. Job xxviii. 16; 1 Kings x. 21, 27; 2 Chron. ix. 20. ' And the king made silver to be in Jerusalem as stones.'—' It was nothing accounted of in the days of Solomon.' From these expressions we see the force of the language of Isaiah—' their land is *full,'* &c. This accumulation of silver and gold was expressly forbidden by the law of Moses ; Deut. xvii. 17 : ' Neither shall he [the king of Israel] greatly multiply to himself silver and gold.' The reason of this prohibition was, that it tended to produce luxury, effeminacy, profligacy, the neglect of religion, and vice. It is on this account that it is brought by the prophet as an *accusation* against them that their land was thus filled. ¶ *Treasures.* Wealth of all kinds ; but chiefly silver, gold, precious stones, garments, &c.; comp. Note, Matt. vi. 19. ¶ *Their land also is full of horses.* This was also forbidden in the law of Moses ; Deut. xvii. 16 : ' But he shall not multiply horses to himself, nor cause the people to return to Egypt, to the end that he should multiply horses.' This law, however, was grossly violated by Solomon ; 1 Kings x. 26: ' And Solomon gathered together chariots and horsemen ; he had a thousand and four hundred chariots, and twelve thousand horsemen.' It is not quite clear *why* the use of horses was forbidden to the Jews. Perhaps several reasons might have concurred:

of their treasures; their land is also full of horses, neither *is there any* end of their chariots:

8 Their land also is full of *a* idols; they worship the work of their

a Jer. 2.28.

(1.) Egypt was distinguished for producing fine horses, and the Egyptians used them much in war (Deut. xvii. 16); and one design of God was to make the Jews distinguished in all respects from the Egyptians, and to keep them from commerce with them. (2.) Horses were chiefly used *in war*, and the tendency of keeping them would be to produce the love of war and conquest. (3.) The tendency of keeping them would be to lead them to put *trust* in them rather than in God for protection. This is hinted at in Ps. xx. 7: ' Some trust in chariots, and some in horses; but we will remember the name of JEHOVAH our God.' (4.) *Horses* were regarded as consecrated *to the sun;* see *Univ. Hist. Anc. P.*, vol. x., 177. Ed. 1780. They were sacrificed in various nations to the sun, their swiftness being supposed to render them an appropriate offering to that luminary. There is no evidence, however, that they were used for sacrifice among the Hebrews. They were probably employed to draw the chariots in the solemn processions in the worship of the sun. The ancient Persians, who were sun-worshippers, dedicated white horses and chariots to the sun, and it is supposed that other nations derived the practice from them. The sun was supposed to be drawn daily in a chariot by four wondrous coursers, and the fate of Phaeton, who undertook to guide that chariot and to control those coursers, is known to all. The use of horses, therefore, among the Hebrews in the time of Ahaz, when Isaiah lived (see 2 Kings xxxiii. 11), was connected with idolatry, and it was mainly on this account that the prophet rebuked their use with so much severity; 2 Kings xxiii. 11. It may be added, that in a country like Judea, abounding in hills and mountains, cavalry could not be well employed even

in war. On the plains of Egypt it could be employed to advantage; or in predatory excursions, as among the Arabs, horses could be used with great success and effect, and Egypt and Arabia therefore abounded with them. Indeed, these may be regarded as the native countries of the horse. As it was the design of God to separate, as much as possible, the Jews from the surrounding nations, the use of horses was forbidden. ¶ *Chariots.* Chariots were chiefly used in war, though they were sometimes used for pleasure. Of those intended for war there were two kinds; one for the generals and princes to ride in, the other to break the enemy's ranks. These last were commonly armed with hooks or scythes. They were much used by the ancients; Josh. xi. 4; Judg. i. 19. The Philistines, in their war against Saul, had 30,000 chariots, and 6000

EGYPTIAN CHARIOT.

horsemen; 1 Sam. xiii. 5. There is no evidence, however, that the Jews used chariots for war. Solomon had many of them (1 Kings x. 26), but they do not appear to have been used in any military expedition, but to have been kept for display and pleasure. Judea was a mountainous country, and chariots would have been of little or no use in war.

8. *Their land also is full of idols;*

own hands, the work which their own fingers have made:

9 And the mean man boweth down, and the great man humbleth himself ; therefore forgive them not

10 Enter [a] into the rock, and hide thee in the dust, for fear of the LORD, and for the glory of his majesty.

a ver.19.21; Rev.6.15,16.

comp. Hos. viii. 4; x. 1. Vitringa supposes that Isaiah here refers to idols that were kept in private houses, as Uzziah and Jotham were worshippers of the true God, and in their reign idolatry was not publicly practised. It is certain, however, that though Uzziah himself did right, and was disposed to worship the true God, yet he did not effectually remove idolatry from the land. The high places were not removed, and the people still sacrificed and burnt incense on them ; 2 Kings xv. 4. It was customary with the heathen to keep in their houses *Penates* or *household gods*—small images, which they regarded as *protectors*, and to which they paid homage : comp. Gen. xxx. 19; Judg. xvii. 5; 1 Sam. xix. 13; Hos. iii. 4. ' This is a true and literal description of India. The traveller cannot proceed a *mile* through an inhabited country without seeing idols, and vestiges of idolatry in every direction. See their vessels, their implements of husbandry, their houses, their furniture, their ornaments, their sacred trees, their *domestic* and public temples ; and they all declare that the land is full of idols.'—*Roberts.* ¶ *The work of their own hands,* &c. Idols. It is often brought as proof of their great folly and degradation that they paid homage to what *they* had themselves made. See this severely satirized in Isa. xl. 18–20; xli. 67; xliv. 9–17.

9. *And the mean man.* That is, the man in humble life, the poor, the low in rank—for this is all that the Hebrew word here—אָדָם—implies. The distinction between the two words here used—אָדָם as denoting a man of humble rank, and אִישׁ as denoting one of elevated rank—is one that constantly occurs in the Scriptures. Our word *mean* conveys an idea of moral baseness and degradation, which is not implied in the Hebrew. ¶ *Boweth down.* That is, before idols. Some commentators, however, have understood this of bowing

down in *affliction,* but the other is probably the true interpretation. ¶ *And the great man.* The men in elevated rank in life. The expressions together mean the same as *all ranks of people.* It was a common or universal thing. No rank was exempt from the prevailing idolatry. ¶ *Therefore forgive them not.* The Hebrew is *future*—לָהֶם וְאַל־תִּשָּׂא. Thou wilt not *bear* for them ; that is, thou wilt not bear away their sins [by an atonement], or ' thou wilt not forgive them ;'—but agreeable to a common Hebrew construction, it has the force of the imperative. It involves a *threatening* of the prophet, in the form of an address to God. ' So great is their sin, that thou, Lord, wilt not pardon them.' The prophet then proceeds, in the following verses, to denounce the certainty and severity of the judgment that was coming upon them.

10. *Enter into the rock.* That is, into the *holes* or *caverns* in the rocks, as a place of refuge and safety; comp. ver. 19, and Rev. vi. 15, 16. In times of invasion by an enemy, it was natural to flee to the fastnesses or to the caverns of rocks for refuge. This expression is highly figurative and poetic. The prophet warns them to flee from danger. The sense is, that such were their crimes that they would certainly be punished ; and he advises them to flee to a place of safety. ¶ *And hide thee in the dust.* In ver. 19, this is ' caves of the dust.' It is parallel to the former, and probably has a similar meaning. But *may* there not be reference here to the mode prevailing in the East of avoiding the monsoon or poisonous heated wind that passes over the desert ? Travellers there, in order to be safe, are obliged to throw themselves down, and to place their mouths close to the earth until it has passed. ¶ *For fear of the Lord.* Heb. ' From the face of the terror of the Lord.' That is, the punishment which God will inflict will sweep over the land, producing fear and terror.

11 The lofty looks *a* of man shall be humbled, and the haughtiness of men shall be bowed down; and the LORD alone shall be exalted in that *b* day.

12 For the day of the LORD of

a ver.17; ch.5,16; Ps.13.27.　*b* Zep.3.11,16; Zec 9.16.

hosts *shall be* upon every *one that is* proud and lofty, and upon every *one that is* lifted up, and he shall be brought low;

13 And upon all the *c* cedars of Lebanon, *that are* high and lifted

c Eze.31.3; Zec.11.1,2.

¶ *And for the glory,* &c. That is, the honour or splendour which will attend him when he comes forth to inflict judgment on the people; ver. 19, 20.

11. *The lofty looks.* Heb. ' The *eyes of pride,*' *i.e.*, the proud eyes or looks. Pride commonly evinces itself in a lofty carriage and supercilious aspect; Ps. xviii. 27. ¶ *Shall be humbled.* By the calamities that shall sweep over the land. This does not mean that he shall be brought *to be* humble, or to have a humble heart, but that that on which he so much prided himself would be taken away. ¶ *The Lord alone,* &c. God will so deal with them as to vindicate his honour; to turn the attention entirely on himself, and to secure the reverence of all the people. So terrible shall be his judgments, and so *manifestly* shall they come from *him,* that they shall look away from every thing else to *him* alone. ¶ *In that day.* In the day of which the prophet speaks, when God would punish them for their sins, Reference is probably made to the captivity at Babylon.—It may be remarked, that one design of punishment is to lead men to regard and honour God. He will humble the pride of men, and so pass before them in his judgments, that they shall be compelled to *acknowledge* him as their just Sovereign and Judge.

12. *The day,* &c. This expression evidently denotes that the Lord would inflict severe punishment upon every one that was lofty. Such a severe infliction is called *the day of the Lord of hosts,* because it would be a time when *he* would particularly manifest himself, and when *he* would be recognised as the inflicter of that punishment. *His* coming forth in this manner would give *character* to that time, and would be the prominent *event.* The punishment of the wicked is thus frequently called *the day of the Lord;* Isa. xiii. 6, 9: ' Behold the day of the

Lord cometh, cruel both with wrath and fierce anger,' &c.; Jer. xlvi. 10: ' The day of the Lord God of hosts, a day of vengeance.' Ezek. xxx. 3; Zeph. i. 7, 14; Joel ii. 31; see also in the New Testament, 1 Thess. v. 2; 2 Pet. iii. 10. ¶ *Every* one that is *proud and lofty.* Or, rather, every *thing* that is high and lofty. The phrase is not restricted to *persons,* though it embraces them. But though the language here is general, the reference is doubtless, mainly, to the princes, magistrates, and nobility of the nation; and is designed not only to designate them as men of rank and power, but as men who were haughty in their demeanour and feelings. At the same time, there is included in the language, as the subsequent verses show, all on which the nation prided itself.

13. *And upon all the cedars of Lebanon.* This is a beautiful specimen of the poetic manner of writing, so common among the Hebrews, where spiritual and moral subjects are represented by grand or beautiful imagery taken from objects of nature. Mount Lebanon bounded Palestine on the north. It was formerly much celebrated for its large and lofty cedars. These cedars were from thirty-five to forty feet in girth, and very high. They were magnificent trees, and were valuable for ceiling, statues, or roofs, that required durable and beautiful timber. The roof of the temple of Diana of Ephesus, according to Pliny, was of cedar, and no small part of the temple of Solomon was of this wood. A few lofty trees of this description are still remaining on Mount Lebanon. ' After three hours of laborious travelling,' says D'Arvieux, ' we arrived at the famous cedars about eleven o'clock. We counted twenty-three of them. The circumference of these trees is thirty-six feet. The bark of the cedar resembles that of the pine;

the leaves and cone also bear considerable resemblance. The stem is upright, the wood is hard, and has the reputation of being incorruptible. The leaves are long, narrow, rough, very green, ranged in tufts along the branches; they shoot in spring, and fall in the beginning of winter. Its flowers and fruit resemble those of the pine. From the full grown trees, a fluid trickles naturally, and without incision; this is clear, transparent, whitish, and after a time dries and hardens; it is supposed to possess great virtues. The place where these great trees are stationed, is in a plain of nearly a league in circumference, on the summit of a mount which is environed on almost all sides by other mounts, so high that their summits are always covered with snow. This plain is level, the air is pure, the heavens always serene.'

LEBANON, AND ITS CEDARS. (*Cedrus Libani Conifera.*)

Maundrell found only sixteen cedars of large growth, and a natural plantation of smaller ones, which were very numerous. One of the largest was twelve yards six inches in girth, and thirty-seven yards in the spread of its boughs. At six yards from the ground, it was divided into five limbs, each equal to a great tree. Dr. Richardson visited them in 1818, and found a small clump of large, tall, and beautiful trees, which he pronounces the most picturesque productions of the vegetable world that he had ever seen. In this clump are two generations of trees; the oldest are large and massy, rearing their heads to an enormous height, and spreading their branches to a great extent. He measured one, not the largest in the clump, and found it thirty-two feet in circumference. Seven of these trees appeared to be very old, the rest younger, though, for want of space, their branches are not so spreading.—Bush's *Illustrations of Scripture.* 'The celebrated cedar-grove of Lebanon,' says Dr. Robinson, 'is at least two days' journey from Beïrût, near the northern, and perhaps the highest summit of the mountain. It has been often and sufficiently described by travellers for the last three centuries; but they

up, and upon all the oaks of Bashan,

14 And upon all the high mountains, and upon all the hills *that
are* lifted up,

15 And upon every high tower,
and upon every fenced wall,

16 And upon all the ships of
Tarshish, and upon all [1]pleasant
pictures.

[1] *pictures of desire.*

---

all differ as to the number of the oldest
trees, inasmuch as in counting, some
have included more and some less of the
younger ones. At present, the number
of trees appears to be on the increase,
and amounts in all to several hundred.
This grove was long held to be the
only remnant of the ancient cedars of
Lebanon. But Seetzen, in 1805, discovered two other groves of greater
extent; and the American Missionaries,
in travelling through the mountains,
have also found many cedars in other
places. The trees are of all sizes, old
and young; but none so ancient and
venerable as those usually visited.'—
Bib. Researches, iii., 440, 441. The
cedar, so large, lofty, and grand, is
used in the Scriptures to represent
kings, princes, and nobles; comp. Ezek.
xxxi. 3; Dan. iv. 20–22; Zech. xi. 1, 2;
Isa. xiv. 8. Here it means the princes
and nobles of the land of Israel. The
Chaldee renders it, 'upon all the strong
and mighty kings of the people.' ¶ *And
upon all the oaks of Bashan.* Bashan
was east of the river Jordan, in the
limits of the half tribe of Manasseh. It
was bounded on the north and east by
Gilead, south by the river Jabbok, and
west by the Jordan. It was celebrated
for pasturage, and for producing fine
cattle; Num. xxi. 33; xxxii. 33; Ps.
xxii. 12; Ezek. xxxix. 18; Amos iv. 1;
Mic. vii. 14. Its lofty oaks are also
particularly celebrated; Ezek. xxvii. 6;
Amos ii. 9; Zech. xi. 2. The sense here
is not different from the former member
of the sentence—denoting the princes
and nobles of the land.

14. *And upon all the high mountains.*
Judea abounded in lofty mountains,
which added much to the grandeur of
its natural scenery. Lowth supposes
that by mountains and hills are meant
here, 'kingdoms, republics, states,
cities;' but there are probably no
parallel places where they have this
meaning. The meaning is probably
this:—high mountains and hills would

not only be objects of beauty or grandeur, but also places of defence, and
protection. In the caverns and fastnesses of such hills, it would be easy for
the people to find refuge when the land
was invaded. The meaning of the
prophet then is, that the day of God's
vengeance should be upon the places of
refuge and strength; the strongly fortified places, or places of sure retreat in
cases of invasion; comp. Notes on ver.
19. ¶ *Hills that are lifted up.* That
is, high, elevated hills.

15. *Every high tower.* Towers, or
fortresses, were erected for defence and
protection. They were made on the
walls of cities, for places of observation
(comp. Note, ch. xxi. 5), or in places
of strength, to be a refuge for an army,
and to be a point from which they
might sally out to attack their enemies.
They were *high* to afford a defence
against being scaled by an enemy, and
also that from the top they might look
abroad for observation; and also to
annoy an enemy from the top, when the
foe approached the walls of a city.
¶ *Every fenced wall.* בְּצוּרָה חוֹמָה.
The word *fenced*, בְּצוּרָה *betzūrâ*, is
from בָּצַר *bâtzăr*, to make inaccessible,
and hence to fortify. It denotes a wall
that is inaccessible, or strongly fortified.
Cities were commonly surrounded by
high and strong walls to defend them
from enemies. The sense is, God would
overturn all their strong places of refuge
and defence.

16. *And upon all the ships of Tarshish.* Ships of Tarshish are often
mentioned in the Old Testament, but
the meaning of the expression is not
quite obvious; see 1 Kings x. 22; 2
Chron. ix. 21; xx. 36, 37; Ps. xlviii. 7,
&c. It is evident that *Tarshish* was
some distant land from which was imported silver, iron, lead, tin, &c. It is
now generally agreed that *Tartessus* in
Spain is referred to by the Tarshish of
Scripture. Bruce, however, supposes

17 And *the loftiness of man shall be bowed down, and the haughtiness of men shall be laid low: and the LORD alone shall be exalted in that day.

18 And the idols ¹he shall utterly abolish.

19 And they shall go into the holes of the rocks, and into the

a ver. 11.   1 or, *shall utterly pass away.*

that it was in Africa, south of Abyssinia; see Note on ch. lx. 9. That it was in the *west* is evident from Gen. x. 4; comp. Ps. lxxxii. 10. In Ezek. xxviii. 13, it is mentioned as an important place of trade; in Jer. x. 9, it is said that silver was procured there; and in Ezek. xxviii. 12, it is said that iron, lead, silver, and tin, were imported from it. In 2 Chron. ix. 21, it is said that the ships of Tarshish returned every three years, bringing gold and silver, ivory, apes and peacocks. These are productions chiefly of India, but they might have been obtained in trade during the voyage. In Isa. xxiii. 1; lx. 9, the phrase, 'ships of Tarshish,' seems to denote ships that were bound on long voyages, and it is probable that they came to denote a particular kind of ships adapted to long voyages, in the same way as the word *Indiaman* does with us. The precise situation of *Tarshish* is not necessary to be known in order to understand the passage here. The phrase, 'ships of Tarshish,' denotes clearly ships employed in foreign trade, and in introducing articles of commerce, and particularly of luxury. The meaning is, that God would embarrass, and destroy this commerce; that his judgments would be on their articles of luxury. The LXX. render it, 'and upon every ship of the sea, and upon every beautiful appearance of ships.' The Targum, 'and upon those who dwell in the isles of the sea, and upon those who dwell in beautiful palaces.' ¶ *And upon all pleasant pictures.* Margin, 'pictures of desire;' that is, such as it should be esteemed desirable to possess, and gaze upon; pictures of value or beauty. Targum, 'costly palaces.' The word rendered 'pictures,' שְׂכִיּוֹת, denotes properly *sights*, or objects to be looked at; and does not designate *paintings* particularly, but every thing that was designed for ornament or luxury. Whether the art of painting was much known among the

Hebrews, it is not now possible to determine. To a certain extent, it may be presumed to have been practised; but the meaning of this place is, that the Divine judgment should rest on all that was designed for mere ornament and luxury; and, from the description in the previous verses, there can be no doubt that such ornaments would abound.

17. *And the loftiness,* &c.; see Note ver. 11. The repetition of this makes it strongly emphatic.

18. *And the idols*; Note, ver. 8. ¶ *Abolish.* Heb. ' Cause to pass away or disappear.' He shall entirely cause their worship to cease. This prediction was most remarkably fulfilled. Before the captivity at Babylon, the Jews were exceedingly prone to idolatry. It is a remarkable fact that no such propensity was ever evinced *after* that. In their own land they were entirely free from it; and scattered as they have been into all lands, they have in every age since kept clear from idolatry. Not an instance, probably, has been known of their relapsing into this sin; and no temptation, or torture, has been sufficient to induce them to bow down and worship an idol. This is one of the few instances that have occurred where affliction and punishment have *completely* answered their design.

19. *And they shall go.* That is, the worshippers of idols. ¶ *Into the holes of the rocks.* Judea was a mountainous country, and the mountains abounded with caves that offered a safe retreat for those who were in danger. Many of those caverns were very spacious. At En-gedi, in particular, a cave is mentioned where David with six hundred men hid himself from Saul in the *sides* of it; 1 Sam. xxiv. Sometimes caves or dens were artificially constructed for refuge or defence in danger; Judg. vi. 2; 1 Sam. xiii. 6. Thus, ' because of the Midianites, the children of Israel made them the dens which are

caves of the [1] earth, for fear of the LORD, and for the glory of his majesty, when he ariseth to shake terribly [a] the earth.

20 In that day a man shall cast

1 or, *dust*.   *a* Hag.2,6,21; He.12.26,27.

his idols of silver,[2] and his idols of gold, which they made [3] *each one* for himself to worship, to the moles and to the bats ;

2 *the idols of his silver*.

3 or, *for him*.

---

in the mountains, and caves, and strong holds.' Judg. vi. 2. To these they fled in times of hostile invasion. 'When the men of Israel saw that they were in a strait (for the people were distressed), then the people did hide themselves in caves, and in thickets, and in rocks, and in high places, and in pits;' 1 Sam. xiii. 6; comp. Jer. xli. 9. Mahomet speaks of a tribe of Arabians, the tribe of Thamud, who 'hewed houses out of the mountains to secure themselves;' Koran, ch. xv. and xxvi. Grots or rooms hewed out of rocks for various purposes are often mentioned by travellers in Oriental regions; see Maundrell, p. 118, and Burckhardt's *Travels in Syria*, and particularly Laborde's *Journey to Arabia Petræa*. Such caves are often mentioned by Josephus as affording places of refuge for banditti and robbers ; *Ant.*, B. xiv. ch. 15, and *Jewish Wars*, B. i. ch. 16. To enter into the caves and dens, therefore, as places of refuge, was a very natural image to denote consternation. The meaning here is, that the worshippers of idols should be so alarmed as to seek for a place of security and refuge; comp. ver. 10. ¶ *When he ariseth*. This is an expression often used in the Scriptures to denote the commencement of doing any thing. It is here derived, perhaps, from the image of one who has been in repose—as of a lion or warrior, rousing up suddenly, and putting forth mighty efforts. ¶ *To shake terribly the earth.* An image denoting the presence of God, for judgment or punishment. One of the magnificent images which the sacred writers often use to denote the presence of the Lord is, that the earth shakes and trembles; the mountains bow and are convulsed ; 2 Sam. xxii. 8: 'Then the earth shook and trembled ; the foundations of heaven moved, because he was wroth ;' see also ver. 9–16; Judg. v. 4; Hab. iii. 6-10: 'The mountains saw thee and trembled;'

Heb. xii. 26: 'Whose voice then shook the earth.' The image here denotes that he would come forth in such wrath that the very earth should tremble, as if alarmed his presence. The mind cannot conceive more sublime images than are thus used by the sacred writers.

20. *In that day.* That is, in the time when God would come forth to inflict punishment. Probably the day to which the prophet refers here was the time of the captivity at Babylon. ¶ *A man shall cast*, &c. That is, *all* who have idols, or who have been trusting in them. Valuable as they may be—made of gold and silver; and much as he may *now* rely on them or worship them, yet he shall then see their vanity, and shall cast them into dark, obscure places, or holes, where are moles and bats. ¶ *To the moles.* לַחְפֹּר פֵּרוֹת. Probably this should be read as a single word, and it is usually interpreted *moles*. Jerome interprets it mice, or moles, from חָפַר *hhâphăr, to dig.* The word is formed by doubling the radical letters to give *intensity*. Similar instances of words being divided in the Hebrew, which are nevertheless to be read as one, occur in 2 Chron. xxiv. 6; Jer. xlvi. 20; Lam. iv. 3; Ezek. xxvii. 6. The mole is a well-known animal, with exceedingly small eyes, that burrows under ground, lives in the dark, and subsists on roots. The bat lives in old ruins, and behind the bark of trees, and flies only in the night. They *resemble* each other, and are used here in connection, because *both* dwell amidst ruins and in obscure places ; both are regarded as animals of the lowest order; both are of the same genus, and both are almost blind. The sense is, therefore, that the idols which had before been so highly venerated, would now be despised, and cast into obscure places, and amidst ruins, as worthless ; see Bochart's *Hieroz.*, P. i., Lib. iii., p. 1032.

21 To go into the clefts of the rocks, and into the tops of the ragged rocks, for fear of the LORD, and for the glory of his majesty,

a Ps.146.3,4; Jer.17.5.

when he ariseth to shake terribly the earth.

22 Cease [a] ye from man, whose breath is in his nostrils; for wherein is he to be accounted of?

Ed. 1663. ¶ *And to the bats.* 'The East may be termed the country of bats; they hang by hundreds and thousands in caves, ruins, and under the roofs of large buildings. To enter such places, especially after rain, is *most* offensive. I have lived in rooms where it was sickening to remain, on account of the smell produced by those creatures, and whence it was almost impossible to expel them. What from the appearance of the creature, its sunken diminutive eye, its short legs (with which it cannot walk), its leather-like wings, its half-hairy, oily skin, its offensive ordure ever and anon dropping on the ground, its time for food and sport, darkness, makes it one of the most disgusting creatures to the people of the East.

GREAT TERNATE BAT (*Pteropus Edwardsii*).

From a Specimen in the British Museum.

No wonder, then, that its name is used by the Hindoos (as by the prophet) for an epithet of contempt. When a house ceases to please the inhabitants, on account of being haunted, they say, Give it to the *bats*. "Alas! alas! my wife and children are dead; my houses, my buildings, are all given to the bats." People ask, when passing a tenantless house, "Why is this habitation given to the bats?"'—*Roberts*. The meaning is, that the man would throw his idols into such places as the bats occupy —he would so see their vanity, and so

despise them, as to throw them into old ruins and dark places.

21. *To go.* That is, that he may go. ¶ *Clefts of the rocks;* see Note on ver. 19. ¶ *Into the tops,* &c. The tops of such rocks were not easily accessible, and were therefore deemed places of safety. We may remark here, how vain were the refuges to which they would resort—as if they were safe from *God,* when they had fled to the places in which they sought safety from *man.* The image here is, however, one that is very sublime. The earth shaking; the consternation and alarm of the people; their renouncing confidence in all to which they had trusted; their rapid flight; and their appearing on the high projecting cliffs, are all sublime and terrible images. They denote the severity of God's justice, and the image is a faint representation of the consternation of men when Christ shall come to judge the earth; Rev. vi. 15–17.

22. *Cease ye from man.* That is, cease to confide in or trust in him. The prophet had just said (ver. 11, 17) that the proud and lofty men would be brought low; that is, the kings, princes, and nobles would be humbled. They in whom the people had been accustomed to confide should show their insufficiency to afford protection. And he calls on the people to cease to put their reliance on any of the devices and refuges of men, implying that trust should be placed in the Lord only; see Ps. cxlvi. 3, 4; Jer. xvii. 5. ¶ *Whose breath is in his nostrils.* That is, who is weak and short-lived, and who has no control over his life. All his power exists only while he breathes, and his breath is in his nostrils. It may soon cease, and we should not confide in so frail and fragile a thing as the breath of man; see Ps. cxlvi. 3–5:

Put not your trust in princes,
Nor in the son of man, in whom there is no help.
His breath goeth forth, he returneth to his earth;
In that very day his thoughts perish.

CHAPTER III.

FOR, behold, the Lord, the LORD of hosts, doth take away *a* from Jerusalem, and from Judah, the stay and the *b* staff, the whole stay

a ch.36.12; Jer.38.9.   *b* Lev.26.26.

Happy is he that hath the God of Jacob for his help,
Whose hope is in the Lord his God.

The Chaldee has translated this verse, ' Be not subject to man when he is terrible, whose breath is in his nostrils; because to-day he lives, and to-morrow he is not, and shall be reputed as nothing.' It is remarkable that this verse is omitted by the LXX., as Vitringa supposes, because it might seem to exhort people not to put confidence in their rulers. ¶ *For wherein,* &c. That is, he is unable to afford the assistance which is needed. When God shall come to judge men, what can *man* do, who is weak, and frail, and mortal? Refuge should be sought in God. The exhortation of the prophet here had respect to a particular time, but it may be applied in general to teach us not to confide in weak, frail, and dying man. For life and health, for food and raiment, for home and friends, and especially for salvation, we are dependent on God. He alone can save the sinner; and though we should treat men with all due respect, yet we should remember that God alone can save us from the great day of wrath.

CHAPTER III.

1. *For.* This is a continuation of the previous chapter. The same prophecy is continued, and the force of the argument of the prophet will not be seen unless the chapters are read together; see the Analysis prefixed to ch. ii. In the close of the second chapter (ver. 22), the prophet had cautioned his countrymen against confiding in man. In this chapter, a reason is given here why they should cease to do it—to wit, that God would soon take away their kings and princes. ¶ *The Lord.* הָאָדוֹן ; see Note on ch. i. 24. ¶ *The Lord of hosts;* see Note ch. i. 9. The prophet calls the attention of the Jews particularly to the fact that this was about to be done by JEHOVAH *of hosts*—a title which he gives

ISAIAH I.

of bread, and the whole stay of water.

2 The mighty *c* man, and the man of war, the judge, and the prophet, and the prudent, and the ancient.

c 2Ki.24.14.

to God when he designs to indicate that that which is to be done implies peculiar strength, power, and majesty. As the work which was now to be done was the removal of the mighty men on which the nation was depending, it is implied that it was a work of power which belonged peculiarly to the God of armies— the Almighty. ¶ *Doth take away.* Is about to remove. In the Hebrew, the word here is a *participle*, and does not mark the precise time. It has reference here, however, to the future. ¶ *From Jerusalem,* &c., Note ch. i. 1. ¶ *The stay.* In the Hebrew, the words translated *stay* and *staff* are the same, with the exception that the former is in the masculine, and the latter is in the feminine gender. The meaning is, that God would remove *all kinds of support,* or *every thing* on which they relied. The reference is undoubtedly to the princes and mighty men on whose counsels and aid the nation was resting for defence; see ver. 2, 3. ¶ *The whole stay of bread.* We use a similar expression when we say that *bread is the staff of life.* The Hebrews often expressed the same idea, representing the *heart* in man as being *supported* or *upheld* by bread, Gen. xviii. 5 (*margin*); Judg. xix. 5 (*margin*); Lev. xxvi. 26; Ps. cv. 16. ¶ *Stay of water.* He would reduce them from their luxuries introduced by commerce (ch. ii.) to absolute want. This often occurred in the sieges and wars of the nation; and in the famines which were the consequence of the wars. The reference here is probably to the invasion of the land by Nebuchadnezzar. The famine consequent on that invasion is described in Jer. xxxviii. 21; xxxviii. 9; Lam. iv. 4: ' The tongue of the sucking child cleaveth to the roof of his mouth for thirst; the young children ask bread, and no man breaketh it unto them."

2. *The mighty man.* The hero. The idea expressed is not simply that of

7

3 The captain of fifty, and the honourable [1] man, and the counsellor, and the cunning artificer, and the [2] eloquent orator.

4 And I will give children [a] *to be* their princes, and babes shall rule over them.

1 *a man eminent in countenance.*
2 *or, skilful of speech.*   *a* Eccl.10.16.

personal strength and prowess, but the higher one of military eminence or heroism.—*Prof. Alexander.* This was fully accomplished in the time of Nebuchadnezzar ; 2 Kings xxiv. 14. ¶ *And the prudent.* This word in the original —ק͏ֹסֵם—means properly *a diviner*, or a *soothsayer.* But it is sometimes used in a good sense : see Prov. xvi. 10, *margin.* The Chaldee understands it of a man *who is consulted*, or whose opinion is asked, in times of perplexity or danger. The word was originally applied to false prophets, diviners, and soothsayers, who claimed the power of looking into futurity. It came, however, to denote also the man of sagacity, the statesman, the experienced counsellor, who from the records of the past could judge of the future, and to whom, therefore, the nation could look in times of perplexity and danger. Vitringa supposes that it may refer here to the false prophets on whose advice the nation might be relying. ¶ *The ancient.* The old man. Such men, especially among the Hebrews, were deemed particularly qualified to give advice. They had experience ; they kept the traditions of their fathers ; they had conversed with the wise of the preceding generation ; and in a land where there were few books, and knowledge was to be gained mainly by conversation and experience, great respect was shown them ; see Lev. xix. 32; 2 Chron. xxxi. 17; 1 Kings xii. 6, 8.

3. *The captain of fifty.* By this was probably denoted an officer in the army. The idea is, that the commanders of the various divisions of the army should be taken away. ¶ *The honourable man.* Heb. נְשׂוּא פָנִים *nĕsū pānīm.* The *man of elevated countenance.* That is, the man high in office. He was so called from the aspect of dignity which a man in office would assume. In the previous chapter, the phrase is used to denote rather the *pride* which attended such officers, than the dignity of the office itself. ¶ *And the counsellor;* Note,

ch. i. 26. ¶ *The cunning artificer.* Heb. The man wise in mechanic arts ; skilled in architecture, &c. ¶ *And the eloquent orator.* וּנְבוֹן לָחַשׁ *nĕbhōn lāhhāsh.* Literally, skilled or learned in whispering, in conjuration, in persuasion. The word לַחַשׁ *lāhhāsh* denotes properly a whispering, sighing, or calling for help ; (Isa. xxvi. 16. 'they have poured out a prayer,' לַחַשׁ—a secret speech, a feeble sigh for aid.) It is applied to the charm of the serpent—the secret breathing or gentle noise by which the charm is supposed to be effected ; Ps. lviii. 6; Jer. viii. 17; Eccl. x. 11. In ver. 20 of this chapter it denotes a charm or amulet worn by females ; see Note on that verse. It is also applied to magic, or conjuration—because this was usually done by gentle whispering, or incantation ; see Note, ch. viii. 19. From this use of the word, it comes to denote one that influences another ; one who persuades him in any way, as an orator does by argument and entreaty. Ancient orators also probably sometimes used a species of recitative, or measured cadence, not unlike that employed by those who practised incantations. Jerome says that it means here, 'a man who is learned, and acquainted with the law, and the prophets.' Chaldee, 'The prudent in council.' It *may be* used in a good sense here ; but if so, it is probably the only place where the word is so used in the Old Testament. A prophecy similar to this occurs in Hos. iii. 4: 'For the children of Israel shall abide many days without a king, and without a prince, and without a sacrifice, and without an image, and without an ephod, and without teraphim.'

4. *And I will give children.* Not children in respect to age so much as in regard to talent for governing. I will commit the land to the government of weak and imbecile princes. This would naturally occur when the wise and great were removed ; comp. Eccl. x. 16: 'Wo to thee, O land, when thy king is a

5 And the people shall be oppressed, every one by another, and every one by his neighbour: the child shall behave himself proudly against the ancient, and the base against the honourable.

6 When a man shall take hold of his brother, of the house of his father, *saying*, Thou hast clothing, be thou our ruler, and *let* this ruin *be* under thy hand:

---

child;' comp. Isa. iii. 12. ¶ *And babes shall rule*, &c. That is, babes in experience and knowledge. This was fully accomplished in the succession of weak and wicked princes that succeeded Isaiah, until the time of Zedekiah, the last of them, when the temple was taken by Nebuchadnezzar.—*Lowth*.

5. *And the people shall be oppressed*. This describes the state of anarchy and confusion which would exist under the reign of children and babes (ver. 4), when all law would be powerless, and all rights violated, and when the feeble would be oppressed and borne down by the strong. The word used here, properly denotes that *unjust exactions or demands* would be made, or that the people would be *urged* to fulfil them. ¶ *Every one by another*. In turn they shall oppress and vex one another. Heb. 'man by man; and man by his neighbour'—a strong mode of expression, denoting that there would be a state of mutual strife, and violation of rights; comp. 1 Kings xx. 20. ¶ *The child*, &c. All ranks of society shall be broken up. All respect due from one rank in life to another shall be violated. ¶ *Shall behave himself proudly*. The word here used means rather to *urge*, or *press on*. The child shall *crowd on* the old man. This was particularly descriptive of a state of anarchy and disorder, from the fact that the Jews inculcated so much respect and deference for age; see Note on ver. 2. ¶ *The ancient*. The old man. ¶ *And the base*. The man of low rank in life. The word properly means the man that is despised, the vile, the ignoble; 1 Sam. xviii. 23; Prov. xii. 9. ¶ *The honourable*. All the forms of respect in life would be broken up; all the proper rules of deference between man and man would be violated. Neither dignity, age, nor honour would be respected.

6. *When a man shall take hold*, &c. In this verse, and the following verses, the prophet continues to describe the calamitous and ruined state that would come upon the Jews; when there would be such a want of wealth and men, that they would seize upon any one that they thought able to defend them. The act of *taking hold* here denotes *supplication* and *entreaty*, as when one in danger or distress clings to that which is near, or which may be likely to aid him; comp. ch. iv. 1; 1 Sam. xv. 27. ¶ *His brother*. His kinsman, or one of the same tribe and family—claiming protection because they belonged to the same family. ¶ *Of the house of his father*. Descended from the same paternal ancestors as himself. Probably this refers to one of an ancient and opulent family—a man who had kept himself from the civil broils and tumults of the nation, and who had retained his property safe in the midst of the surrounding desolation. In the previous verse, the prophet had said that one characteristic of the times would be a want of respect for *the aged* and *the honourable*. He here says that such would be the distress, that a man would be *compelled* to show respect to rank; he would look to the ancient and wealthy families for protection. ¶ *Thou hast clothing*. In ancient times wealth consisted very much in changes of garments; and the expression 'thou hast clothing,' is the same as 'you are *rich*, you are able to assist us;' see Ex. xii. 34; xx. 26; Gen. xlv. 22; 2 Kings v. 5. ¶ *And let this ruin*, &c. This is an expression of entreaty. 'Give us assistance, or defence. We commit our ruined and dilapidated affairs to thee, and implore thy help.' The LXX. read this, 'and let my food,' *i.e.*, my support, 'be under thee'—do thou furnish me food. There are some other unimportant variations in the ancient versions, but the sense is substantially given in our translation. It is expressive of great distress and anarchy—when there would be no ruler, and every man would seek one for himself. The whole deportment evinced

7 In that day shall he [1] swear, saying, I will not be an [2] healer; for in my house *is* neither bread nor clothing: make me not a ruler of the people.

8 For Jerusalem is ruined, *a* and

Judah is fallen; because *b* their tongue and their doings *are* against the LORD, to provoke the *c* eyes of his glory.

9 The show of their *d* countenance doth witness against them, and they

here by the suppliant is one of submission, distress, and humility.

7. *In that day shall he swear.* Hebrew, רִשָּׁא ' Shall he lift up '—*i.e.*, the voice, or the hand. To lift up the hand was one of the modes of taking an oath. Perhaps it means only that he should lift up *the voice—i.e.*, should *answer;* comp. Num. xiv. 1. The Vulgate, the LXX., and the Chaldee, read it simply ' he shall *answer.*' ¶ *I will not be an healer.* Heb. ' *a binder up,*' ch. i. 6. The Vulgate renders it, ' I am not a physician.' The LXX. and the Chaldee, ' I am not sufficient to be a leader.' The meaning is, that the state of affairs was so ruinous and calamitous that he would not attempt to restore them ; as if, in the body, disease should have so far progressed that he would not undertake to restore the person, and have him *die* under his hands, so as to expose himself to the reproach of being an unsuccessful and unskilful physician. ¶ Is *neither bread nor clothing.* I am not rich. I have not the means of providing for the wants of the people, or to maintain the rank of a ruler. ' It is customary,' says Sir John Chardin, ' to gather together an immense quantity of clothes, for their fashions never alter.' ' The kings of Persia have great wardrobes, where they have always many hundreds of habits ready, designed for presents, and sorted.'—*Lowth.* The description here is one of very great calamity and anarchy. So great would be the ruin and danger, that men would be unwilling to be chosen to the office of princes and rulers, and none could be found who would desire to possess the highest honours of the nation. Generally men *aspire* to office ; here they were unwilling, on account of the disordered and ruined state of affairs, even to accept of it.

8. *For Jerusalem, &c.* The prophet proceeds to show the cause of this state

of things. ' These are the words of the *prophet*, and not of him who was chosen leader.'—*Jerome.* ¶ *Is ruined.* It would be so ruined, and the prospect of preserving it would be so completely taken away, that no one could be induced to undertake to defend and protect it. ¶ *Judah.* The kingdom of Judah, of which Jerusalem was the capital ; Note ch. i. 1. ¶ *Is fallen.* Heb. *falls; i.e.*, is about to fall—as a tower or a tree falls to ruin. If the *capital* fell and was ruined, the kingdom would also fall as a matter of course. ¶ *Because their tongue, &c.* This is the *reason* why Judah was ruined. By word and deed —that is, in every way they opposed God. The *tongue* here represents their *language*, their manner of speaking. It was proud, haughty, rebellious, perhaps blasphemous. ¶ *To provoke.* To irritate ; to offend. ¶ *The eyes of his glory.* This is a Hebrew expression to denote *his glorious eyes.* The eye quickly expresses anger or indignation. We perceive these passions in the flashing of the eye sooner than in any other part of the countenance. Hence, to *provoke the eyes*, is an expression signifying simply to excite to anger, or to excite him to punish them. Lowth proposes to render this ' to provoke the *cloud* of his glory '—referring to the Shekinah or cloud that rested over the ark in the temple. By a slight variation of the Hebrew text, reading עֲנָן instead of עֵנִי, it may be so read, and the Syriac so translates it ; but the change in the Hebrew text does not seem to be authorized.

9. *The show of their countenance.* The word rendered *the show* is probably derived from a word signifying *to know*, or *to recognise*, and here denotes *impudence* or *pride.* LXX., ' The *shame* of their face.' ¶ *Doth witness against them. Answers* to them ; or *responds* to them (עָנְתָה). There is a correspondence between the feelings of declare their sin as Sodom, they hide *it* not. Wo unto their soul! for they have rewarded evil unto themselves.

10 Say ye to the righteous, that *it shall be* well *with him:* [a] for they shall eat the fruit of their doings.

11 Wo unto the wicked! *it shall*

be ill *with him:* for the reward of his hands shall be [1] given him.

12 *As for* my people, children *are* their oppressors, and women rule over them. O my people, they which [2] lead thee cause *thee* to err, and [3] destroy the way of thy paths.

the heart and the looks, an *answering* of the countenance to the purposes of the soul that shows their true character, and betrays their plans. The prophet refers here to the great law in physiology that the emotions of the heart will be usually *expressed* in the countenance ; and that by the marks of pride, vanity, and malice there depicted, we may judge of the heart ; or as it is expressed in our translation, that the expression of the face will *witness* against a wicked man. ¶ *They declare*, &c. By their deeds. Their crimes are open and bold. There is no attempt at concealment. ¶ *As Sodom*; see Gen. xix. 5; comp. Note, Isa. i. 10. ¶ *Wo unto their soul.* They shall bring woe upon themselves ; they deserve punishment. This is an expression denoting the highest abhorrence of their crimes. ¶ *They have rewarded evil*, &c. They have brought the punishment upon themselves by their own sins.

10. *Say ye to the righteous.* The meaning of this verse and the following is sufficiently plain, though expositors have given some variety of interpretation. They declare a great principle of the Divine administration similar to what is stated in ch. i. 19, 20. Lowth reads it, ' Pronounce ye a blessing on the just ; verily good (shall be to him).' ¶ *That* it shall be *well*, &c. The word rendered ' well,' means ' good.' The sense evidently is, that in the Divine administration it shall be well to be righteous. The LXX. have rendered this in a remarkable manner, connecting it with the previous verse : ' Wo unto their soul, for they take evil counsel among themselves, saying, *Let us bind the righteous, for he is troublesome unto us;* therefore they shall eat the fruit of their doings.' ¶ *They shall eat*, &c. That is, they shall receive the appro-

priate *reward* of their works, and that reward shall be happiness. As a husbandman who sows his field and cultivates his farm, eats the fruit of his labour, so shall it be with the righteous. A similar expression is found in Prov. i. 31 :

Therefore shall they eat of the fruit of their own way,
And be filled with their own devices.

Also Jer. vi. 19: ' I will bring evil upon this people, *even* the fruit of their thoughts;' comp. Gal. vi. 8.

11. *Wo unto the wicked.* To all the wicked—but here having particular reference to the Jews whom Isaiah was addressing. ¶ It shall be *ill* with him. The word *ill* is the only word here in the original. It is an emphatic mode of speaking—expressing deep abhorrence and suddenness of denunciation. ' Woe to the impious ! Ill !' ¶ *For the reward of his hands.* Of his conduct. The hands are the instruments by which we accomplish any thing, and hence they are put for the whole man. ¶ *Shall be given him.* That is, shall be repaid to him ; or he shall be justly recompensed for his crimes. This is the principle on which God rules the world. It shall be well here and hereafter, with those who obey God ; it shall be ill here and for ever, with those who disobey him.

12. As for *my people, children* are *their oppressors.* This refers, doubtless, to their civil rulers. They who *ought* to have been their *protectors,* oppressed them by grievous taxes and burdens. But whether this means that the rulers of the people were *literally* minors, or that they were so in *disposition* and *character,* has been a question. The original word is in the singular number (מְעוֹלֵל), and means a *child,* or an infant. It may, however, be taken collectively

13 The Lord standeth up to plead,[a] and standeth to judge the people.

14 The Lord will enter into judgment with the ancients of his people, and the princes thereof: for ye have eaten [1] up the [b] vineyard; the spoil of the poor is in your houses.

15 What mean ye that ye beat my people to pieces,[c] and grind the faces of the poor? saith the Lord God of hosts.

16 Moreover, the Lord saith,

---

a Mic.6.2. *1 or, burnt.* *b* Mat.21.33. *c* ch.58.4.

---

as a noun of multitude, or as denoting more than one. To whom reference is made here cannot easily be determined, but possibly to *Ahaz*, who began to reign when he was twenty years old; 2 Kings xvi. 2. Or it may mean that the *character* of the princes and rulers was that of inexperienced children, unqualified for government. ¶ Are *their oppressors*. Literally, 'are their *exactors*,' or their *taxers*—the collectors of the revenue. ¶ And *women rule over them*. This is not to be taken literally, but it means either that the rulers were under the influence of the *harem*, or the females of the court; or that they were effeminate and destitute of vigour and manliness in counsel. The LXX. and the Chaldee render this verse substantially alike: ' Thy exactors strip my people as they who gather the grapes strip the vineyard.' ¶ They *which lead thee*. Heb. *They who bless thee, or call thee blessed*. (See margin.) This refers, doubtless, to the public teachers, and the false prophets, who *blessed* or flattered the people, and who promised them safety in their sins. ¶ Cause *thee to err*. Lead you astray; or lead you into sin and danger. ¶ And *destroy*. Heb. *Swallow up*.

13. *The Lord standeth up*. To *stand up* may mean the same as to *arise*. God would not sit in silence and see their wicked conduct; but he would come forth to inflict on them exemplary and deserved chastisement. ¶ To *plead*. To *litigate*, to contend with, *i.e.*, to condemn, to inflict punishment.

14. *With the ancients*, &c. With the old men, the counsellors. ¶ Ye *have eaten up the vineyard*. Heb. 'Ye have *burnt up*'—that is, you have consumed or destroyed it. By the vineyard is represented the Jewish republic or people; Ps. lxxx. 9–13; comp.

Notes, Isa. v. 1–7. The princes and rulers had, by their exactions and oppressions, ruined the people, and destroyed the country. ¶ The *spoil of the poor*. The *plunder* of the poor; or that which you have taken from the poor by exactions and oppressions. The word *spoil* commonly means the plunder or booty which is obtained in war.

15. *What mean ye*. What is your object? Or, What advantage is it to you? Or, By what right or pretence do you do this? ¶ Beat *my people to pieces*. That is, that you trample on them; or cruelly oppress them; Ps. xciv. 5. ¶ And *grind the faces of the poor* This is an expression also denoting great oppression. It is taken from the act of grinding a substance on a stone until it is worn away and nothing is left. So, by their cruel exactions, by their injustice to the poor, they exhausted their little property until nothing was left. The word *faces* here is synonymous with *persons*—or with the poor themselves. The word *face* is often used in the sense of *person*; Ex. xxxiii. 14; 2 Sam. xviii. 11. A similar description, though in still stronger language, is found in Micah iii. 2, 3:

Who pluck off their skin from off them,
And their flesh from off their bones;
Who also eat the flesh of my people,
And flay their skin from off them;
And they break their bones, and chop them in
  pieces,
As for the pot, and as flesh within the caldron.

16. *Moreover, the Lord saith*. In the previous parts of this prophecy, the prophet had rebuked the princes, magistrates, and the people generally. In the remainder of this chapter, he reproves with great severity the pride, luxury, and effeminacy of the female part of the Jewish community. Some interpreters have understood this as designed to reprove the the pride and luxury of the *cities* and

Because the daughters of Zion are naughty, and walk with stretched-forth necks, and [1] wanton eyes,

[1] *deceiving with their eyes.*

walking and [2] mincing *as* they go, and making a tinkling with their feet.

[2] *tripping nicely.*

towns of Judah, regarded as *daughters of Zion;* see Note, ch. i. 8. But this interpretation is far-fetched and absurd. On this principle everything in the Bible might be turned into allegory. ¶ *The daughters of Zion.* Jewish females; they who dwelt in Zion. Perhaps he means particularly those who dwelt in *Zion,* the capital—or the females connected with the court. It is probable that the prophet here refers to the prosperous reign of Uzziah (2 Chron. xxvi. 5, &c.), when by successful commerce luxury would naturally abound. ¶ *Are haughty.* Are proud. ¶ *And walk with stretched-forth necks.* Displaying the neck ostentatiously ; elevating or extending it as far as possible. Septuagint, ὑψηλῷ τραχήλῳ, with elevated or exalted neck ; *i.e.,* with that indication of pride and haughtiness which is evinced by a lofty demeanour. ' When the females dance [in India], they stretch forth their necks, and hold them away, as if their heads were about to fall from their shoulders.'—*Roberts.* ¶ *And wanton eyes.* וּמְשַׂקְּרוֹת עֵינָיִם. The word שָׁקַר *shâqăr* usually means *to lie, to deceive,* and may here refer to the art of alluring by a wanton or fascinating glance of the eye. There has been great diversity of opinion about the meaning of this expression. Lowth proposes to read it, ' and falsely setting off their eyes with paint,' in allusion to a custom known to prevail in the East, of colouring the eye-lids with stibium, or the powder of lead ore. This was done the better to exhibit the white of the eye, and was supposed by many to contribute to the healthful action of the eye itself. This practice is known to prevail extensively now ; but it is not clear that the prophet here has reference to it. The expression is usually interpreted to mean ' *deceiving with the eyes,*' that is, *alluring* or *enticing* by the motion of the eyes. The *motion* of the eyes is mentioned (Prov. vi. 13, 14) as one mode of *deceiving* a person :

He winketh with his eyes,
He speaketh with his feet,

He teacheth with his fingers ;
Frowardness is in his heart,
He deviseth mischief continually.

Comp. Notes on Job xlii. 14. The meaning here, doubtless, is, that they attempted to entice by the *motion* or *glance* of the eye. The Chaldee seems to have understood this of staining the eyes with stibium. ¶ *Mincing as they go.* Margin, ' Tripping nicely ;' that is, walking with an affected gait—a mode which, unhappily, is too well known in all ages to need a more particular description. Roberts, speaking of the dance in India, says, ' Some parts of the dance consist of a tripping or mincing step, which they call *tatte-tattee.* The left foot is put first, and the inside of the right keeps following the heel of the former.' ¶ *And making a tinkling with their feet.* That is, they adorn themselves with *ankle rings,* and make a tinkling or noise with them to attract attention. The custom of wearing rings on the fingers and wrists has been common every where. In addition to this, Oriental females often wore them on the *ankles*—a custom in

ANKLETS, one-sixth the real size.
From Lane's Egyptians.

itself not more unreasonable or absurd. The custom is mentioned by travellers in Eastern countries in more modern times. Thus, Michaelis says, ' In Syria and the neighbouring provinces, the more opulent females bind ligaments around their feet, like chains, or bracelets, united by small chains of silver and gold, and exhibit them by their sound as they walk.' And Pliny (*Nat. Hist.* lib. xxiii., ch. 12) says, ' Silver has succeeded to gold in the luxury of the females who form bracelets for their feet of that, since an ancient custom forbids

17 Therefore the LORD will smite with a scab the crown of the head of the daughters of Zion, and the LORD will discover¹ their secret parts.

1 *make naked.*

18 In that day the LORD will take away the bravery of *their* tinkling ornaments *about their feet,* and *their* ² cauls, and *their* round tires like the moon,

2 or, *net-works.*

them to wear gold.' Frequent mention is made of these ornaments, says Rosenmüller, in the Arabic and Persian poems. Roberts, speaking of the ornaments on the feet of females in India, says, ' The first is a large silver curb like that which is attached to a bridle ; the second is of the same kind, but surrounded by a great number of small BELLS ; the third resembles a bracelet ; and the fourth is a convex hoop, about two inches deep.'

17. *Therefore the Lord will smite with a scab.* There is some diversity of rendering to this expression. The LXX. read it, ' The Lord will humble the principal daughters of Zion '– those who belong to the court, or to the families of the princes. The Chaldee, ' The Lord will prostrate the glory of the daughters of Zion.' The Syriac is the same. The Hebrew word סִפַּח *s´ippăhh,* translated ' will smite with a scab,' means to *make bald,* particularly to make the hair fall off by sickness. Our translation conveys the idea essentially, that is, that God would visit them with disease that would remove the hair which they regarded as so great an ornament, and on which they so much prided themselves. Few things would be so degrading and humiliating as being thus made bald. The description in this verse means, that God would humble and punish them ; that they who so adorned themselves, and who were so proud of their ornaments, would be divested of their gay attire, and be borne naked into captivity in a foreign land.

18. *In that day.* That is, in the time when he would inflict this exemplary punishment on them — probably the calamitous times of the Babylonish captivity. ¶ *The Lord will take away.* By the agents that he shall choose to employ in this work.—The prophet proceeds to specify the various ornaments that composed the female apparel in his time. It is not easy to describe

them particularly, nor is it necessary. The *general* meaning of the passage is plain : and it is clear from this, that they greatly abounded in ornaments. ¶ *The bravery.* This word *we* apply to valour or courage. The word here used, however, means *ornament, adorning,* or *glory.* ¶ *Of* their *tinkling ornaments.* This is the same word which is used in ver. 16, and refers to the chains or clasps with which they ornamented their feet and ankles, and which made a tinkling noise as they walked. ¶ *And* their *cauls.* Margin, ' *net-works.*' The LXX. is the same. It is commonly supposed to mean *caps of net-work* worn on the head. According to others, the word refers to small *suns* or *spangles* worn on the hair, answering to the following word *moons.* ' The caul is a strap, or girdle, about four inches long, which is placed on the top of the head, and which extends to the brow, in a line with the nose. The one I have examined is made of gold, and has many joints ; it contains forty-five rubies, and nine pearls, which give it a net-work appearance.'—*Roberts.* ¶ Their *round tires like the moon.* Heb. *moons.* This refers to small ornaments in the shape of crescents, or half-moons, commonly worn on the neck. They were also sometimes worn by men, and even by camels ; Judg. viii. 21 (margin), 26. It is probable that these ornaments might originally have had some reference to the moon as an object of worship, but it does not appear that they were so worn by the females of Judea.—They are still worn by the females of Arabia. —*Rosenmüller.* Roberts says of such ornaments in India, ' The crescent is worn by Parvati and Siva, from whom proceed the LINGAM, and the principal impurities of the system. No dancing girl is in full dress without her round tires like the moon.' This ornament is still found in the form which the annexed engraving exhibits—under the

19 The [1] chains, and the brace- | lets, and the [2] mufflers,

1 or, *sweet balls.* | 2 or, *spangled ornaments.*

name of *chumarah.* 'The *chumarah,* which signifies moon, is a splendid orna- | ment worn by the women of western Asia in front of their head-dresses. It

THE CHUMARAH, one-half the real size.—From Lane's Egyptians.

is usually made of gold, set with precious stones and pearls. They are sometimes made of the crescent form, but the most common are such as the engraving represents. They often have Arabic characters inscribed upon them, and sometimes a sentence from the Koran is used by the Mahometan women of Arabia Felix.'

19. *The chains.* Margin, *sweet balls.* The word used here is derived from the verb נָטַף *nâtăph, to drop, to fall in drops,* or *to distil,* as juice from a plant. Hence it means that which *resembles drops*—as pearls, or precious stones, used as ornaments for the neck or ears. We retain a similar word as applicable to the ornaments of the ears, by calling them *drops.* The Chaldee renders this *chains,* and so also the Vulgate. The LXX. understand it of a *hanging* or *pendant* ornament—and this is its undoubted meaning—an ornament pendant like gum distilling from a plant. 'These consist, first, of one most beautifully worked, with a pendant ornament for the neck; there is also a profusion of others which go round the same part, and rest on the bosom. In making curious chains, the goldsmiths of England do not surpass those of the East.'— *Roberts.* ¶ *And the bracelets.* For the wrists. The Chaldee translates it, 'bracelets for the hands.' These ornaments were very ancient; see Gen. xxiv.

22; Num. xxi. 50.—Mahomet promises to those who shall follow him, gold and silver bracelets. 'The bracelets are large ornaments for the wrists, in which are sometimes inclosed small BELLS.'—

ANCIENT BRACELETS, half the real size.

Roberts. ¶ *Mufflers.* Margin, *spangled ornaments.* The word used here is derived from a verb, *to tremble, to shake*—רָעַל *ra'ăl*—and the name is given to the ornament, whatever it was, probably from its *tremulous* motion. Perhaps it means *a light, thin veil;* or possibly, as in the margin, spangled ornaments, producing a tremulous, changing aspect. In Zech. xii. 2, the word is used to denote 'trembling'— giddiness, or intoxication. It was early customary, and is still common in Oriental countries, for the females to wear veils. No female ventures abroad without her veil. That which is supposed to be intended here, is described

20 The bonnets, and the ornaments of the legs, and the head-bands, and the [1] tablets, and the ear-rings.

> [1] houses of the soul.

by the Arabian scholiast Safieri, quoted by Gesenius. It is drawn tight over the upper part of the head, but the part around the eyes is open, and a space

FACE-VEILS AND WALKING-WRAPPERS OF MODERN EGYPTIAN WOMEN.
From Description de l'Egypte.

left to see through, and the lower part is left loose and flowing, and thus produces the *tremulous* appearance indicated in this place; see the Notes and illustrations on ver. 24.

20. *The bonnets.* The *tiara, head-dress,* or *turban.* The word comes from the verb *to adorn.* The *turban* is almost universally worn in the East. It was worn by the priests, Ex. xxxix. 28; by the bridegroom, Isa. lxi. 10; Ezek. xxiv. 17; and by women. Its form is well known. ¶ *And the ornaments for the legs.* The word used here is derived from a verb signifying *to walk, to go,* particularly to walk in a stately and formal manner—with a measured step, הַצְּעָדֹות, from צָעַד; and thus refers to a proud and lofty gait. The *ornament* which is here referred to is supposed to have been a short chain extending from one foot to the other, worn by the Eastern women

to give them a measured and stately gait.—*Gesenius.* This *chain* is supposed to have been attached by hooks or clasps to the 'tinkling ornaments' mentioned in ver. 16. Safieri mentions these ornaments, and thus describes them : ' The word denotes a small chain, with which females, when they walk, connect their feet, in order to make their steps equal.' Happily these ornaments are unknown in modern times, at least in Western countries. They are still retained in the East. ¶ *And the head-bands.* This word means *girdles* of any kind, still commonly worn on the head. The following cut will illustrate one of the usual forms of the head band. ¶ *And the tablets.* The Hebrew is, as in the margin, ' *the houses of the soul.*' The word translated *soul* means also the *breath;* and hence, as one of its meanings, that which is *breathed,* or which is *smelled; scent, fragrancy, odour.* The word *houses* here may denote also *boxes*—as boxes of perfumes. The phrase here means, undoubtedly, *smelling boxes* or *bottles,* containing perfumes or fragrant odours. The word *tablets* has no meaning here. ¶ *And the ear-rings.* It is by no means certain that the original means *ear-rings*

THE KUSSAH OR HEAD-BAND.—From Lane's Modern Egyptians.

The word לְחָשִׁים is derived from the verb לָחַשׁ signifying *to whisper,* and then *to conjure, to charm* (see Note on ver. 3); and here probably denotes precious stones worn by the females as *amulets* or *charms.* The word is often used to denote charming *serpents*—from their *hissing*—and it has been supposed probable that these amulets were small images of serpents. There is no doubt that such ornaments were worn by Oriental females. 'These ornaments seem to have been *amulets,* often gems and precious stones, or plates of gold and silver, on which certain magic formulas were inscribed, which were worn suspended from the neck or ears by Oriental females.'—*Gesenius.*

ORNAMENTED HEAD-DRESS.
From an Egyptian Sculpture.

The following extract will furnish an explanation of these ornaments:—'Besides ornamental rings in the nose and the ears, they [Oriental females] wore others round the legs, which made a tinkling as they went. This custom has also descended to the present times; for Rauwolf met with a number of Arabian women on the Euphrates, whose ankles and wrists were adorned with rings, sometimes a good many together, which, moving up and down as they walked, made a great noise. Chardin attests the existence of the same custom in Persia, in Arabia, and in very hot countries, where they commonly go without stockings, but ascribes the tinkling sound to little bells fastened to those rings. In the East Indies, golden bells adorned the feet and ankles of the ladies from the earliest times; they placed them in the flowing tresses of their hair; they suspended them round their necks, and to the golden rings which they wore on their fingers, to announce their superior rank, and extort the homage which they had a right to expect from the lower orders; and from the banks of the Indus, it is probable the custom was introduced into the other countries of Asia. The Arabian females in Palestine and Syria delight in the same ornaments, and, according to the statements of Dr. Clarke, seem to claim the honour of leading the fashion.'—'Their bodies are covered with a long blue tunic; upon their heads they wear two handkerchiefs, one as a hood, and the other bound over it, as a fillet across the temples. Just above the right nostril, they place a small button, sometimes studded with pearl, a piece of glass, or any other glittering substance; this is fastened by a plug, thrust through the cartilage of the nose. Sometimes they have the cartilaginous separation between the nostrils bored for a ring, as large as those ordinarily used in Europe for hanging curtains; and this pendant in the upper lip covers the mouth; so that, in order to eat, it

21 The rings, and nose-jewels,
22 The changeable suits of appa-

rel, and the mantles, and the wimples, and the crisping-pins,

is necessary to raise it. Their faces, hands, and arms are tatooed, and covered with hideous scars; their eyelashes and eyes being always painted, or rather dirtied, with some dingy black or blue powder. Their lips are dyed of a deep and dusky blue, as if they had been eating blackberries. Their teeth are jet black; their nails and fingers brick red; their wrists, as well as their ankles, are laden with large metal cinctures, studded with sharp pyramidical knobs and bits of glass. Very ponderous rings are also placed in their ears.'—*Paxton.*

21. *The rings.* Usually worn on the fingers. ¶ *And nose-jewels.* The custom of wearing jewels in the *nose* has generally prevailed in savage tribes, and was common, and is still, in Eastern nations—among the Arabians, Persians, &c. Sir John Chardin says, ' It is the custom in almost all the East for the women to wear rings in their noses, in the left nostril, which is bored low down in the middle. These rings are of gold, and have commonly two pearls and one ruby between, placed in the ring. I never saw a girl or young woman in Arabia, or in all Persia, who did not wear a ring in this manner in her nostrils.'—Harmer's *Obs.*, iv., p. 318. The annexed cut will illustrate the usual form of this ornament in the East.

22. The articles which are mentioned

THE KHIZAM OR NOSE-JEWEL OF MODERN EGYPT, one-third the real size.
From Lane's Egyptians.

in the remaining part of this description, are entire articles of apparel; those which had preceded were chiefly single ornaments. ¶ *The changeable suits of apparel.* The word which is used here in the original comes from a verb signifying *to pull of* as a shoe; to unclothe one's-self; and it here denotes the more *costly* or *valuable* garments, which are not worn on common occasions, and which are *laid aside* in ordinary employments. This does not refer to any *particular* article of dress, but to splendid and costly articles in general. ' The Eastern ladies take great pride in having many changes of apparel, because their fashions NEVER alter. Thus the net brocades worn by their grandmothers are equally fashionable for themselves.'—*Roberts.* ¶ *And the mantles.* From the verb *to cover,* or *to clothe.* The word *mantle* does not quite express the force of the original. It means the fuller *tunic* which was worn over the common one, with sleeves, and which reached down to the feet. ' A loose robe,' says Roberts, ' which is gracefully crossed on the bosom.' ¶ *And the wimples.* Our word *wimple* means a *hood,* or *veil,* but this is not the meaning of the Hebrew word in this place. It means a wide, broad garment, which could be thrown over the whole, and in which the individual usually slept. ' Probably the fine muslin which is sometimes thrown over the head and body.'—*Roberts.* ¶ *And the crisping-pins.* This phrase with us would denote *curling-irons.* But the Hebrew here denotes a very different article. It means *money-bags,* or *purses.* These were often made very large, and were highly ornamented; comp. 2 Kings v. 23. Frequently they were attached to the girdle.

23 The glasses, and the fine linen, | and the hoods, and the veils.

23. *The glasses.* These is a great variety of opinion about the expression used here. That the ancient Jews had *looking-glasses,* or mirrors, is manifest from the account in Ex. xxxviii. 8. These *mirrors* were made of polished plates of brass. The Vulgate and Chaldee understand this of *mirrors.* The LXX. understand by it a *thin, transparent covering like gauze,* perhaps like silk. The word is derived from the verb *to reveal, to make apparent,* &c., and applies either to mirrors or to a splendid shining garment. It is probable that their excessive vanity was evinced by carrying small mirrors in their hands—that they might examine and adjust their dress as might be necessary. This is now done by females of Eastern nations. Shaw informs us that, ' In the Levant, looking-glasses are a part of female dress. The Moorish women in Barbary are so fond of their ornaments, and particularly of their looking-glasses, which they hang upon their breasts, that they will not lay them aside, even when, after the drudgery of the day, they are obliged to go two or three miles with a pitcher or a goat-skin to fetch water.' —*Burder.* In Egypt, the mirror was made of mixed metal, chiefly of copper, and this metal was so highly polished, that in some of the mirrors discovered at Thebes, the lustre has been partially restored, though they have been buried in the earth for many centuries. The mirror was nearly round, inserted in a handle of wood, stone, or metal, whose form varied according to the taste of the owner. The following cut will give an idea of the ancient form of the mirror, and will show that they might be easily

ANCIENT METAL MIRRORS.—From Wilkinson's Egyptians.
1, 3. In Mr. Salt's collection.   4. In the museum of Alnwick Castle.
2. In the possession of Dr. Hogg.   5. From a painting at Thebes.

carried abroad as an ornament in public; comp. Wilkinson's *Manners and Customs of the Ancient Egyptians,* vol. iii., pp. 384-386. ¶ *And the fine linen.* Anciently, the most delicate and fine garments were made from linen which was obtained chiefly from Egypt ; see Note, Luke xvi. 19. ¶ *And the hoods.* Or, *turbans.* ¶ *And the veils.* This does not differ probably from the veils worn now, except that those worn by Eastern females are *large,* and made so as to cover

24 And it shall come to pass, *that* instead of sweet smell, there shall be stink; and instead of a girdle, a rent; and instead of well-set hair, baldness;[a] and instead of a stomacher, a girding of sackcloth: *and* burning instead of beauty.

a Mic.1.16.

the head and the shoulders, so that they may be drawn closely round the body, and effectually conceal the person; comp. Gen. xxiv. 65.

24. *And it shall come to pass.* The prophet proceeds to denounce the *judgment* or *punishment* that would come upon them for their pride and vanity. In the calamities that would befall the nation, all their ornaments of pride and vainglory would be stripped off; and instead of them, they would exhibit the marks, and wear the badges of calamity and grief. ¶ *Instead of sweet smell.* Hebrew בֹּשֶׂם *bōsĕm*, aromatics, perfumes, spicy fragrance; such as they used on their garments and persons. 'No one ever enters a company without being well perfumed; and in addition to various scents and oils, they are adorned with numerous garlands, made of the most odoriferous flowers.'—*Roberts.* 'The persons of the Assyrian ladies are elegantly clothed and scented with the richest oils and perfumes. When a queen was to be chosen to the king of Persia, instead of Vashti, the virgins collected at Susana, the capital, underwent a purification of twelve months' duration, to wit: "six months with oil of myrrh, and six months with sweet odours." The general use of such precious oil and fragrant perfumes among the ancient Romans, particularly among the ladies of rank and fashion, may be inferred from these words of Virgil:

Ambrosiaeque comae divinum vertice odorem
Spiravere:—   Æn. i. 403.

"From her head the ambrosial locks breathed divine fragrance." '—*Paxton.* ¶ *A stink.* This word properly means the fetor or offensive smell which attends the decomposition of a deceased body. It means that the bodies which they so carefully adorned, and which they so assiduously endeavoured to preserve in beauty by unguents and perfumes, would die and turn to corruption. ¶ *And instead of a girdle.* Girdles

were an indispensable part of an Oriental dress. Their garments were loose and flowing, and it became necessary to gird them up when they ran, or danced, or laboured. ¶ *A rent.* There has been a great variety of opinion about the meaning of this word. The most probable signification is that which is derived from a verb meaning *to go around, encompass;* and hence that it denotes *a cord.* Instead of the beautiful girdle with which they girded themselves, there shall be *a cord*—an emblem of poverty, as the poor had nothing else with which to gird up their clothes;—a humiliating description of the calamities which were to come upon proud and vain females of the court. ¶ *And instead of well-set hair.* Hair that was curiously braided and adorned. 'No ladies pay more attention to the dressing of the hair than these [the dancing girls of India]; for as they never wear caps, they take great delight in this their natural ornament.' – *Roberts.* Miss Pardoe, in '*The City of the Sultan,*' says, that after taking a bath the slaves who attended her spent an hour and a half in dressing and adorning her hair; comp. 1 Pet. iii. 3. ¶ *Instead of a stomacher.* It is not certainly known what is meant by this, but it probably means some sort of *girdle,* or a plaited or stiffened ornament worn on the breast. 'I once saw a dress beautifully plaited and stiffened for the front, but I do not think it common.'—*Roberts.* ¶ *A girding of sackcloth.* This is a coarse cloth that was commonly worn in times of affliction, as emblematic of grief; 2 Sam. iii. 31; 1 Kings xx. 31; xxi. 27; Job xvi. 15; Isa. xxxii. 11. ¶ *And burning.* The word here used does not occur elsewhere. It seems to denote *a brand, a mark burnt in, a stigma;* pehaps a sun-burnt countenance, indicating exposure in the long and wearisome journey of a captivity over burning sands and beneath a scorching sun. ¶ *Instead of beauty.* Instead of a fair and delicate complexion, cherished and nourished with care. Some of the

25 Thy men shall fall by the sword, and thy [1] mighty in the war.

26 And [a] her gates shall lament and mourn; and she, *being* [2] desolate, shall sit upon [b] the ground.

[1] *might.*
[a] Lam.1.4.   [2] *cleansed,* or *emptied.*   [b] Lam 2.10.

articles of dress here referred to may be illustrated by the following cut [and those p. 106], which exhibit several varieties of the costume of an Oriental female.

A LADY ADORNED WITH THE SAFA AND TURBAN.—From Lane's Modern Egyptians.

To what *particular* time the prophet refers in this chapter is not known, perhaps, however, to the captivity at Babylon. To whatever he refers, it is one of the most striking reproofs of vanity and pride, especially the pride of female ornament, any where to be found. And although he had *particular* reference to the Jewish females, yet there is no impropriety in regarding it as applicable to all such ornaments wherever they may be found. They indicate the same state of the heart, and they must meet substantially the same rebuke from God. The body, however delicately pampered and adorned, must become the prey of corruption. 'The worm shall feed sweetly on it, and the earth-worm shall be its covering;' comp. Isa. xiv. 2; Job xxiv. 20. The single thought that the body must die—that it must lie and moulder in the grave—should check the love of gay adorning, and turn the mind to a far more important matter—the salvation of the soul, which cannot die; to 'the ornament of a weak and quiet spirit, which is in the sight of God of great price;' 1 Pet. iii. 4.[*]

25. *Thy men.* This is an address to Jerusalem itself, by a change not uncommon in the writings of Isaiah. In the calamities coming on them, their strong men should be overcome, and fall in battle.

26. *And her gates.* Cities were sur-

* On this portion of Isaiah (iii. 16-24), the following works may be consulted:—N. G. Schroederi comm. Philo. Crit. de vestitu mulierum Hebraeorum, 1745, 4to.; Disserta Philolo. Polycarpi Lyceri, ad Esa. iii. 16-18 illustrandum, in Thesau. Antiq. Ugolini, tom. xxix., pp. 438-452; also Bynaeus, de Calceis Hebrae. ch. viii.; Thesau. Antiq. Sacr.. tom. xxix., p. 756, *seq.*

CHAPTER IV.

FOR AN ANALYSIS OF THIS CHAPTER,
SEE CH. II.

AND in that day seven women shall take hold of one man, say-ing, We will eat our own bread, and wear our own apparel; only let ¹ us be called by thy name, to take away ² our reproach.

1 *thy name be called upon us.*   2 or, *take thou away.*

rounded with walls, and were entered through gates opening into the principal streets. Those gates became, of course, the places of chief confluence and of business; and the expression here means, that in all the places of confluence, or amidst the assembled people, there should be lamentation on account of the slain in battle, and the loss of their mighty men in war. ¶ *And she.* Jerusalem is often represented as a female distinguished for beauty. It is here represented as a female sitting in a posture of grief. ¶ Being *desolate, shall*

sit upon the ground. To sit on the ground, or in the dust, was the usual posture of grief and mourning, denoting great depression and humiliation; Lam. ii. 10; iii. 28; Jer. xv. 17; Job iii. 13; Ezra ix. 3–5. It is a remarkable coincidence, that in the medals which were made by the Romans to commemorate the captivity of Judea and Jerusalem, Judea is represented under the figure of a female sitting in a posture of grief, under a palm tree, with this inscription —JUDEA CAPTA—in the form which is exhibited in the annexed engraving.

JUDEA MEDALS OF CAPTIVITY.—From Calmet.

The passage here, however, refers not to the captivity by the Romans, but to the first destruction by Nebuchadnezzar. It is a tender and most affecting image of desolation. During the captivity at Babylon, it was completely fulfilled; and for ages since, Judea might be appropriately represented by a captive female sitting pensively on the ground.

CHAPTER IV.

1. *In that day.* The time of calamity referred to in the close of the previous chapter. This is a continuation of that prophecy, and there was no reason why these six verses should have been made a separate chapter. That the passage refers to the Messiah, is apparent from what has been stated in the Notes on the commencement of the prophecy (ch. ii. 1–4), and from the expressions which occur in the chapter itself; see Notes on ver. 2, 5, 6. ¶ *Seven women.* The number *seven* is used often to denote a *large* though *indefinite* number; Lev. xxvi. 28; Prov. xxiv. 16; Zech. iii. 9. It means that so great should be the calamity, so many *men* would fall in battle, that many women would, contrary to their natural modesty, become suitors to a single man, to obtain him as a husband and protector. ¶ *Shall take hold.* Shall apply to. The expression, 'shall take hold,' denotes the *earnestness* of their application. ¶ *We will eat our own bread,* &c. We do not ask this in order to be maintained. We will forego that which the law (Ex. xxi. 10) enjoins as the duty of the husband in case he has more than one wife.

2 In that day shall the *a* branch of the LORD be 1 beautiful and glorious, and the fruit of the earth *shall be* excellent and comely for them 2 that are escaped of Israel.

a Jer.23.5,6; Zec.6.12,13.

1 *beauty and glory.*   2 *the escaping of Israel.*

¶ *Only let us be called by thy name.* Let us be regarded as *thy wives.* The wife then, as now, assumed the name of the husband. A remarkably similar expression occurs in Lucan (B. ii. 342). Marcia there presents a similar request to Cato :

> Da tantum nomen inane
> Connubii; liceat tumulo scripsisse, Catonis
> Marcia.

' Indulge me only with the empty title of wife. Let there only be inscribed on my tomb, " Marcia, wife of Cato." '
¶ *To take away my reproach.* The reproach of being unmarried ; comp. Gen. xxx. 23; 1 Sam. i. 6.

2. *The branch of the* LORD. צֶמַח יְהֹוָה. *The sprout of* JEHOVAH. This expression, and this verse, have had a great variety of interpretations. The LXX. read it, ' In that day God shall shine in counsel with glory upon the earth, to exalt, and to glorify the remnant of Israel.' The Chaldee renders it, ' In that day, the *Messiah* of the Lord shall be for joy and glory, and the doers of the law for praise and honour to those of Israel who are delivered.' It is clear that the passage is designed to denote some signal blessing that was to succeed the calamity predicted in the previous verses. The only question is, to what has the prophet reference ? The word ' branch ' (צֶמַח) is derived from the verb (צָמַח *tzâmăhh*) signifying *to sprout, to spring up,* spoken of plants. Hence the word *branch* means properly that which *shoots up,* or *sprouts* from the root of a tree, or from a decayed tree; comp. Job xiv. 7–9. The Messiah is thus said to be ' a root of Jesse,' Rom. xi. 12; comp. Note, Isa. xi. 1, 10, and ' the root and offspring of David,' Rev. xxii. 16, as being a *descendant* of Jesse ; *i.e.,* as if Jesse should fall like an aged tree, yet the *root* would sprout up and live. The word ' branch ' occurs several times in the Old Testament, and in most, if not all, with express reference to the Messiah ; Jer. xxiii. 5: ' Behold, the days come, saith the Lord, ISAIAH I.

that I will raise unto David a righteous *Branch,* and a king shall reign;' Jer. xxxiii. 15: ' In those days, and at that time, will I cause the Branch of righteousness to grow up unto David;' Zech. iii. 8; vi. 12. In all these places, there can be no doubt that there is reference to him who was *to spring up* from David, as a sprout does from a decayed and fallen tree, and who is therefore called a *root,* a *branch* of the royal stock. There is, besides, a peculiar beauty in the figure. The family of David, when the Messiah was to come, would be fallen into decay and almost extinct. Joseph, the husband of Mary, though of the royal family of David (Matt. i. 20; Luke ii. 4), was poor, and the family had lost all claims to the throne. In this state, as from the decayed root of a fallen tree, a *sprout* or *branch* was to come forth with more than the magnificence of David, and succeed him on the throne. The name ' branch,' therefore, came to be significant of the Messiah, and to be synonymous with ' the son of David.' It is so used, doubtless, in this place, as denoting that the coming of the Messiah would be a joy and honour in the days of calamity to the Jews. Interpreters have not been agreed, however, in the meaning of this passage. Grotius supposed that it referred to Ezra or Nehemiah, but ' mystically to Christ and Christians.' Vogellius understood it of the *remnant* that should return from the Babylonish captivity. Michaelis supposed that it refers to the Jews, who should be a *reformed* people after their captivity, and who should spring up with a new spirit. Others have regarded it as a poetic description of the extraordinary fertility of the earth in future times. The reasons for referring it to the Messiah are plain—(1.) The word has this reference in other places, and the representation of the Messiah under the image of a branch or shoot, is, as we have seen, common in the Scriptures. Thus, also, in ch. liii. 2, he is called also שֹׁרֶשׁ *shŏrĕsh, root,* and

8

יוֹנֵק *yôněq*, a tender plant, a sucker,
sprout, shoot, as of a decayed tree;
comp. Job viii. 16; xiv. 7; xv. 30; Ezek.
xvii. 22. And in reference to the same
idea, perhaps, it is said, Isa. liii. 8,
that he was נִגְזָר *nighzăr, cut off*, as a
branch, sucker, or shoot is cut off by
the vine-dresser or farmer from the
root of a decayed tree. And thus, in
Rev. v. 5, he is called ῥίζα Δαβίδ—the
root of David.   (2.) This interpretation
accords best with the *magnificence* of
the description, ver. 5, 6 ; and, (3.) It
was so understood by the Chaldee inter-
preter, and, doubtless, by the ancient
Jews. ¶ *Shall be beautiful and glorious.* Heb. ' Shall be beauty and glory;'
that is, shall be the chief ornament or
honour of the land ; shall be that which
gives to the nation its chief distinction
and glory. In such times of calamity,
his coming shall be an object of desire,
and his approach shall shed a rich
splendour on that period of the world.
¶ *And the fruit of the earth,* פְּרִי הָאָרֶץ
correctly rendered *fruit of the earth*, or
of the land. The word ' earth ' is often
in the Scriptures used to denote the land
of Judea, and perhaps the article here
is intended to denote that that land is
particularly intended. This is the
parallel expression to the former part
of the verse, in accordance with the
laws of Hebrew poetry, by which one
member of a sentence expresses substantially the same meaning as the former ; see Introduction, § 8. If the
former expression referred to the *Messiah*, this does also. The ' fruit of the
earth ' is that which the earth produces,
and is here not different in signification
from the *branch* which springs out of
the ground. Vitringa supposes that by
this phrase the Messiah, according to
his human nature, is meant. So Hengstenberg (*Christol., in loc.*) understands
it ; and supposes that as the phrase
' branch of Jehovah' refers to his Divine
origin, as proceeding from Jehovah ; so
this refers to his human origin, as proceeding from the earth. But the objections to this are obvious—(1.) The
second phrase, according to the laws of
Hebrew parallelism, is most naturally
an echo or repetition of the sentiment

in the first member, and means substantially the same thing. (2.) The
phrase ' branch of Jehovah ' does not
refer of necessity to his Divine nature.
The idea is that of a decayed tree that
has fallen down, and has left a living
root which sends up a shoot, or sucker ;
and can be applied with great elegance
to the decayed family of David. But
how, or in what sense, can this be
applied to Jehovah ? Is Jehovah thus
fallen and decayed ?   The idea properly
is, that this shoot of a decayed family
should be nurtured up by JEHOVAH;
should be appointed by him, and should
thus be *his* branch. The parallel member denotes substantially the same thing ;
' the fruit of the earth '—the shoot
which the earth produces—or which
springs up from a decayed family, as
the sprout does from a fallen tree. (3.)
It is as true that his human nature
proceeded from God as his Divine. It
was produced by the Holy Ghost, and
can no more be regarded as ' the fruit
of the earth' than his Divine nature ;
Luke i. 35; Heb. x. 5. (4.) This mode
of interpretation is fitted to bring the
whole subject into contempt.   There
are plain and positive passages enough
to prove that the Messiah had a Divine
nature, and there are enough also to
prove that he was a man ; but nothing
is more adapted to produce disgust in
relation to the whole subject, in the
minds of sceptical or of *thinking* men,
than a resort to arguments such as this
in defence of a great and glorious doctrine of revelation. ¶ Shall be *excellent.* Shall be *for exaltation*, or
honour. ¶ *Comely.* Heb. ' For an ornament ;' meaning that *he* would be an
honour to those times. ¶ *For them
that are escaped of Israel.*   Marg.
' The escaping of Israel.' For the remnant, the small number that shall escape the calamities—a description of the
pious portion of Israel which now escaped
from all calamities—would rejoice in
the anticipated blessings of the Messiah's reign, or would participate in the
blessings of that reign. The idea is
not, however, that the number who
would be saved would be *small*, but that
they would be characterized as those who
had *escaped*, or who had been rescued.

3 And it shall come to pass, *that he that is* left in Zion, and *he that* remaineth in Jerusalem, shall be called *a* holy, *even* every one that

a ch.60.21.

is written [1] among the living in Jerusalem:

4 When the LORD shall have washed *b* away the filth of the

[1] or, *to life*, Rev.21.27.   *b* Zec.13.1.

3. *He that is left in Zion.* This *properly* refers to the remnant that should remain after the mass of the people should be cut off by wars, or be borne into captivity. If it refer to the few that would come back from Babylon, it means that they would be reformed, and would be a generation different from their fathers—which was undoubtedly true. If it refer, as the connection seems to indicate, to the times of the Messiah, then it speaks of those who are 'left,' while the great mass of the nation would be unbelievers, and would be destroyed. The mass of the nation would be cut off, and the remnant that was left would be holy; that is, all true friends of the Messiah would be holy. ¶ *Shall be called holy.* That is, shall *be* holy. The expression 'to be called,' is often used in the Scriptures as synonymous with 'to be.' ¶ *Every one that is written among the living.* The Jews were accustomed to register the names of all the people. Those names were written in a catalogue, or register, of each tribe or family. To be written in that book, or register, meant to be alive, for when a death occurred, the name was stricken out; Ex. xxxii. 32; Dan. xii. 1; Ezek. xiii. 9. The expression came also to denote all who were truly the friends of God; they whose names are written in *his* book—the book of life. In this sense it is used in the New Testament; Phil. iv. 3; Rev. iii. 5; xvii. 5. In this sense it is understood in this place by the Chaldee Par.: 'Every one shall be called holy who is written to *eternal* life; he shall see the consolation of Jerusalem.' If the reference here is to the Messiah, then the passage denotes that under the reign of the Messiah, all who should be found enrolled as his followers, would be holy. An effectual separation would subsist between them and the mass of the people. They would be *enrolled* as his friends, and they would be a separate, holy community; comp. 1 Pet. ii. 9.

4. *When the Lord.* That is, *after* God has done this, then all that are written among the living shall be called holy. The prophet in this verse states the benefits of *affliction* in purifying the people of God. He had said, in the previous verse, that all who should be left in Zion should be called holy. He here states that *previous* to that, the defilement of the people would be removed by judgment. ¶ *Shall have washed away.* The expression, *to wash*, is often used to denote to *purify* in any way. In allusion to this fact is the beautiful promise in Zech. xiii. 1; see Note, ch. i. 16. ¶ *The filth.* This word here refers to their *moral* defilement—their pride, vanity, haughtiness; and perhaps to the idolatry and general sins of the people. As the prophet, however, in ch. iii. 16–23, had particularly specified the sins of the female part of the Jewish people, the expression here probably refers especially to them, and to the judgments which were to come upon them; ch. iii. 24. It is not departing from the spirit of this passage to remark, that the church is purified, and true religion is often promoted, by God's humbling the pride and vanity of females. A love of excessive ornament; a fondness for dress and display; and an exhibition of great gaiety, often stand grievously in the way of pure religion. ¶ *The daughters of Zion;* see ch. iii. 16. ¶ *And shall have purged.* This is synonymous with the expression *to wash.* It means to purify, to remove, as one removes blood from the hands by washing. ¶ *Blood of Jerusalem.* Crime, blood-guiltiness—particularly the crime of *oppression, cruelty,* and *robbery,* which the prophet (ch. i. 15) had charged on them. ¶ *By the spirit of judgment.* This refers, doubtless, to the *calamities,* or *punishment,* that would come upon the nation; principally, to the Babylonish captivity. After God should have humbled and reformed the nation by a series of

daughters of Zion, and shall have purged the blood of Jerusalem from the midst thereof by the spirit of judgment, and by the spirit of burning.

5 And the LORD will create upon every dwelling-place of mount Zion, and upon her assemblies, a cloud

a Zec.2.5.　1 or, *above.*　2 *covering.*　*b* ch.25.4.

and smoke by day, and the shining of a flaming fire *a* by night: for upon 1 all the glory *shall be* a 2 defence.

6 And there shall be a tabernacle for a shadow in the day-time from the heat, and for a place of *b* refuge, and for a covert from storm and from rain.

---

judgments, then they who were purified by them should be called holy. The word *spirit* here cannot be shown to be the Holy Spirit; and especially as the Holy Spirit is not represented in the Scriptures as the agent in executing judgment. It perhaps would be best denoted by the word *influence,* or *power.* The word properly denotes *wind, air, motion* (Gen. viii. 1; Job i. 19); then *breathing, exhalation,* or *breath* (Job vii. 7; Ps. xxxiii. 6); hence it means the *soul;* and it means also God's *influence,* or his putting forth his power and life-giving energy in animating and sustaining the universe; and also, as here, his putting forth *any* influence in accomplishing his works and designs. ¶ *And by the spirit of burning. Fire* is often, in the Scriptures, the emblem of punishment, and also of purifying; comp. Note, Matt. iii. 11, 12; see Mal. iii. 2, 3. The Chaldee translates this, ' by the *word* of judgment, and by the *word* of consuming.' The reference is to the *punishments* which would be sent to purify the people *before* the coming of the Messiah.

5. *And the* LORD *will create.* The meaning of this verse and the next is, that God would take his people into his holy care and protection. The idea is expressed by images drawn, in this verse, from the protection which he afforded to the Israelites in their journeying from Egypt. The word *create* means here, he will afford, or furnish, such a defence. ¶ *Upon every dwelling-place, &c.* Upon all the habitations of his people; that is, they shall be secure, and regarded as under his protection. The word *upon* refers to the fact that the pillar of cloud stood *over* the tabernacle in the wilderness, as a symbol of the Divine favour and presence. So his protection should be

on or *over* the houses of all his people; comp. Ps. xcii. 4–6. ¶ *Of mount Zion;* comp. Note, ch. i. 8. ¶ *And upon her assemblies.* Their convocations; their sacred assemblies, such as were called together on the Sabbath; Lev. xxiii. 2; Num. xxviii. 18. It refers here to their *future* assemblies, and therefore includes the Christian church assembled to worship God. ¶ *A cloud and smoke by day.* This refers to the pillar of cloud that went before the Israelites in their journey in the wilderness; Ex. xiii. 21; xiv. 20. ¶ *By day.* By day, this appeared to them as a cloud; by night, as a pillar of fire; Ex. xiii. 21, 22. That is, it was always conspicuous, and could be seen by all the people. A pillar of cloud could not have been seen by night; and God changes the symbols of his presence and protection, so that at all times his people may see them. The meaning here is, that as God gave to the Israelites a symbol of his presence and protection, so he would be the protector and defender of his people hereafter. ¶ *For upon all the glory.* Above all the *glorious object;* that is, his church, his people. It is here called ' the glory,' as being a glorious, or an honourable object. ¶ *A defence.* This word properly means *a covering, a protection,* from the verb *to cover,* and means that God will protect, or defend his people.

6. *And there shall be a tabernacle.* The reference here is to the *tabernacle,* or sacred *tent* that God directed Moses to make in the wilderness. The image of the cloudy pillar mentioned in the previous verses, seems to have suggested to the mind of the prophet the idea of the tabernacle over which that pillar rested. The principal idea here is, however, not a tabernacle as a symbol of the Divine protection, or of Divine

CHAPTER V.

ANALYSIS.

THIS chapter commences a new subject, and is in itself an entire prophecy, having no connection with the preceding or the following chapter. *When* it was delivered is unknown; but from the strong resemblance between the circumstances referred to here, and those referred to in ch. ii., it is probable it was at about the same period. The fact, also, that it is closely connected with that in the place which has been assigned it in the collection of the prophecies of Isaiah, is a circumstance which strongly corroborates that view. The general design of the chapter is to denounce the prevalent vices of the nation, and to proclaim that they will be followed with heavy judgments. The chapter may be conveniently regarded as divided into three parts.

I. A beautiful parable illustrative of the care which God had shown for his people, ver. 1–7. He states what he had done for them; calls on them to judge themselves whether he had not done for them all that he could have done; and, since his vineyard had brought forth no good fruit, he threatens to break down its hedges, and to destroy it.

II. The various vices and crimes which pre-vailed in the nation are denounced, and punishment threatened, ver. 8–23.

1. The sin of covetousness, ver. 8–10.
2. The sins of intemperance, revelry, and dissipation, ver. 11–17.
3. The sin of despising and contemning God, and of practising iniquity as if he did not see it, or could not punish it, ver. 18, 19.
4. The sin of those who pervert things, and call evil good and good evil, ver. 20.
5. The sin of vain self-confidence, pride, and inordinate self-esteem, ver. 21.
6. The sin of intemperance is again reproved, and the sin of receiving bribes; probably because these were in fact connected, ver. 22, 23.

III. Punishment is denounced on the nation for indulgence in these sins, ver. 24–30. The punishment would be, that he would call distant nations to invade their land, and it should be laid waste.

"The subject of this prophecy," says Lowth, "does not differ materially from ch. i., but it is greatly superior to it in force, in severity, in variety, in elegance."

N OW will I sing to my well-beloved a song of my beloved

worship, but of a place of refuge from a tempest; that is, that they should be *safe* under his protection. In Eastern countries they dwelt chiefly in tents. The idea is, therefore, that God would furnish them a place of shelter, a hiding-place from the storm. ¶ *In the day-time from the heat.* The heat in those regions was often very intense, particularly in the vast plains of sand. The *idea* here is, therefore, one that is very striking. It means, that God would furnish to them a refuge that would be like the comfort derived from a tent in a burning desert. ¶ *For a place of refuge.* A place to which to flee in the midst of a storm, as a tent would be. ¶ *A covert.* A place of retreat, a safe place to retire to. The figure here used is not unfrequently employed in the prophets; ch. xxv. 4; xxxii. 2. In eastern countries this idea would be very striking. While traversing the burning sands of a desert, exposed to the rays of a tropical sun, nothing could be more grateful than the cool shadow of a rock. Such figures are therefore common in oriental writings, to denote protection and agreeable shelter from

calamities; see Note on ch. xxxii. 2. The idea in these verses is—(1.) That God will be a defender of his people. (2.) That he will protect their families, and that his blessing will be upon their dwelling-places; comp. Note on ch. lix. 21. (3.) They may expect his blessing on their religious assemblies. (4.) God, through the promised Messiah, would be a refuge and defence. The sinner is exposed to the burning wrath of God, and to the storms of Divine vengeance that shall beat for ever on the naked soul in hell. From all this burning wrath, and from this raging tempest, the Messiah is the only refuge. Through him God forgives sin; and united to him by faith, the soul is safe. There are few images more beautiful than this. Soon the storms of Divine vengeance will beat on the sinner. God will summon him to judgment. But then, he who has fled to the Messiah—the Lord Jesus—as the refuge of his soul, shall be safe. He shall have nothing to fear, and in his arms shall find defence and salvation.

CHAPTER V.

1. *Now will I sing.* This is an indi-

touching his vineyard. My well-
beloved hath a *a* vineyard in *1* a very
fruitful hill :

a Lu.20.9,&c.   1 *the horn of the son of oil.*

2 And he *2* fenced it, and gathered out the stones thereof, and
planted it with the choicest *b* vine,

2 *or, made a wall about it.*   *b* Jer.2.21.

cation that what follows is poetic, or is
adapted to be sung or chanted. ¶ *To
my well-beloved.* The word used here
—דוֹדִי—is a term of endearment. It
properly denotes a friend ; a favourite ;
one greatly beloved. It is applied to
saints as being the beloved, or the
favourites of God, in Ps. cxxvii. 2;
Deut. xxxiii. 12. In this place, it is
evidently applied to JEHOVAH, the God
of the Jewish people. As there is some
reason to believe that the God of the
Jews—the manifested Deity who undertook their deliverance from Egypt, and
who was revealed as *their* God under
the name of 'the Angel of the Covenant'—was the Messiah, so it may be
that the prophet here meant to refer to
him. It is not, however, to the Messiah *to come.* It does not refer to the God
incarnate—to Jesus of Nazareth ; but
to the God of the Jews, in his capacity
as their lawgiver and protector in the
time of Isaiah ; not to him in the capacity of an incarnate Saviour. ¶ *A song
of my beloved.* Lowth, 'A song of
loves,' by a slight change in the Hebrew.
The word דוֹד usually denotes 'an uncle,'
a father's brother. But it also means
one beloved, a friend, a lover ; Cant. i.
13, 14, 16; ii. 3, 8, 9; iv. 16, 17. Here
it refers to Jehovah, and expresses the
tender and affectionate attachment
which the prophet had for his character and laws. ¶ *Touching his vineyard.* The Jewish people are often
represented under the image of a vineyard, planted and cultivated by God ;
see Ps. lxxx; Jer. ii. 21; xii. 10. Our
Saviour also used this beautiful figure
to denote the care and attention which
God had bestowed on his people ; Matt.
xxi. 33, *sq.*; Mark xii. 1, *sq.* ¶ *My
beloved.* God. ¶ *Hath a vineyard in
a very fruitful hill.* Heb. ' On a horn
of the son of oil.' The word *horn* used
here in the Hebrew, denotes the *brow,*
apex, or sharp point of a hill. The
word is thus used in other languages to
denote a hill, as in the Swiss words
shreckhorn, buchorn. Thus *Cornwall,*

in England, is called in the old British
tongue *Kernaw,* as lessening by degrees, like a horn, running out into
promontories, like so many horns ; for
the Britons called a horn *corn,* and in
the plural *kern.* The term ' horn ' is
not unfrequently applied to hills. Thus,
Pococke tells us (vol. ii. p. 67), that
there is a low mountain in Galilee which
has both its ends raised in such a manner
as to look like two mounts, which are
called the ' Horns of Hutin.' Harmer,
however, supposes that the term is used
here to denote the land of Syria, from
its resemblance to the shape of a horn ;
Obs. iii. 242. But the idea is, evidently, that the land on which God
respresents himself as having planted
his vineyard, was like an elevated hill
that was adapted eminently to such a
culture. It may mean either the *top*
of a mountain, or a little mountain, or
a *peak* divided from others. The most
favourable places for vineyards were on
the sides of hills, where they would be
exposed to the sun.—Shaw's *Travels,*
p. 338. Thus Virgil says :

— denique apertos
Bacchus amat colles.

' Bacchus loves open hills;' *Georg.* ii.
113. The phrase, *son of oil,* is used in
accordance with the Jewish custom,
where *son* means descendant, relative,
&c.; see Note, Matt. i. 1. Here it
means that it was so fertile that it
might be called the very *son of oil,* or
fatness, *i.e.,* fertility. The image is
poetic, and very beautiful; denoting that
God had planted his people in circumstances where he had a right to expect
great growth in attachment to him.
It was not owing to any want of care
on his part, that they were not distinguished for piety. The Chaldee renders
this verse, ' The prophet said, I will sing
now to Israel, who is compared to a vineyard, the seed of Abraham my beloved:
a song of my beloved to his vineyard.'
2. *And he fenced it.* Marg. ' Made
a wall about it.' The word used here
is supposed rather to mean *to dig about,*

and built a tower in the midst of it, and also [1] made a wine-press therein: and he looked that it should

bring forth grapes, and it brought forth wild grapes.

1 *hewed.*

to grub, as with a pick-axe or spade.—*Gesenius.* It has this signification in Arabic, and in one place in the Jewish Talmud.—*Kimchi.* The Vulgate and the LXX. understand it of making a hedge or fence, probably the first work in preparing a vineyard. And as 'a hedge' is expressly mentioned in ver. 5, it seems most probable that that is its meaning here. ¶ *And gathered out the stones,* &c. That it might be easily cultivated. This was, of course, a

necessary and proper work. ¶ *And planted it with the choicest vine.* Heb. 'With the sorek.' This was a choice species of vine, the grapes of which, the Jewish commentators say, had very small and scarcely perceptible stones, and which, at this day, is called *serki* in Morocco; in Persia, *kishmis.*—*Gesenius.* ¶ *And built a tower.* For the sake of watching and defending it. These towers were probably placed so as to overlook the whole vineyard, and

WATCH-TOWER IN A VINEYARD.

were thus posts of observation; comp. Note, ch. i. 8; see also Note, Matt. xxi. 33. ¶ *And also made a wine-press.* A place in which to put the grapes for the purpose of expressing the juice; see Note, Matt. xxi. 33. ¶ *And he looked.* He waited in expectation; as a husbandman waits patiently for the vines to grow, and to bear grapes. ¶ *Wild grapes.* The word here used is derived from the verb באַש *bâăsh, to be offensive, to corrupt, to putrify;* and is supposed by Gesenius to mean *monk's-hood,* a poisonous herb, offensive in smell, which produces berries like grapes. Such a meaning suits the connection better than the supposition of grapes that were wild or uncultivated. The Vulgate understands it of the weed

called *wild vine—labruscas.* The LXX. translate it by *thorns, ἄκανθας.* That there were vines in Judea which produced such poisonous berries, though resembling grapes, is evident; see 2 Kings iv. 39–41: 'And one went out into the fields to gather pot herbs, and he found a field vine, and he gathered from it wild fruit.' Moses also refers to a similar vine; Deut. xxxii. 32, 33: 'For their vine is as the vine of Sodom; their grapes are grapes of gall; their clusters are bitter.' Hasselquist thinks that the prophet here means the *nightshade.* The Arabs, says he, call it *wolf-grapes.* It grows much in vineyards, and is very pernicious to them. Some poisonous, offensive berries, growing on wild vines, are doubtless intended here.

3 And now, O inhabitants of Jerusalem, and men of Judah, judge, I pray you, betwixt me and my vineyard.

4 What could have been done more to my vineyard that I have not done in it? Wherefore, when I looked that it should bring forth

The general meaning of this parable it is not difficult to understand; comp. Notes on Matt. xxi. 33. Jerome has attempted to follow out the allegory, and explain the particular parts. He says, ' By the metaphor of the vineyard is to be understood the people of the Jews, which he surrounded or inclosed by *angels;* by gathering out the stones, the removal of *idols;* by the tower, the *temple* erected in the midst of Judea; by the wine-press, the *altar.*' There is no propriety, however, in attempting thus minutely to explain the particular parts of the figure. The general meaning is, that God had chosen the Jewish people; had bestowed great care on them in giving them his law, in defending them, and in providing for them; that he had omitted nothing that was adapted to produce piety, obedience, and happiness, and that they had abused it all, and instead of being obedient, had become exceedingly corrupt.

3. *And now, &c.* This is an appeal which God makes to the Jews themselves, in regard to the justice and propriety of what he was about to do. A similar appeal he makes in Mic. vi. 3: ' O my people, what have I done unto thee? and wherein have I wearied thee? Testify against me.' He intended to *punish* them (ver. 5, 6), and he appeals to them for the justice of it. He would do to them as they would do to a vineyard that had been carefully prepared and guarded, and which yet was valueless. A similar appeal he makes in ch. i. 18; and our Saviour made an application remarkably similar in his parable of the vineyard, Matt. xxi. 40–43. It is not improbable that he had his eye on this very place in Isaiah; and it is, therefore, the more remarkable that the Jews did not understand the bearing of his discourse.

4. *What could I, &c.* As a man who had done what is described in ver. 2, would have done all that *could* be done for a vineyard, so God says that he has done all that he could, in the

circumstances of the Jews, to make them holy and happy. He had chosen them; had given them his law; had sent them prophets and teachers; had defended them; had come forth in judgment and mercy, and he now appeals *to them* to say what *could* have been done more. This important verse implies that God had done all that he could have done; that is, all that he could consistently do, or all that justice and goodness required him to do, to secure the welfare of his people. It cannot, of course, be meant that he had no physical ability to do any thing else, but the expression must be interpreted by a reference to the point in hand; and that is, an appeal to others to determine that he had done all that could be done in the circumstances of the case. In this respect, we may, without impropriety, say, that there *is* a limit to the power of God. It is impossible to conceive that he *could* have given a law more holy; or that he could append to it more solemn sanctions than the threatening of eternal death; or that he could have offered higher hopes than the prospect of eternal life; or that he could have given a more exalted Redeemer. It has been maintained (see the *Princeton Bib. Repert.*, April 1841) that the reference here is to the future, and that the question means, ' what remains now to be done to my vineyard as an expression of displeasure?' or that it is asked with a view to introduce the expression of his purpose to punish his people, stated in ver. 5. But that the above is the meaning or the passage, or that it refers to what God had actually done, is evident from the following considerations:—(1.) He had specified at length (ver. 2) what he had done. He had performed *all* that was usually done to a vineyard; in fencing it, and clearing it of stones, and planting in it the choicest vines, and building a wine-press in it. Without impropriety, it might be said of a man that, whatever wealth he had, or what-grapes, brought it forth wild grapes?

5 And now, go to ; I will tell you what I will do to my vineyard : I will take away the *a* hedge thereof,

a Ps.80.12,13.

and it shall be eaten up ; *and* break down the wall thereof, and it shall be [1] trodden down.

6 And I will lay it waste : it shall not be pruned nor digged ; but there

[1] *for a treading.*

---

ever power he had to do *other* things, he *could do nothing more to perfect a vineyard.* (2.) It is the meaning which is most naturally suggested by the original. Literally, the Hebrew is, ' *What to do more ?* ' — מַה־לַעֲשׂוֹת עוֹד. Coverdale renders this, as it is in our translation, ' What more could have been done for it ?' Luther, ' What should one do more to my vineyard, that I have not done for it?'—Was sollte man doch mehr thun an meinem Weinberge, das ich nicht gethan habe an ihm ? Vulg., Quid est quod debui ultra facere— ' What is there which I *ought* to do more?' Sept., Τί ποιήσω ἔτι—' What shall I do yet?' implying that he had done all that he could for it. The Chaldee renders it, ' What good thing —מַה טָבָא—shall I say that I will do to my people that I have not done for them ?' implying that he had done for them all the good which could be spoken of. The Syriac, ' What remains to be done to my vineyard, and I have not done it?' In all these versions, the sense given is substantially the same— that God had done all that could be done to make the expectation that his vineyard would produce fruit, proper. There is no reference in one of these versions to what he *would* do afterwards, but the uniform reference is to what he *had* done to make the expectation *reasonable,* that his vineyard would produce fruit. (3.) That this is the fair interpretation is apparent farther, because, when, in ver. 5, he says what he *would do,* it is entirely different from what he said he *had done.* He *had* done all that could be done to make it proper to expect fruit; he now *would* do what would be a proper expression of his displeasure that no fruit had been produced. He would take away its hedge; break down its walls, and lay it waste. But in the interpretation of the passage proposed by the *Princeton Repert.,* there is an entire omission of

this part of the verse—' that I have not done in it.' It is not improper, therefore, to use this passage to show that God had done all that could be consistently done for the salvation of man, and the same appeal may now be made to sinners everywhere; and it may be asked, what God *could* have done for their salvation more than has been done? *Could* he have given them a purer law? *Could* he present higher considerations than have been drawn from the hope of an *eternal* heaven, and the fear of an *eternal* hell ? COULD he have furnished a more full atonement than has been made by the blood of his own Son ? The conclusion to which we should come would be in accordance with what is said in the prophet, that God has done *all* for the salvation of sinners that in the circumstances of the case could be done, and that if they are lost, they only will bear the blame.

5. *Go to.* The Hebrew word here is one that is commonly rendered, ' I pray you,' and is used *to call the attention* to what is said. It is the word from which we have derived the adverb *now,* נָא. ¶ *I will take away the hedge.* A *hedge* is a fence of thorns, made by suffering thorn-bushes to grow so thick that nothing can pass through them. Here it means that God would withdraw his protection from the Jews, and leave them exposed to be overrun and trodden down by their enemies, as a vineyard would be by wild beasts if it were not protected. ¶ *The wall,* &c. Vineyards, it seems, had a *double* enclosure.— *Gesenius.* Such a double protection might be necessary, as some animals might scale a wall that would yet find it impossible to pass through a thorn-hedge. The sense here is, that though the Jews had been protected in every way possible, yet that protection would be withdrawn, and they would be left defenceless.

6. *I will lay it waste,* &c. The de-

shall come up briers and thorns; I will also command the clouds that they rain no rain upon it.

7 For the vineyard of the LORD of hosts *is* the house of Israel, and

the men of Judah [1] his pleasant plant; and he looked for judgment, but behold [2] oppression; for righteousness, but behold a cry.

8 Wo unto them that join [a] house

1 *plant of his pleasures.*

2 *a scab.*   a Mic.2.2.

---

scription here is continued from ver. 5. The image is carried out, and means that the Jews should be left utterly without protection. ¶ *I will also command the clouds,* &c. It is evident here, that the parable or figure is partially dropped. A husbandman could not command the clouds. It is God alone who could do that; and the figure of the vineyard is dropped, and God is introduced speaking as a sovereign. The meaning is, that he would withhold his Divine influences, and would abandon them to desolation. The sense of the whole verse is plain. God would leave the Jews without protection; he would remove the guards, the helps, the influences, with which he had favoured them, and leave them to their own course, as a vineyard that was unpruned, uncultivated, unwatered. The Chaldee has well expressed the sense of the passage: 'I will take away the house of my sanctuary [the temple], and they shall be trodden down. I will regard them as guilty, and there shall be no support or defence for them; they shall be abandoned, and shall become wanderers. I will command the prophets, that they shall not prophesy over them.' The lesson taught here is, that when a people become ungrateful, and rebellious, God will withdraw from them, and leave them to desolation; comp. Rev. ii. 3.

7. *For the vineyard,* &c. This is the application of the parable. God had treated the Jews as a husbandman does a vineyard. This was *his* vineyard— the object of his faithful, unceasing care. This was his *only* vineyard; on this people alone, of all the nations of the earth, had he bestowed his peculiar attention. ¶ *His pleasant plant.* The plant in which he delighted. As the husbandman had been at the pains to plant the *sorek* (ver. 2), so had God selected the ancient stock of the Jews as his own, and made the race the object of his chief attention. ¶ *And he looked*

for judgment. For justice, or righteousness. ¶ *But behold oppression.* The word rendered *oppression* means properly *shedding of blood.* In the original here, there is a remarkable *paranomasia,* or play upon words, which is not uncommon in the Hebrew Scriptures, and which was deemed a great beauty in composition:

He looked for	*judgment,*	מִשְׁפָּט *mishpat,*
and lo!	*shedding of blood,*	מִשְׂפָּח *mispáhh;*
For	*righteousness,*	צְדָקָה *tzedhakd,*
but lo!	*a clamour,*	צְעָקָה *tze'akd.*

It is impossible, of course, to retain this in a translation. ¶ *A cry.* A *clamour;* tumult, disorder; the clamour which attends anarchy, and covetousness, and dissipation (ver. 8, 11, 12), rather than the soberness and steadiness of justice.

8. *Wo unto them,* &c. The prophet now proceeds to *specify* some of the crimes to which he had referred in the parable of the vineyard, of which the Jews had been guilty. The first is *avarice.* ¶ *That join house to house.* That seek to possess many houses; or perhaps that seek to live in large and magnificent palaces. A similar denunciation of this sin is recorded in Mic. ii. 2; Neh. v. 1–8. This, together with what follows, was contrary to the law of Moses. He provided that when the children of Israel should enter the land of Canaan, the land should be equitably divided; and in order to prevent avarice, he ordained the *jubilee,* occurring once in fifty years, by which every man and every family should be restored to their former possession; Lev. xxv. Perhaps there could have been no law so well framed to prevent the existence, and avoid the evils of covetousness. Yet, in defiance of the obvious requirements and spirit of that law, the people in the time of Isaiah had become generally covetous. ¶ *That lay field to field.* That purchase one farm after another.

to house, *that* lay field to field, till *there be* no place, that [1] they may be placed alone in the midst of the earth !

9 In mine ears, *said* the LORD of hosts, Of [2] a truth many houses shall be desolate, *even* great and fair, without inhabitant

[1] *ye.*　　　[2] *if not.*

10 Yea, [a] ten acres of vineyard shall yield one bath, and the seed of an homer shall yield an ephah.

11 Wo unto them that rise up early in the morning, *that* they may follow strong drink ; that continue until night, *till* wine [3] inflame them !

[a] Hag.1.9,11.　　　[3] or, *pursue them.*

The words ' that lay,' mean *to cause to approach;* that is, they *join on* one farm after another. ¶ *Till* there be *no place.* Till they reach the *outer limit* of the land ; till they possess all. ¶ *That they may be placed alone.* That they may displace all others ; that they may drive off from their lands all others, and take possession of them themselves. ¶ *In the midst of the earth.* Or rather, in the midst of the *land.* They seek to obtain the whole of it, and to expel all the present owners. Never was there a more correct description of avarice. It is satisfied with no present possessions, and would be satisfied only if *all* the earth were in its possession. Nor would the covetous man be satisfied then. He would sit down and weep that there was nothing more which he could desire. How different this from that *contentment* which is produced by religion, and the love of the happiness of others !

9. *In mine ears.* This probably refers to the prophet. As if he had said, ' God has revealed it to me,' or ' God has said in my ears,' *i.e.,* to me. The LXX. read it, ' These things are heard in the ears of the Lord of hosts,' *i.e.,* the *wishes* of the man of avarice. The Chaldee, ' The prophet said, In my ears I have heard ; a decree has gone from the Lord of hosts,' &c. ¶ *Many houses shall be desolate.* Referring to the calamities that should come upon the nation for its crimes.

10. *Yea, ten acres.* In this verse a reason is rendered why the houses mentioned in the previous verse should become desolate. The reason is, that the land would become sterile and barren, as a Divine judgment for their oppression. To what particular time the prophet refers, here, is not apparent. It is certain, however, that the land of

Canaan was frequently given up to sterility. The withholding of the early and latter rains, or the neglect of cultivation from any cause, would produce this. At present, this formerly fertile country is among the most unproductive on the face of the earth. ¶ *Ten acres.* An *acre,* among the Hebrews, was what could be ploughed by one yoke of oxen in a day. It did not differ materially from our acre. ¶ *Shall yield one bath.* One bath of wine. The *bath* was a Jewish measure for liquids, containing about seven gallons and a half. To say that *ten acres* should produce no more wine than this, was the same as to say that it would produce almost nothing. ¶ *And the seed of an homer.* An *homer* was a Hebrew measure for grain, containing about eight bushels. ¶ *An ephah.* The *ephah* contained about three pecks. Of course, to say that an homer of seed should produce about three pecks, would be the same as saying that it would produce almost nothing.

11. *Wo unto them.* The prophet, having denounced *avarice,* proceeds now to another vice—that of *intemperance,* or *dissipation.* ¶ *That rise up early,* &c. That rise *for this purpose,* when nothing else would rouse them. It may illustrate this somewhat, to remark, that it was not common among the ancients to become intoxicated at an early hour of the day ; see Note on Acts ii. 15 ; comp. 1 Thess. v. 7. It indicated then, as it does now, a confirmed and habitual state of intemperance when a man would do this early in the morning. ' The Persians, when they commit a debauch, arise betimes, and esteem the morning as the best time for beginning to drink wine, by which means they carry on their excess till night.'— *Morier.* ¶ That *they may follow strong*

12 And ᵃthe harp, and the viol, the tabret, and the pipe, and wine, are in their feasts: but they ᵇ regard

not the work of the LORD, neither consider the operation of his hands.

a Amos 6.5,6.   b Ps 28.5.

*drink—*שֵׁכָר shĕkhâr, or sichar. This word is derived from a verb signifying to drink, to become intoxicated. All nations have found out some intoxicating drink. That which was used by the Hebrews was made from grain, fruit, honey, dates, &c., prepared by fermentation. The word sometimes means the same as wine (Num. xxviii. 7), but more commonly it refers to a stronger drink, and is distinguished from it, as in the common phrase, 'wine and strong drink;' Lev. x. 9; Num. vi. 3; Judg. xiii. 4,7. Sometimes it may be used for *spiced wine—*a mixture of wine with spices, that would also speedily produce intoxication. The Chaldee renders the word חֲמַר עַתִּיק 'old fermented liquor;' denoting the *mode* in which strong drink was usually prepared. It may be remarked here, that whatever may be the *form* in which intoxicating drink is prepared, it is substantially the same in all nations. Intoxication is caused by *alcohol,* and that is produced by fermentation. It is never created or increased by distillation. The only effect of distillation is, to collect and preserve the alcohol which existed in the beer, the wine, or the cider. Consequently, the same substance produces intoxication when wine is drank, which does when brandy is drank; the same in cider or other fermented liquor, as in ardent spirits. ¶ *That continue until night.* That drink all day. This shows that the *strong drink* intended here, did not produce *sudden* intoxication. This is an exact description of what occurs constantly in oriental nations. The custom of sitting long at the wine, when they have the means of indulgence, prevails everywhere. D'Arvieux says, that while he was staying among the Arabs on mount Carmel, a wreck took place on the coast, from which one of the emirs obtained two large casks of wine. He forthwith sent to the neighbouring emirs, inviting them to come and drink it. They gladly came, and continued drinking for two days and two nights, till not a

drop of the wine was left. In like manner, Tavernier relates that the king of Persia sent for him early one morning to the palace, when, with other persons, he was obliged to sit all the day, and late at night, drinking wine with the shah; but at last, 'the king growing sleepy, gave us leave to depart, which we did very willingly, having had hard labour *for seventeen hours together.*' ¶ *Inflame them.* Excite them; or stimulate them. We have the same phrase—denoting the *burning* tendency of strong drink. The American Indians appropriately call it *fire-water.*

12. The prophet proceeds to state still further the extent of their crimes. This verse contains an account of their dissipated habits, and their consequent forgetfulness of God. That they commonly had musical instruments in their feasts, is evident from many passages of the Old Testament; see Amos vi. 5, 6. Their feasts, also, were attended with songs; Isa. xxiv. 8, 9. ¶ *The harp—*כִּנּוֹר, *k'innōr.* This is a well-known stringed instrument, employed commonly in sacred music. It is often mentioned as having been used to express the pious feelings of David; Ps. xxxii. 2; xliii. 4; xlix. 5. It is early mentioned as having been invented by Jubal; Gen. iv. 21. It is supposed usually to have had ten strings (Josephus, *Ant.* B. x. ch. xii. § 3). It was played by the hand; 1 Sam. xvi. 23; xviii. 9. The *root* of the word כִּנּוֹר, *k'innōr,* is unknown. The word *kinnor* is used in all the languages cognate to the Hebrew, and is recognised even in the Persian. It is probable that the instrument here referred to was common in all the oriental nations, as it seems to have been known before the Flood, and of course the knowledge of it would be extended far. It is an oriental name and instrument, and from this word the Greeks derived their word κινύρα. The LXX. render it κιθάρα and κινύρα. Once they substitute for it ὄργανον, Ps. cxxxvi. 2; and five times ψαλτήριον, Gen. iv. 20; Ps. xlviii. 4;

lxxx. 2; cxlix. 3; Ezek. xxvi. 13. The harp—*kinnor*—is not only mentioned as having been invented by Jubal, but it is also mentioned by Laban in the description which he gives of various solemnities, in regard to which he assures the fleeing Jacob that it had been his wish to accompany him with all the testimonials of joy—'with music—*toph* and *kinnor*;' Gen. xxxi. 27. In the first age it was consecrated to joy and exultation. Hence it is referred to as the instrument employed by David to drive away the melancholy of Saul (1 Sam. xvi. 16–22), and is the instrument usually employed to celebrate the praises of God ; Ps. xxxiii. 1, 2; xliii. 4; xlix.5; lxxi.22,23. But the harp was not only used on sacred occasions. Isaiah also mentions it as carried about by courtezans (ch. xxiii. 16), and also refers to it as used on occasions of gathering in the vintage, and of increasing the joy of the festival occasion. So also it was used in military triumphs. Under the reign of Jehoshaphat, after a victory which had been gained over the Moabites, they returned in triumph to Jerusalem, accompanied with playing on the *kinnor;* 2 Chron. xx. 27, 28. The harp was generally used on occasions of joy. Only in one place, in Isaiah (xvi. 11), is it referred to as having been employed in times of mourning. There is no ancient figure of the *kinnor* that can be relied on as genuine. We can only say that it was an instrument made of sounding wood, and furnished with strings. Josephus says that it was furnished with ten strings, and was played with the plectrum (*Ant.* B. viii. ch. x.) Suidas, in his explanation of it, makes express mention of strings or sinews (p. 318); and Pollux speaks of goats' claws as being used for the plectrum. David made it out of the *berosh,* or fir, and Solomon out of the almug. Pfeiffer supposes, that the strings were drawn over the belly of a hollow piece of wood, and that it had some resemblance to our violin. But it is more probable that the common representation of the harp as nearly in the form of a triangle, with one side or the front part wanting, is the correct one. For a full discussion of the subject, see Pfeiffer on the Music

of the ancient Hebrews, *Bib. Repos.* vol. vi. pp. 366–373. Montfaucon has furnished a drawing of what was supposed to be the ancient *kinnor,* which is represented in the annexed cut. But, after all, the usual form is not quite certain.

THE HARP OR KINNOR.
From Description de l'Egypte.

Bruce found a sculpture of a harp resembling that usually put into the hands of David, or nearly in the form of a triangle, and under circumstances which led him to suppose that it was as old as the times of Sesostris. ¶ *And the viol.* נֶבֶל *nĕbhĕl.* From this word is derived the Greek word ναβλίον, and the Latin *nablium* and *nabla.* But it is not very easy to form a correct idea of this instrument. The derivation would lead us to suppose that it was something in the shape of a *bottle,* and it is probable that it had a form in the shape of a leathern bottle, such as is used in the East, or at least a vessel in which wine was preserved ; 1 Sam. x. 3; xxv. 18; 2 Sam. xvi. 1. It was at first made of the בְּרוֹשׁ *bĕrōsh* or fir; afterwards it was made of the almug tree, and occasionally it seems to have been made of metal; 2 Sam. vi. 5; 1 Chron. xiii. 8. The external parts of the instrument were of wood, over which strings were drawn in various ways. Josephus says it had twelve strings (*Ant.* B. viii. ch. x.) He says also that it was played with the fingers.— *Ibid.* Hesychius and Pollux reckon it among stringed instruments. The resonance had its origin in the vessel or the bottom part of the instrument, upon which the strings were drawn. According to Ovid, this instrument was played on with both hands:

Quaravis mutus erat, voci favisse putatur
Piscis, Aroniae fabula nota lyrae.
Disce etiam duplicè genialia palmâ
Verrere.   De Arte Amandi, lib. iii. 327.

According to Jerome, Isodorus, and Cassiodorus, it had the form of an inverted Greek Delta ▽. Pfeiffer supposes that this instrument was probably the same as is found represented on ancient monuments. The belly of the instrument is a wooden bowl, having a small hole in the under part, and is covered over with a stretched skin, which is higher in the middle than at the sides. Two posts, which are fastened together at the top by a cross piece, pass obliquely through this skin. Five strings pass over this skin, having a bridge for their support on the cross piece. The instrument has no pins or screws, but every string is fastened by means of some linen wound with it around this cross piece. The description of this instrument is furnished by Niebuhr (Th. i. p. 179). It is played on in two ways, either by being struck with the finger, or by a piece of leather, or perhaps a quill hung at its side and drawn across the strings. It cannot with certainty be determined when this instrument was invented, or when it

LYRE.—From some of the Ancient Sculptures.
came into use among the Hebrews. It is first mentioned in the time of Saul (1 Sam. x. 5), and from this time onward it is frequently mentioned in the Old Testament. It was used particularly in the public worship of God; 2 Sam. vi. 5; 1 Kings x. 12; 2 Chron.

xx. 28; xxix. 25; 1 Chron. xv. 16; xvi. 5. It was usually accompanied with other instruments, and was also used in festivals and entertainments; see Bib.Repos. vol. vi. pp. 357–365. The usual form of representing it is shown in the preceding cut, and is the form in which the lyre appears on ancient monuments, in connection with the statues of Apollo.

The annexed cut is a representation of a lyre from a Jewish shekel of the time of Simon Maccabeus, and may have been, not improbably, a form in frequent use among the Jews.

LYRE.
From the Medals of Simon Maccabeus.

Niebuhr has furnished us with an instrument from the East, which is supposed to have a very near resemblance to that which is referred to by Isaiah. This instrument is represented in the following cut.

EASTERN LYRE.
From Description de l'Egypte.

¶ *The tabret.* תֹף *tŏph.* This was one of the instruments which were struck with the hands. It was the kettle-drum of the ancients, and it is more easy to determine its form and use than it is of most of the instruments used by the Hebrews. The LXX. and other Greek translators render it by τύμπανον. This word, as well as the Latin tympanum, is manifestly derived from the Hebrew. The Arabic word *duf* applied to the same instrument is also derived from the same Hebrew word. It was an instrument of wood, hollowed out, and covered over with leather and struck with the hands—a species of drum. This form of the drum is used by the Spaniards, and they have preserved it ever since the time of the Moors. It was early used. Laban wished to accompany Jacob with its sound; Gen. xxxi. 27. Miriam, the sister of Moses, and the females with her, accompanied the song of victory with this instrument; Ex. xv. 20. Job was acquainted with it (Job xvii. 6; xxi. 12), and David employed it in the festivities of religion; 2 Sam. vi. 5. The occasions on which it is mentioned as being used are joyful occasions, and for the most part those who play on it are females, and on this account they are called 'drum-beating women' (Ps. lxviii. 26)—in our translation, 'damsels playing with timbrels.' In our translation it is rendered *tabret,* Isa. v. 12; 1 Sam. x. 5; Gen. xxxi. 26; Isa. xxiv. 8; xxxi. 22; 1 Sam. xviii. 6; Ezek. xxxviii. 13; Jer. xxxi. 4; Job xvii. 6; *tabcring,* Nah. ii. 7; and *timbrel,* Ps. lxxxi. 2; Ex. xv. 20; Job xxi. 12; Ps. cxlix. 3; cl. 4; Judg. xi. 34; Ps. lxviii. 25. It is no where mentioned as employed in war or warlike transactions. It was sometimes made by merely stretching leather over a wooden hoop, and thus answered to the instrument known among us as the tambourine. It was in the form of a sieve, and is often found on ancient monuments, and particularly in the hands of Cybele. In the East, there is now no instrument more common than this. Niebuhr (*Th.* i. p. 181) has given the following description of it :—' It is a broad hoop covered on one side with a stretched skin. In the rim there are usually thin round pullies or wheels of metal which make some noise, when this drum, held on high with one hand, is struck with the fingers of the other hand. No musical instrument perhaps is so much employed in Turkey as this. When the females in their harems dance or sing, the time is always beat on this instrument. It is called *doff.*' The following figures are representations of it.

TAMBOURINES OF EASTERN ORIGIN.—From Description de l'Egypte.

See *Bib. Repos.* vol. vi. pp. 398–402. It is commonly supposed that from the word *toph,* *Tophet* is derived—a name given to the valley of Jehoshaphat near Jerusalem, because this instrument was used there to drown the cries of children when sacrificed to Moloch. ¶ *And*

pipe. חָלִיל *hhâlil.* This word is derived either from חָלַל *hhâlăl, to bore through,* and thence conveys the idea of a flute bored through, and furnished with holes (*Gesenius*); or from חָלַל *hhâlăl, to leap* or *dance:* and thence it conveys the idea of an instrument that was played on at the dance.—*Pfeiffer*. The Greek translators have always rendered it by αὐλός. There are, in all, but four places where it occurs in the Old Testament; 1 Kings i. 40; Isa. v. 12; xxx. 29; Jer. xlviii. 36; and it is uniformly rendered *pipe* or *pipes*, by our translators. The origin of the pipe is unknown. It was possessed by most ancient nations, though it differed much in form. It was made sometimes of wood, at others of reed, at others of the bones of animals, horns, &c. The *box-wood* has been the common material out of which it was made. It was sometimes used for plaintive music (comp. Matt. ix. 23); but it was also employed in connection with other instruments, while journeying up to Jerusalem to attend the great feasts there; see Note on Isa. xxx. 29. Though employed on plaintive occasions, yet it was also employed in times of joy and pleasure. Hence, in the times of Judas Maccabeus, the Jews complained 'that all joy had vanished from Jacob, and that the flute and cithera were silent;' 1 Mac. iii. 45; see *Bib. Repos.* vol. vi. pp. 387–392. The following graceful figures will show the manner of playing the flute or pipe among the Greeks.

GREEK FLUTE PLAYERS.

It was also a common art to play the double flute or pipe, in the East, in the manner represented in the cut on next page. In the use of these instruments, in itself, there could be no impropriety. That which the prophet rebuked was, that they employed them not for praise, or even for innocent amusement, but that they introduced them to their feasts of revelry, and thus made them the occasion of forgetting God. Forgetfulness of God, in connection with music and dancing, is beautifully described by Job:

They send forth their little ones like a flock,
And their children dance;
They take the timbrel and harp,
And rejoice at the sound of the organ;
They spend their days in mirth,
And in a moment go down to the grave.

And they say unto God—
'Depart from us;
For we know not the knowledge of thy ways.
What is the Almighty, that we should serve him?
And what profit should we have if we pray unto him?'   Job xxi. 11–15.

¶ *In their feasts.* 'The Nabathæans of Arabia Petræa always introduced music at their entertainments (*Strabo*, xvi.), and the custom seems to have been very general among the ancients. They are mentioned as having been essential among the Greeks, from the earliest times; and are pronounced by Homer to be requisite at a feast:

Μολπή τ' ὀρχηστύς τε· τά γάρ τ' ἀναθήματα
δαιτός.   *Od.* i. 152.

Aristoxenus, quoted by Plutarch, *De*

13 Therefore my people are gone into captivity, because ^a*they have no knowledge*; and their ¹honourable men *are* famished, and their multitude dried up with thirst.

<small>a Ho.4.6; Lu.19.44.   1 *glory* are *men of famine*.</small>

14 Therefore hell hath enlarged herself, and opened her mouth without measure : and their glory, and their multitude, and their pomp, and he that rejoiceth, shall descend into it.

Musicâ, says, that 'the music was designed to counteract the effects of ine-

DOUBLE FLUTE PLAYER.

briety ; for as wine discomposes the body and the mind, so music has the power of soothing them, and of restoring their previous calmness and tranquillity.' *See* Wilkinson's *Manners and Customs of the Ancient Egyptians*, vol. ii. pp. 248. 249. ¶ *But they regard not, &c.* The reproof is especially, that they forget him in their entertainments. They employ music to inflame their passions; and amid their songs and wine, their hearts are drawn away from God. That this is the tendency of such feasts, all must know. God is commonly forgotten in such places ; and even the sweetest music is made the occasion for stealing the affections from him, and of inflaming the passions, instead of being employed to soften the feelings of the soul, and raise the heart to God. ¶ *The operation of his hands.* The work of his hands—particularly his dealings

among the people. God is round about them with mercy and judgment, but they do not perceive him.

13. *Therefore my people are gone.* This is evidently used with reference to the *future*. The prophet described events as *passing before his eyes* as a vision (Note, ch. i. 1); and he here seems to *see* the people going into captivity, and describes it as an event actually occurring. ¶ *Into captivity.* Referring, doubtless, to the captivity at Babylon. ¶ *Because* they have *no knowledge.* Because they do not choose to retain the knowledge of God. ¶ *And their honourable men.* The Hebrew is, ' The glory of the people became men of famine;' that is, they shall be destroyed with famine. This was to be a *punishment* for their dissipation at their feasts. ¶ *And their multitude.* The mass, or body of the nation ; the common people. ¶ *Dried up with thirst.* Are punished in this manner for their indulgence in drinking. The punishment here specified, refers particularly to a journey through an arid, desolate region, where drink could be obtained only with difficulty. Such was the route which the nation was compelled afterwards to take in going to Babylon.

14. *Therefore hell.* The word translated *hell*, שְׁאוֹל *sheôl*, has not the same meaning that we now attach to that word ; its usual signification, among the Hebrews, was *the lower world, the region of departed spirits.* It corresponded to the Greek ᾅδης, *hades*, or place of the dead. This word occurs eleven times in the New Testament (Matt. xi. 23; xvi. 18; Luke x. 15; xvi. 23; Acts ii. 27, 31; 1 Cor. xv. 55; Rev. i. 18; vi. 8; xx. 13, 14), in all of which places, except 1 Cor. xv. 55, it is rendered *hell*, though denoting, in most of those places, as it does in the Old Testament, the abodes of the dead. The LXX., in this place, and usually, translate the word *sheol* by ᾅδης, *hades*. In

15 And the mean man shall be brought down, and the mighty man shall be humbled, and the eyes of the lofty shall be humbled :

16 But the LORD of hosts shall be exalted in judgment, and ¹ God,

that is holy, shall be sanctified in righteousness.

17 Then shall the lambs feed after their manner, and the waste places of the fat ones shall strangers eat.

¹ the God the holy, or, the holy God.

was represented by the Hebrews as *low down*, or *deep* in the earth—contrasted with the height of heaven; Deut. xxxii. 22; Job xi. 8; Ps. cxxxix. 7, 8. It was a place where thick darkness reigns; Job x. 21, 22 : 'The land of darkness and the shadow of death; a land of darkness, as darkness itself.' It is described as having *valleys*, or *depths*, Prov. ix. 18. It is represented also as having *gates*, Isa. xxxviii. 10; and as being inhabited by a great multitude, some of whom sit on thrones, occupied in some respects as they were on earth; see Note, Isa. xiv. 9. And it is also said that the wicked descend into it by openings in the earth, as Korah, Dathan, and Abiram did; Num. xv. 30, &c. In this place, it means evidently the *regions of the dead*, without the idea of punishment; and the poetic representation is, that so many of the Jews would be cut off by famine, thirst, and the sword, that those vast regions would be obliged *to enlarge themselves* in order to receive them. It means, therefore, that while many of them would go into captivity (ver. 13), vast multitudes of them would be cut off by famine, thirst, and the sword. ¶ *Opened her mouth.* As if to absorb or consume them; as a *cavern*, or opening of the earth does; comp. Num. xvi. 30. ¶ *Without measure.* Without any limit. ¶ *And their glory.* All that they esteemed their pride and honour shall descend together into the yawning gulf. ¶ *Their multitude.* The multitude of people; their vast hosts. ¶ *Their pomp.* Noise, tumult; the bustle, and shouting, and display made in battle, or war, or victory; Isa. xiii. 4; Amos ii. 2; Hos. x. 14. ¶ *And he that rejoiceth.* All that the nation prided itself on, and all that was a source of joy, should be destroyed.

15, 16. *And the mean man—the mighty man.* The expressions here mean that *all* ranks would be subdued

and punished; see Note, ch. ii. 9. ¶ *The eyes of the lofty*, &c.; see Note, ch. ii. 11, 17. ¶ *Shall be exalted in judgment.* In his justice; he shall so manifest his justice as to be exalted in the view of the people. ¶ *Shall be sanctified.* Shall be *regarded* as holy. He shall so manifest his righteousness in his dealings, that it shall be seen and felt that he is a holy God.

17. *Then shall the lambs feed.* This verse is very variously interpreted. Most of the Hebrew commentators have followed the Chaldee interpretation, and have regarded it as designed to console the pious part of the people with the assurance of protection in the general calamity. The Chaldee is, 'Then the just shall feed, as it is said, to them; and they shall be multiplied, and shall possess the property of the impious.' By this interpretation, *lambs* are supposed, as is frequently the case in the Scriptures, to represent the people of God. But according to others, the probable design of the prophet is, to denote the state of utter desolation that was coming upon the nation. Its cities, towns, and palaces would be destroyed, so as to become a vast pasturage where the flocks would roam at pleasure. ¶ *After their manner.* Heb. 'According to their *word*,' *i.e.*, under their own *command*, or at pleasure. They would go where they pleased without being obstructed by fences. ¶ *And the waste places of the fat ones.* Most of the ancient interpreters suppose, that the waste places of the fat ones here refer to the desolate habitations of the rich people; in the judgments that should come upon the nation, they would become vacant, and strangers would come in and possess them. This is the sense given by the Chaldee. The Syriac translates it, 'And foreigners shall devour the ruins which are yet to be restored.' If this is the sense, then it accords with the *first* interpretation

18 Wo unto them that draw iniquity with cords of vanity, and sin as it were with a cart-rope!

19 That say, ^aLet him make speed, *and* hasten his work, that

a 2 Pe.3.3,4.

we may see *it:* and let the counsel of the Holy One of Israel draw nigh and come, that we may know *it.*

20 Wo unto them that [1] call evil good, and good evil; that put dark-

1 *say concerning evil, it is good.*

---

suggested of the previous verse—that the pious should be fed, and that the proud should be desolate, and their property pass into the hands of strangers. By others (Gesenius, &c.), it is supposed to mean that strangers, or foreigners, would come in, and fatten their cattle in the desert places of the nation. The land would be so utterly waste, that they would come there to fatten their cattle in the rank and wild luxuriancy that would spontaneously spring up. This sense will suit the connection of the passage; but there is some difficulty in making it out from the Hebrew. The Hebrew which is rendered 'the waste places of the fat ones,' may, however, be translated 'the deserts that are rich—rank—luxuriant.' The word *stranger* denotes *foreigners;* or those who are not *permanent* dwellers in the land.

18. *Wo unto them,* &c. This is a new denunciation. It introduces another form of sin, and threatens its appropriate punishment. ¶ *That draw iniquity with cords of vanity.* The general idea in this verse and the next, is, doubtless, that of plunging deeper and deeper into sin. The word *sin* here, has been sometimes supposed to mean *the punishment* for sin. The word has that meaning sometimes, but it seems here to be taken in its usual sense. The word *cords* means strings of any kind, larger or smaller; and the expression *cords of vanity,* is supposed to mean *small, slender, feeble* strings, like the web of a spider. The word vanity שוא, *may,* perhaps, have the sense here of falsehood or deceit; and the cords of deceit may denote the schemes of evil, the plans for deceiving men, or of bringing them into a snare, as the fowler springs his deceitful snare upon the unsuspecting bird. The Chaldee translates it, 'Woe to those who begin to sin by little and little, drawing sin by cords of vanity; these sins grow

and increase until they are strong, and are like a cart-rope.' The LXX. render it, 'Woe to those who draw sin with a long cable;' *i.e.,* one sin is added to another, until it comes to an enormous length, and the whole is drawn along together. Probably the true idea is that of the ancient interpretation of the Rabbins, 'An evil inclination is at first like a fine hair string, but the finishing like a cart-rope.' At first, they draw sin with a slender cord, then they go on to greater deeds of iniquity that urge them on, and draw them with their main strength, as with a cart-rope. They make a strong *effort* to commit iniquity.

19. *That say,* &c. They add one sin to another for the *purpose* of *defying* God, and provoking him to anger. They pretend that he will not punish sin; and hence they plunge deeply into it, and defy him to punish them. ¶ *Let him make speed.* Let him come quick to punish. ¶ *And hasten his work.* His punishment. ¶ *That we may see* it. An expression of defiance. We would like to see him undertake it. ¶ *The counsel of the Holy One,* &c. His threatened purpose to punish. This is the language of all sinners. They plunge deep into sin; they mock at the threatenings of God; they defy him to do his utmost; they do not believe his declarations. It is difficult to conceive more dreadful and high-handed iniquity than this.

20. *Wo unto them that call evil good,* &c. This is the fourth class of sins denounced. The sin which is reprobated here is that of *perverting* and *confounding* things, especially the distinctions of morality and religion. They prefer erroneous and false doctrines to the true; they prefer an evil to an upright course of conduct. The Chaldee renders this, 'Wo to those who say to the impious, who are prospered in this age, You are good; and who say to the meek,

ness for light, and light for darkness; that put bitter for sweet, and
sweet for bitter!

21 Wo unto *them that are* wise in
their own ^aeyes, and prudent ¹in
their own sight!

a Pro.26.12.   1 *before their face.*

22 Wo unto *them that are* mighty
to drink wine, and men of strength
to mingle strong drink:

23 Which justify the wicked for
reward, and take away the righteousness of the righteous from
him!

Ye are impious.' Jarchi thinks that
the prophet here refers to those who
worship idols, but he evidently has a
more general reference to those who
confound all the distinctions of right
and wrong, and who prefer the wrong.
¶ *That put darkness for light. Darkness,* in the Scriptures, is the emblem
of ignorance, error, false doctrine, crime.
Light denotes truth, knowledge, piety.
This clause, therefore, expresses in a
figurative, but more emphatic manner,
what was said in the previous member
of the verse. ¶ *That put bitter.*
Bitter and *bitterness* are often used to
denote *sin;* see Note on Acts viii. 23;
also Rom. iii. 14; Eph. iv. 31; Heb. xii.
15; Jer. ii. 19; iv. 18. The meaning
here does not differ from that expressed
in the other parts of the verse, except
that there is *implied* the additional idea
that sin *is* bitter; and that virtue, or
holiness, is sweet: that is, that the one
is attended with painful consequences,
and the other with pleasure.

21. *Wo unto* them that are *wise,* &c.
This is the fifth crime specified. It
refers to those who are inflated with a
false opinion of their own knowledge,
and who are therefore self-confident and
vain. This is expressly forbidden;
Prov. iii. 7: 'Be not wise in thine own
eyes;' comp. Prov. xxvi. 12. ¶ *In their
own eyes.* In their own opinion, or
estimation. ¶ *And prudent.* Knowing;
self-conceited. This was, doubtless, one
characteristic of the times of Isaiah.
It is known to have been strikingly the
characteristic of the Jews—particularly
the Pharisees—in the time of our
Saviour. The evil of this was, (1.) That
it evinced and fostered *pride.* (2.) That
it rendered them unwilling to be instructed, and especially by the prophets.
As they supposed that they were already
wise enough, they refused to listen to
others. This is always the effect of such
self-confidence: and hence the Saviour

required his disciples to be meek, and
humble, and teachable as children.

22. *Wo unto* them that are *mighty,*
&c. This is the sixth specification of
crime. He had already denounced the
intemperate in ver. 11. But probably
this was a prevailing sin. Perhaps
there was no evidence of reform; and
it was needful to *repeat* the admonition,
in order that men might be brought to
regard it. The prophet repeats a similar
denunciation in ch. lvi. 12. ¶ *Mighty.*
Perhaps those who prided themselves
on their ability to drink *much* without
becoming intoxicated; who had been
so accustomed to it, that they defied its
effects, and boasted of their power to
resist its usual influence. A similar
idea is expressed in ch. lvi. 12. ¶ *Men
of strength.* The Chaldee understands
this of *rich* men; but, probably, the
reference is to those who boasted that
they were able to bear *much* strong
drink. ¶ *To mingle.* To mix wine
with spices, dates, drugs, &c., to make
it more intoxicating; Prov. ix. 2, 5.
They boasted that they were able to
drink, without injury, liquor of extraordinary intoxicating qualities. ¶ *Strong
drink;* Note, ver. 11. On the subject
of the strong drink used in the East,
see Harmer's *Observations,* vol. ii. pp.
140–148. Ed. Lond. 1808.

23. *Which justify.* This refers, doubtless, to magistrates. They gave unjust
decisions. ¶ *For reward.* For bribes,
¶ *And take away the righteousness.*
That is, they do not decide the cause in
favour of those who have just claims,
but are determined by a bribe; see
Note, ch. i. 23. It is remarkable, that
this is introduced in immediate connection with their being mighty to
mingle strong drink. One effect of
intemperance is to make a man ready
to be *bribed.* Its effect is seen as clearly
in courts of justice, and in the decisions
of such courts, as any where. A man

24 Therefore as the [1] fire devour-eth the stubble, and the flame con-sumeth *a* the chaff, *so* their root shall be as rottenness, and their blossom shall go up as dust. Be-cause they have cast away the law of the LORD of hosts, and de-spised the word of the Holy One of Israel;

1 *tongue of fire.*　　　*a* Mat.3.12.

25 Therefore is the anger of the LORD kindled against his people, and he hath stretched forth his hand against them, and hath smitten them : and the hills did *b* tremble, and their carcasses *were* torn [2] in the midst of the streets. For all this *c* his anger is not turned away, but his hand *is* stretched out still.

b Hab.3.6.　　2 or, *as dung.*　　*c* Le.26.14,&c.

that is intemperate, or that indulges in strong drink, is not qualified to be a judge.

24. *Therefore as the fire,* &c. The remainder of this chapter is occupied with predicting *judgments,* or punish-ments, upon the people for their sins which had been specified. The He-brew here is, ' The *tongue* of fire.' The figure is beautiful and obvious. It is derived from the pyramidal, or tongue-like appearance of *flame.* The con-cinnity of the metaphor in the Hebrew is kept up. The word *devoureth* is in the Hebrew *eateth:* ' As the tongue of fire eats up,' &c. The use of the word *tongue* to denote *flame* is common in the Scriptures ; see Note on Acts ii. 3. ¶ *And the flame consumeth the chaff.* The word rendered *chaff* here, means rather *hay,* or *dried grass.* The word rendered ' consumeth,' denotes properly *to make to fall,* and refers to the appearance when a fire passes through a field of grain or grass, consuming the stalks near the ground, so that the upper portion *falls down,* or sinks gently into the flames. ¶ So *their root shall be as rottenness.* Be rotten ; or decayed—of course furnishing no moisture, or suit-able juices for the support of the plant. The idea is, that all the sources of national prosperity among the Jews would be destroyed. The word *root* is often used to denote the source of *strength* or *prosperity;* Is. xiv. 30 ; Hos. ix. 16 ; Job xviii. 16. ¶ *And their blossom.* This word rather means germ, or tender branch. It also means the flower. The figure is kept up here. As the *root* would be destroyed, so would all that was supported by it, and all that was deemed beautiful, or orna-mental. ¶ *As dust.* The Hebrew denotes *fine dust,* such as is easily blown

about. The root would be rotten ; and the flower, wanting nourishment, would become dry, and turn to dust, and blow away. Their strength, and the sources of their prosperity would be destroyed ; and all their splendour and beauty, all that was ornamental, and the source of national wealth, would be destroyed with it. ¶ *They have cast away.* They have refused to *obey* it. This was the cause of all the calamities that would come upon them.

25. *Therefore is the anger of the Lord kindled.* The Lord is *enraged,* or is angry. Similar expressions often occur ; Num. xi. 33 ; 2 Kings xxiii. 26 ; Deut. xi. 17 ; Ps. lvi. 40 ; Job xix. 11, Ps. ii. 12. The *cause* of his anger was the crimes which are specified in this chapter. ¶ *And he hath stretched forth his hand.* To stretch forth the hand may be an action expressive of protection, invitation, or punishment. Here it is the latter ; comp. Isa. xiv. 27. ¶ *And hath smitten them.* Punished them. To what this refers particularly is not clear. Gesenius supposes that the expressions which follow are descriptive of pestilence. Lowth and Rosenmüller suppose that they refer to the earthquakes which occurred in the days of Uzziah, and in the time of the prophets ; Amos i. 1 ; Zech. xiv. 5. The words, perhaps, will bear either construction. ¶ *And the hills did tremble.* This expression is one that is often used in the Scriptures to denote the presence and anger of God. It is well adapted to describe an earthquake ; but it is also often used poetically, to describe the presence and the majesty of the Most High ; comp. Ps. cxliv. 5 ; Job ix. 6 ; xxvi. 11 ; Ps. cxiv. 7 ; Jer. iv. 24 ; Hab. iii. 10 ; Ps. xviii. 7 ; xcvii. 5 ; civ. 32. The image is one that is very sublime. The earth,

26 And he will lift up an ensign to the nations from far, and will hiss unto them from the end of the earth; and, behold, they shall come with speed swiftly.

a Joel 2.3-11.

27 None *a* shall be weary nor stumble among them ; none shall slumber nor sleep ; neither shall the girdle of their loins be loosed, nor the latchet of their shoes be broken :

---

as if conscious of the presence of God, is represented as alarmed, and trembling. Whether it refers here to the earthquake, or to some other mode of punishment, cannot be determined. The fact, however, that such an earthquake had occurred in the time of Isaiah, would seem to fix the expression to that. Isaiah, from that, took occasion also to denounce future judgments. This was but the beginning of woes. ¶ *And their carcasses* were *torn*. The margin here is the more correct translation. The passage means that their dead bodies were strewed, unburied, like filth, through the streets. This expression would more naturally denote a pestilence. But it may be descriptive of an earthquake, or of any calamity. ¶ *For all this.* Notwithstanding all this calamity, his judgments are not at an end. He will punish the nation more severely still. In what way he would do it, the prophet proceeds in the remainder of the chapter to specify; comp. ch. ix. 12; x. 4.

26. *And he will lift up an ensign,* &c. The idea here is, that the nations of the earth are under his control, and that he can call whom he pleases to execute his purposes. This power over the nations he often claims ; comp. Isa. xliv. 28; xlv. 1–7; x. 5–7; ix. 11; viii. 18. An *ensign* is the *standard,* or *flag* used in an army. The elevation of the standard was a signal for assembling for war. God represents himself here as simply raising the standard, expecting that the nations would come at once. ¶ *And will hiss unto them.* This means that he would *collect* them together to accomplish his purposes. The expression is probably taken from the manner in which bees were hived. Theodoret and Cyril, on this place, say, that in Syria and Palestine, they who kept bees were able to draw them out of their hives, and conduct them into fields, and bring them back again, with

the sound of a flute or the noise of hissing. It is certain also that the ancients had this idea respecting bees. Pliny (lib. xi. ch. 20) says : Gaudent plausu, atque tinnitu aeris, eóque convocantur. 'They rejoice in a sound, and in the tinkling of brass, and are thus called together.' Ælian (lib. v. ch. 13) says, that when they are disposed to fly away, their keepers make a musical and harmonious sound, and that they are thus brought back as by a siren, and restored to their hives. So Virgil says, when speaking of bees:

Tinnitusque cie, et Matris quate cymbala circum.
Georg. iv. 64.

' On brazen vessels beat a tinkling sound,
  And shake the cymbals of the goddess round;
  Then all will hastily retreat, and fill
  The warm resounding hollow of their cell.'
Addison.

So Ovid :

Jamque erat ad Rhodopen Pangaeaque flumina ventum,
Acriferae comitum cum crepuere manus.
Ecce! novae coeunt volucres tinnitibus actae
Quosque movent sonitus aera sequuntur apes.
Fastor, lib. iii., 739.

See also Columella, lib. x. ch. 7 ; Lucan, lib. ix. ver. 288 ; and Claudian, *Panegyric. in sextum consul. Honorii,* ver. 259 ; comp. Bochart, *Hieroz.* P. ii. lib. iv. ch. x. pp. 506, 507. The prophets refer to that fact in several places, Isa. viii. 18; Zech. x. 8. The simple meaning is, that God, at his pleasure, would collect the nations around Judea like bees, *i.e.,* in great numbers. ¶ *The end of the earth.* That is, the remotest parts of the world. The most eastern nations known to them were probably the Babylonians, Medes, Persians, and perhaps the inhabitants of India. The general idea is, that he would call in the distant nations to destroy them. In Isa. vii. 18, Egypt and Assyria are particularly specified. This was in accordance with the prediction in Deut. xxviii. 49.

27. *None shall be weary.* In this verse and the following, the prophet

28 Whose arrows *are* sharp, and all their bows bent, their horses' hoofs shall be counted like flint, and their wheels like a whirlwind :
29 Their roaring *shall be* like a

lion, they shall roar like young lions ; yea, they shall roar, and lay hold of the prey, and shall carry *it* away safe, and none shall deliver *it.*

describes the condition of the army that would be summoned to the destruction of Judea. It would be composed of bold, vigorous, courageous men ; they would be unwearied by long and painful journies ; they would be fierce and violent ; they would come fully prepared for conquest. None would be *weary,* *i.e.,* fatigued with long marches, or with hard service ; Deut. xxv. 18 ; 2 Sam. xvi. 14. ¶ *Nor stumble.* They shall be chosen, select men ; not those who are defective, or who shall easily fall by any impediments in the way of their march. ¶ *None shall slumber.* They shall be unwearied, and indefatigable, pursuing their purpose with ever watchful vigilance—so much as not to be off their guard. They cannot be taken by surprise. ¶ *Neither shall the girdle of their loins be loosed.* The ancients wore a loose, large, flowing robe, or upper garment. When they laboured, or ran, it was necessary to *gird* this up round the body, or to lay it aside altogether. The form of expression here may mean, that they will not relax their efforts ; they will not unloose their girdle ; they will not unfit themselves for vigorous action, and for battle. *In* that girdle, with which they bound up their robes, the orientals usually carried their dirks and swords ; see Neh. iv. 18 ; Ezek. xxii. 15. It means that they should be fully, and at all times, prepared for action. ¶ *Nor the latchet of their shoes be broken.* They will be constantly prepared for marches. The shoes, sandals, or *soles* were attached to the feet, not by upper leather, but were girded on by thongs or strings ; see Notes on Matt. iii. 2.

28. *Whose arrows* are *sharp.* Bows and arrows were the common instruments of fighting at a distance. Arrows were, of course, made sharp, and usually pointed with iron, for the purpose of penetrating the shields or coats of mail which were used to guard against them. ¶ *And all their bows bent.* All

ready for battle. ¶ *Their horses' hoofs shall be counted like flint.* It is supposed that the ancients did not usually shoe their horses. Hence a hard, solid hoof would add greatly to the value of a horse. The prophet here means, that their horses would be prepared for any fatigue, or any expedition ; see a full description of horses and chariots in Bochart's *Hieroz.* P. i. lib. ii. ch. viii. ix. ¶ *And their wheels like a whirlwind.* That is, the wheels of their chariots shall be swift as the wind, and they shall raise a cloud of dust like a whirlwind. This comparison was very common, as it is now ; see *Bochart.* See, also, a magnificent description of a war-horse in Job xxxix. 19–25.

29. *Their roaring,* &c. Their battle cry, or their shout as they enter into an engagement. Such a *shout,* or cry, was common at the commencement of a battle. War was very much a personal conflict ; and they expected to accomplish much by making it as frightful and terrible as possible. A shout served not only to excite their own spirits, but to produce an impression of their numbers and courage, and to send dismay into the opposite ranks. Such *shouts* are almost always mentioned by Homer, and by other writers, in their accounts of battles. They are often mentioned, also, in the Old Testament ; Ex. xxxii. 18 ; Jos. vi. 10, 16, 20 ; Jer. l. 15 ; 1 Sam. xvii. 20, 52 ; 2 Chron. xiii. 15 ; Job xxxix. 25. ¶ *Like a lion.* This comparison is common in the Bible ; Jer. li. 38 ; Hos. xi. 10 ; Amos iii. 4 ; comp. Num. xxiii. 24. ¶ *Like young lions.* This variation of the expression, from the lion to the young lion, is very common. It is the Hebrew form of poetry, where the second member expresses little more than the first. Here the description is that of a lion, or more probably a *lioness* and her whelps, all ravenous, and all uniting in roaring for prey. The idea is, that the army that would come up would be

30 And in that day shall they roar against them like the roaring of the sea; and if *one* look unto the land, behold darkness *and* ¹ sorrow, and ² the light is darkened in the heavens thereof.

1 or, *distress.*   2 or, *when it is light, it shall be dark in the destructions thereof.*

greedy of plunder; they would rush on to rapine in a frightful manner.

30. *They shall roar against them.* The army that shall come up shall roar against the Jews. The image of *the roaring of the sea* indicates the great number that would come; that of the roaring of the *lion* denotes their fierceness and terror. ¶ *And if* one *look unto the land.* This expression has given some perplexity, because it is supposed not to be full or complete. The whole image, it has been supposed (see *Lowth*), would be that of looking *upward* to the heaven for help, and then to the land, or *earth;* comp. ch. viii. 22, where the same expression is used. But there is no need of supposing the expression defective. The prophet speaks of the vast multitude that was coming up and roaring like the tumultuous *ocean.* On *that* side there was no safety. The waves were rolling, and every thing was fitted to produce alarm. It was natural to speak of the *other* direction, as the *land,* or the shore; and to say that the people would look there for safety. But, says he, there would be no safety there. All would be darkness. ¶ *Darkness* and *sorrow.* This is an image of distress and calamity. There should be no light; no consolation; no safety; comp. ch. lix. 9; Amos v. 18, 20; Lam. iii. 2. ¶ *And the light is darkened,* &c. That which gave light is turned to darkness. ¶ *In the heavens thereof.* In the *clouds,* perhaps, or by the gloomy thick clouds. Lowth renders it, 'the light is obscured by the gloomy vapour.' The main idea is plain, that there would be distress and calamity; and that there would be no light to guide them on their way. On the one hand a roaring, raging multitude, like the sea; on the other distress, perplexity, and gloom. Thus shut up, they must perish, and their land be utterly desolate.

CHAPTER VI.

ANALYSIS OF THE CHAPTER.

THIS chapter contains a very sublime description of the manifestation of Jehovah to Isaiah, and of a solemn commission to him to declare his purposes to the Jews. It has been supposed by many to be a solemn *inauguration* to the prophetic office, and to have been the *first* of his prophecies. But this supposition is not to be considered as just. It is evident (Isa. i. 1) that he prophesied *before* the death of Uzziah, and there is reason to suppose that the order of *time* is observed in the previous chapters; see Introduction, § 2. The most probable supposition of the occasion of this prophecy, is this, that the people were extremely guilty; that they were strongly indisposed to listen to the message of the prophet, and that he was therefore favoured with this extraordinary commission in order to give his message more success and higher authority in the minds of the people. It is a new commission to make his message as impressive as possible—as if it came direct from the lips of the Almighty. The Jews say, that for this pretension that he had seen Jehovah, he was sawn asunder by *Manasseh.* And to this fact Paul has been supposed to refer in Heb. xi. 37, where he says of those who had been eminent in faith, 'they were sawn asunder;' see Introduction, § 2.

This vision is expressed in the language appropriate to Eastern monarchs. God is represented as sitting on a *throne,* and attended by ministers, here called seraphim. His throne is elevated, and the posture of sitting denotes dignity and majesty. The language of the description is taken from the temple. The image is that of God sitting in the most holy place. Surrounding him are seen the seraphim, and the cloud filling the temple. Isaiah is represented as without the temple, near the altar. The great altar of sacrifice stood directly in front of the temple, so that if the doors of the temple had been open, and the veil separating the holy from the most holy place had been withdrawn, he would have had a distinct view of the mercy-seat. That veil between is supposed to be withdrawn, and he is permitted directly to contemplate the sacred and solemn manifestation made in the immediate dwelling-place of God. The chapter comprises, properly, three parts.

I. The vision, ver. 1-4. Jehovah is seen upon a throne, clad in the manner of an ancient monarch, with a robe and a train which filled the whole temple. He sits as a king, and is adorned in the robes of royalty, ver. 1. He is encompassed with ministering spirits—with the seraphim, in the manner of a magnificent king, ver. 2.

They are seen, by the prophet, to be solemnly engaged in his worship, and to stand in the attitude of the most profound veneration, ver. 3. So awful and sublime was the worship, that even the posts of the temple were moved; the whole sacred edifice trembled at the presence of God, and at the voice of those who were engaged in his praise; and the whole temple was filled with the symbol of the Divine presence and majesty, ver. 4.

II. The *effect on the prophet*, ver. 5–7. He was overcome with a sense of his unworthiness, and felt that he could not live. He had seen Jehovah, and he felt that he was a ruined man, ver. 5. Yet one of the seraphim flew to the altar, and bore thence a live coal, and touched his lips, and assured him that his sin was taken away, and that he was pardoned, ver. 6, 7.

III. The *commission of the prophet*, ver. 8–13.

CHAPTER VI.

1. *In the year.* This naturally denotes a period *after* the death of Uzziah, though in the same year. The mention of the time was evidently made when the prophecy was composed, and it is to be presumed that the death of Uzziah *had* occurred at the time when the prophet saw this vision. If so, it is clear that this was not the *first* of his prophecies, for he saw his visions ' *in the days* of Uzziah;' ch. i. 1. The Chaldee, however, reads this: ' in the year when Uzziah was smitten with the leprosy;' and most of the Jewish commentators so understand it; 2 Chron. xxvi. 19, 20. The Rabbins say that the meaning is, that he then became *civilly* dead, by ceasing to exercise his functions as a king, and that he was cut off as a leprous man from all connection with the people, and from all authority; see Introduction, § 3. This is, doubtless, true; but still, the more natural signification is, that this occurred in the year in which he actually died. ¶ *I saw.* That is, he saw in a *vision;* see Introduction, § 7, (4.) A similar vision is described by Micaiah; 1 Kings xxii. 19; see also Amos vii. 1; viii. 1; ix. 1; Dan. vii. 13, &c. ¶ *The Lord.* In the original here the word is not *Jehovah*, but אֲדֹנָי *ădōnâi;* see Notes on ch. i. 24. Here it is applied to Jehovah; see also Ps. cxiv. 7, where it is also so applied; and see Isa. viii. 7, and Job xxviii. 28, where Jehovah calls

God inquires who will go for him to the people, and bear his message, and the prophet expresses his readiness to do it, ver. 8. The nature of the message is stated, ver. 9, 10. The *duration*— the state of things which he predicted would follow from this—is asked, and the answer is returned, ver. 11–13. It was to be until utter desolation should spread over the land, and the mass of the nation was cut off, and all were destroyed, except the small portion which it was necessary to preserve, in order to prevent the nation from becoming wholly extinct.

IN the year *a* that king Uzziah died, I saw *b* the Lord sitting upon a throne, high and lifted up, and ¹ his train filled the temple.

a 2Ki.15.7.   *b* 1Ki.22.19.   1 or, *the skirts thereof.*

---

himself *Adonai.* The word does not itself denote essential divinity; but it is often applied to God. In some MSS., however, of Kennicott and De Rossi, the word Jehovah is found. We may make two remarks here. (1.) That Isaiah evidently meant to say that it was Jehovah who appeared to him. He is expressly so called in ver. 5, 8, 11. (2.) It is equally clear, from the New Testament, that Isaiah saw The Messiah. John quotes the words in this chapter, ver. 10, as applicable to Jesus Christ, and then adds (John xii. 41), ' these things said Esaias when he saw his glory, and spake of him.' An inspired man has thus settled this as referring to the Messiah, and thus had established the propriety of applying to him the name Jehovah, *i.e.*, has affirmed that the Lord Jesus is Divine. Jerome says, that this vision was designed to represent the doctrine of the Trinity.— In John i. 18, it is said, ' No man hath seen God at any time; the only begotten Son, who is in the bosom of the Father, he hath declared him.' In Ex. xxxiii. 20, God says, ' Thou canst not see my face, for there shall no man see me and live;' see also 1 Tim. vi. 16. These passages may be reconciled with what is here said by Isaiah, in the following manner :—(1.) Isaiah does not say that he saw the Divine essence; and all that his words fairly imply, is, that he saw a manifestation, or vision of Jehovah— some striking symbolical representation

2 Above it stood the seraphims : each one had six wings ; with twain he covered his face, and with twain

he ^a covered his feet, and with twain he did fly.

of him. (2.) It was the manifestation of JEHOVAH in the person of the Messiah, of the 'only begotten Son who hath revealed or declared him,' that he saw. Such manifestations of God have been made often, and all that the declaration of Isaiah implies, of necessity, is, that he had a vision of God incarnate seated in glory, from whom he now received a new commission to go out and proclaim the truth to that wicked and rebellious generation. ¶ *Sitting upon a throne.* God is thus often represented as a king, sitting on a throne; 1 Kings xxii. 19; Ezek. xliii. 7; Jer. xvii. 12. ¶ *High and lifted up.* That is, the *throne ;* an indication of state and majesty. ¶ *And his train.* The word *train* שׁוּלָיו, properly signifies the skirt of a garment, or a robe ; Ex. xxviii. 33, 34. Here it is evidently designed as a representation of a large, flowing robe, that filled all the most holy part of the temple. The Orientals regarded such large robes as indicative of grandeur and state. The Messiah was seen seated on a throne as a king; clothed in a large, loose, flowing robe, in the manner of oriental monarchs, and surrounded by his ministers. The design of this magnificent vision was not only to impress the prophet with a sense of the holiness of God, but also to give additional weight to his commission, as having been derived immediately from the Divine majesty; comp. ver. 9, 10. It is remarkable that Isaiah attempts no representation of JEHOVAH himself. He mentions his robes; the throne; the seraphim; but mentions no form or appearance of God himself. In this there is great sublimity. There is enough mentioned to fill the mind with awe; there is enough concealed to impress as deeply with a sense of the Divine majesty. It is remarkable, also, that it is not the *usual* appearance of God in the temple to which he refers. That was the *Shekinah*, or visible symbol of God. That was on the mercy-seat, this was on a throne ; that was a cloud, of this no form is mentioned ; over that

the cherubim stretched forth their wings, over this stood the seraphim; that had no clothing, this was clad in a full flowing robe. ¶ *Filled the temple.* Probably, the most holy place only is intended. The large, full, magnificent robe seemed to fill up the entire holy of holies. Some have supposed that this vision was represented as appearing in the *heavens.* But the expression here evidently implies, that it was seen in the *temple* at Jerusalem. 2. *Above it.* Either above the throne, or above him. The LXX. render it, 'Round about him '—κύκλῳ αὐτοῦ. The Chaldee, 'The holy ministers stood on high in his presence.' ¶ *The seraphims.* The verb שָׂרַף *sărăph*, from which this word is derived, is uniformly translated *to burn*, and is used frequently ; see *Taylor.* The noun שָׂרָף denotes, according to Bochart, the *chersydros,* a serpent that lives in lakes and moist places ; but when those places are dried up, it becomes a land serpent, and then its bite is very fierce, and is attended with a most dreadful inflammation all over the body. Rabbi Solomon says, that ' serpents are called *seraphim* because they burn men with the poison of their teeth,' perhaps because the idea of *heat* and *poison* were connected. The word is applied to the fiery flying serpents which bit the children of Israel, and in imitation of which a brazen serpent was erected on a pole by Moses. It is translated 'a fiery serpent ' in Num. xxi. 8; Isa. xiv. 29; xxx. 6. In Deut. viii. 15; Num. xxi. 6, it is rendered 'fiery,' and in the passage before us, *seraphims.* The word שָׂרַף often occurs in the sense of *burning ;* Deut. xxix. 23; 2 Chron. xvi. 14; xxi. 19, &c. The LXX. render it *seraphim*, σεραφίμ ; so the Vulgate and the Syriac. The Chaldee, 'his holy ministers.' Probably it is now impossible to tell why this name was given to the representations that appeared to Isaiah. Perhaps it may have been from their *burning* ardour and zeal in the service of God ; perhaps from the *rapidity* of their

3 And [1]one cried unto another, and said, Holy, holy, holy is the

1 this cried to this.

LORD of hosts ; the [2]whole earth is full of his glory.

2 his glory is the fulness of the whole earth.

motion in his service—derived from the rapid motion of the serpent. Gesenius supposes that the name was derived from a signification of the word denoting *noble* or *excellent,* and that it was on this account applied to princes, and to celestial beings. Kimchi says, that the name was given with reference to their bright, shining appearance; comp. Ezek. i. 13; 2 Kings ii. 2; vi. 17. The word is applied to celestial beings no where else, except in this chapter. There is no reason to think that the seraphim described here partook of the *form* of the serpent, as the representation seems to be rather that of a man. Thus each one (ver. 2) is represented as covering his *face* and his *feet* with his wings—a description that does not pertain to the serpentine form. God is usually represented as surrounded or encompassed by heavenly beings, as his ministers ; Ps. civ. 4; Dan. vii. 10; 1 Kings xxii. 19; Ps. lxviii. 17; Heb. xii. 22. The idea is one of peculiar magnificence and grandeur. It is derived especially from the customs of monarchs, particularly Eastern monarchs, who had numerous princes and nobles to attend them, and to give magnificence to their court. ¶ *Each one had six wings.* *Wings* are emblematic of the *rapidity* of their movement; the number here, perhaps, denoting their celerity and readiness to do the will of God. ¶ *With twain he covered his face.* This is designed, doubtless, to denote the *reverence* and *awe* inspired by the immediate presence of God ; comp. Amos vi. 9, 10. The Chaldee adds, 'He covered his face *so that he could not see.*' To cover the face in this manner is the natural expression of reverence ; comp. Note on ch. lii. 15. And if the pure and holy seraphim evinced such reverence in the presence of Jehovah, with what profound awe and veneration should we, polluted and sinful creatures, presume to draw near to him! Assuredly *their* position should reprove our presumption when we rush thoughtlessly and irreverently into his presence, and should teach us to bow with lowly veneration

and deep humility; comp. Rev. iv. 9–11. ¶ *He covered his feet.* In a similar description of the cherubim in Ezek. i. 11, it is said that they covered *their bodies.* In Isaiah, the expression clearly denotes not the feet only, but the lower extremities. This was also an expression of reverence drawn from our conceptions of propriety. The seraphim stood covered, or as if *concealing themselves* as much as possible, in token of their nothingness and unworthiness in the presence of the Holy One. ¶ *He did fly.* He was quick to execute the commands of God. It may be observed, also, that among the ancients, *Mercury,* the messenger of Jupiter, was always represented with wings. Milton has copied this description of the seraphim :

'A seraph winged:—six wings he wore to shade
His lineaments divine; the pair that clad
Each shoulder broad, came mantling o'er his breast
With regal ornament; the middle pair
Girt like a starry zone his waist, and round
Skirted his loins and thighs with downy gold,
And colours dipt in heaven; the third his feet
Shadowed from either heel with feathered mail,
Sky-tinctured grain.'

Par. Lost, Book v.

3. *And one cried to another.* Heb. 'This cried to this.' That is, they cried to each other in alternate responses. One cried ' holy ;' the second repeated it ; then the third; and then they probably united in the grand chorus, ' Full is all the earth of his glory.' This was an ancient mode of singing or recitative among the Hebrews; see Ex. xv. 20, 21, where Miriam is represented as going before in the dance with a timbrel, and the other females as following her, and *answering,* or responding to her, Ps. cxxxvi. 1; comp. Lowth, *on the Sacred Poetry of the Hebrews,* Lect. xix. ¶ *Holy, holy, holy.* The *repetition* of a name, or of an expression, three times, was quite common among the Jews. Thus, in Jer. vii. 4, the Jews are represented by the prophet as saying, ' the temple of the Lord, the temple of the Lord, the temple of the Lord, are these.' Thus, Jer. xxii. 29: 'O earth, earth, earth, hear the word of the Lord ;' Ezek.

4 And the posts of the ¹door moved at the voice of him that cried, and the house was filled with smoke.

5 Then said I, Wo *is* me ! for I am ²undone ; because *a* I *am* a man

1 *thresholds.* 2 *cut off.* a Zec.3.1-7.

xxi. 27 : ' I will overturn, overturn, overturn ;' see also 1 Sam. xviii. 23 : ' O my son Absalom! my son, my son ;' see also the repetition of the form of benediction among the Jews, Num. vi. 24–26:

JEHOVAH bless thee and keep thee;
JEHOVAH make his face to shine upon thee,
 and be gracious unto thee;
JEHOVAH lift up his countenance upon thee,
 and give thee peace.

In like manner, the number *seven* is used by the Hebrews to denote a great, indefinite number ; then a full or complete number ; and then perfectness, completion. Thus, in Rev. i. 4; iii. 1; iv. 5, the phrase, ' the seven spirits of God,' occurs as applicable to the Holy Spirit, denoting his fulness, completeness, perfection. The Hebrews usually expressed the superlative degree by the repetition of a word. Thus, Gen. xiv. 10 : ' The vale of Siddim, *pits*, *pits* of of clay,' *i.e.*, was full of pits; see Nordheimer's *Heb. Gram.* § 822–824. The form was used, therefore, among the Jews, to denote *emphasis ;* and the expression means in itself no more than ' thrice holy ;' that is, supremely holy. Most commentators, however, have supposed that there is here a reference to the doctrine of the Trinity. It is not probable that the Jews so understood it ; but applying to the expressions the fuller revelations of the New Testament, it cannot be doubted that the words will express that. Assuming that that doctrine is true, it cannot be doubted, I think, that the seraphs laid the foundation of their praise in that doctrine. That there was a distinct reference to the second person of the Trinity, is clear from what John says, ch. xii. 41. No *argument* can be drawn directly from this in favour of the doctrine of the Trinity ; for the repetition of such phrases thrice in other places, is merely *emphatic*, denoting the superlative degree. But when the doctrine is *proved* from other places, it may be presumed that the heavenly beings were apprized of it, and that the foundation of their ascriptions of praise was laid in that.

The Chaldee has rendered this, ' Holy in the highest heavens, the house of his majesty ; holy upon the earth, the work of his power ; holy for ever, and ever, and ever, is the Lord of hosts.' The whole expression is a most sublime ascription of praise to the living God, and should teach us in what manner to approach him. ¶ *The* LORD *of hosts;* see Note, ch. i. 9. ¶ *The whole earth.* Marg. ' The earth is the fulness of his glory.' All things which he has made on the earth express his glory. His wisdom and goodness, his power and holiness, are seen every where. The whole earth, with all its mountains, seas, streams, trees, animals, and men, lay the foundation of his praise. In accordance with this, the Psalmist, in a a most beautiful composition, calls upon all things to praise him ; see Ps. cxlviii.

> Praise the Lord from the earth,
> Ye dragons, and all deeps:
> Fire and hail; snow and vapours;
> Stormy wind fulfilling his word:
> Mountains, and all hills;
> Fruitful trees, and all cedars;
> Beasts, and all cattle;
> Creeping things, and flying fowl.

4. *And the posts of the door.* Marg. ' Thresholds.' There is some difficulty in the Hebrew here, but the meaning of the expression is sufficiently apparent. It means that there was a tremour, or concussion, as if by awe, or by the sound attending the cry. It is evidently a poetic expression. ¶ *The house.* The temple. ¶ *Was filled with smoke.* There is here, doubtless, a reference to *the cloud* that is so often mentioned in the Old Testament as the visible symbol of the Divinity; see Note. Isa. iv. 5. A similar appearance is recorded when Solomon dedicated the temple; 1 Kings viii. 10; 2 Chron. v. 13; Ezek. x. 4.

5. *Wo is me !* That is, I am filled with overwhelming convictions of my own unworthiness, with alarm that I have seen JEHOVAH. ¶ *For I am undone.* Marg. ' Cut off.' Chaldee, ' I have sinned.' LXX., ' I am miserable, I am *pierced through.*' Syriac, ' I am

of unclean lips, and I dwell in the midst of a people of unclean lips ; for mine eyes have seen the King, the LORD of hosts.

6 Then flew one of the seraphims

1 *and in his hand a live coal.*

unto me, [1] having a live coal in his hand, *which* he had taken with the tongs from off the [a] altar ;

7 And he [2] laid *it* upon my mouth, and said, Lo, this hath touched thy

a Rev.8.3. 2 *caused it to touch.*

---

struck dumb.' The Hebrew word may sometimes have this meaning, but it also means *to be destroyed, to be ruined, to perish;* see Hos. x. 15; Zeph. i. 2; Hos. iv. 6; Isa. xv. 1. This is probably the meaning here, 'I shall be ruined, or destroyed.' The reason of this, he immediately states. ¶ *A man of unclean lips.* This expression evidently denotes that he was a *sinner,* and especially that he was unworthy either to join in the praise of a God so holy, or to deliver a message in his name. The vision; the profound worship of the seraphim; and the attendant majesty and glory, had deeply impressed him with a sense of the holiness of God, and of his own unfitness either to join in worship so holy, or to deliver the message of so pure a God. A similar effect is recorded in reference to Abraham; Gen. xviii. 27; see also Ex. iv. 10, 12; Jer. i. 6. A deep consciousness of guilt, in view of the holiness and majesty of God, is also described by Job:

I have heard of thee by the hearing of the ear,
But now mine eye seeth thee.
Wherefore I abhor myself,
And repent in dust and ashes.—Job xlii. 5, 6.

An effect also remarkably similar is described in reference to the apostle Peter, Luke v. 8 : " When Simon Peter saw it [the miracle which Jesus had wrought], he fell down at Jesus' knees, saying, Depart from me, for I am a sinful man, O Lord.' ¶ *A people of unclean lips.* A people who are unworthy to celebrate the praises of a God so pure and exalted. ¶ *Mine eyes have seen.* In Ex. xxxiii. 20, it is said: ' Thou canst not see my face ; for there shall no man see me and live ;' comp. John i. 18 ; 1 Tim. vi. 16. Perhaps it was in recollection of this, that Isaiah said he was undone. It is not, however, to be understood that the prophet saw JEHOVAH himself, but only the *symbol* of his presence. It was for this expression, according to the tradition of the Jews, that Manasseh took occasion

to put the prophet to death ; see Introduction, § 2. ¶ *The Lord of hosts.* JEHOVAH of hosts. John applies this to the Lord Jesus, and this proves that he is Divine ; see John xii. 41.

6. *Then flew.* Isaiah is represented as standing *out* of the temple ; the seraphim as *in* it. ¶ *Having a live coal.* The Vulgate renders this, 'A stone.' This is, probably, the original meaning of the word ; see 1 Kings xix. 6. It at first denoted a hot stone which was used to roast meat upon. It may also mean a coal, from its resemblance to such a stone. ¶ *From off the altar.* The altar of burnt-offering. This stood in the court of the priests, in front of the temple; see Notes on Matt. xxi. 12. The fire on this altar was at first kindled by the Lord, Lev. ix. 24, and was kept continually burning ; Lev. vi. 12, 13.

7. *And he laid* it *upon my mouth.* Marg. ' And he caused it to touch my mouth.' This is the more correct rendering. It was a slight, momentary touch, sufficient merely to be a *sign* or *token* that he was cleansed. ¶ *Thine iniquity is taken away.* That is, whatever obstacle there existed to your communicating the message of God to this people, arising from your own consciousness of unworthiness, is taken away. You are commissioned to bear that message, and your own consciousness of guilt should not be a hinderance. To understand this, it should be remembered that *fire,* among the orientals, has been always regarded as an emblem of *purifying.* Thus the Sabeans, the followers of Zoroaster in Persia, worshipped *fire,* as the emblem of a pure divinity ; see Mal. iii. 2, 3 ; comp. Matt. iii. 2. Every minister of the gospel, though conscious of personal unworthiness and unfitness, should yet go freely and cheerfully to his work, if he has evidence that he is called and commissioned by God. ¶ *Is purged.* Is purified, is removed —תְּכֻפַּר from כָּפַר *kâphăr, to cover, to*

lips, and thine iniquity is taken away, and thy sin purged.

8 Also I heard the voice of the

LORD, saying, Whom shall I send, and who will go for us? Then said I, [1] Here *am* I; send me.

[1] *Behold me.*

---

overlay; then to make an atonement for, to expiate, to cover sin, to pardon it, to affect or to procure forgiveness; and then to purify in general, to make whole; comp. Note on ch. xliii. 3. This does not mean, that the fire from the altar had any physical effect to purify him from sin, but that it was *emblematic* of such a purifying; and probably, also, the fact that it was taken from the altar of sacrifice, was to him an indication that he was pardoned through the *atonement*, or expiation there made. The Jews expected pardon in no other mode than by sacrifice; and the offering on their altar pointed to the great sacrifice which was to be made on the cross for the sins of men. There is here a beautiful *union* of the truths respecting sacrifice. The great doctrine is presented that it is only by sacrifice that sin can be pardoned; and the Messiah, the sacrifice himself, is exhibited as issuing the commission to Isaiah to go and declare his message to men.

8. *The voice of the* LORD. Heb. ' The voice of JEHOVAH.' He had before been addressed by one of the seraphim. ¶ *Whom shall I send, and who will go for us?* The change of number here, from the singular to the plural, is very remarkable. Jerome, on this place, says that it indicates the 'sacrament' of the Trinity. The LXX. render it, 'Whom shall I send, and who will go to this people?' The Chaldee, ' Whom shall I send to prophesy, and who will go to teach?' The Syriac, ' Whom shall I send, and who will go?' The Arabic has followed the LXX. The use of the plural pronouns *we* and *us*, as applicable to God, occurs several times in the Old Testament. Thus, Gen. i. 26: ' And God said, Let us make man in our image;' Gen. xi. 6, 7: ' And Jehovah said, Go to, let us go down, and there confound their language.' Such a use of the name of God in the plural is very common, but it is not clear that there is a reference to the doctrine of the Trinity. In some cases, it is evi-

dent that it cannot have such a reference, and that no *argument* can be drawn from the use of that plural form in favour of such a doctrine. Thus, in Isa. xix. 4, the expression ' a cruel lord,' is in the Hebrew in the plural, yet evidently denoting but one. The expression translated ' the most Holy One,' or ' the Holy,' is in the plural in Prov. ix. 10; xxx. 3. In 1 Sam. xix. 13, 16, the plural form is applied to a *household god*, or an image; and the plural form is applied to God in Job xxxv. 20, ' my Makers' (Heb.); Eccl. xii. 1, ' thy Creators' (Heb.); Ps. cxxi. 5, ' JEHOVAH is thy keepers' (Heb.); see also Isa. liv. 5; xxii. 2; xliii. 5; lxii. 5. This is called by grammarians *pluralis excellentiæ*, or the plural form indicating majesty or honour. It is, in all countries, used in reference to kings and princes; and as God often represents himself as a *king* in the Scriptures, and speaks in the language that was usually applied to kings in oriental countries, no argument can be drawn from expressions like these in defence of the doctrine of the Trinity. There are unanswerable arguments enough in support of that doctrine, without resorting to those which are of doubtful authority.

[That there are clearer intimations of the doctrines of the Trinity, than that contained in this and similar texts, is indubitable; but we must not set aside the early and somewhat obscure intimations of a doctrine, simply because it comes afterwards to be exhibited with more fulness. Such is the plan of revelation; and, instead of despising early announcements, or deeming them useless, because better *proofs* of the doctrine in question can be found, we ought to admire the wisdom and goodness of God in this gradual development of truth. The same interest belongs to the work of thus tracing the rise and progress of truth in the Bible, as belongs to that of him who traces rivers to their fountain head, and proves that, far up amid mountains all but inaccessible, rises the tiny stream, on whose broad waters, as it nears the sea, navies float in proud array. No more visible, in its earlier outflowings, is this doctrine of the Trinity; yet by and by it is the element on which Christianity floats, and in which it lives and moves. Thus we see the unity and harmony of revelation in all ages; the doctrine is the same; the degree of manifestation only is different. The necessity of preserving and exhibiting this unity, gives to these early intimations an unspeakable importance; though some, through an excess of candour, would abandon them to the enemy. This text, and its parallels, Gen. i. 26; iii. 22; xi. 7, exhibit the Trinity in Revelation's dawn indistinctly—partially disclosed—revealing only a *plurality* of persons. As the light increases, the *three* persons are seen moving under the lifting shadows, till, in the New Testament, baptism is commanded in the name of the Father, Son, and Holy Ghost; and the existence and functions of each person are clearly unfolded.

The problem is, to account for the use of the plural number in these passages, consistently with the unity of God. The doctrine of the Trinity seems to furnish an easy and beautiful solution; but this solution has been rejected, not by Unitarians only, but by Trinitarians not a few. Various hypotheses have been offered: as, that in the creation of man (Gen. i. 26), God associated with himself the heavens and the earth; or, that he consulted with angels; or, meant simply to indicate the importance of the work; or, perhaps, to supply a lesson of deliberation! These crudities are by most, however, long ago abandoned as untenable; and the solution most generally approved by such as reject that of the Trinity, is that furnished by an appeal to the *style of majesty*. Oriental princes, it is alleged, from the most ancient times, used the plural number in publishing their decrees; and such is the style of royalty to this day. But, unfortunately for this theory, there is no evidence whatever that ancient potentates employed this style. *The use of the plural number by kings and princes, is quite a modern invention.* The Bible does not furnish any example of it. Nor is there any evidence that God himself, on peculiarly solemn occasions, keeping out of sight, of course, the text in question, used such style; there is abundant evidence to the contrary, the singular number being used by Jehovah in the most sublime and awful declarations.

Besides this strange use of the plural number on the part of God himself, plural names (Elohim, Adonim) are frequently given to him by the writers of the Bible; the instances in which these names occur in the singular form, are the exceptions. The name usually rendered *God* in the English Bible, is almost invariably plural—Elohim, Gods. That these plural forms are used of idols, as well as of the true God, is admitted;

but as the peculiar names of the true God came, in process of time, to be applied to idols, so would the peculiar *form* of these names, and to tell us that these forms *are* so applied, is quite beside the question. We wish to know why, originally, such forms were applied to the *true* God; and it is no answer to tell us they are also applied to idols. 'There is nothing more wonderful in the name being so used *in the plural form*, than in its being so used *at all*. The same principle which accounts for the name GOD being given to heathen deities *at all*, will equally well account for its being given to them in the *particular form* in which it is applied to the true God.'—*Wardlaw.* This is pointed and decisive; and renders it needless to speculate here on the *mode* in which the name, or the plural form of it, came to be transferred to false gods, or great men. On this point, see Dr. J. Pye Smith's *Scripture Testimony to the Messiah.* It is further remarkable, that these plural appellatives are, for the most part, combined with verbs and adjectives in *the singular number*; as, 'Gods (he) *created*,' Gen. i. 1; and with plural adjuncts but rarely. Now, the ordinary rule of grammar might have been followed invariably, as well as in these few instances, or the departures from it might have been but few in number. That this is not the case, implies the existence of some very cogent reason, and cannot be regarded as the result, merely, of accident. To account for the use of these plural names, our author has recourse to what is called the *pluralis majestaticus*, or *excellentiæ*, according to which, nouns of dignity and majesty, in Hebrew, are said to be used in the plural form. But the existence of this *pluralis majestaticus* has never been proved. Its defence is now abandoned by the most skilful grammarians. Ewald repudiates it. And it is not a little remarkable, that some of the examples most relied on for proof of this *dignified plural*, are found, on examination, to possess nothing of the dignity, while more exact scholarship has reduced their plurality also. The examples alluded to, are, Exod. xxi. 29, 34; xxii. 10, 13; Isa. i. 3; where the supposed plural form denotes the owner of oxen, of sheep, and of asses!—fit partners, doubtless, to be honoured with the *pluralis majestaticus*. In truth, leaving out of view the plural appellatives applied to the Deity, *i.e.,* the appellatives in question, and which, therefore, cannot be adduced, there is no evidence whatever of this pretended rule. Had any rule of the kind existed, we should, without doubt, have found it exemplified, when kings, princes, nobles, generals, priests, and prophets figure on the sacred pages. That the *pluralis excellentiæ* is not applied to them, is sufficient proof of its non-

9 And he said, Go and tell this people, Hear ye ¹indeed, but understand not; and see ye ² indeed, but perceive not.

10 Make the heart of this people fat, and make their ears heavy,

1 in hearing, or without ceasing.

and shut their eyes: lest they see with their eyes, and hear with their ears, and understand with their heart, and convert, and be healed.

11 Then said I, LORD, how long? And he answered, Until the cities

2 in seeing.

---

existence; and should dispose rational and candid inquirers to acquiesce in the solution of the grammatical anomalies we have been considering, that is furnished by the doctrine of Trinity in Unity—the solution which, to say the least of it, is beset with fewest difficulties.]

The language here indicates the *design* for which this vision was shown to Isaiah. It was to commission him to exhibit truth that would be extremely unpleasant to the nation, and that would have the certain effect of hardening their hearts. In view of the nature and effect of this message, God is represented as inquiring who would be willing to undertake it? Who had courage enough to do it? Who would risk his life? And it indicates, perhaps, that there were *few* in the nation who would be willing to do it, and that it was attended with self-denial and danger. ¶ *Here am I.* This shows at once his confidence in God, and his zeal. He had been qualified for it by the extraordinary commission, and he was now ready to bear the message to his countrymen. In this attitude *we* should stand, prompt to deliver *any* message that God shall intrust to our hands, and to engage in *any* service that he calls on us to perform.

9. *And he said,* &c. The expressions which follow are those which denote hardness of heart and blindness of mind. They would hear the *words* of the prophet, but they would not understand him. They were so obstinately bent on iniquity that they would neither believe nor regard him. This shows the spirit with which ministers must deliver the message of God. It is their business to deliver the message, though they should know that it will neither be understood nor believed. ¶ *Hear ye indeed.* Heb. 'In hearing, hear.' This is a mode of expressing emphasis. This passage is quoted in Matt. xiii. 14; see Note on that place.

10. *Make the heart.* The word *heart*

here is used in the sense of the *mind*—to denote all their mental powers. It is commonly used in this sense in the Scriptures. ¶ *Fat.* Gross, heavy, dull, stupid. That is, go and proclaim such *truth* to them as shall have this effect—as shall irritate, provoke, enrage them; truth, whose delivery shall be attended, in their gross and corrupt hearts, with this blinding and infatuating influence. The effect would be produced by the corrupt state of their hearts, not by any native tendency of the truth, and still less by any direct Divine influence. 'Go, and *proclaim truth* to a corrupt and sensual people, and the *result* will be that they will not hear; they are so wicked that they will not attend to it; they will become even *more* hardened; yet go, and though certain of producing this effect, still proclaim it;' see this passage explained in the Notes on John xii. 40. ¶ *Their ears heavy.* Dull, stupid, insensible. ¶ *And shut their eyes.* The word here used means *to spread over,* and then to close. It denotes here the state of mind which is more and more indisposed to attend to the truth. ¶ *And be healed.* Be restored from the malady of sin; be recovered and pardoned. Sin is often represented as a painful, loathsome malady, and forgiveness as restoration from such a malady; Isa. xxx. 26; Ps. ciii.; xli. 3, 4; 2 Chron. vii. 14; Jer. iii. 22; xvii. 14. We may learn here, (1.) That the effect of truth is often to irritate men and make them more wicked. (2.) The truth must, nevertheless, be proclaimed. This effect is not the fault of the truth; and it is often well that the heart should be known, and the true effect should be seen.

11. *How long.* The prophet did not dare to pray that this effect should not follow. He asked merely therefore *how long* this state of things must continue; how long this message was to be

be wasted without inhabitant. and the houses without man, and the land be ¹utterly desolate ;

12 And the LORD have removed men ª far away, and *there be* a great forsaking in the midst of the land.

1 *desolate with desolation.*   a 2 Ki.25.21.

13 But yet in it *shall be* a tenth, and² *it* shall return, and shall be eaten: as a teil-tree, and as an oak, whose ³substance *is* in them when they cast *their leaves, so* the holy seed *shall be* the substance thereof.

2 or, *when it is returned and hath been broused.*

3 or, *stock* or *stem.*

---

delivered, and how long it should be attended with these painful effects. ¶ *Until the cities,* &c. They will remain perverse and obstinate until the land is completely destroyed by Divine judgments. Still the truth is to be proclaimed, though it is known it will have no effect in reforming the nation. This refers, doubtless, to the destruction that was accomplished by the Babylonians. ¶ *The houses without man.* This is strong language, denoting the certain and wide-spread desolation that should come upon the nation.

12. *And the Lord have removed,* &c. The land shall be given up to desolation. The men—the strength of the nation— shall be taken to a distant land. ¶ *And* there be *a great forsaking.* A great desolation ; the cities and dwellings shall be abandoned by the inhabitants ; comp. Isa. xvii. 2 ; Jer. iv. 29 ; Zeph. ii. 4.

13. *But yet,* &c. The main idea in this verse is plain, though there is much difficulty in the explanation of the particular phrases. The leading thought is, that the land should not be *utterly* and finally abandoned. There would be the remains of life—as in an oak or terebinth tree when the tree has fallen ; comp. Notes on ch. xi. 1. ¶ *A tenth.* That is, a tenth of the inhabitants, or a very small part. Amidst the general desolation, a small part should be preserved. This was accomplished in the time of the captivity of the Jews by Nebuchadnezzar. We are not to suppose that *literally* a tenth part of the nation would remain ; but a part that should bear somewhat the same proportion to the entire nation, in strength and resources, that a tenth does to the whole. Accordingly, in the captivity by the Babylonians we are told (2 Kings xxv. 12), that ' the captain of the guard left the poor of the land to be vinedressers and husbandmen ;' comp. 2 Kings xxiv.

14, where it is said, that ' Nebuchadnezzar carried away all Jerusalem, and all the princes, and all the mighty men of valour, even ten thousand captives, and all the craftsmen and smiths, none remained *save the poorer sort of the people of the land.*' Over this remnant, Nebuchadnezzar made Gedaliah king ; 2 Kings xxv. 22. ¶ *And it shall return.* This expression can be explained by the history. The prophet mentions the *return,* but he has omitted the fact that this remnant should go away ; and hence all the difficulty which has been experienced in explaining this. The history informs us, 2 Kings xxv. 26, that this remnant, this tenth part, ' *arose and came to Egypt, for they were afraid of the Chaldees.*' A part also of the nation was scattered in Moab and Edom, and among the Ammonites ; Jer. xl. 2. By connecting this idea with the prophecy, there is no difficulty in explaining it. It was of the return from Egypt that the prophet here speaks ; comp. Jer. xlii. 4–7. After this flight to Egypt they returned again to Judea, together with those who were scattered in Moab, and the neighbouring regions ; Jer. xl. 11, 12. This remnant thus collected was what the prophet referred to as *returning* after it had been scattered in Egypt, and Moab, and Edom, and among the Ammonites. ¶ *And shall be eaten.* This is an unhappy translation. It has arisen from the difficulty of making sense of the passage, by not taking into consideration the circumstances just adverted to. The word translated ' eaten ' means to feed, to graze, to consume by grazing, to consume by fire, to consume or destroy in any way, to remove.—*Gesenius* on the word בָּעַר. Here it means that this remnant shall be for *destruction ;* that judgments and punishments shall follow them after their return from Egypt and Moab. Even this remnant shall be the object of Divine displeasure, and shall feel the weight of his indignation ; see Jer. xliii.; xliv. ¶ *As a teil-tree.* The word *teil* means the *linden*, though there is no evidence that the linden is denoted here. The word here used—אֵלָה—is translated *elm* in Hos. iv. 13, but generally *oak; Gen.* xxxv. 4 ; Judg. vi. 11, 19 ; 2 Sam. xviii. 9, 14. It is here distinguished from the אַלּוֹן *oak.* It probably denotes the *terebinth*, or turpentine tree; for a description of which, see Notes on ch. i. 29. ¶ *Whose substance.* Marg. 'Stock' or 'Stem.' The margin is the more correct translation. The word usually denotes the upright shaft, stem, or stock of a tree. It means here, whose *vitality* shall remain ; *i.e.*, they do not entirely die. ¶ *When they cast* their leaves. The words 'their leaves' are not in the original, and should not be in the translation. The Hebrew means, 'in their falling '—or when they fall. As the evergreen did *not* cast its leaves, the reference is to the falling of the *body* of the tree. The idea is, that when the tree should fall and decay, still the life of the tree would remain. In the root there would be life. It would send up new *shoots*, and thus a new tree would be produced ; see Notes on ch. iv. 2 ; xi. 1. This was particularly the case with the terebinth, as it is with the fir, the chestnut, the oak, the willow, &c.; see Job xiv. 7. The idea is, that it would be so with the Jews. Though desolate, and though one judgment would follow another, and though even the remnant would be punished, yet the race would not be extinguished. It would spring up again, and survive. This was the case in the captivity of Babylon ; and again the case in the destruction of Jerusalem ; and in all their persecutions and trials since, the same has always occurred. They survive ; and though scattered in all nations, they still live as demonstrative of the truth of the Divine predictions ; Deut xxviii. ¶ *The holy seed.* The few remaining Jews. They shall not be utterly destroyed, but shall be like the life remaining in the root of the tree. No prophecy, perhaps, has been more remarkably fulfilled than that in this verse. 'Though the

cities be waste and the land be desolate, it is not from the poverty of the soil that the fields are abandoned by the plough, nor from any diminution of its ancient and natural fertility, that the land has rested for so many generations. Judea was not forced only by artificial means, or from local and temporary causes, into a luxuriant cultivation, such as a barren country might have been, concerning which it would not have needed a prophet to tell that, if once devastated and abandoned, it would ultimately revert to its original sterility. Phenicia at all times held a far different rank among the richest countries of the world ; and it was not a bleak and sterile portion of the earth, nor a land which even many ages of desolation and neglect could impoverish, that God gave in possession and by covenant to the seed of Abraham. No longer cultivated as a garden, but left like a wilderness, Judea is indeed greatly changed from what it was ; all that human ingenuity and labour did devise, erect, or cultivate, men have laid waste and desolate ; all the "plenteous goods " with which it was enriched, adorned, and blessed, have fallen like seared and withered leaves when their greenness is gone ; and stripped of its " ancient splendour," it is left *as an oak whose leaf fadeth :*—but its inherent sources of fertility are not dried up ; the natural richness of the soil is unblighted ; *the substance is in it,* strong as that of the teil tree or the solid oak, which retain their substance when they cast their leaves. And as the leafless oak waits throughout winter for the genial warmth of returning spring, to be clothed with renewed foilage, so the once glorious land of Judea is yet full of latent vigour, or of vegetative power, strong as ever, ready to shoot forth, even " better than at the beginning," whenever the sun of heaven shall shine on it again, and " the holy seed " be prepared for being finally "the substance thereof." *The substance that is in it*—which alone has here to be proved—is, in few words, thus described by an enemy : " The land in the plains is *fat* and *loamy,* and exhibits every sign of the *greatest fecundity.* Were nature assisted by art, the fruits of the most distant countries might be produced within the distance of

CHAPTER VII.

ANALYSIS.

PROBABLY no portion of the Bible has been regarded as so difficult of interpretation, and has given rise to so great a variety of expositions, as the prophecy which is commenced in this chapter, and which is closed in ch. ix. 7. The importance of the prophecy respecting the Messiah (vii. 14, *sq.*; viii. 7; ix. 1–7), is one reason why interpreters have been so anxious to ascertain the genuine sense; and the difficulties attending the supposition that there is reference to the Messiah, have been among the causes why so much anxiety has been felt to ascertain its true sense.

The prophecy which commences at the beginning of this chapter, is continued to ch. ix. 7. All this was evidently delivered at the same time, and constitutes a single vision, or oracle. This should have been indicated in the division of the chapters. Great obscurity arises from the arbitrary, and, in many instances, absurd mode of division into chapters which has been adopted in the Bible.

This chapter, for convenience of illustration, may be regarded as divided into four parts:—

I. The historical statement with which the whole account is introduced in ver. 1, 2. The principal occurrences referred to in the chapter took place in the time of Ahaz. For an account of his character and reign, see Introduction, § 3. He was an idolater, and erected the images, and altars, and groves of idolatry everywhere. He sacrificed to Baalim, and burned his children in the valley of Hinnom in honour of Moloch, and filled Jerusalem everywhere with abominations, 2 Kings xvi. 2–4; 2 Chron. xxviii. 1–4. For these abominations, he was delivered into the hand of the king of Syria, and was subjected to calamities from the threatened invasion of the united armies of Syria and Samaria. At this time Rezin was king of Syria, of which Damascus was the capital; and Pekah was king of Israel, or Samaria. These kings, during the concluding part of the reign of Jotham, the predecessor of Ahaz, had formed an alliance and had gone up towards Jerusalem to make war upon it, but had not been able to take it. The formation of this confederacy in the time of Jotham is distinctly declared in 2 Kings xv. 37. To this confederacy Isaiah refers in ver. 1, where he says that it occurred in the days of Jotham. The statement is made by Isaiah here, doubtless, in order to trace the important matter to which

he alludes to its commencement, though what he subsequently says had particular relation to Ahaz. Though the confederacy was formed in the time of Jotham, yet the consequences were of long continuance, and were not terminated until the defeat of Sennacherib in the time of Hezekiah; see ch. xxxvii. Isaiah here, in general, says (ver. 1) that they went up against Jerusalem, and could not take it. He may refer here to an expedition which they made in the time of Jotham, or he may design this as a *general* statement, indicating the result of *all* their efforts, that they could not take Jerusalem. If the latter is the proper interpretation, then the statement in ver. 1, was made by Isaiah at a subsequent period, and is designed to state *all* that occurred. It is more natural, however, to suppose that they made an attempt in the time of Jotham to take Jerusalem, but that they were unsuccessful. When Ahaz came to the throne, the alliance was continued, and the effort was renewed to take Jerusalem. Formidable preparations were made for the war, and an invading army came up upon the land. Many of the subjects of Ahaz were taken captive and carried to Damascus. Pekah slew in one day an hundred and twenty thousand men, and took two hundred thousand captives, and carried them towards Samaria. They were released from bondage by the solicitation of Oded, a prophet, who represented to them the impropriety of taking their brethren captive, and they were re-conveyed to Jericho; 2 Chron. xxviii. 5–15. At about the same time, the Assyrians took Elath, and retained it as a city belonging to them; 2 Kings xvi. 6. From the report of this strong alliance, and from the ravages which were committed by their united forces, Ahaz was alarmed, and trembled for the safety of Jerusalem itself, ver. 3. But instead of looking to God for aid, he formed the purpose of securing the alliance of the king of *Assyria*, and for this purpose sent messengers to Tiglath-pileser with professions of deep regard, and with the most costly presents which could be procured by exhausting the treasury (2 Kings xvi. 7, 8), to secure his friendship and co-operation. To this the king of Assyria agreed, and entered into the war by making an assault on Damascus; 2 Kings xvi. 9. It was this alliance, and the confidence which Ahaz had in it, that produced his answer to Isaiah (vii. 12), and his refusal to ask a sign of the Lord; and it was this alliance which subsequently involved Jerusalem in so much difficulty from the invasion of the Assyrians. The Assyrians, as might have been fore-

---

twenty leagues." "Galilee," says Malte Brun, "would be a paradise, were it in- | habited by an industrious people, under an enlightened government."'

seen, consulted their own advantage, and not the benefit of Ahaz. They meant to avail themselves of the opportunity of subduing, if possible, Judea itself; and, consequently, the land was subsequently invaded by them, and Jerusalem itself put in jeopardy. This consequence was distinctly foretold by Isaiah, ch. vii. 17–25; viii. 7, 8. Yet before the alliance was secured, Ahaz was in deep consternation and alarm, and it was at this point of time that Isaiah was sent to him, ver. 2, 3.

II. At this time of consternation and alarm, Isaiah was sent to Ahaz to assure him that Jerusalem would be safe, and that there was no real cause of alarm, ver. 3–9. His main object was to induce the monarch to repose confidence in Jehovah, and to believe that his kingdom, protected by God, could not be overthrown. Isaiah was directed to take with him his son, whose name (Shear-jashub—*the remnant shall return*) was itself a sign or pledge that the nation should not be *utterly* destroyed, and that, consequently, it could not become permanently subject to Syria or Samaria, ver. 3. He went to meet Ahaz at the upper pool, whither, probably, Ahaz had gone, attended by many of the court, to see whether it was practicable to stop the water, so as to prevent an enemy from procuring it; comp. 2 Chron. xxxii. 4. He directed him not to be afraid of the enemies that were coming, for they were like smoking, half-extinguished brands that could do little injury, ver. 4. He assured him that the purpose of the confederated kings should not be accomplished; that Jehovah had said that their design could not be established; and that the limits of their respective kingdoms should be the same that they were then, and should not be enlarged by the conquest and accession of Jerusalem—for that Damascus should still remain the capital of Syria, and Samaria of Ephraim, and that within sixty-five years the kingdom of Ephraim should be totally destroyed, and of course Jerusalem and Judah could not be permanently added to it. So far from having Jerusalem as a tributary and dependent province, as Remaliah had anticipated, his own kingdom was to be completely and finally destroyed, ver. 4–9. The design of all this was to allay the fears of Ahaz, and to induce him to put confidence in God.

III. A sign is promised—a proof or demonstration of the truth of what the prophet had spoken, ver. 10–17. To the assurance which Isaiah (ver. 4–9) had given of the safety of Jerusalem, Ahaz makes no reply. His whole conduct, however, shows that he is wholly unimpressed and unaffected by what he had said,

and that he put no confidence in the assurances of the prophet. He was not looking to God for aid, but to the king of Assyria; and he, doubtless, felt that if his aid was not obtained, his kingdom would be destroyed. He evidently had no belief in God, and no confidence in the prophet. His mind was in a restless, uneasy condition from the impending danger, and from uncertainty whether the aid of the king of Assyria could be procured. In order to induce him to turn his attention to God, the only Protector, and to calm his fears, Ahaz is commanded to ask of Jehovah any sign or miracle which he might desire, in order to confirm what the prophet had spoken, ver. 10, 11. This Ahaz refuses, ver. 12. He does it under the semblance of piety, and an unwillingness to appear to tempt Jehovah. But the *real* cause was, doubtless, that he had no confidence in Jehovah; he had no belief in what he had spoken; and he was secretly depending on the aid of the king of Assyria. His reply was couched in respectful terms, and had the appearance of piety, and was even expressed in language borrowed from the law, Deut. v. 16. Yet important purposes were to be answered, by there being a sign or proof that what the prophet had said should take place. It was important that Ahaz, as the king of Judah, and as the head of the people, should have evidence that what was said was true. It was important that a suitable impression should be made on those who were present, and on the mass of the people, inducing them to put confidence in Jehovah. It was important that they should look to future times; to the certain security of the nation, and to the evidence that the nation *must* be preserved until the great Deliverer should come. A sign is, therefore, forced upon the attention of Ahaz. The prophet tells him that however reluctant he may be to seek a sign, or however incredulous he might be, yet that Jehovah would give a token, proof, or demonstration, which would be a full confirmation of all that he had said. *That would be done which could be done only by Jehovah, and which could be known only by him;* and *that* would be the demonstration that Jerusalem would be safe from this impending invasion. A virgin should bear a son, and before he should arrive at years of discretion, or be able to discern the difference between good and evil—*i.e.*, in a short space of time, the land would be forsaken of both its kings, ver. 14–16. Who this virgin was, and what is the precise meaning of this prediction, has given, perhaps, more perplexity to commentators than almost any other portion of the Bible. The *obvious* meaning seems to be this. Some young female, who was then a virgin, and who was unmarried at the time when the prophet spoke, would conceive, and bear a son. *To* that son a name would be given, or his birth, in the circumstances in which it occurred, would make such a name proper, as would indicate that God was with them, and would be their Protector. Maternal affection would give the child the name Immanuel. The child would be nurtured up in the usual way among the Jews (ver. 15) until he would be able to discern between good and evil —*i e.*, until he should arrive at years of discretion. Between the time which should elapse from the conception of the child, and the time when he should arrive at an age to distinguish good from evil, that is in about three years, the land should be forsaken of the hostile kings, ver. 16. This seems to be the *obvious* meaning of this passage; and in this way only could this be a clear and satisfactory evidence to Ahaz of the certainty that the land would be entirely and permanently free from the invasion. God only could know this; and, therefore, this was a proof of the certainty of what Isaiah had said. But though this is the obvious meaning, and though such an event only could be a sign to Ahaz that the land would be forsaken of both the invading kings, yet there is no reason to doubt that the prophet *so couched* what he said—so expressed this by the direction of the Holy Ghost, as to be applicable also to another much more important event, which was to be *also*, and in a much more important sense, a sign of the protection of God —the birth of the Messiah. He, therefore, selected words which, while they were applicable to the event immediately to occur, would also cover much larger ground, and be descriptive of more important events—and events which were *in the same line and direction* with that immediately to come to pass—the certainty of the Divine protection, and of ultimate freedom from all danger. The language, therefore, has, at the commencement of the prophecy, a fulness of meaning which is not entirely met by the immediate event which was to occur, and which can be entirely fulfilled only by the great event which Isaiah ever had in his eye—the birth of the Messiah. The mind of Isaiah would very naturally be carried forward to that future event. In accordance with the laws of what may be called *prophetic suggestion* or *association*, see Introduction, §7, iii. (3), and which are constantly exemplified in Isaiah, his mind would fix on better times, and more happy events. He saw the birth of a child in a future age, of which this was but the emblem. That was to be born literally of a virgin. His *appropriate* name, from his nature, and from his being the evidence of the Divine favour and presence, would be *Imma-*

nuel—as the appropriate name of this child would be Immanuel, because he would be the pledge of the Divine protection and presence. The idea is, that there is a *fulness of meaning* in the words used, which will apply to future events more appropriately than to the one immediately before the writer. That there is rapid transition—a sudden carrying the mind forward to rest on a future more important event, which has been *suggested* by the language used, and which is in the mind of the speaker or writer so much more important than that which was first mentioned, as completely to absorb the attention. The reasons for the view here given are detailed at length in the Notes on ch. vii. ver. 14-16.

IV. The prophet had thus far directed all his efforts to convince Ahaz that from the quarter from which they had apprehended danger, nothing was to be feared. He now, however (ver. 17-25), proceeds to assure them that danger would come from the quarter where they least expected it—from the very quarter where Ahaz was seeking aid and deliverance—the king of Assyria. He assures him that the king of Assyria would take advantage of the alliance, and, under pretence of aiding him, would turn every thing to his own account, and would ultimately bring desolation on the land of Judah. The calamities which would follow from this unhappy alliance, the prophet proceeds to state and unfold, and with that concludes the chapter. It is evident from 2 Kings xvi. 7, that the discourse of Isaiah made no impression on the mind of Ahaz. He sent messengers with valuable presents to Tiglath-pileser, king of Assyria. Tiglath-pileser professedly entered into the views of Ahaz, and promised his aid. He went up against Damascus and took it (2 Kings xvi. 9), after Ahaz had suffered a terrible overthrow from the united armies of Rezin and Pekah. The land of Samaria was laid waste by him, and a large part of the inhabitants carried captive to Assyria, 2 Kings xv. 29. Thus the prediction of Isaiah, that the land should be forsaken by two kings (ch. vii. 16), was fulfilled. But this deliverance from their invasion was purchased by Ahaz at a vast price. The real purpose of Tiglath-pileser was not to aid Ahaz, but to make him and his kingdom dependent and tributary (2 Chron. xxviii. 21); and this alliance was the first in the succession of calamities which came upon Judah and Jerusalem, and which ended only under Hezekiah by the entire destruction of the army of Sennacherib ; see ch. xxxvii. During the remainder of the reign of Ahaz, he was tributary to Assyria; and when Hezekiah (2 Kings xvii. 7) endeavoured to throw off the yoke of Assyria, the attempt involved him in war; subjected his kingdom to invasion; and was attended with a loss of no small part of the cities and towns of his kingdom; see 2 Kings xviii.; xix.; xx.; Isa. xxxvi.; xxxvii.; comp. Notes on ch. viii.; x. 28–32. Thus the second part of this prophecy was fulfilled. The fuller statement of these important transactions will be found in the Notes on the various passages which relate to these events.

AND *a* it came to pass in the days of Ahaz the son of Jotham, the

CHAPTER VII.

1. *In the days of Ahaz.* Ahaz began to reign about 738 years before Christ. By a comparison of 2 Kings xvi. 5, &c., with 2 Chron. xxviii. 5, &c., it will be seen that Judea was twice invaded by Rezin and Pekah in the reign of Ahaz; see the Analysis of the chapter. ¶ That *Rezin,* &c. This confederacy was formed in the time of Jotham ; 2 Kings xv. 37. But it was not carried into execution during his reign. It is evident from this place, that it was executed in the early part of the reign of Ahaz ; probably in the first or second year of his reign. ¶ *Syria—*אֲרָם *Arâm,* so called from Aram (Gen. x. 22, 23), a son of Shem, and who peopled its chief provinces. It comprehended the country lying between the Euphrates east, the Mediterranean west, Cilicia north, and Phenicia, Judea, and Arabia south ; see Notes on ch. xvii. Syria of the two rivers is Mesopotamia. Syria of Damascus, so called because Damascus was its capital, extended eastward along Mount Libanus, but its limits varied according to the power of the princes of Damascus. After the reign of the Seleucidae, Syria came to denote the kingdom or region of which Antioch was the capital. Here it denotes the Syria lying around Damascus, and of which Damascus was the capital.—*Calmet.* ¶ *King of Israel.* Of the ten tribes, called the kingdom of Israel, or Samaria ; Note, ch. i. 1. ¶ *Went up.* Jerusalem was situated on hills, and on the highest part of the land. But it is possible that this language is derived from the fact that it was the capital. The language is used even when the region from which the traveller comes

son of Uzziah king of Judah, *that* Rezin the king of Syria, and Pekah the son of Remaliah, king of Israel, went up toward Jerusalem, to war against it, but could not prevail against it.

2 And it was told the house of David, saying, Syria [1] is confederate with Ephraim : and his heart was moved and the heart of his

a 2 Kings 16.5.   1 *resteth on.*

does not lie lower than the city. Thus it is not uncommon to speak of *going up* to London, Paris, &c. ¶ *Could not prevail.* Heb. ' Could not fight against it,' *i.e.,* with happy result, or with success. He was not able to take it. That the allied kings really besieged Ahaz, is evident from 2 Kings xvi. 5 : They ' came up to Jerusalem to war, and they besieged Ahaz, but they could not overcome him.' The reason why they could not take Jerusalem was, probably, not only because it was a strong place and well defended, but because there was intelligence that their own dominions were threatened with an invasion by the Assyrians, and they could not protract their siege of Jerusalem long enough to take it.

2. *And it was told the house of David.* That is, the royal family ; or the king and princes ; the government. Ahaz was the descendant and successor of David. ¶ *Syria is confederate with Ephraim.* Ephraim was one of the tribes of Israel, and the kingdom of Israel was often called *Ephraim,* or the kingdom of Ephraim ; in the same way as the tribes of Judah and Benjamin were called the kingdom of Judah. The phrase, ' is confederate with,' is in Hebrew ' resteth on ;' see margin. The meaning is, that Syria was *supported by* Ephraim, or was allied with Ephraim. The kingdom of Israel, or Ephraim, was situated *between* Syria and Jerusalem. Of course, the latter could not be attacked without marching through the former, and without their aid. In this sense it was that Syria, or the Arameans, relied or *rested* on Ephraim. Though Syria was by far the stronger power, yet it was not strong enough to attack Jerusalem

people, as the trees of the wood are moved with the wind.

3 Then said the LORD unto Isaiah, Go forth now to meet Ahaz, thou

1 *i.e., the remnant shall return.*

and [1] Shear-jashub thy son, at the end of the conduit of the upper pool, in the [2] highway of the fuller's field ;

2 or, *causeway.*

---

had the kingdom of Israel been opposed to it. ¶ *And his heart.* The heart of the king—of Ahaz. ¶ *Was moved as the trees of the wood.* This is a very beautiful and striking image. It expresses universal trembling, consternation, and alarm, as the trees are moved *together* when the wind passes violently over them. A similar expression is found in Ovid—in *Canaces*, Epist. xi. ver. 76, 77:

Ut quatitur tepido fraxina virga noto
Sic mea vibrari pallentia membra videres.

3. *Then said the Lord.* In regard to the purposes for which Isaiah was sent to meet Ahaz, and the reason why this place was selected, see the Analysis of the chapter. ¶ *Thou and Shear-jashub.* The meaning of the name *Shear-jashub* is, 'the remnant shall return.' The names which Isaiah gave to his sons were significant or emblematic of some important events which were to occur to the Jews. They were for *signs* to the people, and had been given in order to keep before the nation the great truth that God was their protector, and that however much they might suffer or be punished, yet the nation would not be totally destroyed until the great Deliverer should come ; see Note on ver. 14, and ch. viii. 3. Why this name was given to this son, or on what occasion, is not certainly known. It is probable, however, that was with reference to the future calamities and captivity of the Jews, denoting that a part of the people would return to the land of their fathers ; comp. ch. x. 21, 22. The name was a remembrancer given by him as a prophet, perhaps, some time before this, that the nation was not to be wholly annihilated—a truth which Isaiah everywhere keeps before them in his prophecies ; comp. Note ch. vi. 13. *Why* Shear-jashub accompanied Isaiah now is not recorded. It might be as a pledge to Ahaz of the purpose of the Lord, that the people should not be

destroyed. Ahaz may have been apprized of the reason why the name was given, and his presence might serve to mitigate his fears. ¶ *At the end of the conduit.* A *conduit* is a pipe, or other conductor of water. The water flowed from a fountain, but was conducted to different receptacles for the supply of the city. ¶ *Of the upper pool.* Or the upper receptacle, or pond. Robinson (*Bib. Researches,* i. p. 483) and Pocoke (*Descr. of the East,* ii. p. 25, 26) suppose that the upper and lower pools referred to by Isaiah, were on the west side of the city, the ruins of which now remain. The upper pool is now commonly called by the monks *Gihon,* and by the natives *Birket el Mamilla.* It lies in the basin forming the head of the valley of Hinnom or Gihon, about seven hundred yards west-northwest from the Yâfa gate, on the west of Jerusalem. The sides of this pool are built of hewn stones laid in cement, with steps at the corners by which to descend into it. The bottom is level. The dimensions are as follows :

Length from east to west.....316 Eng. feet.
Breadth at the west end......200
Breadth at the east end.......218
Depth at each end.............. 18

There is no water-course, or other visible means, by which water is now brought into this reservoir, but it is probable that it was filled in the rainy seasons by the waters which flowed from the higher ground round about. From this upper pool a part of the water was conveyed into the city to the pool of Hezekiah, lying within the walls, and situated some distance to the north-eastward of the Yâfa gate. 'Hezekiah stopped the upper water-course of Gihon, and brought it straight down to the west side of the city of David ;' 2 Chron. xxxii. 30 ; comp. Notes on ch. xxii. 9. This upper pool had a trench or 'conduit,' and a considerable part of the waters were allowed to flow through this to the lower pool. The 'lower pool' is

4 And say unto him, Take heed, and be quiet; fear not, [1] neither be faint-hearted for the two tails of these smoking firebrands, for the

fierce anger of Rezin with Syria, and of the son of Remaliah.

5 Because Syria, Ephraim, and

[1] *let not thy heart be tender.*

mentioned in the Old Testament only once, and that by Isaiah (ch. xxii. 9). and there without any hint of its locality. There is now a large lower pool on the western side of Jerusalem, which is not improbably the one intended, and which stands in contrast with the one here mentioned. This pool is called by the Arabs *Birket es-Sultân.* There is, at present, no other pool in the vicinity of Jerusalem to which the description in Isaiah can be well applied. This reservoir is situated in the valley of Hinnom or Gihon, southward from the Yâfa gate. Its northern end is nearly upon a line with the southern wall of the city. The pool was formed by throwing strong walls across the bottom of the valley, between which the earth was wholly removed. A road crosses on the causeway at the southern end. The following are the measurements of this pool:

Length along the middle......592 Eng. feet.
Breadth at the north end.....245
Breadth at the south end.....275
Depth at north end............ 35
Depth at south end............ 42

This reservoir was probably filled from the rains, and from the superfluous waters of the upper pool. It is now in ruins. The water from this pool would flow off into the valley of Hinnom, and thence into the valley of Jehoshaphat or Kedron, or subsequently into the pool of Hezekiah, situated *within* the city; see Notes on ch. xxii. 9, 11. Why Ahaz was at that place, the prophet does not say. It is possible he was examining it, to see whether the fountain could be stopped up, or the water diverted, so that it could not be used by the enemy, and so that they could be prevented from maintaining a protracted siege; comp. 2 Chron. xxxii. 4. It is probable that the king had gone to this place attended by many of his counsellors, and as this was the main source of the supply of water to the city, a multitude would be there, and Isaiah could have an opportunity not only to deliver his message to Ahaz

and his court, but in the presence of a considerable concourse of people, and might thus inspire confidence among the alarmed and dejected inhabitants of the city. ¶ *In the highway of the fuller's field.* In the place occupied as a situation on which to spread, or suspend cloth that was bleached, or dyed. This situation would be chosen because much water was needed in bleaching or dyeing cloth. The name 'highway' denotes the public path, or road that led to this field. Probably, on one side of this highway was the aqueduct, and on the other the fuller's field. Of the fuller's field, Eusebius and Jerome merely say that it was shown in their day in the suburbs of the city.—*Onom.* art. *Ager Fullonis.*

4. *Take heed.* Heb. 'Keep thyself;' that is, from fear. ¶ *Neither be faint-hearted.* Heb. 'Let not thy heart be tender;' that is, let it not be easily moved; be strong, fearless. ¶ *For the tails,* &c. There is much beauty and force in this comparison. The *design* of Isaiah is to diminish the fear of Ahaz. Instead, therefore, of calling them *firebrands*—burning and setting on fire every thing in their way—he calls them the *tails, i.e.,* the *ends,* or remains of firebrands—almost consumed themselves, and harmless. And instead of saying that they were *burning* and *blazing,* he says that they were merely *smoking*—the half-burnt, decaying remains of what might have been once formidable. The prophet also is just about to announce their approaching destruction by the Assyrians; see ver. 8. He therefore speaks of them as already almost extinguished, and incapable of doing extensive injury. ¶ *Son of Remaliah.* Pekah, ver. 1. 'It is by way of contempt that the king of Israel is not called by his own name. The Hebrews and Arabians, when they wish to speak reproachfully of any one, omit his proper name and call him merely the son of this or that, especially when his father is but little known or respected. So Saul names David, in con-

the son of Remaliah have taken evil counsel against thee, saying,

6 Let us go up against Judah, and ¹vex it, and let us make a breach therein for us, and set a king in the midst of it, *even* the son of Tabeal:

7 Thus saith the Lord GOD, It shall not stand, neither shall it come to pass.

8 For the head of Syria *is* Damascus, and the head of Damascus *is* Rezin; and within threescore and five years shall Ephraim be broken, that ²it be not a people.

1 or, weaken.   2 from a.

tempt, the son of Jesse ; 1 Sam. xx. 27, 31.'—*Hengstenberg.*

6. *And vex it.* Marg. ' Weaken it.' Probably the word means to throw into consternation or fear, by besieging it.—*Gesenius.* ¶ *And let us make a breach therein.* Let us break down the walls, &c. ¶ *And set a king.* Subdue it, and make it tributary to the allied kingdoms of Syria and Ephraim. ¶ *The son of Tabeal.* Nothing more is known of this person. He might have been some disaffected member of the royal family of David, who had sought the aid of Rezin and Pekah, and who would be allied to them, or tributary to them. It is possible that he had already a party in Jerusalem in his favour ; comp. ch. viii. 12. Probably, the two kings wished to cut off such portions of the territory of Judah as should be convenient to them, and to set a king over the remainder, who should be under their control ; or to divide the whole between themselves, by setting up a king who would be tributary to both.

8. *For the head of Syria.* The *capital.* The *head* is often used in this sense. ¶ Is *Damascus.* For an account of this city, see Notes on ch. xvii. 1; comp. Notes, Acts ix. 2. The sense of this passage is, ' Do not be alarmed as if Rezin was about to *enlarge* his kingdom, by taking Judea and making Jerusalem his capital. The revolution which these kings contemplate cannot be accomplished. The kingdoms of Syria and Israel shall not be enlarged by the conquest of Judah. The centre of their power shall remain where it is now, and their dominion shall not be extended by conquest. The capital of Syria is, and shall continue to be, Damascus. The king of Syria shall be confined within his present limits, and Jerusalem therefore shall be safe.' ¶ *The head of Damascus.* The *ruler,* or *king* of

Damascus is Rezin. ¶ *And within threescore and five years.* There has been some inquiry why *Ephraim* is mentioned here, as the prophet in the former part of the verse was speaking of *Syria.* But it should be remembered that he was speaking of Syria and Ephraim as *confederate.* It was natural, therefore, to intimate, in close connection, that no fear was to be apprehended from either of them. There has been much difficulty experienced in establishing the fact of the exact fulfilment of this, and in fixing the precise event to which it refers. *One* catastrophe happened to the kingdom of Ephraim or Israel within one or two years of this time, when Tiglath-pileser, king of Assyria, invaded the land and carried no small part of the people to Assyria ; 2 Kings xv. 29. *Another* occurred in the next reign, the reign of Hoshea, king of Israel, when Shalmaneser king of Assyria took Samaria, and carried Israel away captive into Assyria ; 2 Kings xvii. 1–6. This occurred in the twelfth year of Ahaz. But that the Israelites remained in Samaria, and kept up the forms of a civil community, and were not finally carried away until the time of Esarhaddon, is evident ; comp. 2 Chron. xxxiv. 6, 7, 33 ; xxxv. 18 ; 2 Kings xxiii. 19, 20. Manasseh, king of Judah, was taken captive by the king of Assyria's captains (2 Chron. xxxiii. 2) in the twenty-second year of his reign ; that is, sixty-five years from the second year of Ahaz, when this prophecy is supposed to have been delivered. And it is also supposed that at this time Esarhaddon took away the remains of the people in Samaria, and put an end to the kingdom, and put in their place the people who are mentioned in Ezra iv. 3.—*Dr. Jubb, as quoted by Lowth.* The entire extinction of the people of Israel and the kingdom did

9 And the head of Ephraim *is* Samaria, and the head of Samaria *is* Remaliah's son. ¹ If ye will not

believe, surely ye shall not be established.

not take place till Esarhaddon put new colonists from Babylon, and from Cuthah, and from Ava, and from Hamath, and from Sepharvaim in the cities of Samaria, instead of the children of Israel ; 2 Kings xvii. 24 ; comp. Ezra iv. 2, 10. Long before this, indeed, the power of the kingdom had been on the wane ; a large portion of the people had been removed (2 Kings xvii. 5, 6, 18) ; but its *entire* extinction was not accomplished, and the kingdom utterly destroyed, until this was done. Till this occurred, the land might be still regarded as in the possession somewhat of its former people, and all hopes of their rising again to the dignity of a kingdom was not extinguished. But when foreigners were introduced, and took possession of the land ; when all the social organization of the ancient people was dissolved ; then it might be said that ' Ephraim was *for ever* broken,' and that it was demonstrated that it 'should be no more a people.' Its inhabitants were transferred to a distant land, no longer to be organized into a peculiar community, but to mingle with other people, and finally all traces of their origin as Jews were to be lost. This event, of placing the foreigners in the cities of Samaria, occurred just sixty-five years after it had been predicted by Isaiah.—*Archbishop Usher.*

It may be asked here, how the statement of what was to occur at so remote a period as sixty-five years could be any consolation to Ahaz, or any security that the designs of the kings of Syria and Samaria should *then* fail of being accomplished ? To this we may reply, —(1.) It was the assurance that Jerusalem could not be finally and permanently reduced to submission before these dreaded enemies. *Their* power was to cease, and of course Jerusalem had nothing *ultimately* and *finally* to dread. (2.) The design was to inspire confidence in Jehovah, and to lead Ahaz to look directly to him. If these formidable powers could not ultimately prevail, and if there was a certain prediction that they should be destroyed,

then it was possible for God, if Ahaz would look to him, *now* to interpose, and save the city. To inspire that confidence in Jehovah was the leading purpose of Isaiah. (3.) This prediction is in accordance with many which occur in Isaiah, that all the enemies of the people of God would be *ultimately* defeated, and that God, as the head of the theocracy, would defend and deliver his people ; see Notes on ch. xxxiv. A kingdom that was so soon to be destroyed as Ephraim was, could not be an object of great dread and alarm. Rosenmüller conjectures, that Isaiah refers to some unrecorded prophecy made before his time, that in sixty-five years Israel would be destroyed ; and that he refers here to that prophecy to encourage the heart of Ahaz, and to remind him that a kingdom could not be very formidable that was so soon to come to an end. At all events, there is no contradiction between the prophecy and the fulfilment, for *within* the time here mentioned, Ephraim ceased to be a kingdom. The ancient Jewish writers, with one consent, say, that Isaiah referred here to the prophecy of Amos, who prophesied in the days of Uzziah, and whose predictions relate mainly to the kingdom of Israel. But as Amos, does not specify any particular *time* when the kingdom should be destroyed, it is apparent that Isaiah here could not have referred to any *recorded* prophecy of his. ¶ *Be broken.* Its power shall be destroyed ; the kingdom, as a kingdom, shall come to an end.

9. *And the head of Ephraim.* The capital city of Ephraim, or of Israel. ¶ *Is Samaria.* This was long the capital of the kingdom of Israel. For a description of this city, see Notes on ch. xxviii. 1. The meaning of the prophet is, that Samaria should *continue* to be the head of Ephraim ; that is, Jerusalem should not be made its capital. ¶ *If ye will not believe, surely ye shall not be established.* There is considerable variety in the interpretation of these words, though the general sense is evident. The Chaldee renders them,

10 Moreover, [1] the LORD spake
again unto Ahaz, saying,
   11 Ask thee a sign [a] of the LORD
thy God: ask [2] it either in the depth,
or in the height above.

1 *And the LORD added to speak.*
a ch 38.7,22.   2 or, *make thy petition deep.*

' If ye will not believe *the words of the
prophet,* ye shall not remain.' It is
probable that Ahaz, who was greatly
alarmed, and who trembled at the formidable power of Syria and Israel
united, received the annunciation of
the prophet with much distrust. He
was anxious about the means of defence,
but did not trust in the promise of God
by the prophet. Isaiah, therefore, assures him, that if he did not believe
him; if he did not put confidence in
God, and his promises, he *should* not
be protected from Syria and Ephraim.
They would come and destroy his kingdom. ' You have no occasion,' is the
language of the prophet, ' to fear. God
has resolved to protect you, and no portion of your land shall be taken by your
enemies. Nevertheless, in order that
you may obtain deliverance, you must
believe his promise, and put your confidence in him, and not in the aid of the
Assyrians. If you do this, your mind
shall be calm, peaceful, and happy.
But if you do *not* do this; if you rely
on the aid of Assyria, you shall be
troubled, alarmed, unsuccessful, and
bring ruin upon yourself and nation.'
This, therefore, is an exhortation to
confide solely in the promises of God,
and is one of the instances constantly
occurring in the Old Testament and
the New, showing, that by faith or
confidence in God only, can the mind
be preserved calm when in the midst
of dangers.
   11. *Ask thee.* Ask for *thyself;* ask
a sign that shall be convincing to *thyself,* since thou dost not fully credit the
words of the prophet. It is evident
that the words of the prophet had made
no impression on the mind of Ahaz.
God, therefore, proposes to him to ask
any *proof* or *demonstration* which he
might select; any thing that would be
an indication of Divine power that
should put what the prophet had said
beyond doubt. Had Ahaz put confidence in God, he would have believed
what the prophet said without miraculous proof. But he had no such confidence. The prophet, therefore, proposes that he should ask *any* miraculous demonstration that what he said
would come to pass. This proposition
was made, probably, not so much from
respect to Ahaz as to leave him without
excuse, and in order that *the people*
might have the assurance that the city
and kingdom were safe. ¶ *A sign.* A
demonstration that shall confirm the
promise now made, and that shall be
an evidence that Jerusalem shall be
safe. The word used here, and translated *sign*—אוֹת *oth*—means a *flag*, or
standard, Num. ii. 2; a *memorial* or
pledge of a covenant, Gen. xvii. 11 ;
any *pledge, token,* or *proof* of a Divine
mission, Judg. vi. 17; or a miracle
wrought in attestation of a Divine promise or message. This is its sense
here. That which Isaiah had spoken
seemed highly improbable to Ahaz, and
he asked him to seek a proof of it, if
he doubted, by any prodigy or miracle.
It was customary for miracles or prodi-
gies to be exhibited on similar occasions; see ch. xxxviii. 7, where the
shadow on the dial of this same Ahaz
was carried backward ten degrees, in
proof of what the prophet Isaiah had
spoken; comp. 1 Sam. ii. 27–34; 1
Kings xiii. 1–3; Ex. iii. 12; Judg. vi.
36–40. That the word here refers to
some event which could be brought
about only by Divine power, is evident
from the whole connection. No mere
natural occurrence could have satisfied
Ahaz, or convey to the people a demonstration of the truth of what the prophet was saying. And if the prophet
had been unable or unwilling to give a
miraculous sign, where is the fitness of
the answer of Ahaz? How could he be
regarded as in any way tempting God
by asking it, unless it was something
which God only could do? And how
could the prophet bring the charge (ver.
13), that he had not merely offended
men, but God also? It is clear, therefore, that Isaiah was conscious that he
was invested by God with the power of
working a miracle, and that he pro-

12 But Ahaz said, I will not ask, neither will I tempt the LORD.

posed to perform any miracle which Ahaz should suggest that would serve to remove his doubts, and lead him to put confidence in God. ¶ *Ask it either in the depth,* &c. He gave him his *choice* of a miracle—any sign or wonder in heaven, or on earth—above or below; a miracle in the sky, or from beneath the earth. Many of the versions understand the expression 'the depth,' as referring to *the grave,* or to the region of departed souls—*hades.* So the Vulgate, Aquila, Symmachus. The Chaldee reads it, ' Seek that there may be a miracle to thee upon the earth, or a sign in the heavens.' The literal meaning of the Hebrew is, 'make low, ask for ;' that is, ask for a sign below ; obtain, by asking for thyself, a miracle that shall take place below. It may refer to the earth, or to the region under the earth, since it stands in contrast with that which is above. If it refers to the region under the earth, it means that Isaiah would raise the dead to life if Ahaz desired it ; if to the earth, that any wonder or miracle that should take place in the elements—as a tempest, or earthquake—should be performed. ¶ *The height above.* The heaven, or the sky. So the Pharisees desired to see a sign from heaven, Matt. xvi. 1.

12. *I will not ask.* In this case Ahaz assumed the appearance of piety, or respect for the command of God. In Deut. vi. 16, it is written, ' Thou shalt not tempt the Lord thy God ;' and Ahaz perhaps had this command in his eye. It was a *professed* reverence for God. But the *true* reason why he did not seek this sign was, that he had already entered into a negotiation with the king of Assyria to come and defend him ; and that he was even stripping the temple of God of its silver and gold, to secure this assistance ; 2 Kings xvi. 7, 8. When men are depending on their own devices and resources, they are unwilling to seek aid from God ; and it is not uncommon if they excuse their want of trust in him by some appearance of respect for religion. ¶ *Tempt.* Try, or do a thing that shall provoke his displeasure, or seek his interposition in a case where he has not promised it. To tempt God

is the same as to put him to the proof ; to see whether he is able to perform what he proposed. It is evident, however, that here there would have been no *temptation* of God, since a sign had been offered him by the prophet in the name of God. ' The answer of Ahaz can be regarded either as one of bitter scorn, as if he had said, " I will not put thy God to the proof, in which he will be found wanting. I will not embarrass thee by taking thee at thy word ;" or as the language of a hypocrite who assumes the mask of reverence for God and his command.' — *Hengstenberg.* Chrysostom and Calvin regard the latter as the correct interpretation. If it be asked here *why* Ahaz did not put Isaiah to the test, and *secure,* if possible, the Divine confirmation to the assurance that Jerusalem would be safe, the following may be regarded as the probable reasons :—(1.) He was secretly relying on the aid of Assyria. He believed that he could fortify the city, and distress the enemy by turning away the supply of water, so that they could not carry on a siege, and that all the further aid which he needed could be derived from the Assyrians. (2.) If the miracle had been *really wrought,* it would have been a proof that JEHOVAH was the true God—a proof which Ahaz had no desire of witnessing. He was a gross idolater ; and he was not anxious to witness a demonstration which would have convinced him of the folly and sin of his own course of life. (3.) If the miracle could not be wrought, as Ahaz seems to have supposed would be the case, then it would have done much to unsettle the confidence of the people, and to have produced agitation and alarm. It is probable that a considerable portion of the people were worshippers of JEHOVAH, and were looking to him for aid. The pious, and the great mass of those who conformed to the religion of their fathers, would have been totally disheartened ; and this was a result which Ahaz had no desire to produce. (4.) Michaelis has suggested another reason, drawn from the character of idolatry. According to the prevailing notions at that period, every nation had its own gods. Those

13 And he said, Hear ye now, O house of David; *Is it* a small thing for you to weary men, but will ye weary my God also?

a Lu.1.31-35.   b Mat.1.23.

1 or, *thou, O Virgin, shalt.*

14 Therefore the LORD himself shall give you a sign: Behold, *a* a virgin shall conceive, and bear a son, and *b* shall call his ¹name Immanuel.

---

of one people were more, and those of another less powerful; see Isa. x. 10, 11; xxxvi. 18–20; xxxvii. 10–13. If a miracle had been performed, Ahaz *might* have believed that it was performed by the god of the country, who might have had the disposition, but not the power, to defend him. It would have been to the mind of the idolater no proof that the god of Syria or Samaria was not more powerful, and might not have easily overcome him. Ahaz seems to have regarded JEHOVAH as such *a* God—as one of the numerous gods which were to be worshipped, and perhaps as not the most powerful of the tutelary divinities of the nations. This was certainly the view of the surrounding idolaters (ch. x. 10, 11; xxxvi. 18–20); and it is highly probable that this view prevailed among the idolatrous Israelites.

13. *O house of David* (ver. 2). By this is to be understood not only the king himself, but the princes and rulers. Perhaps in addressing him thus, there was implied no small irony and reproach. David confided in God. But *Ahaz*, his descendant, feared to *tempt* God! As if God could not aid him! Worthy descendant he of the pious and devoted David!! ¶ Is it *a small thing.* You are not satisfied with wearying men, but you would also fatigue and wear out the patience of God. ¶ *Weary.* Exhaust their patience; oppose them; prevent their sayings and messages; try their spirits, &c. ¶ *Men.* Prophets; the men who are sent to instruct, and admonish. ¶ *Will ye weary my God also?* Will you refuse to keep his commands; try his patience; and exhaust his long-suffering? comp. ch. i. 14. The sense of this passage seems to be this: When Ahaz refused to believe the bare prediction of the prophet, his transgression was the more excusable. He had wearied and provoked him, but Isaiah had as yet given to Ahaz no direct demonstration that he was from God; no outward proof of his Divine mission; and the offence of

Ahaz might be regarded as in a sense committed against man. It was true, also, that Ahaz had, by his unbelief and idolatry, greatly tried the feelings of the pious, and wearied those who were endeavouring to promote true religion. But now the case was changed. God had offered a sign, and it had been publicly rejected. It was a direct insult to God; and an offence that demanded reproof. Accordingly, the manner of Isaiah is at once changed. Soft, and gentle, and mild before, he now became bold, open, vehement. The honour of God was concerned; a direct affront had been offered to him by the sovereign of the people of God; and it was proper for the prophet to show that *that* was an offence which affected the Divine Majesty, and demanded the severest reproof.

14. *Therefore.* Since you will not *ask* a pledge that the land shall be safe, JEHOVAH will furnish one unasked. A sign or proof is desirable in the case, and JEHOVAH will not withhold it because a proud and contemptuous monarch refuses to seek it. Perhaps there is no prophecy in the Old Testament on which more has been written, and which has produced more perplexity among commentators than this. And after all, it still remains, in many respects, very obscure. Its general original meaning is not difficult. It is, that in a short time—within the time when a young woman, then a virgin, should conceive and bring forth a child, and that child should grow old enough to distinguish between good and evil—the calamity which Ahaz feared would be entirely removed. The confederacy would be broken up, and the land forsaken by both those kings. The conception and birth of a child—which could be known only by him who knows *all* future events—would be the evidence of such a result. His appropriate *name* would be such as would be a *sign*, or an indication that God was the protector of the nation, or was

still with them. In the examination of this difficult prophecy, my first object will be to give an explanation of the meaning of the *words* and *phrases* as they occur in the passage, and then to show, as far as I may be able, what was the design of the passage. ¶ *The* Lord *himself*. Heb. ' Adonai ;' see this word explained in the Note on ch. i. 24. He will do it without being asked to do it ; he will do it though it is rejected and despised ; he will do it because it is important for the welfare of the nation, and for the confirmation of his religion, to furnish a demonstration to the people that he is the only true God. It is clearly implied here, that the sign should be such as Jehovah alone could give. It would be such as would be a demonstration that he presided over the interests of the people. If this refers to the birth of a child, *then* it means that this was an event which could be known only to God, and which could be accomplished only by his agency. If it refers to the miraculous conception and birth of the Messiah, then it means that *that* was an event which none but God could accomplish. The true meaning I shall endeavour to state in the Notes, at the close of ver. 16. ¶ *Shall give you.* Primarily to the house of David ; the king and royal family of Judah. It was especially designed to assure the government that the kingdom would be safe. Doubtless, however, the word ' you ' is designed to include the nation, or the people of the kingdom of Judah. It would be so public a sign, and so clear a demonstration, as to convince *them* that their city and land must be ultimately safe. ¶ *A sign.* A pledge ; a token ; an evidence of the fulfilment of what is predicted. The word does not, of *necessity*, denote a miracle, though it is often so applied ; see Notes on ver. 11. Here it means a proof, a demonstration, a certain indication that what he had said should be fulfilled. As that was to be such a demonstration as to show that he was *able* to deliver the land, the word *here* denotes that which was miraculous, or which could be effected *only* by Jehovah. ¶ *Behold.* הִנֵּה. This interjection is a very common one in the Old Testa-

ment. It is used to arrest attention ; to indicate the importance of what was about to be said. It serves to designate persons and things ; places and actions. It is used in lively descriptions, and animated discourse ; when any thing unusual was said, or occurred ; or any thing which peculiarly demanded attention ; Gen. xii. 19 ; xvi. 16 ; xviii. 9 ; i. 29 ; xl. 9 ; Ps. cxxxiv. 1. It means here, that an event was to occur which demanded the attention of the unbelieving monarch, and the regard of the people—an event which would be a full demonstration of what the prophet had said, that God would protect and save the nation. ¶ *A virgin.* This word properly means a girl, maiden, virgin, a young woman who is unmarried, and who is of marriageable age. The word עַלְמָה, *ălmâ*, is derived from the verb עָלַם, *ălăm*, to conceal, to hide, to cover. The word עֶלֶם, *ĕlĕm*, from the same verb, is applied to a *young man*, in 1 Sam. xvi. 56 ; xx. 22. The word here translated a virgin, is applied to Rebekah (Gen. xxiv. 43), and to Miriam, the sister of Moses, Ex. ii. 8. It occurs in only seven places in the Old Testament. Besides those already mentioned, it is found in Ps. lxviii. 25 ; Cant. i. 3 ; vi. 8 ; and Prov. xxx. 19. In all these places, except, perhaps, in Proverbs, it is used in its obvious natural sense, to denote a young, unmarried female. In the Syriac, the word ܥܠܝܡ, *alĕm*, means to grow up, *juvenis factus est; juvenescere fecit.* Hence the derivatives are applied to youth; to young men; to young women—to those who *are growing up*, and becoming youths. The etymology of the word requires us to suppose that it means one who is growing up to a marriageable state, or to the age of puberty. The word maiden, or virgin, expresses the correct idea. Hengstenberg contends, that it means one *in the unmarried state;* Gesenius, that it means simply the being of marriageable age, the age of puberty. The Hebrews usually employed the word בְּתוּלָה, *bĕthûlâ*, to denote a pure virgin (a word which the Syriac translation uses here) ; but the word here evidently denotes one who was *then* unmarried; and though its primary idea is that of one who is growing up, or in a marriageable state, yet the whole connection requires us to understand it of one who was *not then married*, and who was, therefore, regarded and designated as a virgin. The Vulgate renders it 'virgo.' The LXX. ἡ παρθίνος, *a virgin*—a word which they use as a translation of the Hebrew בְּתוּלָה in Ex. xxii. 16, 17; Lev. xxi. 3, 14; Deut. xxii. 19, 23, 28; xxxii. 25; Judg. xix. 24; xxi. 12; and in thirty-three other places (see Trommius' *Concord.*); of נַעֲרָה, *nāărā̆*, a girl, in Gen. xxiv. 14, 16, 55; xxxiv. 3 (twice); 1 Kings i. 2; and of עַלְמָה, *ălmâ*, only in Gen. xxiv. 43; and in Isa. vii. 14. The word, in the view of the LXX. translators, therefore, conveyed the proper idea of a virgin. The Chaldee uses substantially the same word as the Hebrew. The idea of a *virgin* is, therefore, the most obvious and natural idea in the use of this word. It does not, however, imply that the person spoken of should be a virgin *when* the *child* should be born; or that she should ever after be a virgin. It means simply that one who was *then* a virgin, but who was of marriageable age, should conceive, and bear a son. Whether she was *to be* a virgin *at the time* when the child was born, or was to remain such afterwards, are inquiries which cannot be determined by a philological examination of the word. It is evident, also, that the word is not opposed to *either* of these ideas. *Why* the name which is thus given to an unmarried woman was derived from the verb to *hide*, to *conceal*, is not agreed among lexicographers. The more probable opinion is, that it was because to the time of marriage, the daughter was supposed to be hidden or concealed in the family of the parents; she was kept shut up, as it were, in the paternal dwelling. This idea is given by Jerome, who says, 'the name is given to a virgin because she is said to be hidden or secret; because she does not expose herself to the gaze of men, but is kept with great care under the custody of parents.' The sum of the inquiry here, into the meaning of the word translated *virgin*, is, that it does not differ from that word as used by us. The expression means no more than that one who was then a virgin should have a son, and that this should be a sign to Ahaz. ¶ *And shall call his name.* It was usual for *mothers* to give names to their children; Gen. iv. 1; xix. 37; xxix. 32; xxx. 18. There is, therefore, no reason to suppose, as many of the older interpreters did, that the fact that it is said the mother should give the name, was a proof that the child should have no human father. Such arguments are unworthy of notice; and only show to what means men have resorted in defending the doctrines, and in interpreting the pages of the Bible. The phrase, 'she will name,' is, moreover, the same as 'they shall name,' or he shall be named. 'We are not, then, to suppose that the child should actually receive the name Immanuel as a proper name, since, according to the usage of the prophet, and especially of Isaiah, that is often ascribed to a person or thing as a name which belongs to him in an eminent degree as an attribute; see ch. ix. 5; lxi. 6; lxii. 4.'—*Hengstenberg.* The idea is, that that would be a name that might be *appropriately* given to the child. Another name was also given to this child, expressing substantially the same thing, with a circumstantial difference; see Note on ch. viii. 3. ¶ *Immanuel.* Heb. 'God with us'—עִמָּנוּאֵל—from אֵל, *God*, and עִמָּנוּ, *with us.* The name is designed to denote that God would be with the nation as its protector, and the birth of this child would be a sign or pledge of it. The mere circumstance that this name is given, however, does not imply any thing in regard to the nature or rank of the child; for nothing was more common among the Jews than to incorporate the name, or a part of the name, of the Deity with the names which they gave to their children. Thus, *Isaiah* denotes the salvation of Jehovah; *Jeremiah*, the exaltation or grandeur of Jehovah, each compounded of two words, in which the name Jehovah constitutes a part. Thus, also, in *Elijah*, the two names of God are combined, and it means literally, *God the Jehovah.* Thus, also, *Eliab*, God my father; *Eliada*,

15 Butter and honey shall
he eat, that he may know to

refuse the evil, and choose the
good.

knowledge of God; *Eliakim*, the resurrection of God; *Elihu*, he is my God;
Elisha, salvation of God. In none of
these instances is the fact, that the name
of God is incorporated with the proper
name of the individual, any argument
in respect to his rank or character. It
is true, that Matthew (ch. i. 23) uses
this name as properly expressing the
rank of the Messiah; but all that can
be demonstrated from the use of the
name by Matthew is, that it *properly*
designated the nature and rank of the
Lord Jesus. It was a pledge, then, that
God was with his people, and the name
designated by the prophet had a complete fulfilment in its use as applied to
the Messiah. Whether the Messiah be
regarded as himself a pledge and demonstration of the presence and protection of God, or whether the name be
regarded as descriptive of his nature
and dignity, yet there was an *appro-
priateness* in applying it to him. It
was fully expressive of the event of the
incarnation. Jerome supposes that the
name, Immanuel, denotes nothing more
than Divine aid and protection. Others
have supposed, however, that the name
must denote the assumption of our
nature by God in the person of the
Messiah, *i.e.*, that God became man.
So Theodoret, Irenæus, Tertullian, Lactantius, Chrysostom, Calvin, Rosenmüller, and others. The true interpretation is, that no *argument* to prove
that can be derived from the use of the
name; but when the fact of the incarnation has been demonstrated from other
sources, the *name is appropriately expressive of that event.* So it seems to
be used by Matthew.

[It may be quite true, that no argument can
be founded on the bare name, Immanuel; yet
that name, *in its connection here*, may certainly
be regarded as a designed prediction of the incarnation of Christ. Such a design our author
allows in the prophecy generally. 'The prophet,' says he, '*designedly* made use of language
which would be appropriate to a future and most
glorious event.' Why, then, does he speak of
the most pregnant word in the prophecy as if
Matthew had accidentally stumbled on it, and,

finding it would appropriately express the nature
of Christ, accommodated it for that purpose?
Having originally rejected the Messianic reference, and been convinced only by a more careful examination of the passage, that he was in
error, something of his old view seems still to
cling to this otherwise admirable exposition.
'The name Immanuel,' says Professor Alexander, 'although it might be used to signify God's
providential presence merely (Ps. xlvi. 8, 12;
lxxxix. 25; Josh. i. 5; Jer. i. 8; Isa. xliii. 2), has
a latitude and pregnancy of meaning which can
scarcely be fortuitous; and which, combined with
all the rest, makes the conclusion almost unavoidable, that it was here intended to express
a personal, as well as a providential presence.
. . . When we read in the Gospel of Matthew,
that Jesus Christ was actually born of a virgin,
and that all the circumstances of his birth came
to pass that this very prophecy might be fulfilled,
it has less the appearance of an unexpected
application, than of a conclusion rendered necessary by a series of antecedent facts and rea-
sonings, the last link in a long chain of intimations more or less explicit (referring to such
prophecies as Gen. iii. 15; Micah v. 2). The
same considerations seem to show that the prophecy is not merely accommodated, which is,
moreover, clear from the emphatic form of the
citation (τοῦτο ὅλον γίγονεν ἵνα πληρωθῇ),
making it impossible to prove the existence of
any quotation in the proper sense, if this be not
one.' But, indeed, the author himself admits
all this, though his language is less decided and
consistent than could be wished on so important
a subject.]

15. *Butter and honey.* The word
rendered *butter* (הֶמְאָה *hĕmâh*), denotes
not butter, but thick and curdled milk.
This was the common mode of using
milk as an article of food in the East,
and is still. In no passage in the Old
Testament does butter seem to be meant
by the word. Jarchi says, that this
circumstance denotes a bare state of plenty,
meaning that the land should yield its
usual increase notwithstanding the
threatened invasion. Eustatius on this
place says, that it denotes delicate food.
The more probable interpretation is,
that it was the usual food of children,
and that it means that the child should
be nourished in the customary manner.
That this was the common nourishment

16 For before the child shall
know to refuse the evil, and choose
the good, the land that thou abhor-

rest shall be forsaken of both her
kings.

---

of children, is abundantly proved by
Bochart; *Hieroz.* P. i. lib. xi. ch. li.
p. 630. Barnabas, in his epistle, says,
'The infant is first nourished with honey,
and then with milk.' This was done
usually by the prescription of physi-
cians. Paulus says, 'It is fit that the
first food given to a child be honey, and
then milk.' So Aëtius, 'Give to a child,
as its first food, honey;' see *Bochart.*
Some have, indeed, supposed that this
refers to the fact that the Messiah
should be *man* as well as God, and that
his eating honey and butter was expressive of the fact that he had a *human
nature!* But against this mode of interpretation, it is hoped, it is scarcely
needful now to protest. It is fitted to
bring the Bible into contempt, and the
whole science of exegesis into scorn.
The Bible is a book of sense, and it
should be interpreted on principles that
commend themselves to the sober judgment of mankind. The word rendered
honey—דְּבַשׁ—is the same word—*dibs*—
which is now used by the Arabs to
denote the syrup or jelly which is made
by boiling down wine. This is about
the consistence of molasses, and is used
as an article of food. Whether it was
so employed in the time of Isaiah, cannot now be determined, but the word here
may be used to denote honey; comp.
Note, ver. 22. ¶ *That he may know.*
As this translation now stands, it is
unintelligible. It would *seem* from
this, that his eating butter and honey
would *contribute* to his knowing good
and evil. But this cannot be the meaning. It evidently denotes '*until* he
shall know,' or, 'at his knowing;' Nord.
Heb. Gram., § 1026. 3. He shall be
nourished in the usual way, *until* he
shall arrive at such a period of life as
to know good from evil. The LXX.
render it, Πριν ἢ γνῶναι αὐτὸν—'*Before* he
knows.' The Chaldee, '*Until* he shall
know.' ¶ *To refuse the evil,* &c.
Ignorance of good and evil denotes
infancy. Thus, in Nineveh, it is said
there were 'more than sixscore thousand persons that cannot discern be-

tween their right hand and left hand;'
commonly supposed to denote infants;
Jonah iv. 11; comp. Deut. i. 39. The
meaning is, that he should be nourished
in the usual mode in infancy, and before he should be able to discern right
from wrong, the land should be forsaken
of its kings. At what particular period
of life this occurs, it may not be easy
to determine. A capability to determine, in some degree, between good
and evil, or between right and wrong,
is usually manifest when the child is
two or three years of age. It is evinced
when there is a capability of understanding *law*, and feeling that it is
wrong to disobey it. This is certainly
shown at a very early period of life;
and it is not improper, therefore, to
suppose that here a time was designated
which was not more than two or three
years.

16. *The land that thou abhorrest.*
The land concerning which thou art so
much *alarmed* or *distressed;* that is,
the united land of Syria and Ephraim.
It is mentioned here as 'the land,' or as
one land, because they were united then
in a firm alliance, so as to constitute,
in fact, or for the purposes of invasion
and conquest, one people or nation.
The phrase, 'which thou abhorrest,'
means properly, which thou loathest,
the primary idea of the word—קוץ,
qūtz—being to feel a nausea, or to vomit.
It then means to fear, or to feel alarm;
and this, probably, is the meaning here.
Ahaz, however, evidently looked upon
the nations of Syria and Samaria with
disgust, as well as with alarm. This
is the construction which is given of
this passage by the Vulgate, Calvin,
Grotius, Junius, Gataker, and Piscator, as well as by our common version.
Another construction, however, has been
given of the passage by Vitringa, J. D.
Michaelis, Lowth, Gesenius, Rosenmüller, Hengstenberg, and Hendewerk.
According to this, the meaning is not
that the *land* should be the object of
abhorrence, but that the kings themselves were the objects of dislike or

dread ; and not merely that the two kings should be removed, but that the land itself was threatened with desolation. This construction is free from the objections of an exegetical kind to which the other is open, and agrees better with the idiom of the Hebrew. According to this, the correct translation would be :

> ' For before the child shall learn to refuse the evil and to choose the good,
> Desolate shall be the land, before whose two kings thou art in terror.'

¶ *Of both her kings.* Ahaz took the silver and gold that was found in the temple, and sent it as a present to the king of Assyria. Induced by this, the king of Assyria marched against Damascus and slew Rezin, 2 Kings xvi. 9. This occurred but a short time after the threatened invasion of the land by Rezin and Remaliah, in the *third* year of the reign of Ahaz, and, consequently, about one year after this prophecy was delivered. Pekah, the son of Remaliah, was slain by Hoshea, the son of Elah, who conspired against him, slew him, and reigned in his stead. This occurred in the fourth year of the reign of Ahaz, for Pekah reigned twenty years. Ahaz began to reign in the seventeenth year of the reign of Pekah, and as Pekah was slain after he had reigned twenty years, it follows that he was slain in the fourth year of the reign of Ahaz—perhaps not more than two years after this prophecy was delivered ; see 2 Kings xv. 27, 30 ; xvi. 1. We have thus arrived at a knowledge of the time intended by Isaiah in ver. 16. The whole space of time was not, probably, more than two years.

A great variety of opinions have been entertained by interpreters in regard to this passage (ver. 14–16). It may be useful, therefore, to state briefly what those opinions have been, and then what seems to be the true meaning.

(i.) The first opinion is that which supposes that by the ' virgin ' the wife of Ahaz is referred to, and that by the child which should be born, the prophet refers to Hezekiah. This is the opinion of the modern Jewish commentators

generally. This interpretation prevailed among the Jews in the time of Justin. But this was easily shown by Jerome to be false. Ahaz reigned in Jerusalem but sixteen years (2 Kings xvii. 2), and Hezekiah was twenty-five years old when he began to reign (2 Kings xviii. 2), and of course was not less than nine years old when this prophecy was delivered. Kimchi and Abarbanel then resorted to the supposition that Ahaz had a second wife, and that this refers to a child that was to be born of her. This supposition cannot be *proved* to be false, though it is evidently a *mere* supposition. It has been adopted by the Jews, because they were pressed by the passage by the early Christians, as constituting an argument for the divinity of Christ. The ancient Jews, it is believed, referred it mainly to the Messiah.

(ii.) Others have supposed, that the prophet designated some virgin who was then present when the king and Isaiah held their conference, and that the meaning is, ' as surely as this virgin shall conceive, and bear a son, so surely shall the land be forsaken of its kings.' Thus Isenbiehl, Bauer, Cube, and Steudel held, as quoted by Hengstenberg, *Christol.* i. p. 341.

(iii.) Others suppose that the ' virgin ' was not an actual, but only an ideal virgin. Thus Michaelis expresses it : ' By the time when one who is yet a virgin can bring forth (*i.e.*, in nine months), all will be happily changed, and the present impending danger so completely passed away, that if you were yourself to name the child, you would call him Immanuel.' Thus Eichhorn, Paulus, Hensler, and Ammon understand it ; see *Hengstenberg.*

(iv.) Others suppose that the ' virgin ' was the prophet's wife. Thus Aben Ezra, Jarchi, Faber, and Gesenius. Against this supposition there is only one objection which has been urged that is of real force, and that is, that the prophet already had a son, and of course his wife could not be spoken of as a virgin. But this objection is entirely removed by the supposition, which is by no means improbable, that the former wife of the prophet was dead, and that he was about to be united in marriage to another who was a virgin.

In regard to the prophecy itself, there have been three opinions :—

(i.) That it refers *exclusively* to some event in the time of the prophet ; to the birth of a child then, either of the wife of Ahaz, or of the prophet, or of some other unmarried female. This would, of course, exclude all reference to the Messiah. This was formerly my opinion ; and this opinion I expressed and endeavoured to maintain, in the first composition of these Notes. But a more careful examination of the passage has convinced me of its error, and satisfied me that the passage has reference to the Messiah. The reasons for this opinion I shall soon state.

(ii.) The second opinion is, that it has *exclusive* and *immediate* reference to the Messiah ; that it does not refer at all to any event which was *then* to occur, and that to Ahaz the future birth of a Messiah from a virgin, was to be regarded as a pledge of the Divine protection, and an assurance of the safety of Jerusalem. Some of the objections to this view I shall soon state.

(iii.) The third opinion, therefore, is that which *blends* these two, and which regards the prophet as speaking of the birth of a child which would soon take place of some one who was then a virgin —an event which could be known only to God, and which would therefore constitute a sign, or demonstration to Ahaz of the truth of what Isaiah said ; but that the prophet intentionally so used language which would *also* mark a more important event, and direct the minds of the king and people onward to the future birth of one who should more fully answer to all that is here said of the child that would be born, and to whom the name Immanuel would be more appropriately given. This, I shall endeavour to show, must be the correct interpretation. In exhibiting the reasons for this opinion, we may, FIRST, state the evidence that the prediction refers to some child that would be born *soon* as a pledge that the land would be forsaken of its kings ; and SECONDLY, the evidence that it refers also to the Messiah in a higher and fuller sense.

I. EVIDENCE THAT THE PROPHECY REFERS TO SOME EVENT WHICH WAS SOON TO OCCUR—TO THE BIRTH OF A CHILD OF SOME ONE WHO WAS THEN A VIRGIN, OR UNMARRIED.

(i.) It is the *obvious* interpretation. It is that which would strike the great mass of men accustomed to interpret language on the principles of common sense. If the passage stood by itself ; if the seventh and eighth chapters were *all* that we had ; if there were no allusion to the passage in the New Testament ; and if we were to sit down and merely look at the circumstances, and contemplate the narrative, the unhesitating opinion of the great mass of men would be, that it *must* have such a reference. This is a good rule of interpretation. That which strikes the mass of men ; which appears to men of sound sense as the meaning of a passage on a simple perusal of it, is likely to be the true meaning of a writing.

(ii.) Such an interpretation is demanded by the circumstances of the case. The immediate point of the inquiry was not about the *ultimate* and *final* safety of the kingdom—which would be demonstrated indeed by the announcement that the Messiah would appear—but it was about a present matter ; about impending danger. An alliance was formed between Syria and Samaria. An invasion was threatened. The march of the allied armies had commenced. Jerusalem was in consternation, and Ahaz had gone forth to see if there were any means of defence. In this state of alarm, and at this juncture, Isaiah went to assure him that there was no cause for fear. It was not to assure him that the nation should be ultimately and finally safe— which might be proved by the fact that the Messiah would come, and that, therefore, God would preserve the nation ; but the pledge was, that he had no reason to fear *this* invasion, and that within a short space of time the land would 'be forsaken of both its kings.' How could the fact that the Messiah would come more than seven hundred years afterwards, prove this ? Might not Jerusalem be taken and subdued, as it was afterwards by the

Chaldeans, and yet it be true that the Messiah would come, and that God would manifest himself as the protector of his people? Though, therefore, the assurance that the Messiah would come would be a *general* proof and pledge that the nation would be preserved and ultimately safe, yet it would not be a pledge of the *specific* and *immediate* thing which occupied the attention of the prophet, and of Ahaz. It would not, therefore, be a ' sign' such as the prophet offered to give, or a proof of the fulfilment of the specific prediction under consideration. This argument I regard as unanswerable. It is so obvious, and so strong, that all the attempts to answer it, by those who suppose there was an immediate and exclusive reference to the Messiah, have been entire failures.

(iii.) It is a circumstance of *some* importance that Isaiah regarded himself and his children as ' signs' to the people of his time; see ch. viii. 18. In accordance with this view, it seems he had named one child SHEAR-JASHUB, vii. 3; and in accordance with the same view, he afterwards named another MAHER-SHALAL-HASH-BAZ—both of which names are significant. This would *seem* to imply that he meant here to refer to a similar fact, and to the birth of a son that should be a sign also to the people of his time.

(iv.) An unanswerable reason for thinking that it refers to some event which was soon to occur, and to the birth of a child *before* the land should be forsaken of the two kings, is the record contained in ch. viii. 1–4. That record is evidently connected with this account, and is intended to be a public assurance of the fulfilment of what is here predicted respecting the deliverance of the land from the threatened invasion. In that passage, the prophet is directed to take a great roll (ver. 1), and make a record concerning the son that was to be born; he calls public witnesses, men of character and well-known reputation, in attestation of the transaction (ver. 2); he approaches the prophetess (ver. 3); and it is expressly declared (ver. 4) that before the child should have ' knowledge to say, My father, and my mother,' *i.e.*, be able to discern between good and evil

(ch. vii. 16), ' the riches of Damascus and the spoil of Samaria' should be ' taken away before the king of Assyria.' This is so evidently a completion of the prophecy in ch. vii., and a solemn fulfilling of it in a manner that should be satisfactory to Ahaz and the people, that it is impossible, it seems to me, to regard it any otherwise than as a *real* transaction. Hengstenberg, and those who suppose the prophecy to refer *immediately* and *exclusively* to the Messiah, are obliged to maintain that that was a ' symbolical transaction ' — an opinion which might, with the same propriety, be held of any historical statement in the Bible; since there is nowhere to be found a more simple and unvarnished account of mere matter of historical fact than that. The statement, therefore, in ch. viii., is conclusive demonstration, I think, that there was a reference in ch. vii. 14–16, to a child of the prophet that would be soon born, and that would be a *pledge* of the Divine protection, and a *proof* or *sign* to Ahaz that his land would be safe.

It is no objection to this that Isaiah then had a son (ch. vii. 3), and that therefore the mother of that son could not be a virgin. There is no improbability in the supposition that the mother of that son was deceased, and that Isaiah was about again to be married. Such an event is not so uncommon as to make it a matter of ridicule (see *Hengstenberg*, p. 342); or to render the supposition wholly incredible.

Nor is it any objection that another name was given to the child that was born to Isaiah; ch. viii. 1, 3. Nothing was more common than to give two names to children. It might have been true that the name usually given to him was Maher-shalal-hash-baz; and still true that the circumstances of his birth were such an evidence of the Divine protection, and such an emblem of the Divine guardianship, as to make proper the name Immanuel; see Note on ver. 14. It may be observed, also, that on the supposition of the strict and exclusive Messianic interpretation, the same objection might be made, and the same difficulty would lie. It was no more true of Jesus of Nazareth than of the child of Isaiah, that he was commonly called Immanuel. He had another name also, and was called by that other name. Indeed, there is not the slightest evidence that the Lord Jesus was *ever* designated by the name Immanuel as a proper name. All that the passage means is, that such should be the circumstances of the birth of the child as to render the name Immanuel *proper;* not that it would be applied to him in fact as the usual appellation.

Nor is it any objection to this view, that the mind of the prophet is evidently directed onward *to* the Messiah; and that the prophecy terminates (ch. viii. 8; ix. 1–7) with a reference to him. That this is so, I admit; but nothing is more common in Isaiah than for him to *commence* a prophecy with reference to some remarkable deliverance which was soon to occur, and to *terminate* it by a statement of events connected with a higher deliverance under the Messiah. By the laws of *prophetic suggestion,* the mind of the prophet seized upon resemblances and analogies; was carried on to future times, which were *suggested* by something that he was saying or contemplating as about to occur, until the mind was absorbed, and the primary object forgotten in the contemplation of the more remote and glorious event; see Introduction to Isaiah, § 7. III. (3.)

II. EVIDENCE THAT THE PROPHECY REFERS TO THE MESSIAH.

(i.) The passage in Matt. i. 22, 23, is an evidence that *he* regarded this as having a reference to the Messiah, and that it had a complete fulfilment in him. This quotation of it also shows that that was the common interpretation of the passage in his time, or he would not thus have introduced it. It cannot be *proved,* indeed, that Matthew means to affirm that this was the primary and original meaning of the prophecy, or that the prophet had a direct and exclusive reference to the Messiah; but it proves that in his apprehension the words had a *fulness* of meaning, and an adaptedness to the actual circumstances of the birth of the Messiah, which would accurately and appropriately express that event; see Notes on the passage in Matthew. The prophecy was not completely *fulfilled, filled up, fully and*

adequately met, until applied to the Messiah. That event was so remarkable; the birth of Jesus was so strictly of a virgin, and his nature so exalted, that it might be said to be a *complete* and *entire* fulfilment of it. The language of Isaiah, indeed, was applicable to the event referred to immediately in the time of Ahaz, and expressed that with clearness; but it more appropriately and fully expressed the event referred to by Matthew, and thus shows that the prophet designedly made use of language which would be appropriate to a future and most glorious event.

(ii.) An argument of no slight importance on this subject may be drawn from the fact, that this has been the common interpretation in the Christian church. I know that this argument is not conclusive; nor should it be pressed beyond its due and proper weight. It is of force only because the united and almost uniform impression of mankind, for many generations, in regard to the meaning of a written document, is not to be rejected without great and unanswerable arguments. I know that erroneous interpretations of many passages have prevailed in the church; and that the interpretation of many passages of Scripture which have prevailed from age to age, have been such as have been adapted to bring the whole subject of scriptural exegesis into contempt. But we should be slow to reject that which has had in its favour the suffrages of the unlearned, as well as the learned, in the interpretation of the Bible. The interpretation which refers this passage to the Messiah has been the prevailing one in all ages. It was followed by all the fathers and other Christian expositors until the middle of the eighteenth century (*Hengstenberg*); and is the prevailing interpretation at the present time. Among those who have defended it, it is sufficient to mention the names of Lowth, Koppe, Rosenmüller, and Hengstenberg, in addition to those names which are found in the well-known English commentaries. It has been opposed by the modern Jews, and by German neologists; but has *not* been regarded as false by the great mass of pious and humble Christians. The argument here is simply that which would be applied in the interpretation of a passage in Homer or Virgil ; that where the great mass of readers of all classes have concurred in any interpretation, there is *presumptive evidence* that it is correct—evidence, it is true, which may be set aside by argument, but which is to be admitted to be of *some* account in making up the mind as to the meaning of the passage in question.

(iii.) The reference to the Messiah in the prophecy accords with the *general strain and manner* of Isaiah. It is in accordance with his custom, at the mention of some occurrence or deliverance which is soon to take place, to suffer the mind to fix ultimately on the more remote event of the *same general character*, or lying, so to speak, *in the same range of vision* and of thought ; see the Introduction, § 7. It is also the custom of Isaiah to hold up to prominent view the idea that the nation would not be ultimately destroyed till the great Deliverer should come ; that it was safe amidst all revolutions ; that vitality would remain like that of a tree in the depth of winter, when all the leaves are stripped off (ch. vi. 13); and that all their enemies would be destroyed, and the true people of God be ultimately secure and safe under their great Deliverer ; see Notes on ch. xxxiv.; xxxv. It is true, that this argument will not be *very* striking except to one who has attentively studied this prophecy ; but it is believed, that no one can profoundly and carefully examine the manner of Isaiah, without being struck with it as a very important feature of his mode of communicating truth. In accordance with this, the prophecy before us means, that the nation was safe from this invasion. Ahaz feared the extinction of his kingdom, and the *permanent* annexation of Jerusalem to Syria and Samaria. Isaiah told him that that could not occur ; and proffered a demonstration, that in *a very few years* the land would be forsaken of both its kings. —*On another ground also it could not be.* The people of God were safe. His kingdom could not be permanently destroyed. It must continue until the Messiah should come, and the eye of the prophet, in accordance with his usual custom, glanced to that future event,

and he became *totally* absorbed in its contemplation, and the prophecy is finished (ch. ix. 1–7) by a description of the characteristics of the light that he saw in future times rising in dark Galilee (ch. ix. 1, 2), and of the child that should be born of a virgin then.

In accordance with the same view, we may remark, as Lowth has done, that to a people accustomed to look for a great Deliverer ; that had fixed their hopes on one who was to sit on the throne of David, the *language* which Isaiah here used would naturally suggest the idea of a Messiah. It was so animated, so ill adapted to describe his own son, and so fitted to convey the idea of a most remarkable and unusual occurrence, that it could scarcely have been otherwise than that they should have *thought* of the Messiah. This is true in a special manner of the language in ch. ix. 1–7.

(iv.) An argument for the Messianic interpretation may be derived from the public expectation which was excited by some such prophecy as this. There is a striking similarity between it and one which is uttered by Micah, who was contemporary with Isaiah. Which was penned *first* it would not be easy to show ; but they have internal evidence that they both had their origin in an expectation that the Messiah would be born of a virgin ; comp. Note, ch. ii. 2. In Micah v. 2, 3, the following prediction occurs : ' But thou, Bethlehem Ephratah, though thou be little among the thousands of Judah, yet out of thee shall he come forth unto me that is to be ruler over Israel ; whose goings forth have been from of old, from the days of eternity. Therefore will he give them up, until the time when she which travaileth hath brought forth.' That this passage refers to the birth of the Messiah, is demonstrable from Matt. ii. 6. Nothing can be clearer than that this is a prediction respecting the place of his birth. The Sanhedrim, when questioned by Herod respecting the place of his birth, answered without the slightest hesitation, and referred to this place in Micah for proof. The expression, ' she which travaileth,' or, ' she that bears shall bear '—יָלָדָה or, יוֹלֵדָה, *she bearing shall bear*—refers evidently to some prediction of such a birth; and the word 'she that bears' (יוֹלֶדֶת) seems to have been used somewhat in the sense of a proper name, to designate one who was well known, and of whom there had been a definite prediction. Rosenmüller remarks, 'She is not indeed expressly called a virgin, but that she is so is self-evident, since she shall bear the hero of Divine origin (from everlasting), and consequently not begotten by a mortal. The predictions throw light on each other; Micah discloses the Divine origin of the person predicted, Isaiah the wonderful manner of his birth.'—*Ros.*, as quoted by Hengstenberg. In his first edition, Rosenmüller remarks on Micah v. 2: 'The phrase, "she who shall bear shall bear," denotes the *virgin* from whom, in a miraculous manner, the people of that time hoped that the Messiah would be born.' If Micah refers to a well-known existing prophecy, it must evidently be this in Isaiah, since no other similar prophecy occurs in the Old Testament; and if he wrote subsequently to Isaiah, the prediction in Micah must be regarded as a proof that this was the prevailing interpretation of his time.

That this was the prevailing interpretation of those times, is confirmed by the traces of the belief which are to be found extensively in ancient nations, that some remarkable person would appear, who should be born in this manner. The idea of a Deliverer, to be born of a *virgin*, is one that somehow had obtained an extensive prevalence in Oriental nations, and traces of it may be found almost everywhere among them. In the Hindoo Mythology it is said, respecting *Budhu*, that he was born of *Maya*, a goddess of the imagination—a virgin. Among the Chinese, there is an image of a beautiful woman with a child in her arms, which child, they say, was born of a virgin. The passage in Virgil is well known:

> Jam redit et Virgo, redeunt Saturnia regna:
> Jam nova progenies coelo demittitur alto.
> Tu modo nascenti puero, quo ferrea primum
> Desinet, ac toto surget gens aurea mundo.
> Casta fave Lucina: tuus jam regnat Apollo.
> *Eclog.* iv. 4, *sq.*

> Comes the last age, by Cumæ's maid foretold;
> Afresh the mighty line of years unrolled.

> The Virgin now, now Saturn's sway returns;
> Now the blest globe a heaven-sprung child adorns,
> Whose genial power shall whelm earth's iron race,
> And plant once more the golden in its place.—
> Thou chaste Lucina, but that child sustain,
> And lo! disclosed thine own Apollo's reign.
> *Wrangham.*

This passage, though applied by Virgil to a different subject, has been usually regarded as having been suggested by that in Isaiah. The coincidence of thought is remarkable on any supposition; and there is no improbability in the supposition that the expectation of a great Deliverer to be born of a virgin had prevailed extensively, and that Virgil wrought it up in this beautiful manner, and applied it to a prince in his own time. On the prevalent expectation of such a Deliverer, see Note on Matt. ii. 2.

(v.) But the great and the unanswerable argument for the Messianic interpretation is derived from the conclusion of the prophecy in ch. viii. 8, and especially in ch. ix. 1–7. The prophecy in ch. ix. 1–7 is evidently connected with this; and yet *cannot* be applied to a son of Isaiah, or to any other child that should be then born. If there is any passage in the Old Testament that *must* be applied to the Messiah, that is one; see Notes on the passage. And if so, it proves, that though the prophet at first had his eye on an event which was soon to occur, and which would be to Ahaz full demonstration that the land would be safe from the impending invasion, yet that he employed language which would describe also a future glorious event, and which would be a fuller demonstration that God would protect the people. He became *fully* absorbed in that event, and his language at last referred to that alone. The child then about to be born would, in most of the circumstances of his birth, be an apt emblem of him who should be born in future times, since both would be a demonstration of the Divine power and protection. To both, the name Immanuel, though not the common name by which either would be designated, might be appropriately given. Both would be born of a virgin —the former, of one who was then a virgin, and the birth of whose child could be known only to God,—the

17 The LORD shall bring upon thee, and upon thy people, and upon thy father's house, days that have not come, from the day that

Ephraim departed from Judah; *even* the king of Assyria.

18 And it shall come to pass in that day, *that* the LORD shall hiss

---

latter, of one who should be appropriately called *the* virgin, and who should remain so at the time of his birth. This seems to me to be the meaning of this difficult prophecy. The considerations in favour of referring it to the birth of a child in the time of Isaiah, and which should be a pledge to him of the safety of his kingdom *then*, seem to me to be unanswerable. And the considerations in favour of an ultimate reference to the Messiah—a reference which becomes in the issue total and absorbing — are equally unanswerable ; and if so, then the twofold reference is clear.

17. *The Lord shall bring*, &c. The prophet having assured Ahaz that his kingdom should be free from the invasion that then threatened it, proceeds, however, to state to him that it would be endangered from another source. ¶ *Thy father's house.* The royal family —the princes and nobles. ¶ *Days that have not come.* Times of calamity that have not been equalled. ¶ *From the day that Ephraim departed from Judah.* From the time of the separation of the ten tribes from the tribes of Judah and Benjamin. ¶ Even *the king of Assyria.* This was done in the following manner. Though the siege which Rezin and Pekah had undertaken was not at this time successful, yet they returned the year after with stronger forces, and with counsels better concerted, and again besieged the city. This was in consequence of the continued and increasing wickedness of Ahaz ; 2 Chron. xxviii. 1–5. In this expedition, a great multitude were taken captives, and carried to Damascus; 2 Chron. xxviii. 5. Pekah at this time also slew 120,000 of the Jews in one day (2 Chron. xxviii. 6); and Zichri, a valiant man of Ephraim, slew Maaseiah the son of Ahaz. At this time, also, Pekah took no less than 200,000 of the kingdom of Judah, proposing to take them to Samaria, but was prevented by the influence of the prophet Oded ; 2 Chron. xxviii. 8–15. In this calamity, Ahaz stripped the temple of its treasures and ornaments,

and sent them to Tiglath-pileser, king of Assyria, to induce him to come and defend him from the united arms of Syria and Ephraim. The consequence was, as might have been foreseen, that the king of Assyria took occasion, from this, to bring increasing calamities upon the kingdom of Ahaz. He first, indeed, slew Rezin, and took Damascus; 2 Kings xvi. 7. Having subdued the kingdoms of Damascus and Ephraim, Tiglath-pileser became a more formidable enemy to Ahaz than both of them. His object was not to aid Ahaz, but to distress him (2 Chron. xxviii. 20); and his coming professedly and at the request of Ahaz, to his help, was a more formidable calamity than the threatened invasion of both Rezin and Pekah. God has power to punish a wicked nation in his own way. When they seek human aid, he can make this a scourge. He has kings and nations under his control ; and though a wicked prince may seek earthly alliance, yet it is easy for God to allow such allies to indulge their ambition and love of rapine, and make them the very instruments of punishing the nation which they were called to defend. It should be observed that this phrase, ' even the king of Assyria,' is by many critics thought to be spurious, or a marginal reading, or gloss, that has by some means crept into the text. The ground of this opinion is, that it does not harmonize entirely with the following verse, where *Egypt* is mentioned as well as Assyria, and that it does not agree with the poetical form of the passage.

18. *In that day the Lord shall hiss ;* see Note, ch. v. 26. ¶ *For the fly.* That is, for the army, or the multitude of people. The comparison of a numerous army with *flies* is not uncommon ; *see* Homer's *Iliad*, B. ii. 469, &c.

————— Thick as insects play,
The wandering nation of a summer's day,
That, drawn by milky streams at evening hours
In gathered swarms surround the rural bowers;
From pail to pail with busy murmur run
The gilded legions, glittering in the sun.
                                        Pope.

The comparison is drawn probably from

for the fly that *is* in the uttermost part of the rivers of Egypt, and for the bee that *is* in the land of Assyria:

the *number*, but also is intended to indicate the *troublesome* character, of the invaders. Perhaps, also, there is an allusion here to the well-known fact that one of the ten plagues of Egypt was caused by numerous swarms of flies; Ex. viii. 21–24. An army would be brought up from that country as numerous, as troublesome, and as destructive as was that swarm of flies. The following description, by Bruce, of a species of flies in Abyssinia and the adjacent regions, will give an idea of the character of this calamity, and the force of the language used here:—

' This insect is called Zimb; it has not been described by any naturalist. It is, in size, very little larger than a bee, of a thicker proportion, and has wings, which are broader than those of a bee, placed separate, like those of a fly: they are of pure gauze, without colour or spot upon them; the head is large, the upper jaw or lip is sharp, and has at the end of it a strong pointed hair, of about a quarter of an inch long; the lower jaw has two of these pointed hairs; and this pencil of hairs, when joined together, makes a resistance to the finger, nearly equal to that of a strong hog's bristle; its legs are serrated in the inside, and the whole covered with brown hair or down.

ZIMB OR DOG-FLY OF ABYSSINIA.
From Bruce's Travels.

As soon as this plague appears, and their buzzing is heard, all the cattle forsake their food, and run wildly about the plain, till they die, worn out with fatigue, fright, and hunger. No remedy remains, but to leave the black earth, and hasten down to the sands of Atbara; and there they remain, while the rains last, this cruel enemy never daring to pursue them further. Though his size be immense, as is his strength, and his body covered with a thick skin, defended with strong hair, yet even the camel is not capable to sustain the violent punctures the fly makes with his pointed proboscis. He must lose no time in removing to the sands of Atbara; for when once attacked by this fly, his body, head, and legs, break out into large bosses, which swell, break, and putrefy, to the certain destruction of the creature. Even the elephant and rhinoceros, who, by reason of their enormous bulk, and the vast quantity of food and water they daily need, cannot shift to desert and dry places as the season may require, are obliged to roll themselves in mud and mire, which, when dry, coats them over like armour, and enables them to stand their ground against this winged assassin; yet I have found some of these tubercles upon almost every elephant and rhinoceros that I have seen, and attribute them to this cause. All the inhabitants of the sea-coast of Melinda, down to Cape Gardefan, to Saba, and the south coast of the Red Sea, are obliged to put themselves in motion, and remove to the next sand, in the beginning of the rainy season, to prevent all their stock of cattle from being destroyed. This is not a partial emigration; the inhabitants of all the countries, from the mountains of Abyssinia northward, to the confluence of the Nile, and Astaboras, are once a year obliged to change their abode, and seek protection in the sand of Beja; nor is there any alternative, or means of avoiding this, though a hostile band were in their way, capable of spoiling them or half their substance. This fly has no sting, though he seemed to me to be rather of the bee kind; but his motion is more rapid and sudden than that of the bee, and resembles that of the gad-fly in England. There is something particular in the sound or buzzing of this insect; it is a jarring noise, together with a humming, which induces me to believe it proceeds, at least in part, from a vibration made with the three hairs at his snout.' ¶ *The uttermost part of the rivers of Egypt.* The remotest part of the land—that is, from the whole country. Egypt was watered by a single river; the Nile. But this river emptied into the Medi-

19 And *a* they shall come, and shall rest all of them in the desolate valleys, and in the holes of the rocks, and upon all thorns, and upon all 1 bushes.

a Je.16.16.   1 or, *commendable trees.*

20 In the same day shall the LORD shave with a razor that is hired, *namely*, by them beyond the river, by the king of Assyria, the head, and the hair of the feet: and it shall also consume the beard.

---

terranean by several mouths ; and from this river also were cut numerous canals to water the land. These are intended by the *rivers* of Egypt ; see Notes, ch. xix. 6, 7. Those canals would be stagnant for no small part of the year ; and around them would be produced, as is usual near stagnant waters, great quantities of flies. This prophecy was fulfilled by the invasion of the land in subsequent times by the Egyptians ; 2 Kings xxiii. 33, 34 ; 2 Chron. xxxv. 20, 24 ; xxxvi. 1, 2. ¶ *And for the bee.* That is, for the *army.* An army is compared to *bees* on account of their number ; perhaps also on account of the pungency and severity of the sting. The comparison is common ; see Deut. i. 44; vii. 20; Ps. cxviii. 12. The Chaldee has rendered this verse, ' The Lord shall call to a people girded with the armies of the brave, who are numerous as flies, and shall bring them from the ends of the land of Egypt ; and strong armies, strong as bees, and shall bring them from the land of Assyria.' No prophecy was ever more completely fulfilled than this by the successive invasions of Pharaoh-Necho, Esarhaddon and Nebuchadnezzar ; see Isa. xxxvi.; xxxvii.; 2 Chron. xxxvi. 7–21.

19. *And they shall come.* The idea in this verse is, that they would spread over the land, and lay it waste. The poetic image of flies and bees is kept up ; meaning, that the armies would be so numerous as to occupy and infest all the land. ¶ *And shall rest.* As bees do. Thus the *locusts* are said to have *rested* in all the land of Egypt ; Ex. x. 14. ¶ *In the desolate valleys.* The word translated *valleys* usually means *a valley with a brook,* or a brook itself. The Chaldee translates it, ' In the streets of cities.' But the idea is derived from the habits of flies and bees. The meaning is, that they should fill all the land, as innumerable swarms of flies and bees—would settle down everywhere,

and would infest or consume everything. Bees, probably, chose situations near to running streams. Virgil, in his directions about selecting a place for an apiary, gives the following among others :—

At liquidi fontes, et stagna virentia musco
Adsint, et tenuis fugiens per gramina rivus.
Georg. iv. 18, 19.

But there let pools invite with moss arrayed,
Clear fount and rill that purls along the glade.
Sotheby.

¶ *In the holes of the rocks.* Probably the same image is referred to here. It is well known that in Judea, as well as elsewhere, bees were accustomed to live in the holes or caverns of the rocks. They were very numerous ; and the figure here is, that the Assyrians would be numerous as the swarms of bees were in that land, even in the high and inaccessible rocks ; comp. Isa. ii. 19– 21. ¶ *Upon all thorns.* The image here is kept up of flies and bees resting on everything. *Thorns* here refer to those trees and shrubs that were of little value ; but even on these they would rest. ¶ *All bushes.* Heb. ' All trees that are commendable, or that are to be praised ;' see margin. The word denotes those shrubs and trees that were objects of *praise ;* that is, that were cultivated with great attention and care, in opposition to *thorns* that grew wild, and without cultivation, and that were of little value. The meaning of the passage is, that the land would be invaded in every part, and that everything, valuable or not, would be laid waste.

20. *In the same day, &c.* The idea in this verse is the same as in the preceding, though presented in a different form. The meaning is, that *God* would bring upon them this punishment, but that he would make use of the Assyrian as an *instrument* by which to do it. ¶ *Shave.* The act of shaving off the hair denotes punishment or disgrace ;

21 And it shall come to pass in that day, *that* a man shall nourish a young cow and two sheep:

22 And it shall come to pass, for the abundance of milk *that* they shall give, that he shall eat butter: for butter and honey shall every one eat *that is* left [1] in the land.

1 *in the midst of.*

comp. 2 Sam. x. 4. : 'Hanun took David's servants, and shaved off one half of their beards ;' 1 Chron. xix. 4. ¶ *With a razor.* Using them as an instrument. God here claims the power of directing them, and regards them as employed by him; see ch. x. 5-7. ¶ *That is hired.* This is an allusion to the custom of *hiring* soldiers, or employing *mercenary armies.* Thus Great Britain employed *mercenary* troops, or hired of the Germans bodies of *Hessians* to carry on the war in America. The meaning here is, that God would employ the Assyrians as *his* instruments, to effect *his* purposes, as though they were *hired* and paid by the plunder and spoil of the nation. ¶ *By them beyond the river.* The river *Euphrates.* The Euphrates is usually meant in the Scriptures where '*the river*' is mentioned without specifying the name ; Ps. lxxii. 8; lxxx. 2. This was the river which Abraham had passed ; and this, perhaps, was, for a long time, the eastern boundary of their geographical knowledge ; see Note, ch. xi. 15. ¶ *The head.* The hair of the head. ¶ *The hair of the feet.* Or the other parts of the body ; of the lower parts of the body. ¶ *Shall consume the beard.* Shall cut off the beard. This was esteemed particularly disgraceful among the Jews. It is, at this day, among all Eastern nations. The *beard* is regarded as a distinguished ornament ; among the Mahometans, it is *sworn* by, and no higher insult can be offered than to treat the beard with indignity ; comp. Note, Isa. l. 6. The meaning is here, that God would employ the Assyrian as his instrument to lay waste the land.

21. *In that day.* In the time specified in the previous verses—in the judgments that should be brought upon the land by the Egyptians and Assyrians. ¶ *A man shall nourish.* Heb. 'Make to live ;' that is, he shall own, or feed. ¶ *A young cow.* The Hebrew denotes a heifer that gives milk. The state which is denoted by this is that of great *poverty.* Instead of being engaged in agriculture, of possessing great resources in that time, a man should depend, for the subsistence of himself and his family, on what a single cow and two sheep would yield. Probably this is intended also as a description of the general state of the nation, that it would be reduced to great poverty. ¶ *And two sheep.* Two here seems to be used to denote a very small number. A man, *i.e.,* the generality of men, would be so reduced as to be able to purchase and keep no more.

22. *For the abundance of milk,* &c. On account, or by means of the great quantity of milk. This image also denotes that the land should be desolate, and abandoned by its inhabitants. Such a range would the cow and sheep have in the lands lying waste and uncultivated, that they would yield abundance of milk. ¶ *For butter and honey.* This shall be the condition of all who are left in the land. Agriculture shall be abandoned. The land shall be desolate. The few remaining inhabitants shall be dependent on what a very few cows and sheep shall produce, and on the subsistence which may be derived from honey obtained from the rocks where bees would lodge. Perhaps, also, the swarms of *bees* would be increased, by the fact that the land would be forsaken, and that it would produce abundance of wild flowers for their subsistence. The general idea is plain, that the land would be desolate. Butter and honey, that is, butter mingled with honey, is a common article of food in the East; see Note on ver. 15. D'Arvieux being in the camp of an Arab prince who lived in much splendour, and who treated him with great regard, was entertained, he tells us, the first morning of his being there, with little loaves, *honey, new-churned butter,* and cream more delicate than any he ever saw, together with coffee.—*Voy. dans la Pal.,* p. 24. And in another

23 And it shall come to pass in that day, *that* every place shall be, where there were a thousand vines at a thousand silverlings, it shall *even* be for briers and thorns.

24 With arrows and with bows shall *men* come thither; because all the land shall become briers and thorns. .

25 And *on* all hills that shall be digged with the mattock, there shall not come thither the fear of briers and thorns; but it shall be for the sending forth of oxen, and for the treading of lesser cattle.

---

place, he assures us that one of the principal things with which the Arabs regale themselves at breakfast is cream, or new butter mingled with honey.—P. 197. The statement of the prophet here, that the poor of the land should eat butter and honey, is not inconsistent with this account of D'Arvieux, that it is regarded as an article of food with which even princes treat their guests; for the idea of the prophet is, that when the land should be desolate and comparatively uninhabited, the natural luxuriant growth of the soil would produce an abundance to furnish milk, and that honey would abound where the bees would be allowed to multiply, almost without limit; see Harmer's *Obs.*, vol. ii. p. 55. Ed. Lond. 1808.

23. The remainder of this chapter is a description of great desolation produced by the invasion of the Assyrians. ¶ *Where there were a thousand vines.* Where there was a valuable vineyard. In every place, that is, that was well cultivated and valuable. ¶ *At a thousand silverlings.* The word rendered 'silverlings' here—כֶּסֶף, *kĕsĕph*—denotes, properly, *silver*, of any amount. But it is also used to denote the silver coin which was in use among the Jews, *the shekel.* Perhaps this was the only silver coin which, in early times, they possessed, and hence the word *shekel* is omitted, and so many pieces of *silver* are mentioned. Thus, in Gen. xx. 16, Abimelech says, that he had given Abraham 'a thousand of silver'—that is, a thousand shekels. The shekel was worth about two shillings of our money. It is probable that a vineyard would be valued, in proportion to the number of vines that could be raised on the smallest space; and the meaning is here, that the land that was most fertile, and that produced the most, would be desolate, and would produce only briers and

thorns. The land in Judea admits of a high state of cultivation, and requires it, in order to make it productive. When neglected, it becomes as remarkably sterile. At present, it generally bears the marks of great barrenness and sterility. It is under the oppression of Turkish power and exactions; and the consequence is, that, to a traveller, it has the appearance of great barrenness. But, in the high state to which the Jews brought it, it was eminently fertile, and is capable still of becoming so, if it should be placed under a government that would encourage agriculture and bestow freedom. This is the account which all travellers give of it now.

24. *With arrows and with bows, &c.* This is a continuation of the description of its desolation. So entirely would it be abandoned, so utterly desolate would it be, that it would become *a vast hunting-ground.* It would be covered with shrubs and trees that would afford a convenient covert for wild beasts; and would yield to its few inhabitants a subsistence, not by cultivation, but by the bow and the arrow. There can scarcely be a more striking description of utter desolation. But, perhaps, the long captivity of seventy years in Babylon literally fulfilled it. Judea was a land that, at all times, was subject to depredations from wild beasts. On the banks of the Jordan—in the marshes, and amid the reeds that sprung up in the lower bank or border of the river—the lion found a home, and the tiger a resting-place; comp. Jer. xlix. 19. When the land was for a little time vacated and forsaken, it would be, therefore, soon filled with wild beasts; and during the desolations of the seventy years' captivity, there can be no doubt that this was literally fulfilled.

25. *And on all hills, &c.* All the fertile places in the mountains that

CHAPTER VIII.

ANALYSIS OF THE CHAPTER.

In ch. vii. the prophet had told Ahaz that God would give him a sign that the land of Judah should be safe from the threatened invasion of the united armies of Syria and Israel. In this chapter, there is a record of the primary fulfilment of that promise, ver. 1–4. From ver. 5 to ver. 8, the prophet resumes and repeats what he had said before in ch. vii. 17–25, that although the land should be safe from *this* invasion, yet one more formidable would occur by the armies of Assyria. The cause of this is stated to be, that Judah had despised the Lord, and had sought alliances with Syria and Israel. The prophet then proceeds to exhort the people to put confidence in Jehovah—assuring them that if they refused to confide in him, they must expect to be destroyed, ver. 9–18; and the chapter concludes with denouncing punishment on those that looked to necromancers and diviners, rather than to the true God. The prophecy is intimately connected with that in the previous chapter; and was delivered, evidently, not far from the same time.

MOREOVER the Lord said unto me, Take thee a great roll, and write in it with a man's pen concerning [1] Maher-shalal-hash-baz.

[1] *in making speed to the spoil, he hasteneth the prey,* or, *make speed,* &c.

used to be cultivated with the spade. Vineyards were often planted on the sides of hills; and those places were among the most productive and fertile in the land; see ch. v. 1. ¶ *The mattock.* The spade; the garden hoe; or the weeding-hook. An instrument chiefly used, probably, in vineyards. ¶ *There shall not come thither.* There shall not be. ¶ *The fear of briers and thorns.* This does not make sense; or if it does, it is not a sense consistent with the connection. The idea of the whole passage is, that the land, even the most fertile parts of it, should be given up to briers and thorns; that is, to desolation. The Hebrew here, is ambiguous. It may mean, '*thou* shalt not come there, for fear of the briers and thorns.' That is, the place that was formerly so fertile, that was cultivated with the spade, shall now be so completely covered with thorns, and shall furnish so convenient a resting-place for wild beasts and reptiles, as to deter a man from going there. The LXX., and the Syriac, however, understand it differently—as denoting that those places should be still cultivated. But this is evidently a departure from the sense of the connection. Lowth understands it in the *past* tense; 'where the fear of briers and thorns never came.' The general idea of the passage is plain, that those places, once so highly cultivated, would now be desolate. ¶ *Shall be for the sending forth,* &c. Shall be wild, uncultivated, and desolate—vast *commons* on which oxen and sheep shall feed at large. ¶ *Lesser*

cattle. Heb. 'Sheep, or the flock.' Sheep were accustomed to range in deserts and uncultivated places, and to obtain there, under the guidance of the shepherd, their subsistence. The description, therefore, in these verses, is one of extensive and wide desolation; and one that was accomplished in the calamities that came upon the land in the invasions by the Egyptians and Assyrians.

CHAPTER VIII.

1. *Take thee a great roll.* The word which is here translated 'roll' more properly signifies *tablet.* So the Chaldee renders it. Those *tablets* were made of wood, metal, or stone, for the purpose of writing on; see ch. xxx. 8; Hab. ii. 2. On these tablets, or smooth plates, writing was performed by cutting the letters with an iron *stylus,* or small chisel. The process was slow, but the writing was permanent. They sometimes used the skins of animals, or the bark of trees, and subsequently the *papyrus* of Egypt (comp. Note, ch. xix. 7); and it is possible that Isaiah may have used such a roll or volume on this occasion; comp. ver. 16. ¶ *With a man's pen.* The word *pen* here (חֶרֶט) denotes the iron *stylus,* which was used to *engrave* or *cut* the letters in the metal or wood. The phrase 'a man's pen,' has been variously interpreted. The Chaldee renders it, 'Write in it an open, or clear writing, or an expanded writing;' meaning that he should make it clear and distinct, so as to be easily read. The Syriac, 'Write on it in the [usual] custom of men.' The word which is translated 'man's' (אֱנוֹשׁ)

2 And I took unto me faithful witnesses to record, Uriah *a* the priest, and Zechariah the son of Jeberechiah.

3 And I ¹went unto the pro-

a 2 Ki.16.10.   ¹ approached.

phetess; and she conceived and bare a son. Then said the LORD to me, Call his name Maher-shalal-hash-baz:

4 For *b* before the child shall have

b ch.7.16.

usually denotes *common men*, the lower ranks, in opposition to the higher ranks of society. And probably the direction means simply, 'write on it in letters such as men commonly use ; in a plain, open, distinct manner—without using any mysterious emblems or characters, but so that men may read it distinctly and easily.' A parallel place occurs in Hab. ii. 2 : 'Write the vision and make it plain upon tables, that he may run that readeth it.' ¶ *Concerning.* Heb. ל. This preposition may denote *concerning, of,* or *to.* I understand it here as referring to the *heading* or *title* of the prophecy. This was to be set *over* the prophecy, as a running title, to denote the main subject of it. The subject is indicated in the name which is immediately added. ¶ *Maher.* Hasten ; or, he shall hasten. ¶ *Shalal.* Spoil, or prey. ¶ *Hash.* Hasten, or make speed. ¶ *Baz.* Spoil, or prey. The name used here is a repetition of the same idea—denoting haste in seizing prey, or spoil ; and is repeated to give emphasis, and to excite attention. The idea is, that the Assyrian would hasten to his plunder—that it would be accomplished with speed. This name was to be given to a child of Isaiah ; and this child was to be a *sign* of the event which was signified by the name ; see ver. 18 ; comp. Hab. ii. 2, 3.

2. *And I took unto me faithful witnesses.* What was the precise object in calling in these witnesses is not known. Some have supposed that it was to bear testimony to the marriage of the prophet at that time. But it may have been for the purpose of a public record of the prophecy ; a record so made, that *the precise time* when it was delivered could be attested without dispute. The prophecy was an important one ; and it was important to know, in the most authentic and undisputed manner, that such a prophecy had been delivered. It is probable that the prophecy, attested

by the names of those two men, was suspended in some public place in the temple, so that it might be seen by the people, and allay their fears ; and in order to remove from the multitude every suspicion that it was *a prophecy after the event.* That this was a real, and not a symbolical transaction, is perfectly manifest, not only from the narrative itself, but from ver. 18. They are called 'faithful,' not on account of their private character, but because their public testimony would be credited by the people. ¶ *To record.* To bear witness. ¶ *Uriah the priest.* This is, doubtless, the same man that is mentioned in 2 Kings xvi. 10. He was a man of infamous character ; the accomplice of Ahaz in corrupting the true religion ; but still his testimony might be the more valuable to Ahaz, as he was associated with him in his plans. ¶ *And Zechariah,* &c. It is not certainly known who this was. Perhaps he was one of the Levites whose name is mentioned in 2 Chron. xxix. 13.

3. *Then said the* LORD, &c. The name thus given was to be emblematic of a particular event—that Assyria would soon take away the spoil of Damascus and Samaria. It is not remarkable that the name Immanuel should also be given to the same child, as signifying the presence and protection of God in defending the nation from the invaders ; see Notes on ch. vii. 14, 15. Calvin thinks that all this passed in *a vision* before the prophet ; but it has every mark of being a literal narrative of the birth of a son to Isaiah ; and without this supposition, it is impossible to understand the account contained here.

4. *For before,* &c. This must have occurred in a short time—probably before the expiration of three years. A child would usually learn to address his parents in that time. *In fact,* the event here predicted occurred in less than three years from the time when the prophecy

knowledge to cry, My father, and my mother, the [1] riches of Damascus and the spoil of Samaria shall be taken away [a] before the king of Assyria.

[1] or, he that is *before the king of Assyria shall take away the riches.*

5 The Lord spake also unto me again, saying,

6 Forasmuch as this people refuseth the waters of Shiloah [b] that go softly, and rejoice in Rezin and Remaliah's son;

[a] 2 Ki.15.29; 16.9; 17.3.   [b] Neh.3.15; Jn.9.7.

was spoken; see Notes on ch. vii. 16. ¶ *Before the king of Assyria.* By the king, or by his conquests. By the spoil of Samaria here, is to be understood, not the plunder which should be carried away from the city, but from the kingdom of Samaria. In other places, the land is called by the name of the capital; comp. 2 Kings xvii. 26; xxiii. 19; Jer. xxxi. 5. The *city* of Samaria was not plundered until eighteen years after the time here mentioned by the prophet; 5, 6. These verses introduce again what was predicted in ch. vii. 17, *sq.*, respecting the invasion of the land by the king of Assyria. The *cause* of the invasion is specified, and the consequences are foretold.

6. *Forasmuch as this people.* There has been a considerable difference of opinion among interpreters respecting the 'people' to whom the prophet here refers. Some have supposed that it refers to the kingdom of Judah alone; others to a *party* in that kingdom; and others to the kingdom of Judah in connection with the ten tribes, or the kingdom of Israel also. The latter is probably the correct interpretation. The prophet reproves the *whole* nation of the Jews for despising the mild and gentle reign of the family of David, and for seeking the aid of foreign nations; the ten tribes as seeking an alliance with Rezin and Pekah; and the kingdom of Judah as seeking an alliance with the king of Assyria. It was characteristic of the nation—both of the ten tribes, and of the tribe of Judah—that they forsook the defence which they had in themselves, and sought foreign alliances. Hence God says, that he will bring upon them the judgments which they deserve. That there is a joint reference to both the kingdoms of Israel and Judah, is apparent from ver. 14. It cannot refer to the kingdom of Judah alone, for it could not be brought as an accusation

against them, that they took pleasure in Rezin. In the opinion that it refers to the kingdoms of Israel and of Judah —to the whole Jewish people, Vitringa, Lowth, and Hengstenberg concur. ¶ *The waters of Shiloah that go softly.* That flow gently. The name Siloah, or Siloam, is found only three times in the Scriptures as applied to waters; once in this place, where it is spoken of a running water; once as a pool in Nehemiah —בְּרֵכַת הַשֶּׁלַח—ch. iii. 15, and again as a pool, in the account of the miracle of healing the man who was born blind; John ix. 7, 11. Siloam is on the east side of the city of Jerusalem, to the south-east of the site of the temple, and its waters flow into the valley of Jehoshaphat. The name means *sent*, or *sending*, from שָׁלַח *to send*, and was probably given to it because the waters were *sent* or made to pass through a subterranean passage or aqueduct.

At present, it properly consists of two receptacles or reservoirs, the waters from one of which flow into the other. The first, or upper one, is now called the 'Fountain of the Virgin,' from a tradition that it was here that the Virgin Mary resorted before her purification, in order to wash her child's linen. This fountain is on the west side of the valley of Jehoshaphat, and is about 1550 feet from the south-east corner of the city wall. The cavity of this fountain is wholly excavated in the solid rock. To enter it there is at first a descent of sixteen steps, to a level place or platform of twelve feet in diameter, and then another descent of ten steps to the water, making the whole depth twenty-five feet. The basin here is about fifteen feet long by five or six wide, and the height six or eight feet. There is some reason to suppose that this is supplied by a fountain lying under the mosque of Omar, on the site of the temple of Solomon. From this fountain the water is conducted by a subterranean passage, in a direction a little to the west of south to what is properly called the fountain of Siloam. This passage runs under the extremity of mount Ophel; is cut entirely from the solid rock, and is found by measurement to be 1750 feet in length. At the lower part it is from ten to fifteen feet in height by two in breadth; but in the middle so low, that it can be passed only by creeping on the hands and knees. The passage is partly filled up with sand. From this aqueduct the water is conveyed into the pool of Siloam, situated near where the Ty-

7 Now therefore, behold, the LORD bringeth up upon them the waters of the river, strong and many, *even* *a* the king of Assyria,

and all his glory: and he shall come up over all his channels, and go over all his banks:

a ch.7.1-6.

---

ropeon, or 'valley of cheesemongers,' opens into the valley of Jehoshaphat. This reservoir is

POOL OF SILOAM.—From Forbin.

fifty-three feet long, eighteen feet broad, and nineteen feet deep, though now there is usually no water remaining within it. From this reservoir the water flows off into the vale below, furnishing water for the gardens, which are constructed in terraces on the side of the valley. The water in both these fountains is the same. It is sweet, and slightly brackish, but not disagreeable. It is the common water now used by the inhabitants of the neighbouring village of Kefr Selwâne—or the straggling village of Siloam. For a full description of this fountain, *see* Robinson's *Bib. Researches,* vol. i. pp. 493-514. This fountain was probably formerly included within the walls, and furnished a part of the supply of water to the city.

The meaning of this passage is this. The waters of Siloam denote the reign of JEHOVAH, as manifesting itself in the administration of the family of David—a mild, gentle, and munificent reign, beautifully represented by the unfailing and gently-flowing waters on which the happiness of Jerusalem so much depended. That reign a large part of the nation—the ten tribes—had rejected, and had set up a separate kingdom, and had sought the aid of the king of Damascus. The remainder—the kingdom of Judah—were in like manner now disposed to reject the aid of JEHOVAH, and sought an alliance

with the king of Assyria—beautifully represented here by the river Euphrates. The waters of Siloam—a gentle, small, sweetly-flowing stream, represented the government of JEHOVAH. The waters of the Euphrates—violent, rapid, impetuous, and overflowing, represented the government of Assyria. The one they despised; the other they sought and admired. The power of the kingdom of David was then feeble and decayed. That of the Assyrian monarch was vigorous, mighty, vast. They despised the one, and sought the alliance of the other. ¶ *And rejoice.* That is, they confide in, and feel that in their protection they are safe. ¶ *In Rezin.* King of Syria. ¶ *And Remaliah's son.* Pekah, king of Samaria; ch. vii. 1. The crime here mentioned was peculiar to the kingdom of Israel; showing that the prophet, in part at least, had reference to them.

7. *The waters of the river.* By *the river,* in the Scripture, is commonly meant the river Euphrates, as being, by way of eminence, the largest river with which they were acquainted; and also as being that distinguished by the fact that Abraham had lived beyond it, and crossed it; see Note, ch. vii. 20. In this verse the image is kept up which was commenced in ver. 6. The Jews rejected the gentle waters of Siloah, and sought the alliance of a foreign king, whose kingdom stretched along, and extended beyond the Euphrates. It was natural, therefore, to compare the invasion of the land to the overflowing of mighty waters that would sweep everything away. A similar comparison is found in Juvenal, who, in describing the introduction of Eastern customs into Rome, represents the *Orontes* as flowing into the Tiber :—

Jampridem Syrus in Tiberim defluxit Orontes.

The comparison of an invading army with an overflowing stream, or an inundation, is not uncommon; see Lucan's *Phars.* vi. 272. Hor. *Car.* iv. 14, 15, *sq.* ¶ *Strong and many.* Violent

8 And he shall pass through Judah; he shall overflow and go over; he shall reach *even* to the

1 *fulness of the breadth of thy land shall be the stretchings out of his wings.*

neck: and the 1 stretching out of his wings shall fill *a* the breadth of thy land, O Immanuel.

a ch. 36.1, &c.

waves, and numerous. It means that a mighty host would come up upon the land. ¶ *Even the king of Assyria.* It has been supposed by many that this is a *gloss*, or explanation, which has crept into the text. There is no doubt that it expresses the true sense of the passage, but it is remarkable that Isaiah himself should furnish a *literal* explanation in the midst of a figurative description. ¶ *And all his glory.* Eastern kings marched in the midst of vast splendour. They moved with all the magnificence of the court, and were attended usually with their princes and nobles; with a splendid retinue; and with all the insignia of royalty. Such was the case with Xerxes when he invaded Greece; and such, too, with Darius, and with most of the Oriental conquerors. ¶ *And he shall come up,* &c. The figure of overflowing waters is here retained. To understand this, it is necessary to remark, that the Euphrates annually overflows its banks to a very considerable extent. It rises in the mountains of Armenia, and, flowing for a considerable distance in a region where the mountains are covered with snow, it falls into the level region of Mesopotamia or Syria, and flows through that region, almost parallel with the Tigris, towards the Persian Gulf. From its banks, vast numbers of canals were made, as in Egypt, to receive the water, and to render the country fertile. By the melting of the snows in Armenia, in the summer, the stream becomes greatly enlarged, and overflows vast portions of the adjacent country in a manner similar to the Nile. Usually the river is *not* very large. Otho says, that on the 12th of March, when he crossed the Euphrates, it was not more than 200 paces in width, but in its height, it extends 500 or 600 paces into the plains on the right. Thevenot observes, that near to Bir, the Euphrates seemed no larger than the Seine at Paris, but was very large when it was swollen. At Baby-

lon, it is said to be about four hundred feet in breadth. That it overflows its banks, is abundantly attested by ancient as well as modern travellers; see Rosenmüller and Gesenius on this verse. ¶ *Its channels.* This word means either *brooks*, or *valleys*, or *canals*, or *channels* of a river. The Euphrates flowed through a level region, and it is not improbable that it had at various times made for itself many channels. Besides this, there were many *canals* cut in various directions to convey its waters to the gardens, farms, &c. All these the prophet says would be full—and the water would extend even far beyond them.

8. *He shall*, &c. That is, the Assyrian—though still retaining the idea of an overflowing stream, or a deluge of waters. ¶ *Reach* even *to the neck.* Chaldee, 'They shall come even to Jerusalem.' 'The prophet compares Jerusalem here,' says Kimchi, ' to the head of the human body. As when the waters reach to the *neck* of a man, he is very near drowning, so here, the prophet intimates that the whole land would be deluged, and that it would be nearly *utterly* destroyed.' The figure thus understood is a very sublime one. Jerusalem was situated on hills—elevated above the surrounding country, and, in reference to the whole land, might be aptly compared to the human head. Thus Josephus (*De Bello*, lib. iii. ch. ii.), describing Jerusalem, says,— Ἱεροσόλυμα προανίσχουσα τῆς περιοίκου πάσης, ὥσπερ ἡ κεφαλὴ σώματος—*Jerusalem, eminent above all the surrounding region, as the head of the body.* The country is represented as being laid under water—a vast sea of rolling and tumultuous waves — with Jerusalem alone rising above them, standing in solitary grandeur amidst the heaving ocean, and itself in danger each moment of being ingulphed; see a similar figure, Isa. xxx. 28:

His spirit is like a torrent overflowing
It shall reach to the middle of the neck.

12

9 Associate yourselves, O ye people, and ¹ye shall be broken *a* in pieces; and give ear, all ye of far

1 or, *yet.*   *a* ch.37.36.

countries: gird yourselves, and ye shall be broken in pieces; gird yourselves, and ye shall be broken in pieces.

And so also, Hab. iii. 13:

Thou didst go forth for the salvation of thy people,
For the salvation of thine anointed:
Thou didst smite the head from the house of the wicked,
Destroying the foundation even to the neck.

¶ *And the stretching out of his wings.* This is a continuation of the same idea under a new figure. The term *wings* is often applied to an army, as well in modern as in ancient writings. It denotes that the invading army would be so vast as, when expanded or drawn out, to fill the land. ¶ *Shall fill the breadth.* Shall occupy the entire land, so that there shall be no city or town which he shall not invade. ¶ *Thy land, O Immanuel;* see Note, ch. vii. 14. If this be understood as referring to the son of Isaiah that was to be born, then it means that the child was given as a pledge that the land would be safe from the threatened invasion. It was natural, therefore, to address the child in that manner; as reminding the prophet that this land, which was about to be invaded, belonged to God, and was yet under his protection. Its meaning may be thus paraphrased: 'O thou who art a pledge of the protection of God—whose birth is an assurance that the land is under his care, and who art given as such a sign to the nation. Notwithstanding this pledge, the land shall be full of foes. They shall spread through every part, and endanger all.' Yet the name, the circumstances of the birth, the promise at that time, would all remind the prophet and the king, that, notwithstanding this, the land would be still under the protection of God. If the language be understood as referring to the future Messiah, and as an address made to him then, by calling the land *his* land, it is intimated that it could not be brought to utter desolation, nor could the country where he was to be born remain wasted and ruined. It would be indeed invaded; the armies of the Assyrian would spread over it, but still it was the land of Immanuel; and

was to be the place of his birth, and it was to be secure until the time should arrive for him to come. The probability is, I think, that the address is here solely to the Messiah; and that the purpose of God is to fix the mind of the prophet on the fact that the Messiah must come, as an assurance that the land could not be wholly and perpetually desolate; see Notes on ch. vii. 14.

9. *Associate yourselves.* In the previous verses the prophet had seen the Assyrian coming up on the land like an overwhelming flood. He looked upon the danger, and his mind was turned to the pledge of safety which God had given. The name Immanuel, and the promise connected with the giving of that name (ch. vii. 16), reminded him of the perfect safety of the nation; for it was a pledge that God was with them; see ver. 10. In view of this pledge of the protection of God, this verse is a spirited apostrophe to the mighty host that was about to invade the land. Though confederated and vast, yet they could not prevail. They should be scattered, much as they might be prepared for victory, for God had given a pledge that he would defend his people. ¶ *Associate.* There has been much variety among interpreters about the meaning of the original word used here. It may mean *to be terrified, to be alarmed,* as well as to associate or become confederate. The Vulgate and Chaldee render it, 'Be assembled, or congregated.' The LXX., 'Know, ye nations,' &c. The Syriac, 'Tremble, ye people,' &c. Still the notion of associating, confederating, or entering into an alliance, suits the connection better; answers to the parallelism in the latter part of the verse, and is equally consonant with the original. ¶ *O ye people.* Ye people of Assyria. This is an apostrophe to the mighty multitudes that were to come up upon the land from that country. ¶ *And ye shall be broken in pieces.* That is, though the confederacy be mighty, yet it shall not prevail. It shall not ac-

10 Take counsel together, and it shall come to nought; speak the word, and it shall not stand: for God *a is* with us.

11 For the LORD spake thus to

a Ps.46.1,7.   1 *in strength of.*

me with [1] a strong hand, and instructed me, that I should not walk *b* in the way of this people, saying,

12 Say ye not, A confederacy, to

b Prov.1.15.

complish that which you purpose—the entire destruction of the land of Judah. ¶ *Give ear, all ye of far countries.* That should be particularly engaged in the confederacy—Assyria, and the kingdoms allied with it. ¶ *Gird yourselves.* As if for war; that is, prepare yourselves thoroughly for conquest; see Note, ch. v. 27. The *repetition* of this shows the excited and agitated state of the prophet's mind. It is a strong, emphatic mode of expression—denoting that they should be *certainly* broken in pieces, notwithstanding the strength of their confederacy.

10. *Take counsel together.* This is an address to the same foreign nations. It refers to the designs which they would form to destroy the Jewish state. ¶ *Speak the word.* That is, give the command—to overturn the nation of the Jews. ¶ *It shall not stand.* It shall not be accomplished. ¶ *For God is with us.* Heb. 'For Immanuel.' It indicates the confidence of the prophet in view of the promise and the pledge. His reliance was there. Though the enemies were strong and mighty; though the confederacy was formidable; yet his simple reliance was in the name *Immanuel!* In this he had confidence, in spite of all the violent efforts and designs of the foes of Judah; see Num. xiv. 9:

Only, rebel not ye against the Lord:
Neither fear ye the people of the land;
For they are bread for us;
Their defence is departed from them,
And JEHOVAH *is with us,*
Fear them not.

See also Ps. xlvi. 6, 7:

The heathen raged,
The kingdoms were moved.
He uttered his voice, the earth dissolved.
JEHOVAH *of hosts is with us;*
The God of Jacob is our refuge.

11. *For the* LORD *spake thus.* Spake that which immediately follows in the next verse. Warned him not to unite in the alliance with foreign kingdoms which the nation was about forming. ¶ *With a strong hand.* Marg. 'With

strength of hand.' That is, when the hand of God *urged* me. A strong prophetic impulse is often represented as being produced by God's laying his *hand* on the prophet; or by his being thus, as it were, *urged* or *impelled* to it; Ezek. iii. 14: ' The hand of JEHOVAH was strong upon me ;' 2 Kings iii. 15: 'And it came to pass, that when the minstrel played, the hand of the LORD came upon him ;' Jer. xx. 7: 'O LORD, thou art stronger than I, and hast prevailed ;' see also Eccl. ii. 24; 1 Kings xviii. 46; 2 Kings iii. 15; Ezek. xxxiii. 22; xl. 1; comp. Introduction, § 7. 11. (3.) The meaning is, that the prophet was strongly, and almost irresistibly, urged by the Divine influence, to say what he was about to say. ¶ *That I should not walk,* &c. That I should not approve, and fall in with, the design of Ahaz, and of the nation, in calling in the aid of the Assyrian armies.

12. *Say ye not.* Do not join in their purposes of forming a confederacy. Do not unite with the king and the people of Judah in their alarms about the threatened invasion by the kings of Syria and Samaria, and in their purpose to form an alliance with the king of Assyria. The reason why they should not do this, he states in ver. 13, where he exhorts the nation to put confidence in the Lord rather than in man. There has been, however, great diversity in the interpretation of this passage. The LXX. render the word קֶשֶׁר *qésher,* 'confederacy,' by the word σκληρόν— 'Everything which this people say, is *hard.*' The Syriac, 'Do not say, *rebellion,*' &c. The Chaldee understands the word in the same sense. Lowth proposes to change the word קֶשֶׁר *qésher,* into קָדוֹשׁ *qádhósh,* because Archbishop Secker possessed one MS. in which this reading was found ; and he translates the passage :

' Say ye not it is holy,
Of every thing of which this people shall say it is holy.'

all *them to* whom this people shall say, A confederacy; neither *a* fear ye their fear, nor be afraid.

13 Sanctify the LORD of hosts himself; and *let* him *b be* your fear, and *let* him *be* your dread.

a 1 Pet.3.14,15.   *b* Lu.12.5.

14 And he shall be for a *c* sanctuary; but for a stone of *d* stumbling, and for a rock of offence,*e* to both the houses of Israel; for a *g*in and for a snare to the inhabitants of Jerusalem.

c Eze.11.16.   *d* 1 Pet.2.8.   *e* Mat.13.57.

That is, 'call not their idols holy; nor fear ye the object of their fear; that is, the gods of the idolaters.' But it is plain that this does not suit the connection of the passage, since the prophet is not reproving them for their idolatry, but is discoursing of the alliance between the kings of Syria and Samaria. Besides, the authority of *one* MS., without the concurrence of any ancient version, is not a sufficient authority for changing the Hebrew text. Most commentators have understood this word 'confederacy' as referring to the alliance between the kings of Syria and Samaria; as if the prophet had said, 'Do not join in the cry so common and almost universal in the nation, *There is a confederacy between those two kingdoms; there is an alliance formed which endangers our liberty*—a cry that produces alarm and trepidation in the nation.' Thus Rosenmüller and Gesenius explain it. Aben Ezra and Kimchi, however, understand it of a *conspiracy*, which they suppose was formed in the kingdom of Ahaz, against him and the house of David; and that the prophet warns the people against joining in such a conspiracy. But of the existence of such a conspiracy there is no evidence. Had there *been* such a conspiracy, it is not probable that it would have been so well known as to make it a proper subject of public denunciation. Conspiracies are usually secret and concealed. I regard this, however, as a caution to the prophet not to join in the prevailing demand for an alliance with the king of Assyria. Ahaz trembled before the united armies of Syria and Samaria. He sought, therefore, foreign assistance—the assistance of the king of Assyria. It is probable that in this he was encouraged by the leaders of the people, and that this would be a popular measure with the mass of the nation. Yet it implied distrust of God (Note, ver. 6); and,

therefore, the prophet was directed not to unite with them in seeking this 'confederacy,' or alliance, but to oppose it. The word translated 'confederacy,' קֶשֶׁר, *qĕshĕr*, is derived from the verb קָשַׁר, *qâshăr, to bind, to fetter;* to enter into a conspiracy. It usually refers to a *conspiracy*, but it may mean a combination or alliance of any kind. Or, if it here means a *conspiracy*, a union between Ahaz and the Assyrians may be regarded as a species of *conspiracy*, as it was an unnatural alliance; a species of combination against the natural and proper government of Judah—the theocracy. ¶ *Neither fear ye their fear.* Do not partake of their alarm at the invasion of the land by the united armies of Syria and Samaria. Rather put confidence in God, and believe that he is able to save you; comp. 1 Pet. iii. 13–15.

13. *Sanctify, &c.* Regard JEHOVAH as holy; *i.e.*, worship and honour him with pious fear and reverence. Regard *him* as the source of safety, and the true defence. Ahaz and his people sought for aid from Assyria against the armies of Syria and Samaria. The direction here is rather to seek aid from God. ¶ Let *him* be *your fear.* Do not be alarmed at what man can do (ver. 12), but fear and honour God. Be afraid to provoke his wrath by looking to other sources of help when his aid only should be sought.

14. *And he shall be for a sanctuary.* The word translated *sanctuary* means, literally, *a holy place, a consecrated place,* and is usually applied to the tabernacle, or to the temple; Ex. xxv.8; Lev. xii. 4; xxi. 12; Jer. li. 51. It also means *an asylum,* or *a refuge,* to which one might flee in case of danger, and be safe; see Ezek. xi. 16. Among all ancient nations, *temples* were regarded as safe places to which men might flee when pursued, and when in danger. It

15 And many among them shall stumble, and fall, and be broken, and be snared, and be taken.

16 Bind up the testimony, *a* seal the law among *b* my disciples.

a Rev.5.1,5.   b Prov.8.8,9.

was deemed sacrilege to tear a man away from a temple or an altar. That the temple was so regarded among the Jews is manifest; see 1 Kings i. 50; ii. 28. In allusion to this, the prophet says, that JEHOVAH would be a sanctuary; that is, an asylum, or refuge, to whom they should flee in times of danger, and be safe; see Psal. xlvi. 1: 'God is our refuge and strength;' Prov. xviii. 10: 'The name of the LORD is a strong tower; the righteous runneth into it, and is safe.' It is also well known that temples and altars were regarded as *asyla* among the Greeks and Romans. The reference here is rather to an *altar*, as the asylum, than to a city or temple; as, in the other member of the sentence, the same object is said to be a stone of stumbling— a figure which would not be applicable to a temple or a city. ¶ *A stone of stumbling.* A stone against which one should impinge, or over which he should fall. The idea is, that none could run against a hard, rough, fixed stone, or rock, without injuring himself. So the Jews would oppose the counsels of God; instead of making him their refuge and strength, they would resist his claims and appeals, and the consequence would be their destruction. It is also to be remembered, that God is often represented in the Scriptures as a *rock*, a firm defence, or place of safety, to those who trust in him. But instead of their thus taking refuge in him, they would oppose themselves to this firm rock, and ruin themselves; see Deut. xxxii. 4, 15, 18, 30, 31, 37; Ps. xix. 14; xxviii. 1; xxxi. 2, 3; xli. 2; xlii. 9. Many of the ancient Jewish commentators applied this to the Messiah.—*Gesenius in loco.* It is also applied to Christ in the New Testament, 1 Pet. ii. 8. ¶ *A rock of offence.* A rock over which they should fall. The English word *offence*, had that meaning formerly, and retains it in our translation of the Bible. ¶ *To both the houses of Israel.* To the two kingdoms of Judah and Israel; that is, to the wicked portion of them, not to those who were truly pious. ¶ *For a*

gin. A *net*, or *snare*, to take birds. The idea is the same as in the former part of the verse. By rejecting the counsel of God; by despising his protection, and by resisting his laws, they would be unexpectedly involved in difficulties, as birds which are caught in a snare.

15. *And many among them.* Many by the invasion under the Assyrian. Many were taken captive; many killed, and many were carried to Babylon. The repetition here of so many expressions so nearly synonymous is emphatic, and shows that it would be certainly done.

16. *Bind up.* This expression is one that is applicable to a *volume*, or *roll* of writing. Thus far the prophet seems to have had the *roll* opened, which is mentioned in ver. 1. Now the prophecy is complete, and he directs to bind it up, or close it. Perhaps, also, it is implied that it would be useless any further to address a rebellious and headstrong people. He had delivered his message, but they disregarded it. ¶ *The testimony.* The message; especially that of which Uriah and Zechariah had been called *to bear witness*, ver. 2. Any message from God is, however, sometimes called a *testimony*, as being that to which a prophet bears witness; Ps. xix. 7; 2 Kings xi. 12; Deut. iv. 45; vi. 17, 20; 1 Kings ii. 3; Neh. ix. 34. ¶ *Seal.* Books were made in the form of rolls, and were often sealed when completed—as we seal a letter. The mode of sealing them was not by wax only, but by uniting them by any adhesive matter, as paste, or glue. Wax in warm climates would be generally rendered useless by the heat. The meaning here is, to secure, to close up—perhaps by passing a cord or string around the volume, and making it secure, denoting that it was finished; see Dan. viii. 26; xii. 4. ¶ *The law.* The communication or command which he had delivered, and which, being given by inspiration, had now the force of a *law*. ¶ *Among my disciples.* Most of the Jewish commentators suppose that the volume, when

17 And *a*I will wait upon the Lord, that hideth *b* his face from the house of Jacob, and I will look for him.

18 Behold,*c* I and the children

a ch.50.11; 45.8.   *b* Hab.2.3.   *c* Heb.2.13.

completed by a prophet, was given for safe keeping to his disciples, or to some employed to preserve it securely. The word *disciples* means those who are *taught*, and here means those who were taught by the prophet; perhaps the pious and holy part of the people who would listen to his instructions. The Chaldee translates this verse, ' O prophet, preserve the testimony, lest ye testify to those who will not obey ; seal and hide the law, because they will not learn it.'

17. *And I will wait upon the* Lord. This is the commencement of a new subject. The prophet had closed his former message ; but had seen that in regard to the great mass of the nation, his exhortation had been in vain. He now says, that having delivered his message, he would patiently look to God alone. His hope was in him, though the nation looked elsewhere ; and though calamities were coming, yet he would still trust in God only. ¶ *That hideth his face.* This is a figurative expression, denoting the withdrawing of his favour and protection. He would leave them, and give them to deserved punishment; comp. Job xxiii. 9 ; xiii. 24 ; Ps. xliv. 24 ; x. 1 ; civ. 29. ¶ *And I will look for him.* I will expect aid from him, and will believe that his promises of final protection will yet be fulfilled ; comp. Hab. ii. 3:

For the vision is yet for an appointed time,
But at the end it shall speak, and not lie:
Though it tarry, wait for it;
Because it will surely come, it will not tarry.

18. *Behold, I,* &c. By ' signs and wonders,' here, it is meant that they, by the names given them, were intended to teach important lessons to the Jewish people. Their names were significant, and were designed to illustrate some important truth ; and especially the prophet here intimates that they were to inculcate the truth in regard to the presence and protection of God, to induce the people to look to him. Thus the

whom the Lord hath given me, *are* for signs and for wonders in Israel from the Lord of hosts, which dwelleth in mount Zion.

19 And when they shall say unto you, Seek unto them that have

name *Immanuel*, ' God with us,' ch. vii. 14 ; and *Shear-jashub*, ' the remnant shall return,' ch. vii. 3, were both significant of the fact that none but God could be the protector of the nation. And in like manner, it is possible that his own name, signifying the *salvation of Jehovah*, had been given him with such a reference. But at all events, it was a name which would remind them of the truth that he was *now* inculcating, that salvation was to be found in Jehovah, and that they should look to him. Names of children were often thus emblematic (see Hos. i.) ; and the prophets themselves were regarded as signs of important events ; Ezek. xxiv. 24 ; comp. Note, Isa. xx. 3. This passage is quoted with reference to the Messiah in Heb. ii. 13. ¶ *Which dwelleth in mount Zion.* Mount Zion was the residence of the house of David, or of the court, and it was often used to signify Jerusalem itself. The sense here is, that God was the protector of Jerusalem, or regarded that as his home; see Note, ch. i. 8.

19. *And when they shall say.* When the people, instead of putting confidence in God, shall propose to apply to necromancers. In the time of Ahaz the people were, as they were often, much inclined to idolatry ; 2 Kings xvi. 10. In their troubles and embarrassments, instead of looking to Jehovah, they imitated the example of surrounding nations, and applied for relief to those who professed to be able to hold converse with spirits. That it was common for idolatrous people to seek direction from those who professed that they had the power of divining, is well known ; see Isa. xix. 3 ; xxix. 4. It was expressly forbidden to the Jews to have recourse to those who made such professions ; Lev. xx. 6; Deut. xviii. 10, 11. Yet, notwithstanding this express command, it is evident that it was no uncommon thing for the Jews to make application for such instructions ; see the case of Saul, who made

familiar spirits, and unto wizards
that peep and that mutter; should

application to the woman of Endor,
who professed to have a familiar spirit,
in 1 Sam. xxviii. 7–25. Among heathen
nations, nothing was more common than
for persons to profess to have intercourse
with spirits, and to be under the influence of their inspiration. The oracle at
Delphi, of this nature, was celebrated
throughout Greece, and throughout the
world. Kings and princes, warriors and
nations, sought of the priestess who presided there, responses in undertaking
any important enterprise, and were
guided by her instructions ; *see* the
Travels of Anacharsis, vol. ii. 376, *sq.*
¶ *Seek unto.* Apply to for direction.
¶ *That hath familiar spirits.* Heb.
אֹבוֹת *ōbhōth.* The word 'familiar,'
applied to spirit, is supposed to have
been used by our translators to imply
that they were attended by an invisible
spirit that was subject to their call, or
that would inspire them when they
sought his direction. The Hebrew word
is used to denote a necromancer, a con-
juror ; particularly one who was supposed to have power to call up the
dead, to learn of them respecting future
events ; see 1 Sam. xxviii. 7–19; Deut.
xviii. 11. The word is most commonly
applied to *women ;* as it was almost
entirely confined to women to profess
this power ; Lev. xix. 31 ; xx. 6; 1 Sam.
xxviii. The idea was, that they could
call up the spirits of the dead who were
supposed to have seen objects invisible
to the living, and who could, therefore,
inform them in regard to things which
mortals on earth could not see. The
Vulgate renders this by ' Pythons and
diviners.' A *Python*, among the Greeks
and Romans, denoted one that had the
spirit of prophesying, and was particularly applied to the priestess of Apollo
at Delphi. The LXX. render the place
thus: ' And if they say to you, Seek the
ventriloquists, ἐγγαστριμύθους, and those
speaking from the earth, and speaking
vain things, who speak from the belly,'
οἳ ἐκ τῆς κοιλίας φωνοῦσιν. From this it
is evident, that the art of the *ventrilo-
quist,* so well known now, was known
then; and it is highly probable that the
secret of the art of soothsayers consisted

not a people seek unto their God?
for the living to the dead?

very much in being able to throw the
voice, with various modifications, into
different places, so that it would seem to
come from a grave, or from an image of
a dead person, that was made to appear
at the proper time. ¶ *And unto wizards.* The word used here—יִדְּעֹנִים
—is derived from the verb יָדַע *to know;*
and means *a wise man, a soothsayer, a
magician,* or one possessed with a spirit
of divination. The arts of the magician,
or soothsayer, were often the arts of one
skilled in natural magic ; acquainted
somewhat with the laws of chemistry;
and able, therefore, to produce appearances among an ignorant people that
would surprise them ; *see* Brewster's
Natural Magic, where this art is fully
explained. ¶ *That peep.* This word is
properly used of young birds, and means
to chirp, to pip ; and also to make a
small noise by the gentle opening of the
mouth. It is then applied to the *gentle
whispering* which the ancients ascribed
to departed spirits ; the small, low, shrill
voice which they were supposed to use,
and which, probably, those attempted to
imitate who claimed the power of raising them to the earth. It was believed
among all the ancient nations, that departed spirits did not speak out openly
and clearly, but with an indistinct,
low, gentle, suppressed voice. Thus, in
Virgil :—

—— pars tollere vocem
Exiguam.   *Æneid,* vi. 492.

—— gemitus lachrymabilis imo
Auditur tumulo, et vox reddita fertur ad aures.
Æneid, iii. 39.

Thus Horace :—

Umbræ cum Sagana resonarint triste et acutum.
Sat. lib i. 8, 40.

Thus Homer, speaking of the shade or
spirit of Patroclus, says that it went
with a whizzing sound: Ὤχετο τετριγυῖα.
—*Iliad,* Ψ-101.

He said, and with his longing arms essay'd
In vain to grasp the visionary shade;
Like a thin smoke he sees the spirit fly,
And hears a feeble, lamentable cry.

This night my friend, so late in battle lost,
Stood at my side a pensive, plaintive ghost.
Pope.

So, also, Lucian says of the infernal

20 To ^a the law and to the testimony: if they speak not according

a Lu.16.29; Jn.5.39.

to this word, *it is* because *there is* no ¹ light in them.

¹ *morning.*

---

regions, ' The whizzing shades of the dead fly around us ;' see *Gesenius in loc.* and *Rosenmüller;* also Bochart's *Hieroz.*, Part i. B. iii. ch. ii. p. 731. ¶ *And that mutter.* The word used here—הָגָה *hâghâ*—usually means *to meditate, to consider;* and then *to speak, to utter.* It also means *to sigh, to mourn,* Jer. xlviii. 31; Isa. xvi. 7; *to coo,* as a dove, Isa. xxxvii. 14; lix. 11; and then *to roar* like a lion ; not the *loud roar,* but the *grumbling,* the *suppressed* roar *(Bochart);* Isa. xxxi. 4. The idea here is, probably, that of *gently sighing,* or *mourning*—uttering feeble, plaintive lamentations or sighs, as departed shades were supposed to do ; and this was, probably, imitated by necromancers. By thus feigning that they conversed with the dead, they imposed on the ignorant populace, and led them to suppose that they had supernatural powers. ¶ *Should not a people seek,* &c. Is it not proper that a people should inquire of the God that is worshipped, in order to be directed in perplexing and embarrassing events ? Some have understood this to be a question of the *idolaters,* asking whether it was not right and proper for a people to seek counsel of those whom they worshipped as God. I understand it, however, as a question asked by the prophet, and as the language of strong and severe rebuke. ' You are seeking to idols, to the necromancers, and to the dead. But JEHOVAH is your God. And should not a people so signally favoured, a people under his peculiar care, apply to him, and seek his direction ?' ¶ *For the living.* On account of the affairs of the living. To ascertain what will be their lot, what is their duty, or what will occur to them. ¶ *To the dead.* The necromancers pretended to have intercourse with the spirits of the dead. The prophet strongly exposes the absurdity of this. What could the *dead* know of this ? How could they declare the future events respecting the living ? Where was this authorized? Men should seek God—the living God—and not

pretend to hold consultation with the dead.

20. *To the law,* &c. To the revelation which God has given. This is a solemn call of the prophet to try everything by the revealed will of God ; see ver. 16. ¶ *If they speak not.* If the necromancers—those that pretended to have intercourse with the dead. ¶ *According to this word.* According to what God has revealed. By this standard all their pretended revelations were to be tried. By this standard all doctrines are still to be tried. ¶ *It is because.* There has been a great variety of criticism upon this verse, but our translation expresses, probably, the true idea. The word rendered here ' *because,*' אֲשֶׁר *âshĕr,* commonly denotes ' which;' but it seems here to be used in the sense of the Syriac ? *Dolath,* or the Greek ὅτι. ¶ *No light.* Marg. 'Morning.' Heb. שַׁחַר *shâhhăr.* The word usually means the morning light ; the mingled light and darkness of the aurora; daybreak. It is an emblem of advancing knowledge, and perhaps, also, of prosperity or happiness after calamity, as the break of day succeeds the dark night. The meaning here may be, ' If their teachings do not accord with the law and the testimony, it is proof that they are *totally* ignorant, without even the *twilight* of true knowledge ; that it is *total darkness* with them.' Or it may mean, 'If they do not speak according to this word, *then no dawn will arise, i.e.,* no prosperity will smile upon *this people.*'—*Gesenius.* Lowth understands it of *obscurity, darkness :*—

' If they speak not according to this word,
In which there is no obscurity.'

But there is no evidence that the word is ever used in this sense. Others suppose that the Arabic sense of the word is to be retained here, *deception,* or *magic.* ' If they speak not according to this oracle, in which there is no *deception.*' But the word is not used in this sense in the Hebrew. The meaning is, probably, this : ' The law

21 And they shall pass through it hardly bestead and hungry; and it shall come to pass, that, when they shall be hungry, they shall fret *a* themselves, and curse *b* their

a Prov.19.3.   *b* Rev.16.11.

king and their God, and look upward.

22 And they shall look unto the earth; and behold trouble and darkness, dimness of anguish; and *they shall be* driven to darkness.

of God is the standard by which all professed communications from the invisible world are to be tested. If the necromancers deliver a doctrine which is not sustained by that, and not in accordance with the prophetic communications, it shows that they are in *utter* ignorance. There is not even the *glimmering* of the morning twilight; all is total night, and error, and obscurity with them, and they are not to be followed.'

21. *And they shall pass.* The people who have been consulting necromancers. This represents the condition of those who have sought for counsel and direction, and who have not found it. They shall be conscious of disappointment, and shall wander perplexed and alarmed through the land. ¶ *Through it.* Through the land. They shall wander in it from one place to another, seeking direction and relief. ¶ *Hardly bestead.* Oppressed, borne down, agitated. The meaning is, that the people would wander about, oppressed by the calamities that were coming upon the nation, and unalleviated by all that soothsayers and necromancers could do. ¶ *And hungry.* Famished; as one effect of the great calamities that would afflict the nation. ¶ *They shall fret themselves.* They shall be irritated at their own folly and weakness, and shall aggravate their sufferings by self-reproaches for having trusted to false gods. ¶ *Their king and their God.* The Hebrew interpreters understand this of the *false gods* which they had consulted, and in which they had trusted. But their *looking upward*, and the connection, seem to imply that they would rather curse the *true* God—the 'king and the God' of the Jewish people. They would be subjected to the proofs of his displeasure, and would vent their malice by reproaches and curses. ¶ *And look upward.* For relief. This denotes the condition of those in deep distress,

instinctively casting their eyes to heaven for aid. Yet it is implied that they would do it with no right feeling, and that they would see there only the tokens of their Creator's displeasure.

22. *And they shall look unto the earth.* They would look upward and find no relief, and then in despair cast their eyes to the earth to obtain help there. Yet equally in vain. The whole image is one of intense anguish brought on the nation for leaving the counsel of the true God. ¶ *And behold,* &c.; see Note, ch. v. 30. ¶ *Trouble.* Anguish, oppression, צָרָה *tzârâ,* from צוּר *tzūr,* to oppress, to straiten, to afflict. This is a remarkable instance of the prophet Isaiah's manner—of a rapid, impetuous, and bold style of utterance. He accumulates images; piles words on each other; and deepens the anxiety by each additional word, until we almost feel that we are enveloped by the gloom, and see objects of terror and alarm on every side. ¶ *Dimness of anguish.* These words should be kept separate in the translation—מְעוּף צוּקָה *mĕūph tzūkâ, darkness, oppression*—accumulated epithets to heighten the gloom and terror of the scene. ¶ *And they shall be driven to darkness.* Heb. וַאֲפֵלָה מְנֻדָּה a darkness that is *driven,* or that is urged upon itself; that becomes condensed, accumulated, until it becomes terrible and frightful. The idea is that of a driving tempest, or an involving obscurity (מְנֻדָּה *menŭddâ* from נָדַה *nâdhâ,* to push, thrust, impel, urge on, as a driving storm). The prophet has thus accumulated every possible idea of gloom and obscurity, and probably there is not anywhere a more graphic description of gathering darkness and trouble, and of the consternation of those involved in it, than this. So fearful and terrific are the judgments of God when he comes forth to punish men!

CHAPTER IX.

ANALYSIS.

THIS chapter is a continuation of the prophecy begun in ch. vii., and continued in ch. viii. It is composed of mingled threats and promises. Its characteristic may be said to be *rays of light thrown into the midst of shades.* It promises comfort and deliverance, while at the same time it denounces the sins of the nation, and assures the nation that the anger of the Lord is not turned away. The previous chapter had closed by describing a time of general calamity and darkness. This begins (ver. 1–i) by showing that the calamity would not be so great as in former times. It would be mitigated. There would be light—particularly in the dark regions of Zebulun and Naphtali—the provinces lying most exposed to the Syrian invasion. This light or deliverance was connected with the birth of the promised child (ver. 6, 7); and the mention of this leads the prophet into a magnificent description of his names, character, and reign. The prophet then returns to the threatened destruction of Israel, and denounces the Divine judgment against it. By the Syrians and the Philistines it would be invaded and destroyed, ver. 8–12. The *effects* of this, in cutting off their sources of strength, and producing general dismay and ruin, are described in the remainder of the chapter, ver. 13–21. The chapter, therefore, would impart consolation to the inhabitants of Judah, and is designed to confirm the promise that it should be safe from the threatened invasion; comp. ch. viii. 1–4.

NEVERTHELESS, the dimness *shall* not *be* such as *was* in her vexation, when at the first he lightly afflicted the land of Zebulun and the land of Naphtali, and afterward did

CHAPTER IX.

1. *Nevertheless.* Notwithstanding what is said in the previous chapter of the calamities that are coming upon Israel. Hengstenberg renders this whole verse : 'For darkness shall not be upon the land upon which there is distress ; as the former time has dishonoured the land of Zebulun and the land of Naphtali ; so shall the time come to honour it, the region on the border of the sea, by the side of the Jordan, Galilee of the Gentiles.' ¶ *The dimness.* The Hebrew word here denotes obscurity, or darkness ; and is here used, as the word darkness often is in the Scriptures, to denote calamity or affliction. The dimness, or calamity, here referred to, is that which is threatened, ch. viii. 21, 22. ¶ Shall *not* be *such.* It shall not be unbroken darkness, and unalleviated calamity ; but it shall be interrupted by the rising of the great light that shall shine on the dark land of Zebulun and Naphtali. ¶ *In her vexation.* The word ' her ' refers to the whole land of Palestine, to the afflictions that came upon the whole region. The word *vexation*, מוּצָק, means oppression, calamity, or being *straitened*, or *pressed.* ¶ *When at the first.* In the former time ; on a former occasion. ¶ *He lightly afflicted.* The word here used, קָלַל, means properly, to be, or make light, or small ; and in Hiphil, the form which occurs here, it often means *to esteem lightly, to despise, to hold in contempt;* 2 Sam. xix. 44; Ezek. xxii. 7. It probably has that sense here, as the design of the prophet is evidently to speak, not of a *light* affliction in the former time, but of a grievous, heavy calamity—a calamity which would be well denoted by the expression, 'he made them vile; he exposed them to contempt and derision.' The time to which reference is made here, was probably the invasion of the land by Tiglath-pileser ; 2 Kings xv. 29; 1 Chron. v. 26. In that invasion, the parts of Zebulun and Naphtali were particularly afflicted. ' Tiglath-pileser took Ijon, and Gilead, and Galilee, and all the land of Naphtali, and carried them captive to Assyria ;' 2 Kings xv. 29. This region had also been invaded by Benhadad two hundred years before the time of Isaiah ; 1 Kings xv. 20, and there might have been a reference to these various invasions to which this northern part of the land of Palestine had been subjected. ¶ *The land of Zebulun.* The region occupied by the tribe of Zebulun. This tribe was located between the sea of Tiberias, or the lake Gennesareth, and the Mediterranean. It extended entirely across from the one to the other, and as it was thus favoured with a somewhat extended sea-coast, the people were more given to commerce than the other tribes, and hence mingled

more grievously afflict *her* by the

way of the sea, beyond Jordan, in Galilee 1 of the nations.

---

more with surrounding nations. ¶ *And the land of Naphtali.* The region which was occupied by this tribe was directly north of Zebulun, and of the sea of Galilee, having that sea and the tribe of Zebulun on the south and south-east, Asher on the west, and a part of the tribe of Manasseh, on the east. ¶ *And afterward.* That is, in subsequent times; meaning times that were to come *after* the prophecy here delivered. The previous part of the verse refers to the calamities that had come upon that region in former times. The expression here refers to what was seen by the prophet as *yet* to occur. ¶ *Did more grievously afflict.* הִכְבִּיד. This verb has very various significations. It properly means *to be heavy, to be grievous, to lie* or *fall heavy on any one, to be dull, obstinate;* also, *to be honoured, respected; i.e.,* of *weight,* or influence in society. It means, in Hiphil, the form which is used here, *to make heavy,* or *grievous;* 1 Kings xii. 10; Isa. xlvii. 6; *to oppress,* Neh. v. 15; and it *also* means *to cause to be honoured,* or *distinguished, to favour.* —*Gesenius.* The connection requires that it should have this sense here, and the passage means, that the land which he had *made vile* in former times, or had suffered to be despised, he had purposed to *honour,* or to render illustrious by the great light that should rise on it. So Lowth, Rosenmüller, and Gesenius, translate it; see a similar use of the word in Jer. xxx. 19; 2 Chron. xxv. 19; 1 Sam. ii. 30. ¶ *By the way of the sea.* The sea of Galilee, or Gennesareth. All this region was in the vicinity of that sea. The word *way* here, דֶּרֶךְ *dĕrĕkh,* means *towards,* or *in the vicinity of.* The extensive dark region lying in the vicinity of that sea. Both those tribes bordered on the sea of Tiberias, or had that as a part of their boundary. ¶ *Beyond Jordan.* This expression—עֵבֶר הַיַּרְדֵּן—means in the vicinity of Jordan; the land by the side of the Jordan, or perhaps that large region through which the upper part of the Jordan passed. It does not

mean strictly on the *east* of Jordan, but rather the northern portion of the land. It is such language as a man would use who was describing the upper and imperfectly known regions of the country—the dark, uncivilized region through which the upper part of the Jordan flowed, and the word עֵבֶר, here rendered *beyond,* means *side*—by the side of the Jordan. ¶ *Galilee of the nations.* This was sometimes called *upper Galilee.* It was called ' Galilee of the nations,' or of the *Gentiles,* because it was surrounded by them, and because the heathen were extensively intermingled with the Jews. In this region, Solomon had given to Hiram, king of Tyre, twenty cities; 1 Kings ix. 2. Adjacent to this region were the countries of Phenicia, Tyre, and Sidon; and the people would naturally mingle much with them in commerce. The country abounded with hills and caverns, and, consequently, it was never possible completely to dislodge from the fastnesses the former inhabitants of the land. Strabo enumerates among the inhabitants of Galilee, Arabians and Phenicians. The inhabitants of this country are represented as having been bold and courageous, but as seditious, and prone to insolence and rebellion. If it be asked here, in what way this land had been made contemptible, or why it was regarded as an object of contempt? we may reply, (1.) The district in which these two tribes dwelt constituted the border-land towards the heathen nations. (2.) The Galileans not only dwelt in the vicinity of the heathen, but a large number of them had actually remained in the country, and it had been found impossible to expel them from it; Judg. i. 30–35. (3.) The Phenicians, with whom they held commercial intercourse, and with whom they dwelt intermingled, were among the most corrupt of the heathen nations. To this may be added, (4.) They were far from Jerusalem, and, consequently, the influence of religion may be supposed to have been less felt among them than among the other Jews. The true

2 The *a* people that walked in
darkness have seen a great light:
they that dwell in the land of the

a Mat.4.15,16.   1 or, *to him.*

shadow of death, upon them hath
the light shined.

3 Thou hast multiplied the nation,
and not [1] increased the joy: they

religion was, in a great measure, lost
upon them, and ignorance and superstition took its place. Hence, in the New
Testament, they are spoken of as almost
proverbially rude and ignorant.

2. *The people that walked in darkness.* The inhabitants of the region of
Galilee. They were represented as
walking in darkness, because they were
far from the capital, and from the temple; they had few religious privileges;
they were intermingled with the heathen, and were comparatively rude and
uncultivated in their manners and in
their language. Allusion to this is
several times made in the New Testament; John i. 46: 'Can any good thing
come out of Nazareth?' vii. 52: 'Search
and look, for out of Galilee ariseth no
prophet;' Matt. xxvi. 69; Mark xiv. 70.
The word *walked* here is synonymous
with *lived*, and denotes that thick darkness brooded over the country, so that
they *lived*, or walked amidst it. ¶ *Have
seen a great light. Light* is not only
an emblem of knowledge in the Scriptures, but of joy, rejoicing, and deliverance. It stands opposed to moral darkness, and to times of judgment and calamity. What is the particular reference
here, is not agreed by expositors. The
immediate connection seems to require
us to understand it of deliverance from
the calamities that were impending over
the nation then. They would be afflicted,
but they would be delivered. The tribes
of Israel would be carried captive away;
and Judah would also be removed. This
calamity would particularly affect the
ten tribes of Israel—the northern part
of the land, the regions of Galilee—*for
those tribes would be carried away not
to return.* Yet this region also would
be favoured with a peculiarly striking
manifestation of light. I see no reason
to doubt that the language of the prophet here is adapted to extend into that
future period when the Messiah should
come to that dark region, and become
both its light and its deliverer. Isaiah
may have referred to the immediate
deliverance of the nation from impend-

ing calamities, but there is a fulness and
richness of the language that seems to
be applicable only to the Messiah. So
it is evidently understood in Matt. iv.
13–16. ¶ *They that dwell.* The same
people are referred to here as in the
former member of the verse. ¶ *In the
land of the shadow of death.* This is
a most beautiful expression, and is
peculiar to the Hebrew poets. The
word צַלְמָוֶת *tzălmâvĕth*, is exceedingly
poetical. The *idea* is that of *death*, as
a dark substance or being, casting a
long and chilly *shade* over the land—
standing between the land and the light
—and thus becoming the image of
ignorance, misery, and calamity. It is
often used, in the Scriptures, to describe
those regions that were lying as it were
in the *penumbra* of this gloomy object,
and exposed to all the chills and sorrows
of this melancholy darkness. Death,
by the Hebrews, was especially represented as extending his long and baleful
shadow over the regions of departed
spirits; Job xxxviii. 17:

Have the gates of death been opened to thee?
Hast thou seen the gates of the shadow of death?

Job x. 21:

Before I go—I shall not return—
To the land of darkness
And of the shadow of death.

It is thus an image of chills, and gloom,
and night—of anything that resembles
the still and mournful regions of the
dead. The Chaldee renders these two
verses thus: 'In a former time Zebulun
and Naphtali emigrated; and those who
remained after them a strong king shall
carry into captivity, because they did
not remember the power which was
shown in the Red Sea, and the miracles
which were done in Jordan, and the
wars of the people of the cities. The
people of the house of Israel who walked
in Egypt as in the midst of shades, came
out that they might see a great light.'

3. *Thou hast multiplied the nation.*
Thou hast rendered the nation strong,
powerful, mighty. Several interpreters,
as Calvin, Vitringa, and Le Clerc, sup-

jcy before thee according to the joy
in harvest, *and* as *men* rejoice when
they divide the spoil.

4 For [1] thou hast broken the yoke

of his burden, and the staff of his
shoulder, the rod of his oppressor,
as in the day *a* of Midian.

1 or, *when thou breakest.*　　　*a* Judg.7.21, &c.

pose that the prophet here, and in the
two following verses, speaks in the first
instance of the prosperity near at hand,
and of the rapid increase of the Israelites after the return from the Babylonish
exile, in which the inhabitants of Galilee
must have participated, as may be inferred from the accounts of Josephus
respecting the great population of that
province in his time ; see *Jewish Wars,*
i. 20, 3. Vitringa also directs our
attention to the fact, that the Jewish
people, after the exile, not only filled
Judea, but spread themselves into Egypt,
Syria, Mesopotamia, Asia Minor, Greece,
and Italy. But there seems to be no
necessity for referring it to such an increase of the inhabitants. It may refer
to the great increase of the Messiah's
kingdom, or of the kingdom which he
would set up, and whose commencement
would be in Galilee ; *see* Hengstenberg,
Christol., vol. i. p. 354. ¶ And *not increased the joy.* The Masorites here
read in the margin לוֹ *to it,* instead of
לֹא *not.* Eleven MSS., two of them
ancient, have this reading. This reading is followed by the Chaldee Paraphrase, the Syriac, and the Arabic. The
LXX. seem also to have so understood
it. So also it is in the margin, and so
the connection demands ; and it is unquestionably the correct reading. It
would then read, 'thou hast increased
for it [the nation] the joy.' Hengstenberg, however, suggests that the phrase
may mean, 'whose joy thou didst not
before enlarge,' that is, upon whom thou
hast before inflicted heavy sufferings.
But this is harsh, and I see no reason
to doubt that an error may have crept
into the text. ¶ *They joy before thee
according to the joy of harvest.* This
is a beautiful figure ; and is found frequently in ancient writings. The harvest was a time of exultation and joy,
and was commonly gathered amid songs
and rejoicings, and concluded with a
festival. The phrase ' before thee' refers
to the fact that the first-fruits of the
harvest among the Hebrews were presented with thanksgiving before God

in the temple ; Deut. xii. 7 ; xiv. 22–26.
¶ And *as* men *rejoice,* &c. This is also
an expression of great joy and rejoicing.
Such an occasion, at the close of a battle,
when great spoil or plunder had been
taken, would be one of great rejoicing ;
see Judg. v. 30 ; 1 Sam. xxx. 16 ; 2
Chron. xx. 25–28.

4. *For thou hast broken.* This verse,
and the following, show the way in which
the occasion of the joy had been furnished. The expression ' thou *hast* '
does not necessarily refer to *the past,*
but is a form of expression derived from
the nature of the prophetic visions, where
that is described as *past* which is seen
to pass before the eyes of the prophet ;
see Introduction, § 7. ¶ *The yoke.*
This word is often used to denote *oppression,* or *tyranny;* Lev. xxvi. 13 ; Deut.
xxviii. 48—where oppression is described
as 'an iron yoke;' comp. 1 Kings xii. 4;
Isa. xlvii. 6 ; lviii. 6. ¶ *The staff of
his shoulder.* The word rendered *staff*
here may mean a bough, a branch, a
staff, stick, or rod. Gesenius supposes
that the expression here means the rod
by which punishment is inflicted, and
that the phrase ' rod of, or for the
shoulder,' denotes oppression and servitude. Rosenmüller thinks, that it refers
rather to the custom among the ancients
of placing a piece of wood, not unlike a
yoke, on the necks and shoulders of
slaves, as a mark of servitude. Hengstenberg understands it, ' the staff which
strikes the neck or back.' ¶ *The rod
of his oppressor.* This, doubtless, refers
to the chastisement which was inflicted
on those in bondage, and is a phrase denoting oppression and servitude. The
word ' his' here refers to *Israel.* ¶ *As
in the day of Midian.* This refers to
the deliverance that was accomplished
under Gideon against the Midianites ;
see Judg. vii. ; viii. That deliverance
was a remarkable interposition of God.
It was accomplished not by human
strength ; but was a signal manifestation
of the power of God in delivering the
nation from the long oppression of the
Midianites. So the prophet says here,

5 For [1] every battle of the warrior *is* with confused noise, and garments

1 or, *when the whole.*

rolled in blood; [2] but *this* shall be with burning *and* [3] fuel of fire.

2 or, *and it was.*　　　　3 *meat.*

that the deliverance will be as signal a proof of the presence and power of God as is was in that day. Herder (*Heb. Poetry*, vol. ii. p. 296) says, ' At that period, in the north part of the country, a great deliverance was wrought. Then, in the obscure forests of Naphtali and Zebulun, the light of freedom went forth over all the land. So now, also, in this northern press of nations, in the way along the sea of Galilee, where now the hostile Syrians are exercising their oppressions, the light of freedom is going forth, and there shall be joy and jubilee, like that of the song of Deborah.'

5. *For every battle of the warrior.* The expression used here has caused great difficulty, from the fact that it occurs nowhere else in the Scriptures. The word סְאוֹן *sĕōn*, rendered here *battle*, is supposed to mean rather *greaves*, or the armour of the warrior which covered the feet and the legs. It would be literally translated, ' Every greave of those armed with greaves.'—*Gesenius*. The Chaldee renders it, ' For every gift of theirs is for evil.' The Syriac, ' For every tumult [of battle] is heard with terror.' Hengstenberg renders it, ' For all war-shoes put on at the noise of battle, all garments dipped in blood, shall be burnt, shall be the food of fire.' The idea, according to him, is, that the great future redemption will be like the deliverance under Gideon'; ' because, far from being accomplished by force of arms, with it all contention and war shall cease.' Gesenius regards the figurative expression as a general designation of that peace which shall never end. All the armour used in war shall then be burnt, as being of no further use. ¶ *Is with confused noise.* The word used here—רַעַשׁ *ra'ash*—denotes, properly, a shaking, as of a spear ; a concussion, tumult, noise, as of a battle. Here it is supposed to refer to the noise which the armour of the soldiers made—particularly to the noise made by the *greaves*, or war-shoes, worn on the feet and legs. Those greaves were fitted up, it is said, by numerous large iron hooks, or clasps, and were fastened sometimes

with large nails; comp. Josephus, *Jewish Wars*, B. vi. ch. i. § 8. ¶ *And garments.* This word here refers, doubtless, to the soldier's cloak or blanket. ¶ *Rolled in blood.* This is a description of the usual effect of war. The image of war is that of a clangour made by the armour of soldiers, and by garments that have been dipped in human blood. It is a most revolting but just image. ¶ *But this shall be.* In regard to this threatened invasion and danger, this shall be the result. The meaning is this. The prophet sees the image of war and of threatened invasion. He hears the clangour of their greaves—the sound of their march ; and he sees the usual emblem of battle—bloody garments. But he says here, that this invasion shall not be successful. There was no occasion of alarm. The very armour of the warrior should be burned up. The enemy should be defeated—and their greaves, and their bloody garments, should be consumed. ¶ *With burning.* For burning; that is, it shall be consumed. ¶ And *fuel of fire.* Heb. ' Food of fire.' This is a strong, emphatic expression—' it shall be to be burned—the food of fire.' It denotes the certainty that they would be vanquished; that the invading foe would not be successful ; and that his very armoury and garments would be stripped off and burned. To understand this, it is necessary to remark, that in ancient times it was customary to strip the dead which were slain in a vanquished army, and to collect their armour, their chariots, &c., and consume them. The more valued spoils of battle were reserved as the prey of the victors, or to be suspended in temples consecrated to the gods ; see Ps. xlvi. 9, 10 :

He maketh wars to cease unto the end of the earth;
He breaketh the bow;
And cutteth the spear in sunder;
He burneth the chariot in the fire.

Ezekiel has carried out this description more at length :

And the inhabitants of the cities of Israel shall go forth,
And shall set on fire and burn the weapons,

6 For unto us a child is born, unto *a* us a son is given, and the

a Lu.2.11.

Both the shields and the bucklers,
The bows and the arrows,
And the clubs and the lances.
                Ezek. xxxix. 9.

Zechariah has a similar figure, as descriptive of the time of the Messiah:

Rejoice greatly, O daughter of Zion;
Shout, O daughter of Jerusalem;
Behold, thy king cometh unto thee.

And I will cut off the chariot from Ephraim,
And the horse from Jerusalem,
And the battle bow shall be cut off, &c.
                Zech. ix. 9, 10.

This custom prevailed among several nations. Thus Virgil:

   — scutorumque incendi victor accrvos.
                Æneid, viii. 562.

There can be no doubt, I think, that the prophet here has his eye on the victories of the Messiah, and that he means to say, that in those victories all armour would be for fuel of fire; that is, that they would be achieved without hostile arms. Applied to the Messiah, it means either that his victories would be complete, or that *in* his victories all necessity of such armour would cease. According to this, the passage teaches that peace should be introduced by him without a conflict, and thus harmonizes with the numerous parallel passages in which peace is represented as a characteristic mark of the times of the Messiah, when contention, war, and destruction shall cease; see ch. xi. 6, 7.

6. *For.* This is given as a *reason* of the victories that were predicted in the previous verses. That it has reference to the Messiah has been almost universally conceded; and indeed it does not seem possible to doubt it. The eye of the prophet seems to have been fixed on this great and glorious event—as attracting all his attention. The scenes of coming times, like a *panorama,* or *picture,* passed before him. Most of the picture seems to have been that of battles, conflicts, sieges, dimness, and thick darkness. But in one portion of the passing scene there was light. It was the light that he saw rising in the distant and darkened Galilee. He saw the joy of the people; the armour of

government *b* shall be upon his shoulder; and his name shall be

b Mat.28.18.

war laid aside; the image of peace succeeding; the light expanding and becoming more intense as the darkness retired, until he saw in this region the Prince of Peace—the Sun of Righteousness itself. The eye of the prophet gazed intently on that scene, and was fixed on that portion of the picture: he sees the Messiah in his office, and describes him as already come, and as born unto the nation. ¶ *Unto us.* For our benefit. The prophet saw in vision the darkness and gloom of the nation, and saw also the son that would be born to remove that darkness, and to enlighten the world. ¶ *A child* (יֶלֶד). This word usually denotes a lad, a boy, a youth. It is commonly applied to one in early life; but no particular stress is to be laid on the word. The vision of the prophet is, that the long-expected Messiah is born, and is seen growing up amidst the surrounding darkness of the north of Palestine, ver. 1. ¶ *Is born.* Not that he was born when the prophet spake. But in prophetic vision, as the events of the future passed before his mind, he saw that promised son, and the eye was fixed intently on him; see the Introduction, § 7, and Note, ch. i. 1. ¶ *A son.* בֵּן *bēn.* This word does not differ materially from the word translated *child.* In the future scenes, as they passed before the mind of the prophet, he saw the child, the son that was to be born, and described him as he appeared to his view —as a child. Fixing the eye on him, he proceeds at once to designate his character by stating the appropriate names which he would bear. ¶ *Is given.* The Messiah is often represented as having been *given,* or *sent;* or as the rich gift of God; Note, Acts iv. 12; John iii. 16; Eph. i. 22; John xvii. 4. The Messiah was pre-eminently the *gift* of the God of love. Man had no claim on him, and God voluntarily gave his Son to be a sacrifice for the sins of the world. ¶ *And the government shall be upon his shoulder.* The sense of this passage is, that he shall *rule,* or that the government shall be vested in him. Various called Wonderful, Counsellor, The

a Heb.1.8.   *b* Eph.2.14.

mighty God, *a* The everlasting Father, the Prince of Peace.*b*

interpretations have, however, been given of the phrase 'upon his shoulder.' Some have supposed, that it means simply he shall sustain the government, as the shoulder is that by which we uphold any thing. Pliny and Cicero thus use the phrase ; see Rosenmüller. Others, that it means that he should wear the royal purple from a child.—*Grotius.* Lowth supposes that it refers to the ensign of government—the sceptre, the sword, the keys, or the like, that were borne upon the shoulder, or suspended from it : see Note on ch. xxii. 22. It is evident, from this latter place, that some ensign of office was usually borne upon the shoulder. The sense is, that he should be a king, and under this character the Messiah is often predicted. ¶ *And his name shall be called.* That is, his attributes shall be such as to make all these applications appropriate descriptions of his power and work. *To be called,* and *to be,* in the Hebrew, often mean the same thing. The word אקרא *may* possibly mean, JEHOVAH shall call him ; or it may be regarded as taken impersonally. Such a use of a verb is not uncommon in Isaiah. ' *One calls him,'* is, according to the usage in Isaiah, as much as to say, he will justly bear this name ; or simply, he will be. ¶ *Wonderful.* פלא. This word is derived from the verb פלא *pálâ,* to separate, to distinguish, or to make great. It is applied usually to anything that is great or wonderful, as a miracle ; Ex. xv. 2 ; Lam. i. 9 ; Dan. xii. 6. It is applied here to denote the unusual and remarkable assemblage of qualities that distinguished the Messiah. Those are specified more particularly in the other part of the verse ; such an assemblage of qualities as to make proper the names Mighty God, &c. ' The proper idea of the word,' says Hengstenberg, ' is *miraculous.* It imports that the personage here referred to, in his being and in his works, will be exalted above the ordinary course of nature, and that his whole manifestation will be a miracle.' Yet it seems to me, that the proper idea of the word is not that of *miraculous.* It

is rather that which is *separated* from the ordinary course of events, and which is fitted to excite amazement, wonder, and admiration, whether it be miraculous or not. This will be apparent if the following places are examined, where the word occurs in various forms. It is rendered *marvellous,* Ps. cxviii. 23 ; cxxxix. 14 ; xcviii. 1 ; Job v. 9 ; *wonderful,* 2 Sam. i. 26 ; Ps. cxxxix. 14 ; Prov. xxx. 18 ; Job xlii. 3 ; Ps. lxxii. 18 ; lxxxvi. 10 ; *hidden,* Deut. xxx. 2 ; *things too high,* Ps. cxxxi. 1 ; *miracles,* Judg. vi. 13 ; Ex. xv. 2 ; Ps. lxxvii. 14 ; lxxxviii. 10 ; lxxxix. 5 ; the word is translated *wonders,* in the sense of *miracles,* in several places ; and *hard,* Deut. xvii. 8 ; Jer. xxxii. 17. From these passages, it is clear that it *may* denote that which is miraculous, but that this idea is not necessarily connected with it. Anything which is fitted to excite wonder and amazement, from any cause, will correspond with the sense of the Hebrew word. It is a word which expresses with surprising accuracy everything in relation to the Redeemer. For the Messiah was *wonderful* in all things. It was wonderful love by which God gave him, and by which he came ; the manner of his birth was wonderful ; his humility, his self-denial, his sorrows were wonderful ; his mighty works were wonderful ; his dying agonies were wonderful ; and his resurrection, his ascension, were all fitted to excite admiration and wonder. ¶ *Counsellor.* This word has been sometimes joined with ' wonderful,' as if designed to qualify it thus—*wonderful counsellor ;* but it expresses a distinct attribute, or quality. The name *counsellor* here, יועץ, denotes one of honourable rank ; one who is fitted to stand near princes and kings as their adviser. It is expressive of great wisdom, and of qualifications to guide and direct the human race. The LXX. translate this phrase, ' The angel of the mighty counsel.' The Chaldee, ' The God of wonderful counsel.' ¶ *The mighty God.* Syriac, ' The mighty God of ages.' This is one, and but one out of many, of the instances in which the name *God* is

applied to the Messiah ; comp. John i. 1;
Rom. ix. 5; 1 John v. 20; John xx. 28;
1 Tim. iii. 16; Heb. i. 8. The name
'mighty God,' is unquestionably attributed to the true God in ch. x. 21.
Much controversy has arisen in relation
to this expression ; and attempts have
been made to show that the word translated God, אֵל, may refer to a hero, a
king, a conqueror. Thus Gesenius renders, it 'Mighty hero;' and supposes
that the name 'God' is here used in
accordance with the custom of the Orientals, who ascribe Divine attributes to
kings. In like manner Plüschke (see
Hengstenberg) says, ' In my opinion this
name is altogether symbolical. The
Messiah shall be called strength of God,
or strong God, Divine hero, in order by
this name to remind the people of the
strength of God.' But after all such
controversy, it still remains certain that
the natural and obvious meaning of the
expression is to denote a Divine nature.
So it was evidently understood by the
ancient versions ; and the fact that the
name God is so often applied to Christ
in the New Testament, proves that it
is to be understood in its natural and
obvious signification. ¶ *The everlasting
Father.* The Chaldee renders this expression, ' The man abiding for ever.'
The Vulgate, ' The Father of the future
age.' Lowth, ' The Father of the everlasting age.' Literally, it is the Father
of eternity, אֲבִי עַד. The word rendered *everlasting*, עַד, properly denotes
eternity, and is used to express *for ever;*
see Ps. ix. 6, 19; xix. 10. It is often
used in connection with עוֹלָם, thus,
וְעֶד עוֹלָם, *for ever and ever;* Ps. x. 16;
xxi. 5; xlv. 7. The Hebrews used the
term *father* in a great variety of senses
—as a literal father, a grandfather, an
ancestor, a ruler, an instructor. The
phrase may either 'mean the same as
the Eternal Father, and the sense will
be, that the Messiah will not, as must
be the case with an earthly king, however excellent, leave his people destitute
after a short reign, but will rule over
them and bless them for ever (*Hengstenberg*); or it may be used in accordance with a custom usual in Hebrew
and in Arabic, where he who possesses
a thing is called the father of it. Thus,

the father of strength means strong ; *the
father of knowledge,* intelligent ; *the
father of glory,* glorious ; *the father of
goodness,* good ; *the father of peace,*
peaceful. According to this, the meaning of the phrase, *the Father of eternity,*
is properly *eternal.* The application of
the word here is derived from this usage.
The term *Father* is not applied to the
Messiah here with any reference to the
distinction in the Divine nature ; for
that word is uniformly, in the Scriptures, applied to the *first,* not to the
second person of the Trinity. But it is
used in reference to *duration,* as a Hebraism involving high poetic beauty.
He is not merely represented as everlasting, but he is introduced, by a strong
figure, as even *the Father of eternity,*
as if even *everlasting duration* owed
itself to his paternity. There could not
be a more emphatic declaration of strict
and proper eternity. It may be added,
that *this* attribute is often applied to
the Messiah in the New Testament ;
John viii. 58; Col. i. 17; Rev. i. 11, 17,
18; Heb. i. 10, 11; John i. 1, 2. ¶ *The
Prince of Peace.* This is a Hebrew
mode of expression denoting that he
would be *a peaceful prince.* The tendency of his administration would be
to restore and perpetuate peace. This
expression is used to distinguish him
from the mass of kings and princes who
have delighted in conquest and blood.
In contradistinction from all these, the
Messiah would seek to promote universal
concord, and the tendency of his reign
would be to put an end to wars, and
to restore harmony and order to the
nations ; see the tendency of his reign
still further described in ch. xi. 6–9;
Note, ch. ii. 4; see also Mic. v. 4; Hos.
ii. 18. It is not necessary to insist on
the coincidence of this description with
the uniform character and instructions
of the Lord Jesus. In this respect, he
disappointed all the hopes of the Jewish
nation, who, in spite of the plain prophecies respecting his peaceful character,
expected a magnificent prince, and a
conqueror. The expressions used here
imply that he would be more than
human. It is impossible to believe that
these appellations would be given under
the Spirit of inspiration to a mere man.
They express a higher nature ; and they
13

7 Of the increase of *his* government and peace *there shall be* no end,[a] upon the throne of David, and upon his kingdom, to order it, and to establish it with judgment

a Dan.2.44; 1 Cor.15.25.

coincide with the account in the New Testament throughout, that he would be Divine. It is true, indeed, that expressions of a pompous and high-sounding character were commonly assumed by Oriental princes. The following is a single instance of their arrogance, ostentation, and pride. 'Chosröes, king of kings, lord of lords, ruler of the nations, *prince of peace*, saviour of men ; among the gods, a man good and eternal, but among men, a god most illustrious, glorious, a conqueror rising with the sun, and giving vision at night.'— Theoph. *Simocatta Chron.*, iv. 8, quoted by Gesenius. But it cannot be pretended, that the Spirit of inspiration would use titles in a manner so unmeaning and so pompous as this. Besides, it was one great object of the prophets to vindicate the name and character of the true God, and to show that all such appellations belonged to him alone. However such appellations might be used by surrounding nations, and given to kings and princes by the heathen, yet in the Scriptures they are not given to earthly monarchs. That this passage refers to the Messiah has been generally conceded, except by the Jews, and by a few later critics. Jarchi and Kimchi maintain that it refers to Hezekiah. They have been driven to this by the use which Christians have made of the passage against the Jews. But the absurdity of this interpretation has been shown in the Notes on ch. vii. 14. The *ancient* Jews incontestably referred it to the Messiah. Thus the Targum of Jonathan renders it, 'His name shall be called God of wonderful counsel, man abiding for ever, THE MESSIAH, מְשִׁיחַ, whose peace shall be multiplied upon us in his days.' Thus Rabbi Jose, of Galilee, says, 'The name of the Messiah is שָׁלוֹם *Shâlôm*, as is said in Isa. ix. 6, "Father of Eternity, Prince of Peace."' Ben Sira (fol. 40, of the Amsterdam Edition, 1679) numbers among the eight names of the Messiah those also taken from this passage, Wonderful, Counsellor, Mighty God, Prince of Peace. The

later Jews, however, have rejected this interpretation, because the Messiah is here described as God.

7. *Of the increase*, &c. The word rendered *government* here, מִשְׂרָה, means properly his government *as a prince— his principality*, and is a continuation of the idea in the previous verse, 'the Prince of Peace.' It means that his reign as a prince of peace—in extending and promoting peace, shall be unlimited, ¶ *And peace*. This does not signify in the original, as our translation would seem to do, that there should be no end to the increase of his peace, but that there should be no limit to *peace*, that is, that his reign should be one of unlimited peace. The whole is a description of a prosperous, wide-extended, ever-growing and unlimited empire of peace. ¶ *No end.* The word here used—קֵץ—may refer either to space or time. The connection, however, seems to confine it to *time*, and to mean simply that over his wide-extended and peaceful principality he should reign for ever. ¶ *Upon the throne of David ;* see Note, Acts ii. 30. This was in accordance with the promise made to David ; 1 Kings viii. 25 ; 2 Sam. vii. 12, 13 ; Ps. cxxxii. 11. This promise was understood as referring to the Messiah. The primary idea is, that he should be descended in the line of David, and accordingly the New Testament writers are often at pains to show that the Lord Jesus was of that family ; Luke ii. 4. When it is said that he would sit upon the throne of David, it is not to be taken literally. The peculiarity of the reign of David was, *that he reigned over the people of God.* He was chosen for this purpose from humble life ; was declared in his administration to be a man after God's own heart ; and his long and prosperous reign was a reign over the people of God. To sit upon the throne of David, therefore, means to reign over the people of God ; and in this sense the Messiah sat on his throne. There is also a similarity in the two administrations, in the fact that the Messiah was taken from humble life.

and with justice, from henceforth even for ever. The zeal of the LORD of hosts will perform this.

8 The Lord sent a word into Jacob, and it hath lighted upon Israel.

9 And all the people shall know, *even* Ephraim and the inhabitants

---

and that his reign will be far-extended and prosperous. But the main idea of resemblance is, that the reign of each extended over the people of God. ¶ *And upon his kingdom.* That is, over the kingdom of the people of God. It does not mean particularly the Jews, but all those over whom the Divine administration should be set up. ¶ *To order it.* To raise up, or confirm it. The word, also, is sometimes used to denote to *found* a kingdom. Here it means to *confirm* it, to cause it to stand. ¶ *And to establish it.* To place it on a firm foundation; to make it firm. ¶ *With judgment,* &c. That is, under an administration that shall be just and right. Most kingdoms have been those of blood, and have been established by iniquity, and by the unjust overthrow of others. But the administration of the Messiah shall be established in righteousness, and shall be destined to extend and perpetuate justice and righteousness for ever. ¶ *From henceforth.* That is, from the time which was the period of the prophet's vision, when he saw in vision the Messiah rising in the dark parts of Galilee; Notes, ver. 1, 2. ¶ *The zeal.* The word here used denotes *ardour,* intense desire in accomplishing an object; and means that the establishment of this kingdom was an object of intense and ardent desire on the part of JEHOVAH. It is also implied that nothing else than the zeal of JEHOVAH could do it. We may remark here—(1.) That if JEHOVAH feels so intense a desire for this, then the subjects of the Messiah's reign should also feel this. (2.) If JEHOVAH feels this zeal, and if he will certainly accomplish this, then Christians should be encouraged in their efforts to spread the gospel. His *purpose* to do this is their only encouragement—and a sufficient encouragement—to excite *their* zeal in this great and glorious work.

8. *The Lord sent.* Not JEHOVAH here, but *Adonai.* It is apparent that this verse is the commencement of a new prophecy, that is not connected with that which precedes it. The strain of

the preceding prophecy had respect to Judah; this is confined solely to Israel, or Ephraim. Here the division of the chapter should have been made, and should not have been again interrupted till the 4th verse of ch. x., where the prophecy closes. The prophecy is divided into *four* parts, and each part is designed to threaten a distinct judgment on some particular, prominent vice. I. *Crime—* their pride and ostentation, ver. 8, 9. *Punishment—*the land would be invaded by the Syrians and the Philistines, ver. 11, 12. II. *Crime—*they had apostatized from God, and the leaders had caused them to err, ver. 13, 16. *Punishment—*JEHOVAH would cut off the chief men of the nation, ver. 14, 15, 17. III. *Crime—*prevalent wickedness in the nation, ver. 18. *Punishment —* the anger of JEHOVAH, consternation, anarchy, discord, and want, ver. 19–21. IV. *Crime—*prevalent injustice; ch. x. 1, 2. *Punishment—*foreign invasion, and captivity; ch. x. 3, 4. The poem is remarkably regular in its structure (*Lowth*), and happy in its illustrations. At what *time* it was composed is not certain, but it has strong internal evidence that it immediately followed the preceding respecting Judah. ¶ *A word.* A message, or prediction; Note, ch. ii. 1. ¶ *Into Jacob.* Jacob was the ancestor of the nation. But the name came to be appropriated to the ten tribes, as constituting the majority of the people. It was at first used to denote *all* the Jews (Num. xxiii. 7, 10, 23; xxiv. 17, 19; Deut. xxxii. 9; 1 Chron. xvi. 13; Ps. xiv. 7; xx. 1); but it came, after the revolt of the ten tribes under Jeroboam, to be used often to denote them alone; Amos vi. 8; Mic. i. 5; iii. 1; v. 8. The word or message which was sent, refers undoubtedly to that which immediately follows. ¶ *And it hath lighted upon.* Heb. 'It fell.' This is but a varied expression for, he sent it to Israel. ¶ *Israel.* The same as Jacob—the ten tribes—the kingdom of Ephraim.

9. *And all the people shall know.* Shall know the message; or shall know

of Samaria, that say in the pride and stoutness of heart,

10 The bricks are fallen down,

but we will build with hewn stones: the sycamores are cut down, but we will change *them into* cedars.

the judgment which God denounces against their crimes. The Chaldee renders this, 'All the people have exalted themselves, Ephraim and the inhabitants of Samaria, in their magnitude, and in the pride of the heart.' ¶ *Ephraim.* This is another name for Israel, as Ephraim was the principal tribe ; Note, ch. vii. 2. ¶ *And the inhabitants of Samaria.* The capital of Ephraim or Israel ; Note, ch. vii. 9. ¶ *That say in the pride.* This is a description of general and prevalent pride ; and it is traced to the source of all pride—*the heart.* It was a desire of splendour, power, and magnificence, originating in the heart, and manifesting itself by the language of self-confidence and defiance at the judgments of God. ¶ *Stoutness.* Heb. 'Greatness.' It means a self-confident purpose; and indicates the state of feeling in a man when he trusts to his own resources, and not to God.

10. *The bricks are fallen down.* The language of this verse is figurative ; but the sentiment is plain. It contains the confession of the inhabitants of Samaria, that their affairs were in a ruinous and dilapidated state; but also their self-confident assurance that they would be able to repair the evils, and restore their nation to more than their former magnificence.

Bricks, in oriental countries, were made of clay and straw, and were rarely burned. Hence, exposed to suns and rains, they soon dissolved. Walls and houses constructed of such materials would not be very permanent, and to build with them is strongly contrasted with building in a permanent and elegant manner with hewn stone.

The meaning is, that their former state was one of less splendour than they designed that their subsequent state should be. Desolation had come in upon their country, and this they could not deny. But they confidently boasted that they would more than repair the evil. ¶ *We will build.* Our ruined houses and walls. ¶ *With hewn stones.* At once more permanent and elegant than the structures of bricks had been. ¶ *The sycamores.* These trees grew abundantly on the low lands of Judea, and were very little esteemed ; 1 Ki. x. 27; 2 Ch. i. 15; ix. 27. 'This curious tree seems to partake of the

nature of two different species,' says Calmet, 'the mulberry and the fig; the former in its leaf, and the latter in its fruit. Its Greek name, συκόμορος, is plainly descriptive of its character, being compounded of συκος, a fig tree, and μορος, a mulberry tree. It is thus described by Norden:

SYCAMORE (*Ficus sycomorus*).

"They have in Egypt divers sorts of figs; but if there is any difference between them, a particular kind differs still more. I mean that which the sycamore bears, that they name in Arabic *giomez.* This sycamore is of the height of a beech, and bears its fruit in a manner quite different from other trees. It has them on the trunk itself, which shoots out little sprigs in form of a grape-stalk, at the end of which grows the fruit close to one another, most like bunches of grapes. The tree is always green, and bears fruit several times in the year, without observing any certain seasons, for I have seen some sycamores which had fruit two months after others. This sort of tree is pretty common in Egypt."' They were not highly valued, though it is probable they were often employed in building.

They are contrasted with cedars here— (1.) Because the cedar was a much more rare and precious wood. (2.) Because it was a much more smooth and elegant article of building. (3.) Because it was more permanent. The grain and texture of the sycamore is remarkably coarse and spongy, and could, therefore, stand in no competition with the cedar for beauty and ornament. ¶ *We will change* them. We will employ in their stead.

¶ *Cedars.* The cedar was a remarkably fine, elegant, and permanent wood for building. It was principally obtained on mount Lebanon, and was employed in temples, palaces, and in the houses of the rich; see Note on ch. ii. 18.

The sycamore is contrasted with the cedar in 1 Kings x. 27 : 'Cedars he made

11 Therefore the LORD shall set up the adversaries of Rezin against him, and [1] join his enemies together:

12 The Syrians before, and the Philistines behind ; and they shall devour Israel with [2] open mouth. For all this his anger is not turned

    1 mingle.   2 whole.

away, but his hand is stretched out still.

13 For the people turneth not unto him that smiteth them, neither do they seek the LORD of hosts.

14 Therefore the LORD will cut off from Israel head and tail, branch and rush, in one day.

---

to be as sycamore trees.' The whole passage denotes self-confidence and pride; an unwillingness to submit to the judgments of God, and a self-assurance that they would more than repair all the evils that would be inflicted on them.

11. *Therefore.* This verse indicates the *punishment* that would come upon them for their pride. ¶ *The* LORD *shall set up.* Heb. 'Shall exalt.' That is, they shall overcome and subdue him. ¶ *The adversaries of Rezin.* King of Syria, ch. vii. 1. It should be observed here, that twenty-one MSS., instead of *adversaries*, read *princes* of Rezin. The sense seems to require this ; as in the following verse, it is said that the *Syrians* will be excited against them. ¶ *Against him.* Against Ephraim. ¶ *And join his enemies together.* Heb. 'Mingle them together.' They shall be excited into wild and agitated commotion, and shall pour down together on the land and devour it. In what way this would be done is specified in ver. 12.

12. *The Syrians ;* chap. vii. 1. The Syrians had been the allies of the Israelites. But after the death of Rezin, it is probable that they joined the Assyrians, and united with them in the invasion of Samaria.— *Aben Ezra ; Grotius.* ¶ *Before.* Heb. 'From the east.' Syria was situated to the east of Samaria, and the meaning is here, that they would pour in upon Samaria from that side. ¶ *And the Philistines.* The Philistines occupied the country south-west of Samaria, lying along on the shores of the Mediterranean. It is not particularly mentioned in the Scriptures that they invaded Samaria after this prediction of Isaiah, but such a thing is by no means improbable. They were long unsubdued ; were full of hostility to the Jewish people ; and were many times engaged with them in wars, and several

times subdued them ; Judg. xiii.; xiv. ; 2 Chron. xxviii. 18. The name Palestine is derived from Philistine, although this people occupied but a small part of the country ; *see* Reland's *Palestine*, c. vii. ¶ *Behind.* That is, from *the west*—the region where they dwelt. The sacred writers speak as if looking toward the east, the rising sun, and they speak of the west as the region behind them ; see Notes on Job xxiii. 8, 9. ¶ *And they shall devour.* Heb. ' They shall eat.' This figure is taken from a ravenous beast ; and means that they should come up with raging desires, and fierce impetuosity, to destroy the nation. ¶ *With open mouth.* Heb. ' With the whole mouth.' The metaphor is derived from raging and furious animals. Chaldee, ' In every place.' ¶ *For all this.* Notwithstanding all this. ¶ *His anger,* &c.; see Note, ch. v. 25.

13. *For the people,* &c. This is a reason why his anger would not cease, and it is, at the same time, the suggestion of a new crime for which the Divine judgment would rest upon them. It commences the second part of the oracle. ¶ *Turneth not.* It is *implied* here that it was the design of the chastisement to turn them to God. In this case, as in many others, such a design had not been accomplished. ¶ *Unto him that smiteth them.* To God, who had punished them. ¶ *Neither do they seek.* They do not seek his protection and favour ; they do not worship and honour him. ¶ *The* LORD *of hosts ;* Note, ch. i. 9.

14. *Will cut off head and tail.* This is a proverbial expression, which is explained in the following verse ; see also Deut. xxviii. 13, 14. The head is often used to denote those in honour and authority. The tail is an expression applicable to the lower ranks, and would

15 The ancient and honourable, he *is* the head; and the prophet that teacheth lies, he *is* the tail.

16 For ¹ the leaders of this people cause *them* to err; and *they that are* ² led of them *are* ³ destroyed.

17 Therefore the LORD shall have no joy in their young men, neither shall have mercy on their father-

1 or, *they that call them blessed.*   2 or, *called blessed.*

less and widows: for every one *is* an hypocrite and an evil-doer, and every mouth speaketh ⁴ folly. For all this his anger is not turned away, but his hand *is* stretched out still.

18 For wickedness ᵃ burneth as the fire: it shall devour the briers and thorns, and shall kindle in the

3 *swallowed up.*   4 or, *villany.*   a Mal.4.1.

commonly indicate more than simply the common people. It would imply contempt; a state of great abjectness and meanness. ¶ *Branch and rush.* This is also a proverbial expression, meaning the highest and lowest; see Note, Isa. xix. 15. The word here translated *branch*, means properly the bough or top of the palm tree. The palm grew to a great height before it gave out any branches, and hence the image is a beautiful one to denote those *high* in office and authority. The word *rush* means the coarse, long-jointed reed, that grows in marshes—an apt emblem of the base and worthless classes of society.

15. *The ancient.* The elder; the old man. ¶ *And honourable.* Heb. ' The man of elevated countenance.' The man of rank and office. ¶ *The prophet that teacheth lies.* The false prophet. Of those there were many; and probably at this time many in Samaria.

16. *For the leaders of this people,* &c.; Note, ch. iii. 12. Heb. ' They that call this people blessed '—referring more particularly to the false prophets. ¶ They that are *led of them.* Heb. ' They that are called blessed by them.' ¶ *Are destroyed.* Heb. ' Are swallowed up;' see Note, ch. iii. 12. They are ruined; or swallowed up as in a vast whirlpool or vortex.

17. *Shall have no joy.* He shall not delight in them so as to preserve them. The parallel part of the verse shows that the phrase is used in the sense of having mercy. ¶ *In their young men.* The hope and strength of the nation. The word here used commonly denotes those *who are chosen*, particularly for purposes of war. The sense is, that the hope and strength of the nation, that

on which the chief reliance would be placed, would be cut off. ¶ *Neither shall have mercy,* &c. Judgment would sweep through the nation, even over those who were the usual objects of the Divine protection—widows and orphans; comp. Ps. x. 14, 18; xlviii. 5; Deut. x. 18; Jer. xlix. 11; Hos. xiv. 3. These passages show that the fatherless and the widow are the special objects of the Divine favour; and when, therefore, it is said that the Lord would not have mercy even on these, it shows the extent and severity of the Divine judgments that were coming on the nation. ¶ *For every one* is *a hypocrite.* A deceiver; a dissembler. The word used here, however, חָנֵף *hhânêph*, means rather a profane or profligate man, a man who is *defiled* or *polluted*, than a dissembler. It is applied often to idolaters and licentious persons, but not to hypocrites; see Job viii. 13; xiii. 16; xv. 34; xvii. 8; Dan. xi. 32. ¶ *Every mouth speaketh folly.* The word rendered *folly*, may denote foolishness, but it is also used to denote wickedness or crime; 1 Sam. xxv. 23. Probably this is the meaning here. That the character here given of the Ephraimites is correct, is abundantly shown also by other prophets; see particularly Hosea. ¶ *For all this.* Notwithstanding all the judgments that should come thus upon the young men, and widows, and orphans, still his anger was not turned away. This is the close of the second *strophe* or part of this prophecy.

18. *For wickedness.* This commences the *third* part of the prophecy, which continues to the end of the chapter. It is a description of prevailing impiety. The effects and prevalence of it are described by the image of a raging, burn-

thickets of the forest: and they shall mount up *like* the lifting up of smoke.

19 Through the wrath of the LORD of hosts is the land darkened,[a] and the people shall be as

a Acts 2.20.   1 *meat.*   b Mic.7.2,6.

ing flame, that spreads everywhere; first among the humble shrubbery—the briers and thorns, then in the vast forests, until it spreads over the land, and sends a mighty column of flame and smoke up to heaven. ¶ *Burneth as the fire.* Spreads, rages, extends as fire does in thorns and in forests. In what respects it burns like the fire, the prophet immediately specifies. It spreads rapidly everywhere, and involves all in the effects. Wickedness is not unfrequently in the Scriptures compared to a *fire* that is shut up long, and then bursts forth with raging violence. Thus Hos. vii. 6:

Truly, in the inmost part of it, their heart is like
    an oven,
While they lie in wait;
All the night their baker sleepeth;
In the morning it burneth like a blazing star.

' As an oven conceals the lighted fire all night, while the baker takes his rest, and in the morning vomits forth its blazing flame; so all manner of concupiscence is brooding mischief in their hearts, while the ruling faculties of reason and conscience are lulled asleep, and their wicked designs wait only for a fair occasion to break forth.'—*Horsley* on Hosea; see also Isa. l. 2; lxv. 5. ¶ *It shall devour.* Heb. ' It shall eat.' The idea of devouring or eating, is one which is often given to fire in the Scriptures. ¶ *The briers and thorns.* By the briers and thorns are meant, doubtless, the lower part of the population; the most degraded ranks of society. The idea here seems to be, first, that of impiety spreading like fire over all classes of people; but there is also joined with it, in the mind of the prophet, the idea of punishment. Wickedness would rage like spreading fire; but like fire, also, it would sweep over the nation accomplishing desolation and calamity, and consuming everything in the fire of God's vengeance. The wicked are often

the [1]fuel of the fire: no man shall spare his [b] brother.

20 And he shall [2]snatch on the right hand, and be hungry; and he [c] shall eat on the left hand, and they shall not be satisfied: they

2 *cut.*   c Lev.26.26; Jer.19 9.

compared to thorns and briers—fit objects to be burned up; Isa. xxxiii. 12:

And the people shall be as the burnings of lime;
As thorns cut up shall they be burned in the fire.

¶ *And shall kindle.* Shall burn, or extend, as sweeping fire extends to the mighty forest. ¶ *In the thickets of the forests.* The dense, close forest or grove. The idea is, that it extends to all classes of people—high as well as low. ¶ *And they shall mount up.* The Hebrew word here used—יִתְאַבְּכוּ from אָבַךְ—occurs nowhere else. The image is that of a far-spreading, raging fire, sending columns of smoke to heaven. So, says the prophet, is the rolling, raging, consuming fire of the sins of the nation spreading over all classes of people in the land, and involving all in wide-spread desolation.

19. *Through the wrath.* By the anger, or indignation. This spreading desolation is the proof of his anger. ¶ *Is the land darkened.* The word here used—עָתַם—occurs nowhere else. According to Gesenius, it is the same as הָמַם to be or make complete; and hence means, in this place, to be consumed, or laid waste. Kimchi and Aben Ezra render it, ' The land is darkened.' Sept. Συγκέκαυται. Chald. חֲרוּכַת—' Is scorched.' Jerome renders it, *Conturbata est terra*—' The land is disturbed.' The effect is doubtless such as ascending and spreading columns of fire and smoke would produce, and perhaps the general word *desolate* had better be used in translating the word. ¶ *And the people shall be as fuel of the fire.* This is an image of wide-spread ruin. The idea is, that they shall destroy one another as pieces of wood, when on fire, help to consume each other. The way in which it shall be done is stated more fully in the next verse. ¶ *No man shall spare his brother.* There shall be such a state of wickedness, that it shall lead to anar-

shall eat every man the flesh of his own arm:

21 Manasseh, Ephraim; and Ephraim, Manasseh; *and* they

together *shall be* against Judah. For all this his anger is not turned away, but his hand *is* stretched out still.

chy, and strife, and mutual destruction. The common ties of life shall be dissolved, and a man shall have no compassion on his own brother.

20. *And he shall snatch.* Heb. ' He shall cut off.' Many have supposed that this refers to a state of famine ; but others regard it as descriptive of a state of faction extending throughout the whole community, dissolving the most tender ties, and producing a dissolution of all the bonds of life. The context (ver. 19, 21) shows, that the latter is meant ; though it is not improbable that it would be attended with famine. When it is said that he ' would cut off his right hand,' it denotes a condition of internal anarchy and strife. ¶ *And be hungry.* And not be satisfied. Such would be his rage, and his desire of blood, that he would be insatiable. The murder of those on one side of him would not appease his insatiable wrath. His desire of carnage would be so great that it would be like unappeased hunger. ¶ *And he shall eat.* The idea here is that of contending factions excited by fury, rage, envy, hatred, contending in mingled strife, and spreading death with insatiable desire everywhere around them. ¶ *They shall eat.* Not literally ; but shall destroy. To eat the flesh of any one, denotes to seek one's life, and is descriptive of blood-thirsty enemies ; Ps. xxvii. 2 : ' When the wicked, *even* mine enemies and foes, came upon me *to eat up my flesh*, they stumbled and fell ;' Job xix. 22 :

Why do ye persecute me as God,
And are not satisfied with my flesh?

. comp. Deut. vii. 16; Jer. x. 25; xxx. 15; l. 17; Hos. vii. 7; see Ovid's *Metam.* 8, 867 :

Ipse suos artus lacero divellere morsu
Cœpit; et infelix minuendo corpus alebat.

¶ *The flesh of his own arm.* The Chaldee renders this, ' Each one shall devour the substance of his neighbour.' Lowth proposes to read it, ' The flesh of his

neighbour.' but without sufficient authority. The expression denotes a state of dreadful faction—where the ties of most intimate relationship would be disregarded, represented here by the appalling figure of a man's appetite being so rabid that he would seize upon and devour his own flesh. So, in this state of faction and discord, the rage would be so great that men would destroy those who were, as it were, their own flesh, *i.e.*, their nearest kindred and friends.

21. *Manasseh, Ephraim.* This verse is a continuation of the statement in regard to the extent and fearfulness of the faction. Those who were hitherto most tenderly and intimately allied to each other, would now be engaged in furious strife. Manasseh and Ephraim were the two sons of Joseph (Gen. xlvi. 20), and their names are used as expressive of tender union and friendship; comp. Gen. xlviii. 20. The tribes of Ephraim and Manasseh were near each other, and they always were allied together. The expression here denotes that they who had hitherto been joined in tender alliance, would be rent into contending factions, thirsting for each other's blood. ¶ *And they together.* They would be united in opposing Judah while they were devouring each other, as it is not an uncommon thing for those who are opposed to each other to unite in hostility to a common foe ; comp. Luke xxiii. 12. This is an image that heightens the description of the anarchy — introducing implacable animosity against another tribe, while they were contending among themselves. That such anarchies and factions existed, is apparent from all the history of the kingdom of Israel ; comp. 2 Kings xv 10, *sq.;* 2 Kings xv. 30. In this last passage, the death of Pekah is described as having occurred in a conspiracy formed by Hoshea. ¶ *For all this*, &c.; see ver. 12, Note v. 25. This closes the third *strophe* or part of the prophecy under consideration. The fourth and last strophe occurs in ch. x. 1–4.

CHAPTER X.
ANALYSIS.

This chapter is composed of two parts: the first (ver. 1–4) closes the prophecy commenced in ch. ix. 8, and should have been connected with that in the division into chapters; and the second part commences an entirely *new* prophecy, respecting the destruction of the Assyrians; see the Analysis prefixed to ver. 5. The first four verses of this chapter constitute the *fourth* strophe, or part of the prophecy, commenced in ch. ix. 8, and contains a specification of a crime, and its punishment:—*the crime,* prevalent injustice and oppression (ch. ix. 1, 2);

CHAPTER X.

1. *Wo unto them that decree unrighteous decrees.* To those who frame statutes that are oppressive and iniquitous. The prophet here refers, doubtless, to the rulers and judges of the land of Judea. A similar description he had before given; chap. i. 10, 23, &c. ¶ *And that write,* &c. Heb. 'And to the writers who write violence.' The word translated *grievousness,* עָמָל, denotes properly *wearisome labour, trouble, oppression, injustice.* Here, it evidently refers to the judges who declared oppressive and unjust sentences, and caused them to be recorded. It does not refer to the mere scribes, or recorders of the judicial opinions, but to the judges themselves, who pronounced the sentence, and caused it to be recorded. The manner of making Eastern decrees differs from ours: they are first written, and then the magistrate authenticates them, or annuls them. This, I remember, is the Arab manner, according to D'Arvieux. When an Arab wanted a favour of the emir, the way was to apply to the secretary, who drew up a decree according to the request of the party; if the emir granted the favour, he printed his seal upon it; if not, he returned it torn to the petitioner. Sir J. Chardin confirms this account, and applies it, with great propriety, to the illustration of a passage which I never thought of when I read over D'Arvieux. After citing Isa. x. 1, ' *Wo unto them that decree unrighteous decrees, and to the writers that write grievousness,'* for so our translators have rendered the latter part of the verse in the margin, much

the punishment, foreign invasion, ch. ix. 3, 4; see Note on ch. ix. 8.

WO [a] unto them that decree unrighteous decrees, and [1] that write grievousness *which* they have prescribed;

2 To turn aside the needy from judgment, and to take away the right from the poor of my people, that widows may be their prey, and *that* they may rob the fatherless!

<hr>

[a] Ps. 94. 20.   [1] *to the writers that.*

more agreeably than in the body of the version, Sir John goes on, ' The manner of making the royal acts and ordinances hath a relation to this; they are always drawn up according to the request; the first minister, or he whose office it is, writes on the side of it, " according to the king's will," and from thence it is sent to the secretary of state, who draws up the order in form.' —*Harmer.*

2. *To turn aside.* Their sentences have the effect, and are designed to have, to pervert justice, and to oppress the poor, or to deprive them of their rights and just claims; comp. ch. xxix. 21; Prov. xxvii. 5. ¶ *The needy.* דָּלִים. Those of humble rank and circumstances; who have no powerful friends and defenders. ¶ *From judgment.* From obtaining justice. ¶ *And to take away.* To take away by violence and oppression. The word גָּזַל *gâzăl,* is commonly applied to robbery, and to oppression; to the taking away of spoils in battle, &c. ¶ *That widows may be their prey.* That they may rob widows, or obtain their property. This crime has always been one particularly offensive in the sight of God; see Note, ch. i. 23. The widow and the orphan are without protectors. Judges, by their office, are particularly bound to preserve their rights; and it, therefore, evinces peculiar iniquity when they who should be their protectors become, in fact, their oppressors, and do injustice to them without the possibility of redress. Yet this was the character of the Jewish judges; and for this the vengeance of Heaven was about to come upon the land.

3 And what *a* will ye do in the day of visitation, and in the desolation *which* shall come from far? to whom will ye flee for help? and where will ye leave your glory?

a Job 31.14; Hos.9.7; Rev.6.17.

4 Without me they shall bow down under the prisoners, and they shall fall under the slain. For all this his anger is not turned away, but his hand *is* stretched out still.

---

3. *And what will ye do.* The prophet here proceeds to denounce the judgment, or punishment, that would follow the crimes specified in the previous verses. That punishment was the invasion of the land by a foreign force. 'What will ye do?' To whom will you fly? What refuge will there be?' Implying that the calamity would be so great that there would be no refuge, or escape. ¶ *In the day of visitation.* The word *visitation* (פְּקֻדָּה) is here used in the sense of God's coming to punish them for their sins; comp. Job xxxi. 14; xxxv. 15; Isa. xxvi. 14; Ezek. ix. 1. The idea is probably derived from that of a master of a family who comes to take account, or to investigate the conduct of his servants, and where the visitation, therefore, is one of reckoning and justice. So the idea is applied to God as designing to *visit* the wicked; that is, to punish them for their offences; comp. Hos. ix. 7. ¶ *And in the desolation.* The destruction, or overthrowing. The word used here—שׁוֹאָה—usually denotes a storm, a tempest (Prov. i. 27); and then sudden destruction, or calamity, that sweeps along irresistibly like a tempest; Zeph. i. 15; Job xxx. 3, 14; Ps. xxxv. 8. ¶ *Which shall come from far.* That is, from Assyria, Media, Babylonia. The sense is, 'a furious storm of war is about to rage. To what refuge can you then flee? or where can you then find safety?' ¶ *Where will ye leave your glory.* By the word *glory* here, some have understood the prophet as referring to their aged men, their princes and nobles, and as asking where they would find a safe place for them. But he probably means their *riches, wealth, magnificence.* Thus Ps. xlix. 17:

For when he dieth, he shall carry nothing away; His *glory* shall not descend after him.

See also Hos. ix. 2; Isa. lxvi. 12. The word *leave* here, is used in the sense

of *deposit*, or commit for safe keeping; comp. Job xxxix. 14. 'In the time of the invasion that shall come up like a tempest on the land, where will you deposit your property so that it shall be safe?'

4. *Without me.* בִּלְתִּי. There has been a great variety of interpretation affixed to this expression. The sense in which our translators understood it was, evidently, that they should be forsaken of God; and that, as the effect of this, they should bow down under the condition of captives, or among the slain. The Vulgate and the LXX., however, and many interpreters understand the word here as a simple negative. 'Where will you flee for refuge? Where will you deposit your wealth *so as not* to bow down under a chain?' Vulgate, *Ne incurvemini sub vinculo.* LXX. Τοῦ μὴ ἐμπεσεῖν εἰς ἀπαγωγήν—'Not to fall into captivity.' The Hebrew will bear either mode of construction. Vitringa and Lowth understand it as our translators have done, as meaning that God would forsake them, and that without him, that is, deprived of his aid, they would be destroyed. ¶ *They shall bow down.* They shall be subdued, as armies are that are taken captive. ¶ *Under the prisoners.* That is, under the *condition* of prisoners; or *as* prisoners. Some understand it to mean, that they should bear down *in the place* of prisoners; that is, in prison. But it evidently means, simply, that they should be captives. ¶ *They shall fall under the slain.* They shall be slain. Gesenius renders it, '*Among* the prisoners, and *among* the slain.' The Chaldee reads it, 'You shall be cast into chains out of your own land, and beyond your own cities you shall be cast out slain.' Vitringa supposes that the prophet, in this verse, refers to the custom, among the ancients, of placing prisoners in war under a yoke of wood to indicate their captivity. That such

GENERAL ANALYSIS OF CHAPTERS X. 5–34; XI.; XII.

At ver. 5, in this chapter, there is evidently the commencement of a new prophecy, or vision; and the division into chapters should have indicated such a commencement. The prophecy is continued to the close of the 12th chapter. Its general scope is a threatening against Assyria, and the prediction of ultimate safety, happiness, and triumph to the people of Judah. It has no immediate connection with the previous vision any further than the subjects are similar, and one seems to have suggested the other. In the previous vision, the prophet had described the threatened invasion of *Ephraim* or *Israel*, by the *Syrians;* in this, he describes the threatened invasion of *Judah* by the *Assyrians.* The result of the invasion of Ephraim would be the desolation of Samaria, and the captivity of the people; but the result of the invasion of Judah would be that God would interpose and humble the Assyrian, and bring deliverance to his people. This chapter is occupied with an account of the threatened invasion of Judea by the Assyrian, (ver. 5–7); with a statement of his confident boasting, and defiance of God (ver. 8–14); with encouraging the people to confide in God, and not to be afraid of him; and with the assurance that he would be discomfited and overthrown, ver. 15–34. The mention of this deliverance gives occasion for the elevated and beautiful statement respecting the *future* deliverance of the nation by the Messiah, and the glorious triumph that would attend his reign, which occurs in ch. xi.; xii.

When the prophecy was uttered, and in regard to whom, has been a question. Vitringa supposes that it was uttered in immediate connection with the foregoing, and that it is in fact a part of it. But from ver. 9, 11, it is evident that at the time this prophecy was uttered, Samaria was destroyed; and from ver. 20, it is clear that it was after the ten tribes had been carried into captivity, and when the Assyrian supposed that he could accomplish the same

destruction and captivity, in regard to Jerusalem and Judah, that had taken place in regard to Samaria and Ephraim. As to the remark of Vitringa, that the prophet anticipated these future events, and spoke of them as already passed, it may be observed, that the structure and form of the expressions suppose that they were *in fact* passed at the time he wrote; see the Notes on ver. 9, 11, 20. Lightfoot (*Chronica Temporum*) supposes that the prophet here refers to the threatened invasion of the land by Tiglath-pileser, king of Assyria, after he had destroyed Damascus, and when, being about to advance upon Jerusalem, Ahaz stripped the temple of its valuable ornaments, and sent them to him; 2 Kings xvi. 17, 18. Lowth supposes that the threatened invasion here refers to that of Sennacherib. This is, probably, the correct reference. This took place in the fourteenth year of Hezekiah, 725 years before the Christian era. Hezekiah, alarmed at the approach of Sennacherib, sent messengers to him to Lachish (2 Kings xviii. 14), to obtain a cessation of hostilities. Sennacherib agreed to such a peace, on condition that Hezekiah should pay him three hundred talents of silver, and thirty of gold. In order to meet this demand, Hezekiah was obliged to advance all the silver and gold in the treasury, and even to strip the temple of its ornaments. Having done this, he hoped for safety; and on this occasion, probably, this prophecy was uttered. It was designed to show that the danger of invasion was not passed; to assure them the king of Assyria would still come against the nation (comp. 2 Kings viii. 17, &c.); but that still God would interpose, and would deliver them. A further reference to this is made in Isa. xx., and a full history given in ch. xxxvii.; xxxviii; see Notes on those chapters.

5 ¹O ²Assyrian, the rod *a*of mine anger, ³and the staff in their hand is mine indignation.

> 1 *wo to the Assyrian.*   2 *Asshur.*
> *a* Jer.51.20,21.   3 *or, though.*

a custom obtained, there can be no doubt; but it is not probable that Isaiah refers to it here. The simple idea is, that many of them should be taken captive, and many of them slain. This prediction was fulfilled in the invasion of Tiglath-pileser; 2 Kings xv.; xvi. ¶ *For all this.* Notwithstanding these calamities. The cup of punishment is not filled by these, but the Divine judgment shall still be poured

out further upon the nation. The anger of God shall not be fully expressed by these *minor* inflictions of his wrath, but his hand shall continue to be stretched out until the whole nation shall be overwhelmed and ruined; see Note on ver. 12.

5. *O Assyrian.* The word הוֹי *hō*, is commonly used to denounce wrath, or to indicate approaching calamity; as an interjection of threatening; Isa. i. 4,

6 I will send him against an
hypocritical nation, and against
the people of my wrath will I give
him a charge, *a* to take the spoil,

and to take the prey, and to ¹ tread
them down *b* like the mire of the
streets.

a Jer.47.6,7.　1 *lay them a treading.*　*b* ch.37.26.

'Wo sinful nation;' ver. 8, 11, 18, 20,
21; Jer. xlviii. 1; Ezek. xiii. 2. The
Vulgate so understands it here: '*Væ
Assur;*' and the LXX. Οὐαὶ 'Ασσυρίοις
—'Wo to the Assyrians.' So the Chaldee and the Syriac. It is not then a
simple *address* to the Assyrian; but a
form denouncing wrath on the invader.
Yet it was not so much designed to in-
timidate and appal the Assyrian himself, as to comfort the Jews with the
assurance that calamity should overtake him. The 'Assyrian' referred to
here was the king of Assyria—Sennacherib, who was leading an army to
invade the land of Judea. ¶ *The rod
of mine anger.* That is, the rod, or
instrument, by which I will inflict punishment on a guilty nation. The Hebrew would bear the interpretation that
the Assyrian was an object against
which God was angry; but the former
is evidently the sense of the passage,
as denoting that the Assyrian was the
agent by which he would express his
anger against a guilty people. Wo
might be denounced against him for
his wicked intention, at the same time
that God might design to make use of
his plans to punish the sins of his own
people. The word *anger* here, refers
to the indignation of God against the
sins of the Jewish people. ¶ *And the
staff.* The word *staff* here, is synonymous with *rod*, as an instrument of
chastisement or punishment; ch. ix. 4;
comp. ver. 24; Nah. i. 13; Ezek. vii.
10. ¶ *In their hand.* There has been
considerable variety in the interpretation of this passage. Lowth and Noyes
read it, 'The staff in whose hand is the
instrument of my indignation.' This
interpretation Lowth adopts, by omit-
ting the word הוא on the authority
of the Alexandrine copy of the LXX.,
and five MSS., two of them ancient.
Jerome reads it, 'Wo to the Assyrian!
He is the staff and the rod of my fury;
in their hand is my indignation.' So
Forerius, Ludovicus, de Dieu, Cocceius,
and others. Vitringa reads it, 'And
in the hands of those who are my rod

is my indignation.' Schmidius and
Rosenmüller, 'And the rod which is in
their hands, is the rod of mine indignation.' There is no necessity for any
change in the text. The Hebrew
literally, is, 'Wo to the Assyrian! Rod
of my anger! And he is the staff. In
their hands is my indignation.' The
sense is sufficiently clear, that the Assyrian was appointed to inflict punishment on a rebellious people, as the
instrument of God. The Chaldee renders it, 'Wo to the Assyrian! The
dominion [power, ruler] of my fury,
and the angel sent from my face,
against them, for a malediction. LXX.
'And wrath in their hands.' ¶ *In their
hand.* In the hand of the Assyrians,
where the word 'Assyrian' is taken as
referring to the king of Assyria, as the
representative of the nation.

6. *I will send him.* Implying that
he was entirely in the hand of God, and
subject to his direction; and showing
that God has control over kings and
conquerors; Prov. xxi. 1. ¶ *Against
an hypocritical nation.* Whether the
prophet here refers to Ephraim, or to
Judah, or to the Jewish people in general, has been an object of inquiry among
interpreters. As the designs of Sennacherib were mainly against Judah, it is
probable that that part of the nation
was intended. This is evidently the
case, if, as has been supposed, the prophecy was uttered after the captivity
of the ten tribes; see ver. 20. It need
scarcely be remarked, that it was eminently the characteristic of the nation
that they were hypocritical; comp.
Isa. ix. 17; Matt. xv. 17; Mark vii. 6.
¶ *And against the people of my wrath.*
That is, those who were the objects of
my wrath; or the people on whom I
am about to pour out my indignation.
¶ *To take the spoil.* To plunder them.
¶ *And to tread them down.* Heb. 'And
to make them a treading down.' The
expression is drawn from war, where
the vanquished and the slain are trodden down by the horses of the conquer-
ing army. It means here, that the

7 Howbeit ^ahe meaneth not so. neither doth his heart think so ; but *it is* in his heart to

a Mi.4.12.

destroy and cut off nations not a few.

8 For he saith, *Are* not my princes altogether kings?

Assyrian would humble and subdue the people ; that he would trample indignantly on the nation, regarding them with contempt, and no more to be esteemed than the mire of the streets. A similar figure occurs in Zech. x. 5 : 'And they shall be as mighty men which tread down their enemies in the mire of the streets in battle.'

7. *Howbeit he meaneth not so.* It is not his purpose to be the instrument, in the hand of God, of executing his designs. He has a different plan ; a plan of his own which he intends to accomplish. ¶ *Neither doth his heart think so.* He does not intend or design it. The *heart* here, is put to express *purpose*, or *will*. ¶ It is *in his heart to cut off nations.* Utterly to destroy or to annihilate their political existence. ¶ *Not a few.* The ambitious purpose of Sennacherib was not confined to Judea. His plan was also to invade and to conquer Egypt; and the destruction of Judea was only a part of his scheme ; Isa. xx. This is a most remarkable instance of the supremacy which God asserts over the purposes of wicked men. Sennacherib formed his own plan without compulsion. He devised large purposes of ambition, and intended to devastate kingdoms. And yet God says that he was under his direction, and that his plans would be overruled to further his own purposes. Thus 'the wrath of man would be made to praise him ;' Ps. lxxvi. 10. And from this we may learn—(1.) That wicked men form their plans and devices with perfect freedom. They lay their schemes as if there were no superintending providence ; and feel, correctly, that they are not under the laws of compulsion, or of fate. (2.) That God presides over their schemes, and suffers them to be formed and executed with reference to his own purposes. (3.) That the plans of wicked men often, though they do not intend it, go to execute the purposes of God. Their schemes result in just what they did not intend—the furtherance of his

plans, and the promotion of his glory. (4.) That their plans are, nevertheless, wicked and abominable. They are to be judged according to what they are in themselves, and not according to the use which God may make of them by counteracting or overruling them. *Their* intention is evil; and by that they must be judged. That God brings good out of them, is contrary to their design, and a thing for which *they* deserve no credit, and should receive no reward. (5.) The wicked are in the hands of God. (6.) There is a superintending providence ; and men cannot defeat the purposes of the Almighty. This extends to princes on their thrones ; to the rich, the great, and the mighty, as well as to the poor and the humble— and to the humble as well as to the rich and the great. Over all men is this superintending and controlling providence ; and all are subject to the direction of God. (7.) It has often happened, *in fact*, that the plans of wicked men have been made to contribute to the purposes of God. Instances like those of Pharaoh, of Cyrus, and of Sennacherib ; of Pontius Pilate, and of the kings and emperors who persecuted the early Christian church, show that they are in the hand of God, and that he can overrule their wrath and wickedness to his glory. The madness of Pharaoh was the occasion of the signal displays of the power of God in Egypt. The wickedness, and weakness, and flexibility of Pilate, was the occasion of the atonement made for the sins of the world. And the church rose, in its primitive brightness and splendour, amid the flames which persecution kindled, and was augmented in numbers, and in moral loveliness and power, just in proportion as the wrath of monarchs raged to destroy it.

8. *For he saith.* This verse, and the subsequent verses to ver. 11, contain the vaunting of the king of Assyria, and the descriptions of his own confidence of success. ¶ *Are not my princes altogether kings?* This is a confident

9 [a] *Is* not [b] Calno as [c] Carche- mish? *is* not Hamath as Arpad?
is not Samaria as [d] Damascus?

[a] 2 Ki.18.33;19.12,13.   [b] Amos 6.2.
[c] 2 Chron.35.20.   [d] 2 Ki.16.9.

boast of his *own* might and power. His own dominion was so great that even his princes were endowed with the ordinary power and *regalia* of kings. The word *princes*, may here refer either to those of his own family and court— to the *satraps* and officers of power in his army, or around his throne; or more probably, it may refer to the subordinate governors whom he had set over the provinces which he had conquered. 'Are they not clothed with royal power and majesty? Are they not of equal splendour with the other monarchs of the earth?' How great, then, must have been his *own* rank and glory to be placed *over* such illustrious sovereigns! It will be recollected, that a common title which oriental monarchs give themselves, is that of King of kings; see Ezek. xxvi. 7; Dan. ii. 37; Ezra vii. 12. The oriental princes are still distinguished for their sounding titles, and particularly for their claiming dominion over all other princes, and the supremacy over all other earthly powers.

9. Is *not Calno as Carchemish?* The meaning of this confident boasting is, that none of the cities and nations against which he had directed his arms, had been able to resist him. All had fallen before him; and all were alike prostrate at his feet. Carchemish had been unable to resist him, and Calno had shared the same fate. Arpad had fallen before him, and Hamath in like manner had been subdued. The words which are used here are the same nearly that Rabshakeh used when he was sent by Sennacherib to insult Hezekiah and the Jews; Isa. xxxvi. 19; 2 Kings xviii. 34. *Calno* was a city in the land of Shinar, and was probably the city built by Nimrod, called in Gen. x. 10, *Calneh*, and at one time the capital of his empire. It is mentioned by Ezekiel, xxvii. 23. According to the Targums, Jerome, Eusebius, and others, Calno or Calneh, was the same city as *Ctesiphon*, a large city on the bank of the Tigris, and opposite to Seleucia.— *Gesenius* and *Calmet*. ¶ *Carchemish.* This was a city on the Euphrates, be-

longing to Assyria. It was taken by Necho, king of Egypt, and re-taken by Nebuchadnezzar in the fourth year of Jehoiachin, king of Judah; 2 Kings xxiii. 29. Probably it is the same city as Cercusium, or Kirkisia, which is situated in the angle formed by the junction of the Chebar and the Euphrates; comp. Jer. xlvi. 2; 2 Chron. xxv. 20. ¶ *Hamath.* This was a celebrated city of Syria. It is referred to in Gen. x. 18, as the seat of one of the tribes of Canaan. It is often mentioned as the northern limit of Canaan, in its widest extent; Num. xiii. 21; Josh. xiii. 5; Judg. iii. 3. The Assyrians became masters of this city about 753 years before Christ; 2 Kings xvii. 24. Burckhardt mentions this city as situated on both sides of the river Orontes. The town is at present of considerable extent, and contains about 30,000 inhabitants. There are four bridges over the Orontes, in the town. The trade of the town now is with the Arabs, who buy here their tent-furniture, and their clothes. This city was visited by the Rev. Eli Smith, in 1834. It lies, says he, on the narrow valley of the 'Asy; and is so nearly concealed by the high banks, that one sees little of it until he actually comes up to the gates; *see* Robinson's *Bib. Researches*, vol. iii. App. pp. 176, 177. ¶ *Arpad.* This city was not far from Hamath, and is called by the Greeks Epiphania; 2 Kings xviii. 34. ¶ *Samaria.* The capital of Israel, or Ephraim. From the mention of this place, it is evident that this prophecy was written *after* Samaria had been destroyed; see Notes on ch. vii. 9; xxviii. 1. ¶ *As Damascus.* The capital of Syria; see Note, ch. vii. 9, and the Analysis of ch. xvii. The LXX. have varied in their translation here considerably from the Hebrew. They render these verses, 'And he saith, Have I not taken the region beyond Babylon, and Chalane, where the tower was built? and I have taken Arabia, and Damascus, and Samaria.' The *main idea*, however—the *boast* of the king of Assyria, is retained.

10 As my hand hath found the kingdoms of the idols, and whose graven images did excel them of Jerusalem and of Samaria;

11 Shall I not, as I have done unto Samaria and her idols, so do to Jerusalem and her idols?

12 Wherefore it shall come to pass, *that*, when the LORD hath performed his whole work upon those of Jerusalem. ¶ *Of Jerusalem.*

10, 11. The argument in these two verses is this: 'The nations which I have subdued were professedly under the protection of idol gods. Yet those idols were not able to defend them—though stronger than the gods worshipped by Jerusalem and Samaria. And is there any probability, therefore, that the protection on which you who are Jews are leaning, will be able to deliver you?' Jerusalem he regarded as an idolatrous city, like others; and as all others had hitherto been unable to retard his movements, he inferred that it would be so with Jerusalem. This is, therefore, the confident boasting of *a man* who regarded himself as able to vanquish all *the gods* that the nations worshipped. The same confident boasting he uttered when he sent messengers to Hezekiah; 2 Kings xix. 12: 'Have the gods of the nations delivered them which my father destroyed; as Gozan, and Haran, and Rezeph, and the children of Eden, which were in Thelasar?' Isa. xxxvi. 18–20: 'Hath any of the gods of the nations delivered his land out of the hand of the king of Assyria? Where are the gods of Hamath and of Arphad? Where are the gods of Sepharvaim? And have they delivered Samaria out of my hand?' ¶ *Hath found.* That is, 'I have found them unable to defend themselves by their trust in their idols, and have subdued them.' ¶ *The kingdoms of the idols.* The kingdoms that worship idols. ¶ *And whose graven images.* That is, whose idols; or whose representations of the gods. The word properly signifies that which is hewn or cut out; and then the block of wood, or stone, that is carved into an image of the god. Here it refers to the gods themselves, probably, as having been found to be impotent, though he supposed them to be more powerful than those of Jerusalem and Samaria. ¶ *Did excel.* Heb. 'More than Jerusalem,' where the preposition מ, *mem*, is used to denote comparison. They were *more* to be dreaded; or more mighty than

Jerusalem and Samaria had often been guilty of the worship of idols; and it is probable that Sennacherib regarded them as idolaters in the same sense as other nations. They had given occasion for this suspicion by their having often fallen into idolatrous habits; and the Assyrian monarch did not regard them as in any manner distinguished from surrounding nations. It is not improbable that he was aware that Jerusalem worshipped JEHOVAH (comp. Isa. xxxvi. 20); but he doubtless regarded JEHOVAH as a mere tutelary divinity—the peculiar god of that land, as Baal, Ashtaroth, &c., were of the countries in which they were adored. For it was a common doctrine among ancient idolaters, that each nation had its peculiar god; that the claims of that god were to be respected and regarded *in* that nation; and that thus all nations should worship their own gods undisturbed. JEHOVAH was thus regarded as the tutelary god of the Jewish nation. The sin of Sennacherib consisted in confounding JEHOVAH with false gods, and in then setting him at defiance.

11. *Shall I not*, &c. 'Shall I not meet with the same success at Jerusalem that I have elsewhere? As I have overcome all others, and as Jerusalem has no peculiar advantages; as the gods of other nations were more in number, and mightier than those of Jerusalem, and yet were unable to resist me; what is there in Jerusalem that can stay my progress?'

12. *Wherefore*, &c. In this verse God, by the prophet, threatens punishment to the king of Assyria for his pride, and wicked designs. ¶ *His whole work.* His entire plan in regard to the punishment of the Jews. He sent the king of Assyria for a specific purpose to execute his justice on the people of Jerusalem. That plan he would execute *entirely* by the hand of Sennacherib, and would *then* inflict deserved punishment on Sennacherib himself, for his

mount Zion and on Jerusalem, I will ¹punish ᵃ the fruit of the ²stout heart of the king of Assyria, and the glory of his high ᵇ looks.

1 *visit upon.*　　ᵃ Jer.50.15.

13 For he saith, By the strength of my hand I have done *it*, and by my wisdom; for I am prudent: and I have removed the bounds of the

2 *greatness of the heart.*　　ᵇ Ps.18.27.

wicked purposes. ¶ *Upon mount Zion.* Mount Zion was a part of Jerusalem (see Note, ch. i. 8), but it was the residence of the court, the dwelling-place of David and his successors; and perhaps here, where it is mentioned as distinct from Jerusalem, it refers to the court, the princes, nobles, or the government. 'I will execute my purposes against the government, and the people of the city.' ¶ *I will punish.* Heb. 'I will visit;' but here, evidently used to denote punishment; see Note, ver. 3. ¶ *The fruit of the stout heart.* Heb. 'The fruit of the greatness of the heart.' The 'greatness of the heart,' is a Hebraism for pride of heart, or great swelling designs and plans formed in the heart. *Fruit* is that which a tree or the earth produces; and then anything which is produced or brought forth in any way. Here it means that which a proud heart had produced or designed, that is, plans of pride and ambition; schemes of conquest and of blood. ¶ *The glory of his high looks.* Heb. 'The glory of the lifting up of his eyes'— an expression indicative of pride and haughtiness. The word *glory*, here, evidently refers to the self-complacency, and the air of majesty and haughtiness, which a proud man assumes. In this verse we see—(1.) That God will accomplish all the purposes of which he designs to make wicked men the instruments. *Their* schemes shall be successful just so far as they may contribute to *his* plans, and no further. (2.) When that is done, they are completely in *his* power, and under his control. He can stay their goings when he pleases, and subdue them to his will. (3.) The fact that they have been made to further the plans of God, and to execute his designs, will not free them from deserved punishment. They meant not so; and they will be dealt with according to *their* intentions, and not according to God's design to overrule them. *Their* plans were wicked; and if God brings good out of them, it is

contrary to *their* intention; and hence, they are not to be screened from punishment because he brings good out of their plans, contrary to their designs. (4.) Wicked men *are in fact* often thus punished. Nothing is more common on earth; and all the woes of hell will be an illustration of the principle. Out of all evil God shall educe good; and even from the punishment of the damned themselves, he will take occasion to illustrate his own perfections, and, in that display of his just character, promote the happiness of holy beings.

13. *For he saith.* The king of Assyria saith. This verse and the following are designed to show the reason why the king of Assyria should be thus punished. It was on account of his pride, and wicked plans. He sought not the glory of God, but purposed to do evil. ¶ *For I am prudent.* I am wise; attributing his success to his own understanding, rather than to God. ¶ *I have removed the bounds of the people.* That is, 'I have changed the limits of kingdoms; I have taken away the old boundaries, and made new ones at my pleasure. I have divided them into kingdoms and provinces as I pleased.' No higher assumption of power could have been made than thus to have changed the ancient limits of empires, and remodelled them at his will. It was claiming that he had so extended his own empire, as to have effectually blotted out the ancient lines which had existed, so that they were now all one, and under his control. So a man who buys farms, and annexes them to his own, takes away the ancient limits; he runs new lines as he pleases, and unites them all into one. This was the claim which Sennacherib set up over the nations. ¶ *Have robbed their treasures.* Their hoarded wealth. This was another instance of the claim which he set up, of power and dominion. The treasures of kingdoms which had been hoarded for purposes of peace **or war**, he had plundered, and appropriated to his

people, and have robbed their treasures, and I have put down the inhabitants like [1] a valiant *man:*

14 And my hand hath found, as a nest, the riches of the people: and as one gathereth eggs *that are* left, have I gathered all the earth; and there was none that moved the wing, or opened the mouth, or peeped.

15 Shall the axe boast itself against him that heweth therewith? *or* shall the saw magnify itself against him that shaketh it? as if the [2] rod should shake *itself* against them that lift it up, *or* as if the

---

[1] or, *many people.*

[2] or, *a rod should shake them.*

---

own use; comp. Note on ch. xlvi. 3. ¶ *I have put down the inhabitants.* I have subdued them; have vanquished them. ¶ *As a valiant* man. כַּאבִּיר. Marg. 'Many people.' The Keri, or Hebrew marginal reading, is כְּבִיר, without the א, 'a mighty, or, strong man.' The sense is not materially different. It is a claim that he had evinced might and valour in bringing down nations. Lowth renders it, 'Them that were strongly seated.' Noyes, 'Them that sat upon thrones.' The Chaldee renders the verse, not literally, but according to the sense, 'I have made people to migrate from province to province, and have plundered the cities that were the subjects of praise, and have brought down by strength those who dwelt in fortified places.' Our translation has given the sense correctly.

14. *And my hand hath found, as a nest.* By a beautiful and striking figure here, the Assyrian monarch is represented as describing the *ease* with which he had subdued kingdoms, and rifled them of their treasures. No resistance had been offered. He had taken them with as little opposition as a rustic takes possession of a nest, with its eggs or young, when the parent bird is away. ¶ *Eggs* that are *left.* That is, eggs that are left of the parent bird; when the bird from fright, or any other cause, has gone, and when no resistance is offered. ¶ *Have I gathered all the earth.* That is, I have subdued and plundered it. This shows the height of his self-confidence and his arrogant assumptions. ¶ *That moved the wing.* Keeping up the figure of the nest. There was none that offered resistance; as an angry bird does when her nest is about to be robbed. ¶ *Or opened the mouth.* To make a noise in alarm. The dread of him produced perfect silence and sub-

ISAIAH I.

mission. ¶ *Or peeped.* Or that chirped —the noise made by young birds ; Note, ch. viii. 19. The idea is, that such was the dread of his name and power that there was universal silence. None dared to resist the terror of his arms.

15. *Shall the axe, &c.* In this verse God reproves the pride and arrogance of the Assyrian monarch. He does it by reminding him that he was the mere instrument in his hand, to accomplish *his* purposes ; and that it was just as absurd for him to boast of what he had done, as it would be for the axe to boast when *it* had been wielded with effect. In the axe there is no wisdom, no skill, no power ; and though it may lay the forest low, yet it is not by any skill or power which it possesses. So with the Assyrian monarch. Though nations had trembled at his power, yet he was in the hand of God, and had been directed by an unseen arm in accomplishing the designs of the Ruler of the universe. Though himself free, yet he was under the direction of God, and had been *so* directed as to accomplish his designs. ¶ *The saw magnify itself.* That is, boast or exalt itself *against* or *over* him that uses it. ¶ *That shaketh it.* Or moves it backwards and forwards, for the purpose of sawing. ¶ *As if the rod.* A rod is an instrument of chastisement or punishment ; and such God regarded the king of Assyria. ¶ *Should shake* itself, &c. The Hebrew, in this place, is as in the margin : 'A rod should shake them that lift it up.' But the sense is evidently retained in our translation, as this accords with all the other members of the verse, where the leading idea is, the absurdity that a mere instrument should exalt itself against him who makes use of it. In this manner the preposition עַל *over,* or *against,* is evidently understood

14

staff should lift up [1] *itself, as if it were* no wood.

16 Therefore [a] shall the Lord, the LORD of hosts, send among his fat ones [b] leanness; and under his

So the Vulgate and the Syriac. ¶ *The staff.* This word here is synonymous with *rod*, and denotes an instrument of chastisement. ¶ *As if it were no wood.* That is, as if it were a moral agent, itself the actor or deviser of what it is made to do. It would be impossible to express more strongly the idea intended here, that the Assyrian was a mere instrument in the hand of God to accomplish *his* purposes, and to be employed at his will. The statement of this truth is designed to humble him : and if there be *any* truth that will humble sinners, it is, that they are in the hands of God ; that he will accomplish his purposes by them ; that when they are laying plans against him, he will overrule them for his own glory ; and that they will be arrested, restrained, or directed, just as he pleases. Man, in his schemes of pride and vanity, therefore, should not boast. He is under the God of nations ; and it is one part of his administration, to control and govern ALL THE INTELLECT IN THE UNIVERSE. In all these passages, however, there is not the slightest intimation that the Assyrian was not *free*. There is no fate ; no compulsion. He regarded himself as a free moral agent ; he did what he pleased ; he never supposed that he was urged on by any power that violated his own liberty. If he did what he pleased, he was free. And so it is with all sinners. They do as they please. They form and execute such plans as they choose ; and God overrules *their* designs to accomplish his own purposes. The Targum of Jonathan has given the sense of this passage ; 'Shall the axe boast against him who uses it, saying, I have cut [wood] ; or the saw boast against him who moves it, saying, I have sawed ? When the rod is raised to smite, it is not the rod that smites, but he who smites with it.'

16. *Therefore shall the Lord.* Heb. אָדוֹן *Adōn.* ¶ *The Lord of hosts.* In the present Hebrew text, the original

glory he shall kindle a burning like the burning of a fire.

17 And the light of Israel shall be for a fire, [c] and his Holy One for a flame ; and it shall burn and

word is also אֲדֹנָי *adōnâi*, but fifty-two MSS. and six editions read JEHOVAH. On the meaning of the phrase, *the Lord of hosts*, see Note, ch. i. 9. This verse contains a threatening of the punishment that would come upon the Assyrian for his insolence and pride, and the remainder of the chapter is mainly occupied with the details of that punishment. The punishment here threatened is, that while he appeared to be a victor, and was boasting of success and of his plunder, God would send leanness—as a body becomes wasted with disease. ¶ *His fat ones.* That is, those who had *fattened* on the spoils of victory ; his vigorous, prosperous, and flourishing army. The prophet here evidently intends to describe his numerous army glutted with the trophies of victory, and revelling on the spoils. ¶ *Leanness.* They shall be emaciated and reduced ; their vigour and strength shall be diminished. In Ps. cvi. 15, the word *leanness*, רָזוֹן *rázōn*, is used to denote destruction, disease. In Mic. vi. 10, it denotes diminution, scantiness—'the scant ephah.' Here it denotes, evidently, that the army which was so large and vigorous, should waste away as with a pestilential disease ; comp. ver. 19. The *fact* was, that of that vast host few escaped. The angel of the Lord slew 185,000 men in a single night ; 2 Kings xviii. 35 ; see Notes on ch. xxxviii. 36. ¶ *And under his glory.* That is, beneath the boasted honour, might, and magnificence of the proud monarch. ¶ *He shall kindle.* That is, God shall suddenly and entirely destroy his magnificence and pride, as when a fire is kindled beneath a magnificent temple. A similar passage occurs in Zech. xii. 6 :

In that day I will make the governors of Judah
Like a hearth of fire among the wood,
And like a torch of fire in a sheaf ;
And they shall devour all the people round about.

17. *And the light of Israel.* That is, JEHOVAH. The word *light* here, אוֹר, is used also to denote a *fire*, or that

devour his thorns and his briers in one *a* day.

18 And shall consume the glory of his forest, and of his fruitful field, ¹both soul and body: and they shall be as when a standard-bearer fainteth.

a ch.37.36.   1 *from the soul, and even to the flesh.*

---

which causes light and heat ; see Ezek. v. 2 ; Isa. xliv. 16 ; xlvii. 14. Here it is used in the same sense, denoting that JEHOVAH would be *the fire* (אוֹר) that would cause the *flame* (אֵשׁ) which would consume the Assyrian. JEHOVAH is often compared to a burning flame, or fire ; Deut. iv. 24 ; ix. 3 ; Heb. xii. 29. ¶ *Shall be for a fire.* By his power and his judgment he shall destroy them. ¶ *His Holy One.* Israel's Holy One ; that is, JEHOVAH—often called in the Scriptures the Holy One of Israel. ¶ *And it shall burn.* That is, the flame that JEHOVAH shall kindle, or his judgments that he shall send forth. ¶ *And devour his thorns and his briers.* An expression denoting the utter impotency of all the mighty armies of the Assyrian to resist JEHOVAH. As dry thorns and briers cannot resist the action of heat, so certainly and speedily would the armies of Sennacherib be destroyed before JEHOVAH ; comp. Note, ch. ix. 18. Lowth supposes, that by ' briers and thorns' here, the common soldiers of the army are intended, and by ' the glory of his forest' (ver. 18), the princes, officers, and nobles. This is, doubtless, the correct interpretation ; and the idea is, that all would be completely consumed and destroyed. ¶ *In one day.* The army of Sennacherib was suddenly destroyed by the angel ; see Notes on ch. xxxvii. 36.

18. *The glory of his forest.* In these expressions, the army of Sennacherib is compared with a beautiful grove thick set with trees ; and as all the beauty of a grove which the fire overruns is destroyed, so, says the prophet, it will be with the army of the Assyrian under the judgments of God. If the ' briers and thorns' (ver. 17) refer to the common soldiers of his army, then the glory of the forest—the tall, majestic trees—refer to the princes and nobles. But this mode of interpretation should not be pressed too far. ¶ *And of his fruit-ful field.* וְכַרְמִלּוֹ. The word used here—*carmel*—is applied commonly to

a rich mountain or promontory on the Mediterranean, on the southern boundary of the tribe of Asher. The word, however, properly means a fruitful field, a finely cultivated country, and was given to Mount Carmel on this account, In this place it has no reference to that mountain, but is given to the army of Sennacherib to *keep up the figure* which the prophet commenced in ver. 17. That army, numerous, mighty, and well disciplined, was compared to an extensive region of hill and vale ; of forests and fruitful fields ; but it should all be destroyed as when the fire runs over fields and forests, and consumes all their beauty. Perhaps in all this, there may be allusion to the proud boast of Sennacherib (2 Kings xix. 23), that he would ' go up the sides of Lebanon, and cut down the cedars thereof, and the choice fir-trees thereof, and enter into the forest of Carmel.' In allusion, possibly, to this, the prophet says that God would cut down the tall trees and desolate the fruitful field—the ' carmel' of his army, and would lay all waste. ¶ *Both soul and body.* Heb. ' From the soul to the flesh ;' *i.e.,* entirely. As the soul and the flesh, or body, compose the entire man, so the phrase denotes the *entire-ness* or *totality* of anything. The army would be totally ruined. ¶ *And they shall be as when a standard-bearer fainteth.* There is here a great variety of interpretation. The LXX. read it, ' And he shall flee as one that flees from a burning flame.' This reading Lowth has followed ; but for this there is not the slightest authority in the Hebrew. The Vulgate reads it, ' And he shall fly for terror,' *et erit terrore profugus.* The Chaldee, ' And he shall be broken, and shall fly.' The Syriac, ' And he shall be as if he had never been.' Probably the correct idea is, *and they shall be as when a sick man wastes away.* The words which are used (כִּמְסֹס נֹסֵס) are brought together for the sake of a *para-nomasia*—a figure of speech common in the Hebrew. The word rendered in our

19 And the rest of the trees of his forest shall be [1]few, that a child may write them.

20 And it shall come to pass in that day, *that* the remnant of Israel,

[1] *number.*

and such as are escaped of the house of Jacob, shall no more again stay upon him that smote them; but [a] shall stay upon the [b] LORD, the Holy One of Israel, in truth.

a 2 Chro.28.20.   5 Hos.14.3.

---

version *fainteth* (מָסֹס *měsōs*) is probably the infinitive construct of the verb מָסַס *māsăs*, to melt, dissolve, faint. It is applied to the manna that was dissolved by the heat of the sun, Ex. xvi. 21; to wax melted by the fire, Ps. lxviii. 2; to a snail that consumes away, Ps. lviii. 8; or to water that evaporates, Ps. lviii. 7. Hence it is applied to the heart, exhausted of its vigour and spirit, Job vii. 5; to things decayed that have lost their strength, 1 Sam. xv. 9; to a loan or tax laid upon a people that wastes and exhausts their wealth. It has the general notion, therefore, of melting, fainting, sinking away with the loss of strength; Ps. xxii. 14; cxii. 10; xcvii. 5; Isa. xix. 1; xiii. 7; Josh. ii. 11; v. 1; vii. 5. The word rendered standard-bearer (נֹסֵס) is from the verb נָסַס *nāsăs*. This word signifies sometimes *to lift up*, to elevate, or to erect a flag or standard to public view, to call men to arms; Isa. v. 26; xi. 10, 12; xiii. 2; xviii. 3; xlix. 22; and also to lift up, or to exhibit anything as a judgment or public warning, and may thus be applied to Divine judgments. Gesenius renders the verb, *to waste away, to be sick.* In Syriac it has this signification. Taylor (*Heb. Con.*) says, that it does not appear that this word ever has the signification of a military standard under which armies fight, but refers to a standard or ensign to *call* men together, or to indicate alarm and danger. The probable signification here, is that which refers it to a man wasting away with sickness, whose strength and vigour are gone, and who becomes weak and helpless. Thus applied to the Assyrian army, it is very striking. Though mighty, confident, and vigorous—like a man in full health—yet it would be like a vigorous man when disease comes upon him, and he pines away and sinks to the grave.

19. *And the rest of the trees*, &c. Keeping up still the image of a large

and once dense forest, to which he had likened the Assyrian army. ' *The rest*' here means that which shall be left after the threatened judgment shall come upon them. ¶ *That a child may write them.* That a child shall be able to number them, or write their names; that is, they shall be very few. A child can number or count but few; yet the number of those who would be left, would be so very small that even a child could count them with ease. It is probable that a few of the army of Sennacherib escaped (see Note, ch. xxxvii. 37); and compared with the whole army, the remnant might bear a striking resemblance to the few decaying trees of a once magnificent forest of cedars.

20. *And it shall come to pass.* The prophet proceeds to state the effect on the Jews, of the judgment that would overtake the army of the Assyrian. One of those effects, as stated in this verse, would be, that they would be led to see that it was in vain to look to the Assyrians any more for aid, or to form any further alliance with them, but that they should trust in the Lord alone. ¶ *The remnant of Israel.* Those that would be left after the Assyrian had invaded and desolated the land. ¶ *Shall no more again stay.* Shall no more depend on them. Alliances had been formed with the Assyrians for aid, and they had resulted as all alliances formed between the friends and the enemies of God do. They are observed as long as it is for the interest or the convenience of God's enemies to observe them; and then his professed friends are made the victims of persecution, invasion, and ruin. ¶ *Upon him that smote them.* Upon the Assyrian, who was about to desolate the land. The calamities which he would bring upon them would be the main thing which would open their eyes, and lead them to forsake the alliance. One design of God's permitting the Assyrians to invade the land, was, to punish them

21 The remnant [a] shall return, *even* the remnant of Jacob, unto the mighty God.

22 For though thy people Israel

a ch. 6.13; 65.8,9.   *b* Ro.9.27,28.   1 *in*, or, *among.*

be as the sand of the sea, *yet* [b] a remnant [1] of them shall return: the consumption [c] decreed shall overflow [2] with righteousness.

c ch.28.22; Dan.9.27.   2 or, *in.*

for this alliance, and to induce them to trust in God. ¶ *But shall stay, &c.* They shall depend upon JEHOVAH, or shall trust in him for protection and defence. ¶ *The Holy One of Israel;* see ver. 17. ¶ *In truth.* They shall serve him sincerely and heartily, not with feigned or divided service. They shall be so fully satisfied that the Assyrian cannot aid them, and be so severely punished for ever, having formed an alliance with him, that they shall now return to JEHOVAH, and become his sincere worshippers. In this verse, the prophet refers, doubtless, to the times of Hezekiah, and to the extensive reformation, and general prevalence of piety, which would take place under his reign; 2 Chron. xxxii. 22–33. Vitringa, Cocceius, Schmidius, &c., however, refer this to the time of the Messiah; Vitringa supposing that the prophet refers *immediately* to the times of Hezekiah, but *in a secondary sense,* for the complete fulfilment of the prophecy, to the times of the Messiah. But it is not clear that he had reference to any other period than that which would immediately follow the invasion of Sennacherib.

21. *The remnant, &c.* That is, those who shall be left after the invasion of Sennacherib. ¶ *Shall return.* Shall abandon their idolatrous rites and places of worship, and shall worship the true God. ¶ *The mighty God.* The God that had evinced his power in overcoming and destroying the armies of Sennacherib.

22. *For though, &c.* In this verse, and in ver. 23, the prophet expresses positively the idea that *but* a remnant of the people should be preserved amidst the calamities. He had said (ver. 20, 21), that a remnant should return to God. He now carries forward the idea, and states that *only* a remnant should be preserved out of the multitude, however great it was. Admitting that the number was then very great, yet the great mass of the nation would be cut off, and only a small portion would re-

main. ¶ *Thy people Israel.* Or rather, ' thy people, O Israel,' making it a direct address to the Jews, rather than to God. ¶ *Be as the sand of the sea.* The sands of the sea cannot be numbered, and hence the expression is used in the Bible to denote a number indefinitely great; Ps. cxix. 18; Gen. xxii. 17; xli. 49; Josh xi. 4; Judg. vii. 12; 1 Sam. xiii. 5, &c. ¶ *Yet a remnant.* The word *yet* has been supplied by the translators, and evidently obscures the sense. The idea is, that a remnant ONLY—a very small portion of the whole, should be preserved. Though they were exceedingly numerous as a nation, yet the mass of the nation would be cut off, or carried into captivity, and only a few would be left. ¶ *Shall return.* That is, shall be saved from destruction, and return by repentance unto God, ver. 21. Or, if it has reference to the approaching captivity of the nation, it means that but a few of them would return from captivity to the land of their fathers. ¶ *The consumption.* The general sense of this is plain. The prophet is giving a reason why only a few of them would return, and he says, that the judgment which God had determined on was inevitable, and would overflow the land in justice. As God had determined this, their *numbers* availed nothing, but the consumption would be certainly accomplished. The word *consumption* (כִּלָּיוֹן from כָּלָה *kâlâ* to complete, to finish, to waste away, vanish, disappear) denotes a languishing, or wasting away, as in disease; and then *destruction,* or that which *completes* life and prosperity. It denotes such a series of judgments as would be a *completion* of the national prosperity, or as should *terminate* it entirely. ¶ *Decreed.* חָרוּץ *hhârûtz.* The word here used is derived from חָרַץ *hhârätz,* to sharpen, or bring to a point ; to rend, tear, lacerate ; to be quick, active, diligent; and then to decide, determine, decree ; because that which is decreed is brought to a point, or issue.—*Taylor.*

23 For the Lord God of hosts shall make a consumption, even determined, in the midst of all the land.

24 Therefore thus saith the Lord God of hosts, O my people that dwellest in Zion, be not *a* afraid of the Assyrian: he shall smite thee with a rod, [1] and shall lift up his staff against thee, after the manner of Egypt.

a ch.37.6.   [1] *but he shall.*

It evidently means here, that it was fixed upon or decreed in the mind of God, and that being thus decreed, it must certainly take place. ¶ *Shall overflow.* שׁוֹטֵף *shōtēph.* This word is usually applied to an inundation, when a stream rises above its banks and overflows the adjacent land; Isa. xxx. 28; lxvi. 12; Ps. lxxviii. 20. Here it means evidently, that the threatened judgment would spread like an overflowing river through the land, and would accomplish the devastation which God had determined. ¶ *With righteousness.* With justice, or in the infliction of justice. Justice would abound or overflow, and the consequence would be, that the nation would be desolated.

23. *For the Lord God of hosts;* Note, ch. i. 9. ¶ *Shall make a consumption.* The Hebrew of this verse might be rendered, 'for its [destruction] is completed, and is determined on; the Lord Jehovah of hosts will execute it in the midst of the land.' Our translation, however, expresses the force of the original. It means that the destruction was fixed in the mind or purpose of God, and would be certainly executed. The translation by the LXX., which is followed in the main by the apostle Paul in quoting this passage, is somewhat different. ' For he will finish the work, and cut it short in righteousness; for a short work will the Lord make in the whole habitable world '—ἐν τῇ οἰκουμένῃ ὅλῃ: as quoted by Paul, 'upon the earth' —ἐπὶ τῆς γῆς. For the manner in which this passage is quoted by Paul, see Notes on Rom. ix. 27, 28. ¶ *In the midst of all the land.* That is, the land of Israel, for the threatened judgment extended no further.

24. *Therefore, &c.* In this verse the prophet returns to the main subject of this prophecy, which is to comfort the people of Jerusalem with the assurance that the army of the Assyrian would be destroyed. ¶ *O my people.* An expres-

sion of tenderness, showing that God regarded them as his children, and notwithstanding the judgments that he would bring upon them for their sins. In the midst of severe judgments, God speaks the language of tenderness; and, even when he punishes, has towards his people the feelings of a father; Heb. xii. 5-11. ¶ *That dwelleth in Zion.* Literally, in mount Zion; but here taken for the whole city of Jerusalem; see Note, ch. i. 8. ¶ *Be not afraid, &c.* For his course shall be arrested, and he shall be repelled and punished; ver. 25-27. ¶ *He shall smite thee.* He shall, indeed, smite thee, but shall not utterly destroy thee. ¶ *And shall lift up his staff.* Note, ver. 5. The *staff* here is regarded as an instrument of punishment; comp. Note, ch. ix. 4; and the sense is, that by his invasion, and by his exactions, he would oppress and punish the nation. ¶ *After the manner of Egypt.* Heb. 'In the way of Egypt.' Some interpreters have supposed that this means that Sennacherib would oppress and afflict the Jews in his going down to Egypt, or on his way thither to attack the Egyptians. But the more correct interpretation is that which is expressed in our translation—*after the manner of Egypt.* That is, the nature of his oppressions shall be like those which the Egyptians under Pharaoh inflicted on the Jews. There are *two* ideas evidently implied here. (1.) That the oppression would be heavy and severe. Those which their fathers experienced in Egypt were exceedingly burdensome and cruel. So it would be in the calamities that the Assyrian would bring upon them. But, (2.) their fathers had been delivered from the oppressions of the Egyptians. And so it would be now. The Assyrian would oppress them; but God would deliver and save them. The phrase, ' in the way of,' is used to denote *after the manner of,* or, as an example, in Amos iv. 10, ' I have sent among you

25 For yet a very little while, and the indignation[a] shall cease, and mine anger in their [b] destruction.

26 And the LORD of hosts shall stir up a scourge for him, according to the slaughter of Midian[c] at the

rock of Oreb: and *as* his rod *was* upon the sea, so shall he lift it up after the manner of Egypt.

27 And it shall come to pass in that day, *that* his burden shall [1]be taken away from off thy shoulder, and his yoke from off thy neck, and

a Dan.11.36.   b 2 Ki.19.35.   c Judg.7.25.   1 remove.

the pestilence after the manner of Egypt;' Heb. ' In the way of Egypt;' comp. Ezek. xx. 30.

25. *For yet a very little while.* This is designed to console them with the hope of deliverance. The threatened invasion was brief, and was soon ended by the pestilence that swept off the greater part of the army of the Assyrian. ¶ *The indignation shall cease.* The anger of God against his offending people shall come to an end ; his purposes of chastisement shall be completed; and the land shall be delivered. ¶ *In their destruction.* עַל־תַּבְלִיתָם from בָּלָה *bâlâ,* to wear out ; to consume ; to be annihilated. It means here, that his anger would terminate in the entire annihilation of their power to injure them. Such was the complete overthrow of Sennacherib by the pestilence ; 2 Kings xix. 35. The word here used, occurs in this form in no other place in the Hebrew Bible, though the verb is used, and other forms of the noun. The *verb,* Deut. vii. 4; xxix. 5 ; Josh. ix. 13 ; Neh. ix. 21, &c. *Nouns,* Ezek. xxiii. 43 ; Isa. xxxviii. 17 ; Jer. xxxviii. 11, 12 ; Isa. xvii. 14, *et al.*

26. *And the LORD of hosts shall stir up.* Or shall raise up that which shall prove as a scourge to him. ¶ *A scourge for him.* That is, that which shall punish him. The scourge, or rod, is used to denote severe punishment of any kind. The nature of this punishment is immediately specified. ¶ *According to the slaughter of Midian.* That is, as the Midianites were discomfited and punished. There is reference here, doubtless, to the discomfiture and slaughter of the Midianites by Gideon, as recorded in Judg. vii. 24, 25. That was signal and entire ; and the prophet means to say, that the destruction of the Assyrian would be also signal and total. The country of Midian, or Ma-

dian, was on the east side of the Elanitic branch of the Red Sea ; but it extended also north along the desert of mount Seir to the country of the Moabites ; see Note on ch. lx. 6. ¶ *At the rock of Oreb.* At this rock, Gideon slew the two princes of the Midianites, Oreb and Zeeb (Judg. vii. 25) ; and from this circumstance, probably, the name was given to the rock : Lev. xi. 15; Deut. xiv. 14. It was on the east side of the Jordan. ¶ *And as his rod,* &c. That is, as God punished the Egyptians in the Red Sea. ¶ *So shall he lift it up after the manner of Egypt.* As God overthrew the Egyptians in the Red Sea, so shall he overthrow and destroy the Assyrian. By these two comparisons, therefore, the prophet represents the complete destruction of the Assyrian army. In both of these cases, the enemies of the Jews had been completely overthrown, and so it would be in regard to the hosts of the Assyrian.

27. *His burden shall be taken away.* The oppressions and exactions of the Assyrian. ¶ *From off thy shoulder.* We bear a burden on the shoulder; and hence any grievous exaction or oppression is represented as borne upon the shoulder. ¶ *And his yoke,* &c. Another image denoting deliverance from oppression and calamity. ¶ *And the yoke shall be destroyed because of the anointing.* In the interpretation of these words, expositors have greatly differed. The Hebrew is literally, ' From the face of oil,' מִפְּנֵי־שָׁמֶן. The Vulgate renders it, literally, *à facie olei.* The LXX. ' His fear shall be taken from thee, and his yoke *from thy shoulders.'* The Syriac, ' His yoke shall be broken before the oxen.' The Chaldee Paraphrase, ' The people shall be broken before the Messiah.' Lowth renders it, ' The yoke shall perish from off your shoulders ;' following the Septuagint. Grotius sug-

the yoke shall be destroyed because of the *a* anointing.

28 He is come to Aiath, he is

passed to Migron; at Michmash he hath laid up his carriages:

a Dan.9.24.

gests that it means that the yoke which the Assyrians had imposed upon the Jews would be broken by Hezekiah, the king who had been anointed with oil. Jarchi also supposes that it refers to one who was anointed—to the king; and many interpreters have referred it to the Messiah, as the anointed of God. Vitringa supposes that the Holy Spirit is here intended. Kimchi supposes, that the figure is derived from the effect of oil on wood in destroying its consistency, and loosening its fibres; and that the expression means, that the yoke would be broken or dissolved as if it were penetrated with oil. But this is ascribing a property to oil which it does not possess. Archbishop Secker supposes that, instead of *oil*, the text should read *shoulder*, by a slight change in the Hebrew. But for this conjectural reading there is no authority. Cocceius supposes, that the word *oil* here means *fatness*, and is used to denote prosperity and wealth, and that the prophet means to say, that the Assyrian would be corrupted and destroyed by the great amount of wealth which he would amass. The Rabbins say, that this deliverance was wrought on account of the great quantity of oil which Hezekiah caused to be consumed in the synagogues for the study of the law—a striking instance of the weak and puerile methods of interpretation which they have everywhere evinced. I confess that none of these explanations seem to me to be satisfactory, and that I do not know what is the meaning of the expression.

28. *He is come to Aiath.* These verses (28–32) contain a description of the march of the army of Sennacherib as he approached Jerusalem to invest it. The description is expressed with great beauty. It is rapid and hurried, and is such as one would give who was alarmed by the sudden and near approach of an enemy—as if, while the narrator was stating that the invader had arrived at one place, he had already come to another; or, as if while one messenger should say, that he had come to one

place, another should answer that he was still nearer, and a third, that he was nearer still, so as to produce universal consternation. The prophet speaks of this as if he *saw* it (comp. Note, ch. i.); as if, with the glance of the eye, he sees Sennacherib advancing rapidly to Jerusalem. The general course of this march is from the north-east to the south-west towards Jerusalem, and it is possible still to follow the route by the names of the places here mentioned, and which remain at present. All the places are in the vicinity of Jerusalem, and this shows how much his rapid approach was fitted to excite alarm. The name *Aiath* עַיָּת does not occur elsewhere; but *Ai* עַי is often mentioned, and *Aijah* עַיָּא is found in Neh. xi. 31. Doubtless, the same city is meant. It was situated near Bethel eastward; Josh. vii. 2. It was at this place that Joshua was repulsed on account of the sin of Achaz, though the city was afterwards taken by Joshua, the king seized and hanged, and the city destroyed. It was afterwards rebuilt, and is often mentioned; Ezra ii. 28; Neh. vii. 32. It is called by the LXX. Ἀγγαι; and by Josephus, *Aina*. In the time of Eusebius and Jerome, its site and scanty ruins were still pointed out, not far distant from Bethel towards the east. The name, however, has at present wholly perished, and no trace of the place now remains. It is probable that it was near the modern Deir Diwân, about three miles to the east of Bethel; *see* Robinson's *Bib. Researches*, ii. pp. 119, 312, 313. ¶ *He is passed to Migron.* That is, he does not remain at Aiath, but is advancing rapidly towards Jerusalem. This place is mentioned in 1 Sam. xiv. 2, from which it appears that it was near Gibeah, and was in the boundaries of the tribe of Benjamin, to the southwest of Ai and Bethel. No trace of this place now remains. ¶ *At Michmash.* This was a town within the tribe of Ephraim, on the confines of Benjamin; Ezra ii. 27; Neh. vii. 31. This place is now called Mükhmâs, and is situated on a slope or

29 They are gone over the passage: they have taken up their
lodging at Geba; Ramah *a* is afraid;
Gibeah of Saul is fled.

a Jer.31.15.

low ridge of land between two small
wadys, or water-courses. It is now
desolate, but bears the marks of having
been a much larger and stronger place
than the other towns in the neighbourhood. There are many foundations of
hewn stones; and some columns are
lying among them. It is about nine
miles to the north-east of Jerusalem,
and in the immediate neighbourhood
of Gibeah and Ramah. — Robinson's
Bib. Researches, ii. p. 117. In the
time of Eusebius it was a large village.
— *Onomast.* Art. *Machmas.* ¶ *He
hath laid up his carriages.* Heb.
'He hath deposited his weapons.' The
word rendered *hath laid up*—רְפָּקִיד—
may possibly mean, *he reviewed*, or he
took an account of; that is, he made
that the place of *review* preparatory to
his attack on Jerusalem. Jerome says,
that the passage means, that he had
such confidence of taking Jerusalem,
that he deposited his armour at Michmash, as being unnecessary in the siege
of Jerusalem. I think, however, that
the passage means simply, that he had
made Michmash one of his *stations* to
which he had come, and that the expression 'he hath deposited his armour
there,' denotes merely that he had come
there as one of his stations, and had
pitched his camp in that place on the
way to Jerusalem. The English word
carriage, sometimes meant formerly,
that which is carried, baggage, vessels,
furniture, &c. — *Webster.* In this
sense it is used in this place, and also
in 1 Sam. xvii. 22; Acts xxi. 15.

29. *They are gone over the passage.*
The word *passage* (מַעְבָּרָה) may refer
to any passage or ford of a stream, a
shallow part of a river where crossing
was practicable; or it may refer to any
narrow pass, or place of passing in
mountains. The Chaldee Paraphrase
renders this, 'They have passed the
Jordan;' but this cannot be the meaning, as all the transactions referred to
here occurred in the vicinity of Jerusalem, and long after they had crossed the
Jordan. In 1 Sam. xiii. 23, the 'pas-

sage of Michmash' is mentioned as the
boundary of the garrison of the Philistines. Between Jeb'a and Mŭkhmâs
there is now a steep, precipitous valley,
which is probably the 'passage' here
referred to. This wady, or valley, runs
into another that joins it on the north,
and then issues out upon the plain not
far from Jericho. In the valley are
two hills of a conical form, having steep
rocky sides, which are probably the
rocks mentioned, in connection with
Jonathan's adventure, as a narrow defile
or way between the rock Bozez on the
one side, and Seneh on the other;
1 Sam. xiv. 4, 5. This valley appears
at a later time to have been the dividing line between the tribes of Ephraim
and Benjamin, for Geba on the south
side of this valley was the northern
limit of Judah and Benjamin (2 Kings
xxiii. 8); while Bethel on its north side
was on the southern border of Ephraim;
Judg. xvi. 1, 2.—Robinson's *Bib. Researches*, ii. p. 116. Of course it was
an important place, and could be easily
guarded—like the strait of Thermo-
pylæ. By his having passed this place
is denoted an advance towards Jerusalem, showing that nothing impeded his
progress, and that he was rapidly hastening with his army to the city. ¶ *They
have taken up their lodging at Geba.*
They have pitched their camp there,
being entirely *through* the defile of
Michmash. Heb. 'Geba is a lodging
place for us;' that is, for the Assyrians.
Perhaps, however, there is an error in
the common Hebrew text here, and
that it should be לָמוֹ *lâmō*, 'for them,'
instead of לָנוּ *lânū*, 'for us.' The LXX.
and the Chaldee so read it, and so our
translators have understood it. *Geba*
here is not be confounded with 'Gibeah
of Saul,' mentioned just after. It was
in the tribe of Benjamin (1 Kings xv.
22); and was on the line, or nearly on
the line, of Judah, so as to be its northern boundary; 2 Kings xxiii. 8. It was
not far from Gibeah, or Gibeon. There
are at present no traces of the place
known. ¶ *Ramah.* This city was in

30 Lift [1] up thy voice, O daughter of Gallim: cause it to be heard unto Laish, O poor Anathoth.

the tribe of Benjamin. It was between Geba and Gibea. It was called *Ramah*, from its being on elevated ground ; comp. Note, Matt. ii. 18. Ramah, now called *er-Râm*, lies on a high hill a little east of the road from Jerusalem to Bethel. It is now a miserable village, with few houses, and these in the summer mostly deserted. There are here large square stones, and also columns scattered about in the fields, indicating an ancient place of some importance. A small mosque is here with columns, which seems once to have been a church. Its situation is very conspicuous, and commands a fine prospect. It is near Gibeah, about six Roman miles from Jerusalem. So Jerome, *Comm.* in Hos. v. 8: 'Rama quæ est juxta Gabaa in septimo lapide a Jerosolymis sita.' Josephus places it at forty stadia from Jerusalem ; *Ant.* viii. 12, 3. ¶ *Is afraid.* Is terrified and alarmed at the approach of Sennacherib —a beautiful variation in the description, denoting his rapid and certain advance on the city of Jerusalem, spreading consternation everywhere. ¶ *Gibeah of Saul.* This was called ' Gibeah of Saul,' because it was the birthplace of Saul (1 Sam. xi. 4 ; xv. 34 ; 2 Sam. xxi. 6); and to distinguish it from Gibea in the tribe of Judah (Josh. xv. 57); and also a Gibeah where Eleazar was buried ; Josh. xxiv. 33. Jerome mentions Gibeah as in his day level with the ground.— *Epis.* 86, *ad Eustoch.* It has been almost wholly, since his time, unnoticed by travellers. It is probably the same as the modern village of Jeba, lying in a direction to the southwest of Mŭkhmâs. This village is small, and is half in ruins. Among these there are occasionally seen large hewn stones, indicating antiquity. There is here the ruin of a small tower almost solid, and a small building having the appearance of an ancient church. It is an elevated place from which several villages are visible.—Robinson's *Bib. Researches*, ii. p. 113. ¶ *Is fled.* That is, the inhabitants have fled. Such was the consternation produced by the march of the army of Sennacherib, that the city was thrown into commotion, and left empty.

30. *Lift up thy voice.* That is, cry aloud from alarm and terror. The prophet here changes the manner of describing the advance of Sennacherib. He had described his rapid march from place to place (ver. 28, 29), and the consternation at Ramah and Gibeah ; he now changes the mode of description, and calls on Gallim to lift up her voice of alarm at the approach of the army, so that it might reverberate among the hills, and be heard by neighbouring towns. ¶ *Daughter.* A term often applied to a beautiful city or town ; see Note on ch. i. 8. ¶ *Gallim.* This was a city of Benjamin, north of Jerusalem. It is mentioned only in this place and in 1 Sam. xxv. 44. No traces of this place are now to be found. ¶ *Cause it to be heard.* That is, cause thy voice to be heard. Raise the cry of distress and alarm. ¶ *Unto Laish.* There was a city of this name in the northern part of Palestine, in the bounds of the tribe of Dan ; Judg. xviii. 7, 29. But it is contrary to all the circumstances of the case to suppose, that the prophet refers to a place in the north of Palestine. It was probably a small village in the neighbourhood of Gallim. There are at present no traces of the village ; in 1 Mac. ix. 9, a city of this name is mentioned in the vicinity of Jerusalem, which is, doubtless, the one here referred to. ¶ *O poor Anathoth.* Anathoth was a city of Benjamin (Josh. xxi. 18), where Jeremiah was born ; Jer. i. 1. 'Anàta, which is, doubtless, the same place here intended, is situated on a broad ridge of land, at the distance of one hour and a quarter, or about three miles, from Jerusalem. Josephus describes Anathoth as twenty stadia distant from Jerusalem (*Ant.* x. 7, 3); and Eusebius and Jerome mention it as about three miles to the north of the city. 'Anàta appears to have been once a walled town, and a place of strength. Portions of the wall still remain, built of large hewn stones, and apparently ancient, as are also the foundations of some of the houses. The houses are few, and the people are poor

31 Madmenah is removed; the inhabitants of Gebim gather themselves to flee.

32 As yet shall he remain at Nob that day: he shall shake his hand *against* the mount of the daughter of Zion, the hill of Jerusalem.

and miserable. From this point there is an extensive view over the whole eastern slope of the mountainous country of Benjamin, including all the valley of the Jordan, and the northern part of the Dead Sea. From this place, also, several of the villages here mentioned are visible. — Robinson's *Bib. Researches*, ii. pp. 109–111. The word *poor*, applied to it here (עֲנִיָּה) denotes *afflicted*, oppressed; and the language is that of pity, on account of the impending calamity, and is not designed to be descriptive of its ordinary state. The language in the Hebrew is a paranomasia, a species of writing quite common in the sacred writings; see Gen. i. 2; iv. 12; Isa. xxviii. 10, 13; Joel i. 15; Isa. xxxii. 7; Micah i. 10, 14; Zeph. ii. 4; comp. Stuart's *Heb. Gram.* Ed. 1, § 246. The figure abounded not only in the Hebrew but among the Orientals generally. Lowth reads this, 'Answer her, O Anathoth;' following in this the Syriac version, which reads the word rendered poor (עֲנִיָּה) as a verb from עָנָה *ânâ*, to answer, or respond, and supposes that the idea is retained of an *echo*, or reverberation among the hills, from which he thinks *Anathoth*, from the same verb, took its name. But the meaning of the Hebrew text is that given in our translation. The simple idea is that of neighbouring cities and towns lifting up the voice of alarm, at the approach of the enemy.

31. *Madmenah.* This city is mentioned nowhere else. The city of Madmanna, or Medemene, mentioned in Josh. xv. 31, was in the bounds of the tribe of Simeon, and was far south, towards Gaza. It cannot be the place intended here. ¶ *Is removed.* Or, the inhabitants have fled from fear; see ver. 29. ¶ *Gebim.* This place is unknown. It is nowhere else mentioned. ¶ *Gather themselves to flee.* A description of the alarm prevailing at the approach of Sennacherib.

32. *As yet shall he remain.* This is still a description of his advancing towards Jerusalem. He would make a station at Nob and remain there a day, meaning, perhaps, *only* one day, such would be his impatience to attack and destroy Jerusalem. ¶ *At Nob.* Nob was a city of Benjamin, inhabited by priests; Neh. xi. 32. When David was driven away by Saul, he came to this city, and received supplies from Ahimelech the priest; 1 Sam. xxi. 1–6. Nob must have been situated somewhere upon the ridge of the mount of Olives, to the northeast of the city. So Jerome, professedly from Hebrew tradition, says, 'Stans in oppidulo Nob et procul urbem conspiciens Jerusalem.'—*Comm. in loc.* Messrs. Robinson and Smith sought all along the ridge of the mount of Olives, from the Damascus road to the summit opposite to the city, for some traces of an ancient site which might be regarded as the place of Nob; but without the slightest success.—*Bib. Researches*, ii. p. 150. ¶ *He shall shake his hand.* That is, in the attitude of menace, or threatening. This language implies, that the city of Nob was so near to Jerusalem that the latter city could be seen from it; and the description denotes, that at the sight of Jerusalem Sennacherib would be full of indignation, and utter against it the threat of speedy and complete ruin. ¶ *The mount of the daughter of Zion;* see Note, ch. i. 8. The Chaldee renders this, 'He shall come, and stand in Nob, the city of the priests, over against the wall of Jerusalem, and shall answer and say to his army, " Is not this that city of Jerusalem against which I have assembled all my armies, and on account of which I have made an exaction on all my provinces? And lo, it is less and more feeble than any of the defences of the people which I have subjected in the strength of my hand." Over against that he shall stand, and shake his head, and shall bring his hand against the mount of the sanctuary which is Zion, and against the court which is in Jerusalem.' Jarchi and Kimchi say, that Nob was so near to Jerusalem that it could be seen from

33 Behold, the Lord, the Lord of hosts, shall lop the bough with terror: and the high ones of stature *shall be* hewn down, and the haughty shall be humbled.

34 And he shall cut down the thickets of the forests with iron, and Lebanon shall fall ¹ by a mighty one.

CHAPTER XI.

ANALYSIS OF THE CHAPTER.

THIS chapter is connected with the preceding as part of the same general prophecy. In that, the prophet had described the invasion of Sennacherib, and had given the assurance that Jerusalem should be safe, notwithstanding the threatened invasion. The general design of that

¹ or, *mightily.*

thence; and hence this is mentioned as the last station of the army of the Assyrian, the end of his march, and where the prize seemed to be within his grasp.

33. *Behold, the Lord,* &c. The prophet had described, in the previous verses, the march of the Assyrians towards Jerusalem, station by station. He had accompanied him in his description, until he had arrived in full sight of the city, which was the object of all his preparation. He had described the consternation which was felt at his approach in all the smaller towns. Nothing had been able to stand before him; and now, flushed with success, and confident that Jerusalem would fall, he stands before the devoted city. But here, the prophet announces that his career was to close; and here his arms to be stayed. Here he was to meet with an overthrow, and Jerusalem would still be safe. This is the design of the prophecy, to comfort the inhabitants of Jerusalem with the assurance that they still would be safe. ¶ *Will lop the bough.* The word *bough* here (פֻּארָה) is from פָּאַר to adorn, to beautify; and is given to a branch or bough of a tree on account of its beauty. It is, therefore, descriptive of that which is beautiful, honoured, proud; and is applied to the Assyrian on account of his pride and magnificence. In ver. 18, 19, the prophet had described the army of the Assyrian as a magnificent forest. Here

prophecy was *to console the people with the assurance of their deliverance from impending calamity.* But it was a general principle with the Hebrew prophets, and particularly with Isaiah, when *any* event tending to console the people, or to excite the nation's gratitude, occurred, to cast the eye forward to that great future deliverance which they anticipated under the Messiah; see Introduction, § 7, (3.) The contemplation of *present* objects dies away; the mind fixes more intently on the glories of the Messiah's reign; the prophetic vision ranges over the beauties of his person, and the glories of his kingdom, until the prophet seems to have forgotten the subject with which he commenced. This was perfectly natural. It was by an obvious law of association in the mind, by which the mention of deliverance, in any form, however humble, would suggest that great deliverance on which the eye of every Jew would rest. It

he says that the glory of that army should be destroyed, as the vitality and beauty of the waving bough of a tree is quickly destroyed when it is lopped with an axe. There can scarcely be conceived a description, that would more beautifully represent the fading strength of the army of the Assyrian than this. ¶ *With terror.* In such a way as to inspire terror. ¶ *The high ones of stature.* The chief men and officers of the army.

34. *And he shall cut down the thickets of the forest.* The army of the Assyrians, described here as a thick, dense forest; comp. ver. 18, 19. ¶ *With iron.* As a forest is cut down with an axe, so the prophet uses this phrase here, to *keep up and carry out the figure.* The army was destroyed with the pestilence (2 Kings xix. 35); but it fell as certainly as a forest falls before the axe. ¶ *And Lebanon.* Lebanon is here evidently descriptive of the army of the Assyrian, retaining the idea of a beautiful and magnificent forest. Thus, in Ezek. xxxi. 3, it is said, 'the king of the Assyrians was a cedar of Lebanon with fair branches.' Lebanon is usually applied to the Jews as descriptive of them (Jer. xxii. 6, 23; Zech. x. 10; xi. 1), but it is evidently applied here to the Assyrian army; and the sense is, that that army should be soon and certainly destroyed, and that, therefore, the inhabitants of Jerusalem had no cause of alarm; see Notes on ch. xxxvii.

hence follows, that wherever the prophet *begins*, he usually *ends* with a glowing description of the reign of the Messiah. However far from this central object of revealed religion he may commence, yet there is a tendency everywhere *to it* in the prophetic writings; and the moment that, by any law of association, this object is suggested, or the eye catches a glimpse of it, the former object sinks out of view, and the person and reign of the Messiah becomes the sole theme of the prophetic description. This is the case here. Isaiah had commenced the prophecy with an account of the invasion of Sennacherib; ch. x. 5, &c. He had described the deliverance from that danger; ch. x. 33, 34. The mention of this deliverance directs his thoughts to that far greater deliverance which would take place under the Messiah; and immediately (ch. xi.) he commences a glowing description of his coming and his reign. The *language* with which he commenced the prophecy, is retained; the illustrations are drawn from the subject *before* under consideration; but the description pertains to the glories of the reign of the Mes-

siah. The proof of this will appear in the Notes on particular passages in the chapter. Its general design is, to console the people by the prospect of a great future deliverance under the Messiah, and by a prospect of the glories of his reign. He describes, (i.) The certainty that he would come, and his character; ver. 1-5. (ii.) The peace and prosperity which would follow from his advent; ver. 6-9. (iii.) The fact that the Gentiles would be called to partake of the privileges of his reign; ver. 10. (iv.) The restoration of the exiles to their native land under his reign; ver. 11, 12. (v.) The fact, that his reign would put a period to dissensions and strifes between the contending nations of the Jews; ver. 13; and (vi.) The universal prevalence of his religion, and the deliverance of his people; ver. 14-16.

A ND *a*there shall come forth a rod out of the stem *b* of Jesse, and a branch *c* shall grow out of his roots:

a ch. 53. 2.   b Acts 13. 23; Rev. 22. 16.   c Zec. 6. 12.

CHAPTER XI.

1. *And there shall come forth a rod.* In the previous chapter, the prophet had represented the Assyrian monarch and his army under the image of a dense and flourishing forest, with all its glory and grandeur. In opposition to this, he describes the illustrious personage who is the subject of this chapter, under the image of a slender twig or shoot, sprouting up from the root of a decayed and fallen tree. Between the Assyrian, therefore, and the person who is the subject of this chapter, there is a most striking and beautiful contrast. The one was at first magnificent—like a vast spreading forest—yet should soon fall and decay; the other was the little sprout of a decayed tree, which should yet rise, expand, and flourish. ¶ *A rod* (חֹטֶר *hhōtĕr*). This word occurs in but one other place; Prov. xiv. 3: 'In the mouth of the foolish is *a rod* of pride.' Here it means, evidently, *a branch, a twig, a shoot*, such as starts up from the roots of a decayed tree, and is synonymous with the word rendered *branch* (צֶמַח *tzēmăhh*) in ch. iv. 2; see the Note on that place. ¶ *Out of the stem.* (מִגֶּזַע). This word occurs but three times in the Old Testament; see Job xiv. 8; where it is rendered *stock:*

Though the root thereof wax old in the earth,
And the *stock* thereof die in the ground;

and in Isa. xl. 24: 'Yea, their *stock* shall not take root in the earth.' It means, therefore, the stock or stump of a tree that has been cut down—a stock, however, which may not be quite dead, but where it may send up a branch or shoot from its roots. It is beautifully applied to an ancient family that is fallen into decay, yet where there may be a descendant that shall rise and flourish; as a tree may fall and decay, but still there may be vitality in the root, and it shall send up a tender germ or sprout. ¶ *Of Jesse.* The father of David. It means, that he who is here spoken of should be of the family of Jesse, or David. Though Jesse had died, and though the ancient family of David would fall into decay, yet there would arise from that family an illustrious descendant. The beauty of this description is apparent, if we bear in recollection that, when the Messiah was born, the ancient and much honoured family of David had fallen into decay; that the mother of Jesus, though appertaining to that family, was poor, obscure, and unknown; and that, to all appearance, the glory of the family had departed. Yet from that, as from a long-decayed root in the ground, he

2 And the Spirit of the LORD
shall rest upon *a* him, the spirit of

<small>*a* Mat.3.16; Jn.3.34.</small>

should spring who would restore the
family to more than its ancient glory,
and shed additional lustre on the
honoured name of Jesse. ¶ *And a
branch* (נֵצֶר *nētzĕr*). A twig, branch,
or shoot; a slip, scion, or young sucker
of a tree, that is selected for transplant-
ing, and that requires to be watched
with peculiar care. The word occurs
but four times; Isa. lx. 21: 'They shall
inherit the land for ever, THE BRANCH
of my planting;' Isa. xiv. 19: 'But
thou art cast out of thy grave as an
abominable branch;' Dan. xi. 7. The
word rendered BRANCH in Jer. xxiii. 5;
xxxiii. 15, is a different word in the original (צֶמַח *tzēmăhh*), though meaning
substantially the same thing. The word
branch is also used by our translators,
in rendering several other Hebrew words;
see Taylor's *Concordance*. Here the
word is synonymous with that which is
rendered *rod* in the previous part of the
verse—a shoot, or twig, from the root
of a decayed tree. ¶ *Out of his roots.*
As a shoot starts up from the roots of
a decayed tree. The LXX. render this,
'And a *flower* (ἄνθος) shall arise from
the root.' The Chaldee, 'And a king
shall proceed from the sons of Jesse,
and the Messiah from his sons' sons
shall arise;' showing conclusively that
the ancient Jews referred this to the
Messiah.

That this verse, and the subsequent
parts of the chapter, refer to the Messiah, may be argued from the following
considerations:—(1.) The fact that it is
expressly applied to him in the New
Testament. Thus Paul, in Rom. xv.
12, quotes the tenth verse of this chapter as expressly applicable to the times
of the Messiah. (2.) The Chaldee
Paraphrase shows, that this was the
sense which the ancient Jews put upon
the passage. That paraphrase is of
authority, only to show that this was
the sense which appeared to be the true
one by the ancient interpreters. (3.) The
description in the chapter is not applicable to any other personage than the
Messiah. Grotius supposes that the
passage refers to Hezekiah; though, 'in

wisdom *b* and understanding, the
spirit of counsel and might, the

<small>*b* 1Cor.1.30.</small>

a more sublime sense,' he refers to the Messiah.
Others have referred it to Zerubbabel.
But none of the things here related
apply to either, except the fact that
they had a descent from the family of
Jesse; for neither of those families had
fallen into the decay which the prophet
here describes. (4.) The peace, prosperity, harmony and order, referred to
in the subsequent portions of the chapter, are not descriptive of any portion
of the reign of Hezekiah. (5.) The
terms and descriptions here accord with
other portions of the Scriptures, as applicable to the Messiah. Thus Jeremiah (xxiii. 5; xxxiii. 15) describes the
Messiah under the similitude of a *branch.*
a germ or shoot—using, indeed, a different Hebrew word, but retaining the
same idea and image; comp. Zech. iii.
8. It accords also with the description
by Isaiah of the same personage in ch.
iv. 2; see Note on the place. (6.) I may
add, that nearly all commentators have
referred this to the Messiah; and, perhaps, it would not be possible to find
greater unanimity in regard to the interpretation of any passage of Scripture than on this.

2. *And the Spirit of the* LORD. The
Spirit of JEHOVAH. Chaldee, 'And
there shall rest upon him the spirit of
prophecy from before JEHOVAH.' In the
previous verse, the prophet had announced his origin and his birth. In
this, he proceeds to describe his extraordinary endowments, as eminently
holy, pure, and wise. There can be no
doubt that reference is here had to the
Holy Spirit, the third person of the
sacred Trinity, as descending upon him
in the fulness of his influences, and producing in him perfect wisdom, knowledge, and the fear of the Lord. The
Spirit of JEHOVAH shall rest upon him
—a Spirit producing wisdom, understanding, counsel, might, &c. All these
are in the Scriptures traced to the
agency of the Holy Spirit; see 1 Cor.
xii. 8–11. The meaning here is, that
the Messiah should be endowed with
these eminent prophetic gifts and qualifications for his ministry by the agency

spirit of knowledge, and of the fear of the LORD;

3 And shall make him of ¹ quick

---

¹ *scent, or, smell.*

---

of the Holy Spirit. It was by that Spirit that the prophets had been inspired (see 2 Pet. i. 21; 2 Tim. iii. 16); and as the Messiah was to be a prophet (Deut. xviii. 15, 18), there was a fitness that he should be endowed in the same manner. If it be asked how one, who was Divine in his own nature, could be thus endowed by the aid of the Spirit, the answer is, that he was also to be a man descended from the honoured line of David, and that *as* a man he might be furnished for his work by the agency of the Holy Ghost. His human nature was kept pure; his mind was made eminently wise; his heart always retained the fear and love of God, and there is no absurdity in supposing that these extraordinary endowments were to be traced to God. That he *was* thus under the influence of the Holy Spirit, is abundantly taught in the New Testament. Thus, in Matt. iii. 16, the Holy Spirit is represented as descending on him at his baptism. In John iii. 34, it is said, 'For he whom God hath sent speaketh the words of God; for God giveth not the Spirit by measure unto him;' comp. Col. i. 19. ¶ *Shall rest upon him.* That is, shall descend on him, and remain with him. It shall not merely *come* upon him, but shall attend him permanently; comp. Num. xi. 25, 26. ¶ *The spirit of wisdom.* The spirit producing wisdom, or making him wise. Wisdom consists in the choice of the best means to secure the best ends. This attribute is often given to the Messiah in the New Testament, and was always evinced by him; comp. 1 Cor. i. 30; Eph. i. 17; Col. ii. 3: 'In whom are hid all the treasures of wisdom and knowledge.' ¶ *And understanding.* The difference between the words here rendered *wisdom* and *understanding* is, that the former denotes wisdom properly; and the latter, that judgment resulting from wisdom, by which we distinguish things, or decide on their character. ¶ *The spirit of counsel.* That by which he shall be qualified to *give* counsel or advice; the

understanding in the fear of the LORD: and he shall not judge after the sight of his eyes, neither reprove after the hearing of his ears:

qualification of a public instructor and guide; see Note on ch. ix. 6. ¶ *And might.* Strength, vigour, energy; that strength of heart and purpose which will enable a man to meet difficulties, to encounter dangers, to be bold, open, and fearless in the discharge of his duties. It is not necessary to remark, that this characteristic was found in an eminent degree in the Lord Jesus Christ. ¶ *Of knowledge.* That is, the knowledge of the attributes and plans of JEHOVAH; comp. Matt. xi. 27: 'Neither knoweth any man the Father save the Son.' John i. 18: 'No man hath seen God at any time; the only begotten Son, which is in the bosom of the Father, he hath declared him;' 1 John v. 20. ¶ *And of the fear of the* LORD. The fear of JEHOVAH is often used to denote piety in general, as consisting in a reverence for the Divine commands, and a dread of offending him; *i.e.*, a desire to please him, which is piety; comp. Job xxviii. 28; Ps. xix. 9; cxi. 10; Prov. i. 7; iii. 13; xv. 33; xix. 23. That this characteristic was found eminently in the Lord Jesus, it is not necessary to attempt to prove.

3. *And shall make him of quick understanding.* (וַהֲרִיחֹ.) The LXX. render this, 'And the spirit of the fear of God shall fill him.' The Chaldee, 'And the Lord shall draw him near to him in his fear.' The Syriac, 'And he shall be resplendent (like the sun, or the stars) in the fear of the Lord.' The Hebrew word here used is probably derived from רִיחַ *riăhh*, used only in Hiphil, *to smell;* and is kindred with רוּחַ *ruăh*, *wind, breath*, for fragrant substances *breathe out* an odour.—*Gesenius.* It then denotes *to take delight in smelling* (Ex. xxx. 38; Lev. xxvi. 31); and thence, by an easy transition, to take delight in anything; Amos v. 21. The reason is, that the objects of smell are usually pleasant and agreeable; and especially such as were the aromatics used in public worship. The sense here is, probably, that he would take pleasure

4 But ^awith righteousness shall he judge the poor, and ¹reprove with equity for the meek of the earth: and he shall smite the earth

a Ps.72.2,4; Rev.19 11.

1 argue.

in the fear of JEHOVAH, that is, in piety, and in devoting himself to his service. The interpretation given in our translation, is that given by many expositors; though that above suggested is probably the correct one. The word is used to denote *pleasure* in a thing ; it is not used anywhere, it is believed, to denote a quick understanding ; comp. Ex. v. 21 ; Phil. iv. 18. The idea which is conveyed by our translators is, probably, derived from *the discernment of the quality of objects* by an acute sense of *smell,* and hence they interpreted the word to denote an acute discrimination of any objects. ¶ *And he shall not judge after the sight of his eyes.* He shall not judge of things by their external appearance, or with partiality. This is language which is applicable to a magistrate, and is spoken of the Messiah as the descendant of David, and as sitting on his throne as a ruler of his people. He who judges ' after the sight of his eyes,' does it according to external appearances, showing favour to rank, to the rich, and the great; or judging as things *appear* without a close and careful inquiry into their true nature and bearings ; comp. John vii. 24: 'Judge not according to the appearance, but judge righteous judgment ;' Deut. i. 16, 17. ¶ *Neither reprove.* יוֹכִיחַ. This word means *to show, to prove; to correct, reprove, convince; to reproach, or censure; to punish; to judge, decide,* &c. Here it is evidently used as synonymous with 'shall he judge' in the former part of the parallelism—retaining the idea of a just judge, who decides not according to the hearing of the ears, but according to justice. ¶ *After the hearing of his ears.* Not by plausible statements, and ingenious defences, but by weighing evidence, and by an impartial examination of the true merits of the case. This belonged to the Lord Jesus, because, (1.) He was never influenced by any undue regard to rank, honour, or office. His opinions were always impartial; his judgments without bias or favouritism. (2.) He was able to discern the true merits of every case. He knew what was in man, saw the true state of the heart, and, therefore, was not deceived or imposed upon as human judges are; see John ii. 24, 25 ; comp. Rev. ii. 23; John vi. 64.

4. *Shall he judge the poor.* That is, he shall see that impartial justice is done them ; he shall not take part with the rich against the poor, but shall show that he is the friend of justice. This is the quality of a just and upright magistrate, and this character the Lord Jesus everywhere evinced. He chose his disciples from among the poor ; he condescended to be their companion and friend ; he provided for their wants ; and he pronounced their condition blessed ; Matt. v. 3. There may be a reference here to the poor in spirit—the humble, the penitent ; but the main idea is, that he would not be influenced by any undue regard for the higher ranks of life, but would be the friend and patron of the poor. ¶ *And reprove.* הוֹכִיחַ. And judge, decide, or argue for ; that is, he shall be their friend and their impartial judge ; ver. 3. ¶ *With equity.* With uprightness, or uncorrupted integrity. ¶ *For the meek of the earth.* עֲנְוֵי־אָרֶץ. For the humble, the lower class; referring to those who were usually passed by, or oppressed by those in power. ¶ *And he shall smite the earth.* By the *earth* here, or the land, is meant evidently *the wicked,* as the following member of the parallelism shows. Perhaps it is intended to be implied, that the earth, when he should come, would be eminently depraved ; which was the fact. The characteristic here is that of an upright judge or prince, who would punish the wicked. To *smite* the earth, or the wicked, is expressive of punishment ; and this characteristic is elsewhere attributed to the Messiah; see Ps. ii. 9–12; Rev. ii. 27. The trait is that of a just, upright, impartial exercise of power—such as would be manifested in the defence of the poor and the innocent, and in the punishment of the proud and the

with the ^arod of his mouth, and with the breath of his lips shall he slay the wicked.

5 And righteousness shall be the girdle ^bof his loins, and faithfulness the girdle of his reins.

guilty. ¶ *With the rod of his mouth.* The word שֵׁבֶט here rendered ' rod,' denotes properly a stick, or staff; a rod for chastisement or correction (Prov. x. 13; xiii. 24; Job ix. 34; xxi. 9); the staff, or sceptre of a ruler—as an emblem of office; a measuring rod; a spear, &c.; Note, ch. x. 5. It is not elsewhere applied to the mouth, though it is often used in other connections. It means that which goes out of the mouth—a word, command, threatening, decision; and it is implied that it would go forth to pronounce sentence of condemnation, and to punish. His word would be so just, impartial, and authoritative, that the effect would be to overwhelm the wicked. In a sense similar to this, Christ is said to have been seen by John, when ' out of his mouth went a sharp two-edged sword' (Rev. i. 16); that is, his commands and decisions were so authoritative, and so certain in their execution, as to be like a sharp sword; comp. Heb. iv. 12; Isa. xlix. 2 : ' And he hath made my mouth like a sharp sword.' The discriminating preaching, the pungent discourses, the authoritative commands of the Lord Jesus, when on earth, showed, and his judicial decisions in the day of judgment will show, the manner of the fulfilment of the prediction. ¶ *And with the breath of his lips.* This is synonymous with the previous member of the parallelism. ' The breath of his lips' means that which goes forth from his lips—his doctrines, his commands, his decisions. ¶ *Shall he slay the wicked.* That is, he shall condemn the wicked; or, he shall sentence them to punishment. This is descriptive of a prince or ruler, who by his commands and decisions effectually subdues and punishes the wicked; that is, he does justice to all. Grotius interprets this, ' by his prayers,' referring it to Hezekiah, and to the influence of his prayers in destroying the Assyrians. The Chaldee Paraphrast translates it, ' And by the word of his lips he shall slay the impious Armillus.' By *Armillus*, the Jews mean the last

great enemy of their nation, who would come after Gog and Magog and wage furious wars, and who would slay the Messiah Ben Ephraim, whom the Jews expect, but who would be himself slain by the rod of the Messiah Ben David, or the son of David.—*Castell.*

5. *And righteousness shall be the girdle of his loins.* The sense of this verse is plain. He will always exhibit himself as a just and faithful king. The *girdle of the loins* refers to the cincture, or band, with which the ancients girded themselves. A part of their dress consisted of an outward, loose, flowing robe. This robe it was necessary to gird up, or to confine close to the body in active labour, or in running; and the meaning of the figure here used is, probably, that the virtues of righteousness and justice would *adhere* to him as closely and inseparably as the garment does to the body to which it was bound. The figure of representing the virtues as *clothing*, or describing them as parts of *dress* with which we are invested, is common in the Scriptures :

I put on righteousness, and it clothed me;
My judgment was as a robe and a diadem.
                        Job xxix. 14.
I will greatly rejoice in the Lord,
My soul shall be joyful in my God;
For he hath clothed me with the garments of salvation,
He hath covered me with the robe of righteousness,
As a bridegroom decketh himself with ornaments,
And as a bride adorneth herself with her jewels.
                        Isa. lxi. 10.

Comp. Rev. xix. 8, and Paul's beautiful description in Eph. vi. 13–17. In like manner, vice and wickedness are sometimes represented as so closely *adhering* to a man as to be a part of his very clothing; Ps. cix. 18, 19 :

He clothed himself with cursing, like as with a garment.
Let it be unto him as the garment which covereth him,
And for a girdle, wherewith he is girded continually.

The Chaldee renders this, ' And the just shall be round about him on every side — סָחוֹר סָחוֹר — and the servants

6 The *a* wolf also shall dwell with the lamb, and the leopard shall lie down with the kid; and the calf, and the young lion, and the fatling together; and a little child shall lead them.

a ch.65.25.

of truth shall come near to him.' The idea is, that he shall be distinguished for justice and truth, and that a zeal for these shall make him strong and active in executing the purposes of his reign. This closes the description of the *personal* qualities of the Messiah. The account of the effects of his reign follows in the subsequent verses.

6. *The wolf also.* In this, and the following verses, the prophet describes the effect of his reign in producing peace and tranquillity on the earth. The description is highly poetical, and is one that is common in ancient writings in describing a golden age. The two leading ideas are those of *peace* and *security.* The figure is taken from the condition of animals of all descriptions living in a state of harmony, where those which are by nature defenceless, and which are usually made the prey of the strong, are suffered to live in security. By nature the wolf preys upon the lamb, and the leopard upon the kid, and the adder is venomous, and the bear, and the cow, and the lion, and the ox, cannot live together. But if a state of things should arise, where all this hostility would cease; where the wild animals would lay aside their ferocity, and where the feeble and the gentle would be safe; where the adder would cease to be venomous, and where all would be so mild and harmless that a little child would be safe, and could lead even the most ferocious animals, that state would represent the reign of the Messiah. Under his dominion, such a change would be produced as that those who were by nature violent, severe, and oppressive; those whose disposition is illustrated by the ferocious and blood-thirsty propensities of the lion and the leopard, and by the poison of the adder, would be changed and subdued, and would be disposed to live in peace and harmony with others. This is the *general* idea of the passage. We are not to cut the interpretation to the quick, and to press the expressions to know what particular class of men are

represented by the lion, the bear, or the adder. The *general* image that is before the prophet's mind is that of peace and safety, *such as that would be* if a change were to be produced in wild animals, making them tame, and peaceful, and harmless.

This description of a golden age is one that is common in Oriental writers, where the wild beasts are represented as growing tame; where serpents are harmless; and where all is plenty, peace, and happiness. Thus Jones, in his commentary on Asiatic poetry, quotes from an Arabic poet, *Ibn Onein*, p. 380:

Justitia, a qua mansuetus fit lupus fame astrictus,
Esuriens, licet hinnulum candidum videat—

'Justice, by which the ravening wolf, driven by hunger, becomes tame, although he sees a white kid.' Thus, also, Ferdusi, a Persian poet:

Rerum Dominus, Mahmud, rex potens,
Ad cujus aquam potum veniunt simul agnus et lupus—

'Mahmud, mighty king, lord of events, to whose fountain the lamb and the wolf come to drink.' Thus Virgil, Eclogue iv. 21:

Ipsæ lactæ domum referent distenta capellæ
Ubera; nec magnos metuent armenta leones—

Home their full udders, goats, unurged shall bear,
Nor shall the herd the lordly lion fear.

And immediately after:

Occidet et serpens, et fallax herba veneni
Occidet—

The snake, and poison's treacherous weed shall die.   *Wrangham.*

Again, Eclogue, v. 60:

Nec lupus insidias pecori, nec retia cervis
Ulla dolum mediantur: amat bonus otia Daphnis.

So also Horace, *Epod.* xvi. 53, 54:

Nec vespertinus circumgemit ursus ovile,
Nec intumescit alta viperis humus.

See also *Claudian*, Lib. ii. v. 25, *sq.*; and Theocritus, Idyl xxiv. 84, as quoted by Gesenius and Rosenmüller.

These passages are beautiful, and highly poetic; but they do not equal the beauty of the prophet. There is an exquisite sweetness in the passage of Isaiah—in the picture which he has drawn—particularly in the introduction of the security of the young child, which does not occur in the quotations from the heathen poets.

That this passage is descriptive of the times of the Messiah, there can be no doubt. It has been a question, to what particular part of his reign the prophet has reference. Some have referred it to the time when he came, and to the influence of his gospel in mitigating the ferocity of his enemies, and ultimately disposing them to suffer Christians to live with them—the infuriated enemies of the cross, under the emblem of the wolf, the bear, the leopard, and the adder, becoming willing that the Christian, under the emblem of the lamb, and the kid, should live with them without molestation. This is the interpretation of Vitringa. Others have referred it to the Millennium—as descriptive of a state of happiness, peace, and universal security then. Others have referred it to the second coming of the Messiah, as descriptive of a time when it is supposed that he will reign personally on the earth, and when there shall be universal security and peace, and when the nature of animals shall be so far changed, that the ferocity of those which are wild and ravenous shall cease, and they shall become harmless to the defenceless. Without attempting to examine these opinions at length, we may, perhaps, express the sense of the passage by the following observations :—(1.) The eye of the prophet is fixed upon the reign of the Messiah, not with reference to time, but with reference to the actual facts of that reign. He saw the scene pass before his mind in vision (see the Introduction, § 7, iii. (4.) (5.), and it is not the nature of such descriptions to mark the *time*, but the order, the passing aspect of the scene. *Under the reign of the Messiah*, he saw that this would occur. Looking down distant times, as on a beautiful landscape, he perceived, under the mild reign of the Prince of peace, a state of things which would be well represented by the wolf dwelling with the lamb, the leopard crouching down with the kid,

and a little child safe in their midst. (2.) It was, *in fact*, partially fulfilled in the earliest times of the gospel, and has been everywhere. Under that gospel, the mad passions of men have been subdued ; their wild ferocious nature has been changed ; their love of conquest, and war, and blood taken away ; and the change has been such as would be beautifully symbolized by the change of the disposition of the wolf and the leopard—suffering the innocent and the harmless to live with them in peace. (3.) The scene will not be fully realized until the reign of the Messiah shall be extended to all nations, and his gospel shall everywhere accomplish its full effects. The vision of Isaiah here has not yet received a full completion ; nor will it until the earth shall be full of the knowledge of the Lord, ver. 9. The mind is, therefore, still directed onward. In future times, UNDER THE REIGN OF THE MESSIAH, what is here described shall occur—a state of security, and peace, and happiness. Isaiah saw that splendid vision, as in a picture, pass before the mind ; the wars, and persecutions, and trials of the Messiah's kingdom were, for a time at least, thrown into the back ground, or not represented, and, in that future time, he saw what is here represented. It has been partially fulfilled—in all the changes which the Messiah's reign has made in the natural ferocity and cruelty of men ; in all the peace which at any time the church has been permitted to enjoy ; in all the revolutions promoting human safety, welfare, and happiness, which Christianity has produced. It is to receive the complete fulfilment—τὸ ἀποτελίσμα —only in that future time when the gospel shall be everywhere established on the earth. The essential thing, therefore, in the prophecy, is the representation of the peace, safety, and harmony which shall take place under the Messiah. So to speak, it was a taking out, and causing to pass before the mind of the prophet, all the circumstances of harmony, order, and love in his reign —as, in a beautiful panoramic view of a landscape, the beauties of the whole scene may be made to pass before the mind ; the circumstances that might even then, if surveyed closely, give pain, were hid from the view, or lost in the loveliness of the whole scene. (4.) That it does not refer to any literal change in the nature of animals, so that the ferocity of the untamed shall be wholly laid aside, the disposition to prey on one another wholly cease, and the poisonous nature of the adder be destroyed, seems to me to be evident— (*a*) Because the whole description has a highly figurative and poetical cast. (*b*) Because such figurative expressions are common in all poetry, and especially among the Orientals. (*c*) Because it does not appear how the gospel has any tendency to change the nature of the lion, the bear, or the serpent. It acts on men, not on brutes; on human hearts, not on the organization of wild animals. (*d*) Because such a state of things could not occur without a perpetual miracle, changing the *physical* nature of the whole animal creation, The lion, the wolf, the panther, are made to live on flesh. The whole organization of their teeth and digestive powers is adapted to this, and this alone. To fit them to live on vegetable food, would require a change in their whole structure, and confound all the doctrines of natural history. The adder is poisonous, and nothing but a miracle would prevent the poisonous secretion, and make his bite innocuous. But where is a promise of any such continued miracle as shall change the whole structure of the animal creation, and make the physical world different from what it is? It is indeed probable that wild animals and venomous serpents will wholly retire before the progress of civilization and Christianity, and that the earth may be inhabited everywhere with safety—for such is the tendency of the advance of civilization—but this is a very different thing from a change in the physical nature of the animal creation. The fair interpretation of this passage is, therefore, that revolutions will be produced in the wild and evil passions of men—the only thing with which the gospel has to do—as great *as if* a change were produced in the animal creation, and the most ferocious and the most helpless should dwell together.—*The wolf* (זְאֵב *zĕebh*) is a

well-known animal, so called from his yellow or golden colour. The Hebrew name is formed by changing ה *hē* in the word זָהָב *zâhâbh*, *gold*, to א *aleph*. —Bochart. The wolf, in the Scriptures, is described as ravenous, fierce, cruel; and is the emblem of that which is wild, ferocious, and savage among men; Gen. xlix. 27: 'Benjamin shall ravin as a wolf;' Ezek. xxii. 27: 'Her princes in the midst thereof are like wolves ravening the prey;' Matt. vii. 15: 'Beware of false prophets, which come to you in sheep's clothing, but inwardly they are ravening wolves;' John x. 12; Matt. x. 16; Luke x. 3; Acts xx. 29. The wolf is described as sanguinary and bloody (Ezek. xxii. 27), and as taking its prey by night, and as therefore particularly an object of dread; Jer. v. 6: 'A wolf of the evenings shall spoil them; Hab. i. 8: 'Their horses are more fierce than the evening wolves;' Zeph. iii. 3: 'Her judges are evening wolves, they gnaw not the bones till to-morrow.' In the Scriptures, the wolf is constantly represented in contrast with the lamb; the one the emblem of ferocity, the other of gentleness and innocence; Matt. x. 16; Luke x. 3. The heathen poets also regard the wolf as an emblem of ferocity and cruelty:

Inde lupi ceu
Raptores, atra in nebula, quos improba ventris
Exegit cæcos rabies, etc.—
         (Virg. *Æn.* ii. 355, *sq.*)

As hungry wolves, with raging appetite,
Scour through the fields, nor fear the stormy
      night—
Their whelps at home expect the promised food,
And long to temper their dry chaps in blood—
So rushed we forth at once.   *Dryden.*

Cervi, luporum præda rapacium.
       Hor. *Car.* Lib. iv. Ode iv. 50.

See a full illustration of the nature and habits of the wolf in Bochart, *Hieroz.* Part i. B. iii. ch. x. pp. 821–830. ¶ *Shall dwell.* גָּר. Shall sojourn, or abide. The word usually denotes a residence for a time only, away from home, not a permanent dwelling. The idea here is, that they shall remain peacefully together. The same image occurs in ch. lxv. 25, in another form: 'The wolf and the lamb shall feed together.' ¶ *The lamb.* Everywhere the emblem of mildness, gentleness, and innocence;

7 And the cow and the bear
shall feed; their young ones shall

lie down together: and the lion
shall eat straw like the ox.

and, therefore, applied often to the people of God, as mild, inoffensive, and forbearing; John xxi. 15; Luke x. 3; Isa. xl. 2. It is very often applied, by way of eminence, to the Lord Jesus Christ; John i. 29; Acts viii. 32; Isa. ii. 7; 1 Pet. i. 19; Rev. v. 6, 8, 12, 13; vi. 16; vii. 9, 10, 14, 17, *et al.* ¶ *And the leopard.* נָמֵר *nâmēr.* The leopard, a well-known wild beast, was regarded in Oriental countries as second in dignity only to the lion. The Arabic writers say, 'He is second in rank to the lion, and, as there is a natural hatred between them, victory is alternate between them.' Hence, in the Scriptures, the lion and the leopard are often joined together as animals of the same character and rank; Cant. iv. 8:

From the lions' den,
From the mountains of the leopards.

See Jer. v. 6, and Hos. xiii. 7:

Therefore I will be unto them as a lion,
As a leopard by the way will I observe them.

The leopard is distinguished for his spots; Jer. xiii. 23: 'Can the Ethiopian change his skin, or the leopard his spots?' it has small white eyes, wide jaws, sharp teeth, and is represented as extremely cruel to man. It was common in Palestine, and was an object of great dread. It lurked for its prey like the lion, and seized upon it suddenly (Jer. v. 6; Hos. xiii. 7), and was particularly distinguished for its velocity (Hab. i. 8), and is often referred to in the classic writers as an emblem of fleetness. See *Bochart.* The image here used by Isaiah, that 'the leopard should lie down with the kid,' as an emblem of peace and safety, occurs almost in the same form in the Sybilline oracles, Lib. iii:

παρδάλιές τ' ἐριφοίς ἅμα βοσκήσονται,—

'Leopards shall feed together with kids.' *See* Bochart, *Hieroz.* Part i. B. iii. ch. vii. pp. 786–791. ¶ *With the kid.* The young of the goat; Gen. xxxvii. 21; Lev. xxiii. 19; Luke xv. 29. Like the lamb, it was an emblem of gentleness, mildness, and inoffensiveness. ¶ *And the calf.* Another emblem of inoffen-

siveness and innocence. ¶ *And the young lion.* The Hebrew word here used—כְּפִיר—denotes one that is old enough to go abroad for prey. It is employed as emblematic of dangerous enemies (Ps. xxxiv. 2; xxxv. 17; lviii. 7); and also as emblematic of young heroes, or defenders of a state; Ezek. xxxviii. 15; Nah. ii. 14. ¶ *And the fatling.* The calf or other animal that was well fed, and that would be therefore particularly an object of desire to a wild beast. The beauty of the image is heightened, by the circumstance that now the ravenous beast would live with that which usually excites its keenest appetite, without attempting to injure it. ¶ *And a little child shall lead them.* This is a peculiarly beautiful image introduced into the picture of peace and prosperity. Naturally, the lion and the leopard are objects of dread to a young child. But here, the state of peace and safety is represented as not only so entire that the child might live with them in safety, but their natural ferocity is so far subdued and tamed, that they could be led by him at his will. The verisimilitude of the picture is increased by the circumstance, that these wild beasts *may be* so far tamed as to become subject to the will of a man, and even of a child.

7. *And the cow and the bear shall feed.* That is, together. Animals that by nature do not dwell together, where by nature the one would be the prey of the other, shall dwell together—an image of safety and peace. ¶ *And the lion shall eat straw like the ox.* A representation of the change that will take place under the reign of the Messiah in the natural disposition of men, and in the aspect of society; as great *as if* the lion were to lose his natural appetite for blood, and to live on the usual food of the ox. This cannot be taken literally; for such an interpretation would suppose a change in the physical organization of the lion—of his appetites, his teeth, his digestive organs—a change which it would be absurd to suppose will ever exist. It would in fact make him a different being. And it is clear, therefore, that the whole passage is to be

8 And the sucking child shall play on the hole of the asp, and the weaned child shall put his hand on the [1] cockatrice' den.

[1] or, *adder's.*   [a] Job.5.23; ch.35.9; Rev.21.7.
     [b] Ps.72.19; Hab.2.14.

9 They shall not hurt[a] nor destroy in all my holy mountain: for [b] the earth shall be full of the knowledge of the LORD, as the waters cover the sea.

interpreted in a *moral* sense, as denoting great and important changes in society, and in the hearts of men.

8. *And the sucking child.* An emblem here of harmlessness and innocence. The change in the world, under the Messiah, shall be as great as if a sucking infant should be able to play unharmed with a venomous serpent. ¶ *Shall play.* Shall delight himself (שׁעֲשַׁע) as children usually engage in their sports; comp. Prov. viii. 30, 31; Ps. cxix. 24. ¶ *On the hole of the asp.* Over, or around the cavern, hole, or place of retreat of the asp. He shall play over that place as safely as if the nature of the asp was changed, and it had become innocuous. The Hebrew word here rendered *asp* (פֶּתֶן *pethên*) denotes the serpent usually called the asp, whose poison is of such rapid operation that it kills almost instantly; see Job xx. 14, 16; Ps. lviii. 4; xci. 13; Deut. xxxii. 33. The word occurs in no other places in the Old Testament. This serpent is small. It is found particularly in Egypt, though also in other places; see Note on Job xx. 14. It is here used as the emblem of the more sudden, malignant, and violent passions; and the idea is, that under the Messiah a change would be wrought in men of malignant and deadly passions as signal *as if* the asp or adder were to lose his venom, and become innocuous to a child. ¶ *And the weaned child.* But still, a young and helpless child. The image is varied, but the same idea is retained. ¶ *Shall put his hand.* That is, he shall do it safely, or uninjured. ¶ *On the cockatrice' den.* Marg. 'Adder's.' The word here rendered *cockatrice* (צִפְעֹנִי *tz'phôni*) occurs only in the following places: Isa. xiv. 29; xi. 8; lix. 5; Prov. xxiii. 32; Jer. viii. 17. In all these places, it is rendered cockatrice, except in Prov. xxiii. 32. The *cockatrice* was a fabulous kind of serpent, supposed to be hatched from the

egg of a cock. The serpent here designated is, doubtless, a species of the *adder*, more venomous, perhaps, than the *pethen*, but still belonging to the same species. Bochart (*Hieroz.* P. ii. lib. iii. ch. ix.) supposes that the *basilisk* is intended—a species of serpent that, he says, was supposed to poison even with its breath. The general idea is the same here as above. It is in vain to attempt to spiritualize these expressions, and to show that they refer to certain individuals, or that the animals here designated refer to particular classes of the enemies of the gospel. It is a mere poetic description, denoting great peace and security; and all the changes in the mad, malignant, and envenomed passions of men, that may be necessary to produce and perpetuate that peace. Pope has versified this description in the following beautiful manner:

The lambs with wolves shall graze the verdant
    mead,
And boys, in flowery bands, the tigers lead.
The steer and lion at one crib shall meet,
And harmless serpents lick the pilgrim's feet.
The smiling infant in his hand shall take
The crested basilisk, and speckled snake;
Pleased, the green lustre of the scales survey,
And, with their forked tongue, shall innocently
    play.   *Messiah.*

9. *They shall not hurt.* That is, those who are designated above under the emblems of the lion, the leopard, the bear, and the adder. ¶ *Nor destroy in all my holy mountain.* Mount Zion; here used, as elsewhere, to denote the seat of his reign on the earth, or his church; Notes, ch. i. 8; ii. 4. The disposition of men, naturally ferocious and cruel, shall be changed so entirely, that the causes of strife and contention shall cease. They shall be disposed to do justice, and to promote each other's welfare everywhere. ¶ *For the earth.* That is, in the times of the Messiah. It does not say that it shall be *immediate* under his reign, but *under* his reign this shall occur on the earth.

10 And in that day there shall
be a *a*root of Jesse, which shall
stand for an ensign of the people;

to it shall the *b* Gentiles seek: and
his rest *c* shall be ¹ glorious.

a ver.1.   b Rom.15.9-12.
c Mat.11.28; Heb.4.1 &c.   1 glory.

¶ *The knowledge of the Lord.* This
is put for piety, as the *fear* of the Lord
often is. The earth shall be full of a
correct understanding of the existence,
perfections, plans, and claims of God ;
and shall be disposed to yield to those
claims—thus producing universal peace.
¶ *As the waters cover the sea.* That
is, the depths or the bottom of the sea ;
comp. Hab. ii. 14. The vast waters
of the ocean cover all its depths, find
their way into all the caverns, flow into
all the recesses on the shore—and thus
shall the knowledge of JEHOVAH spread
like deep, flowing waters, until the earth
shall be pervaded and covered with it.
It is evident that a time is here spoken
of which has not yet fully come, and the
mind is still directed onward, as was
that of the prophet, to a future period
when this shall be accomplished. The
prophecy has been indeed in part fulfilled. Wherever the gospel has spread,
its effect has been just that which is
predicted here. It has calmed and
subdued the angry passions of men ;
changed their feelings and their conduct ; disposed them to peace ; and
tended to mitigate national ferocity, to
produce kindness to captives, and to
those who had been oppressed. It has
mitigated laws that were cruel and
bloody ; and has abolished customs,
games, sports, and pastimes that were
ferocious and savage. It has often
changed the bitter persecutor, as it did
Saul of Tarsus, to the mildness and
gentleness of a lamb ; and it has spread
an influence over nations tending to
produce humanity and benevolence.
It has produced mildness, gentleness,
and love, in the domestic circle ; changed
the cruel and lordly husband to a companion and friend ; and the character
of the stern and inexorable father to one
of paternal kindness and peace. Wherever it has spread *in truth* and not *in
form merely*, it has shed a mild, calm-
ing, and subduing influence over the
passions, laws, and customs of men.
But its effects have been but partially
felt ; and we are led, therefore, to look

forward to future times, when the prophecy shall be entirely fulfilled, and the
power of the gospel shall be felt in all
nations.
10. *And in that day.* That future
time when the reign of the Messiah
shall be established ; Note, ch. iii. 2;
iv. 1. The prophet, having described
the birth, and the personal characteristics of the great personage to whom
he referred, together with the peaceful
effects of his reign, proceeds to state
the *result* of that reign in some other
respects. The first is (ver. 10), that
the *Gentiles* would be brought under
his reign ; the second (ver. 14), that it
would be attended with the restoration
of the scattered people of Judea ; and
the third (ver. 15, 16), that it would
be followed by the destruction of the
enemies of the people of God. ¶ *There
shall be a root of Jesse.* There shall
be a sprout, shoot, or scion of the ancient
and decayed family of Jesse ; see Note,
v. 1. Chaldee, ' There shall be a son
of the sons of Jesse.' The word *root*
here—שֹׁרֶשׁ—is evidently used in the
sense of a root that is alive when the
tree is dead ; a root that sends up a
shoot or sprout ; and is thus applied to
him who should proceed from the ancient
and decayed family of Jesse ; see ch. liii.
2. Thus in Rev. v. 5, the Messiah is
called ' the *root* of David,' and in Rev.
xxii. 16, ' the root and the offspring of
David.' ¶ *Which shall stand.* There
is reference here, doubtless, to the fact
that military ensigns were sometimes
raised on mountains or towers which
were *permanent*, and which, therefore,
could be rallying points to an army or
a people. The idea is, that the root of
Jesse, *i.e.*, the Messiah, should be conspicuous, and that the nations should
flee to him, and rally around him as a
people do around a military standard.
Thus the Saviour says (John xii. 32) :
' And I, if I be lifted up from the earth,
will draw all men unto me.' ¶ *For an
ensign.* For a standard, or a sign
around which they shall rally. ¶ *Of
the people.* That is, as the parallelism

11 And it shall come to pass in that day, that the LORD shall set his hand again the second time to recover the remnant of his people, which shall be left, from *a* Assyria, and from Egypt, and from Pathros, and from Cush, and from Elam, and from Shinar, and from Hamath, and from the islands of the sea.

a Zec.10.10,11.

shows, of the Gentiles. ¶ *To it shall the Gentiles seek.* The heathen world shall look to it for safety and deliverance. In the Scriptures, the world is spoken of as divided into Jews and Gentiles. All who are not Jews come under this appellation. This is a distinct prophecy, that other nations than the Jews should be benefited by the work of the Messiah, and constitute a part of his kingdom. This fact is often referred to by Isaiah, and constitutes a very material feature in his prophecies ; ch. xlii. 1, 6; xlix. 22; liv. 3; lx. 3, 5, 11, 16; lxi. 6, 9; lxii. 2; lxvi. 12, 19. The word *seek* here, is used in the sense of seeking as a Deliverer, or a Saviour : they shall apply to him for instruction, guidance, and salvation ; or they shall apply to him as a nation looks to its deliverer to protect it ; comp. ch. viii. 19; 2 Kings i. 3; Isa. lxv. 1. ¶ *And his rest.* The rest, peace, and quietness, which he shall give. This evidently includes *all* the rest or peace which he shall impart to those who seek him. The word מְנוּחָה *mĕnūhhâ* sometimes denotes *a resting-place,* or a habitation (Num. x. 33; Micah ii. 10; Ps. cxxxii. 8); but it also denotes a *state of rest, quietness;* Ruth i. 9 ; Jer. xlv. 3 ; Ps. xxiii. 2 ; xcv. 11 ; Deut. xii. 9 ; Isa. xxviii. 12 ; lxvi. 1. Here it evidently means the latter. It may refer, (1.) To the peace which he gives to the conscience of the awakened and troubled sinner (Matt. xi. 28–30) ; or (2.) to the prosperity and peace which his reign shall produce. ¶ *Shall be glorious.* Heb. ' Shall be glory.' That is, shall be full of glory and honour. It shall be such as shall confer signal honour on his reign. The Chaldee understands this of his *place* of residence, his palace, or court. ' And the place of his abode shall be in glory.' The Vulgate renders it, ' and his sepulchre shall be glorious.'

[' By his rest, we are not to understand his grave—or his death—or his Sabbath—or the rest he gives his people—but his place of rest, his residence. There is no need of supplying a preposition before *glory*, which is an abstract used for a concrete—glory, for glorious. *The church, Christ's home,* shall be glorious from his presence, and the accession of the Gentiles.'—(Alexander.) This is a beautiful rendering; it is, moreover, consistent with the letter and spirit of the passage. Some include both ideas.]

11. *And it shall come to pass.* The prophet having, in the previous verse, stated the effect of the reign of the Messiah on the *Gentile* world, proceeds to state the result on the scattered Jews. Whether it is to be a *literal* re-collecting of the scattered tribes to the land of their fathers, has been a subject of debate, and is still so by expositors. We may be able to determine what is the correct general interpretation after the particular phrases have been examined. ¶ *In that day.* That future time referred to in this whole prophecy. The word *day* is often used to denote a long time—or the time during which anything continues, as *the day* denotes all the hours until it is terminated by night. So *day* denotes the time of a man's life—' his day ;' or time in general ; or the time when one shall be prominent, or be the principal object at that time. Thus it is applied to the time of the Messiah, as being the period of the world in which *he* will be the prominent or distinguished object ; John viii. 56: ' Abraham rejoiced to see my day ;' Luke xvii. 24: ' So shall the Son of man be in his day.' The expression here means, that somewhere in that future time, when the Messiah should appear, or when the world should be put under him as the Mediator, the event would take place which is here predicted. As the word ' day ' includes *all* the time of the Messiah, or all his reign from his first to his second advent, it is not to be supposed that the event would take place when he was personally on earth. Isaiah saw it in vision, as *one* of the

events which was to occur after the 'root of Jesse' should stand as an ensign to the nations. ¶ That *the* LORD *shall set his hand.* That JEHOVAH shall undertake this, and accomplish it. To set the hand to anything is to undertake to perform it. ¶ *The second time.* שֵׁנִית. This word properly means, as it is here translated, the second time, implying that the prophet here speaks of a deliverance which would resemble, in some respects, a *former* deliverance or recovery. By the former recovery to which he here refers, he cannot mean the deliverance from Egypt under Moses, for at that time there was no recovery from scattered and distant nations. Besides, if *that* was the reference by the former deliverance, then that here mentioned as the 'second' deliverance would be that from the Babylonish captivity. But on the return from that captivity, there was *not* a collecting of the Jews from all the nations here specified. When the Jews were led back to Judea under Nehemiah, there is no record of their having been collected from 'Egypt,' or from 'Cush,' or from 'the islands of the sea.' It is evident, therefore, I think, that by the former deliverance to which the prophet here alludes—the deliverance which was to precede that designated here as the *second*—he refers to the return from the captivity of Babylon; and by the 'second,' to some still more future recovery that should take place under the administration of the Messiah. This is further confirmed from the fact that the whole scope of the prophecy points to that future period. ¶ *To recover.* Heb. 'To possess,' or, to obtain possession of—לִקְנוֹת *l'qnoth.* This word properly means to obtain possession of by purchasing or buying anything. But it is also applied to *any* possession obtained of an object by power, labour, skill, or by delivering from bondage or captivity, and is thus synonymous with *redeem* or *deliver.* Thus it is applied to the deliverance of the people from Egypt; Deut. xxxii. 6; Ex. xv. 16; Ps. lxxiv. 2. It means here, that JEHOVAH would redeem, rescue, recover his people; but it does not specify the *mode* in which it would be done. Any mode—

either by collecting and rescuing them from the regions into which they were scattered into one place, or by a *spiritual* turning to him, wherever they might be, would meet the force of this word. If *in* the lands where they were scattered, and where they had wandered away from the true God, they were converted, and should become again his people, the event would correspond with all that is meant by the word here. They would *then* be purchased, possessed, or recovered to himself, by being delivered from their spiritual oppression. It is not necessary, therefore, to resort to the interpretation that they should, in the 'second' deliverance, be restored *literally* to the land of Canaan. Any argument for *that* doctrine from this passage must be drawn from the word here used— 'recover'—and that *that* idea is not necessarily involved in this word is abundantly manifest from its familiar use in the Old Testament. All that that word implies, is, that they should *be possessed* by God as his people ; an idea which is fully met by the supposition that the scattered Jews everywhere will be converted to the Messiah, and thus become his true people. For this use of the word, see Gen. xxv. 10; xlvii. 22; xlix. 30; l. 13; Josh. xxiv. 32; 2 Sam. xii. 3; Ps. lxviii. 54; Lev. xxvii. 24; Neh. v. 8. In no place does it necessarily imply the idea of *collecting* or *restoring* a scattered people to their own land. ¶ *The remnant of his people.* That is, the remnant of the Jews, still called his people. In all the predictions respecting the calamities that should ever come upon them, the idea is *always* held out that the nation would not be wholly extinguished; but that, however great the national judgments, a remnant would still survive. This was particularly true in regard to the fearful judgments which Moses denounced on the nation if they should be disobedient, and which have been so strikingly fulfilled; Deut. xxviii. As the result of those judgments, Moses does not say that JEHOVAH would annihilate the nation, or extinguish their name, but that they would be 'left few in number,' (Deut. xxviii. 62); that JEHOVAH would scatter them among all people, from the one end of the earth even to the other,

(Deut. xxviii. 64); and that among those nations they should find no ease, neither should the sole of their foot have rest, ver. 65. In like manner it was predicted that they should be scattered everywhere. 'I will scatter them also among the heathen, whom neither they nor their fathers have known. I will deliver them to be removed into all the kingdoms of the earth for their hurt, to be a reproach, a proverb, a taunt, and a curse, in all places whither I will drive them;' Jer. ix. 16; xxiv. 9, 10. 'I will execute judgments in thee, and the whole remnant of thee will I scatter into all the winds;' Ezek. v. 10. 'I will also scatter them among the nations, among the heathen, and disperse them in the countries;' Ezek. xii. 15. 'I will sift the house of Israel among the nations, like as corn is sifted in a sieve, yet shall not the least grain fall upon the earth. They shall be wanderers among the nations;' Amos ix. 9. 'I will make a full end of the nations whither I have driven thee, but I will not make a full end of thee, but correct thee in measure; yet will I not leave thee wholly unpunished;' Jer. xlvi. 28. From all these, and from numerous other passages in the Old Testament, it is evident that it was designed that the Jewish nation should never be wholly destroyed; that though they were scattered among the nations, they should still be a distinct people; that while other nations would wholly cease to exist, yet that a *remnant* of the Jewish people, with the national peculiarities and customs, would still survive. How entirely this has been fulfilled, the remarkable history of the Jewish people everywhere testifies. Their present condition on the earth, as a people scattered in all nations, yet surviving; without a king and a temple, yet preserving their national prejudices and peculiarities, is a most striking fulfilment of the prophecy; *see* Keith's *Evidence of the Fulfilment of Prophecy*, p. 64–82. ¶ *From Assyria*. The name Assyria is commonly applied to that region of country which lies between Media, Mesopotamia, Armenia, and Babylon, and which is now called Kurdistan. The boundaries of the kingdom have often varied, and, as a kingdom or separate nation, it has long since ceased to exist. The name *Assyria* in Scripture is given, (1.) To ancient Assyria, lying east of the Tigris, and between Armenia, Susiana, and Media—the region comprising mostly the modern kingdoms and the pashalic of Mosul. (2.) Most generally the name Assyria means *the kingdom of Assyria*, including Babylonia and Mesopotamia, and extending to the Euphrates; Isa. vii. 20; viii. 7. (3.) After the overthrow of the Assyrian empire, the name continued to be applied to those countries which were formerly held under its dominion—including Babylonia (2 Kings xxiii. 29; Jer. ii. 18), Persia (Ezra vi. 22), and Syria.—*Robinson; Calmet*. It is in this place applied to that extensive region, and means that the Jews scattered there—of whom there have always been many—shall be brought under the dominion of the Messiah. If the Nestorian Christians in the mountains of Kurdistan are the descendants of the lost ten tribes (see Note on ver. 12), then the reference here is, doubtless, to them. There are, however, other Jews there, as there always has been; *see* Dr. Grant's work on *'The Nestorians, or, the Lost Ten Tribes,'* New York, 1841. ¶ *And from Egypt.* The well-known country in Africa, watered by the Nile. In all ages, there have been many Jews there. Its vicinity to Palestine; its remarkable fertility, and the advantages which it offered to them, attracted many Jews there; and at some periods they have composed no inconsiderable part of the population. It was in this country that the translation of the Hebrew Scriptures into the Greek language, called the Septuagint, was made, for the use of the numerous Jews residing there. At present they are numerous there, though the exact number is unknown. During the reign of Bonaparte, an estimate was made, for his information, of the number of Jews in the world, and, in that estimate, 1,000,000 was assigned to the Turkish empire—probably about a third part of all on the earth. A large portion of this number is in Egypt. ¶ *And from Pathros.* This was one of the three ancient divisions of Egypt. It was the same as Upper Egypt, or the southern part of Egypt, the *Coptic* portion of that country. The inhabitants of that country are called *Pathrusini.* To that place many of the Jews retired in the calamities of the nation, notwithstanding the remonstrances of Isaiah ; Jer. xliv. 1, 15. For this act God severely threatened them ; see Jer. xliv. 26–29. ¶ *And from Cush.* The Chaldee reads this, 'And from Judea.' The Syriac, ' And from Ethiopia.' This country denotes, properly, the regions settled by the descendants of Cush, the eldest son of Ham ; Gen. x. 8. Commentators have differed very much about the region understood in the Scriptures by the name *Cush.* Bochart supposes that by it the southern parts of Arabia are always meant. Gesenius supposes, that by Cush is always meant a region in Africa. Michaelis supposes that by Cush the southern part of Arabia and the African Ethiopia were both intended. In the Scriptures, however, it is evident that the name is given to different regions. (1.) It means what may be called the *Oriental Cush,* including the region of the ancient Susiana, and bounded on the south by the Persian Gulf, and on the west and southwest by the Tigris, which separates it from the Arabian Irak. This province has the name Chusastan, or Chusistan, and was, probably, the ancient *Cush* mentioned in Zeph. iii. 10 : ' From beyond the rivers of Ethiopia, (Heb. *Cush*), my suppliants, even the daughter of my dispersed, shall bring mine offering.' The principal rivers there were the Ulai, the Kur, the Chobar, and the Choaspes. The same place is referred to in 2 Kings xvii. 24, where the king of Assyria is said to have ' brought men from Babylon, and from *Cuthah,* and from Ava,' where the word *Cuthah* evidently refers to *Cush,* the Armenian mode of pronouncing Cush by exchanging the letters *Shin* for *Tav,* as they always do in pronouncing *Ashur,* calling it *Athur,* &c.; see the Chaldee Paraphrase, and the Syriac version, *passim.* (2.) *Cush,* as employed by the Hebrews, *usually* denoted the southern parts of Arabia, and was situated chiefly along the coast of the Red Sea, since there are several passages of Scripture where the name *Cush* occurs, which can be applied to no other country,

and least of all to the African Cush or Ethiopia ; see Num. xii. 1, where the woman whom Moses married is called an 'Ethiopian,' (Heb. 'Cushite'). It can be scarcely supposed that she came from the distant regions of Ethiopia in Africa, but it is evident that she came from some part of Arabia. Also Habakkuk iii. 7, says :

I saw the tents of *Cushan* in affliction;
And the curtains of the land of Midian did tremble.

From which it is evident, that *Cushan* and *Midian* were countries adjacent ; that is, in the southern part of Arabia ; comp. 2 Chron. xxi. 16 ; xiv. 9. (3.) The word *Cush* is applied to Ethiopia, or the country south of Egypt, now called Abyssinia. This country comprehended not only Ethiopia above Syene and the cataracts, but likewise Thebais, or Upper Egypt ; comp. Jer. xiii. 23; Dan. xi. 3; Ezek. xxx. 4, 5 ; Isa. xliv. 14; see Notes on Isa. xviii. 1. To which of these regions the prophet here refers, it is not easy to determine. As the other countries here mentioned, however, are chiefly in the East, it is most natural to suppose that he refers to *the Oriental Cush* mentioned under the first division. The general idea of the prophet is plain, that the scattered Jews should be gathered back to God. ¶ *And from Elam.* This was the name of a country originally possessed by the Persians, and so called from the son of Shem of the same name ; Gen. xiv. 1. It was the southern part of Persia, situated on the Persian Gulf, and included, probably, the whole of the region now called Susiana or Chusistan. The city Susa or Shushan was in it ; Dan. viii. 2. ¶ *And from Shinar.* This was a part of Babylonia, and is supposed to be the plain lying between the Tigris and the Euphrates ; Gen. x. 10; xi. 2; Dan. i. 2; Zech. v. 11. It was the region elsewhere called Mesopotamia. The LXX. render it, ' And from Babylon ;' and it is remarkable that Luke (Acts ii. 9), where he has reference, probably, to the place, speaks of ' the dwellers in Mesopotamia' as among those who heard ' the wonderful works of God ' in their own language. It was in this plain that the tower of Babel was commenced ; Gen. x. ¶ *And from*

12 And he shall set up an ensign *a* for the nations, and shall assemble the *b* outcasts of Israel,

a ch.18.3.   *b* Ps.147.2; ch.27.13; 56.8.

and gather together the *c* dispersed of Judah from the four corners [1] of the earth.

c Jn.7.35; Js.1.1.   1 *wings.*

Hamath ; see Note, ch. x. 9. ¶ *And from the islands of the sea.* This expression probably denotes the islands situated in the Mediterranean, a part of which were known to the Hebrews. But, as geography was imperfectly known, the phrase came to denote the regions lying west of the land of Canaan ; the unknown countries which were situated in that sea, or west of it, and thus included the countries lying around the Mediterranean. The word translated 'islands' here (אִיִּים) means properly *habitable dry land*, in opposition to water ; Isa. xlii. 13: ' I will make the rivers *dry land ;*' where to translate it *islands* would make nonsense. Hence, it means also land adjacent to water, either washed by it, or surrounded by it, that is, a maritime country, coast, or island. Thus it means *coast* when applied to Ashdod (Isa. xx. 6); to Tyre (Isa. xxii. 2, 6); to Peloponnesus or Greece (called Chittim, Ezek. xxvii. 6). It means an *island* when applied to Caphtor or Crete (Jer. xlvii. 4; Amos ix. 7). The word was commonly used by the Hebrews to denote *distant regions beyond the sea*, whether coasts or islands, and especially the maritime countries of the West, to them imperfectly known through the voyages of the Phenicians ; see Note on ch. xli. 1 ; comp. Isa. xxiv. 15; xl. 15; xlii. 4, 10, 12; li. 5.

12. *And he shall set up an ensign ;* see ver. 10. The Messiah shall stand in view of the nations, as a standard is erected by a military leader. An ensign or standard was usually lifted up on the mountains or on some elevated place (comp. ch. xviii. 3); and the meaning here is, that the Messiah would be the conspicuous object around which the nations would rally. ¶ *And shall assemble.* This word, אָסַף *âsăph*, properly means, to gather, collect, to assemble together, as fruits are collected for preservation (Ex. xxiii. 10); to collect a people together (Num. xxi. 16); to gather or collect gold ; 2 Kings xxii. 4. It may also mean to gather or collect

any thing for destruction (Jer. viii. 13); and hence to take out of the way, to kill, destroy ; 1 Sam. xv. 6; Ezek. xxiv. 29. Here, it is evidently synonymous with the word 'recover' in ver. 11. It cannot be proved that it means that God will *literally* re-assemble all the scattered Jews ; for the *collecting them*, or regathering them to himself *as his people*, though they may be still scattered among the nations, is all that the words necessarily imply. Thus when the word is used, as it is repeatedly, to denote the death of the patriarchs, where it is said they were 'gathered to their fathers,' it does not mean that they were buried in the same grave, or the same vicinity, but that they were united to them in death ; they partook of the same lot ; they all alike went down to the dead ; Gen. xxv. 8; xxxv. 29; xlix. 29; Num. xx. 24; Deut. xxxii. 50. ¶ *The outcasts of Israel.* The name ' Israel,' applied at first to all the descendants of Jacob, came at length to denote the ' kingdom of Israel,' or of the ' ten tribes,' or of ' Ephraim,' as the tribes which revolted under Jeroboam were called. In this sense it is used in the Scriptures after the time of Jeroboam, and thus it acquired a technical signification, distinguishing it from Judah. ¶ *The dispersed of Judah.* ' Judah,' also, though often used in a general sense to denote the Jews as such, without reference to the distinction in tribes, is also used technically to denote the kingdom of Judah, as distinguished from the kingdom of Israel. The tribe of Judah was much larger than Benjamin, and the name of the latter was lost in the former. A considerable part of the ten tribes returned again to their own land, with those of the tribes of Judah and Benjamin ; a portion remained still in the countries of the East, and were intermingled with the other Jews who remained there. All distinctions of the tribes were gradually abolished, and there is no reason to think that the ' ten tribes,' here referred to by the name ' Israel,' have now anywhere a distinct

13 The *a* envy also of Ephraim shall depart, and the adversaries

a Jer.3.18; Eze.37.17,22; Hos.1.11.

of Judah shall be cut off; Ephraim shall not envy Judah, and Judah shall not vex Ephraim.

and separate existence; see this point fully proved in a review of Dr. Grant's work on ' *The Nestorians, or, the Lost Ten Tribes*,' in the *Bib. Rep.* for October 1841, and January 1842, by Prof. Robinson. The literal meaning here then would be, that he would gather the remains of those scattered people, whether pertaining to ' Israel ' or ' Judah,' from the regions where they were dispersed. It does not necessarily mean that they would be regathered in their distinctive capacity *as* ' Israel ' and ' Judah, or that the distinction would be still preserved, but that the people of God would be gathered together, and that all sources of alienation and discord would cease. The meaning, probably, is, that under the Messiah all the remains of that scattered people, in all parts of the earth, whether originally appertaining to ' Israel ' or ' Judah,' should be collected into one spiritual kingdom, constituting one happy and harmonious people. To the fulfilment of this, it is not necessary to be supposed that they would be literally gathered into one place, or that they would be restored to their own land, or that they would be preserved as a distinct and separate community. The leading idea is, that the Messiah would set up a glorious kingdom in which all causes of alienation and discord would cease. ¶ *From the four corners of the earth.* Chaldee, ' From the four *winds* of the earth.' The LXX. render it, ' From the four *wings* (πτερύγων) of the earth.' It means, that they should be collected to God from each of the four parts of the earth—the east, the west, the north, and the south. The Hebrew word here rendered ' corners,' means properly *wings*. It is applied, however, to the *corner*, or border of a thing, as a skirt, or mantle (1 Sam. xxiv. 5, 11; Deut. xxiii. 1); and hence to the boundaries, or corners of the earth, because the earth seems to have been represented as a quadrangular plain; Ezek. vii. 2.

13. *The envy also.* The word *envy* here, is used in the sense of *hatred*, or the hatred which arose from the *ambi-*

tion of Ephraim, and from the *prosperity* of Judah. Ephraim here, is the name for the kingdom of Israel, or the ten tribes. The *reasons* of their envy and enmity towards Judah, all arising from their ambition, were the following:—(1.) This tribe, in connection with those which were allied to it, constituted a very large and flourishing part of the Jewish nation. They were, therefore, envious of any other tribe that claimed any superiority, and particularly jealous of Judah. (2.) They occupied a central and commanding position in Judea, and naturally claimed the pre-eminence over the tribes on the north. (3.) They had been formerly highly favoured by the abode of the ark and the tabernacle among them, and, on that account, claimed to be the natural *head* of the nation; Josh. xviii. 1, 8, 10; Judg. xviii. 31; xxi. 19; 1 Sam. i. 3, 24. (4.) When Saul was king, though he was of the tribe of Benjamin (1 Sam. ix. 2), they submitted peaceably to his reign, because the Benjaminites were in alliance with them, and adjacent to them. But when Saul died, and the kingdom passed into the hands of David, of the tribe of Judah, their natural rival, thus exalting that powerful tribe, they became dissatisfied and restless. David kept the nation united; but on his death, they threw off the yoke of his successor, and became a separate kingdom. From this time, their animosities and strifes became an important and painful part of the history of the Jewish nation, until the kingdom of Ephraim was removed. The language here is evidently figurative, and means, that in the time here referred to UNDER THE MESSIAH, the causes of animosity, before existing, would cease; that contentions between those who are, by nature, brethren, and who ought to evince the spirit of brethren, would come to an end ; and that those animosities and strifes would be succeeded by a state of amity and peace. When the scattered Jews shall be regathered to God under the Messiah, all the contentions among them

14 But they shall fly upon the shoulders of the Philistines toward the west; they shall spoil ¹ them of

¹ *the children.*   ² *Edom and Moab shall be the laying on of their hand.*

the east together; ² they shall lay their hand upon Edom and Moab; and ᵃ the children of Ammon ³ shall obey them.

ᵃ ch.60.14.   ³ *their obedience.*

shall cease, and they shall be *united* under one king and prince. All the causes of contention which had so long existed, and which had produced such disastrous results, would come to an end. The strifes and contentions of these two kingdoms, once belonging to the same nation, and descended from the same ancestors—the painful and protracted *family broil*—was the object that most prominently attracted the attention, then, of the prophets of God. The most happy idea of future blessedness which was presented to the mind of the prophet, was that period when all this should cease, and when, under the Messiah, all should be harmony and love. ¶ *And the adversaries of Judah shall be cut off.* That is, Judah shall be safe; the people of God shall be delivered from their enemies—referring to the future period under the Messiah, when the church should be universally prosperous. ¶ *Judah shall not vex Ephraim.* Shall not oppress, disturb, or oppose. There shall be peace between them. The church prospers only when contentions and strifes cease; when Christians lay aside their animosities, and love as brethren, and are *united* in the great work of spreading the gospel around the world. That time will yet come. *When* that time comes, the kingdom of the Son of God will be established. *Until* that time, it will be in vain that the effort is made to bring the world to the knowledge of the truth; or if not wholly in vain, the efforts of Christians who seek the conversion of the world will be retarded, embarrassed, and greatly enfeebled. How devoutly, therefore, should every friend of the Redeemer pray, that all causes of strife may cease, and that his people may be united, as the heart of one man, in the effort to bring the whole world to the knowledge of the truth.

14. *But they shall fly.* The design of this verse is, to show the rapid and certain spiritual conquests which would

result from the conversion of the scattered Jewish people. The Jews understood this literally, as referring to the conquests over their enemies. But if the exposition which has been given of this chapter thus far is correct, the passage is to be interpreted as a figurative description of the triumph of the people of God under the Messiah. The *time* to which it refers, is that which shall succeed the conversion of the scattered Jews. The *effect* of the gospel is represented under an image which, to Jews, would be most striking—that of conquest over the neighbouring nations with whom they had been continually at war. Philistia, Edom, Moab, and Ammon, had been always the enemies of Judea; and to the Jews, no figurative representation could be more striking than that, *after* the union of Judah and Ephraim, they should proceed in rapid and certain conquest to subdue their ancient and formidable enemies. The meaning of the phrase 'they shall fly,' is, they shall hasten with a rapid motion, like a bird. They shall do it quickly, without delay, as an eagle hastens to its prey. It indicates their *suddenly* engaging in this, and the celerity and certainty of their movements. As the united powers of Judah and Ephraim would naturally make a sudden descent on Philistia, so the Jews, united under the Messiah, would go to the rapid and certain conversion of those who had been the enemies of the cross. ¶ *Upon the shoulders.* בְּכָתֵף. There has been a great variety in the interpretation of this passage; and it is evident that our translation does not express a very clear idea. The LXX. render it, ' And they shall fly in the ships of foreigners, and they shall plunder the sea.' The Chaldee, ' And they shall be joined with one shoulder [that is, they shall be *united* shoulder to shoulder], that they may smite the Philistines who are in the west.' The Syriac, ' But they shall *plough* the Philistines;' that is,

15 And the LORD shall utterly destroy the tongue of the Egyptian

sea; and with his mighty wind shall he shake his hand over tho

---

they shall subdue them, and cultivate their land. The word rendered 'shoulder,' means, properly, *the shoulder*, as of a man or beast (ch. xlvi. 7; xlix. 22; Num. vii. 9; Job xxxi. 22; Ezek. xxiv. 4); the *undersetters* or shoulders to support the lavers (1 Kings vii. 30); a corner or side of a building (Ex. xxxviii. 14); and is applied to *the side* of anything, as the side of a building, the border of a country, a city, or sea (1 Kings vi. 8; vii. 39; Num. xxxiv. 11; Josh. xv. 8, 10, 11, &c.) Here it seems to mean, not that the Jews would be borne *upon* the shoulder of the Philistines, but that they would make a sudden and rapid descent *upon their borders;* they would invade their territory, and carry their conquest 'toward the west.' The construction is, therefore, 'they shall make a rapid descent on the borders of the Philistines,' or, in other words, the spiritual conquest over the enemies of the church of God shall be certain and rapid. ¶ *The Philistines.* Philistia was situated on the southwestern side of the land of Canaan. The Philistines were therefore adjacent to the Jews, and were often involved in war with them. They were among the most constant and formidable enemies which the Jews had. ¶ *Toward the west.* This does not mean that they should be borne on the shoulders of the Philistines *to* the west; but that they should make a sudden and rapid descent on the Philistines, who *were* west of them. It stands opposed to the nations immediately mentioned as lying *east* of the land of Judea. ¶ *They shall spoil.* They shall plunder; or, they shall take them, and their towns and property, as the *spoil* of war. That is, they shall vanquish them, and make them subject to them. According to the interpretation which has been pursued in this chapter, it means, that the enemies of God shall be subdued, and brought to the knowledge of the truth, in a rapid and decisive manner. The *language* is that which is drawn from the idea of conquest; the *idea* is that of a rapid and far-spreading conversion among the na-

tions, to the gospel. ¶ *Them of the east.* Heb. ' The sons of the east;' that is, the nations east of Judea. ¶ *They shall lay their hand.* Heb. ' Edom and Moab shall be the laying on of their hand;' that is, they shall lay their hand on those nations for conquest and spoil; they shall subdue them. ¶ *Edom.* Idumea; the country settled by the descendants of Esau—a country that was south of Judea, and extended from the Dead Sea to the Elanitic gulf of the Red Sea. They were an independent people until the time of David, and were reduced to subjection by him, but they afterwards revolted and became again independent. They were often engaged in wars with the Jews, and their conquest was an object that was deemed by the Jews to be very desirable (see Notes on ch. xxxiv.) ¶ *And Moab.* The country of the Moabites was east of the river Jordan, on both sides of the river Arnon, and adjoining the Dead Sea. Their capital was on the river Arnon. They also were often involved in wars with tho Jews (comp. Deut. xxiii. 3; see Notes on ch. xv., xvi.) ¶ *And the children of Ammon.* The Ammonites, the descendants of Ammon, a son of Lot. Their country lay southeast of Judea (Deut. ii. 19-21). Their territory extended from the river Arnon north to the river Jabbok, and from the Jordan far into Arabia. It was directly north of Moab. They were often engaged, in alliance with the Moabites, in waging war against the Jews. ¶ *Shall obey them.* Heb. ' Shall be their obedience.' All these descriptions are similar. They are not to be interpreted literally, but are designed to denote the rapid triumphs of the truth of God *after* the conversion of the Jews; and the sense is, that tho conquests of the gospel will be as sudden, as great, and as striking over its enemies, as *would have been* the complete subjugation of Philistia, Moab, Ammon, and Edom, to the victorious army of the Jews.

15. *And the* LORD. The prophet goes on with the description of the effect which shall follow the return of

river, and shall smite it in the

seven streams,•and make *men* go over [1]dry-shod.

the scattered Jews to God. The language is figurative, and is here drawn from that which was the great storehouse of all the imagery of the Jews—the deliverance of their fathers from the bondage of Egypt. The general sense is, that all the embarrassments which would tend to impede them would be removed; and that God would make their return as easy and as safe, as *would* have been the journey of their fathers to the land of Canaan, if the ' Egyptian Sea ' had been removed entirely, and if the ' river,' with its ' seven streams,' by nature so formidable a barrier, had been dried up, and a path had been made to occupy its former place. Figuratively, the passage means, that all the obstructions to the peace and safety of the people of God would be removed, and that their way would be easy and safe. ¶ *The tongue.* The Hebrews applied the word ' tongue ' to anything that resembled a tongue—to a bar of gold (Josh. vii. 21, 24); to a flame of fire (Note, Isa. v. 24; comp. Acts ii. 3); to a bay of the sea, or a gulf, from its shape (Josh. xv. 5; xviii. 19). So we speak of a tongue of land. When it is said that the Lord would ' utterly destroy ' it, it is equivalent to saying that it would be entirely dried up; that is, so as to present no obstruction. ¶ *Of the Egyptian Sea.* Some interpreters, among whom is Vitringa, have supposed that by the tongue of the Egyptian Sea here mentioned, is meant the river Nile, which flows into the Mediterranean, here called, as they suppose, the Egyptian Sea. Vitringa observes that the Nile, before it flows into the Mediterranean, is divided into two streams or rivers, which form the Delta or the triangular territory lying between these two rivers, and bounded on the north by the Mediterranean. The eastern branch of the Nile being the largest, he supposes is called the tongue or *bay* of the Egyptian Sea. But to this interpretation there are obvious objections—(1.) It is not known that the Mediterranean is elsewhere called the Egyptian Sea. (2.) This whole description pertains to the departure

of the children of Israel from Egypt. The imagery is all drawn from that. But, in their departure, the Nile constituted no obstruction. Their place of residence, in Goshen, was east of the Nile. All the obstruction that they met with, from any sea or river, was from the Red Sea. (3.) The Red Sea is divided, at its northern extremity, into two bays, or forks, which may be called the *tongues* of the sea, and across one of which the Israelites passed in going from Egypt. Of these branches, the western one was called the Heroöpolite branch, and the eastern, the Elanitic branch. It was across the western branch that they passed. When it is said that Jehovah would ' destroy ' this, it means that he would dry it up so that it would be no obstruction; in other words, he would take the most formidable obstructions to the progress of his people out of the way. ¶ *And with his mighty wind.* With a strong and powerful wind. Michaelis supposes that by this is meant a tempest. But there is, more probably, a reference to a strong and steady *hot* wind, such as blows over burning deserts, and such as would have a tendency to dry up even mighty waters. The illustration is, probably, derived from the fact that a strong east wind was employed to make a way through the Red Sea (Ex. xiv. 21). If the allusion here be rather to a mighty wind or a tempest, than to one that is hot, and that tends to evaporate the waters even of the rivers, then it means that the wind would be so mighty as to part the waters, and make a path through the river, as was done in the Red Sea and at the Jordan. The *idea* is, that God would remove the obstructions to the rapid and complete deliverance and conversion of men. ¶ *Shall he shake his hand.* This is to indicate that the mighty wind will be sent from God, and that it is designed to effect this passage through the rivers. The shaking of the hand, in the Scripture, is usually an indication of anger, or of strong and settled purpose (see ch. x. 32; xiii. 2; Zech. ii. 9). ¶ *Over the*

16 And there shall be an highway for the remnant of his people, which shall be left, from Assyria; like as

it was *a* to Israel in the day that he came up out of the land of Egypt.

a Ex. 14.29.

river. Many have understood this as referring to the Nile; but two considerations show that the Euphrates is rather intended—(1.) The term ' THE river ' (הַנָּהָר, *hannâhâr*) is usually applied to the Euphrates, called THE RIVER, by way of eminence; and when the term is used without any qualification, that river is commonly intended (see Notes, ch. vii. 20; viii. 7; comp. Gen. xxxi. 21; xxxvi. 37; 1 Kings iv. 21; Ezra iv. 10, 16; v. 3). (2.) The effect of this smiting of the river is said to be (ver. 16) that there would be a highway for the people *from Assyria,* which could be caused only by removing the obstruction which is produced by the Euphrates lying between Judea and some parts of Assyria. ¶ *And shall smite it.* That is, to dry it up, or to make it passable. ¶ *In the seven streams.* The word ' streams ' here (נְחָלִים) denotes streams of much less dimensions than a river. It is applied to *a valley* with a brook running through it (Gen. xxvi. 19); and then to any small brook or stream, or rivulet (Gen. xxxii. 24; Ps. lxxiv. 15). Here it denotes brooks or streams that would be fordable. When it is said that the river should be smitten ' *in* the seven streams,' the Hebrew does not mean that it was *already* divided into seven streams, and that God would smite *them,* but it means, that God would smite it *into* seven streams or rivulets; that is, into *many* such rivulets (for the number seven is often used to denote a large indefinite number, Note, ch. iv. 1); and the expression denotes, that though the river presented an obstruction, in its natural size, which they could not overcome, yet God would make new channels for it, and scatter it into innumerable rivulets or small streams, so that they could pass over it dry-shod. A remarkable illustration of this occurs in Herodotus (i. 189): ' Cyrus, in his march to Babylon, arrived at the river Gyndes, which, rising in the mountains of Matiene, and passing through the country of the Dar-

neans, loses itself in the Tigris; and this, after flowing by Opis, is finally discharged into the Red Sea. While Cyrus was endeavouring to pass this river, which could not be performed without boats, one of the white consecrated horses boldly entering the stream, in his attempts to cross it, was borne away by the rapidity of the current, and totally lost. Cyrus, exasperated by the accident, made a vow that he would render this stream so very insignificant, that women should hereafter be able to cross it without so much as wetting their feet. He accordingly suspended his designs on Babylon, and divided his forces into two parts; he then marked out with a line, on each side of the river, one hundred and eighty trenches; these were dug according to his orders, and so great a number of men were employed that he accomplished his purpose; but he thus wasted the whole of that summer' (see also Seneca, *De Ira.* iii. 21). ¶ *Go over dry-shod.* Heb. ' In shoes, or sandals.' The waters in the innumerable rivulets to which the great river should be reduced, would be so shallow, that they could even pass them in their sandals without wetting their feet—a strong figurative expression, denoting that the obstruction would be completely removed. ' The prophet, under these metaphors, intends nothing else than that there would be no impediment to God when he wished to deliver his people from captivity.'—(Calvin.)

16. *And there shall be an highway.* All obstructions shall be removed, and they shall be permitted to return without hinderance (comp. Note on ch. xxxv. 8). ¶ *For the remnant of his people from Assyria* (Note, ver. 11). ¶ *Like as it was to Israel,* &c. That is, God will remove all obstructions as he did at the Red Sea; he will subdue all their enemies; he will provide for their wants; and he will interpose by the manifest marks of his presence and protection, as their God and their friend.—The

CHAPTER XII.

ANALYSIS OF THE CHAPTER.

THIS chapter is a part of the vision which was commenced in ch. x. 5. The prophet had foretold the deliverance of the nation from the threatened invasion of Sennacherib (ch. x.); he had then looked forward to the times of the Messiah, and described the certainty, the character, and the consequences of his reign (ch. xi.) The eleventh chapter closes with a reference to the deliverance of the nation from the oppression of the Egyptians. That deliverance was celebrated with a beautiful ode, which was sung by Miriam and 'all the women,' who 'went out after her with timbrels and with dances' (Ex. xv. 1-21). In imitation of that deliverance, Isaiah says, in this chapter, that the deliverance of which he speaks shall be celebrated also with a song of praise; and this chapter, therefore, is properly an

expression of the feelings of the redeemed people of God, in view of his great mercy in interposing to save them. It should be read in view of the great and glorious deliverance which God has wrought for us in the redemption of his Son; and with feelings of lofty gratitude that he has brought us from worse than Egyptian bondage—the bondage of sin. The song is far better applied to the times of the Messiah, than it could be to anything which occurred under the Jewish dispensation. The Jews themselves appear to have applied it to his time. On the last day of the feast of tabernacles, they brought water in a golden pitcher from the fountain of Siloam, and poured it, mingled with wine, on the sacrifice that was on the altar, with great rejoicing (see Notes, John vii. 14, 37). This custom was not required by Moses, and probably arose from the command in ver. 3 of this chapter. Our Saviour applied it to himself, to the benefits of

general view of the chapter is, therefore, that it refers to the triumph of the Messiah's kingdom; that it is not yet fully accomplished; and that the time is coming when the scattered Jews shall be regathered to God—not returned to their own land, but brought again under his dominion under the administration of the Messiah; and that this event shall be attended with a sudden removal of the obstructions to the gospel, and to its rapid spread everywhere among the nations. Comparing this with the present state of the Jews, we may remark, in regard to this prospect—(1.) That they are now, and will continue to be, scattered in all nations. They have been driven to all parts of the earth—wanderers without a home—yet continuing their customs, rites, and peculiar opinions; and continuing to live, notwithstanding all the efforts of the nations to crush and destroy them. (2.) They speak nearly all the languages of the world. They are acquainted with all the customs, prejudices, and opinions of the nations of the earth. They would, therefore, be under no necessity of engaging in the laborious work of learning language—which now occupies so much of the time, and consumes so much of the strength of the modern missionary. (3.) The law of God is thus in all nations. It is in every synagogue; and it has been well said, that the law there is like extin-

guished candles, and that all that is needful to illuminate the world, is to light those candles. Let the Jew everywhere be brought to see the true meaning of his law; let the light of evangelical truth shine into his synagogue, and the world would be at once illuminated. The truth would go with the rapidity of the sunbeams from place to place, until the whole earth would be enlightened with the knowledge of the Redeemer. (4.) The Jews, when converted, make the best missionaries. There is a freshness in their views of the Messiah when they are converted, which Gentile converts seldom feel. The apostles were all Jews; and the zeal of Paul shows what converted Jews will do when they become engaged in making known the true Messiah. If it has been a characteristic of their nation that they would 'compass sea and land to make one proselyte,' what will their more than three millions accomplish when they become converted to the true faith of the Redeemer? We have every reason, therefore, to expect that God intends to make great use yet of the Jews, whom he has preserved scattered everywhere—though they be but a 'remnant' —in converting the world to his Son. And we should most fervently pray, that they may be imbued with love to their long-rejected Messiah, and that they may everywhere become the missionaries of the cross.

his gospel, and to the influences of the Spirit (John vii.); and the ancient Jews so applied it also. 'Why is it called the house of drawing? Because from thence they draw the Holy Spirit; as it is written, "and ye shall draw water with joy from the fountains of salvation."'—(*Jerusalem Talmud*, as quoted by Lowth.)

A ND in that day thou shalt say, O Lord, I *a* will praise thee:

though *b* thou wast angry with me, thine anger is turned away, and thou comfortedst me.

2 Behold, God *is* my salvation; I will trust, and not be afraid: for the *c* Lord JEHOVAH *is* my strength and *my* song; he also is become my salvation.

a Ps.34.1,&c.   *b* Ps.30.5; ch 54.7,8; Hos.6.1.
c Ps.118.14.

CHAPTER XII.

1. *And in that day.* The day referred to in the previous chapter, the time of the Messiah, when the effects of his reign shall be seen everywhere. The duty of praise, however, is couched in such language as to make it applicable to the event predicted in the former part of the prophecy (ch. x.)—the delivering of the nation from the invasion of Sennacherib, as well as the more glorious event on which the prophet fixed his eye (ch. xi.)—the coming and reign of the Messiah. The language of this song of praise would be appropriate to both these events. ¶ *Thou shalt say.* The address to an individual here, in the term 'thou,' is equivalent to *every one*, meaning that *all* who were thus interested in the Divine interposition should say it. ¶ *O Lord.* O Jehovah —the great author of this interposition. ¶ *I will praise thee: though thou wast angry with me.* If this language is applied to the Jews, and supposed to be used by them in regard to the invasion of Sennacherib, it means, that God suffered their land to be invaded, and to be subjected to calamities, in consequence of their sins (ch. x. 6, *sq.*) If it is supposed to be applied to the time of the Messiah, then it is language which every redeemed sinner may use, that God was angry with him, but that his anger is turned away. As applicable to the redeemed, it is an acknowledgment which they all feel, that they have no claim to his mercy, and that it lays the foundation for unceasing praise that his anger is turned away by the plan of salvation.

2. *Behold, God is my salvation.* Or, God is the author, or source, of my salvation. It has not been brought about by any human hands, but is to be traced directly to him. The value of a gift is

always enhanced by the dignity and excellency of the giver, and it confers an inestimable value on the blessings of salvation, that they are conferred by a being no less than the infinite God. It is not by human or angelic power; but it is to be traced directly and entirely to Jehovah. ¶ *I will trust, and not be afraid.* Since God is its author; since he is able to defend me, and to perfect that which he has begun, I will confide in him, and not be afraid of the power or machinations of any enemy. In his hands I am safe. God is the foundation of our confidence; and trusting in him, his people shall never be moved. ¶ *For the* Lord JEHOVAH. This is one of the four places in which our translators have retained the original word Jehovah, though the Hebrew word occurs often in the Scriptures. The other places where the word Jehovah is retained in our version are, Ex. vi. 3; Ps. lxviii. 18; Isa. xxvi. 4. The original in this place is יָהּ יְהוָֹה (Jah, Jehovah). The word Jah (יָהּ) is an abbreviation of the word Jehovah. The abbreviated form is often used for the sake of conciseness, particularly in the Psalms, as in the expression *Hallelujah* (הַלְלוּ־יָהּ), *i.e.*, praise Jehovah (Ps. lxxxix. 9; xciv. 7, 12; civ. 35; cv. 15; cvi. 1, 48; cxi. 1; cxiii. 1, *et al.*) In this place, and Isa. xxvi. 4, the *repetition* of the name seems to be used to denote *emphasis;* or perhaps to indicate that Jehovah is the same always—an unchangeable God. In two codices of Kennicott, however, the name Jah (יָהּ) is omitted, and it has been conjectured by some that the repetition is an error of transcribers; but the best MSS. retain it. The LXX., the Chaldee, and the Syriac, however, omit it. ¶ *Is my strength and my song.* The same expression occurs in the hymn

3 Therefore with joy *a* shall ye draw water *b* out of the wells of salvation.

4 And in that day shall ye say, Praise *c* the Lord, ¹ call upon his

a Cant.2.3.   *b* Jn.4.10,14.

name, declare his doings among the people, make mention that his name is exalted.

5 Sing *d* unto the Lord; for he

c Ps.145.4-6.   1 or, *proclaim.*

d Ex.15.1,21; Ps.98.1.

---

that Moses composed after the passage of the Red Sea, in imitation of which this song is evidently composed ; Ex. xv. 2 :

JEHOVAH is my strength and my song,
And he is become my salvation.

The word 'strength' means, that he is the source of strength, and implies that all who are redeemed are willing to acknowledge that all their strength is in God. The word 'song' implies that he is the proper object of praise ; it is to celebrate *his* praise that the 'song' is composed. ¶ *He also is become my salvation.* This is also found in the song of Moses (Ex. xv. 2). It means that God had become, or was the author of salvation. It is by his hand that the deliverance has been effected, and to him should be the praise.

3. *Therefore.* In view of all his mercies. The Hebrew is, however, simply, '*and* ye shall draw.' It has already been intimated that the Jews applied this passage to the Holy Spirit : and that probably on this they based their custom of drawing water from the fountain of Siloam at the feast of the dedication (Note, John vii. 37). The fountain of Siloam was in the eastern part of the city, and the water was borne from that fountain in a golden cup, and was poured, with every expression of rejoicing, on the sacrifice on the altar. It is not probable, however, that this custom was in use in the time of Isaiah. The language is evidently figurative ; but the meaning is obvious. A fountain, or a well, in the sacred writings, is an emblem of that which produces joy and refreshment ; which sustains and cheers. The figure is often employed to denote that which supports and refreshes the soul ; which sustains man when sinking from exhaustion, as the bubbling fountain or well refreshes the weary and fainting pilgrim (comp. John iv. 14). It is thus applied to God as an overflowing fountain, fitted to supply the wants of all his creatures (Jer. ii. 13 ; xvii. 13 ;

Ps. xxxvi. 9 ; Prov. xiv. 27) ; and to his plan of salvation—the sources of comfort which he has opened in the scheme of redeeming mercy to satisfy the wants of the souls of men (Zech. xiii. 1 ; Isa. xli. 18 ; Rev. vii. 17). The word 'rivers' is used in the same sense as 'fountains' in the above places (Isa. xlii. 15 ; xliii. 19, 20). Generally, in the Scriptures, streams, fountains, rivers, are used as emblematic of the abundant fulness and richness of the mercies which God has provided to supply the spiritual necessities of men. The idea here is, therefore, that they should partake abundantly of the mercies of salvation ; that it was free, overflowing, and refreshing —like waters to weary pilgrims in the desert ; and that their partaking of it would be with joy. It would fill the soul with happiness ; as the discovery of an abundant fountain, or a well in the desert, fills the thirsty pilgrim with rejoicing.

4. *And in that day* (see ver. 1). ¶ *Call upon his name.* Marg. 'Proclaim.' It denotes to call upon him in the way of celebrating his praise. The whole hymn is one of praise, and not of prayer. ¶ *Declare among the people.* Among all people, that they may be brought to see his glory, and join in the celebration of his praise. ¶ *His doings.* Particularly in regard to the great events which are the subject of the previous predictions—his interposition in saving men by the Messiah from eternal death. ¶ *Make mention.* Heb. 'Cause it to be remembered' (see Note on ch. lxii. 6). ¶ *That his name is exalted.* That it is worthy of adoration and praise. It is worthy to be exalted, or lifted up in view of the nations of the earth (2 Sam. xxii. 47 ; Ps. xxi. 13 ; xlvi. 10).

5. *Sing unto the Lord.* This is the same expression which occurs in the song of Moses (Ex. xv. 21). Isaiah evidently had that in his eye. ¶ *He hath done excellent things.* Things that are exalted (גֵּאוּת) ; that are worthy

hath done excellent things: this *is* known in all the earth.

6 Cry *a* out and shout, thou 1 inhabitant of Zion: for *b* great *is* the Holy One of Israel in the midst of thee.

a Zep.3.14.　　1 *inhabitress.*　　*b* Ps.89.18.

CHAPTER XIII.

ANALYSIS OF CHAPTERS XIII.; XIV. 1–27.

. THE thirteenth chapter of Isaiah commences a new prophecy, and, according to the division of Vitringa, a new book or part of his prophecies. The first book, according to him, extending from ch. i. to the close of ch. xii., is occupied with a series of prophecies respecting the Jews. The second portion, from ch. xiii. to ch. xxxv. inclusive, consists of a number of separate predictions respecting other nations, with which the Jews were in various ways more or less connected. See Introduction.

The thirteenth and the fourteenth chapters, with the exception of the last five verses of ch. xiv., contain one entire prophecy foretelling the destruction of Babylon. The main design is to predict the destruction of that city: but it is also connected with a design to furnish consolation to the Jews. They were to be carried captive there; and the purpose of the prophet was to assure them that the city to which they should yet be borne as exiles would be completely destroyed.

It is not easy to ascertain with certainty the precise time when this prophecy was delivered, nor is it very material. It is certain that it was delivered either during the reigns of Uzziah, Jotham, Ahaz, or Hezekiah (ch. i. 1), the reign of the last of whom closed 710 years before the Christian era; and, since the Jews were carried captive to Babylon 586 years before that era, the prophecy must have been delivered 124 years before that event; and, as Babylon was taken by Cyrus 536 years before Christ, it must have been delivered at least 174 years before its accomplish-

---

to be celebrated, and had in remembrance ; things that are majestic, grand, and wonderful. ¶ *This is known in all the earth.* Or, more properly, 'Let this be known in all the earth.' It is worthy of being celebrated everywhere. It should be sounded abroad through all lands. This expresses the sincere desire of all who are redeemed, and who are made sensible of the goodness and mercy of God the Saviour. The instinctive and the unceasing wish is, that the wonders of the plan of redeeming mercy should be everywhere known among the nations, and that all flesh should see the salvation of our God.

6. *Cry out* (צְהֲלִי). This word is usually applied to the neighing of a horse (Jer. v. 8; viii. 16). It is also used to express joy, pleasure, exultation, by a clear and loud sound of the voice (Isa. x. 30; xii. 6; xiv. 14; liv. 1; Jer. xxxi. 7; l. 11). It is here synonymous with the numerous passages in the Psalms, and elsewhere, where the people of God are called on to exult, to shout, to make a noise as expressive of their joy (Ps. xlvii. 1; cxlviii.; cxlix.; Isa. xlii. 11; xliv. 23; Jer. xxxi. 7; Zeph. iii. 14; Zech. ix. 9). ¶ *And shout* (וָרֹנִּי). This word properly means to cry aloud (Prov. i. 20; viii. 3); to cry for help (Lam. ii. 19); to raise a shout of joy,

to rejoice, or exult (Lev. ix. 24; Job xxxviii. 7); to praise, or celebrate with joy (Ps. xxxiii. 1; li. 15; lix. 17; lxxxix. 13). Here it denotes the joy in view of God's mercies, which leads to songs of exalted praise. ¶ *Thou inhabitant of Zion.* Thou that dwellest in Zion ; that is, thou who art numbered with the people of God (Note, ch. i. 8). The margin here is in accordance with the Hebrew — 'Inhabitress of Zion ;' and the word here used is applicable to *the people*, rather than to an individual. ¶ *For great is the Holy One of Israel.* That is, God has shown himself great and worthy of praise, by the wonderful deliverance which he has wrought for his people. Thus closes this beautiful hymn. It is worthy of the theme —worthy to be sung by all. O, may all the redeemed join in this song of deliverance ; and may the time soon come, when the beautiful vision of the poet shall be realized, in the triumphant song of redemption echoing around the world :

'One song employs all nations; and all cry,
 "Worthy the Lamb, for he was slain for us!"
The dwellers in the vales and on the rocks
Shout to each other, and the mountain-tops
From distant mountains catch the flying joy;
Till, nation after nation taught the strain,
Earth rolls the rapturous hosanna round.'

　　　　　　　　　The Task, Book vi.

ment. Theodoret supposed that this prophecy was published during the latter part of the reign of Hezekiah. Cocceius and Lightfoot supposed that it was delivered about the same period as the former, and this also is the opinion of Vitringa. All that is of importance, is, that if it was a true prophecy of Isaiah, as there is the fullest demonstration, it must have been delivered *at least* 170 years before the event which it foretells was accomplished. The *material* points to settle in regard to the prophecies are— (1) Whether they were delivered before the event; (2) whether the things predicted could have been foreseen by human sagacity; (3) whether the prediction is so clear, and particular, as to correspond with the event, or not to be mere vague conjecture; and (4) whether there is such an occurrence of events as to constitute in fact a fulfilment of the prophecy. If these things meet, there is the fullest evidence that the prediction was from God.

At the time when this prophecy was delivered, the Jews were in the secure possession of their own capital and country. They were harassed, indeed, by surrounding nations, but they were still free. They had no controversy with Babylon; nor had they reason to apprehend danger from that distant people. Their being borne to that land, was itself, in the time of Isaiah, a distant event, and one that then was not likely to occur. It is remarkable that Isaiah does not distinctly *foretell* that event here, but throws himself to a period of time *beyond* that, when they *would be* in captivity, and predicts their deliverance. His prophecy *supposes* that event to have occurred. It is a vision passing before his mind *after* that event had taken place; when they would be *in* Babylon; and when they would be sighing for deliverance (ch. xiv. 1, 2). The prophet, therefore, may be conceived in this vision as taking his stand *beyond* an event which had not yet occurred—the captivity of the Jews and their removal to Babylon—and predicting *another* event still more future, which would result in their deliverance—the complete overthrow of the city, and the consequent deliverance of the Jewish people. We are to conceive him standing, as it were, amidst the captive Jews, and directing his eye onward to the complete recovery of the nation by the destruction of Babylon itself (ch. xiv. 1, 2). See Introduction, § 7, III. (4.)

This prophecy of the destruction of Babylon was delivered, we have seen, at least 174 years before the event occurred. At the time when it was delivered, nothing was more improbable than the ruin of that city as described by Isaiah (ch. xiii. 19-22). It was one of the largest, most flourishing, and perhaps the most strongly fortified city of the world. The prediction that it should be like 'Sodom and Gomorrah;' that it should 'never be inhabited;' that the wild beast of the desert should lie there; and that dragons should be in their pleasant palaces, was wholly improbable; and could have been foreseen *only* by God. There were no natural causes that were leading to this which man could perceive, or of which a stranger and a foreigner, like Isaiah, could have any knowledge. This will appear evident by a brief description of the condition of this celebrated city.—BABYLON (derived from BABEL, and probably built on the same spot as the tower of Babel) was the capital of Babylonia, or Chaldea, and was probably built by Nimrod; but it was a long period before it obtained its subsequent size and splendour. It was enlarged by Belus, and so greatly beautified and improved by Semiramis, that she might be called not improperly the foundress of it. It was subsequently greatly increased and embellished by Nebuchadnezzar. It stood in the midst of a large plain, and on a very deep and fertile soil. It was on both sides of the river Euphrates, and of course was divided by that river into two parts. The two parts were connected by a bridge near the centre of the city; and there is also said to have been a *tunnel*, or subterranean passage, made from the palace on the east of the river to the palace on the west, made under the river. The old city was on the east, and the new city, built by Nebuchadnezzar, was on the west. Both these divisions were enclosed by one wall, and the whole formed a complete square, which Herodotus, who visited it, and who is the most ancient author who has written on it, says, was 480 furlongs in compass, or 120 furlongs on each side: that is, it was fifteen miles on each side, or sixty miles in compass. Public belief has been greatly staggered by the accounts which are thus given of the size of Babylon. But the account of the extent of the walls given, by ancient authors, is nearly uniform. Thus Herodotus says it was 480 stadia, or furlongs, in circumference. Pliny and Solinus make it the same. Strabo says it was 385 stadia in circumference; Diodorus, 360; Clitarchus, who accompanied Alexander, says it was 365, and Curtius says it was 368. According to the lowest of these estimates, it could not have been less than twelve miles square, or forty-eight miles in circumference; and was at least eight times as large in extent as London and its appendages; and somewhat larger than the entire district of Columbia.—(Calmet, and *Edin. Ency.*) It is not to be inferred, however, that all this vast space was compactly built. It was enclosed with a wall; but a considerable portion of it might have been occupied with the public squares, with palaces, and with hanging gardens, or, possibly, might have been unoccupied.

The walls of Babylon are said by Herodotus to have been eighty-seven feet thick, and 350 high. They were built of brick, or clay dried in the sun, and not burned; and were cemented by a kind of glutinous earth, or bitumen, with which the adjacent region abounded. The whole city was surrounded by an immense ditch, from which this clay had been taken to make the walls of the city, and which, being always filled with water, contributed materially to its defence. There were 100 gates to the city, twenty-five on each side. These gates were of solid brass. Between every two of them there were three towers, raised ten feet above the walls. From the gates there were streets, each 151 feet in width, which ran through the city, so that there were fifty streets in all, cutting each other at right angles, and forming 676 squares in the city. A bridge sixty feet in width crossed the Euphrates in the centre of the city, and at the extremities of the bridge were two palaces, the old palace on the east, and the new palace on the west. The temple of Belus, which occupied almost a square, was near the old palace on the east. Babylon was celebrated for its hanging gardens, built on arches, near 400 feet square, and which were elevated one above another, by terraces, until they reached the height of the walls of the city. On the highest terrace was an aqueduct for watering the gardens, supplied with water by a pump, or probably by the *Persian wheel*, by which the water of the Euphrates was raised to this extraordinary height. In order to prevent the danger of being overflown by the rise in the Euphrates, two canals were cut from the river at a considerable distance above the town, by which the superabundant waters were carried into the Tigris. It is to be borne in mind, however, in order to a just view of this prophecy, that Babylon did not attain its highest splendour and magnificence until *after* the time of Isaiah. It was under Nebuchadnezzar, who ascended the throne of Babylon about 100 years after Isaiah died, that it rose to its highest degree of splendour and power. When Isaiah lived, though it was a city of great wealth and power, and distinguished for great commercial advantages, yet it was then dependent on Assyria. It did not become the capital of the vast kingdom of Chaldea until 680 years before Christ, according to the chronology of Hales, when Assaradon became master of Babylon, and reunited the empires of Assyria and Chaldea.

Babylon was the natural seat of empire in the East, and was early distinguished for its commercial advantages. A simple glance at the map of Asia will convince any one that somewhere in the vicinity of Babylon is the natural seat of power in the East, and that few places on the globe are more eligibly situated for a vast trade, as it was conducted before the discovery of the Cape of Good Hope. The commerce from the rich regions of Asia naturally passed through Babylon on its way to Europe, and to Western Asia. It was the centre of a vast fertile region, the productions of which were conveyed to Babylon, and from which they would naturally be borne down on the Euphrates to the ocean; see Note on ch. xliii. 14. The first empire of which the earliest historians furnish any trace, was in the land of Shinar, the land of the Chaldeans (Gen. x. 8–10; xi. 1–9). Syria, Arabia, Tyre with all her wealth, and distant Egypt, were subject and tributary to it. The natural advantages of that *region* for a vast capital, are shown by the fact, that amidst all changes and revolutions, empire has been disposed to fix her permanent seat somewhere on the banks of the Tigris or the Euphrates. Thus, Nineveh, the capital of Assyria, was long a mighty and magnificent commercial city, as well as the proud capital of a vast empire. Thus, when Babylon fell, Seleucia rose on the banks of the Tigris, as if prosperity and power were unwilling to leave the fertile plains watered by those rivers. Thus, near Seleucia, arose Ctesiphon, the winter residence of the Parthian monarchs. And thus, under the sway of the Arabians, long after Nineveh, and Babylon, and Seleucia had fallen, Bagdad and Ormus rivalled Babylon and Seleucia, and 'became, like them, the resort of the merchant, and the home of the learned.' 'At this time Bagdad and Bussora are faded tokens of the splendour of those which have faded and fallen.' The fact that there was in that vicinity such a succession of celebrated cities, demonstrates that there were there some important commercial advantages. Among those advantages respecting Babylon, was the fact that it was the centre of a vast fertile region; that it naturally received the productions of Armenia on the north; and that its midway position rendered it the natural thoroughfare for the caravan trade between Eastern and Western Asia. Accordingly, Babylon was early distinguished for its commerce and manufactures. Babylonian garments, of uncommon value, had made their way to Palestine as early as the times of Joshua (Josh. vii. 21). Tapestries embroidered with figures of griffons, and other monsters of Eastern imagination, were articles of export. Carpets were wrought there of the finest material and workmanship, and formed an article of extensive exportation. They were in high repute in the time of Cyrus, whose tomb at Pasargada was adorned with them.— (Arrian, *Exped. Alex.*, vi. 29.) Babylonian robes were also highly esteemed for the fineness of their texture and the brilliancy of their purple, and were used by the royal family of Persia. The *commerce* of that city and of Babylonia consisted in the traffic in emeralds and other precious stones; silver and gold; carpets, tapestries, and other manufactured cloths; cotton and pearls; cinnamon and other spicery, obtained from the East; and, in general, of whatever articles were produced in the eastern parts of Asia, which were naturally brought to Babylon on the way to Western Asia and to Europe. For a learned and interesting article on the commerce of Babylon, see *Bib. Rep.* vol. vii. pp. 364–390. Thus, by the fertility of the soil; by its size and strength; by its strong and lofty walls; by its commercial advantages; and by everything that could contribute to the defence of an ancient city, Babylon seemed to be safe; and if there was any ancient city that appeared to bid defiance to the attacks of enemies, or to the ravages of time, it was Babylon. Yet Isaiah said that it should be destroyed; and in the course of our exposition we shall be greatly struck, not only with the certain fulfilment of the prediction, but with the wonderful accuracy and minuteness of the entire prophetic statement.

The vision opens (ch. xiii. 2, 3), with the command of God to assemble his forces to go forth, and accomplish his work in regard to the city. By a beautiful poetic image, the prophet represents himself as *immediately*, on the issuing of this command, listening to the tumult and noise caused by those who were assembling for war; by the gathering together of nations; by their assembling from a far country to destroy the whole land (ver. 4, 5). He then proceeds to depict the consternation that would follow; the alarm of the people; and their distress, when the day of the Lord should come (6–10). Then, changing the mode of address from himself to God, he sets forth, in a variety of the most distressing and appalling images, the destruction that would come upon the *inhabitants* of Babylon—the humbling of their pride (11); the almost entire destruction of the men (12); the flight of the inhabitants (13, 14); the murder of those who should flee; and the destruction of their wives and children (15, 16). He then specifies (17) the instruments by which this should be done, and closes the chapter (19–22) with a minute and most particular account of the complete and final overthrow of the city; of its entire and everlasting desolation. The subsequent chapter, which is a continuation of this prophecy, is occupied with an account of the deliverance of the Jews from their captivity, and with a further description of the humbling of that proud city and of its monarch. See an analysis of it at the commencement of the chapter.

The thirteenth chapter 'is one of the most beautiful examples that can be given of elegance of composition, variety of imagery, and sublimity of sentiment and diction in the prophetic style.' —(Lowth.) It may be added, that it is one of the clearest predictions of a future event that can anywhere be found; and that the exact and minute fulfilment of it furnishes the highest possible evidence that Isaiah 'spake as he was moved by the Holy Ghost.'

THE burden of Babylon,*a* which Isaiah the son of Amoz did see.

a ch.xxi.; xlvii.; Jer. l.; li.

CHAPTER XIII.

1. *The burden of Babylon.* Or, the burden *respecting*, or *concerning* Babylon. This prophecy is introduced in a different manner from those which have preceded. The terms which Isaiah employed in the commencement of his previous prophecies, were VISION (see Note, ch. i. 1), or WORD (ch. ii. 1). There has been considerable diversity of opinion in regard to the meaning of the word 'burden,' which is here employed. The Vulgate renders it, *Onus*—' Burden,' in the sense of *load*. The LXX. "Ορασις— ' Vision.' The Chaldee, ' The burden of the cup of malediction which draws near to Babylon.' The Hebrew word (מַשָּׂא *mâssâ*, from נָשָׂא *nâsâ*, to lift,

to raise up, to bear, to bear away, to suffer, to endure), means properly that which is borne ; that which is heavy ; that which becomes a burden ; and it is also applied to a gift or present, as that which is borne *to* a man (2 Chron. xvii. 11). It is also applied to a proverb or maxim, probably from the *weight* and *importance* of the sentiment condensed in it (Prov. xxx. 1; xxxi. 1). It is applied to an oracle from God (2 Kings iv. 25). It is often translated ' burden' (Isa. xv. ; xix. 1; xxi. 11, 13; xxii. 1 ; xxiii. 1 ; xxx. 6 ; lxvii. 1 ; Jer. xxiii. 33, 34, 38 ; Neh. i. 1 ; Zech. i. 1 ; xii. 1 ; Mal. i. 1). By comparing these places, it will be found that the term is applied to those oracles or prophetic declarations

2 Lift ye up a banner upon the high mountain, exalt the voice unto them, shake the hand, that they may go into the gates of the nobles.

which contain sentiments peculiarly weighty and solemn; which are employed chiefly in denouncing wrath and calamity; and which, therefore, are represented as weighing down, or *oppressing* the mind and heart of the prophet. A similar usage prevails in all languages. We are all familiar with expressions like this. We speak of news or tidings of so melancholy a nature as to weigh down, to sink, or depress our spirits; so heavy that we can scarcely bear up under it, or endure it. And so in this case, the view which the prophet had of the awful judgments of God, and of the calamities which were coming upon guilty cities and nations, was so oppressive, that it weighed down the mind and heart as a heavy burden. Others, however, suppose that it means merely a message or prophecy which is *taken up*, or borne, respecting a place, and that the word indicates nothing in regard to the nature of the message. So Rosenmüller, Gesenius, and Cocceius, understand it. But it seems to me the former interpretation is to be preferred, Grotius renders it, ' A mournful prediction respecting Babylon.' ¶ *Did see*. Saw in a vision; or in a scenical representation. The various events were made to pass before his mind in a vision, and he was permitted to see the armies mustered; the consternation of the people; and the future condition of the proud city. This verse is properly the *title* to the prophecy.

2. *Lift ye up a banner*. A military ensign or standard. The vision opens here; and the first thing which the prophet hears, is the solemn command of God addressed to the nations as subject to him, to rear the standard of war, and to gather around it the mighty armies which were to be employed in the destruction of the city. This command, ' Lift ye up a banner,' is addressed to the leaders of those armies to assemble them, and to prepare them for war. ¶ *Upon the high mountain*. It was customary for military leaders to plant a standard on a tower, a fortress, a city, a high mountain, or any elevated spot, in order that it might be seen afar, and be the rallying point for the people to

collect together (see Note, ch. xi. 10). Here, the prophet does not refer to any particular *mountain*, but means simply, that a standard should be raised, around which the hosts should be assembled to march to Babylon. The Chaldee renders it, ' Over the city dwelling in security, lift up the banner.' ¶ *Exalt the voice*. Raise up the voice, commanding the people to assemble, and to prepare for the march against Babylon. Perhaps, however, the word ' voice ' here (קוֹל *qōl*) refers to the *clangour*, or sound, of a trumpet used for mustering armies. The word is often used to denote *any* noise, and is frequently applied to thunder, to the trumpet, &c. ¶ *Unto them*. That is, to the Medes and Persians, who were to be employed in the destruction of Babylon. ¶ *Shake the hand*. In the way of *beckoning;* as when one is at so great a distance that the voice cannot be heard, the hand is waved for a sign. This was a command to *beckon* to the nations to assemble for the destruction of Babylon. ¶ *That they may go into the gates of the nobles*. The word here rendered ' nobles ' (נְדִיבִים) means, properly, *voluntary, free, liberal;* then those who are noble, or liberally-minded, from the connection between nobleness and liberality; then those who are noble or elevated in rank or office. In this sense it is used here; comp. Job xii. 21; xxxiv. 18; 1 Sam. ii. 8; Ps. cvii. 40; and Prov. viii. 16, where it is rendered ' princes;' Num. xxi. 18, where it is rendered ' nobles.' Lowth renders it here ' princes.' Noyes renders it ' tyrants '—a sense which the word has in Job xxi. 28 (see Note on that place). There is no doubt that it refers to Babylon; and the prophet designs probably to speak of Babylon as a magnificent city—a city of princes, or nobles. The Chaldee renders it, ' That they may enter its gates, which open to them of their own accord;' retaining the original signification of *voluntariness* in the Hebrew word, and expressing the idea that the conquest would be easy. Our common translation has expressed the correct sense.

3 I have commanded my sanctified ones, I have also called my
mighty *a* ones for mine anger, *even*
them that rejoice in my highness.

4 The noise of a multitude in the

mountains, 1 like as of a great people ; a tumultuous noise of the kingdoms of nations gathered together:
the LORD of hosts mustereth the
host of the battle.

---

a Joel 2.11.

1 *the likeness.*

---

3. *I have commanded.* This is the
language of God in reference to those
who were about to destroy Babylon.
He claimed the control and direction of
all their movements ; and though the
command was not understood by *them*
as coming from him, yet it was by his
direction, and in accordance with his
plan (comp. Notes on ch. x. 7 ; xlv. 5,
6). The *command* was not given by
the prophets, or by an audible voice ;
but it was his secret purpose and direction that led them to this enterprise.
¶ *My sanctified ones.* The Medes and
Persians ; not called 'sanctified' because they were holy, but because they
were *set apart* by the Divine intention
and purpose to accomplish this. The
word 'sanctify' (קָדַשׁ) often means *to
set apart*—either to God ; to an office ;
to any sacred use ; or to any purpose
of religion, or of accomplishing any of
the Divine plans. Thus, it means to
dedicate one to the office of priest (Ex.
xxviii. 41) ; to set apart or dedicate an
altar (Ex. xxxix. 36) ; to dedicate a
people (Ex. xix. 10–14) ; to appoint, or
institute a fast (Joel i. 14 ; ii. 15) ; to
sanctify a war (Joel iii. 9), that is, to
prepare one's-self for it, or make it
ready. Here it means, that the Medes
and Persians were *set apart*, in the purpose of God, to accomplish his designs
in regard to Babylon (comp. Note, ch.
x. 5, 6). ¶ *My mighty ones.* Those
who are strong ; and who are so entirely
under my direction, that they may be
called mine. ¶ *For mine anger.* To
accomplish the purposes of my anger
against Babylon. ¶ *Even them that
rejoice in my highness.* It cannot be
supposed that the Medes and Persians
really exulted, or rejoiced in God or in
his plans ; for it is evident that, like
Sennacherib (ch. x.), they were seeking
to accomplish their *own* purposes, and
were not solicitous about the plans of
God (comp. Note on ch. xlvii. 6). The
word rendered 'my highness' (גַּאֲוָתִי)

means, properly, *my majesty*, or *glory.*
When applied to men, as it often is, it
means pride or arrogance. It means
here, the high and exalted plan of God
in regard to Babylon. It was a mighty
undertaking ; and one in which the
power, the justice, and the dominion of
God over nations would be evinced. In
accomplishing this, the Medes and Persians would rejoice or exult, not *as* the
fulfilling of the plan of God ; but they
would exult *as if* it were their *own*
plan, though it would be *really* the glorious plan of God. Wicked men often
exult in their success ; they glory in
the execution of their purposes ; but
they are really accomplishing the plans
of God, and executing his great designs.

4. *The noise of a multitude in the
mountains.* The prophet here represents himself as hearing the confused
tumult of the nations assembling to the
standard reared on the mountains (ver.
2). This is a highly beautiful figure—
a graphic and vivid representation of
the scene before him. Nations are seen
to hasten to the elevated banner, and to
engage in active preparations for the
mighty war. The sound is that of a *tumult*, an *excited multitude* hastening to
the encampment, and preparing for the
conquest of Babylon. ¶ *Like as of a great
people.* Heb. 'The likeness of a great
people.' That is, such a confused and
tumultuous sound as attends a great
multitude when they collect together.
¶ *A tumultuous noise.* Heb. ' The
voice of the tumultuous noise of the
kingdoms of nations gathered together.'
¶ *The* LORD *of hosts.* JEHOVAH, the
God of hosts, or armies (Note, ch. i. 9).
¶ *Mustereth.* Collects ; puts in military array. Over all this multitude of
nations, hastening with confused sounds
and tumult like the noise of the sea,
putting themselves in military array,
God, unseen, presides, and prepares
them for his own great designs. It is
not easy to conceive a more sublime

5 They come from a far country, from the end of heaven, *even* the LORD and the weapons of his indignation, to destroy the whole land.

6 Howl ye: for the day *a* of the

a Zep.1.7; Rev.6.17.

LORD *is* at hand; it shall come as a destruction from the Almighty.

7 Therefore shall all hands 1 be faint, and every man's heart shall melt:

1 or, *fall down.*

---

image than these mighty hosts of war, unconscious of the hand that directs them, and of the God that presides over them, moving as he wills, and accomplishing his plans.

5. *They come.* That is, 'JEHOVAH and the weapons of his indignation'— the collected armies come. The prophet sees these assembled armies with JEHOVAH, as their leader, at their head. ¶ *From a far country.* The country of the Medes and Persians. These nations, indeed, bordered on Babylonia, but still they stretched far to the north and east, and, probably, occupied nearly all the regions to the east of Babylon which were then known. ¶ *From the end of heaven.* The LXX. render this, 'Aπ' ἄκρου θεμελίου τοῦ οὐρανοῦ— ' From *the extreme foundation* of the heaven.' The expression in the Heb., 'From the end, or extreme part of heaven,' means, the distant horizon by which the earth appears to be bounded, where the sky and the land seem to meet. In Ps. xix. 6, the phrase ' from the end of the heaven' denotes the east, where the sun appears to rise ; and ' unto the ends of it' denotes the west:

His going forth is from the end of the heaven;
And his circuit unto the ends of it.

It is here synonymous with the phrase, ' the end of the earth,' in Isa. v. 26. ¶ *Even the* LORD. The word ' even,' introduced here by the translators, weakens the force of this verse. The prophet means to say that JEHOVAH is coming at the head of those armies, which are the weapons of his indignation. ¶ *The weapons of his indignation.* The assembled armies of the Medes and Persians, called ' the weapons of his indignation,' because by them he will accomplish the purposes of his anger against the city of Babylon (see Note, ch. x. 5). ¶ *To destroy the whole land.* The whole territory of Babylonia, or Chaldea. Not only the city, but the nation and kingdom.

6. *Howl ye.* Ye inhabitants of Babylon, in view of the approaching destruction. ¶ *The day of the* LORD. The time when JEHOVAH will inflict vengeance on you draws near (see Note, ch. ii. 12; comp. ver. 9). ¶ *As a destruction from the Almighty.* Not as a desolation from man, but as destruction sent from him who has all power in heaven and on earth. Destruction meditated by man might be resisted ; but destruction that should come from the Almighty must be final and irresistible. The word ' Almighty' (שַׁדַּי *Shăddai*), one of the names given to God in the Scriptures, denotes, properly, *one who is mighty,* or who has all power ; and is correctly rendered Almighty, or Omnipotent ; (Gen. xvii. 1 ; xxviii. 3; xlviii. 3; Ex. vi. 3; Ruth i. 20; Job v. 17; vi. 4, 14; viii. 3, 5; xi. 7; xiii. 4; xv. 25). In the Hebrew here, there is a paronomasia or *pun*—a figure of speech quite common in the Scriptures, which cannot be retained in the translation— ' It shall come as a *destruction* (כְּשֹׁד *keshōdh*) from the Almighty (מִשַּׁדַּי *m'sshăddai*).'

7. *Therefore shall all hands be faint.* This is designed to denote the consternation and alarm of the people. They would be so terrified and alarmed that they would have no courage, no hope, and no power to make resistance. They would abandon their plans of defence, and give themselves up to despair (comp. Jer. l. 43: ' The king of Babylon hath heard the report of them, and his hands waxed feeble ; anguish took hold of him, and pangs as of a woman in travail ;' Ezek. vii. 17; Zeph. iii. 16). ¶ *And every man's heart shall melt.* Or, shall faint, so that he shall have no courage or strength (comp. Deut. xx. 8). The fact was, that the destruction of Babylon took place in the night. It came suddenly upon the city, while Belshazzar was at his impious feast ; and the alarm was so unexpected

8 And they shall be afraid: pangs and sorrows shall take hold of them; they shall be in pain as a woman that travaileth; they shall be [1] amazed [2] one at another; their faces *shall be as* [3] flames.

1 *wonder.* 2 *every man at his neighbour.*

9 Behold, the day [a] of the LORD cometh, cruel both with wrath and fierce anger, to lay the land desolate; and he shall destroy the sinners thereof out of it.

10 For the stars of heaven, and

3 *faces of the flames.* a Mal.4.1.

and produced such consternation, that no defence was attempted (see Dan. v. 30; comp. Notes on ch. xlv. 1).

8. *They shall be in pain as a woman that travaileth.* This comparison is often used in the Scriptures to denote the deepest possible pain and sorrow, as well as the *suddenness* with which any calamity comes upon a people (Ps. xlviii. 6; Isa. xxi. 3; xlii. 14; Jer. vi. 24; xiii. 21; xxii. 33; xlix. 24; l. 43; Hos. xiii. 13; Mic. iv. 9, 10; John xvi. 21; Gal. iv. 19; 1 Thess. v. 3). ¶ *They shall be amazed one at another.* They shall stare with a stupid gaze on one another, indicating a state of great distress, anxiety, and alarm. They shall look to each other for aid, and shall meet in the countenances of others the same expressions of wonder and consternation. ¶ *Their faces* shall be as *flames.* Their faces shall glow or burn like fire. When grief and anguish come upon us, the face becomes inflamed. The face *in fear* is usually pale. But the idea here is not so much that of *fear* as of *anguish;* and, perhaps, there is mingled also here the idea of *indignation* against their invaders.

9. *The day of the* LORD *cometh;* see ver. 6. ¶ *Cruel* (אַכְזָרִי). This does not mean that *God* is cruel, but that the 'day of JEHOVAH' that was coming should be unsparing and destructive to them. It would be the exhibition of *justice,* but not of *cruelty;* and the word stands opposed here to *mercy,* and means that God would not spare them. The *effect* would be that the inhabitants of Babylon would be destroyed. ¶ *Fierce anger.* Heb. (אַף חָרוֹן) 'A glow, or burning of anger.' The phrase denotes the most intense indignation (comp. Num. xxv. 4; xxxii. 14; 1 Sam. xxviii. 18). ¶ *To lay the land desolate.* Chaldea (ver. 5).

10. *For the stars of heaven.* This verse cannot be understood literally,

but is a metaphorical representation of the calamities that were coming upon Babylon. The meaning of the figure evidently is, that those calamities would be such as would be appropriately denoted by the sudden extinguishment of the stars, the sun, and the moon. As nothing would tend more to anarchy, distress, and ruin, than thus to have all the lights of heaven suddenly and for ever quenched, this was an apt and forcible representation of the awful calamities that were coming upon the people. Darkness and night, in the Scriptures, are often the emblem of calamity and distress (see Note, Matt. xxiv. 29). The revolutions and destructions of kingdoms and nations are often represented in the Scriptures under this image. So respecting the destruction of Idumea (Isa. xxxiv. 4):

And all the hosts of heaven shall be dissolved,
And the heavens shall be rolled together as a scroll;
And all their host shall fall down,
As the leaf falleth from off the vine,
And as a falling fig from the fig-tree.

So in Ezek. xxxii. 7, 8, in a prophecy respecting the destruction of Pharaoh, king of Egypt:

And when I shall put thee out,
I will cover the heavens, and make the stars thereof dark,
I will cover the sun with a cloud,
And the moon shall not give her light.
And the bright lights of heaven will I make dark over thee,
And set darkness upon thy land.

(comp. Joel ii. 10; iii. 15, 16.) Thus in Amos viii. 9:

I will cause the sun to go down at noon,
And I will darken the earth in a clear day.

see also Rev. vi. 12–14:

And I beheld when he had opened the sixth seal, and lo,
The sun became black as sackcloth of hair,
And the moon became as blood;
And the stars of heaven fell unto the earth,
Even as a fig-tree casteth her untimely figs
When she is shaken of a mighty wind;
And the heaven departed as a scroll when it is rolled together.

the constellations thereof, shall not give their light: the sun shall be darkened in his going forth, and the moon shall not cause her light to shine.

11 And I will punish the world for *their* evil, and the wicked for their iniquity; and I will cause the arrogancy of the proud to cease, and will lay low the haughtiness of the terrible.

12 I will make a man more precious than fine gold; even a man than the golden wedge of Ophir.

Many have supposed that these expressions respecting the sun, moon, and stars, refer to kings, and princes, and magistrates, as the *lights* of the state; and that the sense is, that their power and glory should cease. But it is rather a figurative representation, denoting calamity *in general*, and describing a state of extreme distress, such as *would be* if all the lights of heaven should suddenly become extinct. ¶ *And the constellations thereof* (וּכְסִילֵיהֶם). The word (כְּסִיל *khesil*) means properly *a fool;* Prov. i. 32; x. 1, 18; xiii. 19, 20, *et al.* It also denotes *hope, confidence, expectation* (Job xxxi. 24; Prov. iii. 26; Job viii. 14); also the *reins*, the *flanks* or *loins* (Lev. iii. 4, 10, 15; Ps. xxxviii. 7). It is also, as here, applied to a constellation in the heavens, but the connection of this meaning of the word with the other significations is uncertain. In Job ix. 9, and xxxviii. 31, it is translated 'Orion.' In Amos v. 8, it is translated the 'seven stars'—the Pleiades. In Arabic, that constellation is called 'the giant.' According to an Eastern tradition, it was Nimrod, the founder of Babylon, afterwards translated to the skies; and it has been supposed that the name *the impious* or *foolish one* was thus given to the deified Nimrod, and thus to the constellation. The Rabbins interpret it *Simis*. The word 'constellations' denotes clusters of stars, or stars that appear to be near to each other in the heavens, and which, on the celestial globe, are reduced to certain figures for the convenience of classification and memory, as the bear, the bull, the virgin, the balance. This arrangement was early made, and there is no reason to doubt that it existed in the time of Isaiah (comp. Notes on Job ix. 9).

11. *And I will punish the world.* By the 'world' here is evidently meant the Babylonian empire, in the same way as 'all the world' in Luke ii. 1, means Judea; and in Acts xi. 28, means the Roman empire. Babylonia, or Chaldea, was the most mighty empire then on earth, and might be said to comprehend the whole world. ¶ *And I will cause the arrogancy.* This was the prevailing sin of Babylon, and it was on account of this *pride* mainly that it was overthrown (see Notes on ch. xiv.; xlvii. 1–7; comp. Dan. iv. 22, 30).

12. *I will make a man, &c.* I will so cut off and destroy the men of Babylon, that a single man to defend the city will be more rare and valuable than fine gold. The expression indicates that there would be a great slaughter of the men of Babylon. ¶ *Than fine gold.* Pure, unalloyed gold. The word here used (פָּז *pâz*) is often distinguished from common gold (Ps. xix. 11; cxix. 127; Prov. viii. 19). ¶ *Than the golden wedge of Ophir.* The word (כֶּתֶם *kĕthĕm*) rendered 'wedge' means properly *gold;* yellow gold; what is hidden, precious, or hoarded; and is used only in poetry. It indicates nothing about the *shape* of the gold, as the word *wedge* would seem to suppose. 'Ophir' was a country to which the vessels of Solomon traded, and which was particularly distinguished for producing gold; but respecting its particular situation, there has been much discussion. The 'ships of Tarshish' sailed from Ezion-geber on the Red Sea, and went to Ophir (1 Kings ix. 26; x. 22; xxii. 48). Three years were required for the voyage; and they returned freighted with gold, peacocks, apes, spices, ivory, and ebony (1 Kings ix. 28; x. 11, 12; comp. 2 Chron. viii. 18). The gold of that country was more celebrated than that of any other country for its purity. Josephus supposes that it was in the East Indies; Bruce that it was in South Africa; Rosenmüller and others suppose that it was in Southern Arabia. It is probable

13 Therefore [a] I will shake the heavens, and the earth [b] shall remove out of her place, in the wrath of the Lord of hosts, and in the day of his fierce anger.

a Hag. 2.6.

14 And it shall be as the chased roe, and as a sheep that no man taketh up: they shall every man turn to his own people, and flee every one into his own land.

b 2 Pet. 3.10,11.

---

that the situation of Ophir must ever remain a matter of conjecture. The Chaldee Paraphrase gives a different sense to this passage. ' I will love those who fear me, more than gold in which men glory ; and those who observe the law more than the tried gold of Ophir.' (On the situation of Ophir the following works may be consulted :— *The Pictorial Bible*, vol. ii. pp. 364–369; Martini Lipenii, *Dissert. de Ophir;* Joan. Christophori Wichmanshausen *Dissert. de Navig. Ophritica ;* H. Relandi, *Dissert. de Ophir :* Ugolini, *Thes. Sac. Ant.* vol. viii.; and Forster *On Arabia.*)

13. *Therefore I will shake the heavens.* A strong, but common figure of speech in the Scriptures, to denote great commotions, judgments, and revolutions. The figure is taken from the image of a furious storm and tempest, when the sky, the clouds, the heavens, appear to be in commotion ; comp. 1 Sam. xxii. 8:

Then the earth shook and trembled,
The foundation of heaven moved and shook,
Because he was wroth.

See also Isa. xxiv. 19, 20; Hag. ii. 6, 7. ¶ *And the earth shall remove out of her place.* A common figure in the Scriptures to denote the great effects of the wrath of God ; as if even the earth should be appalled at his presence, and should tremble and flee away from the dread of his anger. It is a very sublime representation, and, as carried out often by the sacred writers, it is unequalled in grandeur, probably, in any language. Thus the hills, the mountains, the trees, the streams, the very heavens, are represented as shaken, and thrown into consternation at the presence of God ; see Hab. iii. 6, 10 :

He stood and measured the earth ;
He beheld and drove asunder the nations;
And the everlasting mountains were scattered.
The perpetual hills did bow;
His ways are everlasting.

The mountains saw thee and they trembled;
The overflowing of the water passed by;
The deep uttered his voice,
And did lift up his hands on high.

See Rev. xx. 11: ' And I saw a great white throne, and him that sat on it, from whose face the earth and the heaven fled away.' The figure in Isaiah is a strong one to denote the terror of the anger of God against Babylon.

14. *And it shall be.* Babylon shall be. ¶ *As the chased roe.* Once so proud, lofty, arrogant, and self-confident ; it shall be as the trembling gazelle, or the timid deer pursued by the hunter, and panting for safety. The word (צְבִי *tzĕbhī*) denotes a deer of the most delicate frame ; the species that is most fleet and graceful in its movements ; properly the *gazelle* (see Bochart's *Hieroz.* i. 3. 25). ' To hunt the antelope is a favourite amusement in the East, but which, from its extraordinary swiftness, is attended with great difficulty. On the first alarm, it flies like an arrow from the bow, and leaves the best-mounted hunter, and the fleetest dog, far behind. The sportsman is obliged to call in the aid of the falcon, trained to the work, to seize on the animal, and impede its motions, to give the dogs time to overtake it. Dr. Russel thus describes the chase of the antelope: '' They permit horsemen, without dogs, if they advance gently, to approach near, and do not seem much to regard a caravan that passes within a little distance ; but the moment they take the alarm, they bound away, casting from time to time a look behind : and if they find themselves pursued, they lay their horns backwards, almost close on the shoulders, and flee with incredible swiftness. When dogs appear, they instantly take the alarm ; for which reason the sportsmen endeavour to steal upon the antelope unawares, to get as near as possible before slipping the dogs ; and then, pushing on at full speed, they throw off the falcon, which being taught to strike or fix upon the cheek of the game, retards its course by repeated attacks, till the greyhounds have time to get up.'' '—(Burder's *Orient. Cus.*)

15 Every one that is found shall be thrust through; and every one that is joined *unto them* shall fall by the sword.

16 Their children also shall be dashed *a* to pieces before their eyes;

their houses shall be spoiled, and their wives ravished.

17 Behold, I will stir up the Medes *a* against them, which shall not regard silver; and *as for* gold, they shall not delight in it.

¶ *As a sheep.* Or like a scattered flock of sheep in the wilderness that has no shepherd, and no one to collect them together; an image also of that which is timid and defenceless. ¶ *That no man taketh up.* That is astray, and not under the protection of any shepherd. The meaning is, that that people, once so proud and self-confident, would become alarmed, and scattered, and be afraid of everything. ¶ *They shall every man turn unto his own people.* Babylon was the capital of the heathen world. It was a vast and magnificent city; the centre of many nations. It would be the place, therefore, where numerous foreigners would take up a temporary residence, as London and other large cities are now. Jeremiah (ch. l. 37) describes Babylon as containing a mingled population—'and upon all the mingled people that are in the midst of her'— *i.e.*, the *colluvies gentium*, as Tacitus describes Rome in his time. Jeremiah also (ch. l. 28) describes this mingled multitude as fleeing and escaping out of the land of Babylon, when these calamities should come upon them. The idea in Isaiah is, that this great and mixed multitude would endeavour to escape the impending calamities, and flee to their own nations.

15. *Every one that is found.* In Babylon, or that is overtaken in fleeing from it. This is a description of the capture of the city, and of the slaughter that would ensue, when the invaders would spare neither age nor sex. ¶ *Every one that is joined* unto them. Their allies and friends. There shall be a vast, indiscriminate slaughter of all that are found in the city, and of those that attempt to flee from it. Lowth renders this, 'And all that are collected in a body;' but the true sense is given in our translation. The Chaldee renders it, 'And every one who enters into fortified cities shall be slain with the sword.'

16. *Their children also shall be dashed to pieces.* This is a description of the horrors of the capture of Babylon; and there can be none more frightful and appalling than that which is here presented. That this is done in barbarous nations in the time of war, there can be no doubt. Nothing was more common among American savages, than to dash out the brains of infants against a rock or a tree, and it was often done before the eyes of the afflicted and heart-broken parents. That these horrors were not unknown in Oriental nations of antiquity, is evident. Thus, the Psalmist implies that it would be done in Babylon, in exact accordance with this prediction of Isaiah; Ps. cxxxvii. 8, 9:

O daughter of Babylon, who art to be destroyed:
Happy shall he be who rewardeth thee as thou hast served us;
Happy shall he be who taketh and dasheth thy little ones against the stones.

Thus, also, it is said of Hazael, that when he came to be king of Syria, he would be guilty of this barbarity in regard to the Jews (2 Kings viii. 13; comp. Nahum iii. 10). It was an evidence of the barbarous feelings of the times; and a proof that they were far, very far, from the humanity which is now deemed indispensable even in war. ¶ *Their houses shall be spoiled.* Plundered. It is implied here, says Kimchi, that this was to be done also 'before their eyes,' and thus the horrors of the capture would be greatly increased.

17. *Behold, I will stir up.* I will cause them to engage in this enterprise. This is an instance of the control which God claims over the nations, and of his power to excite and direct them as he pleases. ¶ *The Medes.* This is one of the places in which the prophet specified, *by name,* the instrument of the wrath of God. Cyrus himself is subsequently mentioned (Isa. xliv. 28; xlv. 1) as the agent by which God

would accomplish his purposes. It is remarkable, also, that 'the Medes' are here mentioned many years before they became a separate and independent nation. It was elsewhere predicted that the Medes would be employed in this siege of Babylon ; thus, in Isa. xxi. 2 : ' Go up, O Elam (that is, Persia), besiege, O Media;' Jer. li. 11 : 'Jehovah hath raised up the spirit of the kings of the Medes, for his device is against Babylon to destroy it.' Media was a country east of Assyria, which is supposed to have been peopled by the descendants of Madai, son of Japheth (Gen. x. 2). Ancient Media extended on the west and south of the Caspian Sea, from Armenia, on the north, to Faristan or Persia proper, on the south. It was one of the most fertile regions of Asia. It was an ancient kingdom. Ninus, the founder of the Assyrian monarchy, is said to have encountered one of its kings, whom he subdued, and whose province he made a part of the Assyrian empire. For 520 years, the Medes were subject to the Assyrians ; but, in the time of Tiglath-pileser and Shalmaneser, they revolted, and, by the destruction of the army of Sennacherib before Jerusalem—an event which was itself *subsequent* to the delivery of this prophecy respecting Babylon—they were enabled to achieve their independence. At the time when this prophecy was uttered, therefore, Media was a dependent province of the kingdom of Assyria. Six years they passed in a sort of anarchy, until, about 700 years B.C., they found in Dejoces an upright statesman, who was proclaimed king by universal consent. His son and successor, Phraortes, subdued the Persians, and all upper Asia, and united them to his kingdom. He also attacked Assyria, and laid siege to Nineveh, the capital, but was defeated. Nineveh was finally taken by his successor, Cyaxares, with the aid of his ally, the king of Babylon ; and Assyria became a province of Media. This widely-extended empire was delivered by him to his son Astyages, the father of Cyrus. Astyages reigned about 35 years, and then delivered the vast kingdom to Cyrus, about 556 years B.C., under whom the prediction of Isaiah respecting Babylon

was fulfilled. In this way arose the Medo-Persian kingdom, and henceforward *the laws of the Medes and Persians* are always mentioned together (Est. i. 9; x. 2 ; Dan. vi. 8, 12). From this time, all their customs, rites, and laws, became amalgamated.—(Herod. i. 95–130). In looking at this prophecy, therefore, we are to bear in mind—(1.) the fact that, when it was uttered, Media was a dependent province of the .kingdom of Assyria ; (2.) that a long time was yet to elapse before it would become an independent kingdom ; (3.) that it was yet to secure its independence by the aid of that very Babylon which it would finally destroy ; (4.) that no human foresight could predict these revolutions, and that every circumstance conspired to render this event *improbable*. The great strength and resources of Babylon ; the fact that Media was a dependent province, and that such great revolutions must occur *before* this prophecy *could* be fulfilled, render this one of the most striking and remarkable predictions in the sacred volume. ¶ *Which shall not regard silver,* &c. It is remarkable, says Lowth, that Xenophon makes Cyrus open a speech to his army, and, in particular, to the Medes, who made the principal part of it, with praising them for their disregard of riches. ' Ye Medes and others who now hear me, I well know, that you have not accompanied me in this expedition with a view of acquiring wealth.'—(*Cyrop.* v.) That this was the character of the Medes, is further evident from several circumstances. ' He reckoned, says Xenophon, that his riches belonged not any more to himself than to his friends. So little did he regard silver, or delight in gold, that Crœsus told him that, by his liberality, he would make himself poor, instead of storing up vast treasures for himself. The Medes possessed, in this respect, the spirit of their chief, of which an instance, recorded by Xenophon, is too striking and appropriate to be passed over. When Gobryas, an Assyrian governor, whose son the king of Babylon had slain, hospitably entertained him and his army, Cyrus appealed to the chiefs of the Medes and Hyrcanians, and to the noblest and

18 *Their* bows also shall dash the young men to pieces; and they shall have no pity on the fruit of the womb; their eye shall not spare children.

1 *the overthrowing of.*

19 And Babylon, the glory of kingdoms, the beauty of the Chaldees' excellency, shall be ¹ as when God ªoverthrew Sodom and Gomorrah.

a Gen.19.24.

most honourable of the Persians, whether, giving first what was due to the gods, and leaving to the rest of the army their portion, they would not overmatch his generosity by ceding to him their whole share of the first and plentiful booty which they had won from the land of Babylon. Loudly applauding the proposal, they immediately and unanimously consented; and one of them said, "Gobryas may have thought us poor, because we came not loaded with coins, and drink not out of golden cups; but by this he will know, that men can be generous even without gold." ' (*See* Keith *On the Prophecies*, p. 198, Ed. New York, 1833.) This is a remarkable prediction, because this is a very unusual circumstance in the character of conquerors. Their purpose has been chiefly to obtain plunder, and, especially, gold and silver have been objects to them of great value. Few, indeed, have been the invading armies which were not influenced by the hope of spoil; and the want of that characteristic among the Medes is a circumstance which no human sagacity could have foreseen.

18. Their *bows also*. Bows and arrows were the usual weapons of the ancients in war; and the Persians were particularly skilled in their use. According to Xenophon, Cyrus came to Babylon with a great number of archers and slingers (*Cyrop.* ii. 1). ¶ *Shall dash the young men*, &c. That is, they shall dash the young men to pieces, or kill them by their bows and arrows. Vulgate, ' And with their arrows shall they slay the young.' The meaning of the word here rendered ' dash to pieces,' is to smite suddenly to the ground.

19. *And Babylon, the glory of kingdoms.* That is, the capital, or chief ornament of many nations. Appellations of this kind, applied to Babylon, abound in the Scriptures. In Dan. iv. 30, it is called ' great Babylon;' in

Isa. xiv. 4, it is called ' the golden city;' in Isa. xlvii. 5, ' the lady of kingdoms;' in Jer. li. 13, it is spoken of as ' abundant in treasures;' and, in Jer. li. 41, as ' the praise of the whole earth.' All these expressions are designed to indicate its immense wealth and magnificence. It was the capital of a mighty empire, and was the chief city of the heathen world. ¶ *The beauty of the Chaldees' excellency.* Heb. ' The glory of the pride of the Chaldees;' or the ornament of the proud Chaldees. It was their boast and glory; it was that on which they chiefly prided themselves. How well it deserved these appellations we have already seen. ¶ *Shall be as when God overthrew Sodom and Gomorrah* (Gen. xix. 24). That is, shall be completely and entirely overthrown; shall cease to be inhabited, and shall be perfectly desolate. It does not mean that it shall be overthrown in the same manner as Sodom was, but that it should be as completely and entirely ruined. The successive steps in the overthrow of Babylon, by which this prophecy was so signally fulfilled, were the following: (1.) The taking of the city by Cyrus. This was accomplished by his clearing out the *Pallacopas*, a canal that was made for the purpose of emptying the superfluous waters of the Euphrates into the lakes and marshes formed by it in the south-west borders of the province towards Arabia. Into this canal he directed the waters of the Euphrates, and was thus enabled to enter the city in the channel of the river under the walls (see Notes on ch. xlv. 1, 2). He took the city by surprise, and when the inhabitants, confident of security, had given themselves up to the riot of a grand public festival; and the king and the nobles were revelling at a public entertainment. From this cause, also, it happened that the waters, which were thus diverted from their usual channel, converted the whole country into a vast, unhealthy morass, that contributed greatly to the decline of Babylon. (2.) The *second* capture of Babylon by Darius Hystaspes. Cyrus was not the destroyer of the city, but he rather sought to preserve its magnificence, and to perpetuate its pre-eminence among the nations. He left it to his successor in all its strength and magnificence. But, after his death, it rebelled against Darius, and bade defiance to the power of the whole Persian empire. Fully resolved not to yield, they adopted the resolution of putting every woman in the city to death, with the exception of their mothers and one female, the best beloved in every family, to bake their bread. All the rest, says Herodotus (iii. 150), were assembled together and strangled. The city was taken at that time by Darius, by the aid of Zopyrus, son of Megabyzus, who, in order to do it, mutilated himself beyond the power of recovery. He cut off his nose and ears, and having scourged himself severely, presented himself before Darius. He proposed to Darius to enter the city, apparently as a deserter who had been cruelly treated by Darius, and to deliver the city into his hands. He was one of the chief nobles of Persia; was admitted in this manner within the walls; represented himself as having been punished because he advised Darius to raise the siege; was admitted to the confidence of the Babylonians; and was finally intrusted with an important military command. After several successful conflicts with the Persians, and when it was supposed his fidelity had been fully tried, he was raised to the chief command of the army; and was appointed to the responsible office of τειχοφύλαξ, or guardian of the walls. Having obtained this object, he opened the gates of Babylon to the Persian army, as he had designed, and the city was taken without difficulty (Herod. iii. 153-160). As soon as Darius had taken the city, he 'levelled the walls, and took away the gates, neither of which things had Cyrus done before. Three thousand of the most distinguished of the nobility he ordered to be crucified; the rest he suffered to remain.'—(Herod. iii. 159.) (3.) After

its conquest by Darius, it was alway? regarded by the Persian monarchs with a jealous eye. Xerxes destroyed the temples of the city, and, among the rest, the celebrated temple or tower of Belus (Strabo, xvi. 1, 5.) 'Darius,' says Herodotus, 'had designs upon the golden statue in the temple of Belus, but did not dare to take it; but Xerxes, his son, took it, and slew the priest who resisted its removal.' (4.) The city was captured a third time, by Alexander the Great. Mazæus, the Persian general, surrendered the city into his hands, and he entered it with his army —*velut in aciem irent*—'as if they were marching to battle.'—(Q. Curtius, v. 3.) It was afterwards taken by Antigonus, by Demetrius, by Antiochus the Great, and by the Parthians; and each successive conquest contributed to its reduction. (5.) Cyrus transferred the capital from Babylon to *Susa* or Shusan (Neh. i. 1; Ezra ii. 8; iv. 16; ix. 11, 15), which became the capital of the kingdom of Persia, and, of course, contributed much to diminish the importance of Babylon itself. (6.) Seleucus Nicator founded Seleucia in the neighbourhood of Babylon, on the Tigris, chiefly with a design to draw off the inhabitants of Babylon to a rival city, and to prevent its importance. A great part of its population migrated to the new city of Seleucia (Plin. *Nat. Hist.* vi. 30). Babylon thus gradually declined until it lost all its importance, and the very place where it stood was, for a long time, unknown. About the beginning of the first century, a small part of it only was inhabited, and the greater portion was cultivated (Diod. Sic. ii. 27). In the second century, nothing but the walls remained (Pausanius, *Arcad.* c. 33). It became gradually a great desert; and, in the fourth century, its walls, repaired for that purpose, formed an enclosure for wild beasts, and Babylon was converted into a hunting place for the pastime of the Persian monarchs. After this, there is an interval of many ages in the history of its mutilated remains, and of its mouldering decay (Keith, *On the Prophecies*, p. 216; Jerome, *Comm. on Isa.* ch. xiv.) Benjamin of Tudela vaguely alludes to the palace of Nebuchadnez-

20 It [a] shall never be inhabited, neither shall it be dwelt in from generation to generation; neither shall the Arabian pitch tent there; neither shall the shepherds make their fold there:

zar, which, he says, could not be entered, on account of its being the abode of dragons and wild beasts. Sir John Maundeville, who travelled over Asia, A.D. 1322, says, that 'Babylone is in the grete desertes of Arabye, upon the waye as men gon towarde the kyngdome of Caldee. But it is full longe sithe ony man durste neyhe to the toure; for it is alle deserte and full of dragons and grete serpentes, and fulle dyverse veneymouse bestes all abouten.'

20. *It shall never be inhabited.* This has been completely fulfilled. It is now, and has been for centuries, a scene of wide desolation, and is a heap of ruins, and there is every indication that it will continue so to be. From Rauwolff's testimony it appears, that in the sixteenth century 'there was not a house to be seen;' and now the 'eye wanders over a *barren desert*, in which the ruins are nearly the only indication that it had ever been inhabited. It is impossible to behold this scene and not be reminded how exactly the predictions of Isaiah and Jeremiah have been fulfilled, even in the appearance Babylon was doomed to present, *that she should never be inhabited*.'—(Keppel's *Narrative*, p. 234.) 'Babylon is spurned alike by the heel of the Ottoman, the Israelites, and the sons of Ishmael.'—(Mignan's *Travels*, p. 108.) 'It is a *tenantless* and desolate metropolis.'—(Ibid. p. 235; see Keith *On Prophecy*, p. 221.) ¶ *Neither shall it be dwelt in*, &c. This is but another form of the expression, denoting that it shall be utterly desolate. The following testimonies of travellers will show *how* this is accomplished:—'Ruins composed, like those of Babylon, of heaps of rubbish impregnated with nitre, cannot be cultivated.'—(Rich's *Memoir*, p. 16.) 'The decomposing materials of a Babylonian structure doom the earth on which they perish, to lasting sterility. On this part of the plain, both where traces of buildings are left, and where none stood, all seemed equally *naked* of vegetation; the whole ground appearing as if it had been washed over and over again by the coming and receding waters, till every bit of genial soil was swept away; its half-clay, half-sandy surface being left in ridgy streaks, like what is often seen on the flat shores of the sea after the retreating of the tide.'—(Sir R. K. Porter's *Travels*, vol. ii. p. 392.) 'The ground is low and marshy, and presents not the slightest vestige of former buildings, of any description whatever.'—(Buckingham's *Travels*, vol. ii. p. 278.) 'The ruins of Babylon are thus *inundated* so as to render many parts of them inaccessible, by converting the valleys among them into morasses.'—(Rich's *Memoir*, p. 13.) ¶ *Neither shall the Arabian pitch tent there.* The Arabians dwelt chiefly in tents; and were a wandering people, or engaged in traffic which was conducted in caravans travelling from place to place. The idea here is, that Babylon, so far from being occupied as a *permanent* residence for any people, would be unfit even for a resting place. It would be so utterly desolate, so forsaken, and so unhealthy, that the caravan would not even stop there for a night. What a change this from its former splendour! How different from the time when it was the place of magnificent palaces, when strangers flocked to it, and when people from all nations were collected there! ¶ *Neither shall the shepherds*, &c. This is an additional image of desolation. Babylon was situated in the midst of a most fertile region. It might be supposed that, though it was to be destroyed, it would still furnish pasturage for flocks. But no, says the prophet, it shall be so utterly and entirely desolate, that it shall not even afford pasturage for them. The reasons of this are—(1) that the whole region round about Babylon was laid under water by the Euphrates after the city was taken, and became a stagnant pool, and of course an unfit place for flocks; and (2) that Babylon was reduced to an extended scene of ruins; and on those ruins—those extended wastes of broken walls, of bricks and cement—no grass would grow. The

21 But [1] wild beasts of the desert shall lie there: and their houses shall be full of [2] doleful creatures: | and [3] owls shall dwell there, and satyrs shall dance there.

[1] *ziim.*   [2] *ochim,* or, *ostriches.*   [3] *daughters of the owl.*

prophecy has been remarkably fulfilled. It is said that the Arabs cannot be persuaded to remain there even for a night. They traverse these ruins by day without fear ; but at night the superstitious dread of evil spirits deters them from remaining there. 'Captain Mignan was accompanied by six *Arabs* completely armed, but he " could not induce them to remain towards night, from the apprehension of evil spirits. It is impossible to eradicate this idea from the minds of these people, who are very deeply imbued with superstition. . . And when the sun sunk behind the Mujelibé, and the moon would have lighted his way among the ruins, it was with infinite regret that he obeyed the summons of his guides." ' —(Mignan's *Travels,* as quoted by Keith, pp. 221, 222.) ' All the people of the country assert that it is extremely dangerous to approach the mound ' [the mound in Babylon called Kasr, or Palad] 'after nightfall, on account of the multitude of evil spirits by which it is haunted.'—(Rich's *Memoir on the Ruins of Babylon,* p. 27.) The Rev. Joseph Wolff, speaking of his visit to Babylon, says, ' I inquired of them (the Yezeedes), whether the Arabs ever pitched their tents among the ruins of Babylon. No, said they, the Arabs believe that the ghost of Nimrod walks amidst them in the darkness, and no Arab would venture on so hazardous an experiment.'

21. *But wild beasts of the desert shall lie there.* Heb. צִיִּים (*tziyim*). This word denotes properly those animals that dwell in *dry* and desolate places, from צִי, *a waste, a desert.* The ancient versions have differed considerably in the interpretation. The LXX. in different places render it, Θηρία —' Wild animals ;' or δαιμόνια —' Demons.' The Syriac, 'Wild animals, spirits, sirens.' Vulg. ' Beasts, demons, dragons.' Abarbanel renders it, ' Apes.' This word is applied to *men,* in Ps. lxx. 9 ; lxxiv. 14; to *animals,* Isa. xxiii. 13; xxxiv. 14; Jer. l. 39. Bochart supposes that *wild cats* or *catamounts* are here intended. He has

proved that they abound in eastern countries. They feed upon dead carcasses, and live in the woods, or in desert places, and are remarkable for their howl. Their yell resembles that of infants. (*See* Bochart's *Hieroz.* i. 3. 14. pp. 860–862.) ¶ *And their houses shall be full of doleful creatures.* Marg. ' Ochim,' or ' Ostriches.' אֹחִים. The LXX. render this 'Clamours,' or ' Howlings,' without supposing that it refers to any particular animals. The Hebrew word is found nowhere else. Bochart supposes that the yell or howl of wild animals is intended, and not animals themselves (*Hieroz.* i. 3. 15). ¶ *And owls shall dwell there.* Heb. ' Daughters of the owl or ostrich.' The owl is a well-known bird that dwells only in obscure and dark retreats, giving a doleful screech, and seeking its food only at night. It is not certain, however, that the owl is intended here. The LXX. render it, Σειρῆνες —' Sirens.' The Chaldee, ' The daughter of the ostrich.' Bochart has gone into an extended argument to prove that the ostrich is intended here (*Hieroz.* xi. 2. 14). The Hebrew does not particularly denote the kind of bird intended, but means those that are distinguished for their sound—' the daughters of sound or clamour.' ' The ostrich is a sly and timorous creature, delighting in solitary barren deserts. In the night they frequently make a very doleful and hideous noise ; sometimes groaning as if they were in the greatest agonies.'—(Shaw's *Travels,* vol. ii. p. 348, 8vo ; Taylor's *Heb. Con.;* see Job xxx. 29 ; Isa. xxxiv. 13; xliii. 20; Jer. l. 39; Mic. i. 8; Lev. xi. 16; Deut. xiv. 15; Lam. iv. 3.) The word does not elsewhere occur. ¶ *And satyrs shall dance there* (שְׂעִירִים). A *satyr,* in mythology, was a sylvan deity or demigod, represented as a monster, half man and half goat, having horns on his head, a hairy body, with the feet and tail of a goat (Webster). The word here used properly denotes that which is *hairy,* or *rough,* and is applied to *goats* in Gen. xxv. 25; Ps. lxviii. 21; Lev. xiii. 10, 25, 26, 30,

22 And ¹the wild beasts of the islands shall cry in their ²desolate houses, and dragons in *their*

1 *Jim.*   2 or, *palaces.*

pleasant palaces: and her time *is* near *ᵃ* to come, and her days shall not be prolonged.

a Deut.32.35,36.

---

32. It is often rendered *hair* (*see* Taylor). In Isa. xxxiv. 14, it is rendered 'satyr;' in Deut. xxxii. 2, it is rendered 'the small ram;' in Lev. xvii. 7, and 2 Chron. xi. 15, it is rendered 'the devils,' meaning objects of worship, or idols. Bochart supposes that it refers to the idols that were worshipped among the Egyptians, who placed *goats* among their gods. Döderlin supposes that it means either *fawns,* or a species of the monkey tribe, resembling in their rough and shaggy appearance the wild goat. They are here represented as 'dancing;' and in Isa. xxxiv. 14, as 'crying to each other.' It is evident that the prophet intends animals of a rough and shaggy appearance; such as are quick and nimble in their motions; such as dwell in deserts, in forests, or in old ruins; and such as answer to each other, or chatter. The description would certainly seem more applicable to some of the *simia* or monkey tribe than to any other animals. It is *possible,* indeed, that he means merely to make use of language that was well known, as describing animals that the ancients *supposed* had an existence, but which really had not, as the imaginary beings called satyrs. But it is possible, also, that he means simply wild goats (comp. Bochart's *Hieroz.* xi. 6. 7). The LXX. render it, Δαιμόνια—'Demons, or devils.' The Vulgate, *Pilosi*—'Shaggy, or hairy animals.' The Chaldee, ' Demons.' The essential idea is, that such wild animals as are supposed to dwell in wastes and ruins, would hold their revels in the forsaken and desolate palaces of Babylon. The following remarks of the Rev. Joseph Wolff may throw light on this passage : ' I then went to the mountain of Sanjaar, which was full of Yezeedes. One hundred and fifty years ago, they believed in the glorious doctrine of the Trinity, and worshipped the true God ; but being severely persecuted by the neighbouring Yezeedes, they have now joined them, and are worshippers of the devil. These men frequent the ruins of Babylon, and

dance around them. On a certain night, which they call the Night of Life, they hold their dances around the desolate ruins, in honour of the devil. The passage which declares that "satyrs shall dance there," evidently has respect to this very practice. The original word translated "satyr," literally means, according to the testimony of the most eminent Jewish Rabbins, *devil worshippers.*' ' It is a curious circumstance,' says Mr. Rich, in his *Memoir on the Ruins of Babylon,* p. 30, in describing the Mujelibé, ' that here I first heard the oriental account of satyrs. I had always imagined the belief of their existence was confined to the mythology of the west; but a Chôadar who was with me when I examined this ruin, mentioned by accident, that in this desert an animal is found resembling a man from the head to the waist, but having the thighs and legs of a sheep or a goat; he said also that the Arabs hunt it with dogs, and eat the lower parts, abstaining from the upper on account of their resemblance to the human species.' ' The Arabians call them Sied-as-sad, and say that they abound in some woody places near Semava on the Euphrates.'

22. *And the wild beasts of the islands* (אִיִּים) ; see Notes, ch. xi. 11; xli. 1, on the word rendered ' islands.' The word denotes islands, or coasts, and as those coasts and islands were unknown and unexplored, the word seems to have denoted unknown and uninhabited regions in general. Bochart supposes that by the word here used is denoted a species of wolves, the jackal, or the *thoes.* It is known as a wild animal, exceedingly fierce, and is also distinguished by alternate howlings in the night (*see* Bochart's *Hieroz.* i. 3. 12). The word wolf probably will not express an erroneous idea here. The Chaldee renders it, ' Cats.' ¶ *Shall cry.* Heb. ' Shall answer, or respond to each other.' This is known to be the custom of wolves and some other wild animals, who send forth those dismal howls in alternate responses

at night. This alternation of the howl
or cry gives an additional impressiveness to the loneliness and desolation of
forsaken Babylon. ¶ *And dragons*
(תַּנִּים). This word, in its various forms
of *tannim, taninim, tannin,* and *tan-
noth,* denotes sometimes *jackals* or
thoes, as in Job xxx. 29 ; Ps. xliv. 19 ;
Micah i. 8 ; Mal. i. 3. But it also denotes a great fish, a whale, a sea monster, a dragon, a serpent. It is translated ' a whale ' in Gen. i. 21 ; Job vii.
12 ; Ezek. xxxii. 2 ; ' serpents,' Ex.
vii. 9, 10, 12 ; ' dragons,' or ' dragon,'
Deut. xxxii. 33 ; Neh. ii. 13 ; Ps. xliv.
19 ; lxxiv. 13 ; xci. 13 ; cxlviii. 7 ; Isa.
xxvii. 1 ; li. 9 ; Jer. xiv. 6 ; li. 34 ;
Mal. i. 3, *et al.;* and once ' sea monsters,' Lam. iv. 3. A *dragon* properly
means a kind of winged serpent much
celebrated in the dark ages. Here it
may not improperly be rendered *jackal
(see* Bochart's *Hieroz.* i. 1. 9, p. 69).
¶ *In* their *pleasant palaces.* Heb.
' Their palaces of luxury and pleasure.'
The following testimonies from travellers will show how minutely this was
accomplished :—' There are many dens
of wild beasts in various parts.' ' There
are quantities of porcupine quills.' ' In
most of the cavities are numberless bats
and owls.' ' These caverns, over which
the chambers of majesty may have been
spread, are now the refuge of jackals
and other savage animals. The mouths
of their entrances are strewed with the
bones of sheep and *goats ;* and the
loathsome smell that issues from most
of them is sufficient warning not to
proceed into the den.'—(Sir R. K. Porter's *Travels,* vol. ii. p. 342.) ' The
mound was full of large holes ; we entered some of them, and found them
strewed with the carcasses and skeletons
of animals recently killed. The ordure
of wild beasts was so strong, that pru-
dence got the better of curiosity, for we
had no doubt as to the savage nature of
the inhabitants. Our guides, indeed,
told us that all the ruins abounded in
lions and other wild beasts ; so literally
has the Divine prediction been fulfilled,
that wild beasts of the deserts should
lie there.'—(Keppel's *Narrative,* vol. i.
pp. 179, 180.) ¶ *And her time is near
to come.* This was spoken about 174
years before the destruction of Babylon.

But we are to bear in mind that the
prophet is to be supposed to be speaking
to the captive Jews *in* Babylon, and
speaking to them respecting their release (see ch. xiv. 1, 2 ; comp. remarks
on the Analysis of this chapter). Thus
considered, supposing the prophet to be
addressing the Jews in captivity, or
ministering consolation to them, the
time was near. Or if we suppose him
speaking as in his own time, the period
when Babylon was to be destroyed was
at no great distance.

On this whole prophecy, we may observe—(1.) That it was uttered at least
170 years before it was fulfilled. Of
this there is all the proof that can be
found in regard to any ancient writings.
(2.) When uttered, there was the
strongest improbability that it would be
fulfilled. This improbability arose from
the following circumstances : (*a*) The
Jews were secure in their own land, and
they had no reason to dread the Babylonians ; they had no wars with them,
and it was improbable that they would
be plucked up as a nation and carried
there as captives. Such a thing had
never occurred, and there were no circumstances that made it probable that
it would occur. (*b*) The great strength
and security of Babylon rendered it improbable. It was the capital of the
heathen world ; and if there was any
city that seemed impregnable, it was
this. (*c*) It was improbable that it
would be overthrown by *the Medes.*
Media, at the time when the prophecy
was uttered, was a dependent province
of Assyria (Note, ver. 17), and it was
wholly improbable that the Medes would
revolt ; that they would subdue their
masters ; that they would be united to
the Persians, and that thus a *new* kingdom would arise, that should overthrow
the most mighty capital of the world.
(*d*) It was improbable that Babylon
would become uninhabitable. It was
in the midst of a most fertile country ;
and by no human sagacity could it have
been seen that the capital would be removed to Susa, or that Seleucia would
be founded, thus draining it of its inhabitants ; or that by the inundation
of waters it would become unhealthy.
How could mere human sagacity have
foreseen that there would not be a house

CHAPTER XIV.

ANALYSIS.

This chapter is a continuation of the prophecy respecting Babylon, which was commenced in the previous chapter. The prophecy is concluded at ver. 27. A considerable portion of the chapter is a poem of unequalled beauty and sublimity. It is to be remembered that this prophecy was uttered at least 174 years before they were carried into captivity; and the design of the prophet is, to declare the *certainty* of their release after they should be subjected to this bondage. He, doubtless, intended that this prophecy should be borne with them, in memory at least, to Babylon, and that it should comfort and sustain them when there (see Introduction to ch. xiii). He, therefore, opens the vision by a summary statement of the *certainty* of their deliverance (1–3). This general declaration respecting the deliverance of the Jews, is followed by a triumphant song on that subject, that is singularly beautiful in its imagery, and sublime in its conception. 'It moves in lengthened elegiac measure, like a song of lamentation for the dead, and is full of lofty scorn and contumely from beginning to the end.'—(Herder's *Spirit of Hebrew Poetry*, by Marsh, vol. ii. p. 206.) It may be called *the triumphal song of the Jews when delivered from their long and oppressive bondage.* The parts and design of this poem may be thus expressed:

I. A chorus of Jews is introduced, expressing their surprise at the sudden and entire downfall of Babylon, and the complete destruction of the proud and haughty city. The whole earth is full of joy and rejoicing that the city, so long distinguished for oppressions and arrogance, is laid low; and even *the cedars* of Lebanon are introduced as uttering a most severe taunt over the fallen tyrant, and expressing their security now that he is no more (4–8).

II. The scene is immediately changed from earth to hell. Hades, or the region of the dead, is represented as moved at the descent of the haughty king of Babylon to those abodes. Departed monarchs rise from their thrones, and insult him on being reduced from his pride and magnificence to the same low state as themselves (9–11). This portion of the ode is one of the boldest personifications ever attempted in poetry: and is executed with remarkable brevity and force—so much so that we almost seem to *see* the illustrious shades of the dead rise from their couches to meet the descending king of Babylon.

III. The Jews now resume the speech (12–17). They address the king of Babylon as fallen from heaven—like the bright star of the morning. They speak of him as the most magnificent and proud of the monarchs of the earth. They introduce him as expressing the most extravagant purposes of ambition; as designing to ascend to heaven, and to make his throne above the stars; and as aiming at equality with God.

in it in the sixteenth century; or that now, in 1839, it would be a wide and dreary waste? Can any man now tell what London, or Paris, or New York, or Philadelphia, will be two years hence? Yet a prediction that those cities shall be the residence of 'wild beasts of the desert,' of 'satyrs'.and 'dragons,' would be as probable now as was the prediction respecting Babylon at the time when Isaiah uttered these remarkable prophecies. (3.) The prophecy is not vague conjecture. It is not a *general* statement. It is minute, and definite, and particular; and it has been as definitely, and minutely, and particularly fulfilled. (4.) This is one of the evidences of the Divine origin of the Bible. How will the infidel account for this prophecy and its fulfilment? It will not do to say that it is *accident*. It is too minute, and too particular. It is not *human sagacity*. No human sagacity could have foretold it. It is not *fancied fulfilment*. It is real, in the most minute particulars. And if so, then Isaiah was commissioned by Jehovah as he claimed to be—for none but the omniscient Jehovah can foresee and describe future events as the destruction of Babylon was foreseen and described. And if *this* prophecy was inspired by God, by the same train of reasoning it can be proved that the whole Bible is a revelation from heaven. For a very interesting account of the present state of the ruins of Babylon, furnishing the most complete evidence of the fulfilment of the prophecies in regard to it, the reader may consult an article in the *Am. Bib. Rep.*, vol. viii, pp. 177–189. (See also the two *Memoirs on the Ruins of Babylon*, by C. J. Rich, Esq. London, 1816 and 1818.) The frontispiece to this volume, compiled from the sketches of recent travellers, gives accurate and interesting views of those ruins.

They then speak of him as cast down to hell, and as the object of reproach by all those who shall behold him.

IV. The scene is again changed. Certain persons are introduced who are represented as seeing the fallen king of Babylon—as looking narrowly upon him, to make themselves sure that it was he—and as taunting him with his proud designs and his purposes to make the world a wilderness (15-20). They see him cast out and naked; lying among the undistinguished dead, and trodden under feet; and contrast his condition with that of monarchs who are usually deposited in a splendid mausoleum. But the once haughty king of Babylon is represented as denied even a common burial, and as lying undistinguished in the streets.

V. The whole scene of the poem is closed by introducing God as purposing the certain ruin of Babylon; as designing to cut off the whole of the royal family, and to convert the whole city into pools of water, and a habitation for the bittern (21-23). This is declared to be the purpose of JEHOVAH; and a solemn declaration is made, that when he makes a purpose none can disannul it.

VI. A confirmation of this is added (24-27) in a fragment respecting the destruction of the army of the Assyrian under Sennacherib, by

which the exiles in Babylon would be comforted with the assurance, that he who had destroyed the Assyrian host with such ease could also effect his purposes respecting Babylon (see the remarks introductory to ver. 24).

'I believe it may be affirmed,' says Lowth, that there is no poem of its kind extant in any language, in which the subject is so well laid out, and so happily conducted, with such a richness of invention, with such a variety of images, persons, and distinct actions, with such rapidity and ease of transition in so small a compass, as in this ode of Isaiah. For beauty of disposition, strength of colouring, greatness of sentiment, brevity, perspicuity, and force of expression, it stands, among all the monuments of antiquity, unrivalled.'

The king of Babylon, who was the subject of this prediction, and who reigned when Babylon was taken, was Belshazzar (see Dan. v.; and Notes on ver. 22).

FOR *a* the LORD will have mercy on Jacob, and will yet *b* choose Israel, and set them in their own land: and the strangers shall be joined with them, and they shall cleave to the house of Jacob.

a Ps.102.13.　　　　　*b* Zec.1.17; 2.12.

CHAPTER XIV.

1. *For the* LORD *will have mercy on Jacob.* That is, he will pity the captive Jews in Babylon. He will not abandon them, but will remember them, and restore them to their own land. ¶ *And will yet choose Israel.* Will show that he regards them as still his chosen people; or will again *choose* them by recovering them from their bondage, and by restoring them to their country as his people. The names 'Jacob' and 'Israel' here simply denote the Jews. They do not imply that *all* of those who were to be carried captive would return, but that as a people they would be restored. ¶ *And set them,* &c. Heb. 'Will cause them to rest in their own country;' that is, will give them peace, quietness, and security there. ¶ *And the stranger shall be joined to them.* The 'stranger,' here, probably refers to those foreigners who would become proselytes to their religion, while they were in Babylon. Those proselytes would be firmly united with them, and would return with them to their own land. Their captivity would be attended

with this advantage, that many even of those who led them away, would be brought to embrace their religion, and to return with them to their own country. If it is asked what *evidence* there is that any considerable number of the people of Chaldea became Jewish proselytes, I answer, that it is expressly stated in Esther viii. 17: 'And many of the people of the land became Jews; for the fear of the Jews fell upon them.' Ezra, indeed, has not mentioned the fact, that many of the people of Babylonia became proselytes to the religion of the Jews, but it is in accordance with all that we know of their history, and their influence on the nations with which, from time to time, they were connected, that many should have been thus joined to them. We know that in subsequent times many of other nations became proselytes, and that multitudes of the Egyptians, the Macedonians, the Romans, and the inhabitants of Asia Minor, embraced the Jewish religion, or became what were called 'proselytes of the gate.' They were circumcised, and were regarded as entitled to a part

2 And the people shall take them, and bring *a* them to their place: and the house of Israel shall possess them in the land of the Lord for servants and handmaids: and they shall take them captives, whose captives ¹they were; and they shall rule over their oppressors.

a ch.18.7; 60.4,&c.; 66.20.
1 that had taken them captives.

3 And it shall come to pass in the day that the Lord shall give thee rest *b* from thy sorrow, and from thy fear, and from the hard bondage wherein thou wast made to serve.

4 That *c* thou shalt take up this proverb ² against the king of Ba-

b Eze.28.24.　　c Hab.2.6.
2 or, taunting speech.

of the privileges of the Jewish people (see Acts ii. 9-11; comp. Acts xvii. 4, 17). Tacitus, speaking of his time, says, that 'every abandoned man, despising the religion of his country, bears tribute and revenue to Jerusalem, whence it happens that the number of the Jews is greatly increased.'—(*Hist.* v. 5.) That the Jews, therefore, who were in Babylon should induce many of the Chaldeans during their long captivity to become proselytes, is in accordance with all their history.

2. *And the people shall take them.* That is, the people in Babylon. ¶ *And bring them to their place.* That is, they shall attend them to the land of Judea, and aid in restoring them to their own country. There is reference here, doubtless, to the fact that Cyrus would assist them (comp. Ezra ch. i.), and that many of the inhabitants of Chaldea who would become proselytes, would be willing to accompany them to their own land. ¶ *And the house of Israel shall possess them in the land of the* Lord. Not in a foreign land, and among strangers and foes, but in their own land, and among the institutions of their own religion. They would be willing to return with them, and occupy a humble place among them, as servants, for the sake of enjoying the privileges of the true religion. It was a matter of course among the Hebrews, that proselytes would be regarded as occupying a less elevated place in society than native-born Jews. ¶ *And they shall take them captive,* &c. That is, they shall induce them to become proselytes; to be willing to accompany them to their own homes, and to become their servants there. It does not mean that they would subdue them by force; but they would *be* able, by their influence

there, to disarm their opposition; and to induce them to become the friends of their religion. ¶ *And they shall rule over their oppressors.* This is one instance where the people of God would show that they could disarm their oppressors by a mild and winning demeanour, and in which they would be able to induce others to join with them. Such would be the force of their example and conduct, of their conversation and of their deportment, even in the midst of proud and haughty Babylon, that their oppressors would be won to embrace the religion of their captives. If, in proud and haughty Babylon, those who loved the Lord could thus do good; if, when they were *captives,* they could have such an influence over their haughty masters, where is there a place in which the friends of God may not be useful by their example, their conversation, and their prayers?

3. *And it shall come to pass.* That is, then thou shalt take up a taunting song against the king of Babylon (ver. 4). ¶ *That the* Lord *shall give thee rest* (comp. ch. xxxviii. 12). The nature of this predicted rest, is more fully described in Ezek. xxviii. 25, 26. ¶ *From thy sorrow.* The long pain of thy captivity in Babylon. ¶ *And from thy fear.* Heb. 'Trembling.' That is, the apprehension of the ills to which they were continually exposed. Trembling is usually one effect of fear. ¶ *And from thy hard bondage.* The severe and galling servitude of seventy years.

4. *That thou shalt take up.* Thou shalt utter, declare, or commence. The word 'take up,' is used in the sense of utter, speak, or declare, in Ex. xx. 7; xxiii. 1; Ps. xv. 2. ¶ *This proverb* (הַמָּשָׁל). Vulg. 'Parable.' Sept. Τὸν θρῆνον,—'Lamentation.' The Hebrew

bylon, and say, How hath the oppressor ceased! the ¹golden ᵃ city
ceased!

5 The LORD hath broken the staff

1 or, *exactress of gold.*   ᵃ Rev.18.16.

of the wicked, *and* the sceptre of
the rulers.

6 He who smote ᵇ the people in
wrath with a ²continued stroke, he

ᵇ ch.33.1.   2 *a stroke without removing.*

word *mâshâl*, usually rendered *proverb*,
is also rendered *a parable*, or *a by-word*.
It properly denotes *a metaphor, a comparison, a similitude;* and is applied
usually to a brief and pungent sentiment
or maxim, where wisdom is embodied
in few words. In these the ancients
abounded. They had few books; and
hence arose the necessity of condensing
as much as possible the sentiments of
wisdom, that they might be easily
remembered, and transmitted to future
times. These maxims were commonly
expressed in figurative language, or by
a brief comparison, or short parable, as
they are with us. The word also means,
figurative discourse generally; and
hence, a song or poem (Num. xxiii. 7,
18; Job xxvii. 1; xxix. 1; Ps. xlix. 5).
It is also used to denote a *satire*, or a
song of triumph over enemies (Micah
ii. 4; Heb. iv. 6; Joel ii. 17). It is
evidently used in this sense here—to
denote a taunting speech, a song of
triumph over the prostrate king of
Babylon. In this beautiful song, there
are all the elements of the most pungent
satire, and all the beauties of the highest
poetry. ¶ *Against the king of Babylon.*
Over the king of Babylon, or in regard
to him. It is not certain that any
particular king of Babylon is here intended. If there was, it was probably
Belshazzar, in whose reign the city was
taken (see Notes on ver. 22). It may,
however, be designed to denote the
Babylonian empire—the kingdom that
had oppressed the Jews; and thus *the
king* may be referred to as the head of
the nation, and as the representative of
the whole people. ¶ *How hath the
oppressor ceased!* The word 'oppressor'
(נֹגֵשׂ) denotes, properly, *the exactor of
tribute,* and refers here to the fact that
Babylon had oppressed its dependent
provinces, by exacting large revenues
from them, and thus cruelly oppressing
them. ¶ *Ceased.* Ceased to exact
tribute; or (Heb.) 'is at rest.' It is
now at rest, and no more puts forth its

power in oppressing its dependent provinces. ¶ *The golden city.* Babylon.
The word used here (מַדְהֵבָה) occurs
nowhere else in the Bible. According
to the Jewish Commentators, it means
an exactress of gold, as if derived from
דְּהַב (*děhâbh*), used for זָהָב (*zěhâbh*), gold.
Gesenius and Michaelis prefer another
reading (מַרְהֵבָה *mărhêbhâ*, from רָהַב
râhâbh), and suppose that it means
oppression. The Vulgate renders it
tribute—'The tribute hath ceased.'
The LXX. 'Ἐπισπουδαστής—'Solicitor,
or exactor (of gold).' Vitringa supposes
that the word means *gold,* and that it
refers to the golden sceptre of its kings
that had now ceased to be swayed over
the prostrate nations. The most probable sense is, that it means the exactress
of gold, or of tribute. This best expresses
the force of the word, and best agrees
with the parallelism. In this sense it
does not refer to the magnificence of the
city, but to its oppressive acts in de-
manding tribute of gold from its dependent provinces.

5. *The LORD hath broken.* JEHOVAH,
by the hand of Cyrus. ¶ *The staff of
the wicked.* That is, the sceptre of the
king of Babylon. The word rendered
'staff' (מַטֶּה) may mean either a bough,
stick, staff, rod, or a sceptre. The sceptre
was the symbol of supreme power. It
was in the form of a staff, and was made
of wood, ivory, or gold. It here means
that JEHOVAH had taken away the power
from Babylon, and destroyed his dominion.

6. *He who smote.* This may either
refer to the king of Babylon, or to the
rod or sceptre which he had used, and
which was now broken. Herder refers
it to the sceptre, 'that which smote the
nations.' (On the meaning of the word
smote, see Notes on ch. x. 20.) ¶ *The
people.* The nations that were subject
to his authority. ¶ *With a continual
stroke.* Marg. 'A stroke without removing.' Vulg. *Plagâ insanabili—*

that ruled the nations in anger, is persecuted, *and* none hindereth.

7 The whole earth is at rest, *and* is quiet ; they break forth into singing.

8 Yea, the fir trees [a] rejoice at thee, *and* the cedars of Lebanon, *saying,* Since thou art laid down, no feller is come up against us.

'With an incurable plague.'—Sept. the same—Πληγῇ ἀνιάτῳ. The Hebrew is, as in the margin, 'A smiting without removing,' or without cessation. There was no relaxation in its oppressions, it was *always* engaged in acts of tyranny. ¶ *He that ruled the nations.* Babylon was the capital of a vast empire, and that empire was composed of many dependent nations. ¶ *Is persecuted.* By those that make war upon it. *Its* turn had come to be oppressed, and overthrown. ¶ And *none hindereth.* No nation opposes the invader. None of the dependent kingdoms of Babylon have any real attachment to it, but all rejoice at its downfall. The most mighty kingdom of the earth is helpless and ruined. What a change was this ! How sudden and striking the revolution ! And what a warning to proud and guilty cities !

7. *The whole earth is at rest.* The kingdom of Babylonia, or Chaldea, extended nearly over the whole heathen world. Now that Babylon was fallen, and that those oppressions would cease, the world is represented as in peace and quietness. ¶ *They break forth into singing.* That is, the inhabitants of all the nations that were subject to Babylon now rejoice that they are released from its galling and oppressive yoke.

8. *Yea, the fir trees rejoice at thee.* They join with the inhabitants of the nations in rejoicing at thy downfall— for they now, like those inhabitants, are suffered to remain undisturbed. (On the word rendered *fir trees,* see Notes on ch. i. 29.) It is evident that a species of evergreen is meant ; and probably some species that grew in Syria or Palestine. The idea is plain. The very forest is represented as rejoicing. It would be safe from the king of Babylon. He could no longer cut it down to build his palaces, or to construct his implements of war. This figure of representing the hills and groves, the trees, the mountains, and the earth, as exulting,

or as breaking forth into joy, is common in the Scriptures :

Let the heavens rejoice, and let the earth be glad ;
Let the sea roar, and the fulness thereof.
Let the field be joyful, and all that is therein :
Then shall all the trees of the wood rejoice
Before the Lord.   Ps. xcvi. 11–13.

Let the floods clap their hands ;
Let the hills be joyful together
Before the Lord.   Ps. xcviii. 8, 9.

Praise the Lord from the earth,
Ye dragons and all deeps ;
Fire and hail ; snow and vapour ;
Stormy wind fulfilling his word :
Mountains and all hills ;
Fruitful trees and all cedars.
          Ps. cxlviii. 7–12.

(Comp. 1 Chron. xvi. 31 ; Hab. iii. 10, 11.) ¶ *The cedars of Lebanon* (Note, ch. x. 34). The cedars of Lebanon were much celebrated for building ; and it is not impossible that the king of Babylon had obtained timber from that mountain with which to construct his palaces at Babylon. They are now represented as rejoicing that he is fallen, since they would be safe and undisturbed. A similar figure of speech occurs in Virgil, *Ecl.* v. 68 :

Peace, peace, mild Daphnis loves ; with joyous cry
The untill'd mountains strike the echoing sky ;
And rocks and towers the triumph spread abroad—
'A god ! Menalcas ! Daphnis is a god !'
          Wrangham.

It is a beautiful figure ; and is a fine specimen of the poetry of the Hebrews, where everything is animated, and full of life. ¶ *Since thou art laid down.* Since thou art dead. ¶ *No feller.* No one to cut us down. Jowett (*Chris. Res.*) makes the following remarks on this passage on his visit to Lebanon :— 'As we passed through the extensive forest of fir trees situated between Deirel-Kamr and Ainep, we had already heard, at some distance, the stroke of one solitary axe, resounding from hill to hill. On reaching the spot, we found a peasant, whose labour had been so far successful, that he had felled his tree and lopped his branches. He was now

9 ¹ Hell *ᵃ*from beneath is moved
for thee to meet *thee* at thy coming:
it stirreth up the dead for thee,

1 or, *the graves.*   *ᵃ* Eze.32.21.

even all the ² chief ones of the earth:
it hath raised up from their thrones
all the kings of the nations.

2 *leaders,* or, *great goats.*

hewing it in the middle, so as to balance
the two halves upon his camel, which
stood patiently by him waiting for his
load. In the days of Hiram, king of
Tyre, and subsequently under the kings
of Babylon, this romantic solitude was
not so peaceful; that most poetic image
in Isaiah, who makes these very trees
vocal, exulting in the downfall of the
destroyer of nations, seems now to be
almost realized anew—*Yea, the fir
trees rejoice at thee, and the cedars of
Lebanon, saying, Since thou art laid
down, no feller is come up against us.*'

9. *Hell from beneath.* The scene is
now changed. The prophet had represented the people of all the subject
nations as rejoicing that the king of
Babylon had fallen, and had introduced
even the trees of the forest as breaking
forth into joy at this event. He now
transfers the scene to the mournful regions of the dead; follows the spirit of
the departed king of Babylon—the man
who once gloried in the magnificence of
his kingdom and his court, and who was
more distinguished for pride and arrogance than all other monarchs—down to
the land of darkness, and describes his
reception there. This portion of the
ode is signally sublime, and is managed
with great power and skill. It is unequalled, perhaps, by any writings for
boldness, majesty, and, at the same time,
for its severe sarcasm. The word 'hell'
here (שְׁאוֹל *sheōl*) is rendered by the
Vulgate *infernus ;* and by the LXX.
'Ο ᾅδης—*Hades.* It properly means the
grave, and then the dark regions of the
lower world—the region of ghosts and
shades: a place where thick darkness
reigns. The verb from which it is derived means, properly, *to ask, to demand,
to require, to seek ;* and this name (*sheol*)
is supposed to have been given to the
grave, and to the regions of departed
spirits, from the insatiable *demand*
which they are constantly making of
the living (see Note on ch. v. 14, where
the word is explained). The word denotes, says Taylor (*Heb. Con.*), 'The
underground parts of the earth, other-

wise called the nether, or lower parts
of the earth; the earth beneath in opposition to the earth above, where men
and other animals live. In *sheol*
are the foundations of the mountains
(Deut. xxxii. 22). In *sheol* men pene-
trate by digging into the earth (Amos
ix. 2). Into *sheol* the roots of trees do
strike down (Ezek. xxxi. 16). Into
sheol, Korah, Dathan, and Abiram
went down alive (Num. xvi. 30, 33).
In *sheol* the body is corrupted and consumed by worms (Job xvii. 13, 14; Ps.
xvi. 10; xlix. 14). They that rest together in the dust are said to go down
to the bars, or *strong gates of sheol* (Job
xvii. 16). In *sheol* there is no knowledge, nor can any praise God or give
thanks there (Ps. vi. 5; Eccl. ix. 10;
Isa. xxxviii. 10, 11). *Sheol* and the
pit, death, and corruption, are synonymous (Ps. xvi. 10; lxxxix. 48; Prov. i.
12; vii. 27; Ezek. xxxi. 16; Hos. xiii.
14). A grave is one particular cavity
purposely digged for the interment of a
dead person; *sheol* is a collective name
for all the graves. He that is in the
grave is in *sheol ;* but he that is in *sheol*
may not be in a grave, but in any pit,
or in the sea. In short, it is the region
of the dead; which is figuratively considered as a city or large habitation with
gates and bars in which there are many
chambers (Prov. vii. 27).' *Sheol* is
never full, but is always asking or crav-
ing more (Prov. xxvii. 20; Heb. ii. 5).
Here it means, not a place of punishment, but the region of the dead, where
the ghosts of the departed are considered
as residing together. ¶ *From beneath.*
From beneath the earth. *Sheol* was
always represented as being *in* or *under*
the ground, and the grave was the avenue
or door that led to it (see Note on ch.
v. 14. ¶ *Is moved for thee.* Is roused
to meet thee; is surprised that a monarch
once so proud and magnificent is descending to it. The image here is taken from
the custom of the ancients in burying,
especially of burying princes and kings.
This was usually done in caves or sepulchres excavated from a rock (see the

Notes and illustrations on ch. lxvi. 4). Mr. Stephens, in his *Travels in Egypt, Arabia Petrea, and the Holy Land,* has given an account of the manner in which he passed a night in Petra, which may serve to illustrate this passage : ' We ascended the valley, and rising to the summit of the rocky rampart [of Petra], it was almost dark when we found ourselves opposite a range of tombs in the suburbs of the city. Here we dismounted ; and selecting from among them one which, from its finish and dimensions, must have been the last abode of some wealthy Edomite, we prepared to pass the night within its walls. In the front part of it was a large chamber, about twenty-five feet square, and ten feet high ; and behind this was another of smaller dimensions, furnished with receptacles of the dead, not arranged after the manner of shelves along the wall, as in the catacombs I had seen in Italy and Egypt, but cut lengthwise in the rock, like ovens, so as to admit the insertion of the body with the feet foremost. My plans for the morrow being all arranged, the Bedouins stretched themselves out in the outer chamber, while I went within ; and seeking out a tomb as far back as I could find, I crawled in feet first, and found myself very much in the condition of a man buried alive. I had just room enough to turn round ; and the worthy old Edomite for whom the tomb was made, never slept in it more quietly than I did.'—(Vol. ii. pp. 82, 83, 86.) To understand the passage before us, we are to form the idea of an immense and gloomy cavern, all around which are niches or cells made to receive the bodies of the dead. In this vast vault monarchs repose in grandeur suitable to their former rank, each on his couch, ' in glory,' with their arms beside them (see ver. 18). These mighty shades— these departed monarchs—are represented as rising from their couches to meet the descending king of Babylon, and receive him with insults on his fall. —The Hebrew word for *moved* denotes more than our translation conveys. It means that they were *agitated*—they *trembled*—they advanced towards the descending monarch with trepidation. The idea of the shades of the mighty

dead thus being troubled, and rising to meet the king of Babylon, is one that is exceedingly sublime. ¶ *It stirreth up. Sheol* stirreth up ; that is, they are stirred up or excited. So the LXX. render it ' All the giants who rule the earth rise up to thee.' ¶ *The dead* Heb. רְפָאִים (*rĕphâim*). The LXX. render this, Οἱ γίγαντες—' Giants.' So the Vulgate and the Chaldee. The meaning of this word has been a subject of great difference of opinion among lexicographers. It is sometimes found as a gentile noun to denote the sons of Raphah, called *Rephaim* (2 Sam. xxi. 16, 18), a Canaanitish race of giants that lived beyond Jordan (Gen. xiv. 5 ; xv. 20), from whom Og the son of Bashan was descended (Deut. iii. 11). It is sometimes used to denote all the giant tribes of Canaan (Deut. ii. 11, 20) ; and is particularly applied to men of extraordinary strength among the Philistines (2 Sam. xxi. 16, 18.) Vitringa supposes that the term was given to the spirits of the dead on account of the fact that they appeared to be *larger* than life ; that they in their form and stature resembled giants. But a more probable opinion is, that it is applied to the shades of the dead as being weak, feeble, or without power or sensation, from the word רָפָא (*râphâ*), weak, feeble, powerless. This interpretation is strongly confirmed by the place before us (ver. 10), ' Art thou become weak as we ? ' The word is rendered ' giants ' in the following places : Deut. ii. 11, 20 ; iii. 13 ; Josh. xii. 4 ; xv. 8 ; xvii. 15 ; xviii. 16 ; 2 Sam. xxi. 16, 18, 20, 22 ; 1 Chron. xx. 5, 6, 8. It is rendered ' Rephaims,' Gen. xiv. 5 ; xv. 20 ; 2 Sam. v. 18, 22 ; xxiii. 13. It is rendered ' the dead ' Job xxvi. 5 ; Ps. lxxxviii. 10 ; Prov. ii. 18 ; ix. 18 ; xxi. 16 ; Isa. xxvi. 29 ; and once it is rendered ' deceased,' Isa. xxvi. 14. It here means the departed spirits of the dead—the inhabitants of that dark and dismal region, conceived by the Hebrews to be situated beneath the ground, where dwell the departed dead before their final destiny is fixed— called *sheol* or *hades.* It is not the residence of the wicked only—the place of punishment—but the place where *all* the dead are supposed to be

10 All they shall speak and say unto thee, Art thou also become weak as we? art thou become like unto us?

11 Thy pomp is brought down to the grave, *and* the noise of thy viols: the worm is spread under thee, and the worms cover thee.

congregated before their final doom is pronounced.

[The author entertains peculiar views of the state of knowledge among the Hebrews regarding the future world—views which will be found fully canvassed in the preface to the volumes on Job. As to the alleged notion of *all* the dead dwelling in some dismal region before their final doom is pronounced, we have there taken pains to show that the righteous in ancient times entertained no such gloomy expectations. The opinions of the ancient Hebrews on this subject, must be taken from passages in which they expressly treat of it, and intimate plainly what their belief is, and not from passages confessedly full of poetical imagery. Nor are we to construe popular and poetical phraseology so strictly and literally as to form a theological creed out of it, in contradiction to the actual belief of those who daily used that phraseology. Because Englishmen speak of the dead *indiscriminately* as having *gone to the grave, and to the land of spirits,* must we, out of this, construct a Popish purgatory as the national belief? Yet this would be just as reasonable in the case of the English, as in the case of the Jews. The reader will appreciate the following observations of Professor Alexander on the place:—'Two expressions have been faithfully transcribed by interpreters, from one another, in relation to this passage, with a very equivocal effect upon its exposition. The one is, that it is full of biting sarcasm—an unfortunate suggestion of Calvin's, which puts the reader on the scent for irony, and even wit, instead of opening his mind to impressions of sublimity and tragic grandeur. The other, for which Calvin is in no degree responsible, is, that we have before us not a mere prosopopeia, or poetical creation of the highest order, but a chapter from the popular belief of the Jews, as to the locality, contents, and transactions of the unseen world. Thus Gesenius, in his Lexicon and Commentary, gives a minute topographical description of *Sheol*, as the Hebrews believed it to exist. With equal truth, a diligent compiler might construct a map of hell, as conceived of by the English Puritans, from the descriptive portions of the Paradise Lost. The infidel interpreters of Germany regard the scriptural and classical mythology precisely in the same light. But when Christian writers copy their expressions or ideas, they should take pains to explain whether the popular belief of which they speak was true or false, and, if false, how it could be countenanced and sanctioned by inspired writers. This kind of exposition is, moreover, chargeable with a rhetorical incongruity, in lauding the creative genius of the poet, and yet making all his grand creations commonplace articles of popular belief. The true view of the matter, as determined both by piety and taste, appears to be, that the passage now before us comprehends two elements, and only two religious verities or certain facts, and poetical embellishments. The admission of a *tertium quid*, in the shape of superstitious fables, is as false in rhetoric as in theology.']

¶ *The chief ones of the earth.* Marg. 'Leaders,' or 'great goats.' The Hebrew word means properly *great goats*, or goats that are leaders of the flock. Perhaps there is intended to be a slight degree of sarcasm in applying this word to princes and monarchs. It is nowhere else applied to princes, though the word is often used or applied to *rams*, or to the chief goats of a flock. ¶ *From their thrones.* In *hades*, or *sheol*. They are there represented as occupying an eminence similar to that which distinguished them on earth.

10. *All they shall speak*, &c. Language of astonishment that one so proud, and who apparently never expected to die, should be brought down to that humiliating condition. It is a severe taunt at the great change which had taken place in a haughty monarch.

11. *Thy pomp.* Thy magnificence (see Note on ch. v. 14). ¶ *The noise of thy viols.* Instruments of music were often used in their feasts; and the meaning here is, that instead of being surrounded with splendour, and the instruments of music, the monarch was now brought down to the corruption and stillness of the grave. The instrument referred to by the word 'viol' (נבֶל *neb-hēl*, plur. *nebhâlim*, Gr. νάβλα, Lat. *nablium*), was a stringed instrument usually with twelve strings, and played by the pecten or by the hand (see Notes and illustrations on ch. v. 12). Addi-

12 How art thou fallen from heaven, O ¹ Lucifer, son of the morning! *how* art thou cut down to the

1 *or, day star.*

ground, which didst weaken the
nations!
13 For thou hast said in thine
heart, I will ascend into heaven,

---

tional force is given by all these expressions if they are read, as Lowth reads
them, as questions asked in suprise, and
in a taunting manner, over the haughty
king of Babylon—'Is thy pride then
brought down to the grave?' &c. ¶ *The
worm*. This word, in Hebrew (רִמָּה
rĭmmă), denotes a worm that is found
in putrid substances (Ex. xvi. 25; Job
vii. 5; xxi. 26). ¶ *Is spread under
thee*. Is become thy couch—instead of
the gorgeous couch on which thou wert
accustomed to repose. ¶ *And the worm*
(תּוֹלֵעָה *tōlĕā*)—the same word which
occurs in ch. i. 18, and there rendered
crimson (see Note on that verse). This
word is usually applied to the insect from
which the crimson dye was obtained;
but it is also applied to the worm which
preys upon the dead (Ex. xvi. 20; Isa.
lxvi. 24). ¶ *Cover thee*. Instead of the
splendid covering which was over thee
when reposing on thy couch in thy palace.
What could be more humiliating than
this language? How striking the contrast between his present situation and
that in which he reposed in Babylon!
And yet this language is as applicable
to all others as to that proud and haughty
king. It is equally true of the great
and mighty everywhere; of the rich,
the gay, the beautiful, and the proud,
who lie on beds of down, that they will
soon lie where worms shall be their couch
and their covering. How ought this
reflection to humble our pride! How
should it lead us to be prepared for that
hour when the grave shall be our bed;
and when far away from the sound of
the viol and the harp; from the sweet
voice of friendship and the noise of
revelry, we shall mingle with our native
dust!

12. *How art thou fallen from heaven.*
A new image is presented here. It is
that of the bright morning star; and a
comparison of the once magnificent monarch with that beautiful star. He is
now exhibited as having fallen from his
place in the east to the earth. His glory
is dimmed; his brightness quenched.

Nothing can be more poetic and beautiful than a comparison of a magnificent monarch with the bright morning
star! Nothing more striking in representing his death, than the idea of that
star falling to the earth! ¶ *Lucifer*.
Marg. 'Day-star' (הֵילֵל *hēlēl*, from
הָלַל *hālăl, to shine*). The word in Hebrew occurs as a noun nowhere else.
In two other places (Ezek. xxi. 12;
Zech. xi. 2), it is used as a verb in the
imperative mood of Hiphil, and is
translated 'howl' from the verb יָלַל
(*yālăl*), *to howl* or *cry*. Gesenius and
Rosenmüller suppose that it should be
so rendered here. So Noyes renders it,
'Howl, son of the morning!' But the
common translation seems to be prefer-
able. The LXX. render it, 'Εωσφόρος,
and the Vulgate, 'Lucifer, the morning
star.' The Chaldee, 'How art thou
fallen from high, who wert splendid
among the sons of men.' There can be
no doubt that the object in the eye of
the prophet was the bright morning
star; and his design was to compare
this magnificent oriental monarch with
that. The comparison of a monarch
with the sun, or the other heavenly
bodies, is common in the Scriptures.
¶ *Son of the morning*. This is a Hebraism (see Note, Matt. i. 1), and signifies that that bright star is, as it were,
the production, or the offspring of morning; or that it *belongs to* the morning.
The word 'son' often thus denotes *possession*, or that one thing belongs to
another. The same star in one place
represents the Son of God himself; Rev.
xxi. 16: 'I am—the bright and morning star.' ¶ *Which didst weaken the
nations*. By thy oppressions and exactions, rendering once mighty nations
feeble.

13. *For thou hast said in thine heart.*
It was thy purpose or design. ¶ *I will
ascend into heaven*. Nothing could
more strikingly show the arrogance of
the monarch of Babylon than this impious design. The meaning is, that he
intended to set himself up as supreme;

1 will exalt my throne above the stars *a* of God : I will sit also upon

a Dan.8.10.

the mount of the congregation, in the sides *b* of the north:

b Ps.48.2.

---

he designed that all should pay homage to him ; he did not intend to acknowledge the authority of God. It is not to be understood literally ; but it means that he intended *not* to acknowledge any superior either in heaven or earth, but designed that himself and his laws should be regarded as supreme. ¶ *Above the stars of God.* The stars which God has made. This expression is equivalent to the former that he would ascend into heaven. ¶ *I will sit also upon the mount of the congregation.* The word rendered 'congregation' (מוֹעֵד from יָעַד *to fix, appoint*), properly means a fixed or definite time; then an *appointed* place of meeting ; then a meeting itself ; an assembly, a congregation. What is referred to here it is difficult to determine. The LXX. render it, ' On a high mountain, on the lofty regions which lie to the north.' The Chaldee, ' I will sit in the mount of covenant, in the regions of the north.' Grotius supposes that when the king of Babylon said he would ascend into heaven, he meant the land of Judea, which was called heaven because it was dedicated to God ;—that when he said he would ascend above the stars, he meant to denote those ' who were learned in the law ; ' that by the ' mount of the congregation,' he meant mount Moriah where was the temple ; and that by the ' side of the north,' he meant mount Zion, which, he says, was on the north of Jerusalem. It is remarkable that the usually accurate Grotius should have fallen into this error, as mount Zion was not on the north of Jerusalem, but was south of mount Moriah. Vitringa defends the same interpretation in the main, but supposes that by the ' mount of the congregation ' is meant mount Zion, and by ' the sides of the north,' is meant mount Moriah lying north of Zion. He supposes that mount Zion is called ' the mount of the congregation,' not because the congregation of Israel assembled there, but because it was the *appointed place* where God met his people, or where he manifested himself to them, and appeals to the following places where the word which is here

rendered ' congregation ' is applied, in various forms, to the manifestation which God thus made (Ex. xxv. 22 ; xxix. 42, 43; Ps. lxxiv. 8). So Lowth supposes that it refers to the place where God promised to meet with his people (Ex. xxv. 22; xxix. 42, 43), and to commune with them, and translates it ' the mount of the Divine presence.' But to this interpretation there are great objections —(1.) The terms here employed ' the mount of the congregation,' ' the sides of the north,' are not elsewhere applied to mount Zion, and to mount Moriah. (2.) It does not correspond with the evident design of the king of Babylon. His object was not to make himself master of Zion and Moriah, but it was to exalt himself above the stars ; to be elevated above *all* inferior beings ; and to be above the gods. (3.) It is a most forced and unnatural interpretation to call the land of Judea ' heaven,' to speak of it as being ' above the stars of God,' or as ' above the heights of the clouds ;' and it is clear that the king of Babylon had a much higher ambition, and much more arrogant pretensions, than the conquest of what to him would be the comparatively limited province of Judea. However important that land appeared to the Jews as their country and their home ; or however important it was as the place of the solemnities of the true religion, yet we are to remember that it had no such consequence in the eyes of the king of Babylon. He had no belief in the truth of the Jewish religion, and all Judea compared with his other vast domains would appear to be a very unimportant province. It is evident, therefore, I think, that the king of Babylon did not refer here to Judea, or to Zion. The leading idea of his heart, which ought to guide our interpretation, was, that he designed *to ascend in authority over all inferior beings, and to be like the Most High.* We are to remember that Babylon was a city of idolatry ; and it is most probable that by ' the mount of the congregation, in the sides of the north,' there is reference to a belief prevalent in

Babylon that the gods had their residence on some mountain of the north. This was a common opinion among the ancients. The Hindoos call that mountain *Meru;* the Persians, who are followers of Zoroaster, *Al Bordsch;* the Arabs, *Kafe;* and the Greeks, *Olympus.* The common opinion was that this mountain was in the centre of the world, but the Hindoos speak of it as to the north of themselves in the Himalaya regions; the followers of Zoroaster in the mountains of Caucasus, lying to the north of their country; and the Greeks speak of Olympus, the highest mountain north of them in Thessaly. The Hindoo belief is thus referred to by Ward :—' In the book of Karma-Vipaka, it is said that the heavenly Vishnu, Brahma, and Siva, are upon the three peaks of the mountain Su-Meru, and that at the foot of this mountain are the heavens of twenty-one other gods.'—(*View of the History, Literature, and Religion of the Hindoos,* vol. i. p. 13.) So Wilford, in a Treatise on the mountain Caucasus, in the *Asiatic Researches,* vol. vi. p. 488, says, ' The Hindoos regard the mountain Meru as the dwelling-place of the gods. In the Puranas it is said, that upon the mountain Meru there is eternal day, for a space of fourteen degrees around the mountain Su-Meru, and consequently eternal night for the same space on the opposite side; so the Hindoos are constrained to admit that Su-Meru is directly upon the top of the shadow of the earth, and that from the earth to that peak there is a vast cone-formed hill, dense as other earthly bodies, but invisible, impalpable, and impassable by mortals. On the side of this hill are various abodes, which, the higher one ascends, become the more beautiful, and which are made the dwellings of the blessed, according to the degrees of their desert. God and the most exalted of the divine beings have their abodes on the sides of the north, and on the top of this mountain.' According to the Zendavesta, the Al Bordsch is the oldest and the highest of the mountains; upon that is the throne of Ormuzd, and the assemblage of the heavenly spirits (Feruer; see Rosenmüller, *Alter-thumskunde,* vol. i. pp. 154-157). Thus in Babylon, some of the mountains north

in Armenia may have been supposed to be the peculiar dwelling-place of the gods. Such a mountain would *appear* to be under the north pole, and the constellations would seem to revolve around it. It is not improbable that the Aurora Borealis, playing often as it does in the north with peculiar magnificence, might have contributed to the belief that this was the peculiar abode of the gods. Unable to account—as indeed all moderns are—for these peculiar and magnificent lights in the north, it accorded with the poetic and mythological fancy of the ancients to suppose that they were designed to play around, and to adorn the habitation of the gods. This disposition to make the mountains of the north the seat of the gods, may have arisen also in part from the fact that the country on the north of Babylon was a volcanic region, and that the light emitted from volcanoes was an appropriate manifestation of the glory of superior invisible beings. ' On the borders of the Caspian [Sea], in the country around the Bakir, there is a tract called The Field of Fire, which continually emits inflammable gas, while springs of naphtha and petroleum occur in the same vicinity, as also mud volcanoes. In the chain of Elburs, to the south of this sea, is a lofty mountain, which, according to Morier, sometimes emits smoke, and at the base of which there are several craters where sulphur and saltpetre are procured in sufficient abundance to be used in commerce.'— (Lyell's *Geology,* vol. i. p. 297.) We find some traces of these ideas in the Scriptures. The *north* is often mentioned as the seat of the whirlwind, the storm, and especially as the residence of the cherubim. Thus in Ezekiel's vision of the cherubim, the whole magnificent scene is represented as coming from the *north*—as if the appropriate abode of the cherubim:

' I looked, and lo! a whirlwind *from the north*
Came sweeping onward, a vast cloud that rolled
In volumes, charged with gleaming fire, along,
And cast its splendours all around.
Now from within shone forth, what seemed
  the glow
Of gold and silver molten in the flame,
And in the midst thereof the form expressed,
As of a fourfold living thing—a shape
That yet contained the semblance of a man.'
   Ezek. i. 4, 5, trans. in Marsh's *Herder.*

14 I will ascend above the heights of the clouds: I will be *a* like the Most High.

15 Yet *b* thou shalt be brought down to hell, to the sides of the pit.

a 2 Thes.2.4.

16 They that see thee shall narrowly look upon thee, and consider thee, *saying, Is* this the man that made the earth to tremble, that did shake kingdoms;

b Mat.11.23.

Thus, in Ezek. xxviii. 14, Tyre is said to be 'the anointed cherub that covereth,' and to have been 'upon the holy mountain of God,' or *the gods*—evidently meaning, not Zion, but some mountain in the vicinity of Eden (see ver. 13). Thus also, in Zech. vi. 1–8, four chariots are represented as coming out of the mountains, the first chariot with red horses, the second with black horses, the third with white horses, and the fourth with bay horses. The horses that have gone through the earth are (ver. 8) represented as going to the *north* as their place of rest. These passages, particularly the one from Ezekiel, show that the northern regions were regarded as the seat of striking and peculiar manifestations of the Divine glory (comp. Notes on Job xxiii. 9; xxxvii. 22). And it is probable that, in the view of the Babylonians, the northern mountains of Armenia, that seemed to be near the north pole, around which the constellations revolved, and that appeared to be surmounted and encompassed by the splendid light of the Aurora Borealis, were regarded as the peculiar place where the gods held their assemblies, and from whence their power went forth through the nations. Over all their power it was the intention of the king of Babylon to ascend, and even to rise above the stars that performed their revolutions around the seats of the gods in the north; to be *supreme* in that assembly of the gods, and to be regarded there as the supreme and incontrollable director of even all the gods. It is probable, says Mitford (*Life of Milton*, vol. i. p. 73), that from this scarcely intelligible hint Milton threw up his palace for his fallen angels—thus:

At length into the limits of the north
They came, and Satan to his royal seat,
High on a hill, far blazing as a mount
Raised on a mount, with pyramids and towers,
From diamond quarries hewn, and rocks of gold.
The palace of great Lucifer, so call

That structure in the dialect of men
Interpreted; which not long after he
Affecting an equality with God,
In imitation of that mount, whereon
Messiah was declared in sight of heaven,
The mountain of the congregation called, &c.

14. *I will be like the Most High.* There is a remarkable resemblance between this language and that used in 2 Thess. ii. 4, in regard to Antichrist: 'He, as God, sitteth in the temple of God, showing himself that he is God.' And this similarity is the more remarkable, because Antichrist is represented, in Rev. xvii. 4, 5, as seated in BABYLON—the spiritual seat of arrogance, oppression, and pride. Probably Paul had the passage in Isaiah in his eye when he penned the description of Antichrist.

15. *Yet thou shalt be brought down to hell.* Heb. 'To sheol' (comp. ver. 9). ¶ *To the sides of the pit.* The word 'pit,' here, is evidently synonymous with *hell* or *hades*, represented as a deep, dark region under ground. The dead were often buried in caves, and the descent was often dark and dreary, to the vaults where they reposed. Hence it is always represented as going *down;* or, as the *inferior* regions. The 'sides of the pit' here stand opposed to the 'sides of the north.' He had sought to *ascend* to the one; he should be *brought down* to the other. The reference here is, doubtless, to the land of shades; to the dark and dismal regions where the departed dead are supposed to dwell—to *sheol.* So the parallelism proves. But the image or figure is taken from the custom of burying, where, in a deep natural cavern, or a sepulchre excavated from a rock, the dead were ranged around the *sides* of the cavern in niches or recesses excavated for that purpose (see Note on ver. 9).

16. *They that see thee.* That is, after thou art dead. The scene here changes, and the prophet introduces those who would contemplate the body

17 *That* made the world as a wilderness, and destroyed the cities thereof; [1] *that* opened not the house of his prisoners?

18 All the kings of the nations, *even* all of them, lie in glory, every one in his own house:

1 or, *did not let his prisoners loose homewards.*

of the king of Babylon after he should be slain—the passers-by arrested with astonishment, that one so proud and haughty was at last slain, and cast out among the common dead (ver. 19). ¶ *Shall narrowly look upon thee.* To be certain that they were not deceived. This denotes great astonishment, as if they could scarcely credit the testimony of their senses. It also expresses insult and contempt. They ask whether it is possible that one who so recently shook the kingdoms of the earth should now lie cast out as unworthy of a burial. ¶ *That made the earth to tremble.* That agitated the world by his ambition. 17. That *made the world as a wilderness.* That made cities and kingdoms desolate. ¶ That *opened not the house of his prisoners.* This is a description of his oppression and cruelty. Of course many prisoners would be taken in war. Instead of giving them liberty,

he threw them into prison and kept them there. This may be rendered, 'his prisoners he did not release that they might return home' (see the Margin). The Chaldee renders it, 'To his prisoners he did not open the door.' The sense is substantially the same. The idea is, that he was cruel and oppressive. He threw his captives into dungeons, and found pleasure in retaining them there. 18. *All the kings of the nations.* That is, this is the common way in which the kings are buried. ¶ *Lie in glory.* They lie in a magnificent mausoleum; they are surrounded with splendour even in their tombs. It is well known that vast sums of money were expended to rear magnificent mausoleums as the burial place of kings. With this design, probably, the pyramids of Egypt were reared; and the temple of Bel in Babylon, we are told, was employed for this purpose. Jose-

THE PYRAMIDS OF GHIZEH, LOWER EGYPT.

phus says that vast quantities of money were buried in the sepulchre of David. The kings of Israel were buried in a

royal burying place on Mount Zion (2 Chron. xxi. 20; xxxv. 24; Neh. iii. 16). For a description of the sepul-

19 But thou art cast out of thy grave like an abominable branch, *and as* the raiment of those that are slain, thrust through with a sword, that go down to the stones of the pit; as a carcase trodden under feet.

20 Thou shalt not be joined with them in burial, because thou hast destroyed thy land, *and* slain thy people: the *a* seed of evil-doers shall never be renowned.

a Job 18.16; Ps.37.28.

chre of David, and of sepulchres in general, *see* Calmet's *Dict.* Art. *Sepulchre* (comp. Ezek. xxxii.) ¶ *Every one in his own house.* In a sepulchre constructed for himself. It was usual for kings to have a splendid tomb constructed for themselves.

19. *But thou art cast out of thy grave.* Thou art not buried like other kings in a magnificent sepulchre, but art cast out like the common dead. This was a mark of the highest infamy (see Isa. xxxiv. 3; Ezek. xxix. 5; Jer. xxii. 19). Nothing was considered more disgraceful than to be denied the privileges of an honourable burial (see Note on ch. liii. 9). On the fulfilment of this prophecy, see Note on ver. 20. ¶ *As an abominable branch* (כְּנֵצֶר נִתְעָב). The LXX. render this, 'And thou shalt be cast upon the mountains as a dead body that is abominable, with many dead that are slain by the sword, descending to Hades.' The Chaldee, 'And thou shalt be cast out of thy sepulchre as a branch that is hid.' Lowth supposes that by 'abominable branch' there is allusion to a tree on which a malefactor was hanged, that was regarded as detestable, and cursed. But there are obvious objections to this interpretation. One is, that the word *branch* (*netzer*) is never applied to a *tree*. It means *a shoot, a slip, a scion* (Note, ch. xi. 1). Another objection is, that there seems here to be no necessary allusion to such a tree; or to anything that would lead to it. Jerome says, that the word *netzer* denotes a shoot or sucker that starts up at the root of a plant or tree, and that is useless to the husbandman, and which he therefore cuts off. So, says he, the king of Babylon shall be cast off—as the farmer throws away the useless sucker. This is probably the correct idea. The word *abominable* means, therefore, not only that which is *useless,* but indicates that the shoot or sucker is *troublesome* to

the husbandman. It is an object that he *hates,* and which he gets clear of as soon as possible. So the king of Babylon would be cast out as useless, hateful, abominable; to be thrown away, as the noxious shoot is, as unfit for use, and unworthy to be preserved. ¶ As *the raiment of those that are slain.* As a garment that is all defiled with gore, and that is cast away and left to rot. The garments of those slain in battle, covered with blood and dirt, would be cast away as polluted and worthless, and so would be the king of Babylon. Among the Hebrews such garments were regarded with peculiar abhorrence (Rosenmüller); perhaps from the dread which they had of touching a dead body, and of course of anything that was found on a dead body. ¶ *Thrust through with a sword.* That is, the slain thrust through. The effect of this was to pollute the garment with blood, and to render it useless. ¶ *That go down to the stones of the pit.* The 'pit' here means the grave or sepulchre (ver. 15). The phrase 'stones of the pit,' conveys the idea that the grave or sepulchre was usually either excavated from the solid rock, or constructed of stones. The idea is simply, that those who were slain with the sword were buried in the usual manner, though their bloody garments defiled were cast away. But the king of Babylon should not have even the honour of such a burial as was given to those who fell in battle. ¶ *As a carcase trodden under foot.* Unburied; as the body of a brute that is exposed to the air, and denied the honour of a sepulchre.

20. *Thou shalt not be joined with them in burial.* That is, even with those who are slain with the sword in battle, and to whom is granted the privilege of a decent burial. ¶ *Hast destroyed thy land.* Hast been a cruel, harsh, and oppressive prince. ¶ *The seed of evil-doers.* The posterity of

21 Prepare slaughter for his children ^a for the iniquity of their fathers; that they do not rise, nor possess the land, nor fill the face of the world with cities.

22 For I will rise up against them, saith the LORD of hosts, and cut off from Babylon the name, and remnant, and son, and nephew, saith the LORD.

---

the wicked. ¶ *Shall never be renowned.* Heb. 'Shall never be called,' or 'named' (לֹא־יִקָּרֵא); that is, shall never be distinguished, celebrated, or honoured. This is a general proposition; but the prophet here possibly designs to apply it to the king of which he is speaking, as having been descended from ancestors that were wicked; or more probably it is a new circumstance, more fully explained in the following verse, that *his* posterity should be cut off from the honour of succeeding him on the throne, and that they, as well as he, should be loaded with disgrace. The design is to affirm the fact that the Babylonian dynasty would end with him; and that his posterity would be reduced from the honours which they had hoped to have inherited. At the same time, the general proposition is applicable not only to the posterity of the king of Babylon, but to all. It is a great truth pertaining to the Divine administration, that the descendants of wicked men shall be dishonoured. So it is with the posterity of a traitor, a pirate, a drunkard, a man of profligacy. They are involved in disgrace, poverty, and calamity, as the result of the sin of their ancestor.

21. *Prepare slaughter for his children.* That is, cut them off not only from inheriting the honour of their father, but from life. This command seems to be directed to the Medes and Persians, and denotes that they *would* thus cut off his children. ¶ *For the iniquity of their fathers.* On account of the crimes of their ancestors—the pride, haughtiness, and oppression of the kings of Babylon. This is the statement of a general principle of the Divine administration, that the consequences of crime often pass over from the perpetrator, and impinge on his descendants (see Ex. xx. 5). ¶ *That they do not rise.* That they do not rise to occupy the places of their fathers; that they be degraded and reduced from

their elevation and honours. ¶ *Nor fill the face of the world with cities.* The LXX. render this, 'And fill the land with wars.' The Chaldee, 'And fill the face of the world with *enemies.*' The Syriac, 'And fill the face of the earth with *war.*' These versions evidently took the word עָרִים (*ârim*) to mean *enemies* or *wars*—a sense which the word sometimes may have. But the common interpretation is to be preferred. The apprehension was, that they would fill the land, if they lived, with such cities of pride, magnificence, and wickedness, as *Babylon* was, and that thus crimes would be multiplied and prolonged; and hence the purpose of God was not only to cut off Babylon—the *model* of all cities of arrogance and pride—but also to cut off those who would be disposed to rear similar cities, and to fill the land again with crime.

22. *For I will rise up against them, saith the* LORD *of hosts.* That is, against the family of the king of Babylon. ¶ *And cut off from Babylon the name.* That is, all the *males* of the royal family, so that the name of the monarch shall become extinct (comp. Ruth iv. 5; Isa. lvi. 5). ¶ *And remnant.* All that is left of them; so that the family shall cease to exist. ¶ *The son and nephew.* Every one of the family who could claim to be an heir of the throne. The dynasty shall cease; and the proud and haughty family shall become wholly extinct. This is the solemn purpose in regard to the *family* of the monarch of Babylon. It only remains to inquire when and how it was fulfilled.

The circumstances which it was said would exist in regard to the king of Babylon here spoken of, are the following:—(1.) That he would be a proud, haughty, and oppressive prince (ver. 17, and throughout the prophecy). (2.) That when he died he would be cast out with the common dead, and denied the common honours of the sepulchre—

especially the honours which all other monarchs have in their burial (ver. 18–20). (3.) That his posterity would be cut off, and that he would have no one to succeed him on his throne; or that the dynasty and the kingdom would terminate in him (ver. 21, 22).

In regard to the application and the fulfilment of this prophecy there have been three opinions.

I. That it does not refer to an *individual* sovereign, but to the kings of Babylon in general; that the description is designed to be applicable to the succession or the dynasty, as signally haughty, proud, and oppressive; and that the prophet means to say that that haughty and wicked reign of kings should cease. To this, the objections are obvious—(1.) The whole aspect and course of the prophet seems to have reference to an *individual*. Such an individual the prophet seems to have constantly in his eye. He descends to *sheol* (ver. 9); he is proud, ambitious, oppressive, cast out; all of which circumstances refer naturally to an individual, and not to a *succession* or dynasty. (2.) The main circumstance mentioned in the prophecy is applicable only to an individual—that he should be *unburied* (ver. 18–21). It was not true of *all* the kings of Babylon that they were unburied, and how could it be said respecting a *succession* or a dynasty at all that it should be cast out of the grave as an abominable branch; and that it should not be joined with others in burial? All the circumstances, therefore, lead us to suppose that the prophet refers to an individual.

II. The Jews, in general, suppose that it refers to Nebuchadnezzar. But to this interpretation, the objections are equally obvious—(1.) It was not true that Nebuchadnezzar had no one to succeed him on the throne; or that his family was totally cut off, as it was foretold of this king of Babylon that his would be (ver. 21, 22). (2.) It was not true that he was denied the privileges of a burial which kings commonly enjoy. To meet this difficulty, the Jews have invented the following story. They say that when Nebuchadnezzar was driven from men during his derangement (Dan. iv.), and when he was with the beasts

of the field seven years, the people made his son, Evil-Merodach, king; but that when Nebuchadnezzar was restored to his right mind and to his throne, he threw Evil-Merodach into prison, where he lay until he died. At the death of Nebuchadnezzar, the people released him to make him king, but he refused because he did not believe that his father was dead, and said that if his father should find him he would kill him; and that in order to convince him that his father was dead he was taken out of the grave. But this is manifestly a fiction. Besides, the prophecy was not that the king should be taken out of the grave, but that he should not be buried. Nebuchadnezzar was succeeded in the kingdom by his son Evil-Merodach, and he by Belshazzar, in whom the line of kings ended.

III. The only other interpretation of which this is susceptible, is that which refers it to Belshazzar, in whose reign the city of Babylon was taken. This king, called in Scripture Belshazzar (Dan. v.), was the son of Evil-Merodach, and the grandson of Nebuchadnezzar. His name, as it occurs in heathen writers, was *Nabonadius*. In him the circumstances of the prophecy agree—(1.) He was an impious prince (Xen. *Cyr.* vii. Dan. v). (2.) In his reign the city and the kingdom came to an end, as it was foretold. (3.) Every circumstance of the taking of Babylon would lead us to suppose that he was denied the privilege of a magnificent sepulture. (*a.*) He was slain in the night (Dan. v. 30). (*b.*) It was in the confusion of the capture of the city—amidst the tumult caused by the sudden and unexpected invasion of Cyrus. It is therefore altogether improbable that he had a regular and an honoured burial. Like the common dead, he would lie in the palace where he fell, or in the street. (*c.*) There is no evidence that Cyrus gave him an honourable sepulchre. (4.) None of his posterity occupied the throne to give honour to the memory of their father. (5.) In him the dynasty and the kingdom ended. Immediately the kingdom on his death was given to the Medes and Persians (Dan. v. 28–31). None of the names of his posterity, if he had any, are known; and God cut off from

23 I will also make it a possession for the bittern and pools of
water; and I will sweep it with the

him 'the name and remnant, the son and
nephew,' as was predicted (see Prideaux's
Connection, i. 2. 257–271, Ed. 1815).

23. *I will also make it a possession
for the bittern.* The word ' bittern,' in
English, means a bird with long legs
and neck, that stalks among reeds and
sedge, feeding upon fish. The Hebrew

THE BITTERN. *(Ardea Stellaries)*

word (קִפֹּד *q'ppōdh*), occurs but five times
(Isa. xxxiv. 11; Zeph. ii. 14). According to Bochart and Gesenius, it means
the hedgehog. It has been variously
rendered. Some have supposed it to be
a land animal; some an aquatic animal;
and most have regarded it as a fowl.
Bochart has proved that the hedgehog
or porcupine is found on the shores of
the Euphrates. He translates this place,
' I will place Babylon for an habitation
of the porcupine, *even* the pools of
water;' that is, the pools that are round
about Babylon shall become so dry that
porcupines may dwell there (see Bochart,
Hieroz. iii. 36. pp. 1036–1042). ¶ *And
pools of water.* Bochart supposes this
means, *even* the pools of water shall become dry. But the common interpretation is to be preferred, that Babylon
itself should become filled with pools of
water. This was done by Cyrus' directing the waters of the Euphrates from

besom of destruction, saith the
LORD of hosts.
24 The LORD of hosts hath sworn,

their channel when the city was taken,
and by the fact that the waters never
returned again to their natural bed, so
that the region was overflowed with
water (see Notes on ch. xiii.) ¶ *And I
will sweep it with the besom of destruction.* A *besom* is a broom; and the
sense here is, that God would entirely
destroy Babylon, and render it wholly
uninhabitable.

24. *The* LORD *of hosts* (see Note on
ch. i. 9). It is evident that this verse
and the three following, is not directly
connected with that which goes before,
respecting Babylon. This pertains to
the Assyrian; that had relation to Babylon. Vitringa says that this is attached to the prophecy respecting Babylon, and is a peculiar yet not altogether
foreign argument, and is a sort of epilogue to the prophecy respecting Babylon. The design, he says, is this. As the
events which had been foretold respecting Babylon seemed so great and wonderful as to be almost incredible, the
prophet, in order to show the Jews how
easily it could be accomplished, refers
them to the case of Sennacherib, and
the ease with which he and his army
had been destroyed. Lowth supposes
that the Assyrians and Babylonians here
are one people. Rosenmüller supposes
that this prophecy respecting Sennacherib has been *displaced* by the collector of the prophecies of Isaiah, and
that it should have been attached to the
prophecy respecting the Assyrian monarch (see ch. x.) The probable sense
of the passage is that which makes it
refer to the predicted destruction of
Sennacherib (ch. x.); and the design of
the prophet in referring to that here is,
to assure the Jews of the certain destruction of Babylon, and to comfort them
with the assurance that they would be
delivered from their captivity there.
The prophecy respecting Babylon was
uttered *before* the destruction of Sennacherib; but it is to be remembered that
its design was to comfort the Jews *in*
Babylon. The prophet therefore throws
himself *beyond* the period of their captivity—though it was to occur many

saying, Surely as I have thought, so shall it come to pass; and as I have purposed, *so* shall it stand;

25 That I will break the Assyrian in my land, and upon my mountains tread him under foot: then *a* shall his yoke depart from off them, and his burden depart from off their shoulders.

26 This *is* the purpose that is purposed, upon the whole earth; and this *is* the hand that is stretched out upon all the nations.

27 For *b* the LORD of hosts hath purposed, and who shall disannul *it?* and his hand *is* stretched out, and who shall turn it back?

a ch.10.27.　　*b* 2 Ch.20.6; Job 23.13; Pr.21.30; Dan.4.35.

---

years *after* the prophecy respecting Babylon was uttered; and with this view he introduces the subject of the Assyrian. At that future time, Sennacherib would have been destroyed. And as God would have fulfilled the prophecy respecting the proud and self-confident Assyrian, so they might have the assurance that he *would* fulfil his predictions respecting the *no less* proud and self-confident king of Babylon; and as he would have delivered his people from the invasion of the Assyrian, even when he was at the gates of Jerusalem, so he *would* deliver them in their captivity in Babylon. ¶ *Hath sworn* (see Gen. xxiv. 7; Ex. xiii. 5, 11; xxxiii. 1; Num. xxxii. 10; Heb. iii. 18; vi. 13). JEHOVAH is often represented as making use of an oath to denote the strong confirmation, the absolute certainty of what he utters. The oath here was designed to comfort the Jews, when they should be in Babylon, with the assurance that what he had thus solemnly promised would assuredly come to pass. ¶ *As I have thought.* As I have designed, or intended. God's promises never fail; his purposes shall all be accomplished (comp. ch. xlvi. 10, 11). This passage is full proof that God does not *change:* that whatever his purposes are, they are inflexible. Change supposes imperfection; and it is often affirmed that God is immutable (1 Sam. xv. 29; Mal. iii. 6; James i. 17.) 25. *That I will break.* That I will break his power; that I will discomfit and destroy his army. ¶ *The Assyrian.* Sennacherib (see ch. x.) ¶ *In my land.* That is, in the land of Canaan. This is often called his land; and this expression shows that the passage does not and cannot refer to the king of Babylon, for he was destroyed in his own city (Dan. v.) ¶ *And upon my mountains.* That is, upon the mountains of Palestine.

The army of Sennacherib was destroyed on the mountains that were near to Jerusalem (see Notes on ch. x. 33, 34). ¶ *Then shall his yoke.* The yoke of the Assyrian (see Note on ch. x. 27).

26. *This* is *the purpose.* This is the sum of the whole design—a design that embraces the destruction both of the king of Assyria, and of Babylon. ¶ *Upon the whole earth.* The successive kingdoms of Assyria and Babylonia embraced the whole earth, and to destroy them would in fact affect all the nations.

27. *For the* LORD *of hosts* (see Note on ch. i. 9). ¶ *Who shall disannul* it? Who has power to defeat his purposes? Difficult as they may be in appearance, and incredible as their fulfilment may seem, yet his purposes are formed in full view of all the circumstances; and there is no power to resist his arm, or to turn him aside from the execution of his designs. By this assurance God designed to comfort his people when they should be in Babylon in a long and dreary captivity (comp. Psal. cxxxvii.) And by the same consideration his people may be comforted at all times. His plans shall stand. None can disannul them. No arm has power to resist him. None of the schemes formed against him shall ever prosper. Whatever ills, therefore, may befall his people; however thick, and gloomy, and sad their calamities may be; and however dark his dispensations may appear, yet they may have the assurance that all his plans are wise, and that they all shall stand. No matter how many, or how mighty may be the foes of the church; no matter how strong their cities, or their ramparts; no matter how numerous their armies, or how self-confident may be their leaders, they have no power to resist God. If *their* plans are in his way they will be thrown down; if revolutions are

28 In the year that *a* king Ahaz died was this burden.

29 Rejoice not thou, whole Palestina, because *b* the rod of him that

a 2 Ki.16.20.   *b* 2 Ch.26.6.

needful among men to accomplish *his* purposes, they will be brought about ; if cities and armies need to be destroyed in order that *his* plans may succeed, and his church be safe, they will be demolished, just as the army of Sennacherib was laid pale in death, and as Babylon—the haughtiest of cities—was overthrown. Who can stand against God? and who can resist the execution of his will?

28. *In the year that king Ahaz died.* This is the caption or title to the following prophecy, which occupies the remainder of this chapter. This prophecy has no connection with the preceding ; and should have been separated from it in the division into chapters. It relates solely to Philistia ; and the design is to comfort the Jews with the assurance that they had nothing to apprehend from them. It is not to call the Philistines to lamentation and alarm, for there is no evidence that the prophecy was promulgated among them (Vitringa); but it is to assure the Jews that they would be in no danger from their invasion under the reign of the successor of Ahaz, and that God would more signally overthrow and subdue them than had been done in his time. It is not improbable that at the death of Ahaz, and with the prospect of a change in the government on the accession of his successor, the Philistines, the natural enemies of Judah, had meditated the invasion of the Jews. The Philistines had been subdued in the time of Azariah (2 Kings xv. 1–7), or Uzziah, as he is called in 2 Chron. xxvi. 1, who was the son and successor of Amaziah. He broke down the wall of Gath, and the wall of Gabneh, and the wall of Ashdod, and effectually subdued and humbled them (2 Chron. xxvi. 6). In the time of Ahaz, and while he was engaged in his unhappy controversies with Syria and Ephraim, the Philistines took advantage of the enfeebled state of Judah, and made successful war on it, and took several of the towns (2 Chron. xxviii. 18); and at his death they had

smote thee is broken : for out of the serpent's root shall come forth a cockatrice,[1] and his fruit *c shall be* a fiery flying serpent.

[1] or, *adder.*   *c* 2 Ki.18.3.

hope of being able to resist Judah, perhaps the more so as they apprehended that the reign of Hezekiah would be mild, peaceable, and unwarlike. Isaiah, in the prophecy before us, warns them not to entertain any such fallacious expectations, and assures them that his reign would be quite as disastrous to them as had been the reign of his predecessors. ¶ *Was this burden* (see Note on ch. xiii. 1).

29. *Rejoice not thou.* Rejoice not at the death of Ahaz, king of Judah. It shall be no advantage to thee. It shall not be the means of making an invasion on Judah more practicable. ¶ *Whole Palestina.* We apply the name *Palestine* to the whole land of Canaan. Formerly, the name referred only to Philistia, from which we have derived the name *Palestine.* The word פְּלֶשֶׁת (*Peleshĕth*) means properly the land of sojourners or strangers, from פָּלַשׁ (*pălăsh*), *to rove about, to wander, to migrate.* The LXX. render it, 'Αλλοφυλοι—' Strangers,' or ' Foreigners,' and Γῆ ἀλλοφύλων—'Land of strangers.' Philistia was situated on the south-western side of the land of Canaan, extending along the Mediterranean Sea from Gaza on the south, to Lydda on the north. The Philistines were a powerful people, and had often been engaged in wars with Judah. They had made a successful attack on it in the time of Ahaz ; and amidst the feebleness and distractions which they supposed might succeed on the change of the government of Judah, and the administration of an inexperienced prince like Hezekiah, they hoped to be still more successful, and would naturally rejoice at the death of Ahaz. When the prophet says '*whole* Palestina,' he means to say that no part of Philistia would have occasion to rejoice at the succession of Hezekiah (see ver. 31). ¶ *Because the rod of him that smote thee is broken.* It was not true that they had been smitten during the reign of Ahaz, but it had been done by his predecessor Uzziah. Perhaps the prophet refers to

30 And the first-born of the poor shall feed, and the needy shall lie down in safety: and I will kill thy root with famine, and he shall slay thy remnant.

31 Howl, O gate; cry, O city;

that prince, and to his death. He had smitten and subdued them. At his death they would rejoice; and their joy had been continued during the reigns of Jotham and Ahaz. They would now rejoice the more that a young and inexperienced prince was to ascend the throne. Their joy had been that *Uzziah* had died, and that joy had been augmenting since his death. But the prophet now tells them that they will have no further occasion for such joy. ¶ *For out of the serpent's root.* That is, there shall spring forth from the serpent, or shall succeed the serpent, as a shoot or sprout springs from the root of a decayed tree (see Note on ch. xi. 1). By the serpent here, is undoubtedly intended king Uzziah, who had so severely chastised the Philistines. The word 'serpent' (נָחָשׁ) denotes a serpent of any kind, and usually one far less venomous than that which is meant by the word translated cockatrice. Probably the prophet does not give this name *serpent* to Uzziah or to Ahaz, or the name *cockatrice* to Hezekiah, because *he* regarded the names as properly descriptive of their character, but because they were so regarded by the Philistines. They were as odious and offensive to them, and as destructive of their plans, as venomous reptiles would be. ¶ *Shall come forth a cockatrice* (see Note on ch. lix. 5). A basilisk, or adder, a serpent of most venomous nature (see Note on ch. xi. 8). That is, though Uzziah is dead, yet there shall spring up from him one far more destructive to you than he was; one who shall carry the desolations of war much further, and who shall more effectually subdue you. Most commentators have concurred in supposing that Hezekiah is here referred to, who 'smote the Philistines even unto Gaza and the borders thereof, from the tower of the watchmen to the fenced city' (2 Kings xviii. 8). This is, doubtless, the correct interpretation. The Chaldee renders it, however, 'Because there shall proceed from the descendants of Jesse the Messiah, and his works shall be among

you as a flying serpent.' This interpretation Rosenmüller supposes is correct; but it is evidently foreign to the scope of the passage.

30. *And the first-born of the poor shall feed.* That is, there shall be safety to those parts of Judah which have long been exposed to the invasions of the Philistines. Philistia bordered on Judea, and was constantly making wars upon it, so that there was no safety felt. Isaiah now says, that Hezekiah would so effectually and completely subdue them that there should be no danger from their invasion. The phrase 'the first-born of the poor' is an Hebraism, a strong, emphatic expression, denoting those who are the most poor; the most abject sons of poverty; those who have an eminence or a double portion of want, as the first-born among the Hebrews were entitled to peculiar distinctions and privileges. The idea is, that even the most poor and defenceless would be safe. ¶ *Shall feed.* That is, they shall be supplied with food; they shall feed safely as a flock does that is guarded from wild beasts. They shall be no longer alarmed, but shall dwell in security, peace, and plenty. ¶ *And I will kill thy root.* The word rendered 'root' denotes properly the root of a plant, which being dried up or killed, the plant of course withers and dies. So God says that he would effectually and entirely destroy the power of the Philistines. ¶ *Slay thy remnant.* That is, shall slay all that appertains to thee. Or, he shall dry up the root, and the branches shall wither and die also. The whole power of the nation shall be withered and destroyed.

31. *Howl, O gate.* That is, ye who throng the gate. The *gates* of a city were the chief places of concourse. ¶ *Cry, O city.* The prophet here fixes the attention upon some principal city of Philistia, and calls upon it to be alarmed in view of the judgments that were about to come upon the whole land. ¶ *Art dissolved.* The word 'dissolved' (מוּג) is applied to that which melts, or which wastes away gradually, and then

thou, whole Palestina, *art* dissolved: for there shall come from the north a smoke, and ¹none *shall be* alone in his ²appointed times.

32 What shall *one* then answer

1 or, he shall *not.*   2 or, *assemblies.*

the messengers of the nation? That *ᵃ* the LORD hath founded Zion, and the *ᵇ* poor of his people shall 3 trust in it.

a Ps.87.1-6.   b Zep.3.12.

3 *betake themselves unto.*

---

to that which faints or disappears. It means here that the kingdom of Philistia would disappear, or be destroyed. It probably conveys the idea of its fainting, or becoming feeble from fear or apprehension. ¶ *From the north a smoke.* From the regions of Judah, which lay north and east of Philistia. The 'smoke' here probably refers to a cloud of dust that would be seen to rise in that direction made by an invading army. ¶ *And none* shall be *alone in his appointed times.* There has been a great variety of interpretation in regard to this passage. Lowth renders it, 'And there shall not be a straggler among his levies.' The Hebrew is, as in the margin, 'And not solitary in his assemblies.' The LXX. render it, Καὶ οὐκ ἔσται τοῦ εἶναι—'And it is not to be endured.' The Chaldee, 'And there shall be none who shall retard him in his times.' The Arabic, 'Neither is there any one who can stand in his footsteps.' The Vulgate, 'Neither is there any one who can escape his army.' Aben Ezra renders it, 'No one of the Philistines shall dare to remain in their palaces, as when a smoke comes into a house all are driven out.' Probably the correct idea is given by Lowth; and the same interpretation is given by Gesenius, Rosenmüller, Dathe, and Michaelis. No one of the invading army of Hezekiah shall come by himself; no one shall be weary or be a straggler: the army shall advance in close military array, and in dense columns; and this is represented as the cause of the cloud or smoke that the prophet saw rising, the cloud of dust that was made by the close ranks of the invading host (comp. Isa. v. 27).

32. *What shall one then answer.* The design of this verse is obvious. It is to show that Judea would be safe from the invasions of the Philistines, and that God was the protector of Zion. For this purpose the prophet refers to messengers or ambassadors who should be sent for any purpose to Jerusalem, either

to congratulate Hezekiah, or to form an alliance with the Jews. The prophet asks what answer or information should be given to such messengers when they came respecting their state? The reply is, that JEHOVAH had evinced his purpose to protect his people. ¶ *Of the nation.* Of any nation whose ambassadors should be sent into Judea. ¶ *That the LORD hath founded Zion.* That he is its original founder, and that he has now shown his regard for it by protecting it from the Philistines. It would be safe from their attacks, and JEHOVAH would thus show that he had it under his own protection. The LXX. render this, 'And what shall the kings of the Gentiles then answer? That the Lord hath founded Zion.' The scope of the passage is the assurance that Zion would be safe, being founded and preserved by JEHOVAH; and that the Philistines had no cause of triumph at the death of Ahaz, since God would still be the protector of his people. The doctrine established by this passage is, that in all the changes which take place by the death of kings, princes, magistrates, and ministers; and in all the revolutions which occur in kingdoms, the enemies of the people of God have no cause for rejoicing. God is the protector of his church; and he will show that he has founded Zion, and that his people are safe. No weapon that is formed against his people shall prosper, and the gates of hell shall not prevail against his church. ¶ *Shall trust in it.* In Zion. It was a strongly fortified city, God was its protector, and in times of calamity his people could betake themselves there in safety. In this strong place the most weak and defenceless—the poorest of the people, would be safe. In the church of God, the poor are the objects of as deep regard as the rich; the humble, the meek, the weak, the feeble, are there safe, and no power of an enemy can reach or affect them. God is their defender and their friend; and in his arms they are secure.

CHAPTER XV.

ANALYSIS OF CHAPTERS XV., XVI.

§ I. *The time of the prophecy.*

THIS and the following chapter make one entire prophecy, and should not have been divided. At what time it was delivered is unknown. The only period which is designated is, that it was to be fulfilled in three years from the time when it was uttered (ch. xvi. 14). Lowth supposes that it was delivered soon after the former, in the first years of the reign of Hezekiah, and that it was fulfilled in the fourth year of his reign, when Shalmanezer invaded the kingdom of Israel. He supposes that he might have marched through Moab, and secured its strong places on his way to Judea. Gesenius supposes that it was uttered by some contemporary of Isaiah, or by some earlier prophet, without the epilogue (ch. xvi. 14), as a general denunciation against Moab; and that it was adopted by Isaiah and applied to the Moabites during his own time. This he argues because of the repetition of geographical names; the play upon those names; the roughness and harshness of the expressions; and many favourite phrases which, he says, are foreign to 'the genuine Isaiah.' He supposes that it had its origin in the national animosity which subsisted between the Jews and the Moabites; and that it might have been composed on account of the tribute which had been withheld, B.C. 896; or on account of the corruption of the Moabites, B.C. 949; or on the taking possession of the territory by Reuben and Gad. But this is evidently conjectural. It is fair to presume that it is a production of Isaiah himself, unless it can be proved that he did not write it; and the argument from the style, to prove that it was written by some other person than Isaiah, does not seem to be sufficient. It *may* have been written by Isaiah at an early period of his life, and subsequently incorporated into his prophecies, and adapted by himself to a state of things existing in an advanced period of his prophetic life (see Note on ch. xvi. 14). Compare, however, the arguments of Gesenius in his Commentary, and in the *Bib. Rep.*, vol. vii. pp. 120, 121. It is *certain* that it was composed when the tribute was withheld from Judah which was due from the Moabites (see ch. xvi. 1).

§ II. *History of Moab.*

THE land of Moab, so called from Moab the son of Lot, by his eldest daughter (Gen. xix. 31–37), was situated on the east side of the river Jordan, and adjacent to the Dead Sea, and on both sides of the river Arnon, although, strictly and properly speaking, the river Arnon was re-

garded as its northern boundary. Its capital city was on the river Arnon. The first residence of Lot, after fleeing from Sodom, was *Zoar* (Gen. xix. 30), on the south-east of the Dead Sea; from thence he removed into the mountainous region where his two sons were born (Gen. xix. 30). The country was originally occupied by a race of giants called *Emim* (Deut. ii. 10), whom the Moabites conquered and expelled. A considerable part of this country was subsequently conquered by Sihon, king of the Amorites, who made the Arnon the boundary of the land of Moab, and Heshbon his capital (Num. xxi. 26; comp. Num. xxi. 13; Judg. xi. 18). The Israelites passed by their land in journeying to Canaan, without distressing or embarrassing them; because God had said that he had given 'Ar to the children of Lot for a possession' (Deut. ii. 9). But the adjacent region in the possession of the Amorites, the Israelites took, after a signal victory, and gave to the tribes of Reuben and Gad (Num. xxi. 31–35). Thus the territory of the Jews, being bounded by the river Arnon, was adjacent to that of Moab. It is evident, however, though the Arnon was the proper boundary of Moab, yet that a considerable portion of country on the north of that river was usually regarded as lying in the land of Moab, though strictly within the limits of the territory formerly of the Amorites, and subsequently of the tribes of Reuben and Gad. Thus mount Nebo is said to be in the land of Moab (Deut. xxxii. 49; xxxiv. 1), though it was properly within the limits of the Amorites. And thus many of the places in the prophecy before us were on the north of that river, though specified as in the country of Moab. It is probable that the boundary was never regarded as permanently fixed, though the river Arnon was its natural and usual limit.

There was always a great antipathy between the Jews and the Moabites, and they were the natural and constant enemies of the Jewish nation. The foundation of the enmity was laid far back in their history. Balaam seduced the Israelites to sin by means of the daughters of Moab (Num. xxv. 1, 2); and God ordered that this people should not enter into the congregation of his people, or be capable of office, to the tenth generation, because they had the inhumanity to refuse the children of Israel a passage through their land in their journey to Canaan (Deut. xxiii. 3).

Eglon, king of the Moabites, was the first who oppressed Israel after the death of Joshua. Ehud killed him and subdued the Moabites (Judg. iii. 21). Toward the end of this period, however, peace and friendship were restored, mutual honours were reciprocated, as the history of Ruth shows, and Moab appears to have been a place of refuge for outcasts and emigrant Hebrews (Ruth i. 1; 1 Sam. xxii. 3; Jer. xl. 11; Isa. xvi. 3). David subdued Moab and Ammon, and made them tributary (2 Sam. viii. 2-12; xxiii. 20). The right to levy this tribute seems to have been transferred to Israel after the division of the kingdom; for after the death of Ahab, they refused to pay the customary tribute of 100,000 lambs and as many rams (2 Kings i. 1; iii. 4; Isa. xvi. 1). Soon after the death of Ahab they began to revolt (2 Kings iii. 4, 5). They were subsequently engaged in wars with the Jews. Amos (i. 13, *sq.*) denounced great calamities on them, which they probably suffered under Uzziah and Jotham, kings of Judah (2 Chron. xxvi. 7, 8; xxvii. 5). Calmet supposes that they were carried captive by Nebuchadnezzar beyond the Euphrates, as the prophets had threatened (Jer. ix. 26; xii. 14, 15; xxv. 11, 12; xlviii. 47; xlix. 3, 6, 39; l. 16); and that they were restored by Cyrus to their land, as many other captive nations were. It is probable that, in the latter times, they were subject to the Asmonean kings, and finally to Herod the Great.—(Robinson; Calmet.) It is remarkable that Jeremiah has introduced much of this chapter into his prophecy in his 48th chapter.

§ III. *Comparison of Isaiah with Jeremiah.*

In order to see the resemblance between the two prophecies, I insert here a comparison of the corresponding parts, following the order of Isaiah.

ISAIAH XV.	JEREMIAH XLVIII.
2. On all their heads shall be baldness, And every beard cut off.	37. For every head shall be bald, And every beard clipped. Upon all the hands shall be cuttings, And upon the loins sackcloth.
3. In their streets they shall gird themselves with sackcloth; On the tops of their houses, and in their streets, every one shall howl.	38. There shall be lamentations, generally, upon the housetops of Moab, and in the streets thereof.
4. And Heshbon shall cry, and Elealeh; Their voice shall be heard unto Jahaz: Therefore the armed soldiers of Moab shall cry out: His life shall be grievous unto him.	34. From the cry of Heshbon even unto Elealeh And unto Jahaz have they uttered their voice.
5. His fugitives shall flee unto Zoar, an heifer of three years old; For by the mounting up of Luhith with weeping shall they go it up; For in the way of Horonaim they shall raise up a cry of destruction.	34. From Zoar even unto Horonaim, As an heifer of three years old; For in the going up of Luhith, Continual weeping shall go up.
	3. A voice of crying shall be from Horonaim.
	5. For in the going down of Horonaim, The enemies have heard a cry of destruction
6. For the waters of Nimrim shall be desolate.	34. For the waters also of Nimrim shall be desolate.
7. Therefore the abundance they have gotten, And that which they have laid up, Shall they carry away to the brook of the willows.	36. Because the riches that he hath gotten is perished.
[3, 9; xvi. 1-5, are wanting in Jeremiah.]	
xvi. 6. We have heard of the pride of Moab; He is very proud; Even his haughtiness, and his pride, and his wrath; But his lies shall not be so.	29. We have heard of the pride of Moab; he is exceeding proud; His loftiness and his arrogancy, And his pride and the haughtiness of his heart:
	30. I know his wrath, saith the Lord; But it shall not be so: His lies shall not so effect it.
7. Therefore shall Moab howl for Moab, Every one shall howl: For the foundation of Kir-hareseth shall ye mourn; Surely are they stricken.	31. Therefore will I howl for Moab, And I will cry out for all Moab; Mine heart shall mourn for the men of Kir-heres.
8. As to the vine of Sibmah, the lords of the heathen have broken down the principal plants thereof; They have come even unto Jazer, They wandered through the wilderness; Her branches are stretched out, They are gone over the sea.	32. O vine of Sibmah! Thy plants are gone over the sea; They reach even unto the sea of Jazer.

9. Therefore I will bewail with the weeping of
   Jazer, the vine of Sibmah;
   For the shouting of thy summer fruits,
   And for thy harvest is fallen.

10. And gladness is taken away, and joy out of
    the plentiful field;
    The treaders shall tread out no wine in their
    presses;
    I have made their vintage-shouting to cease.

11. Wherefore my bowels shall sound like an
    harp for Moab.
    And mine inward parts for Kir-haresh.

§ IV. *Moab after the exile.*

AFTER the exile, intimate connections took
place between the Jews and the Moabites by
marriages (Ezra ix. 1, *sq.*; Neh. xiii. 1). These
marriages, however, were dissolved by Ezra as
being, in his view, contrary to the law of Moses.
In the time of the Maccabees little mention is
made of them (comp. Dan. xi. 41); but Josephus
mentions them in the history of Alexander Jan-
næus. Heshbon and Nadaba, Lemba and
Oronas, Gelithon and Zara, cities of Moab, are
there mentioned as being at that time in the
possession of the Jews (Jos. *Ant.* xiii. 15. 4).
After that, their name is lost under that of the
Arabians, as was also the case with Edom and
Ammon. At the time of Abulfeda, Moab proper, south of the river Arnon, bore the name of
Karrak, from the city of that name (comp. Note
on ch. xv. 1); the territory north of the Arnon,
the name of Belka, which includes also the
country of the Amorites. Since that time the
accounts of the country are exceedingly meagre,
and it is only until quite recently that the state
of Moab has attracted the attention of travellers.
It has been ranged and ravaged by the predatory tribes of Arabs, and, through fear of them,
few travellers have ventured to visit it. In
February and March, 1806, however, Mr. Seetz-
en, not without danger of losing his life, undertook a tour from Damascus down to the south
of the Jordan and the Dead Sea, and thence to
Jerusalem; and, in his journey, threw much
unexpected light on the prophecy before us,
especially in regard to the places here mentioned. He found a multitude of places, or the
ruins of places, still bearing the old names, and
thus has set bounds to the perfectly arbitrary
designations of the old maps. In September
1812, that distinguished German traveller, I. L.
Burckhardt, made the same tour from Damascus
down to Karrak, whence he pursued his journey
over Wady Mousa, or Petra, and thence to Cairo
in Egypt. In 1818, a company of intelligent
English travellers (Bankes, Irby, Mangles, and
Legh), made a journey from Karrak to the land
of the Edomites, particularly to Petra, and

32. O vine of Sibmah!
    I will weep for thee with the weeping of Jazer:
    The spoiler is fallen upon thy summer fruits
    and upon thy vintage.

33. And joy and gladness is taken from the plen-
    tiful field, and from the land of Moab;
    And I have caused wine to fail from the
    wine presses;
    None shall tread with shouting;
    Their shouting shall be no shouting.

36. Therefore my heart shall sound for Moab
    like pipes;
    And mine heart shall sound like pipes for
    the men of Kir-heres.

thence back, on the other side of the Jordan, to
Tiberius. In some respects they confirmed,
and, in others, extended the accounts of Seetzen
(see Gesenius' *Commentary*). In the Notes on
these chapters, I have endeavoured to embody
the principal information found in these writers
on the topography of Moab.

§ V. *Analysis of this prophecy.*

'THE prophecy,' says Prof. Stuart (*Bib. Rep.*,
vii. 110), 'is a piece replete with vivid description, with animated and impassioned thought,
with poetic diction, and with scenes which are
adapted to make a deep impression on the mind
of the reader.' The prophecy in the two chapters contains the following parts:—

I. The capitals of Moab are destroyed suddenly in one night (ch. xv. 1).

II. In the midst of the consternation, the
people hasten to the high places, and to the
altars and temples of the gods, to implore protection. They are seen in the streets with sackcloth, and on the tops of the houses, crying out
with loud lamentations, and every expression
of sorrow and despair (xv. 2–4).

III. Some of the fugitives flee to Zoar for protection, and others to Luhith and Horonaim,
hastening to countries beyond their own borders, because everything in their own land was
withered and dried up (xv. 5–7).

IV. Consternation and desolation are spread
throughout the land, and even the streams are
full of blood, and wild beasts are seen coming
up upon the land (xv. 8, 9).

V. The prophet pities them, weeps with them
(xv. 5; xvi. i. 11), and advises them to seek the
favour of Judah by sending to them the customary tribute which was due, and which had
been for a long time withheld (xvi. 1).

VI. Some of the fugitives are seen at the
fords of Arnon endeavouring to escape to Judea,
and making supplication for reception, and imploring blessings on the land (xvi. 2–6). But
see the Notes on ch. xvi. 2–7, for another view of
the design of this passage. The view here given
is that suggested by Gesenius and Prof. Stuart.

VII. They are repulsed, and the answer to their supplication is given in such a tone as to show the deep sense of the injury received from Moab which the Jewish people entertained (xvi. 7).

VIII. The prophet then proceeds in his description of the utter wasting of the country of Moab—desolation which excited the deepest feelings in his heart, and so great as to move his most tender compassion (xvi. 8–12).

CHAPTER XV.

1. *The burden of Moab* (see Note on ch. xiii. 1). This is the *title* of the prophecy. The Chaldee renders this, 'The burden of the cup of malediction which is to come upon Moab.' ¶ *Because in the night.* The fact that this was to be done in the night denotes the *suddenness* with which the calamity would come upon them. Thus the expression is used in Job to denote the suddenness and surprise with which calamities come:

Terrors take hold on him as waters,
A tempest stealeth him away in the night.
　　　　　　　　　Job xxvii. 20.

So a thief is represented as coming in the night—in a sudden and unexpected manner (Job xxiv. 14):

The murderer in the night is as a thief.

See also Matt. xxiv. 43; 1 Thess. v. 2; 2 Pet. iii. 10; Rev. iii. 3; xvi. 15. ¶ *Ar of Moab.* This was the capital of Moab. It was situated on the south of the river Arnon. It was sometimes called *Rabbath Moab.* Isaiah (ch. xvi. 7–11) calls it the city 'with walls of burnt brick.' Under the name of Areopolis it occurs in Eusebius and Stephen of Byzantium, and in the acts of many Synods of the fifth and sixth centuries, when it was the seat of a bishop (Reland's *Palestine,* pp. 577, 578). Abulfeda says that in his time it was a small town. Jerome says that the city was destroyed by an earthquake when he was young, probably about A.D. 315. Burckhardt found a place called Rabba about twenty miles south of the river Arnon, which he supposed to be the ancient Ar. Seetzen found there ruins of considerable compass; especially the ruins of an old palace or temple, of which portions of the wall and some pillars are still standing. Legh says, 'There are no traces of fortifications to be seen; but, upon an eminence, were a dilapidated Roman

IX. Then follows a limitation of the time when all this would take place. Within three years all this would be fulfilled (xvi. 13, 14).

THE [a] burden of Moab. Because in the night Ar of Moab is laid waste, *and* brought [1] to silence; because in the night Kir of Moab is laid waste, *and* brought to silence;

a Jer.48; Eze.25.8–11; Amos 21.3.　　1 or, *cut off.*

temple and some tanks.' ¶ *Is laid waste.* That is, is about to be laid waste. This passed before the mind of Isaiah in a vision, and he represents it as it appeared to him, as already a scene of desolation. ¶ And *brought to silence.* Marg. 'Cut off.' The word may mean either. The sense is, that the city was to be destroyed, for so the word דָּמָה (*dâmâ*) often means (Hos. iv. 5, 6; x. 7, 15; Jer. vi. 2; xlvii. 5; Zeph. i. 11). ¶ *Kir of Moab.* Probably this city was the modern *Kerek* or *Karak.* The Chaldee renders it by the name כְּרַכָּא (*Kĕrăkkâ*), or 'fortress,' hence the name *Kerek* or *Karak.* According to Burckhardt, it lies about three hours, and according to Abulfeda twelve Arabic miles, south of Ar Moab, upon a very high and steep rocky hill, from which the prospect extends even to Jerusalem, and which, formed by nature for a fortress, overlooks the whole surrounding country. In the wars of the Maccabees (2 Macc. xii. 17) it is mentioned under the name of Κάρακα (*Karaka*), and it is now known by the name of *Kerek* or *Karak.* In the time of the crusades, a heathen prince built there under king Fulco (in the year 1131) a very important castle, which was very serviceable to the Franks, and in 1183 it held out successfully against a formidable siege of a month by Saladin. Abulfeda speaks of it as so strong a fortress that one must abandon even the wish to take it. It has been visited in modern times by Seetzen, Burckhardt, and the company of English travellers referred to above. The place has still a castle, into which the whole surrounding country brings its grain for safe keeping. The small and poor town is built upon the remains of once important edifices, and is inhabited by Moslems and Christians. It is the seat of a bishop, though the

2 He is gone up to Bajith, and to Dibon, the high places, to weep: Moab shall howl over Nebo, and over Medeba: on all their heads *shall be* baldness, *and* every beard cut off.

---

bishop resides at Jerusalem (see Gesenius, *Comm. in loc.*)

2. *He is gone up.* That is, the inhabitants of Moab in consternation have fled from their ruined cities, and have gone up to other places to weep. ¶ *To Bajith, and to Dibon.* Lowth supposes that these two words should be joined together, and that one place is denoted. The Chaldee renders it, 'Ascend into the houses of Dibon.' Kimchi supposes that the word (בַּיִת) denotes a temple. It usually means *house*, and hence may mean a temple of the gods; that is, the principal *house* in the land. This interpretation is adopted by Gesenius and Noyes. Vitringa supposes it to mean Beth-Meon (Jer. xlviii. 24), or Beth-Baal-Meon (Josh. xiii. 17), north of the Arnon, now *Macin*. I have adopted the translation proposed by Kimchi as better expressing the sense in my view than that which makes it a proper name. Dibon, perhaps the same place as Dimon in ver. 9, was a city given by Moses to Gad, and afterwards yielded to Reuben (Num. xxxii. 3, 33, 34; Josh. xiii. 9). It was again occupied by the Moabites (Jer. xlviii. 18, 22). Eusebius says it was a large town on the north of the river Arnon. Seetzen found there ruins under the name of Dibân in a magnificent plain. Hence *Dibon* is here appropriately described as *going up* from a plain to weep; and the passage may be rendered, 'Dibon is weeping upon the high places.' ¶ *To weep.* Over the sudden desolation which has come upon the principal cities. ¶ *Moab shall howl over Nebo.* Nebo was one of the mountains on the east of the Jordan. It was so high that from it an extended view could be taken of the land of Canaan opposite. It was distinguished as being the place where Moses died (Deut. xxii. 49; xxxiv. 1). The meaning of this is, that *on* mount Nebo, Moab should lift up the voice of wailing. Jerome says that the idol Chamos, the principal idol of Moab, was on mount Nebo, and that this was the place of its worship. This mountain was near the northern extremity of the Dead Sea. Mount Nebo was completely barren when Burckhardt passed over it, and the site of the ancient city had not been ascertained (*Travels in Syria*, p. 370.) On its summit, says Burckhardt, was a heap of stones overshadowed by a very large wild pistacia tree. At a short distance below, to the south-west, is the ruined place called Kereyat. ¶ *And over Medeba.* This was a city east of the Jordan in the southern part of the territory allotted to Reuben. It was taken from the Reubenites by the Moabites. Burckhardt describes the ruins of this town, which still bears the same name. He says of it, it is 'built upon a round hill; but there is no river near it. It is at least half an hour in circumference. I observed many remains of private houses, constructed with blocks of silex; but not a single edifice is standing. There is a large birket [tank, or cistern], which, as there is no spring at Medeba, might be still of use to the Bedouins, were the surrounding ground cleared of the rubbish to allow the water to flow into it; but such an undertaking is far beyond the views of the wandering Arab. On the west side of the town are the foundations of a temple built with large stones, and apparently of great antiquity. A part of its eastern wall remains, constructed in the same style as the castle wall at Ammon. At the entrance to one of the courts stand two columns of the Doric order. In the centre of one of the courts is a large well.'—(*Travels in Syria*, pp. 366, 367.) ¶ *On all their heads* shall be *baldness*, &c. To cut off the hair of the head and the beard was expressive of great grief. It is well known that the Orientals regard the beard with great sacredness and veneration, and that they usually dress it with great care. Great grief was usually expressed by striking external acts. Hence they lifted up the voice in wailing; they hired persons to howl over the dead; they rent their garments; and for the same reason, in times of great

3 In their streets they shall gird themselves with sackcloth: on the tops of their houses, and in their

1 *descending into weeping,* or, *coming down with weeping.*

streets, every one shall howl, 1 weeping abundantly.

4 And Heshbon shall cry, and Elealeh; their voice shall be heard *even* unto Jahaz: therefore the

calamity or grief, they cut off the hair, and even the beard. Herodotus (ii. 36) speaks of it as a custom among all nations, except the Egyptians, to cut off the hair as a token of mourning. So also Homer says, that on the death of Patroclus they cut off the hair as expressive of grief (*Iliad,* xxiii. 46, 47) :

Next these a melancholy band appear,
Amidst lay dead Patroclus on a bier;
O'er all the course their scattered locks they
    threw.   *Pope.*

See also *Odyss.* iv. 197. This was also the custom with the Romans (Ovid. *Amor.* 3, 5, 12); the Egyptians (Diod. i. 84); the Scythians (Herod. iv. 71); and the modern Cretans. The *principle* on which this is done is, that thereby they are deprived of what is esteemed the most beautiful ornament of the body ; an idea which lies at the foundation of mourning in all countries and ages. The loss of the beard, also, was the highest calamity, and would be expressive of the deepest grief. 'It is,' says D'Arvieux, who has devoted a chapter to the exposition of the sentiments of the Arabs in regard to the *beard,* 'a greater mark of infamy in Arabia to cut a man's beard off, than it is with us to whip a fellow at the cart's tail, or to burn him in the hand. Many people in that country would far rather die than incur that punishment. I saw an Arab who had received a musket shot in the jaw, and who was determined rather to perish than to allow the surgeon to cut his beard off to dress his wound. His resolution was at length overcome ; but not until the wound was beginning to gangrene. He never allowed himself to be seen while his beard was off; and when at last he got abroad, he went always with his face covered with a black veil, that he might not be seen without a beard ; and this he did till his beard had grown again to a considerable length.'—(*Pic. Bib.,* vol. ii. p. 109.) Burckhardt also remarks, that the Arabs who have, from any cause, had the misfortune to lose

their beards invariably conceal themselves from view until their beards are grown again (comp. Isa. iii. 24; xxii. 12; Jer. xli. 5; Micah i. 16). The idea is, that the Moabites would be greatly afflicted. Jeremiah has stated the same thing of Moab (xlviii. 37):

For every head shall be bald, and every beard
    be clipt;
And upon all hands shall be cuttings,
And upon the loins sackcloth.

3. *In their streets.* Publicly. Everywhere there shall be lamentation and grief. Some shall go into the streets, and some on the tops of the houses. ¶ *They shall gird themselves with sackcloth.* The common token of mourning ; and also worn usually in times of humiliation and fasting. It was one of the outward acts by which they expressed deep sorrow (Gen. xxxvii. 34 ; 2 Sam. iii. 31 ; 1 Kings xxi. 27 ; 2 Kings xix. 1 ; Job xvi. 15 ; Note on ch. iii. 24). ¶ *On the tops of the houses.* The roofs of the houses in the East were, and still are, made flat, and were places of resort for prayer, for promenade, &c. The prophet here says, that all the usual places of resort would be filled with weeping and mourning. In the streets, and on the roofs of the houses, they would utter the voice of lamentation. ¶ *Shall howl.* It is known that, in times of calamity in the East, it is common to raise an unnatural and forced howl, or long-continued shriek. Persons are often hired for this purpose (Jer. ix. 17). ¶ *Weeping abundantly.* Heb. 'Descending into weeping ;' *i.e.,* going, as we would say, *deep into it,* or weeping much ; immersed as it were in tears (comp. Jer. xiii. 17; xiv. 17).

4. *And Heshbon shall cry.* This was a celebrated city of the Amorites, twenty miles east of the Jordan (Josh. xiii. 17). It was formerly conquered from the Moabites by Sihon, and became his capital, and was taken by the Israelites a little before the death of Moses (Num. xxi. 25). After the carrying away of the ten tribes it was re-

armed soldiers of Moab shall cry out; his life shall be grievous unto him.

5 My ^aheart shall cry out for

a ch.16.11.

Moab;[1] his fugitives *shall flee* unto Zoar, an heifer of three years old: for by the mounting up of Luhith with weeping shall they go it up;

1 or, *to the borders thereof, even as an heifer.*

---

covered by the Moabites. Jeremiah (xlviii. 2) calls it 'the pride of Moab.' The town still subsists under the same name, and is described by Burckhardt. He says, it is situated on a hill, south-west from El Aal [Elealeh]. 'Here are the ruins of an ancient town, together with the remains of some edifices built with small stones; a few broken shafts of columns are still standing, a number of deep wells cut in the rock, and a large reservoir of water for the summer supply of the inhabitants.' —(*Travels in Syria*, p. 365.) ¶ *And Elealeh.* This was a town of Reuben about a mile from Heshbon (Num. xxxii. 37). Burckhardt visited this place. Its present name is El Aal. 'It stands on the summit of a hill, and takes its name from its situation—Aal, meaning "the high." It commands the whole plain, and the view from the top of the hill is very extensive, comprehending the whole of the southern Belka. El Aal was surrounded by a well built wall, of which some parts yet remain. Among the ruins are a number of large cisterns, fragments of walls, and the foundations of houses, but nothing worthy of notice. The plain around it is alternately chalk and flint.'—(*Travels in Syria*, p. 365.) ¶ *Even unto Jahaz.* This was a city east of Jordan, near to which Moses defeated Sihon. It was given to Reuben (Deut. ii. 32), and was situated a short distance north of Ar, the capital of Moab. ¶ *The armed soldiers of Moab.* The consternation shall reach the very army. They shall lose their courage, and instead of defending the nation, they shall join in the general weeping and lamentation. ¶ *His life shall be grievous.* As we say of a person who is overwhelmed with calamities, that his life is wearisome, so, says the prophet, shall it be with the whole nation of Moab.

5. *My heart shall cry out for Moab.* This is expressive of deep compassion; and is proof that, in the view of the prophet, the calamities which were coming

upon it were exceedingly heavy. The same sentiment is expressed more fully in ch. xvi. 11; see also Jer. xlviii. 36: 'My heart shall sound for Moab like pipes.' The phrase denotes great inward pain and anguish in view of the calamities of others; and is an expression of the fact that we feel ourselves oppressed and borne down by sympathy on account of their sufferings (see Note on ch. xxi. 3). It is worthy of remark, that the LXX. read this as if it were '*his* heart'—referring to the Moabites, 'the heart of Moab shall cry out.' So the Chaldee; and so Lowth, Michaelis, and others read it. But there is no authority for this change in the Hebrew text; nor is it needful. In the parallel place in Jer. xlviii. 36, there is no doubt that the heart of the prophet is intended; and here, the phrase is designed to denote the deep compassion which a holy man of God would have, even when predicting the ills that should come upon others. How much compassion, how much deep and tender feeling should ministers of the gospel have when they are describing the final ruin —the unutterable woes of impenitent sinners under the awful wrath of God in the world of woe! ¶ *His fugitives.* Marg. 'Or to the borders thereof, even as an heifer' (בְּרִיחֶהָ). Jerome and the Vulgate render this 'her *bars*,' and it has been explained as meaning that the voice of the prophet, lamenting the calamity of Moab, could be heard as far as the *bars*, or gates, of Zoar; or that the word *bars* means *princes, i.e.*, protectors, a figure similar to *shields of the land* (Ps. xlvii. 10; Hos. iv. 18.) The LXX. render it, 'Εν αὐτῇ—'The voice of Moab in her is heard to Zoar.' But the more correct rendering is, undoubtedly, that of our translation, referring to the fugitives who should attempt to make their escape from Moab when the calamities should come upon her. ¶ *Unto Zoar.* Zoar was a small town in the southern extremity of the Dead Sea, to which Lot fled when Sodom was for in the way of Horonaim they shall raise up a cry of [1] destruction.

6 For the waters of Nimrim shall

1 *breaking.*

be desolate: [2] for the hay is withered away, the grass faileth, there is no green thing.

2 *desolations.*

overthrown (Gen. xix. 23). Abulfeda writes the name Zoghar, and speaks of it as existing in his day. The city of Zoar was near to Sodom, so as to be exposed to the danger of being overthrown in the same manner that Sodom was, Zoar being exempted from destruction by the angel at the solicitation of Lot (Gen. xix. 21). That the town lay on the east side of the Dead Sea, is apparent from several considerations. Lot ascended from it to the mountain where his daughters bore each of them a son, who became the ancestors of the Moabites and the Ammonites. But these nations both dwelt on the east side of the Dead Sea. Further, Josephus, speaking of this place, calls it Ζοάρων τῆς Ἀραβίας—'Zoar of Arabia' (*Bell. Jud.* iv. 8, 4). But the Arabia of Josephus was on the east of the Dead Sea. So the crusaders, in the expedition of King Baldwin, A.D. 1100, after marching from Hebron, proceeded around the lake, and came, at length, to a place called *Segor*, doubtless the Zoghar of Abulfeda. The probability, therefore, is, that it was near the southern end of the sea, but on the eastern side. The exact place is now unknown. In the time of Eusebius and Jerome, it is described as having many inhabitants, and a Roman garrison. In the time of the crusaders, it is mentioned as a place pleasantly situated, with many palm trees. But the palm trees have disappeared, and the site of the city can be only a matter of conjecture (see Robinson's *Bib. Researches*, vol. ii. pp. 648–651). ¶ *An heifer of three years old.* That is, their fugitives flying unto Zoar shall lift up the voice like an heifer, for so Jeremiah in the parallel place explains it (xlviii. 34). Many interpreters have referred this, however, to Zoar as an appellation of that city, denoting its flourishing condition. Bochart refers it to Isaiah, and supposes that he designed to say that *he* lifted his voice as an heifer. But the more obvious interpretation is that given above, and is that which

occurs in Jeremiah. The expression, however, is a very obscure one. See the various senses which it may bear, examined in Rosenmüller and Gesenius *in loc.* Gesenius renders it, 'To Eglath the third ;' and supposes, in accordance with many interpreters, that it denotes a place called *Eglath,* called the third in distinction from two other places of the same name ; though he suggests that the common explanation, that it refers to a heifer of the age of three years, may be defended. In the third year, says he, the heifer was most vigorous, and hence was used for an offering (Gen. xv. 9). Until that age she was accustomed to go unbroken, and bore no yoke (Pliny, 8, 4, 5). If this refers to Moab, therefore, it may mean that hitherto it was vigorous, unsubdued, and active; but that now, like the heifer, it was to be broken and brought under the yoke by chastisement. The expression is a very difficult one, and it is impossible, perhaps, to determine what is the true sense. ¶ *By the mounting up of Luhith.* The *ascent* of Luhith. It is evident, from Jer. xlviii. 5, that it was a mountain, but where, is not clearly ascertained. Eusebius supposes it was a place between Areopolis and Zoar (see Reland's *Palestine,* pp. 577–579). The whole region there is mountainous. ¶ *In the way of Horonaim.* This was, doubtless, a town of Moab, but where it was situated is uncertain. The word means *two holes.* The region abounds to this day with caves, which are used for dwellings (Seetzen). The place lay, probably, on a declivity from which one descended from Luhith. ¶ *A cry of destruction.* Heb. 'Breaking.' A cry *appropriate to* the great calamity that should come upon Moab.

6. *For the waters of Nimrim.* It is supposed by some that the prophet here states the cause why the Moabites would flee to the cities of the south, to wit, that the *waters* of the northern cities would fail, and the country become desolate, and that they would

7 Therefore the abundance they
have gotten, and that which they
have laid up, shall they carry away
to the ¹ brook of the willows.

8 For the cry is gone round about
the borders of Moab, the howling

1 or, *valley of the Arabians.*   2 *additions.*
a 2 Ki. 17. 25.

thereof unto Eglaim, and the howling thereof unto Beer-elim.

9 For the waters of Dimon shall
be full of blood: for I will bring
more ² upon Dimon, lions *a* upon
him that escapeth of Moab, and
upon the remnant of the land.

seek support in the south. But it is
more probable that he is simply continuing the description of the desolation that would come upon Moab.
Nimrah, or Beth Nimra, meaning *a
house of limpid waters*, was a city of
Reuben east of the Dead Sea (Num.
xxxii. 3; comp. Jer. xlviii. 34). It
was, doubtless, a city celebrated for its
pure fountains and springs of water.
Here Seetzen's chart shows a brook
flowing into the Jordan called *Nahr
Nimrim*, or *Wady Shoaib*. 'On the
east of the Jordan over against Jericho,
there is now a stream called *Nimlim*—
doubtless the ancient *Nimrim*. This
flows into the Jordan, and as it flows
along gives fertility to that part of the
country of Moab.'—(Rev. Eli Smith.)
It is possible that the waters failed by
a common practice in times of war,
when an enemy destroyed the fountains
of a country by diverting their waters,
or by casting into them stones, trees,
&c. This destructive measure of war
occurs, with reference to Moab, in
2 Kings iii. 25, when the Israelites,
during an incursion into Moab, felled
the fruit trees, cast stones into the
ploughed grounds, and *closed the fountains*, or *wells*. ¶ *For the hay is withered away.* The waters are dried up, and
the land yields nothing to support life.

7. *Therefore the abundance they have
gotten.* Their wealth they shall remove
from a place that is utterly burnt up
with drought, where the waters and the
grass fail, to another place where they
may find water. ¶ *To the brook of
willows.* Marg. 'The valley of the
Arabians.' The LXX. render it, 'I
will lead them to the valley of the Arabians, and they shall take it.' So Saadias. It might, perhaps, be called the
valley of the Arabians, because it was
the boundary line between them and
Arabia on the south. Lowth renders
it, 'To Babylon.' The probability is,

that the prophet refers to some valley
or brook that was called the brook of
the willows, from the fact that many
willows grew upon its bank. Perhaps
it was the small stream which flows into
the southern extremity of the Dead
Sea, and which forms the boundary of
Arabia Petrea of the province of Jebal.
They withdrew towards the south, where
towards Petra or Sela they had their
property in herds (ch. xvi. 1); for probably the invader came from the north,
and drove them in this direction. Lowth,
and most commentators, suppose that
'they' in this verse refers to the enemies of Moab, and that it means that
they would carry away the property of
Moab to some distant place. But the
more probable meaning is, that when
the waters of the Nimrim should fail,
they would remove to a place better
watered; that is, they would leave
their former abode, and wander away.
It is an image of the desolation that
was coming upon the land.

8. *For the cry is gone round about*,
&c. The cry of distress and calamity
has encompassed the whole land of Moab.
There is no part of the land which is
not filled with lamentation and distress.
¶ *The howling.* The voice of wailing
on account of the distress. ¶ *Unto Eglaim.* This was a city of Moab east of
the Dead Sea, which, Eusebius says,
was eight miles south of Ar, and hence,
says Rosenmüller, it was not far from
the south border of Moab. It is mentioned by Josephus (*Ant.* xiv. 1), as one
of the twelve cities in that region which
was overthrown by Alexander the Great.
¶ *Unto Beer-elim.* Literally, *the well
of the princes.* Perhaps the same as that
mentioned in Num. xxi. 14–18, as being
in the land of Moab, and near to Ar:

The princes digged the well,
The nobles of the people digged it.

9. *For the waters of Dimon.* Probably the same as *Dibon* (ver. 2). Euse-

CHAPTER XVI.

ANALYSIS.

THIS chapter is a continuance of the former, and the scope of it is, to give advice to the Moabites, and to threaten them with punishment in case, as the prophet foresaw, they should neglect or refuse to follow it. The advice was (1–5), to send the customary tribute to the king of Judah; to seek his protection, and to submit themselves to him. But the prophet foresaw that, through the pride of Moab

(6), they would refuse to recognize their subjection to Judah, and that, as a consequence, they would be doomed to severe punishment (7–11), and to a certain overthrow within a specified time (12–14). See the *Analysis* prefixed to ch. xv.

SEND ye the lamb *a* to the ruler of the land from ¹ Sela to the wilderness, unto the mount of the daughter of Zion.

a 2 Ki.3.4.   1 a rock, or, Petra.

bius says it was a large town on the northern bank of the river Arnon. Jerome says that the letters *m* and *b* are often interchanged in oriental dialects (see Note on ver. 2). ¶ *Shall be full of blood.* That is, the number of the slain of Moab shall be so great, that the blood shall colour the waters of the river—a very common occurrence in times of great slaughter. Perhaps by the *waters* of Dimon the prophet does not mean the river Arnon, but the small rivulets or streams that might flow into it near the city of Dibon. Probably there were winter brooks there, which do not run at all seasons. The Chaldee renders it, ' The waters of Dimon shall be full of blood, because I will place upon Dimon an assembly of armies.' ¶ *For I will bring more upon Dimon.* Heb. ' I will bring *additions;*' that is, I will bring upon it additional calamities. Jerome says, that by those additional calamities, the prophet refers to the *lions* which are immediately after mentioned. ¶ *Lions upon him that escapeth of Moab.* Wild beasts upon those who escaped from the slaughter, and who took refuge in the wilderness, or on the mountains. The Chaldee renders it, ' A king shall ascend with an army, and shall destroy the remainder of their land.' Aben Ezra interprets it of the king of Assyria; and Jarchi of Nebuchadnezzar, who is called a lion in Jer. iv. 7. Vitringa also supposes that Nebuchadnezzar is meant. But it is more probable that the prophet refers to wild beasts, which are often referred to in the Scriptures as objects of dread, and as bringing calamities upon nations (see Lev. xxvi. 22; Jer. v. 6; xv. 3; 2 Kings xviii. 25). ¶ *Upon the remnant of the land.* Upon all those who escaped the desolation of the war. The LXX. and the

Arabic render this, ' Upon the remnant of *Adama,*' understanding the word rendered ' land' (הָמָדְאַ *ădhámá*), as the name of a city. But it more probably means the land.

CHAPTER XVI.

1. *Send ye the lamb.* Lowth renders this, ' I will send forth the son from the ruler of the land ;' meaning, as he supposes, that under the Assyrian invasion, even the young prince of Moab would be obliged to flee for his life through the desert, that he might escape to Judea ; and *that* thus God says that *he* would send him. The only authority for this, however, is, that the LXX. read the word ' send ' in the future tense (ἀποστιλῶ) instead of the imperative ; and that the Syriac reads רַבּ (*băr*) instead of רַכּ (*kăr*), a lamb. But assuredly this is too slight an authority for making an alteration in the Hebrew text. This is one of the many instances in which Lowth has ventured to suggest a change in the text of Isaiah without sufficient authority. The LXX. read this, ' I will send reptiles (ἑρπετὰ) upon the land. Is not the mountain of the daughter of Zion a desolate rock ?' The Chaldee renders it, ' Bear ye tribute to the Messiah, the anointed of Israel, who is powerful over you who were in the desert, to Mount Zion.' And this, understanding by the Messiah the anointed king of Israel, is probably the true rendering. The word ' lamb' (רַכּ *kăr*) denotes, properly, a pasture lamb, a fat lamb, and is usually applied to the lamb which was slain in sacrifice. Here it probably means a lamb, or *lambs* collectively, as a tribute, or acknowledgment of subjection to Judah. Lambs were used in the daily sacrifice in the temple, and in the other sacrifices of the Jews. Large numbers

of them would, therefore, be needed, and it is not improbable that the *tribute* of the nations subject to them was often required to be paid in animals for burnt offering. Perhaps there might have been this additional reason for that—that the sending of such animals would be a sort of incidental acknowledgment of the truth of the Jewish religion, and an offering to the God of the Hebrews. At all events, the word here seems to be one that designates *tribute*; and the counsel of the prophet is, that they should send their *tribute* to the Jews. ¶ *To the ruler of the land.* To the king of Judah. This is proved by the addition at the close of the verse, 'unto the mount of the daughter of Zion.' It is evident from 2 Sam. viii. 2, that David subdued the Moabites, and laid them under tribute, so that the 'Moabites became David's servants, and brought gifts.' That *lambs* were the specific kind of tribute which the Moabites were to render to the Jews as a token of their subjection, is clearly proved in 2 Kings iii. 4: 'And Mesha, king of Moab, was a sheep-master, and rendered unto the king of Israel an hundred thousand rams, with the wool.' This was in the time of Ahab. But the Moabites after his death revolted from them, and rebelled (2 Kings iv. 5). It is probable that as this tribute was laid by *David* before the separation of the kingdoms of Judah and Israel, and as the kings of Judah claimed to be the true successors of David and Solomon, they demanded that the tribute should be rendered to *them*, and not to the kings of Israel, and this is the claim which Isaiah enforces in the passage before us. The command of the prophet is to regain the lost favour of Israel by the payment of the tribute that was due.—The territory of Moab was in early times, and is still, rich in flocks of sheep. Seetzen made his journey with some inhabitants of Hebron and Jerusalem who had purchased sheep in that region. Lambs and sheep were often demanded in tribute. The Persians received fifty thousand sheep as a tribute annually from the Cappadocians, and one hundred thousand from the Medes (Strabo, ii. 362). ¶ *From Sela in the wilderness.* The word 'Sela'

(סֶלַע) means *a rock;* and by it here there can be no doubt that there is intended the city of that name which was the capital of *Arabia Petrea.* The city was situated within the bounds of Arabia or Idumea, but was probably at this time in the possession of the Moabites. It was, therefore, the remotest part of their territory, and the sense may be, 'Send tribute even from the remotest part of your land;' or it may be, that the region around that city was particularly favourable to pasturage, and for keeping flocks. To this place they had fled with their flocks on the invasion from the north (see Note on ch. xv. 7). Vitringa says that that desert around Petra was regarded as a vast common, on which the Moabites and Arabians promiscuously fed their flocks. The situation of the city of *Sela,* or (πέτρα) *Petra,* meaning the same as *Sela,* a rock, was for a long time unknown, but it has lately been discovered. It lies about a journey of a day and a half south-east of the southern extremity of the Dead Sea. It derived its name from the fact that it was situated in a vast hollow in a rocky mountain, and consisted almost entirely of dwellings hewn out of the rock. It was the capital of the Edomites (2 Kings xix. 7); but might have been at this time in the possession of the Moabites. Strabo describes it as the capital of the Nabatheans, and as situated in a vale well watered, but encompassed by insurmountable rocks (xvi. 4), at a distance of three or four days' journey from Jericho. Diodorus (19, 55) mentions it as a place of trade, with caves for dwellings, and strongly fortified by nature. Pliny, in the first century, says, 'The Nabatheans inhabit the city called Petra, in a valley less than two [Roman] miles in amplitude, surrounded by inaccessible mountains, with a stream flowing through it' (*Nat. Hist.* vi. 28). Adrian, the successor of Trajan, granted important privileges to that city, which led the inhabitants to give his name to it upon coins. Several of these are still extant. In the fourth century, Petra is several times mentioned by Eusebius and Jerome, and in the fifth and sixth centuries it appears as the metropolitan see of the Third

Palestine (see the article *Petra* in Reland's *Palestine*). From that time, Petra disappeared from the pages of history, and the metropolitan see was transferred to Rabbah. In what way Petra was destroyed is unknown. Whether it was by the Mahometan conquerors, or whether by the incursions of the hordes of the desert, it is impossible now to ascertain. All Arabian writers of that period are silent as to Petra. The name became changed to

VIEW OF PETRA (SELA) FROM THE TOP OF THE THEATRE.—LABORDE.

that which it bears at present—Wady Musa, and it was not until the travels of Seetzen, in 1807, that it attracted the attention of the world. During his excursion from Hebron to the hill Madŭrah, his Arab guide described the place, exclaiming, 'Ah! how I weep when I behold the ruins of Wady Musa.' Seetzen did not visit it, but Burckhardt passed a short time there, and described it. Since his time it has been repeatedly visited (see Robinson's *Bib. Researches*, vol. ii. pp. 573–580).

This city was formerly celebrated as a place of great commercial importance, from its central position and its being so securely defended. Dr. Vincent (in his *Commerce of the Ancients*, vol. xi. p. 263, quoted in Laborde's *Journey to Arabia Petrea*, p. 17) describes Petra as the capital of Edom or Sin, the Idumea or Arabia Petrea of the Greeks, the Nabatea considered both by geographers, historians, and poets, as the source of all the precious commodities of the East. The caravans in all ages, from Minea in the interior of Arabia, and from Gerka on the gulf of Persia, from Hadramont on the ocean, and some even from Sabea in Yemen, appear to have pointed to Petra as a common centre ; and from Petra the trade seems to have branched out into every direction—to Egypt, Palestine, and Syria, through Arsinoe, Gaza, Tyre, Jerusalem, Damascus, and a variety of intermediate roads that all terminated on the Mediterranean. Strabo relates, that the merchandise of India and Arabia was transported on camels from Leuke Kome to Petra, and thence to Rhinocolura and other places (xvi. 4, 18, 23, 24). Under the Romans the trade was still more prosperous. The country was rendered more accessible, and the passage of merchants facilitated by military ways, and by the establishment of military posts to keep in check the predatory hordes of the neighbouring deserts. One great road, of which

RUINS OF A TRIUMPHAL ARCH (PETRA).

traces still remain, went from Petra to Damascus ; another went off from this road west of the Dead Sea to Jerusalem, Askelon, and other parts of the Mediterranean (Laborde, p. 213 ; Burckhardt, 374, 419). At a period subsequent to the Christian era there always reigned at Petra, according to Strabo, a king of the royal lineage, with whom a prince was associated in the government (Strabo, p. 779). The very situation of this city, once so celebrated, as

has been remarked above, was long unknown. Burckhardt, under the assumed name of Sheikh Ibrahim, in the year 1811, made an attempt to reach Petra under the pretext that he had made a vow to sacrifice a goat in honour of Aaron on the summit of Mount Hor near to Petra. He was permitted to enter the city, and to remain there a short time, and to *look* upon the wonders of that remarkable place, but was permitted to make no notes or drawings on the spot. His object was supposed to be to obtain treasures, which the Arabs believe to have been deposited there in great abundance, as all who visit the ruins of ancient cities and towns in that region are regarded as having come there solely for that purpose. If assured that they have no such design, and if the Arabs are reminded that they have no means to remove them, it is replied ' that, although they may not remove them in their presence, yet when they return to their own land, they will have the power of *commanding* the treasures to be conveyed to them, and it will be done by magic.'—(Burckhardt's *Travels in Syria*, pp. 428, 429.)

Burckhardt's description of this city, as it is brief, may be here given *verbatim* :—' Two long days' journey northeast from Akaba [a town at the extremity of the Elanitic branch of the Red Sea, near the site of the ancient Eziongeber], is a brook called Wady Musa, and a valley of the same name. This place is very remarkable for its antiquities, and the remains of an ancient city, which I take to be Petra, the capital of Arabia Petrea, a place which, so far as I know, no European traveller has ever explored. In the red sandstone of which the vale consists, there are found more than two hundred and fifty sepulchres, which are entirely hewn out of the rock, generally with architectural ornaments in the Grecian style. There is found there a mausoleum in the form of a temple [obviously the same which Legh and Laborde call the temple of victory], on a colossal scale, which is likewise hewn out of the rock, with all its apartments, portico, peristylum, &c. It is an extremely fine monument of Grecian architecture, and in a fine state of preservation. In the same place there are yet other mausoleums with obelisks, apparently in the Egyptian style ; a whole amphitheatre hewn out of the solid rock, and the remains of a palace and many temples.'

TEMPLE IN ROCK (PETRA).

Mr. Bankes, in company of Mr. Legh, and Captains Irby and Mangles, have the merit of being the first persons who, as Europeans, succeeded to any extent in making researches in Petra. Captains Irby and Mangles spent two days amongst its temples, tombs, and ruins, and have furnished a description of what they saw. But the most full and satisfactory investigation which has been made of these ruins, was made by M. de Laborde, who visited the city in 1829, and was permitted to remain there eight days, and to examine it at leisure. An account of his journey, with splendid plates, was published in Paris in 1830, and a translation in London in 1836. To this interesting account the reader must be referred. It can only be remarked here, that Petra, or Sela, was a city entirely encompassed with lofty rocks, except in a single place, where was a deep ravine between the rocks which constituted the principal entrance. On the east and west it was enclosed with lofty rocks, of from three to five hundred feet in height ; on the north and south the ascent was gradual from the city to the adjacent hills. The ordinary entrance was through a deep ravine, which has been, until lately, supposed to have been the only way of access to the city. This ravine approaches it from the east, and is about a mile in length. In the narrowest part it is twelve feet in width, and the rocks are on each side about three hundred feet in height. On the northern side, there are tombs excavated in the rocks nearly the entire distance. The stream which watered Petra runs along in the bottom of the ravine, going through the city, and descending through a ravine to the west (see Robinson's *Bib. Researches*, vol. ii. pp. 514, 538). Of this magnificent entrance, the following cut will furnish an illustration. The city is wholly uninhabited, except when the wandering Arab makes use of an excavated tomb or palace in which to pass the night, or a caravan pauses there. The rock which encompasses it is a soft freestone. The tombs, with which almost the entire city was encompassed, are cut in the solid rock, and are adorned in the various modes of Grecian and Egyptian architecture. The surface of the solid rock was first made smooth, and then a plan of the tomb or temple was drawn on the smoothed surface, and the workmen began at the top and cut the various pillars, entablatures, and capitals. The tomb was then excavated from the rock, and was usually entered by a single door. Burck-

ENTRANCE TO A ROCK-HEWN TOMB (PETRA).

hardt counted two hundred and fifty of these tombs, and Laborde has described minutely a large number of them. For a description of these splendid monuments, the reader must be referred to the work of Laborde, pp. 152–193. Lond. Ed.

2 For it shall be, *that* as a wandering bird cast [1] out of the nest, *so* the daughters of Moab shall be at the fords of *a* Arnon.

1 or, *a nest forsaken.*   a Num.21.13.   2 *bring.*

That this is the Sela referred to here there can be no doubt; and the discovery of this place is only one of the instances out of many, in which the researches of oriental travellers contribute to throw light on the geography of the Scriptures, or otherwise illustrate them. For a description of this city, see Stephen's *Incidents of Travel in Egypt, Arabia Petrea, and the Holy Land,* vol. ii. ch. iv. p. 65, *sq.;* the work of Laborde referred to above; and Robinson's *Bib. Researches,* vol. ii. pp. 573–580, 653–659. ¶ *To the mount of the daughter of Zion.* To Mount Zion; *i.e.,* to Jerusalem (Note, ch. i. 8). The meaning of this verse, therefore, is, 'Pay the accustomed tribute to the Jews. Continue to seek their protection, and acknowledge your subjection to them, and you shall be safe. They will yield you protection, and these threatened judgments will not come upon you. - But refuse, or withhold this, and you will be overthrown.'

2. *For it shall be.* It shall happen in the time of the calamity that shall come upon Moab. ¶ *As a wandering bird.* (See ch. x. 14.) The same idea is presented in Prov. xxvii. 8:

As a bird that wanders from her nest,
So is a man that wandereth from his place.

The idea here is that of a bird driven away from her nest, where the nest is destroyed, and the young fly about without any home or place of rest. So would Moab be when the inhabitants were driven from their dwellings. The reason why this is introduced seems to be, to enforce what the prophet had said in the previous verse—the duty of paying the usual tribute to the Jews, and seeking their protection. The time is coming, says the prophet, when the Moabites shall be driven from their homes, and when they will need that protection which they can obtain by paying the usual tribute to the Jews. ¶ *The daughters of Moab.* The females shall be driven from their homes, and

3 Take [2] counsel, execute judgment; make thy shadow as the night in the midst of the noonday; hide the outcasts, bewray not him that wandereth.

shall wander about, and endeavour to flee from the invasion which has come upon the land. By the apprehension, therefore, that their wives and daughters would be exposed to this danger, the prophet calls upon the Moabites to secure the protection of the king of Judah. ¶ *At the fords of Arnon.* Arnon was the northern boundary of the land of Moab. They would endeavour to cross that river, and thus flee from the land, and escape the desolations that were coming upon it. The river Arnon, now called Mujeb, flows in a deep, frightfully wild, and rocky vale of the same name (Num. xxi. 15; Deut. ii. 24; iii. 9), in a narrow bed, and forms at this time the boundary between the provinces of Belka and Karrak (Seetzen). Bridges were not common in the times here referred to; and, indeed, permanent bridges among the ancients were things almost unknown. Hence they selected the places where the streams were most shallow and gentle, as the usual places of crossing.

3. *Take counsel.* Heb. 'Bring counsel;' or cause it to come (הָבִיאוּ, or as it is in the *keri,* הביאי). The Vulgate renders this in the singular number, and so is the *keri,* and so many MSS. J. D. Michaelis, Lowth, Eichhorn, Gesenius, and Noyes, regard verses 3–5 as a supplicatory address of the fugitive Moabites to the Jews to take them under their protection, and as imploring a blessing on the Jewish people if they would do it; and ver. 6 as the negative answer of the Jews, or as a refusal to protect them on account of their pride. But most commentators regard it as addressed to the Moabites by the prophet, or by the Jews, calling upon the Moabites to afford such protection to the Jews who might be driven from their homes as to secure their favour, and confirm the alliance between them; and ver. 6 as an intimation of the prophet, that the pride of Moab is such that there is no reason to suppose the

4 Let mine outcasts dwell with thee, Moab: be thou a covert to them from the face of the spoiler:

1 *wringer.*

for the [1] extortioner is at an end, the spoiler ceaseth, the [2] oppressors are consumed out of the land.

2 *treaders down.*

advice will be followed. It makes no difference in the sense here, whether the verb 'give counsel' be in the singular or the plural number. If singular, it may be understood as addressed to *Moab* itself; if plural, to the *inhabitants* of Moab. Vitringa supposes that this is an additional advice given to the Moabites by the prophet, or by a chorus of the Jews, to exercise the offices of kindness and humanity towards the Jews, that thus they might avoid the calamities which were impending. The *first* counsel was (ver. 1), to pay the proper tribute to the Jewish nation; *this* is (ver. 3–5) to show to those Jews who might be driven from their land kindness and protection, and thus preserve the friendship of the Jewish nation. This is, probably, the correct interpretation, as if he had said, 'take counsel; seek advice in your circumstances; be not hasty, rash, impetuous, unwise; do not cast off the friendship of the Jews; do not deal unkindly with those who may seek a refuge in your land, and thus provoke the nation to enmity; but let your land be an asylum, and thus conciliate and secure the friendship of the Jewish nation, and thus mercy shall be reciprocated and shown to you by him who shall occupy the throne of David' (ver. 5). The *design* is, to induce the Moabites to show kindness to the fugitive Jews who might seek a refuge there, that thus, in turn, the Jews might show them kindness. But the prophet foresaw (ver. 6) that Moab was so proud that he would neither pay the accustomed tribute to the Jews, nor afford them protection; and therefore the judgment is threatened against them which is finally to overthrow them. ¶ *Execute judgment.* That is, do that which is equitable and right; which you would desire to be done in like circumstances. ¶ *Make thy shadow.* A *shadow* or *shade,* is often in the Scriptures an emblem of protection from the burning heat of the sun, and thence of those burning, consuming judgments, which

are represented by the intense heat of the sun (Note on Isa. iv. 6 ; comp. Isa. xxv. 4 ; xxxii. 2 ; Lam. iv. 20). ¶ *As the night.* That is, a deep, dense shade, such as the night is, compared with the intense heat of noon. This idea was one that was very striking in the East. Nothing, to travellers crossing the burning deserts, could be more refreshing than the shade of a far-projecting rock, or of a grove, or of the night. Thus Isaiah counsels the Moabites to be to the Jews—to furnish protection to them which may be like the grateful shade furnished to the traveller by the rock in the desert. The figure here used is common in the East. Thus it is said in praise of a nobleman: 'Like the sun, he warmed in the cold ; and when Sirius shone, then was he coolness and shade.' In the *Sunna* it is said: 'Seven classes of men will the Lord overshadow with his shade, when no shade will be like his ; the upright Imam, the youth,' &c. ¶ *Hide the outcasts.* The outcasts of Judah— those of the Jews who may be driven away from their own homes, and who may seek protection in your land. Moab is often represented as a place of refuge to the outcast Hebrews (see the Analysis to ch. xv.) ¶ *Bewray not him that wandereth.* Reveal not (תְּגַלִּי), do not show them to their pursuer ; *i.e.,* give them concealment and protection.

4. *Let mine outcasts.* This may be understood as the language of Judea, or of God. '*Mine* outcasts' may mean the exiles of Judea, or God may call them *his.* The sense is essentially the same. It denotes those who were fugitives, wanderers, exiles from the land of Judea, and who took refuge in the land of Moab ; and God claims for them protection. ¶ *Dwell with thee.* Not dwell permanently, but sojourn (יָגוּרוּ), let them remain with you as exiles ; or let them find a refuge in your land. ¶ *Be thou a covert to them.* A refuge ; a hiding-place ; a place of secresy (סֵתֶר *sēthĕr*). ¶ *From the face*

5 And in mercy shall the throne be [1] established ; and [a] he shall sit upon it in truth in the tabernacle of David, [b] judging and seeking

1 or, *prepared.*　a Dan.7.14,27; Mic.4.7; Lu.1.32,33.

of the spoiler. That is, the conqueror from whose desolating career they would seek a refuge in the land of Moab. Who this *spoiler* would be, is not known. It would seem to be some invader who was carrying desolation through the land of Judea. It may be observed, however, that Lowth, by setting the points aside, supposes that this should be read, 'Let the outcasts of Moab sojourn with thee, O Zion.' So Noyes. But this seems to me not to suit the connection and the design ; which is, to persuade the Moabites to conciliate the favour of the Jews by affording a hiding-place to their fugitives. ¶ *For the extortioner is at an end.* Literally, 'there is an end, or there will be an end of the oppressor ; or he will be wanting.' The Chaldee renders it, 'The *enemy* is at an end.' The idea here seems to be, that the oppressor in the land of Judea would not continue there always ; the exiles of the Jews might soon return ; and Judea be able *then* to return kindness to Moab. Judea did not ask that her exiles should permanently abide in Moab, but asked only a temporary refuge, with the certainty that she would be soon delivered from her oppressions, and would then be able to furnish aid to Moab in return. ¶ *The oppressors are consumed.* Or, 'the treader down,' he that has trodden down the nations *shall* soon be removed, and *then*, in turn, Judea will be able to repay the kindness which is now asked at the hand of Moab, in permitting her exiles to remain in their land.

5. *And in mercy.* In benignity ; kindness ; benevolence. ¶ *Shall the throne be established.* The throne of the king of Judah. That is, he that shall sit upon the throne of David shall be disposed to repay the kindness which is now sought at the hand of Moab, and shall be able to do it. ¶ *And he shall sit upon it.* The king of Israel. ¶ *In truth.* In faithfulness ; that is, shall be true and faithful. His character shall be such that he will do justice,

judgment, and hasting righteousness.

6 We have heard of the pride of Moab ; *he is* very proud : *even* of

b Ps.72.2.

and will furnish protection and aid to the Moabites, if they now receive the fugitives of Israel. ¶ *In the tabernacle of David.* In the dwelling place ; the palace of David ; for so the word *tabernacle,* or *tent* (אֹהֶל *ōhĕl*) seems to be used here. It means *temple* in Ezek. xli. 1. It denotes a habitation, or dwelling place, in general, in Prov. xiv. 11 ; Ps. lii. 7; xci. 10. The palace, court, or *citadel* of David, was on mount Zion ; and the sense here is, that the king to whom Israel refers would be a worthy successor of David—just, true, faithful, benignant, and disposed to repay the favours now sought at the hand of Moab. ¶ *Seeking judgment.* Anxious to do right ; and seeking an opportunity to recompense those who had shown any favour to the people of the Jews. Moab, therefore, if she would now afford protection to the Jews, might be certain of a recompense. ¶ *And hasting righteousness.* Not tardy and slow in doing what should be done—anxious to do justice to all. It is implied here also, that a king who would be so just, and so anxious to do *right* to all, would not only be ready to show kindness to the Moabites, if they protected the fugitives of Judea, but would also be disposed to do *right* if they refused that protection ; that is, would be disposed to inflict *punishment* on them. Alike, therefore, by the hope of the protection and favour of the king of the Jews, and by the dread of punishment, the prophet endeavours to persuade Moab now to secure their favour by granting protection to their exiles.

6. *We have heard of the pride of Moab.* We Jews ; we have *all* heard of it ; that is, we *know* that he is proud. The evident design of the prophet here is, to say that Moab was so proud, and was well known to be so haughty, that he would *reject* this counsel. He would neither send the usual tribute to the land of Judea (ver. 1), thus acknowledging his dependence on them ; nor would he give protection to the exiled

his haughtiness, and his pride, and his wrath : *but* his lies *shall* not be so.

7 Therefore shall Moab howl for Moab ; every one shall howl: for

the foundations of ^aKir-hareseth shall ye ¹mourn ; surely *they are* stricken.

8 For the fields of Heshbon lan-

a 2 Ki.3.25.   1 or, mutter.

Jews as they should wander through his land, and *thus* endeavour to conciliate their favour, and secure their friendship. As a consequence of this, the prophet proceeds to state that heavy judgments would come upon Moab as a nation. ¶ He is *very proud.* The same thing is stated in the parallel place in Jer. xlviii. 29 (comp. ver. 11). Moab was at ease ; he was confident in his security ; he feared nothing ; he sought *no* means, therefore, of securing the friendship of the Jews. ¶ *And his wrath.* As the result of pride and haughtiness. Wrath or indignation is excited in a proud man when he is opposed, and when the interests of others are not made to give way to his. ¶ But *his lies* shall *not* be so. The Hebrew phrase (לֹא־כֵן—'not so') here seems to be used in the sense of 'not right ;' 'not firm, or established ;' that is, his vain boasting, his false pretensions, his *lies* shall not be confirmed, or established ; or they shall be vain and impotent. In the parallel place in Jeremiah, it is, 'But it shall not be so ; his lies shall not effect it.' The word rendered 'his lies' here (בַּדָּיו), means his boasting, or vain and confident speaking. In Isa. xliv. 25, it is connected with the vain and confident responses of diviners and soothsayers. Here it means that Moab boasted of his strength and security, and did not feel his need of the friendship of the Jews ; but that his security was false, and that it should not result according to his expectations. That Moab was proud, is also stated in ch. xxv. 8 ; and that he was disposed to give vent to his pride by reproaching the people of God, is apparent from Zech. ii. 8 :

I have heard the reproach of Moab,
And the revilings of the children of Ammon,
Whereby they have reproached my people,
And boasted themselves upon their border.

7. *Therefore shall Moab howl for Moab.* One part of the nation shall mourn for another ; they shall howl, or

lament, in alternate responses. Jerome renders it, 'the people (shall howl) to the city ; the city to the provinces.' The general idea is, that there would be an universal lamentation throughout the land. This would be the punishment which would result from their pride in neglecting to send the tribute and seeking the favour of the Jews ; or they would lament because the expectation of finding a refuge among the Israelites was taken away. ¶ *For the foundations.* On account of the foundations of Kir-hareseth, for they shall be overthrown ; that is, that city shall be destroyed. The word here rendered 'foundations' (אֲשִׁישֵׁי), occurs nowhere else but in this place, and in Hos. iii. 1. The LXX. render it, 'The inhabitants.' The Chaldee, 'Men.' Jeremiah, in the parallel place, renders it also 'men' (xlviii. 31). In Hos. iii. 1, it is rendered 'flagons of wine'—and it has been supposed by many that it has this sense here, as this would agree with what is immediately added of the fields of Heshbon, and the vine of Sibmah. Rosenmüller renders it by 'strong men, or *heroes;*' and supposes that it means that the *strong* men of Kir-hareseth would be destroyed, and that they would mourn on that account. The probable sense is, that that on which the city rested, or was based, was to be destroyed. So Kimchi, Jarchi, and the Syriac understand it. ¶ *Kir-hareseth.* Literally, *wall of potsherds,* or *of bricks.* Aquila renders it, Τοιχῳ ὀστρακίνῳ. Symmachus, Τείχει ὀστρακίνῳ. This was a city of Moab, but where it was situated is unknown. Vitringa supposes that it was the same as Kir Moab (ch. xv. 1), which, Gesenius says, is not improbable, for it is now mentioned as in ruins, and as one of the chief cities.

8. *For the fields of Heshbon.* (See Note, ch. xv. 4.) ¶ *Languish.* They are parched up with drought. The 'fields' here evidently mean *vineyards,*

guish, *and* the vine of Sibmah : the lords of the heathen have broken down the principal plants thereof, they are come *even* unto Jazer, they wandered *through* the wilderness: her branches are [1]stretched out, they are gone over the sea :

1 or, *plucked up.*

for so the parallelism demands. So in Deut. xxxii. 32 :

Their vine is of the vine of Sodom,
And of the fields of Gomorrah.

¶ And *the vine of Sibmah.* Sibmah, or Shibmah, was a city of Reuben (Num. xxxii. 38; Josh. xiii. 19). Jeremiah, in the parallel place (xlviii. 32) speaks of the vine of Sibmah also. He also says that the enemies of Moab had taken Sibmah, and that the vine and wine had been destroyed (xlviii. 33). There was no more certain mode of producing desolation in a land where grapes were extensively cultivated than to cut down the vines. The Turks constantly practise that in regard to their enemies, and the result is, that wide desolation comes upon the countries which they invade. At this time it is probable that Sibmah belonged to the Moabites. It is mentioned here as being distinguished for the luxuriant production of the grape. Seetzen still found the vine cultivated in that region. Jerome says, that between Sibmah and Heshbon there was scarcely a distance of five hundred paces, half a Roman mile. ¶ *The lords of the heathen.* The princes of the heathen nations that had come to invade Moab. The words ' have broken down ' (הָלְמוּ) may be taken in either of two senses, either to beat, strike, or break down, as in our version ; or *to be* beaten, or smitten with wine—*i.e.,* to become intoxicated—like the Greek οἰνοπλὴξ—*smitten withwine.* The former is doubtless the sense here. ¶ *The principal plants thereof.* The choice vines of it—*her sorek* (שֹׂרֵקֶיהָ). (See Notes on ch. v. 2.) ¶ *They are come.* That is, the vines of Sibmah had spread or extended themselves even to Jazer, indicating their great luxuriance and fertility. Jazer was a city at the foot of the mountains of Gilead which was given to Gad, and afterwards to the Levites (Josh. xxi. 39). Jerome says it was about fifteen miles from Heshbon. Seetzen found the ruins of a city called Szâr, and another place called

Szir, from which a small stream (Nahar Szir) flows into the Jordan (Gesenius). That the shoots of the vine of Sibmah reached unto Jazer and the desert, is a beautiful poetic expression for the extensive spread and luxuriance of the vine in that region. ¶ *They wandered.* The vines *wandered* in the desert. They found no twig or tree to which they could attach themselves, and they spread around in wild luxuriancy. ¶ Through *the wilderness.* The wilderness or desert of Arabia, which encompassed Moab. ¶ *Her branches are stretched out.* Are extended far, or are very luxuriant. ¶ *They are gone over the sea.* Called in the parallel place in Jer. xlviii. 32, ' the Sea of Jazer ;' probably some lake that had that name near the city of Jazer. It may *possibly* mean the Dead Sea, but that name is not elsewhere given to the Dead Sea in the Scriptures. It has been objected by some to this statement that modern travellers have not found any such place as the ' Sea of Jazer ;' or any lake in the vicinity of Jazer. But we may observe—(1.) that Seetzen found a stream flowing into the Jordan near Jazer ; and (2.) that it is possible that a pond or lake may have once there existed which may have been since, in the course of ages, filled with sand. It is known, for example, that in the vicinity of Suez the ancient narrow gulf there, and the large inland sea made by the Bitter lakes, have been choked up by the sand of the desert. Seetzen also says that he saw some pools near the source of the stream called Nahar Szir (*river Szir*).—Prof. Stuart. *Bib. Rep.* vol. vii. p. 158. The whole description of the vines of Sibmah is poetic ; designed, not to be literally understood, but to denote their remarkable luxuriance and fertility. A similar description of a *vine*—though there used to denote the Jewish people—occurs in Psal. lxxx. 8–11 :

Thou hast brought a vine out of Egypt;
Thou hast cast out the heathen and planted it;
Thou preparedst room before it,
And didst cause it to take deep root,
And it filled the land.

9 Therefore *a* I will bewail with the weeping of Jazer the vine of Sibmah: I will water thee with my tears, O Heshbon, and Elealeh; for ¹ the shouting for thy summer fruits and for thy harvest is fallen.

10 And *b* gladness is taken away, and joy out of the plentiful field;

a Jer.48.32, &c. 1, or, *the alarm is fallen upon.*

and in the vineyards there shall be no singing, neither shall there be shouting: the treaders shall tread out no wine in *their* presses; I have made *their vintage* shouting to cease.

11 Wherefore my bowels *c* shall sound like an harp for Moab, and mine inward parts for Kir-haresh.

b ch.24.8. *c* ch.63.15.

The hills were covered with the shadow of it,
And the boughs thereof were like the goodly
    cedars.
She sent out her boughs unto the sea,
And her branches unto the river.

9. *Therefore I will bewail.* So great is the desolation that I, the prophet, will lament it, though it belongs to another nation than mine own. The expression indicates that the calamity will be great (see Note on ch. xv. 5). ¶ *With the weeping of Jazer.* That is, I will pour out the same lamentation for the vine of Sibmah which I do for Jazer; implying that it would be deep and bitter sorrow (see Jer. xlviii. 32). ¶ *I will water thee with my tears.* Indicating the grievous calamities that were coming upon those places, on account of the pride of the nation. They were to Isaiah foreign nations, but he had a heart that could feel for their calamities. ¶ *For the shouting for thy summer fruits.* The shouting attending the ingathering of the harvest (Note on ch. ix. 3). The word used here (הֵידָד), denotes, properly, a joyful acclamation, a shout of joy or rejoicing, such as was manifested by the vintager and presser of grapes (Jer. xxv. 30; xlviii. 33); or such as was made by the warrior (Jer. li. 14). Here it means, that in the time when they would expect the usual shout of the harvest, it should not be heard, but instead thereof there should be the triumph of the warrior. Literally, 'upon thy summer fruits, and upon thy harvests has the shouting fallen;' that is, the shout of the warrior has fallen upon that harvest instead of the rejoicing of the husbandman. So Jeremiah evidently understands it (xlviii. 32): 'The *spoiler* is fallen upon thy summer fruits, and upon thy vintage.' Lowth proposes here a correction of the Hebrew text, but without necessity or authority.

10. *And gladness,* &c. The gladness

and joy that was commonly felt in the field producing a rich and luxuriant harvest. ¶ *Out of the plentiful field.* Heb. 'From Carmel;' but Carmel means a fruitful field as well as the mountain of that name (see Note on ch. x. 18). ¶ *I have made* their vintage *shouting to cease.* That is, by the desolation that has come upon the land. The vineyards are destroyed; and of course the shout of joy in the vintage is no more heard.

11. *Wherefore my bowels.* This is also an expression of the deep grief of the prophet in view of the calamities which were coming upon Moab. The *bowels* in the Scriptures are everywhere represented as the seat of compassion, pity, commiseration, and tender mercy (Gen. xiii. 30): 'His bowels did yearn upon his brother'—he deeply felt for him, he greatly pitied him (1 Kings iii. 26; Ps. xxv. 6; Prov. xii. 10; Cant. v. 4; Isa. lxiii. 15; Jer. iv. 19; xxxi. 20; Phil. i. 8; ii. 1). In classic writers, the word 'bowels' denotes the *upper* viscera of victims—the heart, the lungs, the liver, which were eaten during or after the sacrifice (Robinson, *Lex.,* on the word σπλάγχνον). In the Scriptures, it denotes the *inward parts*—evidently also the upper viscera, regarded as the seat of the emotions and passions. The word as we use it—denoting the lower viscera—by no means expresses the sense of the word in the Scriptures, and it is this change in the signification which renders the use of the very language of the Bible unpleasant or inappropriate. We express the idea by the use of the word *heart*—the seat of the affections. ¶ *Shall sound like an harp.* The *bowels* are represented in the Scriptures as affected in various modes in the exercise of pity or compassion. Thus, in Lam. i. 20, Jeremiah says, 'My bowels are troubled' (see Lam. ii. 1; Jer. xxxi. 20). Job (ch. xxx. 27,) says, 'My

12 And it shall come to pass, when it is seen that Moab is *a* weary on the high place, that he shall
a ch.26.16.

bowels *boiled*, and rested not;' there was great agitation; deep feeling. Thus, Jer. iv. 19:

My bowels! My bowels! I am pained at my very heart.
My heart *maketh a noise* in me.

So Isa. lxiii. 15: 'Where is the *sounding* of thy bowels and mercies?' The word 'sound' here means to make a tumultuous noise; and the whole expression here denotes that his heart was affected with the calamities of Moab as the strings of the harp vibrate when beaten with the plectrum or the hand. His heart was deeply pained and affected by the calamities of Moab, and responded to those calamities, as the strings of the harp did to the blow of the plectrum. ¶ *Mine inward parts.* The expressions here used are somewhat analogous to ours of the *beating of the heart*, to denote deep emotion. Forster says of the savages of the South Sea that they call compassion *a barking of the bowels.* ¶ *For Kirharesh.* (See Note on ver. 7.)

12. *When it is seen.* When it occurs; that is, when Moab actually *becomes* weary. ¶ *Is weary on the high place.* The *high place* denotes the place of idolatrous worship, and here means the same as the temple of Chemosh or his sanctuary. Temples and altars were usually constructed on such places, and especially the temples of the heathen gods. Moab is represented here as looking to her gods for protection. Weary, exhausted, worn down with calamities, she is represented as fleeing from the desolate towns and cities, and taking refuge at the altar, and seeking assistance there. This, says Jerome, is the final misery. She is now forsaken of those aids to which she had always trusted, and on which she had relied. Her men slain; her towns destroyed; her strong places broken down; her once fertile fields languishing and desolate, she flees to the shrine of her god, and finds even her god unable to aid and defend her. ¶ *Shall come to his sanctuary.* To his *principal* sanctuary; or

come to his sanctuary to pray; but he *b* shall not prevail.
13 This *is* the word that the
b Pr.1.28.

to the temple of the principal god which they worshipped — the god *Chemosh* (1 Kings xi. 7). This does not mean the temple at Jerusalem, though Kimchi so understands it; but the temple of the chief divinity of Moab. Jerome says that this temple was on mount Nebo. ¶ *Shall not prevail.* That is, her prayer shall not be heard.

13. *This is the word.* This is the substance of the *former* predictions respecting Moab. This has been the *general course* or sense of the prophecies respecting Moab, during all its history. ¶ *Since that time.* Formerly; from former times. There had been a course of predictions declaring in general that Moab should be destroyed, and the prophet says here that he had expressed their general sense; or that *his* predictions accorded with them all —for they all predicted the complete overthrow of Moab. He now says (ver. 14) that these general prophecies respecting Moab which had been of so long standing were now to be speedily accomplished. The prophecies respecting Moab, foretelling its future ruin, may be seen in Ex. xv. 15; Num. xxi. 29; xxiv. 17; Ps. lx. 8; cviii. 9; Amos ii. 2; Zeph. ii. 9. It *may*, however, be intended here that the former portion of this prophecy had been uttered by Isaiah himself during the early part of his prophetic life. He is supposed to have prophesied some sixty or more years (*see* Introduction, § 3); and it may be that the prophecy in the fifteenth and the previous part of the sixteenth chapter had been uttered during the early part of his life without specifying the time when it would be fulfilled; but now he says, that it would be accomplished in three years. Or it may be that some other prophet had uttered the prediction which he now repeats with additions at the close. The fact that Isaiah had done this on some occasions seems probable from the beginning of ch. ii., which appears to be a quotation from Mic. iv. 1–3 (see the Analysis to ch. xv., and Notes on ch. ii. 2).

LORD hath spoken concerning Moab since that time.

14 But now the LORD hath spoken, saying, Within three years, as the *a* years of an hireling, and the glory of Moab shall be contemned, with all that great multitude ; and the remnant *shall be* very small *and* feeble.[1]

a ch.21.16.   [1] or, *not many.*

---

14. *But now the* LORD *hath spoken.* This refers to the particular and specific prophecy of Isaiah that destruction should come upon them in three years. Instead of a *general* but *indefinite* prediction of calamity to the Moabites, such as had been uttered by the former prophets, or by Isaiah himself before, it was now specific and definite in regard to the *time* when it should be fulfilled. ¶ *Within three years.* We have no means of ascertaining the exact fulfilment of this prediction, nor do we certainly know by whom it was accomplished. ¶ *As the years of an hireling.* A man that is hired has a certain time specified during which he is to labour ; the years, the months, the days for which he is engaged are agreed on, nor will he suffer any addition to be made to it. So the prophet says that the very time is fixed. It shall not be varied. It will be adhered to by God—as the time is adhered to between a man who employs another and him who is hired. And it means, that *exactly at the time* which is here specified, the predicted destruction should come upon Moab. ¶ *The glory of Moab.* That in which it glories, or boasts—its wealth, its armies, its cities, towns, &c. ¶ *Shall be contemned.* Shall be esteemed of no value ; shall be destroyed. ¶ *And the remnant.* There shall be few cities, few men, and very little wealth that shall escape the desolation (comp. ch. x. 25 ; xxiv. 6). Jerome says that 'this prophecy was delivered after the death of Ahaz, and in the reign of Hezekiah, during whose reign the ten tribes were led by Sennacherib, king of the Assyrians, into captivity. And therefore after three years, the Assyrians came and destroyed Moab, and very few were left in the land who could inhabit the deserted cities, or cultivate the desolate fields.' But it is not certainly known to what particular time the prophecy refers.—In regard to the present state of Moab, and the complete fulfilment of the prophecies respecting it, the following works may be consulted:—Newton, *On the Prophecies;* Keith, *On the Prophecies;* Burckhardt's *Travels in Syria;* and Captains Irby and Mangles' *Travels.* In regard to the fulfilment of these predictions respecting the destruction of Moab, it may be sufficient to refer to the remarks which I have made on the particular places which are mentioned in these two chapters, and to the writers mentioned above. All travellers concur in the general desolation of that country which was once so thickly studded with towns, and that abounded so richly in flocks, and produced so luxuriantly the grape. It is now strewed with ruins. All the cities of Moab have disappeared. Their place is characterized in the map of Volney's *Travels,* by *the ruins of towns.* Burckhardt, who encountered many difficulties in so desolate and dangerous a land, thus records the brief history of a few of them : 'The ruins of Eleale, Heshbon, Meon, Medaba, Dibon, Arver, all situated on the north side of the Arnon, still subsist to illustrate the history of the Beni-Israel' (*Life and Travels,* prefixed to the *Travels in Nubia,* pp. 48, 49). 'And it might be added,' says Keith, 'that they still subsist to confirm the inspiration of the Jewish Scriptures, for the desolation of each of these cities was the theme of a distinct prediction' (*Prophecies,* p. 129). Within the boundaries of Moab, Burckhardt enumerates about *fifty* ruined cities, many of them extensive. In general they are a broken down and undistinguishable mass of ruins ; but, in some instances, there are remains of temples, sepulchral monuments, traces of hanging gardens, entire columns lying on the ground, and dilapidated walls made of stones of large dimensions (see *Travels in Syria,* pp. 311–456).

In view of these two chapters, constituting one prophecy, and the facts in regard to the present state of the country of Moab, we may observe that we

CHAPTER XVII.

ANALYSIS.

THE prophecy which comprises verses 1-11 of this chapter, professes, by its title, to be against Damascus only. But it relates to the kingdom of Samaria no less than to Damascus. The reason is, that the kingdoms of Israel and Damascus were confederated against the king-

dom of Judah. The design of the prophecy may have been to warn the kingdom of Israel of the approaching destruction of the city of Damascus, and, by this means, to keep them from forming an alliance with them against Judah. When it was delivered is unknown. Lowth supposes that it was immediately after the prophecies in the seventh and eighth chapters, in the reign of Ahaz, and this supposition

have here clear and unanswerable evidence of the genuineness and truth of the sacred records. That evidence is found in the *particularity* with which *places* are mentioned ; and in the fact that impostors would not *specify* places, any further than was unavoidable. Mistakes, we all know, are liable to be made by those who attempt to describe the *geography* of places which they have not seen. Yet here is a description of a land and its numerous towns, made nearly three thousand years ago, and in its *particulars* it is sustained by all the travellers in modern times. The ruins of the same towns are still seen ; their places, in general, can be designated ; and there is a moral certainty, therefore, that this prophecy was made by one who *knew* the locality of those places, and that, therefore, the prophecy is ancient and genuine. An impostor would never have attempted such a description as this ; nor could he have made it so accurate and true. In the language of Prof. Stuart (*Bib. Rep.*, vol. vii. pp. 108, 109), we may say, ' How obviously everything of this kind serves to give confirmation to the authority and credibility of the sacred records ! Do sceptics undertake to scoff at the Bible, and aver that it is the work of impostors who lived in later ages? Besides asking them what *object* impostors could have in forging a book of such high and lofty principles, we may ask—and ask with an assurance that need not fear the danger of being put to the blush—whether impostors of later ages could possibly have so managed, as to preserve all the *localities* in complete order which the Scriptures present? Rare impostors they must indeed have been—men possessed of more knowledge of antiquity than we can well imagine could ever be possessed by such as would condescend to

an imposition of such a character. In fact the thing appears to be morally impossible, if one considers it in the light of *antiquity*, when so little knowledge of a geographical kind was in existence, and when mistakes respecting countries and places with which one was not personally familiar, were almost, if not altogether, unavoidable. ' How happens it, now, that the authors of the Old Testament Scriptures should have possessed such a wonderful tact in geography, as it would seem they did, unless they lived at the time and in the countries of which they have spoken? This happens not elsewhere. It is but yesterday since one of the first scientific writers on geology in Great Britain, published to the world the declaration that our Mississippi and Missouri rivers *belong to the tropics.* Respectable writers, even in Germany, the land of classical attainments, have sometimes placed Cœlo-Syria on the east of the Anti-Libanus ridge, or even seemed to transfer Damascus over the mountains, and place it between the two Lebanon ridges in the valley.' No such mistakes occur in the sacred writers. They write as men who were familiar with the geography of places named ; they mention places with the utmost familiarity ; and, after a lapse of three thousand years, every successive traveller who visits Moab, Idumea, or Palestine, does something to confirm the accuracy of Isaiah. Towns, bearing the same name, or the ruins of towns, are located in the same relative position in which he said they were ; and the ruins of once splendid cities, broken columns, dilapidated walls, trodden down vineyards, and half-demolished temples, proclaim to the world that those cities are what he said they would be, and that he was under the inspiration of God.

is not improbable, though it is not quite certain. He also supposes that it was fulfilled when Damascus was taken captive by Tiglath-pileser, and its inhabitants carried to Kir (2 Kings xvi. 9), and when he overran, also, a great part of the kingdom of Israel, and carried its inhabitants captive to Assyria.

In regard to the *time* when it was uttered, there can be little doubt that it was when the alliance existed between Damascus and the kingdom of Ephraim, or Samaria, for on no other supposition can it be accounted for, that the two kingdoms were united in the prophecy (see ver. 3). The scope or design of the prophecy is indicated in the close (ver. 14): 'This is the portion of them that spoil us, and the lot of them that rob us;' and one design, at least, was to give an assurance to the kingdom of Judah, that the alliance between Damascus and Samaria was not to be dreaded, but that the kingdom of Judah would be safe. No alliance formed against them would be successful; no purpose to destroy them should be an object of dread.

The prophecy may be regarded as consisting of three parts. I. The prediction of the Divine judgment against Damascus (1, 2). II. The prediction respecting Ephraim, the ally of Damascus, and its fulfilment (3–11). III. A prediction respecting the Assyrians, and the calamities that should come upon them as a nation (12–14).

The kingdom of Syria, or Damascus, was overthrown in the fourth year of the reign of Ahaz. It is clear, therefore, that the prophecy was delivered before that time. And if so, its proper place, in the collection of the prophecies of Isaiah, would have been immediately after the ninth chapter. The reason why it is placed here, Lightfoot supposes to be, that in the seventh and eighth chapters the special design was to denounce judgment on the two kingdoms of Damascus and Ephraim; but that the design here was to connect the prediction of those judgments with the surrounding kingdoms, and to show how they would be affected by it. The prophecy is, therefore, placed amidst those which relate to foreign nations; or to kingdoms out of the land of Canaan.

Damascus was a celebrated city of Syria, and was long the capital of the kingdom of Damascus. It was a city in the time of Abraham, for the steward in his house, Eliezer, was said to be of Damascus (Gen. xv. 2). It is situated in a very fertile plain at the foot of mount Anti-Libanus, and is surrounded by hills. It is watered by a river which the ancients called *Chrysorrhoas*, as if it flowed with gold. This

river was divided into several canals, which were conducted to various parts of the city. It rose in the mountains of Anti-Libanus, and it is probable that the branches of that river were anciently called Abana and Pharpar (2 Kings v. 12). This river is now called the Barraday, and the peculiar beauty and fertility of Damascus is owing wholly to it. It rises in the adjacent mountains of Anti-Libanus, and, by numerous natural and artificial channels, is made to spread over the plain on which the city stands. It waters the whole extent of the gardens—an extent of country about nine miles in diameter, in the midst of which the city is situated—and when this is done, the water that is left flows off to the south-east through the plain, where, amid the arid sands, it is soon absorbed or evaporated, and the river disappears. The gardens are planted with all kinds of trees; mostly such as produce fruit, among which the apricot holds the ascendancy. Pomegranate, orange, lemon, and fig trees abound, and rising above these are other trees of huge proportions, intermingled with the poplar and sometimes the willow. Into every garden of the city water is carried, and this river, thus divided, gives to Damascus the beauty for which it has been so celebrated. The Persian geographers say, that the plain of Damascus is one of the four paradises of the East, and it is now said that there is not in all Syria a more delightful place.

From the time of Abraham until David, the Scripture says nothing of Damascus. In his time it was subdued, and brought under his authority. Towards the end of the reign of Solomon, the authority of the Jews was cast off by Rezin, and Damascus became again independent. Jeroboam, king of Israel, again conquered Damascus, and brought Syria into subjection (2 Kings xiv. 25); but after his death the Syrians again established their independence. Rezin became king of Damascus, and entered into an alliance with Pekah, king of Israel, and, unitedly, they invaded Judah, and made great havoc in its territories (see Notes on ch. vii.; comp. 2 Kings xvi. 5). Tiglath-pileser, however, king of Assyria, came to the assistance of the king of Judah and took Damascus, and destroyed it, and killed Rezin, and carried the Syrians into captivity beyond the Euphrates. To this event, probably, Isaiah refers in the prophecy before us. He, however, did not foretell its utter and *perpetual* ruin as he did that of Babylon. Damascus again recovered from its calamities. Holofernes again took it (Judith ii. 27). It is spoken of as flourishing in the time of Ezekiel (xxvii. 2). The Romans took it in the time, and by the agency, of Pompey the Great, about sixty years before Christ. It afterwards fell into the hands of the Arabians. It was taken by the Ottomans A.D. 1517; and has since been in the possession of the Turks. At present, it has a population of about 100,000. The name by which it is now known is *El-Sham*. It is a part of the pashalic of Damascus, which extends to the southern extremity of the Dead Sea. Mehemet Ali of Egypt obtained possession of it without resistance, in June 1832, and since that time it has been under the jurisdiction of his son Ibrahim. It is regarded by Mussulmans as a place of peculiar sanctity. According to them, Mecca has the first place, Jerusalem the next, and Damascus the third.

The prophecy respecting Damascus occupies verses 1–11 of the chapter. The general sense is, that Damascus and its allies would be greatly enfeebled and almost destroyed. Its fulfilment is to be referred to the invasion of Damascus by

CHAPTER XVII.

1. *The burden of Damascus.* The oracle indicating calamity or destruction to Damascus (see Note on ch. xiii. 1). ¶ *Damascus is taken away.* That is, it shall be destroyed. It was represented to the prophet in vision as destroyed (see Note on ch. i. 1). ¶ *And it shall be a ruinous heap* (see ch. xxxv. 2.) This took place under the kings of Assyria, and particularly under Tiglath-pileser. This was in the fourth year of Ahaz (2 Kings xvi. 9).

2. *The cities of Aroer.* By *Aroer* here seems to be meant a tract or region of country pertaining to Damascus, in which were situated several cities. Grotius supposes that it was a tract of country in Syria which is called by Ptolemy *Aueira* — Αΰιρα Vitringa supposes that one part of Damascus is meant by this, as Damascus was divided by the river in the same manner that Babylon was. There were several cities of the name of *Aroer.* One was on the river Arnon in the land of Moab (Deut. ii. 36; iii. 12; Josh. xii. 3). Burckhardt found this city under the name of Araayr. There was another city of this name further north, over against Rabbath-Ammon (Josh. xiii. 25). There was a third city of this name in the tribe of Judah (1 Sam. xxx. 28). Of the city of Araayr which Burckhardt visited, nothing is now remarkable but its entire desolation. Gesenius supposes

Tiglath-pileser and the Assyrians. The remainder of the chapter (12–14) is a distinct prophecy (see Notes on ver. 12).

THE *a* burden of Damascus. Behold, *b* Damascus is taken away from *being* a city, and it shall be a ruinous heap.

2 The cities of Aroer *are* forsaken; they shall be for flocks which shall lie down, and none *c* shall make *them* afraid.

3 The fortress also shall cease from Ephraim, and the kingdom from Damascus, and the remnant of Syria: they shall be as the glory of the children of Israel, saith the LORD of hosts.

a Jer.49.23,&c.; Amos 1.3-5; Zec.9.1, fulfilled.
b 2 Ki.16.9.　　　*c* Jer.7.33.

(*Comm. in loc.*) that the phrase ‘the cities of Aroer’ means the cities round about Aroer, and that were connected with it, similar to the phrase ‘daughters of a city.’ This city he supposes was near the river Arnon, within the limits of Moab, and that the prediction here was fulfilled by Tiglath-pileser, when he carried away the inhabitants of Galilee, Gilead, and other places mentioned in 2 Kings xv. 29. There can be no doubt that it was under the jurisdiction of Damascus. ¶ *Are forsaken.* Are desolate, and the inhabitants have fled. ¶ *They shall be for flocks*, &c. (See Note on ch. v. 17.)

3. *The fortress.* The strong place of defence; the fortified place. ¶ *Shall cease.* Shall come to an end; shall cease to be, for so the word רבַשָׁ (*shâbath*) is often used, (Gen. viii. 22; Isa. xxiv. 8; Lam. v. 15). ¶ *From Ephraim.* The name given to the kingdom of Israel, or to the ten tribes, because Ephraim was the largest of the ten, and was a leading tribe in their councils (see Note on ch. vii. 2). Ephraim, or the kingdom of Samaria, is here mentioned in connection with Damascus or Syria, because they were confederated together, and would be involved in the same overthrow. ¶ *And the remnant of Syria.* That which is left of the kingdom of Syria after the capital Damascus shall be destroyed. ¶ *They shall be as the glory of the children of Israel.* That

4 And in that day it shall come to pass, *that* the glory of Jacob shall be made thin, and *ª* the fatness of his flesh shall wax lean.

5 And *ᵇ* it shall be as when the harvest-man gathereth the corn,

and reapeth the ears with his arm ; and it shall be as he that gathereth ears in the valley of Rephaim.

6 Yet gleaning-grapes shall be left in it, as the shaking of an olive-tree, two *or* three berries in the top of the uppermost bough, four *or*

---

is, as the defences, or the strongly fortified towns and fastnesses of the kingdom of Israel shall pass away or be destroyed, so shall it be with the kingdom of Damascus. As they are allied with each other, they shall fare alike. The Chaldee reads this, ' And the dominion shall cease from Ephraim, and the kingdom from Damascus.'

4. *The glory of Jacob.* Jacob is here used to denote the kingdom of Israel, or Samaria. The word ' glory ' here denotes dignity, power ; that on which they relied, and of which they boasted. ¶ *Shall be made thin.* Shall be diminished, as a body wastes away by disease, and becomes feeble. The prophet sets forth the calamities of Ephraim by two figures ; the first is that of a *body* that becomes emaciated by sickness, the other that of the harvest when all the fruits are gathered except a few in the upper branches (ver. 5, 6). ¶ *And the fatness of his flesh shall wax lean.* He shall become feeble, as a man does by wasting sickness. Chaldee, ' The riches of his glory shall be removed.'

5. *And it shall be,* &c. This is the other figure by which the prophet sets forth the calamities that were coming upon Ephraim—an image designed to denote the fact that the inhabitants and wealth of the land would be collected and removed, as the husbandman gathers his harvest, and leaves only that which is inaccessible in the upper boughs of the tree, or the gleanings in the field. ¶ *As when the harvest-man gathereth the corn.* The wheat, the barley, &c.; for so the word *corn*—now applied by us almost exclusively to maize — means in the Scriptures. The sense in this passage is plain. As the farmer cuts down and collects his grain and removes it from the harvest field, so the enemies of Ephraim would come and remove the people and their wealth to a distant land. This received a complete fulfil-

ment when the ten tribes were removed by the Assyrians to a distant land. This was done by Tiglath-pileser (2 Kings xv. 29), and by Shalmaneser (2 Kings xvii. 6). ¶ *And reapeth the ears with his arm.* As he collects the standing grain with one arm so that he can cut it with the sickle in the other hand. The word rendered 'reapeth' (קָצַר) means here *to collect together* as a reaper does the standing grain in his arm. The word rendered 'ears' (שִׁבֳּלִים *shibbolim*), means here rather the spires or stalks of standing grain. ¶ *In the valley of Rephaim.* The valley of Rephaim is mentioned in 2 Sam. v. 18, 22 ; xxiii. 13 ; 1 Chron. xi. 15 ; xiv. 9. The name means ' the Giants ;' but why it was given to it is now unknown. In passing from Bethlehem to Jerusalem, it lies on the left, and descends gradually to the south-west, until it contracts in that direction into a deeper and narrower valley, called wady el - Werd, which unites further on with wady Ahmed, and finds its way to the Mediterranean. The plain extends nearly to Jerusalem, and is terminated by a slight rocky ridge forming the brow of the valley of Hinnom (see Josephus, *Ant.* vii. 4. 1 ; viii. 12. 4 ; also Robinson's *Bib. Researches,* vol. i. pp. 323, 324). It seem to have been distinguished for its fertility, and is here used to denote a fertile region in general.

6. *Yet gleaning-grapes,* &c. They shall not all be removed, or destroyed. A *few* shall be left, as a man who is gathering grapes or olives will leave a few that are inaccessible on the topmost boughs, or the furthest branches. Those would be usually the poorest, and so it may be implied that those left in Israel would be among the poorer inhabitants of the land. ¶ *Two or three.* A very few—such as would be left in gathering grapes, or in endeavouring to shake olives from a tree. ¶ *Four or five.* A

five in the outmost fruitful branches thereof, saith the LORD God of Israel.

7 At that day shall a man *a* look to his Maker, and his eyes shall have respect to the Holy One of Israel.

8 And he shall not look to the

altars, the work of his hands, neither shall respect *that* which his fingers have made, either the groves or the [1] images.

9 In that day shall his strong cities be as a forsaken bough, and an uppermost branch, which they

a Mic.7.7.   1 or, *sun images*, Jer.17.13.

very few that would remain on the furthest branches, and that could not be shaken off or reached.

7. *At that day shall a man look to his Maker.* Instead of confiding in their strongly fortified places and armies, they shall look for aid and protection to the God that made them, and who alone can help them. National afflictions and judgments often have the effect to turn the eyes of even a wicked and rebellious people to God. They feel their danger; they are convinced of their guilt; they see that no one but God can protect them; and for a time they are willing, even by humiliation and fasting, to seek the Divine protection. ¶ *His eyes shall have respect*, &c. He shall look up to, or regard. ¶ *The Holy One of Israel.* The God of Israel; the true God. As the Syrians were allied with the kingdom of Samaria or Ephraim, they were, of course, acquainted with the true God, and in some sense acknowledged him. In these times of impending calamity, they would be led to seek him, and implore his aid and protection. There is no reason to believe, however, that they would turn permanently to him, or become his true worshippers.

8. *And he shall not look to the altars.* That is, the altars of the gods which the Syrians worshipped, and the altars of the false gods which had been erected in the land of Israel or Samaria by its wicked kings, and particularly by Ahaz. Ahaz fancied an altar which he saw at Damascus when on a visit to Tiglath-pileser, and ordered Urijah the priest to construct one like it in Samaria, on which he subsequently offered sacrifice (2 Kings xvi. 10–13). It is well known, also, that the kings of Israel and Judah often reared altars to false gods in the high places and the groves of the land (see 2 Kings xxi. 3, 4, 5). The Ephraimites were particularly guilty in this respect

(Hos. viii. 11): 'Because Ephraim hath made many altars to sin, altars shall be unto him to sin.' ¶ *Which his fingers have made.* Perhaps indicating that the idols which they worshipped had been constructed with special art and skill (see ch. ii. 8). ¶ *Either the groves.* The altars of idols were usually erected in groves, and idols were worshipped there before temples were raised (see Ex. xxxiv. 13; Deut. vii. 5; xii. 3; Judg. iii. 7; 1 Kings xiv. 23; xviii. 19; 2 Chron. xxxiii. 3; comp. Notes on ch. i. 29). ¶ *Or the images.* Marg. 'Sun images' (חַמָּנִים *hhămmânîm*). This word is used to denote idols in general in Lev. xxvi. 30; 2 Chron. xxiv. 4. But it is supposed to denote properly images erected to the sun, and to be derived from חַמָּה (*hhămma*), *the sun.* Thus the word is used in Job xxx. 28; Isa. xxiv. 23; xxx. 26; Cant. vi. 10. The word, according to Gesenius, is of Persian origin (*Comm. in loc.*) The sun was undoubtedly worshipped by the ancient idolaters, and altars or images would be erected to it (see Notes on Job xxxi. 26).

9. *His strong cities.* The cities of the united kingdoms of Damascus and Samaria. ¶ *Be as a forsaken bough.* There has been much difficulty in the interpretation of this passage. Lowth says, 'No one has ever been able to make any tolerable sense of these words;' and proposes himself the translation,

In that day shall his strongly fenced cities become

Like the desertion of the Hivites and the Amorites;

following in this the translation of the LXX., but doing violence to the Hebrew text. Rosenmüller translates it, 'As the remnant of a grove when the thicket is cut down, and when few trees are left.' The word rendered 'bough' (חֹרֶשׁ *hhōrĕsh*) means, properly, a thicket, or thick foliage, a wood that is entangled

left because of the children of Israel:
and there shall be desolation.

10 Because ^a thou hast forgotten
the God of thy salvation, and hast
not been mindful of the Rock of
thy strength; therefore shalt thou

a Jer.17.13.

plant pleasant plants, and shalt set
it with ^b strange slips:

11 In the day shalt thou make
thy plant to grow, and in the morning shalt thou make thy seed to
flourish; *but* the harvest *shall be*

b Jer.5.21.

---

or intricate (1 Sam. xxiii. 15, 16, 18;
2 Chron. xxvii. 4); and probably this is
the idea here. The phrase may be
rendered, 'as the *leavings* or *residue* of
a grove, copse, or entangled wood;' and
the idea is, that as a *few* trees might
be left when the axeman cuts down the
grove, so a few inferior and smaller
towns should be left in the desolation
that would come upon Damascus. ¶ *And
an uppermost branch* (ver. 6). As a
few berries are left in the topmost
branch of the olive, or the vine, so shall
a few cities or people be left in the general desolation. ¶ *Which they left.*
Which *are* left, or which the invaders
would leave. ¶ *Because of the children
of Israel.* Literally, 'from the face,'
i.e., before the children of Israel. Lowth
supposes that it refers to the Amorites,
who left their land before the Israelites,
or gave up their land for them. Vitringa
renders it, ' On account of the children
of Israel;' and supposes that it means
that a few cities were spared by the
purpose of God in the invasion by Tiglath-pileser, to be a residence of the
Israelites that should remain; or that,
for some reason which is not known,
the Assyrians chose to spare a few
towns, and not wholly to destroy the
country. The *general* idea is plain,
that a few towns would be left, and that
it would be *before* the children of Israel,
or in their presence, or in order that
they might continue to dwell in them.
Jerome interprets the whole as referring
to the time when the land of Judea was
forsaken on the invasion of the Romans.
¶ *And there shall be desolation.* The
land shall be desolated, except the few
cities and towns that shall be left, like
the gleaning of the olive tree.

10. *Because thou,* &c. Because the
kingdom of Israel or Samaria had done
it. ¶ *The God of thy salvation.* The
God in whom alone was salvation; or
who alone could protect thee (comp.
Mic. vii. 7. Hos. ii. 15). ¶ *The rock of*

thy strength. God. A rock of strength
is a strongly fortified place; or a rock
which an enemy could not successfully
assail. High rocks were selected as a
place of refuge from an invading foe
(see Notes on ch. i. 10, 21). In allusion
to this, God is often called *a Rock*, and
a strong tower (Deut. xxxii. 4, 15, 18,
30, 31, 37; 1 Sam. ii. 2; 2 Sam. xxii. 2,
3, 32; Ps. xviii. 31, 46; xix. 14; xxviii. 1;
xxx. 1, 2). ¶ *Shalt thou plant pleasant plants.* Plants that are fitted to
produce pleasure or delight; that is, you
shall cultivate your fields, and set them
out with choice vines and plants in
hope of a future harvest, but you shall
be disappointed. ¶ *And shall set it
with strange slips.* The word 'slips'
means the *cuttings* of the vine that are
set in the ground to grow; or the shoot
or sucker that is taken off and *set out,*
or put in the earth to take root and
grow, as is often done by farmers and
gardeners. The word 'strange' here
means *foreign*, those which are procured
from a distance, and which are therefore esteemed valuable; plants selected
with care. This does not mean, as
Lowth supposes, strange and idolatrous
worship, and the vicious practices connected with it; but it means that,
though they should be at great pains
and expense in cultivating their land,
yet the enemy would come in and make
it desolate.

11. *In the day,* &c. Thou shalt cultivate it assiduously and constantly.
Thou shalt be at special pains that it
may be watered and pruned, in order
that it may produce abundantly. ¶ *And
in the morning.* With early care and
attention—denoting the pains that
would be bestowed on the young plant.
¶ *The harvest* shall be *a heap.* The
margin reads this, 'the harvest shall be
removed in the day of inheritance,'
rendering it as if the word נֵד (*nēdh*)
usually meaning a heap, were derived
from נוּד (*nūdh*), to shake, move, wan-

a¹ heap in the day of grief and of desperate sorrow.

12 Wo to the ² multitude of many people, *which* make a noise like the noise of the seas; and to the rushing of nations, *that* make

1 or, *removed in the day of inheritance, and there shall be deadly sorrow.*

a rushing like the rushing of mighty ³ waters!

13 The nations shall rush like the rushing of many waters: but God *a* shall rebuke them, and they shall flee far off, and shall be chased as the chaff of the mountains be-

2 or, *noise.*   3 or, *many.*   a Ps.9.5.

der; or, as if it were to be removed. Probably the translation in the text is correct; and the sense is, 'When from the plant which was so beautiful and valuable, and which you cherished with so much care, you expected to obtain a rich harvest, you had only sorrow and inexpressible disappointment.' The figure used here is supposed by Rosenmüller to be that of hendiadys ($\tilde{\epsilon}\nu$ $\delta\iota\grave{\alpha}$ $\delta\nu o\tilde{\iota}\nu$), by which the phrases 'shall be an heap,' and 'desperate sorrow,' are to be taken together, meaning 'the heap of the harvest shall be inexpressible sorrow.' ¶ *In the day of grief.* The word rendered 'grief' here (נַחֲלָה) means, properly, *inheritance, heirship, possession,* and should have been so rendered here. It means that in the day when they *hoped* to possess the result of their planting, or in the time of the usual harvest, they would obtain only grief and disappointment. ¶ *And desperate sorrow.* The word rendered 'desperate' (אָנוּשׁ, *ânush*), denotes that which is *weak, mortal, incurable* (Job xxxiv. 6; Jer. xvii. 16; xxx. 12, 15). The sense here is, that there would be grievous disappointment, and that there would be no remedy for it; and the idea of the whole is, that calamities were coming upon the nation which would blast all their hopes, and destroy all their prospects. The prophecy was fulfilled in the invasion by Tiglath-pileser, and the army of the Assyrians.

The twelfth verse commences a new prophecy, which has no connection with that which precedes it; and which in itself gives no certain indication of the time when it was uttered, or of the people to which it relates. It is a broken and detached piece, and is evidently the description of some army rushing to conquest, and confident of success, but which was to be overtaken with sudden calamity. The entire

description is so applicable to the invasion of the land of Judah by the army of Sennacherib, and his overthrow by the angel of JEHOVAH, that by the common consent of interpreters it has been regarded as referring to it (see Notes on ch. x). But when it was spoken, or why it was placed here, is unknown. It may be added that many commentators and, among the rest, Gesenius, have supposed that the following chapter is a part of this prophecy. The general sense of the prophecy is, that numerous hostile nations would overrun Palestine, but that JEHOVAH would destroy them all.

12. *Wo to the multitude,* &c. The word 'wo' (הוֹי *hō*) may be either an interjection simply directing the attention to them, or it may be a word indicating approaching calamity and judgment (see Note on ch. v. 6). Gesenius supposes that it is rather the language of compassion, on account of the evil which they threatened to bring upon the people of God, like 1 Kings xiii. 30, 'Ah! wo, my brother!' ¶ *The multitude of many people.* Or, the tumult of many nations—a description of the noise attending an invading army made up of many nations mingled together, such as was that of Sennacherib. ¶ *Which make a noise,* &c. This is a beautiful description of a vast army, and of the shouting, the tumult, the din, which attends its march. The same comparison occurs in Jer. vi. 23; Psal. lxv. 7 (see Ezek. xliii. 2; Rev. i. 15; xiv. 2; xix. 6). ¶ *And to the rushing of nations.* The rushing of mighty armies to conquest.

13. *God shall rebuke them.* The word 'God' is not here in the original, but is evidently to be supplied. The word 'rebuke' means that he would disarrange their plans, prevent their success, and defeat their purposes. It

fore the wind, and like [1] a rolling thing before the whirlwind.

14 And, behold, at evening-tide trouble; *and* before the morning he *is* not. This *is* the portion of them [a] that spoil us, and the lot of them that rob us.

CHAPTER XVIII.

ANALYSIS.

'THE eighteenth chapter of Isaiah,' says bishop Horsley, 'is one of the most obscure passages of the ancient prophets. It has been considered as such by the whole succession of interpreters from Jerome to Bishop Lowth.' 'The object of it,' says Bishop Lowth, 'the end and design of it; the people to whom it is addressed; the history to which it belongs; the person who sends the messengers; and the nation to whom they are sent, are all obscure and doubtful. Much of the obscurity lies in the highly figurative cast of the language, and in the ambiguity of some of the principal words, arising from the great variety of the senses often comprehended under the primary meaning of a single root.'

Lowth supposes that Egypt is the country referred to; that the prophecy was delivered before the return of Sennacherib's expedition to Egypt; and that it was designed to give to the Jews, and perhaps likewise to the Egyptians, an intimation of the destruction of their great

1 or, *thistle-down.*   a Jer.2 3.

and powerful enemy. Taylor, the editor of Calmet's *Dictionary*, supposes that it relates to a people lying in southern, or Upper Egypt, or the country above the cataracts of the Nile, *i.e.*, Nubia; and that the people to whom the message is sent are those who were situated north on the river Nile, where the various streams which go to form the Nile become a single river; and that the nation represented as 'scattered and peeled,' or as he renders it, 'a people contracted and deprived,' *i.e.*, in their persons, refers to the Pigmies, as they are described by Homer, Strabo, and others (see this view drawn out in the *Fragments* appended to Calmet's *Dict.* No. cccxxii.) Rosenmüller says of this prophecy, that 'it is involved in so many, and so great difficulties, on account of unusual expressions and figurative sentences, and the history of those times, so little known to us, that it is impossible to explain and unfold it. We seem to be reading mere *enigmas*, in explaining which, although many learned interpreters have taken great pains, yet scarcely two can be found who agree.' Gesenius connects it with the closing verse of the previous chapter; and so does also Vitringa. Gesenius supposes that it refers to a nation in distant Ethiopia in alliance with Israel. To this, says he, and to all the nations of the earth, the prophet addresses himself, in order to draw their attention to the sudden overthrow which God would bring upon the enemy, after he has quietly looked upon their violence for a long time. According to this view, the prophecy belongs to the period immediately pre-

shows the great power of God, that he can thus by a *rebuke*—a word—arrest mighty nations, and discomfit them when they are tumultuously hastening onward in the confidence of victory. This discomfiture refers, doubtless, to the overthrow of Sennacherib and his army by the pestilence (2 Kings xix. 35; see Notes on ch. xxxvii. 36). ¶ *And they shall flee far off.* The whole army of Sennacherib was not destroyed, but a part with himself returned to Assyria (2 Kings xix. 36). ¶ *And shall be chased as the chaff,* &c. Denoting the ease with which God would do it, and the certain and entire discomfiture of the army. The figure is one that is very striking in describing an army that is routed, and that flies in disorder (comp. Job xxi. 18; Ps. i. 4; xxxv. 5; Isa. xxix. 5; Hos. xiii. 3). ¶ *And like a rolling thing.* Marg. 'Thistle-down.' It means, literally, anything that *rolls* (בַּלְגַּל *găl-*

găl, from בָּלַל *gălăl,* to roll). It is applied to chaff, stubble, or anything that is driven about by a whirlwind (Psal. lxxxiii. 14).

14. *At evening-tide trouble.* In the time of evening—that is, in the night. ¶ *Before the morning he is not.* That is, he is destroyed. This is strikingly descriptive of the destruction of the army of Sennacherib on that fatal night when the angel of the Lord slew one hundred and eighty-five thousand men (see Note on ch. xxxvii. 36). ¶ *This is the portion of them that spoil us.* Of those who would plunder us. This is a *general* declaration in regard to the enemies of the Jewish people. This is the lot, the end, the destiny of all who attempt to destroy them. That is, the people of God shall be safe whoever rises up against them; and whatever may be the number, or the power of their foes, they shall be overthrown.

ceding the 14th year of Hezekiah, when the Assyrian armies had already overrun, or were about to overrun Palestine on their way to Egypt, and the prophet confidently predicts their destruction. At this time, he remarks, Tirhakah, king of Ethiopia, with a part of Egypt, had armed himself against the Assyrians; for which purpose he had probably entered into an alliance with the Hebrews. To this friend and ally of Israel, the prophet gives the assurance that God was about to destroy completely the common enemy, the Assyrian.—By some, the land here referred to has been supposed to be Egypt; by others, Ethiopia in Africa; by others, Judea; by others, the Roman empire; and others have supposed that it refers to the destruction of Gog and Magog in the times of the Messiah. Vitringa supposes that the prophecy must be referred either to the Egyptians or the Assyrians; and as there is no account, he says, of any calamity coming upon the Egyptians like that which is described in ver. 4–6, and as that description is applicable to the destruction of the Assyrians under Sennacherib, he regards it as referring to him. Calvin says that many have supposed that the Troglodytes of Upper Egypt are meant here, but that this is improbable, as they were not known to have formed any alliances with other nations. He supposes that some nation is referred to in the vicinity of Egypt and Ethiopia, but what people he does not even conjecture. Amidst this diversity of opinion, it may seem rash to hazard a

conjecture in regard to the situation of the nation who *sent* the messengers, and the nation to whom they were sent; and it is obviously improper to hazard such a conjecture without a careful examination of the phrases and words which occur in the prophecy. When that is done—when the characteristics of the nation have been fully determined, then, perhaps, we may be able to arrive at some satisfactory conclusion in regard to this very difficult portion of the Bible. The prophecy consists of the following parts:—1. The prophet addresses himself to the nation here described as a 'land shadowing with wings,' and as sending ambassadors, in a manner designed to call their attention to the great events soon to occur (1, 2). 2. He addresses all nations, calling upon them also to attend to the same subject (3). 3. He says that God had revealed to him that destruction should come upon the enemies here referred to, and that the immense host should be left to the beasts of the earth, and to the fowls of the mountains (4–6). 4. The consequence, he says, of such events would be, that a present would be brought to Jehovah from the distant nation 'scattered and peeled,' and whose land the rivers had spoiled (7).

WO to the land shadowing with wings, which *is* beyond the rivers[a] of Ethiopia:

a ch.20.3-5; Eze.30.4-9; Zep.2.12.

CHAPTER XVIII.

1. *Woe to the land* (הוֹי). This word, as has been already remarked (Note on ch. xvii. 12), may be a mere interjection or salutation, and would be appropriately rendered by 'Ho!' Or it may be a word denouncing judgment, or wrath, as it is often used in this prophecy (Note on ch. v. 8). ¶ *Shadowing with wings* (צִלְצַל כְּנָפָיִם). This is one of the most difficult expressions in the whole chapter; and one to which as yet, probably, no satisfactory meaning has been applied. The LXX. render it, Οὐαὶ γῆς πλοίων πτέρυγες—'Ah! wings of the land of ships.' The Chaldee, 'Woe to the land in which they come in ships from a distant country, and whose sails are spread out as an eagle which flies upon its wings.' Grotius renders it, 'The land whose extreme parts are shaded by mountains.' The word rendered 'shadowed' (צִלְצַל *tzĭl-tzăl*), occurs only in this place, and in

Job xli. 7, where it is translated 'fish-spears'—but as we know nothing of the *form* of those spears, that place throws no light on the meaning of the word here. The word is derived, evidently, from צָלַל (*tzâlăl*), which has three significations :—(1.) *To be shady, dark, obscure;* and hence its derivatives are applied to anything that *makes* a shade or shadow—particularly *shady trees* (Job xl. 21, 22); the shades of night (Cant. ii. 17; iv. 6); or anything that produces obscurity, or darkness, as a tree, a rock, a wing, &c. (2.) It means *to tingle,* spoken of the ears (1 Sam. iii. 11; 2 Kings xxi. 13); *to quiver,* spoken of the lips (Hab. iii. 16); and hence its derivatives are applied to anything that makes a sound by *tinkling*—an instrument of music; a cymbal made of two pieces of metal that are struck together (2 Sam. vi. 5; 1 Chron. xv. 16; xvi. 42; xxv. 6; 2 Chron. v. 12; Neh. xii. 27; Ps. cl. 5.) (3.) It means *to sink*

(Ex. xv. 10).—From the sense of making a *shade*, a derivative of the verb צֵלָצַל (*tzĕlâtzâl*)—the same as used here except the points—is applied to locusts, because they appear in such swarms as to obscure the rays of the sun, and produce an extended shade, or shadow, over a land as a cloud does ; or because they make a rustling with their wings. The word here used, therefore, may mean either *shaded*, or *rustling*, or *rattling*, in the manner of a cymbal or other tinkling instrument. It may be added, that the word *may* mean a *double shade*, being a doubling of the word צֵל (*tzēl*), a *shade*, or *shadow*, and it has been supposed by some to apply to Ethiopia as lying between the tropics, having a *double shadow;* that is, so that the shadow of objects is cast one half of the year on the north side, and the other half on the south. The word ‘ wings ’ is applied in the Scriptures to the following things, viz.—(1.) The wing of a fowl. This is the literal, and common signification. (2.) The skirts, borders, or lower parts of a garment, from the resemblance to wings (Num. xv. 38 ; 1 Sam. xxiv. 5, 11 ; Zech. viii. 13). Also a bed-covering (Deut. xxxiii. 1). (3.) The extremities or borders of a country, or of the world (Job xxxvii. 3 ; Isa. xxiv. 16 ; Ezek. xvii. 3, 7). (4.) The *wing* or extremity of an army, as we use the word *wing* (Isa. viii. 8 ; Jer. xlviii. 40 ; Dan. ix. 27). (5.) The expanding rays of the morning, because the light *expands* or *spreads* out like wings (Ps. cxxxix. 9 ; Mal. iv. 2). (6.) The *wind*—resembling wings in rapid motion (Ps. xviii. 10, 21 ; civ. 3 ; Hos. iv. 19). (7.) The battlement or pinnacle of the temple—or perhaps the porches extended on each side of the temple like wings (Dan. ix. 27 ; comp. Matt. iv. 5). (8.) *Protection*—as wings are a protection to young birds in their nest (see Ps. xviii. 8 ; xxxvi. 7 ; lxi. 4 ; xci. 4 ; Matt. xxiii. 37). It has been proposed by some to apply this description to *ships*, or the sails of vessels, as if a land was designated which was covered with *sails*, or the *wings* of vessels. So the LXX., and the Chaldee. But there is no instance in which the word *wings* is so applied in the Scriptures.

The expression here used *may*, therefore, be applied to many things ; and it is not easy to determine its signification. The *general* idea is, that of *something* that abounds in the land that is stretched out or expanded ; that, as it were, *covers* it, and so abounds as to make a shade or shadow everywhere. And it may be applied—(1.) to a nation that abounds with birds or fowls, so that they might be said to shade the land ; (2.) to a nation abounding with locusts, shading the land or making a rustling noise ; or (3.) to a nation furnishing protection, or stretching out its wings, as it were, for the defence of a feeble people. So Vitringa interprets this place, and supposes that it refers to Egypt, as being the nation where the Hebrews sought protection. Or (4.) to a country that is shaded with trees, mountains, or hills. So Grotius supposes it means here, and thinks that it refers to Ethiopia, as being bounded by high hills or mountains. (5.) It *may* mean a people distinguished for navigation—abounding in *sails* of vessels—as if they were everywhere spread out like wings. So the LXX. and the Chaldee understand this ; and the interpretation has some plausibility, from the fact that light vessels are immediately mentioned. (6.) The editor of Calmet's *Dictionary* supposes that it refers to the *winged Cnephim* which are sculptured over the temple gates in Upper Egypt. They are emblematic representatives of the god *Cneph*, to which the temples are dedicated, and abound in Upper Egypt. The symbol of the *wings* is supposed to denote the *protection* which the god extended over the land. (7.) Gesenius (*Com. on Isaiah*) renders it, ‘ Land rustling with wings,’ and supposes that the word rendered ‘ shadowing,’ denotes the *rustling* sound that is made by the clangour of weapons of war. Amidst this variety of interpretation, it is, perhaps, not possible to determine the meaning of the phrase. It has no parallel expression to illustrate it ; and its meaning must be left to conjecture. Almost any one of the above significations will suit the connection ; and it is not very material which is chosen. The one that, perhaps, best suits the connection, is that of the LXX.

2 That sendeth ambassadors by
the sea, even in vessels of bulrushes
upon the waters, *saying*, Go, ye
swift messengers, to a nation [1] scattered and peeled, to a people terri-

1 or, *outspread and polished.*

ble from their beginning hitherto:
a nation [2] meted out and trodden
down, whose land the rivers [3] have
spoiled !

2 *of line line, and treading under foot,* or, *that meteth
out and treadeth down.*   3 or, *despise.*

and the Chaldee, which refers it to the
multitude of ships that expand their
sails, and appear to fill all the waters
of the land with wings. ¶ *Which* is
beyond (מֵעֵבֶר). This does not, of necessity, mean *beyond*, though that is its
usual signification. It properly means
*from the passing, the passages, the
crossing over,* of a river ; and may be
rendered what is on the other side ; or
over against. It sometimes means on
this side, as if used by one living on the
other side (Deut. iv. 49 ; Josh. xiii. 27 ;
1 Kings iv. 24) ; in which places it has
not the sense of *beyond*, but means
either on this side, or lying alongside.
The sense here is, probably, that this
country was situated *not far* from the
rivers of Cush, *probably* beyond them,
but still it is implied that they were
not *far* beyond them, but were rather
at their passings over, or crossing-
places ; that is, near them. ¶ *The
rivers of Ethiopia.* Heb. ' Rivers of
Cush.' (On the meaning of the word
' Cush,' see Note on ch. xi. 11.) It is
sometimes applicable to Ethiopia or
Nubia—that is, the portion of Egypt
above the cataracts of the Nile. Comp.
Jer. xiii. 23 : ' Can the Ethiopian [the
Cushite] change his skin ?' (see also
Ezek. xxix. 10). This word does not
determine with certainty the country to
which reference is made—for the country of Cush *may* mean that east of the
Euphrates, or southern Arabia, or
southern Egypt. Egypt and Cush are,
however, sometimes connected (2 Kings
xix. 9 ; Ps. lxviii. 31 ; Isa. xx. 3 ; xliii.
3 ; Nah. iii. 9 ; comp. Dan. xi. 43).
The *probability* from the use of this
word is, that some part of Upper Egypt
is intended. Ethiopia in part lies
beyond the most considerable of the
streams that make up the river Nile.
2. *That sendeth ambassadors.* That
is, *accustomed* to send messengers.
What was the design of their thus sending ambassadors does not appear. The

prophet simply intimates the fact ; a
fact by which they were well known.
It may have been for purposes of commerce, or to seek protection. Bochart
renders the word translated ' ambassadors ' by *images*, and supposes that it
denotes an image of the god Osiris made
of the papyrus ; but there does not seem
to be any reason for this opinion. The
word צִיר (*tzir*) *may* mean an idol or
image, as in Isa. xlv. 16 ; Ps. xlix. 15.
But it usually denotes ambassadors, or
messengers (Josh. ix. 4 ; Prov. xxv.
13 ; xiii. 17 ; Isa. lvii. 9 ; Jer. xlix. 14 ;
Obad. 1). ¶ *By the sea.* What *sea* is
here meant cannot be accurately determined. The word ' sea ' (יָם) is applied
to various collections of water, and may
be used in reference to a sea, a lake, a
pond, and even a large river. It is
often applied to the Mediterranean ;
and where the phrase *Great Sea* occurs,
it denotes that (Num. xxxiv. 6, 7 ; Deut.
xi. 24). It is applied to the Lake of
Gennesareth or the Sea of Galilee (Num.
xxxiv. 11) ; to the Salt Sea (Gen. xiv.
3) ; to the Red Sea often (Ex. xiii. 10 ;
Num. xiv. 25 ; xxi. 4 ; xxxiii. 10, *et al.*)
It is also applied to *a large river*, as,
e.g., the *Nile* (Isa. xix. 5 ; Neh. iii. 8) ;
and to the Euphrates (Jer. li. 36). So
far as this *word* is concerned, therefore,
it may denote either the Mediterranean,
the Red Sea, the Nile, or the Euphrates.
If the country spoken of is Upper Egypt
or Nubia, then we are naturally led to
suppose that the prophet refers either
to the Nile or the Red Sea. ¶ *Even
in vessels of bulrushes.* The word rendered ' bulrushes ' (גֹּמֶא) is derived
from the verb גָּמָא (*gâmâ*), *to swallow,
sip, drink ;* and is given to a reed or
bulrush, from its *imbibing* water. It is
usually applied in the Scriptures to the
Egyptian *papyrus*—a plant which grew
on the banks of the Nile, and from
which we have derived our word *paper.*
' This plant,' says Taylor (*Heb. Con.*),

'grew in moist places near the Nile, and was four or five yards in height. Under the bark it consisted wholly of thin skins, which being separated and spread out, were applied to various uses. Of these they made boxes and chests, and even boats, smearing them over with pitch.' These *laminæ,* or skins, also served the purpose of paper, and were used instead of parchment, or plates of lead and copper, for writing on. This plant, the *Cyperus Papyrus* of modern botanists, mostly grew in Lower Egypt, in marshy land, or in shallow brooks and ponds, formed by the inundation of the Nile. ' The papyrus,'

PAPYRUS (*Cyperus Papyrus*).

says Pliny, ' grows in the marsh lands of Egypt, or in the stagnant pools left inland by the Nile, after it has returned to its bed, which have not more than two cubits in depth. The root of the plant is the thickness of a man's arm ; it has a triangular stalk, growing not higher than ten cubits (fifteen feet), and decreasing in breadth towards the summit, which is crowned with a thyrsus, containing no seeds, and of no use except to deck the statues of the gods. They employ the roots as firewood, and for making various utensils. They even construct small boats of the plant ; and out of the rind, sails, mats, clothes, bedding, ropes ; they eat it either crude or cooked, swallowing only the juice ;

and when they manufacture paper from it, they divide the stem by means of a kind of needle into thin plates ; or laminæ, each of which is as large as the plant will admit. All the paper is woven upon a table, and is continually moistened with Nile water, which being thick and slimy, furnishes an effectual species of glue. In the first place, they form upon a table, perfectly horizontal, a layer the whole length of the papyrus, which is crossed by another placed transversely, and afterwards enclosed within a press. The different sheets are then hung in a situation exposed to the sun, in order to dry, and the process is finally completed by joining them together, beginning with the best. There are seldom more than twenty slips or stripes produced from one stem of the plant.' —(Pliny, xiii. 11, 12.) Wilkinson remarks, that ' the mode of making papyri was this : the interior of the stalks of the plant, after the rind had been removed, was cut into thin slices in the direction of their length, and these being laid on a flat board, in succession, similar slices were placed over them at right angles, and their surfaces being cemented together by a sort of glue, and subjected to the proper degree of pressure, and well dried, the papyrus was completed.'—(*Ancient Egyptians,* vol. iii. p. 148.) The word here used is translated ' bulrushes ' in Ex. ii. 3, where the little ark is described in which Moses was laid near the Nile ; the 'rush' in Job viii. 11 ; and 'rushes,' in Isa. xxxv. 7. It does not elsewhere occur. That the ancients were in the practice of making light boats or vessels from the papyrus is well known. Thus Theophrastus (in the *History of Plants,* iv. 9) says, that ' the papyrus is useful for many things ; for from this they make vessels,' or ships (πλοῖα). Thus, Pliny (xiii. 11, 22) says, *ex ipso quidem papyro navigia texunt*—'from the papyrus they weave vessels.' Again, (vi. 56, 57) : ' Even now,' says he, ' in the Britannic Ocean useful vessels are made of bark ; on the Nile from the papyrus, and from reeds and rushes.' Plutarch describes Isis going in search of the body of Osiris, ' through the fenny country in a bark made of the papyrus (ἐν βαρίδι παπυρίνη) ; where it is supposed that persons using boats of this description (ἐν παπυρίνοις ὀκαφίσι πλέοντας) are never attacked by crocodiles out of respect to the goddess,' (*De Is.* 18.) Moses, also, it will be remembered, was exposed on the banks of the Nile in a similar boat or ark. 'She took for him an ark of bulrushes, and daubed it with slime and with pitch, and put the child therein' (Ex. ii. 3). The same word occurs here (גֹּמֶא) which is used by Isaiah, and this fact shows that such boats were known as early as the time of Moses. Lucan also mentions boats made of the papyrus at Memphis:

Conseritur bibula Memphitis cymba papyro.—
Phar. iv. 136.

At Memphis boats are woven together from the marshy papyrus

The sculptures of Thebes, Memphis, and other places, abundantly show that they were employed as punts, or canoes for fishing, in all parts of Egypt, during the inundation of the Nile.'—(Wilkinson's *Ancient Egyptians,* vol. iii. p. 186.) In our own country, also, it will be remembered, the natives were accustomed to make canoes, or vessels, of the bark of the birch, with which they often adventured on even dangerous navigation. The circumstance here mentioned of the גֹּמֶא (the papyrus), seems to fix the scene of this prophecy to the region of the Nile. This reed grew nowhere else; and it is natural, therefore, to suppose, that some nation living near the Nile is intended. Taylor, the editor of Calmet, has shown that the inhabitants of the upper regions of the Nile were accustomed to form floats of hollow earthen vessels, and to weave them together with rushes, and thus to convey them to Lower Egypt to market. He

EGYPTIAN POTTERY FLOAT ON THE NILE.

supposes that by 'vessels of bulrushes,' or rush floats, are meant such vessels. (For a description of the *floats* made in Upper Egypt with *jars,* see Pococke's *Travels,* vol. i. p. 84, Ed. London, 1743.) 'I first saw in this voyage [on the Nile] the large floats of earthenware; they are about thirty feet wide, and sixty long, being a frame of palm boughs tied together about four feet deep, on which they put a layer of large jars with the mouths uppermost; on these they make another floor, and then put on another layer of jars, and so a third, which last are so disposed as to trim the float, and leave room for the men to go between. The float lies across the river, one end being lower down than the other; toward the lower end on each side they have four long poles with which they row and direct the boat, as well as forward the motion down.' Mr. Bruce, in his *Travels,* mentions vessels made of the papyrus in Abyssinia. ¶ *Upon the waters.* The waters of the Nile, or the Red Sea.

¶ *Saying.* This word is not in the Hebrew, and the introduction of it by the translators gives a peculiar, and probably an incorrect, sense to the whole passage. As it stands here, it would seem to be the language of the inhabitants of the land who sent the ambassadors, usually saying to their messengers to go to a distant nation; and this introduces an inquiry into the characteristics of the nation to *whom* the ambassadors are sent, as if it were a *different* people from those who are mentioned in ver. 1. But probably the words which follow are to be regarded as the words of the prophet, or of God (ver. 4), giving commandment to those messengers to *return* to those who sent them, and deliver the message which follows : ' You send messengers to distant nations in reed boats upon the rivers. Return, says God, to the land which sent you forth, and announce to them the will of God. Go rapidly in your light vessels, and bear this message, for it shall speedily be executed, and I will sit calmly and see it done' (ver. 4– 6). A remarkably similar passage, which throws great light on this, occurs in Ezek. xxx. 9 : ' In that day shall messengers go forth from me [God] in ships to make the careless Ethiopians afraid, and great pain shall come upon them, as in the day of Egypt ; for lo, it cometh.' ¶ *Go, ye swift messengers.* Heb. ' Light messengers.' This is evidently addressed to the boats. Achilles Tatius says that they were frequently so light and small, that they would carry but one person (Rosenmüller). ¶ *To a nation.* What nation this was is not known. The *obvious* import of the passage is, that it was some nation to whom they were *accustomed* to send ambassadors, and that it is here added merely as *descriptive* of the people. Two or three characteristics of the nation are mentioned, from which we may better learn what people are re- ferred to. ¶ *Scattered* (מְמֻשָּׁךְ). This word is derived from מָשַׁךְ (*mâshăkh*), *to seize, take, hold fast;* to draw out, extend, or prolong ; to make double or strong ; to spread out. The LXX. render it, "Εθνος μετέωρον—' A lofty na- tion.' Chaldee, ' A people suffering

violence.' Syriac, ' A nation distorted.' Vulg., ' A people convulsed, and lacer- ated.' It *may* denote a people *spread out* over a great extent of country ; or a people *drawn out in length*—*i.e.,* ex- tended over a country of considerable length, but of comparatively narrow breadth, as Egypt is ; so Vitringa un- derstands it. Or it may mean a people *strong, valiant;* so Gesenius under- stands it. This best suits the connec- tion, as being a people ' terrible hitherto.' Perhaps all these ideas may be united by the supposition, that the nation was drawn out or extended over a large re- gion, and was *therefore* a powerful or mighty people. The idea of its being *scattered* is not in the text. Taylor renders it, ' A people of short stature ; contracted in height ; that is, dwarfs.' But the idea in the text is not one that is descriptive of *individuals,* but of the *collected* nation ; the people. ¶ *And peeled* (מֹרָט, from מָרַט [*mârăt*] *to make smooth,* or *sharpen,* as a sword, Ezek. xxi. 14–32; then, to make smooth the head of any one, to pluck off his hair, Ezra ix. 3; Neh. xiii. 25; Isa. l. 6). The LXX. render it, Ξένον λαὸν καὶ χαλεπόν—' A foreign and wicked people.' Vulg., ' To a people lacerated.' The Syriac renders the whole verse, ' Go, swift messengers, to a people perverse and torn ; to a people whose strength has been long since taken away ; a people defiled and trodden down ; whose land the rivers have spoiled.' The word here used is capable of two significa- tions :—(1.) It may denote a people who are shaved or made smooth by re- moving the hair from the body. It is known to have been the custom with the Egyptians to make their bodies smooth by shaving off the hair, as He- rodotus testifies (xi. 37). Or, (2.) It may be translated, as Gesenius proposes, a people valiant, fierce, bold, from the sense which the verb has *to sharpen* a sword (Ezek. xxi. 15, 16). The former is the most obvious interpretation, and agrees best with the proper meaning of the Hebrew word ; the latter would, perhaps, better suit the connection. The editor of Calmet supposes that it is to be taken in the sense of *diminished, small, dwarfish,* and would apply it to the *pigmies* of Upper Egypt. ¶ *To a people terrible.* That is, warlike, fierce, cruel. Heb. ' A people feared.' If the Egyptians are meant, it may refer to the fact that they had always been an object of terror and alarm to the Israelites from their early oppressions there before their deliverance under Moses. ¶ *From their beginning hitherto.* Heb. ' From this time, and formerly.' It has been their general character that they were a fierce, harsh, oppressive nation. Gesenius, however, renders this, ' To the formidable nation (and) further beyond;' and supposes that two nations are referred to, of which the most remote and formidable one, whose land is washed by streams, is the proper Ethiopian people. By the other he supposes is meant the Egyptian people. But the scope of the whole prophecy rather requires us to understand it of one people. ¶ *A nation meted out.* Heb. ' Of line line ' (קַו־קָו *qǎv-qǎv*). Vitringa renders this, ' A nation of precept and precept ;' that is, whose religion abounded with rites and ceremonies, and an infinite multitude of *precepts* or *laws* which prescribed them. Michaelis renders it, ' A nation measured by a line ;' that is, whose land had been divided by victors. Döderlin renders it, ' A nation which uses the line ;' *i.e.*, as he supposes, which extended its dominion over other provinces. The LXX. render it, *"Εθνος ἀνέλπιστον*—' A nation without hope.' Aquila, *"Εθνος ὑπόμενον*—' A nation enduring or patient.' Jonathan, the Chaldee, עַמָּא אֲגִירָא וּבְזִירָא—' A nation oppressed and afflicted.' Aben Ezra explains it as meaning ' A nation like a school-boy learning line after line.' Theodore Hasæus endeavours to prove that the reference here is to Egypt, and that the language is taken from the fact that the Egyptians were early distinguished for surveying and mensuration. This science, he supposes, they were led to cultivate from the necessity of ascertaining the height of the Nile at its annual inundation, and from the necessity of an accurate survey of the land in order to preserve the knowledge of the right of property in a country inundated as this was. In support of this, he appeals to Servius (*ad* Virg.

Ecl. iii. 41), where he says of the *radius* mentioned there, ' The Radius is the rod of the philosophers, by which they denote the lines of geometry. This art was invented in the time when the Nile, rising beyond its usual height, confounded the usual marks of boundaries, to the ascertaining of which they employed philosophers who divided the land by *lines*, whence the science was called geometry.' Comp. Strabo (*Geo.* xvii. 787), who says that Egypt was divided into thirty *nomes*, and then adds, ' that these were again subdivided into other portions, the smallest of which were *farms* (αἱ ἄρουραι). But there was a necessity for a very careful and subtle division, on account of the continual confusion of the limits which the Nile produced when it overflowed, adding to some, taking away from others, changing the forms, obliterating the signs by which one farm was distinguished from another. Hence it became necessary to re-survey the country ; and hence, they suppose, originated the science of geometry ' (see also Herodot. *Euterpe*, c. 109). Hence it is supposed that Egypt came to be distinguished by the use of *the line*—or for its skill in surveying, or in geometry—or a nation *of the line* (see the Dissertation of Theodore Hasæus, גּוֹי קַו קַו—*De Gente kav kav*, in Ugolin's *Thes. Ant. Sac.* vii. 1568–1580). The word קַו (*qǎv*) means, properly, *a cord, a line*, particularly a measuring line (Ezek. xlvii. 3 ; 2 Kings xxi. 13): ' I will stretch over Jerusalem the measuring line of Samaria,' *i.e.*, I will destroy it like Samaria. Hence the phrase here may denote a people accustomed *to stretch out such lines* over others ; that is, to lay them waste. It is applied usually to the line connected with a plummet, which a carpenter uses to mark out his work (comp. Job xxxviii. 5 ; Isa. xxviii. 17 ; xxxiv. 11 ; Zeph. ii. 1) ; or to a line by which a land or country is measured by the surveyor. Sometimes it means *a precept*, or *rule*, as Vitringa has rendered it here (comp. Isa. xxviii. 10). But the phrase ' to stretch out a line,' or ' to measure a people by a line,' is commonly applied to their destruction, as if a conqueror used a line to mark out what he had to

3 All ye inhabitants of the world, and dwellers on the earth, see ye, when he lifteth up an ᵃ ensign on the mountains; and when he bloweth a trumpet, hear ye.

ᵃ ch.5.26.

do (see this use of the word in 2 Kings xxi. 13; Isa. xxviii. 17; xxxiv. 11; Lam. ii. 8; Zech. i. 16). This is probably its sense here—a nation terrible in all its history, and which had been distinguished for stretching lines over others; that is, for marking them out for destruction, and dividing them as it pleased. It is therefore a simple description, not of the nation as *being itself* measured out, but as extending its dominion over others. ¶ *And trodden down* (מְבוּסָה). Marg. 'And treading under foot,' or, 'that meteth out and treadeth down.' The margin here, as is frequently the case, is the more correct rendering. Here it does not mean that *they were trodden down*, but that it was a characteristic of their nation that *they trod down others;* that is, conquered and subdued other nations. Thus the verb is used in Psal. xliv. 6; Isa. xiv. 25; liii. 6; lxiii. 18; Jer. xii. 10. Some, however, have supposed that it refers to the fact that the land was trodden down by their feet, or that the Egyptians were accustomed to lead the waters of the Nile, when it overflowed, by *treading* places for it to flow in their fields. But the former is the more correct interpretation. ¶ *Whose land the rivers have spoiled.* Marg. 'Despise.' The Hebrew word (בָּזְאוּ) occurs nowhere else. The Vulgate renders it, *Diripuerunt*—'Carry away.' The Chaldee reads it, 'Whose land the people plunder.' The word is probably of the same signification as בָּזַז (*bâzăz*), to plunder, lay waste. So it was read by the Vulgate and the Chaldee; and this reading is found in four MSS. The word is in the present tense, and should be rendered not 'have spoiled,' but 'spoil.' It is probably used to denote a country the banks of whose rivers are washed away by the floods. This description is particularly applicable to Nubia or Abyssinia—the region above the cataracts of the Nile. One has only to remember that these streams continually wash away the banks and bear the earth to deposit it *on* the lands of

Lower Egypt, to see that the prophet had this region particularly in his eye. He could not have meant Egypt proper, because instead of *spoiling* the lands, or washing them away, the Nile constantly brings down a deposit from the upper regions that constitutes its great fertility. The *rivers* that are here mentioned are doubtless the various branches of the Nile (see Bruce's *Travels*, ch. iii., and Burckhardt's *Travels in Nubia.* The Nile is formed by the junction of many streams or branches rising in Abyssinia, the principal of which are the Atbara; the Astapus or Blue River; and the Astaboras or White River. The principal source of the Nile is the Astapus or Blue River, which rises in the Lake Coloe, which Bruce supposes to be the head of the Nile. This river on the west, and the various branches of the Atbara on the east, nearly encompass a large region of country called Meroë, once supposed to be a large island, and frequently called such. The whole description, therefore, leads us to the conclusion that a region is mentioned *in* that country called in general *Cush;* that it was a people living on rivers, and employing reed boats or skiffs; that they were a fierce and warlike people; and that the country was one that was continually washed by streams, and whose soil was carried down by the floods. All these circumstances apply to Nubia or Abyssinia, and there can be little doubt that this is the country intended.

3. *All ye inhabitants of the world.* These are to be regarded as the words of the prophet summoning all nations to attend to that which was about to occur. Grotius, however, and some others, suppose that they are the words of the Ethiopians. The meaning is, that the events which are here predicted would be of so public a nature as to attract the attention of all the world. ¶ *When he.* Vitringa supposes that this means the Assyrians lifting up a standard on the mountains of Judea. But the better interpretation is that which refers it to the people of Nubia,

4 For so the Lord said unto me,
I will take my rest, and I will
consider¹ in my dwelling-place like

a clear heat ² upon herbs, *and* like a
cloud of dew in the heat of harvest:

1 or, *regard my set dwelling.*   2 or, *after rain.*

mustering their forces for war. 'All
nations behold when that people collects
an army; sounds the trumpet for war;
and arrays its military forces for battle.
See then the judgments that God will
inflict on them—their discomfiture (ver.
4–7), and their turning to Jehovah,
and sending an offering to him (ver.
7).' According to this interpretation,
it will refer to the people making preparation for battle; and perhaps it may
mean that they were preparing to join
the enemies of Judea—*not improbably
preparing to join the forces of Sennc-
cherib, and to invade Judea.* For this
purpose it may have been that the
messengers were sent to negotiate the
terms of alliance with Sennacherib;
and the object of the prophecy is, to
assure the Jews that this people, as
well as Sennacherib, would be discomfited, and that they would yet bring an
offering to God (ver. 7). ¶ *Lifteth
up an ensign.* A military standard
(see Note on ch. v. 26). ¶ *And when
he bloweth a trumpet.* Also a signal
for an army to assemble (see Note on
ch. xiii. 2).

4. *For so the* Lord *said unto me.*
So Jehovah has revealed his purpose,
that is, to execute punishment on the
people who have been described in the
previous verses. Their state as there
described is that of a fierce people
making ready for war, and probably
designing an alliance with the enemies
of Judea, and marshalling their armies
for that purpose. Jehovah here reveals
to the prophet that they shall be discomfited, and shows the manner in
which it will be done. He says he
will sit calm while these preparations
are going on—as the sun shines serenely on the earth while the harvest
is growing, and the dew falls gently on
the herb;—but that *before* their plans
are completed, he will interpose and
destroy them, as if one should appear
suddenly before the harvest is ripe and
cut it down. The *design*, therefore,
of this part of the prophecy is to comfort the Jews, and to assure them that
there is no danger to them from the

preparations which were made against
them—for Jehovah calmly beholds the
proud rage of the enemy. ¶ *I will
take my rest.* I will not interpose. I
will remain calm—not appearing to
oppose them, but keeping as calm, and
as still, as if I seemed to favour their
plans—as the sun shines on the herb,
and the gentle dew falls on the grass,
until the proper time for me to interpose and defeat them shall arise (ver.
5, 6). ¶ *I will consider.* I will look
on; that is, I will not now interpose
and disarrange their plans before they
are complete. We learn here, (1.) that
God sees the plans of the wicked;
(2.) that he sees them *mature* them
without attempting then to interpose to
disarrange them; (3.) that he is calm
and still, because he designs that those
plans shall be developed; and (4.) that
the wicked should not indulge in any
dreams of security and success because
God does not interpose to thwart their
plans while they are forming them.
He will do it in the proper time. ¶ *In
my dwelling-place.* In heaven. I will
sit in heaven and contemplate leisurely
the plans that are going forward.
¶ *Like a clear heat.* A serene, calm,
and steady sunshine, by which plants
and herbs are made to grow. There
seem to be two ideas blended here:
the first, that of the *stillness* with
which the sun shines upon the herbs;
and the other, that of the fact that the
sun shines that the herbs *may grow.*
¶ *Upon herbs.* Marg. 'After rain'
(אֹור־עֲלֵי). The word אֹור usually signifies *light*, or *fire.* The plural form
(אֹורֹת) is used to denote herbs or vegetables in two places, in 2 Kings iv. 39,
and Isa. xxvi. 19. For in the Shemitic
languages the ideas of *sprouting, being
grown, growing,* &c., are connected
with that of the shining of the sun, or
of light; that which grows in the light;
that is, vegetables. But in the singular
form the word is not thus used, unless
it be in this place. That it may have
this signification cannot be doubted;
and this interpretation makes good
sense, and suits the connection. The

5 For afore the harvest, when the bud is perfect, and the sour grape is ripening in the flower, he shall both cut off the sprigs with pruning-hooks, and take away *and* cut down the branches.

6 They shall be left together unto the fowls of the mountains, and to

---

Rabbins generally interpret it as it is in the margin—'rain.' In proof of this they appeal to Job xxxvi. 30, and xxxvii. 11; but the word in these passages more properly denotes a cloud of light or of lightning, than rain. The common interpretation is probably correct, which regards the word אוֹר here as the same as אוֹרָה — 'herbs' (see Vitringa). The Syriac reads it עַל יְאֹר —'upon the river.' The parallelism seems to require the sense of *herb*, or something that shall answer to 'harvest' in the corresponding member. ¶ *And like a cloud of dew.* Such a dew was still, and promoted the growth of vegetables. The idea is that of stillness and rest : where there is no storm or tempest to dissipate the gently-falling dew. This is an emblem of the perfect quietness with which God would regard the preparations for war until the proper time would come for him to interpose. The whole passage is similar to Ps. ii. 4, 5 :

He that sitteth in the heavens shall laugh;
Jehovah shall have them in derision.
Then shall he speak unto them in his wrath,
And vex them in his hot displeasure.

The idea is, that he would be as calm as the sun is upon the herb, or the dew upon the harvest field, until the time should come when it would be proper for him to interpose, and disconcert their counsels. When and how this would be done is stated in the following verses ; and the whole passage is a most striking illustration of the manner with which God contemplates the machinations and evil designs of the wicked.

5. *For afore the harvest.* This verse is evidently figurative, and the image is drawn from that which is commenced in the previous verse. There, God is represented as calmly regarding the plans of the people here referred to— as the sun shines serenely on the herb, or the dew falls on the grass. *That* figure supposes that they had *formed* plans, and that they were advancing to maturity, like a growing harvest, while God surveyed them without interposition. This verse continues the figure, and affirms *that those plans shall not be mature ;* that God will interpose and defeat them *while* they are maturing—as if a man should enter the harvest field and cut it down after it had been sown, or go into the vineyard, and cut down the vines while the green grape was beginning to ripen. It is, therefore, a most beautiful and expressive figure, intimating that all their plans would be foiled even when they had the prospect of a certain accomplishment. ¶ *When the bud is perfect.* The word 'bud' here (פֶּרַח) denotes either a *blossom,* or a sprout, shoot, branch. Here it denotes probably the *blossom* of the grain ; or it may be the grain when it is *set.* Its meaning is, when their plans are maturing, and there is every human prospect that they will be successful. ¶ *And the sour grape is ripening.* Begins to turn ; or is becoming mature. ¶ *In the flower* (נִצָּה). The blossom. This should be read rather, 'and the flower is becoming a ripening grape.' The common version does not make sense ; but with this translation the idea is clear. The sense is the same as in the former phrase—when their plans are maturing. ¶ *He shall cut off the sprigs.* The shoots ; the small limbs on which the grape is hanging, as if a man should enter a vineyard, and, while the grape is ripening, should not only cut off the grape, but the small branches that bore it, thus preventing it from bearing again. The idea is, not only that God would disconcert their *present* plans, but that he would prevent them from forming any in future. Before their plans were matured, and they obtained the anticipated triumph, he would effectually prevent them from forming such plans again.

6. *They shall be left together.* The figure here is dropped, and the literal

the beasts of the earth: and the fowls shall summer upon them, and all the beasts of the earth shall winter upon them.

7 In that time shall the *a* present be brought unto the LORD of hosts of a people scattered ¹ and peeled,

and from a people terrible from their beginning hitherto; a nation meted out and trodden under foot, whose land the rivers have spoiled, to the place of the name of the LORD of hosts, the mount Zion.

a Ps.68.31; 72.10; ch.16.1.
1 or, *outspread and polished.*

---

narration is resumed. The sense is, that the army shall be slain and left unburied. Perhaps the *branches* and *twigs* in the previous verse denoted military leaders, and the captains of the armies, which are now represented as becoming food for beasts of the field and for birds of prey. ¶ *To the fowls of the mountains.* Their dead bodies shall be unburied, and shall be a prey to the birds that prey upon flesh. ¶ *And to the beasts of the earth.* The wild animals; the beasts of the forest. ¶ *And the fowls shall summer upon them.* Shall pass the summer, *i.e.*, they shall continue to be unburied. ¶ *And the beasts of the earth shall winter upon them.* They shall be unburied through the winter; probably indicating that they would furnish food for the fowls and the wild beasts for a long time. On the multitude of carcases these animals will find nourishment for a whole year, *i.e.*, they will spend the summer and the winter with them. When this was fulfilled, it is, perhaps, not possible to tell, as we are so little acquainted with the circumstances of the people in relation to whom it was spoken. If it related, as I suppose, to the people of Nubia or Ethiopia forming an alliance with the Assyrians for the purpose of invading Judea, it was fulfilled probably when Sennacherib and his assembled hosts were destroyed. Whenever it was fulfilled, it is quite evident that the design of the prophecy was to give comfort to the Jews, alarmed and agitated as they were at the prospect of the preparations which were made, by the assurance that those plans would fail, and all the efforts of their enemies be foiled and disconcerted.

7. *In that time.* When their plans shall thus be disconcerted, and their armies be overthrown. ¶ *Shall the present be brought,* &c. The word

'present' (שַׁי) denotes a gift, and is found only in the phrase 'to bring gifts,' or 'presents' (Ps. lxviii. 30; lxxvi. 11). It means here evidently a tribute, or an offering to JEHOVAH as the only true God; and possibly may mean that the people would be converted to him, and embrace the true religion. ¶ *Of a people,* &c. From a people. The description which follows is the same precisely as in ver. 2. Numerous repetitions of this kind will be recollected by the classic reader in the *Iliad.* ¶ *To the place of the name,* &c. The place where JEHOVAH is worshipped, *i.e.*, Jerusalem (comp. Notes, ch. i. 8, 9). We have no means of knowing with certainty when or how this prophecy was fulfilled. That the Jewish religion spread into Upper Egypt, and that the Christian religion was afterwards established there, there can be no doubt. The Jews were scattered into nearly every nation, and probably many of this people became proselytes, and went with them to Jerusalem to worship (see Acts ii. 10; viii. 27). 'The Abyssinian annals represent the country as converted to Judaism several centuries before the Christian era; and it certainly retains many appearances bearing the stamp of that faith. In the fourth century, the nation was converted to Christianity by the efforts of Frumentius, an Egyptian, who raised himself to high favour at court. Abyssinia remained impenetrable to the arms or the creed of the followers of Mahomet, and, affording shelter to the refugees from Egypt and Arabia, it became more decidedly Christian.'— 'The Abyssinians profess the same form of Christianity with the Copts of Egypt, and even own the supremacy of the Patriarch at Cairo. They combine with their Christian profession many Judaical observances, such as circumcision, abstinence from meats,

CHAPTER XIX.

ANALYSIS.

This prophecy respecting Egypt extends only through this chapter. Its general scope and design is plain. It is intended to describe the calamities that would come upon Egypt, and the effect which they would have in turning the people to God. The scene is laid *in* Egypt; and the following things passed before the mind of the prophet in vision:—1. He sees JEHOVAH coming in a cloud to Egypt (1). 2. The effect of this is to produce alarm among the idols of that nation (2). 3. A state of internal commotion and discord is described as existing in Egypt; a state of calamity so great that they would seek relief from their idols and necromancers (2, 3). 4. The consequence of these dissensions and internal strifes would be, that they would be subdued by a foreign and cruel prince (4). 5. To these political calamities there would be added *physical* sufferings (5–10)—the Nile would be dried up, and all that grew on its banks would wither (5–7); those who had been accustomed to fish in the Nile would be thrown out of employment (8); and those that were engaged in the manufacture of linen had been made, as a consequence, be driven from employment (9, 10). 6. All counsel and wisdom would fail from the nation, and the kings and priests be regarded as fools (11–16). 7. The land of Judah would become a terror to them (17). 8. This would be followed by the conversion of many of the Egyptians to the true religion (18–20); JEHOVAH would become their protector, and would repair the breaches that had been made, and remove the evils which they had experienced (21, 22), and a strong alliance would be formed between the Egyptians, the Assyrians, and the Jews, which should secure the Divine blessing and favour (23–25).

This is the outline of the prophecy. In regard to the *time* when it was delivered, we have no certain knowledge. Lowth supposes that it refers to times succeeding the destruction of the army of Sennacherib. After that event, he says, the affairs of Egypt were thrown into confusion; intestine broils succeeded; these were followed by a tyranny of twelve princes, who

divided the country between them, until the distracted affairs settled down under the dominion of Psammetichus, who held the sceptre for fifty-four years. Not long after this, the country was invaded and conquered by Nebuchadnezzar; and then by the Persians under Cambyses, the son of Cyrus. Alexander the Great subsequently invaded and took the country, and made Alexandria the capital of his empire. Many Jews were invited thither by Alexander, and under the favour of the Ptolemies they flourished there; the true religion became prevalent in the land, and multitudes of the Egyptians, it is supposed, were converted to the Jewish faith. Bishop Newton (*Diss.* xii. *on the Prophecies*) supposes, that there was a *general* reference here to the conquest by Nebuchadnezzar, and a *particular* reference to the conquest under Cambyses the son of Cyrus. He supposes that the anarchy described in ver. 2, refers to the civil wars which arose between Apries and Amasis in the time of Nebuchadnezzar's invasion, and the civil wars between Tachos, Nectanebus, and the Mendesians, a little before the country was subdued by Ochus. The cruel king mentioned in ver. 4, into whose hands they were delivered, he supposes was Nebuchadnezzar, or more probably Cambyses and Ochus, one of whom put the yoke on the neck of the Egyptians, and the other riveted it there. The Egyptians say that Cambyses, after he killed Apis, a god worshipped in Egypt, was stricken with madness; but his actions, says Prideaux, show that he was mad long before. Ochus was the most cruel of the kings of Persia. The final deliverance of the nation, and the conversion to the true God, and the alliance between Egypt, Assyria, and Israel (18–25), he supposes, refers to the deliverance that would be introduced by Alexander the Great, and the protection that would be shown to the Jews in Egypt under the Ptolemies.

Vitringa, Gesenius, Grotius, Rosenmüller, and others, suppose that the anarchy described in ver. 2, refers to the discord which arose in the time of the δωδεκαρχία (*dodekarchy*), or the reign of the twelve kings, until Psammetichus prevailed over the rest, and that he is intended by the 'cruel lord' and 'fierce king,' described in ver. 4. In other respects, their interpretation

and the observance of Saturday as well as Sunday as a Sabbath.'—(*Encyc. of Geography*, vol. ii. pp. 585, 588.) In these facts—in the prevalence of the true religion there in former periods, the prophecy may be regarded as having been in part fulfilled. Still, as is the case with a large portion of the

prophecies of Isaiah, we must regard this as having reference to a period of greater light and truth than has yet existed there; and as destined to receive a more complete fulfilment when all lands shall be full of the knowledge of the Lord.

of the prophecy coincides, in the main, with that proposed by Bishop Newton.

A slight glance at some of the leading events in the history of Egypt, may enable us more clearly to determine the application of the different parts of the prophecy.

Egypt, a well-known country in Africa, is, for the most part, a great valley through which the Nile pours its waters from south to north, and is skirted on the east and west by ranges of mountains which approach or recede more or less from the river in different parts. Where the valley terminates towards the north, the Nile divides itself, about forty or fifty miles from the Mediterranean, into several parts, enclosing the territory called the Delta—so called because the various streams flowing from the one river diverge as they flow towards the sea, and thus form with the coast a triangle in the shape of the Greek letter Δ. The southern limit of Egypt proper is Syene (Ezek. xxix. 10; xxx. 6), or Essuan, the border of Ethiopia. Here the Nile issues from the granite rocks of the cataracts and enters Egypt proper. This is N. lat. 24°.

Egypt was anciently divided into forty-two *nomes* or districts, which were little provinces or counties. It was also divided into Upper and Lower Egypt. Upper Egypt was called Thebais, from Thebes the capital, and extended south to the frontier of Ethiopia. Lower Egypt contained principally the Delta and the parts on the Mediterranean. The capital was Cairo.

The most common division, however, was into three parts, Lower, Middle, and Upper Egypt. In Lower Egypt, lying on the Mediterranean, were the cities of Pithon, Raamses, Heliopolis, &c. In this division, also, was the land of Goshen. In Middle Egypt was Moph, or Memphis, Hanes, &c. In Upper Egypt was No-Ammon, or Thebes, and Syene, the southern limit of Egypt.

The ancient history of Egypt is obscure. It is agreed on all hands, however, that it was the early seat of civilization; and that this civilization was introduced from the south, and especially from Meroë. The country in the earliest times was possessed by several kings or states, which were at length united into one great kingdom. Not long after the death of Joseph, it came into the possession of the Hyksos or Shepherd kings, probably an Arabian nomadic tribe. After they were driven out, the whole country came again under one sovereign, and enjoyed great prosperity. The first king of the 19th dynasty, as it is called by Manetho, was the celebrated Sesostris, about 1500 years B.C. His successors were all called by the general name of Pharaoh, *i.e.*, kings. The first who is mentioned by his proper name is Shishak (1 Kings xiv. 25, 26), supposed to be the Sesonchosis of Manetho, who reigned about 970 years B.C. Gesenius says, that in the time of the Jewish king Hezekiah, there reigned at the same time in Egypt three dynasties; an Ethiopic (probably over Upper Egypt), a Saïtish, and a Tanitish dynasty—of which at last sprung the dodekarchy, and whose dominion ultimately lost itself in the single reign of Psammetichus. The Ethiopic continued forty years, and consisted of three kings—Sabaco, Sevechus, and Tarakos, or Tearko—of which the two last are mentioned in the Bible, Sevechus under the name of So, סוֹא probably כָּוֶא Sevechus—as the ally of Hosea, king of Israel (2 Kings xvii. 4), 722 B.C., and Tarakos, the same as Tirhakah, about the time of the 16th year of the reign of Hezekiah (714 B.C.) Instead of this whole dynasty, Herodotus (ii. 137, 139), and Diodorus (i. 65), give us only one name, that of Sabaco. Contemporary with these were the four, or according to Eusebius, five, first kings of the dynasty of Saïte, Stephinates, Nerepsus, Nichao I., who was slain by an Ethiopian king, and Psammetichus, who made an end of the dodekarchy, and reigned fifty-four years. Of the Tanitish dynasty, Psammus and Zeth are mentioned (Introduction to ch. xix.) Different accounts are given of the state of things by Herodotus and by Diodorus. The account by Diodorus, which is the most probable, is, that a state of anarchy prevailed in Egypt for two whole years; and that the troubles and commotions suggested to the chief men of the country the expediency of assuming the reins of government, and restoring order to the state. With this view, twelve of the most influential men were chosen to preside with regal power. Each had a particular province allotted to him, in which his authority was permanent; and though independent of one another, they bound themselves with mutual oaths to concord and fidelity.

During fifteen years, their relations were maintained with entire harmony: but during that time Psammetichus, whose province extended to the Mediterranean, had availed himself of his advantages, and had maintained extensive commercial intercourse with the Phenicians and Greeks, and had amassed considerable wealth. Of this his colleagues became jealous, and supposing that he meant to secure the government of the whole country, they resolved to deprive him of his province. They therefore prepared to attack him, and he was thrown upon the necessity of self defence.

Apprised of their designs, he sent to Arabia, Caria, and Ionia, for aid, and having secured a large body of troops, he put himself at their head, and gave battle to his foes at Momemphis, and completely defeated them, drove them from the kingdom, and took possession of an undivided throne (Diod. i. 66). The account of Herodotus may be seen in his history (ii. 154). Psammetichus turned his attention to the internal administration of the country, and endeavoured to ingratiate himself with the priesthood and the people by erecting splendid monuments, and beautifying the sacred edifices. There was a strong jealousy, however, excited by the fact that he was indebted for his crown to foreign troops, and from the fact that foreigners were preferred to office over the native citizens (Diod. i. 67). A large part of his troops—to the number, according to Diodorus, of 240,000—abandoned his service at one time, and moved off in a body to Ethiopia, and entered the service of the monarch of that country. His reign appears to have been a military despotism, and though liberal in its policy towards foreign governments, yet the severity of his government at home, and the injustice which the Egyptians supposed he showed to them in relying on foreigners, and preferring them, justified the appellation in ver. 4, that he was a 'cruel lord.'

Egypt was afterwards conquered by Cambyses, and became a province of the Persian empire about 525 B.C. Thus it continued until it was conquered by Alexander the Great, 350

B.C., after whose death it formed, together with Syria, Palestine, Lybia, &c., the kingdom of the Ptolemies. After the battle of Actium, 30 B.C., it became a Roman province. In A.D. 640, it was conquered by the Arabs, and since that time it has passed from the hands of the Caliphs into the hands of the Turks, and since A.D. 1517 it has been regarded as a province of the Turkish empire. This is an outline of the principal events of the Egyptian history. The events predicted in this chapter will be stated in their order in the comments on the particular verses. The two leading points which will guide our interpretation will be, that Psammeticlius is intended in ver. 4, and that the effects of Alexander's conquest of Egypt are denoted from ver. 18 to the end of the chapter. Keeping these two points in view, the interpretation of the chapter will be easy. On the history of Egypt, and the commotions and revolutions there, the reader may consult Wilkinson's *Manners and Customs of the Ancient Egyptians*, vol. i., particularly pp. 143–180.

THE burden of *a* Egypt. Behold, the LORD rideth *b* upon a swift cloud, and shall come into Egypt; and the idols *c* of Egypt shall be moved at his presence, and the heart of Egypt shall melt in the midst of it.

a Jer.46; Eze.xxix. & xxx.　　b Ps.18,10; 104 3.
c Ex.12.12; Jer.43.12.

CHAPTER XIX.

1. *The burden of Egypt.* This is the title to the prophecy. For the meaning of the word *burden*, see Note on ch. xiii. 1. The word 'Egypt' in the original is מִצְרַיִם (*Mitzraim*); and it was so called after Mizraim the second son of Ham, and grandson of Noah. Sometimes it is called Mazor (2 Kings xix. 24; Isa. xix. 6; xxxvii. 25; Mic. vii. 12); where, however, our English version has rendered the word by *besieged place* or *fortress*. The ancient name of the country among the inhabitants themselves was *Chimi* or *Chami* (Χημυ). The Egyptian word signified *black*, and the name was probably given from the black deposit made by the slime of the Nile. 'Mizraim, or Misrim, the name given to Egypt in the Scriptures, is in the plural form, and is the Hebrew mode of expressing the "two regions of Egypt" (so commonly met with in

the hieroglyphics), or the "two Misr," a name still used by the Arabs, who call all Egypt, as well as Cairo, Musr or Misr.'—(Wilkinson's *Ancient Egyptians*, vol. i. p. 2). The origin of the name 'Egypt' is unknown. Egyptus is said by some to have been an ancient king of this country. ¶ *Behold, the* LORD. This is a bold introduction. JEHOVAH is seen advancing to Egypt for the purpose of confounding its idols, and inflicting punishment. The leading idea which the prophet wishes probably to present is, that national calamities—anarchy, commotion, revolution, as well as physical sufferings—are under the government and direction of JEHOVAH. ¶ *Rideth upon a swift cloud.* JEHOVAH is often thus represented as riding on a cloud, especially when he comes for purposes of vengeance or punishment:

And he rode upon a cherub and did fly,
Yea, he did fly upon the wings of the wind.
　　　　　　　　　　Ps. xviii. 10.

2 And I will ¹set the Egyptians against the Egyptians; and they shall fight every one against his brother, and every one against his

1 *mingle.*

neighbour; city against city, *and* kingdom against kingdom.

3 And the spirit of Egypt shall fail² in ªthe midst thereof; and I

2 *be emptied.*   a Eze.22.14.

Who maketh the clouds his chariot,
Who walketh upon the wings of the wind.
Ps. civ. 3.

'I saw in the night visions, and behold, one like the Son of Man came with the clouds of heaven' (Dan. vii. 13). So the Saviour is represented as coming to judgment in the clouds of heaven (Matt. xxiv. 30). Compare the sublime description in Hab. iii. 3–10. ¶ *And the idols of Egypt.* It is well known that Egypt was celebrated for its idolatry. They worshipped chiefly the heavenly bodies; but they worshipped also all kinds of animals, probably as living symbols of their gods. ¶ *Shall be moved.* That is, shall tremble, be agitated, alarmed; or shall be removed from their place, and overthrown. The word will bear either construction. Vitringa inclines to the latter. ¶ *And the heart of Egypt.* The strength; the courage; the vigour. We use the word *heart* in the same sense now, when we speak of a stout heart; a courageous heart, &c. ¶ *Shall melt.* The word here used denotes *to dissolve;* and is applied to the heart when its courage fails—probably from the sensation of weakness or fainting. The fact alluded to here was probably the disheartening circumstances that attended the civil commotions in Egypt, when the people felt themselves oppressed by cruel rulers. See the Analysis of the chapter.

2. *And I will set* (סִכְסַכְתִּי). This word (from סָכַךְ) means properly *to cover,* to spread over, to hide, conceal, to protect. Another signification of the verb is, to weave, to intermingle. It may mean here, 'I will *arm* the Egyptians against each other' (Gesenius); or, as in our version, 'I will mingle, confound, or throw them into discord and strife.' The LXX. render it, Ἐπεγερθήσονται — 'They shall be excited,' or, 'raised up.' Symmachus, Συμβαλῶ. Syriac and Chaldee, 'I will excite.' The sense is, that there would

be discord and civil war, and this is traced to the agency or overruling providence of God—meaning that he would *permit* and *overrule* it. Compare Notes on Isa. xlv. 7: 'I make peace, and I create evil; I, JEHOVAH, do all these things;' Amos iii. 6: 'Shall there be evil in a city and JEHOVAH hath not done it?' The civil war here referred to was probably that which arose between the twelve kings in the time of the dodekarchy (see the Analysis to the chapter), and which resulted in the single dominion of Psammetichus. Bishop Newton (*On the Prophecies,* xii.) supposes, however, that the prophet refers to the civil wars between Apries and Amasis at the time of the invasion by Nebuchadnezzar. But it agrees much better with the former discord than with this. The description which follows is that of anarchy or civil strife, where *many* parties are formed, and would naturally lead to the supposition that there were more than two engaged. ¶ And *kingdom against kingdom.* Sept. Νόμος ἐπὶ νόμον—'Nome against nomes.' Egypt was formerly divided into forty-two *nomes* or districts. The version by the LXX. was made in Egypt, and the translators would naturally employ the terms which were in common use. Still the event referred to was probably not that of one *nome* contending against another, but a civil war in which one dynasty would be excited against another (Gesenius), or when there would be anarchy and strife amongst the different members of the dodekarchy. See the Analysis of the chapter.

3. *And the spirit of Egypt* (see ver. 1). They shall be exhausted with their long internal contentions and strifes; and seeing no prospect of deliverance, and anxious that the turmoils should end, they shall seek counsel and refuge in their gods and necromancers, but in vain. ¶ *Shall fail* (נָבְקָה). Marg. 'Be emptied.' The word means, literally, *to pour out, empty, depopu-*

will [1] destroy the counsel thereof; and they shall seek *a* to the idols, and to the charmers, and to them that have familiar spirits, and to the wizards.

4 And the Egyptians will I [2] give over into the hands of a cruel *b* lord; and a fierce king shall rule over them, saith the LORD, the LORD of hosts.

1 swallow up.　　a ch.8.19; 47.12.

2 or, shut up.　　b ch.20.4.

---

late. Here it means that they would become disheartened and discouraged. ¶ *And I will destroy.* Marg., as the Heb., 'I will swallow up.' So the word is used in Ps. cvii. 27, ' All their wisdom is destroyed' (Heb. 'swallowed up').' ¶ *And they shall seek to the idols.* According to Herodotus (ii. 152), Psammetichus had consulted the oracle of Latona at Butos, and received for answer that the sea should avenge his cause by producing brazen men. Some time after, a body of Ionians and Carians were compelled by stress of weather to touch at Egypt, and landed there, clad in brazen armour. Some Egyptians, alarmed at their appearance, came to Psammetichus, and described them as brazen men who had risen from the sea, and were plundering the country. He instantly supposed that this was the accomplishment of the oracle, and entered into an alliance with the strangers, and by their aid was enabled to obtain the victory over his foes. Compare the different accounts of Diodorus in the Analysis of this chapter. The whole history of Egypt shows how much they were accustomed to consult their idols (see Herodot. ii. 54, *sq.*, 82, 83, 139, 152). Herodotus says (ii. 83), that the art of divination in Egypt was confined to certain of their deities. There were in that country the oracles of Hercules, of Apollo, of Mars, of Diana, and of Jupiter; but the oracle of Latona in Butos was held in greater veneration than any of the rest. ¶ *And to the charmers* (אִטִּים). This word occurs nowhere else. The root אָטַט, in Arabic, means *to mutter, to make a gentle noise;* and this word probably denotes conjurors, diviners (see Note on ch. viii. 19). The LXX. render it, ' Their idols.' ¶ *And to them that have familiar spirits* (see Note on ch. viii. 19). The LXX. render this, ' Those who speak from the ground.' ¶ *And to*

the wizards. LXX., Ἐγγαστριμύθους —'Ventriloquists.' The Hebrew word means a wise man, a soothsayer, a magician (יִדְּעֹנִים from יָדַע *to know;* see Lev. xix. 31; xx. 6; Deut. xviii. 11). This false science abounded in Egypt, and in most Oriental countries. 4. *And the Egyptians.* The Egyptian nation; the entire people, though divided into factions and contending with each other. ¶ *Will I give over.* Marg. ' Shut up.' The Hebrew word (סָכַר) usually has the sense of shutting up, or closing. Here it means that these contentions would be *closed* or concluded by their being delivered to the dominion of a single master. The LXX. render it, Παραδώσω—'I will surrender.' ¶ *Into the hands of a cruel lord.* Heb. ' Lords of cruelty, or severity.' The word rendered ' lord,' meaning master, is in the Hebrew in the plural number (אֲדֹנִים). It is, however, generally supposed that it is *pluralis excellentiæ* —denoting majesty and dignity, and applicable to a *single* monarch. The connection requires this, for the state here described would be different from that where *many* rule, and it seems to suppose that *one* should succeed to the many who had been contending. In the parallel member, also, a name in the singular number is used—' a fierce king;' and as this evidently denotes the same, it follows that the word here is used to denote a single monarch. The plural form is often thus used in the Hebrew (see Ps. vii. 10; Ezek. xxix. 3; Hos. xii. 1). God here claims jurisdiction over the nation, and says that he will do it—a most striking illustration of the power which he asserts over contending people to deliver them to whomsoever he will. Bishop Newton supposes that this was Nebuchadnezzar, or more properly Cambyses, by whom Egypt was made subject to the authority of Persia, and who was eminently a cruel man, a

5 And the waters shall fail from the sea, and the river shall be wasted and dried up.

6 And they shall turn the rivers far away, *and* the brooks *a* of de-

a 2 Ki.19.24.

madman. But the more probable interpretation is that which refers it to Psammetichus. Twelve kings were in contention, of whom he was one. He called in the aid of the Arabians, and the pirates of Caria and Iona (Herodot. ii. 152; see the Analysis of the chapter; Diod. i. 66). This was in the twentieth year of the reign of Manasseh. Psammetichus reigned fifty-four years and was succeeded by Nechus his son, called in Scripture Pharaoh-Necho, and often mentioned under that name. Psammetichus, during a considerable part of his reign, was engaged in wars with Assyria and Palestine. He is here called a 'cruel lord;' that is, an oppressive monarch, probably because he secured the kingdom by bringing in to his aid foreign mercenaries—robbers and pirates, and because his wars made his government oppressive and burdensome. ¶ *A fierce king.* Heb. ' A king of strength '—a description particularly applicable to one who, like Psammetichus, had subdued eleven rivals, and who had obtained the kingdom by conquest.

5. *And the waters shall fail.* Here commences a description of the *physical* calamities that would come upon the land, which continues to ver. 10. The previous verses contained an account of the national calamities by civil wars. It may be observed that discord, anarchy, and civil wars, are often connected with physical calamities ; as famine, drought, pestilence. God has the elements, as well as the hearts of men, under his control ; and when he chastises a nation, he often mingles anarchy, famine, discord, and the pestilence together. Often, too, civil wars have a *tendency* to produce these calamities. They annihilate industry, arrest enterprise, break up plans of commerce, and divert the attention of men from the cultivation of the soil. This might have been in part the case in Egypt ; but it would seem also that God, by direct agency, intended to afflict them by drying up

their streams in a remarkable manner. ¶ *From the sea.* The parallelism here, as well as the whole scope of the passage, requires us to understand this of the Nile. The word רָם is sometimes used to denote a large river (see Notes on ch. xi. 15; xviii. 2). The Nile is often called a sea. Thus Pliny (*Nat. Hist.* ii. 35) says, ' The water of the Nile resembles the sea.' Thus, Seneca (*Quæst. Nat.* v. 2) says, ' By continued accessions of water, it stagnates (*stagnat*) into the appearance of a broad and turbid sea.' Compare Herodot. ii. 97; Diod. i. 12, 96 : ' To this day in Egypt, the Nile is named *el-Bahr*, " the sea," as its most common appellation.' ' Our Egyptian servant,' says Dr. Robinson, ' who spoke English, always called it " the sea." '—(*Bib. Researches*, vol. i. p. 542). ¶ *And the river.* The Nile. ¶ *Shall be wasted.* This does not mean *entirely*, but its waters would fail so as to injure the country. It would not *overflow* in its accustomed manner, and the consequence would be, that the land would be desolate. It is well known that Egypt derives its great fertility entirely from the overflowing of the Nile. So important is this, that a public record is made at Cairo of the daily rise of the water. When the Nile rises to a less height than twelve cubits, a famine is the inevitable consequence, for then the water does not overflow the land. When it rises to a greater height than sixteen cubits, a famine is almost as certain—for then the superabundant waters are not drained off soon enough to allow them to sow the seed. The height of the inundation, therefore, that is necessary in order to insure a harvest, is from twelve to sixteen cubits. The annual overflow is in the month of August. The prophet here means that the Nile would not rise to the height that was desirable—or the waters should *fail*— and that the consequence would be a famine.

6. *And they shall turn the rivers far away* (הֶאֶזְנִיחוּ), probably from זָנַח, *to*

fence shall be emptied and dried up: the reeds and flags shall wither.

7 The paper reeds by the brooks, by the mouth of the brooks, and everything sown by the brooks,

shall wither, be driven away, and be [1] no *more*.

8 The fishers also shall mourn, and all they that cast angle into

1 *shall not be.*

---

have an offensive smell; to be rancid, or putrid. The word in this form occurs nowhere else. It is in the Hiphil conjugation, and is probably a form made from a mixture with the Chaldee. The sense is not doubtful. It means 'the rivers shall become putrid—or have an offensive smell;' that is, shall become stagnant, and send forth unwholesome *miasmata* producing sickness, as stagnant waters often do. The Vulgate renders it, 'And the rivers shall fail.' The LXX., 'And the Egyptians shall drink the waters from the sea, but the river shall fail, and be dried up, and the rivers shall fail, and the streams (διῶϱυχες) of the river, and all the assembling (συναγωγὴ) of waters shall be dried up.' ¶ And *the brooks of defence*. Heb. 'The rivers of מָצוֹר (*mâtzōr*).' The word מָצוֹר often means *straitness, affliction;* then a siege, a wall, a bulwark, a fortification. But, probably, it here means *Egypt*, or the same as מִצְרַיִם (*Mitzrāim*) (comp. ch. xxxvii. 25; 2 Kings xxx. 24; Mark vii. 12). Perhaps the Hebrews may have thought of Egypt as a strongly fortified place, and thus have given the name to it; or possibly this may have been a modification of the name *Mitzraim*. ¶ *The reeds and flags*. Which grew on the banks of the Nile—the papyrus, &c. (see Note on ch. xviii. 2.)

7. *The paper reeds* (עָרוֹת *ârōth*). This is not the word which occurs in ch. xviii. 2, and which, it is supposed, means there the papyrus (see Note on that place). Interpreters have been divided in regard to the meaning of the word here. Gesenius derives it from עָרָה (*ârâ*), *to be naked, open, bare;* and supposes that it means an open place, a place naked of wood, and that it here denotes the pastures on the banks of the Nile. So Rosenmüller interprets it of the green pastures on the banks of the Nile; and the Hebrew commentators generally so understand it. The

Vulgate renders it, 'And the bed (*alveus*) of the river shall be dried up from the fountain.' So the Chaldee, 'And their streams shall be desolate.' It probably denotes, not paper reeds, but the green pastures that were beside the brooks, or along the banks of the Nile. ¶ *By the brooks*. Heb. 'Rivers' (יְאֹרֵי). By the 'brooks' here, in the plural number, the prophet probably means the artificial canals which were cut in every direction from the Nile for the purpose of conveying the waters to various parts of the land. ¶ *By the mouth of the brooks*. At the mouth of the canals, or where they emptied into the Nile. Such meadows, being *near* the Nile, and most sure of a supply of water, would be more valuable than those which were remote, and are, therefore, particularly specified. ¶ *Shall wither*, &c. That is, there shall be utter and entire desolation. If the Nile ceased to overflow; if the streams, reservoirs, and canals, could not be filled, this would follow as a matter of course. Everything would dry up.

8. *The fishers also*. In this verse, and the two following, the prophet describes the calamities that would come upon various classes of the inhabitants, as the consequence of the failing of the waters of the Nile. The first class which he mentions are the fishermen. Egypt is mentioned (Num. xi. 5), as producing great quantities of fish. 'We remember the fish which we did eat in Egypt freely.' 'The Nile,' says Diodorus (i.), 'abounds with incredible numbers of all sorts of fish.' The same was true of the artificial canals, and lakes, and reservoirs of water (ver. 10). Herodotus (ii. 93) says that large quantities of fish were produced in the Nile: 'At the season of spawning,' says he, 'they move in vast multitudes towards the sea.—As soon as that season is over they leave the sea, return up the river, and endeavour to regain their accustomed haunts.'—As a specimen of his

the brooks shall lament, and they that spread nets upon the waters shall languish.

a 1 Ki.10.28.

credulity, however, and also of the attention which he bestowed on natural history, the reader may consult the passage here referred to in regard to the mode of their propagation.—He also says that it is observed of the fish that are taken in their passage to the sea, that they have ' the left part of their heads depressed.' Of those that are taken on their return, the *right* side of the head is found to be depressed. This he accounts for by observing, that ' the cause of this is obvious : as they pass to the sea they rub themselves on the banks on the left side ; as they return they keep closely to the same bank, and, in both instances, press against it, that they may not be obliged to deviate from their course by the current of the stream.' Speaking of the Lake Moeris, Herodotus says, that ' for six months the lake empties itself into the Nile, and the remaining six, the Nile supplies the lake. During the six months in which the waters ebb, the fishing which is here carried on furnishes the royal treasury with a talent of silver (about £180) every day' (ii. 149). ' The silver which the fishery of this lake produced, was appropriated to find the queen with clothes and perfumes.'—(Diod. i. 52.) The Lake Moeris is now farmed for 30 purses (about £193) annually. Michaud says that the Lake Menzaleh now yields an annual revenue of 800 purses,' about £5364. ' The great abundance of fish produced in the Nile was an invaluable provision of nature, in a country which had neither extended pasture grounds, nor large herds of cattle, and where corn was the principal production. When the Nile inundated the country, and filled the lakes and canals with its overflowing waters, these precious gifts were extended to the most remote villages in the interior of the valley, and the plentiful supply of fish which they obtained was an additional benefit conferred upon them at this season of the year.'—(Wilkinson's *Ancient Egyptians,* vol. iii. pp. 62, 63.) Hence the great-

9 Moreover they that work in fine *a* flax, and they that weave net-works,[1] shall be confounded.

1 or, *white-works.*

ness of the calamity here referred to by the prophet when the lakes and canals should be dried up. The whole country would feel it. ¶ *And all they that cast angle.* Two kinds of fishermen are mentioned—those who used a hook, and those who used the net. The former

FISHING WITH THE HOOK.
From Wilkinson's Ancient Egyptians.

FISHING WITH THE NET.
From Wilkinson's Ancient Egyptians.

would fish mainly in the *brooks* or canals that were cut from the Nile to water their lands. For the various methods of fishing, illustrated by drawings, the reader may consult Wilkinson's *Ancient Egyptians,* vol. ii. p. 21 ; vol. iii. p. 53, *sq.*

9. *Moreover.* In addition to the calamities that will come upon the fishermen, the drying up of the river will affect all who are supported by that which the overflowing of its waters produced. ¶ *They that work in fine flax.* Egypt was celebrated anciently for producing flax in large quantities, and of a superior quality (see Ex. ix. 31; 1 Kings x. 28). The fine linen of Egypt which was manufactured from this is celebrated in Scripture (Prov. vii. 16; Ezek. xxvii. 7). The Egyptians had early carried the art of manufacturing linen to a great degree of per-

fection. As early as the exode of the Hebrews, we find that the art was known by which stuffs made of linen or other materials were curiously worked and embroidered. ' And thou shalt make an hanging for the door of the tent, of blue, and purple, and scarlet, and *fine-twined linen, wrought with needle-work* ' (Ex. xxvi. 36; comp. xxvii. 16; xxxvi. 37). So Ezek. xxvii. 7: ' Fine linen, with broidered work from Egypt.' So also Martial refers to embroidery with the needle in Egypt:

Hæc tibi Memphitis tellus dat munera; victa est
Pectine Niliaco jam Babylonis acus.
Martial, xiv. Ep. 50.

In regard to the *fineness* of the linen which was produced and wrought in Egypt, we may introduce a statement made by Pliny when speaking of the *nets* which were made there. ' So delicate,' says he, ' were some of them, that they would pass through a man's ring, and a single person could carry a sufficient number of them to surround a whole wood. Julius Lupus, who died while governor of Egypt, had some of those nets, each string of which consisted of 150 threads ; a fact perfectly surprising to those who are not aware that the Rhodians preserve to this day, in the temple of Minerva, the remains of a linen corslet, presented to them by Amasis, king of Egypt, whose threads are composed each of 365 fibres.'— (Pliny, xix. 1.) Herodotus also mentions this corslet (iii. 47), and also another presented by Amasis to the Lacedemonians, which had been carried off by the Samians : ' It was of linen, ornamented with numerous figures of animals, worked in gold and cotton. Each thread of the corslet was worthy of admiration. For though very fine, every one was composed of 360 other threads, all distinct ; the quality being similar to that dedicated to Minerva at Lindus, by the same monarch.' Pliny (xix. 1) mentions four kinds of linen that were particularly celebrated in Egypt—the Tanitic, the Pelusiac, the Butine, and the Tentyritic. He also says that the quantity of flax cultivated in Egypt was accounted for, by their exporting linen to Arabia and India.—It is now known, also, that the cloth used for

enveloping the dead, and which is now found in abundance on the mummies, was *linen*. This fact was long doubted, and it was until recently supposed by many that the cloth was made of cotton. This fact that it is linen was settled beyond dispute by some accurate experiments made by Dr. Ure, Mr. Bauer, and Mr. Thompson, with the aid of powerful microscopes. It was found that linen fibres uniformly present a cylindrical form, transparent, and articulated, or jointed like a cane, while the fibres of cotton have the appearance of a flat ribbon, with a hem or border at the edge. In the mummy cloths, it

FIBRES OF COTTON AND LINEN.

was found, without exception, that the fibres were linen. Vast quantities of linen must, therefore, have been used. —The linen of the mummy cloths is generally coarse. The warp usually contains about 90 threads in the inch ; the woof about 44. Occasionally, however, very fine linen cloth is found, showing the skill with which the manufacture was executed. Sir J. G. Wilkinson observes, that a piece of linen in his possession from Egypt had 540 (or 270 double) threads in one inch in the warp. Some of the cambric which is now manufactured has but 160 threads in the inch in the warp, and 140 in the woof. It is to be remembered, also, that the linen in Egypt was spun by hand, and without the aid of machinery (see, on this whole subject, Wilkinson's *Ancient Egyptians*, vol. iii. pp. 113–142. Ed. Lond. 1837). The word rendered ' fine ' here denotes, according to Gesenius, *combed* or *hatchelled*. The word ' fine,' however, expresses the idea with sufficient accuracy. Fine linen was used for clothing ; but was so expensive that it was worn chiefly

10 And they shall be broken in
1 *foundations.*　　2 *of living things.*

the purposes [1] thereof, all that make
sluices *and* ponds [2] for fish.

by the rich and by princes (Luke xvi.
19). ¶ *They that weave networks.*
Marg. 'White-works.' According to
Gesenius the word חוֹרָי means *white
linen*—that which is fully bleached.
The word חוֹר means *a hole* or *cavern*,
but is not applied to cloth. The parallelism seems rather to require that the
word should mean 'white,' or that which
would correspond to 'fine,' or valuable ;
and it is not known that the Egyptians
had the art of working lace from linen.
Saadias supposes that *nets* are meant,
as being made with holes or meshes ;
but it is evident that a finer work is intended than that. ¶ *Shall be confounded.* Heb. 'Shall be ashamed.' That is,
they shall be thrown out of employment,
and not know what to do.

10. *And they shall be broken.* There
has been a great variety of opinion in
regard to the interpretation of this
verse, and much difficulty in the construction of the Hebrew words. The
Vulgate renders it, 'And its wet places
shall fail ; all who make ponds to take
fish.' The LXX. 'And all who make
beer (ζῦθον) shall lament, and shall afflict
their souls.' This ζῦθον was a sort of
malt liquor made of fruits by fermentation, and was used in Egypt in the
place of wine, as the grape did not
flourish there. Jerome on this place
says, that this was much used also in
Dalmatia and Pannonia, and was commonly called *Sabaium.* The Chaldee
renders this, ' And the place where they
weave cloth shall be trodden down, and
the place where they make fish ponds,
and where they collect waters, each one
for his own life.' This variety of reading arises chiefly from the different
modes of *pointing* the Hebrew words.
The word rendered 'broken' (מְדֻכָּאִים)
means *trodden down*, from דָּכָא *to tread*,
or *trample down*, and agrees in the
Hebrew with the word rendered 'purposes'—'the purposes shall be trodden
down.' The word 'purposes' (שָׁתֹתֶיהָ)
is found only in the plural, and is translated in Ps. xi. 3, 'foundations,' from
שִׁית, *foundation* or *pillar.* According
to this, it would mean that all *the pillars*

or *foundations, i.e.,* probably all the
nobles of Egypt, would be trodden down.
But this does not well suit the connection. Others derive it from שָׁתָה
(*shâthâ*), *to drink ;* and suppose that it
means that which is prepared for drink
shall be trodden down or destroyed.
Others suppose that it is derived from
שָׁתָה (*shâthâ*), *to weave*, and that it refers to the places where they wove the
cloth, *i.e.,* their looms ; or to the places
where they made their nets. And others
suppose that it is not the *places* where
they wove which are intended, but the
weavers themselves. Forerius supposes
it to be derived from שִׁתַת (*shâthǔth*), *to
place, lay,* and that it refers to the
banks or *dykes* that were made to retain the waters in the canals, and that
these would be trodden down. This,
it seems to me, is the most probable
interpretation, as it suits the connection,
and agrees with the derivation of the
word. But the meaning cannot be
certainly ascertained. ¶ *All that make
sluices.* There has been quite as great
a variety in the intepretation of this
passage as in the former. The word
rendered 'sluices' (שֶׂכֶר), our translators
understand in the sense of places where
the water would be retained for fish
ponds—made by artificial banks confin-
ing the waters that overflow from the
Nile. This sense they have given to
the word, as if it were derived from סָכַר
(*sâkhǎr*), *to shut up, to enclose.* The
LXX. read it as if it meant the Hebrew
שֵׁכָר (*shēkhâr*), or strong drink ; and so
also the Syriac renders it—as if from
שָׁכַר (*shâkhǎr*), *to drink.* There is no
doubt that by a difference of pointing
it may have this signification. But the
most probable interpretation, perhaps, is
that which derives it from שָׂכַר (*sâkhǎr*),
to hire, and means that they made those
places for reward, or for gain. They
thus toiled for hire ; and the prophet
says, that they who thus made enclosures
for fish in order to make a livelihood,
would be trodden down—that is, they
would fail of their purposes. ¶ *Ponds
for fish.* The word rendered 'fish'

11 Surely the princes of *a*Zoan *are* fools, the counsel of the wise counsellors of Pharaoh is become brutish : how say ye unto Pharaoh, I *am* the son of the wise, the son of ancient kings ?

12 Where *b* are they ? where *are* thy wise *men ?* and let them tell

thee now, and let them know what the *c* Lord of hosts hath purposed upon Egypt.

13 The princes of Zoan are become fools, *d* the princes of Noph are *c* deceived ; they have also seduced Egypt, *even* ¹ *they that are* the stay of the tribes thereof.

(נֶפֶשׁ *nêphêsh*), denotes properly any living thing (*see marg.*), but if the usual interpretation is given of this verse, it is evident that fish are intended. The description, therefore, in this entire passage, from verse fifth to verse tenth, is designed to denote the calamities which would come upon Egypt from the failure of the waters of the Nile ; and the slightest knowledge of the importance of the Nile to that country will show that all these calamities would follow from such a failure.

11. *Surely the princes.* The following verses, to ver. 16, are designed to describe further the calamities that were coming upon Egypt by a want of wisdom in their rulers. They would be unable to devise means to meet the impending calamities, and would actually increase the national misery by their unwise counsels. The word 'princes' here is taken evidently for the rulers or counsellors of state. ¶ *Of Zoan.* The Vulgate, LXX., and Chaldee, render this 'Tanis.' Zoan was doubtless the Tans of the Greeks (Herod. ii. 166), and was a city of Lower Egypt, built, according to Moses (Num. xiii. 22), seven years after Hebron. It is mentioned in Ps. lxxviii. 12; Isa. xix. 11, 13; xxx. 4; Ezek. xxx. 14. It was at the entrance of the Tanitic mouth of the Nile, and gave name to it. Its ruins still exist, and there are seen there at present numerous blocks of granite, seven obelisks of granite, and a statue of Isis. It was the capital of the dynasty of the Tanitish kings until the time of Psammetichus ; it was at this place principally that the miracles wrought by Moses were performed. 'Marvellous things did he in the sight of their fathers in the land of Egypt; in the field of Zoan' (Ps. lxxviii. 12). Its ruins are still called *San*, a slight change

of the word *Zoan*. The Ostium Taniticum is now the *Omm Faredje*. ¶ Are *fools.* They are unable to meet by their counsels the impending calamities. Perhaps their folly was evinced by their flattering their sovereign, and by exciting him to plans that tended to the ruin, rather than the welfare of the kingdom. ¶ *The wise counsellors of Pharaoh.* Pharaoh was the common name of the kings of Egypt in the same way as *Cæsar* became afterwards the common name of the Roman emperors—and the king who is here intended by Pharaoh is probably Psammetichus (see Note on ver. 4). ¶ *How say ye, &c.* Why do you *flatter* the monarch ? Why remind him of his ancestry ? Why attempt to inflate him with the conception of his own wisdom ? This was, and is, the common practice of courtiers ; and in this way kings are often led to measures most ruinous to their subjects.

12. *Where* are *they ?* This whole verse is an appeal by the prophet to the king of Egypt respecting the counsellors and soothsayers of his kingdom. The sense is, ' a time of distress and danger is evidently coming upon Egypt. They pretend to be wise ; and there is now occasion for all their wisdom, and opportunity to evince it. Let them show it. Let them declare what is coming upon the nation, and take proper measures to meet and remove it ; and they will then demonstrate that it would be proper for Pharaoh to repose confidence in them.' But if they could not do this, then he should not suffer himself to be deluded, and his kingdom ruined, by their counsels.

13. *The princes of Zoan* (Note on ver. 11). This *repetition* is intensive and emphatic, and shows the deep conviction of the prophet of their folly. The design is to show that *all* the counsellors

14 The ^a Lord hath mingled a perverse ¹ spirit in the midst thereof: and they have caused Egypt to err in every work thereof, as a drunken *man* staggereth in his vomit.

15 Neither shall there be *any* work for Egypt, which the head or tail, branch or rush, may do.

a 1 Ki.22.22,23. 1 *spirit of perverseness.*

---

on which the Egyptians depended were fools. ¶ *The princes of Noph.* The Vulgate, the LXX., and the Chaldee, render this ' Memphis,' and there is no doubt that this is the city intended. The name Memphis may have easily arisen from Noph. It was written also *Moph*, and hence Memphis. It is called *Menouf* by the Copts and Arabians. According to Plutarch, the name Memphis means *the port of the good.* The situation of Memphis has been a subject of considerable dispute, and has afforded matter for long and laborious investigation. Sicard and Shaw fix its site at Djezeh or Ghizeh, opposite to old Cairo. Pococke, D'Anville, Niebuhr, and other writers and travellers, place Memphis more in the direction of Mitraheny, about fifteen miles further south, on the banks of the Nile, at the entrance of the plain of the mummies, at the north of which the pyramids are placed. It was the residence of the ancient kings of Egypt until the time of the Ptolemies, who commonly resided at Alexandria. Memphis retained its splendour until it was conquered by the Arabians, about A.D. 641. At the supposed site of Memphis south of Ghizeh, there are large mounds of rubbish, a colossal statue sunk in the ground, and a few fragments of granite, which remain to test the existence of this renowned capital. In Strabo's time, although partly in ruins, it was yet a populous city, second only to Alexandria. The total disappearance of the ancient edifices of Memphis is easily accounted for by the circumstance, that the materials were employed for the building of adjacent cities. Fostât rose out of the ruins, and when that city was again deserted, these ruins migrated again to the more modern Cairo (see Robinson's *Bib. Researches*, vol. i. p. 40). ¶ *They have also seduced Egypt.* That is, they have by their counsels caused it to err, and have led it into its present embarrassment. ¶ *The stay, &c.* Heb. פִּנָּה (*p'nnâ*)—the cor-

ner; *i.e.*, those who should have been the support. So the word is used to denote the head or leader of a people in Judg. xx. 2, 14; 1 Sam. xiv. 38; Ps. cxviii. 22; Isa. xxviii. 16; Zec. x. 4.

14. *The Lord hath mingled.* The word מָסַךְ (*mâsăkh*), *to mingle*, is used commonly to denote the act of mixing spices with wine to make it more intoxicating (Prov. ix. 2, 5; Isa. v. 22). Here it means, that Jehovah has poured out into the midst of them a spirit of giddiness; that is, has produced consternation among them. National commotions and calamities are often thus traced to the overruling providence of God (see Note on ver. 2; comp. ch. x. 5, 6). ¶ *A perverse spirit.* Heb. ' A spirit of perverseness.' The word rendered ' perverse ' is derived from עָוָה, *to be crooked* or *perverted.* Here it means, that their counsels were unwise, and such as tended to error and ruin. ¶ *To err as a drunken* man, &c. This is a very striking figure. The whole nation was reeling to and fro, and unsettled in their counsels, as a man is who is so intoxicated as to reel and to vomit. Nothing could more strikingly express, first, the *fact* of their perverted counsels and plans, and secondly, God's deep abhorrence of the course which they were pursuing.

15. *Neither shall there be any work.* The sense is, that there shall be such discord that no man, whether a prince, a politician, or a priest, shall be able to give any advice, or form any plan for the national safety and security, which shall be successful. ¶ *Which the head or tail.* High or low; strong or weak: those in office and those out of office; all shall be dispirited and confounded. Rosenmüller understands by the head here, the *political* orders of the nation, and by the tail the *sacerdotal* ranks. But the meaning more probably is, the highest and the lowest ranks—all the politicians, and priests, and princes, on

16 In that day shall Egypt be like *a* unto women ; and it shall be afraid and fear, because of the shaking of the hand of the LORD of hosts, which he shaketh over it.

17 And the land of Judah shall be a terror unto Egypt: every one that maketh mention thereof shall

be afraid in himself, because of the counsel of the LORD of hosts, which he hath determined against it.

18 In that day shall five cities in the land of Egypt speak [1] the language *b* of Canaan, and swear to the LORD of hosts: one shall be called, The city of [2] destruction.

a Jer.51.30; Nah.3.13.   1 *lip.*

b Zep.3.9.   2 or, *Heres*, or, *the sun.*

---

the one hand, as the prophet had just stated (ver. 11–15); and all the artificers, fishermen, &c., on the other, as he had stated (ver. 8–10). This verse, therefore, is a *summing up* of all he had said about the calamities that were coming upon them. ¶ *Branch or rush.* See these words explained in the Note on ch. ix. 14.

16. *In that day shall Egypt be like unto women.* Timid ; fearful; alarmed. The Hebrews often, by this comparison, express great fear and consternation (Jer. li. 30; Nah. iii. 13). ¶ *Because of the shaking of the hand.* The shaking of the hand is an indication of threatening or punishment (Note on ch. x. 32; xi. 15).

17. *And the land of Judah.* The fear and consternation of Egypt shall be increased when they learn what events are occurring there, and what JEHOVAH has purposed in regard to it. ¶ *Shall be a terror.* This cannot be understood to mean that they were in danger from an invasion by the Jews, for at that time they were not at war, and Judah had no power to overrun Egypt. Jarchi and Kimchi suppose that the passage means that the Egyptians would hear what had occurred to the army of Sennacherib on its overthrow, and that they would be alarmed as if a similar fate was about to come upon them. But the more probable interpretation is that which refers it to the *invasion* of Judah by Sennacherib. The Egyptians would know of that. Indeed, the leading design of Sennacherib was to invade Egypt, and Judah and Jerusalem were to be destroyed only *in the way* to Egypt. And when the Egyptians heard of the great preparations of Sennacherib, and of his advance upon Judah (see ch. x. 28–31), and knew that his design was to invade

them, 'the land of Judah' would be 'a terror,' because they apprehended that he would make a rapid descent upon them. Vitringa, however, supposes that the sense is, that the Egyptians in their calamities would remember the prophecies of Jeremiah and others, of which they had heard, respecting their punishment; that they would remember that the prophecies respecting Judah had been fulfilled, and that thus Judah would be a terror to them *because* those predictions had come out of Judah. This is plausible, and it may be the correct explanation. ¶ *Which he hath determined against it.* Either against Judah, or Egypt. The Hebrew will bear either. It may mean that they were alarmed at the counsel which had been formed by JEHOVAH against Judah, and which was apparently about to be executed by the invasion of Sennacherib, and that thus they feared an invasion themselves, or that they learned that a purpose of destruction was formed by JEHOVAH against themselves, and that Judah became thus an object of terror, because the prophecies which were spoken there were certain of being fulfilled. The latter is the interpretation given by Vitringa, and perhaps is the most probable.

18. *In that day.* The word 'day' is used in Scripture in a large signification, *as including the whole period under consideration,* or the whole time that is embraced in the scope of a prophecy. In this chapter it is used in this sense ; and evidently means that the event here foretold would take place *somewhere* in the period that is embraced in the design of the prophecy. That is, the event recorded in this verse would occur in the series of events that the prophet saw respecting

Egypt (see ch. iv. 1). The sense is, that somewhere in the general time here designated (ver. 4-17), the event here described would take place. There would be an extensive fear of JEHOVAH, and an extensive embracing of the true religion, in the land of Egypt. ¶ *Shall five cities.* The number 'five' here is evidently used to denote an *indefinite* number, in the same way as 'seven' is often used in the Scriptures (see Lev. xxvi. 8). It means, that several cities in Egypt would use that language, one of which only is specified. ¶ *The language of Canaan.* Marg. 'Lip of Canaan.' So the Hebrew; but the word often means 'language.' The language of Canaan evidently means the *Hebrew* language; and it is called 'the language of Canaan' either because it was spoken by the original inhabitants of the land of Canaan, or more probably because it was used by the Hebrews who occupied Canaan as the promised land; and then it will mean the language spoken in the land of Canaan. The phrase here used is employed probably to denote that they would be converted to the Jewish religion; or that the religion of the Jews would flourish there. A similar expression, to denote conversion to the true God, occurs in Zeph. iii. 9: 'For there I will turn to the people a pure language, that they may call upon the name of the Lord, to serve him with one consent.' ¶ *And swear to the* LORD *of hosts.* That is, they shall *devote* themselves to him; or they shall bind themselves to his service by solemn covenant; compare Deut. x. 20; Isa. xlv. 20, where conversion to God, and a purpose to serve him, is expressed in the same manner by *swearing* to him, *i.e.*, by solemnly devoting themselves to his service. ¶ *One shall be called.* The name of one of them shall be, &c. Why *one* particularly is designated is not known. ¶ *The city of destruction.* There has been a great variety of interpretation in regard to this expression. Marg. 'Heres,' or, 'The sun.' The Vulgate, 'The city of the sun;' evidently meaning Heliopolis. The LXX. Ασεδίκ—'The city Asedek.' The Chaldee, 'The city of the house of the sun (בֵּית שֶׁמֶשׁ), which is to be destroyed.'

The Syriac, 'The city of *Heres.*' The common reading of the Hebrew text is, עִיר הַהֶרֶס ('*Ir Hääres*). This reading is found in most MS. editions and versions. The word הֶרֶס (*hěrěs*) commonly means *destruction*, though it may also mean *deliverance*; and Gesenius supposes the name was to be given to it because it was to be a *delivered* city; *i.e.*, it would be the city to which 'the saviour' mentioned in ver. 20, would come, and which he would make his capital. Ikenius contends that the word '*Heres*' is taken from the Arabic, and that the name is the same as Leontopolis—'The city of the lion,' a city in Egypt. But besides other objections which may be made to this interpretation, the signification of *lion* is not given to the word in the Hebrew language. The common reading is that which occurs in the text—the city of *Heres.* But another reading (הַחֶרֶס) is found in sixteen MSS., and has been copied in the Complutensian Polyglot. This word (הֶרֶס *Hhěrěs*) properly means the *sun*, and the phrase means the city of the sun; *i.e.*, Heliopolis. Onias, who was disappointed in obtaining the high-priesthood (B.C. 149) on the death of his uncle Menelaus, fled into Egypt, and ingratiated himself into the favour of Ptolemy Philometer and Cleopatra, and was advanced to the highest rank in the army and the court, and made use of his influence to obtain permission to build a temple in Egypt like that at Jerusalem, with a grant that he and his descendants should always have a right to officiate in it as high priests. In order to obtain this, he alleged that it would be for the interest of Egypt, by inducing many Jews to come and reside there, and that their going annually to Jerusalem to attend the great feasts would expose them to alienation from the Egyptians, to join the Syrian interest (*see* Prideaux's *Connection*, under the year 149 B.C. Josephus expressly tells us (*Ant.* xiii. 3. 1-3), that in order to obtain this favour, he urged that it had been predicted by Isaiah six hundred years before, and that in consequence of this, Ptolemy granted him permission to build the temple, and that it was built at Leontopolis. It resembled that at Jerusalem, but was smaller and less splendid. It was within the Nomos or prefecture of Heliopolis, at the distance of twenty-four miles from Memphis. Onias pretended that the very place was foretold by Isaiah; and this would seem to suppose that the ancient reading was that of 'the city of the sun.' He urged this prediction in order to reconcile the Jews to the idea of another temple besides that at Jerusalem, because a temple erected in Egypt would be an object of disapprobation to the Jews in Palestine. Perhaps for the same reason the translation of Isaiah in the Septuagint renders this, 'Ασεδέκ—' The city of Asedek,' as if the original were צֶדֶק tzedâkâ—' The city of righteousness '—i.e., a city where righteousness dwells; or a city which was approved by God. But this is manifestly a corruption of the Hebrew text. It may be proper to remark that

the change in the Hebrew between the word rendered 'destruction' (חֶרֶס hĕrĕs), and the word 'sun' (חֶרֶס hhĕrĕs), is a change of a single letter where one might be easily mistaken for the other— the change of ה into ח. This might have occurred by the error of a transcriber, though the circumstances would lead us to think it not improbable that it may have been made designedly, but by whom is unknown. It may have been originally as Onias pretended, and have been subsequently altered by the Jews to counteract the authority which he urged for building a temple in Egypt; but there is no certain evidence of it. The evidence from MSS. is greatly in favour of the reading as in our translation (חֶרֶס hĕrĕs), and this may be rendered either 'destruction,' or more probably, according to Gesenius, 'deliverance,' so called from the *deliverance* that would be brought to it by the

PLAIN AND OBELISK OF HELIOPOLIS.

promised saviour (ver. 20). It may be added, that there is no evidence that Isaiah meant to designate the city where Onias built the temple, but

merely to predict that many cities in Egypt would be converted, one of which would be the one here designated. Onias took *advantage* of this, and made an

19 In that day shall there be an altar to the LORD in the midst of

the land of Egypt, and a pillar *a* at the border thereof to the LORD.

a Gen.28.18; Ex.24.4.

artful use of it, but it was manifestly not the design of Isaiah. Which is the true reading of the passage it is impossible now to determine; nor is it important. I think the most probable interpretation is that which supposes that Isaiah meant to refer to a city *saved* from destruction, as mentioned in ver. 20, and that he did not design to designate any particular city by name.—The city of Heliopolis was situated on the Pelusian branch of the Nile, about five miles below the point of the ancient Delta. It was deserted in the time of Strabo; and this geographer mentions its mounds of ruin, but the houses were shown in which Eudoxus and Plato had studied. The place was celebrated for its learning, and its temple dedicated to the sun. There are now no ruins of ancient buildings, unless the mounds can be regarded as such; the walls, however, can still be traced, and there is an entire obelisk still standing. This obelisk is of red granite, about seventy feet high, and from its great antiquity has excited much attention among the learned. In the neighbouring villages there are many fragments which have been evidently transferred from this city. Dr. Robinson, who visited it, says, that 'the site is about two hours N.N.E. from Cairo. The way thither passes along the edge of the desert, which is continually making encroachments, so soon as there ceases to be a supply of water for the surface of the ground.—The site of Heliopolis is marked by low mounds, inclosing a space about three quarters of a mile in length, by half a mile in breadth, which was once occupied by houses, and partly by the celebrated temple of the sun. This area is now a ploughed field, a garden of herbs; and the solitary obelisk which rises in the midst is the sole remnant of the splendour of the place.—Near by it is a very old sycamore, its trunk straggling and gnarled, under which legendary tradition relates that the holy family once rested.'—(*Bib. Researches*, vol. i. pp. 36, 37.) The preceding cut, from the

Pictorial Bible, will give an idea of the present appearance of Heliopolis.

19. *In that day shall there be an altar.* An *altar* is properly a place on which sacrifices are offered. According to the Mosaic law, but one great altar was to be erected for sacrifices. But the word 'altar' is often used in another sense to denote a place of *memorial;* or a place of worship in general (Josh. xxii. 22–26). It is clear that Isaiah did not intend that this should be taken *literally*, or that there should be a rival temple and altar erected in Egypt, but his description is evidently taken in part from the account of the religion of the patriarchs who erected altars and pillars and monuments to mark the places of the worship of the true God. The parallelism here, where 'pillars' are mentioned, shows in what sense the word 'altar' is used. It means that the worship of the true God would be established in Egypt, and that certain *places* should be set apart to his service. *Altars* were among the first places reared as connected with the worship of God (see Gen. viii. 20; xii. 7; xxxv. 1; Ex. xvii. 15). ¶ *To the* LORD. To JEHOVAH—the true God. ¶ *And a pillar.* That is, a memorial to God. Thus Jacob set up the stone on which he had lain 'for a pillar,' and poured oil on it (Gen. xxviii. 18). Again (Gen. xxxv. 14), he set up a pillar to mark the place where God met him and talked with him (comp. Gen. xxxi. 13; Lev. xxvi. 1; Deut. xvi. 22). The word 'pillar,' when thus used, denotes a stone, or column of wood, erected as a monument or memorial; and especially a memorial of some manifestation of God or of his favour. Before temples were known, such pillars would naturally be erected; and the description here means simply that JEHOVAH would be worshipped in Egypt. ¶ *At the border thereof.* Not in one place merely, but in all parts of Egypt. It is not improbable that the *name* of JEHOVAH, or some rude designation of the nature of his worship, would be inscribed on such pillars. It

20 And it shall be for a *a* sign and for a witness unto the LORD of hosts in the land of Egypt: for

a Jos. 4. 20.

they shall cry unto the LORD because of the oppressors, and he shall send them a saviour, and a great one, and he shall deliver them.

is known that the Egyptians were accustomed to rear pillars, monuments, obelisks, &c., to commemorate great events, and that the names and deeds of illustrious persons were engraven on them; and the prophet here says, that such monuments should be reared to JEHOVAH. In regard to the fulfilment of this prophecy, there can be no question. After the time of Alexander the Great, large numbers of Jews were settled in Egypt. They were favoured by the Ptolemies, and they became so numerous that it was deemed necessary that their Scriptures should be translated into Greek for their use, and accordingly the translation called the Septuagint was made. See Introduction, § 8, 1, (1).

20. *And it shall be for a sign.* The altar, and the pillar. This shows that the altar was not to be for sacrifice, but was a *memorial,* or designed to designate a place of worship. ¶ *They shall cry to the* LORD *because of the oppressors.* That is, oppressed and borne down under the exactions of their rulers, they shall seek deliverance from the true God—one instance among many of the effect of affliction and oppression in leading men to embrace the true religion. ¶ *And he shall send them a saviour.* Who this *saviour* would be, has been a subject on which there has been a great difference of opinion. Grotius supposes that it would be *the angel* by which the army of Sennacherib would be destroyed. Gesenius thinks it was Psammetichus, who would deliver them from the tyranny of the eleven kings who were contending with each other, or that, since in ver. 4, he is called a 'severe lord,' it is probable that the promise here is to be understood of a delivering or protecting angel. But it is evident that some person is here denoted who would be sent *subsequently* to the national judgments which are here designated. Dr. Gill supposes that by the saviour here is meant the Messiah; but this interpretation does not suit the connection,

for it is evident that the event here predicted, was to take place before the coming of Christ. Vitringa and Bishop Newton suppose with more probability that Alexander the Great is here referred to, who took possession of Egypt after his conquest in the East, and who might be called *a saviour,* inasmuch as he delivered them from the reign of the oppressive kings who had tyrannized there, and inasmuch as his reign and the reigns of those who succeeded him in Egypt, would be much more mild than that of the former kings of that country. That Alexander the Great was regarded by the Egyptians as a saviour or deliverer, is apparent from history. Upon his coming to Egypt, the people submitted to him cheerfully, out of hatred to the Persians, so that he became master of the country without any opposition (Diod. Sic. xvii. 49; Arrian, iii. 3, 1; Q. Curtius, iv. 7, 8, as quoted by Newton). He treated them with much kindness; built the city of Alexandria, calling it after his own name, designing to make it the capital of his empire; and under him and the Ptolemies who succeeded him, trade revived, commerce flourished, learning was patronized, and peace and plenty blessed the land. Among other things, Alexander transplanted many Jews into Alexandria, and granted them many privileges, equal to the Macedonians themselves (Jos. *Bell. Jud.* ii. 18. 7; *Contra Ap.* ii. 4). 'The arrival of Alexander,' says Wilkinson (*Ancient Egyptians,* vol. i. pp. 213, 214), 'was greeted with universal satisfaction. Their hatred of the Persians, and their frequent alliances with the Greeks, who had fought under the same banners against a common enemy, naturally taught the Egyptians to welcome the Macedonian army with the strongest demonstrations of friendship, and to consider their coming as a direct interposition of the gods; and so wise and considerate was the conduct of the early Ptolemies, that they almost ceased to regret the period when they were

21 And the LORD shall be known to Egypt, and the Egyptians shall know the LORD in that day, and shall do *a* sacrifice and oblation ; yea, they shall vow a vow unto the LORD, and perform *it.*

22 And the LORD shall smite Egypt; he shall smite and heal *it :* and they shall return *even* to the LORD, and he shall be entreated of them, and shall heal them.

23 In that day shall there be a highway *b* out of Egypt to Assyria ; and the Assyrian shall come into Egypt, and the Egyptian into Assyria ; and the Egyptians shall serve with the Assyrians.

<hr>

a Mal.1.11.　　　　　*b* ch.11.16.

<hr>

governed by their native princes.' Under the Ptolemies, large numbers of the Jews settled in Egypt. For their use, as has been remarked, the Old Testament was translated into Greek, and a temple was built by Onias, under the sixth Ptolemy. Philo represents the number of the Jews in Egypt in his time at not less than one million. They were settled in nearly all parts of Egypt; but particularly in Heliopolis or the city of the sun, in Migdol, in Tahpanes, in Noph or Memphis, in Pathros or Thebais (Jer. xliv. 1)—perhaps the five cities referred to in ver. 18. ¶ *And a great one* (רָב). A mighty one ; a powerful saviour. The name 'great' has been commonly assigned to Alexander. The LXX. render this, ' Judging (κρίνων), he shall save them ;' evidently regarding רִב as derived from רִיב, *to manage a cause,* or *to judge.* Lowth renders it, ' A vindicator.' The word means *great, mighty ;* and is repeatedly applied to a prince, chief, or captain (2 Kings xxv. 8; Esth. i. 8; Dan. i. 3; ii. 48; v. 11).

21. *And the* LORD *shall be known to Egypt.* Shall be worshipped and honoured by the Jews who shall dwell there, and by those who shall be proselyted to their religion. ¶ *And the Egyptians shall know the* LORD. That many of the Egyptians would be converted to the Jewish religion there can be no doubt. This was the result in all countries where the Jews had a residence (comp. Notes on Acts ii. 9–11). ¶ *And shall do sacrifice.* Shall offer sacrifices to JEHOVAH. They would naturally go to Jerusalem as often as practicable, and unite with the Jews there, in the customary rites of their religion. ¶ *And oblation.* The word מִנְחָה (*minhha*) 'oblation,' denotes any

offering that is not a *bloody* sacrifice— a thank-offering ; an offering of incense, flour, grain, &c. (see Notes on ch. i. 13.) The sense is, that they should be true worshippers of God. ¶ *They shall vow a vow,* &c. They shall be sincere and true worshippers of God. The large numbers of the Jews that dwelt there ; the fact that many of them doubtless were sincere ; the circumstances recorded (Acts ii. 9–11), that Jews were in Jerusalem on the day of Pentecost ; and the fact that the true religion was carried to Egypt, and the Christian religion established there, all show how fully this prediction was fulfilled.

22. *And the* LORD *shall smite Egypt.* That is, in the manner described in the previous part of this prophecy (ver. 2–10). ¶ *And heal* it. Or restore it to more than its former splendour and prosperity, as described in the previous verses (18–20). He shall send it a saviour ; he shall open new sources of prosperity ; and he shall cause the true religion to flourish there. These advantages would be more than a compensation for all the calamities that he would bring upon it. ¶ *And they shall return,* &c. These calamities shall be the means of their conversion to JEHOVAH.

23. *There shall be a highway.* A communication ; that is, there shall be an alliance between Egypt and Assyria, as constituting parts of one empire, and as united in the service of the true God. The same figure of a *highway* is found in ch. xi. 16 (see Note on that place). The truth was, that Alexander, by his conquests, subjected Assyria and Egypt, and they constituted parts of his empire, and were united under him. It was true, also, that there were large numbers of Jews in both these countries, and

24 In that day shall Israel be the third with Egypt and with Assyria, even a blessing in the midst of the land.

25 Whom the LORD of hosts shall bless, saying, Blessed be Egypt my people, *a* and Assyria the work *b* of my hands, and Israel mine inheritance.

CHAPTER XX.

ANALYSIS.

THIS prophecy occupies this single chapter. Its design and scope it is not difficult to understand. The time when it was delivered is designated in ver. 1, and was manifestly in the reign

a 1 Pet.2.10.　　　　*b* Eph.2.10.

of Hezekiah. The Assyrian empire had extended its conquests over Syria, Damascus, and Ephraim or Samaria (2 Kings xviii. 9–12). The king of Assyria had sent Tartan to take possession of Ashdod, or Azotus, the maritime key of Palestine, and there was evident danger that the Assyrians would overthrow the government of Judah, and secure also the conquest of Egypt. In these circumstances of danger, the main reliance of Judah was on the aid which they hoped to derive from Egypt and Ethiopia (ver. 5), as being alone able to repel the Assyrians. They relied rather on that aid than on God. To *recall* them from this, and to show them the vanity of such a dependence, and to lead them to rely on God, Isaiah was sent to them to be a sign; or to indicate by a symbolical action what would be the fate of the Egyptians on whom they were placing their reliance (ver. 4). By

that they were united in the service of the true God. They worshipped him *in* those countries; and they met at Jerusalem at the great feasts, and thus Judah, Assyria, and Egypt, were united in his worship. ¶ *And the Assyrian shall come into Egypt.* There shall be free and uninterrupted intercourse between the two nations, as parts of the same empire. ¶ *And the Egyptians shall serve with the Assyrians.* In the same armies; under the same leader. This was the case under Alexander the Great. Or the word 'serve' may mean that they would serve God unitedly. So Lowth and Noyes render it.

24. *In that day shall Israel be the third.* That is, the three shall be united as one people. Instead of being rival, hostile, and contending kingdoms, they shall be united and friendly; and instead of having different and jarring religions, they shall all worship the same God. The prophecy rather refers to the spread of the true religion, and the worship of the true God, than to a political or civil alliance. ¶ *Even a blessing.* It shall be a source of blessing, because from Judea the true religion would extend into the other lands. ¶ *In the midst of the land.* That is, *the united land*—composed of the three nations now joined in alliance. Judea was situated in the *midst* of this united land, or occupied a central position between the two. It was also true that it occupied a central position in regard to the whole earth, and that from

it, as a radiating point, the true religion was disseminated throughout all nations.

25. *Whom the* LORD *of hosts shall bless.* That is, which united country he shall acknowledge as truly worshipping him, and on which he shall bestow his favours as his favoured people. ¶ *Assyria the work of my hands.* This is synonymous with the expression 'my people.' It means that the arrangements by which the true religion would be established among them, were the work of God. Conversion to God is everywhere in the Scriptures spoken of as his work, or creation; see Eph. ii. 10: 'For we are his workmanship; created in Christ Jesus unto good works' (comp. 2 Cor. v. 17; Ps. c. 3). ¶ *Israel mine inheritance.* The land and people which is peculiarly my own —a name not unfrequently given to Israel. For a learned examination of the various hypotheses in regard to the fulfilment of this prophecy, see Vitringa. He himself applies it to the times succeeding Alexander the Great. Alexander he regards as the 'saviour' mentioned in ver. 20; and the establishment of the true religion referred to by the prophet as that which would take place under the Ptolemies. Vitringa has proved—what indeed is known to all who have the slightest knowledge of history—that there were large numbers of Jews under the Ptolemies in Egypt, and that multitudes became proselytes to the Jewish faith.

showing the Jews what would be the destiny of Egypt, he designed to withdraw them from resting on their assistance, and to turn them to God for protection and aid.

IN the year *a* that Tartan came unto Ashdod, (when Sargon the king of Assyria sent him,) and

a 2 Ki. 18. 17.   1 *by the hand of.*

CHAPTER XX.

1. *In the year that Tartan came unto Ashdod.* Tartan was one of the generals of Sennacherib. Ashdod, called by the Greeks Azotus, was a seaport on the Mediterranean, between Askelon and Ekron, and not far from Gaza (Reland's *Palestine,* iii.) It was one of the five cities of the Philistines, assigned to the tribe of Judah, but never conquered by them (Josh. xiii. 8; xv. 46, 47). The temple of Dagon stood here; and hither the ark of God was brought after the fatal battle of Eben-ezer (1 Sam. v. 1, *sq.*) It sustained many sieges, and was regarded as an important place in respect to Palestine, and also to Egypt. It was taken by Tartan, and remained in the possession of the Assyrians until it was besieged by Psammetichus, the Egyptian king, who took it after a siege of twenty-nine years (Herod. ii. 157). It was about thirty miles from Gaza. It is now a small village, and is called *Esdud.* It was besieged and taken by Tartan as preparatory to the conquest of Egypt; and if the king who is here called *Sargon* was Sennacherib, it is probable that it was taken before he threatened Jerusalem. ¶ *Sargon the king of Assyria.* Who this *Sargon* was is not certainly known. Some have supposed that it was Sennacherib; others that it was Shalmaneser the father of Sennacherib, and others that it was Esar-haddon the successor of Sennacherib—(Michaelis). Rosenmüller and Gesenius suppose that it was a king who reigned *between* Shalmaneser and Sennacherib. Tartan is known to have been a general of Sennacherib (2 Kings xviii. 17), and it is natural to suppose that he is here intended. Jerome says that Sennacherib had seven names, and Kimchi says that he had eight; and it is not improbable that *Sargon* was one of those names. Oriental princes often

fought against Ashdod and took it;

2 At the same time spake the LORD 1 by Isaiah the son of Amoz, saying, Go, and loose the sackcloth from off thy loins, and put off thy shoe from thy foot. And he did so, walking naked and barefoot.

had several names; and hence the difficulty of identifying them. See Vitringa on this place.

2. *By Isaiah.* Marg. 'By the hand of Isaiah.' So the Hebrew. That is, by the instrumentality of Isaiah. He sent him to make known the fate of the Egyptians, and the folly of trusting in them on this occasion. ¶ *Go, and loose the sackcloth.* For the meaning of the word *sackcloth,* see Note on ch. iii. 24. It was commonly worn as an emblem of mourning. But there is reason to believe that it was worn also by the prophets, and was regarded, in some degree, as their appropriate dress. It was made usually of the coarse hair of the goat, and was worn as a zone or girdle around the loins. That this was the dress of Elijah is apparent from 2 Kings i. 8: 'He was an hairy man, and girt with a girdle of leather;' that is, he was clothed in a garment made of hair. The same was true of John the Baptist (Matt. iii. 4). That the prophets wore 'a rough garment' is apparent also from Zech. xiii. 4: 'Neither shall they (the false prophets) wear a rough garment (Heb. A garment of hair) to deceive;' *i.e.,* the false prophets shall not assume the dress of the true prophets for the purpose of deluding the people, or to make them think that they are true prophets. It is evident, therefore, that this hairy garment was regarded as a dress that appertained particularly to the prophets. It is well known, also, that the ancient Greek philosophers had a peculiar dress to distinguish them from the common people. Probably the custom of wearing *hair cloth* among the monks of later ages took its rise from this example of the prophets. His removing this garment was designed to be a sign or an emblem to show that the Egyptians should be stripped of all their possessions, and

3 And the Lord said, Like as ┊ my servant Isaiah hath walked

carried captive to Assyria. ¶ *Walking naked.* That is, walking *without this peculiar prophetic garment.* It does not mean that he was in a state of entire nudity ; for all that he was directed to do was to lay this garment—this emblem of his office—aside. The word *naked,* moreover, is used in the Scriptures, not to denote an absolute destitution of clothing, but that the *outer* garment was laid aside (see Note on John xxi. 7). Thus it is said of Saul (1 Sam. xix. 24) that he 'stripped off his clothes also, and prophesied before Samuel, and lay down naked all that day ;' *i.e.,* he stripped off his royal robes, and was *naked* or *unclothed* in that respect. He removed his *peculiar* dress as a king, or military chieftain, and appeared in the ordinary dress. It cannot be supposed that the king of Israel would be seen literally without raiment. So David is said to have danced *naked* before the ark, *i.e.,* with his royal robes laid aside. How *long* Isaiah walked in this manner has been a matter of doubt (see Note on ver. 3). The prophets were accustomed to use symbolical actions to denote the events which they foretold (see Note on ch. viii. 18). Thus the children of Isaiah, and the names given to them, were significant of important events (ch. viii. 1, 2, 3 ; comp. Jer. xviii. 1-6 ; xliii. 8, 9) ; in both of which places he used emblematic actions to exhibit the events concerning which he prophesied in a striking manner. Thus also the prophets are expressly called '*signs and wonders*' (Zech. iii. 8 ; Ezek. xii. 6).

3. *Like as.* That is, ' as Isaiah has gone stripped of his peculiar garment as a prophet, so shall the Egyptians and Ethiopians be stripped of all that they value, and be carried captive into Assyria.' ¶ *Hath walked—three years.* A great deal of difficulty has been felt in the interpretation of this place, from the strong improbability that Isaiah should have gone in this manner for a space of time so long as our translation expresses. The LXX. render this, ' As my servant Isaiah hath walked naked and barefoot three years, three years shall be for signs and wonders to the

Egyptians and Ethiopians.' The phrase in the Hebrew, 'three years,' *may* either be taken in connection with the preceding part of the sentence, as in our translation, meaning that he actually walked so long ; or it may be taken with that which follows, and then it will denote that he was a sign and wonder with reference to the captivity of the Egyptians and Ethiopians ; and that by this symbolical action he in some way indicated that they would be carried away captive for that space of time ; or, as Aben Ezra and Abarbanel suppose, that he signified that their captivity would commence after three years. Lowth supposes that it means that his walking was for three days, and that the Hebrew text has been corrupted. Vitringa also seems to suppose that this is possible, and that a day was a symbolical sign for a year. Rosenmüller supposes that this prophetic action was continued during three years *at intervals,* so that the subject might be kept before the mind of the people. But the supposition that this means that the symbolic action of walking naked and barefoot continued for so long a time in any manner, is highly improbable. (1.) The Hebrew does not necessarily require it. It *may* mean simply that his actions were a sign and wonder with reference to a three years' captivity of the Egyptians. (2.) It is in itself improbable that he should so long a time walk about Jerusalem expressly as a sign and wonder, when a much shorter period would have answered the purpose as well. (3.) Such a sign would have hardly met the circumstances of the case. Ashdod was taken. The Assyrian king was advancing. The Jews were in consternation and looking to Egypt for help ; and amidst this agitation and alarm, there is the highest improbability that Isaiah would be required to remain a sign and wonder for the long space of three years, when decided action was needed, and when, unless prevented, the Jews would have formed a speedy alliance with the Egyptians. I suppose, therefore, that the entire sense of the phrase will be expressed by translating it, 'my servant Isaiah hath walked **naked and** naked and barefoot three years *for* a sign and wonder upon Egypt and upon Ethiopia ;

4 So shall the king of Assyria lead away the [1] Egyptians prisoners, and the Ethiopians captives, young and old, naked and barefoot, even with *their* buttocks uncovered, to the [2] shame of Egypt.

5 And they shall be afraid and ashamed of Ethiopia their expectation, and of Egypt their glory.

6 And the inhabitant of this isle [3] shall say in that day, Behold, such *a is* our expectation, whither we flee for help to be delivered from the king of Assyria : and how shall we escape ?

[1] *captivity of Egypt.*　　　[2] *nakedness.*

[3] or, *country,* Jer. 47. 4.　　　*a* Job 6. 20.

barefoot, *a three years' sign and wonder ;'* that is, a sign and indication that *a three years' calamity* would come upon Egypt and Ethiopia. Whether this means that the calamity would *commence* in three years from that time, or that it should *continue* three years, perhaps we cannot determine. Grotius thinks that it means that it would occur *after* three years ; that is, that the war between the Assyrians and Ethiopians would continue during that time only. In what manner Isaiah indicated this, is not certainly known. The conjecture of Lowth is not improbable, that it was by appearing three *days* naked and barefoot, and that each day denoted a year. Or it may have been that he appeared in this manner for a short period—though but once—and *declared* that this was the design or purport of the action. ¶ *Upon Egypt,* &c. With reference to ; or as a sign in regard to Egypt. It does not mean that he was *in* Egypt, but that his action *had reference to* Egypt. ¶ *And Ethiopia.* Heb. כוּשׁ—*Cush* (see Note on ch. xi. 11). Whether this denotes the African Cush or Ethiopia, or whether it refers to the *Cush* in Arabia, cannot be determined. The latter is the more probable supposition, as it is scarcely probable that the Assyrian would extend his conquests south of Egypt so as to subdue the African Ethiopia. Probably his conquest embraced the *Cush* that was situated in the southern regions of Arabia.

4. *So shall the king of Assyria.* The emphasis here is on the word *so.* As Isaiah has walked naked, *i.e.,* stripped off his usual clothing, *so* shall the Egyptians and Ethiopians be led away *stripped* of all their possessions. ¶ *The Egyptians prisoners, and the Ethiopians captives.* The Egyptians

and Ethiopians, or Cushites, were often united in an alliance, and appear to have been when this prophecy was delivered. Thus Nahum iii. 8 :

Ethiopia and Egypt were her strength, and it was infinite ;
Put and Lubim were thy helpers.

¶ *To the shame of Egypt.* It shall be a disgrace to them to be subdued, and to be carried captive in so humiliating a manner. It is remarked by Belzoni ('*Operations and Recent Discoveries in Egypt and Nubia*'), that in the figures on the remains of their temples, prisoners are often represented as naked, or only in aprons, with dishevelled hair, and with their hands chained. He also remarks, that on a *bas-relief,* on the recently-discovered graves of the kings of Thebes, a multitude of *Egyptian* and *Ethiopian prisoners* are represented— showing that Egypt and Ethiopia were sometimes *allied,* alike in mutual defence and in bondage (comp. Isa. xlvii. 2, and Nah. iii. 5).

5. *And they shall be afraid.* The Jews, or the party or faction among the Jews, that were expecting aid from allied Ethiopia and Egypt. When they shall see them vanquished, they shall apprehend a similar danger to themselves ; and they shall be ashamed that they ever confided in a people so little able to aid them, instead of trusting in the arm of God. ¶ *Egypt their glory.* Their boast, as if Egypt was able to save them. The word here rendered 'glory' (תִּפְאָרָת) means properly, *ornament, praise, honour ;* and then it may mean the *object* of glory, or that in which men boast or confide. That is its sense here (comp. Isa. x. 12 ; xiii. 19 ; Zech. xii. 7).

6. *And the inhabitant.* The dwellers generally. ¶ *Of this isle.* The word

CHAPTER XXI.

ANALYSIS OF VER. 1–10.

THE prophecy which commences this chapter occupies the first ten verses. That it relates to Babylon is apparent from ver. 2 and 9. The object is to foretell the destruction of that city by the Medes and Persians, and the design is the same as in the more extended and minute description of the same event in ch. xiii., xiv. Whether it was delivered at the same, or at another time, cannot be determined from the prophecy. The purpose, however, of the prophecy is the same as there—to give consolation to the Jews who should be carried captive to that city; to assure them that Babylon would be destroyed, and that they would be delivered from their long and severe bondage. This is indicated in a brief and graphic manner in ver. 10.

This oracle, or ode, is one of singular beauty. It is distinguished for its brevity, energy, and force; for the variety and the rapidity of the action, and for the vivid manner in which the events are made to pass before the mind. It is the language of strong excitement and of alarm; language that expresses rapid and important movements; and language appropriate to great vigour of conception and sublimity in description. In the oracle the prophet supposes himself in Babylon, and the events which are described are made to pass rapidly in vision (see Intro. § 7, 4) before him. He first sees (ver. 1) the dreadful storm coming at a distance (the hostile armies), approaching like a whirlwind and threatening destruction to everything in its way. He then (ver. 2) hears God's direction to the invading armies; represents himself as made acquainted with the design of the vision, and

hears the command of God to Elam (Persia) and Media to go up and commence the siege. Regarding himself as among the exiles in the midst of Babylon, he (ver. 3, 4) describes himself as deeply affected in view of this sudden invasion, and of the calamities that were coming upon Babylon. In ver. 5, he describes the state of the Babylonians. They are represented, first as preparing the table, making ready for feasting and revelry, setting the watch on the watchtower, and giving themselves up to dissipation; and secondly, as suddenly alarmed, and summoned to prepare for war. He then (ver. 6–9) declares the way in which the princes of Babylon would be roused from their revelry. But it is described in a very remarkable manner. He does not *narrate* the events, but he represents himself as directed to appoint a watchman (ver. 6) to announce what he should see. That watchman (ver. 7) sees two chariots—representing two nations coming rapidly onward to execute the orders of God. So rapid is their approach, so terrible their march, that the watchman cries out (ver. 9) that Babylon is fallen, and will be inevitably destroyed. The prophecy is then closed (ver. 10) by an address to the afflicted Jews whom God had 'threshed,' or punished by sending them captive to Babylon, and with the declaration that this was intended by the Lord of hosts to be declared unto them. The whole design of the prophecy, therefore, is to console them, and to repeat the assurance given in ch. xiii., xiv., that Babylon would be destroyed, and that they would be delivered from bondage.

T HE burden of the desert of the
　sea. As whirlwinds *a* in the
south pass through; *so* it cometh
　　　　a Zec.9.14.

ℵ (*isle*) is used here in the sense of *coast*, or *maritime* country, and is evidently applied to Palestine, or the land of Canaan, which is a narrow coast lying on the Mediterranean. That the word is often used in this sense, and may be applied to a maritime country, see Notes on ch. xiii. 22; xli. 1. The connection here requires us to understand it of Palestine. ¶ *Shall say*, &c. Shall condemn their own folly in trusting in Egypt, and seeking deliverance there. ¶ *And how shall we escape?* They shall be alarmed for their own safety, for the very nation on which they had relied had been made captive. And when the *stronger* had been subdued, how could the feeble

and dependent escape a similar overthrow and captivity? All this was designed to show them the folly of trusting in the aid of another nation, and to lead them to put confidence in the God of their fathers.

CHAPTER XXI.

1. *The burden* (see Note on ch. xiii. 1). ¶ *Of the desert.* There have been almost as many interpretations of this expression, as there have been interpreters. That it means Babylon, or the country about Babylon, there can be no doubt; but the question why this phrase was applied, has given rise to a great diversity of opinions. The term 'desert' (מִדְבָּר) is usually applied to a wilderness, or to a comparatively

from the desert, from a terrible land.

2 A ¹ grievous vision is declared unto me; the treacherous ª dealer

¹ *hard.*   ª ch.33.1.

dealeth treacherously, and the spoiler spoileth. Go ᵇ up, O Elam: besiege, O Media: all the sighing thereof have I made to cease.

ᵇ ch.13.17; Jer.49.34.

barren and uncultivated country—a place for flocks and herds (Ps. lxv. 13; Jer. ix. 9, &c.); to an actual waste, a sandy desert (Isa. xxxii. 15; xxxv. 1); and particularly to the deserts of Arabia (Gen. xiv. 6; xvi. 7; Deut. xi. 24). It may here be applied to Babylon either historically, as having been *once* an unreclaimed desert: or by *anticipation*, as descriptive of what it *would be* after it should be destroyed by Cyrus, or possibly both these ideas may have been combined. That it was *once* a desert before it was reclaimed by Semiramis is the testimony of all history; that it is *now* a vast waste is the united testimony of all travellers. There is every reason to think that a large part of the country about Babylon was formerly overflowed with water *before* it was reclaimed by dykes; and as it was naturally a waste, when the artificial dykes and dams should be removed, it would again be a desert. ¶ *Of the sea* (יָם). There has been also much difference of opinion in regard to this word. But there can be no doubt that it refers to the Euphrates, and to the extensive region of marsh that was covered by its waters. The name 'sea' (יָם) is not unfrequently given to a large river, to the Nile, and to the Euphrates (see Note on ch. xi. 15; comp. ch. xix. 5). Herodotus (i. 184), says, that 'Semiramis confined the Euphrates within its channel by raising great dams against it; for before, it overflowed the whole country like a sea.' And Abydenus, in Eusebius, (*Prepara.Evang.*, ix. 457) says, respecting the building of Babylon by Nebuchadnezzar, that 'it is reported that all this was covered with water, *and was called a sea*'—λέγεται δὲ πάντα μὲν ἐξ ἀρχῆς ὕδωρ εἶναι, θαλασσαν καλουμένην. (Comp. Strabo, *Geog.* xvi. 9, 10; and Arrianus, *De Expedit. Alexandri*, vii. 21). Cyrus removed these dykes, reopened the canals, and the waters were suffered to remain, and again converted the whole country into a vast marsh (**see** Notes on ch. xiii., xiv.) ¶ *As whirl-*

winds. That is, the army comes with the rapidity of a whirlwind. In ch. viii. 8 (comp. Hab. i. 11), an army is compared to an overflowing and rapid river. ¶ *In the south.* Whirlwinds or tempests are often in the Scriptures represented as coming from the south, Zech. ix. 14; Job xxxvii. 9:

Out of the south cometh the whirlwind,
And cold out of the north.

So Virgil:

——creberque procellis
Africus—   *Æneid*, i. 85.

The deserts of Arabia were situated to the south of Babylon, and the south winds are described as the winds of the desert. Those winds are represented as being so violent as to tear away the tents occupied by a caravan (Pietro della Valle, *Travels*, vol. iv. pp. 183, 191). In Job i. 19, the whirlwind is represented as coming 'from the wilderness;' that is, from the *desert* of Arabia (comp. Jer. xiii. 24; Hos. xiii. 15). ¶ *So it cometh from the desert* (see ch. xiii. 4, and the Note on that place). God is there represented as collecting the army for the destruction of Babylon 'on the mountains,' and by mountains are probably denoted the same as is here denoted by the desert. The country of the *Medes* is doubtless intended, which, in the view of civilized and refined Babylon, was an uncultivated region, or a vast waste or wilderness. ¶ *From a terrible land.* A country rough and uncultivated, abounding in forests or wastes.

2. *A grievous vision.* Marg. as in Heb. 'Hard.' On the word 'vision,' see Note on ch. i. 1. The sense here is, that the vision which the prophet saw was one that indicated great calamity (ver. 3, 4). ¶ *Is declared unto me.* That is, is caused to pass before me, and its meaning is made known to me. ¶ *The treacherous dealer* (הַבּוֹגֵד). The perfidious, unfaithful people. This is the usual signification of the word; but the connection here does not seem to require the signification of treachery

3 Therefore *a* are my loins filled
with pains ; pangs have taken hold
upon me, as the pangs of a woman

a ch.15.5.

that travaileth : I was bowed down
at the hearing *of it ;* I was dismayed
at the seeing *of it.*

---

or perfidy, but of *violence.* The word
has this meaning in Hab. ii. 5, and in
Prov. xi. 3, 6. It refers here to the
Medes ; and to the fact that oppression
and violence were now to be exercised
towards Babylon. Lowth renders this :
'The plunderer is plundered, and the destroyer
is destroyed ;'
but the authority for so rendering it is
doubtful. He seems to suppose that it
refers to Babylon. The Hebrew evidently means, that there is to be plundering and devastation, and that this is
to be accomplished by a nation accustomed to it, and which is immediately
specified ; that is, the united kingdom
of Media and Persia. The Chaldee
renders it, ' They who bring violence,
suffer violence ; and the plunderers are
plundered.' Jarchi says, that the sense
of the Hebrew text according to the
Chaldee is, ' Ah ! thou who art violent !
there comes another who will use thee
with violence ; and thou plunderer,
another comes who will plunder thee,
even the Medes and Persians, who will
destroy and lay waste Babylon.' But
the Hebrew text will not bear this interpretation. The sense is, that desolation was about to be produced by a
nation *accustomed* to it, and who would
act towards Babylon in their true character. ¶ *Go up.* This is an address
of God to Media and Persia (see Note
on ch. xiii. 17). ¶ *O Elam.* This was
the name of the country originally possessed by the Persians, and was so called
from Elam a son of Shem (Gen. x. 22).
It was east of the Euphrates, and comprehended properly the mountainous
countries of Khusistan and Louristan,
called by the Greek writers *Elymais.*
In this country was Susa or Shushan,
mentioned in Dan. viii. 2. It is here
put for Persia in general, and the call
on Elam and Media to go up, was a
call on the united kingdom of the Medes
and Persians. ¶ *Besiege.* That is,
besiege Babylon. ¶ *O Media* (see Note
on ch. xiii. 17). ¶ *All the sighing
thereof have I* made *to cease.* This
has been very differently interpreted by

expositors. Some understand it (as
Rosenmüller, Jerome, and Lowth,) as
designed to be taken in an *active* sense ;
that is, all the groaning *caused* by
Babylon in her oppressions of others,
and particularly of God's people, would
cease. Others refer it to the army of
the Medes and Persians, as if *their*
sighing should be over ; *i.e.,* their
fatigues and labours in the conquest of
Babylon. Calvin supposes that it
means that the Lord would be deaf to
the sighs of Babylon ; that is, he would
disregard them and would bring upon
them the threatened certain destruction. The probable meaning is that
suggested by Jerome, that God would
bring to **an** end all the sighs and groans
which Babylon had caused in a world
suffering under her oppressions (comp.
ch. xiv. 7, 8).

3. *Therefore.* In this verse, and the
following, the prophet represents himself as *in* Babylon, and as a witness
of the calamities which would come
upon the city. He describes the
sympathy which he feels in her sorrows, and represents himself as deeply
affected by her calamities. A similar
description occurred in the pain which
the prophet represents himself as enduring on account of the calamities of
Moab (see Note on ch. xv. 5 ; xvi. 11).
¶ *My loins* (see Note on ch. xvi. 11).
¶ *With pain.* The word here used
(חַלְחָלָה) denotes properly the pains of
parturition, and the whole figure is
taken from that. The sense is, that
the prophet was filled with the most
acute sorrow and anguish, in view of
the calamities which were coming on
Babylon. That is, the sufferings of
Babylon would be indescribably great
and dreadful (see Nah. ii. 11 ; Ezek.
xxx. 4, 9). ¶ *I was bowed down.* Under the grief and sorrow produced by
these calamities. ¶ *At the hearing of
it.* The Hebrew may have this sense,
and mean that these things were made
to pass before the eye of the prophet,
and that the sight oppressed him, and
bowed him down. But more probably

4 My [1] heart panted, fearfulness affrighted me: the *a* night of my pleasure hath he [2] turned into fear unto me.

5 Prepare the table, watch in the watch-tower, eat, drink: arise, ye princes, *and* anoint the shield.

1 or, *my mind wandered.*   *a* Dan.5.5,&c.   2 *put.*

the מ in the word מְשׁוֹמֵעַ is to be taken *privatively*, and means, 'I was so bowed down or oppressed that I *could not* see; I was so dismayed that *I could not hear :*' that is, all his senses were taken away by the greatness of the calamity, and by his sympathetic sufferings. A similar construction occurs in Ps. lxix. 23: 'Let their eyes be darkened that they see not' (מֵרְאוֹת) *i.e., from* seeing.

4. *My heart panted.* Marg. 'My mind wandered.' The Hebrew word rendered 'panted' (תָּעָה) means to wander about ; to stagger ; to be giddy ; and is applied often to one that staggers by being intoxicated. Applied to the heart, it means that it is disquieted or troubled. The Hebrew word *heart* here is to be taken in the sense of *mind.* ¶ *The night of my pleasure.* There can be no doubt that the prophet here refers to the night of revelry and riot in which Babylon was taken. The prophet calls it the night of *his* pleasure, because he represents himself as being *in* Babylon when it should be taken, and therefore uses such language as an inhabitant of Babylon would use. *They* would call it the night of their pleasure, because it was set apart to feasting and revelry. ¶ *Hath he turned into fear.* God has made it a night of consternation and alarm. The prophet here refers to the fact that Babylon would be taken by Cyrus during that night, and that consternation and alarm would suddenly pervade the affrighted and guilty city (see Dan. v).

5. *Prepare the table.* This verse is one of the most striking and remarkable that occurs in this prophecy, or indeed in any part of Isaiah. It is language supposed to be spoken in Babylon. The first direction—perhaps supposed to be that of the king—is to prepare the table for the feast. Then follows a direction to set a watch—to make the city safe, so that they might revel without fear. Then a command to eat and drink : and then immediately a sudden order, as if alarmed at an unexpected attack, to arise and anoint the shield, and to

prepare for a defence. The *table* here refers to a feast—that impious feast mentioned in Dan. v. in the night in which Babylon was taken, and Belshazzar slain. Herodotus (i. 195), Xenophon (*Cyr.* 7, 5), and Daniel (v.) all agree in the account that Babylon was taken in the night in which the king and his nobles were engaged in feasting and revelry. The words of Xenophon are, ' But Cyrus, when he heard that there was to be such a feast in Babylon, in which all the Babylonians would drink and revel through the whole night, on that night, as soon as it began to grow dark, taking many men, opened the dams into the river ;' that is, he opened the dykes which had been made by Semiramis and her successors to confine the waters of the Euphrates to one channel, and suffered the waters of the Euphrates again to flow over the country so that he could enter Babylon beneath its wall in the channel of the river. Xenophon has also given the address of Cyrus to the soldiers. ' Now,' says he, ' let us go against them. Many of them are asleep ; many of them are intoxicated ; and all of them are unfit for battle (ἀσύντακτοι).' Herodotus says (i. 191), ' It was a day of festivity among them, and while the citizens were engaged in dance and merriment, Babylon was, for the first time, thus taken.' Compare the account in Daniel v. ¶ *Watch in the watch-tower.* Place a guard so that the city shall be secure. Babylon had on its walls many *towers*, placed at convenient distances (see Notes on ch. xiii.), in which guards were stationed to defend the city, and to give the alarm on any approach of an enemy. Xenophon has given a similar account of the taking of the city : ' They having arranged their guards, drank until light.' The annexed group of oriental watch-towers is introduced here for the purpose of illustrating a general subject often referred to in the Scriptures. ¶ *Eat, drink.* Give yourselves to revelry during the night (see Dan. v.) ¶ *Arise, ye princes.* This language indicates sudden alarm. It is the language either of the prophet, or more probably of the king of Babylon, alarmed at the sudden approach of the enemy, and calling upon his nobles to arm themselves and make, a defence. The army of Cyrus entered Babylon by two divisions—one on the north where the waters of the Euphrates

GROUP OF ORIENTAL WATCH TOWERS, SELECTED FROM EXAMPLES IN THE TOWNS OF LOWER EGYPT.

entered the city, and the other by the channel of the Euphrates on the south. Knowing that the city was given up to revelry on that night, they had agreed to imitate the sound of the revellers until they should assemble around the royal palace in the centre of the city. They did so. When the king heard the noise, supposing that it was the sound of a drunken mob, he ordered the gates of the palace to be opened to ascertain the cause of the disturbance. When they were thus opened, the army of Cyrus rushed in, and made an immediate attack on all who were within. It is to this moment that we may suppose the prophet here refers, when the king, aroused and alarmed, would call on his

6 For thus hath the LORD said unto me, Go, set a watchman, let him declare what he seeth.

7 And he saw a chariot *with* a couple of horsemen, a chariot of asses, *and* a chariot of camels; and he hearkened diligently with heed.

---

nobles to arm themselves for battle (see Jahn's *Hebrew Commonwealth*, p. 153, Ed. Andover, 1828). ¶ *Anoint the shield.* That is, prepare for battle. Gesenius supposes that this means to rub over the shield with oil to make the leather more supple and impenetrable (comp. 2 Sam. i. 21). The Chaldee renders it, 'Fit, and polish your arms.' The LXX. 'Prepare shields.' Shields were instruments of defence prepared to ward off the spears and arrows of an enemy in battle. They were usually made of a rim of brass or wood, and over this was drawn a covering of the skin of an ox or other animal in the manner of a drum-head with us. Oc-

ANCIENT LEATHER SHIELDS.

casionally the hide of a rhinoceros or an elephant was used. Burckhardt (*Travels in Nubia*) says that the Nubians use the hide of the hippopotamus for the making of shields. But whatever skin might be used, it was necessary occasionally to rub it over with oil lest it should become hard, and crack, or lest it should become so rigid that an arrow or a sword would easily break through it. Jarchi says, that 'shields were made of skin, and that they anointed them with the oil of olive.' The sense is, 'Prepare your arms! Make ready for battle!'

6. *Go, set a watchman.* This was said to Isaiah in the vision. He represents himself as in Babylon, and as hearing God command him to set a watchman on the watch-tower who would announce what was to come to pass. All this is designed merely to bring the manner of the destruction of the city more vividly before the eye.

7. *And he saw a chariot* with *a couple of horsemen.* This passage is very obscure from the ambiguity of the word רֶכֶב (rĕkhĕbh)—'chariot.' Gesenius contends that it should be rendered 'cavalry,' and that it refers to cavalry two abreast hastening to the destruction of the city. The word רֶכֶב denotes properly a chariot or waggon (Judg. v. 28); a collection of waggons (2 Chron. i. 14; viii. 6; ix. 25); and sometimes refers to the *horses* or *men* attached to a chariot. 'David houghed all the chariots' (2 Sam. viii. 4); that is, all the *horses* belonging to them. 'David killed of the Syrians seven hundred chariots' (2 Sam. x. 18); that is, all *the men* belonging to seven hundred chariots. According to the present Masoretic pointing, the word רֶכֶב does not mean, perhaps, anything else than a chariot strictly, but other forms of the word with the same letters denote *riders* or *cavalry.* Thus, the word רַכָּב denotes a horseman (2 Kings ix. 17); a charioteer or driver of a chariot (1 Kings xxii. 34; Jer. li. 21). The verb רָכַב means *to ride,* and is usually applied to riding on the backs of horses or camels; and the sense here is, that the watchman saw *a riding,* or persons riding two abreast; that is, *cavalry,* or men borne on horses, and camels, and asses, and hastening to attack the city. ¶ With *a couple of horsemen.* The word 'couple' (צֶמֶד tzemĕdh) means properly a *yoke* or *pair;* and it means here that the cavalry was seen *in pairs, i.e.,* two abreast. ¶ *A chariot of asses.* Or rather, as above, *a riding* on asses —an approach of men in this manner to battle. Asses were formerly used in war where horses could not be procured. Thus Strabo (xv. 2, 14) says of the inhabitants of Caramania, 'Many use asses for war in the want of horses.' And Herodotus (iv. 129) says expressly that Darius Hystaspes employed asses in a battle with the Scythians. ¶ And *a chariot of camels.* A *riding* on camels. Camels also were used in war, perhaps

8 And he cried, ¹ A lion: My lord, I stand continually upon the watch-tower in *a* the day-time, and I am set in my ward ² whole nights ;

9 And, behold, here cometh a chariot of men, *with* a couple of horsemen. And he answered and said, Babylon *b* is fallen, is fallen ; and *c* all the graven images of her gods he hath broken unto the ground.

1 or, *as a lion.*
a Hab.2.1.	2 or, *every night.*
b Jer.51.8,&c.; Rev.14.8.	*c* Jer.50.2.

usually to carry the baggage (see Diod. ii. 54; iii. 44; Livy, xxxvii. 40; Strabo, xvi. 3). They are used for all purposes of burden in the East, and particularly in Arabia.

8. *And he cried, A lion.* Marg. ' As a lion.' This is the correct rendering. The particle כ — 'as,' is not unfrequently omitted (see Isa. lxii. 5 ; Ps. xi. 1). That is, ' I see them approach with the fierceness, rapidity, and terror of a lion ' (comp. Rev. x. 3). ¶ *My lord, I stand continually upon the watch-tower.* This is the speech of the watchman, and is addressed, not to JE- HOVAH, but to him that appointed him. It is designed to show the *diligence* with which he had attended to the object for which he was appointed. He had been unceasing in his observation ; and the result was, that now at length he saw the enemy approach like a lion, and it was certain that Babylon now must fall. The language here used has a striking resemblance to the opening of the *Agamemnon* of Æschylus ; being the speech of the watchman, who had been very long upon his tower looking for the signal which should make known that Troy had fallen. It thus commences :

' For ever thus ! O keep me not, ye gods,
For ever thus, fixed in the lonely tower
Of Atreus' palace, from whose height I gaze
O'erwatched and weary, like a night-dog, still
Fixed to my post ; meanwhile the rolling year
Moves on, and I my wakeful vigils keep
By the cold star-light sheen of spangled skies.'
Symmons, quoted in the *Pictorial Bible.*

¶ *I am set in my ward.* My place where one keeps watch. It does not mean that he was confined or imprisoned, but that he had kept his watch station (מִשְׁמְרֶת from שָׁמַר. *to watch, to keep, to attend to*). ¶ *Whole nights.* Marg. ' Every night.' It means that he had not left his post day or night.

9. *And, behold—a chariot of men.* This place shows that the word 'chariot' (רֶכֶב) may denote something else than

ISAIAH I.

a waggon or carriage, as a chariot drawn by men cannot be intended. The sense can be expressed, perhaps, by the word *riding,* ' I see a *riding* of men approach ;' that is, I see *cavalry* drawing near, or men riding and hastening to the battle. ¶ With *a couple of horsemen.* The word ' with ' is not in the Hebrew. The meaning is, ' I see a riding of men, or cavalry ; and they come in pairs, or two abreast.' A part of the sentence is to be supplied from ver. 7. He saw not only horsemen, but riders on asses and camels. ¶ *And he answered.* That is, the watchman answered. The word ' answer,' in the Scriptures, means often merely to commence a discourse after an interval ; to begin to speak (Job iii. 2 ; Dan. ii. 26 ; Acts v. 8). ¶ *Babylon is fallen.* That is, her ruin is certain. Such a mighty army is drawing near, and they approach so well prepared for battle, that the ruin of Babylon is inevitable. The *repetition* of this declaration that ' Babylon is fallen,' denotes emphasis and certainty. Comp. Ps. xcii. 9 :

For lo, thine enemies, O Lord,
For lo, thine enemies shall perish.

Ps. xciii. 3 :

The floods have lifted up, O Lord ;
The floods have lifted up their waves.

A similar description is given of the fall of Babylon in Jer. l. 32 ; li. 8 ; and John has copied this description in the account of the overthrow of the mystical Babylon (Rev. xviii. 1, 2). Babylon was distinguished for its pride, arrogance, and haughtiness. It became, therefore, the emblem of all that is haughty, and as such is used by John in the Apocalypse ; and as such it was a most striking emblem of the pride, arrogance, haughtiness, and oppression which have always been evinced by Papal Rome. ¶ *And all the graven images.* Babylon was celebrated for its idolatry, and perhaps was the place where the worship of idols commenced.

28

10 O my threshing, and the ¹ corn of my floor: that which I have heard of the LORD of hosts, the God of Israel, have I ᵃ declared unto you.

ANALYSIS OF VER. 11, 12.—VISION XVII.

Dumah, or *Idumea*.

THIS prophecy is very obscure. It comprises but two verses. When it was delivered, or on what occasion, or what was its design, it is not easy to determine. Its brevity has contributed much to its obscurity; nor, amidst the variety of interpretations which have been proposed, is it possible to ascertain with entire certainty the true explanation. Perhaps no portion of the Scriptures, of equal length, has been subjected to a greater variety of exposition. It is not the design of these Notes to go at length into a detail of opinions which have been proposed, but to state as accurately as possible the sense of the prophet. Those who wish to see at

¹ *son.*　　ᵃ Eze.3.17-19; Acts 20.26,27.

length the opinions which have been entertained on this prophecy, will find them detailed in Vitringa and others.

The prophecy relates evidently to Idumea. It stands in connection with that immediately preceding respecting Babylon, and it is probable that it was delivered at that time. It has the appearance of being a reply by the prophet to language of *insult* or *taunting* from the Idumeans, and to have been spoken when calamities were coming rapidly on the Jews. But it is not certain that that was the time or the occasion. It is certain only that it is a prediction of calamity succeeding to prosperity—perhaps prosperity coming to the afflicted Hebrews in Babylon, and of calamity to the taunting Idumeans, who had exulted over their downfall and captivity, and who are represented as sneeringly inquiring of the prophet what was the prospect in regard to the Jews. This is substantially the view given by Vitringa, Rosenmuller, and Gesenius.

According to this interpretation, the scene is laid in the time of the Babylonish captivity. The prophet is represented as having been

---

The principal god worshipped there was Belus, or Bel (see Note on ch. xlvi. 1). ¶ *Are broken*, &c. That is, shall be destroyed; or, in spite of its idols, the whole city would be ruined.

10. *O my threshing.* The words 'to thresh,' 'to tread down,' &c., are often used in the Scriptures to denote punishments inflicted on the enemies of God. An expression like this occurs in Jer. li. 33, in describing the destruction of Babylon: 'The daughter of Babylon is like a threshing floor; it is time to thresh her.' In regard to the mode of threshing among the Hebrews, and the pertinency of this image to the destruction of the enemies of God, see Note on Isa. xxviii. 27. Lowth, together with many others, refers this to Babylon, and regards it as an address of God to Babylon in the midst of her punishment: 'O thou, the object on which I shall exercise the severity of my discipline; that shall lie under my afflicting hand like corn spread out upon the floor to be threshed out and winnowed, to separate the chaff from the wheat.' But the expression can be applied with more propriety to the Jews; and may be regarded as the language of *tenderness* addressed by God through the prophet to his people when they should be oppressed and

broken down in Babylon: 'O thou, my people, who hast been afflicted and crushed; who hast been under my chastening hand, and reduced to these calamities on account of your sins; hear what God has spoken respecting the destruction of Babylon, and your consequent certain deliverance.' Thus it is the language of consolation; and is designed, like the prophecies in ch. xiii., xiv., to comfort the Jews, when they should be in Babylon, with the certainty that they would be delivered. The language of *tenderness* in which the address is couched, as well as the connection, seems to demand this interpretation. ¶ *And the corn of my floor.* Heb. 'The son of my threshing floor'—a Hebraism for grain that was on the floor to be threshed. The word 'son' is often used in this peculiar manner among the Hebrews (see Note on Matt. i. 1). ¶ *That which I have heard*, &c. This shows the scope or design of the whole prophecy—to declare to the Jews the destruction that would come upon Babylon, and their own consequent deliverance. It was important that they should be *assured* of that deliverance, and hence Isaiah *repeats* his predictions, and minutely states the manner in which their rescue would be accomplished.

placed on a watch-tower long and anxiously looking for the issue. It is night; *i e.*, it is a time of calamity, darkness, and distress. In this state of darkness and obscurity, some one is represented as calling to the prophet from Idumea, and tauntingly inquiring, what of the night, or what the prospect was. He asks, whether there was any prospect of deliverance; or whether these calamities were to continue, and perhaps whether Idumea was also to be involved in them with the suffering Jews. To this the prophet answers, that the morning began to dawn—that there *was* a prospect of deliverance. But he adds that calamity was also coming;—calamity probably to the nation that made the inquiry—to the land of Idumea —*perhaps* calamity that should follow the deliverance of the Hebrew captives, who would thus be enabled to inflict vengeance on Edom, and to overwhelm it in punishment. The morning dawns, says the watchman; but there is darkness still beyond. Light is coming— but there is night also: light for us—darkness for you. This interpretation is strengthened by a remarkable coincidence in an independent source, and which I have not seen noticed, in the 137th Psalm. The irritated and excited feelings of the captive Jews against Edom; their indignation at the course which Edom pursued when Jerusalem was destroyed; and their desire of vengeance, are all there strongly depicted, and accord with this interpretation, which supposes the prophet to say that the glad morning of the deliverance of the *Jews* would be succeeded by a dark night to the taunting Idumean. The feelings of the captured and exiled Jews were expressed in the following language in Babylon (Ps. cxxxvii. 7):—

Remember, O JEHOVAH, the children of Edom
  in the day of Jerusalem;
Who said, Rase it, rase it, even to the foundation.

That is, we desire vengeance on Idumea, who joined with our enemies when Jerusalem was destroyed; and when Jerusalem shall be again rebuilt, we pray that they may be remembered, and that punishment may be inflicted on them for exulting over our calamities. The watchman adds, that if the Idumean was disposed to inquire further, he could. The result could be easily ascertained. It was clear, and the watchman would be disposed to give the information. But he adds, 'return, come;' perhaps meaning,

'repent; then come and receive an answer;'— denoting that if the Idumeans *wished* a favourable answer, they should repent of their treatment of the Jews in their calamities, and that *then* a condition of safety and prosperity would be promised them.

As there is considerable variety in the ancient versions of this prophecy, and as it is brief, they may be presented to advantage at a single view. The Vulgate does not differ materially from the Hebrew. The following are some of the other versions:

Septuagint.

The vision of Idumea. —Unto me he called out of Seir, Guard the fortresses — ($\Phi\upsilon\lambda\acute{\alpha}\sigma\sigma\epsilon\tau\epsilon$ $\dot{\epsilon}\pi\acute{\alpha}\lambda\xi\epsilon\iota\varsigma$). I guard morning and night. If you inquire, inquire, and dwell with me. In the grove ($\delta\rho\upsilon\mu\tilde{\omega}$) thou shalt lie down, and in the way of Dedan ($\Delta\alpha\iota\delta\acute{\alpha}\nu$).

Chaldee.

The burden of the cup of malediction which is coming upon Duma.—He cries to me from heaven, O prophet, prophesy; O prophet, prophesy to them of what is to come. The prophet said, There is a reward to

the just, and revenge to the unjust. If you will be converted, be converted while you can be converted.

Syriac.

The burden of Duma. —The nightly watchman calls to me out of Seir. And the watchman said, The morning cometh and also the night. If ye will inquire, inquire, and then at length come.

Arabic.

A prophecy respecting Edom and Seir, the sons of Esau.—Call me from Seir. Keep the towers. Guard thyself morning and evening. If you inquire, inquire.

It is evident, from this variety of translation, that the ancient interpreters felt that the prophecy was enigmatical and difficult. It is not easy, in a prophecy so brief, and where there is scarcely any clue to lead us to the historical facts, to give an interpretation that shall be entirely satisfactory and unobjectionable. Perhaps the view given above may be as little liable to objection as any one of the numerous interpretations which have been proposed.

11 The burden of ^a Dumah. He calleth to me out of Seir, Watchman, what of the night? Watchman, what of the night?

a 1 Ch.1.30; Jer.49.7,&c.; Eze.35.2,&c.; Ob.1,&c.

---

11. *The burden* (see Note on ch. xiii. 1). This word 'burden' naturally leads to the supposition that *calamity* in some form was contemplated in the prophecy. This is also indicated in the prophecy by the word 'night.'   ¶ *Of Dumah.*

Dumah (דּוּמָה) is mentioned in Gen. xxv. 14, and 1 Chron. i. 30, as one of the twelve sons of Ishmael. It is known that those sons settled in Arabia, and that the Arabians derive their origin from Ishmael. The name

'Dumah,' therefore, properly denotes one of the wandering tribes of the Ishmaelites. The LXX. evidently read this as if it had been אֱדֹם—Edom or Idumea—Ἰδουμαία. Jakut mentions two places in Arabia to which the name 'Dumah' is given, Dumah Irak, and Dumah Felsen. The former of these, which Gesenius supposes is the place here intended, lies upon the borders of the Syrian desert, and is situated in a valley seven days' journey from Damascus, according to Abulfeda, in lon. 45° E.; and in lat. 29° 30′ N; and about three and a half days' journey from Medina. Niebuhr mentions Dumah as a station of the Wehabites (see Gesenius, *Comm. in loc.*) There can be little doubt that the place referred to is situated on the confines of the Arabian and Syrian deserts, and that it is the place called by the Arabians *Duma the stony*, or *Syrian Duma* (Robinson's Calmet). It has a fortress, and is a place of strength. Jerome says, 'Duma is not the whole province of Idumea, but is a certain region which lies toward the south, and is twenty miles distant from a city of Palestine called Eleutheropolis, near which are the mountains of Seir.' It is evident from the prophecy itself that Idumea is particularly referred to, for the prophet immediately adds, that the voice came to him from mount 'Seir,' which was the principal mountain of Idumea. Why the name 'Dumah' is used to designate that region has been a matter on which critics have been divided. Vitringa supposes that it is by a play upon the word 'Dumah,' because the word *may* be derived from דָּמַם (dâmăm) to be silent, to be still; and that it is used to denote the *silence*, or the *night*, which was about to come upon Idumea; that is, the calamity of which this was a prediction. Kocher supposes that the prophet used the word denoting '*silence*' (דוּמָה) by a paranomasia, and by derision for אֱדֹם, as if Idumea was soon to be reduced to silence, or to destruction. Idumea, or the country of Edom, is frequently referred to by the prophets (see Jer. xlix. 7–10, 12–18; Ezek. xxxv. 1–4, 7, 9, 14, 15; Joel iii. 19; Amos i. 11; Obad. 2–18; Mal. i.

3, 4).—For a description of Idumea, and of the prophecies respecting it, see Notes on Isa. xxxiv. ¶ *He calleth.* One calleth; there is a voice heard by me from Seir. Lowth renders it, 'A voice crieth unto me.' But the sense is, that the prophet hears one crying, or calling (קֹרֵא) to him from the distant mountain. ¶ *Unto me.* The prophet Isaiah. ¶ *Out of Seir.* The name 'Seir' was given to a mountainous tract or region of country that stretched along from the southern part of the Dead Sea, to the eastern branch of the Red Sea, terminating near Ezion-geber. Mount Hor formed a part of this range of mountains. Esau and his descendants possessed the mountains of Seir, and hence the whole region obtained the name of Edom or Idumea. Mount Seir was anciently the residence of the *Horites* (Gen. xiv. 6), but Esau made war upon them and destroyed them (comp. Gen. xxxvi. 8, 9; Deut. ii. 5, 12). Here it is put for the country of Idumea, and the sense is, that the whole land, or the inhabitants of the land, are heard by the prophet in a taunting manner asking him what of the night. ¶ *Watchman* (see Note on ver. 6). The prophet Isaiah is here referred to (comp. ch. lii. 8; lvi. 10). He is represented as being in the midst of the calamities that had come upon Judea, and as having his station in desolate Jerusalem, and looking for the signs of returning day. The eye is turned towards the east—the source whence light comes, and whence the exiles would return to their own land. Thus anxiously waiting for the indications of mercy to his desolate country, he hears this taunting voice from Idumea, asking him what was the prospect? what evidence there was of returning prosperity? ¶ *What of the night?* (comp. Hab. ii. 1). 'How stands the night? What is the prospect? What have you to announce respecting the night? How much of it is passed? And what is the prospect of the dawn?' 'Night' here is the emblem of calamity, affliction, oppression, as it often is in the Scriptures (comp. Job xxxv. 10; Mic. iii. 6); and it refers here probably to the calamities which had come upon Judea. The

12 The watchman said, The morning cometh, and also the night:

if ye will inquire, inquire ye: return, come.

---

inquiry is, How much of that calamity had passed? What was the prospect? How long was it to continue? How far was it to spread? The inquiry is *repeated* here to denote *intensity* or *emphasis*, manifesting the deep interest which the inquirer had in the result, or designed to give emphasis and point to the cutting taunt.

12. *The watchman said.* Or rather *saith ;* indicating that this is the answer which the prophet returned to the inquiry from Idumea. ¶ *The morning cometh.* There are signs of approaching day. The 'morning' here is an emblem of prosperity; as the light of the morning succeeds to the darkness of the night. This refers to the deliverance from the captivity of Babylon, and is to be supposed as having been spoken near the time when that captivity was at an end ;—or nearly at break of day after the long night of their bondage. This declaration is to be understood as referring to a different people from those referred to in the expression which immediately follows— 'and also the night.' 'The morning cometh'—to the captive Jews ; '*and also the night*'—to some other people— to wit, the Idumeans. It *might* mean that the morning was to be succeeded by a time of darkness to the same people ; but the connection seems to demand that we understand it of others. ¶ *And also the night.* A time of calamity and affliction. This is emphatic. It refers to the Idumeans. 'The morning cometh to the captive Jews ; it shall be *closely* succeeded by a night—a time of calamity—to the taunting Idumeans.'—During the captivity of the Jews in Babylon, the Idumeans invaded and took possession of the southern part of Judea. The prophet here refers to the fact, perhaps, that on the return of the Jews to their native land, they would revenge this by expelling them, and by inflicting punishment on the land of Edom. For a full proof that calamities came upon the land of Idumea, see Keith *On the Prophecies*, Art. *Idumea*, and Notes on Isa. xxxiv.) ¶ *If ye will inquire, in-*

quire ye. If you choose to ask anything further in regard to this, you can. The sense is probably this : ' You Idumeans have asked respecting *the night* in derision and reproach. An answer has been given somewhat agreeably *to* that inquiry. But if you seriously wish to know anything further respecting the destiny of your land, you can ask me (Isaiah) or any other prophet, and it will be known. But ask it in seriousness and earnestness, and with a suitable regard for the prophetic character and for God. And especially if you wish a more favourable answer to your inquiries, it is to be obtained only by forsaking sin and turning to God, and *then* you may come with the hope of a brighter prospect for the future.' The design of this is, therefore—(1) to *reprove* them for the manner in which they had asked the question ; (2) to assure them that God was willing to direct humble and serious inquirers ; and (3) to show in what way a favourable answer could be obtained—to wit, by repentance. And this is as true of sinners now as it was then. *They* often evince the reproachful and taunting spirit which the Idumeans did. *They* hear only a similar response—that prosperity and happiness await the Christian, though now in darkness and affliction ; and that calamity and destruction are before the guilty. They *might* have the same answer—an answer that God would bless them and save them, if they would inquire in a humble, serious, and docile manner. ¶ *Return.* Turn from your sins ; come back to God, and show respect for him and his declarations. ¶ *Come. Then* come and you shall be accepted, and the watchman will also announce *morning* as about to dawn on you.—This seems to be the sense of this very dark and difficult prophecy. It is brief, enigmatical, and obscure. Yet it is beautiful ; and if the sense above given be correct, it contains most weighty and important truth—alike for the afflicted and persecuted friends, and the persecuting and taunting foes of God. With reference to the interpretation here pro-

ANALYSIS OF VER. 13–17.—VISION XVIII.

Arabia.

THE remainder of this chapter is occupied with a single prophecy respecting Arabia. It was *probably* delivered about the time that the former was uttered—during the reign of Hezekiah, and before the invasion of Sennacherib. It had reference, I suppose, to Sennacherib; and was designed to foretell the fact that, either in his march to attack Judea, or on his return from Egypt, he would pass through Arabia, and perhaps oppress and overthrow some of their clans. At all events, it was to be fulfilled within a year after it was uttered (ver. 16), and refers to *some* foreign invasion that was to come upon their land. Rosenmüller supposes that it relates to the same period as the prophecy in Jer. xlix. 28, *sq.*, and refers to the time when Nebuchadnezzar sent Nebuzaradan to overrun the lands of the Ammonites, the Moabites, the Philistines, the Arabians, the Idumeans, and others who had revolted from him, and who had formed an alliance with Zedekiah.

The sentiment of the prophecy is simple—that within a year the country of Arabia would be overrun by a foreign enemy. The form and

manner of the prophecy is highly poetic and beautiful. The images are drawn from customs and habits which pertain to the Arabians, and which characterize them to this day. In ver. 13, the prophecy opens with a declaration that the caravans that were accustomed to pass peacefully through Arabia would be arrested by the apprehension of war. They would seek a place of refuge in the forests and fastnesses of the land. Thither also the prophet sees the Arabians flocking, as if to exercise the rites of hospitality, and to minister to the wants of the oppressed and weary travellers. But the reasons why *they* are there, the prophet sees to be that *they* are oppressed and driven out of their land by a foreign invader, and *they* also seek the same places of security and of refuge (ver. 14, 15). All this would be accomplished within a year (ver. 16); and the result would be, that the inhabitants of Arabia would be greatly diminished (ver. 17).

13 The burden upon Arabia. In the forest in Arabia shall ye lodge, O ye travelling companies of Dedanim.

For the day of the LORD is near upon all the heathen;
As thou hast done, it shall be done unto thee;
Thy reward shall return upon thine own head,
&c.

In this prophecy these circumstances are all to be found: (1) The hostility of the Edomites against Jerusalem, and the part which they took in the destruction of the city, in ver. 10–14; (2) the fact of the deliverance of the Jews from captivity, in ver. 17; (3) the consequent vengeance upon the Idumeans (ver. 18–21). This remarkable coincidence in an independent prophecy is a strong circumstance to prove that the interpretation above proposed is correct. In regard to the general reasons for the interpretation here proposed, and the lessons which the prophecy is fitted to convey, I may be permitted to refer to my *Practical Sermons*, pp. 325–341.

13. *The burden* (see Note on ch. xiii. 1). ¶ *Upon Arabia* (בְּעְרָב). This is an unusual form. The title of the prophecies is usually without the בְ, rendered 'upon.' Lowth supposes this whole title to be of doubtful authority, chiefly because it is wanting in most MSS. of the LXX. The LXX. connect it with the preceding prophecy respect-

posed, which supposes, as will have been seen—(1) a state of excited feeling on the part of the Jews towards the Idumeans, for the part which they took in the destruction of their city; (2) the prospect of speedy deliverance to the Jews in Babylon; and (3) a consequent desolation and vengeance on the Idumeans for the feelings which they had manifested in the destruction of Jerusalem, see the prophecy of Obadiah, ver. 8–21:—

Shall I not in that day, saith the LORD,
Even destroy the wise men out of Edom,
And understanding out of the mount of Esau?
And thy mighty men, O Teman, shall be dismayed,
To the end that every one of the mount of Esau may be cut off by slaughter.
For thy violence against thy brother Jacob shame shall cover thee,
And thou shalt be cut off for ever.
In the day that thou stoodest on the other side;
In the day that the stranger carried away captive his forces;
And foreigners entered into his gates, and cast lots upon Jerusalem;
Even thou wast as one of them.
But thou shouldest not have looked on the day of thy brother in the day that he became a stranger;
Neither shouldest thou have rejoiced over the children of Judah in the day of their destruction;
Neither shouldest thou have spoken proudly in the day of distress.

*   *   *   *

ing Dumah, and make this a continuance of that. The preposition (ב)—'upon,' means here *respecting, concerning*, and is used instead of עַל, as in Zech. ix. 1. Arabia is a well-known country of western Asia, lying south and southeast of Judea. It was divided into three parts, Arabia Deserta, on the east; Arabia Petrea, lying south of Judea; and Arabia Felix, lying still further south. What part of Arabia is here denoted it may not be easy to determine. It is probable that it was Arabia Petrea, because this lay between Judea and Egypt, and would be exposed to invasion by the Assyrians should they invade Egypt; and because this part of Arabia furnished, more than the others, such retreats and fastnesses as are mentioned in ver. 13–15. ¶ *In the forest* (בַּיַּעַר). The word (יַעַר) 'forest' usually denotes a grove, a collection of trees. But it may mean here, any place of refuge from a pursuing foe; a region of thick underwood; an uncultivated, inaccessible place, where they would be concealed from an invading enemy. The word rendered 'forest' is commonly supposed to mean a forest in the sense in which that word is now used by us, meaning an extensive wood —a large tract of land covered with trees. It is doubtful, however, whether the word is so used in the Bible. The Rev. Eli Smith stated to me that he had visited several of the places in Palestine to which the word (יַעַר) 'forest' or 'grove' is given, and that he was satisfied that there never was a forest there in our use of the word. The same word *vaar*—the ר not being used to begin a word in Arabic, but the ן being used instead of it—occurs often in Arabic. It means, as used by the Arabs, a rough, stony, impassable place; a place where there are no roads; which is inaccessible; and which is a safe retreat for robbers—and it is not improbable that the word is so used here. ¶ *In Arabia* (בַּעְרָב). The LXX., the Vulgate, and the Chaldee, understand this of the *evening*—'in the evening.' The word עֶרֶב, with different points from those which the Masorites have used here, means *evening*, but there is no

necessity of departing from the translation in our English version. The sense would not be materially affected whichever rendering should be preferred. ¶ *Shall ye lodge*. Shall you pass the night. This is the usual signification of the word. But here it may be taken in a larger sense, as denoting that they would pitch their tents there, or that they would seek a refuge there. The sense I suppose to be this : 'O ye travelling caravans of Dedan! Ye were accustomed to pass through Arabia, and to find a safe and hospitable entertainment there. But now, the Arabians shall be overrun by a foreign enemy; they shall be unable to show you hospitality, and to insure your safety in their tents, and for fear of the enemy still in the land you will be obliged to seek a lodging in the inaccessible thickets of the forests.' The passage is intended to denote the *change* that had taken place, and to show the *insecurity* for caravans. ¶ *O ye travelling companies*. Ye *caravans* (אֹרְחוֹת). This word usually signifies *ways, paths, cross roads*. But it is here used evidently to denote those who *travelled* in such ways or paths; that is, caravans of merchants. So it is used in Job vi. 19: 'The *caravans* of Tema.' It is well known that in the East it is usual for large companies to travel together, called *caravans*. Arabia Petrea was a great thoroughfare for such companies. ¶ *Of Dedanim*. Descendants of *Dedan*. There are two men of this name mentioned in the Old Testament—the son of Raamah, the son of Cush, mentioned in Gen. x. 7; and the son of Jokshan, the son of Abraham by Keturah (Gen. xxv. 3). The descendants of the latter settled in Arabia Petrea, and the descendants of the former near the Persian Gulf. It is not easy to determine which is here intended, though most probably those who dwelt near the Persian Gulf, because they are often mentioned as merchants. They dealt in ivory, ebony, &c., and traded much with Tyre (Ezek. xxvii. 21), and doubtless also with Egypt. They are here represented as passing through Arabia Petrea on their way to Egypt, and as compelled by the calamities in the

14 The inhabitants of the land of Tema brought ¹water to him

1 or, *bring ye.*

that was thirsty, they prevented with their bread him that fled.

country to find a refuge in its fastnesses and inaccessible places.

14. *Of the land of Tema.* Tema was one of the sons of Ishmael (Gen. xxv. 15), and is supposed to have peopled the city of Thema in Arabia Deserta. The word denotes here one of the tribes of Ishmael, or of the Arabians. Job speaks (vi. 19) of 'the troops of Tema,' and Jeremiah (xxv. 23) connects Tema and Dedan together. Jerome and Eusebius say that the village of Theman (Θαιμάν) existed in their time. It was, according to Jerome, five, and according to Eusebius, fifteen miles from Petra, and was then occupied as a Roman garrison (*Onomas Urb. et Locor*). Ptolemy speaks of a city called Themme (Θέμμη) in Arabia Deserta. This city lies, according to D'Anville, in lon. 57° E., and lat. 27° N. According to Seetzen, it is on the road usually pursued by caravans from Mecca to Damascus. Lowth renders it 'The southern country,' but without authority. The LXX. render it, Θαιμάν —'Thaiman.' ¶ *Brought water.* Marg. 'Bring ye.' This might be rendered in the imperative, but the connection seems rather to require that it be read as a declaration that they did so. To bring water to the thirsty was an act of hospitality, and especially in eastern countries, where water was so scarce, and where it was of so much consequence to the traveller in the burning sands and deserts. The idea is, that the inhabitants of the land would be oppressed and pursued by an enemy; and that the Arabians, referred to by the prophet (ver. 13), would be driven from their homes; and be dependent on others; that they would wander through the vast deserts, deprived of the necessaries of life; and that they would be dependent on the charity of the people of Tema for the supply of their wants. The following illustration of this passage has been kindly furnished me by the Rev. Eli Smith, missionary to Syria, showing that Isaiah, in mentioning *hospitality* as one of the virtues of the inhabitants of Tema, drew from

the life. 'Even in Hebrew prophecy hospitality is distinctly recognized as a trait in the Arab character. Isaiah says, "the inhabitants of Tema," &c. Tema is known as an oasis in the heart of Arabia, between Syria and Mecca. And among the scraps of ante-Mahometan poetry that have reached us, is one by Samaciel, a prince of this same Tema. In extolling the virtues of his tribe he says—

وما أُحمِدَت نارُلنا دونَ طارق
ولا ذَمَّنا فِى النازلِينَ خَزِيل

"No fire of ours was ever extinguished at night without a guest, and of our guests never did one disparage us."

'In the passage quoted from Isaiah, it is to the thirsty and hungry in flight, that the inhabitants of Tema are represented as bringing water and bread, as if hastening to afford them protection. The extent to which this protection is sometimes carried, is finely illustrated by a traditional anecdote in the life of Samaciel, the prince and poet of Tema just mentioned. In some feud among the tribes in his neighbourhood, a prince [Amru el-Keis] fled to Samaciel, left with him his treasures, and was conducted by him beyond the reach of his enemies. They assembled their forces, and marched upon Tema. On their way Samaciel's son fell into their hands. Presenting the young man before his castle, they proposed to the father the dreadful alternative, of delivering up to them what his guest had left, or seeing his son massacred. Samaciel's sense of honour dictated the reply—

اجلِدَ ى فاجلِدَه . . . . الثَّار
طوق لا يبلى

"He honoured me, and I'll honour him ... Treachery is a chain to the neck that never wears out." So he defended the rights of his guest, and his son was

15 For ^athey fled ¹from the swords, from the drawn sword, and from the bent bow, and from the grievousness of war.

16 For thus hath the LORD said unto me, Within a year, according to the years of an hireling, ^b and all the glory of Kedar ^c shall fail.

17 And the residue of the number of ² archers, the mighty men of the children of Kedar, shall be diminished: for the LORD God of Israel hath spoken it.

CHAPTER XXII.
ANALYSIS OF VER. 1–14.

THIS chapter is made up of *two* prophecies, one comprising the first fourteen verses, and addressed to the city of Jerusalem; and the other (ver. 15-25) relating to the fall of Shebna, the prefect of the palace, and to the promotion of Eliakim in his place. They may have been delivered nearly at the same time, but the subjects are distinct.

a Job 6.19,20.   1 *from the face of,* or, *for fear.*
b Job 7.1.   *c* ch.60.7.   2 *bows.*

---

slain.' ¶ *They prevented.* Our word 'prevent' usually means at present, to hinder, to obstruct. But in the Scriptures, and in the old English sense of the word, it means to anticipate, to go before. That is the sense of the word קִדְּמוּ here. They *anticipated* their wants by bread; that is, they supplied them. This was an ancient and an honourable rite of hospitality. Thus Melchizedek (Gen. xiv. 17, 18) is said to have come out and met Abraham, when returning victorious from the slaughter of Chedorlaomer, with bread and wine. ¶ *Him that fled.* The inhabitant of the land of Arabia that fled before the invader, perhaps the inhabitants of Kedar (ver. 16), or of some other part of Arabia. It is not meant that the *whole* land of Arabia would be desolate, but that the invasion would come upon certain parts of it; and the inhabitants of other portions—as of Tema—would supply the wants of the fugitives.

15. *For they fled.* The inhabitants of one part of the land. ¶ *The grievousness of war.* Heb. כֹּבֶד—the *weight,* the *heaviness,* the *oppression* of war; probably from the calamities that would result from the march of the Assyrian through their land, either on his way to Judea or to Egypt.

16. *Within a year.* What has been said before was figurative. Here the prophet speaks without a metaphor, and fixes the time when this should be accomplished. It is not usual for the prophets to designate the exact *time* of the fulfilment of their prophecies in this manner. ¶ *According to the years of an hireling.* Exactly; observing

the precise time specified (Job vii. 1). See the phrase explained on ch. xvi. 14. ¶ *All the glory.* The beauty, pride, strength, wealth, &c. ¶ *Of Kedar.* Kedar was a son of Ishmael (Gen. xxv. 15). He was the father of the Kedarencans or *Cedrai,* mentioned by Pliny (*Nat. Hist.* v. 11). They dwelt in the neighbourhood of the Nabatheans, in Arabia Deserta. These people lived in tents, and were a wandering tribe, and it is not possible to fix the precise place of their habitation. They resided, it is supposed, in the south part of Arabia Deserta, and the north part of Arabia Petrea. The name 'Kedar' seems to be used sometimes to denote Arabia in general, or Arabia Deserta particularly (see Ps. cxx. 5; Cant. i. 5; Isa. xlii. 11; lx. 7; Jer. ii. 10; xlix. 28; Ezek. xxvi. 21). ¶ *Shall fail.* Shall be consumed, destroyed (כָּלָה).

17. *And the residue of the number.* That is, those who shall be left in the invasion. Or perhaps it may be read, 'There shall be a remnant of the number of bowmen; the mighty men of Kedar shall be diminished.' ¶ *Of archers.* Heb. 'Of the bow;' that is, of those who use bows in war. The bow was the common instrument in hunting and in war among the ancients. ¶ *Shall be diminished.* Heb. 'Shall be made small;' they shall be reduced to a very small number. We cannot indeed determine the precise historical event to which this refers, but the whole connection and circumstances seem to make it probable that it referred to the invasion by the Assyrian when he went up against Judah, or when he was on his way to Egypt.

The first (ver. 1-14) relates to Jerusalem. It has reference to some period when the city was besieged, and when universal consternation spread among the people. The prophet represents himself as in the city, and as a witness of the alarm. 1. He describes (1-3) the consternation that prevailed in the city at the approach of the enemy. The inhabitants flee to the tops of the houses, either to observe the enemy or to make a defence, and the city is filled with distress, mingled with the tumultuous mirth of a portion who regard defence as hopeless, and who give themselves up to revelry and gluttony, because they apprehended that they must at all events soon die. 2. The prophet then describes (4-8) his own grief at the impending calamity, and especially at the state of things within the city. He portrays the distress; describes those who cause it, and the people engaged in it; and says that the valleys around the city are filled with chariots, and that the horsemen of the enemy have come to the very gate. 3. He then describes the preparations which are made in the city for defence (9-11). The inhabitants of the city had endeavoured to repair the breaches of the walls; had even torn down their houses to furnish materials, and had endeavoured to secure the *water* with which the city was supplied from the enemy; but they had not looked to God as they should have done for protection. The scope of the prophecy therefore is, to reprove them for not looking to God, and also for their revelry in the very midst of their calamities. 4. The prophet then describes the state of *morals* within the city (12-14). It was a time when they should have humbled themselves, and looked to God. He called them to fasting and to grief; but they supposed that the city *must* be taken, and that they must die, and a large portion of the inhabitants, despairing of being able to make a successful defence, gave themselves up to riot and drunkenness. To reprove this, was one design of the prophet; and perhaps, also, to

teach the general lesson that men, in view of the certainty of death, should *not* madly and foolishly give themselves to sensual indulgence.

There has been a difference of opinion in regard to the event to which this prophecy refers. Most have supposed that it relates to the invasion by Sennacherib; others have supposed that it relates to the destruction of the city by Nebuchadnezzar. Vitringa and Lowth suppose that the prophet had *both* events in view; the former in ver. 1-5, and the latter in the remainder of the prophecy. But it is not probable that it has a twofold reference. It has the appearance of referring to a *single* calamity; and this mode of interpretation should not be departed from without manifest necessity. The general aspect of the prophecy has reference, I think, to the invasion by Sennacherib. He came near the city; the city was filled with alarm; and Hezekiah prepared himself to make as firm a stand against him as possible, and put the city in the best possible state of defence. The description in ver. 9-11 agrees exactly with the account given of the defence which Hezekiah made against Sennacherib in 2 Chron. xxxii. 2, *sq.*; and particularly in regard to the effort made to secure the fountains in the neighbourhood for the use of the city, and to prevent the Assyrians from obtaining it. In 2 Chron. xxxii. 2, *sq*, we are told that Hezekiah took measures to stop all the fountains of water without the city, and the brook 'that ran through the midst of the land,' in order that the Assyrians under Sennacherib should not find water; and that he repaired the walls, and built new towers of defence in the city, and placed guards upon them. These circumstances of *coincidence* between the history and the prophecy, show conclusively that the reference is entirely to the invasion under Sennacherib. This occurred B.C. 710.

T HE burden of the valley of vision. What aileth thee now,

CHAPTER XXII.

1. *The burden* (see Note on ch. xiii. 1). ¶ *The valley* (גיא). Sept. Φάραγγος—' Valley.' Chaldee, ' The burden of the prophecy respecting the city which dwells (*i.e.*, is built) in the valley, which the prophets have prophesied concerning it.' There can be no doubt that Jerusalem is intended (see ver. 9, 10). It is not usual to call it *a valley*, but it may be so called, either (1.) because there were several valleys *within* the city and adjacent to it, as the vale between mount Zion and Moriah; the

vale between mount Moriah and mount Ophel; between these and mount Bezetha; and the valley of Jehoshaphat, without the walls of the city; or (2.) more probably it was called *a valley* in reference to its being *encompassed with hills*, rising to a considerable elevation above the city. Thus mount Olivet was on the east, and overlooked the city. Jerusalem is also called a *valley*, and a *plain*, in Jer. xxi 13: 'Behold, I am against thee, O inhabitant of the valley, and rock of the plain, saith the Lord.' Thus it is described in Reland's *Pales-*

that thou art wholly gone up to the house-tops? [a]

2 Thou that art full of stirs, a

tumultuous city, a [b]joyous city: thy slain *men are* not slain with the sword, nor dead in battle.

tine:—' The city was in the mountain region of Judea, in an elevated place, yet so that in respect to the mountains by which it was surrounded, it seemed to be situated in a humble place, because mount Olivet, and other mountains surrounding it, were more elevated.' So Phocas says, ' The holy city is placed in the midst of various valleys and hills, and this is wonderful (θαυμαστόν) in it, that at the same time the city seems to be elevated and depressed; for it is elevated in respect to the region of Judea, and depressed in respect to the hills around it.' — (Reland's *Palestine*, iii. 802, in Ugolini's *Thesaurus*, vi.) It was common with Isaiah and the other prophets to designate Jerusalem and other places, not by their proper names, but by some appellation that would be descriptive (see ch. xxi. 1; xxix. 1). ¶ *Of vision* (see Note on ch. i. 1). The word here means that Jerusalem was eminently the place where God made known his will to the prophets, and manifested himself to his people by *visions.* ¶ *What aileth thee now?* What is the cause of the commotion and tumult that exists in the city? The prophets throws himself at once into the midst of the excitement; sees the agitation and tumult, and the preparations for defence which were made, and asks the *cause* of all this confusion. ¶ *That thou art wholly gone up to the house-tops.* That all classes of the people had fled to the house-tops, so much that it might be said that all the city had gone up. Houses in the East were built in a uniform manner in ancient times, and are so to this day. (See a description of the mode of building in Notes on

Matt. ix. 1, *sq.*) The roofs were always flat, and were made either of earth that was trodden hard, or with large flat stones. This roof was surrounded with a balustrade (Deut. xxii. 8), and furnished a convenient place for walking, or even for eating and sleeping. Whenever, therefore, anything was to be seen in the street, or at a distance; or when there was any cause of alarm, they

HOUSE TOPS IN THE EAST.

would naturally resort to the roof of the house. When there was a tower in the city, the inhabitants fled to that, and took refuge on its top (see Judg. x. 50 –53). The image here is, therefore, one of consternation and alarm, as if on the sudden approach of an enemy.

2. *Thou that art full of stirs.* Of tumult, of commotion, of alarm. Or, perhaps, this whole description may mean that it was formerly a city distinguished for the hum of business, or for pleasure; a busy, active, enterprising city. The Hebrew will bear this, but I prefer the former interpretation, as indicating mingled alarm and consternation, and at the same time a disposition to engage in riot and revelry. ¶ *A joyous city.* A city exulting; rejoicing; given to pleasure, and to riot. (See

3 All thy rulers are fled *a to-gether, they are bound ¹ by the archers : all that are found in thee are bound together, *which* have fled from far.

a 2 Ki.25.5,11.   1 *of the bow.*

the description of Nineveh in Zeph. ii. 15.) It is remarkable that the prophet has blended these things together, and has spoken of the tumult, the alarm, and the rejoicing, in the same breath. This may be either because it was the *general* character of the city thus to be full of revelry, dissipation, and riot, and he designates it by that which *usually* and *appropriately* described it ; or because it was, even then, notwithstanding the general consternation and alarm, given up to revelry, and the rather on account of the approaching danger. So he describes the city in ver. 12, 13. ¶ *Thy slain* men are *not slain with the sword.* The words ' thy slain ' here (הַלָלַיִךְ), seem to be intended to be applied to the soldiers on whom the defence of the city rested ; and to mean those who had not died an honourable death *in* the city in its defence, but who had *fled* in consternation, and who were either taken in their flight and made captive, or who were pursued and put to death. To be slain with the sword here is equivalent to being slain in an honourable engagement with the enemy. But here the prophet speaks of their consternation, their cowardice, and of their being partly trampled down in their hasty and ignominious flight by each other ; and partly of the fugitives being overtaken by the enemy, and thus put to death.

3. *All thy rulers are fled together.* The general idea in this verse is plain. It is designed to describe the consternation which would take place on the approach of the invader, and especially the timidity and flight of those on whom the city relied for protection and defence. Hence, instead of entering calmly and firmly on the work of defence, no inconsiderable part of the rulers of the city are represented as fleeing from the city, and refusing to remain to protect the capital. The word rendered ' thy rulers ' (קְצִינַיִךְ) denotes either the civil rulers of the city, or military leaders. It is most usually applied to the latter (Josh. x. 24 ; Judg. xi. 6, 11 ; Dan. xi. 18), and probably refers here to military

commanders. ¶ *They are bound by the archers.* Heb. as in the margin, ' Of the bow.' There has been a great variety in the interpretation of this passage. The LXX. read it, Σκληρῶς δεδέμενοι εἰσί—' And the captives are bound with severity.' The Chaldee, ' And the captives migrate from before the extending of the bow.' Jarchi renders it, ' Who from the fear of arrows were bound so that they shut themselves up in the city.' Houbigant and Lowth render it, ' They are fled from the bow,' reading it הָסָרוּ instead of the present Hebrew text אֻסָרוּ, but without the slightest authority. Vitringa renders it, ' They were bound from treading, *i.e.*, extending, or using the bow ;' or ' They were bound *by* those who tread, *i.e.*, use the bow ;' indicating that they were so bound that they could not use the bow in defence of the city. I think that the *connection* here requires that the word אֻסָרוּ should be used in the sense of being *bound* or influenced by fear— they were so intimidated, so much under the influence of terror, so entirely unmanned and disabled by alarm, that they could not use the bow ; or this was caused *by* the bow, *i.e.*, by the bowmen or archers who came to attack the city. It is true that no other instance occurs in which the word is used in precisely this sense, but instances in abundance occur where strong passion is represented as having a controlling or disabling influence over the mind and body ; where it takes away the energy of the soul, and makes one timid, feeble, helpless, *as if* bound with cords, or made captive. The word אָסַר commonly means to bind with cords, or to fetter ; to imprison (Gen. xlii. 24 ; Judg. xvi. 5 ; 2 Kings xvii. 4) ; to yoke (1 Sam. vi. 7, 10) ; and then to bind with a vow (Num. xxx. 3). Hence it may mean to *bind* with fear or consternation. ¶ Which *have fled from far.* That is, either they have fled far away ; or they had fled *from* far in order to reach Jerusalem as a place of safety. Probably the latter is the sense.

4 Therefore said I, Look away from me; I will [1] weep bitterly, labour [a] not to comfort me; because of the spoiling of the daughter of my people.

5 For *it is* a day of trouble, and of treading down, and of perplexity

1 *be in bitter weeping.*   a Jer.4 19; 9.1; Lam.1.2.

by the LORD God of hosts in the valley of vision, breaking down the walls, and of crying to the mountains.

6 And Elam [b] bare the quiver with chariots of men *and* horsemen, and Kir [2] uncovered the shield.

b Jer.49.35.   2 *made naked.*

---

4. *Look away from me.* Do not look upon me—an indication of deep grief, for sorrow seeks to be alone, and grief avoids publicity and exposure. ¶ *I will weep bitterly.* Heb. ' I will be bitter in weeping.' Thus we speak of *bitter* sorrow, indicating excessive grief (see Note on ch. xv. 5; comp. Jer. xiii. 17; xiv. 17; Lam. i. 16; ii. 11; Mic. i. 8, 9). ¶ *Labour not.* The sense is, ' My grief is so great that I cannot be comforted. There are no topics of consolation that can be presented. I must be alone, and allowed to indulge in deep and overwhelming sorrow at the calamities that are coming upon my nation and people.' ¶ *Because of the spoiling.* The desolation; the ruin that is coming upon them. ¶ *The daughter of my people.* Jerusalem (see Note on ch. i. 8; comp. Jer. iv. 11; vi. 14; viii. 19, 21, 22; Lam. ii. 11; iv. 3, 6, 10).

5. *For* it is *a day of trouble and of treading down.* When our enemies trample on everything sacred and dear to us, and endanger all our best interests (see Ps. xliv. 6; Luke xxi. 24). ¶ *And of perplexity.* In which we know not what to do. We are embarrassed, and know not where to look for relief. ¶ *By the* LORD *God of hosts.* That is, he is the efficient cause of all this. It has come upon us under his providence, and by his direction (see Note on ch. x. 5). ¶ *In the valley of vision.* In Jerusalem (see Note on ver. 1). ¶ *Breaking down the walls.* There has been much variety in the interpretation of this place. The LXX. render it, ' In the valley of Zion they wander, from the least to the greatest; they wander upon the mountains.' See a discussion of the various senses which the Hebrew phrase may admit, in Rosenmüller and Gesenius. Probably our common version has given the true sense, and the reference is to the fact that the walls of the city be-

came thrown down, either in the siege or from some other cause. If this refers to the invasion of Sennacherib, though his army was destroyed, and he was unable to take the city, yet there is no improbability in the supposition that he made some breaches in the walls. Indeed this is implied in the account in 2 Chron. xxxii. 5. ¶ *And of crying to the mountains.* Either for help, or more probably of such a loud lamentation that it reached the surrounding hills, and was re-echoed back to the city. Or perhaps it may mean that the shout or clamour of those engaged in building or defending the walls, reached to the mountains. Comp. Virg. *Æneid,* iv. 668:

— resonat magnis plangoribus æther.

Rosenmüller renders it, ' A cry—to the mountains!' That is, a cry among the people to escape to the hills, and to seek refuge in the caves and fastnesses there (comp. Judg. vi. 2; Matt. xxiv. 16; Mark xiii. 14).

6. *And Elam.* The southern part of Persia, perhaps here used to denote Persia in general (see Note on ch. xxi. 2). Elam, or Persia, was at this time subject to Assyria, and their forces were united doubtless in the invasion of Judea. ¶ *Bare the quiver.* A ' quiver ' is a case in which arrows are carried. This was usually hung upon the shoulders, and thus *borne* by the soldier when he entered into battle. By the expression here, is meant that Elam was engaged in the siege, and was distinguished particularly for skill in shooting arrows. That the Elamites were thus distinguished for the use of the bow, is apparent from Ezek. xxxii. 24, and Jer. xlix. 35. ¶ *With chariots of men* and *horsemen.* Lowth proposes, instead of ' men,' to read אָרָם, *Syria,* instead of אָדָם, *man,* by the change of the single letter ד into ר   This mis-

7 And it shall come to pass, *that* thy [1] choicest valleys shall be full of chariots, and the horsemen shall set themselves in array [2] at the gate

8 And he discovered the covering of Judah, and thou didst look in that day to the armour of the house *a* of the forest.

a 1 Ki.7.2; 10.17.

take might have been easily made where the letters are so much alike, and it would suit the parallelism of the passage, but there is no authority of MSS. or versions for the change. The words 'chariots of men—horsemen,' I understand here, as in ch. xxi. 7, to mean *a troop* or *riding* of men who were horsemen. Archers often rode in this manner. The Scythians usually fought on horseback with bows and arrows. ¶ *Kir.* Kir was a city of Media, where the river Kyrus or Cyrus flows (2 Kings xvi. 9; Amos i. 5; ix. 7). This was evidently then connected with the Assyrian monarchy, and was engaged with it in the invasion of Judea. Perhaps the name 'Kir' was given to a region or province lying on the river Cyrus or Kyrus. This river unites with the Araxes, and falls into the Caspian Sea. ¶ *Uncovered the shield* (see Note on xxi. 5). Shields were protected during a march, or when not in use, by a covering of cloth. Among the Greeks, the name of this covering was Σάγμα. Shields were made either of metal or of skin, and the object in covering them was to preserve the metal untarnished, or to keep the shield from injury. To *uncover the shield*, therefore, was to prepare for battle. The Medes were subject to the Assyrians in the time of Hezekiah (2 Kings xvi. 9; xvii. 6), and of course in the time of the invasion of Judea by Sennacherib.

7. *Thy choicest valleys.* Heb. 'The choice of thy valleys;' meaning the most fertile and most valued lands in the vicinity of the city. The rich and fertile vales around Jerusalem would be occupied by the armies of the Assyrian monarch. What occurs in this verse and the following verses to ver. 14, is a prophetic description of what is presented historically in Isa. xxxvi., and 2 Chron. xxxii. The coincidence is so exact, that it leaves no room to doubt that the invasion here described was that which took place under Sen-

nacherib. ¶ *Set themselves in array.* Heb. 'Placing shall place themselves;' *i.e.*, they shall be drawn up for battle; they shall besiege the city, and guard it from all ingress or egress. Rabshakeh, sent by Sennacherib to besiege the city, took his station at the upper pool, and was so near the city that he could converse with the people on the walls (Isa. xxxvi. 11–13).

8. *And he discovered.* Heb. וַיְגַל —'He made naked, or bare.' The expression, 'He discovered,' means simply that it *was* uncovered, without designating the agent. ¶ *The covering of Judah.* The word here used (מָסָךְ) denotes properly *a covering*, and is applied to the *curtain* or vail that was before the tabernacle (Ex. xxvi. 36: xxxix. 38); and to the curtain that was before the gate of the court (Ex. xxxv. 17; xxxix. 40). The LXX. understand it of the *gates* of Judah, 'They revealed the gates (τὰς πύλας) of Judah.' Many have understood it of the defences, ramparts, or fortifications of Judah, meaning that they were laid open to public view, *i.e.*, were demolished. But the more probable meaning, perhaps, is, that the invading army exposed Judah to every kind of reproach; stripped off everything that was designed to be ornamental in the land; and thus, by the figure of exposing one to reproach and shame by stripping off all his clothes, exposed Judah in every part to reproach. Sennacherib actually came up against all the fortified cities of Judah, and took them and dismantled them (2 Kings xviii. 13; Isa. xxxvi. 1). The land was thus laid bare, and unprotected. ¶ *And thou didst look.* Thou Judah; or the king of Judah. Thou didst cast thine eyes to that armoury as the last resort, and as the only hope of defence. ¶ *To the armour.* Or rather, perhaps, the *armoury*, the *arsenal* (נֶשֶׁק). The LXX. render it, 'To the choice houses of the city' (comp. Neh. iii. 19). ¶ *Of the house*

9 Ye [a] have seen also the breaches of the city of David, that they are many; and ye gathered together the waters of the lower pool:

10 And ye have numbered the

houses of Jerusalem, and the houses have ye broken down to fortify the wall.

11 Ye made also a ditch between the two walls for the water of the old pool: but ye have not looked

a 2 Ch.32.4.

---

of the forest. This was built within the city, and was called the house of the forest of Lebanon, probably from the great quantity of cedar from Lebanon which was employed in building it (1 Kings vii. 2–8). In this house, Solomon laid up large quantities of munitions of war (1 Kings x. 16, 17); and this vast storehouse was now the principal reliance of Hezekiah against the invading forces of Sennacherib.

9. *Ye have seen also the breaches.* You who are inhabitants of the city. That such breaches were actually made, see 2 Chron. xxxii. 5. ¶ *Of the city of David.* Of Jerusalem, so called because it was the royal residence of David. Zion was usually called the city of David, but the name was given also to the entire city. ¶ *And ye gathered together,* &c. That is, Hezekiah and the people of the city collected those waters. ¶ *Of the lower pool.* (For a description of the upper and lower pool, see Notes on ch. vii. 3). The superfluous waters of the lower pool usually flowed into the valley of Hinnom, and thence into the valley of Jehoshaphat, mingling with the waters of the brook Kedron. It would seem from the passage here that those waters were not usually retained for the use of the city, though it was possible to retain them in case of a drought or a siege. At present, the lower pool is without the walls, but Hezekiah appears to have extended a temporary wall around it so as to enclose it (see Note on ver. 11). This he did, probably for two purposes; (1.) to cut off the Assyrians from the supply of water; and (2.) to retain *all* the water in the city to supply the inhabitants during the siege; see 2 Chron. xxxii. 4, where it is expressly declared that Hezekiah took this measure to distress the Assyrians.

10. *And ye have numbered the houses of Jerusalem.* That is, you have taken

an estimate of their number so as to ascertain how many can be spared to be pulled down to repair the walls; or you have made an estimate of the amount of materials for repairing the walls, which would be furnished by pulling down the houses in Jerusalem. ¶ *To fortify the wall.* The houses in Jerusalem were built of stone, and therefore they would furnish appropriate materials for repairing the walls of the city. In 2 Chron. xxxii. 5, it is said that Hezekiah not only repaired the broken walls of the city on the approach of Sennacherib, but 'raised up the towers, and another wall without, and repaired Millo in the city of David, and made darts and shields in abundance.'

11. *Ye made also a ditch.* That is, they made a *reservoir* to retain the water. The word 'ditch,' however, will well describe the character of the pool of Gihon on the west side of the city (see Notes on ch. vii. 3). ¶ *Between the two walls for the water of the old pool.* Hezekiah built one of these walls himself (2 Chron xxxii. 5, 30; comp. 2 Kings xxv. 5, and Jer. xxxix. 4). Between these two walls the water would be collected so as to be accessible to the inhabitants of the city in case of a siege. Before this, the water had flowed without the walls of the city, and in a time of siege the inhabitants would be cut off from it, and an enemy would be able easily to subdue them. To prevent this, Hezekiah appears to have performed two works, one of which was particularly adapted to the times of the siege, and the other was of permanent utility. (1.) He made a wall on the west side of Gihon, so as to make the pool accessible to the inhabitants of the city, as described here by Isaiah; and (2.) he 'stopped the upper water-course of Gihon, and brought it straight down to the west side of the city of David' (2 Chron.

unto the maker thereof, neither had respect unto him that fashioned it long ago.

12 And in that day did the Lord God of hosts call [a] to weeping, and to mourning, and to

baldness,[b] and to girding with sackcloth:

13 And behold, joy and gladness, slaying oxen and killing sheep, eating flesh and drinking wine: let us [c] eat and drink, for to-morrow we shall die.

a Jo.11.13.　*b* Job 1.20; Mic.1.16.　*c* ch.56.12.

---

xxxii. 30). By this is not improbably meant that he constructed the pool which is now known as the 'pool of Hezekiah.' This reservoir lies within the walls of the city, some distance north-eastward of the Yâfa Gate, and just west of the street that leads to the church of the Holy Sepulchre. Its sides run towards the cardinal points. Its breadth at the north end is 144 feet, its length on the east side about 240 feet. The depth is not great. The bottom is rock, and is levelled and covered with cement. The reservoir is now supplied with water during the rainy season by the small aqueduct or drain brought down from the upper pool, along the surface of the ground and under the wall at or near the Yâfa Gate (comp. Robinson's *Bib. Researches*, vol. i. p. 487). This was deemed a work of great utility, and was one of the acts which particularly distinguished the reign of Hezekiah. It is not only mentioned in the Books of Kings and Chronicles, but the son of Sirach has also mentioned it in his encomium on Hezekiah: 'Hezekiah fortified his city, and brought in water into the midst thereof; he digged the hard rock with iron, and made wells for water' (Ecclus. xlviii. 17). ¶ *But ye have not looked.* You have not relied on God. You have depended on your own resources; and on the defences which you have been making against the enemy. This probably described the *general* character of the people. Hezekiah, however, was a pious man, and doubtless really depended on the aid of God. ¶ *The maker thereof.* God; by whose command and aid all these defences are made, and who has given you ability and skill to make them. ¶ *Long ago.* God had made this fountain, and it had *long* been a supply to the city. He had a claim, therefore, to their gratitude and respect.

12. *And in that day.* In the invasion of Sennacherib. It might be rendered, 'And the Lord, Jehovah of hosts, *on such a day calls* to weeping;' intimating that in such a time it was a general truth that God required those who were thus afflicted to weep, and fast, and pray. ¶ *Call to weeping.* That is, by his providence; or, it was *proper* that at such a time they should weep. Affliction, oppression, and calamity are indications from God *always* that we ought to be humbled, and to prostrate ourselves before Him. ¶ *And to baldness.* To plucking off the hair, or shaving the head—one of the emblems of grief among the ancients (Job i. 20; Micah i. 16). ¶ *And to girding with sackcloth* (see Note on ch. iii. 24).

13. *And behold, &c.* When they ought to give themselves to fasting and prayer, they gave themselves up to revelry and riot. ¶ *Let us eat and drink.* Saying, Let us eat and drink. That is, it is inevitable that we must soon die. The army of the Assyrian is approaching, and the city cannot stand against him. It is in vain to make a defence, and in vain to call upon God. Since we *must* soon die, we may as well enjoy life while it lasts. This is always the language of the epicure; and it seems to be the language of no small part of the world. Probably if the *real* feelings of the great mass of worldly men were expressed, they could not be better expressed than in this passage of Isaiah: 'We must soon die at all events. We cannot avoid that, for it is the common lot of all. And since we have been sent into a dying world; since we had no agency in being placed here; since it is impossible to prevent this doom, we may as well *enjoy* life while it lasts, and give ourselves to pleasure, dissipation, and revelry. While we can, we will take our com-

fort, and when death comes we will
submit to it, simply because we cannot
avoid it.' Thus, while God calls men
to repentance and seriousness; and
while he would urge them, by the consideration that this life is short, to prepare for a better ; and while he designs
that the nearness of death should lead
them to think solemnly of it, they abuse
all his mercies, endeavour to thwart all
his arrangements, and live and die like
the brutes.—This passage is quoted by
Paul in his argument on the subject of
the resurrection in 1 Cor. xv. 32. Sentiments remarkably similar to this occur in the writings of the Greek and
Roman poets. Among the Egyptians,
the fact that life is short was urged as
one argument for promoting soberness
and temperance, and in order to produce this effect, it was customary at
their feasts to have introduced, at some
part of the entertainment, a wooden
image of Osiris in the form of a human
mummy standing erect, or lying on a
bier, and to show it to each of the
guests, warning him of his mortality,
and of the transitory nature of human
pleasures. He was reminded that one
day he would be like that ; and was
told that men ' ought to love one another, and to avoid those evils which
tend to make them consider life too
long, when in reality it is too short,
and while enjoying the blessings of this
life, to bear in mind that life was pre-
carious, and that death would soon close
all their comforts.' (See Wilkinson's
Ancient Egyptians, vol. ii. pp. 409–
411.) With the Greeks and Romans,
however, as well as the Jews in the
time of Isaiah, the fact of the shortness
of life was used to produce just the contrary effect—to prompt them to dissipation and licentiousness. The fact
of the temporary pilgrimage of man
served as an inducement to enjoy the
pleasures of life while they lasted, since
death was supposed to close the scene,
and no prospect was held out of happiness in a future state. This sentiment was expressed in their songs at
their entertainments to urge themselves on to greater indulgence in wine
and in pleasure. Thus, in Anacreon,
Ode 4 :

Εις εαυτον.

Ο δ' Ερως χιτωνα δησ ις
Υπερ αυχενος παπυρω
Μεθυ μοι διηκονειτο·

Τροχος αρματος γαρ οια
Βιοτος τρεχει κυλισθεις
Ολιγη δε κεισομεσθα
Κονις, οστεων λυθεντων·

Τι σε δει λιβον μυριζειν ;
Τι δε γη χεειν ματαια ;
Εμε μαλλον, ως ετι ζω,
Μυριζον, καλει δ' εταιρην.

Πριν, Ερως, εκει με απελθειν
Υπο νερτερων χορειας,
Σκεδασαι θελω μεριμνας.

' In decent robe behind him bound,
Cupid shall serve the goblet round ;
For fast away our moments steal,
Like the swift chariot's rolling wheel;
The rapid course is quickly done,
And soon the race of life is run.
Then, then, alas! we droop, we die;
And sunk in dissolution lie:
Our frame no symmetry retains,
Nought but a little dust remains.
Why o'er the tomb are odours shed ?
Why poured libations to the dead?
To me, far better, while I live,
Rich wines and balmy fragrance give.
Now, now, the rosy wreath prepare,
And hither call the lovely fair.
Now, while I draw my vital breath,
Ere yet I lead the dance of death,
For joy my sorrows I'll resign,
And drown my cares in rosy wine.'

A similar sentiment occurs in Horace,
Od. iii. 13 :

Huc vina, et unguente, et nimium brevis
Flores amœnos ferre jube rosæ.
Dum res, et ætas, et sororum
Fila trium patiuntur atra.

And still more strikingly in Petronius,
Satyric. c. 34, *ad finem :*

Heu, heu, nos miseros, quam totus homuncio nil
    est!
Sic erimus cuncti, postquam nos auferat Orcus :
    Ergo vivamus, dum licet esse, bene.

The same sentiments prevailed among
the Jews in the time of the author of
the Book of Wisdom (xi. 1–9) :—' Our
life is short and tedious, and in the death
of a man there is no remedy : neither
was there any man known to have returned from the grave. For we are
born at all adventure ; and we shall be
hereafter as though we had never been,
for the breath in our nostrils is as smoke,
and a little spark in the moving of our
heart. Come on, therefore, let us enjoy
the good things that are present ; let us

14 And it was revealed in mine ears by the Lord of hosts, Surely this iniquity shall not be purged from you till ye die, saith the Lord God of hosts.

ANALYSIS OF VER. 15–25.—VISION XX.

The remainder of this chapter (ver. 15–25) is occupied with a prediction respecting Shebna, and the promotion of Eliakim in his place. From the prophecy itself it appears that Shebna was prefect of the palace (15), or that he was in the highest authority in the time of Hezekiah. That he was an unprincipled ruler is evident from the prophecy, and hence Isaiah was directed to predict his fall, and the elevation of another in his place. Whether this Shebna is the same that is mentioned in ch. xxxvi. 3, is not known. The Shebna there mentioned is called a *scribe* (22), and that was *after* the fall of Shebna here mentioned, for it occurred after Eliakim had been placed over the palace. Eliakim was then in office, and was sent on that

embassy to Sennacherib (xxxvi. 2, 22; xxxvii. 2). The probability is, therefore, that this was some other man of the same name, unless it may have been that *Shebna*, after being degraded from the rank of prefect of the palace or prime minister, became *a scribe*, or had an inferior office under Eliakim. The prophecy contains the following things:—1. A *command* to Isaiah to go to Shebna, and to reprove him for his self-confidence in his sin (15, 16). 2. A declaration that he should be carried captive to a foreign land (17, 18). 3. A declaration that he should be deposed and succeeded by Eliakim (20). 4. A description of the character and honours of Eliakim, and his qualifications for the office (21–24), and 5. A confirmation of the whole prophecy, or a summing up the whole in a single declaration (25).

15 Thus saith the Lord God of hosts, Go, get thee unto this treasurer, *even* unto Shebna, [a]which *is* over the house, *and say*,

a 2 Ki.18.37.

fill ourselves with costly wine and ointments, and let no flower of the spring pass by us ; let us crown ourselves with rose buds before they be withered ; let none of us go without his part of our voluptuousness ; let us leave tokens of our joyfulness in every place.' It was with reference to such sentiments as these, that Dr. Doddridge composed that beautiful epigram which Dr. Johnson pronounced the finest in the English language :

'Live while you live,' the sacred preacher cries,
'And give to God each moment as it flies ;'
'Live while you live,' the Epicure would say,
'And seize the pleasures of the present day.'
Lord, in my view, let both united be,
I live to pleasure when I live to thee.

14. *It was revealed in mine ears, Surely this iniquity shall not be purged from you till ye die.* That is, the sin is so aggravated that it shall never be expiated or pardoned. Few sins can be more aggravated than revelry and riot, thoughtlessness and mirth over the grave. Nothing can show a more decided disregard of God, and nothing a more grovelling and sensual disposition. And yet, it is the common sin of the world ; and there can be nothing more melancholy than that a race hastening to the grave should give itself to riot and dissipation. One would think that the

prospect of a speedy and certain death would deter men from sin. But the very reverse is true. The nearer they approach death, the more reckless and abandoned do they often become. The *strength* and *power* of depravity is thus shown in the fact that men CAN sin thus when near the grave, and with the most fearful warnings and assurances that they are soon to go down to eternal wo.

15. *Thus saith the Lord God of hosts* (see Note on ch. i. 9). ¶ *Go, get thee.* Heb. ' Go, come to.' This was one of the instances in which the prophets were directed to go personally, and even at the hazard of their life, to those who were high in office, and to denounce on them the Divine judgment for their sins. ¶ *Unto this treasurer* (הַסֹּכֵן). The Vulgate renders this, ' To him who dwells in the tabernacle.' The LXX. render it, Εἰς τὸ παστοφόριον, denoting properly what is borne into a recess, cell, or chapel, and referring properly to a place where an idol was placed in a temple ; and then any recess, or chamber, as a treasury, and referring here to the room which the treasurer of the temple occupied. The Hebrew word סָכַן means *to dwell with any one ;* then to be an associate or friend, and hence the participle is applied to one intrusted

16 What hast thou here, and whom hast thou here, that thou hast hewed thee out a sepulchre here, [1] *as* he that heweth him out a sepulchre on high, *and* that graveth an habitation for himself in a rock ?

with the care of anything, a steward, a treasurer. Jerome explains this in his Commentary as meaning, ' go to him who dwells in the tabernacle, which in Hebrew is called *Sochen.*' He understands by this some room, or recess in the temple, where the treasurer or the prefect of the temple dwelt. Our translators have expressed probably the true sense by the word ' treasurer.' ¶ *Which is over the house.* That is, either who is over the temple, or over the palace. I understand it of the latter. Shebna was not high priest, and the expression, ' over the house,' more properly denotes one who had the rule of the palace, or who was the principal minister of the king. See 1 Kings xviii. 3 : ' And Ahab called Obadiah, which was the governor of his house.' What was the offence or crime of Shebna, it is impossible to say. The Jewish commentators say that he was intending to betray the city to Sennacherib, but although this is possible it has no direct proof.

16. *What hast thou here ?* This verse contains a severe repoof of the pride and ostentation of Shebna, and of his expectation that he would be buried where he had built his own tomb. It also contains an *implied* declaration that he would not be permitted to lie there, but would be removed to a distant land to be buried in some less honourable manner. It is probable that Isaiah met him when he was *at* the sepulchre which he had made, and addressed this language to him there : ' What hast thou here ? What right to expect that thou wilt be buried here, or why do you erect this splendid sepulchre, as if you were a holy man, and God would allow you to lie here ?' Probably his sepulchre had been erected among the sepulchres of holy men, and perhaps in some part of the royal burying place in Jerusalem. ¶ *And whom hast thou here ?* Who among the dead that are entombed here are connected with you, that you should deem yourself entitled to lie with them ? If this was the royal cemetery, these words might be designed to intimate that he had no connection with the royal family ; and thus his building a tomb there was an evidence of vainglory, and of an attempt to occupy a place, even in death, to which he had no title. ¶ *That thou hast hewed thee out a sepulchre here.* Sepulchres were hewn or cut out of rocks (see Note on ch. xiv. 9). It was usual also for princes and rich men to have their sepulchres or tombs constructed while they were themselves alive (see Matt. xxvii. 60). Shebna was doubtless a man of humble birth, none of whose ancestors or family had been honoured with a burial in the royal cemetery, and hence the prophet reproves his pride in expecting to repose with the royal dead. ¶ *He that heweth him out a sepulchre on high.* On some elevated place, that it might be more conspicuous. Thus Hezekiah (2 Chron. xxxii. 33) was buried ' in the chiefest of the sepulchres of the sons of David.' Heb. בְּמַעֲלֵה—'In the highest.' LXX. Ἐν ἀναβάσει. Such sepulchres are still found in Persia. They consist of several tombs, each hewn in a high rock near the top, the front of the rock being adorned with figures in *relievo.* ' Sepulchres of this kind are remarkably exemplified in the very ancient tombs excavated in the cliffs of the mountain of sepulchres at Naksh-i-Roustan, a full description of which may be found in Sir Robert Ker Porter's *Travels.* They are excavated in an almost perpendicular cliff of about 300 feet high. There are two rows, of which the uppermost are the most ancient and interesting, presenting highly sculptured fronts about fifty-three feet broad, crowned by a representation of an act of Sabean worship. To the lowest of them, which, however, he describes as not less than sixty feet from the ground, Sir Robert could gain access only by being drawn up by means of a rope fastened around his waist, by some active natives who had contrived to clamber up to the ledge in front of the tomb. These appear to be royal sepul-

17 Behold, the LORD [1] will carry thee away with a [2] mighty captivity, and will surely cover thee.

18 He will surely violently turn,

and toss thee *like* a ball into a large [3] country : there shalt thou die, and there the chariots of thy glory *shall be* the shame of thy lord's house.

1 or, *who covered thee with an excellent covering, and clothed thee gorgeously, shall surely*, ver.18.

2 *the captivity of a man.*   3 *large of spaces.*

chres, and probably not later than the time of the kings of Persia mentioned in Scripture.' — (*Pict. Bible.*) Two

objects were probably contemplated by such sepulchres. One was security from desecration. The other was ostentatio.

TOMBS IN THE ROCKS AT NASKI ROUSTAN.—From Flandin, Voyage en Perse.

—sepulchres thus excavated furnishing an opportunity for the display of architectural taste in front, and being conspicuous objects. Such sepulchres are found at Petra (see Notes on ch. xvi. 1), and it is probable that Shebna sought this kind of immortality.—Many a man who has done nothing to deserve celebrity by his noble deeds while living, seeks it by the magnificence of his tomb.

17. *Behold, the* LORD *will carry thee away.* Of the historical fact here referred to we have no other information. To what place he was to be carried, we know not. It is probable, however, that it was to Assyria. ¶ *With a mighty captivity.* Heb. גֶּבֶר—'Of a man,' or perhaps, ' O man.' If it means ' the captivity of a man,' the sense is, a strong, irresistible, mighty captivity, where the word *man* is emphatic, and means such as a mighty man would make. Comp. Job xxxviii. 3 : ' Gird up now thy loins like a man.' The margin reads this, he ' who covered thee with an excellent covering, and clothed thee gorgeously, shall surely turn and toss thee.' But the text conveys more nearly the idea of the Hebrew word,

which denotes the action of *casting away*, or *throwing* from one as a man throws a stone. See the same use of the word טוּל in 1 Sam. xviii. 2; xx. 33; Jer. xvii. 13; xxii. 26, 28; Jonah i. 5, 12, 16. *And will surely cover thee.* ' Thy face,' says Lowth ; for this was the condition of mourners. The Chaldee is, ' Shall cover thee with confusion.' So Vitringa, who supposes that it means that although Shebna was endeavouring to rear a monument that should perpetuate his name and that of his family, God would cover them with ignominy, and reduce them to their primitive, obscure, and humble condition.

18. *He will surely violently turn.* Lowth has well expressed the sense of this :

He will whirl thee round and round, and cast thee away.

Thus it refers to the action of throwing a stone with a *sling*, when the sling is whirled round and round several times before the string is let go, in order to increase the velocity of the stone. The idea is here, that God designed to cast him into a distant land, and that he would give such an *impulse* to him that

19 And I will drive thee from thy station, and from thy state shall he pull thee down.

20 And it shall come to pass in that day, that I will call my servant *a* Eliakim, the son of Hilkiah:

a 2 Ki.18.18.

21 And I will clothe him with thy robe, and strengthen him with thy girdle, and I will commit thy government into his hand; and he shall be a father to the inhabitants of Jerusalem, and to the house of Judah.

---

he would be sent afar, so far that he would not be able to return again. ¶ Like *a ball*. A stone, ball, or other projectile that is cast from a sling. ¶ *Into a large country*. Probably Assyria. When this was done we have no means of determining. ¶ *And there the chariots of thy glory* shall be *the shame of thy lord's house*. Lowth renders this,

—— and there shall thy glorious chariots
Become the shame of the house of thy lord.

Noyes renders it,

There shall thy splendid chariots perish,
Thou disgrace of the house of thy lord.

The Chaldee renders it, 'And there the chariots of thy glory shall be converted into ignominy, because thou didst not preserve the glory of the house of thy lord.' Probably the correct interpretation is that which regards the latter part of the verse, 'the shame of thy lord's house,' as an address to him as the shame or disgrace of Ahaz, who had appointed him to that office, and of Hezekiah, who had continued him in it. The phrase 'the chariots of thy glory,' means splendid or magnificent chariots; and refers doubtless to the fact that in Jerusalem he had affected great pride and display, and had, like many weak minds, sought distinction by the splendour of his equipage. The idea here is, that the 'chariot of his glory,' *i.e.*, the vehicle in which he would ride, would be in a distant land, not meaning that *in* that land he would ride in chariots as magnificent as those which he had in Jerusalem, but that he would be conveyed there, and probably be borne in an ignominious manner, instead of the splendid mode in which he was carried in Jerusalem. The Jews say that when he left Jerusalem to deliver it into the hands of the enemy, they asked him where his army was; and when he said that they had turned back, they said,

'thou hast mocked us;' and that thereupon they bored his heels, and tied him to the tails of horses, and that thus he died.

19. *And from thy state*. From thy office; thy place of trust and responsibility. ¶ *Shall he pull thee down*. That is, *God* shall do it. The prophet here uses the third person instead of the first. Such a change of person is very common in the writings of the prophets (see Stuart's *Heb. Gram.* § 563–565, sixth Ed.)

20. *My servant Eliakim*. A man who will be faithful to me; who will be trustworthy, and to whom the interests of the city may be safely confided; a man who will not seek to betray it into the hands of the enemy. Of Eliakim we know nothing more than what is stated here, and in ch. xxxvi. From that account it appears that he was prefect of the palace; that he was employed in a negotiation with the leader of the army of the Assyrians; and that he was in all things faithful to the trust reposed in him. ¶ *The son of Hilkiah*. Kimchi supposes that this was the same as Azariah the son of Hilkiah, who might have had two names, and who was a ruler over the house of God in the time of Hezekiah (1 Chron. vi. 13).

21. *And I will clothe him with thy robe*. He shall succeed thee in the office, and wear the garments which are appropriate to it. ¶ *And strengthen him with thy girdle*. That is, he shall wear the same girdle that thou didst (see Note on ch. iii. 24). In that girdle was usually the purse, and to it was attached the sword. Often, among the Orientals, the girdle was adorned with gold and precious stones, and was regarded as the principal embellishment of the dress. ¶ *And he shall be a father*, &c. A counsellor; a guide; one who can be trusted in time of danger and difficulty. We use the word

22 And the key of the house of David will I lay upon his shoulder : so [a] he shall open, [b] and none shall shut ; and he shall shut, and none shall open.

23 And I will fasten him *as* a nail [c] in a sure place ; and he shall be for a glorious throne to his father's house.

[a] ch.9.6.   [b] Job 12.14; Rev.3.7   [c] Ezra 9.8.

father in the same sense, when we speak of the 'father of his country.'

22. *And the key.* A key is that by which a house is locked or opened. To possess that is, therefore, to have free access to it, or control over it. Thus we give possession of a house by giving the *key* into the hands of a purchaser, implying that it is his ; that he has free access to it ; that he can close it when he pleases, and that no other one, without his permission, has the right of access to it. ¶ *Of the house of David.* Of the house which David built for his royal residence ; that is, of the palace. This house was on Mount Zion ; and to have the key of that house was to have the chief authority at court, or to be prime minister (see Note on ver. 15). To be put in possession of that key, therefore, was the mark of office, or was a sign that he was intrusted with the chief authority in the government. ¶ *Will I lay upon his shoulder* (see ch. ix. 6). This seems to have been designed as an emblem of office. But in what way it was done is unknown. Lowth supposes that the key was of considerable magnitude, and was made crooked, and that thus it would lie readily on the shoulder. He has observed also, that this was a well-known badge or emblem of office. Thus the priestess of Ceres is described as having a key on the shoulder (Callim. *Ceres*, ver. 45); and thus in Æschyl. *Supp.* 299, a female high in office is described as having a key. But it is not known in what way the key was borne. It may have been borne on the shoulder, being so made as to be easily carried there ; or it may have been attached to the shoulder by a belt or strap, as a sword is ; or it may have been a mere emblem or figure inwrought into the robe, and worn as a sign of office ; or the figure of a key may have been worn on the shoulder as an epaulet is now, as a sign of office and authority. If the locks were made of wood, as

we have reason to suppose, then the key was probably large, and would answer well for a sign of office. 'How much was I delighted when I first saw the people, especially the Moors, going along the streets with each his key on his shoulder. The handle is generally made of brass (though sometimes of silver), and is often nicely worked in a device of filigrane. The way it is carried is to have the corner of a kerchief tied to the ring ; the key is then placed on the shoulder, and the kerchief hangs down in front. At other times they have a bunch of large keys, and then they have half on one side of the shoulder, and half on the other. For a man thus to march along with a large key on his shoulder, shows at once that he is a person of consequence. " Raman is in great favour with the Modeliar, for he now carries the key." " Whose key have you got on your shoulder ?" " I shall carry my key on my own shoulder." '—(Roberts.) ¶ *So he shall open,* &c. This phrase means, that he should have the highest authority in the government, and is a promise of unlimited power. Our Saviour has made use of the same expression to denote the unlimited power conferred on his apostles in his church (Matt. xvi. 19); and has applied it also to himself in Rev. iii. 7.

23. *And I will fasten him* as *a nail in a sure place.* The word 'nail' here (יָתֵד) means properly a peg, pin, or spike ; and is applied often to the pins or large spikes which were used to drive into the ground to fasten the cords of tents. It is also applied to the nails or spikes which are driven into walls, and on which are suspended the garments or the utensils of a family. In ancient times, every house was furnished with a large number of these pegs, or nails. They were not *driven* into the walls after the house was made, but they were *worked in* while the walls were going up. The houses were usually made of stone ; and strong iron hooks,

24 And they shall hang upon him all the glory of his father's house, the offspring and the issue, all ves-

sels of small quantity, from the vessels of cups, even to all the vessels [1] of flagons.

1 or, *instruments of viols.*

or spikes, were worked into the mortar while soft, and they answered the double purpose of nails to hang things on, and of cramp-irons, as they were so bent as to hold the walls together. These spikes are described by Sir John Chardin (Harmer's *Observations*, vol. i. p. 191) as 'large nails with square heads like dice, well made, the ends being so bent as to make them cramp-irons. They commonly,' says he, ' place them at the windows and doors, in order to hang upon them, when they like, veils and curtains.' It was also the custom to suspend in houses, and especially temples, suits of armour, shields, helmets, swords, &c., that had been taken in war as spoils of victory, or which had been used by illustrious ancestors, and these spikes were used for that purpose also. The word is here applied to a leader, or officer ; and it means that he would be fixed and permanent in his plans and office ; and that as a pin in the wall sustained the ornaments of the house *safely*, so all the glory of the house of David, all that was dear and valuable to the nation, might be reposed on him (ver. 24). ¶ *And he shall be for a glorious throne to his father's house.* A glorious seat ; that is, all his family and kindred would be sustained, and honoured by him ; or their honour and reputation might rest securely on him, and his deeds would diffuse a lustre and a glory over them all. Every virtuous, patriotic, benevolent, and pious son diffuses a lustre on all his kindred ; and this is one of the incitements to virtuous and elevated deeds which God has presented in the government of the world.

24. *And they shall hang upon him.* This figure is a continuation of that commenced in the previous verse ; and is derived from the custom of *hanging* clothes or ornaments on the spikes that were fixed in the walls ; and, perhaps, more particularly from the custom of suspending shields, swords, suits of armour, &c., taken in battle, around the walls of a temple. A great portion of the wealth of the ancients consisted

in gold and silver vessels, and in changes of raiment. These would be hung around a house in no inconsiderable degree for ostentation and parade. ' Solomon's drinking vessels were of gold ; and all the vessels of the forest of Lebanon were of pure gold ; none were of silver ' (1 Kings x. 21). ' The vessels in the house of the forest of Lebanon were two hundred targets and three hundred shields of beaten gold ' (1 Kings x. 16, 17). That these were hung on spikes or pins around the house is apparent from Cant. iv. 4 : ' Thy neck is like the tower of David, builded for an armoury, whereon there hang a thousand bucklers, all shields of mighty men.' Eliakim is considered as a principal support like this, whereon would be suspended all the glory of his father's family, and all the honour of his house ; that is, he would be the principal support of the whole civil and ecclesiastical polity. ¶ *The offspring and the issue.* All that proceeded from the family ; all that were connected with it. Kimchi and Aben Ezra render it, ' Sons and daughters.' The LXX. ' From the least to the greatest.' The Chaldee, ' Sons and grandsons, youth and children.' The idea is, that all the prosperity, near and remote, would depend on him ; and that his character would sustain and give dignity to them all. The word which is rendered ' issue ' (הַצֶּפִעוֹת), according to Vitringa and Rosenmüller, denotes those that were of humble condition ; and the passage means that honour would be conferred even on these by the virtues of Eliakim. ¶ *From the vessels of cups.* Literally, goblets, or bowls (אֲגָנוֹת). The idea probably is, simply that of vessels of *small capacity*, whatever was the material of which they were composed ; and hence the reference here is to those of the family of Eliakim who were of humble rank, or who were poor. ¶ *To all the vessels of flagons.* Marg. ' Instruments of viols.' Heb. נְבָלִים. This word is often applied to instruments of music, the *nebel*,

25 In that day, saith the LORD of hosts, shall the nail that is fastened in the sure place be removed, and be cut down, and fall ; and the burden that *was* upon it shall be cut off : for the LORD hath spoken *it.*

CHAPTER XXIII.

ANALYSIS.

THIS prophecy respects Tyre, and extends only to the end of this chapter. It is made up of a succession of *apostrophes* directed either to Tyre itself, or to the nations with which it was accustomed to trade. The first part of the prophecy (1-13) is occupied with the account of the *judicial sentence* which God had passed upon Tyre. This is not done in a direct and formal manner, but by addresses to the various people with whom the Tyrians had commercial intercourse, and who would be particularly affected by its destruction. Thus (1) the prophet calls on the ships of Tarshish to 'howl' because their advantageous commerce with Tyre must cease. This intelligence respecting the calamities that had come upon Tyre, he says would be brought to them 'from the land of Chittim' (1), that is, from the islands and coasts of the Mediterra-

nean. In ver. 2, the calamity is described as coming directly on the island on which Tyre was built. In the subsequent verses, the prophet describes the sources of the wealth of Tyre (3), and declares that her great luxury and splendour would be destroyed (5-12). In ver. 13, the prophet says that this would be done by the 'Chaldeans;' and this verse serves to fix the time of the fulfilment to the siege of Tyre by Nebuchadnezzar. In this all commentators probably (except Grotius, who supposes that it refers to Alexander the Great) are agreed. Indeed, it seems to be past all doubt, that the events here referred to pertain to the siege of Tyre by Nebuchadnezzar. In the remainder of the prophecy (ver. 14 to the end of the chapter), the prophet declares the *time* during which this calamity would continue. He declares that it would be only for seventy years (14), and that after that, Tyre would be restored to her former splendour, magnificence, and successful commerce (16, 17); and that then her wealth would be consecrated to the service of Jehovah (18).

The *design* of the prophecy is, therefore, to foretell the calamities that would come upon a rich, proud, and luxurious city; and thus to show that God was Governor and Ruler over the nations of the earth. Tyre became distinguished for pride, luxury, and consequent

---

viol (see it described in Notes on ch. v. 12 ; xiv. 11) ; but it properly denotes a bottle made of skin for holding wine, and which, being made of the whole skin of a goat or sheep, indicated the vessels of large dimensions. Here it refers to the members of the family of Eliakim who were more wealthy and influential than those denoted by the small vessels. The glory of the whole family would depend on him. His virtues, wisdom, integrity, and valour in defending and saving the Hebrew commonwealth, would diffuse honour over the whole family connection, and render the name illustrious.

25. *In that day shall the nail.* Not Eliakim, but Shebna. Eliakim was to be fastened, *i.e.*, confirmed in office. But Shebna was to be removed. ¶ *That is fastened in the sure place.* Or, that was once fastened, or was supposed to be fastened—a phrase appropriate to an office which the incumbent supposed to be firm or secure. It here refers to Shebna. He was regarded as having a permanent hold on the office, and was making provisions for ending his days in it. ¶ *Be removed.* To a distant

land (ver. 17, 18), or simply taken down. ¶ *And be cut down, and fall.* As a spike, pin, or peg would be taken away from the wall of a house. ¶ *And the burden that* was *upon it.* All that it sustained—as the spikes in the wall of a house sustained the cups of gold, the raiment, or the armour that belonged to the family. Here it means, all that was dependent on Shebna—the honour of his family, his emoluments, his hope of future fame, or of an honoured burial. All these would fail, as a matter of course, when he was removed from his office. This is one instance of the usual mode of the Divine administration. The errors of a man intrusted with office entail poverty, disgrace, and misery on all who are connected with him. Not only is his own name disgraced, but his sin *diffuses itself*, as it were, on all connected with him. It involves them in want, and shame, and tears ; and the design is to deter those in office from sin, by the fact that their crimes and errors *will* thus involve the innocent in calamity, and shed disgrace and woe on those whom they love.

dissipation; and the destruction that was to come upon it was to be a demonstration that wicked nations and cities would incur the displeasure of God, and would be destroyed.

Tyre, the subject of the prophecies, particularly of Isaiah and Ezekiel, who both predicted its overthrow (Isa. xxiii.; Ezek. xxvi.–xxix.), was a celebrated city of Phenicia, and is usually mentioned in connection with Sidon (Matt. xi. 21, 22; xv. 21; Mark iii. 8; vii. 24, 31; Luke x. 13, 14). It was on the coast of the Mediterranean, about lat. 33° 20′ N., and was about twenty miles south of Sidon. It was one of the cities allotted to the tribe of Asher (Josh. xix. 29), but it is probable that the ancient inhabitants were never driven out by the Israelites. It seems to have been occupied by the Canaanites, and is always mentioned as inhabited by a distinct people from the Jews (2 Sam. xxiv. 7; 1 Kings vii. 13, 14; ix. 12; Ezra iii. 7; Neh. xiii. 16; Ps. lxxxiii. 7; lxxxvii. 4). It was probably built by a colony from Sidon, since Isaiah (xxiii. 12) calls it the 'daughter of Zidon,' and it is said (ver. 2) to have been replenished by Sidon. That Sidon was the most ancient city there can be no doubt. *Sidon* was the eldest son of Canaan (Gen. x. 15), and the city of Sidon is mentioned by the patriarch Jacob (Gen. xlix. 13), and in the time of Joshua it is called 'Great Sidon' (Josh. xi. 8). Strabo affirms that *after Sidon*, Tyre was the most celebrated city of the Phenicians. Justin (xviii. 1, 5), expressly declares that the Sidonians, being besieged by the king of Ascalon, went in ships and built Tyre. But though Tyre was the 'daughter' of Sidon, yet it soon rivalled it in importance, and in commercial enterprise.

Among the ancient writers, Tyre is mentioned as Palæo-Tyrus (Παλαί τυρος), or ancient Tyre, and as Insular Tyre. The former was built on the *coast*, and was doubtless built first, though there is evidence that the latter was early used as a place for anchorage, or a harbour. In Old Tyre, or Tyre on the coast, undoubtedly also the most magnificent edifices would be built, and the principal business would there be at first transacted. Probably Insular Tyre was built either because it furnished a better harbour, or because, being inaccessible to an invading army, it was more secure. Insular Tyre, as the name imports, was built on an island, or a *rock*, about three quarters of a mile from the coast, or from Old Tyre. Probably the passage from one to the other was formerly by a ferry, or in boats only, until Alexander the Great, in his siege of the city, built a mole from the ruins of the old city to the new. This mole, or embankment, was not less than 200 feet in breadth, and con-

stituted a permanent connection between Tyre and the mainland. Insular Tyre was remarkably safe from the danger of invasion. It commanded the sea, and of course had nothing to dread from that quarter; and the only mode in which it could become accessible to Alexander, was to build this gigantic causeway from the mainland.

Tyre was distinguished for its enterprise, its commercial importance, its luxury, and its magnificence. Few, perhaps none, of the cities of antiquity, were more favourably situated for commerce. It was the natural seaport of Palestine and Syria, and it was favourably situated for commerce with all the cities and states bordering on the Mediterranean, and, indeed, with all the known world. The luxuries of the East passed through Tyre (see Ezek. xxvii., where there is an extended description of the various nations that trafficked with and enriched it), and the productions of distant climes from the West were introduced to the East through this seaport. It rose, therefore, to great opulence, and to consequent luxury and sin.

It was also a place of great strength. Old Tyre was defended by a wall, which was regarded as impregnable, and which is said to have resisted the attacks of Nebuchadnezzar for thirteen years. New, or Insular Tyre, was inaccessible, until Alexander constructed the immense mole by which he connected it with the mainland, and as they had the command of the sea, the city was regarded unapproachable. Alexander could not have taken it had he not possessed resources, and patience, and power, which perhaps no other ancient conqueror possessed; and had he not engaged in an enterprise which perhaps all others would have regarded as impracticable and hopeless. Josephus, indeed, states, that Shalmaneser, king of Assyria, made war against the Tyrians, with a fleet of sixty ships, manned by 800 rowers. The Tyrians had but twelve ships, yet they obtained the victory, and dispersed the Assyrian fleet, taking 500 prisoners. Shalmaneser then besieged the city for five years, but was unable to take it. This was in the time of Hezekiah, A.M. 3287, or about 717 B.C.

Nebuchadnezzar took the city after a siege of thirteen years, during the time of the Jewish captivity, about 573 years before Christ. This was in accordance with the prophecy in this chapter (see Note, ver. 13), and according to the predictions also of Ezekiel. The desolation was entire. The city was destroyed, and the inhabitants driven into foreign lands (see Notes, ver. 7, 12). The city lay desolate for seventy years (see Note on ver. 15, 17), and Old Tyre was in ruins in the time of the invasion of Alexander the Great. A new city had risen, however, on the island, called New Tyre, and this city was taken by Alexander, after a siege of eight months. Near the shore the water is said to have been shallow, but near the new city it was three fathoms, or nineteen feet in depth. The city of Tyre was taken by Alexander 332 B.C., and 241 years after its destruction by Nebuchadnezzar, and consequently about 170 years after it had been rebuilt. It was not, however, entirely destroyed by Alexander, and became an object of contention to his successors. It was successively invested by Antigonas and Ptolemy, and fell into the hands of the latter. In the apostolic age it seems to have regained somewhat of its ancient splendour. There were some Christians here (Acts xxi. 3, 4). At present it belongs to Syria. It was often an object of contention during the crusades, and was distinguished as the first archbishopric under the patriarchate of Jerusalem. It gradually sunk into decay, lost its importance, and became a place of utter ruin. Volney noticed there, in 1784, the choir of the ancient church, the remains of the walls of the city which can still be traced, and some columns of red granite, a species unknown in Syria. In the time when it was visited by Volney and Maundrell, it was a miserable village, where the inhabitants subsisted chiefly by fishing. Its exports consist only of a few sacks of corn and cotton; and the only merchant of which it could boast in the time when Volney was there, was a solitary Greek, who could hardly gain a livelihood. At present, Tyre, or, as it is called, *Sur*, is nothing more than a mar-

ket town, a small seaport, hardly deserving the name of a city. Its chief export is the tobacco raised on the neighbouring hills; with some cotton, and also charcoal and wood from the more distant mountains. The houses are for the most part mere hovels, very few being more than one story high, with flat roofs. The streets are narrow lanes, crooked, and filthy. Yet the many scattered palm trees throw over the place an oriental charm; and the numerous Pride of India trees interspersed among the houses and gardens, with their beautiful foliage, give it a pleasing aspect. It has a population of less than three thousand souls. In 1837, an earthquake was felt here to a very considerable extent. A large part of the eastern wall was thrown down, and the southern wall was greatly shattered, and several houses were destroyed (see Robinson's *Bib. Researches*, vol. iii. p. 400; Robinson's Calmet; *Edin. Ency.*; Newton, *On the Prophecies*, vol. xi.; Keith, *On the Prophecies*; and the *Travels* of Volney and Maundrell. On the ancient commercial importance of Tyre, also, and its present situation, and the *cause* of its decline, the reader may consult an article in the *Am. Bib. Rep.* for October 1840).

THE burden of Tyre. *a* Howl, ye ships of Tarshish; for it is laid waste so that there is no house, no entering in : from the land of Chittim *b* it is revealed to them.

a Jer.25.22;47.4; Eze.26.28; Amos 9.10; Zec.9.2-4.
b ver.12; Jer.2.10.

CHAPTER XXIII.

1. *The burden of Tyre* (see Note on ch. xiii. 1). ¶ *Howl.* This is a highly poetic description of the destruction that was coming on Tyre. The ships of Tarshish traded there ; and the prophet now addresses the ships, and calls upon them to lament because the commerce by which they had been enriched was to be destroyed, and they were to be thrown out of employ. ¶ *Ye ships of Tarshish* (see Note on ch. ii. 16). The 'Tarshish' here referred to, was doubtless a city or country in Spain (Ταρτησσὸς, *Tartessus*), and was the most celebrated emporium to which the Phenicians traded. It is mentioned by Diod. Sic., v. 35-38; Strabo, iii. 148; Pliny, *Nat. Hist.* iii. 3. According to Jer. x. 9, it exported silver; according to Ezek. xxvii. 12, 25, it exported silver, iron,

tin, and lead, to the Tyrian market. In this chapter (ver. 1, 6, 10), it is represented as an important Phenician or Tyrian colony. All the circumstances agree with the supposition that *Tartessus* in Spain is the place *here* referred to. The name 'Tartessus' (Ταρτησσὸς) is derived from the Hebrew תַּרְשִׁישׁ by a change simply in the pronunciation (see Bochart, *Geo. Sacra*, iii. 7, and J. D. Michaelis, *Spicileg. Geo. Heb.* i. 82–103). ¶ *For it is laid waste.* Tyre is laid waste; that is, in vision it was made to pass before the mind of the prophet *as* laid waste, or as it *would* be (see Notes on ch. i. 1). ¶ *So that there is no house.* It would be completely destroyed. This was the case with old Tyre after the conquest by Nebuchadnezzar, and it remained so. See the analysis of the chapter. ¶ *No entering in.* No harbour; no port; where the ships could remain, and with which they could continue to trade. Tyre was once better situated for commerce, and had greater natural advantages, than any port in the Mediterranean. Those advantages have, however, to a great extent passed away, and natural causes combine to confirm the truth of the Divine predictions that it should cease to be a place of commerce. The merchandise of India, which was once conveyed overland through Babylon and Palmyra, and which found its natural outlet at Tyre, is now carried around the Cape of Good Hope, and will never again be restored to its old channel. Besides, Tyre itself, which once had so fine a harbour, has ceased to be a safe haven for large vessels. Robinson (George) says of its harbour, in 1830, ' It is a small circular basin, now quite filled up with sand and broken columns, leaving scarcely space enough for small boats to enter. The few fishing boats that belong to the place are sheltered by some rocks to the westward of the island '—(*Travels in Syria and Palestine*, vol. i. p. 269). Shaw, who visited Tyre in 1738, says of the harbour, ' I visited several creeks and inlets, in order to discover what provision there might have been formerly made for the security of their vessels. Yet, notwithstanding that Tyre was the chief maritime power of this country, I could not discover the least token of either *cothon* or harbour that could have been of extraordinary capacity. The coasting ships, indeed, still find a tolerably good shelter from the northern winds, under the southern shore, but are obliged immediately to return when the winds change to the west or south ; so that there must have been some better station than this for their security and reception. In the N.N.E. part, likewise, of the city, we see the traces of a safe and commodious basin, lying within the walls ; but which, at the same time, is very small, scarce forty yards in diameter. Yet even this port, small as it is at present, is, notwithstanding, so choked up with sand and rubbish, that the boats of those poor fishermen who now and then visit this renowned

emporium, can, with great difficulty, only be admitted ' (*Travels*, pp. 330, 331. Ed. fol. Oxon. 1738). Dr. Robinson says of the port of Tyre, ' The inner port or basin on the north was formerly enclosed by a wall, running from the north end of the island in a curve towards the main land. Various pieces and fragments of this wall yet remain, sufficient to mark its course ; but the port itself is continually filling up more and more with sand, and now-a-days boats only can enter it. Indeed, our host informed us, that even within his own recollection, the water covered the open place before his own house, which at present is ten or twelve rods from the sea, and is surrounded with buildings ; while older men remember, that vessels formerly anchored where the shore now is ' (*Bib. Researches*, vol. iii. p. 397). ¶ *From the land of Chittim.* This means, probably, from the islands and coasts of the Mediterranean. In regard to the meaning of the word *Chittim*, the following is the note of Gesenius on this verse : ' Among the three different opinions of ancient and modern interpreters, according to which they sought for the land of Chittim in Italy, Macedonia, and Cyprus, I decidely prefer the latter, which is also the opinion of Josephus (*Ant.* i. 6. 1). According to this, Chittim is the island Cyprus, so called from the Phenician colony Κίτιον (Citium), in the southern part of the island, but still in such a sense, that this name Chittim was, at a later period, employed also in a wider sense, to designate other islands and countries adjacent to the coasts of the Mediterranean, as, *e.g.*, Macedonia (Dan. xi. 30 ; 1 Mac. i. 1 ; viii. 5). This is also mentioned by Josephus. That Κίτιον (Citium) was sometimes used for the whole island of Cyprus, and also in a wider sense for other islands, is expressly asserted by Epiphanius, who himself lived in Cyprus, as a well-known fact (*Adv. Hæres.* xxx. 25) ; where he says, " it is manifest to all that the island of Cyprus is called Κίτιον (Citium), for the Cyprians and *Rhodians* ('Ρόδιοι) are called *Kitians* (Κίτιοι)." It could also be used of the Macedonians, because they were descended from the Cyprians and Rho-

2 Be ¹ still, ye inhabitants of the isle ; thou whom the merchants of

¹ *silent.*

Zidon, that pass over the sea, have replenished.

3 And by great waters the seed

---

dians. That most of the cities of Cyprus were Phenician colonies, is expressly affirmed by Diodorus (ii. 114; comp. Herod. vii. 90), and the proximity of the island to Phenicia, together with its abundant supply of productions, especially such as were essential in shipbuilding, would lead us to expect nothing else. One of the few passages of the Bible which give a more definite hint in regard to Chittim is Ezek. xxvii. 6, which agrees very well with Cyprus : " Of the oaks of Bashan do they make them oars ; thy ships' benches do they make of ivory, encased with cedar from the isles of Chittim." The sense of this passage is, that the fleets coming from Tarshish (Tartessus) to Tyre, would, on their way, learn from the inhabitants of Cyprus the news of the downfall of Tyre.' ¶ *It is revealed to them.* If we understand *Chittim* to denote the islands and coasts of the Mediterranean, it means that the navigators in the ships of Tarshish would learn the intelligence of the destruction of Tyre from those coasts or islands where they might stop on their way. Tyre was of so much commercial importance that the news of its fall would spread into all the islands of the Mediterranean.

2. *Be still.* This is the description of a city which is destroyed, where the din of commerce, and the sound of revelry is no longer heard. It is an address of the prophet to Tyre, indicating that it would be soon still, and destroyed. ¶ *Ye inhabitants of the isle* (of Tyre). The word ' isle ' (אִי) is sometimes used to denote a *coast* or *maritime region* (see Note on ch. xx. 6), but there seems no reason to doubt that here it means the island on which New Tyre was erected. This may have been occupied even before Old Tyre was destroyed by Nebuchadnezzar, though the main city was on the coast. ¶ *Thou whom the merchants of Zidon.* Tyre was a colony from Sidon ; and the merchants of Sidon would trade to Tyre as well as to Sidon. ¶ *Have replen-*

ished. Heb. ' Have filled,' *i.e.,* with merchandise, and with wealth. Thus, in Ezek. xxvii. 8, Tyre is represented as having derived its seamen from Sidon : ' The inhabitants of Sidon and of Arvad were thy mariners.' And in Ezek. xxvii. 9–23, Tyre is represented as having been filled with shipbuilders, merchants, mariners, soldiers, &c., from Gebal, Persia, Lud, Phut, Tarshish, Javan, Tubal, Mesheck, Dedan, Syria, Damascus, Arabia, &c.

3. *And by great waters.* That is, by the abundant waters, or the overflowing of the Nile. Tyre was the mart to which the superabundant productions of Egypt were borne (see Ezek. xxvii.) ¶ *The seed of Sihor.* There can be no doubt that by 'Sihor' here is meant the river Nile in Egypt (see Josh. xiii. 3 ; 1 Chron. xiii. 5 ; Jer. ii. 18). The word שִׁיחֹר (*Shihhōr*) is derived from שָׁחַר (*Shâhhăr*), *to be black* (Job xxx. 30), and is given to the Nile from its colour when it brings down the slime or mud by which Egypt is rendered so fertile. The Greeks gave to the river the name Μέλας (*black*), and the Latins call it *Melo*—(Serv. ad Virg. *Geor.* iv. 291). It was called *Siris* by the Ethiopians ; perhaps the same as Sihor. The upper branches of the Nile in Abyssinia all receive their names from the *colour* of the water, and are called the White River, the Blue River, &c. ¶ *The harvest of the river.* The productions caused by the overflowing of the river. Egypt was celebrated for producing grain, and Rome and Greece derived no small part of their supplies from that fertile country. It is also evident that the inhabitants of Palestine were early accustomed to go to Egypt in time of scarcity for supplies of grain (see Gen. xxxvii. 25, 28, and the history of Joseph, Gen. xli.–xliii.) That the *Tyrians* traded with Egypt is also well known. Herodotus (ii. 112) mentions one entire quarter of the city of Memphis that was inhabited by the Tyrians. ¶ Is *her revenue.* Her re-

of Sihor, the harvest of the river, *is* her revenue ; and she is a mart of nations.

4 Be thou ashamed, O Zidon ; for the sea hath spoken, *even* the strength of the sea, saying, I travail not, nor bring forth chil-

dren, neither do I nourish up young men, *nor* bring up virgins.

5 As at the report *a* concerning Egypt, *so* shall they be sorely pained at the report of Tyre.

6 Pass ye over to Tarshish ; howl, ye inhabitants of the isle.

---

sources are brought from thence. ¶ *She is a mart of nations.* How true this was, see Ezek. xxvii. No place was more favourably situated for commerce ; and she had engrossed the trade nearly of all the world.

4. *Be thou ashamed, O Zidon.* Tyre was a colony of Sidon. Sidon is here addressed as the *mother* of Tyre, and is called on to lament over her daughter that was destroyed. In ver. 12, Tyre is called the ' daughter of Sidon ;' and such appellations were commonly given to cities (see Note on ch. i. 8). Sidon is here represented as *ashamed*, or grieved—as a mother is who is bereft of all her children. ¶ *The sea hath spoken.* New Tyre was on a rock at some distance from the land, and seemed to *rise out* of the sea, somewhat as Venice does. It is described here as a production of the sea, and the sea is represented as speaking by her. ¶ Even *the strength of the sea.* The fortress, or strong place (מָעוֹז) of the sea. Tyre, on a rock, might be regarded as the strong place, or the defence of the Mediterranean. Thus Zechariah (ix. 3) says of it, ' And Tyrus did build herself a stronghold ' (מָצוֹר). ¶ *Saying, I travail not.* The expressions which follow are to be regarded as the language of Tyre—the founder of colonies and cities. The sense is, ' My wealth and resources are gone. My commerce is annihilated. I cease to plant cities and colonies, and to nourish and foster them, as I once did, by my trade.' The idea of the whole verse is, that the city which had been the mistress of the commercial world, and distinguished for founding other cities and colonies, was about to lose her importance, and to cease to extend her colonies and her influence over other countries. Over this fact, Sidon, the mother and founder of Tyre herself,

would be humbled and grieved that her daughter, so proud, so rich, and so magnificent, was brought so low.

5. *As at the report concerning Egypt.* According to our translation, this verse would seem to mean that the Sidonians and other nations had been pained or grieved at the report of the calamities that had come upon Egypt, and that they would be similarly affected at the report concerning Tyre. In accordance with this, some (as Jarchi) have understood it of the plagues of Egypt, and suppose that the prophet means to say, that as the nations were astonished at that, *so* they would be at the report of the calamities that would come upon Tyre. Others refer it to the calamities that would come upon Egypt referred to in ch. xix., and suppose that the prophet means to say, that as the nations would be amazed at the report of these calamities, so they would be at the report of the overthrow of Tyre. So Vitringa. But the sense of the Hebrew may be expressed thus : ' As the report, or tidings of the destruction of Tyre shall reach Egypt, they shall be pained at the tidings respecting Tyre.' So Lowth, Noyes, Rosenmüller, Grotius, Calvin. They would be grieved, either (1) because the destruction of Tyre would injure the commerce of Egypt ; or (2) because the Egyptians might fear that the army of Nebuchadnezzar would come upon them, and that they would share the fate of Tyre. ¶ *Sorely pained.* The word here used (יָחִילוּ) is commonly applied to the severe pain of parturition.

6. *Pass ye over.* That is, ye inhabitants of Tyre. This is an address to Tyre, in view of her approaching destruction ; and is designed to signify that when the city was destroyed, its inhabitants *would* flee to its colonies, and seek refuge and safety there. As

7 *Is* this your joyous *city*, whose antiquity *is* of ancient days? her own feet shall carry her ¹ afar off to sojourn.

1 *from afar off.*

8 Who hath taken this counsel against Tyre, the crowning *city*, whose merchants *are* princes, whose traffickers *are* the honourable of the earth?

Tarshish was one of its principal colonies, and as the ships employed by Tyre would naturally sail to Tarshish, the inhabitants are represented as fleeing there on the attack of Nebuchadnezzar. That the inhabitants of Tyre did flee in this manner, is expressly asserted by Jerome upon the authority of Assyrian histories which are now lost. 'We have read,' says he, 'in the histories of the Assyrians, that when the Tyrians were besieged, after they saw no hope of escaping, they went on board their ships, and fled to Carthage, or to some islands of the Ionian and Ægean Sea' (Jerome *in loco*.) And again (on Ezek. xxix.) he says, 'When the Tyrians saw that the works for carrying on the siege were perfected, and the foundations of the walls were shaken by the battering rams, whatever precious things in gold, silver, clothes, and various kinds of furniture the nobility had, they put them on board their ships, and carried to the islands. So that the city being taken, Nebuchadnezzar found nothing worthy of his labour.' Diodorus (xvii. 41) relates the same thing of the Tyrians during the siege of Alexander the Great, where he says that they took their wives and children to Carthage. ¶ *Howl.* Deep grief among the Orientals was usually expressed by a loud, long, and most dismal howl or shriek (see Note on ch. xv. 2). ¶ *Ye inhabitants of the isle.* Of Tyre. The word 'isle,' however, *may* be taken as in ch. xx. 6 (see Note on that place), in the sense of *coast*, or *maritime country* in general, and possibly may be intended to denote Old Tyre, or the coast of Phenicia in general, though most naturally it applies to the city built on the island.

7. Is *this your joyous* city. Is this the city that was just now so full of happiness, of revelry, of business, of gaiety, of rejoicing? (see Note on ch. xxii. 2.) ¶ *Whose antiquity* is *of ancient days.* Strabo (xvi. 756) says, 'After Sidon, Tyre, a splendid and

most ancient city, is to be compared in greatness, beauty, and antiquity, with Sidon.' Curtius (*Hist. Alex.* iv. 4) says, 'The city was taken, distinguished both by its antiquity, and its great variety of fortune.' Arrian (ii. 16) says, that 'the Temple of Hercules at Tyre was the most ancient of those which the memory of men have preserved.' And Herodotus (ii. 44) says, that in a conversation which he had with the priest of that Temple, he informed him that it had then existed for 2300 years. Josephus, indeed, says (*Ant*. viii. 3. 1) that Tyre was built but 240 years before the temple was built by Solomon—but this was probably a mistake. Justin (xviii. 3) says that Tyre was founded in the year of the destruction of Troy. Its very high antiquity cannot be doubted. ¶ *Her own feet shall carry her afar off.* Grotius supposes that by *feet* here, the 'feet of ships' are intended, that is, their sails and oars. But the expression is designed evidently to stand in contrast with ver. 6, and to denote that a part of the inhabitants would go by land into captivity. Probably many of them were taken prisoners by Nebuchadnezzar; and perhaps many of them, when the city was besieged, found opportunity to escape and flee by land to a distant place of safety.

8. *Who hath taken this counsel?* To whom is this to be traced? Is this the work of man, or is it the plan of God?—questions which would naturally arise at the contemplation of the ruin of a city so ancient and so magnificent. The object of this question is to trace it all to God; and this perhaps indicates the scope of the prophecy—to show that God reigns, and does all his pleasure over cities and kingdoms. ¶ *The crowning* city. The distributer of crowns; or the city from which dependent towns, provinces, and kingdoms had arisen. Many colonies and cities had been founded by Tyre. Tartessus in Spain, Citium in Cyprus,

9 The LORD of hosts hath purposed it, to [1] stain the pride of all glory, and to bring *a* into contempt all the honourable of the earth.

10 Pass through thy land as a river, O daughter of Tarshish: *there is* no more [2] strength.

1 *pollute.*   *a* 1 Cor 1.28,29.   2 *girdle.*

Carthage in Africa, and probably many other places were Phenician colonies, and derived their origin from Tyre, and were still its tributaries and dependants (comp. Ezek. xxvii. 33). ¶ *Whose merchants are princes.* Princes trade with thee ; and thus acknowledge their dependence on thee. Or, thy merchants are splendid, gorgeous, and magnificent like princes. The former, however, is probably the meaning. ¶ *Whose traffickers* (כְּנָעֶיהָ, *Canaanites*). As the ancient inhabitants of Canaan were *traffickers* or *merchants,* the word came to denote merchants in general (see Job xli. 6; Ezek. xvii. 4; Hos. xii. 7; Zeph. i. 11). So the word *Chaldean* came to mean *astrologers,* because they were celebrated for astrology.

9. *The* LORD *of hosts hath purposed it* (see Note on ch. i. 9). It is not by human counsel that it has been done. Whoever is the instrument, yet the overthrow of wicked, proud, and vicious cities and nations is to be traced to the God who rules in the empires and kingdoms of the earth (see Notes on ch. x. 5–7). ¶ *To stain the pride of all glory.* Marg. 'Pollute.' The Hebrew' word (חָלַל) means properly *to bore,* or *pierce through;* to open, make common (Lev. xix. 29); then to profane, defile, pollute, as, *e.g.,* the sanctuary (Lev. xix. 8; xxi. 9), the Sabbath (Exod. xxxi. 14), the name of God (Lev. xviii. 21; xix. 12). Here it means that the destruction of Tyre would show that God could easily level it all with the dust. The destruction of *Tyre* would show this in reference to *all* human glory, because (1) it was one of the most *ancient* cities ; (2) it was one of the most magnificent ; (3) it was one of the most strong, secure, and inaccessible ; (4) it was the one of most commercial importance, most distinguished in the view of nations ; and (5) its *example* would be the most striking and impressive. God often selects the most distinguished and important cities and men to make them examples to others, and to show

the case with which he can bring all down to the earth. ¶ *To bring into contempt,* &c. To bring their plans and purposes into contempt, and to show how unimportant and how foolish are their schemes in the sight of a holy God.

10. *Pass through thy land as a river.* This verse has been very variously understood. Vitringa supposes that it means that all that held the city together —its fortifications, walls, &c., would be laid waste, and that as a river flows on without obstruction, so the inhabitants would be scattered far and near. Everything, says he, would be levelled, and the field would not be distinguishable from the city. Grotius thus renders it : ' Pass to some one of thy colonies ; as a river flows from the fountain to the sea, so do you go to the ocean.' Lowth understands it also as relating to the time of the destruction of Tyre, and to the escape which the inhabitants would then make.

' Overflow thy land like a river,
O daughter of Tarshish ; the mound [that kept
    in thy waters] is no more.'

The LXX. render it, ' Cultivate ('Εργάζου) thy land, for the ships shall no more come from Carthage' (Καρχηδόνος). Probably the true meaning is that which refers it to the time of the siege, and to the fact that the inhabitants would seek other places when their defence was destroyed. That is, ' Pass through thy *territories,* thy dependent cities, states, colonies, and seek a refuge there ; or wander there like a flowing stream.' ¶ *As a river.* Perhaps the allusion is to the Nile, as the word יְאֹר is usually given to the Nile ; or it may be to *any* river that flows on with a mighty current when all obstructions are removed. The idea is, that as waters *flow on* when the barriers are removed, so the inhabitants of Tyre would *pour forth* from their city. The idea is not so much that of *rapidity,* as it is they should go like a stream that has no dikes, barriers, or obstacles now to confine its flowing waters. ¶ *O daughter of Tarshish.* Tyre ; so called either be-

11 He stretched out his hand over the sea ; he shook the kingdom : the LORD hath given a command-ment ¹ against ² the merchant *city*, to destroy the ³ strong holds thereof.

12 And he said, Thou shalt *ᵃ* no more rejoice, O thou oppressed virgin, daughter of Zidon ; arise, pass over to *ᵇ* Chittim ; there also shalt thou have no rest.

cause it was in some degree *sustained* and supplied by the commerce of Tar-shish ; or because its inhabitants would become the inhabitants of Tarshish, and it is so called by anticipation. The Vul-gate renders this, *Filia maris*—'Daugh-ter of the sea.' Junius supposes that the prophet addresses those who were then in the city who were natives of Tarshish, and exhorts them to flee for safety to their own city. ¶ There is *no more* strength. Marg. 'Girdle.' The word מָזִיחַ means properly a *girdle* (Job xii. 31). It is applied to that which *binds* or secures the body ; and *may* be applied here perhaps to that which *secured* or *bound* the city of Tyre ; that is, its forti-fications, its walls, its defences. They would all be levelled ; and nothing would *secure* the inhabitants, as they would flow forth as waters that are pent up do, when every barrier is removed.

11. *He stretched out his hand.* That is, JEHOVAH (see ver. 9). To stretch out the hand is indicative of punishment (see Notes on ch. v. 25, and ix. 12), and means that God has resolved to inflict exemplary punishment on Tyre and its dependent colonies. ¶ *Over the sea.* That is, over the *sea coast* of Phenicia ; or over the cities that were built on the coast. This alludes to the fact that Nebuchadnezzar would lay siege to these cities, and would ravage the maritime coast of Phenicia. It is not improbable also that, having taken Tyre, he would extend his conquests to *Citium*, on the island of Cyprus, and destroy as many of the dependent cities of Tyre as pos-sible. ¶ *The* LORD *hath given a com-mandment.* The control here asserted over Nebuchadnezzar is similar to that which he asserted over the Assyrian Sennacherib (see Note on ch. x. 5). ¶ *Against the merchant* city. Heb. 'Against Canaan' (אֶל-כְּנַעַן). The word ' *Canaan* ' *may* here be used as in ver. 8, to denote a place given to merchandise or traffic, since this was the principal

employment of the inhabitants of this region ; but it is rather to be taken in its obvious and usual sense in the Scrip-tures, as denoting the land of Canaan, and as denoting that Nebuchadnezzar would be sent against that, and espe-cially the maritime parts of it, to lay it waste. ¶ *To destroy the strongholds thereof.* That is, the strongholds of Canaan ; as Tyre, Sidon, Accho, &c. Tyre, especially, was strongly fortified, and was able long to resist the arms of the Chaldeans.

12. *And he said.* God said (ver. 9). ¶ *Thou shalt no more rejoice.* The sense is, that Tyre was soon to be de-stroyed. It does not mean that it should *never* afterwards exult or rejoice, for the prophet says (ver. 17), that *after* its destruction it would be restored, and again be filled with exultation and joy. ¶ *O thou oppressed virgin.* Lowth renders this, 'O thou deflowered virgin,' expressing the sense of the word הַמְעֻשָּׁקָה. ¶ *O daughter of Zidon* (ver. 4). ¶ *Pass over to Chittim* (see Note on ver. 1). The idea is, that under the siege the inhabitants of Tyre would seek refuge in her colonies, and the cities that were dependent on her. ¶ *There also shalt thou have no rest.* It is not improbable that Nebuchadnezzar would carry his arms to Cyprus—on which the city of Citium was—where the Tyrians would take refuge first. Megasthenes, who lived about 300 years before Christ, says of Nebuchadnezzar that he subdued a great part of Africa and Spain, and that he carried his arms so far as the Pillars of Hercules (see Newton, *On the Prophecies,* xi. 11). But whether this refers to the oppressions which Nebu-chadnezzar would bring on them or not, it is certain that the colonies that sprung from Phenicia were exposed to constant wars after this. Carthage was a colony of Tyre, and it is well known that this city was engaged in hostility with the Romans until it was utterly destroyed.

13 Behold, the land of the Chaldeans : this people was not *till* the | Assyrian founded it for them [a] that

a Ps.72.9.

Indeed all the dependent colonies of ancient Tyre became interested and involved in the agitations and commotions which were connected with the conquests of the Roman empire.

13. *Behold the land of the Chaldeans.* This is a very important verse, as it expresses the source whence these calamities were coming upon Tyre ; and as it states some historical facts of great interest respecting the rise of Babylon. In the previous verses the prophet had foretold the certain destruction of Tyre, and had said that whoever was the agent, it was to be traced to the overruling providence of God. He here states distinctly that the agent in accomplishing all this would be the Chaldeans—a statement which fixes the time to the siege of Nebuchadnezzar, and proves that it does not refer to the conquest by Alexander the Great. A part of this verse should be read as a parenthesis, and its general sense has been well expressed by Lowth, who has followed Vitringa :—

'Behold the land of the Chaldeans ;
This people was of no account ;—
(The Assyrian founded it for the inhabitants of the desert ;
They raised the watch towers, they set up the palaces thereof ;)
This people hath reduced her to a ruin.'

¶ *Behold.* Indicating that what he was about to say was something unusual, remarkable, and not to be expected in the ordinary course of events. That which was so remarkable was the fact that a people formerly so little known, would rise to such power as to be able to overturn the ancient and mighty city of Tyre. ¶ *The land of the Chaldeans.* Nebuchadnezzar was the king of Chaldea or Babylonia. The names Babylon and Chaldea are often interchanged as denoting the same kingdom and people (see ch. xlviii. 14, 20 ; Jer. l. 1 ; li. 24 ; Ezek. xii. 13). The sense is, 'Lo ! the power of Chaldea shall be employed in your overthrow.' ¶ *This people.* The people of Babylonia or Chaldea. ¶ *Was not.* Was not known ; had no government or power ; was a rude, nomadic, barbarous, feeble, and illiterate people. The same phrase occurs in Deut. xxxii.

21, where it also means a people unknown, rude, barbarous, wandering. That this was formerly the character of the Chaldeans is apparent from Job i. 17, where they are described as a nomadic race, having no established place of abode, and living by plunder. ¶ *Till the Assyrian.* Babylon was probably founded by Nimrod (see Notes on ch. xiii.), but it was long before it rose to splendour. Belus or Bel, the Assyrian, is said to have reigned at Babylon A.M. 2682, or 1322 B.C., in the time of Shamgar, judge of Israel. He was succeeded by Ninus and Semiramis, who gave the principal celebrity and splendour to the city and kingdom, and who may be said to have been its founders. They are probably referred to here. ¶ *Founded it.* Semiramis reclaimed it from the waste of waters ; built dikes to confine the Euphrates in the proper channel ; and made it the capital of the kingdom. This is the account given by Herodotus (*Hist.* i.) :—' She (Semiramis) built mounds worthy of admiration, where before the river was accustomed to spread like a sea through the whole plain.' ¶ *For them that dwell in the wilderness.* Heb. לְצִיִּים—' For the tziim.' This word (from צִי or צִיָּה, *a waste* or *desert*) denotes properly the inhabitants of the desert or waste places, and is applied to men in Ps. lxxii. 9 ; lxxiv. 14 ; and to animals in Isa. xiii. 21 (Notes) ; xxxiv. 14. Here it denotes, I suppose, those who had been formerly inhabitants of the deserts around Babylon—the wandering, rude, uncultivated, and predatory people, such as the Chaldeans were (Job i. 17) ; and means that the Assyrian who founded Babylon collected this rude and predatory people, and made use of them in building the city. The same account Arrian gives respecting Philip of Macedon, the father of Alexander the Great, who says, that 'Philip found them wandering and unsettled (πλανήτας καὶ ἀπόρευς), feeding small flocks of sheep upon the mountains, that he gave them coats of mail instead of their shepherd's dress, and led them from the mountain to the plain, and gave them cities to dwell in, and established them with good dwell in the wilderness : they set up the towers thereof ; *and* he brought it to ruin.

14 Howl, ye ships of Tarshish : for your strength is laid waste.

15 And it shall come to pass in that day that Tyre shall be for-

gotten seventy years, according to the days of one king : after the end of seventy years ¹ shall Tyre sing as an harlot.

16 Take an harp, go about the city, thou harlot that hast been

1 *it shall be unto Tyre as the song of.*

---

and wholesome laws.'—(*Hist. Alex.* vii.) ¶ *They set up the towers thereof.* That is, the towers in Babylon, not in Tyre (see Notes on ch. xiii.) Herodotus expressly says that the Assyrians built the towers and temples of Babylon (i. 84). ¶ *And he brought it to ruin.* That is, the Babylonian or Chaldean brought Tyre to ruin : to wit, Nebuchadnezzar, the king of a people formerly unknown and rude, would be employed to destroy the ancient and magnificent city of Tyre.

14. *Howl, &c.* (ver. 1). ¶ *For your strength.* That which has been your support and strength ; to wit, Tyre (comp. Ezek. xxvi. 15–18).

15. *Tyre shall be forgotten.* Shall cease to be a place of importance in commerce ; shall be unheard of in those distant places to which ships formerly sailed. ¶ *Seventy years, according to the days of one king.* ' That is, of one kingdom (see Dan. vii. 17 ; viii. 20).' —(Lowth.) The word ' king ' may denote dynasty, or kingdom. The duration of the Babylonian monarchy was properly but seventy years. Nebuchadnezzar began his conquest in the first year of his reign, and from thence to the taking of Babylon by Cyrus was seventy years. And at that time the nations that had been conquered and subdued by the Babylonians would be restored to liberty. Tyre was, indeed, taken towards the middle of that period, and its subjugation referred to here was only for the remaining part of it. ' All these nations,' says Jeremiah (xxv. 11), 'shall serve the king of Babylon seventy years.' Some of them were conquered sooner, and some later ; but the end of this period was the common time of deliverance to them all. So Lowth, Newton, Vitringa, Aben Ezra, Rosenmüller, and others, understand this. That ' the days of one king ' may denote here kingdom or dynasty, and be applied to the duration of the kingdom of Babylon, is

apparent from two considerations, viz. (1.) The word ' king ' must be so understood in several places in the Scriptures ; Dan. vii. 17 : ' These great beasts which are four, are four great *kings* which shall arise out of the earth,' that is, dynasties, or *succession* of kings (Dan. viii. 20 ; so Rev. xvii. 12). (2.) The expression is peculiarly applicable to the Babylonian monarchy, because, during the entire seventy years which that kingdom lasted, it was under the dominion of one family or dynasty. Nebuchadnezzar founded the Babylonian empire, or raised it to so great splendour, that he was regarded as its founder, and was succeeded in the kingdom by his son Evil-Merodach, and his grandson Belshazzar, in whose reign the kingdom terminated ; comp. Jer. xxvii. 7 : ' And all nations shall serve him, and his son, and his son's son.' The period of seventy years is several times mentioned, as a period during which the nations that were subject to Babylon would be oppressed, and *after* that they should be set at liberty (see Jer. xxv. 11, 12 ; xxix. 10 ; comp. Jer. xlvi. 26). ¶ *Shall Tyre sing as an harlot.* Marg. as the Hebrew, ' It shall be unto Tyre as the song of an harlot.' That is, Tyre shall be restored to its former state of prosperity and opulence ; it shall be adorned with the rich productions of other climes, and shall be gay and joyful again. There are two ideas here ; one that Tyre would be again prosperous, and the other that she would sustain substantially the same character as before. It was common to compare cities with females, whether virtuous or otherwise (see Note on ch. i. 8). The same figure which is here used occurs in Rev. xvii. 3–19 (comp. Isa. xlvii. 1 ; Nah. iii. 4 ; Rev. xviii. 3, 9).

16. *Take an harp.* This is a continuation of the figure commenced in the previous verse, a direct command to

forgotten : make sweet melody, sing many songs, that thou mayest be remembered.

17 And it shall come to pass, after the end of seventy years, that the LORD will visit Tyre, and she shall turn to her hire, and *a* shall commit fornication with all the king-

a Rev.17.2.   *b* Zec.14.20,31.   1 *old.*

doms of the world upon the face of the earth.

18 And her merchandise and her hire shall be holiness *b* to the LORD: it shall not be treasured nor laid up ; for her merchandise shall be for them that dwell before the LORD, to eat sufficiently, and for 1 durable clothing.

Tyre as an harlot, to go about the city with the usual expressions of rejoicing. Thus Donatus, in *Terent. Eunuch.*, iii. 2, 4, says :—

'Fidicinam esse meretricum est ;'

And thus Horace :—

'Nec meretrix tibicina, cujus
   Ad strepitum salias.'   1 *Epis.* xiv. 25.

¶ *Thou harlot that hast been forgotten.* For seventy years thou hast lain unknown, desolate, ruined. ¶ *Make sweet melody*, &c. Still the prophet keeps up the idea of the harlot that had been forgotten, and that would now call her lovers again to her dwelling. The sense is, that Tyre would rise to her former splendour, and that the nations would be attracted by the proofs of returning prosperity to renew their commercial intercourse with her.

17. *The* LORD *will visit Tyre.* He will restore her to her former wealth and magnificence. ¶ *And she shall turn to her hire.* The word 'hire' here denotes the wages or reward that is given to an harlot ; and the idea which was commenced in the previous verses is here continued—of Tyre as an harlot—gay, splendid, licentious, and holding intercourse with strangers and foreigners. The *gains* of that commerce with other nations are here represented as her *hire.* ¶ *And shall commit fornication*, &c. Shall again be the mart of commerce (ver. 3) ; shall have intercourse with all the nations, and derive her support, splendour, luxury, from all. The idea is, that she would be restored to her former commercial importance, and perhaps, also, the prophet intends to intimate that she would procure those gains by dishonest acts, and by fraudulent pretexts. After the destruction of Tyre by Nebuchadnezzar, it remained desolate until the close of the Babylonian monarchy. Then a new city was

built on the island, that soon rivalled the former in magnificence. That new city was besieged and taken by Alexander the Great, on his way to the conquests of the East.

18. *And her merchandise.* The prophecy here does not mean that this would take place *immediately* after her rebuilding, but that *subsequent* to the seventy years of desolation this would occur. ¶ *Shall be holiness to the* LORD. This undoubtedly means, that at some future period, after the rebuilding of Tyre, the true religion would prevail there, and her wealth would be devoted to his service. That the true religion prevailed at Tyre subsequently to its restoration and rebuilding there can be no doubt. The Christian religion was early established at Tyre. It was visited by the Saviour (Matt. xv. 21), and by Paul. Paul found several disciples of Christ there when on his way to Jerusalem (Acts xxi. 3–6). It suffered much, says Lowth, under the Diocletian persecution. Eusebius (*Hist.* x. 4.) says that 'when the church of God was founded in Tyre, and in other places, much of its wealth was consecrated to God, and was brought as an offering to the church, and was presented for the support of the ministry agreeable to the commandments of the Lord.' Jerome says, 'We have seen churches built to the Lord in Tyre ; we have beheld the wealth of all, which was not treasured up nor hid, but which was given to those who dwelt before the Lord.' It early became a Christian bishopric ; and in the fourth century of the Christian era, Jerome (*Comm.* in Ezek. xxvi. 7 ; xxvii. 2) speaks of Tyre as the most noble and beautiful city of Phenicia, and as still trading with all the world. Reland enumerates the following list of bishops as having been present from Tyre at

CHAPTER XXIV.

ANALYSIS.

THE previous chapters, from the thirteenth to the twenty-third inclusive, have been occupied mainly in describing the destruction of nations that were hostile to the Jews, or great and distressing calamities that would come upon them. The prophet had thus successively depicted the calamities that would come upon Babylon, Damascus, Moab, Nubia, Egypt, Dumah, and Tyre. In ch. xxii., he had, however, described the calamities which would come upon Judea and Jerusalem by the invasion of Sennacherib.

In this chapter, the prophet returns to the calamities which would come upon the people of God themselves. This chapter, and the three following, to the end of the twenty-seventh, seem to have been uttered about the same time, and perhaps may be regarded as constituting one vision, or prophecy. So Noyes, Lowth, and Rosenmuller, regard it. If these chapters be included in the prophecy, then it consists (1) of a description of *calamities* in ch. xxiv., (2) of a song of praise expressive of deliverance from those calamities, and of the consequent spread of the true religion, in ch. xxv.; (3) of a song of praise suitable to celebrate the triumphs of the true religion in ch. xxvi.; and (4) of the effect of this deliverance in purifying the Jews in ch. xxvii.

When the prophecy was uttered is wholly unknown. In regard to the *events* to which it relates, there has been a great diversity of opinion, and scarcely are any two interpreters agreed. Grotius regards it as relating to the carrying away of the ten tribes by Shalmaneser. Hensler supposes that it refers to the invasion of Sennacherib. Vitringa supposes that it relates to the times of the Maccabees, and to the trials and calamities which came upon the Jews under the persecutions of Antiochus Epiphanes. Noyes regards it as descriptive of the destruction of

the land by Nebuchadnezzar, and of the return of the Jews from exile. Calvin considers the account in these four chapters as a *summing up*, or *recapitulation* of what the prophet had said in the previous prophecies respecting Babylon, Moab, Egypt, &c.; and then of the prosperity, and of the spread of the true religion which would succeed these general and far-spread devastations. Subsequently to *each* of these predictions respecting calamity, the prophet had foretold prosperity and the advance of truth; and he supposes that this is a mere condensing or summing up of what he had said more at length in the preceding chapters. Lowth supposes that it may have a reference to *all* the great desolations of the country by Shalmaneser, by Nebuchadnezzar, and by the Romans, especially to that of the Romans, to which some parts of it, he says, seem to be peculiarly applicable. It is certain that the prophet employs *general* terms; and as he gives no *certain* indications of the time, or the circumstances under which it was delivered, it is exceedingly difficult to determine either. The *general* drift of the prophecy is, however, plain. It is a prediction of prosperity, and of the prevalence of true religion *after* a series of oppressive judgments should have come upon the land. It is designed, therefore, to be *consolatory* to the Jews under impending calamities, and to convey the assurance that though they would be oppressed, yet their sufferings would be succeeded by occasions of gratitude and joy. In this respect, it accords with the general strain of the prophecies of Isaiah, that the people of God would be protected; that their name and nation should not be wholly obliterated; and that the darkest seasons of trial would be succeeded by deliverance and joy.

On the whole, it seems to me, that the prophecy relates to the calamities that would come upon the nation by the invasion of Nebuchadnezzar, and the carrying away to Babylon, and the sub-

---

various councils; viz., Cassius, Paulinus, Zeno, Vitalis, Uranius, Zeno, Photius, and Eusebius (see Reland's *Palestine*, pp. 1002–1011, in Ugolin vi.) Tyre continued Christian until it was taken by the Saracens in A.D. 639; but was recovered again by Christians in 1124. In 1280, it was conquered by the Mamelukes, and was taken by the Turks in 1516. It is now under the dominion of the Sultan as a part of Syria. ¶ *It shall not be treasured,* &c. It shall be regarded as consecrated to the Lord, and freely expended in his

service. ¶ *For them that dwell before the* LORD. For the ministers of religion. The *language* is taken from the custom of the Jews, when the priests *dwelt* at Jerusalem. The meaning is, that the wealth of Tyre would be consecrated to the service and support of religion. ¶ *For durable clothing.* Wealth formerly consisted much in changes of raiment; and the idea here is, that the wealth of Tyre would be devoted to God, and that it would be furnished for the support of those who ministered at the altar.

sequent deliverance from the oppressive bondage, and the joy consequent on that. According to this interpretation, the twenty-fourth chapter is occupied mainly with the description of the *calamities* that would come upon the land by the invasion of Nebuchadnezzar; the twenty-fifth describes the *deliverance* from that oppressive bondage, and the re-establishment of the true religion on Mount Zion, with a rapid glance at the ultimate prevalence of religion under the Messiah, suggested by the deliverance from the Babylonish bondage; the twenty-sixth chapter is a *song* expressive of joy at this signal deliverance—in language, in the main, so general that it is as applicable to the redemption under the Messiah as to the deliverance from Babylon; and the twenty-seventh chapter is descriptive of the *effect* of this captivity and subsequent deliverance in purifying Jacob (ch. xxvii. 6-9), and recovering the nation to righteousness.

The twenty-fourth chapter is composed of three parts. The first (1–12) contains a description of the calamities that would come upon the whole land, amounting to far-spread and wide desolation—with a graphic description of the effects of it on the inhabitants (2), on the land (3–6), on the amusements, the song, &c. (7–12), causing all gaiety and prosperity to come to an end. The second (13–17) contains a statement by the prophet that a *few* would be left in the land amidst the general desolation, and that they would be filled with joy that they had escaped. From their retreats and refuges, their fastnesses and places of security, they would lift up the song of praise that they had been preserved. The third (18–23) contains a further description of augmented judgment that

would come upon the land—a more severe and lengthened calamity stretching over the country, agitating it like an earthquake. Yet there is even here (22, 23), an indication that there would be deliverance, and that the Lord of hosts would reign on Mount Zion—a description which is extended through the next chapter, and which constitutes the scope and substance of that chapter. In the division of the prophecy into chapters, that chapter should have been connected with this as a part of the same prophecy, and a continuance of the same subject. Indeed, but for the *length* of the prophecy, these four chapters should have been thrown into one, or if the prophecy had been broken up into chapters, important aids would have been rendered to a correct understanding of it had there been some indication in the margin that they constituted one prophecy or vision.

B EHOLD, the Lord maketh the earth empty; and maketh it waste, and turneth [1] it upside down, and scattereth abroad the inhabitants thereof.

2 And it shall be, as with the people, so with [a] the [2] priest; as with [b] the servant, so with his master; as with the maid, so with her mistress; as with the buyer, so with the seller; as with the lender, so with the borrower; as with the taker of usury, so with the giver of usury to him.

1 *perverteth the face thereof.*　a Hos.4.9.
2 or, *prince*; Gen.41.45.　b Ep.6.8,9.

CHAPTER XXIV.

1. *Maketh the earth empty.* That is, will depopulate it, or take away its inhabitants, and its wealth. The word 'earth' here (אֶרֶץ) is used evidently not to denote the whole world, but the land to which the prophet particularly refers —the land of Judea. It should have been translated *the land* (see Joel i. 2). It is possible, however, that the word here may be intended to include so much of the nations that surrounded Palestine as were allied with it, or as were connected with it in the desolations under Nebuchadnezzar. ¶ *And turneth it upside down.* Marg. 'Perverteth the face thereof.' That is, everything is thrown into confusion; the civil and religious institutions are disorganized, and de-

rangement everywhere prevails. ¶ *And scattereth abroad*, &c. This was done in the invasion by the Chaldeans by the carrying away of the inhabitants into their long and painful captivity.

2. *As with the people, so with the priest.* This does not mean in moral character, but in destiny. It does not mean that the character of the priest would have any influence on that of the people, or that because the one was corrupt the other would be; but it means that all would be involved in the same calamity, and there would be no favoured class that would escape. The prophet, therefore, enumerates the various ranks of the people, and shows that all classes would be involved in the impending calamity. ¶ *As with the taker of usury.*

3 The land shall be utterly emptied, and utterly spoiled : for the LORD hath spoken this word.

4 The earth mourneth, *and* fadeth away : the world languisheth and fadeth away ; the haughty people [1] of the earth do languish.

5 The earth also is defiled under the inhabitants thereof, because

they [a] have transgressed the laws, changed the ordinance, broken the everlasting covenant.

6 Therefore [b] hath the curse devoured the earth, and they that dwell therein are desolate : therefore the inhabitants of the earth are burned, [c] and few men left.

1 *height of the.*   *a* Gen.3.17; Num.35.33.
b Mal.4.6.   *c* 2 Pet.3.10.

He who lends his money at interest. It was contrary to the Mosaic law for one Israelite to take interest of another (Lev. xxv. 36 ; Deut. xxiii. 19 ; Neh. v. 7, 10) ; but it is not probable that this law was very carefully observed, and especially in the corrupt times that preceded the Babylonian captivity.

3. *The land.* Heb. ' The earth,' as in ver. 1. It is here rendered correctly ' the land,' as it should have been there —meaning the land of Canaan. ¶ *And spoiled.* Its valuable possessions shall become the prey of the invading foe. This is an emphatic repetition of the declaration in ver. 1, to show the absolute certainty of that which was threatened.

4. *The earth mourneth.* The word ' earth ' here, as in ver. 1, means the land of Judea, or that and so much of the adjacent countries as would be subject to the desolation described. The figure here is taken from flowers when they lose their beauty and languish ; or when the plant that lacks moisture, or is cut down, loses its vigour and its vitality, and soon withers (comp. Note, ch. i. 30 ; ch. xxxiv. 4 ; Ps. i. 3). ¶ *The world* (תֵּבֵל) Literally, the inhabitable world, but used here as synonymous with the ' land,' and denoting the kingdoms of Judah and Israel (comp. Note, ch. xiii. 11). ¶ *The haughty people.* Marg. as in the Hebrew, ' Height of the people.' It denotes the great, the nobles, the princes of the land. The phrase is expressive of *rank*, not of their moral character.

5. *The earth also is defiled under the inhabitants thereof.* The statements in this verse are given as a reason why the curse had been pronounced against them, and why these calamities had come upon them, ver. 6. The first reason is, that the very earth had become polluted by their crimes. This phrase may denote

that injustice and cruelty prevailed to such an extent that the very earth was stained with gore, and covered with blood *under* the guilty population. So the phrase is used in Num. xxxiii. 33 ; Ps. cvi. 38. Or it may mean in general, that the wickedness of the people was great, and was accumulating, and the very earth under them was polluted by sustaining such a population. But the former is probably the correct interpretation. ¶ *Changed the ordinance.* Or, the *statute* (חֹק). This word, from חָקַק, *to engrave*, and then to make or institute a law or an ordinance, is usually applied to the *positive* statutes appointed by Moses. The word *statute* accurately expresses the idea. These they had changed by introducing new statutes, and had in fact, if not in form, repealed the laws of Moses, and introduced others. ¶ *Broken the everlasting covenant.* The word ' covenant ' here is evidently used, as it is often, in the sense of *law.* By the term ' everlasting covenant,' Vitringa correctly supposes is denoted the laws of nature, the immutable laws of justice and right, which are engraven on the conscience, and which are inflexible and perpetual.

6. *Therefore hath the curse devoured.* Eaten it up ; a figurative expression that is common in the Scriptures, denoting that the desolation is wide-spread and ruinous. ¶ *Are burned* (חָרוּ). Instead of this reading, Lowth proposes to read חָרְבוּ, ' Are destroyed.' The LXX. read it, ' Therefore the inhabitants of the land shall be poor.' The Syriac, ' The inhabitants of the land shall be slain.' But there is no authority from the MSS. to change the text as proposed by Lowth. Nor is it necessary. The prophet does not mean that the inhabitants of the land were *consumed by fire.*

7 The ᵃ new wine mourneth, the vine languisheth, all the merry-hearted do sigh.

8 The mirth of ᵇ tabrets ceaseth, the noise of them that rejoice end-eth, the joy of the harp ceaseth.

ᵃ ch.16.8,9; Joel 1.10,12.

9 They shall not drink wine with a song; strong drink shall be bitter to them that drink it.

10 The city of confusion is broken down: every house is shut up, that no man may come in.

ᵇ Jer.7.34; Hos.2.11; Rev.18.22.

The expression is evidently figurative. He is speaking of the effect of *wrath* or the *curse*, and that effect is often de-scribed in the Scriptures as burning, or consuming, as a fire does. The sense is, that the inhabitants of the land are brought under the withering, burning, consuming effect of that wrath; and the same effects are produced by it as are seen when a fire runs over a field or a forest. Hence the word here used (חָרָה, *to burn, to be kindled*) is often used in connection with wrath, to denote burning or raging anger. Ex. xxii. 23: 'His anger burns.' Gen. xxx. 2: 'And the anger of Jacob was kindled against Rachel; Gen. xliv. 18; Job xxvii. 2, 3; xlii. 7; Gen. xxxi. 6: 'His anger was kindled.' (Ps. xxxvii. 1, 7, 8; Prov. xxiv. 19.) Comp. Job xxx. 30:

My skin is black upon me,
And my bones are burnt with heat.

The sense is, that the inhabitants of the land were wasted away under the wrath of God, so that few were left; as the trees of the forest are destroyed before a raging fire. ¶ *And few men are left.* This was literally true after the invasion of the land by the Chaldeans (2 Kings xxiv. 14–16).

7. *The new wine languisheth.* The new wine (תִּירוֹשׁ, *tīrōsh*), denotes pro-perly *must*, or wine that was newly ex-pressed from the grape, and that was not fermented, usually translated 'new wine,' or 'sweet wine.' The expression here is poetic. The wine languishes or mourns because there are none to drink it; it is represented as grieved because it does not perform its usual office of exhilarating the heart, and the figure is thus an image of the desolation of the land. ¶ *The vine languisheth.* It is sickly and unfruitful, because there are none to cultivate it as formerly. The idea is, that all nature sympathizes in the general calamity. ¶ *All the merry-hearted.* Probably the reference is

mainly to those who were once made happy at the plenteous feast, and at the splendid entertainments where wine abounded. They look now upon the wide-spread desolation of the land, and mourn.

8. *The mirth of tabrets.* The joy and exultation which is produced by tabrets. On the words 'tabret' (תֹּף) and 'harp' (כִּנּוֹר), see Notes on ch. v. 12.

9. *Drink wine with a song.* That is, accompanied with a song, as the usual mode was in their feasts. ¶ *Strong drink.* On the word שֵׁכָר, see Note on ch. v. 11. ¶ *Shall be bitter,* &c. They shall cease to find pleasure in it in con-sequence of the general calamities that have come upon the nation.

10. *The city of confusion.* That Jerusalem is here intended there can be no doubt. The name 'city of confusion.' is probably given to it by *anticipation* of what it would be; that is, as it ap-peared in prophetic vision to Isaiah (see Note on ch. i. 1). He gave to it a name that would describe its state when these calamities should have come upon it. The word rendered 'confusion' (תֹּהוּ, *tōhū*) does not denote *disorder* or *anarchy*, but is a word expressive of emptiness, vanity, destitution of form, waste. It occurs Gen. i. 2: 'And the earth was *without form.*' In Job xxvi. 7, it is rendered 'the empty place;' in 1 Sam. xii. 21; Isa. xlv. 18, 19, 'in vain;' and usually 'emptiness,' 'vanity,' 'confusion' (see Isa. xxiv. 10; xl. 17; xli. 29). In Job xii. 24; Ps. cvii. 40, it denotes a wilderness. Here it means that the city would be desolate, empty, and depopulated. ¶ *Is broken down.* Its walls and dwellings are in ruins. ¶ *Every house is shut up.* That is, either because every man, fearful of danger, would fasten his doors so that enemies could not enter; or more pro-bably, the entrance to every house would be so obstructed by ruins as to render it impossible to enter it.

11 *There is* a crying for wine in the streets ; all joy is darkened, the mirth of the land is gone.

12 In *ª* the city *is* left desolation, and the gate *b* is smitten with destruction.

13 When thus it shall be in the midst of the land among the people, *there shall be c* as the shaking of an

olive-tree, and as the gleaning-grapes when the vintage is done.

14 They *d* shall lift up their voice, they shall sing for the majesty of the LORD, they shall cry aloud from the sea.

15 Wherefore *e* glorify ye the LORD in the ¹ fires, *even* the name of the LORD God of Israel in the isle *f* of the sea.

---

a Lam.1.1.   *b* Lam.2.9.
c ch.6; 13; 17.5,6; Mic.2.12.   *d* Zep.2.14,15.

e 1 Pe.3.15.   1 or, *valleys.*   *f* Zep.2.11.

---

11. There is *a crying for wine in the streets.* The inhabitants of the city, turned from their dwellings, would cry for wine to alleviate their distress, and to sustain them in their calamity (comp. ch. xvi. 8–10). ¶ *All joy is darkened.* Is gone, or has departed, like the joyful light at the setting of the sun.

12. *And the gate is smitten with destruction.* The word rendered 'destruction' may denote 'a crash' (Gesenius). The idea is, that the gates of the city, once so secure, are now battered down and demolished, so that the enemy can enter freely. Thus far is a description of the calamities that would come upon the nation. The following verses show that, though the desolation would be general, a few of the inhabitants would be left—a circumstance thrown in to mitigate the prospect of the impending ruin.

13. *In the midst of the land.* That is, in the midst of the land of Canaan. ¶ There shall be *as the shaking of an olive-tree.* A few shall be left, as in gathering olives a few will remain on the highest and outermost boughs (see Notes on ch. xvii. 5, 6).

14. *They shall lift up their voice.* They who are left in the land ; or who are not carried away to Babylon. ' To lift up the voice ' in the Scriptures may denote either grief or joy ; compare Gen. xxi. 6 ; 1 Sam. xxiv. 16 ; Judg. ii. 4 ; Ruth i. 9, &c., where to lift up the voice is conected with weeping ; and Ezek. xxi. 22 ; Ps. xciii. 3 ; Isa. xl. 29 ; xlii. 11, &c., where it is connected with exultation and joy. The latter is evidently the idea here, that the few who would escape from captivity by fleeing to neighbouring countries, would lift up their voice with exultation that they

had escaped. ¶ *They shall sing for the majesty of the* LORD. They shall sing on account of the glory, or goodness of JEHOVAH, who had so mercifully kept and preserved them. ¶ *They shall cry aloud from the sea.* From the isles and coasts of the Mediterranean whither they would have escaped, and where they would find a refuge. No doubt many of the inhabitants adjacent to the sea, when they found the land invaded, would betake themselves to the neighbouring islands, and find safety there until the danger should be overpast. Lowth renders this,

'The waters shall resound with the exaltation of Jehovah,'

where he supposes מים should be rendered as if pointed מַיִם, 'waters,' not as it is in the present Hebrew text, מִיָּם, 'from the sea.' The sense is not materially different ; but there seems to be no good reason for departing from the usual interpretation.

15. *Wherefore glorify ye the* LORD. The prophet, in this verse, calls upon the people to join in the praise of JEHOVAH wherever they are scattered. In the previous verse he describes the scattered few who were left in the land, or who had escaped to the adjacent islands in the sea, as celebrating the praises of God where they were. In this verse he calls on *all* to join in this wherever they were scattered. ¶ *In the fires.* Marg. ' Valleys.' The LXX. read, Ἐν τοῖς νήσοις—' In the islands.' The Chaldee, ' Therefore, when light shall come to the just, they shall glorify the Lord.' Lowth supposes that the word בָּאֻרִים should have been בָּאִיִּים, ' in the islands,' or ' coasts.' But the MSS. do not give authority for this reading ; the only authority which Lowth

16 From the [1] uttermost part of
the earth have we heard songs, *even*
glory to the righteous. But I said,
My [2] leanness, my leanness, woe

unto me! the treacherous dealers
have dealt treacherously; [a] yea, the
treacherous dealers have dealt very
treacherously.

[1] *wing.*　　[2] *leanness to me, or, my secret to me.*

[a] ch.48.8; Jer.5.11.

---

refers to being that of the LXX. Other
conjectures have been made by others,
but all without any authority from MSS.
The Hebrew word in the plural form
does not occur elsewhere in the Scriptures. The proper signification of the
word אוֹר (*ōr*) is *light*, and it is applied
(*a*) to *daylight*, or daybreak, 1 Sam.
xiv. 36; Neh. viii. 3; (*b*) to light from
daybreak to mid-day, Job xxiv. 14; (*c*)
the sun, Job xxxi. 26; xxxvii. 21; (*d*)
light as the emblem of happiness; (*e*)
light as the emblem of knowledge. It
is also used to denote *fire*, Ezek. v. 2;
Isa. xliv. 16; xlvii. 14. In the plural
form it is applied, in connection with
the word *Thummim*, to the gems or
images which were on the breastplate
of the high priest, and from which responses were obtained. Ex. xxviii. 30:
'And thou shalt put in the breastplate
of judgment the Urim (הָאוּרִים) and the
Thummim' (comp. Lev. viii. 8; Ezra ii.
63). Probably it was thus used to denote
the *splendour* or beauty of the gems there
set, or perhaps the *light* or instruction
which was the result of consulting the
oracle. The proper meaning of the
word is, however, *light*, and it usually
and naturally suggests the idea of the
morning light, the aurora; perhaps,
also, the *northern* light, or the aurora
borealis. It in no instance means *caves*,
or *valleys*. Vitringa supposed it referred to *caves*, and that the address
was to the *Troglodytes*, or those who
had been driven from their homes, and
compelled to take up their residence in
caves. The word probably refers either
to the regions of the morning light, the
rising of the sun; or of the northern
light, the aurora borealis; and in either
case, the reference is doubtless to those
who would be carried away to Babylon,
and who were called on there by the
prophet to glorify God. 'In those regions
of *light*, where the morning dawns; or
where the northern skies are illuminated at night, there glorify God' (see
Note on ch. xiv. 13). The reasons for

this opinion are, (1.) That such is the
natural and proper sense of the word.
It properly refers to light, and *not* to
caves, to valleys, or to islands. (2.)
The parallelism, the construction, demands such an interpretation. It would
then be equivalent to calling on the
scattered people to glorify God in the
East, and in the West; in the regions
of the rising sun and in the coasts of the
sea; or wherever they were scattered.
And the sense is, (1) that they should
be *encouraged* to do this by the prospect
of a return; (2) that it was their *duty*
still to do this wherever they were; and
(3) that the worship of the true God
would be in fact continued, and celebrated, though his people were scattered,
and driven to distant lands. ¶ *In the
isle of the sea.* The coasts and islands
of the Mediterranean (ver. 14).

16. *From the uttermost part of the
earth.* The word 'earth' here seems to
be taken in its usual sense, and to denote countries without the bounds of
Palestine, and the phrase is equivalent
to *remote regions*, or *distant countries*
(see Note on ch. xi. 12). The prophet
here represents himself as *hearing*
those songs from distant lands as a
grand chorus, the sound of which came
in upon and pervaded Palestine. The
worship of God would be still continued,
though the temple should be destroyed,
the inhabitants of the land dispersed,
and the land of Judea be a wide-spread
desolation. Amidst the general wreck
and woe, it was *some* consolation that
the worship of JEHOVAH was celebrated
anywhere. ¶ *Have we heard songs.*
Or, we *do* hear songs. The distant
celebrations of the goodness of God
break on the ear, and amidst the general calamity these songs of the scattered people of God comfort the heart.
¶ *Glory to the righteous.* This is the
burden and substance of those songs.
Their general import and design is, to
show that there shall be honour to the
people of God. They are now afflicted

17 Fear, *a* and the pit, and the snare, *are* upon thee, O inhabitant of the earth.

a Jer.48.43,44.

and scattered. Their temple is destroyed, their land waste, and ruin spreads over the graves of their fathers. Yet amidst these desolations, their confidence in God is unshaken; their reliance on him is firm. They still believe that there shall be honour and glory to the just, and that God will be their protector and avenger. These assurances served to sustain them in their afflictions, and to shed a mild and cheering influence on their saddened hearts. ¶ *But I said.* But I, the prophet, am constrained to say. This the prophet says respecting *himself*, viewing himself as left in the land of Canaan; or more probably he personifies, in this declaration, Jerusalem, and the inhabitants of the land that still remained there. The songs that came in from distant lands; the echoing praises from the exiles in the east and the west seeming to meet and mingle over Judea, only served to render the abounding desolation more manifest and distressing. Those distant praises recalled the solemn services of the temple, and the happiness of other times, and led each one of those remaining, who witnessed the desolations, to exclaim, 'my leanness.' ¶ *My leanness, my leanness.* The language of Jerusalem, and the land of Judea. This language expresses calamity. The loss of flesh is emblematic of a condition of poverty, want, and wretchedness—as sickness and affliction waste away the flesh, and take away the strength; Ps. cix. 24:

> My knees are weak through fasting,
> And my flesh faileth of fatness.

Ps. cii. 5:

> By reason of the voice of my groaning
> My bones cleave to my flesh.

See also Job vi. 12; xix. 20; Lam. iii. 4. Leanness is also put to denote the displeasure of God, in Ps. cvi. 15:

> And he gave them their request;
> But sent leanness into their soul.

Comp. Isa. x. 16. ¶ *The treacherous dealers.* The foreign nations that disregard covenants and laws; that pursue their object by deceit, and stratagem, and fraud. Most conquests are made by what are called the *stratagems* of war; that is, by a course of perfidy and deception. There can be no doubt that the usual mode of conquest was pursued in regard to Jerusalem. This whole clause is exceedingly emphatic. The word implying *treachery* (בָּגַד) is repeated no less than *five* times in various forms in this single clause, and shows how strongly the idea had taken possession of the mind of the prophet. The passage furnishes one of the most remarkable examples of the *paronomasia* occurring in the Bible. בֹּגְדִים בָּגָדוּ וּבֶגֶד בּוֹגְדִים —*Baghadu boghedim baghadu ubegehd boghedhim.* In fact, this figure abounds so much in this chapter that Gesenius contends that it is not the production of Isaiah, but a composition belonging to a later and less elegant period of Hebrew literature.

17. *Fear, and the pit.* This verse is an explanation of the cause of the wretchedness referred to in the previous verse. The same expression is found in Jer. xlviii. 43, in his account of the destruction that would come upon Moab, a description which Jeremiah probably copied from Isaiah.— There is also here in the original a *paronomasia* that cannot be retained in a translation—פַּחַד וָפַחַת וָפָח *pāhhădh vâpahhăth vâpāhh*—where the form *pahh* occurs in each word. The sense is, that they were nowhere safe; that if they escaped one danger, they immediately fell into another. The expression is equivalent to that which occurs in the writings of the Latin classics:

Incidit in Scyllam cupiens vitare Charybdin.

The same idea, that if a man should escape from one calamity he would fall into another, is expressed in another form in Amos v. 19:

As if a man did flee from a lion, and a bear met him;
Or went into a house, and leaned his hand on the wall,
And a serpent bit him.

18 And it shall come to pass, *that* he who fleeth from the noise of the fear shall fall into the pit ; and he that cometh up out of the midst of the pit shall be taken in the snare : for the *ᵃ* windows from

a Gen.7.11.   *b* Ps.18.7.

on high are open, and the foundations *ᵇ* of the earth do shake.

19 The earth *ᶜ* is utterly broken down, the earth is clean dissolved, the earth is moved exceedingly.

20 The earth shall reel *ᵈ* to and

c Jer.4.23.   *d* ch.19.14.

In the passage before us, there is an *advance* from one danger to another, or the subsequent one is more to be dreaded than the preceding. The figure is taken from the mode of taking wild beasts, where various nets, toils, or pitfalls were employed to secure them. The word 'fear' (פַּחַד), denotes anything that was used to frighten or arouse the wild beasts in hunting, or to drive them into the pitfall that was prepared for them. Among the Romans the name 'fears' (*formidines*) was given to lines or cords strung with feathers of all colours, which, when they fluttered in the air or were shaken, frightened the beasts into the pits, or the birds into the snares which were prepared to take them (Seneca, *De Ira*, ii. 12 ; Virg. *Æn*. xii. 749 ; *Geor*. iii. 372). It is possible that this may be referred to here under the name of 'fear.' The word 'pit' (פַּחַת) denotes the pitfall ; a hole dug in the ground, and covered over with bushes, leaves, &c., into which they might fall unawares. The word 'snare' (פָּה) denotes a net, or gin, and perhaps refers to a series of nets enclosing at first a large space of ground, in which the wild beasts were, and then drawn by degrees into a narrow compass, so that they could not escape.

18. *From the noise of the fear.* A cry or shout was made in hunting, designed to arouse the game, and drive it to the pitfall. The image means here that calamities would be multiplied in all the land, and that if the inhabitants endeavoured to avoid one danger they would fall into another. ¶ *And he that cometh up out of the midst of the pit.* A figure taken still from hunting. It was *possible* that some of the more strong and active of the wild beasts driven into the pitfall would spring out, and attempt to escape, yet they might be secured by snares or gins purposely con-

trived for such an occurrence. So the prophet says, that though a few might escape the calamities that would at first threaten to overthrow them, yet they would have no security. They would immediately fall into others, and be destroyed. ¶ *For the windows on high are open.* This is evidently taken from the account of the deluge in Gen. vii. 11: ' In the six hundredth year of Noah's life, in the second month, the seventeenth day of the month, the same day were all the fountains of the great deep broken up, and the windows (or *flood-gates*, Margin) of heaven were opened.' The word 'windows' here (אֲרֻבּוֹת) is the same which occurs in Genesis, and properly denotes *a grate, a lattice, a window*, and then any opening, as a sluice or floodgate, and is applied to a tempest or a deluge, because when the rain descends, it seems like opening sluices or floodgates in the sky. The sense here is, that calamities had come upon the nation *resembling* the universal deluge. ¶ *And the foundations of the earth do shake.* An image derived from an earthquake —a figure also denoting far-spreading calamities.

19. *The earth is utterly broken down.* The effect as it were of an earthquake where everything is thrown into commotion and ruin. ¶ *The earth is moved exceedingly.* Everything in this verse is intense and emphatic. The verbs are in the strongest form of emphasis : ' By breaking, the land is broken ;' ' by scattering, the land is scattered ;' ' by commotion, the land is moved.' The repetition also of the expression in the same sense three times, is a strong form of emphasis ; and the whole passage is designed to denote the utter desolation and ruin that had come upon the land.

20. *The earth shall reel to and fro like a drunkard.* This is descriptive of the agitation that occurs in an earthquake when everything is shaken from

fro like a drunkard, and shall be removed *a* like a cottage ; and the transgression thereof shall be heavy upon *b* it : and it shall fall, and not rise again.

a Rev.21.1.   b Zec.5.5-8.

21 And it shall come to pass in that day, *that* the LORD shall punish *1* the host of the high ones *that are* on high, and the kings of *c* the earth upon the earth.

1 *visit upon.*   c Ps.76.12.

its foundation, and when trees and towers are shaken by the mighty concussion. The same figure is used in ch. xxix. 9. See also the description of a tempest at sea, in Ps. cvii. 27 :

> They reel to and fro,
> And stagger like a drunken man,
> And are at their wit's end.

¶ *And shall be removed like a cottage.* Or rather, shall *move* or *vacillate* (הִתְנוֹדְדָה) like a cottage. The word cottage (מְלוּנָה from לוּן, *to pass the night, to lodge for a night*) means properly a temporary shed or lodge for the watchman of a garden or vineyard (see Note on ch. i. 8). Sometimes these cottages were erected in the form of a hut ; and sometimes they were a species of *hanging bed* or *couch*, that was suspended from the limbs of trees. They were made either by interweaving the limbs of a tree, or by suspending them by cords from the branches of trees, or by extending a cord or cords from one tree to another, and laying a couch or bed on the cords. They were thus made to afford a convenient place for observation, and also to afford security from the access of wild beasts. Travellers in the East even now resort to such a temporary lodge for security (see Niebuhr's *Description of Arabia*). These lodges were easily moved to and fro, and swung about by the wind—and this is the idea in the verse before us. The whole land was agitated as with an earthquake ; it reeled like a drunkard ; it moved, and was unsettled, as the hanging couch on the trees was driven to and fro by the wind. ¶ *And the transgression thereof shall be heavy upon it.* Like a vast incumbent weight on a dwelling which it cannot sustain, and beneath which it is crushed. ¶ *And it shall fall, and not rise again.* This does not mean, as I apprehend, that the nation should never be restored to its former dignity and rank as a people ; for the prophet immediately (ver. 23) speaks of such a

restoration, and of the re-establishment of the theocracy ; but it must mean that IN *those convulsions* it would not rise. It would not be able to recover itself ; it *would certainly* be prostrated. As we say of a drunkard, he may stumble often, and partially recover himself, yet he will certainly fall so as not then to be able to recover himself, so it would be with that agitated and convulsed land. They would make many efforts to recover themselves, and they would partially succeed, yet they would ultimately be completely prostrate in the dust.

21. *In that day.* In the time of the captivity at Babylon. ¶ *Shall punish.* Heb. as the Marg., 'Shall visit upon' (see Note on ch. x. 12). ¶ *The host of the high ones.* There have been various interpretations of this expression. Jerome understands it of the host of heaven, and thinks it refers to the fact that in the day of judgment God will judge not only earthly things but celestial, and especially the sun and moon and stars, as having been the objects of idolatrous worship (see Deut. iv. 19 ; Dan. viii. 10 ; xi. 13). Comp. Ps. xviii. 17 ; Jer. xxv. 30, where the words 'on high' are used to denote heaven. Aben Ezra supposes that by the phrase is meant *angels*, who preside over the governors and kings of the earth, in accordance with the ancient opinion that each kingdom was under the tutelage of guardian angels. To this Rosenmüller seems to assent, and to suppose that the beings thus referred to were *evil* spirits or demons to whom the kingdoms of the world were subject. Others, among whom is Grotius, have supposed that the reference is to the images of the sun, moon, and stars, which were erected in high places, and worshipped by the Assyrians. But probably the reference is to those who occupied places of power and trust in the *ecclesiastical* arrangement of Judea, the high priest and priests, who exercised a vast dominion over the nation, and who, in many respects, were re-

22 And they shall be gathered together ¹ *as* prisoners are gathered in ² the pit, and shall be shut up in the prison, and after many days shall they be ³ visited.

1 *with the gathering of prisoners.* 2 or, *dungeon.*

23 Then ᵃ the moon shall be confounded, and the sun ashamed, when the LORD of hosts shall reign in mount Zion, and in Jerusalem, and ⁴ before his ancients, gloriously.

3 or, *found wanting.* a Eze.32.7.
4 or, *there shall be glory before his ancients*

garded as elevated even over the kings and princes of the land. The comparison of rulers with the sun, moon, and stars, is common in the Scriptures; and this comparison was supposed peculiarly to befit *ecclesiastical* rulers, who were regarded as in a particular manner the lights of the nation. ¶ *Upon the earth.* Beneath, or inferior to those who had places of the highest trust and honour. The ecclesiastical rulers are represented as occupying the superior rank; the princes and rulers in a civil sense as in a condition of less honour and responsibility. This was probably the usual mode in which the ecclesiastical and civil offices were estimated in Judea.

22. *And they shall be gathered together.* That is, those who occupy posts of honour and influence in the ecclesiastical and civil polity of the land. ¶ *As prisoners.* Margin, as in the Heb. 'With the gathering of prisoners.' The reference is to the custom of collecting captives taken in war, and chaining them together by the hands and feet, and thrusting them in large companies into a prison. ¶ *In the pit.* Marg. 'Dungeon.' The sense is, that the rulers of the land should be made captive, and treated as prisoners of war. This was undoubtedly true in the captivity under Nebuchadnezzar. The people were assembled; were regarded as captives; and were conveyed together to a distant land. ¶ *And shall be shut up in the prison.* Probably this is not intended to be taken *literally*, but to denote that they would be as secure as *if* they were shut up in prison. Their prison-house would be Babylon, where they were enclosed *as in a prison* seventy years. ¶ *And after many days.* If this refers, as I have supposed, to the captivity at Babylon, then these 'many days' refer to the period of seventy years. ¶ *Shall they be visited.* Marg. 'Found wanting.' The word here used (פָּקַד) may be used either in a good or bad

sense, either to visit for the purpose of reviewing, numbering, or aiding; or to visit for the purpose of punishing. It is probably, in the Scriptures, most frequently used in the latter sense (see 1 Sam. xv. 2; Job xxxi. 14; xxxv. 15; Ps. lxxxix. 33; Isa. xxvi. 14; Jer. ix. 24). But it is often used in the sense of taking account of, reviewing, or mustering as a military host (see Num. i. 44; iii. 39; 1 Kings xx. 15; Isa. xiii. 4). In this place it may be taken in either of these senses, as may be best supposed to suit the connection. To me it seems that the connection seems to require the idea of a visitation for the purpose of relief or of deliverance; and to refer to the fact that at the end of that time there would be a reviewing, a mustering, an enrolment of those who should have been carried away to their distant prison-house, to ascertain how many remained, and to *marshal* them for their return to the land of their fathers (see the books of Ezra and Nehemiah). The word here used has *sometimes* the sense expressed in the margin, 'found wanting' (comp. 1 Sam. xx. 6; xxv. 15; Isa. xxxviii. 10); but such a sense does not suit the connection here. I regard the verse as an indication of future mercy and deliverance. They would be thrown into prison, and treated as captives of war; but after a long time they would be visited by the Great Deliverer of their nation, their covenant-keeping God, and reconducted to the land of their fathers.

23. *Then the moon shall be confounded.* The heavenly bodies are often employed in the sacred writings to denote the princes and kings of the earth. These expressions are not to be pressed *ad unguem* as if the sun denoted one thing and the moon another; but they are *general* poetic expressions designed to represent rulers, princes, and magistrates of all kinds (comp. Ezek. xxxii. 7; Joel ii. 30, 31). ¶ *Shall be confounded.* Shall be covered with shame.

CHAPTER XXV.

ANALYSIS.

For the general design and scope of this chapter, see the Analysis to ch. xxiv. It is a song of praise to God for the anticipated deliverance of his people from the bondage in Babylon. The desolation of Jerusalem and Judah had been described in ch. xxiv.; that chapter had closed with an intimation that Jehovah would again reign in glory on Mount Zion (ver. 23); and in view of this future deliverance the prophet breaks out into this beautiful song of praise. It was not unusual for the prophets to express, by anticipation, such songs of praise as would be celebrated by the people in times of signal deliverance (see Notes on ch. xii.) This song of praise is one of the most beautiful that is to be found in the writings of Isaiah. The essential idea is that which was hinted at in ch. xxiv. 23, that Jehovah would reign with a glory that would obscure the brightness of the sun and the moon on Mount Zion. Filled with the idea, the prophet fixes the eye on those future glories, and declares

what shall occur *under* that reign. He sees Jehovah reigning there for a long series of years; and *during* that reign he sees (6) that he would provide a way by which the darkness might be removed from all nations (7); that he would originate that plan by which death would be swallowed up in victory (8); and that there he would execute a plan by which all his enemies would be laid low (9–12). The hymn is designed, therefore, to celebrate the faithfulness of God in fulfilling his ancient promises, and delivering his people from their long captivity by the destruction of Babylon (1–5); and the future glories that would shine forth under the reign of Jehovah on Mount Zion, including the arrangements of redeeming mercy for the world.

O LORD, thou *art* my God; I will *ᵃ* exalt thee, I will praise thy name: for thou hast done wonderful *things*; *thy* counsels of old *are* faithfulness *ᵇ and* truth.

ᵃ Ps.46.10.   ᵇ Num.23.19.

That is, shall appear to shine with diminished beauty, as if it were *ashamed* in the superior glory that would shine around it. The sense is, that when the people should be returned to their land, the theocracy would be restored, and the magnificence of the kings and other civil rulers would be dimmed in the superior splendour of the reign of God. Probably there is reference here to the time when Jehovah would reign in Jerusalem through, or by means of, the Messiah. ¶ *In Mount Zion* (see Note on ch. i. 8). This would take place subsequently to the captivity, and pre-eminently under the reign of the Messiah. ¶ *And before his ancients.* That is, before the elders of the people; in the presence of those intrusted with authority and rule. ¶ *Gloriously.* He would reign gloriously when his laws should be respected and obeyed; when his character as King and Ruler should be developed; and, when, under his sceptre, his kingdom should be augmented and extended. On this glad prospect the eye of the prophet was fixed; and this was the bright and splendid object in the 'vision' that served to relieve the darkness that was coming upon the nation. Present calamities may be borne, with the hope that Jehovah will reign more gloriously hereafter; and when the effect of all

shall be such as to exalt Jehovah in the view of the nations. It may be added that when Jehovah, by the Messiah, shall reign over all the earth, all the glory of princes and monarchs shall be dimmed; the celebrity of their wisdom and power and plans shall be obscured in the superior splendour of the wisdom of God, in reigning through his Son over the human race. Come that blessed day; and speedily let the glory of the moon be confounded, and the sun be ashamed, and all inferior magnificence fade away before the splendour of the Sun of righteousness!

CHAPTER XXV.

1. *O Lord, thou art my God.* The prophet speaks, not in his own name, but in the name of the people that would be delivered from bondage. The sense is, that Jehovah had manifested himself as their covenant-keeping God; and that in view of his faithfulness in keeping his promises, they now had demonstration that he was *their* God. ¶ *I will exalt thee.* A form of expression often used to denote *praise* (Ps. cxviii. 28; cxlv. 1), meaning that the worshipper would exalt God in the view of his own mind, or would regard him as above all other beings and objects. ¶ *For thou hast done wonderful* things. On the meaning of the Heb. אלפ—'wonderful,'

2 For thou hast made of a city an heap ; *of* a defenced city a ruin : a *a* palace of strangers to be no city ; it shall never be built.

a Jer.51.37.　　　*b* Rev.11.13.

3 Therefore shall the strong people glorify *b* thee, the city of the terrible nations shall fear thee.

4 For thou hast been a strength to the poor, a strength to the needy

see Note on ch. ix. 6. ¶ Thy *counsels of old.* Which were formed and revealed long since. The counsels referred to are those respecting the delivery of his people from bondage, which had been expressed even long before their captivity commenced, and which would be now completely and triumphantly fulfilled. ¶ Are *faithfulness.* Have been brought to pass ; do not fail. ¶ And *truth.* Heb. אָמֵן—whence our word *Amen.* LXX. Γένοιτο — ' Let it be.' The word denotes that the purposes of God were *firm,* and would certainly be fulfilled.

2. *For thou hast made.* This is supposed to be uttered by the Jews who should return from Babylon, and therefore refers to what *would have been* seen by them. In their time it would have occurred that God had made of the city an heap. ¶ *Of a city.* I suppose the whole scope of the passage requires us to understand this of Babylon. There has been, however, a great variety of interpretation of this passage. Grotius supposed that Samaria was intended. Calvin that the word is used *collectively,* and that various cities are intended. Piscator that Rome, the seat of Antichrist, was intended. Jerome says that the Jews generally understand it of Rome. Aben Ezra and Kimchi, however, understand it to refer to many cities which they say will be destroyed in the times of Gog and Magog. Nearly all these opinions may be seen subjected to an examination, and shown to be unfounded, in Vitringa. ¶ *An heap.* It is reduced to ruins (see Notes on ch. xiii., xiv.) The ruin of Babylon *commenced* when it was taken by Cyrus, and the Jews were set at liberty ; it was not *completed* until many centuries after. The form of the Hebrew here is, ' Thou hast placed *from* a city *to* a ruin ;' that is, thou hast changed it *from* being a city *to* a pile of ruins. ¶ Of a *defenced city.* A city fortified, and made strong against the approach of an enemy. How

true this was of Babylon may be seen in the description prefixed to chapter xiii. ¶ *A palace.* This word properly signifies the residence of a prince or monarch (Jer. xxx. 18 ; Amos i. 4, 7, 10, 12). Here it is applied to Babylon on account of its splendour, as if it were a vast palace, the residence of princes. ¶ *Of strangers.* Foreigners ; a term often given to the inhabitants of foreign lands, and especially to the Babylonians (see Note on ch. i. 7 ; comp. Ezek. xxviii. 7 ; Joel iii. 17). It means that this was, by way of eminence, THE city of the foreigners ; the capital of the whole Pagan world ; the city where foreigners congregated and dwelt. ¶ *It shall never be built.* (See Notes on ch. xiii. 19–22.)

3. *The strong people.* The reference here is not probably to the Babylonians, but to the surrounding nations. The deliverance of the Jews, and the destruction of Babylon, would be such striking events that they would lead the surrounding nations to acknowledge that it was the hand of God. ¶ *The city of the terrible nations.* The word ' city ' here is taken probably in a collective sense, to denote the *cities* or the strong places of the surrounding nations which would be brought thus to tremble before God. The destruction of a city so proud and wicked as Babylon would alarm *them,* and would lead them to *fear* that they might share the same fate, especially as many of them had been associated in oppressing the now delivered people of the land of Judea.

4. *For thou hast been a strength to the poor.* Thou hast sustained and upheld them in their trials, and hast delivered them. God is often spoken of as the *strength* of his people. Isa. xxvi. 4 : ' In the Lord JEHOVAH is everlasting strength.' Ps. xxvii. 1 : ' The Lord is the strength of my life, of whom shall I be afraid ? ' Ps. xxviii. 8 ; xxix. 11 ; xxxi. 2 ; xlvi. 1 ; Isa. xlv. 24.—By the ' poor ' and the ' needy ' here undoubtedly are meant the captive Jews

in his distress, a refuge from the storm, a shadow from the heat, when the blast of the terrible ones *is* as a storm *against* the wall.

5 Thou shalt bring down the noise of strangers, as the heat in a dry place; *even* the heat with the shadow of a cloud: the branch

of the terrible ones shall be brought low.

6 And in this mountain *a* shall the LORD of hosts make unto all people a feast *b* of fat things, a feast of wines on the lees, of fat things full of marrow, of *c* wines on the lees well refined.

who had been stripped of their wealth, and carried from their homes, and confined in Babylon. ¶ *A refuge.* A place of safety; a retreat; a protection. God is often spoken of as such a *refuge;* Deut. xxxiii. 27: 'The eternal God is thy refuge.' (2 Sam. xxii. 3; Ps. ix. 9; xiv. 6; xlvi. 1, 7, 11; lvii. 1; lix. 16.) ¶ *From the storm.* This word (זֶרֶם) usually denotes a tempest of wind and rain. Here it is put for calamity and affliction. The figure is common in all languages. ¶ *A shadow from the heat.* (See Note on ch. iv. 6; xvi. 3; comp. ch. xxxii. 2.) ¶ *When the blast of the terrible ones.* Of the fierce, mighty, invading enemies. When they sweep down all before them as a furious tempest does. ¶ Is *as a storm* against *the wall.* For 'wall' here (קיר), Lowth proposes to read קֹר, from קָרַר, *to be cold* or *cool,* and supposes that this means a winter's storm. In this interpretation also Vitringa and Cappellus coincide. But there is no need of supposing an error in the text. The idea is, probably, that of a fierce driving storm that would prostrate walls and houses; meaning a violent tempest, and intending to describe in a striking manner the severity of the calamities that had come upon the nation.

5. *Thou shalt bring down the noise.* The tumult; the sound which they make in entering into battle; or the note of triumph, and the sound of revelry. The phrase may refer either to their shout of exultation over their vanquished foes; or to the usual sound of revelry; or to the hum of business in a vast city. ¶ *Of strangers.* Of foreigners (see Note on ver. 2). ¶ *As the heat in a dry place.* The parallelism here requires that we should suppose the phrase ' with the shadow of a cloud ' to be supplied in this hemistich, as it is obscurely ex-

pressed in our translation by the word ' even,' and it would then read thus:

As the heat in a dry place [by the shadow of a cloud],
The noise of the strangers shalt thou humble;
As the heat by the shadow of a cloud,
The exultation of the formidable ones shalt thou bring low.

The idea thus is plain. Heat pours down intensely on the earth, and if unabated would wither up every green thing, and dry up every stream and fountain. But a cloud intervenes, and checks the burning rays of the sun. So the wrath of the ' terrible ones,' the anger of the Babylonians, raged against the Jews. But the mercy of God interposed. It was like the intervening of a cloud to shut out the burning rays of the sun. It stayed the fury of their wrath, *and rendered them impotent to do injury, just as the intense burning rays of the sun are completely checked by an interposing cloud.* ¶ *The branch of the terrible ones.* This is a very unhappy translation. The word זָמִיר (*zâmīr*) is indeed used to denote a branch, or bough, as derived from זָמַר, *to prune a vine;* but it also has the sense of *a song;* a song of praise, or a song of exultation, from a second signification of זָמַר, *to sing; perhaps* from the song with which the work of the vineyard was usually accompanied. See the verb used in this sense in Judg. v. 3; Ps. ix. 12; xxx. 5; xlvii. 7; and the word which occurs here (*zâmīr*) used in the sense of *a song* in Ps. cxix. 54; 2 Sam. xxiii. 1; Job xxxv. 10. Here it is undoubtedly used in the sense of *a song,* meaning either a shout of victory or of revelry; and the idea of the prophet is, that this would be brought low by the destruction of Babylon, and by the return of the captive Jews to their own land.

6. *And in this mountain.* In mount

7 And he will ¹destroy in this
mountain the face of the covering
cast² over all people, and the vail
that ᵃ is spread over all nations.

1 *swallow up.*   2 *covered.*   ᵃ 2 Cor.3.16,18.

Zion, *i.e.*, in Jerusalem. The following
verses undoubtedly refer to the times of
the Messiah. Several of the expressions
used here are quoted in the New Testament, showing that the reference is to
the Messiah, and to the fact that his
kingdom would commence in Jerusalem,
and then extend to all people. ¶ *Shall
the* LORD *of hosts.* (See Note on ch. i.
9.) ¶ *Make unto all people.* Provide
for all people. He shall adapt the provisions of salvation not only to the Jews,
but to men everywhere. This is one
of the truths on which Isaiah loved to
dwell, and which in fact constitutes one
of the peculiarities of his prophecy. It
is one of the chief glories of the gospel,
that it is *unto all people.* See Isa. lvii.
7; Dan. v. 19; vii. 14; comp. Luke ii.
10: 'I bring you good tidings of great
joy, which shall be *unto all people.*'
¶ *A feast.* A feast, or entertainment,
was usually observed, as it is now, on
occasion of a great victory, or any other
signal success. It is, therefore, emblematic of an occasion of joy. Here it is
used in the twofold sense of an occasion
of joy, and of an abundance of provisions for the necessities of those who
should be entertained. This feast was
to be prepared on mount Zion—in the
provision which would be made in Jerusalem by the Messiah for the spiritual
wants of the whole world. The arrangements for salvation are often represented
under the image of an ample and rich
entertainment (see Luke xiv. 16; Rev.
xix. 19; Mat. xiii. 11). ¶ *Of fat things.*
Of rich delicacies. Fat things and
marrow are often used as synonymous
with a sumptuous entertainment, and
are made emblematic of the abundant
provisions of Divine mercy (see Isa. lv.
2; Ps. lxiii. 5; xxxvi. 8: 'I shall be
satisfied with the fatness of thy house.')
¶ *A feast of wines on the lees.* The
word which is here used (שְׁמָרִים) is derived from שָׁמַר, *to keep, preserve, retain,*
and is applied usually to the *lees* or
dregs of wine, because they *retain* the
strength and colour of the wine which
is left to stand on them. It is also in

this place applied to *wine* which has
been kept on the lees, and is therefore
synonymous with *old wine ;* or wine of
a rich colour and flavour. This fact,
that the colour and strength of wine are
retained by its being suffered to remain
without being poured from one vessel
into another, is more fully expressed in
Jer. xlviii. 11:

Moab hath been at ease from his youth,
And he hath settled on his lees,
And hath not been emptied from vessel to vessel,
Neither hath he gone into captivity ;
Therefore his taste remaineth in him,
And his scent is not changed.

Comp. Zeph. i. 12. It is well known
that wines, unless retained for a considerable time on the lees, lose their
flavour and strength, and are much less
valuable (comp. Notes on John ii. 10,
11). ¶ *Of fat things full of marrow.*
Marrow is also an emblem of richness,
or the delicacy of the entertainment
(Ps. lxiii. 5). ¶ *Of wines on the lees
well refined.* The word rendered 'well
refined' (מְזֻקָּקִים) is usually applied to
the purifying of metals in a furnace
(1 Chron. xxviii. 18; xxix. 4; Job
xxviii. 1). When applied to wine, it
denotes that which has been suffered to
remain on the lees until it was entirely
refined and purified by fermentation,
and had become perfectly clear.

7. *And he will destroy.* Heb. 'He
will swallow up,' that is, he will abolish,
remove, or take away. ¶ *In this mountain the face of the covering.* In mount
Zion, or in Jerusalem. This would be
done in Jerusalem, or on the mountains
of which Jerusalem was a part, where
the great transactions of the plan of
redemption would be accomplished. The
word 'face' here is used as it is frequently among the Hebrews, where the
face of a thing denotes its aspect, or
appearance, and then the thing itself.
Thus 'the face of God' is put for God
himself ; the 'face of the earth' for the
earth itself ; and the 'face of the vail'
means the vail itself, or the appearance
of the vail. To cover the head or the
face was a common mode of expressing
grief (see 2 Sam. xv. 30; xix. 5; Es.

26

8 He will ^aswallow up death in victory ; and the LORD God will wipe ^baway tears from off all faces ;

and the rebuke of his people shall be taken away ^cfrom off all the earth : for the LORD hath spoken *it*.

^a Hos.13.14; 1Cor.15.54.　　^b Rev.21.4.　　^c Mal.3.17,18.

vi. 12). It is probable that the expression here is taken from this custom, and the vail over the nations here is to be understood as expressive of the ignorance, superstition, crime, and wretchedness that covered the earth.

8. *He will swallow up.* This image is probably taken from a whirlpool or mælstrom in the ocean that absorbs all that comes near it. It is, therefore, equivalent to saying he will destroy or remove (ver. 7). In this place it means that he will abolish death ; that is, he will cause it to cease from its ravages and triumphs. This passage is quoted by Paul in his argument respecting the resurrection of the dead (1 Cor. xv. 54). He does not, however, quote directly from the Hebrew, or from the LXX., but gives the substance of the passage. His quoting it is sufficient proof that it refers to the resurrection, and that its primary design is to set forth the achievements of the gospel—achievements that will be fully realized only when death shall cease its dominion, and when its reign shall be for ever at an end. ¶ *Death.* Vitringa supposes that by ' death ' here is meant the wars and calamities with which the nation had been visited, and which would cease under the Messiah. In this interpretation Rosenmüller concurs. It is possible that the word may have this meaning in some instances ; and it is possible that the calamities of the Jews may have *suggested* this to the prophet, but the primary sense of the word here, I think, is death in its proper signification, and the reference is to the triumphs of God through the Messiah in completely abolishing its reign, and introducing eternal life. This was designed, doubtless, to comfort the hearts of the Jews, by presenting in a single graphic description the gospel as adapted to overcome *all* evils, and even to remove the greatest calamity under which the race groans—DEATH. ¶ *In victory.* Heb. לָנֶצַח. Paul, in 1 Cor. xv. 54, has translated this, Εἰς νῖκος—' Unto victory.' The word νῖκος (victory) is often

the translation of the word (see 2 Kings ii. 26; Job xxxvi. 7; Lam. iii. 18; Amos i. 2; viii. 7); though here the LXX. have rendered it ' strong (or prevailing) death shall be swallowed up.' The word may be derived from the Chaldee verb נְצַח, *to conquer, surpass ;* and then may denote *victory.* It often, however, has the sense of permanency, duration, completness, eternity ; and may mean *for ever,* and then *entirely* or *completely.* This sense is not materially different from that of Paul, ' unto victory.' Death shall be completely, permanently, destroyed ; that is, a complete *victory* shall be gained over it. The Syriac unites the two ideas of victory and perpetuity. ' Death shall be swallowed up *in victory for ever.*' This will take place under the reign of the Messiah, and shall be completed only in the morning of the resurrection, when the power of death over the people of God shall be completely and for ever subdued. ¶ *Will wipe away tears from off all faces.* This is quoted in Rev. xxi. 4, as applicable to the gospel. The sense is, that JEHOVAH would devise a plan that would be fitted to furnish perfect consolation to the afflicted ; to comfort the broken-hearted ; and that would in its final triumphs remove calamity and sorrow from men for ever. The *fulness* of this plan will be seen only in heaven. In anticipation of heaven, however, the gospel now does much to alleviate human woes, and to wipe away tears from the mourner's eyes. This passage is exquisitely beautiful. The poet Burns once said that he could never read it without being affected to tears. It may be added that nothing but the gospel will do this. No other religion can furnish such consolation ; and no other religion is, therefore, adapted to man. ¶ *And the rebuke of his people.* The reproach ; the contempt ; the opposition to them. This refers to some future period when the church shall be at peace, and when pure religion shall everywhere prevail. Hitherto the people of God have been

9 And it shall be said in that day, Lo, this *is* our God; we have waited *a* for him, and he will save us : this *is* the LORD; we have waited for him, we will be glad and rejoice in his salvation.

10 For in this mountain shall the hand of the LORD rest, and Moab shall be trodden [1] down under

him, even as straw [2] is trodden down for the dunghill.

11 And he shall spread forth his hands in the midst of them, as he that swimmeth spreadeth forth *his hands* to swim : and he shall bring down their pride together with the spoils of their hands.

a Tit.2.13. 1 *threshed.* 2 or, *threshed in Madmenah.*

---

scorned and persecuted, but the time will come when persecution shall cease, the true religion shall everywhere prevail, the church shall have rest, and its triumphs shall spread everywhere on the earth.

9. *And it shall be said in that day.* By the people of God. This shall be the language of exultation and joy which they shall use. ¶ *Lo, this* is *our God.* This is the language of those who now see and hail their Deliverer. It implies that *such* deliverance, and *such* mercy could be bestowed only by God, and that the fact that such mercies had been bestowed was proof that he was *their* God. ¶ *We have waited for him.* Amidst many trials, persecutions, and calamities, we have looked for the coming of our God to deliver us, and we will rejoice in the salvation that he brings. ¶ *This* is *the* LORD. This is JEHOVAH. It is JEHOVAH that has brought this deliverance. None but he could do it. The plan of redeeming mercy comes from him, and to him is to be traced all the benefits which it confers on man.

10. *For in this mountain.* In mount Zion. ¶ *Shall the hand of the* LORD *rest.* The *hand* in the Scriptures is often used as the symbol of protection and defence. By the expression that the hand of JEHOVAH should REST on mount Zion, is meant probably that he would be its defender; his protection would not be withdrawn, but would be *permanent* there. For an illustration of the phrase, see a similar use of the word *hand* as denoting protection, in Ezra vii. 6, 28; viii. 18, 22, 31; Neh. ii. 8. ¶ *And Moab.* (For an account of Moab, see Notes on ch. xv., xvi.) Moab here seems to be used in a general sense to denote the enemies of God, and the declaration that it would be

trodden down seems designed to indicate that the foes of God and his people would all be destroyed (comp. Notes on ch. xxxiv.) ¶ *Under him.* The Chaldee renders this, ' In his own place.' The phrase has the sense of 'in his place,' in Ex. xvi. 29; 2 Sam. ii. 23. Here it may mean that Moab, or the enemies of God, would be trodden down and destroyed in their own land. ¶ *As straw is trodden down for the dunghill.* As straw is suffered to lie in the yard where cattle lie, to be trodden down by them for the purpose of making manure. Lowth renders this,

'As the straw is threshed under the wheels of the car.'

The LXX. render it in the same way. Lowth supposes that there has been an error in transcribing the Hebrew text, and that the former reading was מרכבה instead of מדמנה. But there is not the slightest evidence from the MSS. that any such mistake has occurred. Nor is it necessary to suppose it. The image is one that is not of unfrequent occurrence in the Scriptures, to denote the complete and disgraceful prostration of an enemy (see Ps. lxxxiii. 10; 2 Kings ix. 37; Jer. viii. 2; ix. 22; xvi. 4; xxv. 33).

11. *And he shall spread forth his hands.* The sense is, that JEHOVAH would stretch out his hands everywhere, prostrating his enemies, and the enemies of his people. Lowth, however, applies this to Moab, and supposes that it is designed to represent the action of one who is in danger of sinking, and who, in swimming, stretches out his hands to sustain himself. In order to this, he supposes that there should be a slight alteration of a single letter in the Hebrew. His main reason for suggesting this change is, that he cannot conceive how the act of the stretch-

12 And the fortress of the high fort of thy walls shall he bring down, lay low, *and* bring to the ground, *even* to the dust.

CHAPTER XXVI.

ANALYSIS.

FOR the general scope and design of this chapter, see the remarks at the commencement of ch. xxiv. and xxv. It is a song of praise supposed to be sung by the Jews on their return to their own land, and in the re-establishment of the government of God with the ordinances of worship on Mount Zion. It was usual, as has been already remarked, to celebrate any great event with a song of praise, and the prophet supposes that the recovered Jews would thus be disposed to celebrate the goodness of JEHOVAH in again restoring them to their own land, and to the privileges of their own temple service. There are some indications that this was designed to be sung with a chorus, and with alternate responses, as many of the Psalms were. The ode opens with a view of Jerusalem as a strong city, in which they might find protection under the guardianship of God (1). Then there is a response, or a call, that the gates of the strong city should be open to receive the return-

ing nation (2). This is followed by a declaration of the safety of trusting in JEHOVAH, and a call on all to confide in him (3, 4). The reason of this is stated (5–7), that JEHOVAH humbled the proud, and guarded the ways of the just. The confidence of the Jews in JEHOVAH is next described (8, 9); and this is followed by a declaration (10, 11) that the wicked would not recognize the hand of God; and by an assertion that all their deliverance had been wrought by God (12). This is succeeded by an acknowledgment that they had submitted to other lords than JEHOVAH; but that now they would submit to him alone (13, 14). The declaration succeeds that God had enlarged their nation (15); and this is followed by a description of their calamities, and their abortive efforts to save themselves (16–18). Many had died in their captivity, yet there is now the assurance that they should live again (19); and a general call on the people of God to enter into their chambers, and hide themselves there until the indignation should be overpast (20), with the assurance that JEHOVAH would come forth to punish the oppressors for their iniquity (21). With this assurance the poem closes.

IN that day shall this song be sung in the land of Judah ; We

out of the hands of a swimmer can be any illustration of the action of God in extending his hands over Moab to destroy it. It must be admitted that the figure is one that is very unusual. Indeed it does not anywhere else occur. But it is the obvious meaning of the Hebrew text ; it is so understood in the Vulgate, the Chaldee, the Syriac, and the figure is one that is not unintelligible. It is that of a swimmer who extends his hands and arms as far as possible, and who by force removes all that is in his way in passing through the water. So JEHOVAH would extend his hands over all Moab. He would not confine the desolation to any one place, but it would be complete and entire. He would subject all to himself, as easily as a swimmer makes his way through the waters. ¶ *With the spoils of their hands.* The word here rendered 'spoils' (אָרְבֹת), Lowth renders, ' The sudden gripe.' The Chaldee renders it substantially in the same manner, 'With the laying on of his hands,' *i.e.*, with all his might. Kim-

chi also understands it of the gripe of the hands or the arms. The LXX. render it, ' Upon whatsoever he lays his hands,' *i.e.*, God shall humble the pride of Moab in respect to everything on which he shall lay his hands. The word properly and usually signifies *snares, ambushes, craft;* and then, by a natural metonymy, the plunder or spoils which he had obtained by snares and ambushes—which seems to be the sense here. It would all perish with Moab, and the land would thus be completely subdued.

12. *And the fortress,* &c. Thy strong defences shall be destroyed. This is spoken of Moab (comp. Notes on ch. xv., xvi.), and is designed to be emblematic of the enemies of the people of God (comp. Notes on ch. xxxiv.) The *repetition* of the expressions ' bring down,' ' lay low,' and ' bring to the ground,' is designed to make the sentence emphatic, and to indicate that it would certainly be accomplished.

CHAPTER XXVI.

1. *In that day shall this song be*

have a strong *a* city ; salvation will God appoint *for* walls *b* and bulwarks.

2 Open *c* ye the gates, that the

a Ps. 31.21.   *b* ch.60.18.   *c* Ps.118.19.
1 *truths.*   2 *peace, peace.*   *d* Ph.4.7.

righteous nation which keepeth the truth 1 may enter in.

3 Thou wilt keep *him* 2 in perfect peace, *d whose* 3 mind *is* stayed *on thee :* because he trusteth in thee.

3 or, *thought,* or, *imagination.*

---

sung. By the people of God, on their restoration to their own land. ¶ *We have a strong city.* Jerusalem. This does not mean that it was then strongly fortified, but that God would guard it, and that thus it would be strong. Jerusalem was easily capable of being strongly fortified (Ps. xxv. 2) ; but the idea here is, that Jehovah would be a protector, and that this would constitute its strength. ¶ *Salvation will* God *appoint* for *walls*. That is, he will himself be the defender of his people in the place of walls and bulwarks. A similar expression occurs in ch. lx. 18 (see also Jer. iii. 23, and Zech. ii. 5). ¶ *Bulwarks.* This word means properly bastions, or ramparts. The original means properly a *pomœrium*, or antemural defence ; a space without the wall of a city raised up like a small wall. The Syriac renders it, *Bar shuro*, —' Son of a wall,' meaning a small wall. It was usually a breastwork, or heap of earth thrown up around the city, that constituted an additional defence, so that if they were driven from that they could retreat within the walls.

2. *Open ye the gates.* This is probably the language of a chorus responding to the sentiment in ver. 1. The captive people are returning ; and this cry is made that the gates of the city may be thrown open, and that they may be permitted to enter without obstruction (comp. Ps. xxiv. 7, 9 ; cxviii. 19). ¶ *That the righteous nation which keepeth the truth.* Who, during their long captivity and intercourse with heathen nations, have not apostatized from the true religion, but have adhered firmly to the worship of the true God. This was doubtless true of the great body of the captive Jews in Babylon.

3. *Thou wilt keep* him. The following verses to ver. 11, contain moral and religious reflections, and seem designed to indicate the resignation

evinced by the ' righteous nation ' during their long afflictions. Their own feelings they are here represented as uttering in the form of *general truths* to be sources of consolation to others. ¶ *In perfect peace.* Heb. as in the Marg., ' Peace, peace ;' the repetition of the word denoting, as is usual in Hebrew, emphasis, and here evidently meaning undisturbed, perfect peace. That is, the mind that has confidence in God shall not be agitated by the trials to which it shall be subject ; by persecution, poverty, sickness, want, or bereavement. The inhabitants of Judea had been borne to a far distant land. They had been subjected to reproaches and to scorn (Ps. cxxxvii.) ; had been stripped of their property and honour ; and had been reduced to the condition of prisoners and captives. Yet their confidence in God had not been shaken. They still trusted in him ; still believed that he could and would deliver them. Their mind was, therefore, kept in entire peace. So it was with the Redeemer when he was persecuted and maligned (1 Pet. ii. 23 ; comp. Luke xxiii. 46). And so it has been with tens of thousands of the confessors and martyrs, and of the persecuted and afflicted people of God, who have been enabled to commit their cause to him, and amidst the storms of persecution, and even in the prison and at the stake, have been kept in perfect peace. ¶ *Whose mind is stayed* on thee. Various interpretations have been given of this passage, but our translation has probably hit upon the exact sense. The word which is rendered ' mind ' (יֵצֶר) is derived from יָצַר (*yâtzăr*) *to form, create, devise ;* and it properly denotes that which *is* formed or made (Ps. ciii. 14 ; Isa. xxix. 16, Heb. ii. 18). Then it denotes anything that is formed by the mind — its thoughts, imaginations, devices (Gen. viii. 21 ; Deut. xxxi. 21). Here it may

4 Trust *a* ye in the LORD for
ever: *b* for in the LORD JEHOVAH
is ¹ everlasting strength.

5 For he bringeth down them
that dwell on high ; the lofty city,
he layeth it low ; he layeth it low,

a Ps.62.8.　　*b* Ps.125.1.　　¹ *the rock of ag. s.*

even to the ground ; he bringeth it
even to the dust.

6 The foot *c* shall tread it down,
even the feet of the poor, *and* the
steps of the needy.

7 The way *d* of the just *is* upright-

c Mal.4.3.　　　　*d* Ep.2.10.

mean the *thoughts* themselves, or the
mind that forms the thoughts. Either
interpretation suits the connection, and
will make sense. The expression, ' is
stayed on thee,' in the Hebrew does
not express the idea that the mind is
stayed *on God*, though that is evidently
implied. The Hebrew is simply, whose
mind is *stayed, supported* (סָמוּךְ) ; that
is, evidently, supported by God. There
is no other support but that ; and the
connection requires us to understand
this of him.

4. *Trust ye in the Lord for ever.*
The sense is, ' Let your confidence in
God on no occasion fail. Let no calamity, no adversity, no persecution, no
poverty, no trial of any kind, prevent
your reposing entire confidence in him.'
This is spoken evidently in view of the
fact stated in the previous verse, that
the mind that is stayed on him *shall*
have perfect peace. ¶ *For in the* LORD
JEHOVAH. This is one of the four
places where our translators have retained the original word JEHOVAH
(comp. Ex. vi. 3 ; Ps. lxxxiii. 18 ; Notes
on Isa. xii. 2). The original is יְהוָה
בְּיָהּ (BeJah Jehovah) ; the first word,
יָהּ (Jah), (comp. Ps. lxviii. 4), being
merely an abridged form of Jehovah.
The same form occurs in ch. xii. 2.
The *union* of these two forms seems
designed to express, in the highest sense
possible, the majesty, glory, and holiness of God ; to excite the highest
possible reverence where language fails
of completely conveying the idea. ¶ Is
everlasting strength. Heb. as in the
Marg., ' The rock of ages ;' a more
poetic and beautiful expression than in
our translation. The idea is, that God
is firm and unchangeable like an eternal
rock ; and that in him we may find
protection and defence for everlasting
ages (see Deut. xxxii. 4, *et al.* ; 1 Sam.
ii. 2 ; 2 Sam. xxii. 32, 47 ; xxiii. 3 ;

Ps. xviii. 31 ; xix. 14 ; xxviii. 1 ; xlii. 9 ;
lxii. 2, 6, 7, &c., where God is called
' a rock').

5. *The lofty city, he layeth it low.*
The city of Babylon (see Note on ch.
xxv. 12 ; comp. Notes on ch. xiii., xiv.)

6. *The foot shall tread it down,* even
the feet of the poor. That is, evidently,
those who had been despised by them,
and who had been overcome and oppressed by them. The obvious reference here is to the Jews who had been
captives there. The idea is not necessarily that the ' poor ' referred to here
would be among the conquerors, but
that *when* the Babylonians should be
overcome, and their city destroyed,
those who were then oppressed should
be in circumstances of comparative
prosperity. No doubt the Jews, who
in subsequent times travelled to the
site of Babylon for purposes of traffic,
would trample indignantly on the remains of the city where their fathers
were captives for seventy years, and
would exult in the idea that their own
once down-trodden city Jerusalem was
in a condition of comparative prosperity.
That there were many Jews in Babylon
after that city began to decline from its
haughtiness and grandeur, we learn
expressly from both Philo and Josephus.
Thus Philo (*De Legatione ad Caium*,
p. 792) says, that ' it is known that
Babylon and many other satraps were
possessed by the Jews, not only by
rumour, but by experience.' So Josephus
(*Ant.* xv. 2.) says, that there were in
the time of Hyrcanus many Jews at
Babylon.

7. *The way of the just* is *uprightness.* The Hebrew is literally, ' The
way *to* the just is uprightness ;' the
word ' way ' probably refers to God's
way, or his dealings with the righteous. The sentiment is, that his dealings with them are just ; that though
they are afflicted and oppressed, yet that

ness : ᵃthou, most upright, dost weigh the path of the just.

8 Yea, in the way of thy ᵇ judgments, O Lord, have we waited for thee ; the desire ᶜof our soul is to thy name, and to the remembrance of thee.

a Ps.37.23.	b Ps.65.6.	c Ps.63.1,6.

9 With my soul have I desired thee in the night ; ᵈyea, with my spirit within me will I seek thee early ; for when ᵉthy judgments are in the earth, the inhabitants of the world will learn righteousness.

d Ca.3.1.	e Ps.58.11.

his ways are right, and they will yet perceive it. This is language supposed to be used by the captive Jews after they had seen the proud city of Babylon taken, and after God had come forth to restore them to their own land. The word 'uprightness' in the original is in the plural number, but is often used in the sense of *straightness* (Prov. xxiii. 31; Cant. vii. 10) ; of sincerity, or uprightness (Cant. i. 4) ; or of righteousness as a judge (Ps. ix. 9 ; lviii. 2 ; xcix. 4). ¶ *Thou most upright.* Evidently an address to God, as being most just, and as having now evinced his uprightness in the deliverance of his people. The same epithet is applied to him in Deut. xxxii. 4 ; Ps. xxv. 8; xcii. 16. ¶ *Dost weigh the path of the just.* The word here used (פָּלַס) may mean to weigh as in a balance (Ps. lviii. 3) ; but it may also mean, and does usually, to make straight or smooth ; to beat a path ; to make level (Ps. lxxviii. 50; Prov. iv. 26; v. 21). Here it probably means, that God had made the way smooth, or exactly level. He had removed all obstacles, and had conducted his people in a plain and levelled way (see Notes on ch. xl. 3, 4).

8. *Yea, in the way of thy judgments.* The word 'judgments' often refers to the statutes or laws of God. But it may also refer to the afflictions and trials with which he visits or judges men ; the punishments which they endure for their sins. In which sense the word is used here it is not easy to determine. Lowth understands it of the 'laws' of Jehovah. So Kimchi, who says that the sense is, that during their captivity and trials, they had not remitted anything of their love and piety towards God. I am inclined to the belief that this is the true interpretation, because in the corresponding member of the parallelism they are

represented as saying that the desire of their soul was to God, and to the remembrance of him, implying that they sought by an observance of his laws to please him, and to secure his favour. ¶ *The desire of our soul is to thy name.* The word 'name' is here used, as it is often, to denote God himself. They desired that he would come and deliver them ; they earnestly wished that he would manifest himself to them as their friend. ¶ *And to the remembrance of thee.* The word 'remembrance' (זֵכֶר) is often equivalent to *name, appellation,* or that by which any one is remembered, or known. Thus Ex. iii. 15 :

This is my name for ever;
And this is my memorial זִכְרִי unto all generations.

So Ps. xxx. 4 :

Sing unto Jehovah, O ye saints of his;
And give thanks at the remembrance of his holiness;

that is, at his holy memorial (Marg.) or name. In the place before us it seems to be used in the sense of *name* or *appellation ;* that is, that by which God would be remembered or known.

9. *With my soul—in the night.* By desiring God in the night, and by seeking him early, is meant that the desire to seek him was unremitted and constant. The prophet speaks of the pious Jews who were in captivity in Babylon ; and says that it was the object of their unremitted anxiety to please God, and to do his will. ¶ *For when thy judgments* are *in the earth.* This is given as a reason for what had just been said, that in their calamity they had sought God without ceasing. The reason is, that the punishments which he inflicted were intended to lead men to learn righteousness. The sentiment is expressed in a general form, though there is no doubt that the immediate

10 Let *a* favour be shewed to the wicked, *yet* will he not learn righteousness : in *b* the land of uprightness will he deal unjustly, and will not behold the majesty *c* of the LORD.

a Ec.8.11; Re.2.21.　*b* Ec.3.16.　*c* ch.2.10.　*d* Je.5.3.

11 LORD, *when* thy hand is lifted up, they *d* will not see : *but* they shall *e* see, and be ashamed for *their* envy ¹ at the people ; yea, the fire *f* of thine enemies shall devour them.

e Re.1.7.　1 or, *toward thy.*　*f* Da.3.22,25.

reference is to the calamities which the Jews had suffered in their removal to Babylon as a punishment for their sins. ¶ *Learn righteousness.* The design is to warn, to restrain, and to reform them. The immediate reference here was undoubtedly to the Jews, in whom this effect was seen in a remarkable manner in their captivity in Babylon. But it is also true of other nations ; and though the effect of calamity is not always to turn a people to God, or to make them permanently righteous, yet it restrains them, and leads them at least to an external reformation. It is also true in regard to nations as well as individuals, that they make a more decided advance in virtue and piety in days of affliction than in the time of great external prosperity (comp. Deut. vi. 11, 12).

10. *Let favour be showed to the wicked.* This is designed as an illustration of the sentiment in the previous verse —that judgments were needful in order that wicked men might be brought to the ways of righteousness. The truth is general, that though wicked men are favoured with success in their enterprises, yet the effect will not be to lead them to the ways of virtue and religion. How often is this illustrated in the conduct of wicked men ! How often do they show, when rolling in wealth, or when surrounded with the comforts of the domestic circle, that they feel no need of the friendship of God, and that their heart has no response of gratitude to make for all his mercies ! Hence the necessity, according to the language of the song before us, that God should take away their property, remove their friends, or destroy their health, in order that they may be brought to honour him. To do this, is benevolence in God ; for whatever is needful to bring the sinner to the love of God and to the ways of virtue, is kindness to his soul. ¶ *In*

the land of uprightness. Even when others are just and pious around him ; when this is so much the general characteristic that it may be called ' the land of integrity,' yet he will pursue his way of iniquity, though in it he may be solitary. Such is his love of sin, that neither the favour of God nor the general piety around him—neither the mercy of his Maker nor the influence of holy examples, will lead him in the way of piety and truth. ¶ *Will not behold the majesty of the* LORD. Will not see that which makes the Lord glorious in his dealings with men, so as to love and adore him. He is blind, and sees no evidence of loveliness in the character of God.

11. LORD, when *thy hand is lifted up.* This is an explanation of the sentiment expressed in the former verse. The lifting up of the hand here refers, doubtless, to the manifestations of the majesty and goodness of the Lord. ¶ *They will not see.* They are blind to all the exhibitions of power, mercy, and goodness. ¶ But *they shall see.* They shall yet be brought to recognize thy hand. They shall see thy favour towards thy children, and thy judgment on thy foes. The Divine dealings will be such that they shall be constrained to recognize him, and to acknowledge his existence and perfections. ¶ *And be ashamed.* Be confounded because they did not sooner recognize the Divine goodness. ¶ *For* their *envy at thy people.* The word ' their ' is not in the Hebrew, and the sense is, that they shall see the zeal of JEHOVAH in behalf of his people, and shall be ashamed that they did not sooner recognize his hand. The word rendered 'envy' (קִנְאַת) may mean envy (Eccl. iv. 4 ; ix. 6), but it more properly and frequently means *zeal, ardour* (2 Kings x. 16 ; Isa. ix. 6). ¶ *Yea, the fire of thine enemies shall devour them.* Or rather, ' Yea, the fire in regard to

12 LORD, thou wilt ordain peace for *a* us: for thou also hast **wrought** all our works [1] in us.

13 O LORD our God, *other* *b* lords beside thee have had dominion over us: *but* *c* by thee only will we make mention of thy name.

a ver.3.   1 or, *for.*

14 *They are* dead, they shall not live; *they are* deceased, they shall not rise: therefore hast thou visited and destroyed them, and made all their memory to perish.

15 Thou hast increased the nation, O LORD, thou hast increased

b 2 Ch.28.5,6; Ro.6.16-18.   *c* Ps.71,15,16.

---

thy enemies shall devour them.' The sense is, that when his people were delivered, his foes would be destroyed; his zeal for his people would also be connected with indignation against his foes. The deliverance of his people from Babylon, and the commencement of the downfall of that city, were simultaneous, and the cause was the same.

12. *Thou wilt ordain peace.* The word 'peace' here seems to stand opposed to the evils of various kinds which they had experienced in the captivity at Babylon; and to refer not only to peace, but also to prosperity, and to the continued Divine favour. ¶ *For thou hast wrought all our works in us.* Or rather, '*for* us' (לָֽנוּ). It is owing to thy hand that we are saved.

13. Other *lords beside thee have had dominion.* The allusion here is to the kings of Babylon who had subdued and oppressed them, and who in their long captivity had held them in subjection to their laws. ¶ But *by thee only will we make mention of thy name.* This may be better rendered, '*but* only thee, thy name will we henceforward commemorate.' The words 'by thee,' and 'thy name,' are put in apposition, and denote the same thing. The word 'make mention' (נַזְכִּיר) means literally to cause to be remembered; to commemorate; to celebrate. The idea is, that during their long captivity they had been subject to the dominion of other lords than JEHOVAH; but now that they were restored to their own land, they would acknowledge only JEHOVAH as their Lord, and would henceforward celebrate only his name.

14. They are *dead.* That is, the kings and tyrants to whom reference is made in ver. 13. The principal enemies of the Jews, who had oppressed them, were slain when Babylon was

taken by Cyrus (see Notes on ch. xiii., xiv.) ¶ *They shall not live.* They shall not again live, and be permitted to harass and enslave us. ¶ They are *deceased.* Heb. רְפָאִים—a name given to the *shades* or *manes* of the dead, from an idea that they were weak and powerless (see Notes on ch. xiv. 9, 10; comp. Ps. lxxxviii. 11; Prov. ii. 18; ix. 18; xxi. 16). The sense here is, that they had died and gone to the land of shades, and were now unable any more to reach or injure the people of God. ¶ *Therefore.* Or rather, *for;* the word לָכֵן being used evidently in the sense of *because that,* as in Gen. xxxviii. 26; Num. xi. 31; xiv. 13; Ps. xlii. 7; xlv. 3. The declaration that follows is given as the reason why they were dead, and incapable of again injuring or annoying them. ¶ *Hast thou visited,* &c. (see Note on ch. xxiv. 22.) The word 'visit' here is used in the sense of *to punish.* ¶ *And made all their memory to perish.* Hast blotted out their name; hast caused their celebrity to cease.

15. *Thou hast increased the nation.* That is, the Jewish nation (see Note on ch. ix. 3). The nation was not only enlarged by its regular increase of population, but many converts attended them on their return from Babylon, and probably many came in from surrounding nations on the rebuilding of their capital. ¶ *Thou hadst removed* it *far,* &c. Or rather, thou hast extended far all the borders of the land. The word rendered 'removed' (רָחַק) means usually to put far away, and here it may mean to put far away the borders or boundaries of the nation; that is, to extend them far. The word 'unto' is not in the original; and the phrase rendered 'ends of the earth,' may mean the borders, or boundaries of the land. The parallelism requires

the nation: thou art glorified: thou
hadst removed *it* far *unto* all the
ends of the earth.

16 LORD, in trouble *a* have they
visited thee, they poured out a
prayer[1] *when* thy chastening *was*
upon them.

17 Like as a woman with child,
that draweth near the time of her
delivery, is in pain, *and* crieth out

a Hos.5,15.   1 *secret speech.*

this construction, and it is indeed the
obvious one, and has been adopted by
Lowth and Noyes.

16. *Poured out a prayer.* Marg.
'Secret speech.' The Hebrew word צֻּן
means properly a whispering, mutter-
ing; and then a sighing, a calling for
help. This is the sense here. In their
calamity they sighed, and called on
God for help.

17. *Like as a woman with child,* &c.
This verse is designed to state their
griefs and sorrows during the time of
their oppression in Babylon. The
comparison here used is one that is
very frequent in the sacred writings to
represent any great suffering (see Ps.
xlviii. 6; Jer. vi. 24; xiii. 21; xxii. 23;
xlix. 24; l. 43; Mic. iv. 9, 10).

18. *We have been,* &c. This refers
to sorrows and calamities which they
had experienced in former times, when
they had made great efforts for deliverance, and when those efforts had
proved abortive. Perhaps it refers to
the efforts of this kind which they had
made during their painful captivity of
seventy years. There is no direct
proof, indeed, that during that time
they attempted to revolt, or that they
organized themselves for resistance to
the Babylonish power; but there can
be no doubt that they earnestly desired
deliverance, and that their condition
was one of extreme pain and anguish
—a condition that is strikingly represented here by the pains of childbirth.
Nay, it is not improbable that during
that long period there may have been
abortive efforts made at deliverance,
and that here they refer to those efforts
as having accomplished nothing. ¶ *We
have as it were brought forth wind.*
Our efforts have availed nothing. Mi-

in her pangs; so have we been in
thy sight, O LORD.

18 We have been with child, we
have been in pain, we have as it
were brought forth wind; we have
not wrought any deliverance in the
earth, neither have the inhabitants
of the world fallen.

19 Thy dead *men* shall live,
together with my dead body shall
they arise.   Awake and sing, ye

chaelis, as quoted by Lowth, explains
this figure in the following manner:
' Rariorem morbum describi, empneu-
matosin, aut ventosam molam dictum;
quo quæ laborant diu et sibi, et peritis
medicis gravidæ videntur, tandemque
post omnes veræ gravitatis molestias
et labores ventum ex utero emittant;
quem morbum passim describunt me-
dici.'—(*Syntagma Comment.* vol. ii. p.
165.) Grotius thinks that the reference is to birds, ' Quæ edunt ova sub-
ventanea,' and refers to Pliny x. 58.
But the correct reference is, doubtless,
that which is mentioned by Michaelis.
¶ *Neither have the inhabitants of the
world fallen.* We had no power to
subdue them; and notwithstanding all
our exertions their dominion was unbroken. This refers to the Babylonians
who had dominion over the captive
Jews.

19. *Thy dead* men *shall live.* Very
various interpretations have been given
of this verse, which may be seen at
length by comparing Vitringa, Rosenmüller, Gesenius, and Poole's *Synopsis.*
In ver. 14, the chorus is represented as
saying of the dead men and tyrants of
Babylon that had oppressed the captive
Jews, that they should not rise, and
should no more oppress the people of
God. In contradistinction from this
fate of their enemies, the choir is
here introduced as addressing JEHOVAH
(comp. ver. 16), and saying ' THY dead
shall live;' that is, thy people shall
live again; shall be restored to vigour,
and strength, and enjoyment. They
had been dead; that is, *civilly* dead in
Babylon; they were cut off from their
privileges, torn away from their homes,
made captives in a foreign land. Their
king had been dethroned; their temple

that *a* dwell in dust; for thy dew

a Dan. 12.2.

is as the dew of herbs, and the earth shall cast out the dead.

demolished; their princes, priests, and people made captive; their name blotted from the list of nations; and to all intents and purposes, as a people, they were *deceased.* This figure is one that is common, by which the loss of privileges and enjoyments, and especially of civil rights, is represented as *death.* So we speak now of a man's being dead in law; dead to his country; spiritually dead; dead in sins. I do not understand this, therefore, as referring primarily to the doctrine of the resurrection of the dead; but to the captives in Babylon, who were civilly dead, and cut off by their oppressors from their rights and enjoyments as a nation. ¶ *Shall live.* Shall be restored to their country, and be reinstated in all their rights and immunities as a people among the nations of the earth. This restoration shall be as striking as would be the resurrection of the dead from their graves. Though, therefore, this does not refer primarily to the resurrection of the dead, yet the illustration is drawn from that doctrine, and implies that that doctrine was one with which they were familiar. An image which is employed for the sake of illustration must be one that is familiar to the mind, and the reference here to this doctrine is a demonstration that the doctrine of the resurrection was well known. ¶ *Together with my dead body shall they arise.* The words 'together with' are not in the original. The words rendered 'my dead body' (וּבְלָתִי) literally means, 'my dead body,' and may be applied to a man, or to a beast (Lev. v. 2; vii. 24). It is also applied to the dead in general; to the deceased; to carcasses, or dead bodies (see Lev. xi. 11; Ps. lxxix. 2; Jer. vii. 33; ix. 22; xvi. 18; xxvi. 23; xxxiv. 20). It may, therefore, be rendered, 'My deceased, my dead;' and will thus be parallel with the phrase 'thy dead men,' and is used with reference to the same species of resurrection. It is not the language of the prophet Isaiah, as if he referred to *his* own body when it should be

dead, but it is the language of the *choir* that sings and speaks in the name of the Jewish people. *That people* is thus introduced as saying *my* dead, that is, *our* dead, shall rise. Not only in the address to JEHOVAH is this sentiment uttered when it is said '*thy* dead shall rise,' but when the attention is turned to themselves as a people, they say '*our* dead shall rise;' those that appertain to our nation shall rise from the dust, and be restored to their own privileges and land. ¶ *Awake and sing.* In view of the cheering and consolatory fact just stated that the dead shall rise, the chorus calls on the people to awake and rejoice. This is an address made directly to the dejected and oppressed people, as if the choir were with them. ¶ *Ye that dwell in dust.* To sit in dust, or to dwell in the dust, is emblematic of a state of dejection, want, oppression, or poverty (Ps. xliv. 25; cxix. 25; Isa. xxv. 12; xxvi. 5; xlvii. 1). Here it is supposed to be addressed to the captives in Babylon, as oppressed, enslaved, dejected. The *language* is derived from the doctrine of the resurrection of the body, and proves that that doctrine was understood and believed; the *sense* is, that those who were thus dejected and humbled should be restored to their former elevated privileges. ¶ *For thy dew.* This is evidently an address to JEHOVAH. *His* dew is that which he sends down from heaven, and which is under his direction and control. Dew is the emblem of that which refreshes and vivifies. In countries where it rains but seldom, as it does in the East, the copious dews at night supply in some sense the want of rain. Thence *dew* is used in Scripture as an emblem of the graces and influences of the Spirit of God by which his people are cheered and comforted, as the parched earth and the withered herbs are refreshed by the copious dews at night. Thus in Hos. xiv. 5:

I will be as the dew unto Israel;
He shall grow as the lily,
And cast forth his roots as Lebanon.

The prophet here speaks of the captivity in Babylon. Their state is repre-

20 Come, my people, enter thou into thy chambers, and shut thy doors about thee : hide thyself as it were for a little moment, until the indignation be overpast.

21 For, behold, the LORD cometh out *a* of his place to punish the inhabitants of the earth for their iniquity : the earth also shall disclose her [1] blood, and shall no more cover her slain.

a Jude 14,15.   1 *bloods.*

---

sented as a state of death—illustrated by the parched earth, and the decayed and withered herbs. But his grace and favour would visit them, and they would be revived. ¶ As *the dew of herbs.* As the dew that falls on herbs. This phrase has, however, been rendered very variously. The Vulgate renders it, 'Thy dew is as the dew of light.' The LXX. 'Thy dew shall be healing (*ἴαμα*) unto them.' The Chaldee, 'Thy dew shall be the dew of light.' But the most correct and consistent translation is undoubtedly that which renders the word אֹרֹת, *herbs* or *vegetables* (comp. 2 Kings ix. 19). ¶ *And the earth shall cast out the dead.* This is language which is derived from the doctrine of the resurrection of the body ; and shows also that that doctrine was understood by the Hebrews in the time of Isaiah. The sense is, that as the earth shall cast forth its dead in the resurrection, so the people of God in Babylon should be restored to life, and to their former privileges in their own land.

20. *Come, my people.* This is an *epilogue* (Rosenmüller), in which the choir addresses the people, and entreats them to be tranquil during that convulsion by which their oppressors would be punished, and the way made for their deliverance. The image is taken from seeking a shelter when a storm rages, until its fury is spent. The address is to the captive Jews in Babylon. The tempest that would rage would be the wars and commotions by which Babylon was to be overthrown. While that storm raged, *they* were exhorted to be calm and serene. ¶ *Enter thou into thy chambers.* Into places of retirement, where the storm of indignation on your enemies shall not reach or affect you. ¶ *Hide thyself as it were, &c.* Do not mingle in the scenes of battle, lest you should partake of the general calamity. ¶ *For a little mo-*

ment. Implying that the war would not rage long. Babylon was taken in a single night (see Notes on ch. xiii., xiv.), and the call here is for the people of God to be calm while this battle should rage in which the city should be taken. ¶ *Until the indignation, &c.* Not, as Lowth supposes, the indignation of God against his people, but the storm of his indignation against their enemies the Babylonians. That would be soon 'overpast,' the city would be taken, the storms of war would cease to rage, and *then* they would be delivered, and might safely return to their own land.

21. *For, behold, the LORD cometh out of his place.* That is, from heaven, which is the dwelling-place or residence of God (Ps. cxv. 3 ; Ezek. iii. 12 ; Mic. i. 3). When God executes vengeance, he is represented as coming from his abode, his dwelling-place, his capitol, as a monarch goes forth to war to destroy his foes. ¶ *To punish the inhabitants of the earth.* The land of Chaldea, or of Babylon. ¶ *The earth also shall disclose her blood.* Blood, in the Scriptures, often denotes *guilt.* The sense here is, that the land of Chaldea would reveal its guilt ; that is, the punishment which God would inflict would be a revelation of the crimes of the nation. There is a resemblance here to the language which was used respecting the blood of Abel, Gen. iv. 10 : 'The voice of thy brother's blood (Heb. as here, *bloods*) crieth unto me from the ground.' ¶ *And shall no more cover her slain.* Shall no more be able to conceal its guilt in slaying the people of God. By these hopes, the Jews were to be comforted in their calamity ; and no doubt this song was penned by Isaiah long before that captivity, in order that, in the midst of their protracted and severe trials, they might be consoled with the hope of deliverance, and might know what to

CHAPTER XXVII.

ANALYSIS.

For the general design of this chapter, see the analysis of ch. xxiv. Many different expositions have been given of its design, and indeed almost every commentator has had his own theory, and has differed from almost every other. Some of the different views which have been taken may be seen in the Notes on ver. 1, and may be examined at length in Vitringa. I regard the most simple and obvious interpretation as the correct one; and that is, that it is a continuation of the vision commenced in ch. xxiv., and referring to the same great event—the captivity at Babylon and the deliverance from that captivity. This subject has been pursued through the 24th, the 25th, and the 26th chapters. In the 25th and the 26th chapters, the main design was to show the joy which would be evinced on their rescue from that land. The main purpose of this is to show the effect of that captivity and deliverance in purifying the Jews themselves, and in overcoming their propensity to idolatry, on account of which the captivity had been suffered to take place. The *design* of the chapter is, like that of many others in Isaiah, to comfort

them when they should be oppressed during their long and painful exile. The general plan of the chapter is—1. A statement that their great enemy, the leviathan, should be destroyed (1); and, 2. A song, in alternate responses, respecting the people of God, under the image of a vineyard yielding rich wines (2–13). In this song Jehovah's protection over the vineyard is shown (3); he declares that he is not actuated by fury (4); his people are exhorted to trust in him (5); a full promise that the Jews shall yet flourish is given (6); Jehovah says that his judgments are mild on them (7, 8), and that the design is to purify his people (9); for their sins they should be punished (10, 11); yet that they should be restored to their own land, and worship him in the holy mount at Jerusalem (12, 13).

IN that day the Lord, with his sore, and great, and strong sword, shall punish leviathan *a* the piercing 1 serpent, even leviathan that crooked serpent; and he shall slay the dragon that *is* in the sea.

a Ps.74.14.　　　1 or, *crossing like a bar.*

CHAPTER XXVII.

1. *In that day.* In that future time when the Jews would be captive in Babylon, and when they would sigh for

do when the storms of war should rage around the place of their captivity, and when the proud city was to fall. They were not to mingle in the strife; were to take no part with either their foes or their deliverers; but were to be calm, gentle, peaceful, and to remember that all this was to effect their deliverance. Compare Ex. xiv. 13, 14: 'Fear ye not, stand still, and see the salvation of Jehovah; Jehovah shall fight for you, and ye shall hold your peace.'—There are times when the children of God should look calmly on the conflicts of the men of this world. They should mingle with neither party; for they should remember that Jehovah presides over these agitations, and that their ultimate end is to bring deliverance to his church, and to advance the interests of his kingdom on the earth. Then they should be mild, gentle, prayerful; and should look up to God to make all these agitations and strifes the means of advancing the interests of his kingdom.

deliverance (see Note on ch. xxvi. 1). This verse might have been connected with the previous chapter, as it refers to the same event, and then this chapter would have more appropriately commenced with the poem or song which begins in ver. 2. ¶ *With his sore.* Heb. הַקָּשָׁה—'Hard.' Sept. Τὴν ἁγίαν—'Holy.' The Hebrew means a sword that is hard, or well-tempered and trusty. ¶ *And great, and strong sword.* The sword is an emblem of war, and is often used among the Hebrews to denote war (see Gen. xxvii. 40; Lev. xxvi. 25). It is also an emblem of justice or punishment, as punishment then, as it is now in the Turkish dominions, was often inflicted by the sword (Deut. iii. 41, 42; Ps. vii. 12; Heb. xi. 37). Here, if it refers to the overthrow of Babylon and its tyrannical king, it means that God would punish them by the armies of the Medes, employed as his sword or instrument. Thus in Ps. xvii. 13, David prays, 'Deliver my soul from the wicked, which is thy sword' (comp. Notes on ch. x. 5, 6). ¶ *Leviathan* (לִוְיָתָן). The LXX. render this, Τὸν δράκοντα—'The dragon.' The word 'leviathan' is probably derived from לָוָה in Arabic, *to weave, to twist* (Gesenius); and literally means, *the twisted animal*. The word occurs in six places in the Old Testament, and is translated in Job iii. 8, 'mourning,' Marg. 'leviathan;' in Job xli. 1, 'leviathan'—in which chapter is an extended description of the animal; in Ps. lxxiv. 14, it is rendered 'leviathan,' and seems to be applied to Pharaoh; and in Ps. civ. 26, and in the passage before us, where it is twice also rendered 'leviathan.' Bochart (*Hieroz.* ii. 5. 16–18) has gone into an extended argument to show that by the leviathan the *crocodile* is intended; and his argument is in my view conclusive. On this subject, Bochart, Dr. Good (on Job xli.), and Robinson's Calmet, may be consulted. The crocodile is a natural inhabitant of the Nile and of other Asiatic and African rivers; is of enormous voracity and strength, as well as of fleetness in swimming; attacks mankind and all animals with prodigious impetuosity; and is furnished with a coat of mail so scaly and callous that it will resist the force of a musket ball in every part except under the belly. It is, there-

CROCODILE.

fore, an appropriate image by which to represent a fierce and cruel tyrant. The sacred writers were accustomed to describe kings and tyrants by an allusion to strong and fierce animals. Thus, in Ezek. xxix. 3–5, the dragon, or the crocodile of the Nile, represents Pharaoh; in Ezek. xxii. 2, Pharaoh is compared to a young lion, and to a whale in the seas; in Ps. lxxiv. 13, 14, Pharaoh is compared to the dragon, and to the leviathan. In Dan. vii., the four monarchs that should arise

are likened to four great beasts. In Rev. xii., Rome, the new Babylon, is compared to a great red dragon. In the place before us, I suppose that the reference is to Babylon; or to the king and tyrant that ruled there, and that had oppressed the people of God. But among commentators there has been the greatest variety of explanation. As a *specimen* of the various senses which commentators often assign to passages of Scripture, we may notice the following views which have been taken of this passage. The Chaldee Paraphrast regards the leviathans, which are twice mentioned, as referring, the first one to some king like Pharaoh, and the second to a king like Sennacherib. Rabbi Moses Haccohen supposes that the word denotes the most select or valiant of the rulers, princes, and commanders that were in the army of the enemy of the people of God. Jarchi supposes that by the first-mentioned leviathan is meant Egypt, by the second Assyria, and by the dragon which is in the sea, he thinks *Tyre* is intended. Aben Ezra supposes that by the dragon in the sea, Egypt is denoted. Kimchi supposes that this will be fulfilled only in the times of the Messiah, and that the sea monsters here mentioned are Gog and Magog—and that these denote the armies of the Greeks, the Saracens, and the inhabitants of India. Abarbanel supposes that the Saracens, the Roman empire, and the other kingdoms of Gentiles, are intended by these sea monsters. Jerome, Sanctius, and some others suppose that *Satan* is denoted by the leviathan. Brentius supposes that this was fulfilled in the day of Pentecost when Satan was overcome by the preaching of the gospel. Other Christian interpreters have supposed, that by the leviathan first mentioned *Mahomet* is intended; by the second, *heretics ;* and by the dragon in the sea, *Pagan India.* Luther understood it of Assyria and Egypt; Calvin supposes that the description properly applies to the king of Egypt, but that under this image other enemies of the church are embraced, and does not doubt that *allegorically* Satan and his kingdom are intended. The more simple interpretation, however, is that which refers

2 In that day sing ye unto her, | A vineyard *a* of red wine.

a Lu.20.9,&c.

it to Babylon. This suits the connection; accords with the previous chapters; agrees with all that occurs in this chapter, and with the image which is here used. The crocodile, the dragon, the sea monster—extended, vast, unwieldy, voracious, and odious to the view—would be a most expressive image to denote the abhorrence with which the Jews would regard Babylon and its king. ¶ *The piercing serpent.* The term 'serpent' (נָחָשׁ) may be given to a dragon, or an extended sea monster. Comp. Job xxvi. 13. The term 'piercing,' is, in the Marg., 'Crossing like a bar.' The LXX. render it, Ὄφιν φεύγοντα—'Flying serpent. The Heb. בָּרִיחַ, rendered 'piercing,' is derived from בָּרַח, *to flee;* and then to stretch across, or pass through, as a bar through boards (Ex. xxxvi. 33). Hence this word may mean fleeing; extended; a cross bar for fastening gates; or the cross piece for binding together the boards for the tabernacle of the congregation (Ex. xxvi. 26; xxxvi. 31). Lowth renders it, 'The rigid serpent;' probably with reference to the hard scales of the crocodile. The word *extended, huge, vast,* will probably best suit the connection. In Job xxvi. 13, it is rendered, 'the crooked serpent;' referring to the constellation in the heavens by the name of the Serpent (see Notes on that place). The idea of *piercing* is not in the Hebrew word, nor is it ever used in that sense. ¶ *That crooked serpent.* This is correctly rendered; and refers to the fact that the monster here referred to throws itself into immense volumes or folds, a description that applies to all serpents of vast size. Virgil has given a similar description of sea monsters throwing themselves into vast convolutions:

'Ecce autem gemini a Tenedo tranquilla per alta —— immensis orbibus angues.'—*Æn.* ii. 203.

And again:

'Sinuantque immensa volumine terga.'
Idem. 208.

The reference in Isaiah, I suppose, is not to *different* kings or enemies of the people of God, but to the same. It is customary in Hebrew poetry to refer to the same subject in different members of the same sentence, or in different parts of the same parallelism. ¶ *The dragon.* Referring to the same thing under a different image—to the king of Babylon. On the meaning of the word 'dragon,' see Note on ch. xiii. 22. ¶ *In the sea.* In the Euphrates; or in the marshes and pools that encompass Babylon (see Notes on ch. xi. 15; xviii. 2). The sense of the whole verse is, that God would destroy the Babylonish power that was to the Jews such an object of loathsomeness and of terror.

2. *Sing ye unto her.* That is, sing unto, or respecting the vineyard. The word rendered 'sing' (עָנָה) signifies properly, *answer, respond to;* and then, sing a responsive song, where one portion of the choir responds to another (see Ex. xv. 21). This has been well expressed here by Lowth in his translation:

'To the beloved Vineyard, sing ye a responsive song.'

It is the commencement of a song, or hymn respecting Judea, represented under the image of a vineyard, and which is probably continued to the close of the chapter. ¶ *A vineyard* (see Notes on ch. v. 1, &c.) The Hebrew phrase rendered 'a vineyard of red wine' is the title to the song; or the responsive song respects the 'vineyard of red wine.' ¶ *Of red wine* (חֶמֶר, *hhĕmer*). Lowth proposes to read instead of this, חֶמֶד (*hhĕmedh*), *pleasantness, beauty,* or *beloved.* He observes that many MSS. have this meaning, and that it is followed by the LXX. and the Chaldee. The LXX. read it, Ἀμπελὼν καλλός—'Beautiful vineyard.' This would well suit the connection, and this slight error in transcribing might have easily occurred. But the authority in the MSS. for the change is not conclusive. The word which now occurs in the text denotes properly *wine,* from חָמַר, *to ferment.* The word חָמַר also has the signification *to be red* (Ps. lxxv. 9; Job

3 I *a* the LORD do keep it ; I will water it every moment ; lest *any* hurt it, I will keep it night and day.

4 Fury *is* not in me : who would set the briers *and* thorns against

me in battle ? I would [1] go through them, I would burn them together.

5 Or let him take hold of my strength, *b that* he may make peace *c* with me ; *and* he shall make peace with me.

a Ps.121.4,5.   1 or, *march against.*

b ch.45.24.   c Job 22.21.

xvi. 16); and according to this, our translators have rendered it ' of red wine.' Bochart (*Geog. Sac.* ii. 1, 29) renders it, ' A vineyard fertile in producing wine.' The correct translation would be one that would not seem very congruous in our language, ' a vineyard of wine,' or ' a wine-vineyard.'

3. *I the* LORD *do keep it.* There is understood here or implied an introduction ; as ' JEHOVAH said ' (comp. Ps. cxxi. 35). ¶ *I will water it every moment.* That is, constantly, as a vine-dresser does his vineyard.

4. *Fury* is *not in me.* That is, I am angry with it no more. He had punished his people by removing them to a distant land. But although he had corrected them for their faults, yet he had not laid aside the affection of a Father. ¶ *Who would set.* Heb. ' Who would give me.' The LXX. render this, ' Who would place me to keep the stubble in the field ? ' Great perplexity has been felt in regard to the interpretation of this passage. Lowth translates it :

' O that I had a fence of the thorn and the brier;'

evidently showing that he was embarrassed with it, and could not make of it consistent sense. The whole sentence must refer either to the people of God, or to his enemies. If to his people, it would be an indication that they were like briers and thorns, and that if his fury should rage they would be consumed, and hence he calls upon them (ver. 5) to seize upon his strength, and to be at peace with him. If it refers to his enemies, then it expresses a *wish* that his enemies were in his possession ; or a purpose to go against them, as fire among thorns, and to consume them if they should presume to array themselves against his vineyard. This latter I take to be the true sense of the passage. The phrase ' who would set me,' or in Heb. ' who will give me,' may be ex-

pressed by *utinam,* indicating strong desire ; and may be thus paraphrased : ' I retain no anger against my people. I have indeed punished them ; but my anger has ceased. I shall now defend them. If they are attacked by foes, I will guard them. When their foes approach, *I desire, I earnestly wish,* that they may be in my possession, that I may destroy them—as the fire rages through briers and thorns.' It expresses a firm determination to defend his people and to destroy their enemies, unless (ver. 5), which he would prefer, they should repent, and be at peace with him. ¶ *The briers* and *thorns.* His enemies, and the enemies of his people (comp. Notes on ch. ix. 17 ; x. 17). Perhaps the phrase is here used to denote enemies, because briers and thorns are so great enemies to a vineyard by impeding growth and fertility. ¶ *I would go through them.* Or, rather, I would go against them in battle to destroy them. ¶ *I would burn them up together.* As fire devours the thorns and briers ; that is, I would completely destroy them.

5. *Or let him.* The Hebrew word rendered here ' or ' (אוֹ) means *unless;* and the sense is, the enemies of the Jewish people shall be completely destroyed as briers are by fire, *unless* they flee to God for a refuge. ¶ *Take hold of my strength.* That is, let the enemy take hold of me to become reconciled to me. The figure here is taken probably from the act of fleeing to take hold of the horns of the altar for refuge when one was pursued (comp. 1 Kings i. 50 ; ii. 28) ¶ *That he may make peace with me.* With me as the guardian of the vineyard. If this were done they would be safe. ¶ *And he shall make peace with me.* That is, even the enemy of me and of my vineyard *may* be permitted to make peace with me. Learn, (1.) That God is willing to be reconciled to his enemies. (2.) That that peace

6 He shall cause them that come of Jacob to take root : *a* Israel shall blossom and bud, and *b* fill the face of the world with fruit.

7 Hath he smitten him, 1 as he smote those that smote him ? *or* is

a Ps.92.13-15; Hos.14.5,6.　　　*b* Rom.11.12.

1 *according to the stroke of.*

he slain according to the slaughter of them that are slain by him ?

8 In measure, when 2 it shooteth forth, thou wilt debate with it : he 3 stayeth his *c*rough wind in the day of the east wind.

2 or, *thou sendest it forth.*

3 or, *when he removeth it.*　　*c* ch.57.16.

---

must be obtained by seeking his protection ; by submitting to him, and laying hold of his strength. (3.) That if this is not done, his enemies must be inevitably destroyed. (4.) He will defend his people, and no weapon that is formed against them shall prosper.

6. *He shall cause them that come of Jacob to take root.* This language is derived from the vine, as the shoots or cuttings of the vine take root and flourish. To take root, therefore, is an emblem denoting that the descendants of Jacob, or the people of God, would increase and prosper. ¶ *Shall blossom and bud.* An image also taken from the vine, or from fruit trees in general, and meaning that they should greatly flourish in the time succeeding their return from the captivity. ¶ *And fill the face of the world with fruit.* On the meaning of the word 'face,' see Note on ch. xxv. 7. The sense is, that the people of God would so increase and flourish that the true religion would ultimately fill the entire world. The same idea of the universal prevalence of the true religion is often advanced by this prophet, and occurs in various parts of the hymns or songs which we are now considering (see ch. xxv. 6–8). The figure which is here used, drawn from the vine, denoting prosperity by its increase and its fruit, is beautifully employed in Ps. xcii. 13, 14 :

Those that be planted in the house of Jehovah,
Shall flourish in the courts of our God.
They shall still bring forth fruit in old age ;
They shall be rich and green.

7. *Hath he smitten him, as he smote those that smote them ?* Has God punished his people in the same manner and to the same extent as he has their enemies? It is implied by this question that he had not. He had indeed punished them for their sins, but he had not destroyed them. Their enemies

he had utterly destroyed. ¶ *According to the slaughter of those that are slain by him.* Heb. 'According to the slaying of his slain.' That is, not as our translation would seem to imply, that their enemies had been slain BY them ; but that they were '*their* slain,' inasmuch as they had been slain on their account, or to promote their release and return to their own land. It was not true that their enemies had been slain *by* them ; but it was true that they had been *slain on their account,* or in order to secure their return to their own country.

8. *In measure, &c.* This verse in our translation is exceedingly obscure, and indeed almost unintelligible. Nor is it much more intelligible in Lowth, or in Noyes ; in the Vulgate, or the Septuagint. The various senses which have been given to the verse may be seen at length in Vitringa and Rosenmüller. The idea, which I suppose to be the true one, without going into an examination of others which have been proposed, is the following, which is as near as possible a literal translation :

In moderation in sending her [the vineyard]
　　away didst thou judge her,
Though carrying her away with a rough tempest
　　in the time of the east wind.

The word rendered ' measure ' (כַּאסְאָה) occurs nowhere else in the Scriptures. It is probably derived from סְאָה, a *measure ;* usually denoting a measure of grain, containing, according to the Rabbins, a third part of an ephah, *i.e.,* about *a peck.* The word here used is probably a contraction of סְאָה סְאָה, literally, *measure by measure,* i.e., *moderately,* or in moderation. So the Rabbins generally understand it. The idea is ' small measure by small measure,' not a large measure at a time ; or, in other words, *moderately,* or in moderation. It refers, I suppose, to

9 By this therefore shall the iniquity of Jacob be purged; *a* and this *is* all the fruit to take away his sin; when he maketh all the stones of the altar as chalk stones that are beaten in sunder, the groves and [1] images shall not stand up.

10 Yet the defenced city *shall*

a Heb.12.6.   1 or, *sun images.*

the fact that in inflicting judgment on his people, it had not been done with intolerable severity. The calamity had not been so overwhelming as entirely to cut them off, but had been tempered with mercy. ¶ *When it shooteth forth.* This expression does not convey an intelligible idea. The Hebrew בְּשַׁלְחָהּ —literally, *in sending her forth*, from שָׁלַח *to send*, or *to put forth*—refers, I suppose, to the fact that God had sent her, *i.e.*, his vineyard, his people, forth to Babylon; he had cast them out of their own land into a distant country, but when it was done it was tempered with mercy and kindness. In this expression there is indeed a mingling of a metaphor with a literal statement, since it appears rather incongruous to speak of sending forth *a vineyard;* but such changes in expressions are not uncommon in the Hebrew poets. ¶ *Thou wilt debate with it.* Or, rather, thou hast *judged* it; or hast *punished* it. The word רִיב means sometimes to debate, contend, or strive; but it means also to take vengeance (1 Sam. xxv. 39), or to punish; to contend with any one so as to overcome or punish him. Here it refers to the fact that God *had* had a contention with his people, and had punished them by removing them to Babylon. ¶ *He stayeth* (הָגָה). This word means in one form *to meditate*, to think, to speak; in another, *to separate*, as dross from silver, to remove, to take away (Prov. xxv. 4, 5). Here it means that he *had* removed, or separated his people from their land as with the sweepings of a tempest. The word 'stayeth' does not express the true sense of the passage. It is better expressed in the margin, 'when he removeth it.' ¶ *His rough wind.* A tempestuous, boisterous wind, which God sends. Winds are emblematic of judgment, as they sweep away everything before them. Here the word is emblematic of the calamities which came upon Judea by which the nation was removed to

Babylon; and the sense is, that they were removed *as in* a tempest; they were carried away as if a violent storm had swept over the land. ¶ *In the day of the east wind.* The east wind in the climate of Judea was usually tempestuous and violent; Job xxvii. 21:

The east wind carrieth him away and he departeth;
And, as a storm, hurleth them out of his place.

Jer. xviii. 17:

I will scatter them as with an east wind before the enemy.

(Comp. Gen. xli. 6; Ex. x. 13; xiv. 21; Job xxxviii. 24; Ps. lxxviii. 26; Hab. i. 6). This wind was usually hot, noxious, blasting, and scorching (Taylor).

9. *By this.* This verse states the whole design of the punishment of the Jews. They were taken away from their temple, their city, and their land; they were removed from the groves and altars of idolatry by which they had been so often led into sin; and the design was to preserve them henceforward from relapsing into their accustomed idolatry. ¶ *The iniquity of Jacob.* The sin of the Jewish people, and particularly their tendency to idolatry, which was their easily besetting sin. ¶ *Be purged* (see Note on ch. i. 25). ¶ *And this is all the fruit.* And this is all the *object* or *design* of their captivity and removal to Babylon. ¶ *When he maketh all the stones of the altar as chalk stones.* That is, JEHOVAH shall make the stones of the altars reared in honour of idols like chalk stones; or shall throw them down, and scatter them abroad like stones that are easily beaten to pieces. The sense is, that JEHOVAH, during their captivity in Babylon, would overthrow the places where they had worshipped idols. ¶ *The groves and images shall not stand up.* The groves consecrated to idols, and the images erected therein (see Note on ch. xvii. 8).

10. *Yet the defenced city.* Gesenius supposes that this means Jerusalem. So Calvin and Piscator understand it.

be desolate, *and* the habitation forsaken, and left like a wilderness: there shall the calf feed, and there shall he lie down and consume the branches thereof.

11 When the boughs thereof are withered, they shall be broken off: the women come *and* set them on fire ; for *a* it *is* a people of no understanding : therefore he that made

them will not have mercy on them, and he that formed them will shew them no favour.

12 And it shall come to pass in that day, *that* the LORD shall beat off from the channel of the river unto the stream of Egypt, and *b* ye shall be gathered one by one, O ye children of Israel.

a De.32.28; Ho.4.6. b Jn.6.37.

Others understand it of Samaria, others of Babylon (as Vitringa, Rosenmüller, and Grotius), and others of cities in general, denoting those in Judea, or in other places. To me it seems plain that Babylon is referred to. The whole description seems to require this; and especially the fact that this song is supposed to be sung *after* the return from the captivity to celebrate their deliverance. It is natural, therefore, that they should record the fact that the strong and mighty city where they had been so long in captivity, was now completely destroyed. For the meaning of the phrase 'defenced city,' see Note on ch. xxv. 2. ¶ Shall be *desolate* (see ch. xxv. 2; comp. Notes on ch. xiii.) ¶ *The habitation forsaken.* The *habitation* here referred to is Babylon. It means the habitation or dwelling-place where *we* have so long dwelt as captives (comp. Prov. iii. 33; xxi. 20; xxiv. 15). ¶ *And left like a wilderness.* See the description of Babylon in the Notes on ch. xiii. 20–22. ¶ *There shall the calf feed.* It shall become a vast desert, and be a place for beasts of the forest to range in (comp. ch. vii. 23; see Note on ch. v. 17). ¶ *And consume the branches thereof.* The branches of the trees and shrubs that shall spring up spontaneously in the vast waste where Babylon was.

11. *When the boughs thereof are withered.* This is a further description of the desolation which would come upon Babylon. The idea is, that Babylon would be forsaken until the trees should grow and decay, and the branches should fall to be collected for burning. That is, the desolation should be entire, undisturbed, and long continued. The idea of the desolation is, therefore, in this verse carried forward, and a new

circumstance is introduced to make it more graphic and striking. Lowth, however, supposes that this refers to the vineyard, and to the fact that the vine-twigs are collected in the East from the scarcity of fuel for burning. But it seems to me that the obvious reference is to Babylon, and that it is an image of the great and prolonged desolation that was coming upon that city. ¶ *They shall be broken off.* That is, by their own weight as they decay, or by the hands of those who come to collect them for fuel. ¶ *The women come.* Probably it was the office mainly of the women to collect the fuel which might be necessary for culinary purposes. In eastern climates but little is needed; and that is collected of the twigs of vineyards, of withered stubble, straw, hay, dried roots, &c., wherever they can be found. ¶ And *set them on fire.* That is, to burn them for fuel. ¶ *Of no understanding.* Of no right views of God and his government— wicked, sinful (Prov. vi. 32; xviii. 2; Jer. v. 21).

12. *And it shall come to pass in that day,* that *the Lord shall beat off.* The word which is here used (חָבַט) means properly to beat off with a stick, as fruit from a tree (Deut. xx. 20). It also means to beat out grain with a stick (Judg. vi. 11; Ruth xi. 17). The word which is rendered in the other member of the sentence, 'shall be gathered' (לָקַט), is applied to the act of collecting fruit after it has been beaten from a tree, or grain after it has been threshed. The use of these words here shows that the image is taken from that of collecting fruit or grain after the harvest; and the expression means, that as the husbandman gathers in his fruit, so God would gather in his people. In the

13 And it shall come to pass in that day, *that* the great trumpet shall *a* be blown, and they shall come which were ready to perish in the land of Assyria, and the outcasts in the land of Egypt, and shall worship the LORD in the holy mount at Jerusalem.

CHAPTER XXVIII.

ANALYSIS.

THIS chapter comprises a new prophecy and

a Mat.24.31; 1 Thes.4.16; Rev.11.15.

figure, it is supposed that the garden or vineyard of JEHOVAH extends from the Euphrates to the Nile; that his people are scattered in all that country; that there shall be agitation or a shaking in all that region as when a farmer beats off his fruit from the tree, or beats out his grain; and that the result would be that all those scattered people would be gathered into their own land. The time referred to is, doubtless, after Babylon should be taken; and in explanation of the declaration it is to be remembered that the Jews were not only carried to Babylon, but were scattered in large numbers in all the adjacent regions. The promise here is, that from all those regions whither they had been scattered they should be re-collected and restored to their own land. ¶ *From the channel of the river.* The river here undoubtedly refers to the river Euphrates (see Note on ch. xi. 15). ¶ *Unto the stream of Egypt.* The Nile. ¶ *And ye shall be gathered one by one.* As the husbandman collects his fruits one by one—collecting them carefully, and not leaving any. This means that God will not merely collect them as a nation, but as *individuals.* He will see that none is overlooked, and that all shall be brought in safety to their land.

13. *The great trumpet shall be blown.* This verse is designed to describe in another mode the same fact as that stated in verse 12, that JEHOVAH would re-collect his scattered people. The figure is derived from the trumpet which was blown to assemble a people for war (Grotius); or from the blowing of the trumpet on occasion of the great feasts and festivals of the Jews (Vitringa). The idea is, that God would summon

relates to a new subject. Gesenius supposes that it is to be connected with the following to to the close of ch. xxxiii., and that they relate to the same subject, and were delivered at the same time. Munster supposes that the prophecy here commenced continues to the close of ch. xxxv., and that it relates to the Assyrian war in which the ten tribes were carried away captive. Dœderlin supposes that this chapter and the two following were uttered at the same time, and relate to the same subject; Hensler, that the prophecy closes at the 33d chapter.

It is not improbable that this chapter and the following were delivered at the same time, and the scattered people to return to their own land. The *way* in which this was done, or in which the will of God would be made known to them, is not specified. It is probable, however, that the reference here is to the decree of Cyrus (Ezra i. 1), by which they were permitted to return to their own country. ¶ *Which were ready to perish.* Who were reduced in numbers, and in power, and who were ready to be annihilated under their accumulated and long-continued trials. ¶ *In the land of Assyria.* The ten tribes were carried away into Assyria (2 Kings xvii. 6); and it is probable that many of the other two tribes were also in that land. A portion of the ten tribes would also be re-collected, and would return with the others to the land of their fathers. Assyria also constituted a considerable part of the kingdom of the Chaldeans, and the name Assyria may be given here to that country in general. ¶ *And the outcasts.* Those who had fled in consternation to Egypt and to other places when these calamities were coming upon the nation (see Jer. xli. 17, 18; xlii. 15–22). ¶ *And shall worship the LORD.* Their temple shall be rebuilt; their city shall be restored; and in the place where their fathers worshipped shall they also again adore the living God.—This closes the prophecy which was commenced in ch. xxiv.; and the design of the whole is to comfort the Jews with the assurance, that though they were to be made captive in a distant land, yet they would be again restored to the land of their fathers, and again worship God there. It is almost needless to say that this prediction was completely fulfilled by the return of the Jews to their own country under the decree of Cyrus.

that they relate to the same general subject—the approaching calamities and wars with the Assyrians, which would terminate only in the removal of the people to a distant land, and in the destruction of the entire city and nation. But the prophecy in this chapter has not any necessary connection with those which follow, and it may be regarded as separate.

When it was uttered is not certainly known. It is clear, however, that it was before the carrying away of the ten tribes, or while the kingdom of Ephraim or Samaria was still standing. Yet it would seem that it was when that kingdom was exceedingly corrupt, and was hastening to a fall (ver. 1–4). Perhaps it was in the time of Ahaz, or in the beginning of the reign of Hezekiah, when Samaria or Ephraim had entered into a league with Rezin, king of Damascus, and may therefore synchronize with ch. vii., viii. Whenever it was uttered, it is certain that its purpose was to predict the overthrow of Ephraim or Samaria, and the fact, that when that kingdom should be overthrown, the kingdom of Judah would still survive.

The prophecy consists of two parts:—1. The overthrow of Samaria or Ephraim (1–4). 2. The fact that JEHOVAH would preserve and defend a portion of his people—those who comprise the kingdom of Judah (5–29). The following brief view will present an analysis of the prophecy:—

I. Ephraim or Samaria, for its sins, particularly for intemperance, would be overthrown (1–4).

II. God would preserve the residue of his people, yet they also deserved rebuke, and would be also subjected to punishment (5–29). 1. He would preserve them (5, 6) and be their glory and strength. 2. Yet they deserved, on many accounts, to be reproved, particularly because many even of the priests and prophets were intemperate (7–8). 3. They also disregarded the

messengers of God, and treated their messages with contempt and scorn, as being vain repetitions and a mere stammering (9–13). 4. They regarded themselves as safe, since they were firm and united, and had as it were made a league with death (14, 15). 5. God, in view of their sins, threatens them with deserved punishment (16–21). This would occur in the following manner:—(a.) He would lay in Zion a corner stone, tried and precious, and all that regarded that should be safe (16). (b.) Yet heavy judgments would come upon the guilty and the unbelieving. Judgment would be laid to the line, and the storms of Divine vengeance would sweep away their false refuges, and their covenant with death should not avail them (17–21). (c.) The people are therefore admonished to attend to this, for the destruction was determined upon the whole land (22). (d.) The whole account of their punishment is concluded by a reference to the conduct of a husbandman, and an illustration is drawn from the fact that he takes various methods to secure his harvest. He ploughs, he sows, and in various ways he thrashes his grain. So in various ways God would deal with his people. He would instruct, admonish, correct, and punish them, in order that he might secure the *greatest amount of piety and good fruits from them*. Chastisement was just as necessary for them as it was for the husbandman in various modes to beat out his grain (23–29).

W O to the crown of pride, to the drunkards of Ephraim, whose glorious beauty *is* a fading flower, which *are* on the head of the fat valleys of them that are overcome [1] with wine !

1 *broken.*

CHAPTER XXVIII.

1. *Wo* (see Note on ch. xviii. 1). The word here is used to denounce impending judgment. ¶ *To the crown of pride.* This is a Hebrew mode of expression, denoting the *proud* or *haughty crown*. There can be no doubt that it refers to the capital of the kingdom of Ephraim ; that is, to Samaria. This city was built by Omri, who purchased ' the hill Samaria ' of Shemer, for two talents of silver, equal in value to £792, 11s. 8d., and built the city on the hill, and called it, after the name of Shemer, Samaria (1 Kings xvi. 24). Omri was king of Israel (B.C. 925), and he made this city the capital of his kingdom. The city was built on a pleasant and fertile hill,

and surrounded with a rich valley, with a circle of hills beyond ; and the beauty of the hill on which the city was built suggested the idea of a wreath or chaplet of flowers, or a *crown*. After having been destroyed and reduced to an inconsiderable place, it was restored by Herod the Great, B.C. 21, who called it *Sebaste* (Latin, *Augusta*), in honour of the Emperor Augustus. It is usually mentioned by travellers under the name of Sebaste. Maundrell (*Travels*, p. 58) says, ' Sebaste, the ancient Samaria, is situated on a long mount of an oval figure ; having first a fruitful valley, and then a ring of hills running round it.' The following is the account which is given by Richardson :—' Its situation

2 Behold, the LORD hath a mighty and strong one, *which* as

is extremely beautiful, and strong by nature; more so, I think, than Jerusalem. It stands on a fine large insulated hill, compassed all round by a broad, deep valley. The valley is surrounded by four hills, one on each side, which are cultivated in terraces to the top, sown with grain, and planted with fig and olive trees, as is also the valley. The hill of Samaria, likewise, rises in terraces to a height equal to any of the adjoining mountains.' Dr. Robinson, who visited this place in 1838, says, ' The find round swelling hill, or almost mountain of Samaria, stands alone in the midst of the great basin of some two hours [seven or eight miles] in diameter, surrounded by higher mountains on every side. It is near the eastern side of the basin; and is connected with the eastern mountains, somewhat after the manner of a promontory, by a much lower ridge, having a wady both on the south and on the north. The mountains and the valleys around are to a great extent arable, and enlivened by many villages and the hand of cultivation. From all these circumstances, the situation of the ancient Samaria is one of great beauty. The hill itself is cultivated to the top; and, at about midway of the ascent, is surrounded by a narrow terrace of level land like a belt, below which the roots of the hill spread off more gradually into the valleys. The whole hill of Sebästich [the Arabic form for the name Sebaste] consists of fertile soil; it is cultivated to the top, and has upon it many olive and fig trees. It would be difficult to find, in all Palestine, a situation of equal strength, fertility, and beauty combined. In all these particulars, it has very greatly the advantage over Jerusalem.'—(*Bib. Researches*, vol. iii. pp. 136—149). Standing thus by itself, and cultivated to the top, and exceedingly fertile, it was compared by the prophet to a crown, or garland of flowers—such as used to be worn on the head, especially on festival occasions. ¶ *To the drunkards of Ephraim.* Ephraim here denotes the kingdom of Israel, whose capital was Samaria (see Note on ch. vii. 2). That intemperance was the prevailing sin in

the kingdom of Israel is not improbable. It prevailed to a great extent also in the kingdom of Judah (see ver. 7, 8; comp. Notes on ch. v. 11, 22). ¶ *Whose glorious beauty* is *a fading flower.* That is, it shall soon be destroyed, as a flower soon withers and fades away. This was fulfilled in the destruction that came upon Samaria under the Assyrians when the ten tribes were carried into captivity (2 Kings xvii. 3–6). The allusion in this verse to the ' crown' and ' the fading flower' encircling Samaria, Grotius thinks is derived from the fact that among the ancients, drunkards and revellers were accustomed to wear a crown or garland on their heads, or that a wreath or chaplet of flowers was usually worn on their festival occasions. That this custom prevailed among the Jews as well as among the Greeks and Romans, is apparent from a statement by the author of the Book of Wisdom:

' Let us fill ourselves with costly wine and ornaments,
And let no flower of the spring pass by us;
Let us crown ourselves with rose-buds before they are withered.'—*Wisdom*, ii. 7, 8.

¶ *Which* are *on the head.* Which flowers or chaplets are on the eminence that rises over the fat valleys; that is, on Samaria, which seemed to stand as the head rising from the valley. ¶ *Of the fat valleys of them that are overcome with wine.* That are occupied by, or in the possession of, those who are overcome with wine. Marg. ' Broken' with wine. Heb. (הֲלוּמֵי יָיִן) ' Smitten with wine;' corresponding to the Greek οἰνοπλὴξ; that is, they were overcome or subdued by it. A man's reason, conscience, moral feelings, and physical strength are all overcome by indulgence in wine, and the entire man is prostrate by it. This passage is a proof of what has been often denied, but which further examination has abundantly confirmed, that the inhabitants of wine countries are as certainly intemperate as those which make use of ardent spirits.

2. *Behold, the* LORD *hath a mighty and strong one.* The Hebrew of this passage is, ' Lo! there is to the Lord (לַאדֹנָי) mighty and strong.' Lowth renders it,

a tempest *a* of hail, *and* a destroying storm, as a flood of mighty
waters overflowing, shall cast down
to the earth with the hand.

3 The crown of pride, the drunkards of Ephraim, shall be trodden
under ¹ feet.

a Ezek.13.11.   1 *with.*

4 And the glorious beauty which
is on the head of the fat valley shall
be *b* a fading flower, *and* as the
hasty fruit before the summer;
which *when* he that looketh upon
it seeth, while it is yet in his hand
he eateth ² it up.

b Ps.73.19,20.   2 *swalloweth.*

'Behold the mighty one, the exceedingly strong
one,'

and supposes that it means the Lord
himself. It is evident, however, that
something must be understood as being
that which the Lord ' hath,' for the
Hebrew properly implies that there is
something strong and mighty which is
under his control, and with which, as
with a tempest, he will sweep away
and destroy Ephraim. Jarchi supposes
that רוּחַ (*wind*) is understood; Kimchi
that the word is יוֹם (*day*); others that
חַיִל (*an army*) is understood. But I
think the obvious interpretation is to
refer it to the Assyrian king, as the
agent by which JEHOVAH would destroy
Samaria (2 Kings xvii. 3–6). This
power was entirely under the direction
of JEHOVAH, and would be employed by
him in accomplishing his purpose on
that guilty people (comp. Notes on ch.
x. 5, 6). ¶ *As a tempest of hail.* A
storm of hail is a most striking representation of the desolation that is produced by the ravages of an invading
army (comp. Job xxvii. 21; Note on ch.
xxx. 30; also Hos. xiii. 15). ¶ *A flood
of mighty waters.* This is also a striking description of the devastating effects
of an invading army (comp. Ps. xc. 5;
Jer. xlvi. 7, 8. ¶ *Shall cast down to
the earth.* To cast it to the earth means
that it should be entirely humbled and
destroyed (see Note on ch. xxv. 12).
¶ *With the hand.* LXX. Βίᾳ—' Force,'
' violence.' This is its meaning here;
as if it were taken in the hand, like a
cup, and dashed indignantly to the
ground.

4. *As the hasty fruit before the summer.* The word rendered ' hasty fruit '
(בִּכּוּרָה *bikkurah;* in Arabic, *bokkore;*
in Spanish, *albacore*), denotes the *early
fig.* This ripens in June; the common
fig does not ripen until August. Shaw,

in his *Travels,* p. 370, says: ' No sooner
does the *boccore* (the early fig) draw
near to perfection in the middle or latter
end of June, than the *kermez* or summer fig begins to be formed, though it
rarely ripens before August, about which
time the same tree frequently throws
out a third crop, or the winter fig, as
we may call it. This is usually of a
much longer shape and darker complexion than the kermez, hanging and
ripening on the tree after the leaves are
shed; and provided the winter be mild
and temperate it is gathered as a delicious morsel in the spring.' Robinson
[George], (*Travels in Palestine and
Syria,* vol. i. p. 354), says, ' The fig
tree, which delights in a rocky and
parched soil, and is therefore often found
in barren spots where nothing else will
grow, is very common in Palestine and
the East. The fruit is of two kinds,

Fig (*Ficus carica*).

the *boccore* and the *kermouse.* The
black and white boccore, or early fig, is
produced in May; but the kermouse, or
the fig properly so called, which is preserved and exported to Europe, is rarely
ripe before September.' Compare Hos.
ix. 10. The phrase ' before the summer '
means before the heat of the summer,
when the common fig was usually ripe.

5 In that day shall the Lord of hosts be for a crown of glory, and for a diadem of beauty, unto the residue of his people.

6 And for a spirit of judgment to him that sitteth in judgment, and for strength to them that turn the battle to the gate.

7 But they also have erred through wine, *a* and through strong drink are out of the way : the priest *b* and the prophet have erred through strong drink, they are swallowed up of wine, they are out of the way through strong drink ; they err in vision, they stumble *in* judgment.

a Ho.4.11.   *b* ch.56.10-12.

The idea here is this, the early fig would be plucked and eaten with great greediness. So the city of Samaria would be seized upon and destroyed by its enemies. ¶ *Which* when *he that looketh upon it seeth*, &c. That is, as soon as he sees it he plucks it, and eats it at once. He does not lay it up for future use, but as soon as he has it in his hand he devours it. So soon as the Assyrian should see Samaria he would rush upon it, and destroy it. It was usual for conquerors to *preserve* the cities which they took in war for future use, and to make them a part of the strength or ornament of their kingdom. But Samaria was to be at once destroyed. Its inhabitants were to be carried away, and it would be demolished as greedily as a hungry man plucks and eats the first fig that ripens on the tree.

5. *In that day.* This verse commences a new subject, and affirms that while the kingdom of Israel should be destroyed, the kingdom of Judah would be preserved, and restored (comp. ch. vii.-ix.) ¶ *Be for a crown of glory.* He shall reign there as its king, and he shall guard and defend the remnant of his people there. This reign of Jehovah shall be to them better than palaces, towers, walls, and fruitful fields, and shall be a more glorious ornament than the proud city of Samaria was to the kingdom of Israel. ¶ *And for a diadem of beauty.* A beautiful garland. The phrase stands opposed to the wreath of flowers or the diadem which was represented (ver. 1, 3) as adorning the kingdom and capital of Israel. Jehovah and his government would be to them their chief glory and ornament. ¶ *Unto the residue of his people.* To the kingdom of Judah, comprising the two tribes of Judah and Benjamin. This doubtless refers to the comparatively pros-

perous and happy times of the reign of Hezekiah.

6. *And for a spirit of judgment* (comp. Note on ch. i. 26 ; ch. xi. 2). The sense of this passage is, that Jehovah would enlighten the judges of the land, so that they should understand what was right, and be disposed to do it. ¶ *To him that sitteth in judgment.* This is to be understood *collectively*, and means those who sat upon the bench of justice ; that is, the magistracy in general. ¶ *And for strength to them that turn the battle to the gate.* That is, to the very gate of their enemies ; who not only repel their foes from their own city, but who drive them even to the gates of their own cities, and besiege them there. Thus 2 Sam. xi. 23 : 'And we were upon them even unto the entering of the gate ;' that is, we drove them back unto their own gates.

7. *But they also have erred through wine.* In the previous verses the prophet had said that the kingdom of Judah should be saved, while that of Ephraim should be destroyed. Yet he does not deny that they also were guilty of crimes for which punishment would come upon them. To portray these crimes, and to declare the certain judgment which awaited them, is the design of the remainder of the chapter. The word rendered 'have erred' (שָׁגוּ) refers usually to the fact that men *stagger* or *reel* through wine, and is applied commonly to those who are intoxicated (Prov. xx. 1). The subsequent part of this verse shows, however, that it does not refer merely to the fact that they stagger and reel as intemperate men do, but that it had an effect on their 'vision' and 'judgment ;' that is, it disqualified them for the discharge of their duties as priests and as prophets. In this part of the verse, however, the simple idea

8 For all tables are full of vomit *and* filthiness, *so that there is* no place *clean.*

9 Whom *ª* shall he teach know-

ª Jer.6.10.

ledge ? and whom shall he make to understand doctrine ? ² *them that are* weaned from the milk, *and* drawn from the breasts.

² the hearing.

---

is, that they reel or stagger through wine, *i.e.,* they are addicted to intoxication. In the subsequent part of the verse the prophet states the effect in producing indistinctness of vision and error of judgment. ¶ *And through strong drink* (see Note on ch. v. 11). ¶ *They are out of the way* (תָעוּ). They wander ; stagger ; reel (comp. Notes on ch. xix. 14). ¶ *The priest and the prophet.* Probably these persons are specified to denote the higher classes of society. It is probable that the prophet also designs to indicate the enormity of the sins of the nation, from the fact that those who were specially devoted to religion, and who were supposed to have immediate communication with God, were addicted to intemperance. ¶ *They are swallowed up of wine.* They are completely absorbed by it (see Note on ch. xxv. 7); they not only themselves indulge in its use, but they are themselves, as it were, swallowed up by it, so that their reason, and strength, and virtue are all gone—as a vessel is absorbed in a mælstrom or whirlpool. ¶ *They err in vision.* For the sense of the word ' vision,' see Note on ch. i. 1. The prophet here states the effect of the use of wine and strong drink on their mental and moral powers. It was the office of the prophets to declare the will of God ; probably also to explain the sense of the sacred Scriptures, and to address the people on their duty. Here the prophet says that the effect of their intemperance was that they had themselves no correct and clear views of the truth, and that they led the people into error. ¶ *They stumble* in *judgment.* There were many important subjects on which the priests sat in judgment among the Hebrews, particularly in all matters pertaining to religion. By the influence of intoxicating liquors they were disqualified for the high and holy functions of their office ; and the consequence was, that the nation was corrupt, and was exposed to the heavy judgments of God.

8. *For all tables,* &c. The tables at

which they sit long in the use of wine (see Note on ch. v. 11). There was no place in their houses which was free from the disgusting and loathsome pollution produced by the use of wine.

9. *Whom shall he teach knowledge?* This verse commences a statement respecting another form of sin that prevailed among the people of Judah. That sin was contempt for the manner in which God instructed them by the prophets, and a disregard for his communications as if they were suited to children and not to adults. That *scoffing* was the principal sin aimed at in these verses, is apparent from ver. 14. Vitringa supposes that these words (ver. 9, 10) are designed to describe the manner of teaching by the priests and the prophets as being puerile and silly, and adapted to children. Michaelis supposes that the prophet means to signify that it would be a vain and fruitless labour to attempt to instruct these persons who were given to wine, because they were unaccustomed to sound and true doctrine. Others have supposed that he means that these persons who were thus given to wine and strong drink were disqualified to instruct others, since their teachings were senseless and incoherent, and resembled the talk of children. But the true sense of the passage has undoubtedly been suggested by Lowth. According to this interpretation, the prophet speaks of them as deriders of the manner in which God had spoken to them by his messengers. ' What !' say they, ' does God treat us as children ? Does he deal with us as we deal with infants just weaned, perpetually repeating and inculcating the same elementary lessons, and teaching the mere rudiments of knowledge?' The expression, therefore, ' Whom shall he teach knowledge ?' or, ' Whom does he teach ?' is an expression of contempt supposed to be spoken by the intemperate priests and prophets—the leaders of the people. ' Whom does God take us to be ?

10 For precept ¹must be upon precept, precept upon precept; line upon line, line upon line; here a little, and there a little :

11 For with ²stammering lips, and another tongue, ³will he speak to his people.

12 To whom he said, This is the

Does he regard us as mere children? Why are we treated as children with an endless repetition of the same elementary instruction?' ¶ To understand doctrine. Heb. as Marg. 'Hearing,' or 'report' (Isa. liii. 1). The sense is, For whom is that instruction intended? Whom does he wish to be taught by it? ¶ Them that are weaned from the milk, &c. Does he regard and treat us as mere babes?

10. For precept must be upon precept. This is probably designed to ridicule the concise and sententious manner of the prophets, and especially the fact that they dwelt much upon the same elementary truths of religion. In teaching children we are obliged to do it by often repeating the same simple lesson. So the profane and scoffing teachers of the people said it had been with the prophets of God. It had been precept upon precept, and line upon line, in the same way as children had been instructed. The meaning is, 'there is a constant repetition of the command, without ornament, imagery, or illustration; without an appeal to our understanding, or respect for our reason; it is simply one mandate after another, just as lessons are inculcated upon children.' ¶ Line upon line. This word (קָו qăv), properly means a cord, a line; particularly a measuring cord or line (2 Kings xxi. 13; Ezek. xlvii. 13; see Note on ch. xviii. 2). Here it seems to be used in the sense of a rule, law, or precept. Grotius thinks that the idea is taken from schoolmasters who instruct their pupils by making lines or marks for them which they are to trace or imitate. There is a repetition of similar sounds in the Hebrew in this verse which cannot be conveyed in a translation, and which shows their contempt in a much more striking manner than any version could do—

קַו לָקָו קַו לָקָו צַו לָצָו צַו לָצָו כִּי
—kĭ tzăv lătzăv tzăv lătzăv qăv lâqăv qăv lâqăv. ¶ Here a little and there

a little. In the manner of instructing children, inculcating elementary lessons constantly. It may be observed here that God's method of imparting religious truth has often appeared to a scoffing world to be undignified and foolish. Sinners suppose that he does not sufficiently respect their understanding, and pay a tribute to the dignity of their nature. The truths of God, and his modes of inculcating them, are said to be adapted to the understandings of childhood and of age; to imbecility of years, or to times when the mind is enfeebled by disease.

11. For. This verse is to be understood as a response to what the complaining and dissatisfied people had said, as expressed in the previous verse. God says that he will teach them, but it should be by another tongue—a foreign language in a distant land. Since they refused to hearken to the messages which he sent to them, and which they regarded as adapted only to children, he would teach them in a manner that should be much more humiliating; he would make use of the barbarous language of foreigners to bring them to the true knowledge of God. ¶ With stammering lips. The word which is used here is derived from a verb (לָעַג), which means to speak unintelligibly: especially to speak in a foreign language, or to stammer; and then to mock, deride, laugh at, scorn (comp. Isa. xxxiii. 19; Prov. i. 26; xvii. 5; Ps. ii. 4; lix. 9; Job xxii. 19). Here it means in a foreign or barbarous tongue; and the sense is, that the lessons which God wished to teach would be conveyed to them through the language of foreigners—the Chaldeans. They should be removed to a distant land, and there, in hearing a strange speech, in living long among foreigners, they should learn the lesson which they refused to do when addressed by the prophets in their own land.

12. To whom he said. To whom

rest *wherewith* ye may cause the weary to rest ; and this *is* the refreshing ; yet they would not hear.

13 But *a* the word of the LORD was unto them precept upon precept, precept upon precept ; line upon line; line upon line ; here a little, *and* there a little ; that *b* they might go, and fall backward, and be broken, and snared, and taken.

14 Wherefore hear the word of

the LORD, ye scornful men, that rule this people which *is* in Jerusalem.

15 Because ye have said, We have made a covenant with death, and with hell are we at agreement ; when the overflowing scourge shall pass through, it shall not come *c* unto us : for we have made lies our refuge, and under falsehood have we hid ourselves.

a Ho.6.5; 8.12.   *b* Mat.13.14.

c Eccl.8.8.

God had said ; *i.e.*, to the Jews. He *had* taught them the way of rest through the prophets, but they had refused to learn. ¶ *This* is *the rest*. That is, this is the true way of happiness, to wit, by keeping the commands of God which had been so often repeated as to become to them objects of satiety and disgust. ¶ *This* is *the refreshing*. This is the way in which the mind may be comforted.

13. *But the word of the* LORD *was unto them*. Or, rather, but the word of JEHOVAH *shall be* unto them. This refers to the mode in which God said he would instruct them in a foreign land. They had complained (ver. 9, 10) that his instructions had been like a short lesson constantly repeated, as we instruct children. God here says that it should be as they said it was— they would be carried away to a distant land, and long abide among strangers ; they would have ample time there to acquire instruction, and all that they would receive would be lesson after lesson of the same kind—line upon line, one judgment following another, until the lesson of their disobedience had been fully inculcated, and they had been brought to true repentance. ¶ *Here a little*, and *there a little*. So they had said (ver. 10) the lessons of God were to them by the prophets. So God says his lessons *shall be* to them by judgment. It shall not come in one sudden and overpowering burst of indignation, but it shall be, as it were, dealt out to them in small portions that it may not be soon exhausted. ¶ *That they might go*, &c. That they may go into captivity, and stumble, and be broken by the judgments of God. God will so

deal out the lessons of his judgment and wrath, that as a people they shall be broken up, and made prisoners, and be borne to a distant land.

14. *Wherefore*, &c. This verse commences a direct address to the scoffing and scornful nation, which is continued to the close of ver. 22. It is addressed particularly to the rulers in Jerusalem, as being the leaders in crime, and as being eminently deserving of the wrath of God. ¶ *Ye scornful men*. Ye who despise and reproach God and his message ; who fancy yourselves to be secure, and mock at the threatened judgments of the Almighty.

15. *We have made a covenant with death*. We are not to suppose that they had formally said this, but that their conduct was *as if* they had said it ; they lived as securely as if they had entered into a compact with death not to destroy them, and with hell not to devour them. The figure is a very bold one, and is designed to express the extraordinary stupidity of the nation. It is most strikingly descriptive of the great mass of men. They are as little anxious about death and hell as if they had made a compact with the king of terrors and the prince of darkness not to destroy them. They are as little moved by the appeals of the gospel, by the alarms of God's providence, by the preaching of his word, and by all the demonstrations that they are exposed to eternal death, as though they had proved that there was no hell, or had entered into a solemn covenant that they should be unmolested. A figure similar to this occurs in Job v. 23:

For thou shalt be in league with the stones of
       the field;

16 Therefore thus saith the Lord God, Behold I lay in Zion for a foundation a stone, *a* a tried stone, a precious corner-*stone*, a sure foundation : he *b* that believeth shall not make haste.

a Ps.118.22; Mat.21.42; Acts 4.11; Rom.9.33; Eph.2.20.

b Rom.10.11.

And the beasts of the field shall be at peace with thee. Comp. Hos. ii. 18. ¶ *And with hell.* Heb. 'Sheol'—the land of shades, or of departed spirits (see Note on ch. v. 14). It is nearly synonymous here with death. ¶ *When the overflowing scourge shall pass through.* There is here, in our translation, a little confusion of metaphor, since we speak usually of an overflowing *stream*, and not of an overflowing *scourge.* The word 'scourge' (שׁוֹט) means usually *a whip, a scourge,* the same as שׁוֹט, and then means any punishment or calamity (see Note on ch. x. 26; comp. Job ix. 23; v. 21. Here its means severe judgments or calamities, as *overflowing* like water, or inundating a people. ¶ *We have made lies*, &c. That is, they acted *as if* they had a safe refuge in falsehood. They sought security in false doctrines, and regarded themselves as safe from all that the prophets had denounced.

16. *Therefore thus saith the Lord God.* This verse is introductory to the solemn threatening which follows. Its design seems to be this. The prophet was about to utter an awful threatening of the judgment of God upon the nation. It might be supposed, perhaps, that the intention was completely to sweep them, and destroy them—that the threatened calamity would remove every vestige of the Jewish people and of the true religion together. To meet this supposition, God says that this should not occur. Zion was founded on a rock. It should be like an edifice that was reared on a firm, well-tried corner-stone—one that could endure all the storms that should beat around it, and be unmoved. The general sentiment of the verse is, therefore, that though a tempest of calamity was about to beat upon the people for their sins ; though the temple was to be destroyed, the city laid in ashes, and many of the people slain ; yet it was the purpose of God that his empire on earth should not be destroyed. A foundation, a corner-stone was to be laid that would

be unshaken and unmoved by all the assaults of the foes of God, and all who were truly resting on that should be safe. The perpetuity of his kingdom, and the safety of his true people, is, therefore, the essential idea in this passage. That it refers to the Messiah, and is designed to show that his kingdom will be perpetual *because* it is reared on him, we shall see by an examination of the words which occur in the verse. ¶ *In Zion* (see Note on ch. i. 8). Zion here is put for his empire, kingdom, or church in general on earth. To lay a corner-stone in Zion, means that his kingdom would be founded on a rock, and would be secure amidst all the storms that might beat upon it. ¶ *For a foundation a stone.* That is, I lay a firm foundation which nothing can move ; I build it on a rock so that the storms and tempests of calamity cannot sweep it away (comp. Matt. vii. 24, 25). The Targum renders this, 'Lo! I appoint in Zion a king, a strong, mighty, and terrible king.' That the passage before us has reference to the Messiah there can be no doubt. The writers of the New Testament so understood and applied it. Thus it is applied by Peter (1 Pet. ii. 6), 'Wherefore, also, it is contained in the Scripture, Behold I lay in Zion a chief corner-stone, elect, precious ; and he that believeth on him shall not be confounded' (see Notes on Rom. ix. 33 ; comp. Rom. x. 11; Matt. xxi. 42; Luke xx. 17, 18; ii. 34; Eph. ii. 20). Such a reference also exactly suits the conception. The stability of the kingdom of God on earth rests on the Messiah. God had determined to send him ; and, consequently, amidst all the agitations and revolutions that could take place among his ancient people, this promise was sure, and it was certain that he would come, and that his church would be preserved. ¶ *A tried stone.* The word which is used here is applied commonly to *metals* which are tried in the fire to test their quality (see Job xxiii. 10; Ps. lxvi. 10; Jer ix. 6; Zech. xiii.

17 Judgment also will I lay to the line, and righteousness to the plummet ; and the hail shall sweep away the refuge of lies, and the waters shall overflow the hiding-place.

1 *a treading down to it.*

18 And your covenant with death shall be disannulled, and your agreement with hell shall not stand ; when the overflowing scourge shall pass through, then ye shall be ¹ trodden down *a* by it.

a Mal.4.3.

---

9). The idea is, that God would lay for a foundation not a stone whose qualities are unknown, and whose stability might be doubtful, but one whose firmness and solidity were so fully known, that the foundation and the superstructure would be secure. ¶ *A precious corner*-stone. The word ' precious ' (LXX., and 1 Pet. ii. 6, ἔντιμον) refers to the fact that the most solid stone would be used to sustain the corner of the edifice. The principal weight of the superstructure rests on the corners, and hence, in building, the largest and firmest blocks are selected and placed there. ¶ *He that believeth.* He that confides in that ; he that believes that that foundation is firm, and that he is secure in trusting in that, shall not make haste. The great doctrine of faith in the Messiah as a ground of security and salvation, on which so much stress is laid in the New Testament, is here distinctly adverted to. The sense is, that confidence in him should keep the mind firm, and preserve him that believes in safety. ¶ *Shall not make haste.* The LXX. render it, Οὐ μὴ καταισχυνθῇ —' Shall not be ashamed.' So Peter, 1 Pet. ii. 6 ; and Paul, Rom. ix. 33. The Hebrew word יָחִישׁ, from חִישׁ, means properly *to make haste ;* and then to urge on ; and then to be afraid, to flee. The idea is derived from one who is alarmed, and flees to a place of safety. The specific thought here is that of a man on whose house the tempest beats, and who apprehends that the foundation is insecure, and leaves it to seek a more safe position. The prophet says here, that the foundation on which Zion was reared would be so firm that if a man trusted to that he would have no cause of alarm, however much the storms should beat around it. The same idea essentially is conveyed in the version of the LXX., and by Paul and Peter, where it is ren-

dered ' shall not be ashamed,' or ' confounded.' That is, he shall have no reason to be ashamed of his confidence in the firm foundation ; he shall not flee from it as a man does who puts his trust in that which fails him in the day of trial.

17. *Judgment also will I lay to the line.* The sense of this is, I will judge them *according to the exact rule of law,* as an architect frames everything according to the rule which he uses. In other words, there shall be no mercy intermingled. The *line* is used by a carpenter for measuring ; the plummet consists of a piece of lead attached to a string, and is also used by carpenters to obtain a perpendicular line. A carpenter works exactly according to the lines which are thus indicated, or his frame would not be properly adjusted. So God says that he would judge the people of Jerusalem according to the exact rule, without any intermingling of mercy. ¶ *And the hail,* &c. (see Note on ver. 2). Hail, hailstones, and floods of waters are frequent images of the Divine vengeance and wrath (Ps. cv. 32 ; Isa. xxii. 19 ; xxx. 30 ; Ezek. xiii. 13 ; xxxviii. 22 ; Rev. viii. 7 ; xi. 19 ; xvi. 21).

18. *And your covenant with death* (see Note on ver. 15). ¶ *Shall be disannulled.* The word rendered ' shall be disannulled,' (וְכֻפַּר from כָּפַר), properly means *to cover, overlay ;* then to pardon, forgive ; then to make atonement, to expiate. It has the idea of blotting out, forgiving, and obliterating—because a writing in wax was obliterated or *covered* by passing the *stylus* over it. Hence, also, the idea of abolishing, or rendering nought, which is the idea here. ¶ *When the overflowing scourge* (see Note on ver. 15). ¶ *Then ye shall be trodden down by it.* There is in this verse a great intermingling of metaphor, not less than three figures

19 From the time that it goeth
forth it shall take you : for morning by morning shall it pass over,
by day and by night ; and it shall
be a vexation only [1] *to* understand
the report.

20 For the bed is shorter than
that *a man* can stretch himself
on it; and the covering narrower

than that he can wrap himself
in it.

21 For the LORD shall rise up
as *a in* mount Perazim, he shall
be wroth as *b in* the valley of
Gibeon, that he may do his work,
his strange *c* work ; and bring to
pass his act, his strange act.

1 or, when *he shall make* you *to understand doctrine.*
a 2 Sa. 5. 20.　　b Jos. 10. 10, &c.; 1 Ch. 14 16.　c La. 3. 33.

---

being employed to denote the calamity.
There is first the scourge, an instrument of punishment , there is then the
idea of inundating waters or floods ;
then there is also the idea of a warrior
or an invading army that treads down
an enemy. All the images are designed to denote essentially the same
thing, that the judgments of God would
come upon the land, and that nothing
in which they had trusted would constitute a refuge.

19. *From the time that it goeth forth
it shall take you.* It shall not delay, or
be hindered, or put back. As soon as
the judgment is sent forth from God it
shall come upon you. ¶ *For morning
by morning.* Continually ; without intermission. It shall be like floods and
tempests that have no intermission ;
that are repeated every day, and continued every night, until everything is
swept before them. ¶ *And it shall be
a vexation.* It shall be an object of
alarm, of agitation, of distress—זְוָעָה;
from זוּעַ, *to move one's self;* to tremble with alarm ; to be troubled (Eccl.
xii. 3; Dan. v. 19; vi. 27; Heb. ii. 7).
Here it means that the calamity would
be so great that it would fill the mind
with horror only to hear of it. For
similar expressions denoting the effect
of hearing a report of the judgments
of God, see 1 Sam. iii. 11; 2 Kings
xxi. 12; Jer. xix. 3. ¶ *The report.*
Marg. ' Doctrine ' (see Note on ver. 9).

20. *For the bed is shorter,* &c. This
is evidently a proverbial saying, and
means that they would find all their
places of defence insufficient to secure
them. They seek repose and security
—as a man lies down to rest at night.
But they find neither. His bed furnishes no rest ; his scanty covering furnishes no security from the chills of the

night. So it would be with those who
sought protection in idols, in the promises of false prophets, and in the aid
which might be obtained from Egypt.
—So it is with sinners. Their vain
refuges shall not shield them. The
bed on which they seek rest shall give
them no repose ; the covering with
which they seek to clothe themselves
shall not defend them from the wrath
of God.

21. *For the* LORD *shall rise up.* To
rise up is indicative of going forth to
judgment, as when one rises from his
seat to accomplish anything. ¶ *As* in
mount Perazim. There is reference
here, doubtless, to the event recorded in
2 Sam. v. 20, 21, and 1 Chron. xiv. 11,
where David is said to have defeated
the Philistines at Baal-Perazim. This
place was near to the valley of Rephaim
(2 Sam. v. 19), and not far from Jerusalem. The word ' Perazim ' is from
פָּרַץ (*părătz*), *to tear,* or *break forth,* as
waters do that have been confined ; and
is indicative of sudden judgment, and
of a complete overthrow. It was on
that account given to the place where
David obtained a signal and complete
victory (2 Sam. v. 20) ; and it is here
referred to, to denote that God would
come forth in a sudden manner to destroy Jerusalem and Judea. He would
come upon them like bursting waters,
and sweep them away to a distant land.
¶ *As* in *the valley of Gibeon.* In
1 Chron. xiv. 16, it is said that after
the victory of Baal-Perazim, ' David
smote the host of the Philistines from
Gibeon even to Gaza.' This victory is
doubtless referred to here, and not the
victory of Joshua over the Gibeonites
(Josh. x. 10), as Vitringa and others
suppose. ¶ *That he may do his work,
his strange work.* This is called his

22 Now therefore be ye not mockers, lest your bands be made strong: for I have heard from the Lord God of hosts a consumption,

a Dan.9.27.

even [d] determined upon the whole earth.

23 Give ye ear, and hear my voice; hearken, and hear my speech.

---

strange work because it would be inflicted on his people. He had destroyed their enemies often, but now he was about to engage in the unusual work of coming forth against his own people, and sweeping them away to a distant land. The work of judgment and punishment may be called the *strange* work of God always, inasmuch as it is not that in which he delights to engage, and is foreign to the benevolence of his heart. It is peculiarly so when his own people are the objects of his displeasure, and when their sins are such as to demand that he should visit them with the tokens of his wrath.

22. *Now therefore.* In view of the certain judgment which God will bring upon you. ¶ *Be ye not mockers.* This was the prevailing sin (ver. 9–14), and on account of this sin in part the judgment of God was about to come upon the guilty nation. ¶ *Lest your bands be made strong.* Lest your confinement should be more severe and protracted. God would punish them according to their sins, and if they now ceased to mock and deride him it would greatly mitigate the severity of their punishment (comp. ch. xxiv. 22). ¶ *For I have heard,* &c. I, the prophet, have heard Jehovah of hosts threaten a consumption. ¶ *A consumption,* &c. (see this phrase explained in the Note on ch. x. 23.) ¶ *Upon the whole earth.* The whole land of Judea (see Note on ch. xxiv. 1).

23. *Give ye ear.* In this verse the prophet introduces an important and striking illustration drawn from the science of agriculture. It is connected with the preceding part of the chapter, and is designed to show the propriety of what the prophet had said by an appeal to what they all observed in the cultivation of their lands. The previous discourse consists mainly of reproofs, and of threatenings of punishment on God's people for their profane contempt of the messengers of God. He had threatened to destroy their nation, and

to remove them for a time to a distant land. This the prophet had himself said (ver. 21) was his 'strange work.' To vindicate this, and to show the propriety *of God's adopting every measure, and of not always pursuing the same course in regard to his people,* he draws an illustration from the farmer. He is not always doing the same thing. He adopts different methods to secure a harvest. He adapts his plans to the soil and to the kind of grain; avails himself of the best methods of preparing the ground, sowing the seed, collecting the harvest, and of separating the grain from the chaff. He does not *always* plough; nor *always* sow; nor *always* thresh. He does not deal with all kinds of land and grain in the same way. Some land he ploughs in one mode, and some in another; and in like manner, some grain he threshes in one mode, and some in another — adapting his measures to the nature of the soil, and of the grain. Some grain he beats out with a flail; some he bruises; but yet he will be careful not to break the kernel, or destroy it in threshing it. However severe may appear to be his blows, yet his object is not to crush and destroy it (ver. 28), but it is to remove it from the chaff, and to save it. In all this he acts the part of wisdom, for God has taught him what to do (ver. 26, 29). So, says the prophet, God will not deal with all of his people in the same manner, nor with them always in the same mode. He will *vary* his measures as a husbandman does. When mild and gentle measures will do, he will adopt them. When severe measures are necessary, he will resort to them. His object is not to destroy his people, any more than the object of the farmer in threshing is to destroy his grain. The general design of this allegory is, therefore, to vindicate the propriety of God's engaging in what the prophet calls his 'strange act,' and 'strange work,' in punishing his people. The allegory is one of great

24 Doth the ploughman plough all day to sow? doth he open and break the clods of his ground?

25 When he hath made plain the face thereof, doth he not cast

1 or, *the wheat in the principal* place, *and barley in the appointed* place.

abroad the fitches, and scatter the cummin, and cast in 1 the principal wheat, and the appointed barley, and the 2 rye, in their place 3 ?

2 or, *spelt.*   3 *border.*

beauty, and its pertinency and *keeping* are maintained throughout; and it furnishes a most important practical lesson in regard to the mode in which God deals with his people.

24. *Doth the ploughman*, &c. The question here asked implies that he does *not* plough all the day. The interrogative form is often the most emphatic mode of affirmation. ¶ *All day.* The sense is, does he do nothing else but plough? Is this the only thing which is necessary to be done in order to obtain a harvest? The idea which the prophet intends to convey here is this. A farmer does not suppose that he can obtain a harvest by doing nothing else but plough. There is much else to be done. So it would be just as absurd to suppose that God would deal with his people always in the same manner, as it would be for the farmer to be engaged in nothing else but ploughing. ¶ *Doth he open*, &c. That is, is he always engaged in opening, and breaking the clods of his field? There is much else to be done besides this. The word ' open ' here refers to the *furrows* that are made by the plough. The earth is laid open as it were to the sunbeams, and to the showers of rain, and to the reception of seed. The word rendered ' break ' (יְשַׂדֵּד) properly means *to harrow*, that is, to break up the clods by harrowing (Job xxxix. 10; Hos. x. 11).

25. *When he hath made plain*, &c. That is, when he has *levelled*, or made smooth the surface of the ground by harrowing, or rolling it. ¶ *Doth he not scatter abroad.* He does not sow one kind of grain merely, but different species according to the nature of the soil, or according to his wishes in regard to a crop. ¶ *The fitches* (קֶצַח). Vulg. *Gith;* a kind of cockle (*Nigella Romana*), an herb of sweet savour. LXX. Μικρὸν μελάνθιον. The word ' fitch ' denotes a small species of pea. The Hebrew word, however, which occurs

nowhere else but here, probably denotes fennel, or dill, an herb whose seed the ancients mixed with their bread in order to give it a more agreeable relish. ¶ *And scatter the cummin* (כַּמֹּן). Vulg. *Cyminum*—' Cummin.' LXX. Κύμινον —also ' Cummin.' The word properly denotes an annual plant whose seeds have a bitterish warm taste with an aromatic flavour (Webster). The seeds of this plant were used as a condiment in sauces. ¶ *And cast in the principal wheat.* Marg. ' The wheat in the principal place.' Vulg. *Per ordinem*—' In its proper order, place, proportion.' So Lowth, ' In due measure.' So Aben Ezra and Kimchi render it, ' By measure;' and they suppose it means that if too much wheat be sown on the land, it will grow too thick, and that the spires will crowd and suffocate each other. Our translators have rendered the word שׂוֹרָה, ' principal,' as if it were derived from שׂוּר, *to rule*, and seem to have supposed that it denoted wheat that was peculiarly excellent, or distinguished for its good qualities. Ge-

EGYPTIAN WHEAT (*Triticum compositum*).

senius supposes that it means ' fat wheat,' from an Arabic signification of

26 For ¹his GOD doth instruct him to discretion, *and* doth teach him.

1 or, *and he bindeth it in such sort as his God doth teach him.*

27 For the fitches are not

the word. Probably the word is designed to denote *quality*, and to convey the idea that wheat is the principal, or chief grain that is sown ; it is that which is most valued and esteemed. ¶ *And the appointed barley.* The barley is a well-known grain. The word rendered 'appointed' (נִסְמָן), occurs nowhere else in the Scriptures. Castellio, Taylor, Grotius, Calvin, our translators, and others, suppose that it is derived from a Hebrew word which does not now occur —סָמַן, *to designate, to mark, to seal ;* and that it means barley that had been put aside and *marked* as peculiarly excellent, or seed-barley. In Chaldee, the word סְמַן occurs in the sense of *to seal, to mark, to designate* (Chaldee Par. Num. xvii. 3; 2 Kings ix. 13; Esth. v. 1). The LXX., who translated it κέγχρον, and the Vulgate, Aquila, and Theodotion, understand the word as denoting a species of grain, *the millet.*

MILLET (*Holcus sorghum*).

The idea is probably that expressed by Grotius, and in our version—of barley that had been selected as seed-barley on account of its excellent quality. ¶ *And the rye.* Marg. 'Spelt.' The word usually denotes *spelt*—a kind of wheat now found in Flanders and Italy, called German wheat. It may, however, denote rye. ¶ *In their place.* Literally, 'In the border.' LXX. 'Εν τοῖς ὁρίοις σου—'In thy borders.' The

ISAIAH I

idea seems to be that the spelt or rye was sown in the borders of the field while the wheat was sown in the middle; or that the rye was sown in its *proper bounds*, or in the places which were adapted to it, and best fitted to promote its growth.

26. *For his* GOD *doth instruct him*, &c. Marg. 'He bindeth it in such sort as his God doth teach him.' The more correct idea is conveyed in the text. The word יְסְרוֹ, properly means, he instructs, admonishes, or teaches him. The idea that skill in agriculture is communicated by God is not one that is discordant to reason, or to the general teachings of the Bible. Thus the architectural and mechanical skill of Bezaleel and Aholiab, by which they were enabled to make the tabernacle, is said expressly to have been imparted to them by God (Ex. xxxi. 2–6). Thus also Noah was taught how to build the ark (Gen. vi. 14–16). We are not, indeed, to suppose that the farmer is inspired ; or that God communicates to him by special revelation where, and when, and how he shall sow his grain, but the sense is, that God is the author of all his skill. He has endowed him with understanding, and taught him by his providence. It is by the study of what God teaches in the seasons, in the soil, in the results of experience and observation, that he has this art. He teaches him also by the example, the counsel, and even by the failures of others ; and all the knowledge of agriculture that he has is to be traced up to God.

27. *For the fitches are not threshed with a threshing instrument.* The word here used (חָרוּץ) denotes properly that which is pointed or sharp, and is joined with מוֹרַג in Isa. xli. 15— meaning there the threshing dray or sledge ; a plank with iron or sharp stones that was drawn by oxen over the grain (comp. 2 Sam. xxiv. 22 ; 1 Chron. xxi. 23). In the passage before us, several methods of threshing are mentioned as adapted to different

threshed with a threshing instrument, neither is a cart wheel turned about upon the cummin; but the fitches are beaten out with a staff, and the cummin with a rod.

kinds of grain, all of which are at the present time common in the East. Those which are mentioned under the name of the 'threshing instrument,' and 'a cart wheel,' refer to instruments which are still in use in the East. Niebuhr, in his *Travels in Arabia*, says, (p. 299,) 'In threshing their corn, the Arabians lay the sheaves down in a certain order, and then lead over them two oxen dragging a large stone.' 'They use oxen, as the ancients did, to beat out their corn, by trampling on the sheaves, and dragging after them a clumsy machine. This machine is not a stone cylinder; nor a plank with sharp stones, as in Syria; but a sort of sledge consisting of three rollers, fitted with irons, which turn upon axles. A farmer chooses out a level spot in his fields, and has his corn carried thither in sheaves, upon asses or dromedaries. Two oxen are then yoked in a sledge; a driver then gets upon it, and drives them backwards and forwards upon the sheaves; and fresh oxen succeed in the yoke from time to time. By this operation the chaff is very much cut down; it is then winnowed, and the grain thus separated.' 'This machine,' Niebuhr adds, 'is called Nauridj. It has three rollers which turn on three axles; and each of them is furnished with some irons which are round and flat. Two oxen were made to draw over the grain again and again the sledge above mentioned, and this was done with the greatest convenience to the driver; for he was seated in a chair fixed on a sledge.' The annexed cut

THRESHING WITH THE SLEDGE.—From *Description de l'Egypte.*

will give an idea of this mode of threshing, and of the instruments that were employed. ¶ *Neither is a cart wheel.* This instrument of threshing is described by Bochart (*Hieroz.* i. 2. 32. 311), as consisting of a cart or waggon fitted with wheels adapted to crush or thresh the grain. This, he says, was used by the Carthagenians who came from the vicinity of Canaan. It

28 Bread *corn* is bruised; because he will not ever be threshing it, nor

break it *with* the wheel of his cart, nor bruise it *with* his horsemen.

appears to have been made with serrated wheels, perhaps almost in the form of circular saws, by which the straw was cut fine at the same time that the grain was separated from the chaff. ¶ *But the fitches are beaten out with a staff.* With a stick, or flail. That is, pulse in general, beans, pease, dill, cummin, &c., are easily beaten out with a stick or flail. This mode of threshing is common everywhere. It was also practised, as with us, in regard to barley and other grain, where there was a small quantity, or where there was need of special haste (see Ruth ii. 17; Judg. vi. 11).

28. *Bread* corn. Heb. לֶחֶם—'Bread.' But the word evidently denotes the material from which bread is made. The word is used in the same sense in ch. xxx. 23. ¶ *Is bruised.* That is, is more severely bruised than the dill and the cummin; it is pressed and crushed by passing over it the sledge, or the wain with serrated wheels. The word דָּקַק means often to break in pieces; to make small or fine. It is, however, applied to threshing, as consisting in beating, or crushing (Isa. xli. 15: 'Thou threshest the mountains,

and beatest them small'—וְהֲדִק. ¶ *Because he will not ever be threshing it.* The word rendered 'because' (כִּי) evidently here means *although* or *but;* and the sense is, that he will not *always* continue to thresh it; this is not his only business. It is only a *part* of his method by which he obtains grain for his bread. It would be needless and injurious to be *always* engaged in rolling the stone or the sledge over the grain. So God takes various methods with his people. He does not always pursue the same course. He sometimes smites and punishes them, as the farmer beats his grain. But he does not *always* do it. He is not engaged in this method alone; nor does he pursue this constantly. It would crush and destroy them. *He, therefore, smites them just enough to secure, in the best manner, and to the fullest extent, their obedience; just as the farmer bruises his sheaves enough to separate all the grain from the chaff.* When this is done, he pursues other methods. Hence the various severe and heavy trials with which the people of God are afflicted. ¶ *Nor bruise it* with *his horsemen.* Lowth renders this, 'With

TREADING OUT CORN IN THE EAST BY HORSES.—From *Description de l'Egypte.*

the hoofs of his cattle;' proposing to read פֵּרָסִין instead of פָּרָשָׁיו by a

change of a single letter ס *Samekh,* instead of שׁ *Shin.* So the Syriac and

29 This also cometh forth from the LORD of hosts, *which* is won-derful *a*in counsel, *and* excellent in working.

a Ps.92.5; Jer.32.19; Rom.11.33.

the Vulgate ; and so Symmachus and Theodotion. But the word פָּרָשׁ may denote not only a *horseman*, but the *horse* itself on which one rides (see Bochart, *Hieroz.* i. 2, 6. p. 98. Comp. Note on Hab. i. 8; 2 Sam. i. 6; Isa. xxi. 7, 9). That horses were used in treading out grain there can be no doubt. They are extensively used in this country ; and though in Palestine it is probable that oxen were chiefly employed (Deut. xxv. 4) in the early times, yet there is no improbability in supposing that in the times subsequent to Solomon, when horses abounded, they were preferred. Their more rapid notion, and perhaps the hardness of their hoofs, makes them more valuable for this service (see Michaelis' *Commentary on the Laws of Moses*, vol. ii. App. pp. 430–514, Lond. Ed. 1814). There are here, therefore, four modes of threshing mentioned, all of which are common still in the East. 1. The sledge with rollers, on which were pieces of iron, or stone, and which was dragged over the grain. 2. The cart or wain, with serrated wheels, and which was also drawn over the grain. 3. The flail, or the stick. 4. The use of cattle and horses.

29. *This also cometh*, &c. That is, these various devices for threshing his grain comes from the Lord no less than the skill with which he tills his land. (see ver. 26). ¶ And *excellent in working*. Or rather, who magnifies (הִגְדִּיל) his wisdom (תּוּשִׁיָּה). This word properly means wisdom, or understanding (Job xi. 6; xii. 16; xxvi. 3; Prov. iii. 21; viii. 14; xviii. 1). The idea of the prophet is, that God, who had so wisely taught the husbandman, and who had instructed him to use such various methods in his husbandry, would also be himself wise, and would pursue similar methods with his people. He would not always pursue the same unvarying course, but would vary his dispensations as they should need, and as would best secure their holiness and happiness. We see—1. The reason of afflictions. It is for the same cause

which induces the farmer to employ various methods on his farm. 2. We are not to expect the same unvarying course in God's dealings with us. It would be as unreasonable to expect that the farmer would be always ploughing, or always threshing. 3. We are not to expect always the same *kind* of afflictions. The farmer uses different machines and modes of threshing, and adapts them to the nature of the grain. So God uses different modes, and adapts them to the nature, character, and disposition of his people. One man requires one mode of discipline, and another another. At one time we need one mode of correction to call us from sin and temptation ; at another another. We may lay it down as a general rule, that *the Divine judgments are usually in the line of our offences ;* and by the nature of the judgment we may usually ascertain the nature of the sin. If a man's besetting sin is *pride*, the judgment will usually be something that is fitted to humble his pride ; if it be covetousness, his property may be removed, or it may be made a curse ; if it be undue attachment to children or friends, they may be removed. 4. God will not crush or destroy his people. The farmer does not crush or destroy his grain. In all the various methods which he uses, he takes care not to pursue it too far, and not to injure the grain. So with God's dealings with his people. His object is not to destroy them, but it is to separate the chaff from the wheat ; and he will afflict them only so much as may be necessary to accomplish this. He will not be *always* bruising his people, but will in due time remit his strokes—just as the thresher does. 5. We should, therefore, bear afflictions and chastisements with patience. God deals with us in mercy—and the design of all his dispensations toward us in prosperity and adversity ; in sickness and in health ; in success and in disappointment, is to produce the richest and most abundant fruits of righteousness, and to prepare us to enter into his kingdom above.

CHAPTER XXIX.

ANALYSIS.

This chapter relates solely to Jerusalem—here called Ariel (see Note on ver. 1). It is not immediately connected with the preceding or the following chapters, though it is not improbable they were delivered about the same time. At what time this .was delivered is not known, though it is evident that it was before the invasion by Sennacherib, and probably before the time of Hezekiah. The prophecy in the chapter consists of two parts:—I. The invasion of Judea by Sennacherib, and its sudden deliverance (1–8). II. A reproof of the Jews for their infidelity and impiety.

I. The invasion of Judea, and the distress that would be brought upon Jerusalem, and its sudden deliverance (1–8). 1. Ariel would be filled with grief and distress (1, 2). 2. Jehovah would encamp against it and besiege it, and it would be greatly straitened and humbled (3, 4). 3. Yet the besieging army would be visited with sudden calamity and destruction—represented here by thunder, and tempest, and flame (5, 6). 4. The enemy would vanish as a dream, and all his hopes would be disappointed, as the hopes of a hungry and thirsty man are disappointed who dreams of having satisfied his hunger and thirst (7, 8).

There can be no doubt, I think, that this portion of the prophecy refers to the sudden and dreadful overthrow of Sennacherib; and the design of this portion of the prophecy is to give the assurance, that though Jerusalem would be in imminent danger, yet it would be suddenly delivered.

II. The second part consists of reproofs of the inhabitants of Jerusalem for their infidelity and impiety. 1. They were full of error, and all classes of people were wandering from God—reeling under error like a drunken man (9). 2. A spirit of blindness and stupidity everywhere prevailed among the people (10–12). 3. Formality and external regard for the institutions of religion prevailed, but without its life and power (13). 4. They attempted to lay deep and skilful plans to hide their wickedness from Jehovah (15). 5. They were unjust in their judgments, making a man an offender for a word, and perverting just judgment (21). 6. For all this they should be punished. (a.) The wisdom of their wise men should fail (14). (b.) The scorner would be consumed (20). 7. There would be an overturning, and the people would be made acquainted with the law of God, and the truly pious would be comforted (16–19). Those who had erred would be reformed, and would come to the true knowledge of God (22–24).

W O [1] to Ariel, to Ariel, [2] the city where [a] David dwelt! add ye year to year; let them [3] kill sacrifices.

1 or, *O Ariel, i.e., the lion of God.*
2 or, *of the city.*　　a 2 Sam.5.9.　　3 *cut off the heads.*

CHAPTER XXIX.

1. *Wo* (comp. Note on ch. xviii. 1). ¶ *To Ariel.* There can be no doubt that Jerusalem is here intended. The declaration that it was the city where David dwelt, as well as the entire scope of the prophecy, proves this. But still, it is not quiet clear why the city is here called *Ariel.* The margin reads, 'O Ariel, *i.e.,* the lion of God.' The word *Ariel* (אֲרִיאֵל) is compounded of two words, and is usually supposed to be made up of אֲרִי, *a lion,* and אֵל, *God;* and if this interpretation is correct, it is equivalent to a strong, mighty, fierce lion—where the word 'God' is used to denote greatness in the same way as the lofty cedars of Lebanon are called cedars of God ; *i.e.,* lofty cedars. The *lion* is an emblem of strength, and a strong lion is an emblem of a mighty warrior or hero. 2 Sam. xxiii. 20 : 'He slew two *lion-like* (אֲרִיאֵל) men of Moab' (1 Chron. xi. 22). This use of the word to denote a hero is common in Arabic (see Bochart, *Hieroz.,* i. 3. 1). If this be the sense in which it is used here, then it is applied to Jerusalem under the image of a hero, and particularly as the place which was distinguished under David as the capital of a kingdom that was so celebrated for its triumphs in war. The word 'Ariel' is, however, used in another sense in the Scriptures, to denote an *altar* (Ezek. xliii. 15, 16), where in the Heb. the word is *Ariel.* This name is given to the altar, because Bochart supposes (*Hieroz.,* i. 3. 1), because the altar of burnt-offering *devours* as it were the sacrifices as a lion devours its prey. Gesenius, however, has suggested another reason why the word is given to the altar, since he says that the word אֲרִי is the same as one used in Arabic to denote a *fire-hearth,* and that the altar was so called because it was the place of perpetual burnt-offering. The name *Ariel,* is, doubtless, given in

2 Yet I will distress Ariel, and there shall be heaviness and sor- | row : and it shall be unto me as Ariel.

Ezekiel to an altar; and it may be given here to Jerusalem because it was the place of the altar, or of the public worship of God. The Chaldee renders it, 'Wo to the altar, the altar which was constructed in the city where David dwelt.' It seems to me that this view better suits the connection, and particularly ver. 2 (see Note), than to suppose that the name is given to Jerusalem because it was like a lion. If this be the true interpretation, then it is so called because Jerusalem was the place of the burnt-offering, or of the public worship of God; the place where the fire, as on a hearth, continually burned on the altar. ¶ *The city* where *David dwelt.* David took the hill of Zion from the Jebusites, and made it the capital of his kingdom (2 Sam. v. 6–9). Lowth renders this, 'The city which David besieged.' So the LXX. 'Ἐπολέμησε; and so the Vulgate, *Expugnavit.* The word חָנָה properly means *to encamp,* to pitch one's tent (Gen. xxvi. 17), to station one's self. It is also used in the sense of encamping *against* any one, that is, to make war upon or to attack (see ver. 3, and Ps. xxvii. 3; 2 Sam. xii. 28); and Jerome and others have supposed that it has this meaning here in accordance with the interpretation of the LXX. and the Vulgate. But the more correct idea is probably that in our translation, that David pitched his tent there; that is, that he made it his dwelling-place. ¶ *Add ye year to year.* That is, 'go on year after year, suffer one year to glide on after another in the course which you are pursuing.' This seems to be used ironically, and to denote that they were going on one year after another in the observance of the feasts; walking the round of external ceremonies as if the fact that David had dwelt there, and that that was the place of the great altar of worship, constituted perfect security. One of the sins charged on them in this chapter was *formality* and *heartlessness* in their devotions (ver. 13), and this seems to be referred to here. ¶ *Let them kill sacrifices.* Marg. 'Cut off the heads.' The word here rendered 'kill' (נָקַף) may mean to

smite; to hew; to cut down (Isa. x. 34; Job xix. 26). But it has also another signification which better accords with this place. It denotes to make a circle, to revolve; to go round a place (Josh. vi. 3, 11); to surround (1 Kings vi. 24; 2 Kings vi. 14; Ps. xvii. 9; xxii. 17; lxxxviii. 18). The word rendered 'sacrifices' (חַגִּים) may mean a sacrifice (Ex. xxiii. 18; Ps. cxviii. 27; Mal. ii. 3), but it more commonly and properly denotes feasts or festivals (Ex. x. 9; xii. 14; Lev. xxiii. 39; Deut. xvi. 10, 16; 1 Kings viii. 2, 65; 2 Chron. vii. 8, 9; Neh. viii. 14; Hos. ii. 11, 13). Here the sense is, 'let the festivals go round;' that is, let them revolve as it were in a perpetual, unmeaning circle, until the judgments due to such heartless service shall come upon you. The whole address is evidently ironical, and designed to denote that all their service was an unvarying repetition of heartless forms.

2. *Yet I will distress Ariel.* The reference here is doubtless to the siege which God says (ver. 3) he would bring upon the guilty and formal city. ¶ *And there shall be heaviness and sorrow.* This was true of the city in the siege of Sennacherib, to which this probably refers. Though the city was delivered in a sudden and remarkable manner (see Note on ver. 7, 8), yet it was also true that it was reduced to great distress (see ch. xxxvi., xxxvii.) ¶ *And it shall be unto me as Ariel.* This phrase shows that in ver. 1 Jerusalem is called 'Ariel,' because it contained the great altar, and was the place of sacrifice. The word *Ariel* here is to be understood in the sense of *the hearth of the great altar;* and the meaning is, 'I will indeed make Jerusalem like the great altar; I will make it the burning place of wrath where my enemies shall be consumed as if they were on the altar of burnt sacrifice.' Thus in ch. xxx. 9, it is said of JEHOVAH that his 'fire is in Zion, and his furnace in Jerusalem.' This is a strong expression, denoting the calamity that was approaching; and though the main reference in this whole passage is to the distress that would

3 And I will camp against thee round about, and will lay siege against *a* thee with a mount, and I will raise forts against thee.

4 And thou shalt be brought down, *b and* shalt speak out of the ground, and thy speech shall be low out of the dust, and thy voice shall be as of one that hath a fa-

miliar spirit, out of the ground, and thy speech shall [1] whisper out of the dust.

5 Moreover the multitude of thy strangers shall be like small dust, and the multitude of the terrible ones *shall be* as chaff *c* that passeth away : yea, it shall be at an instant suddenly.*d*

a 2 Ki.25.1,&c.   *b* La.1.9.   1 *peep,* or, *chirp.*   *c* Job 21.18.   *d* 1 Th.5.3.

come upon them in the invasion of Sennacherib, yet there is no impropriety in supposing that there was presented to the mind of the prophet in vision the image of the total ruin that would come yet upon the city by the Chaldeans—when the temple, the palaces, and the dwellings of the magnificent city of David would be in flames, and like a vast blazing altar consuming that which was laid upon it.

3. *And I will camp against thee.* That is, I will cause an army to pitch their tents there for a siege. God regards the armies which he would employ as under his control, and speaks of them as if he would do it himself (see Note on ch. x. 5). ¶ *Round about* (בַדּוּר). As in a circle ; that is, he would encompass or encircle the city. The word here used (דוּר) in ch. xxii. 18, means *a ball,* but here it evidently means a circle ; and the sense is, that the army of the besiegers would encompass the city. A similar form of expression occurs in regard to Jerusalem in Luke xix. 43 : ' For the days shall come upon thee, that thine enemies shall cast a trench (χάρακα—*a rampart, a mound*) about thee (σοι *against thee*), and *compass thee round* (περικυκλώσουσί σι, *encircle thee*).' So also Luke xxi. 20. The LXX. render this, ' I will encompass thee as David did ;' evidently reading it as if it were בַדּוּד; and Lowth observes that two MSS. thus read it, and he himself adopts it. But the authority for correcting the Hebrew text in this way is not sufficient, nor is it necessary. The idea in the present reading is a clear one, and evidently means that the armies of Sennacherib would encompass the city. ¶ *With a mount.* A rampart ; a fortification. Or, rather, perhaps, the word מֻצָּב means a post, a military sta-

tion, from רָצַב, *to place, to station.* The word in this form occurs nowhere else in the Scriptures, but the word מַצָּב occurs in 1 Sam. xiii. 23; xiv. 1, 4; 2 Sam. xxiii. 14, in the sense of a military post, or garrison. ¶ *I will rise forts.* That is, ramparts, such as were usually thrown up against a besieged city, meaning that it should be subjected to the regular process of a siege. The LXX. read, Πύργους—' Towers ;' and so also two MSS. by changing the letter ד into ר. But there is no necessity for altering the Hebrew text. Lowth prefers the reading of the LXX.

4. *And shalt speak out of the ground* (see Note on ch. viii. 19). The sense here is, that Jerusalem, that had been accustomed to pride itself on its strength would be greatly humbled and subdued. Its loud and lofty tone would be changed. It would use the suppressed language of fear and alarm as if it spoke from the dust, or in a shrill small voice, like the pretended conversers with the dead. ¶ *And thy speech shall whisper out of the dust.* Marg. ' Peep,' or ' Chirp,' (see Note on ch. viii. 19).

5. *Moreover.* These verses (5, 7, 8) contain a beautiful description of the destruction of the army of Sennacherib. Though they had laid the plan of a regular siege ; though the city, in itself, would not be able to hold out against them, and all was alarm and conscious imbecility within ; yet in an instant the siege would be raised, and the advancing hosts of the Assyrians would all be gone. ¶ *The multitude of thy strangers.* The multitude of the strangers that shall besiege thee ; called ' *thy* strangers,' because they besieged, or oppressed thee. The word ' strangers ' here, as elsewhere, means *foreigners* (see Note on ch. i. 7; comp. ch. ii. 6 ; v. 17; xiv. 1; xxv. 2, 5;

6 Thou ^ashalt be visited of the LORD of hosts with thunder, and with earthquake, and great noise, with storm and tempest, and the flame of devouring fire.

7 And the multitude of all the nations that fight against Ariel, even all ^b that fight against her and her munition, and that distress her, shall be as a dream ^c of a night vision.

8 It shall even be as when an hungry *man* dreameth, and, behold, he eateth ; but he awaketh, and his soul is empty : or when a thirsty man dreameth, and, behold, he drinketh ; but he awaketh, and behold, *he is* faint, and his soul hath appetite : so shall the multitude of all the nations be that fight against mount Zion.

a ch.30.30.   *b* ch.41.11,12.   *c* ch.37.36.

xxix. 5; lx. 10). ¶ *Shall be like small dust.* Light, fine dust that is easily dissipated by the wind. ¶ *Of the terrible ones.* Of the invading, besieging army, that is so much the object of dread. ¶ *As chaff that passeth away* (see Note on ch. xvii. 13). This image of chaff driven before the wind, to denote the sudden and entire discomfiture of enemies, is common in the Scriptures (see Job xxi. 18; Ps. i. 4; xxxv. 5; Hos. xiii. 13). ¶ *Yea, it shall be at an instant suddenly.* The forces of Sennacherib were destroyed in a single night by the angel of the Lord (Isa. xxxvii. 36; Notes on ch. x. 12, 28–34), and the siege of Jerusalem was of course immediately raised.

6. *Thou shalt be visited.* This is an address to the mighty army of the Assyrian. Such transitions are not uncommon in the writings of Isaiah. His eye seems to have been directed in vision to the hosts of Sennacherib, and to their sudden dispersion and destruction (ver. 5), and by a sudden, but not unnatural transition, he turns and addresses the army itself, with the assurance that it should be punished (comp. ch. xxx. 30). ¶ *With thunder,* &c. The army of the Assyrian was cut off by an angel sent forth from God (ch. xxxvii. 36). It is *possible* that all the agents here referred to may have been employed in the destruction of the Assyrian host, though they are not particularly specified in the history. But it is not absolutely necessary to understand this verse in this manner. The image of thunder, earthquakes, and lightning, is an impressive representation of sudden and awful judgment in any manner. The sense is, that they should be suddenly destroyed by the direct visitation of

God (see ch. ix. 5; xxvi. 11). ¶ *And the flame of devouring fire.* Lightning, that seems to *devour,* or that suddenly consumes.

7. *And the multitude of all the nations.* The Assyrians, and their allied hosts. ¶ *And her munition.* Her fortresses, castles, places of strength (2 Sam. v. 7; Eccl. ix. 14; Ezek. xix. 9). ¶ *Shall be as a dream of a night vision.* In a dream we seem to see the objects of which we think as really as when awake, and hence they are called *visions,* and *visions of the night* (Gen. xlvi. 2; Job iv. 13; vii. 14; Dan. ii. 28; iv. 5; vii. 1, 7, 13, 15). The specific idea here is not that of the *suddenness* with which objects seen in a dream appear and then vanish, but it is that which occurs in ver. 8, of one who dreams of eating and drinking, but who awakes, and is hungry and thirsty still. So it was with the Assyrian. He had set his heart on the wealth of Jerusalem. He had earnestly desired to possess that city—as a hungry man desires to satisfy the cravings of his appetite. But it would be like the vision of the night; and on that fatal morning on which he should awake from his fond dream (ch. xxxvii. 36), he would find all his hopes dissipated, and the long-cherished desire of his soul unsatisfied still.

8. *It shall even be,* &c. This is a most striking figure representing the earnest desire of the Assyrian to possess the city of Jerusalem, and his utter disappointment. The comparison is elegant and beautiful in the highest degree. It is wrought up to great perfection ; and is perfectly suited to illustrate the object in view. The same image substantially is found in the

9 Stay yourselves, and wonder; cry[1] ye out, and cry: they are

1 or, *take your pleasure and riot.*

drunken, [a] but not with wine; they stagger, but not with strong drink.

a ch.51.21.

---

classic writers; and this, says Lowth, may, for beauty and ingenuity, fairly come in competition with one of the most elegant of Virgil (greatly improved from Homer, *Iliad* xxii. 119), where he has applied to a different purpose, but not so happily, the same image of the ineffectual workings of the imagination in a dream:

Ac veluti in somnis oculos ubi languida pressit
Nocte quies, nequicquam avidos extendere cursus
Velle videmur, et in mediis conatibus ægri
Succidimus; non lingua valet, non corpore notæ
Sufficiunt vires; nec, vox, nec verba sequuntur.
                                        Æniad xii. 908.

And as when slumber seals the closing sight,
The sick wild fancy labours in the night,
Some dreadful visionary foe we shun,
With airy strides, but strive in vain to run;
In vain our baffled limbs their powers essay,
We faint, we struggle, sink, and fall away;
Drained of our strength we neither fight nor fly,
And on the tongue the struggling accents die.
                                        Pitt.

See also Lucretius (iv. 10–19), who also expresses the same image as Isaiah. As the simile of the prophet is drawn from nature, an extract which describes the actual occurrence of such a circumstance will be agreeable. 'The scarcity of water,' says Park, 'was greater here at Bubaker than at Benown. Day and night the wells were crowded with cattle lowing, and fighting with each other to come at the trough. Excessive thirst made many of them furious; others being too weak to contend for the water, endeavoured to quench their thirst by devouring the black mud from the gutters near the wells; which they did with great avidity, though it was commonly fatal to them. This great scarcity of water was felt by all the people of the camp; and by none more than myself. I begged water from the negro slaves that attended the camp, but with very indifferent success; for though I let no opportunity slip, and was very urgent in my solicitations both to the Moors and to the negroes, I was but ill supplied, and frequently passed the night in the situation of Tantalus. No sooner had I shut my eyes, than fancy would convey me to the streams and rivers of my native

land; there, as I wandered along the verdant bank, I surveyed the clear stream with transport, and hastened to swallow the delightful draught; but alas! disappointment awakened me, and I found myself a lonely captive, perishing of thirst amid the wilds of Africa.'—(*Travels in Africa*).

9. *Stay yourselves.* Thus far the prophet had given a description of the siege of Jerusalem by Sennacherib, and of his sudden overthrow. He now turns to the Jews, and reproves their stupidity, formality, and hypocrisy; and the remainder of the chapter is occupied with a statement of the prevalence of these sins, of the judgments that must follow, and of the fact that there should yet be an extensive reformation, and turning to the Lord. The word rendered 'stay yourselves' (הִתְמַהְמְהוּ) means properly *to linger*, tarry, delay (Gen. xix. 16; xliii. 10; 2 Sam. xv. 28). Here it seems to denote that state of mind in which any one is *fixed in astonishment;* in which one stops, and stares at some strange and unexpected occurrence. The object of amazement which the prophet supposes would excite astonishment, was the stupidity, dulness, and hypocrisy of a people who had been so signally favoured (comp. Hab. i. 5). ¶ *Cry ye out, and cry.* There is in the original here a paronomasia which cannot be conveyed in a translation. The word which is used (הִשְׁתַּעַשְׁעוּ) is one form of the verb שָׁעַע, which means, usually, to make smooth, rub, spread over; hence, in the Hithpael form which is here used, to be spread over; and hence is applied to the eyes (Isa. vi. 10), to denote blindness, *as if* they were overspread with something by reason of which they could not see. Here it probably means, 'be ye dazzled and blinded,' that is, ye be astonished, as in the former part of the verse. The idea seems to be that of some object of sudden astonishment that dims the sight, and takes away all the powers of vision. The word is used in the same sense in

10 For ^athe Lord hath poured
out upon you the spirit of deep
sleep, and hath closed your eyes ;
the prophets and your ¹rulers the
seers ^b hath he covered.

11 And the vision of all is become
unto you as the words of a ²book
that is sealed, ^c which *men* deliver

a Ro.11.8.   1 *heads.*   *b* 1 Sa.9.9.

to one that is learned, saying, Read
this, I pray thee : and he saith, I
cannot ; for it *is* sealed.

12 And the book is delivered to
him that is not learned, saying,
Read this, I pray thee : and he
saith, I am not learned.

13 Wherefore the Lord said,

2 or, *letter.*   *c* Da.12.4,9; Re.5.1-9.

ch. xxxii. 3; comp. ch. xxxv. 5; xlii.
19. Probably the idea here would be
well expressed by our word *stare,* ' stare
and look with a stupid surprise ;' denoting the attitude and condition of a
man who is amazed at some remarkable
and unlooked for spectacle. ¶ *They
are drunken, but not with wine.* The
people of Jerusalem. They reel and
stagger, but the cause is not that they
are drunken with wine. It is a moral
and spiritual intoxication and reeling.
They err in their doctrines and practice ; and it is with them as it is with
a drunken man that sees nothing clearly
or correctly, and cannot walk steadily.
They have perverted all doctrines ; they
err in their views of God and his truth,
and they are irregular and corrupt in
their conduct.

10. *For the* Lord *hath poured out
upon you.* The word rendered ' hath
poured out ' (נָסַךְ) is usually referred
to the act of pouring out a libation, or
drink-offering in worship (Ex. xxx. 9;
Hos. ix. 4 ; Isa. xxx. 1). Here it means
that Jehovah had, as it were, *drenched
them* (LXX. πεπότικε) with a spirit of
stupefaction. This is traced to God in
accordance with the usual custom in
the Bible, by which his providential
agency is recognized in all events (see
Notes on ch. vi. 9, 10). Compare Notes
on Rom. xi. 8), where this passage is
quoted from the LXX., and is applied
to the Jews in the time of the apostle
Paul. ¶ *The spirit of deep sleep.*
The word rendered ' deep sleep,' is the
same as is used in Gen. ii. 21, to denote
the sleep that God brought on Adam ;
and in Gen. xv. 12, to denote the deep
sleep that fell on Abraham, and when
a horror of great darkness fell upon
him ; and in 1 Sam. xxvi. 12, to denote
the deep sleep that came upon Saul
when David approached and took away

the spear and the cruise of water from
his bolster. Here it means spiritual
sluggishness, inactivity, stupidity, that
prevailed everywhere among the people
in regard to the things of religion.
¶ *The seers.* Those that see visions,
another name for the prophets (see
Note on ch. i. 1). ¶ *Hath he covered.*
That is, he has covered their eyes ; or
they are all blind.

11. *And the vision of all.* The
vision of all the prophets ; that is, all
the revelations which God has made to
you (see Note on ch. i. 1). The prophet refers not only to his own communications, but to those of his contemporaries, and of all who had gone
before him. The sense is, that although
they had the communications which
God had made to them, yet they did
not understand them. They were as
ignorant of their true nature as a man
who can read is of the contents of a letter that is sealed up, or as a man who
cannot read is of the contents of a book
that is handed to him. ¶ *As the words
of a book.* Marg. ' Letter.' The word
סֵפֶר may mean either. It properly
means anything which is *written* (Deut.
xxiv. i. 3; Jer. xxxii. 11; Dan. i. 4),
but is commonly applied to a book
(Ex. xvii. 14 ; Josh. i. 8; viii. 34 ; Ps.
xl. 8). ¶ *That is sealed* (see Note on
ch. viii. 16).

12. *And the book is delivered,* &c.
That is, they are just as ignorant of the
true nature and meaning of the revelations of God as a man is of the contents
of a book who is utterly unable to read.

13. *Wherefore the Lord said.* This
verse, with the following, is designed to
denounce the Divine judgment on their
formality of worship. They kept up
the forms of religion, but they withheld
the affections of their hearts from God ;
and he, therefore, says that he will pro-

Forasmuch as this people draw near *me* with their mouth, *ª* and with their lips do honour me, but have removed their heart far from me, and their fear toward me is taught by the precept of *ᵇ* men :

14 Therefore, behold, I will proceed[1] to do a marvellous *ᶜ* work among this people, *even* a marvellous work and a wonder : for *ᵈ* the wisdom of their wise *men* shall

perish, and the understanding of their prudent *men* shall be hid.

15 Wo unto them that seek deep to hide *ᵉ* their counsel from the LORD, and their works are in the dark, and they say, Who *ƒ* seeth us ? and who knoweth us ?

16 Surely your turning of things upside down shall be esteemed as the potter's clay : for *ᵍ* shall the work say of him that made it, He

---

ª Eze.33.31; Mat.15.6-9. *ᵇ* Col.2.22. [1] *add*.
ᶜ Hab.1.5. *ᵈ* Jer.49.7; Ob.8; 1 Co.1.19.

ᵉ Ps.139.7,&c.; ch.30.1. *ƒ* Ps.94.7.
ᵍ ch.45.9; Ro.9.20.

---

ceed to inflict on them exemplary and deserved punishment. ¶ *This people draw near* me. That is, in the temple, and in the forms of external devotion. ¶ *And with their lips do honour me.* They professedly celebrate my praise, and acknowledge me in the forms of devotion. ¶ *But have removed their heart.* Have withheld the affections of their hearts. ¶ *And their fear toward me.* The worship of God is often represented as *fear* (Job xxviii. 28; Ps. xix. 9; xxxiv. 11; Prov. i. 7). ¶ *Is taught by the precept of men.* That is, their views, instead of having been derived from the Scriptures, were drawn from the doctrines of men. Our Saviour referred to this passage, and applied it to the hypocrites of his own time (Matt. xv. 8, 9). The latter part of it is, however, not quoted literally from the Hebrew, nor from the LXX., but retains the sense : 'But in vain do they worship me, teaching for doctrines the commandments of men.' He quoted it as strikingly descriptive of the people when he lived, not as saying that Isaiah referred directly to his times.

14. *I will proceed to do.* Heb. 'I will add to do ;' that is, I will do it. ¶ *For the wisdom of their wise men shall perish.* I will bring calamity upon them which shall baffle all the skill and wisdom of their wise men. ¶ *Shall be hid.* That is, shall not appear ; shall vanish. It shall not be sufficient to prevent the calamities that shall come upon the nation.

15. *Wo unto them that seek deep, &c.* That is, who attempt to conceal their *real* intentions under a plausible exterior, and correct outward deportment.

This is most strikingly descriptive of the character of a hypocrite who seeks to conceal his plans and his purposes from the eyes of men and of God. His external conduct is fair ; his observance of the duties of religion exemplary ; his attendance on the means of grace and the worship of God regular ; his professions loud and constant, but the whole design is to *conceal* his real sentiments, and to accomplish some sinister and wicked purpose by it. ¶ *From the* LORD. This proves that the design of the hypocrite is not always to attempt to deceive his fellow-men, but that he also aims to deceive God.

16. *Surely your turning of things upside down.* Your *perversion* of all things. They had no just views of truth. They deemed mere formality to be all that was required. They attempted to conceal their plans even from JEHOVAH ; and everything in the opinions and practice of the nation had become perverted and erroneous. There has been much diversity in rendering this phrase. Luther renders it, 'O how perverse ye are.' Lowth renders it,

'Perverse as ye are! shall the potter be esteemed as the clay ?'

Rosenmüller also accords with this interpretation, and renders it, 'O your perversity,' &c. The sense of the passage seems to be this : 'Your *changing of things* is just as absurd as it would be for the thing formed to say to him that formed it, why hast thou made me thus? It is as absurd for you to find fault with the government of God as it would be for the clay to complain of made me not? or shall the thing framed say of him that framed it, He had no understanding?

17 *Is* it not yet a very little while,

and Lebanon shall be turned *a* into a fruitful field, and the fruitful field shall be esteemed as a forest?

want of skill in the potter. You complain of God's laws, and worship him according to the commandments of men. You complain of his requirements, and offer to him the service of the mouth and the lip, and withhold the heart. You suppose that God does not see you, and do your deeds in darkness. All this supposes that God is destitute of wisdom, and cannot see what is done, and it is just as absurd as it would be in the clay to complain that the potter who fashions it has no understanding.' ¶ *Shall be esteemed, &c.* The *literal* translation of this passage would be, 'Your perverseness is as if the potter should be esteemed as the clay;' that is, as if he was no more qualified to form anything than the clay itself. ¶ *For shall the work, &c.* This passage is quoted by the apostle Paul (Rom. ix. 20, 21) to show the right which God has to do with his creatures as shall seem good in his sight, and the impropriety of complaining of his distinguishing mercy in choosing to life those whom he pleases. The sense of the passage is, that it would be absurd for that which is made to complain of the maker as having no intelligence, and no right to make it as he does. It would be absurd in the piece of pottery to complain of the potter as if he had no skill; and it is equally absurd in a man to complain of God, or to regard him as destitute of wisdom.

17. Is *it not yet a very little while.* The idea here is, 'you have greatly perverted things in Jerusalem. The time is at hand when there shall be *other* overturnings—when the wicked shall be cut off, and when there shall be poured out upon the nation such judgments that the deaf shall hear, and the blind see, and when those who have erred in spirit shall come to understanding' (ver. 18–24). ¶ *And Lebanon shall be turned into a fruitful field.* This is evidently a proverbial expression, denoting any great revolution of things. It is probable that in the times

of Isaiah the whole chain of Lebanon was uncultivated, as the word is evidently here used in opposition to a fruitful field (see Note on ch. ii. 13). The word which is rendered 'fruitful field' (כַּרְמֶל, *carmel*) properly denotes *a fruitful field,* or a finely cultivated country (see Isa. x. 18). It is also applied to a celebrated mountain or promontory on the Mediterranean Sea, on the southern boundary of the tribe of Asher. It runs north-west of the plain of Esdraelon, and ends in a promontory or cape, and forms the bay of Acco. The mountain or promontory is about 1500 feet high; and abounds in caves or grottoes, and was celebrated as being the residence of the prophets Elijah and Elisha (see 1 Kings xviii. 19, 42; 2 Kings ii. 25; iv. 25; xix. 23; comp. Note on Isa. xxxv. 2). More than a thousand caves are said to exist on the west side of the mountain, which it is said were formerly inhabited by monks. But the word here is to be taken, doubtless, as it is in our translation, as denoting a well-cultivated country. Lebanon, that is now barren and uncultivated, shall soon become a fertile and productive field. That is, there shall be changes among the Jews that shall be as great *as if* Lebanon should become an extensively cultivated region, abounding in fruits, and vines, and harvests. The idea is this: 'The nation is now perverse, sinful, formal, and hypocritical. But the time of change shall come. The wicked shall be reformed; the number of the pious shall be increased; and the pure worship of God shall succeed this general formality and hypocrisy.' The prophet does not say *when* this would be. He simply affirms that it would be before *a great while*—and it may, perhaps, be referred to the times succeeding the captivity (comp. ch. xxxii. 15; xxxv. i. 6). ¶ *And the fruitful field be esteemed as a forest.* That is, there shall be great changes in the nation, *as if* a well-cultivated field should be

18 And ^ain that day shall the deaf hear the words of the book, and the eyes of the blind shall see out of obscurity, and out of darkness.

19 The meek ^balso shall ¹increase *their* joy in the Lord, and the poor ^camong men shall rejoice in the Holy One of Israel.

^a ch.35.5; Lu.7.22.　　^b ch.61.1.　　1 *add.*
^c Ja.2,5.

20 For the terrible one is brought to nought, ^dand the scorner is consumed, and all that watch ^efor iniquity are cut off ;

21 That make a man an offender for a word, and ^flay a snare for him that reproveth in the gate, and turn aside the just for a thing of nought.

^d ch.51.13; Re.12.10.　　^e Ps.64.6; Jer.20.10.
^f Amos 5.10,12.

allowed to lie waste, and grow up into a forest. Perhaps it means that that which was then apparently flourishing would be overthrown, and the land lie waste. Those who were apparently in prosperity, would be humbled and punished. The effect of this revolution is stated in the following verses.

18. *Shall the deaf hear the words of the book.* They who now have the law and do not understand it, the people who seem to be deaf to all that God says, shall hear and understand it. ¶ *Shall see out of obscurity,* &c. That is, the darkness being removed, they shall see clearly the truth of God, and discern and love its beauty. Their eyes are now blinded, but then they shall see clearly.

19. *The meek.* The word 'meek' usually refers to those who are patient in the reception of injuries, but the Hebrew word used here (עֲנָוִים) means properly the oppressed, the afflicted, the unhappy (Ps. ix. 13; x. 12, 17; Prov. iii. 34; Isa. xi. 4). It involves usually the idea of humility or *virtuous suffering* (comp. Ps. xxv. 9; xxxvii. 11; lxix. 33). Here it may denote the pious of the land who were oppressed, and subjected to trials. ¶ *Shall increase.* Marg., as in Heb. 'Add.' It means, that they should greatly rejoice in the Lord. They should see the evidence of the fulfilment of his predictions ; they should see the oppressors punished (ver. 20, 21), and Jehovah coming forth to be their protector and defender (ver. 22–24). ¶ *And the poor among men.* The poor men ; or the needy. Doubtless the idea is that of the pious poor ; those who feared God, and who had been subjected to the trials of oppression and poverty.

20. *For the terrible one.* The violent one (עָרִיץ), the oppressor, who had exercised cruelty over them. This, I suppose, refers to the haughty among the Jews themselves ; to those who held offices of power, and who abused them to oppress the poor and needy. ¶ *And the scorner* (see ch. xxviii. 14, 22). ¶ *Is consumed.* Shall be entirely destroyed. ¶ *And all that watch for iniquity.* That is, who anxiously seek for opportunities to commit iniquity.

21. *That make a man an offender.* Literally, 'who cause a man to sin ' (מַחֲטִיאֵי) ; that is, who hold a man to be guilty, or a criminal. Lowth renders this singularly enough :

'Who bewildered the poor man in speaking.'

Grotius supposes it means, ' Who on account of the word of God, that is, the true prophecy, treat men as guilty of crime.' Calvin supposes it means, ' Who bear with impatience the reproofs and denunciation of the prophets, and who endeavour to pervert and distort their meaning.' Hence, he supposes, they proposed artful and captious questions by which they might ensnare them. Others suppose that it refers to the fact that they led men into sin by their new doctrines and false views. The connection, however, seems to require that it should be understood of judicial proceedings, and the sense is probably correctly expressed by Noyes:

'Who condemned the poor man in his cause.'

This interpretation is also that which is proposed by Rosenmüller and Gesenius. According to the interpretation above suggested, the word rendered ' who make an offender,' means the same as who holds one guilty, that is, condemns. ¶ *A man* (אָדָם). It is

22 Therefore thus saith the Lord, *a* who redeemed Abraham, concerning the house of Jacob,

a Jos 24.3

Jacob shall not *b* now be ashamed, neither shall his face now wax pale.

b ch.54.4.

well known that this word stands in contradistinction to אִישׁ, and denotes usually a poor man, a man in humble life, in opposition to one who is rich or of more elevated rank. This is probably the sense here, and the meaning is, that they condemned the poor man; that is, that they were partial in their judgments. ¶ *For a word* (בְּדָבָר). *In* a word; denoting the same as *a cause* that is tried before a court of justice. So Ex. xviii. 16: 'When they have *a matter* (דָּבָר *a word*), they come unto me.' So Ex. xviii. 22: 'And it shall be that every great *matter* (Heb. every great *word*) that they shall bring unto me.' So Ex. xxii. 8 (in the English version 9): 'For all manner of trespass,' Heb. for every *word* of trespass; *i.e.*, for every suit concerning a breach of trust. So also Ex. xxiv. 14: 'If any man have *any matters* to do,' (Heb. 'any *words*,') that is, if any one has a law suit. ¶ *And lay a snare.* To lay a snare is to devise a plan to deceive, or get into their possession; as birds are caught in snares that are concealed from their view. ¶ *That reproveth.* Or rather, that *contended* or *pleaded*; that is, that had a cause. The word יָכַח means often to contend with any one; to strive; to seek to confute; to attempt to defend or justify, as in a court of law (Job xiii. 15; xix. 5; xvi. 21; xxii. 4). It is also applied to deciding a case in law, or pronouncing a decision (Isa. xi. 3, 4; Gen. xxxi. 37; Job ix. 33). Here it means one who has brought a suit, or who is engaged in a legal cause. ¶ *In the gate.* Gates of cities being places of concourse, were usually resorted to for transacting business, and courts were usually held in them (Gen. xxiii. 10, 18; Deut. xvii. 5, 8; xxi. 19; xxii. 15; xxv. 6, 7; Ruth iv. 1). The sense is, they endeavoured to pervert justice, and to bring the man who had a cause before them, completely within their power, so that they might use him for their own purposes, at the same time that they *seemed* to

be deciding the cause justly. ¶ *And turn aside the just.* The man who has a just or righteous cause. ¶ *For a thing of nought.* Or a decision which is empty, vain (בַּתֹּהוּ), and which should be regarded as null and void.

22. *Therefore.* In consequence of the happy change which shall take place in the nation when the oppressor shall be removed (ver. 20, 21), and when the poor and the meek shall rejoice (ver. 19), and the ignorant shall be instructed (ver. 18), Jacob shall not be ashamed of his descendants as he was before, nor have cause to blush in regard to his posterity. ¶ *Who redeemed Abraham.* That is, who brought him out of a land of idolaters, and rescued him from the abominations of idolatry. The word 'redeem,' here (פָּדָה), properly denotes *to ransom, i.e.*, to redeem a captive, or a prisoner with a price paid (Ex. xiii. 13; xxxiv. 20). But it is also used as meaning to deliver in general, without reference to a price, to free in any manner, to recover (2 Sam. iv. 9; 1 Kings i. 29; Job v. 20; Ps. lxxi. 23). It is used in this general sense here; and means that Jehovah had rescued Abraham from the evils of idolatry, and made him his friend. The connection, also, would seem to imply that there was a reference to the promise which was made to Abraham that he should have a numerous posterity (see ver. 23). ¶ *Jacob shall not now be ashamed.* This is a poetical introduction of Jacob as the ancestor of the Jewish people, *as if* the venerable patriarch were looking upon his children. Their deportment *had* been such as would suffuse a father's cheeks with shame; henceforward in the reformation that would occur he would *not* be ashamed of them, but would look on them with approbation. ¶ *Neither shall his face wax pale.* The face usually becomes pale with fear; but this may also occur from any strong emotion. *Disappointment* may produce paleness as well as fear; and perhaps the idea may be that the face of Jacob

23 But when he seeth his children, the work ^aof mine hands, in the midst of him, they shall sanctify my name, and sanctify the Holy One of Jacob, and shall fear the God of Israel.

24 They ^b also that erred in spirit shall ¹ come to understanding, and they that murmured shall learn doctrine.

CHAPTER XXX.
ANALYSIS.

It is probable that the prophecy in this chapter was delivered about the same time as that in the previous chapter, and on the same general occasion. It is evident that it refers to the time of Hezekiah, when the Jews were alarmed by an apprehended invasion of the king of Assyria. Hezekiah had revolted from the king of Assyria (2 Kings xviii. 7); and it is probable that many of the leaders of the Jews began to be alarmed at the prospect that their land would be invaded by him, especially as it was known that it was the intention of Sennacherib to make war on Egypt, and that he could easily take Judea in his way. In such circumstances it was natural that they should propose an alliance with the Egyptians, and seek to unite their forces with theirs to repel the common danger. Instead of looking to God, and relying on his aid, they had probably entered into such an alliance, offensive and defensive (ch. xxxi. 1). To see the impropriety of such a league, it is to be remembered that God had promised to be the protector of his people, and that he had prohibited alliances with the surrounding nations; that it was a leading part of the Jewish policy,

a ch 60.21; Eph.2.10.   *b* 1 Co.6.11.
          1 *know understanding.*

as instituted by Moses, to keep them a distinct and independent people; and that special care had been exercised to keep them from returning to the customs, or depending on the aid of the Egyptians. This alliance had been formed unquestionably contrary to the solemn counsel and warning of Isaiah (ch. xx.), and he now reproves them for it, and endeavours to recall them again to confidence in God.

The following is a summary of the contents of the chapter:—I. The prophet denounces 'wo' on them for seeking the aid of Egypt (1, 2). II. He assures them that Egypt would be unable to help them, and that the effect would be that they would yet be ashamed themselves of the alliance (3–7). III. The prophet is directed to make a solem record that the prevailing character of the Jews was that of a rebellious people (8–11). IV. The judgment of God is denounced against them for forming this alliance, under the image of a wall that is ready to fall on them, and destroy them (12–14). V. The prophet tells them of the true way in which they may have peace and confidence, and that is, by putting their trust in God, and assures them that God waits to become their defender (15–18). VI. God *would* yet bless them. The people would see the vanity of their reliance on Egypt, and would turn unto God, and their turning to him would be attended with most rich and valuable blessings. These blessings are described in highly figurative and beautiful language (19–26) VII. Jehovah would show himself the protector of his people; and would, in a signal and sudden manner, overthrow and destroy the Assyrian, and deliver his people (27–33). The *scope*, therefore, of the chapter is to lead them to look away from Egypt, and to put confidence in God, at whose hand they were about to experience so signal a deliverance from the much dreaded invasion of Sennacherib.

---

should no more become pallid *as if* he had been disappointed in regard to the hopes which he had cherished of his sons.

23. *But when he seeth his children.* The sense is, 'he shall not be ashamed of his sons, for he shall see them henceforward walking in the ways of piety and virtue.' ¶ *The work of my hands.* That is, this change (ver. 17–19) by which the nation will be reformed, will be produced by the agency of God himself. The sentiment is in accordance with the doctrines of the Scriptures everywhere, that men are recovered from sin by the agency of God alone (comp. Isa. lx. 21; Eph. ii. 10). ¶ *In*

the midst of him. In the midst of his people. The name Jacob is often employed to denote all his posterity, or the whole nation of the Jews.

24. *They also that erred in spirit* (see ver. 9, 10). ¶ *Shall learn doctrine.* *When* this would occur the prophet does not state. It *may* be intended to denote the times of Hezekiah ; or the times subsequent to the captivity ; or possibly it may refer to the times under the Messiah. All that the prophet teaches is, that at some future period in the history of the Jews, there would be such a reform that they should be regarded as the worthy descendants of the pious patriarch Jacob.

WO *a* to the rebellious children, saith the LORD, that take counsel, but not of me ; and that cover *b* with a covering, but not of my Spirit, that they may add *c* sin to sin :

2 That *d* walk to go down into Egypt, and have not asked at my

a De.29.19.　　*b* ch.29.15.　　*c* Ro.2.5.　　*d* ch.31.1.

mouth ; to strengthen themselves in the strength of Pharaoh, and to trust in the shadow of Egypt !

3 Therefore shall the strength of Pharaoh be your shame, and the trust in the shadow of Egypt *your* confusion.

4 For his princes were at Zoan, and his ambassadors came to Hanes.

CHAPTER XXX.

1. *Wo* (see Note on ch. xviii. 1). ¶ *To the rebellious children.* To those whom he had nourished as children, and who had rebelled against him (see Note on ch. i. 23). ¶ *That take counsel, but not of me.* They look to Egypt, and depend on a human arm. ¶ *And that cover with a covering.* The idea here, according to our translation, is, that they seek protection or a covering from the impending calamity. Lowth renders this, 'Who ratify covenants ;' supposing that the reference is to the fact that in ancient times compacts were formed by offering sacrifices, and by pouring out libations. The Hebrew, according to Lowth, means, 'who pour out a libation.' So the LXX. render it, Συνθήκας—'And thou hast made covenants.' The Syriac renders it, 'Who pour out libations.' The Hebrew word נָסַךְ (*nâsăkh*) properly conveys the idea of *pouring out*, and is applied—(1) to the act of pouring out wine as a drink offering, or as a libation to God (Gen. xxxv. 14 ; Ex. xxx. 9 ; 1 Chron. xi. 18 ; Hos. ix. 4) ; (2) to the act of pouring out oil, that is, to anointing kings and rulers (Ps. ii. 6 ; Dan. xi. 8) ; (3) to the act of pouring out melted metals, that is, to cast them (Isa. xl. 19 ; xliv. 10). The word also may have a meaning kindred to סָכַךְ (*săkhăkh*), and denote *to cover*, as in Isa. xxv. 7. Various derivatives from the word are rendered 'to cover withal' (Num. iv. 7); 'the covering' (Isa. xxviii. 20); 'the web,' that is, that which is woven for a covering (Judg. xvi. 13, 14). The idea, however, which best suits the connection here is probably that suggested by Lowth, in accordance with the LXX., and the Syriac, and adopted by Rosenmüller, Gesenius, and others, *to make a libation;* that is, to ratify a covenant,

or compact. ¶ *But not of my Spirit.* It was not such as was suggested by his Spirit, and not such as he would approve. ¶ *That they may add sin to sin.* They add to the sin of rebellion against God that of forming an alliance. Sins do not usually stand alone. When one is committed, it is often necessary to commit others in order to carry out and complete the plan which that contemplated.

2. *That walk to go down to Egypt.* Heb. 'Going in the descent to Egypt.' That is, they do it by their ambassadors (ver. 4). The journey to Egypt from Palestine is always represented as going down (Gen. xii. 10 ; xlii. 3 ; xliii. 15 ; Num. xx. 15 ; Deut. x. 22). ¶ *To strengthen themselves in the strength of Pharaoh.* To form an alliance with Pharaoh, that thus they might be able to repel the threatened invasion. Pharaoh was the general name of the kings of Egypt, in the same manner as *Cæsar* was the common name of the emperors of Rome. ¶ *To trust in the shadow of Egypt.* A 'shadow' (צֵל) is an emblem of protection and defence, as a shade is a protection from the burning rays of the sun (see Note on ch. iv. 6).

3. *Therefore shall the strength of Pharaoh be your shame* (see Note on ch. xx. 5). ¶ *Your confusion.* Heb. 'For reproach.' It would either occur that the Egyptians *would* not enter into an alliance ; or that if they did, they *could* not defend them, and in either case it would be the source of deep regret and shame.

4. *For his princes.* The sense of this verse seems to be this. The prophet is stating the fact that the Jews would be ashamed of their attempted alliance with Egypt. In this verse, and the following, he states the manner in which they would be made sensible of their

5 They were all ashamed *a* of a people *that* could not profit them, nor be an help nor profit, but a shame, and also a reproach.

6 The burden of the beasts of the south : into the land of trouble

a Jer. 2. 36.

and anguish, from whence *come* the young and old lion, the viper and fiery flying serpent, they will carry their riches upon the shoulders of young asses, and their treasures upon the bunches of camels, to a people *that* shall not profit *them*.

---

folly in seeking this alliance. He therefore enumerates several circumstances in regard to the manner in which the alliance had been sought, and the disappointment that would follow after all their vain confidence. He therefore states (ver. 4), that the Jews had employed persons of the highest respectability and honour, even princes, to secure the alliance ; that they had gone to Egypt with much difficulty—through a land where lions, and vipers, and fiery serpents abounded ; that they had at much hazard taken their treasures down to Egypt in order to secure the alliance (ver. 5, 6), and that after all, the Egyptians could not aid them. The phrase ' his princes,' refers to the princes of Judah, the ambassadors that the Jews sent forth, and the idea is, that they regarded the alliance as of so much importance that they had employed their most honourable men—even their princes—to secure it. ¶ *Were at Zoan.* Had come to Zoan, or were there on the business of their embassy. On the situation of Zoan, see Notes on ch. xix. 11, 13. It was the residence of the kings in Lower Egypt, and would be the place to which the ambassadors would naturally resort to negotiate an alliance. ¶ *Came to Hanes.* Respecting the situation of this place there has been much diversity of opinion among interpreters. The Chaldee renders it by the more full word *Tahpanhes ;* and Grotius supposes that the word is contracted from Tahpanhes (Jer. xliii. 7, 8), and that the name was sometimes abbreviated and written חֲנֵס (*Hanes*). Vitringa supposes that it was Anusis, situated in the Delta of the Nile, and the residence of the king of the same name. Herodotus (ii. 137) mentions a city of that name, "Ἄνυσις. Anusis was a king of Egypt before the irruption of the Ethiopians, and it was not uncommon for a king to give his own name to a

Isaiah 1.

city. Probably Anusis is the city intended here ; and the sense is, that they had come to the royal residence for the purpose of negotiating an alliance. It is known that in the time of Jeremiah (588 years before Christ) *Tahpanhes* was the capital of the nation (see Jer. xliii. 9).

5. *They were all ashamed.* That is, all the legates or ambassadors. When they came into Egypt, they found them either unwilling to enter into an alliance, or unable to render them any aid, and they were ashamed that they had sought their assistance rather than depend on God (comp. Jer. ii. 36).

6. *The burden of the beasts of the south.* The word ' south ' here refers doubtless to the country to the south of Judea, and particularly to Egypt. Thus it is used in Dan. xi. 5, 6. The phrase ' beasts of the south,' here refers to the animals that were travelling to Egypt. Isaiah, in vision, sees the caravan heavily laden with treasures pursuing a southern direction on its way to Egypt. The word ' burden ' is used in two senses, to denote that which is borne, a heavy burden ; or an oracle, a solemn prophetic message (see Notes on ch. xv. 1 ; xvii. 1 ; xix. 1). Many understand the word here in the latter sense, and regard this as the title of a prophetic message similar to those in ch. xv. 1 ; xvii. 1 ; xix. 1. But the word is doubtless used here in its ordinary signification, to denote the load which is borne on animals, and here especially the treasures which were borne down to Egypt, for the purpose of securing their friendly alliance. The prophet sees the caravan, or the beasts of the ambassadors heavily laden with rich treasures, travelling southward towards Egypt, and cries out, ' O the heavy burden, the load of treasures going to the south !' ¶ *Into the land of trouble and anguish.* Egypt ; so called either because it was the land where the He-

29

7 For *a* the Egyptians shall help in vain, and to no purpose: there-

fore have I cried 1 concerning this, Their *b* strength *is* to sit still.

brews had formerly suffered so severe oppressions; or because it was a land where the subjects were now grievously oppressed, and borne down with cruel laws; or because it was yet to be a land of trouble, from which the Jews could expect no aid. The general idea is, that Egypt was not a land of liberty and happiness, but a country where cruelty, oppression, and woe abounded. One source of trouble, as emblematic of all, the prophet immediately mentions when he designates that it abounded with venomous reptiles. ¶ *The viper* (אֶפְעֶה, *epheh*). LXX. 'Ασπίδες—'Asps' (see Isa. lix. 5). This is a well-known species of serpent. It is probably the same as the *El-Effah* of the Arabs, which is thus described by Mr. Jackson: 'It is remarkable for its quick and pene-trating poison; it is about two feet long and as thick as a man's arm, beautifully spotted with yellow and brown, and sprinkled over with blackish specks, similar to the horn-nosed snake. They have a wide mouth, by which they in-hale a great quantity of air, and when inflated therewith they eject it with such force as to be heard at a consider-able distance.' It is well known that

VIPER (*El-Effah*).

Egypt produced venomous reptiles in abundance. Cleopatra destroyed herself with the bite of an asp which she had concealed for that purpose. ¶ *And fiery flying serpent* (שָׂרָף מְעוֹפֵף). LXX. Ἔκγονα ἀσπίδων πετομένων. This is the flying serpent so often referred to in the Scriptures. See a description of it in Notes on ch. xiv. 29. It is known to have abounded in the Arabian deserts, and was doubtless found also in Egypt as being in the same latitude, and in-

fested with similar reptiles. Niebuhr thus describes a species of serpent which answers to this account. 'There is at Bakra a sort of serpents which they call *Heie Sursurie*, or *Heie Thiàre*. They commonly keep upon the date trees; and as it would be laborious for them to come down from a very high tree in order to ascend another, they twist themselves by the tail to a branch of the former, which, making a spring, by the motion they give it, throw them-selves to the second. Hence it is that the modern Arabs call them the flying serpents—*Heie Thiàre.*' Lord Anson, as quoted by Niebuhr, also speaks of them as follows:—' The Spaniards in-formed us that there was often found in the woods a most mischievous serpent, called the flying snake, which, they said, darted itself from the boughs of trees on either man or beast that came within its reach, and whose sting they took to be inevitable death.' There was a species of serpent which the Greeks called *Acontias*, and the Roman *Jaculus*, from their *swift darting motion*, and perhaps the same species is here referred to which Lucan calls *Jaculique volucres*. That these venomous reptiles abounded in Egypt is expressly testified by pro-fane writers. Thus Ammianus says (xxii. 15), that 'Egypt nourishes innu-merable serpents, basilisks, and two-headed serpents [amphisbænas], and the scytalus [a serpent of a glistening col-our], and the acontias [Latin, *Jacu-lus*], and adders, and vipers, and many others.' ¶ *They will carry their riches.* Presents, designed to induce the Egyp-tians to enter into the alliance. That it was a common custom to make pre-sents when one king sent an embassy to another, whether the design was to show friendship or civility, or to form an alliance, is well known in regard to all the nations of the East. The custom prevails at the present day, and is often referred to in Scripture (see 1 Kings xv. 19; 2 Kings xvi. 8; xviii. 14, 15).

7. *For the Egyptians shall help in vain.* That is, if they enter into the alliance, they shall not be able to defend

8 Now go, write it before them in a table, and note it in a book, that it may be for the [1]time to come for ever and ever.

1 *latter day.*

you from the invader. The other member of the sentence would seem to imply that they would make promises of aid, and would even boast of being able to deliver them, but that they would fail in their promises. ¶ *Therefore have I cried.* Therefore have I the prophet cried, *i.e.*, I do call her so. ¶ *Concerning this.* Concerning this country; that is, Egypt. Some have understood this as referring to Jerusalem, but the connection requires us to understand it of Egypt. ¶ *Their strength is to sit still.* This is evidently designed to be an expressive appellation of Egypt. The word here rendered, without much propriety, 'strength' (רַהַב, *rǎhǎbh*) is a proper name of Egypt, and is several times applied to it; Isa. li. 9:

> Art thou not it that hath cut *Rahab*
> And wounded the dragon?

In this passage there can be no doubt that it refers to Egypt. So in Ps. lxxxvii. 4; lxxxix. 10 (see margin). Why it was given to Egypt is unknown, and can only be conjectured. Bochart (*Geog. Sacra*, i. 4. 24) supposes that it is derived from the word βίβι, which signifies *a pear*, and that it was given to the Delta or Lower Egypt on account of its form, as somewhat resembling a pear. But there is not clear evidence that such was the meaning of the word, and there is no reason why we should forsake the usual sense of the Hebrew word. The verb רָהַב (*rǎhǎbh*) means to urge, press on, attack (Prov. vi. 3); to be high-spirited, fierce, full of courage; to behave proudly (Isa. iii. 5); and has, in most instances, a relation to pride, to arrogance, to boasting (Job ix. 13; Ps. xl. 4). The noun *Rahab* indicates ferocity, haughtinesss, boasting, insolence; and the name was doubtless given to Egypt on account of its insolence and pride. It is used here because Egypt would be full of self-confidence, and would boast that she could aid the suppliant Jews, and deliver them from the threatened invasion. The

phrase rendered 'to sit still,' is a part of the name which the prophet gave to her. Though she boasted, yet would she sit still; she would be inefficient, and would do nothing; and the whole name, therefore, may be rendered, 'I call her the blusterer that sitteth still;' that is, 'they are courageous in talking; cowards in acting.'—(Taylor.)

8. *Now go.* This is a direction to the prophet to make a permanent record of the character of the Jewish people. The fact to be recorded was, that they were rebellious (ver. 9); the design for which the record was to be made was to show to future times that this had been the uniform character of the nation. The record was to be preserved that it might be a proof of the care of God towards the nation even in the midst of their long-continued and obstinate perverseness. ¶ *Write it before them.* Before the Jews themselves, that they may see the record, and may have it constantly before them. ¶ *In a table.* Or *on* a table. The word לוּחַ denotes a tablet either of stone to engrave upon (Deut. ix. 9; Ex. xxxi. 18); or of wood (1 Kings vii. 36). It is not improbable that this was to be exposed to public view in

ANCIENT ROLL AND SEAL.

ANCIENT STYLES.

some conspicuous place near the temple. ¶ *And note it.* Engrave it; that is, record it. ¶ *In a book.* On parchment, or in the usual way of writing (see Note

9 That this *is* a rebellious *a* people, lying children, children *that* will not hear the law of the LORD:

10 Which say *b* to the seers, See not; and to the prophets, Prophesy not unto us right things; speak unto us *c* smooth things, prophesy deceits:

11 Get ye out of the way, turn

a De.32.20; Mic.2 6,11.   *b* Jer.11.21; Amos2.12; 7.13.

aside out of the path, cause the Holy One of Israel to cease from before us.

12 Wherefore thus saith the Holy One of Israel, Because ye despise this word, and trust *d* in 1 oppression and perverseness, and stay thereon:

c 1 Ki.22.13.   *d* Ps.62.10.   1 or, *fraud*.

---

on ch. viii. 1). ¶ *For the time to come.* Heb. as Marg. ' The latter day.' It was to be made in order that future ages might know what had been the character of that people, and what had been the patience and forbearance of God in regard to them.

9. *That this* is *a rebellious people* (see Note on ch. i. 2). ¶ *Lying children.* They had promised in solemn covenant to take JEHOVAH as their God, but they had been unfaithful to their vows.

10. *Which say to the seers.* The prophets (see Note on ch. i. 1). ¶ *See not.* They desire not that they should communicate to them the will of JE-HOVAH. ¶ *Prophesy not unto us right things.* It is not probable that they *openly* demanded of the prophets that they should declare falsehood and deceit, but their conduct was *as if* they had required that. The sense is, they bore with impatience the threatenings and commands of the true prophets; they were offended at their plainness and their reproofs of their vices; and they preferred the false prophets, who fell in with their prejudices, and who did not denounce the judgment of God for their crimes. ¶ *Speak unto us smooth things.* That is, those things which are in accordance with our feelings, prejudices, and desires; which assure us of prosperity and success, and which will not disturb us with the apprehension of punishment. This was spoken *particularly* of their desire to make a league with Egypt, an enterprise for which the true prophets threatened them with the Divine displeasure, but which probably the false prophets encouraged. ¶ *Prophesy deceits.* Not that they would openly and avowedly demand to be deceived, but they demanded that which the prophet says *would be* deceits. No man *professedly*

desires to be deceived; but many a man is willing to put himself under that kind of teaching which *is* deceit, and which he might know to be falsehood if he would examine it.

11. *Get ye out of the way.* Or, rather, ' Recede from the way;' or ' Turn aside from the way.' The words *way* and *path* are used to denote the true religion, or the true doctrines of God (Matt. vii. 14; xxii. 16; John xiv. 4; Acts xviii. 26; xix. 9, 23; 2 Pet. ii. 15). The request here was that the true prophets would recede from the stern and true precepts of religion, and turn to the ways of falsehood and deceit. ¶ *Cause the Holy One of Israel to cease from before us.* The sense of this is, ' Let us hear no more of this name. We are weary of constantly hearing it, as if there was nothing else but the ceaseless repetition of the name *The Holy One of Israel.*' It is to be remembered that the prophets spoke in this name, and often commenced their prophecies with the announcement, 'thus saith the Holy One of Israel.' No one more frequently used this than Isaiah (see ver. 12, 15; comp. ch. i. 4; v. 19, 24; x. 20; xii. 6; xvii. 7; xxix. 19; xxxi. 1; xli. 14). It is probable that a reference constantly to the fact that he was HOLY, was that which most troubled them. How descriptive of the feelings of sinners! How striking an illustration of the fact that they do not wish to hear of the name or laws of the Holy Lord God! And what a melancholy proof of depravity is it when men pursue such a course that they do not wish to hear of him, and desire no more to be troubled with his name and laws!

12. *Wherefore thus saith the Holy One.* JEHOVAH. There may be some reference here to the fact adverted to in ver. 11, that they were weary of the

13 Therefore this iniquity shall
be to you as a breach *a* ready to
fall, swelling out in a high wall,
whose breaking cometh suddenly
at an instant.

14 And he shall break *b* it as the

a Ps.62.3.　　　　*b* Ps.2.9; Jer.19.11.

breaking of the [1] potter's vessel that
is broken in pieces ; he shall not
spare : so that there shall not be
found in the bursting of it a sherd
to take fire from the hearth, or to
take water *withal* out of the pit.

1 *bottle of potters.*

name of the Holy One of Israel, and
of the perpetual reiteration of his commands. Isaiah, as if to show them
how little he was disposed to comply
with their prejudices, again makes an
appeal to that name, and urges the
authority of Jehovah. It is often proper to *repeat* the very doctrine to which
sinners object, and which has given
them offence. That they are offended,
shows that their minds are *awake* to
the truth, and gives some indication
that their consciences trouble them.
Ministers of God should never shrink
from their duty because men oppose
them ; they should never cease to speak
in the name and by the authority of the
Holy One of Israel, because that name
may excite opposition and disgust.
¶ *Ye despise this word.* That is, the
word or message of Jehovah (ch. xxviii.
13, 14) ; or perhaps it means the word
' Holy One of Israel.' The sense is,
that they did not trust in the promise
and protection of Jehovah, but relied
on human aid. ¶ *And trust in oppression.* Marg. ' Fraud.' The word עָשֶׁק
properly denotes oppression, or extor-
tion (Eccl. v. 7 ; Ezek. xxii. 7, 12) ;
then, that which is obtained by extor-
tion, and also by fraud (Lev. vi. 4 ;
Ps. lxii. 11 ; Eccl. vii. 7). It may refer
here to the fact that they had, by unjust and oppressive exactions, obtained
the treasures referred to in ver. 6, by
which they hoped to conciliate the
favour of Egypt ; or it may mean
that they trusted in their fraudulent
purposes towards God, that is, to a
false and perfidious course, by which
they were unfaithful to him. ¶ *Perverseness.* A crooked, perverse, rebellious course. They refused submission
to Jehovah, and relied on the aid of
strangers.

13. *Therefore this iniquity.* That
is, this refusing to trust in Jehovah,
and this intention to seek the alliance

of Egypt. The general sense of the
figure here is, that their depending on
Egypt would involve them ultimately
in complete and awful ruin—ruin that
should come upon them as suddenly as
when a wall that had been long swelling out gives way. ¶ *As a breach
ready to fall.* Like a breaking forth,
or a bursting in a wall. ¶ *Swelling out
in a high wall.* That is, where the
foundation is not firm, and where one
part of the wall sinks, and it inclines to
one side until it suddenly bursts forth.
A similar figure is used by the Psalmist (lxii. 3) :

Ye shall be slain all of you
As a bowing wall shall ye be, and as a tottering
fence.

¶ *Whose breaking cometh suddenly.*
Though it has been long leaning and
swelling, yet the actual bursting forth
would be in an instant. So would it
be with the destruction that would
come upon the Jews. Though by their
sins they had been long preparing for
it, yet it would come upon them by a
sudden and tremendous crash. So it
will be with all sinners. Destruction
may seem to be long delayed—as a
wall may be long inclining, and may
seem to prepare imperceptibly to fall ;
but in due time it will come suddenly
upon them, when too late to obtain
relief.

14. *And he shall break it as the
breaking.* That is, its breaking shall
be like the breaking of a potter's vessel. The LXX. read it, ' And its fall
(τὸ πτῶμα) shall be like the breaking
of an earthen vessel,' ¶ *As the breaking of the potter's vessel.* That is, as
an earthen, fragile vessel, which is easily
dashed to pieces. The image here is
all drawn from the bursting forth, or
the complete ruin of the swelling wall ;
but the sense is, that the Jewish republic would be entirely broken, scattered,
demolished. ¶ *He shall not spare
in the bursting of it.* Figuratively in

15 For thus saith the Lord God, the Holy One of Israel, In return-ing and rest *a* shall ye be saved; in

a ver.7.

the bursting of the wall; literally in the destruction of the Jewish state and polity. ¶ *A sherd.* A piece of pot-tery; a fragment. ¶ *To take fire from the hearth.* Large enough to carry coals on. ¶ *Or to take water* withal *out of the pit.* Out of the fountain, or pool; that is, it shall be broken into small fragments, and the ruin shall be complete — as when a wall tumbles down and is completely broken up. The sense is, that the republic of Israel would be completely ruined, so that there should not be found a man of any description who could aid them. The prophet does not specify when this would be. It is not necessary to sup-pose that it would occur on the invasion of Sennacherib, or that it would be the *immediate* consequence of seeking the aid of Egypt, but that it would be *a* consequence, though a remote one. Perhaps the figure used would lead us to look to some remote period. A high wall will begin to give way many years before its fall. The swell will be gra-dual, and perhaps almost imperceptible. For some time it may appear to be sta-tionary; then perhaps some new cause will produce an increase of the project-ing part, until it can no longer sustain itself, and then the ruin will be sudden and tremendous. So it would be with the Jews. The seeking of the alliance with Egypt was *one* cause—though a remote one—of their final ruin. Their forsaking God and seeking human aid, was gradually but certainly *undermin-ing* the foundations of the state—as a wall may be gradually undermined. Frequent repetitions of that would more and more impair the real strength of the republic, until, for their accumu-lated acts of want of confidence, the pa-tience of God would be exhausted, and the state would fall like a mighty, bursting wall. The prophecy was ful-filled in the invasion of Jerusalem by the Chaldeans; it had a more signal and awful fulfilment in its destruction by the Romans.

quietness and in confidence shall be your strength; and ye would not.

16 But ye said, No; for we will flee upon horses; therefore shall ye

15. *For thus saith the Lord* God. The design of this verse is to give a *reason* for the destruction that should come upon them. That reason was, that God had indicated to them the path of truth and safety, but they chose not to follow it, and refused to put con-fidence in him. ¶ *In returning.* In returning to God; that is, if you are converted to him. ¶ *And rest.* That is, by calmly reposing on God for as-sistance, and not seeking the alliance of Egypt (see Ex. xiv. 13). ¶ *In quiet-ness.* In a collected, quiet state of mind. ¶ *In confidence.* By putting simple trust in God. ¶ *Shall be your strength.* You shall be safe; your ene-mies shall not be able to overcome and subdue you. ¶ *But ye would not.* When Jerusalem was threatened by Sennacherib, Hezekiah *did* put this confidence in God, and reposed calmly and securely on his promises (Isa. xxxvi. 15, 18, 21); but it is not improbable that when the city was first threatened, and Hezekiah heard of the preparations made by the Assyrians, he had joined with the party in Jerusalem who pro-posed an alliance with Egypt, and that this was known to Sennacherib (Isa. xxxvi. 6). Probably, however, before the invasion had actually commenced he had seen the impropriety of this, either because the aid of Egypt could not be secured, or because Isaiah had warned him of this, and had been brought to put his trust entirely in Je-hovah. Yet the offence *had been* com-mitted of refusing to put implicit con-fidence in Jehovah, and of seeking the aid of Egypt, and for that the punish-ment is threatened in this chapter (ver. 16, 17).

16. *But ye said, No.* Ye who pro-posed an alliance with Egypt. ¶ *For we will flee upon horses.* The word 'flee' (נוס), usually signifies to flee be-fore or from any person or thing. But here it seems to have the notion of making a rapid motion in general, and not to refer to the fact that they ex-

flee: and, We will ride upon the swift; therefore shall they that pursue *a* you be swift.

17 One thousand *b shall flee* at the rebuke of one; at the rebuke of

a 2 Ki.25.5.   *b* De.32.30.

five shall ye flee; till ye be left as a beacon [1] upon the top of a mountain, and as an ensign on an hill.

18 And therefore will the LORD wait, *c* that he may be gracious

1 or, *a tree bereft of branches, or, boughs:* or, *a mast.*
c Ho.5.15.

pected to flee *from* their enemy, for it does not seem to have been a part of their expectation. The idea seems to be that by their alliance with Egypt they would secure the means of *rapid motion*, whatever might be the necessity or occasion for it, whether against or from an enemy. The sense is, 'we will by this alliance secure the assistance of cavalry;' and, doubtless, the design was to employ it in the attack and discomfiture of their foes. It will be recollected that Moses (Deut. xvii. 16) strictly forbade that the future monarch of the Jews should 'multiply horses to himself, to cause the people to return to Egypt,' and that consequently the employment of cavalry was against the laws of the nation. For the reasons of this prohibition, see Note on ch. ii. 7. The attempt, therefore, in the time of Hezekiah to call in the aid of the cavalry of Egypt, was a violation of both the letter and the spirit of the Jewish institutions (comp. ch. xxxi. 1; Hos. xiv. 4). ¶ *Therefore shall ye flee.* You shall fly before your enemies; you shall be defeated and scattered. ¶ *We will ride upon the swift.* That is, upon fleet horses or coursers. Arabia was celebrated, and is still, for producing fleet coursers, and the same was formerly true of Egypt (see Note on ch. ii. 7).

17. *One thousand,* &c. The sense of this is, that you shall be easily alarmed and overcome by those who are inferior in numbers and strength. The number 'one thousand,' is put for a large indefinite number; probably meaning all. ¶ *At the rebuke of one.* The number *one* here is put to denote a very small number; a number in the ordinary course of warfare entirely disproportionate to those who would be vanquished. There is probably a reference here to the prediction in Deut. xxxii. 30:

How should one chase a thousand,
And two put ten thousand to flight,

Except their Rock had sold them,
And JEHOVAH had shut them up?

¶ *At the rebuke of five.* Of a very small number. ¶ *Till ye be left as a beacon upon the top of a mountain.* The word rendered 'beacon' (תֹּרֶן), [Gr. ἰστός, *a mast*], denotes properly the mast of a ship (Isa. xxxiii. 23; Ezek. xxvii. 5); then anything resembling a mast, a flagstaff, or a beacon of any kind. It may refer to a staff or mast erected on a promontory to warn sailors, or to be a landmark—as it is not improbable that the *masts* of ships would be employed for that purpose; or it may refer to a flagstaff, erected on a conspicuous place, to which the nation could rally in time of war. On the sea coasts of America such beacons are often erected. Those which I have seen consist of a pole erected on an eminence or rising ground, with a cask or barrel painted white on the top. The idea seems to be, that of a long pole erected for any purpose, and which was standing alone, stripped of its leaves and branches, and without ornament. So would be the few, solitary, and scattered Jews when driven before their enemies. ¶ *And as an ensign on a hill* (see Note on ch. v. 26; xi. 12). The idea is, that those who should escape would be few in number, and would stand alone, as a beacon in view of all the nations, to admonish them of the justice of God, and the truth of his threatenings—like an ensign floating on a hill that can be seen from afar. What a striking description is this of the condition of the Jews in our times, and indeed in all ages since their dispersion! Their strength, and influence, and power as a people are gone. They stand as beacons to warn the nations of the evils of a want of confidence in God, and of his justice.

18. *And therefore.* The sense of the words rendered 'and therefore,' may be better expressed by the phrase, 'yet

unto you, and therefore will he be exalted, that he may have mercy upon you; for the LORD *is* a God of judgment: *a* blessed *are* all they that wait for him.

19 For the people shall dwell *b* in Zion at Jerusalem; thou shalt weep no more: he will be very gracious unto thee at the voice of thy cry;

when *c* he shall hear it, he will answer thee.

20 And *though* *d* the LORD give you the bread of adversity, and the water of affliction,1 yet shall not thy teachers be *e* removed into a corner any more, but thine eyes shall see thy teachers:

a Ps.34.8.　　*b* ch.65.9,24.　　*c* Jer.29.12-14.
d Ps.30.5. 1 or, *oppression.* *e* Ps.74.8; Am.8.11,12.

---

moreover,' meaning, that notwithstanding their sins, and the necessity of punishing them, JEHOVAH would be long-suffering, and would yet bring the nation to repentance. ¶ *And therefore will he be exalted.* Lowth renders this in accordance with a conjecture of Houbigant, ' Shall he expect in silence,' by reading רָדֹם instead of רָרֹם. But there is no authority for this except a single MS. Rosenmüller supposes it means, in accordance with the interpretation of Jarchi, that he would delay, *i.e.*, that his mercy would be *long* or his judgment remote. But the sense seems to be, that God would be so forbearing that his character would be *exalted, i.e.*, that men would have more elevated conceptions of his truth, mercy, and faithfulness. ¶ *For the* LORD is *a God of judgment.* He will do what is right. He will spare the nation still; and yet establish among them the true religion, and they shall flourish. ¶ *Blessed* are *all they that wait for him.* This seems to have been recorded to encourage them, when the threatened calamities should come upon them, to put their confidence in God, and to trust that he would yet appear and restore the nation to himself. This verse is the commencement of the annunciation of the blessings which should yet be conferred on them. The description of these blessings is continued to ver. 26.

19 *For the people shall dwell in Zion* (see Note on ch. i. 8). The *language* here is evidently adapted to a return from the captivity. The whole design of the passage (ver. 19–26) is to describe a future state of prosperity by images mainly drawn from the idea of temporal enjoyment. The sense is, that in some period subsequent to the calami-

ties that would befall them for their improper reliance on the aid of Egypt (ver. 16, 17), there would be prosperity, peace, and joy in Jerusalem. The order of events, as seen by the prophet in vision, seems to be this. He sees the people threatened with an invasion by Sennacherib. He sees them forget their reliance on God and seek the aid of Egypt. He sees, as a consequence of this, a long series of calamities resulting in the downfall of the republic, the destruction of the city, and the captivity at Babylon. Yet he sees, in the distant prospect, prosperity, happiness, security, piety, the blessing of God, and rich and abundant future mercies resting on his people. That the blessings under the Messiah constitute a part of this *series* of mercies no one can doubt who attentively considers the language in ver. 25, 26. ¶ *Thou shalt weep no more* (see Note on ch. xxv. 8). ¶ *He will be very gracious unto thee at the voice of thy cry.* When in your calamities you shall cry unto him for deliverance, he shall hear you, and restore you to your own land. This is in accordance with the statements in ch. xxvi. 8, 9 (see Notes on these verses), that in their captivity in Babylon they would seek God. ¶ *He will answer thee* (see Jer. xxix. 12–14).

20. *And though the* LORD *give you the bread of adversity.* The bread that is eaten in a time of calamity; that is, he would bring upon them sore distress and want. ¶ *The water of affliction.* Marg. ' Oppression.' That is, water drank in times of affliction and oppression, or in the long and weary days of captivity. ¶ *Yet shall not thy teachers.* Your public instructors and guides (Ps. lxxiv. 9; Isa. xliii. 27; Dan. xii. 3; Amos viii. 11, 12). This refers to *all*

21 And thine ears shall hear a word behind thee, saying, This *is the way, walk ye in it, when ye turn to the right hand, and when ye turn to the left.

22 Ye shall defile also the cover-

a Ps.32.8.   1 *the graven images of thy silver.*

ing of thy [1] graven images of silver, and the ornament of thy molten images of gold: thou shalt [2] cast them away as a menstruous cloth; thou shalt say unto it, Get thee hence.*b*

2 *scatter.*   *b* Ho.14.8.

those who would be the true guides and teachers of the people of God in subsequent times; and relates, therefore, not only to prophets and pious men whom God would raise up under their own dispensation, but also to all whom he would appoint to communicate his will. It is a promise that the church of God should never want a pious and devoted ministry qualified to make known his will and defend his truth. ¶ *Be removed into a corner.* The word here used (רָכַף from כָּנַף) occurs nowhere else in the Scriptures. It is probably derived from כָּנָף, *a wing;* and in the Syriac and Chaldee, it means to collect together. The LXX. render this, 'And they who deceived thee shall no more come near unto thee.' The Syriac, 'And he (*i.e.*, the Lord) shall no more collect thy seducers.' The Chaldee, 'And he shall no more take away his own glory from the house of his sanctuary.' Rosenmüller, in accordance with Schultens, renders it, 'And thy teachers shall no more hide themselves,' referring to the fact that the wing of a fowl furnishes a hiding-place or shelter. This would accord with the general idea that they should not be removed from public view. Lowth, singularly, and without authority from the versions or MSS., renders it,

'Yet the timely rain shall no more be restrained.'

The general idea is, evidently, that they should be no more taken away; and probably the specific idea is that proposed by Taylor (*Heb. Con.*), that thy teachers shall no more, as it were, *be winged,* or fly away; that is, be removed by flight, or as a flock of birds moving together rapidly on the wing.

21. *And thine ears shall hear a word.* A command or admonition. You shall not be left without spiritual guides and directors. ¶ *Behind thee* That is,

says Vitringa, the voice of conscience, as an *invisible* guide, shall admonish you. The idea, however, seems to be that if they were ignorant of the way, or if they were inclined to err, they should be admonished of the true path which they ought to pursue. The idea is taken either from the practice of teachers who are represented as *following* their pupils and admonishing them if they were in danger of going astray (Grotius); or from shepherds, who are represented as following their flocks, and directing them when they wandered. The Jews understand this voice 'from behind' to be the *Bath Kol*—'the daughter of the voice;' a Divine admonition which they suppose attends the pious. The essential thought is, that they would not be left without a guide and instructor; that, if they were inclined to go astray, they would be recalled to the path of truth and duty. *Perhaps* there is the idea, also, that the admonition would come from some *invisible* influence, or from some unexpected quarter, as it is often the case that those who are inquiring on the subject of religion receive light from quarters where they least expected, and from sources to which they were not looking. It is also true that the admonitions of Providence, of conscience, and of the Holy Spirit, seem often to come from *behind us;* that is, they *recall* us from the path in which we were going, and restrain us from a course that would be fraught with danger. ¶ *When ye turn to the right hand,* &c. When you shall be in danger of wandering from the direct and straight path. The voice shall recall you, and direct you in the way in which you ought to go.

22. *Ye shall defile also.* That is, you shall regard them as polluted and abominable. This is language which is often used respecting their treatment of the images and altars of idolatry when they became objects of abomina-

23 Then shall he give the rain of thy seed, that thou shalt sow the ground withal; and bread of the increase of the earth, and it shall be fat and plenteous: in that day shall thy cattle feed in large pastures.

24 The oxen likewise, and the young asses that ear the ground, shall eat clean[1] provender which hath been winnowed with the shovel and with the fan.

1 *leavened,* or, *savoury.*

---

tion, and when they were induced to abandon them (see 2 Kings xxiii. 8, 10, 16). It is not improbable that before destroying them they would express their abhorrence of them by some act of polluting or defiling them, as significant of their contempt for the objects of degraded idolatry (see Note on ch. ii. 20). The sense of the whole passage is, that the effect of the judgments which God was about to bring upon the nation would be, to turn them from idolatry, to which as a nation they had been signally prone. ¶ *The covering.* The images of idols were usually made of wood or clay, and overlaid with gold. That gold and silver were used *to plate* them is apparent from Deut. vii. 25; and the whole process of making them from wood, and then of overlaying them with plates of gold and silver is described with graphic power and severity of irony in Isa. xl. 19, 20; xli. 6, 7. ¶ *Thy graven images of silver.* Marg. ' The graven images of thy silver.' Probably the construction in the text is correct, as meaning that the images were not made of entire silver, but of wood or clay, plated with silver. ¶ *And the ornament.* The golden plates or the covering of the images. ¶ *Thy molten images.* The word 'molten' refers to those which were made by *casting* (see Notes on ch. xl. 19, 20). ¶ *Thou shalt cast them away* (see Note on ch. ii. 20). This would be in accordance with the express direction of Moses; Deut. vii. 25: 'The graven images of their gods shall ye burn with fire; thou shalt not desire the silver or gold that is on them, nor take it unto thee, lest thou be snared therein; for it is an abomination unto the Lord thy God.'

23. *Then shall he give the rain of thy seed.* That is, he shall send rain on the seed which is sown. You will be allowed to cultivate the soil without molestation, and God will give you

fruitful seasons and abundant harvests. This is a poetic description of a happy or golden age, when there would be peace and prosperity (comp. Notes on ch. xi. 6, 7). ¶ *And bread of the increase of the earth.* And bread which the ground shall produce. ¶ *And it shall be fat and plenteous.* It shall be rich and abundant; that is, there shall be prosperity and an ample supply for your wants. ¶ *Feed in large pastures.* This is a description of security when their cattle should be permitted to roam at large, and have abundant pasturage —an image of prosperity that would be very gratifying to a people whose main conception of wealth consisted in abundance of flocks and herds.

24. *The young asses that ear the ground.* Heb. ' Labouring,' or ' cultivating the ground,' that is, ploughing it. The old English word *ear* (from the Latin *aro*) meant to till, to cultivate. The word is now obsolete, but this is the sense which it has in the Bible (Gen. xlv. 6; Ex. xxxiv. 21; Deut. xxi. 4; 1 Sam. viii. 12). ¶ *Shall eat clean provender.* Marg. 'Leavened,' or ' savoury.' The word rendered ' provender ' (בְּלִיל) is a verbal from בָּלַל, *to mix, mingle, confuse;* and denotes provender that is made by *mixing* various substances, *maslin* or *farago,* a mixture of barley, oats, vetches, and beans, which seem to have been sown together, and reaped at the same time (Job vi. 5; xxiv. 6). The word rendered ' clean,' (חָמִיץ) is not quite so plain in its signification. Kimchi explains it by נָקִי, *pure, clean.* Gesenius renders it ' salted,' and supposes that it refers to fodder that was mixed with salted hay. The LXX. render it, ' Provender mixed with winnowed barley.' But the real notion of the word is that which is *fermented,* from הָמֵץ, *to be sour;* to be leavened. Lowth renders it, ' well fermented.' Noyes, ' well seasoned.' The

25 And there shall be upon every high mountain, and upon every [1] high hill, rivers *and* streams of waters in the day of the great slaughter, when the towers fall.

26 Moreover, the light *a* of the

1 *lifted up.*   *a* ch 60,19,26.

moon shall be as the light of the sun, and the light of the sun shall be seven-fold, as the light of seven days, in the day that the LORD bindeth up the breach of his people, and healeth the stroke of their wound.

---

idea seems to be that of a provender made of a mixture of various substances—as of grain, beans, vetches, herbs, hay, and probably salt, which, when mixed, *would* ferment, and which was regarded as nutritious and wholesome for cattle. A similar compound is used by the Arabs still (see Bochart, i. 2, 7; and Faber, and Harmer's *Observations*, i. 409). ¶ *Which hath been winnowed.* That is, which is the pure grain, which is not fed to them as it is sometimes, before it is separated from the chaff. Grain shall be so abundant in that time of prosperity that even the cattle may be fed with grain prepared as it is usually for man. ¶ *With the shovel.* The large shovel by which the grain in the chaff was thrown up in the wind that the grain might be separated from the chaff. ¶ *The fan.* This word properly means that by which any thing is *scattered*—a shovel by which the grain is thrown or tossed into the wind. ' Those who form their opinion of the latter article by an English *fan*, will entertain a very erroneous notion. That of the East is made of the fibrous part of the palmirah or cocoa-tree leaves, and measures about a yard each way.' —(Roberts).

25. *In the day of the great slaughter.* When the enemies of the people of God shall have been destroyed—probably in a time subsequent to the slaughter of the army of the Assyrians. ¶ *When the towers fall.* The towers of the enemy; perhaps referring here to the towers of Babylon. After they should fall, the Jews would be favoured with the time of prosperity to which the prophet here refers.

26. *Moreover.* In addition to all the blessings which are enumerated above. ¶ *The light of the moon.* Light is in the Scriptures an emblem of purity, intelligence, happiness, prosperity; as darkness is an emblem of ignorance,

calamity, and sin. This figure is often used by the poets. Thus Horace:

Soles melius nitent.   *Carm.* liv.: *Od.* v. 8.

The figure of augmenting light to denote the blessings of religion, and especially of the gospel, is often employed by Isaiah (comp. Notes on ch. ii. 5; ix. 2; x. 17; xiii. 10; lviii. 8, 10; lx. 1, 3, 19, 20). The sense of this passage is, that in those future days the light would shine intensely, and without obscurity; that though they had been walking in the light of the true religion, yet that their light would be greatly augmented, and that they would have much clearer views of the Divine character and government. That this refers to the times of the Messiah there can be little or no room to doubt. It is language such as Isaiah commonly employs to describe those times; and there is a fulness and splendour about it which can suit no other period. There is nothing in the connection, moreover, which forbids such an interpretation of the passage. ¶ *Shall be as the light of the sun.* Shall be clear, bright, intense. The sense is, there shall be a great increase of light, as if the light of the moon were suddenly increased to the brightness of the meridian sun. ¶ *Shall be seven-fold.* Seven times as intense and clear as usual, as if the light of seven days were concentrated into one. The word 'seven' in the Scriptures often denotes a complete or perfect number; and indicates *completeness* or *perfection.* The phrase ' as the light of seven days,' Lowth supposes is a gloss which has been introduced into the text from the margin. The reasons which he adduces for this supposition are, that it is wanting in the LXX., and that it interrupts the rhythmical construction. But this is not sufficient authority for rejecting the words from the text. No authority of MSS. is adduced for thus rejecting them, and they are found in the Vulgate,

27 Behold, the name of the LORD
cometh from far, burning *with* his
anger, and ¹the burden *thereof is*
heavy; ² his lips are full of indignation, and his tongue as a devouring
fire: *a*

1 or, *grievousness of flame.*   2 *heaviness.*

28 And his breath, as an overflowing stream, shall reach to the
midst of the neck, to sift *b* the nations with the sieve of vanity: and
there shall be a bridle *c* in the jaws of
the people, causing *them* to err.

a Zep.3.8.   *b* Lu.22.31.   *c* ch.37.29.

the Chaldee, and the Syriac. They are
wanting, however, in the Arabic. ¶ *In
the day.* Vitringa supposes that this refers to the time of the Maccabees; but
although there may be a reference to
that time, yet the idea is evidently designed to include the future times of the
Messiah. The sense of the prophet is,
that *subsequent* to the great calamities
which were to befall them, there would
be a time of glorious prosperity, and the
design of this was to comfort them with
the assurance that their nation would
not be wholly destroyed. ¶ *Bindeth
up the breach of his people.* Or the
wound. The calamity that should come
upon them is thus represented as a
wound inflicted on them by the stripes
of punishment (see Notes on ch. i. 5).
JEHOVAH would heal it by restoring them
to their own land, and to their former
privileges.

27. *Behold, the name of the* LORD
cometh (comp. Notes on ch. xix. 1). The
verses following, to the end of the chapter,
are designed evidently to describe the
destruction of the army of Sennacherib.
This is expressly declared in ver. 31,
and all the circumstances in the prediction accord with that event. There is
no necessity of supposing that this is the
commencement of a new prophecy, for it
is connected with the main subject in
the previous part of the chapter. The
whole prophecy was composed evidently
in view of that threatened invasion. In
the apprehension of that, they sought
the aid of Egypt (ver. 1–6); for that,
the prophet denounces judgment on them
(ver. 8, *et sq.*); in view of these judgments, however, he promises a more
happy state (ver. 18–26); and now, in
the close of the chapter, in order to deter
them from the alliance, he assures them
that, without any foreign aid, the Assyrian would be destroyed by JEHOVAH
himself. The phrase 'name of JEHOVAH,'
is probably another mode of designating

JEHOVAH himself; as the *name* of God
is often put for God himself (see Acts
iii. 6, 7, 12, 30; iv. 10; 1 Cor. i. 10).
The idea is, that the destruction of the
Assyrian hosts would be accomplished
by the immediate power of JEHOVAH
himself without any need of the aid of
the Egyptian or of any foreign alliances.
¶ *From afar.* That is, from heaven
(comp. Note on ch. xix. 1). ¶ *Burning
with his anger.* Or, rather, his anger
is enkindled. ¶ *And the burden* thereof.
Marg. 'Grievousness of flame.' Lowth
renders it, 'The flame rageth violently.'
Noyes, 'Violent is the flame.' The
LXX. render it, 'A burning wrath.' The
word מַשְּׂאָה, from נָשָׂא *to bear, lift up,
carry,* means properly a lifting up (Ps.
cxli. 2); a burden (Zeph. iii. 18); then
a mounting up, particularly of a flame
or smoke in a conflagration (Judg. xx.
38). This seems to be the idea here,
that the anger of God would be like a
heavy, dark column of mingled smoke
and flame bursting out, and rising up
over a city. ¶ *His lips are full of indignation.* All this language is of course
figurative, and means that he would
issue a command to destroy the Assyrians, or that they would be destroyed
in such a manner as most effectively to
exhibit his displeasure. ¶ *And his
tongue as a devouring fire.* That is,
he shall issue a command that shall
destroy like a raging and devouring
fire.

28. *And his breath.* The word רוּחַ
properly means *wind,* air in motion;
then a breathing, an exhalation, a breath;
then the soul, spirit, &c. The idea here
seems to be that of excited, and rapid,
and agitated breathing, as when one is
in anger (comp. Judg. viii. 3; Zech. vi.
8). ¶ *As an overflowing stream.* This
figure is common to express desolating
judgments (see Notes on ch. viii. 8; x.
22; xxviii. 17; comp. Ps. lxix. 2, 15).
¶ *Shall reach to the midst of the neck.*

29 Ye shall have a song, as ^a in the night, *when a holy solemnity is kept; and gladness of heart, as when one goeth with a pipe to come into the mountain of the LORD, to the* ¹ Mighty One of Israel.

a Ps.42.4.   1 *Rock.*   2 *the glory of his voice.*

Isaiah (ch. viii. 8), in describing the invasion of Sennacherib, and comparing it to an overflowing torrent, says it would 'reach even to the neck;' that is, it would overflow the land, and even approach the head, the capital, but that that would be spared. By the use of a similar figure, and perhaps referring to that, he here says, that the judgment of God would overflow the army of the Assyrians, but that it would approach *only* to the neck, the head would still be spared; the commander and sovereign would not be destroyed. In accordance with this prediction, the angel in one night, as with an overflowing flood, cut off the army, and yet spared the sovereign, Sennacherib, who escaped with his life (Isa. xxxvii. 36, 37). The word rendered 'shall reach' (רֶחֱצֶה) properly means *shall divide*, or cut into two parts (Gen. xxxiii. 8; Num. xxxi. 37, 42; Judg. ix. 43); and the idea here seems to be that a man who is in the water seems to be *divided* into two parts, one part above, and one in the water. ¶ *To sift the nations.* Doubtless many nations were laid under requisition to furnish an army so large as that of Sennacherib, as the kingdom of Assyria was made up of a number of tributary people and provinces. The word rendered 'to sift' refers to the act of winnowing or fanning grain, in which the grain is *tossed* or thrown from the shovel into the air. As the chaff is driven away by the wind, so the nations in the army of Sennacherib would be scattered. ¶ *With the sieve of vanity.* That is, of emptiness or perdition; he would so scatter them that nothing would be left. ¶ *A bridle in the jaws of the people.* The idea is, that he had all these nations as much under his control as a man has a horse with a bridle in his mouth. The same idea the prophet has used in reference to the same subject in ch. xxxvii. 29:

30 And the LORD shall cause ² his glorious voice to be heard, and shall show the lighting down of his arm, with the indignation of *his* anger, and *with* the flame of a devouring fire, *with* scattering, and tempest, and hailstones.

I will put my bridle in thy jaws,
And I will turn thee back by the way by which thou camest.

¶ *Causing* them *to err.* That shall cause them to wander; that is, he would turn them from the path in which they had designed to go. They had purposed to go to Jerusalem, but he would lead them *back* to their own land, discomfited and disheartened (see ch. xxxvii. 29).

29. *Ye shall have a song.* That is, ye inhabitants of Jerusalem shall rejoice when the army of the Assyrian is destroyed. ¶ *As in the night, when a solemnity is kept.* The word 'solemnity' here (חַג) denotes a festival, or feast; and refers, by way of eminence, to the Passover, which is usually designated as THE *feast;* that is, the principal festival of the Jews (see Matt. xxvii. 15; John v. 1, 11, 13, 23). This festival was kept at first at night, and was required to be so celebrated ever afterwards (Ex. xii. 42; Deut. xvi. 1–6). ¶ *As when one goeth with a pipe.* Music was used in the daily service of the temple, and their processions and celebrations were all with instrumental music. The simple idea is, that the sudden and complete destruction of the army of Sennacherib would be the occasion of the highest joy.

30. *And the LORD shall cause his glorious voice to be heard.* That is, he would give command to destroy them. They could not fail to recognize his voice, and to feel that it was accomplished by him. ¶ *The lighting down of his arm.* The descent of his arm—alluding to the act of striking, as with a sword, by which an army is cut down. ¶ With *the flame* (see Note on ch. xxix. 6). ¶ *And tempest, and hailstones.* With us it is rare that a storm of hail would be severe enough to destroy an army. But in oriental countries and in tropical climates, storms of hail are not unfrequently of sufficient violence to do it if the army were encamped in the open

31 For through the voice of the
LORD shall the Assyrian be beaten
down, *which* smote with a rod.

32 And [1] *in* every place where the

1 *every passing of the rod founded.*

grounded staff shall pass, which the
LORD shall [2] lay upon him, *it* shall be
with tabrets and harps: and in battles
of shaking will he fight [3] with it.

2 *cause to rest.*   3 or, *against them.*

field. The following extract of a letter
from one of our own countrymen, will
show that this would be by no means an
improbable occurrence :—' We had got
perhaps a mile and a half on our way,
when a cloud rising in the west gave
indications of approaching rain. In a
few minutes we discovered something
falling from the heavens with a heavy
splash, and with a whitish appearance.
I could not conceive what it was, but
observing some gulls near, I supposed
it to be them darting for fish ; but soon
after discovered that they were large
balls of ice falling. Immediately we
heard a sound like rumbling thunder, or
ten thousand carriages rolling furiously
over the pavement. The whole Bos-
phorus was in a foam, as though heaven's
artillery had been charged upon us and
our frail machine. Our fate seemed
inevitable ; our umbrellas were raised
to protect us, the lumps of ice stripped
them into ribbons. We fortunately had
a bullock's hide in the boat, under which
we crawled and saved ourselves from
further injury. One man of the three
oarsmen had his hand literally smashed,
another much injured in the shoulder,
Mr. H. received a blow on the leg, my
right hand was somewhat disabled, and
all more or less injured. It was the
most awful and terrific scene I ever
witnessed, and God forbid that I should
be ever exposed to another. Balls of
ice as large as my two fists fell into the
boat, and some of them came with such
violence as certainly to have broken an
arm or leg, had they struck us in those
parts. One of them struck the blade
of an oar and split it. The scene lasted
perhaps five minutes ; but it was five
minutes of the most awful feeling I ever
experienced. When it passed over, we
found the surrounding hills covered with
masses of ice, I cannot call it hail, the
trees stripped of their leaves and limbs,
and everything looking desolate. The
scene was awful beyond all description.
I have witnessed repeated earthquakes ;
the lightning has played, as it were,

about my head ; the wind roared, and
the waves at one moment have thrown
me to the sky, and the next have sunk
me into a deep abyss. I have been in
action, and have seen death and destruction around me in every shape of horror ;
but I never before had the feeling of
awe which seized upon me on this occasion, and still haunts, and I fear for ever
will haunt me. My porter, the boldest
of my family, who had ventured an instant from the door, had been knocked
down by a hailstone, and had they not
dragged him in by the heels, would have
been battered to death. Two boatmen
were killed in the upper part of the village, and I have heard of broken bones
in abundance. Imagine to yourself the
heavens suddenly frozen over, and as
suddenly broken to pieces in irregular
masses of from half a pound to a pound
weight, and precipitated to the earth.'
—(Commodore Porter's *Letters from
Constantinople and its Environs*, vol. i.
p. 44.)

31. *For through the voice of the* LORD
By the command of the Lord ; that is,
his voice going forth in the manner
specified in ver. 30. ¶ Which *smote
with a rod.* Who was accustomed to
smite as with a rod ; that is, his government was tyrannical and severe. As
he had been accustomed to smite in
that manner, so he would now meet the
proper reward of his oppression of the
nations.

32. *And* in *every place.* Marg.' Every
passing of the rod founded.' Lowth renders it, ' Whenever shall pass the rod of
correction.' The whole design of the
passage is evidently to foretell the sudden
destruction of the army of the Assyrians,
and to show that this would be accomplished by the agency of God. The
idea seems to be, that in all those places
where the rod of the Assyrian would
pass, that is, where he would cause devastation and desolation, there would
be the sound of rejoicing with instruments of music when he should be overthrown. ¶ *The grounded staff.* The

33 For Tophet ^a *is* ordained[1] of old; yea, for the king it is prepared; he hath made *it* deep *and* large: the

a Jer.7.31. 1 *from yesterday.*

pile thereof *is* fire and much wood; the breath of the LORD, like a stream of brimstone, ^b doth kindle it.

b Rev.14.9,10.

word 'staff' here, or *rod*, seems to refer to that by which the Assyrian smote the nations (ver. 31); or rather perhaps the Assyrian king himself as a rod of correction in the hand of JEHOVAH (see ch. x. 5). The word rendered 'grounded' (מוּסָדָה, *mūsâdhâh*) has given great perplexity to commentators. Lowth supposes it should be מוּסָרָה (*correction*), according to a conjecture of Le Clerc. Two MSS. also read it in the same way. But the authority from the MSS. is not sufficient to justify a change in the present Hebrew text. This word, which is not very intelligibly rendered 'grounded,' is derived from יָסַד (*yâsâdh*), *to found, to lay the foundation of a building* (Ezra iii. 12; Isa. liv. 11); then to establish, to appoint, to ordain (Ps. civ. 8; Hab. i. 12). The idea here is, therefore, that the rod referred to had been *appointed, constituted, ordained* by God; that is, that the Assyrian had been designated by him to accomplish important purposes *as a rod*, or as a means of punishing the nations. ¶ *Shall pass.* In his march of desolation and conquest. ¶ *Which the* LORD *shall lay upon him.* Or rather, as it should be translated, 'upon which JEHOVAH should lay,' *i.e.,* the rod, meaning that in all those places where JEHOVAH should lay this appointed scourge there would be yet rejoicing. ¶ *It shall be with tabrets and harps.* Those places where he had passed, and which he had scourged, would be filled with joy and rejoicing at his complete overthrow, and at their entire deliverance from the scourge. For a description of the tabret and harp, see Notes on ch. v. 12. ¶ *And in battles of shaking.* In the Hebrew there is an allusion here to what is said in ver. 28, that he would 'sift,' that is, agitate or toss the nations as in a winnowing shovel. ¶ *Will he fight with it.* Marg. 'Against them.' JEHOVAH would fight against the 'rod,' to wit, the Assyrian, and destroy him (see ch. xxxvii. 36).

33. *For Tophet.* The same idea is conveyed in this verse as in the pre-ceding, but under another form, and with a new illustration. The sense is, that the army of the Assyrians would be completely destroyed, as if it were a large pile of wood in the valley of Hinnom that should be fired by the breath of God. The word 'Tophet' (תָּפְתֶּה with ה paragogic), denotes properly what causes loathing or abhorrence; that which produces disgust and vomiting (from the Chaldee תּוּף (*Tūph*) to spit out); Job xvii. 6, 'I was an *abhorrence*' (תֹּפֶת), improperly rendered in our version, 'I was among them as a tabret.' The word occurs only in 2 Kings xxiii. 10; Jer. vii. 31, 32; xix. 6, 11, 13, 14, and in this place. It is applied to a deep valley on the south-east of Jerusalem, celebrated as the seat of idolatry, particularly of the worship of Moloch. The name also of 'the valley of Hinnom' was given to it; and hence the name *Gehenna* (γέεννα, Matt. v. 22, 29, 30; x. 28; xviii. 9; xxiii. 15, 33; Mark ix. 43, 45, 47; Luke xii. 5; James iii. 6), as denoting the place of future torments, of which the valley of Hinnom, or Tophet, was a striking emblem. This valley was early selected as the seat of the worship of Moloch, where his rites were celebrated by erecting a huge brazen image with a hollow trunk and arms, which was heated, and within which, or on the arms of which, children were placed as a sacrifice to the horrid idol. To drown their cries, drums were beaten, which were called תֹּף (*Toph*), or תֻּפִּים (*Tophim*), and many suppose the name Tophet was given to the place on this account (see 2 Kings xvi. 3; xxi. 6; xxiii. 10). The name 'valley of Hinnom,' or Gehenna, was probably from the former possessor or occupier of that name. In subsequent times, however, this place was regarded with deep abhorrence. It became the receptacle of all the filth of the city; and hence, in order to purify the atmosphere, and prevent contagion, it was needful to keep fires there continually burning. It was thus

CHAPTER XXXI.

ANALYSIS.

It is evident that this chapter was composed at about the same time as the preceding, and relates to the same subject. The general object, like the former, is to dissuade the Jews from their contemplated alliance with Egypt, and to lead them to rely on God. In doing this, the prophet first denounces a woe on those who went down to Egypt to seek aid (1); he then states that God will punish them for it (2); he then urges the utter inability of the Egyptians to furnish the aid which was needed, since JEHO-VAH was about to stretch out his arm over them also, and they, as well as those who sought their aid, should suffer under his displeasure (3). The prophet then, in order to recall them from this contemplated alliance, and to induce them to put confidence in JEHOVAH, assures them by two most beautiful figures (4, 5) that God would protect their city in the threatened invasion, and save it from destruction. He calls on them, therefore (6), to turn unto God; assures them (7) that at that time every man would see the folly of trusting in idols; and finally (8, 9), assures them of the complete overthrow of the army of the Assyrian. The scope of the prophecy is, therefore, simple and direct; the argument condensed, impressive, and beautiful. It is not improbable, by any means, that these exhortations of Isaiah had a sensible effect on the conduct of

a most striking emblem of hell-fire, and as such is used in the New Testament. Hezekiah was firmly opposed to idolatry; and it is not improbable that he had removed the images of Moloch, and made that valley the receptacle of filth, and a place of abomination, and that the prophet refers to this fact in the passage before us. ¶ Is *ordained*. Was fitted up, appointed, constituted. The prophet by a figure represents Hezekiah as having *fitted up* this place as if for the appropriate punishment of the Assyrians. ¶ *Of old*. Marg. as in Heb. 'From yesterday.' This expression may mean simply 'formerly, some time since,' as in Ex. iv. 10; 2 Sam. iii. 17. The idea here seems to be, that Tophet had been formerly, or was already prepared *as if* for the destruction of Sennacherib and his army. His ruin would be as certain, and as sudden, *as if*, in the valley of Tophet, the breath of JE-HOVAH should set on fire the vast materials that had been collected, and were ready to be kindled. It does not mean that Tophet had actually been prepared *for* the army of Sennacherib; it does not mean that his army would actually be destroyed there—for it was on the other side of the city that they were cut off (see Notes on ch. x. 32); it does not mean that they would be consigned to hell-fire;—but it means that that place had been fitted up *as if* to be an emblematic representation of his ruin; that the consuming fires in that valley were a striking representation of the sudden and awful manner in which the abhorred enemies of God would be destroyed. ¶ *For the king it is prepared*. For Hezekiah; as if the place had been fitted up for his use in order to consume and destroy his enemies. It is not meant that Hezekiah actually had this in view, but the whole language is figurative. It was *as if* that place had been fitted up by Hezekiah as a suitable place in which entirely to destroy his foes. ¶ *He hath made* it *deep* and *large*. Vast; as if able to contain the entire army that was to be destroyed. ¶ *The pile thereof*. The wood that was collected there to be consumed. ¶ *The breath of the* LORD. As if JEHOVAH should breathe upon it, and enkindle the whole mass, so that it should burn without the possibility of being extinguished. The meaning is, that the destruction of the Assyrian would as really come from JEHOVAH as if he should, by his own agency, ignite the vast piles that were collected in the valley of Hinnom. ¶ *Like a stream of brimstone*. Brimstone, or sulphur, is used in the Scriptures to denote a fire of great intensity, and one that cannot be extinguished (Gen. xix. 24; Ps. xi. 6; Ezek. xxxviii. 22; Rev. ix. 17, 18). Hence it is used to denote the eternal torments of the wicked in hell (Rev. xiv. 10; xix. 20; xxi. 8). ¶ *Doth kindle it*. The army of the Assyrians would be destroyed in a manner which would be well represented by JEHOVAH's sending down upon a vast pile collected in the valley of Hinnom, a burning stream of sulphurous flame that should ignite and consume all before it (see Notes on ch. xxxvii. 36).

Hezekiah. The whole narrative respecting the invasion of Sennacherib would lead to the conclusion, that at first Hezekiah himself joined in the purpose of seeking the alliance with Egypt, but that he was afterwards led to abandon it, and to use all his influence to induce his people also to rely on the aid of God; compare ch. xxxvi. 6, with ver. 18.

WO to them that go down to Egypt for help, and stay on horses, and trust in chariots, because *they are* many ; and in horsemen, because they are very strong : but *a* they look not unto the Holy One of Israel, neither seek the LORD.

2 Yet he also *is* wise, and will bring evil, and will not *1* call back his words : but will arise against the house of the evil-doers, and against the help of them that work iniquity.

3 Now the Egyptians *are* men, and not God ; and their horses flesh, and not spirit. When the LORD shall stretch out his hand, both he that helpeth shall fall, and he that is holpen shall fall down, and they all shall fail together.

4 For thus hath the LORD spoken unto me, Like as the lion *b* and the young lion roaring on his prey, when a multitude of shepherds is called forth against him, *he* will not be afraid of their voice, nor abase himself for the *2* noise of them : so shall the LORD of hosts come down to fight for mount Zion, and for the hill thereof.

a Ho.7.7.   1 *remove.*   *b* Ho.11.10.   2 *or, multitude.*

CHAPTER XXXI.

1. *Wo* (see Note on ch. xxx. 1). ¶ *To them that go down to Egypt* (see Note on ch. xxx. 2). ¶ *And stay on horses* (see Note on ch. xxx. 16). ¶ *And trust in chariots* (see Note on ch. xxi. 7). That they were often used in war, is apparent from the following places (Josh. xi. 4 ; Judg. i. 19 ; 1 Sam. xiii. 5 ; 2 Sam. viii. 4). ¶ *Because* they are *many.* Because they hope to secure the aid of many. See the references above. It is evident that their confidence in them would be in proportion to the number which they could bring into the field. ¶ *But they look not,* &c. (see Note on ch. xxx. 1.)

2. *Yet he also* is *wise.* God is wise. It is in vain to attempt to deceive him, or to accomplish such purposes without his knowledge. ¶ *And will bring evil.* The punishment which is due to such want of confidence in him. ¶ *But will arise against the house of the evil-doers.* This is a general proposition, and it is evidently just as true now as it was in the time of Isaiah.

3. *Now the Egyptians* are *men.* They are nothing but men ; they have no power but such as other men possess. The idea here is, that the case in reference to which they sought aid was one in which *Divine* help was indispensable, and that, therefore, they relied on the aid of the Egyptians in vain. ¶ *And their horses flesh, and not spirit.* There is need, not merely of *physical* strength, but of wisdom, and intelligence, and it is in vain to look for that in mere brutes. ¶ *Both he that helpeth.* Egypt, whose aid is sought. ¶ *And he that is holpen.* Judah, that had sought the aid of Egypt. Neither of them would be able to stand against the wrath of God.

4. *For thus hath the* LORD *spoken.* The design of this verse and the following is to assure the Jews of the certain protection of JEHOVAH, and thus to induce them to put their trust in him rather than to seek the alliance with Egypt. To do this the prophet makes use of two striking illustrations, the first of which is, that JEHOVAH would be no more alarmed at the number and power of their enemies than a fierce lion would be that was intent on his prey, and could not be frightened from it by any number of men that should come against him. The *point* of this comparison is, that as the lion that *was intent on his purpose* could not be frightened from it by numbers, so it would be with JEHOVAH, who *was equally intent on his purpose*—the defence of the city of Jerusalem. It does not mean, of course, that the purpose of God and of the lion resembled each other, but merely that there was simi-

5 As birds flying, so will the LORD of hosts defend *a* Jerusalem ; defending also he will deliver *it, and* passing over he will preserve *it.*

6 Turn *b* ye unto *him from* whom

the children of Israel have deeply revolted. *c*

7 For in that day every man shall cast away his idols of silver,

a Ps.46.5.   *b* Jer.3.12.   *c* He.9.9.

---

lar *intensity of purpose,* and similar adherence to it notwithstanding all opposition. The figure is one that denotes the highest vigilance, firmness, steadiness, and a determination on the part of JEHOVAH that Jerusalem should not fall into the hands of the Assyrians. ¶ *Like as the lion.* The Divine nature and purposes are often represented in the Scriptures by metaphors, allegories, and comparisons taken from animals, and especially from the lion (see Deut. xxxiii. 20; Job x. 16; Ps. vii. 2; Hos. xi. 10). ¶ *And the young lion.* The vigorous, strong, fierce lion. The use of the two here, gives intensity and strength to the comparison. It is observable that the lion is seldom mentioned alone in the Scriptures. ¶ *Roaring on his prey.* Roaring as he seizes on his prey. This is the moment of the greatest *intensity of purpose* in the lion, and it is therefore used by Isaiah to denote the intense purpose of JEHOVAH to defend Jerusalem, and not to be deterred by any number of enemies. ¶ *When a multitude of shepherds is called forth.* When the neighbourhood is alarmed, and all the inhabitants turn out to destroy him. This comparison is almost exactly in the spirit and language of Homer, *Il.* xii. 209, *sq.* :

So pressed with hunger from the mountain's brow,
Descends a lion on the flocks below ;
So stalks the lordly savage o'er the plain,
In sullen majesty and stern disdain :
In vain loud mastiffs bay him from afar ;
And shepherds gall him with an iron war ;
Regardless, furious, he pursues his way ;
He foams, he roars, he rends the panting prey.
                         Pope.

So also *Il.* xviii. 161, 162 :

—But checked he turns ; repulsed attacks again.
With fiercer shouts his lingering troops he fires,
Nor yields a step, nor from his post retires ;
So watchful shepherds strive to force in vain,
The hungry lion from the carcass slain.   *Pope.*

¶ He *will not be afraid.* He will be so intent on his prey that he will not heed their shouting. ¶ *Nor abase himself.* That is, he will not be frightened, or disheartened. ¶ *So shall the*

LORD *of hosts.* That is, with the same intensity of purpose ; with the same fixedness of design. He will be as little dismayed and diverted from his purpose by the number, the designs, and the war-shout of the Assyrian armies.

5. *As birds flying.* This is another comparison indicating substantially the same thing as the former, that JEHOVAH would protect Jerusalem. The idea here is, that He would do it in the same manner as birds defend their young by hovering over them, securing them under their wings, and leaping forward, if they are suddenly attacked, to defend them. Our Saviour has used a similar figure to indicate his readiness to have defended and saved the same city (Matt. xxiii. 27), and it is possible that he may have had this passage in his eye. The phrase 'birds flying,' may denote the *rapidity* with which birds fly to defend their young, and hence the rapidity with which God would come to defend Jerusalem ; or it may refer to the fact that birds, when their young are attacked, fly, or flutter around them to defend them ; they will not leave them. ¶ *And passing over* (פָּסֹחַ, *pâsōăhh*). Lowth renders this, 'Leaping forward.' This word, which is usually applied in some of its forms to the Passover (Ex. xii. 13, 23, 27 ; Num. ix. 4 ; Josh. v. 11 ; 2 Chron. xxx. 18), properly means, as a verb, *to pass over,* and hence to preserve or spare. The idea in the passage is, that JEHOVAH would protect Jerusalem, as a bird defends its young.

6. *Turn ye unto* him. In view of the fact that he will assuredly defend Jerusalem, commit yourselves unto him rather than seek the aid of Egypt. ¶ *Have deeply revolted.* For the meaning of this phrase, see Note on ch. xxix. 15.

7. *For in that day.* That is, in the invasion of Sennacherib, and the events that shall be consequent thereon. ¶ *Every man shall cast away his idols*

and [1] his idols of gold, which your own hands have made unto you *for* a sin.

8 Then shall the Assyrian *a* fall with the sword, not of a mighty man ; and the sword, not of a mean man, shall devour him: but he shall

1 *the idols of his gold.*   *a* ch.87.63.
2 or, *for fear of.*
3 *for melting,* or, *tribute,* or, *tributary.*

(see Note on ch. xxx. 22; comp. Note on ch. ii. 20). ¶ For *a sin.* Or rather, the sin which your own hands have made. The sense is, that the making of those idols had been a sin, or sin itself. It had been *the* sin, by way of eminence, which was chargeable upon them.

8. *Then shall the Assyrian fall with the sword.* The *sword* is often used as an instrument of punishment. It is not meant here literally that the sword would be used, but it is employed to denote that complete destruction would come upon them. ¶ *Not of a mighty man.* The idea here is, that the army should not fall by the valour of a distinguished warrior, but that it should be done by the direct interposition of God (see ch. xxxvii. 36). ¶ *Of a mean man.* Of a man of humble rank. His army shall not be slain by the hand of mortals. ¶ *But he shall flee.* The Assyrian monarch escaped when his army was destroyed, and fled towards his own land ; ch. xxxvii. 37. ¶ *From the sword.* Marg. ' For fear of.' The Heb. is ' From the face of the sword ;' and the sense is, that he would flee in consequence of the destruction of his host, here represented as destroyed by the sword of JEHOVAH. ¶ *And his young men.* The flower and strength of his army. ¶ *Shall be discomfited.* Marg. ' For melting ;' or ' tribute,' or ' tributary.' LXX. Εἰς ἥττημα—' For destruction.' The Hebrew word (מַס *măs,* derived probably from מָסַס *măsăs, to melt away, to dissolve*) is most usually employed to denote a levy, fine, or tax— so called, says Taylor, because it *wastes* or *exhausts* the substance and strength of a people. The word is often used to denote that men become tributary, or vassals, as in Gen. xlix. 15; Deut. xx. 11; comp. Josh. xvi. 10; 2 Sam. xx. 24; 1 Kings iv. 6; v. 13; Esth. x. 1. Pro-

flee [2] from the sword, and his young men shall be [3] discomfited.

9 And [4] he shall pass over to his [5] stronghold for fear, and his princes shall be afraid of the ensign, saith the LORD, whose fire *is* in Zion, and his furnace in Jerusalem.

4 *his rock shall pass away for fear.*   5 or, *strength.*

bably it does not here mean that the strength of the Assyrian army would become literally tributary to the Jews, but that they would be *as if* they had been placed under a levy to them ; their vigour and strength would melt away ; as property and numbers do under taxation and tribute.

9. *And he shall pass over.* Marg. ' His rock shall pass away for fear.' The Hebrew would bear this, but it does not convey a clear idea. The sense seems to be this. The word rendered ' stronghold ' (Heb. ' His rock ') denotes his fortifications, or the places of strength in which he trusted. Probably the Assyrian monarch had many such places which he regarded as perfectly secure, both in the limits of his own kingdom, and on the line of his march towards Judea. Those places would naturally be made strong, in order to afford a refuge in case of a defeat. The idea here is, that so great would be his alarm at the sudden destruction of his army and the failure of his plans, that in his flight he would *pass over* or *beyond* these strong places ; he would not even stop to take refuge there and reorganize his scattered forces, but would flee with alarm *beyond* them, and make his way to his own capital. This appears to have been most strikingly fulfilled (see ch. xxxvii. 37). ¶ *And his princes.* Those, perhaps, that ruled over his dependent provinces. ¶ *Shall be afraid of the ensign.* That is, of *any* standard or banner that they saw. They would suppose that it was the standard of an enemy. This denotes a state of great consternation, when all the princes and nobles under the command of the Assyrian would be completely dismayed. ¶ *Whose fire is in Zion, &c.* That is, whose altar is there, and always burns there. That was the place where he

CHAPTER XXXII.

ANALYSIS

THIS chapter has been regarded by many as a continuation and conclusion of the prediction commenced in the preceding chapter. Though it was, however, probably uttered at about the same time, and with reference to the same general subject, yet there is no impropriety in its being separated. The previous chapter closes with a prediction that the Assyrian army, which had been so much the object of dread, would be totally destroyed. This would be of course followed with important consequences, some of which are depicted in this chapter. The prophet, therefore, states (1–8) that the defeat of Sennacherib would be followed by the peaceful and prosperous state of the kingdom under a righteous prince;—under whose reign there would be ample protection (2); at which time the advantages of instruction would prevail, and the ignorant would be enlightened (3, 4); when there would be a proper estimate put on moral worth, and when illiberality, hypocrisy, and falsehood would be no longer held in repute (5–7); and when the character of the nation would be that of a people which devised and executed large and liberal purposes (8). That this has a reference to the reign of Hezekiah, has been abundantly shown by Vitringa; and, indeed, must be obvious on the slightest inspection. For, 1. It is immediately connected with the account of the destruction of Sennacherib, and evidently means that the state of things here described would immediately succeed that. 2. There is nothing in the account that does not fully accord with the prosperous and happy times of the reign of Hezekiah. 3. There are statements in it which cannot be applied directly, or with propriety literally to the times of the Messiah. For example, the statement in the first verse that 'princes shall' rule in judgment' cannot be applied with any propriety to the apostles, since they are not anywhere designated by that name.

That, after the usual manner of Isaiah, he might not also, in the progress of this description, have glanced at the times of the Messiah, perhaps there can be no reason to doubt. But the main and leading purpose was, doubtless, to give a description of the happy times that would succeed the destruction of the army of the Assyrian. Calvin supposes, not improbably, I think, that this prophecy may have been uttered in the time of Ahaz, in whose reign wickedness so much abounded, and ignorance and idolatry so much prevailed. But whether the prophecy was actually *uttered* in the time of Ahaz or not—which cannot now be determined—yet it may have been uttered in view of the ignorance, and superstition, and hypocrisy, which prevailed in his reign, and which extended their influence into the time of his successor, and on account of which the nation was to be subjected to the calamities arising from the invasion of Sennacherib. After that, the king Hezekiah would rule in righteousness, and his kingdom would enjoy the blessings of his mild and virtuous reign.

The prophet then (10–14) proceeds to show, that *previous* to the prosperous times predicted, there would be a state of desolation and alarm. This is indicated by his calling on the daughters of luxury and fashion, who were reposing in security and confidence, to rise up in consternation at the calamities which were impending (10, 11), and by the assurance that there would be a time when they would sigh for the luxuries which they had before enjoyed (12–14). This is descriptive of the calamities which would attend the invasion of the Assyrian. Yet the prophet says, as is usual with him, that these calamities would be succeeded by more happy times (15–20). They would continue until the Spirit should be poured out from on high (15), and the result of this would be the prevalence of righteousness in the nation (16), and peace and safety (17,18); there would be safety, and the privilege of pursuing the peaceful pursuits of agriculture, and of cultivating the entire land without molestation (19, 20).

---

was worshipped, and it was a place, therefore, which he would defend. The meaning is, that they would be as certainly destroyed as the God whose altar was in Jerusalem was a God of truth, and would defend the place where he was worshipped. ¶ *And his furnace, &c.* (see Note on ch. xxix. 1). Where his altar continually burns. The word rendered 'furnace' (תַּנּוּר) means properly *a baking oven* (Ex. vii. 28; Lev. ii. 4; vii. 9; xi. 35). This was either a large conical pot which was heated, in

which the cakes were baked at the sides; or an excavation made in the earth which was heated by putting wood *in* it, and when that was removed, the dough was put in it. Perhaps the whole idea here is, that JEHOVAH had a home in Jerusalem, with the usual appendages of a house; that his fire and his oven were there, an expression descriptive of a dwelling-place. If so, then the meaning is, that he would defend his own home, and that the Assyrian could not expect to prevail against it.

BEHOLD, a king shall reign in
righteousness, ª and princes
shall rule in judgment.

2 And a man shall be as an
hiding-place from the wind, and
a covert ᵇ from the tempest; as
rivers ᶜ of water in a dry place; as
the shadow of a ¹ great rock in a
weary land.

ª Ps.45.6,7; Jer.23.5,6.

ᵇ ch.4.6.   ᶜ ch.44.3.   1 *heavy.*

CHAPTER XXXII.

1. *Behold, a king.* That is, Hezekiah. That it refers to him is apparent
from the connection. The reign of
Ahaz had been one of oppression and
idolatry. This was to be succeeded by
the reign of one under whom the rights
of the people would be secured, and
under whom there would be a state of
general prosperity. This *may* have
been uttered while Ahaz was on the
throne, or it may have been when Hezekiah began to reign. Perhaps the latter
is the more probable, as Ahaz might not
have tolerated anything that would have
looked like a reflection on his own reign;
nor, perhaps, while he was on the throne
would Isaiah have given a description
that would have been a contrast between his reign and that of his successor.
¶ *Shall reign in righteousness.* That
is, a righteous king shall reign; or his
administration shall be one of justice,
and strongly in contrast with that of
his predecessor. This was certainly the
general characteristic of the reign of
Hezekiah. ¶ *And princes shall rule.*
Heb. 'For princes,' or, 'as to princes'
(לְשָׂרִים). Lowth proposes to read this
without the ל, as the ancient versions
do. But it is not necessary to change
the text. It may be rendered, 'As to
princes, they shall rule' (comp. Ps. xvi.
3). The 'princes' here denote the various officers of government, or those to
whom the administration was confided.
¶ *In judgment.* That this is a just
description of the reign of Hezekiah is
apparent from the history, see 2 Kings
xviii. 3–6: 'He removed the high places,
and broke the images, and cut down the
grove. He trusted in the LORD God of
Israel, so that after him was none like
him among all the kings of Judah, nor
any that were before him, for he clave
unto the LORD, and departed not from
following him.'

2. *And a man.* That is, evidently,
the man referred to in the previous
verse, to wit, Hezekiah. ¶ *Shall be as
an hiding-place from the wind.* A
place where one may take refuge from
a violent wind and tempest (see Note
on ch. xxv. 4). ¶ *A covert.* A place
of shelter and security. Wind and tempest are emblematic of calamity and
oppression; and the sense is, that Hezekiah would be the protector of his
people, and would save them from the
calamities to which they had been subjected in former reigns. ¶ *As rivers
of water.* This figure is often used in
Isaiah (see ch. xxxv. 6, 7; and Notes
on xli. 18). It means that the blessings
of such a reign would be as grateful
and refreshing as gushing fountains
and running streams were to a thirsty
traveller. Here it refers to the benefits
that would be conferred by the reign of
Hezekiah—a reign which, compared with
that of his father, would be like a refreshing fountain to a weary pilgrim in
a pathless desert. ¶ *As the shadow of
a great rock.* In a burning desert of
sand nothing is more grateful than the
cooling shade of a far-projecting rock.
It not only excludes the rays of the sun,
but it has itself a refreshing coolness
that is most grateful to a weary traveller. The same figure is often used by
the classic writers (see Virgil, *Georg.*
iii. 145; Hesiod, ii. 106). ¶ *In a weary
land.* A land where there is fatigue
and weariness. Probably here it is
used to denote a land destitute of trees,
and groves, and pleasant abodes; a
land where one expects weariness and
fatigue without any refreshment and
shelter. The following description from
Campbell's *Travels in Africa* will explain this: 'Well does the traveller
remember a day in the wilds of Africa,
where the country was chiefly covered
with burning sand; when, scorched with
the powerful rays of an almost vertical
sun, the thermometer in the shade standing at 100°. He remembers long looking hither and thither for something
that would afford protection from the

3 And the eyes of them that see shall not be dim : and the ears of them that hear shall hearken.

4 The heart also of the [1] rash

shall understand knowledge, and the tongue of the stammerers shall be ready to speak [2] plainly.

1 hasty.　　2 or, elegantly.

almost insupportable heat, and where the least motion of air felt like a flame coming against the face. At length he espied a huge loose rock leaning against the front of a small cliff which faced the sun. At once he fled for refuge underneath its inviting shade. The coolness emitted from this rocky canopy he found exquisitely exhilarating. The wild beasts of the deserts were all fled to their dens, and the feathered songsters were all roosting among the thickest foliage they could find of the evergreen trees. The whole creation around seemed to groan, as if their vigour had been entirely exhausted. A small river was providentially at hand, to the side of which, after a while, he ventured, and sipped a little of its cooling water, which tasted better than the best Burgundy, or the finest old hock in the world. During all this enjoyment, the above apropos text was the interesting subject of the traveller's meditation ; though the allusion as a figure, must fall infinitely short of that which is meant to be prefigured by it. '

[The whole of this passage is capable of beautiful application to the Messiah and his times; while the language of the second verse cannot be supposed descriptive of any *creature*; it is so associated in our minds with the character and functions of the Divine Redeemer, that we cannot easily acquiesce in any meaner application. 'To interpret the sublime imagery of this verse (2) in application to a mere human being, would be quite repugnant to the spirit of the sacred writers, by whom Jehovah alone is represented as the source of protection and refreshment to his people, and all trust in creatures solemnly interdicted' (Henderson). Doubtless, if Hezekiah be at all intended, it is in a typical or inferior sense only. A greater than Hezekiah is here ; the language and figures used are precisely such as are elsewhere by the prophet applied to Jehovah (ch. iv. 6; xxv. 4); while the particulars characteristic of the times predicted, are just such as elsewhere he connects with gospel times (comp. ch. xxix. 18; xxxv. 5). The things predicted, according to this view, are a righteous administration under Messiah the prince (1); protection and refreshment to his subjects; protection from 'the

wrath of God and the temptations of Satan, and the rage of the world; refreshment by the consolations and graces of his Spirit, which are as rivers of water in this dry land' (2); a desire for knowledge and such facility in the acquisition of it, that even persons ordinarily supposed disqualified should both clearly understand, and easily and accurately express the truth (3, 4); a just appreciation of character and estimation of men in accordance therewith (5); and, finally, the prevalence of a loving, liberal spirit, setting itself to devise and execute plans of benevolence on a scale hitherto unprecedented (8); Ps. cx. 3; Acts ii. 44, 45; 2 Cor. viii. 1, 4; ix. 2.]

3. *And the eyes of them that see,* &c. The sense of this verse is, that there shall be, under the reign of this wise and pious prince, on the part of the prophets and teachers, a clear view of Divine truth, and on the part of the people who hear, a disposition to hearken and to attend to it. The phrase ' of them that see,' refers probably to the *prophets,* as those who were called *seers* (see Notes on ch. xxix. 10; xxx. 10; comp. 1 Sam. ix. 9), or those who had *visions* (see Note on ch. i. 1) of the things that God would communicate to men. The word rendered ' be dim ' (תִּשְׁעֶינָה), is derived from שָׁעָה, which usually signifies *to see, to look,* but it also has a meaning similar to שָׁעַע, *to spread over, to close, to make blind.* Of this fact Lowth seems not to have been aware when he proposed, without the authority of any MS., to change the text. The sense is, that those who were prophets and religious teachers should no more see obscurely, but should have clear and just views of Divine truth. ¶ *And the ears of them that hear.* Of the people who were instructed by their religious teachers. ¶ *Shall hearken.* It shall be a characteristic of those times that they shall be disposed to attend to the truth of God.

4. *The heart also of the rash.* Marg. 'Hasty.' The Hebrew word denotes *those who hasten;* that is, those who are precipitate in forming a judgment, or deciding on a course of action. They

5 The vile person shall be no more called liberal, nor the churl said *to be* bountiful.

6 For the vile person will *a* speak villany, and his heart will work iniquity, to practise hypocrisy, and to utter error against the LORD, to make empty the soul of the hungry;

and he will cause the drink of the thirsty to fail.

7 The instruments also of the churl *are* evil: he deviseth wicked devices to destroy the poor with lying words, even when 1 the needy speaketh right.

a Jer.13.23.
1 or, *he speaketh* against *the poor in judgment.*

do not take time to deliberate, and consequently they are led headlong into error, and into improper courses of life. ¶ *Shall understand knowledge.* They shall take time to deliberate; and they shall consequently form a more enlightened judgment. ¶ *And the tongue of the stammerers.* The 'stammerers' (comp. Note, ch. xxviii. 11) seem here to denote those who had indistinct and confused views of subjects, or who were incapable of expressing clear and intelligible views of Divine truth. ¶ *Shall be ready to speak plainly.* Marg. 'Elegantly.' The Hebrew is צחות 'clear,' 'white,' usually applied to a bright, clear, white light. The sense is, that there should be no indistinctness or obscurity in their views and modes of utterance.

5. *The vile person.* Heb. 'Fool.' But the connection requires us to understand this as the opposite of *liberal;* and it means a person who is close, miserly, narrow-minded, covetous. This person is designated, very appropriately, as a fool. ¶ *Shall be no more called liberal.* It is probable that under the reign of former princes, when all views of right and wrong had been perverted, men of unprincipled character had been the subjects of flattery, and names of virtue had been attributed to them by their friends and admirers. But it would not be so under the virtuous reign of the prince here celebrated. Things would be called by their right names, and flattery would not be allowed to attribute to men qualities which they did not possess. ¶ *Nor the churl.* The word 'churl' means properly a rude, surly, ill-bred man; then a miser, a niggard. The Hebrew word means properly a deceiver, a fraudulent man (Gesenius). The word *avaricious,* however, seems to suit the connection. Lowth renders it, 'Niggard.' Noyes, 'Crafty.'

¶ *Bountiful.* Flattery shall no more ascribe to a miserly man a character which does not belong to him.

6. *For the vile person.* Heb. 'The fool.' This word more properly expresses the idea than 'vile person.' The Hebrews used the name *fool* to denote not only one destitute of understanding, but a knave, a dishonest man—regarding sin as the highest folly (see 1 Sam. xxv. 25; 2 Sam. iii. 33; Job ii. 10). ¶ *Will speak villany.* Heb. 'Will speak folly.' That is, he will act in accordance with his nature; it is his nature to speak folly, and he will do it. Under a wicked and unjust administration such persons might be the subjects of flattery (ver. 5), and might be raised to office and power. But under the administration of a virtuous king they would not be admitted to favour; and the reason was, that they would act out their nature, and would corrupt all around them. A monarch, therefore, who regarded the honour of his own throne, and the welfare of his subjects, would exclude them from his counsels. ¶ *To make empty the soul of the hungry.* Probably this refers to spiritual hunger and thirst; and means that such a person would take away the means of knowledge from the people, and leave them to error, ignorance, and want. The sense is, that if such persons were raised to office, they would corrupt the nation and destroy their confidence in God; and *this* was a reason why a virtuous prince would exclude them from any participation in his government.

7. *The instruments also.* In the Hebrew here there is a *paronomasia* which cannot be imitated in a translation. The word 'instruments' here denotes evidently *the means* by which the churl accomplishes his object; whether it be by words, by judicial decisions, or by crafty devices. This is also a kind of proverbial expression, and is given as a

8 But the liberal deviseth liberal things; and by liberal things shall he [1] stand.

9 Rise up, ye women that are at

1 or, *be established*.   *a* Amos 6.1.

further reason why such a person would not be employed by a wise and virtuous prince. ¶ *Are evil.* He will make use of any unprincipled means, any wicked plan or device, to accomplish his purpose. ¶ *With lying words.* With false representations; or with deceitful promises and assurances. His aim would be particularly directed to the poor and humble, as more easily deprived of their rights than the rich and powerful. It was also of greater importance to defend the rights of the poor, and therefore the prophet says that such a person should not be in the employ of a just and virtuous ruler. ¶ *Even when the needy speaketh right.* That is, although the cause of the needy is one of truth and equity. When this would be manifest, the unprincipled man in power would deprive him of his rights, and, therefore, under a wise and virtuous administration, such a person should not be employed.

8. *But the liberal.* This seems also to have the force of a proverbial expression. The word ' liberal' means generous, noble, large-hearted, benevolent; a man of large views and of public spirit; a man above covetousness, avarice, and self-seeking; a man who is willing to devote himself to the welfare of his country, and to the interests of his fellow-men. It is *implied* here that such persons would be selected to administer the affairs of the government under the wise and virtuous prince of whom the prophet speaks. ¶ *Deviseth liberal things.* He purposes those things which will tend to promote the public welfare, and not those merely which will conduce to his private ends and gratification. ¶ *And by liberal things shall he stand.* Marg. ' Be established.' That is, according to the connection, he shall be confirmed, or approved in the government of the virtuous king referred to. It is, however, a proposition in a general form, and means also that a man by a liberal course shall be established; that is, his character, reputation, hopes, shall be established by it. This is true

ease; [a] hear my voice, ye careless daughters; give ear unto my speech.

10 Many [2] days and years shall ye be troubled, ye careless women:

2 *days above a year*.

now. If a man wishes to obtain permanent peace and honour, the esteem of his fellow-men, or the evidence of Divine approbation, it can be best done by large and liberal schemes to advance the happiness of a dying world. He who is avaricious and narrow-minded has no happiness, and no durable reputation; he who is large-hearted and benevolent, has the approbation of the wise and good, the favour of God, and a firm and unshaken support in the trials of life, and in the agonies of death.

9. *Rise up, &c.* Rosenmüller supposes that this commences a new vision or prophecy; and that the former part (ver. 9–14) refers to the desolation of Judea by the invasion of Sennacherib, and the latter (ver. 15–20) to the prosperity which would succeed that invasion. It cannot be doubted that this is the general reference of the passage, but there does not seem to be a necessity of making a division here. The entire prophecy, including the whole chapter, relates in general to the reign of Hezekiah; and as these events were to occur during his reign, the prophet groups them together, and presents them as constituting important events in his reign. The general design of *this* portion of the prophecy (ver. 9–14) is to show the desolation that would come upon the land of Judea in consequence of that invasion. This he represents in a poetical manner, by calling on the daughters of fashion and ease to arouse, since all their comforts were to be taken away. ¶ *Ye women that are at ease.* They who are surrounded by the comforts which affluence gives, and that have no fear of being reduced to want (comp. ch. iii. 16–26). ¶ *Ye careless daughters.* Heb. ' Daughters confiding;' that is, those who felt no alarm, and who did not regard God and his threatenings.

10. *Many days and years.* Marg. ' Days above a year.' This is a literal translation of the Hebrew. LXX. ' Make mention of a day of a year in sorrow, with hope.' Targum, ' Days

for the vintage shall fail, the gathering shall not come.

11 Tremble, ye women that are at ease ; be troubled, ye careless ones ; strip ye, and make ye bare, and gird *sackcloth* upon *your* loins.

12 They shall lament for the

1 *fields of desire.* a Ho.10.8. 2 or, *burning upon.*

teats, for the [1] pleasant fields, for the fruitful vine.

13 Upon the land of my people shall come up thorns *a and* briers, yea, [2] upon all the houses of joy in the joyous city.

14 Because the palaces shall be forsaken ; the multitude of the city

with years.' Kimchi supposes it means 'two years.' Grotius supposes it means 'within three years.' Various other interpretations may be seen in Poole's *Synopsis.* Gesenius renders it, 'For a year's time,' according to the vulgar expression 'a year and a day,' denoting a complete year, and supposes that it means a considerable time, a long period. The phrase literally means 'the days upon [or beyond] a year,' and may denote a long time; as the entire days in a year would denote a long period of suffering. Lowth renders it, not in accordance with the Hebrew, 'Years upon years.' Noyes, 'One year more, and ye shall tremble.' *Perhaps* this expresses the sense; and *then* it would denote not the length of time which they would suffer, but would indicate that the calamities would soon come upon them. ¶ *For the vintage shall fail.* A large part of the wealth and the luxury of the nation consisted in the vintage. When the vine failed, there would be, of course, great distress. The sense is, that in consequence of the invasion of the Assyrians, either the people would neglect to cultivate the lands, or they would fail to collect the harvest. This might occur either from the dread of the invasion, or because the Assyrian would destroy everything in his march.

11. *Strip ye, and make ye bare.* That is, take off your gay and splendid apparel, and put on the habiliments of mourning, indicative of a great calamity. ¶ *And gird* sackcloth (see Note on ch. iii. 24).

12. *They shall lament for the teats.* Interpreters have been not a little perplexed by this expression. Lowth supposes it is to be taken in connection with the previous verse, and that it denotes that sackcloth was to be girded upon the breast as well as upon the loins.

Others have supposed that it denotes to 'smite upon the breasts,' as a token of grief ; others, that the word 'breast' here denotes children by a *synecdoche,* as having been nourished by the breast, and that the women here were called to mourn over their children. But it is evident, I think, that the word *breasts* here is used to denote that which nourishes or sustains life, and is synonymous with fruitful fields. It is so used in Homer (*Iliad,* ix. 141), where οἴθαρ ἀρούρης denotes fertility of land. And here the sense doubtless is, that they would mourn over the fields which once contributed to sustain life, but which were now desolate. In regard to the *grammatical* difficulties of the place, Rosenmüller and Gesenius may be consulted. ¶ *The pleasant fields.* Marg. as in Heb., 'Fields of desire.'

13. *Upon the land of my people.* A description similar to this, in regard to the consequences of the invasion of Sennacherib, is given in ch. vii. 20–25 (see Notes on that passage). ¶ *Yea, upon all the houses of joy.* Marg. 'Burning upon.' The marginal reading has originated from the supposition that the word כִּי is derived from כָּרָה, *to be burned.* This conjecture has been adopted by Junius and Tremellius, and by some others. But it is evidently mere conjecture, and is not demanded. The word 'yea' will express the sense, meaning that desolation, indicated by the growth of thorns and briers, would come upon the cities that were then filled with joy. This does not refer to Jerusalem, which was not taken by Sennacherib, but to the other cities that were destroyed by him in his march, and this account accords with the statement in ch. vii. 20–25.

14. *Because the palaces shall be forsaken.* That is, the palaces in the cities and towns which Sennacherib would

shall be left: the [1] forts and towers shall be for dens for ever, a joy of wild asses, a pasture of flocks ;

15 Until the Spirit *a* be poured

1 or, *cliffs and watch-towers.*

upon us from on high, and the wilderness be a fruitful field, and the *b* fruitful field be counted for a forest.

a Joel 2.28.   *b* Ps.107.33,&c.

lay waste. Or, if it refers, as Lowth supposes, to the invasion of the land in the time of the Chaldeans, then it relates to the palaces in Jerusalem. Vitringa supposes that the temple at Jerusalem is particularly designated by the word rendered *palaces.* But that is not the usual word to denote the temple, and it is not necessary to suppose that that is particularly referred to. The word אַרְמוֹן usually denotes a *palace,* or royal residence in some part of the royal citadel (see 1 Kings xvi. 18; Isa. xxv. 2; Jer. xxx. 18; Amos i. 4, 7, 10, 12). ¶ *The forts.* Marg. ' Cliffs and watch-towers.' Heb. עֹפֶל (*ophel*). This word properly denotes a hill or a cliff, such as is an advantageous situation for fortresses. It is translated in Mic. iv. 8, ' the stronghold ;' in 2 Kings v. 24, ' the tower;' in 2 Chron. xxvii. 3; xxx. 14; Neh. iii. 27; xi. 21, ' Ophel.' With the article (THE *hill*) it was given, by way of eminence, to a bluff or hill lying north-east of mount Zion, and south of mount Moriah, which was surrounded and fortified with a wall (Jos. *Jewish Wars,* vi. 6). It extends south from mount Moriah, running down to the fountain of Siloam, lying between the valley of Jehoshaphat on the east, and the Tyropeon or valley of Cheesemongers on the west. It terminates over the pool of Siloam in a steep point of rock forty or fifty feet high. The top of the ridge is flat, and the ground is now tilled, and planted with olive and other fruit trees (see Robinson's *Bib. Researches,* vol. i. pp. 341, 394). It may be used here, however, to denote a hill or cliff, a strongly-fortified place in general, without supposing of necessity that it refers to the mountain in Jerusalem. ¶ *Towers.* Towers were erected on the walls of cities at convenient distances for purposes of observation. ¶ *Shall be for dens.* Shall become places where banditti and robbers may abide, and secure themselves. ¶ *For ever.* This is evidently one instance in

which the word ' for ever ' (עַד־עוֹלָם), denotes a *long time,* because in the verse following there is a *period* specified when the desolation would terminate. When the word is used without any such limitation, it denotes proper eternity. ¶ *A joy of wild asses.* A place where wild animals will have unlimited range.

15. *Until the Spirit.* The Spirit of God, as the source of all blessings, and especially as able to meet and remove the ills of the long calamity and desolation. This evidently refers to some future period, when the evils which the prophet was contemplating would be succeeded by the spread of the true religion. If the prophet meant to confine his description of calamities to those which would attend the invasion of Sennacherib, then this refers to the piety and prosperity which would prevail after that during the reign of Hezekiah. If he designed, as Lowth supposes, to describe the calamities which would attend the invasion of the Chaldeans and the desolation of the city of Jerusalem during the captivity, then this refers to the prosperous times that would occur after their return to their own land. And if he looked forward beyond even that, then this refers to the times of the Messiah also, and he designed to describe the happy period when the Messiah should have come, and when the Spirit should be poured out. Vitringa supposes that all three of these events are referred to. But although the *expressions* are such as are used in reference to the times of the Messiah, yet the word ' until ' seems to limit the prediction to some event previous to that. The plain sense of the passage is, that the city would lie waste, and would be a pasture for flocks, *until* the Spirit should be poured out ; that is, would lie waste a long time, and then be succeeded by the merciful interposition of God restoring them to their land and privileges. This idea would seem to limit it, at the utmost, to the return

16 Then judgment shall dwell in the wilderness, and righteousness remain in the fruitful field.

17 And the work of righteousness shall be peace ; *a* and the effect of righteousness, quietness and assurance for ever.

a Ps.85.10; Ja.3.18.   *b* Heb.4.9.

18 And my people shall dwell in a peaceable *b* habitation, and in sure dwellings, and in quiet resting-places,

19 When it shall hail, *c* coming down on the forest ; and the city shall be ¹ low in a low place.

c ch.30.30.   1 or, *utterly abased.*

from Babylon. ¶ *Be poured out.* This is a common and usual mode of indicating that the influences of the Spirit of God would be imparted (Isa. xliv. 3; Ezek. xxxix. 29; Joel ii. 28, 29; Acts ii. 17, 18). ¶ *From on high.* From heaven (comp. Luke xxiv. 49). ¶ *And the wilderness be a fruitful field.* Until that change shall come when the places that are desolate shall become fertile, and the places which are now fertile and prosperous shall become desolate and barren. This may refer to the time when Jerusalem, that would have lain so long waste, would be again inhabited and cultivated, and when Babylon, then so prosperous, would become desolate and ruined. The expression has a proverbial cast, and denotes change and revolution (see Note on ch. xxix. 17).

16. *Then judgment shall dwell.* Or, justice shall make its appropriate dwelling-place there. ¶ *In the wilderness.* In the place that *was* a wilderness, but that shall now be turned to a fruitful field. ¶ *In the fruitful field.* In the nation that is like a fruitful field; in Judea restored.

17. *And the work of righteousness.* That which righteousness produces; or the effect of the prevalence of righteousness on the nation. ¶ *Shall be peace.* There shall be no internal agitation, and no conflicts with foreign nations. ¶ *Quietness and assurance.* This is a beautiful description of the happy effect of the prevalence of piety; and it is as true now as it was in the time of Isaiah. True religion would put an end to strifes and litigations; to riots and mobs; to oppressions and tumults; to alarms and robbery; to battle, and murder, and conflict.

18. *And my people shall dwell in a peaceable habitation.* In cities and towns that would not be alarmed by internal or external foes. ¶ *And in*

sure dwellings. In dwellings that would be secure from invasion.—All this is descriptive of the peaceful times, and the general security which followed the return from Babylon. To this period of happiness and prosperity, Isaiah, as well as the other prophets, often refers.

19. *When it shall hail.* Heb. בְּרֶדֶת בָּרָד—'And it shall hail in coming down.' There is a *paranomasia* in the original here, which cannot be expressed in a translation—a figure of speech, which, as we have seen, is common in Isaiah. 'Hail' is an image of Divine vengeance or punishment; and the reference here is, doubtless, to the storms of indignation that would come on the enemies of the Jews, particularly on the Assyrians (see Notes on ch. xxx. 30). ¶ *Coming down on the forest.* Coming down on the army of the Assyrian, which is here called 'a forest.' The same term 'forest' is given to the army of the Assyrians in ch. x. 18, 19, 33, 34. The sense is, that the Divine judgment would come down on that army with as much severity as a storm of hail descends on a forest—stripping the leaves from the trees, destroying its beauty, and laying it waste. ¶ *And the city.* According to Gesenius, this is Nineveh, the capital of the Assyrian empire. According to Rosenmüller, Grotius, and others, it is Babylon. Hensler supposes that it is Jerusalem, and that the sense is, that as a city that is situated in a valley is safe when the storm and tempest sweep over the hills, so would it be to Jerusalem when the storm of wrath should sweep away the army of the Assyrian. But the connection evidently requires us to understand it of the capital of the enemy; though whether it be Nineveh or Babylon perhaps cannot be determined. ¶ *Shall be low in a low place.*

20 Blessed *are* ye that sow beside all waters, *a* that send forth *thither* the feet of the ox and the ass.

CHAPTER XXXIII.

ANALYSIS.

THIS chapter comprises a new and distinct prophecy, though manifestly relating to the same general subject as the preceding. In ver. 19 of the previous chapter, the prophet had foretold the destruction of the army of Sennacherib; and this chapter is designed still further to set forth the circumstances and the effects of that destruction. That it refers to Sennacherib is apparent from the whole structure of the prophecy. So it is understood by Lowth, Rosenmüller, Grotius, and Calvin, though Vitringa supposes that it refers to the destruction of the Syrians, instead of the *Assyrians*, and particularly after the time, and for the crimes of Anti-

a Ec.11.1,2.

ochus Epiphanes. All the circumstances, as well as the connection, however, agree with the invasion by Sennacherib, and agree far better with that than either with the destruction of Babylon, or the judgments that came upon the *Syrians*. The *design* of the prophecy is to assure the Jews that their nation and city would be safe notwithstanding the invasion of the Assyrian, and that JEHOVAH would be to them a source of constant protection and consolation (21). The object of the prophecy, therefore, is to comfort them in this threatened invasion, and to lead them to look up to God.

The prophecy, or poem, is one of uncommon beauty in its structure, and is peculiarly elegant in its expressions. It abounds, indeed, in transitions; but they are easily seen, and can be distinctly marked. The structure and design of the poem may be seen in the following analysis:—

I. Woe is denounced against the Assyrian who had invaded Judea without provocation, and who

---

Marg. 'Utterly abased.' Heb. 'In humility shall be humbled.' The sense is, shall be completely prostrate. Those who refer this to Jerusalem suppose it refers to the time when God should humble it by bringing the enemy so near, and exciting so much consternation and alarm. Those who refer it to Babylon suppose it relates to its destruction. If referred to Nineveh, it must mean when the pride of the capital of the Assyrian empire should be humbled by the complete overthrow of their army, and the annihilation of their hopes. The connection seems to require us to adopt this latter interpretation. The whole verse is very obscure; but perhaps the above will express its general sense.

20. *Blessed* are *ye*. The sense of this verse is, that while the enemies of the Jews would be overthrown, they themselves would be permitted to cultivate their lands in security. Instead of *predicting* this directly, the prophet *implies* that this would occur, by declaring that those who were permitted to do this were happy. ¶ *That sow beside all waters*. Heb. 'Upon (על) all waters.' This *may* mean that they selected places near running streams as being most fertile; or it may refer, as Lowth supposes, to the manner of sowing grain, and particularly rice, in east-

ern countries. This is done by casting the seed upon the water. This custom is referred to in Eccl. xi. 1: 'Cast thy bread,' *i.e.*, thy seed, 'upon the waters, for thou shalt find it after many days;' —that is, cast thy seed upon the waters when the river overflows the banks, and the seed will sink into the slime and mud, and will spring up when the waters subside, and you will find it again after many days in a rich and luxuriant harvest. Sir John Chardin thus describes this mode of sowing: 'They sow it (the rice) upon the water; and before sowing, while the earth is covered with water, they cause the ground to be trodden by oxen, horses, and asses, who go mid-leg deep; and this is the way they prepare the ground for sowing' (Harmer's *Obs.* vol. i. p. 280). ¶ *That send forth* thither *the feet of the ox and the ass.* That is, for the purpose of treading the earth while the water is on it, and preparing it for the seed. In this way the ground would need no ploughing, but the seed would fall into the slime, and be sufficiently covered when the waters should subside. The idea in this verse is, that there would be a state of security succeeding the destruction of their enemies; and that they would be permitted to pursue the cultivation of the soil, unannoyed and undisturbed.

was spreading desolation over a nation that had not injured him (1). This contains the *general* scope and *purport* of the chapter.

II. The Jews are introduced (2) as offering up supplications to JEHOVAH in view of the threatened invasion, and beseeching him to be merciful to them, and expressing their confidence in him.

III. God himself is introduced declaring the overthrow of Sennacherib (3, 4). This he represents (3) under the image of the people—that is, the people in his army—fleeing at the noise of the tumult caused by the desolating tempest that should sweep them away, and at the act of God's lifting up himself to scatter the nations.

IV. A chorus of Jews is introduced (5, 6) extolling the greatness and mercy of God (5); and also celebrating the wisdom and piety of Hezekiah, who had put his confidence in God (6).

V. In ver. 7–9, the despair and alarm of the Jews are described on the approach of Sennacherib. This is exhibited in the following manner: —1. The messengers whom Hezekiah had sent to Sennacherib with three hundred talents of silver and thirty talents of gold, to propitiate his favour (2 Kings xviii. 14–16), return without success and weeping bitterly (7). 2. The desolation is described that attended the march of Sennacherib—a desolation that extended to the highways, the cities, and to the most beautiful and fertile places, represented by hewing down Lebanon, and turning Carmel into a wilderness 8, 9).

VI. God is now introduced (10–13) as saying that he would take the work of the destruction of the Assyrian into his own hand, and showing that he would be himself exalted (10); that he would disappoint their expectations (11); that they should be totally destroyed as if by fire (12), and calling on the nations near and remote to hear what he had done (13).

VII. The various effects of the invasion on the inhabitants of Jerusalem are 'described (14–19). 1. The effect on the hypocrites, producing consternation and alarm of the highest degree (14). 2. This is finely contrasted with the confidence and security of the righteous in that time. They would confide in God (15, 16); they would see the king in his beauty (17); and they would see their foe completely destroyed (18, 19).

VIII. The whole account is closed with a statement of the fact that Jerusalem was safe, and that the enemy would be completely destroyed (20–24).

W O to thee that spoilest, *a* and thou *wast* not spoiled ; and dealest treacherously, and they dealt not treacherously with thee ! when thou shalt cease to spoil, thou shalt *b* be spoiled ; *and* when thou shalt make an end to deal treacherously, they shall deal treacherously with thee.

a ch.21.2; Hab.2.8.   *b* Rev.13.10.

CHAPTER XXXIII.

1. *Wo to thee that spoilest.* This description accords entirely with Sennacherib and his army, who had plundered the cities and countries which they had invaded, and who were about to advance to Jerusalem for the same purpose (comp. ch. xxix. 7, 8; xxxvii. 11). ¶ *And thou* wast *not spoiled.* That is, thou hadst not been plundered by the Jews against whom thou art coming. It was because the war was so unprovoked and unjust, that God would bring so signal vengeance on them. ¶ *And dealest treacherously* (see Note on ch. xxi. 2). The treachery of the Assyrians consisted in the fact that when their assistance was asked by the Jews, in order to aid them against the combined forces of Syria and Samaria (see ch. vii. 1, 2), they had taken occasion from that invitation to bring desolation on Judah (see ch. vii. 17, 20 ; Notes on ch. viii. 6–8 ; x. 6). Hezekiah

also gave to Sennacherib thirty talents of gold and three hundred talents of silver, evidently with an *understanding* that this was all that he demanded, and that if this was paid, he would leave the nation in peace. But this implied promise he perfidiously disregarded (see 2 Kings xviii. 14, 15). ¶ *When thou shalt cease to spoil.* This does not refer to his having *voluntarily* ceased to plunder, but to the fact that God would put an end to it. ¶ *Thou shalt be spoiled.* This was literally fulfilled. The Assyrian monarchy lost its splendour and power, and was finally merged in the more mighty empire of Babylon. The nation was, of course, subject to the depredation of the conquerors, and compelled to submit to them. ¶ *When thou shalt make an end.* The idea is, that there would be a *completion*, or a finishing of his acts of treachery towards the Jews, and that would be when God should overthrow him and his army.

2 O Lord, be gracious unto us; we have waited for thee: be thou their arm every morning, our salvation also in the time of trouble.

3 At the noise of the tumult the people fled ; at the lifting up of thyself the nations were scattered.

¶ *They shall deal treacherously with thee.* The words 'they shall,' are here equivalent to, 'thou shalt be dealt with in a treacherous manner.' The result was, that Sennacherib was treacherously slain by his own sons as he was 'worshipping in the house of Nisroch his god' (Isa. xxxvii. 38), and thus the prophecy was literally fulfilled. The sense of the whole is, that God would reward their desire of plundering a nation that had not injured them by the desolation of their own land ; and would recompense the perfidiousness of the kings of Assyria that had sought to subject Jerusalem to their power, by perfidiousness in the royal family itself.

2. *O Lord.* This is a solemn prayer to Jehovah, made by the Jews in the apprehension of the invasion of the Assyrian. It is not meant that this prayer was actually offered, but it is a prophetic representation indicating the alarm of the Jews at his approach, and their disposition to throw themselves upon the mercy of God. ¶ *We have waited for thee.* That is, we have looked for deliverance from this threatened invasion from thy hand (comp. Note on ch. xxvi.8). ¶ *Be thou their arm.* The *arm* is a symbol of *strength.* It is used in the Scriptures as emblematic of the Divine protection, or of the interposition of God in time of calamity and danger (Ex. xv. 16 ; Job xl. 9 ; Ps. xliv. 3 ; lxxvii. 15 ; lxxxix. 21 ; xcviii. 1). Lowth proposes to read 'our arm' instead of 'their arm ;' and the connection would seem to demand such a reading. The Vulgate and the Chaldee read it in this manner, but there is no authority from MSS. for a change in the text. The truth seems to be, that Isaiah, impelled by prophetic inspiration, here interposes *his own* feelings as a Jew, and offers *his own* prayer that God would be the strength of the nation. The form, however, is *immediately* changed, and he presents the prayer of the people. ¶ *Every morning.* Constantly ; at all times. ¶ *In the time*

of trouble. Referring particularly to the trouble consequent on the invasion of the Assyrians.

3. *At the noise of the tumult.* Lowth supposes that this is addressed by the prophet in the name of God, or rather by God himself to the Assyrian, and that it means that notwithstanding the terror which he had caused the invaded countries, he would himself fall and become an easy prey to those whom he intended to subdue. But probably it should be regarded as a part of the address which the Jews made to Jehovah (ver. 2), and the word ' tumult '—הָמוֹן, *sound, noise,* as of rain (1 Kings xviii. 41), or of music (Ezek. xxvi. 13 ; Amos v. 23), or the bustle or tumult of a people (1 Sam. iv. 11 ; xiv. 19 ; Job xxxix. 7)— refers here to the voice of God by which the army was overthrown. Jehovah is often represented as speaking to men in a voice fitted to produce consternation and alarm. Thus it is said of the vision which Daniel saw of a man by the side of the river Hiddekel, 'his words' were 'like the voice of a multitude' (הָמוֹן), (Dan. x. 6). And thus, in Rev. i. 10, the voice of Christ is said to have been 'like the voice of a trumpet ;' and in ver. 15, 'like the sound of many waters.' It will be recollected also that it was said that God would send upon the Assyrian army 'thunder, and an earthquake, and a great noise, with storm and tempest, and a flame of devouring fire' (Isa. xxix. 6 ; comp. ch. xxx. 30) ; and it is doubtless to this prediction that the prophet refers here. God would come forth with the voice of indignation, and would scatter the combined armies of the Assyrian. ¶ *The people fled.* The people in the army of the Assyrian. A large part of them were slain by the angel of the Lord in a single night, but a portion of them with Sennacherib escaped and fled to their own land (Isa. xxxvii. 36, 37). ¶ *At the lifting up of thyself.* Of Jehovah ; as when one rouses himself to strike. ¶ *The nations.* The army of Sennacherib was doubtless

4 And your spoil shall be gathered *like* the gathering of the caterpillar; as the running to and fro of locusts shall he run upon them.

5 The LORD is exalted ; *a* for he

a Ps.97.9.　　*b* Ro.3.26.　　1 *salvations.*
c Pr.14.27.　　2 or, *messengers.*

made up of levies from the nations that had been subdued, and that composed the Assyrian empire.

4. *And your spoil.* The booty that the Assyrian army had gathered in their march towards Jerusalem, and which would now be left by them to be collected by the Jews. ¶ *Shall be gathered* like *the gathering of the caterpillar.* The grammatical construction here is such that this may admit of two interpretations. It may either mean, as the caterpillar or the locust *is* gathered ; or it may mean, as the caterpillar gathers its spoil. It often occurred that in countries where the locust was an article of food, they were scraped together in large quantities, and thrown into ditches, or into reservoirs, and retained to be eaten. This is the custom in some parts of Africa. But the meaning here

LOCUST (*Gryllus migratorius*).

is, undoubtedly, that the plunder of the Assyrian army would be collected by the Jews, as the locust gathered its food. The sense is, that as locusts spread themselves out over a land, as they go to and fro without rule and without molestation, gathering whatever is in their way, and consuming everything, so the Jews in great numbers, and without regular military array, would run to and fro collecting the spoils of the Assyrian army. In a country where such devastation was made by the caterpillar and locust as in Palestine, this was a very striking figure. The word rendered 'caterpillar' here (חָסִיל from חָסַל *to cut off, consume*), properly de-

dwelleth on high : he hath filled Zion with judgment *b* and righteousness.

6 And wisdom and knowledge shall be the stability of thy times, *and* strength of 1 salvation ; the fear *c* of the LORD is his treasure.

7 Behold their 2 valiant ones

notes *the devourer*, and is applied usually to a species of locust. So it is understood here by most of the versions. The LXX. render it, ' As if one were gathering locusts, so will they insult you.'

5. *The LORD is exalted* (comp. Ps. xcvii. 9). The prophet here introduces a chorus of the Jews, celebrating the praises of God for delivering them from the Assyrian. ¶ *He hath filled Zion with judgment.* That is, the effect of his destroying his enemies will be to fill Jerusalem with reverence for his name. The deliverance would be so signal, and the manifestation of the Divine mercy so great, that the effect would be that the nation would turn to God, and acknowledge his gracious interposition (see ch. xxx. 22–26, 29 ; xxxi. 6 ; xxxii. 15–18).

6. *And wisdom and knowledge shall be.* This verse contains evidently an address to Hezekiah, and asserts that his reign would be characterized by the prevalence of piety and knowledge. This chapter abounds in sudden transitions ; and it accords with its general character that when JEHOVAH had been addressed (ver. 5), there should then be a direct address to Hezekiah. ¶ *The stability.* This word denotes firmness, steadiness, constancy ; and means that in his times knowledge and the fear of the Lord would be settled on a firm foundation. The whole history of the virtuous reign of Hezekiah shows that this was fulfilled (see 2 Kings xviii.) ¶ And *strength of salvation.* Or saving strength ; that is, mighty or distinguished salvation. Thy times shall be distinguished for great reforms, and for the prevalence of the doctrines of salvation. ¶ *The fear of the* LORD *is his treasure.* The principal riches of Hezekiah. His reign shall not be distinguished for wars and conquests, for commercial enterprise, or for external splendour, but for the prevalence of piety, and the fear of the LORD.

7. *Behold.* This verse introduces a

shall cry without; the ambassadors of peace shall weep bitterly.

8 The highways lie waste, the way-

faring man ceaseth: he hath broken the covenant, he hath despised the cities, he regardeth no man.

new subject by a very sudden transition. It is designed, with the two following, to exhibit the desolation of the land on the invasion of Sennacherib, and the consternation that would prevail. For this purpose, the prophet introduces (ver. 7) the ambassadors who had been sent to sue for peace, as having sought it in vain, and as weeping now bitterly; he represents (ver. 8) the desolation that abounded, and the fact that Sennacherib refused to come to any terms; and (ver. 9) the extended desolations that had come upon the fairest portions of the land. ¶ *Their valiant ones.* The 'valiant ones' of the Jews who had been sent to Sennacherib to obtain conditions of peace, or to enter into a negotiation with him to spare the city and the nation. The word which is here rendered 'valiant ones' (אֶרְאֶלָּם) has given great perplexity to expositors. It occurs nowhere else in the Scriptures. The LXX. render the verse, 'With the dread of you shall they be terrified; they, of whom you have been afraid, will, for fear of you, raise a grievous cry.' Jerome renders it, 'Behold, they seeing, cry without,' as if the word was derived from רָאָה, *to see.* The Chaldee renders it, 'And when it shall be revealed to them, the messengers of the people who went to announce peace, shall cry bitterly.' The Syriac, 'If he shall permit himself to be seen by them, they shall weep bitterly.' Symmachus and Theodotion render it, 'Ἰδοὺ ὀφθήσομαι αὐτοῖς—' Lo, I will appear to them.' So Aquila, 'Ὁραθήσομαι αὐτοῖς. Most or all the versions seem to have read it as if it were compounded of אֶרְאֶה לם—' I will appear to them.' But probably the word is formed from אֲרִיאֵל, the same as אֲרִיאֵל (*Ariel*), 'a hero' (see Note ch. xxix. 1), and means *their hero* in a collective sense, or *their heroes;* that is, their men who were distinguished as military leaders, and who were sent to propose terms of peace with Sennacherib. The most honourable and valiant men would be selected, of course, for this purpose (comp. Note on ch. xxx. 4), but they had

made the effort to obtain peace in vain, and were returning with consternation and alarm. ¶ *Shall cry without.* They would lift up their voice with weeping as they returned, and publicly proclaim with bitter lamentation that their efforts to obtain peace had failed. ¶ *The ambassadors of peace.* When Sennacherib invaded the land, and had advanced as far as to Lachish, Hezekiah sent messengers to him with a rich present, having stripped the temple of its gold, and sent him all the silver which was in his treasury, for the purpose of propitiating his favour, and of inducing him to return to his own land (2 Kings xviii. 14–16). But it was all in vain. Sennacherib sent his generals with a great host against Jerusalem, and was unmoved by all the treasures which Hezekiah had sent to him, and by his solicitations for peace (2 Kings xviii. 17). It was to the *failure* of this embassy that Isaiah refers in the passage before us.

8. *The highways lie waste.* This verse contains a description of the desolations that had been caused by the invasion of Sennacherib. Some have understood it as containing the account which the ambassadors sent by Hezekiah gave of the effects of the invasion. Thus Grotius interprets it. But it is probably a description made by the prophet himself, and is designed to state *one cause* why the messengers that had been sent out wept bitterly. They had not only failed of inducing Sennacherib to abandon his purpose of attacking Jerusalem, but they had witnessed the effects of his invasion already. The public ways were desolate. In the consternation and alarm that was produced by his approach, the roads that had been usually thronged were now solitary and still. A mournful desolation already prevailed, and they apprehended still greater calamities, and hence they wept. ¶ *The wayfaring man ceaseth.* Heb. 'He that passes along the road ceases.' That is, there is a cessation of travel. No one is seen passing along the streets that used to

9 The earth mourneth *and* languisheth ; Lebanon is ashamed *and* hewn[1] down ; Sharon is like a wil-

1 or, *withered away.*

derness ; and Bashan and Carmel shake off *their fruits.*

10 Now will I rise, saith the

---

be thronged. ¶ *He hath broken the covenant.* This may either mean that the Assyrian king had violated the compact which had been made with him by Ahaz, by which he was to come and *aid* Jerusalem against the allied armies of Syria and Samaria (see Notes on ch. vii.), or it may mean that he had violated an implied compact with Hezekiah. When Judea was threatened with an invasion by Sennacherib, Hezekiah had sent to him when he was at Lachish, and had sought for peace (2 Kings xviii. 14). In that embassy Hezekiah said, 'I have offended, return from me ; that which thou puttest on me I will bear. And the king of Assyria appointed unto Hezekiah king of Judah three hundred talents of silver and thirty talents of gold.' To pay this, Hezekiah exhausted his treasury, and even stripped the temple of its golden ornaments (2 Kings xviii. 15, 16). A compact was thus made by which it was understood that Sennacherib was to withdraw his army, and depart from the land. But notwithstanding this, he still persisted in his purpose, and immediately despatched a part of his army to lay siege to Jerusalem. *All* the treaties, therefore, had been violated. He had disregarded that which was made with Ahaz, and that which he had now himself made with Hezekiah, and was advancing in violation of all to lay siege to the city. ¶ *He hath despised the cities.* That is, he disregards their defences, and their strength ; he invades and takes all that comes in his way. He *speaks* of them with contempt and scorn as being unable to stand before him, or to resist his march. See his vain and confident boasting in ch. x. 9, and xxxvi. 19. ¶ *He regardeth no man.* He spares no one, and he observes no compact with any man.

9. *The earth mourneth.* The land through which he has passed. For the sense of this phrase, see Note on ch. xxiv. 4. ¶ *Lebanon is ashamed and hewn down.* For the situation of Lebanon, see Note on ch. x. 34. Lebanon

Isaiah I.

was distinguished for its ornaments of beautiful cedars. Here it is represented as being stript of these ornaments, and as covered with shame on that account. There is not any direct historical evidence that Sennacherib *had* advanced to Lebanon, though there are some intimations that this had occurred (see Note on ch. xiv. 8), and it was certainly a part of his boast that he had done it (see ch. xxxvii. 24). There is no improbability in supposing that he had sent a part of his army to plunder the country in the vicinity of Lebanon (see ch. xx. 1). ¶ *Sharon is like a wilderness.* Sharon was the name of a district south of mount Carmel along the coast of the Mediterranean, extending to Cesarea and Joppa. The name was almost proverbial to express any place of extraordinary beauty and fertility (see 1 Chron. v. 16 ; xxvii. 29 ; Cant. ii. 1 ; Isa. xxxv. 2 ; lxv. 10). There was also another Sharon on the east side of the Jordan, and in the vicinity of Bashan, which was also a fertile region (1 Chron. v. 16). To this, it is more probable that the prophet here refers, though it is not certain. The *object* seems to be to mention the most fertile places in the land as being now desolate. ¶ *Bashan.* For an account of the situation of Bashan, subsequently called Batanea, see Note on ch. ii. 13. ¶ *And Carmel* (see Note on ch. xxix. 17). ¶ *Shake off* their fruits. The words 'their fruits,' are not in the Hebrew. The LXX. read this, 'Galilee and Carmel are made bare' (φανερὰ ἔσται, κ.τ.λ.) The Hebrew word נֹעֵר probably means *to shake ; to shake out* or *off* ; and refers here to the fact probably that Bashan and Carmel are represented as having shaken off *their leaves,* and were now lying desolate as in winter.

10. *Now.* This verse commences another transition. In the previous verses, the desolation of the land had been described, and the hopelessness of obtaining any terms of favour from Sennacherib, or of binding him to any

31

LORD ; now will I be exalted ;
now *a* will I lift up myself.

11 Ye shall conceive chaff ; ye
shall bring forth stubble : your
breath *as* fire shall devour you.

12 And the people shall be *as* the
burnings of lime ; *as* thorns cut up
shall they be burned in the fire.

a Ps.46.10.   *b* Mat.22.12.

13 Hear, ye *that are* far off, what
I have done ; and ye *that are* near,
acknowledge my might.

14 The sinners in Zion are afraid;
fearfulness hath surprised *b* the hypocrites : who among us shall dwell
with the devouring fire? who among
us shall dwell with everlasting burnings ?

compact, had been stated. In this state
of things, when inevitable ruin seemed
to be coming upon the nation, God said
that he would interpose. ¶ *Will I
rise.* To vengeance ; or to punish the
invading host. The emphasis in this
passage should be placed on ' I,' indicating that JEHOVAH would himself do
what could not be effected by men.
¶ *Now will I be exalted.* That is,
God would so interpose that it should
be manifest that it was *his* hand that
brought deliverance.

11. *Ye shall conceive chaff.* An
address of God to the Assyrians. The
figure is one that denotes that their
counsels would be in vain. Chaff and
stubble are used in the Scriptures, in
contrast with grain, to denote anything
which is not solid, nutritious, or sub-
stantial ; then anything which is frivol-
ous, useless, vain. A similar image
occurs in ch. xxvi. 18 (see Note on that
place ; comp. ch. lix. 4). ¶ *Your breath*
as *fire shall devour you.* The word
' breath ' here (רוּחַ, *spirit*) is evidently
used in the sense of the θυμός, and denotes *anger*, as in ch. xxx. 28. It
refers to the haughty and arrogant
spirit of Sennacherib ; the enraged and
excited mind intent on victory and
plunder. The sense is, that his mind,
so intent on conquest—so proud, excited, and angry, would be the means
of his own destruction. Lowth proposes to read ' my spirit,' but for this
change there is no authority from
MSS. (see Notes on ch. i. 31).

12. *And the people.* In the army of
Sennacherib. ¶ As *the burnings of lime.*
As if placed in a burning lime-kiln,
where they must certainly be destroyed
(see ch. xxx. 33 ; comp. Amos ii. 1).
¶ As *thorns cut up.* As thorns, or small
brushwood, that has been long cut up
and perfectly dried are speedily con-

sumed, so shall it be with the Assyrian
army. This is an image like many that
are employed, denoting that the destruction of the army of the Assyrians would
be sudden and entire.

13. *Hear, ye* that are *far off.* This
is an address of JEHOVAH, indicating
that the destruction of the Assyrian
army would be so signal that it would
be known to distant nations, and would
constitute an admonition to them. ¶ *Ye*
that are *near.* Ye Jews ; or the nations
immediately adjacent to Judea. The
phrase ' far and near,' is equivalent to
all.

14. *The sinners in Zion are afraid.*
This verse is evidently designed to describe the alarm that was produced in
Jerusalem on impenitent sinners and
hypocrites by a view of the judgment
of God on the army of Sennacherib.
They would see his wrath on his enemies then, and in view of the terrors
of his indignation in relation to that
army they would be alarmed, and would
ask how it would be possible for them
to endure such wrath for ever. If the
effect of the wrath of God even *for a
night*, when it should blaze against that
great army, was so terrible, how could
it be borne for ever ? This seems to be
the general idea of the passage. A great
variety of interpretations have been
proposed, which may be seen in Vitringa
and Poole. The phrase, ' sinners in
Zion ' here refers to the wicked and rebellious in Jerusalem. ¶ *Fearfulness
hath surprised the hypocrites.* Those
who professed to serve God, and yet who
were secretly depending on the aid of
Egypt (see ch. xxxi.; comp. Note on ch.
ix. 17). The sentiment here is, that
those who professedly are the friends of
God, but who are secretly and really
his enemies, are often alarmed at his
judgments. When the judgments of

15 He ^a that walketh ¹ righteously and speaketh ² uprightly ; he that despiseth the gain of ³ oppressions, that shaketh his hands from holding of bribes, that stoppeth his ears from hearing of ⁴ blood, and shutteth his eyes ^b from seeing evil ;

^a Ps.15.2.   1 *in righteousness.*   2 *uprightness.*
3 or, *deceits.*   4 *bloods.*   ^b Ps.119.37.

God overtake sinners, they are conscious that they deserve also his wrath, and their minds are filled with consternation. So in a time of prevailing sickness, or of pestilence, they who have really no confidence in God, and no evidence that they are prepared to die, are filled with alarm. A true friend of God will be calm in such scenes ; a hypocrite will show by his consternation that he has no religion. ¶ *Who among us shall dwell with the devouring fire?* Some have understood this as referring to the fires which they supposed the Assyrian would kindle in Jerusalem, apprehending that he would take and burn the city. But the more probable interpretation is that which refers it to the judgment that would be brought upon the Assyrians—the burning wrath of God like fire that would consume them. The destruction of the Assyrians is repeatedly represented under the image of a storm and tempest, where there would be the ' flame of devouring fire ' (see Note on ch. xxix. 6). The sense is this : ' God has suddenly consumed that immense army of his foes. Such must be the awful punishment of the wicked. How can *we* abide it? We also, though among his people, are his foes, and are exposed to his wrath. How *can* we endure the terrors of that day when his burning indignation shall also overtake us?' ¶ *Shall dwell with everlasting burnings.* Who among us could endure to suffer amid such burning wrath for ever? If that wrath is so fierce as to consume such an immense host in a single night, who could abide it should it be continued for ever and for ever? This is the obvious sense of this passage ; and it implies—1. That hypocrites will be greatly alarmed when they see punishment come upon the open and avowed enemies of God. 2. That in such times they will have none of the peace and quiet confidence which his true friends have. 3. That such an alarm is evidence of conscious guilt and hypocrisy. 4. That the persons here spoken of had a belief of the doctrine of eternal punishment — a belief which hypocrites and sinners always have, else why should they be alarmed? 5. That the punishment of hypocrites in the church will be dreadful and terrific. This seems to have been the conviction here. They saw that if *such* judgments came upon those who had no knowledge of the true God, it must be infinitely more terrible on those who had been trained amidst the institutions of religion, and who had professed attachment to JEHOVAH. And so it will be in a preeminent degree among those who have been trained in the Christian church, and who have been the professed but insincere followers of the Lord Jesus Christ.

15. *He that walketh righteously.* In this and the following verses the prophet presents, in contrast, the confidence and the security of the righteous. He first, in this verse, describes the characteristics of the righteous, and in the following verses their confidence in God, and their security and safety. The first characteristic of the righteous man is that he walks righteously ; that is, he *lives* righteously ; he does right. ¶ *And speaketh uprightly.* The second characteristic—his *words* are well-ordered. He is not false, perfidious, slanderous, or obscene in his words. If a private individual, his words are simple, honest, and true ; if a magistrate, his decisions are according to justice. ¶ *He that despiseth the gain of oppressions.* Marg. ' Deceits.' The third characteristic— he abhors the gain that is the result of imposition, false dealing, and false weights. Or if it mean *oppressions*, as the word usually does, then the sense is, that he does not oppress the poor, or take advantage of their needy condition, or affix exorbitant prices, or extort payment in a manner that is harsh and cruel. ¶ *That shaketh his hands from holding of bribes.* The fourth characteristic — this relates particularly to magistrates. They adjudge causes ac-

16 He shall dwell on ¹high; his place of defence *shall be* the munitions of rocks; bread shall be given him, his waters *shall be* sure.

1 *heights,* or, *high places.*

17 Thine eyes shall see ª the king in his beauty: they shall behold the land that ² is very far off.

18 Thine heart shall meditate terror.

ª Jn.17.24.　2 *of far distances.*

cording to justice, and do not allow their judgment to be swayed by the prospect of reward. ¶ *That stoppeth his ears from hearing of blood.* This is the fifth characteristic. It means, evidently, he who does not listen to a proposal to shed blood, or to any scheme of violence, and robbery, and murder (see Note on ch. i. 15). ¶ *And shutteth his eyes from seeing evil.* He does not *desire* to see it; he is not found in the places where it is committed. A righteous man should not only have no part in evil, but he will keep himself if possible from being a witness of it. A man who sees all the evil that is going forward; that is present in every brawl and contention, is usually a man who has a fondness for such scenes, and who may be expected to take part in them. It is a remarkable fact that very few of the Society of Friends are ever seen in courts of justice as *witnesses.* The reason is, that they have no fondness for seeing the strifes and contentions of men, and are not found in those places where evil is usually committed. This is the sixth characteristic of the righteous man; and the sum of the whole is, that he keeps himself from all forms of iniquity.

16. *He shall dwell on high.* See the margin. Heights, or high places, were usually places of safety, being, inaccessible to an enemy. The sense here is, that such a man as is described in ver. 15, should be preserved from alarm and danger, *as if* his habitation were on a lofty cliff or rock. The particular and special meaning is, that he should be safe from the anger, wrath, and consuming fire, which the sinner and the hypocrite dreaded (ver. 14). ¶ *The munitions of rocks.* The literal translation of this place would be, ' The strongholds of the rocks shall be his lofty fortress ' (comp. Note on ch. ii. 21). ¶ *Bread shall be given him.* He shall be sustained, and his life shall be preserved.

17. *Thine eyes.* The eyes of the righteous, described in ver. 15. ¶ *Shall*

see the king in his beauty. Some understand this of the Assyrian king. Thus Kimchi understands it, and supposes it means that they shall see him at the walls of Jerusalem; that is, shall see him destroyed. Vitringa supposes it means JEHOVAH himself, as the king of his people, and that they should see him in his glory. Others suppose it refers to the Messiah. But the immediate connection requires us to understand it of Hezekiah (comp. Note on ch. xxxii. 1, 2). The sense is, ' You shall be defended from the hostile army of the Assyrian. You shall be permitted to live under the peaceful and prosperous reign of your pious monarch, and shall see him, not with diminished territory and resources, but with the *appropriate* magnificence which becomes a monarch of Israel.' ¶ *The land that is very far off.* You shall be permitted to look to the remotest part of the land of Judea as delivered from enemies, and as still under the happy sceptre of your king. You shall not be confined by a siege, and straitened within the narrow walls of Jerusalem. The empire of Hezekiah shall be extended over the wide dominions that appropriately belong to him, and you shall be permitted to range freely over the whole land, even over the parts that are now occupied by the forces of the Assyrian. Virgil has a beautiful passage remarkably similar to this:

—— juvat ire, et Dorica castra,
Desertosque videre locos, litusque relictum.
　　　　　　　　　　Æn. ii. 28.

18. *Thine heart.* The heart of the people of Jerusalem. ¶ *Shall meditate terror.* This is similar to the expression in Virgil:

— forsan et hæc olim meminisse juvabit.
　　　　　　　　　　Æn. ii. 203.

The sense here is, ' You shall hereafter *think over* all this alarm and distress. When the enemy is destroyed, the city saved, and the king shall reign in magnificence over all the nation then enjoying peace and prosperity, you shall ror. Where *is* the scribe? where *is* the ¹receiver? where *is* he that counted the towers?

19 Thou shalt not see a fierce people; a people of a deeper speech than thou canst perceive; of a stammering ² tongue, *that thou canst not understand.*

20 Look upon Zion, the city of our solemnities: thine eyes shall see Jerusalem a quiet habitation, a tabernacle *that* shall not be taken down; not one of the stakes thereof shall ever ᵃ be removed, neither shall any of the cords thereof be broken.

1 *weigher.*　　2 *or, ridiculous.*　　ᵃ Rev.3,12.

recall these days of terror and alarm, and shall then ask with gratitude and astonishment, Where are they who caused this alarm? Where are now they who so confidently calculated on taking the city? They are all gone—and gone in a manner fitted to excite astonishment and adoring gratitude.' 'Sweet is the recollection,' says Rosenmüller, 'of dangers that are passed.' ¶ *Where* is *the scribe?* How soon, how suddenly has he vanished! The word 'scribe' here (סֹפֵר) evidently refers to some prominent class of officers in the Assyrian army. It is from סָפַר, *to count, to number, to write;* and probably refers to a secretary, perhaps a secretary of state or of war, or an inspector-general, who had the charge of reviewing an army (2 Kings xxv. 19; Jer. xxxvii. 15; lii. 25). ¶ *Where* is *the receiver?* Marg. as in Heb. 'Weigher.' Vulg. 'Where is he that ponders the words of the law?' The LXX. 'Where are the counsellors (συμβουλεύοντες)?' Probably the word refers to him who *weighed* the tribute, or the pay of the soldiers; and means, doubtless, some officer in the army of the Assyrian; probably one whose office it was to have charge of the *military chest,* and to pay the army. ¶ *Where* is *he that counted the towers?* That is, who made an estimate of the strength of Jerusalem—either Sennacherib, or some one appointed by him to reconnoitre and report on the means which the city had of defence (comp. ch. xxxvi. 4).

19. *Thou shalt not see a fierce people.* Or, rather, 'this fierce and boasting people you shall not see.' They shall not enter the city; but though they are advancing with so much confidence, they shall be suddenly cut off and destroyed. The word rendered 'fierce,' (נוֹעָז from יָעַז), probably means *strong,* or *wicked.*

Lowth renders it, 'barbarous people,' as if it were לֹעֵז. Michaelis also adopts this reading by supposing an error in transcribing, a change of נ into ל. Such a change *might* have easily occurred, but there is no authority from the MSS. for making an alteration in the text. The word *strong,* or *mighty,* agrees well with the connection. ¶ *A people of a deeper speech.* A people whose language is so *deep,* i.e., so dark, or obscure, that it cannot be understood by you. This refers to the army of the Assyrians, who spoke the Syrian language, which was understood by some of the Jews, but which was unintelligible to the mass (see ch. xxxvi. 11). ¶ *Than thou canst perceive.* Than you can understand. ¶ *Of a stammering tongue* (see Note on ch. xxviii. 11). Marg. 'Ridiculous;' a sense which the Hebrew will bear, but the more appropriate meaning is that of a barbarous, or unintelligible foreign language.

20. *Look upon Zion.* Lowth renders this, 'Thou shalt see Zion,' by changing the Hebrew text in conformity with the Chaldee. There is no doubt that this accords with the sense of the passage, but there is no authority for the change. It stands in contrast with what had been said in ver. 19. There, the prophet had said that they should no more see those foreign armies that were coming to invade them. Here he directs them to look upon Zion, implying that they should be permitted to behold Zion in a situation such as he proceeds to describe it. 'You shall not see that foreign army carrying desolation as they design through the city and the land. They shall be destroyed. But behold Zion! Her you shall see quiet, prosperous, happy, peaceful.' ¶ *The city of our solemnities.* Where the religious solemnities of the nation were celebrated.

21 But there the glorious LORD *will be* unto us a place ¹of broad

1 *broad of spaces,* or, *hands.*

¶ *A quiet habitation.* Free from invasion, and from the terrors of war. ¶ *A tabernacle.* A tent; a dwelling, such as was common in the nomadic mode of life in the East. The whole city is described under the image of a *tent* that is fixed and undisturbed, where the family may reside in safety and comfort. ¶ *Not one of the stakes thereof.*

rivers and streams; wherein shall go no galley with oars, neither shall gallant ship pass thereby.

The 'stakes' here refer to the poles or fixtures which were driven into the ground in order to fasten the tent, to enable them to spread it, or to the small stakes or pins that were driven in the ground in order to secure the cords by which the tent was extended. The following cut will give an idea of the mode in which tents were commonly

ARABS PITCHING THEIR TENT.—From Laborde.

pitched, and will serve to explain this passage, as well as the similar passage in ch. liv. 2. ¶ *Shall ever be removed.* It shall be a fixed and permanent habitation. The word 'ever' must mean an indefinite period of duration. Sennacherib had designed to blot out the name of the people of God, and destroy their separate and independent existence. The prophet says that that should never be done. Jerusalem, the residence of his people and the emblem of his church, would be safe, and would not be destroyed. There would *always* be a safe and quiet abode for the friends of the Most High. In this sense it accords with the declaration of the Saviour, that the gates of hell should not prevail

against his church. ¶ *Neither shall any of the cords thereof be broken.* Cords were used in tents to fasten the cloth to the poles, or to fasten it to the pins which had been driven into the ground, in order to extend the cloth, and to make it firm.

21. *But there.* In Jerusalem; or in his church, of which Jerusalem was the emblem. ¶ *The glorious* LORD. Lowth renders it, 'The glorious name of JEHOVAH,' taking שֵׁם to be a noun, as if it were pointed שֵׁם. So the Syriac and the LXX. read it. The word 'glorious' (אַדִּיר) means magnificent; denoting that JEHOVAH would manifest himself there as magnificent or great in the destruction

22 For the LORD *is* our judge, the
¹ *statute-maker.*

LORD *is* our ¹ law-giver, the LORD
is our king ; he will save us.

of his enemies, and in the protection of his people. ¶ *Will be unto us a place.* It seems to be harsh to say that JEHOVAH would be *a place ;* but the meaning is, that he would be to them *as* such a place ; that is, his presence and blessing would be such as would be represented by broad rivers and streams flowing through a land, or encompassing a city. Rivers and streams are sources of fertility, the channels of commerce, and objects of great beauty. Such seems to be the idea here. The presence of JEHOVAH would be to them a source of great prosperity and happiness ; and a beauty would be thrown around the city and nation like majestic and useful rivers. It is *possible* that there may have been some allusion here to cities that were encompassed or penetrated by rivers and canals, like Babylon, or Thebes in Egypt. Such cities derived important advantages from rivers. But Jerusalem had nothing of this nature to contribute to its prosperity or beauty. The prophet says, that the presence of JEHOVAH would be to them what these rivers were to other cities. ¶ *Of broad rivers and streams.* Heb. ' Rivers, streams broad of hands.' The sense seems to be, broad rivers that are made up of confluent streams ; or rivers to which many streams are tributary—like the Nile—and which are therefore made *broad,* and capable of navigation. The phrase here used—in the Heb. ' broad of hands ' — properly denotes *broad on both hands,* or as we would say, *on both sides ;* that is, the shores would be separated far from each other. The word *hand* is often used in Hebrew to denote the *side,* the shore, or the bank of a river. The following extract will show the importance of such rivers : ' In such a highly cultivated country as England, and where great drought is almost unknown, we have not an opportunity to observe the fertilizing influence of a broad river ; but in South Africa, where almost no human means are employed for improving the land, the benign influence of rivers is most evident. The Great, or Orange River, is a remarkable instance of this. I travelled

on its banks, at one time, for five or six weeks, when, for several hundred miles, I found both sides of it delightfully covered with trees of various kinds, all in health and vigour, and abundance of the richest verdure ; but all the country beyond the reach of its influence was complete desert. Everything appeared to be struggling for mere existence ; so that we might be said to have had the wilderness on one side, and a kind of paradise on the other.'—(Campbell.) ¶ *Wherein shall go.* The mention of broad rivers here seems to have suggested to the prophet the idea that navigable rivers, while they were the channels of commerce, also gave to an enemy the opportunity of approaching easily with vessels of war, and attacking a city. He therefore says that no such consequence would follow, from the fact that JEHOVAH would be to them in the place of broad rivers. No advantage could be taken from what was to them a source of prosperity and happiness. While other cities were exposed to an enemy from the very sources from which they derived their wealth and prosperity, it would not be so with them. From what constituted their glory—the protection of JEHOVAH—no danger ever could be apprehended. It had all the advantages of broad rivers and streams, but with none of their attendant exposures and perils. ¶ *No galley with oars.* That is, no *small* vessel—for larger vessels were propelled by sails. Still the reference is doubtless to a vessel of war ; since vessels of commerce would be an advantage, and it would not be an object of congratulation that none of them should be there. ¶ *Neither shall gallant ship.* No *great* (אַדִּיר) or magnificent ship ; no ship fitted out for purposes of war. The sense is, therefore, that though Jerusalem should be thus favoured, yet it would not be unapproachable by an enemy.

22. *For the* LORD *is our judge.* JEHOVAH will be to us nothing but a source of happiness, truth, and prosperity. His presence will be to us only a blessing, and a means of success and joy. The

23 Thy [1] tacklings are loosed ; they could not well strengthen their mast, they could not spread the sail ; then is the prey of a great spoil divided ; the lame *a* take the prey.

24 And the inhabitant shall not say, I am sick ; *b* the people that dwell therein *shall be* forgiven *c their* iniquity.

1 or, *they have forsaken thy tacklings.*
a 1 Cor.1.27.   b Rev.21.4.   c Jer.50.20.

repetition of the name JEHOVAH *three times* is common in the Scriptures.

23. *Thy tacklings.* This is evidently an address to Sennacherib. The mention of the war-galley and the ship seems to have suggested the application of the figure to the enemies of the Jews, and particularly to Sennacherib. The prophet, therefore, compares the Assyrian to a ship that was rendered unserviceable; whose sails were unfastened, and whose mast could not be made firm, and which was therefore at the mercy of winds and waves. The Hebrew which is here rendered 'thy tacklings are loosed,' means 'thy cords are let go;' that is, the cords or ropes that fastened the sails, the masts, and the rudder, were loosened. In such a condition the ship would, of course, go to ruin. ¶ *They could not well strengthen their mast.* They could not fix it firm or secure. It is evident that if the *mast* cannot be made firm, it is impossible to navigate a ship. It is to be observed here, however, that the word which our translators have rendered 'well' (נֵס), not only signifies 'well' as an adverb, but is also used as a noun, and means a stand or station (Gen. xl. 13; xli. 13; Dan. xi. 20, 21); and also a base or pedestal (Ex. xxx. 18, 28; xxxi. 9; xxxv. 16; xxxviii. 8; Lev. viii. 11; 1 Kings vii. 31. It may be used here to denote the *socket* or *base* of the ship's mast; or the cross beam which the mast passed through, and which held it firm. This was called by the Greeks ἱστοπέδη (*Odys.* xii. 51), or μεσόδμη, ἱστοδόκη (*Iliad* i. 434). The translation, therefore, 'They could not make fast the base of their mast,' would better express the sense of the Hebrew. The LXX. render it, 'Thy mast gave way.' ¶ *They could not spread the sail.* Of course, as the ropes were all loosened, and the mast could not be made firm, it would be in vain to attempt to spread a sail. The sense is, that the plan of the Assyrian would be disconcerted, his scheme discomfited, and his enterprise would come to naught. He and his army would be like a vessel at sea without sails. ¶ *Then is the prey of a great spoil divided.* The word 'divided' here means shall be distributed or apportioned, as plunder was usually among victors. The sense is, that much booty would be taken from the army of the Assyrian and distributed among the Jews (see Note on ver. 4). It is certain that Hezekiah had given to Sennacherib three hundred talents of silver, and thirty talents of gold, and had stripped the temple, and given the gold that was on the temple to him (2 Kings xviii. 14–16), and this treasure was doubtless in the camp of the Assyrians. And it is certain that *after* this invasion of Sennacherib, the treasures of Hezekiah were replenished, and his wealth so much abounded, that he made an improper and ostentatious display of it to the ambassadors that came from Babylon (2 Kings xx. 13–15); and there is every presumption, therefore, that a great amount of spoil was collected from the camp of the Assyrian. ¶ *The lame take the prey.* It shall be so abundant, and shall be so entirely abandoned by the Assyrians, that even the feeble and the defenceless shall go forth to the camp and take the spoil that is left.

24. *And the inhabitant.* The inhabitant of Jerusalem. ¶ *Shall not say, I am sick.* That is, probably, the spoil shall be so abundant, and the facility for taking it so great, that even the sick, the aged, and the infirm shall go forth nerved with new vigour to gather the spoil. ¶ *The people that dwell therein.* In Jerusalem. ¶ *Shall be forgiven their iniquity.* This is equivalent to saying that the calamities of the invasion would be entirely removed. This invasion is represented as coming upon them as a judgment for their sins. When the Assyrian should be overthrown, it would be a proof that the sin which had been the cause of the inva-

CHAPTER XXXIV.

ANALYSIS.

THE thirty-fourth and thirty-fifth chapters make one distinct and beautiful prophecy, consisting of two parts; the first containing a denunciation of judgment on the enemies of the Jews, particularly Edom (ch. xxxiv.); and the second a most beautiful description of the flourishing state of the people of God which would follow these judgments (ch. xxxv.)

At what time the prophecy was delivered it is uncertain, and, indeed, can be determined by nothing in the prophecy itself. It is observable, however, that it is the close of the first part of the *prophecies* of Isaiah, the remaining chapters to the fortieth, which commences the second part of the prophecies, being occupied with an historical description of the invasion of Sennacherib and his army. It has been supposed (see Introd. § 2, 3,) that between the delivery of the prophecies in the first and second portion of Isaiah, an interval of some years elapsed, and that the second part was delivered for his own consolation, and the consolation of the people, near the close of his life.

A somewhat similar purpose, as I apprehend, led to the composition and publication of the prophecy before us. The *general strain* of his prophecies thus far has been, that however numerous and mighty were the enemies of the Jews, the people of God would be delivered from them all. Such was the case in regard to the allied armies of Syria and Samaria (ch. vii., viii.); of the Assyrian (ch. x.); of Babylon (ch. xiii., xiv.); of Moab (ch. xv., xvi.); of Damascus and Ethiopia (ch. xvii., xviii.); of Egypt (xix., xx.); and more particularly of the Assyrians under Sennacherib (ch. xxv., xxix.–xxxiii.) The prophecy before us I regard as a kind of *summing up*, or recapitulation of all that he had delivered; and the general idea is, *that the people of God would be delivered from all their foes, and that happier times under the Messiah would succeed all their calamities.* This he had expressed often in the *particular* prophecies; he here expresses it in a summary and condensed manner.

Keeping this general design of the prophecy in view, we may observe that it consists of the following parts:—

I. A *general statement* that all the enemies of the people of God would be destroyed (ch. xxxiv. 1–4). 1. The nations of the earth are summoned to see this, and to become acquainted with the purpose of God thus to destroy all his enemies (1). 2. The destruction of the enemies of God described under the image of a great slaughter (2,3). 3. The same destruction described under the image of the heavens rolled together as a scroll (4).

II. This *general truth* paricularly applied to Edom or Idumea as among the most virulent of their enemies (5–17). 1. JEHOVAH's vengeance would come upon the land of Idumea, and the land would be covered with the slain, and soaked in blood (5–8). 2. The entire and utter desolation of the land of Idumea is foretold. The kingdom should be destroyed, the land laid waste, and the whole country become a dwelling-place of wild beasts (9–17).

III. The happy times that would succeed—the times of the Messiah—are exhibited (ch. xxxv.) in language of great beauty and sublimity. This is the substance of all that the prophet had predicted, and all his visions terminate there. The wilderness shall blossom; and the sick and afflicted shall be healed; the desolate lands shall be fertile; there shall be no enemy to annoy, and the ransomed of the Lord shall return and come to Zion with songs and everlasting joy upon their heads.

As so large a part of this prophecy relates to Edom, or Idumea, it may be proper to preface the exposition of the chapter with a brief notice of the history of that country, and of the causes for which God denounced vengeance upon it.

Idumea was the name given by the Greeks to the land of Edom, the country which was settled by Esau. The territory which they occupied extended originally from the Dead Sea to the Elanitic gulf of the Red Sea. Their territory, however, they extended considerably by conquest, and carried their arms to the east and north-east of Moab, and obtained possession of the country of which Bozrah was the chief city. To this they had access through the intervening desert without crossing the country of the Moabites or Ammonites. The capital of East Idumea was Bozrah; the capital of South Edom was Petra or Selah, called, in 2 Kings xiv. 7, Joktheel (see Notes on ch. xvi. 1).

sion had been forgiven, and that God was now disposed to show them favour and mercy. It is common in the Scriptures to represent any calamity as the consequence of sin, to identify the removal of the calamity and the forgiveness of the sin. Thus the Saviour said

(Mark ii. 5) to the man afflicted with the palsy, ' Son, thy sins be forgiven thee.' And when the scribes murmured, he urged that the power of forgiving sins and of healing disease was the same, or that the forgiveness of sin was equivalent to the removal of disease (Mark ii. 9).

This country received its name from Esau, the son of Isaac, and the twin brother of Jacob. He was called Edom, which signifies *red*, from the colour of the red pottage which he obtained from Jacob by the sale of his birthright (Gen. xxv. 30). After his marriage, he removed to mount Seir, and made that his permanent abode, and the country adjacent to it received the name of Edom. Mount Seir had been occupied by a people called Horites, who were displaced by Esau, when he took possession of their country and made it his own (Deut. ii. 12). The Edomites were at first governed by princes, improperly translated 'dukes' in Gen. xxxvi. 9–31. They were an independent people until the time of David. They seem to have continued under the government of separate princes, until the apprehension of foreign invasion compelled them to unite under one leader, and to submit themselves to a king, When the children of Israel were passing through the wilderness, as the land of Edom lay between them and Canaan, Moses sent ambassadors to the king of Edom soliciting the privilege of a peaceful passage through their country, on the ground that they were descended from the same ancestor, and promising that the property of the Edomites should not be injured, and offering to pay for all that they should consume (Num. xx. 14–19). To this reasonable request the king of Edom sent a positive refusal, and came out with a strong army to resist them (Num. xx. 20). This refusal was long remembered by the Jews, and was one cause of the hostile feeling which was cherished against them. The kingdom of Edom seems to have risen to a considerable degree of prosperity. There is, indeed, no direct mention made of it after this until the time of David; but it seems to have then risen into so much importance as to have attracted his attention. David carried his arms there after having obtained a victory over the Syrians, Moabites, and Ammonites. It is not known, indeed, what was the cause of this war, but it is known that he slew eighteen thousand Edomites in the valley of Salt (2 Sam. viii. 13; 1 Chron. xviii. 12), and the rest of them were either brought into subjection under Joab, or forced to fly into foreign countries. Hadad, their young king, fled to Egypt, and was favourably received by Pharaoh, and was highly honoured at his court. He was married to the sister of Tahpanes, who was the queen of Egypt (1 Kings xi. 15–20). Yet though he lived at the court of Pharaoh, he waited only for an opportunity to recover his kingdom, and when David and Joab were dead, he proposed to the king of Egypt to make an effort to accomplish it. He returned to Idumea, but was unsuccessful in his attempts to overcome the garrisons which David had stationed to guard and secure the country (Jos. *Ant.* viii. 2). The kingdom of Edom continued under the house of David until the time of Jehoshaphat, and was probably governed by deputies or viceroys appointed by the kings of Judah. In the reign of Jehoshaphat they joined the Moabites and Ammonites in an attempt to recover their freedom, but they were unsuccessful. In the reign of Jehoram, the son of Jehoshaphat, however, they rose in a body, and though they suffered great slaughter, yet they regained their liberty (2 Chron. xxi. 8–10). After this, no attempts were made to subdue them for more than sixty years. In the reign of Amaziah, king of Judah, however, they were attacked, and ten thousand of them fell in battle in the valley of Salt, and many were made prisoners; their capital, Selah, was taken by storm, and the two thousand captives were by Amaziah's orders thrown down the ragged precipices near the city, and dashed in pieces (2 Kings xiv. 7; 2 Chron. xxv. 12; *Universal History*, vol. i. p. 380; Ed. Lond. 1779, 8vo). When the Jews were subdued by the Babylonians, and carried captive, they seem to have regarded it as a favourable opportunity to avenge all the injustice which they had suffered from the hands of the Jews. They joined the Babylonians in their attempts to subdue Jerusalem, and exulted in the fall and ruin of the city.

Remember, O LORD, the children of Edom
In the day of Jerusalem; who said
Rase it, rase it, even to the foundation thereof.
            Ps. cxxxvii. 7.

They seem to have resolved to take full vengeance for the fact that their nation had been so long subjected by David and his successors; to have cut off such of the Jews as attempted to escape; to have endeavoured to level the whole city with the ground; to have rejoiced in the success of the Babylonians, and to have imbrued their hands in the blood of those whom the Chaldeans had left—and were thus held to be guilty of the crime of fratricide by God (see particularly Obad. 10–12, 18; Ezek. xxv. 12–14; xxxv. 3–15). It was *for this especially* that they were denounced and threatened by the prophets with heavy judgment, and with the utter destruction of the nation (Isa. xxxiv. 5, 10–17; Jer. xlix. 7–10, 12–18; Ezek. xxv. 12–15; xxxv. 1–15; Joel iii. 19; Amos i. 11; Obad. 2, 3, 8, 17, 18; Mal. i. 3, 4). This refusing to aid their brethren the Jews, and joining with the enemies of the people of God, and exulting in their success, was the great crime in their history which was to call down the Divine vengeance, and terminate in their complete and utter ruin.

But their exultation does not long continue, and their cruelty to the Jews did not long remain unpunished. Five years after the taking of Jerusalem, Nebuchadnezzar humbled all the states around Judea, and particularly Idumea (Jer. xxv. 15-26; Mal. i. 3, 4).

During the Jewish exile, it would appear the Edomites pressed forward into the south of Palestine, of which they took possession as far as to Hebron. Here they were subsequently attacked and subdued by John Hyrcanus, and compelled to adopt the laws and customs of the Jews. The name Idumea was transferred to this part of the land of Judea which they occupied, and this is the Idumea which is mentioned by Pliny, Ptolemy, Strabo, and other ancient writers. Indeed the name Idumea was sometimes given by the Roman writers to the whole of Palestine (Reland's *Palestine*). Idumea, including the southern part of Judea, was henceforth governed by a succession of Jewish prefects. One of these, Antipater, an Idumean by birth, by the favour of Cæsar, was made procurator of all Judea. He was the father of Herod the Great, who become king of Judea, including Idumea. While the Edomites had been extending themselves to the north-west, they had in in turn been driven out from the southern portion of their own territory, and from their chief city itself, by the Nabatheans, an Arabian tribe, the descendants of Nebaioth, the eldest son of Ishmael. This nomadic people had spread themselves over the whole of desert Arabia, from the Euphrates to the borders of Palestine, and finally to the Elanitic gulf of the Red Sea. They thus grew up into the kingdom of Arabia Petrea, occupying very nearly the same territory which was comprised within the limits of ancient Edom. A king of this country, Aretas, is mentioned as cotemporary with Antiochus Epiphanes, about B.C. 166. From this time to the

destruction of Jerusalem, the sovereigns of Arabia Petrea came into frequent contact with the Jews and Romans, both in war and peace. —The nominal independence of this kingdom continued for some thirty years after the destruction of Jerusalem. Under the reign of Trajan, about A.D. 105, it was overrun and conquered by Cornelius Palma, then governor of Syria, and formally annexed to the Roman empire (Dio. Cass. lxviii. 14; Amm. Marcell. xiv. 8).—The kingdom of Edom was thus blotted out, and their name was lost. In their own land they ceased to be a separate people, and mingled with the other descendants of Ishmael; in Judea they became, under John Hyrcanus, converts to the Jewish faith; received the rite of circumcision; and were incorporated with the Jews. Very interesting remains of cities and towns of Idumea, and particularly of Petrea, have been recently discovered by the travellers Burckhardt, and Seetzen (see *Universal History*, vol. i. pp. 370-383; *Amer. Bib. Repository*, vol. iii. pp. 247-270; Gesenius's Introduction to his *Com.* on this chapter; the *Travels* of Burckhardt, Legh, Laborde, and Stephens; Keith, *On Prophecy*, pp. 135-168; and Robinson's *Bib. Researches*, vol. ii. p. 551, *sq.*)

COME *a* near, ye nations, to hear; and hearken, ye people: let the earth *b* hear, and 1 all that is therein; the world, and all things that come forth of it.

2 For *c* the indignation of the LORD *is* upon all nations, and *his* fury upon all their armies: he hath utterly destroyed them, he hath delivered them to the slaughter.

a Ps.49.1.   *b* De.32.1.   1 *the fulness thereof.*
c Zep.3.8.

CHAPTER XXXIV.

1. *Come near, ye nations, to hear.* That is, to hear of the judgments which God was about to execute, and the great purposes which he was about to accomplish. If the supposition be correct, that this and the following chapter contain a *summing up* of all that the prophet had thus far uttered; a declaration that ALL the enemies of the people of God would be destroyed—the most violent and bitter of whom was Idumea; and that this was to be succeeded by the happy times of the Messiah, then we see a plain reason why all the nations are summoned to hear and attend. The

events pertain to them all; the truths communicated are of universal interest. ¶ *And all that is therein.* Heb. as in Marg., 'fulness thereof;' that is, all the inhabitants of the earth. ¶ *All things that come forth of it.* All that proceed from it; that is, all the inhabitants that the world has produced. The LXX. render it, 'The world and the people (ὁ λαὸς) who are therein.'

2. *For the indignation of the* LORD. JEHOVAH is about to express his wrath against all the nations which are opposed to his people. ¶ *He hath utterly destroyed them.* In his purpose, or intention. The prophet represents this

3 Their slain also shall be cast out, and their stink shall come up out of their carcases, and the mountains shall be melted with their blood.

4 And *a* all the host of heaven shall be dissolved, and the heavens

a Ps.102.26; Exo.32.7,8; Joel2.31; 3.15,16; Mat.24.29; 2 Pet.3.10; Rev.6.13,14.

shall be rolled together as a scroll: and all their host shall fall down, as the leaf falleth off from the vine, and as a falling *fig* from the fig-tree.

5 For my sword shall be bathed in heaven: behold, it shall come down upon Idumea, *b* and upon the people of my curse, to judgment.

b Jer.49.7.

---

as so certain that it may be exhibited as already done.

3. *Their slain also shall be cast out.* They would lie unburied. The slaughter would be so extensive, and the desolation would be so entire, that there would not remain enough to bury the dead (comp. Notes on ch. xiv. 19). ¶ *And the mountains shall be melted with their blood.* The expression here is evidently hyperbolical, and means that as mountains and hills are wasted away by descending showers and impetuous torrents, so the hills would be washed away by the vast quantity of blood that would be shed by the anger of JEHOVAH.

4. *And all the host of heaven.* On the word 'host' (צָבָא), see Note on ch. i. 9. The heavenly bodies often represent kings and princes (comp. Note on ch. xxiv. 21). ¶ *Shall be dissolved* (וְנָמַקּוּ). This figure Vitringa supposes to be taken from the vulgar prejudice by which the stars appear to be crystals, or gems, set in the azure vault of heaven, which may *melt* and flow down by the application of heat. The sense is, that the princes and nobles who had opposed God and his people would be destroyed, *as if* the sparkling stars, like gems, should *melt* in the heavens, and flow down to the earth. ¶ *And the heavens shall be rolled together as a scroll.* The word 'scroll' here (סֵפֶר *sēphĕr*) means *a roll,* or a book. Books were made of parchment, leaves, &c., and were *rolled together* instead of being *bound,* as they are with us. The figure here is taken from what strikes the eye, that the heaven above us is *an expanse* (רָקִיעַ) Gen. i. 8; Ps. civ. 2,) which is *spread out;* and which might be *rolled together,* and thus pass away. It is possible that there may be a reference also to the fact, that in a

storm, when the sky is filled with dark rolling clouds, the heavens seem to be *rolled together,* and to be passing away. The sense is, that there would be great destruction among those high in office and in power—a destruction that would be well represented by the rolling up of the firmament, and the destruction of the visible heavens and their host, and by leaving the world to ruin and to night. ¶ *And all their host shall fall down.* That is, their stars; either by being as it were *melted,* or by the fact that the *expanse* in which they are apparently located would be rolled up and removed, and there being no *fixtures* for them they would fall. The same image occurs in Rev. vi. 13. One somewhat similar occurs in Virgil, *Georg.* i. 365, *sq.* ¶ *As the leaf falleth off from the vine,* &c. That is, in a storm, or when violently shaken.

5. *For my sword shall be bathed in heaven.* A sword is an instrument of vengeance, and is often so used in the Scriptures, because it was often employed in capital punishments (see Note on ch. xxvii. 1). This passage has given much perplexity to commentators, on account of the apparent want of meaning of the expression that the sword would be *bathed in heaven.* Lowth reads it:

For my sword is made bare in the heavens;

following in this the Chaldee which reads תִּתְגַּלִּי 'shall be revealed.' But there is no authority from MSS. for this change in the Hebrew text. The Vulgate renders it, *Quoniam inebriatus est in cœlo gladius meus*—' My sword is intoxicated in heaven.' The LXX. render it in the same way, 'Εμεθύσθη ἡ μάχαιρά μου ἐν τῷ οὐρανῷ; and the Syriac and Arabic in the same manner. The Hebrew word רִוְּתָה, from רָוָה, means properly *to drink to the full;* to be

6 The sword of the LORD is filled with blood; it is made fat with fatness, *and* with the blood of lambs and goats, with the fat of the kid-

neys of rams: for the LORD hath a sacrifice in Bozrah, *a* and a great slaughter in the land of Idumea.

a ch.63.1,&c.

satisfied, or sated with drink ; and then to be full or satiated with intoxicating liquor, to be drunk. It is applied to the sword, as satiated or made drunk with blood, in Jer. xlvi. 10 :

And the sword shall devour,
And it shall be satiate, and made drunk with
    their blood.

And thus in Deut. xxxii. 42, a similar figure is used respecting arrows, the instruments also of war and vengeance :

I will make mine arrows drunk with blood;
And my sword shall devour flesh.

A similar figure is often used in Oriental writers, where the sword is represented as glutted, satiated, or made drunk with blood (see Rosenmüller on Deut. xxxii. 42). Thus Bohaddinus, in the life of Saladin, in describing a battle in which there was a great slaughter, says, 'The swords drank of their blood until they were intoxicated.' The idea here is, however, not that the sword of the Lord was made drunk *with blood* in heaven, but that it was intoxicated, or made furious with wrath ; it was excited as an intoxicated man is who is under ungovernable passions ; it was in heaven that the wrath commenced, and the sword of Divine justice rushed forth as if intoxicated, to destroy all before it. There are few figures, even in Isaiah, that are more bold than this. ¶ *It shall come down upon Idumea* (see the Analysis of the chapter for the situation of Idumea, and for the causes why it was to be devoted to destruction). ¶ *Upon the people of my curse.* The people devoted to destruction.

6. *The sword of the* LORD *is filled with blood.* The idea here is taken from the notion of sacrifice, and is, that God would devote to sacrifice, or to destruction, the inhabitants of Idumea. With reference to that, he says, that his sword, the instrument of slaughter, would be satiated with blood. ¶ *It is made fat with fatness.* The allusion here is to the sacrifices which were made for sin, in which the blood

and the fat were devoted to God as an offering (see Lev. vii.) ¶ *With the blood of lambs and goats.* These were the animals which were usually offered in sacrifice to God among the Jews. and to speak of a *sacrifice* was the same as to speak of the offering of rams, lambs, bullocks, &c. Yet it is evident that they denote here *the people* of Idumea, and that these terms are used to keep up the image of *a sacrifice.* The idea of sacrifice was always connected with that of *slaughter,* as the animals were slaughtered before they were offered. So here, the idea is, that there would be a great *slaughter* in Idumea ; that it would be so far of the nature of a sacrifice that they would be *devoted* to God and to his cause. It is not probable that any particular classes of people are denoted by the different animals here mentioned, as the animals here mentioned include all, or nearly all those usually offered in sacrifice, the expressions denote simply that all classes of people in Idumea would be devoted to the slaughter. Grotius, however, supposes that the following classes are intended by the animals specified, to wit, by *the lambs,* the people in general ; by *the goats,* the priests ; by *the rams,* the opulent inhabitants. ¶ *For the* LORD *hath a sacrifice in Bozrah.* Bozrah is here mentioned as one of the chief cities of Idumea. It was a city of great antiquity, and was known among the Greeks and Romans by the name of BOSTRA. It is generally mentioned in the Scriptures as a city of the Edomites (Isa. lxiii. 1; Jer. xlix. 13, 22; Amos i. 12); but once it is mentioned as a city of Moab (Jer. xlviii. 24). It probably belonged at different periods to both nations, as in their wars the possession of cities often passed into different hands. Bozrah lay south-east of Edrei, one of the capitals of Bashan, and was thus not properly within the limits of the Edomites, but was north of the Ammonites, or in the region of Auranitis, or in what is now called the

7 And the ¹unicorns shall come down with them, and the bullocks with the bulls; and their land shall be ²soaked with blood, and their dust made fat with fatness.

1 or, *rhinoceros.*   2 or, *drunken.*

Houran.* It is evident, therefore, that in the time of Isaiah, the Edomites had extended their conquests to that region. According to Burckhardt, who visited the Houran, and who went to Bozrah, it is at this day one of the most important cities there. 'It is situated,' says he, 'in the open plain, and is at present the last inhabited place in the south-east extremity of the Houran; it was formerly the capital of the *Arabia Provincia*, and is now, including its ruins, the largest town in the Houran. It is of an oval shape, its greatest length being from east to west; its circumference is three quarters of an hour. It was anciently encompassed with a thick wall, which gave it the reputation of great strength. Many parts of this wall, especially on the west side, remain; it was constructed of stones of moderate size, strongly cemented together. The south, and south-east quarters are covered with ruins of private dwellings, the walls of many of which are still standing, but the roofs are fallen in. The style of building seems to have been similar to that observed in all the other ancient towns of the Houran. On the west side are springs of fresh water, of which I counted five beyond the precincts of the town, and six within the walls; their waters unite with a rivulet whose source is on the north-west side, within the town, and which loses itself in the southern plain at several hours' distance; it is called by the Arabs, El Djeheir. The principal ruins of Bozrah are the following :—A square building which within is circular, and has many arches and niches in the wall. The diameter of the rotunda is four paces; its roof has fallen in, but the walls are entire. It appears to have been a Greek church.—An oblong square building, called by the natives Deir Boheiry, or the Monastery of the priest Boheiry. —The gate of an ancient house com-

municating with the ruins of an edifice, the only remains of which is a large semicircular vault.—The great mosque of Bozrah, which is certainly coeval with the first era of Mahometanism, and is commonly ascribed to Omar el Khattab. The walls of the mosque are covered with a fine coat of plaster, upon which are many Cufic inscriptions in bas-relief, running all round the wall. The remains of a temple, situated on the ·side of a long street which runs across the whole town, and terminates at the western gate,' &c. Of these, and other magnificent ruins of temples, theatres, and palaces, all attesting its former importance, Burckhardt has given a copious description in his *Travels in Syria,* pp. 226–235, Quarto Ed. Lond. 1822.

7. *And the unicorns.* Marg. 'Rhinoceros' (רְאֵמִים from רְאֵם). This was evidently an animal well known in Palestine, since it is frequently mentioned in the Old Testament (Num. xxiii. 22; Deut. xxxiii. 17; Job xxxix. 9, 10; Ps. xxii. 21; xxix. 6; xcii. 10, in all which places it is translated *unicorn,* or *unicorns*). The derivation of the word is uncertain, and it has been regarded as doubtful what animal is intended. The corresponding Arabic word denotes the *oryx,* a large and fierce species of the antelope. Gesenius, Schultens, De Wette, and Rosenmüller suppose that the *buffalo* is intended by the word. Bochart regards it as denoting the *gazelle,* or a species of the antelope. It can hardly, however, be regarded as so small an animal as the *gazelle.* The gazelle is common in the neighbourhood of mount Sinai; and when Laborde passed through that region his companions killed four, 'the father and mother, and two little animals a fortnight old.' He says of them : 'These creatures, which are very lively in their movements, endeavoured to bite when they were caught; their hair is a brown yellow, which becomes pale and long as the animals grows old. In appearance they resemble the Guinea pig. Their legs are of the same height,

* Burckhardt and many others spell this word *Haouran.* The Rev. E. Smith, however, says that it should be spelled without the *a—Houran.*

8 For *it is* the day *a* of the LORD's vengeance, *and* the year of recompenses for the controversy *b* of Zion.

9 And *c* the streams thereof shall

a Jer.46.10. b Mic.6.1.

but the form of their feet is peculiar; instead of nails and claws, they have three toes in front and four behind, and they walk, like rabbits, on the whole length of the foot.

GAZELLES.

The Arabs call it El Oueber, and know no other name for it. It lives upon the scanty herbage with which the rain in the neighbourhood of springs supplies it. It does not burrow in the earth, its feet not being calculated for that purpose; but it conceals itself in the natural holes or clefts which it finds in the rocks.' —(*Journey through Arabia Petrea*, pp. 106, 107. Lond. 8vo. 1836.) Taylor (*Heb. Con.*) supposes it means the rhinoceros; a fierce animal that has a single horn on the nose, which is very strong, and which sometimes grows to the height of thirty-seven inches. The ancient versions certainly regarded the word as denoting an animal with a single horn. It denotes here, evidently, some strong, fierce, and wild animal that was horned (Ps. xxii. 21), but perhaps it is not possible to determine precisely what animal is meant. For a more full investigation in reference to the kind of animal denoted by the word *reem*, see Notes on Job xxxix. 9. Here it represents that portion of the people which was strong, warlike, and hitherto unvanquished, and who regarded themselves as invincible. ¶ *Shall come down.* Shall be subdued, humbled, destroyed. ¶ *With them.* With the lambs and goats mentioned in ver. 6. All classes of the people shall be subdued and

be turned into pitch, and the dust thereof into brimstone, and the land thereof shall become burning pitch.

10 It shall not be quenched night

c De.29.33.

subjected to the slaughter. ¶ *And the bullocks with the bulls.* The young bulls with the old. All shall come down together—the fierce and strong animals representing the fierce and strong people. ¶ *And their land shall be soaked with blood.* Marg. 'Drunken;' the same word which is rendered 'bathed' in ver. 5. ¶ *Their dust made fat.* Their land manured and made rich with the slain. A battle-field is usually distinguished afterwards for its fertility. The field of Waterloo has thus been celebrated, since the great battle there, for producing rank and luxuriant harvests.

8. *For it is the day of the* LORD's *vengeance.* A time when JEHOVAH will take vengeance. ¶ *The year of recompenses for the controversy of Zion.* The time when he will recompense, *i.e.*, punish those who have had a controversy with Zion.

9. *And the streams thereof.* The idea here is, that there would be as great and awful a destruction as if the streams everywhere should become pitch or resin, which would be set on fire, and which would fill the land with flame. This image is very striking, as we may see by supposing the rivers and streams in any land to flow not with water, but with heated pitch, turpentine, or tar, and that this was all suddenly kindled into a flame. It cannot be supposed that this is to be taken literally. The image is evidently taken from the destruction of Sodom and Gomorrah (Gen. xix, 25–28), an image which is more fully used in reference to the same subject in Jer. xlix. 17, 18 : 'And Edom shall be a desolation ;...as in the overthrow of Sodom and Gomorrah, and the neighbour cities thereof, saith the LORD, no man shall abide there, neither shall a son of man dwell in it.' ¶ *And the dust thereof into brimstone.* The ruin shall be as entire as if all the soil were turned into brimstone, which should be ignited and left burning.

10. *It shall not be quenched night nor day.* That is, the burning brimstone

nor day; the [a]smoke thereof shall go up for ever: from generation to generation it shall lie waste; none

and pitch (ver. 9), the emblem of perpetual and entire desolation, shall not be extinguished. ¶ *The smoke thereof shall go up for ever.* Every river and rivulet is supposed to be heated pitch, and every particle of dust sulphur, and all on fire, sending up from an extended region dense columns of smoke to heaven. No idea of ruin could be more sublime; no idea of the vengeance of God more terrible. This image has been copied by John to describe the future woes of the wicked (Rev. xiv. 11), and of mystical Babylon (Rev. xviii. 9, 18; xix. 2. 3). ¶ *From generation to generation it shall lie waste.* Full confirmation of this may be seen in the travels of Seetzen, of Burckhardt, of Volney, of Irby, and Mangles, extracts of which have been collected and arranged by Keith (*Evidences of Prophecy*, pp. 135–168). Thus Volney says, 'From the reports of the Arabs of Bakir, and the inhabitants of Gaza, who frequently go to Maan and Karak, on the road of the pilgrims, there are to the south-east of the lake Asphaltites (Dead Sea), *within three days' journey*, upwards of thirty ruined towns, *absolutely deserted*. Several of them have large edifices, with columns that may have belonged to the ancient temples, or at least to Greek churches. The Arabs sometimes make use of them to fold cattle in; but, in general, avoid them on account of the enormous scorpions with which they swarm.'—(Volney's *Travels*, vol. ii. pp. 344–346.) It is remarkable that an *infidel*, as Volney was, should in this, as in numerous other instances, have given a minute confirmation of the ancient prophecies. Seetzen says (*Travels*, p. 46), that he was told, that, 'at the distance of two days and a half from Hebron he would find considerable ruins of the ancient city of Abde, and that for all the rest of the journey he would see *no place of habitation;* he would meet only with a few tribes of wandering Arabs.' Burckhardt has given the following description of the eastern boundary of Edom, and of the adjoining part of Arabia Petrea: —' It might with truth be called Petrea,

shall pass through it for ever and ever:

not only on account of its rocky mountains, but also of the elevated plain already described' [*i.e.*, Shera (*Seir*), the territory of the Edomites, *Travels*, pp. 410, 435], 'which is so much covered with stones, especially flints, that it may with great propriety be called a stony desert, although susceptible of culture; in many places it is grown over with wild herbs, and must once have been thickly inhabited, for the traces of many towns and villages are met with on both sides of the Hadj road between Maan and Akaba, as well as between Maan and the plains of Houran, in which direction also are many springs. At present all this country is a desert, and Maan is the only inhabited place in it.'—(Burckhardt's *Travels*, p. 436.) Of the remains of ancient cities still exposed to view in different places throughout Idumea, Burckhardt describes the ruins of a large town, of which nothing remains but broken walls and heaps of stones; the ruins of several villages in its vicinity (p. 418); the ruins of an ancient city, consisting of large heaps of hewn blocks of siliceous stone; and the extensive ruins of Arindela, an ancient town of Palestina Tertia (p. 441). 'The following ruined places are situated in Djebal Shera (Mount Seir), to the south and southwest of Wady Musa,—Kalaat Beni Madha, Djerba, Basta, Eyl, Ferdakh, Anyk, Bir el Beytar, Shemakh, and Syk' (p. 444). Burckhardt also gives a most interesting description of the ruins of the ancient Petra which he discovered, the ancient capital of Edom, but which is too long to be transcribed here (see his *Travels*, pp. 422–432; comp. Note on ch. xvi. 1). ¶ *None shall pass through it for ever and ever.* That is, it shall not be a country through which caravans shall pass; there shall be no roads, and it shall not be deemed safe to travel through it. It will be recollected that the original source of all their calamities, and the cause of all the judgments that came upon them, was the fact that they would not let the children of Israel pass peaceably through

11 But the [1] cormorant [a] and the bittern shall possess it ; the owl also and the raven shall dwell in it : and

1 or, *pelican*.   a Zep.2.14; Rev.18.2.

he shall stretch out upon it the [b] line of confusion and the stones of emptiness.

b 2 Ki.21.13.

their land on their way to Canaan (see the Introduction to the chapter). As a punishment for this, God now says that their land shall *not be passed through;* it shall not be a thoroughfare; there shall be no travellers in it. —God usually directs his punishment of individuals and of nations *in the line of their offences,* and thus his judgments become commonly *a recompence in kind.* Thus in 2 Sam. xxii. 26, 27, it is said :—

With the merciful, thou wilt show thyself merciful;
And with the upright man thou wilt show thyself upright.
With the pure thou wilt show thyself pure;
And with the froward thou wilt show thyself unsavoury.

In accordance with this prediction that no one should pass through Edom, Volney (*Travels,* vol. ii. p. 344) says, 'The country has *not been visited by any traveller,* but it well merits such an attention.' Thus Burckhardt (*Travels,* p. 421) says, after he had entered, on the *north-east,* the territories of the Edomites, that he ' was without protection in the midst of a desert *where no traveller had ever before been seen.* It was then,' he adds, 'that for the first time he had ever felt fear during his travels in the desert, and his route thither was the most dangerous he had ever travelled ' (p. 400). ' Seetzen, on a piece of paper pasted against the wall, notified his having penetrated the country in a direct line between the Dead Sea and Mount Sinai (through Idumea), *a route never before accomplished.*'—(Burckhardt's *Syria,* p. 553.) Burckhardt had determined to attempt to pass the same way as being the shortest way to Jerusalem; but he was repeatedly told it was *impossible;* and the difficulty of the journey is illustrated in the *Travels* of Captains Irby and Mangles. They offered five hundred piastres to an Arab tribe if they would conduct them to Wady Musa, but nothing would induce them to consent. 'They said they would not go if we would give them five thousand piastres, observing that money was

ISAIAH I.

of no use to a man if he lost his life ' (p. 349). So strikingly has this prediction been fulfilled.

11. *But the cormorant.* This and the following verses contain a description of the desolations of Edom in language remarkably similar to that employed in the account of the destruction of Babylon (ch. xiii. 20–22; xiv. 23). The word here translated 'cormorant' (קָאַת), occurs in this place and in Zeph. ii. 14, where it is rendered ' cormorant,' and in Lev. xi. 18; Deut. xiv. 17; Ps. cii. 6, where it is rendered ' pelican.' Bochart supposes it is the *ardea stellaris,* or *bitoun,* which frequents watery places in deserts, and makes a horrible noise. The pelican is a sea-fowl, and cannot be intended here. The cormorant or water raven is a large fowl of the pelican kind, which occupies the cliffs by the sea, feeds on fish, and which is extremely voracious, and which is the emblem of a glutton. It is not

CORMORANT.

certain *what* fowl is intended here, but the word properly denotes a water-fowl, and evidently refers to some bird that inhabits desolate places. ¶ *And the bittern shall possess it.* For a description of the *bittern,* see Note on ch. xiv. 23. ¶ *The owl also and the raven.* Well known birds that occupy deserts,

32

12 They shall call the nobles thereof to the kingdom, but none *shall be* there, and all her princes shall be nothing.

13 And thorns shall come up in her palaces, nettles and brambles in the fortresses thereof; and it shall be an habitation of dragons, *and* a court for [1] owls.

1 *daughters of the owl,* or, *ostriches;* ch.13.21,22.

and old ruins of houses or towns. The image here is that of desolation and ruin; and the sense is, that the land would be reduced to a waste that would not be inhabited by man, but would be given up to wild animals. How well this agrees with Edom, may be seen in the *Travels* of Burckhardt, Seetzen, and others. In regard to the fact that the cormorant (קָאַת, *kââth*) should be found there, it may be proper to introduce a remark of Burckhardt, who seems to have had no reference to this prophecy. 'The bird *katta*,' says he, 'is met with in immense numbers. They fly in such large flocks that the boys often kill two or three of them at a time, merely by throwing a stick among them.' So also in regard to the fact that the owl and the raven shall dwell there, the following statements are made by travellers :—Captain Mangles relates that while he and his fellow-travellers were examining the ruins and contemplating the sublime scenery of Petra, 'the screaming of the eagles, hawks, and owls, which were soaring above their heads in considerable numbers, seemingly annoyed at any one approaching their lonely habitation, added much to the singularity of the scene.' So says Burckhardt : 'The fields of Tafyle (situated in the immediate vicinity of Edom) are frequented by an immense number of crows.' ¶ *And he shall stretch out upon it.* This is an illusion to the fact that an architect uses a *line*, which is employed to lay out his work (see Note on ch. xxviii. 17). ¶ *The line of confusion.* A similar expression occurs in 2 Kings xxi. 13 : 'I will stretch over Jerusalem the line of Samaria, and the plummet of the house of Ahab;' *i.e.,* I will apply the same measure and rule of destruction to Jerusalem that has been applied to Samaria. So Edom would be marked out for desolation. It was the work which God had *laid out,* and which he intended to perform. ¶ *And the stones of emptiness.* Prob-

ably the *plummet* which the architect commonly employed with his line (see Note on ch. xxviii. 17). It is a fact, however, that Edom is at present an extended waste of stones and barren rocks. ' We had before us an immense expanse of dreary country, entirely covered with black flints, with here and there some hilly chain rising from the plain.'— (Burckhardt's *Travels in Syria*, p. 445.)

12. *They shall call the nobles thereof to the kingdom.* A more correct rendering of this would be, 'As to the nobles, they shall call them, but there shall be there no kingdom.' The idea is, that the kingdom would be desolate; there would be no people to rule. Or, there will be no nobles there who shall survive the destruction, and who can undertake the government of the state. The idea is taken from a government or constitution where the monarch is chosen from the ranks of the nobility. Idumea was formerly governed, as we have seen (see the Introduction to the chapter), by *dukes* or princes ; and it is probable that when it became a monarchy it was a part of the constitution that the sovereign should be chosen from their ranks. The idea here is, that none would be left who could be called to the throne ; or if any were left, they would be unwilling to undertake the government of a country where all was disorder and confusion. ¶ *And all her princes shall be nothing.* Long since Idumea has ceased to be a kingdom, and there are neither nobles nor princes there, nor are there any remains of an organized and independent government.

13. *And thorns, &c.* (see Note on ch, v. 6.) ¶ *It shall be an habitation of dragons.* On the meaning of the word 'dragons,' see Note on ch. xiii. 22, ¶ *Court for owls.* A place of resort, a residence of owls. The word rendered 'court' (חָצִיר) means a dwelling-place, a habitation, as well as an enclosure or court. The margin is, 'Daughters of

14 The [1] wild beasts of the desert shall also meet with [2] the wild beasts of the island, and the satyr shall cry to his fellow ; the [3] screech-owl also shall rest there, and find for herself a place of rest.

15 There shall the great owl make her nest, and lay, and hatch, and gather under her shadow ; there shall the vultures also be gathered, every one with her mate.

1 Ziim.　　2 Ijim.　　3 or, night-monster.

the owl,' or 'ostriches' (see Note on ch. xiii. 21).—'I would,' says Stephens, when standing amidst the ruins of Petra, the capital of Idumea (see Note on ch. xvi. 1), and with this passage of Isaiah in his eye, 'I would that the sceptic could stand as I did, among the ruins of this city among the rocks, and there open the sacred book, and read the words of the inspired penman, written when this desolate place was one of the greatest cities in the world. I see the scoff arrested, his cheek pale, his lip quivering, and his heart quaking with fear, as the ancient city cries out to him in a voice loud and powerful as one risen from the dead ; though he would not believe Moses and the prophets, he believes the hand-writing of God himself, in the desolation and eternal ruin around him.' —(*Incidents of Travel in Egypt*, &c., vol. ii. p. 76.)

14. *The wild beasts of the desert.* There is in the original here a paronomasia, which cannot be conveyed in a translation.—The word rendered ' wild beasts of the desert' (צִיִּים), is rendered by the LXX., δαιμόνια, ' demons.' On the meaning of the word, see Note on ch. xiii. 21. ¶ *The wild beasts of the island.* Marg. ' Ijim.' Heb. אִיִּים (see Note on ch. xiii. 22). Probably the term denotes the *jackal.* Gesenius supposes it is so called from its howl, or nocturnal cry—from an Arabic word signifying to *howl.* ¶ *And the satyr* (see Note on ch. xiii. 21). ¶ *Shall cry to his fellow.* A most striking description of the desolation, when all that is heard among the ruins shall be the doleful cry of wild beasts. ¶ *The screech-owl.* Marg. ' Night-monster.' The word לִילִית (from לַיְל, *night*) properly denotes a *night-spectre*—a creature of Jewish superstition. The Rabbins describe it in the form of a female elegantly dressed that lay in wait for children at night—either to carry them off, or to murder them. The Greeks

had a similar idea respecting the female ἔμπουσα, and this idea corresponds to the Roman fables respecting the *Lamiæ,* and *Striges,* and to the Arabic notions of the *Ghûles,* whom they described as female monsters that dwell in deserts, and tear men to pieces (see Gesenius, *Com. in loco;* and Bochart, *Hieroz.* ii. 831). The margin in our version expresses the correct idea. All this is descriptive of utter and perpetual desolation—of a land that should be full of old ruins, and inhabited by the animals that usually make such ruins their abode.

15. *There shall the great owl* (קִפּוֹז). Gesenius supposes that this is the *arrow-snake,* so called from its *darting* or springing, in the manner of the rattle-snake—from an obsolete root *to draw one's self together, to contract.* Bochart (*Hieroz.* ii. 3. 11. 408–419) has examined the meaning of the word at length, and comes to the conclusion that it means the serpent which the Greeks called *acontias,* and the Latins, *jaculus*—the arrow-snake. The serpent is oviparous, and nourishes its young. The ancient versions, however,

EGYPTIAN VULTURE (Nephron perenopterous).

understand it in the same sense as the *kippod* in ver. 11—the hedgehog or por-

16 Seek ^a ye out of the book of the LORD, and read : no one ^b of these shall fail, none shall want

a Is.8.20; Jn.5.39; 2 Pe.1.19.

her mate: for my mouth it hath commanded, and his spirit it hath gathered them.

b Mat.5.18; Lu 21.33.

cupine. ¶ *Under her shadow.* This might be done by the serpent that should coil up and cherish her young. ¶ *The vultures,* &c. The black vulture, ac-

ASH VULTURE (*Vultur cinereus*).

cording to Bochart ; according to Gesenius, the kite, or falcon—so called from its swift flight. Either of them will suit the connection. ¶ *Also be gathered, every one with her mate.* They shall make their nests there ; that is, this shall be their secure, undisturbed retreat.

16. *Seek ye out.* Look carefully at the prediction, and its fulfilment. This seems to be addressed to the inhabitants of that land, or to any who might doubt, or be disposed to examine. They were invited to compare the prediction with the fulfilment, and see how literally all would be fulfilled—an examination which may be made now, and the prediction will be seen to have been accomplished with most surprising particularity and accuracy. ¶ *The book of the* LORD. The book of JEHOVAH, which he has caused to be written, referring, perhaps, especially to what Isaiah has here recorded ; including also what had been uttered by the other prophets in regard to Edom. The main reference is, however, doubtless, to what Isaiah has written ; and the invitation is to compare his predictions with the certain and remarkable evidence of the fulfilment. 'The pro-

phet evidently contemplated the insertion of his prophecy among the sacred books of the Jews, from which those that followed him might judge of the correctness of the prophecy ' (Noyes). That a collection of the various prophetic books was made, constituting one book or volume, and regarded as the work of inspiration, is well known, and is referred to during the captivity in Babylon by Daniel (ch. ix. 2). The direction to search that book accords with the command of the Saviour (John v. 39), and the direction of Nicodemus (John vii. 32), to search the Scriptures. ¶ *No one of these shall fail.* Not one of these predictions, or these things which have been spoken. ¶ *None shall want her mate.* That is, none of the things which I have spoken shall want a fulfilment as its companion. The *language* is here evidently taken from the *pairing* of animals, and denotes that all that is spoken shall be entirely fulfilled. Some have understood this as referring to the wild animals of which he had spoken, and as meaning that in desolate Idumea they should be appropriately paired, and should breed and increase in abundance. But the more natural interpretation is to refer it to the predictions of the prophet, as meaning that no one thing which he had uttered should want a complete fulfilment. ¶ *For my mouth.* The word ' my ' is not in the Hebrew. The Hebrew phrase is כִּי־פִי הוּא, ' For the mouth, he hath commanded.' The word הוּא stands for *He,* that is, JEHOVAH, and the phrase means the same as *his* mouth, that is, the mouth of God. The LXX. render it, 'For the Lord hath commanded them.' Lowth renders it, ' For the mouth of JEHOVAH,' changing הוּא into יְהֹוָה in accordance with five MSS. and the translation of the LXX. ¶ *And his spirit.* The Spirit of God ; that is, JEHOVAH himself. ¶ *Hath gathered them.* Will collect, or assemble ; *i.e.,* the wild beasts spoken of in the previous verses that shall occupy

17 And he hath cast the lot for them, and his hand hath divided it unto them by line : they shall possess it for ever, from generation to generation shall they dwell therein.

CHAPTER XXXV.
ANALYSIS.

THIS chapter is a continuation of the prophecy commenced in the previous chapter. See the Analysis of ch. xxxiv. for a general view of the design of the prophecy. The object of the whole is, to show that all the enemies of the people of God, and particularly Edom, which had so peculiarly and grievously offended them, would be destroyed; and that the destruction of their foes would be followed by times of security, prosperity, and joy.

That this chapter refers to the Messiah is apparent from the slightest inspection of it. It so clearly describes the times of the gospel; so distinctly speaks of the very works which the Redeemer in fact performed; and is so full, and rich, and beautiful, that it cannot be regarded as referring to any other period. It has, in many respects, a strong resemblance to the predictions in ch. xi. and xii., and is incontestably among the most beautiful of the prophecies of Isaiah.

The chapter may be divided into the following portions :—

I. The consolations which would follow the destruction of all their enemies—as great a change as if the wilderness were to blossom like the rose, and the glory and beauty of Lebanon and Carmel were given to the desert (1, 2).

II. The exhortation addressed to those in office and authority to comfort the feeble, and strengthen the weak, with the assurance that those blissful times would come (3, 4).

III. The description of the actual condition of the future period of happiness which is foretold. 1. The eyes of the blind would be opened, the deaf made to hear, and the lame man be cured (5–7). 2. It would be a time of holiness. The way of access to these blessings would be open and free to all—even to all nations, but it would be a way for the pure only (8). 3. It would be a time of safety. There would be no enemy that could overcome and subdue them (9). 4. It would be a time of elevated joy—represented by the return to Zion from a long and painful captivity (10). In the fulness of the blessings of the reign of the Messiah all their sorrow and sighing would flee away (10).

THE wilderness and the solitary place shall be glad for them ; and *a* the desert shall rejoice, and blossom as the rose.

a ch.55.12,13.

---

desolate Idumea. It shall be the agency of God that shall bring them up upon the land to occupy it for ever.

17. *And he hath cast the lot for them.* He hath assigned to them the land of Edom to be occupied by them as their portion. This *language* is taken from the fact that countries were commonly apportioned, particularly among conquerors, by the lot. In this way Judea was divided among the tribes of Israel (Num. xxvi. 55, 56). ¶ *His hand hath divided it unto them by line.* He has marked out, as a surveyor does, the land of Edom as the dwelling-place of the beasts of the forest. A land was usually surveyed and divided into proper parts or portions before the lot was cast (Josh. xviii. 4–6). ¶ *They shall possess it.* The wild beasts mentioned in the previous verses. The testimony of all travellers demonstrates that thus far this prediction has been strikingly fulfilled.

CHAPTER XXXV.

1. *The wilderness and the solitary*

place. This is evidently figurative language, such as is often employed by the prophets. The word rendered ' solitary place ' (צִיָּה), denotes properly a *dry place*, a place without springs and streams of water; and as such places produce no verdure, and nothing to sustain life, the word comes to mean a desert. Such expressions are often used in the Scriptures to express *moral* or *spiritual desolation;* and in this sense evidently the phrase is used here. It does not refer to the desolations of Judea, but to all places that might be properly called a moral wilderness, or a spiritual desert; and thus aptly expresses the condition of the world that was to be benefited by the blessings foretold in this chapter. The parallel expressions in ch. xli. 17–19 ; xliv. 3, 4, show that this is the sense in which the phrase is here used; and that the meaning is, that *every* situation which might be appropriately called a moral wilderness— that is, the whole heathen world—would ultimately be made glad. The sense is,

2 It shall blossom abundantly, and rejoice even with joy and singing : the glory of Lebanon *a* shall

a Ho.14.5,6.

be given unto it, the excellency of Carmel and Sharon ; they shall see the glory of the LORD, *and* the excellency of our God.

---

that as great and happy changes would take place in regard to those desolations *as if* the wilderness should become a vast field producing the lily and the rose; or as if (ver. 2) there should be imparted to such places the glory of Lebanon, and the beauty of Sharon and Carmel. ¶ *Shall be glad for them.* This is evidently a personification, a beautiful poetic figure, by which the wilderness is represented as expressing joy. The sense is, the desolate moral world would be filled with joy on account of the blessings which are here predicted. The phrase 'for them,' expressed in Heb. by the affix ם, means, doubtless, *on account* of the blessings which are foretold in this prophecy. Lowth supposes, however, that the letter has been added to the word 'shall be glad' (יָשִׂישׂ), by mistake, because the following word begins with a מ. The reading of the present Hebrew text is followed by none of the ancient versions; but it is nevertheless probably the correct reading, and there is no authority for changing it. The sense is expressed above by the phrase 'shall rejoice on account of the things contained in this prophecy;' to wit, the destruction of all the foes of God, and the universal establishment of his kingdom. Those who wish to see a more critical examination of the words here used, may find it in Rosenmüller and Gesenius. ¶ *And blossom as the rose.* The word rendered 'rose' (חֲבַצָּלֶת) occurs only here and in Cant. ii. 1, where it is also rendered a 'rose.' The LXX. render it, Κρίνον—'Lily.' The Vulgate also renders it, *Lilium*—the lily. The Syriac renders it also by a word which signifies the lily or narcissus; or, according to the Syriac lexicographers, ' the meadow-saffron,' an autumnal flower springing from poisonous bulbous roots, and of a white and violet colour. The sense is not, however, affected materially whatever be the meaning of the word. Either the rose, the lily, or the saffron, would convey the idea of beauty compared with

the solitude and desolation of the desert. The word 'rose' with us, as being a flower better known, conveys a more striking image of beauty, and there is no impropriety in retaining it.
2. *It shall blossom abundantly.* Heb. ' Blossoming it shall blossom '—a common mode of expression in Hebrew, denoting *certainty, abundance, fulness*—similar to the expression (Gen. ii. 17), ' Dying thou shalt die,' *i.e.,* thou shalt surely die. The sense here is, it shall blossom in abundance. ¶ *And rejoice even with joy.* Strong figurative language, denoting the greatness of the blessings; *as* great as if in the waste wilderness there should be heard the voice of joy and rejoicing. The LXX. render this, ' The deserts *of Jordan* also bloom and rejoice;' and Jerome applies this to the preaching of John in the wilderness adjacent to Jordan. The LXX. evidently read יַרְדֵּן instead of the Hebrew וְרַנֵּן. Lowth has followed this, and rendered it, ' The well-watered plain of Jordan shall rejoice,' but without any authority from Heb. MSS. for the change. ¶ *The glory of Lebanon.* The glory or ornament of Lebanon was its cedars (see Note on ch. x. 34). The sense here is, that the change would be as great under the blessings of the Messiah's reign *as if* there should be suddenly transferred to the waste wilderness the majesty and glory of mount Lebanon. ¶ *The excellency of Carmel.* Carmel was emblematic of beauty, as Lebanon was of majesty, and as Sharon was of fertility. For a description of Carmel, see Note on ch. xxix. 17; of Sharon, see Note on ch. xxxiii. 9. The sense is clear. The blessings of the times of the Messiah would be as great, compared with what had existed before, as if the desert were made as lovely as Carmel, and as fertile as Sharon. The world that, in regard to comfort, intelligence, and piety, might be compared to a pathless desert, would be like the beauty of Carmel and the fertility of Sharon. ¶ *They shall see the glory of*

3 Strengthen ^a ye the weak hands, and confirm the feeble knees.

4 Say to them *that are* of a fearful ¹ heart, Be strong, fear ^b not; behold, your God will come *with*

<small>a He.12.12.   1 *hasty.*   b ch.44.2.</small>

vengeance, *even* God *with* a recompence ; he will come and save ^c you.

5 Then ^d the eyes of the blind shall be opened, and the ears of the deaf shall be unstopped.

<small>c ch.25.9; Lu.21.28.   d Mat 11.5.</small>

the LORD. As manifested under the Messiah.

3. *Strengthen ye.* That is, you who are the religious teachers and guides of the people. This is an address made by the prophet *in view* of what he had said and was about to say of the promised blessings. The sense is, strengthen and sustain the feeble and the desponding by the promised blessings; by the assurances (ch. xxxiv.) that all the enemies of God and his people will be destroyed; and that he will manifest himself as their Protector, and send upon them the promised blessings. Or it may be regarded as addressed to the officers and ministers of religion *when* these blessings should have come ; and as being an exhortation to them to make use of the influences, the promises, and the consolations which would attend the coming of the Messiah, to strengthen the feeble, and confirm those who were faint-hearted. ¶ *The weak hands, and confirm the feeble knees.* Strength resides mainly in the arms, and in the lower limbs, or the knees. If these are feeble, the whole frame is feeble. *Fear* relaxes the strength of the arms, and the firmness of the knees; and the expressions 'weak hands,' and 'feeble knees,' become synonymous with saying, of a *timid, fearful,* and *desponding* frame of mind. Such were to be strengthened by the assurance of the favour of God, and by the consolations which would flow from the reign of the Messiah. The Jews, who looked abroad upon the desolations of their country, were to be comforted by the hope of future blessings ; those who lived in those future times were to be consoled by the assurances of the favour of God through the Messiah (comp. Notes on ch. xl. 1).

4. *Say to them.* This is still an address to the ministers of religion, to make use of all the consolations which these truths and predictions furnish to confirm and strengthen the people of God. ¶ *Of a fearful heart.* Of a timid, pusillanimous heart; those who tremble before their enemies. The Hebrew is, as in the Marg., 'Of a *hasty* heart;' that is, of those who are disposed to *flee* before their enemies (see Note on ch. xxx. 16). ¶ *Behold, your God will come* with *vengeance.* That is, in the manner described in the previous chapter ; and, *generally,* he will take vengeance on *all* the enemies of his people, and they shall be punished. The language in this chapter is, in part, derived from the captivity at Babylon (ver. 10), and the general idea is, that God would take vengeance on *all* their enemies, and would bring them complete and final deliverance. This does not mean that when the Messiah should come *he* would be disposed to take vengeance ; nor do the words 'your God' here refer to the Messiah ; but it is meant that their God, JEHOVAH, would certainly come and destroy all their enemies, and prepare the way thus for the coming of the Prince of peace. The general promise is, that however many enemies might attack them, or however much they might fear them, yet that JEHOVAH would be their protector, and would completely humble and prostrate all their foes.—The Hebrew will admit of a somewhat different translation, which I give in accordance with that proposed by Lowth. The sense is not materially varied.

Say ye to the faint-hearted, Be ye strong; fear
   ye not; behold your God !
Vengeance will come ; the retribution of God:
He himself will come, and will deliver you.

5. *Then the eyes of the blind shall be opened.* The images in this verse and the following are those of joy and exultation. They describe the times of happiness when God would come to save them from their foes. This passage is so accurate a description of what the Messiah, the Lord Jesus, did, that it doubtless refers to the miracles which he would perform. In not a few instances did he in fact restore the

6 Then shall the lame *man* leap as an hart, and the tongue of the dumb sing : for in the wilderness shall waters ^abreak out, and streams in the desert.

a ch.43.19.

7 And the parched ground shall become a pool, and the thirsty land springs ^b of water : in the habitation of dragons where each lay, *shall be* grass,¹ with reeds and rushes.

b Jn.4.14; 7.38. 1 or, *a court for.*

blind to sight, giving thus the most unequivocal proof that he was the Messiah sent from God (Matt. ix. 27; xx. 30; Mark viii. 23; x. 46; Luke vii. 21). It is a full confirmation of the opinion that this passage refers to Christ, that the Saviour himself appeals to the fact that he restored the blind to sight, as demonstration that he was the Messiah, implying that it was predicted that this would be a part of his appropriate work (Matt. xi. 5; comp. Luke iv. 18). ¶ *And the ears of the deaf be unstopped.* Another demonstration of Divine power, and another proof that would be furnished that the Messiah was from God. The Lord Jesus often gave this demonstration that he was invested with Divine power (Matt. xi. 5 ; Mark vii. 32, 37; ix. 25).

6. *Then shall the lame* man *leap.* This was literally fulfilled after the coming of the Messiah (Acts xiv. 10; iii. 8). It is an *emblem* of the general joy which the coming of the Messiah would impart, and is an *instance* of the blessings which it would convey. ¶ *As an hart.* The word here used denotes the stag, or male deer. In Arabic it denotes the wild, or mountain-goat. The word sometimes refers to any species of deer or antelope, and this is referred to here from its quick and sprightly nature. ¶ *And the tongue of the dumb sing.* Shall be able to sing, and to praise God. On the restoration of the dumb to the benefits of language, see Matt. ix. 32, 33; xii. 22; xv. 30, 31; Mark ix. 17; Luke xi. 14. ¶ *For in the wilderness shall waters break out.* The joy shall be as great, and the blessings as numerous and refreshing, *as if* running fountains should suddenly break out in the desert, and the thirsty and weary traveller should be thus unexpectedly and fully supplied. The world, in regard to its real comforts without the gospel, may be not unaptly compared to a vast waste of pathless sands and arid plains. Nothing will more strongly

express the blessings of the gospel than the idea of cool, refreshing, abundant fountains and streams bursting forth in such pathless wastes. This is an image which would be very expressive to those who were accustomed to cross such deserts, and it is one which is frequently employed by the sacred writers, and especially by Isaiah (see ch. xliii. 19, 20; xlviii. 21; xlix. 10, 11; lv. 1; lviii. 11). 'Lameness and dumbness are the uniform effects of long walking in a desert; the sand and gravel produce the former, fatigue the latter. In such cases some of us have walked hours together without uttering a sentence ; and all walked as if crippled, from the sand and gravel getting into the shoes ; but the sight of water, especially if unexpected, unloosed every tongue, and gave agility to every limb; men, oxen, goats, sheep, and dogs, ran with speed and expressions of joy to the refreshing element.' —(Campbell's *Travels in Africa.*) The Chaldee Paraphrast understands this as referring entirely to the return from the captivity at Babylon. 'Then shall they see the exiles of Israel assembled, ascend to their own land as the swift stags, so that they shall not be hindered.'

7. *And the parched ground shall become a pool.* The idea is the same here as in the previous verse, that under the Messiah there would be blessings as great *as if* ' the parched ground ' should become a lake of pure and refreshing water. The words ' parched ground,' however, probably do not convey the sense which Isaiah intended. The image which he had in his eye is much more beautiful than that which is denoted by the ' parched ground.' Lowth translates it, ' The glowing sand.' The LXX. Ἄνυδρος — ' The dry place. The Hebrew word (שָׁרָב *shârâb*), properly denotes the heat of the sun (Isa. xlix. 10); and then the phenomenon which is produced by the refraction of the rays of the sun on the glowing sands of a desert, and which gives the appearance of a sea

or lake of water. This phenomenon is witnessed in the deserts of Arabia and Egypt, and has been also seen occasionally in the south of France and in Russia. We have no word in English to express it. The French word by which it is commonly designated is *mirage*. It is caused by the refraction of the rays of the sun, an explanation of which may be found in the *Edin. Encyclopædia*, vol. xiv. pp. 753–755. It is often described by travellers, and is referred to in the Koran, ch. xxiv. 39:

The works of unbelievers are like *the serab* in a plain,
Which the thirsty man takes to be water, until he comes to it, and finds that it is not.

Mr. Sale's Note on this place in the Koran is, ' The Arabic word *serab* signifies that false appearance which in the eastern countries is often seen in sandy plains about noon, resembling a large lake of water in motion, and is occasioned by the reverberation of the sunbeams, " by the quivering undulating motion of that quick succession of vapours and exhalations which are extracted by the powerful influence of the sun " (Shaw's *Travels*, p. 378). It sometimes tempts thirsty travellers out of their way, but deceives them when they come near, either going forward (for it always appears at the same distance), or quite vanishes.' Q. Curtius (vii. 5) also has mentioned it, in the description of the march of Alexander the Great across the Oxus to Sogdiana: ' The vapour of the summer sun inflamed the sands, which when they began to be inflamed all things seemed to burn. A dense cloud, produced by the unusual heat of the earth, covered the light, and the *appearance of the plains was like a vast and deep sea*.' The Arabians often refer to this in their writings, and draw images from it. ' Like the serab of the plain, which the thirsty take to be water.' ' He runs for the spoil of the serab ;' a proverb. ' Deceitful as the appearance of water ;' also a proverb. ' Be not deceived by the glimmer of the serab ;' another proverb. This appearance has been often described by modern travellers (see Shaw's *Travels*, p. 375 ; Clarke's *Travels*, vol. ii. p. 295; Belzoni's *Travels and Operations in Egypt*

and *Nubia*, p. 196). The same appearance has been observed in India, and in various parts of Africa. ' During the French expedition to Egypt, the phenomena of unusual refractions were often seen. The uniformity of the extensive sandy plains of Lower Egypt interrupted only by small eminences, on which the villages are situated, in order to escape the inundations of the Nile. In the morning and the evening, as many have remarked, objects appear in their natural position ; but when the surface of the sandy ground is heated by the sun, the land seems at a certain distance terminated by a general inundation. The villages which are beyond it appear like so many islands situated in the middle of a great lake ; and under each village is an inverted image of it. As the observer approaches the limits of the apparent inundation, the imaginary lake which seemed to encircle the village withdraws itself, and the same illusion is reproduced by another village more remote.'—(*Edin. Encyclopædia*, vol. xiv. p. 754.) ' In the desert,' says Prof. Robinson, ' we had frequent instances of the *mirage* presenting the appearance of lakes of water and islands; and as we began to descend towards Suez, it was difficult to distinguish between these appearances and the distant real waters of the Red Sea.'—(*Travels in Palestine and the adjacent regions, in* 1838, *Bib. Repos.* April, 1839, p. 402.) Major Skinner, in his recently published *Journey Overland to India*, describes the appearance of the serab in that very desert, between Palestine and the Euphrates, which probably supplied the images which the prophet employs: ' About noon the most perfect deception that can be conceived exhilarated our spirits, and promised an early resting-place. We had observed a slight *mirage* two or three times before, but this day it surpassed all I have ever fancied. Although aware that these appearances have often led people astray, I could not bring myself to believe that this was unreal. The Arabs were doubtful, and said that, as we had found water yesterday, it was not improbable that we should find some to-day. The seeming lake was broken in several parts by little islands of sand that gave strength

8 And an high way shall be

to the delusion. The dromedaries of the Sheikhs at length reached its borders, and appeared to us to have commenced to ford as they advanced, and became more surrounded by the vapour. I thought they had got into deep water, and moved with greater caution. In passing over the sand banks their figures were reflected in the water. So convinced was Mr. Calmun of its reality, that he dismounted and walked towards the deepest part of it, which was on the right hand. He followed the deceitful lake for a long time, and to our sight was strolling on the bank, his shadow stretching to a great length beyond. There was not a breath of wind ; it was a sultry day, and such an one as would have added dreadfully to our disappointment if we had been at any time without water.'

Southey has beautifully described this appearance and its effects on the traveller :—

Still the same burning sun! no cloud in heaven!
The hot air quivers, and the sultry mist
Floats o'er the desert, with a show
Of distant waters mocking their distress.

The idea of the prophet, if he refers to this phenomenon, is exceedingly beautiful. It is that the *mirage*, which has the appearance only of a sheet of water, and which often deceives the traveller, shall become a *real* lake; that there shall be hereafter no deception, no illusion; that man, like a traveller on pathless sands, weary and thirsty, shall no more be deceived by false appearances and unreal hopes. The hopes and promises which this world can furnish are as delusive as is the *mirage* to the exhausted and thirsty traveller. Man approaches them, and, like that delusive appearance, they recede or vanish. If they are still seen, they are always at a distance, and he follows the false and deceptive vision till he comes to the end of life. But the promises of God through the Messiah, are like *real* lakes of water and running streams to the thirsty traveller. They never deceive, never recede, never vanish, never are unsatisfactory. Man may approach them, knowing that there is no illusion ; he may satisfy his wants, and still the sup-

there, and a way, and it shall be

ply is unexhausted and inexhaustible. Others also may approach the same fountain of pure joy, with as much freedom as travellers may approach the running stream in the desert. ¶ *In the habitation of dragons* (see Note on ch. xiii. 22). The sense of this is, that the blessings which are promised shall be as great as if in such dry and desolate places there should be verdure and beauty. ¶ *Where each lay.* In every place which the wild beast had occupied. ¶ Shall be *grass.* Marg. ' A court for.' The Hebrew word (הָצִיר) may mean either *grass,* or *a court,* or habitation. The latter is undoubtedly the meaning of the word here, and thus it responds in the parallelism to the ' *habitation* of dragons.'

In *the habitation* where each lay,
Shall be a *court* for reeds and rushes.

¶ *Reeds and rushes.* These usually grew by ponds and marshes. The image which the prophet had been employing was that of a desert of sands and arid plains. He here says, that there would be *verdure.* In those pathless wastes there would spring up that which was nourished by water. The sense is, that those portions of the earth which are covered with moral desolation, like the pathless wastes of the desert, shall put on the appearance of moral cultivation and verdure.

8. *And an highway shall be there* (see Note on ch. xi. 16). This is *language* which is derived from the return of the Jews from captivity. The idea is, that there would be easy and uninterrupted access to their own land. The more remote, though main idea in the mind of the prophet seems to have been, that the way of access to the blessings of the Messiah's reign would be open and free to all (comp. ch. xl. 3, 4). ¶ *And a way.* It is not easy to mark the difference between the word *way* (דֶּרֶךְ) and a *highway* (מַסְלוּל). Probably the latter refers more particularly to a *raised* way (from סָלַל, *to cast up*), and would be expressed by our word *causeway* or *turnpike.* It was such a way as was usually made for the march of armies by removing obstructions, filling valleys, &c. The

called, The way of holiness; the unclean *shall not pass over it; but 1 it *shall be* for those : the wayfaring men, though fools, shall not err *therein*.

word *way* (דֶּרֶךְ) is a more general term, and denotes a path, or road of any kind. ¶ *And it shall be called the way of holiness.* The reason why it should be so called is stated ; — no impure person should travel it. The idea is, that all who should have access to the favour of God, or who should come into his kingdom, should be holy. ¶ *The unclean shall not pass over it.* There shall be no idolater there ; no one shall be admitted who is not a pure worshipper of JEHOVAH. Such is the design of the kingdom which is set up by the Messiah, and such the church of Christ should be (see ch. xl. 3, 4 ; xlix. 11 ; lxii. 10). ¶ *But it* shall be *for those.* For those who are specified immediately ; for the ransomed of the Lord. The Margin is, ' For he shall be with them.' Lowth reads it,

But he himself shall be with them, walking in the way.'

And this, it seems to me, is the more probable sense of the passage, indicating that they should not go alone or unprotected. It would be a holy way, because their God would be with them ; it would be safe, because he would attend and defend them. ¶ *The wayfaring men.* Heb. ' He walking in the way.' According to the translation proposed above, this refers to God, the Redeemer, who will be with his people, walking in the way with them. ¶ *Though fools.* Heb. ' And fools.' That is, the simple, the unlearned, or those who are regarded as fools. It shall be a highway thrown up, so direct, and so unlike other paths, that there shall be no danger of mistaking it.—The friends of God are often regarded as fools by the world. Many of them *are* of the humbler class of life, and are destitute of human learning, and of worldly wisdom. The sense here is, that the way of salvation shall be so plain, that no one, however ignorant and unlearned, need err in regard to it. In accordance with this, the

9 No *b*lion shall be there, nor *any* ravenous beast shall go up thereon, it shall not be found there : but the redeemed shall walk *there :*

Saviour said that the gospel was preached to the poor ; and he himself always represented the way to life as such that the most simple and unlettered might find it.

9. *No lion shall be there.* Lions abounded in all the countries adjacent to Palestine. They are, therefore, often referred to by the sacred writers, as objects of dread and alarm. The leading idea in the *language* of Isaiah in this whole passage, is that of a way constructed from Babylon to Judea, so straight and plain that the most simple of the people might find it and walk in it. But *such* a path would lie through desert sands. It would be in the region infested with lions and other wild beasts. The prophet, therefore, suggests that there should be no cause for such dread and alarm. The sense is, that in that kingdom to which he had made reference all would be *safe.* They who entered it should find security and defence as they travelled that road. And it *is* true. They who enter the path that leads to life, find there no cause of alarm. Their fears subside ; their apprehensions of punishment on account of their sins die away ; and they walk that path with security and confidence. There is nothing *in* that way to alarm them ; and though there may be many foes—fitly represented by lions and wild beasts—lying *about* the way, yet no one is permitted to ' go up thereon.' This is a most beautiful image of the safety of the people of God, and of their freedom from all enemies that could annoy them. ¶ *But the redeemed shall walk* there. The *language* here referred at first doubtless to those who would be rescued from the captivity at Babylon ; but the main reference is to those who would be redeemed by the blood of the atonement, or who are properly called ' the redeemed of the LORD.' That Isaiah was acquainted with the doctrine of redemption is apparent from his fifty-third chapter. There is not here, in-

10 And the ransomed *a* of the
LORD shall return, and come to
Zion with songs, *b* and everlasting

a ch.51.11.   *b* Rev.5.9.

joy *c* upon their heads : they shall
obtain joy and gladness, and sorrow *d* and sighing shall flee away.

c Jude 24.   *d* Rev.7.17; 21.4.

deed, any express mention made of the
means by which they would be redeemed, but the language is so general that
it may refer either to the deliverance
from the captivity at Babylon, or the
future more important deliverance of
his people from the bondage of sin by
the atoning sacrifice of the Messiah.
On the word rendered 'redeem,' see
Note on ch. xliii. 1. The idea is, that
the path here referred to is appropriately designed only for the redeemed of
Lord. It is not for the profane, the
polluted, the hypocrite. It is not for
those who live for this world, or for
those who love pleasure more than they
love God. The church should not be
entered except by those who have evidence that they are redeemed. None
should make a profession of religion
who have no evidence that they belong
to 'the redeemed,' and who are not
disposed to walk in the way of holiness.
But, *for* all such it is a highway on
which they are to travel. It is made
by levelling hills and elevating valleys ;
it is made across the sandy desert and
through the wilderness of this world ;
it is made through a world infested
with the enemies of God and his people.
It is made straight and plain, so that
none need err ; it is defended from
enemies, so that all may be safe ; it is
rendered secure, because 'He,' their
Leader and Redeemer, shall go with
and guard that way.

10. *And the ransomed of the* LORD.
The word here rendered 'ransomed,' is
different from the word rendered 'redeemed' in ver. 9. This word is פְּדוּיֵי
from פָּדָה ; though it is not easy, perhaps not possible, to designate the
difference in the sense. Doubtless
there was a shade of difference among
the Hebrews, but what it was is not
now known. See this word explained
in the Note on ch. i. 27. The *language*
here is all derived from the deliverance
from Babylon, and the images employed by the prophet relate to that event.
Still, there can be no doubt that he
meant to describe the deliverance under

the Messiah. ¶ *Shall return, and come
to Zion.* This language also is that
which expresses the return from Babylon. In a more general sense, and in
the sense intended particularly by the
prophet, it means, doubtless, that *all*
who are the redeemed of God shall be
gathered under his protection, and shall
be saved. ¶ *With songs.* With rejoicing—as the ransomed captives would
return from Babylon, and as all who
are redeemed enter the church on earth,
and will enter into heaven above.
¶ *And everlasting joy upon their heads.*
This *may be* an expression denoting the
fact that joy is manifest in the face and
aspect (Gesenius). Thus we say that
joy lights up the countenance, and it is
possible that the Hebrews expressed
this idea by applying it to the head.
Thus the Hebrews say (Ps. cxxvi. 2):

Then was our mouth filled with laughter.
And our tongue with singing.

Or it may refer to the practice of *anointing* the head with oil and perfume in
times of festivity and joy—in contrast
with the custom of throwing ashes on
the head in times of grief and calamity
(Rosenmüller). Or it may refer to a
custom of wearing a wreath or chaplet
of flowers in times of festivity, as is
often done now, and as was commonly
done among the ancients in triumphal
processions (Vitringa). Whichever exposition be adopted, the idea is the
same, that there would be great joy,
and that that joy would be perpetual
and unfading. This is true of all who
return to Zion under the Messiah. *Joy*
is one of the first emotions ; joy at redemption, and at the pardon of sin ; joy
in view of the hopes of eternal life, and
of the everlasting favour of God. But
this joy is not short-lived and fading,
like the garland of flowers on the head ;
it is constant, increasing, everlasting.
¶ *And sorrow and sighing shall flee
away* (see Note on ch. xxv. 8).

This is a most beautiful close of the
series or succession of prophecies which
we have been thus far contemplating.
The result of all is, that the redeemed

of the Lord shall have joy and rejoicing; that all their enemies shall be subdued, and that they shall be rescued from all their foes. In the analysis of the prophecy contained in the thirty-fourth and thirty-fifth chapters, it was stated that this prophecy seemed to be a *summary* of all that Isaiah had before uttered, and was designed to show that all the enemies of the people of God would be destroyed, and that they would be triumphantly delivered and saved. All these minor deliverances were preparatory to and emblematic of the greater deliverance under the Messiah; and accordingly all his predictions look forward to, and terminate in that. In the portions of prophecy which we have been over, we have seen the people of God represented as in danger from the Syrians, the Assyrians, the Egyptians, the Moabites, the Edomites, the Babylonians; and in reference to them *all*, the same result has been predicted, that they would be delivered from them, and that their enemies would be destroyed. This has been, in the chapters which we have passed over, successively foretold of Damascus, of Egypt; of Moab, of Ethiopia, of Babylon, of Edom, and of Sennacherib; and the prophet has reached the conclusion that ALL the enemies of God's people would ultimately be destroyed, and that they would be safe under the reign of the Messiah, to which all their deliverances were preparatory, and in which they all would terminate. Having pursued this course of the prophecy; having looked at all these foes; having seen them in vision all destroyed; having seen the Prince of Peace come; having seen the wonders that he would perform; having seen all danger subside, and the preparation made for the eternal security and joy of all his people, the prophet closes this series of predictions with the beautiful statement now before us, 'the redeemed of JEHOVAH shall return, and come to Zion with songs, and everlasting joy; and sorrow and sighing shall flee away.'

END OF VOLUME I.